THE POLICE
AND CRIMINAL EVIDENCE
ACT 1984

AUSTRALIA
Law Book Co.
Sydney

CANADA and USA
Carswell
Toronto

HONG KONG
Sweet & Maxwell Asia

NEW ZEALAND
Brookers
Wellington

SINGAPORE and MALAYSIA
Sweet & Maxwell Asia
Singapore and Kuala Lumpur

THE POLICE
AND CRIMINAL EVIDENCE
ACT 1984
(Fifth Edition)

BY

MICHAEL ZANDER Q.C.
Emeritus Professor of Law, London School of Economics and
Political Science

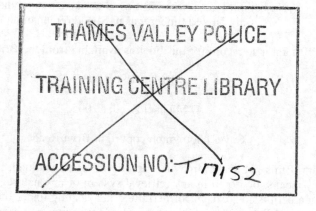

THOMSON

™

SWEET & MAXWELL

First Edition 1985
Second Edition 1990
Third Edition 1995
Reprinted 1997
Reprinted 1999
Reprinted 2001
Fourth Edition 2003

This edition published in 2005 by Sweet & Maxwell Ltd
100 Avenue Road
London NW3 3PF

www.sweetandmaxwell.co.uk

Typeset by J&L Composition Ltd, Filey, North Yorkshire
Printed and bound in great Britain by
TJ International

No natural forests were destroyed to make this product;
only farmed timber was used and replanted

A CIP catalogue record for this book is available from the British Library

ISBN 0421 905 808

FOREWORD TO THE FOURTH EDITION
by Lord Woolf of Barnes,
Lord Chief Justice of England and Wales

This new edition of Michael Zander's most authoritative work on the Police and Criminal Evidence Act 1984 (PACE) will be warmly welcomed by all those engaged in the criminal justice system. PACE is central to the working of the criminal justice system. Together with its Codes, it has a fundamental effect, not only on what happens during a trial, but also on what happens during the investigations into a crime prior to the commencement of proceedings. It sets out standards of conduct with which the police, the Crown Prosecution Service, the lawyers and judges are required to comply. It reflects Parliament's intention as to what should be the balance between, on the one hand, the necessary protection of the rights of the individual citizen and, on the other, the right of the public as a whole that those who commit crimes should be convicted and then punished.

Since the last edition, there have been numerous amendments to PACE and its Codes, and much new case law. In addition, there has been the implementation of the Human Rights Act 1998. The new edition explains clearly the implications of these changes. It does so whilst maintaining the high standards that Michael Zander set in his previous editions. It does so realistically, accepting that, until issues as to the impact of the Human Rights Act on PACE have been authoritatively decided by the courts, it should be assumed that PACE will meet human rights standards. Michael Zander is well aware that quite independently of the Human Rights Act, the courts have historically given full effect to the principles of the right to a fair trial, enshrined in Art.6 of the European Convention on Human Rights, by conferring wide discretion on the trial judge to do justice, according to the circumstances of the particular case, when applying section 78 of PACE.

I have already benefited from the previous editions of this book and, I am sure, will benefit even more from an updated version. Certainly, I foresee that my copy will be regularly in use. I warmly congratulate Michael Zander on this new edition. Practitioners will have reason to be grateful to him for a job well done.

Harry Woolf
February 2003

PREFACE TO THE FIFTH EDITION

The purpose of this book remains what it has been since it was first published in 1985—to provide a work on the Police and Criminal Evidence Act 1984 (PACE) which is useful to practitioners, police officers, judges, academic lawyers and law students. It is not a book that offers the author's critical reflections as to the merits or otherwise of the law. It attempts only to unravel the complexities of the Act.

There was a gap of eight years between the third edition (1995) and the fourth (2003). The chief reason was that the Home Office delayed and delayed in producing its major revision of the PACE Codes of Practice. The revised Codes were originally planned for 2000 but in the event they were not approved by Parliament until 2002 and only became operational as from April 2003, a few days after the fourth edition of this work was published.

The Preface to the fourth edition indicated that there would soon be a need for a further edition to take account of developments that had at that time already emerged and others that were then contemplated.

The changes made in the fifth edition flow primarily from the Criminal Justice Act 2003 and the revised Codes of Practice which came into effect as from August 1, 2004. But there were also a variety of other sources, including new cases and new literature. The opportunity was also taken to make other improvements. The new system for charging brought in by the Criminal Justice Act 2003 is informed by Guidance issued by the DPP. With the Director's permission, the book includes the second version of his Guidance, dated January 2005, as an appendix. The book also takes account of the changes made in 2004 to the service that can be provided at public expense by solicitors in the police station.

In August 2004 the Home Office issued a Consultation Paper, *Policing: Modernising Police Powers to Meet Community Needs,* canvassing a variety of possible further amendments to PACE. These are covered in the book. The closing date for the consultation exercise was October 8, 2004. A little more than a month later, on November 24, the second day of the new session of Parliament, the Home Office published the Serious Organised Crime and Police Bill which incorporated many of the changes in the Consultation Paper. Many of these are significant. One with relevance for many passages in the book, is the abolition of the special category of serious arrestable offences and the application of the powers hitherto only available for such offences to all indictable offences. Although the book was then already in the hands of the publishers for processing there was just time to take account of the provisions of the Bill both in the commentary and in the text of the legislation — PACE and the Police Reform Act 2002. (The text of the statute printed here shows the changes (italicised) that would result from implementation of the Bill as it then stood.) There was of course no way of knowing whether, and if so, when, the Bill would in fact become law or what changes might be made to the provisions in the Bill before Royal Assent.

Despite the fact that not much time has elapsed since the previous edition, the changes for this edition are therefore extensive. Not all are additions. It was decided to drop the material on the admissibility of documents previously dealt with in Part VII of the Act. This is now dealt with in Part 11 of the Criminal Justice Act 2003. Since the subject no longer has any connection with PACE, there seemed to be no sufficient reason for retaining it in this book. Overall the book is more than 100 pages longer than the last edition—of which nearly half (40 pages) is Commentary and a third is made up of the additions to the Police Reform Act made by the Serious Organised Crime and Police Bill 2004–2005 (17 pages) and the DPP's Guidance on charging (16 pages). The additions to PACE itself amount to some 14 pages.

The book proceeds in the same way as the previous editions—a commentary on the sections of the Act in chronological order and on their corresponding provisions in the Codes of Practice, with full references, followed at the end of each Chapter by a Question and Answer section. Since PACE was largely based on the report of the Philips Royal Commission on Criminal Procedure, the commentary still includes the state of the law at the time when the Philips Commission reported in 1981, the Commission's recommendations and, where relevant, an account of the parliamentary debates on the two PACE bills.

With the kind permission of the Controller of Her Majesty's Stationery Office, the book reprints the statute itself as amended (on buff coloured pages), and the Codes of Practice (on blue pages). A new appendix shows the provisions of the statute that had not come into force by the time the book went to press in January 2005.

The book again deals also with the position in Northern Ireland—mainly in footnotes. Broadly it is the same as that in England and Wales, though the legislation there and, even more, the Codes have lagged several years behind. The original Northern Ireland Order[1] reflecting the 1984 Act was passed in 1989. It is referred to here as the 1989 N.I. PACE Order. It came into effect with the Codes of Practice[2] on January 1, 1990, four years to the day after implementation of PACE. Five years later, the Police (Amendment) (Northern Ireland) Order 1995[3] (referred to as the 1995 Order) brought Northern Ireland into line in three areas—police powers, police discipline and police complaints. In regard to police powers, the changes were mainly based on the provisions of the Criminal Justice and Public Order Act 1994. For police discipline, the changes were based mainly on the Police and Magistrates' Courts Act 1994. In regard to police complaints, the Order revoked and re-enacted the provisions of the Police (Northern Ireland) Order 1987 but it also gave effect to the government's decisions on the recommendations of the Independent Commission for Police Complaints. Recent legislation which has effected PACE amendments in Northern Ireland includes the Police (Northern Ireland) Act 2003, the Criminal Justice Act 2003 and the Criminal Justice (Northern Ireland) Order 2004 (SI 2004/1500).

So far as concerns the Codes, the 1995 Northern Ireland Order came into force on July 29, 1996 together with revised Codes of Practice similar to those introduced in 1995 in Great Britain. However, revisions in the Codes of Practice similar to those introduced in England and Wales in 2003 and 2004 have still not been made and it is now expected that it may take until 2006 before they are operational.

---

[1] The Police and Criminal Evidence (Northern Ireland) Order 1989, SI 1989/1341 (N.I. 12).
[2] Codes A to D; there was at that time no Code E on Tape Recording.
[3] The Police (Amendment) (Northern Ireland) Order 1995, SI 1995/2993 (N.I. 17).

Preface to the Fifth Edition

Chapter 12, introduced in the fourth edition, is on civilian staff with PACE police powers under the Police Reform Act 2002. This topic will be of growing importance as the number of Community Support Officers is likely to increase exponentially. The book also deals with two topics derived from other legislation that is integrally related to PACE. One is the "right to silence" provisions in the Criminal Justice and Public Order Act 1994 and the mass of case law spawned by those provisions (Chapter 13). The other is the special provision for terrorism investigations, where these cover the same ground as PACE. They were previously to be found mainly in the Prevention of Terrorism (Temporary Provisions) Act (PTA) first passed in 1974 and re-enacted from time to time, most recently in 1989—as amended by the Criminal Justice (Terrorism and Conspiracy) Act 1998. In Northern Ireland they were to be found latterly in the Northern Ireland (Emergency Provisions) Act 1996 (EPA). The basic legislation is now to be found in the Terrorism Act 2000. That Act reformed and extended previous counter-terrorist legislation and put it largely onto a permanent basis. The 2000 Act applies to all forms of terrorism: Irish, international and domestic. The subject is dealt with throughout the book, wherever the topic arises.

The book also deals with judicial decisions interpreting the European Convention on Human Rights that affect PACE and the right of silence—both those given by the European Court of Human Rights (ECHR) in Strasbourg and those given by domestic courts under the Human Right Act 1998. (A short introduction to the Human Rights Act (HRA) for the uninitiated is to be found in Chapter 14.) Some of the writing on the impact of the HRA on policing and criminal justice has taken an unduly defensive view and the same is true of some of the advice given to the police by their own trainers and advisers. The writer shares the more robust view that until there is an actual judicial decision to the contrary, "there is no reason at all why police officers should not continue to rely on long-established, tried and tested tactics and procedures, especially when they are within a legislative framework . . .".[4] It is time enough to give up what seems to be a sensible rule, procedure or practice when it is judicially declared to be unlawful. This book at all events deals with the effect of the HRA only where there are actual relevant judicial decisions.

The index to the book includes references in different printing styles for the author's text, the Act and the Codes. As before, marginal vertical lines in the text of the Codes of Practice indicate wholly new material. (Changes in the 2003 version of the Codes are indicated by a single line; changes in the 2004 version are indicated by a double line.) The footnotes to the text of the Codes indicate when new material is based on previous provisions and when there has simply been renumbering. The book has been brought up-to-date to January 2005.

I include here the Foreword kindly written for the fourth edition by Lord Woolf, Lord Chief Justice. I express again my gratitude to him for writing it and for its generous terms.

MZ
London
January 2005

---

[4] Pickover, *Police Review*, August 31, 2001, p.31.

THE BACKGROUND AND THE FUTURE

The Police and Criminal Evidence Act was the result of more than 10 years' travail. Official dissatisfaction with the rules of the criminal process goes back in fact even further to the mid-1960s when the Home Office asked the Criminal Law Revision Committee to inquire into the rules of evidence in criminal cases. Their eight year study culminated in 1972 with the publication of the ill-fated 11th Report of that prestigious Committee. Their report[1] was received with a barrage of criticism most of which was actually directed at only one of the Committee's many recommendations, that the right to silence in the police station should be abolished. This proposal led to such a storm of abuse that the report was effectively still-born. No government could implement even the uncontroversial recommendations of a report so widely regarded as fatally flawed.[2]

For some years the Home Office shelved the whole topic. But in June 1977 the Labour Government announced that it was setting up a Royal Commission on Criminal Procedure whose terms of reference were to consider the investigation of offences in the light of police powers and duties as well as the rights and duties of suspects. The Philips Royal Commission was asked to examine the issues, "having regard both to the interests of the community in bringing offenders to justice and to the rights and liberties of persons suspected or accused of crime, and taking into account also the need for the efficient and economical use of resource". (The Philips Royal Commission was also asked to look into the problem of the responsibility for the prosecution process, but that part of the Commission's report is not dealt with in this book since the topic was treated separately in the Prosecution of Offences Act 1985.) The Philips Royal Commission's remit was to attempt to reach an agreed solution to a series of highly contentious issues. Its members included representatives of many of the interested groups—a judge, two police officers, a Queen's Counsel, a stipendiary magistrate who had formerly been a justices' clerk, a defence lawyer, and several lay magistrates. The lay members included the chairman, Sir Cyril Philips, a Professor of History and former Vice-Chancellor of London University. Under his unassuming but effective leadership the Commission achieved the almost impossible task of obtaining unanimity or near unanimity on all the topics in their report. On many issues there were one or two (unidentified) dissenters. But virtually all the recommendations in the report were endorsed by the overwhelming majority of the 15 members.

The report was well received by the police and tolerably well received by the legal profession. It was condemned as too prosecution-minded by the political Left including organisations like the National Council for Civil Liberties and the Legal Action Group, as well as the official Labour Opposition. The Home

---

[1] *Evidence (General)*, Cmnd.4991 (1972).
[2] See Zander, "The CLRC report—a survey of reactions", *Law Society Gazette*, October 2, 1974, p.954.

Office showed every sign of wanting to legislate to implement the report. It set up internal working parties to consider the proposals and issued a long list of examination-type specific questions for comment by interested groups and persons. In November 1982, only 20 or so months after the Philips Royal Commission had reported, the then Home Secretary Mr William Whitelaw introduced the first version of the Police and Criminal Evidence Bill. Broadly, it was based on the report of the Philips Royal Commission, though in many respects the Government had exercised its political right to discriminate as to what it would and would not accept of the Philips Royal Commission's proposals. To some extent therefore the carefully constructed package of proposals hammered out over three years around the Philips Royal Commission's table became unstitched. The Government had put together its own, somewhat different, package.

The Bill proved to be highly controversial and during its passage through the House of Commons in the winter of 1982–1983 it was subject to fierce criticism. The debate on the right to silence which sunk the 11th Report of the Criminal Law Revision Committee was barely mentioned. The Philips Royal Commission had decided that the right to silence in the police station should stay—because it was too important to abolish and moreover so few people were actually silent that it would achieve little to abolish it. (As will be seen, the right to silence question was however re-opened dramatically in July 1987, and in 1994 in the Criminal Justice and Public Order Act the so-called right to silence was abolished.[3])

In 1982–1983 the furious debate over the Bill was mainly about whether the police should have the right to ask to see a doctor's files or the priest's notes of what transpired in the confessional or the records of a citizen's advice bureau. The number of times per year that the police would want to exercise such powers must be rather small, but the heat of the debate suggested that the Government were proposing a serious invasion of fundamental principles. Even the bishops got involved. Eventually the Government retreated and, in addition, amended the Bill on many other less highly publicised issues. The first Bill failed to pass however because the Prime Minister called a General Election in May 1983 when it was just completing its Report stage in the House of Commons. At that point a very large number of government amendments had been incorporated in the Bill but a large number of other government amendments which were already tabled had not been reached.

The new Home Secretary Mr Leon Brittan then spent the summer months considering the Bill. In October 1983 when he unveiled his Bill Mark II it was found to have included not only all the government amendments that had already been tabled but a considerable number of further amendments which in some respects departed from policies of his predecessor in office. Thereafter the process of argument and debate continued with interest groups such as the National Council for Civil Liberties assisting the Labour Opposition to mount a sustained campaign against the Bill. The Committee stage in the House of Commons broke the record for the highest number of sittings. But, in spite of all the sound and fury in both Houses and in spite of the fact that the Government moved hundreds of amendments to its own Bill, on the whole they were of relatively minor import. The Act as it finally emerged at the end of October 1984 was very recognisable as the Bill which was first unveiled a year previously in October 1983.

---

[3] See Chapter 13.

The whole exercise was an impressive example of the democratic system working. The subject was taken off the shelf by the Labour Government when it set up the Philips Royal Commission in 1977. The Commission had its first meeting in early 1978 and three years later, after taking vast quantities of evidence, it had produced a report together with a substantial series of research volumes. There was extensive debate about the proposals before the Conservative Government introduced first one and then a second Bill. Both Bills were massively amended by the Government itself. In a few instances the amendments were made because the Government was swept off course by political tides that were too strong to resist. This was true in particular of the changes made to the first Bill in regard to the search for confidential material and the change in the second Bill giving police officers appealing from serious disciplinary proceedings the right to legal representation (on which the Police Federation formed an unholy alliance with the Law Society and the National Council for Civil Liberties!). But, the vast majority of the amendments were moved by the Government because ministers and officials were persuaded that they represented genuine improvements in the proposed legislation. The Home Office, throughout, showed itself willing to listen and to respond constructively to suggestions from a wide variety of bodies and individuals.

Now, after the Act has been in force for many years, it is possible to get a sense of its impact—partly from the case law, partly from empirical research and partly from the views about the Act's operation expressed by a variety of commentators and concerned organisations. In 1991 the Government established the Runciman Royal Commission on Criminal Justice.[4] Its very wide terms of reference were to "examine the effectiveness of the criminal justice system in England and Wales in securing the conviction of those guilty of criminal offences and the acquittal of those who are innocent, having regard to the efficient use of resources". The Runciman Royal Commission, of which the writer was a member, received mountains of evidence. None of that evidence called into question the basic structure created by PACE. It had clearly been accepted by all as legislation that will be with us into the indefinite future.

The Joint Home Office and Cabinet Office Review of PACE

In May 2002 Mr David Blunkett, the Home Secretary, unexpectedly announced what he called "a fundamental review of PACE" to be conducted jointly by the Home Office and the Cabinet Office. The terms of reference were:

"To undertake a review of the requirements of the Police and Criminal Evidence Act 1984 (PACE), with particular emphasis on, but not limited to, those aspects which govern detention and the custody process. Without compromising the rights of those that the Act protects, the purpose of the review is to identify possible changes to the rules that could: simplify police procedures; reduce procedural or administrative burdens on the police; save police resources; speed up the process of justice."

---

[4] The Runciman Royal Commission's Report was published in July 1993—Cm.2263, HMSO.

The Joint Review team consisted of four officials from the Police Leadership and Powers Unit in the Home Office and three members of the Cabinet Office's Public Sector Team Regulatory Impact Unit. Their Report stated (p.49) that initially interviews were conducted with PACE "experts"[5] and with "frontline staff working in the criminal justice system" (p.10). There were three "stakeholder workshops"—respectively with the police,[6] the "legal profession",[7] and the "wider criminal justice/civil liberties community".[8] The academic "PACE experts" were not invited to the workshops.

The Joint Review's Report (referred to throughout this work as the "Joint Review"), published on November 18, 2002, concluded:

"The general view of the concept of PACE is positive, especially in terms of the way it is viewed as having standardised and professionalised police work. The police are given a clear framework within which to operate, while the provisions of the Act protect the individual. However, there has also been a recognition that PACE requires updating and reorganizing to ensure that it reflects changes in society over the last twenty years. In particular, to address (*sic*) the commonly held observation that PACE has become increasingly rigid over time as a result of the influence of caselaw and the accumulation of additional legislation."[9]

The last sentence of the above paragraph was the subject of the following puzzling development in the Introduction:

"Frontline staff from both the police and legal profession suggested that a return to the original fluidity of the PACE framework was desirable. This could be achieved by allowing the police more discretion, and encouraging them to use their professional judgment, although clear boundaries would have to be retained. Other commentators suggested allowing the judges more discretion to interpret PACE principles."[10]

There was no explanation of what was meant by the "original fluidity of the PACE framework", nor were examples given of matters on which either the police or the judges might usefully be given more discretion.

The Joint Review addressed a total of 43 separate issues. In regard to each topic it briefly indicated the nature of the issue, the "Options Proposed" for dealing with it (presented in bullet point form), the recommended action ("Preferred Actions") and the proposed timescale. (As already noted, some items were included in the Criminal Justice Act 2003.) Each topic was despatched tersely in summary form with no discussion of pros and cons nor argument to justify conclusions.[11]

---

[5] The writer was one of the eight listed. The interview lasted about ten minutes on the telephone.

[6] Including the Association of Police Authorities, the Association of Chief Police Officers (ACPO), the Superintendents' Association and the Police Federation.

[7] Including the CPS, the Law Society and the Magistrates' Association but not the Criminal Bar Association or the Bar Council.

[8] Including JUSTICE, Liberty, the Police Complaints Authority, and the Criminal Cases Review Commission.

[9] Joint Review, Executive Summary, para.5.

[10] Joint Review, Ch.1, para.6.

[11] See further Zander, "The Joint Review of PACE—a Deplorable Report", *New Law Journal*, February 14, 2003, p.204.

One of the more remarkable passages in the Report of the Joint Review was the 15 lines or so (p.35) on the caution and the right to silence. The issue was posed in four short sentences:

"Police suggested to the Review that the capacity to draw inferences from silence is rarely used in practice. Both police and legal professionals stated that they felt judges were unwilling to direct a jury towards adverse inferences from silence. Additionally, police suggested that solicitors have found a way around this by using prepared statements. Legal professionals agreed that prepared statement were used by some 'unscrupulous solicitors' to protect their clients."

There were two Options Proposed: "Strengthen the police/CPS's ability to have adverse inferences drawn to the attention of the court. Issue clearer guidelines on the caution." The Review's Preferred Action: "There is need for a definitive discussion on this matter with key stakeholders, mediated by a recognised authoritative figure to determine a clear course of action." The Timescale: "Discussion should be completed and a way forward decided by early 2003." (The Report it will be recalled was published in November 2002.) Those words represent the totality of the Joint Review's consideration of this large and important topic.

So far as this writer is aware no such meeting to discuss the matter has been held. Nor has the suggestion that the form and nature of the PACE Codes of Practice be radically altered (yet) been acted upon. But, as was noted in the Preface, in August 2004 the Home Office produced its Consultation Paper, *Policing: Modernising Police Powers to Meet Community Needs*, making a raft of new proposals for changes to PACE many of which are reflected in the Serious Organised Crime and Police Bill introduced by the Government in November 2004.

And so the story continues.

CONTENTS

Contents

TABLE OF CASES

Table of Cases

Table of Cases

Table of Cases

Table of Cases

Table of Cases

Table of Cases

Table of Cases

Table of Cases

Table of Cases

Table of Cases

Table of Cases

Table of Cases

Table of Cases

TABLE OF STATUTES

Table of Statutes

Table of Statutes

Table of Statutes

COMMENTARY ON THE ACT

POWERS TO STOP AND SEARCH

Stop and search is a contentious topic that bristles with problems—though few of these have so far reached the courts. The problems are mainly in the domain of application of the law on the street.   **1–01**

Human Rights Act 1998

There is no provision of the European Convention on Human Rights (ECHR) that deals specifically with stop and search. Article 5 which deals with arrest and detention might be relevant in the rare case where a person is stopped for a sufficiently significant time for it to count as a deprivation of liberty. Article 14 provides that the rights and freedoms of the Convention are to be secured without discrimination on any grounds including sex, race, colour, language, religion, national or social origin or association with a national minority. Since allegations of discrimination, especially on grounds of race, are frequently an issue in debates on stop and search, Art.14 might possibly be relevant to a claim of infringement of one's Art.5 right to liberty and security of person or one's Art.8 right to enjoy privacy.   **1–02**

Definition of powers of stop and search: s.1[1]

The Philips Royal Commission's Report

Powers of stop and search have been given by statute for centuries.[2] A common modern example is the power under the Misuse of Drugs Act 1971, s.23 which gives a constable the power to search someone and to detain him for that purpose if he has reasonable grounds to suspect him of being in possession of a controlled drug.   **1–03**

---

[1] In the Police and Criminal Evidence (Northern Ireland) Order 1989 the equivalent numbered article is art.3. (The Order is referred to throughout the book as the "1989 N.I. PACE Order".)
[2] For a full list at that time see Philips Royal Commission on Criminal Procedure, *Law and Procedure Volume* (Cmnd.8092–1 (1981)). (The Philips Royal Commission's Report is referred to throughout in the footnotes as "Philips Report".)

The Philips Royal Commission identified two main defects in the existing law. First, police powers to stop and search varied from one part of the country to another. In London, for instance, the police could use the powers under s.66 of the Metropolitan Police Act 1839 to stop and search for stolen goods and similar local powers existed in Birmingham, Manchester, Liverpool and Rochdale, but equivalent powers did not exist in most other parts of the country. Secondly, existing powers were either inadequate or at best uncertain and required clarification or redefinition. There were some statutes that gave the police powers to stop and search but in other situations the police lacked powers they needed. The police said, "they frequently [had] to lay themselves open to the risk of civil action by stopping and searching in circumstances where they [had] no power to do so but where equally they [would] be criticised for failing to act. One example cited [was] the carrying of offensive weapons by football supporters."[3]

1–04 The Philips Royal Commission proposed, first, that the police should be given a uniform power of stop and search throughout England and Wales and, secondly, that this should replace all existing powers. The new power would cover searches in a public place of anyone reasonably suspected of conveying stolen goods or of being in possession of anything whose possession in a public place was of itself a criminal offence—for example, prohibited drugs, firearms or housebreaking implements.[4] The main innovation, the Philips Royal Commission said, would be in relation to offensive weapons, though the Prevention of Crimes Act 1953 already gave the police some powers in this regard. That Act made it an offence to carry offensive weapons in a public place without lawful authority or reasonable excuse but the police power of arrest in this connection arose only if the suspect's name and address could not be ascertained or to prevent an offence in which an offensive weapon might be used. The proposed new power permitted search simply on the basis that someone was reasonably suspected of being in possession of offensive weapons.

The topic of stop and search led to the biggest row in the deliberations of the Philips Royal Commission, with two members (Mr Jack Jones, former General Secretary of the Transport and General Workers Union, and Canon Wilfrid Wood, a black magistrate) dissenting. They were concerned that the majority's proposal created a danger of random and discriminatory searches "which could further worsen the relationship between the police and young people, particularly black youth".[5] The majority of the Philips Royal Commission thought, however, that safeguards could be introduced to reduce the danger of random and discriminatory searches. They took the view that "if Parliament has made it an offence to be in possession of a particular article in a public place, the police should be able to stop and search persons suspected on reasonable grounds of committing that offence".[6]

PACE and Code A

1–05 The Government accepted the Philips Royal Commission's recommendation that stop and search powers should extend to offensive weapons. It also accepted that

---

[3] Philips Report, para.3.15.
[4] Philips Report, para.3.20.
[5] Philips Report, para.3.21.
[6] Philips Report, para.3.21.

stop and search powers should be uniform throughout the country. But it did not agree with the Commission's recommendation that one single new statutory provision should replace all existing statutory powers of stop and search.

The Act gives the police the power to search "any person or vehicle" and "anything which is in or on a vehicle, for stolen or prohibited articles" and to detain a person or vehicle for the purpose of such a search (s.1(2)). A constable may not, however, search a person or vehicle under s.1 "unless he has reasonable grounds for suspecting that he will find stolen or prohibited articles" (s.1(3)). Any stolen or prohibited article found in the course of such a search may be seized (s.1(6)). The section does not deal with anything else found in the course of such a search.

The phrase "stolen articles" is not defined. It is not clear whether it includes not only articles acquired contrary to ss.1–7 of the Theft Act 1968, but also those obtained or acquired contrary to s.15 which covers obtaining by criminal deception and s.22 which covers handling stolen goods.

An article is defined as being "prohibited" for the purpose of the statute if it is either an offensive weapon or it is "made or adapted for use" in the course of or in connection with burglary, theft, taking a motor vehicle or other conveyance (such as a bicycle) without authority or obtaining property by deception or is intended by the person having it with him for such use by him or by some other person (s.1(7)). (The fact that obtaining property by deception is specifically mentioned here rather suggests that "stolen articles" in s.1(2) does not include property obtained by deception.) An offensive weapon is defined as meaning "any article made or adapted for use for causing injury to persons or intended by the person having it with him for such use by him or by some other person" (s.1(9)). This definition was taken from the Prevention of Crime Act 1953, s.1. It has two categories—items that are offensive weapons *per se* and items that are not offensive weapons but that are intended to be used as such. If the item is in the former category, the prosecution need only prove that the defendant had it with him to put the onus onto the accused to show that he had a lawful excuse. (There has been a considerable case law as to what counts as an offensive weapon *per se*.[7]) If it is in the second category, the prosecution has to prove also that the accused intended it to be used to cause injury by himself or someone else. **1–06**

The Criminal Justice Act 1988, s.139 expanded the concept of offensive weapons. The object was to make unlawful *per se* mere possession, in a public place without lawful authority or reasonable excuse, of most knives. The onus is therefore on the carrier to show that he had a reasonable excuse. It applies to any article which has a blade or is sharply pointed—with the exception of folding pocket knives with a blade of less than three inches. Subsection (5) states that, without prejudice to the generality of the defence of good reason or lawful authority in subs.(4), it would be a valid defence to have such a knife for use at work or for religious reasons or as part of any national costume. There is no specific exception for items carried in connection with sports such as javelins, darts or fishing tackle.

The case law on the Prevention of Crime Act 1953[8] makes it clear that the courts will not countenance the carrying of offensive weapons for generalised self-defence unless there is some immediate and identifiable threat. Women are **1–07**

---

[7] See Smith and Hogan, *Criminal Law* (10th ed., Butterworths, 2002), pp.458–460.
[8] *ibid.*

therefore acting unlawfully if they carry knives or other offensive weapons to deal with the possibility of attack in the street. Section 140 of the Criminal Justice Act 1988 added the items covered by s.139 to the list of those for which a stop and search could be made under PACE, s.1.

The Criminal Justice Act 2003, s.1(2) added a provision adding a new category of prohibited article—"offences under section 1 of the Criminal Damage Act 1971 (destroying or damaging property)".[9] The amendment, which was proposed by the Joint Home Office/Cabinet Office Review of PACE,[10] was aimed especially at spray cans used for graffitti. The Serious Organised Crime and Police Bill introduced in November 2004 would add prohibited fireworks to the items that can be the subject of stop and search.[11]

"Reasonable suspicion"

1–08   The Act (s.1(3)) requires that stops and searches be based on reasonable grounds and the requirement of reasonable grounds and reasonable suspicion are critical to the operation of this power. (As will be seen, later statutes[12] now give the police the right, in some circumstances, to stop and search without reasonable suspicion (see paras 1–13, 1–38 below).)

"Reasonable suspicion" is not defined in the Act but the subject is dealt with in detail in Code A, the Code of Practice on stop and search. Code A was re-issued as from April 1, 2003, in a revised form in light of new research on stop and search (see paras 1–46—1–52 below).

The basic rule is that stop and search must be based on some objective evidence and not on hunch, instinct or stereotyping. ("Reasonable grounds for suspicion depend on the circumstances in each case. There must be an objective basis for that suspicion based on facts, information, and/or intelligence which are relevant to the likelihood of finding an article of a certain kind" (Code A, para.2.2[13]).)

1–09   Paragraph 2.2 goes on to specify what cannot amount to reasonable suspicion. It states that "reasonable suspicion can never be supported on the basis of personal factors alone without reliable[14] supporting intelligence or information or some specific behaviour by the person concerned" (para.2.2[15]). So, for example, "a person's race, age, appearance, or the fact that the person is known to have a previous conviction, cannot be used alone or in combination with each other as

---

[9] Adding new subs.(e) to s.1(8) of PACE.
[10] Joint Review, 2002, para.12, p.16.
[11] New subss.1(8B) and (8C) inserted by cl.106 of the Bill.
[12] Criminal Justice and Public Order Act 1994, s.60; Knives Act 1997, s.8; Terrorism Act 2000, s.45(1)(b) (formerly Prevention of Terrorism (Temporary Provisions) Act 1989, s.13A (as amended by s.81 of the Criminal Justice and Public Order Act 1994 and s.1 of the Prevention of Terrorism (Additional Powers) Act 1996), and s.13B (as inserted by s.1 of the Prevention of Terrorism (Additional Powers) Act 1996)).
[13] Formerly para.1.6.
[14] "Reliable" was added in the 2003 version of former para.1.7.
[15] 2003 redraft of former para.1.7.

the reason for searching that person" (para.2.2[16]). Equally, "Reasonable suspicion cannot be based on generalisations[17] or stereotypical images of certain groups or categories of people as more likely to be involved in criminal activity" (*ibid.*).

Reasonable suspicion can sometimes exist without specific information or intelligence and on the basis of some level of generalisation stemming from the behaviour of a person—for instance, where a person is seen at night obviously trying to hide something that may, depending on other circumstances, be related to stolen or prohibited articles being carried (para.2.3[18]).

As from 2003, Code A cautions that reasonable suspicion should normally, however, be linked to "accurate and current intelligence or information, such as information describing an article being carried, a suspected offender, or a person who has been seen carrying a type of article known to have been stolen recently from premises in the area" (para.2.4). Searches based on accurate and current intelligence or information, it says, "are more likely to be effective" (*ibid.*). Targeting searches in an area at specified crime problems increases their effectiveness and minimises the inconvenience to law-abiding members of the public (*ibid.*). Officers are advised that searches are more likely to be effective, legitimate and secure public confidence when reasonable suspicion is based on a range of factors, when up-to-date and accurate intelligence or information is communicated to officers and they are well informed about local crime patterns (para.2.5).

Where there is reliable information or intelligence that members of a group or **1–10** gang habitually carry knives unlawfully or other weapons or controlled drugs and wear distinctive clothing or jewellery, insignias, tattoos or other identifying features, their members can be identified by such distinctive clothing or other features (para.2.6 and Note 9[19]). The implication is that mere membership of the group or gang is sufficient to found reasonable suspicion.

In the 2003 Code an important new introductory section headed "Principles governing stop and search" stated that power to stop and search must be used "fairly, responsibly, with respect for people being searched and without unlawful discrimination" (para.1.1[20]). Officers were reminded that the Race Relations (Amendment) Act 2000 makes it unlawful for police officers to discriminate on the grounds of race, colour, ethnic origin, nationality or national origin when using their powers (*ibid.*). The primary purpose of stop and search powers, it is stated, "is to enable officers to allay or confirm suspicion about individuals without exercising their power of arrest" (para.1.4). Any misuse of the powers is "likely to be harmful to policing and lead to mistrust of the police" (*ibid.*). Officers must also "be able to explain their actions to the member of the public searched" (*ibid.*).

Note 1 states that the Code does not affect the ability of officers to speak to or question a person in the ordinary course of the officer's duties without detaining him or exercising any element of compulsion. ("It is not the purpose of the code to prohibit such encounters between the police and the community with the co-operation of the person concerned and neither does it affect the principle that all

---

[16] 2003 redraft of former para.1.7.
[17] Added in slight redraft of last sentence of former para.1.7.
[18] Redraft of former para.1.6.
[19] Formerly para.1.7AA and Note 1H.
[20] A strengthened version of the opening of former Note 1AA.

citizens have a duty to help police officers to prevent crime and discover offenders" (*ibid.*[21]).) The Code also makes it clear that the fact that a person is thought to be in innocent possession of a stolen or prohibited article does not prevent him being stopped and searched (para.2.7[22]).

"Voluntary searches"

1–11   The police sometimes operate on the basis that if a person consents to a search, PACE does not apply. This concept is plainly open to abuse and could drive the proverbial "coach and four" through the provisions on stop and search. The original Home Office Circular on PACE issued to the police and the courts in 1985[23] said on this subject:

> "In any situation where a constable exercises a power of search under this Act, the co-operation of the citizen should not be taken as implying consent, and the exercise of the power should be noted in the appropriate record. Whilst it is legitimate to invite co-operation from the public in circumstances where there is no power to require it, the subject of a voluntary search must properly understand the position and not be left with the impression that a power is being exercised. Voluntary search must not be used as a device for circumventing the safeguards established in Part I of the Act."

However, not all forces and all personnel concerned took this message to heart. In too many situations the concept of the consensual or voluntary search was used as a way of avoiding the main thrust of the safeguards. An attempt to address this issue was first made in 1991 by a requirement that "in these circumstances, an officer should always make it clear that he is seeking the consent of the person concerned".[24] In 1995, an amendment went considerably further by requiring the officer to say not only that the person need not consent but "*that without his consent he will not be searched*" (*ibid.*[25])! The 1995 version also added, "Juveniles, people suffering from a mental handicap or mental disorder and others who appear not to be capable of giving an informed consent should not be subject to a voluntary search".[26]

1–12   The 2003 version of the Code dropped both the requirement that the person be told that without his consent he cannot be searched, and the specific ban on voluntary searches of juveniles and others deemed incapable of giving consent. Instead, the new preliminary "Principles governing stop and search" state unambiguously:

> "An officer must not search a person, even with his or her consent, where no power to search is applicable. Even where a person is prepared to submit to a search voluntarily, the person must not be searched unless the necessary legal

---

[21] Formerly Note 1B.
[22] Formerly para.1.7A.
[23] No.88/1985, para.1.
[24] Code A, Note 1D(b).
[25] Emphasis supplied.
[26] Note 1E.

power exists, and the search must be in accordance with the relevant power and the provisions of this Code" (para.1.5).

The only exception where an officer does not require a specific power to search applies to searches of persons entering sports grounds or other premises "carried out with their consent given as condition of entry" (*ibid.*).

The position as stated in the Principles means that the concept of voluntary search is now effectively banned for adults as much as for juveniles. A search can only be done lawfully if there is the legal power, including reasonable suspicion, and if the Code is complied with. Note however that the prohibition of voluntary searches applies to "persons". It would seem that it does not apply to other searches—*e.g.* of vehicles.

Stop and search powers without reasonable suspicion

The Criminal Justice and Public Order Act 1994, s.60 gave a police officer in uni- **1–13** form a new power to stop and search pedestrians, vehicles,[27] and their drivers and passengers for offensive weapons or "dangerous instruments"[28] "whether or not he has any grounds for suspecting that the person or vehicle is carrying weapons or articles of that kind" (subss.(4), (5)). These 1994 provisions were enlarged by the Knives Act 1997, s.8,[29] which, *inter alia*, extended the power to Scotland. The power was extended to Northern Ireland by the Anti-terrorism, Crime and Security Act 2001.[30] The pre-conditions for the valid exercise of this power (set out in the Act and in Code A, paras 2.12–2.14) are that:

(1) an officer of the rank of inspector[31] or above reasonably believes that "incidents involving serious violence may take place in any locality in his police area" and that it is expedient to authorise such powers to prevent their occurrence (subs.(1)(a)) or that persons are carrying dangerous instruments or offensive weapons in any locality in his police area without good reason (subs.(1)(b), Code A, para.2.12);

(2) such authority is given in regard to any place in that locality for a period up to 24 hours (*ibid.*, Code A, para.2.13);

(3) the period authorised should be no longer than appears reasonably necessary to prevent incidents of serious violence (Code A, para.2.13);

---

[27] The section extends also to ships, aircraft and hovercraft (s.60(7)).

[28] "Dangerous instruments" are defined as "instruments which have a blade or are sharply pointed" (s.60(11)).

[29] This section was brought into force as from March 1, 1999.

[30] s.96 of the 2001 Act inserted a new Art.23B into the Public Order (Northern Ireland) Order 1987 (SI 1987/463). Art.23C, added by s.97 of the 2001 Act, enabled the Secretary of State to make regulations to govern the retention and disposal of things seized under new Arts 23A and 23B.

[31] Originally the power normally required the authorisation of a superintendent—see Knives Act 1997, s.8(2) and (3).

> (4) the authority is given in written form specifying the locality, the period covered and the grounds[32] (subs.(9), Code A, para.2.13).

The power applies therefore in two situations. One is where serious violence in that locality is predicted in the very near future. The other is in the much more nebulous situation where people are known to be carrying knives or other "dangerous instruments" in the area.

1–14   The power does not apply retrospectively to incidents that have already occurred. It applies only prospectively to incidents that it is thought will occur. However, incidents that have occurred may provide a basis for a concern that they will occur again. Situations involving racial violence would be an obvious example.

The Code (Note 11) states that authorisation under s.60 must have an objective basis, for instance, intelligence or relevant information such as a history of antagonism between particular groups or previous incidents of violence at or connected with particular events or locations.

It is for the authorising officer to determine what may reasonably constitute a locality. The Code says that in deciding this the officer "may wish to take into account factors such as the nature and venue of the anticipated incident, the number of people who may be in the immediate area of any possible incident, their access to surrounding areas and the anticipated level of violence" (Code A, Note 13[33]). He should not set a wider area than he believes necessary for the purpose of preventing the anticipated violence (*ibid.*).

1–15   If the authorising officer is an inspector, he must, as soon as practicable, ensure that an officer of the rank of superintendent or above is notified.[34] The authorisation can be extended for up to 24 hours[35] if it appears to an officer of the rank of superintendent that it is expedient to do so "having regard to offences which have, or are reasonably suspected to have, been committed in connection with any activity[36] falling within the authorisation" (subs.(3)). Only one extension is permitted, so further use of the power requires fresh authorisation (Code A, Note 12).

The original authorisation and any extension must be in writing (subs.(9)) but where advance written authority for an extension is not practicable, it must be recorded in writing as soon as practicable (*ibid.*).

A similar power to stop and search persons and vehicles without reasonable grounds to suspect exists in regard to prevention of terrorism. It exists in regard to ports and airports[37] and in regard to stop and search in the street provided a specific area has been earmarked by a senior officer—see para.1–38 below.

---

[32] The grounds were added by Knives Act 1997, s.8(6).
[33] Formerly Note 1G.
[34] Knives Act 1997, s.8(5) inserting a new subs.(3A) into s.60 and Code A, para.2.18.
[35] Knives Act 1997, s.8(4), Code A, para.2.18. Previously, the maximum was six hours.
[36] Knives Act 1997, s.8(4)(b). Previously, "any incident".
[37] Terrorism Act 2000, Sch.7, para.8(a).

Search of persons in the exercise of the power to search premises

There are also situations where an officer has power to search persons without **1–16**
prior specific grounds to suspect anything arising out of the power to search
premises. Under the Criminal Justice Act 1988, s.139B a constable may enter
school premises and search both the school and anyone there for any bladed or
pointed article or offensive weapon. Equally, under a warrant issued under the
Misuse of Drugs Act 1971, s.23(3) officers searching premises for drugs may also
search persons if the warrant specifically authorises it. Code A as revised in 2003
states that although no specific grounds to suspect are required "it is still necessary to ensure that the selection and treatment of those searched under these powers is based upon objective factors connected with the search of the premises, and
not upon personal prejudice" (para.2.29).

Not a power to stop and question but . . .

The power conferred by PACE, s.1 is a power to stop and search—not a power to **1–17**
stop and question. (Terrorism legislation specifically includes a power to stop and
question.[38]) However, a police officer can always try to engage a citizen in conversation and it is obviously desirable that the citizen not be subjected to a search
if the officer's suspicions can be allayed. In *Daniel v Morrison*[39] the Divisional
Court held that the power under s.66 of the Metropolitan Police Act 1839 to stop,
search and detain anyone suspected of having stolen goods included the power to
question him as well, though only briefly. See to the same effect *Green*[40] in relation to stop and search for prohibited drugs under the Misuse of Drugs Act 1971.
Code A says, "Before carrying out a search the officer may ask questions about
the person's behaviour or presence in circumstances which gave rise to the suspicion" (para.2.9[41]). Section 2(1) of the Act makes the same point when it says
that a constable need not conduct a search of someone whom he has detained if
it appears to him subsequently that no search is required. (See to like effect, Code
A, para.2.10.[42]) The police are therefore not legally at fault if they stop and do not
search, but the legality of the stop depends on whether there were or were not
grounds for reasonable suspicion before the stop was made.

Code A makes it clear that a person should only be detained against his will if
there are grounds for suspicion beforehand. ("Reasonable grounds for suspicion
however cannot be provided retrospectively by such questioning during a person's detention or by refusal to answer any questions put"[43] and "There is no
power to stop or detain a person in order to find grounds for a search".[44])

This rule is, however, commonly honoured in the breach. ("By now, custom **1–18**
and practice seem generally to sanction searches where the grounds developed

---

[38] The Terrorism Act 2000, s.89 gives the police the power to stop a person for "so long as is necessary to question him to ascertain (a) his identity and movements; (b) what he knows about a recent
explosion . . .; (c) what he knows about a person killed or injured in a recent explosion . . .".
[39] (1979) 70 Cr.App.R. 142.
[40] [1982] Crim.L.R. 604.
[41] Formerly para.2.2.
[42] Formerly para.2.2.
[43] Para.2.9. Formerly para.2.3.
[44] Para.2.11. Formerly para.2.1.

following a stop."[45]) The issue of retrospective justification for search of the person was the subject in *Black v DPP*.[46] The Court of Appeal quashed the conviction on the ground that merely arriving at the premises of a relative who was a drug dealer was not sufficient ground to suspect that he was in possession of a controlled drug and that subsequent conduct could not provide such ground to suspect. Police officers had a search warrant to search the brother's home. The defendant arrived during the search. The police said they thought he might have come for the purpose of buying or selling drugs. They invited him in with a view to his being searched. He became aggressive and tried to leave. He was arrested and charged with obstruction under the Misuse of Drugs Act 1971. The Court of Appeal said that on the facts, the police did not have reasonable grounds for suspicion when they detained him and that the defendant's behaviour after he was detained could not retrospectively provide reasonable grounds. Similarly, in *Samuels v Commissioner of the Police for the Metropolis*[47] the Court of Appeal allowed an appeal in a civil action for damages by the defendant who had forcibly resisted an officer who tried to search him for suspected possession of a prohibited article, a screwdriver. The issue was whether the officer had had reasonable grounds for suspicion. The court held that if the officer did not have such grounds before he came up to the suspect, the fact that the suspect walked away without answering the officer's question as to where he was going could not turn an unreasonable suspicion into a reasonable one. (When asked where he was going, he just said "It's a free country. I can go where I want.")

On the other hand, the 2003 Code added a new provision to cover the situation where suspicion justifying a search emerges during the course of an encounter which did not begin as stop and search. ("Police officers have many encounters with members of the public which do not involve detaining people against their will. If reasonable grounds for suspicion emerge during such an encounter, the officer may search the person, even though no grounds existed when the encounter began" (para.2.11).) Thus, "If an officer is detaining someone for the purpose of a search he or she should inform the person as soon as the detention begins". (*ibid.*).

The line that divides a stop and search that is unlawful because there was no prior reasonable ground of suspicion and a stop and search that is lawful because the encounter started as mere questioning which then generated reasonable grounds of suspicion is rather thin.

Where a stop and search can be conducted

1–19 The power of stop and search can be exercised:

"(a)   in any place to which at the time . . . , the public or any section of the public has access, on payment or otherwise, as of right or by virtue of express or implied permission; or

---

[45] See Marian Fitzgerald, *Searches in London under s.1 of the Police and Criminal Evidence Act 1984* (Metropolitan Police, December 1999), p.66 (emphasis in the original).
[46] [1995] C.O.D. 381, QBD.
[47] Unreported, Case No.CCRTF 98/0410/2, March 3, 1999, CA.

(b)   in any other place to which people have ready access . . . but which is
        not a dwelling" (s.1(1)).

Subsection (a) would cover places such as parks, streets, roads and car parks and,
while open to the public, shops, pubs and sports grounds. Subsection (b) would
cover places such as school yards or gardens that are readily accessible from the
street. So the police can stop and search someone who has aroused reasonable
suspicion who is lurking in a garden next to the road. However, the section makes
it clear that if a person is in a garden or yard or other land attached to a dwelling-
house, the officer cannot search him unless he has reason to believe that he does
not live there and that he does not have the express or implied permission of the
person who lives there to be on the premises (s.1(4)). Similar provisions apply
equally to a search of a vehicle (s.1(5)). In other words, people and their cars are
not to be searched on their own private land.

Safeguards regarding stop and search powers: s.2[48] and Code A, s.3

Section 2 sets out the procedural safeguards relating to stop and search powers,   **1–20**
both under the Act and under any other statutory provisions. These procedural
safeguards apply therefore not only to the police exercising their powers under
PACE, but also to all the various other statutory powers of stop and search and to
similar powers enjoyed by other forces such as the British Transport Police and
the Port of London Police. They do not apply, however, to police at airports, ports
and similar places ("statutory undertakers") where vehicles come in and out constantly and routine checks are a regular feature of the movements of such vehicles (s.2(2)(b) and s.6). Nor do they apply to stop and search under the Aviation
Act 1982, s.27(2).

The provisions of s.2 and Code A broadly followed the recommendations of
the Philips Royal Commission. The first is that before searching a person or vehicle or detaining a person or vehicle for the purpose of such a search, the officer
must take reasonable steps to bring to the person's attention the fact that he is
being detained for that purpose, give his name (in terrorism cases or otherwise
where the officer reasonably believes that giving his name would put him in danger, his number[49]), the legal search power being exercised and a clear explanation
of the purpose of the search (in terms of the articles being sought). Where the
search requires reasonable suspicion, the grounds of that suspicion must be
stated. Where the search does not require reasonable suspicion, the nature of the
power and that necessary authorisation has been given must be explained (s.2(3);
Code A, para.3.8[50]).

The courts take this requirement seriously. In *Fennelley*[51] the prosecution was   **1–21**
unable to establish that the defendant had been told why he was stopped,
searched and arrested in the street. The evidence of the search which produced

[48] See 1989 N.I. PACE Order, Art.4.
[49] Code A, para.3.8(b).
[50] A redraft of former para.2.4.
[51] [1989] Crim.L.R. 142 (Crown Court at Acton).

some jewellery was excluded at the trial. The evidence of two packets of heroin found in his underpants during a strip search at the police station was also excluded for the same reason. In *Osman*[52] the officers had failed to inform O of their names and station before forcibly searching him, in breach of s.2(3)(a). O had resisted and had been charged with assault on two police officers in execution of their duty. The stop and search was one not requiring reasonable grounds to suspect.[53] The Divisional Court quashed the conviction. The words of s.2(3)(a) were mandatory, so any search initiated without prior compliance with the duty to provide the required information was unlawful. Any search, even one on reasonable suspicion, was a trespass requiring proper justification and doubly so when the search was conducted under powers that did not require reasonable suspicion. The officers had not been acting in the course of their duty.[54]

If the officer is not in uniform, he must produce documentary evidence that he is a police officer (para.3.9[55]). The officer must also inform the person being searched (or the owner or person in charge of the vehicle to be searched) that he is entitled to a record of the search and, if it is not given immediately, to which police station he should apply to get the record (para.3.10[56]). However, this duty need not be performed if it appears to the officer that it is not practicable to make a record—for instance because of the size of the group involved (s.2(4)). If the person to be searched, or in charge of the vehicle to be searched, does not understand what is being said, the officer must take "reasonable steps" to bring the information to his attention (para.3.11[57]).

If the search is of an unattended vehicle, the officer must leave a notice stating that he has searched the vehicle, giving the name of his police station, stating that an application for compensation for any damage done should be made to that station and that the owner can request a copy of the record of the search (s.2(6)).

Length of detention for stop and search

1–22 The time for which someone may be detained is limited to such time as is reasonably necessary to permit the search to be carried out there or nearby (s.2(8)). The time must be kept to a minimum (Code A, para.3.3[58]). Code A (para.3.3) states that where the power of stop and search requires reasonable suspicion, the thoroughness of the search depends on what is suspected of being carried. If it relates to an article which is seen to be slipped into a pocket, the search should be limited to that pocket, unless there are other grounds of suspicion or there has been an opportunity for the item to have been moved elsewhere. In the case of a small article, such as drugs, capable of being easily concealed, a more extensive

[52] *Osman (Mustapha) v Southwark Crown Court*, unreported, Case No.CO/2318/98, 1999, DC.
[53] Under the Criminal Justice and Public Order Act 1994, s.60 (see para.1–13 above).
[54] In *McCarthy* [1996] Crim.L.R. 818, CA the police stopped a vehicle as a result of a surveillance operation in a drugs investigation but told the occupants that it was a routine stop. The Court of Appeal upheld the trial judge's decision that the subterfuge was not a substantial breach of the Act or the Code and that evidence of £50,000 in cash in the car was admissible. But there was reasonable suspicion from the outset.
[55] Formerly para.2.5.
[56] Formerly para.2.6.
[57] Formerly para.2.7.
[58] Changed from it should not extend beyond the time for the search—former para.3.3.

search may be necessary. Where the search does not require reasonable suspicion, officers "may make any reasonable search to look for items which they are empowered to search for" (*ibid.*).

Manner of search

The Code states that all stops and searches "must be carried out with courtesy, consideration and respect for the person concerned" and that "every reasonable effort must be made to minimise the embarassment that a person being searched may experience" (para.3.1[59]). The person's co-operation must always be sought. A forcible search may only be made if it has been established that the person is unwilling to co-operate or resists (para.3.2). **1–23**

Nature of search

A search in public of a person's clothing must be restricted to a superficial exam- **1–24** ination of outer garments. The 2003 redraft of the Code says that this does not prevent an officer from "placing his or her hand inside the pockets of the outer clothing, or feeling round the inside of the collar, socks and shoes if this is reasonably necessary in the circumstances to look for the object of the search or to remove and examine any item reasonably suspected to be the object of the search" (para.3.5). Where on reasonable grounds it is considered necessary to conduct a more thorough search (for instance by requiring a person to take off a T-shirt), this must be done out of public view, for instance in a police van or at a nearby police station (para.3.6[60]). Any search involving removal of more than outer coat, jacket, gloves, headgear or footwear or any item concealing identity can only be conducted by an officer of the same sex and may not even be made in the presence of the opposite sex unless this is specifically requested (para.3.6[61]).

Removal of clothing and face covering

It is specifically stated (s.2(9)(a)) that no power to stop and search short of arrest **1–25** authorises a police officer to require a person to remove any of his clothing in public other than an outer coat, jacket or gloves (and in Northern Ireland, head-gear[62]). There is, however, nothing to prevent an officer from asking someone to take off more than the statutory minimum voluntarily (Code A, Note 7[63]). There are some statutes that go beyond what PACE permits by way of removal of outer clothing, etc.—see in particular Misuse of Drugs Act 1971, s.23.

In any locality where an authority under s.60 of the Criminal Justice and Public Order Act 1994 (para.1–13 above) has been given, an officer can also demand the removal of a mask or other face covering where he reasonably believes it is being

---

[59] Expanded version of former para.3.1.
[60] Formerly para.3.5.
[61] Formerly para.3.5.
[62] See 1989 N.I. PACE Order, Art.4(10)(a).
[63] Formerly Note 3A.

worn or carried for the purpose of concealing identity.[64] Moreover, the exercise of this power is technically not a search and therefore does not have to comply with the PACE procedural requirements (giving name, name of police station and grounds of search).[65]

The s.60 power can only be exercised on the basis of reasonable belief that incidents of serious violence may take place in the locality. But the power was extended by s.60AA.[66] This provides that an officer of the rank of inspector or above can authorise an officer in uniform to require removal of face coverings concealing identity and the seizure of items used for the purpose in any area if he reasonably believes that "activities may take place in any locality in the officer's police area that are likely to involve commission of offences"[67] and that it is expedient to prevent or control such offences to give such authorisation (Code A, para.2.16). It applies to the commission of any offence. The authorisation is limited to 24 hours but it can be extended for a further 24 hours by a superintendent.[68] The inspector's authorisation must be in writing signed by the officer giving it and stating the grounds on which it is given, the locality and the period covered.[69] The officer exercising the power must reasonably believe that the person is wearing the disguise for the purpose of concealing identity. Where there may be religious sensitivities about asking someone to remove a face covering (or headgear) the officer should permit the item to be removed out of public view. Where practicable it should be an officer of the same sex.[70] A person failing to remove an item when required to do so is liable, on conviction, to imprisonment for a maximum of one month or a level 3 fine.[71] The powers also apply to the British Transport Police Force.[72]

Place of search

1–26   The basic rule of stop and search is that, "The search must be carried out at or near the place where the person or vehicle was first detained" (Code A, para.3.4). This is the case even if it is necessary to search out of public view. A new Note for Guidance states that a person may be detained for the purpose of a search at a place other than where he was first detained "only if that place, be it a police station or elsewhere, is nearby" (Note 6). It should be "within a reasonable travelling distance" by foot or car (*ibid.*)—whatever that means.

A search that goes beyond what is permitted in exercise of the power of stop and search must take place out of public view, for instance, in a police van. The fact that the street is empty at the time does not mean that it is not a public place

---

[64] Power first given by Crime and Disorder Act 1998, s.25(1) but then replaced by the Anti-terrorism, Crime and Security Act 2001, s.94 inserting s.60AA into the 1994 Act.

[65] *DPP v Avery* [2001] EWHC Admin 748; [2002] 1 Cr.App.R. 31; [2002] Crim.L.R. 142.

[66] s.95(1) of the Anti-terrorism, Crime and Security Act 2001 inserted equivalent provisions in the form of new Art.23A into the Public Order (Northern Ireland) Order 1987 (SI 1987/463). See also Code A, paras 2.15–2.18.

[67] s.60AA, subs.(3)(a).

[68] s.60AA, subs.(4).

[69] s.60AA, subs.(6).

[70] Code A, Notes 4 and 8.

[71] subs.(7). Currently £1,000.

[72] s.60AA, subs.(8).

(Note 7). If there is no suitable place for a more extensive search to be conducted, it can only be done at a police station—and, as already stated, that can only be done if one is nearby.

Searches of intimate parts of the body

Searches involving exposure of intimate parts of the body must not be conducted **1–27** during stop and search as a routine extension of a less thorough search simply because nothing is found in the course of an initial search (para.3.7).[73] If the search involves exposure of intimate parts of the body and a police station is not nearby, particular care must be taken to ensure that the location is suitable in the sense that the search can be conducted in accordance with the requirements of the Code.[74] Such a search may not take place in a police vehicle (para.3.7[75]). An intimate search (of bodily orifices) cannot in any circumstances be carried out as part of stop and search (para.3.7).

As will be seen, the police are permitted to search an arrested person's mouth in public.[76] It would seem that this cannot, however, be construed so as to apply also to stop and search. By ordinary canons of statutory interpretation, the fact that the legislature specifically considered the point in regard to search after arrest implies that it intended not to extend search in public where the stop and search powers are being used. If a search of the mouth is indicated by the situation—for instance, the suspect is seen to put a package in his mouth—the officer could arrest him on suspicion of possession and then search him under the s.32 power (see para.3–34 below).

Road traffic stops

PACE, s.2(9)(b) also makes it clear that only a police officer in uniform can law- **1–28** fully require a person driving a vehicle to stop for the purpose of any exercise of a power of stop and search (s.2(9)(b)). The power to require a driver to stop, now under s.163 of the Road Traffic Act 1988, is not affected by s.1 and stopping a vehicle under that provision therefore still does not require the test of reasonable suspicion to be satisfied.

Subsection (10) of s.2 extends the power of stop and search to vessels, aircraft and hovercraft.

Stop and search by Military Police

Each of the armed forces has a force of Service police—the Royal Military **1–29** Police, the Royal Air Force Police, the Royal Navy Regulating Branch and the

---

[73] A new provision introduced in 2003.

[74] Note 6. The requirements of the Code for such a search are set out in Code C, Annex A, dealt with at para.5–08 below.

[75] Formerly para.3.5

[76] By virtue of an amendment to s.32 of PACE in the Criminal Justice and Public Order Act 1994, s.59(2).

Royal Marines Police. Service police cannot exercise statutory powers conferred on constables unless they are specifically applied to them. PACE originally allowed the Secretary of State to apply some of the civilian powers of investigation of offences under military law (see para.11–01 below). The Armed Forces Act 2001 for the first time provided a coherent source of primary legislation for investigative powers including powers of stop and search similar to those in PACE.

Section 2 of the Act gives the Service police the power to stop and search anyone reasonably believed to be subject to the Service Discipline Acts (SDAs)—the Army Act 1955, the Air Force Act 1955 and the Naval Discipline Act 1957. Stop and search applies also to the person's vehicle, whether or not it is a Service vehicle[77] and to Service vehicles driven by a civilian. (Civilian drivers however are not subject to Service law and therefore cannot be searched by Service police.)

The power may only be exercised if the Service policeman has reasonable grounds for believing that he will find stolen or prohibited articles (defined much as in PACE though obviously excluding offensive weapons possessed for Service reasons), unlawfully obtained stores or controlled drugs (subs.(3)). If found, they can be seized (subs.(7)).

1–30   Like s.1 of PACE the power can be exercised in public places or places to which the public have ready access. It can also be exercised in premises occupied or controlled by any of the armed forces (including vessels, aircraft and hovercraft, other than service living accommodation[78] (subs.(1))). However, a person or vehicle in a garden or yard attached to service living accommodation can be searched if the person (or in the case of the vehicle, the person in charge of it) does not live there and is not there with the permission of someone who lives there.[79]

Section 3 is the equivalent of s.2 of PACE. It provides, for instance, that a person or vehicle may only be detained for a period reasonably required to make a search (subs.(1)); that persons cannot be required to remove anything other than an outer coat, jacket or gloves in public (subs.(2)); and that the Secretary of State may make regulations similar to those in ss.2 and 3 of PACE regarding the information to be communicated to the person prior to a search (subs.(3)).

The power to search applies to vessels, aircraft and hovercraft (subs.(5)). They do not apply, however, to premises used for custody, detention or imprisonment (subs.(6)).

Section 4 gives emergency powers of stop and search to the commanding officer or anyone under his command authorised by him. The power can only be exercised by an order for the search of a particular person or vehicle and only if the person giving the order has reasonable grounds for believing that waiting for the service or civilian police would result in a criminal offence being committed or an offender avoiding arrest.

---

[77] s.2(2)(a)(ii), (iii).
[78] Defined in s.15(1) to include the garage, and any room, structure or area used as sleeping accommodation on land (as in barracks) or on a Service vessel, and any locker provided elsewhere for use in connection with such sleeping accommodation.
[79] subss.(4), (5).

Duty to make records concerning searches: s.3[80] and Code A, s.4

The Philips Royal Commission recommended that as a further control against   **1–31**
arbitrary and discriminatory searches, police officers should be under a duty to
make records of what transpired.[81] Also, the individual, it thought, should have a
right to a copy of such a record. The Government accepted both recommendations. An officer who has searched someone under statutory powers of stop and
search (other than a search by a statutory undertaker—for which, see s.6), must
make a written record of the search, "unless there are exceptional circumstances
which make it wholly impracticable",[82] for instance, because of the numbers
involved or in situations of disorder. If the officer is under a duty to make a record
but it is not practicable to make such a record at the time, it must be done "as soon
as practicable afterwards".[83]

A provision added to Code A in the 2003 revision states that if the record is
made at the time, a copy must be given to the person searched (para.4.2).

The Joint Home Office/Cabinet Office Review of PACE reported the police
fear that this stronger onus on providing records to persons on the spot would
"add unnecessarily to burdens on officers". On the other hand, research showed
that "those who are searched strongly welcome the provision of a record on the
spot". Also, being given a credible reason for a search was "important in securing the confidence of the person being searched". The issue, it suggested, should
be monitored and reviewed after a year of operation.[84]

The officer must ask for the name, address and date of birth of the person   **1–32**
searched but, as the Code makes clear, "there is no obligation on a person to provide those details and no power of detention if the person is unwilling to do so".[85]
The written record must always state the following information "even if the person does not wish to provide any personal details"[86]: name (failing which, a
description) of the person searched[87]; the person's self-defined ethnic origin[88];
where a vehicle is searched, its description and registration number; the date,
time and place of the detention and, if different, of the search; the purpose of the
search; the grounds for making it (or where reasonable suspicion was not
required, the nature of the power and of any necessary authorisation); its outcome
(*e.g.* items found, arrest or no further action); details of any injury or damage to
property caused; and the identity of the constable(s) involved, save that in terrorism cases or other cases where officers reasonably believe that recording names

---

[80] See 1989 N.I. PACE Order, Art.5.
[81] Philips Report, para.3.26.
[82] s.3(1); Code A, para.4.1. In s.3(1) it is merely "unless it is not practicable to do so".
[83] Code A, para.4.1, based on s.3(2).
[84] Joint Review, 2002, p.17.
[85] Code A, para.4.2. See also s.3(3).
[86] para.4.3, formerly para.4.5.
[87] s.3(3) and (4).
[88] Note 18 of the 2003 Code states that the person should be asked to select one of the five main categories of ethnic groups (White, Mixed, Asian, Black, Other) and then a more specific cultural background from within this group as set out in the new Annex B (*e.g.* White British, Black Caribbean,
Black African, etc.).

might endanger them,[89] where the warrant or other identification number may be given.

A record is generally required for each person and each vehicle searched—though one record is sufficient if a person and his vehicle are searched and the object and grounds of the search are the same (para.4.5). Where officers detain someone for the purposes of a search but it does not take place because preliminary questions dispel suspicion, the record must still be made (para.4.7, added in the 2003 redraft of Code A).

Anyone who, or whose vehicle, has been searched under stop and search powers is entitled to ask for a copy of the record made (if any is made), providing he asks for it within 12 months (s.3(7), (8) and (9)).

A new duty to record stops not involving a search

1–33   The requirement under PACE to make a record did not apply where a stop did not lead to a search. The Philips Royal Commission took the view that it would not be desirable, practicable or necessary to require the police to record each occasion on which they stop a member of the public, possibly for an informal conversation. ("It is a search following upon a stop and based upon reasonable suspicion that is the main intrusion upon the person and it is that and the reason for it which should be recorded."[90]) The Macpherson Report on the Stephen Lawrence murder recommended that all stops under legislative provisions, including voluntary stops, should be recorded.[91] The Government accepted the recommendation in principle subject to feasibility trials.

The draft Code A circulated for consultation in March 2002 made provision in paras 4.11–4.18 for the recording of stops without searches. They attracted considerable criticism[92] and when Code A was laid before Parliament on November 7, 2002, these paragraphs had been dropped. The Government decided that instead of including them in the 2003 revised version of Code A, they would first be tested in pilots in a number of police areas: Merseyside, Nottinghamshire, West Midlands, Sussex, North Wales and one borough in the Metropolitan Police area. The pilot began on April 1, 2003. Its main aim was to test whether the recording of stops could be made to work in a way that did not unduly increase bureaucracy. (Announcing the pilots, Mr John Denham, Home Office Minister, said the system needed to be implemented "in a way that is least inconvenient and time-consuming for both the police and the individuals concerned". Phased implementation would allow forces to evaluate at each stage the best way to achieve this.[93])

1–34   When the revised Codes were laid before Parliament in April 2004, the recording of stops as provided for in the pilot was included and it became effective as from August 1, 2004. Code A, para.4.11 said that it was left to individual forces

---

[89] An extension from terrorism cases introduced in the 2003 redraft of the Code.
[90] Philips Report, para.3.26.
[91] Report of the Inquiry into the Matters Arising from the Death of Stephen Lawrence, 1999, Recommendation 61.
[92] See for instance, Zander, "One Stop Beyond", *Police Review*, May 3, 2002, p.29.
[93] Home Office Press Release, 292/2002, November 8, 2002.

to decide when to implement the recording of stops providing that all forces did so by April 1, 2005.

It requires a record to be made not of *all* stops, but "when an officer requests a person in a public place to account for themselves, *i.e.* their actions, behaviour, presence in an area or possession of anything" (para.4.12). Unless it is impracticable to do so, a record of the encounter must be made at the time and a copy given to the person questioned (*ibid.*). The Code specifically says that the requirement does not apply to general conversations such as giving directions or seeking witnesses (para.4.13). Nor does it apply where the police are simply seeking general or background information about an incident (*ibid.*), or when a breath specimen is required from a motorist or a fixed penalty ticket is issued (para.4.14). But it does apply even though the person does not provide his personal details (para.4.18). The record must show the identity of the officer, though not of the person stopped; the date, time and place; the registration number of the person's vehicle, if any; the reason for the stop; the person's ethnic background; and the outcome of the encounter (para.4.17). The person must be told that he has a right to a copy of the record of the encounter (para.4.15). If the person requests a record, one must always be made even if the officer thinks the case is outside the criteria (para.4.19).

Monitoring of the records

The Philips Royal Commission recommended that supervising police officers **1–35** should scrutinise figures of searches and their results. They should watch for signs "that searches are being carried out at random, arbitrarily or in a discriminatory way" [94] Moreover, HM Inspectors of Constabulary should give attention to this matter on their annual inspection of each force. Nothing of this appears in the Act. It is obviously appropriate to deal with such matters by internal police regulation, and training. Numbers of stop and searches must be contained in the chief constable's annual report so as to make the application of the powers subject to scrutiny by the police authority, as will be seen in s.5 of the Act. (See further para.1–41 below.)

The former version of Code A said that supervising officers, in monitoring the exercise of officers' stop and search powers, "should consider in particular whether there is any evidence that officers are exercising their discretion on the basis of stereotyped images of certain persons or groups" and that it was important that any such evidence should be addressed (Note 4DA). The 2003 version of Code A had four separate paragraphs on the topic. The first (para.5.1) is an expanded version of former Note 4DA. The second (para.5.2) states that monitoring should also be undertaken by senior officers with area or force-wide responsibilities. The third (para.5.3) says that supervision and monitoring must be backed by comprehensive statistical records at force, area and local level and that any apparently disproportionate use of the powers by particular officers or groups of officers should be the subject of investigation. The fourth (para.5.4) requires that in order to promote public confidence in the use of the powers, forces must, in consultation with police authorities, arrange for the records to be

[94] Philips Report, para.3.26.

scrutinised by community representatives—though the records should not reveal names (Note 19).

The Philips Commission proposed that failure to provide reasons for a search should make the search unlawful which would entitle the person concerned to resist and also to sue for assault. This recommendation was not reflected in the Act.

Road checks: s.4[95]

1–36   The pre-PACE police power to set up road blocks derived from s.159 of the Road Traffic Act 1972 which required drivers to stop when requested to do so by a constable in uniform. There was no mention in the section as to the purpose for which the power could be used. The police used it not only to set up road blocks for road traffic or vehicle excise purposes but also where they believed it to be necessary in connection with a serious crime or when they were hunting an escaped prisoner. Section 159 did not give any power to search a vehicle. The 1972 Act has been repealed and the powers contained in s.159 are now to be found in s.163 of the Road Traffic Act 1988.

Road blocks are inevitably random in their effect and the Philips Royal Commission said that, in general, such powers should not be used in connection with crime. "Infringement of a person's liberty to go about his business should be allowed only on suspicion of his involvement in an offence."[96] But an exception should be made, it thought, for special emergencies. An officer of the rank of assistant chief constable or above should have the power to authorise in writing road checks in two kinds of situation. One would be when a person wanted in connection with a grave offence was thought to be in the area. Secondly, where it was reasonably thought that a grave offence might be committed in a defined area during a specified period. But the power to establish road blocks should not give the police any right to search vehicles. "That would have to be justified in each case by reference to a suspicion on reasonable grounds that there was evidential material in the vehicle."[97]

1–37   The Government departed from the Philips Royal Commission's approach in two main particulars. First, the Act allows authorisation by an officer of the rank of superintendent, or in a case of urgency by an officer of any rank providing it is subsequently reported to a superintendent or above as soon as practicable.[98]

Secondly, the Act substituted the concept of a "serious arrestable offence" for the Philips Royal Commission's concept of a "grave offence". This has relevance at various points in a comparison between the Act and the Royal Commission's report. (For discussion of "serious arrestable offences" including the radical proposal to abolish the concept in the Serious Organised Crime and Police Bill 2004–2005, see paras 11–09—11–12 below. For definition see s.116 and Sch.5.)

---

[95] See 1989 N.I. PACE Order, Art.6.
[96] Philips Report, para.3.30.
[97] Philips Report, para.3.32.
[98] s.4(3), (5), (6) and (7).

The provisions of PACE apply whenever a road check is made to stop all vehicles or vehicles selected by any criterion—such as, for example, all blue Cortinas.[99]

The Act divides road checks under s.163 of the Road Traffic Act 1988 into those involving serious arrestable offences for which the special rules of s.4 are applicable and any other checks. The s.4 road check is permitted to see if a vehicle is carrying someone who has committed a serious arrestable offence, or is a witness to such an offence or someone intending to commit such an offence, or an escaped prisoner.[1] An officer may only authorise a road check under s.4 where it is reasonably suspected that a person suspected of having committed a serious arrestable offence or who is unlawfully at large is or is about to be in the locality; or where the search is for someone intending to commit a serious arrestable offence, that he is or is about to be in the locality.[2] When the road check is for potential witnesses it is only necessary for the superintendent to have reasonable grounds for believing that the offence is a serious arrestable one. Authorisation can only be given for seven days at a time but this can be renewed in writing from time to time for a further period.[3]

There seems little doubt that the s.4 road check is intended to apply where a serious arrestable offence is involved. But it is arguable that (due perhaps to legislative oversight) such a road check could be set up by an officer of a rank below that of superintendent for any offence. As has been seen, subs.(3) requires the authority of a superintendent save where an officer of a lower rank sets up a road block as a matter of urgency under subs.(5). This can be done for one of the purposes specified in subs.(1)—which makes no reference to serious arrestable offences. If a court had to consider the matter, this interpretation might be held to be wrong as contrary to the purpose and thrust of the system of controls established by the section.

Every authorisation of a road check must specify the ground, the period covered, the locality to which it relates and the name of the officer authorising it. It must also mention the serious arrestable offence in question.[4] Where a vehicle is stopped, the person in charge of it is entitled to a written statement of the reason for the road check if he asks for it within 12 months[5] But there is no requirement that he be told of this right.

Road checks which are not under s.4 continue to be legitimate under s.163 of the Road Traffic Act 1988.[6]   **1–38**

It is doubtful whether the provisions of s.4 legitimised the "ring of steel" road blocks set up in the City of London in November/December 1992 to combat an IRA bombing campaign—unless it could be supposed that the police had information that wanted terrorists were or were about to be in the area. The reality was rather that the police had no knowledge of any actual immediate planned bombings but hoped that the road blocks would act as a general deterrent and that

---

[99] s.4(2).
[1] s.4(1).
[2] s.4(4)(c)(ii).
[3] subss.(11), (12).
[4] s.4(10), (13) and (14).
[5] s.4(15).
[6] See *Lodwick v Saunders* [1985] 1 W.L.R. 382.

possibly, by good luck, they might catch some terrorists.[7] Such objectives could hardly be brought within the very restricted terms of s.4.

The position was regularised, first, by s.81 of the Criminal Justice and Public Order Act 1994[8] and then by the Prevention of Terrorism (Additional Powers) Act 1996, s.1(1).[9] The 1989 provisions gave a power to search vehicles and items such as bags carried by pedestrians. The 1996 provision extended the power of search to pedestrians themselves. The power in regard to both is now to be found in the Terrorism Act 2000[10] and Code A.[11] The 2000 Act also has a power to prohibit or restrict parking on roads specified in the authorisation.[12]

In order to prevent acts of terrorism, a senior officer[13] may now therefore authorise stops and searches of persons and vehicles in a specified locality for a period of up to 28 days without any need to have reasonable grounds to suspect. Authorisation cannot be for more than 28 days at a time but it can be renewed.[14] However, the person who gives such authorisation must inform the Secretary of State before the expiry of 48 hours, beginning with the time it was given, and the authorisation lapses at the expiry of the 48 hours unless it is confirmed before then by the Secretary of State.

1–39   Such stops and searches can be carried out by any constable in uniform. It is a summary only offence to fail to stop or wilfully to obstruct a constable in the exercise of these powers.[15] Both the driver and the pedestrian who has been stopped under these powers can ask for a written statement about the search, provided it is asked for within 12 months.[16]

A challenge to the legality of the provisions for random stop and searches under the Terrorism Act by reference to the Human Rights Act failed. The Court of Appeal held that, given the actual possibility of terrorist attacks, the courts would not question the decision of the authorities that a threat existed in a particular place. But the courts had a role in judging the proportionality of the exercise of the power. The onus of demonstrating that the power was used properly lay on the police. In this instance it had not been shown that the police were given specific instructions regarding the way they should exercise the power. The court made no order but urged the Commissioner to take account of the court's ruling.[17]

Is there a general power to set up police cordons?

1–40   It is common for the police to set up a cordon around a crime scene but the legality of this practice is uncertain. Curiously, there is little or no authority on the

---

[7] For a description of other exceptional measures taken to protect the city see Kelly, "By all means necessary", *Police Review*, April 15, 1994. Mr Kelly was the former Commissioner of the City Police.

[8] This added a new s.13A to the Prevention of Terrorism (Temporary Provisions) Act 1989.

[9] This added a new s.13B.

[10] ss.44–47.

[11] paras 2.19–2.26.

[12] ss.48–52.

[13] In the Metropolitan area and the City of London, of the rank of commander or above; elsewhere, of the rank of assistant chief constable or above (Terrorism Act 2000, s.44(4)).

[14] Terrorism Act 2000, s.45(3) and (7).

[15] s.47.

[16] s.45(5).

[17] *R. (Gillan and Quinton) v Commissioner of the Metropolitan Police*, *The Times*, August 12, 2004.

point. The question was explored by the Divisional Court in *DPP v Morrison*.[18] After an incident involving a stabbing, the police set up a cordon in a private shopping mall. M, who tried to enter the cordoned off area, was arrested and charged with an offence under the Public Order Act 1986, ss.5(1) and (6). In the magistrates' court he was convicted but the Crown Court upheld an appeal on the ground that the police had no power to cordon off an area open to the public. On further appeal the prosecution persuaded the Divisional Court that the Crown Court was mistaken. Hooper J. for the Court said:

> "it would be surprising if, having regard to the duty of the police to bring offenders to justice, officers could not preserve intact the scene of a serious offence, such as a wounding, until that scene could be examined by specialist scenes of crime officers, and it is common knowledge that when an incident occurs in a public place police officers do habitually seek to preserve the scene, either by asking people to keep away or by erecting some form of barrier to cordon off the area or areas they want to preserve. The detailed analysis of a scene of crime for weapons, fingerprints, footprints, DNA, the distribution of blood, fibres etc is vital both in the interests of the public, of the victim of a crime or his family and of any potential defendant. All could have a legitimate right to complain if vital evidence was not preserved." ([15])

Of course, the fact that common sense suggested the desirability of such a power did not mean that it existed. The Divisional Court held however that the police were entitled to proceed on the assumption that the owner of the private land would consent to the setting up of the cordon and would want to assist the police. It even suggested that maybe such consent could not lawfully be withheld.[19] In any event, the Court said, it was "very probable" that a temporary obstruction of the right of public access for this purpose was lawful. ([23])

Reports of recorded searches and road checks: s.5[20]

The chief officer's annual report must contain information about the use made by   **1–41** his force of powers of stop and search and of road checks set up for purposes other than those of road traffic and vehicle excise duties. As the Philips Royal Commission said, this would make the exercise of such powers subject to the independent scrutiny of the police authority and of HM Inspectors. Information about searches does not give details of individual cases but it includes the total number of searches in each month for stolen articles and offensive weapons and for other prohibited articles and the total numbers arrested in each month in respect of each such category (s.5(2)). The information about road blocks must include the reasons for and the result of each road check (s.5(3)).

---

[18] [2003] EWHC 683 Admin. For discussion see the note after the report of the decision [2003] Crim.L.R. 727 at 728–730.
[19] The Court cited Lord Denning's dictum in *Ghani v Jones* [1970] 1 Q.B. 693 at 708 that "the police should be able to do whatever is necessary and reasonable to preserve the evidence of the crime".
[20] See 1989 N.I. PACE Order, Art.7.

Statistics and research

(1) Stop and search under PACE

1–42   The Home Office produces an annual Statistical Bulletin giving the data required by the Act.[21] At the time of writing, the latest of these, giving the figures for 2003–2004 was published in December 2004.

There are two problems with these figures. The first is that the police record only a proportion (and probably a fairly small proportion) of the stops and searches they are required to record.[22] Secondly, as noted above, to date, the requirement has been to record only stops and searches—not stops which do not lead to searches. The 1983 pre-PACE Home Office research study (Willis, 1983) suggested (p.22) that only a quarter of stops led to searches being carried out.

Whatever they mean, the official statistics for the first 13 years showed a consistent annual increase in the numbers of recorded stops and searches[23]—rising from some 110,000 in 1986 to just over a million in 1998–1999. But the figures for the two subsequent years showed a drop to 857,000 in 1999–2000 and to 714,000 in 2000–2001.[24] It was widely believed that the drop in the use of stop and search was at least in part a reaction to the strictures about racially discriminatory policing made by the Macpherson Report into the Stephen Lawrence case. For whatever reason, in 2001–2002 the number rose to 741,000 including 27,000 stops and searches of vehicles and the following year rose again to 895,000, but in 2003–2004 it dropped back to 730,000.[25]

1–43   The reasons recorded for stops and searches have remained remarkably stable over the years. The most common reasons are drugs (in 2003–2004, 43 per cent) and stolen property and "going equipped" (40 per cent). All the other categories (firearms, offensive weapons and miscellaneous) account in aggregate for around 17 per cent. Offensive weapons, which provoked such controversy at the time of the Philips Royal Commission's Report, currently accounts for a mere 8 per cent.

The overall "hit-rate", namely the proportion of stops and searches leading to an arrest, has fluctuated slightly from year to year. In the period 1986 to 1990 it was 15 to 18 per cent. It then steadily declined. In the years 1991 to 1993 it was between 15 and 13 per cent, and between 1994 and 1998–1999 it was between 12 and 10 per cent. In 1999–2000 and again in 2000–2001 and 2001–2002 it was up

---

[21] Formerly called *Operation of Certain Police Powers under PACE* but as from October 2001 entitled *Arrests for Notifiable Offences and Operation of Certain Police Powers under PACE, England and Wales.*

[22] Dixon *et al.* (1990) reported that officers said they might carry out up to four or five stops and searches in one shift. Yet the national figures for stops and searches show under 10 per officer per year.

[23] There is no way of knowing whether this reflects more stops and searches or only more recording of stops and searches—or both. See also the periodic British Crime Survey; the two surveys conducted in Islington (Crawford *et al.*, 1990); the survey conducted in Hammersmith and Fulham (Painter *et al.*, 1989); and the study by Professor Keith Bottomley and colleagues (Bottomley *et al.*, 1991).

[24] Home Office Statistical Bulletin, *Operation of Certain Police Powers under PACE, England and Wales 2003–2004* (Home Office, 2004), Table PA, p.9.

[25] *ibid.*

to 13 per cent which the Statistical Bulletin suggested might be due to a more targeted approach following the Macpherson Report. However, the proportion varies considerably from one offence category to another.

Overall, under a tenth of all arrests are the result of stop and search—though in London it is rather more and outside London somewhat less.[26]

A Home Office study of over 3,000 arrests showed that stop and search accounted for 11 per cent.[27]

The Home Office Statistical Bulletins show wide variations in the policy of different forces in regard to stop and search (or at least the recording of stop and search) as judged by the number per 100,000 of the population.

(2) Stops and searches under other powers

As has been seen (see para.1–13 above), the Criminal Justice and Public Order **1–44**
Act 1994, s.60 introduced new powers to stop vehicles and persons in anticipation of violence without reasonable grounds to suspect. The annual total number of such stops and searches for the years from 1996 to 2000 was of the order of 5,000–8,000, some 3 per cent of which led to an arrest. In 2000–2001, however, the number increased to 11,300 and in 2001–2002 it rose to 18,900.[28] The following year, no doubt reflecting heightened concerns in the aftermath of "9/11", it more than doubled to 44,100, and in 2003–2004 it was 40,000.[29] The proportion of such stops and searches leading to an arrest was 6 per cent[30] in 2000–2001 and 2002–2003 and 4 per cent in 2001–2002 and 2003–2004.[31] Similar powers to make random stops and searches of vehicles, their occupants and of pedestrians in order to prevent acts of terrorism[32] were used in over 40,000 instances in 1996 and 1997. In 1999–2000 there were only 1,900 such stops and searches, reflecting the lower level of terrorist violence—but in 2000–2001 it went up to 6,400 and in 2001–2002 rose sharply to 10,200. Again no doubt because of "9/11" it rose sharply in 2002–2003 to 32,100 and in 2003–2004 to 33,800.[33] Understandably, the proportion of stops and searches resulting in arrests under these powers is very low. In each of the years from 2001–2002 to 2003–2004 it was under 2 per cent—the majority not related to terrorism.[34]

(3) Road checks

The number of road checks is generally of the order of 100 to 450 per annum— **1–45**
though in 1993 and 1994, because of increased IRA activity on the mainland, it

---

[26] In 2003–2004 it was 7% nationally, 15% in the Metropolitan Police District, and 6% elsewhere (*op.cit.*, n.24 above, Table AC and para.15).
[27] Phillips and Brown (1998), Fig. 2.1, p.35.
[28] The increase was mainly due to a rise of 4,000 searches in the West Midlands force under Operation Safer Streets—*op.cit.*, n.21 above, para.22.
[29] *op.cit.*, n.24 above, Table PB, p.13.
[30] *ibid.*
[31] *ibid.*
[32] Previously under ss.13A and 13B of the Prevention of Terrorism (Temporary Provisions) Act 1989 and now under ss.44(1) and 44(2) of the Terrorism Act 2000.
[33] *op. cit.*, n.24 above, Table PC, p.14.
[34] *ibid.*

rose to over 3,000. In 2003–2004 it was 68 resulting in some 7,500 vehicles being stopped—an average of some 110 per road check.

The number of arrests resulting from the reason for the road checks is always very small. (In 2003–2004, the stopping of 7,500 vehicles resulted in only one arrest connected with the reasons for the road check and another six for other reasons.[35])

Home Office post-Macpherson research on stop and search

1–46 As part of its response to the Stephen Lawrence case, the Home Office commissioned a series of research reports on stop and search. Six reports were published in September 2000 in the Home Office Police Research Series.[36] (See also Marian Fitzgerald, *Searches in London*, Final Report, (Metropolitan Police, London, December 1999) (*www.met.police.uk*) and Jordan, *Stop/Search: Impact on crime and impact on public opinion*, (Police Foundation, 2000) (*www.police-foundation.org.uk*). For previous research see, for instance, Dixon *et al.* (1986b), Dixon (1990) and Bottomley *et al.* (1991a).)

A Briefing Note summarised the research results, conclusions and recommendations of the six Home Office reports.[37]

1–47 1. *The Impact of Stops and Searches on Crime and the Community* by Miller, Bland and Quinton (Paper 127)

- *Detection* Searches[38] probably detect offenders for only a small proportion of all the crimes they address. But they can make a more notable contribution to arrests.

- *Disruption* Searches can disrupt criminal activities but this effect is likely to be small in relation to overall crime.

- *Deterrence* There is little evidence of a deterrence effect though police stops[39] may have a role in preventing crime.

- *Order maintenance* The role and effectiveness of stop and search on preventing more serious crime is unknown.

- *Intelligence* Information gained from stops and searches can be fed back into police work.

---

[35] *op. cit.*, n.24 above, Table PD, p.15.
[36] The six projects drew on police statistics, research visits to six police forces, interviews with 100 operational police officers, over 340 hours of observations of routine patrol work and in-depth interviews with 55 people stopped and searched and 12 discussion groups with 104 people from the wider community.
[37] Miller, Quinton, Bland, *Police Stops and Searches: Lessons from a Programme of Research* (Home Office Policing and Reducing Crime Unit, 2000).
[38] "Searches" here mean stop and search.
[39] "Stops" here mean stops that do not result in a search.

The research suggested, not surprisingly, that the effectiveness of searches is greatest when they are based on strong grounds for suspicion and make the best use of intelligence. Higher levels of dissatisfaction with encounters among ethnic minority people appeared to occur because they disproportionately experienced poor practice—such as not being given proper explanations, or not being treated politely.

2. *Upping the PACE? An evaluation of the recommendations of the Stephen Lawrence Inquiry on stops and searches* by Bland, Miller, Quinton (Paper 128)   **1–48**

As has been seen, the Macpherson Report recommended that all stops be recorded and that the record—including the reason for the stop, the outcome and the person's self-defined ethnicity—should be given to the person stopped. This recommendation was piloted in five sites for at least six months.

- *Recording practices* No more than a third of encounters were recorded. The reasons included difficulties in defining the range of encounters to be recorded, the brevity of some stops and the different approaches of officers.

- *Monitoring records* The recorded reasons and outcomes precluded easy coding for statistical purposes. The quality of written reasons varied widely.

- *Recording self-defined ethnicity* This was sometimes problematic. It might be wise to retain officer-based classification in parallel with any new self-defined monitoring.

- *Officer practice* The number of searches conducted or their effectiveness was not obviously affected.

- *Public confidence* Members of the public welcomed the new form but public trust was based primarily on being treated fairly and politely and being given a good reason rather than on changes in procedure.

3. *The Views of the Public on Stops and Searches* by Stone and Pettigrew (Paper 129)   **1–49**

- Being stopped was a familiar experience for some across all ethnic groups. Those stopped regularly felt victimised.[40]

- "There was a very strong perception that the way in which stops and searches are currently handled causes more distrust, antagonism, and

---

[40] "Stops" here mean stops that do not result in a search.

resentment than any of the positive effects they can have." But despite this, all ethnic groups felt that there was a role for stop and search if there were fundamental changes in the way they are done (p.52).

1–50   4. *Police Stops, Decision-making and Practice* by Quinton, Bland and Miller (paper 130)

- There was a wide variation in officers' understanding of the concept of reasonable suspicion.

- Low levels of information were recorded on grounds for searches.

- The legal requirement of reasonable suspicion was not fulfilled for all searches.

1–51   5. *Profiling Populations Available for Stops and Searches* by MVA and Miller (Paper 131)

- A significant body of survey-based research shows a higher rate of stops and searches for minority ethnic groups and especially black people.[41]

- The Macpherson report said "discrimination is a major element in the stop and search problem".[42]

- The higher rates could be due to a variety of factors—to bias on the part of individual officers, targeting areas that have high concentrations of people from ethnic minorities, or to the population "available" for stop and search including larger proportions of people from ethnic minority backgrounds than resident populations or to more crimes of a certain kind being committed by persons of ethnic minority background—or to a mix of these, and other, reasons.

- Being available to be stopped and searched means being out and about on the streets.

- In areas of high stop and search young people and people from ethnic minority backgrounds were over-represented in the available population.

- The research did not suggest any general pattern of bias against people from ethnic minority background either as a whole or for particular

---

[41] Willis (1983); Smith and Gray (1985); Young (1994); Bucke and Brown (1997).
[42] On this see also the report of HM Inspectorate of the Constabulary, *Policing London: Winning Consent* (2000), and Jordan, *op. cit.*, para.1 46 above.

groups—whites tended to be stopped and searched at a higher rate to the available population, Asians were stopped and searched at a lower rate and black people were sometimes over-represented and sometimes under-represented.

- Stops and searches tended to be targetted at areas that had higher than average proportions of people from ethnic minorities. Broadly, this was consistent with the geographic pattern of crime but not wholly.

- Forces should monitor populations available for searches in order to assess and monitor officer practice.

6. *Managing the Use and Impact of Searches: A review of force interventions* by Bland, Miller and Quinton (Paper 132)   **1–52**

- Management interventions can improve arrest rates for searches—notably by an intelligence-led approach. It is vital that the information be up-to-date and accurate.

In regard to the sensitive question of discrimination in the use of the power of stop and search, it seems to be increasingly clear that for a variety of reasons it is not statistically valid to compare the ethnic data in the search figures with local population statistics. But no alternative basis from which to draw valid inferences regarding discrimination has yet been devised.

See also Fitzgerald, Hough, Joseph, Qureshi, *Policing for London* (Willan, 2002), especially pp.54–64.

Special provisions for statutory undertakers: s.6[43]

Constables employed by a railway, canal, dock or harbour undertaking are given a power under the Act to stop, search and detain for the purpose of searching any vehicle before it leaves parts of the undertaker's premises used for the storage and handling of goods. The special feature of the power is that there is no requirement that the constable have any reasonable suspicion that the vehicle is carrying stolen or prohibited goods. Also, it extends the power beyond public places.   **1–53**

Its object is to make it possible for statutory undertakings to check outgoing loaded lorries on a random or routine basis as a means of reducing the practice of pilfering. The power is not one that would be likely to affect ordinary members of the public. The power was based on similar provisions in s.27 of the Aviation Security Act 1982 in regard to airports. Statutory undertakings for the purposes of this section are defined in s.7(3). The section does not, however, confer any

---

[43] See 1989 N.I. PACE Order, Art.8.

power to search the person. This therefore requires reasonable suspicion. Subsection (3) extends the power to the United Kingdom Atomic Energy Authority's constables in relation to property owned or controlled by British Nuclear Fuels Ltd and subs.(4) extends the application of subs.(3) to Northern Ireland.

Repeals of existing stop and search powers: s.7[44]

1–54 Section 7 repealed six statutory provisions giving constables stop and search powers which are now superseded by s.1. The best known was s.66 of the Metropolitan Police Act 1839. The section also repealed stop and search powers under Acts promoted by local authorities. Other stop and search powers in public general Acts were preserved.[45] Stop and search powers conferred on statutory undertakings were preserved and need not any longer be renewed periodically.[46]

Subsection 7(3) defines "statutory undertakers".

[44] See 1989 N.I. PACE Order, Art.9.
[45] s.7(2)(a)(i).
[46] s.7(2)(a)(ii) and (b).

QUESTIONS AND ANSWERS

1. STOP AND SEARCH

Who can exercise the power of stop and search under PACE?   **1–55**

Any police officer whether in uniform or not. (Note that powers under other statutes to stop and search without reasonable suspicion can only be carried out by officers in uniform.)

Where can the power be exercised?   **1–56**

Any place to which the public have access whether for payment or not (a street, park or football ground, but not a private club, school or university); and any other place which is not a dwelling to which people have ready access (*e.g.* a garden next to the street). But a person cannot be searched in a garden or a yard attached to a dwelling unless it appears that he is not the owner and that he does not have the owner's permission to be there.

What does the power consist of?   **1–57**

To stop someone and to speak briefly to him before deciding whether or not to search him. If the decision is to search him he can only be searched superficially. He cannot be required to take off any garments other than his outer coat, his jacket and his gloves—and in Northern Ireland, his headgear. A person suspected of involvement in terrorism can also be asked to remove headgear and footwear. In some circumstances (see para.1–25 above) the police can require the removal of face-covering worn to conceal identity.

He can be asked to remove other items of clothing but if he refuses he cannot be compelled to do so. The stop and search power is intended to be restricted in public to a superficial search in the form of a "patting down". If the police want to conduct a more extensive search it must be done "not in public". Code A (para.3.6) says that where, on reasonable grounds, it is considered necessary to conduct a more thorough search ("*e.g.* by requiring a person to take off a T-shirt") this must be done out of public view, for instance in a police van or police station. It is unlikely that the courts would in any circumstances permit the stop and search power to be used for an extensive search of the person.

1–58   On what grounds can a person be stopped in order to be searched?

Before stopping the person concerned, the police officer must normally have reasonable grounds for suspecting that he will find either stolen goods or "prohibited articles" on him or his vehicle. But there are also some circumstances in which the police have the power to stop and search persons without having reasonable grounds of suspicion. Such powers are restricted to particular localities identified by the police for a limited period in connection with prevention of terrorism or where outbreaks of violence are anticipated or there is a reasonable belief that people are carrying dangerous instruments or offensive weapons.

1–59   What amounts to reasonable grounds to suspect?

The concept of reasonable grounds to suspect is somewhat imprecise, but it means basically that there must be some objective grounds for suspecting that particular individual himself. It is not enough to feel that he is one of a group of a particular type who might be prone to commit that sort of offence—skinheads, young blacks, yobbos or any other category. There must be something about that individual which sparks off suspicion. The concept of "reasonable" suspicion means fairly strong suspicion with a concrete basis that could be evaluated by a third person.

1–60   Can reasonable suspicion be based on the knowledge that the person concerned has committed offences before?

The short answer is no. There must be something about his conduct, manner, appearance, way of moving or other surrounding circumstances which suggests that he has done something recently or is about to do something—or reliable supporting intelligence or information that he is currently in possession of prohibited articles. However, where there is reliable information or intelligence that members of a group or gang habitually carry knives unlawfully or other weapons or controlled drugs and wear distinctive clothing or jewellery, insignias, tattoos or other identifying features, their members can be identified by such distinctive clothing or other features. So just being identified in that way may be a sufficient basis for reasonable suspicion.

1–61   In what circumstances can stop and search be conducted without reasonable suspicion?

There are now two categories of situation. One is where a locality has been designated by the police based on a reasonable belief that incidents involving serious violence may take place there or that people in that area are carrying dangerous instruments or offensive weapons (see para.1–13 above). The second is under the special terrorism legislation in designated localities or at ports and airports (see para.1–38 above). Police officers in uniform are given these powers to stop and search both persons and vehicles.

What are "prohibited articles"? 1–62

The Act established two categories of prohibited items. One is something made or adapted for use in connection with burglary, theft, taking a motor vehicle or other conveyance (including a bicycle) without authority or obtaining property by deception. The other is "offensive weapons". The Criminal Justice Act 1988 added an article with a blade or point other than a short bladed folding penknife. But many other statutes give the police power to stop and search, *e.g.* for drugs, for explosives, for firearms, etc.

What is meant by an offensive weapon? 1–63

An offensive weapon is either something made or adapted for use for causing injury (such as a flick-knife, cosh or knuckle-duster) or something which in itself is innocent but which is intended by the person having it to be used by him or others to cause someone injury.

What must the officer do before carrying out a search? 1–64

It is an absolute rule that before searching anyone the officer must do his best to inform the person concerned by telling him:

(1) that he is detained for the purpose of a search;

(2) his own name unless that would put him at risk (in Northern Ireland his number) and that of his police station;

(3) the legal search powers being exercised;

(4) the object of the proposed search;

(5) the officer's grounds or reasons for wanting to make it;

(6) that the person searched has the right to ask for a copy of the record of the search at the police station within 12 months.

If the officer is in plain clothes he must also first produce evidence that he is in fact a police officer.

1–65   What happens if the person concerned does not understand English? Is any search therefore unlawful?

No. The duty is not to inform the person but to "take reasonable steps" (Code A, para.3.8) to bring the information to his attention. If everything has been done that could reasonably be done to get him to understand the relevant information, the officer can proceed to carry out a search.

1–66   What if the officer wants to search a number of persons in a short space of time which would make it difficult to conform to the duty to give each of them the requisite information?

He must nevertheless do his best to inform them of his name and the name of his station, the object of the search and the reason why he wants to make it. But he is not under a duty to mention the person's right to get a record of the search if the circumstances are such as to make it impracticable to make a record.

1–67   For how long can a person be detained under the stop and search power?

No longer than is reasonably necessary to carry out the search. (The 2003 revised Code A states, "The length of time for which a person or vehicle may be detained must be reasonable and kept to a minimum" (para.3.3).) Once the person has been searched, it would therefore not be legitimate to keep him waiting against his will for 15–20 minutes whilst the control room does Police National Computer checks or checks on other local or national computerised databases. The power is only to detain for the purposes of a physical search.

1–68   When must a record be made of a stop and search?

A record must be made at the time unless it is not practicable to do so, *e.g.* because considerable numbers have been stopped and searched, for instance outside a football ground. But the officer is not exonerated from the duty to make a record where he can in practice make a record later, only if he cannot make one at all. If made then, it must be given immediately to the person. If it is not practicable to make the record on the spot but it is feasible to make it later, the duty is to make it "as soon as practicable".

Must a record be made if there is no search? **1–69**

Previously the duty to make a record only arose if there was a search. The Macpherson Report into the Stephen Lawrence case recommended that it should cover all stops! The draft Code A issued by the Home Office in March 2002 modified this proposal. It suggested that a record should have to be made if an officer requires a person to account for themselves—*i.e.* their actions, behaviour, presence in an area or possession of something. After being piloted, the proposal was included in the revised Code A which came into force on August 1, 2004. As noted above, this stated that it is up to individual forces to decide when to implement the proposal providing all have done so by April 1, 2005.

What has to be included in the record? **1–70**

    (a) *Search* The name of the person searched, if known, and, if not, some description of him including details of his race; the object of the search; the grounds for making it; the date and time; the place; whether anything and, if so, what was found; and the identity of the officer who made the search.

    (b) *An encounter when there is no search* Basically the same information including the reason why the officer questioned the person and the outcome of the encounter. However, the requirement to include the name of the person searched, which was in the pilot, was dropped.

Do the powers to stop and search a person apply to stopping and searching a vehicle? **1–71**

They apply in much the same way. But there are some differences. One is that a police officer in uniform has the power to stop any vehicle under s.163 of the Road Traffic Act 1988. That Act does not require the police officer to be suspicious of anything in particular. But a stop under the Road Traffic Act does not entitle the officer to search the vehicle. A search under PACE normally requires reasonable grounds to suspect that the vehicle is carrying stolen goods or prohibited articles.

Another difference is that the Act makes special provision for the search of an unattended vehicle where reasonable grounds for suspicion exist. In that case the officer must leave a notice in or on the vehicle stating that he has searched it, giving the name of his police station and stating that the owner can get a copy of the record of the search if he applies within 12 months. The record of a search of a vehicle should describe it.

1–72 **Are there any stop and search powers apart from the 1984 Act?**

There are many statutes which give the police stop and search powers, most of which continue to exist. The PACE procedures and safeguards apply to all stop and search powers.

But the 1984 Act has repealed some of these powers, such as the power of the Metropolitan Police dating from 1839 to stop and search persons on reasonable suspicion that they are carrying stolen goods.

1–73 **Can a person be stopped and searched by consent?**

Formerly, the Code recognised the concept of a voluntary search when the PACE safeguards did not apply. The difficulty was in knowing whether a stop was by consent. Code A tried to clarify matters by stating that when a police officer was searching someone on the street on a voluntary basis he should always make it clear to the person concerned that he would not be searched unless he consented (former Note 1Db). In regard to juveniles and other persons requiring special protection, the Code went further in banning searches by consent. (Note 1E stated that "juveniles, persons suffering from a mental handicap or mental disorder and others who appear not to be capable of giving an informed consent should not be subject to a voluntary search".)

The 2003 redraft of Code A changed the whole approach to the idea of searching with consent. Code A now provides (para.1.5) that "an officer must not search a person even with his or her consent, where no power to search is applicable". Even where a person is prepared to submit to a search voluntarily, the person "must not be searched unless the legal power exists" and the search must be in accordance with the relevant power and the provisions of the Code.

The only exception is a search of persons entering sports grounds or other premises where their consent is given as a condition of entry (para.1.5).

2. ROAD CHECKS

1–74 **The police had an unlimited right to stop any vehicle under the Road Traffic Act. How was that right affected by PACE?**

The 1984 Act set up a procedure for establishing a road check when the purpose is to discover whether a vehicle is carrying someone who has committed a serious criminal offence or someone who is a witness to such an offence or someone intending to commit such an offence or an escaped prisoner.

What is the procedure?   1–75

The road check must normally be authorised in advance and in writing by an officer of the rank of superintendent or above. The authorisation must specify the
period for which it is to operate (up to a maximum of one week at a time) and the
locality in which it is to operate. It must also state the name of the officer giving
it; the purpose of the road check; and the nature of the offence in question.

In an emergency, where no superintendent is available, an officer of any rank
can authorise a road check, but he must then as soon as is practicable notify a
superintendent and make a record of the time at which he granted authority for
the road block. The superintendent can then authorise the continuation of the
check or can order that it be discontinued. The person in charge of any vehicle
that is stopped in the course of such a check has the right to a written statement
as to the grounds for the road check providing he applies for it within 12 months.

What grounds justify the setting up of a road block?   1–76

There are five possible grounds:

(1) That there are reasonable grounds for believing that someone who has
     committed a "serious arrestable offence" (for discussion see paras
     11 09—11–12 below) is or is about to be in the area.

(2) That the police are looking for a witness to a "serious arrestable
     offence". In this category there is no requirement that they expect to
     find a witness in the area. They can therefore try their luck without any
     commitment.

(3) That they are looking for a person who intends to commit a "serious
     arrestable offence" and that there are reasonable grounds for suspect-
     ing that the person is or is about to be in the locality.

(4) That there are reasonable grounds to believe that an escaped prisoner is
     in the area.

(5) That it is a road block set up under powers to prevent acts of terrorism
     in a specified locality authorised by a very senior officer for periods of
     up to 28 days at a time.

Does the power of setting up road blocks include a power of search?   1–77

Section 4 of PACE speaks only of stopping vehicles and says nothing of a power
of search. The power to search must therefore arise under s.1 (on reasonable

suspicion that the vehicle is carrying stolen or prohibited articles) or s.17 (on reasonable suspicion that there is in the vehicle a person who has committed an arrestable offence).

1–78 Can civilian Community Support Officers take part in road checks and stop vehicles?

Community Support Officers employed under the Police Reform Act 2002 can be given the same power as constables to carry out road checks and for that purpose can also be given the power of constables in uniform to stop a vehicle—see Sch.4, Pt I, paras 10 and 13. But neither they nor Civilian Investigating Officers have been given the power to carry out stop and search.

PART II

POWERS OF ENTRY, SEARCH AND SEIZURE

Entry, search and seizure by the police is a topic that raises important issues con- **2–01**
cerning the proper balance between police powers and protection of the citizen.
The provisions of PACE are based largely on the recommendations of the Philips
Royal Commission though, as will be seen, in some important respects they differ
from what the Royal Commission proposed.

A very significant development of the powers of entry, search and seizure came
with the enactment of the Police Reform Act 2002 which extended to authorised
civilians most of the powers previously limited to police officers.[1]

As will be seen, the Serious Organised Crime and Police Bill introduced in
November 2004, would make a number of important changes in regard to search
warrants.[2]

The Philips Royal Commission's Report

The Philips Royal Commission recommended[3] that existing powers of entry and **2–02**
search under warrant needed to be supplemented. The existing powers were
somewhat haphazard and there were surprising omissions. There was, for
instance, no power to get a search warrant to search the scene of a murder or a
kidnap, apart from the power to search premises after an arrest. In the Philips
Royal Commission's view a new compulsory power of search for evidence
should be available, though it should be a limited power and one subject to stringent safeguards. ("A compulsory power of search for evidence should be available only as a last resort. It should be granted only in exceptional circumstances
and in respect only of grave offences."[4])

Under the then existing law the police had authority to enter to search premises under different levels of supervision. In most cases the supervising authority
was a magistrate but, in some circumstances, authority for a search could be
given by a senior police officer and in others there had to be the permission of a
judge. In the view of the Philips Royal Commission, in general the appropriate
supervision could continue to be provided by the magistracy. But in cases of great

---

[1] On these provisions of the Police Reform Act see generally Ch.12 below and for the text of the 2002
Act itself see the end of that Chapter.
[2] Para.2–43 below summarises the changes.
[3] Philips Report, para.3.42.
[4] Philips Report, para.3.42.

urgency in searching for prohibited goods, a police officer not below the rank of superintendent should be able to authorise a search. When, however, it came to searches for evidence, the Commission thought that supervision should be by a judge. The procedure should have two stages. The police should first have to apply for a court order similar to a witness summons in a criminal case or an order for discovery in a civil case. Such an order would require the person to whom it was directed to allow the police to look at the items covered by the order. There should be a right of appeal to the court against the order. If the person refused to comply with the order, the police should have the right to get a search warrant. They should also have a right to ask for a warrant forthwith "where there [was] reason to believe that the evidence [would] disappear, or be disposed of if the person concerned [was] alerted to the police interest in it".[5]

An order should be made by a judge only if he was satisfied that other methods of investigation had failed, that the nature of the items was specified with some precision, that there were reasonable grounds for thinking that the items would be found at those premises and that the evidence would be of substantial value to identify those responsible for the crime or to determine the particulars of offences.[6]

The PACE Bills

2–03   The Government only gave partial effect to these proposals. It did not accept the Philips Royal Commission's recommendation that a senior officer should, in an emergency, be permitted to authorise a search for prohibited goods. Nor did it agree with the Commission that searches for evidence should always require the authority of a judge subject to a two-stage process of an order and a warrant. It accepted that if the evidence was held on a confidential basis a judge's authority would have to be obtained but in other circumstances it would be enough to get a magistrate's permission. (The Home Office made the point that there were already some 40 statutes which gave magistrates powers to authorise searches of premises, including in some instances searches for evidence.[7])

When the first PACE Bill was published it gave the police the right to seek a search warrant from a justice of the peace to look for evidence of a serious arrestable offence. The only qualification was that the application to the magistrate had to indicate how the evidence in question related to the inquiry. Where, however, the evidence was held on a confidential basis the first Bill provided a special procedure by way of application to a circuit judge. This was in two stages. In the first instance, the police would normally have to ask for an order to produce. If this had already proved abortive or if the order was bound to fail, the police could ask for a search warrant.

2–04   These provisions were subjected to fierce criticism especially by the medical profession, the clergy, lawyers, journalists, Citizens' Advice Bureaux and other advisory agencies. All were concerned that the powers as they stood would have permitted a judge to authorise a search of any records held in confidence. As a

---

[5] Philips Report, para.3.42.
[6] Philips Report, para.3.43.
[7] The list was set out in the Commission's *Law and Procedure Volume* (Cmnd. 8092–1 (1981), App.5).

result of the pressure placed upon it the Government made a series of concessions, the most important of which were:

(1) to provide that the hearing before the judge would normally have to be *inter partes* (*i.e.* with both sides present), though not if the police could satisfy the judge that there was reason to believe that the person holding the material in question was in some way implicated in the crime;

(2) that certain categories of material could be generally exempt from any police scrutiny—notably the records of doctors, clergymen and advisory agencies; and

(3) that enforcement of a judicial order to produce confidential material which was not exempt would be by proceedings for contempt and not by a search warrant.

The categories of material exempted were those subject to legal professional privilege, and "excluded material"—namely confidential personal records of doctors and caring professions and advisory agencies, and material held in confidence by journalists. Material held in confidence that was not exempt was called "special procedure" material, access to which had to be sought from a circuit judge[8] rather than from a magistrate. The relevant provisions are in ss.8–14 of the Act.

Human Rights Act 1998

Entry, search and seizure raise issues that are covered by Art.8 of the ECHR. **2–05**
Article 8(1) provides that "Everyone has the right to respect for his private life and family life, his home and his correspondence". Article 8(2) provides that:

"There shall be no interference by a public authority with the exercise of this right except such as is in accordance with the law and is necessary in a democratic society in the interests of national security, public safety or the economic well-being of the country, for the prevention of disorder or crime, for the protection of health or morals, or for the protection of the rights and freedoms of others."[9]

Applications to justices of the peace for search warrants: s.8[10]

Section 8 provides for the issue by a magistrate of a warrant to enter and search **2–06**
premises for evidence of serious arrestable offences. (As will be seen, the Serious

---

[8] In Northern Ireland, a county court judge.
[9] For an example of a successful action brought under the Convention for a breach of Art.8 see *McLeod v United Kingdom* (1998) 27 E.H.R.R. 493, para.2–62, n.89 below.
[10] See 1989 N.I. PACE Order, Art.10.

Organised Crime and Police Bill introduced in November 2004 changes serious arrestable offences to any indictable offence—see para.11–09 below.)

The section gives a justice of the peace, on written application from a constable or an authorised civilian investigating officer,[11] power to issue a search warrant to search premises. Such a civilian may also be named as a person entitled to enter and search under the authority of the warrant.[12]

If the written information provided by the police covers all the material necessary to satisfy them that a search warrant should be issued, the magistrates are not required by the Human Rights Act 1998 to make a written record of their reasons or of the oral exchanges leading to its issue.[13]

The warrant has to be directed against named premises. (See however, para.2–43 below for the new type of warrant known as an "all premises warrant" introduced by the Serious Organised Crime and Police Bill 2004–2005.)

2–07 The recommendation made by the Joint Home Office/Cabinet Office Review of PACE that magistrates should be permitted to authorise search warrants by telephone, fax or video link was not included in the Criminal Justice Act 2003 nor in the Serious Organised Crime and Police Bill.

The justice of the peace must be satisfied:

(1) that there is material on the premises likely to be of substantial value to the investigation (s.8(1)(b));

(2) that it is likely to be "relevant evidence" (*i.e.* admissible as evidence— ss.8(1)(c) and 8(4));

(3) that it is not and does not include "excluded material" (see s.11), or "special procedure material" (see s.14); or material subject to legal privilege (s.10); and

(4) that any of the conditions in subs.(3) applies.

The conditions in subs.(3) are basically that it is not practicable to gain entry to the premises in question without a search warrant. Examples are where entry has been refused or no one with authority to grant access can be reached or the purpose of the search may be frustrated unless an officer can gain immediate entry.

2–08 The applicant for the warrant should inform the magistrates if any of the material "consists of or includes items subject to legal privilege" (s.8(1)(d)). If there is no mention of the fact, the magistrates should inquire to satisfy themselves as to that.[14] If in doubt whether material is covered by legal privilege or is special

---

[11] Police Reform Act 2002, Sch.4, Pt 2, para.16(a). See generally Ch.12 on the Police Reform Act 2002.

[12] Police Reform Act 2002, Sch.4, Pt 2, para.16(b).

[13] *R. (Cronin) v Sheffield Magistrates' Court* [2002] EWHC 2568 Admin; [2003] 1 W.L.R.752.

[14] [2000] Q.B. 576 at 583; *R. v Chesterfield Justices and another, Ex p. Bramley* [2000] 2 W.L.R. 409 at 415; [2000] 1 All E.R. 411 at 417, *per* Kennedy L.J., DC.

procedure material, the magistrates should refuse the application under s.8 and leave the applicant to make a special procedure application to a circuit judge—*R. v Guildhall Magistrates' Court, Ex p. Primlaks Holdings Co. (Panama) Inc.*[15] Granting judicial review, the Divisional Court held that it was impossible to believe that Parliament could have intended that a magistrate should be able, on an *ex parte* application, to authorise a search for and seizure of documents from solicitors' firms, when it had created a procedure in which any question of privilege being lost could be dealt with by a circuit judge. Section 8 conferred a draconian power and it was for the magistrate to satisfy himself that there were reasonable grounds for believing the matters set out. The fact that a police officer stated that there were reasonable grounds was not enough. In this case the magistrate could not have been satisfied that there were reasonable grounds for believing that the conditions specified in s.8(3) applied. The decision is a helpful reminder to magistrates (and their clerks) that when deciding whether to grant a police application for a search warrant, magistrates must not allow themselves to act as rubber stamps for the police. All too often, it seems, this is what happens in practice.

In contrast to applications for access to special procedure material under s.9 (see below), it is not however necessary for the magistrates to be persuaded that other methods of obtaining the sought material have been tried without success.[16]   **2–09**

Does the seizure that subsequently takes place have to be authorised by the search warrant? Section 8(2) states that a constable "may seize and retain anything for which a search has been authorised under subs.(1)". (That power also applies to authorised civilian investigating officers.[17]) Seizure is dealt with in s.19 (see para.2–67 below). In *R. v Chief Constable of Warwickshire, Ex p. Fitzpatrick*,[18] the Divisional Court held that it was not sufficient that the material seized should be covered by the warrant, it also had to be authorised under s.8(1). In other words, there had to be reasonable grounds for believing that it was likely to be of substantial value to the investigation and be evidence of the stated offence and not consist of or include special procedure material or material covered by legal professional privilege. "The effect of s.8(1) and (2) is to limit what may be seized under a search warrant issued under s.8."[19] The judge said that this point was especially important in a case in which it was difficult to identify with any precision the material to be sought.

But this interpretation was inconsistent with the plain terms of s.19—as the Divisional Court later decided in *R. v Chesterfield Justices, Ex p. Bramley*[20] when Jowitt J. admitted that what he had said in this regard in *Ex p. Fitzpatrick* "went too far" and "was wrong" (see para.2–70 below).[21]

---

[15] [1989] 2 W.L.R. 841, DC.
[16] *R. v Billericay Justices and Dobbyn, Ex p. Frank Harris (Coaches) Ltd* [1991] Crim.L.R. 472, DC; *cf.* s.9 applications *R. v Crown Court at Leeds, Ex p. Hill* (1990) 93 Cr.App.R. 60, DC.
[17] Police Reform Act 2002, Sch.4, Pt 2, para.16(c).
[18] [1998] 1 All E.R. 65.
[19] [1998] 1 All E.R. 65 at 74, *per* Jowitt J.
[20] [2000] 1 All E.R. 411, DC.
[21] See also *R. v Customs and Excise Commissioners, Ex p. Popely* [1999] STC 1016, DC. It was held that a search warrant cannot authorise seizure of items held under legal professional privilege but if in the course of a lawful search of a solicitors' office, especially if the solicitor is himself suspected of involvement, the officer inadvertently seizes material which includes items subject to legal privilege, the execution of the warrant is not thereby rendered unlawful.

Subsection (5) of s.8 makes it clear that the power to issue a search warrant under subs.(1) is in addition to any existing power to issue warrants. Existing provisions for the issue of search warrants (which were listed in Appendix 5 to the Philips Royal Commission's *Law and Procedure Volume*), include powers to search for evidence of various offences.

Applies also to investigations on behalf of authorities abroad

2–10   Under the Criminal Justice (International Co-operation) Act 1990, s.8, the whole of Pt II of PACE (entry, search and seizure)[22] can be used in the UK on behalf of authorities wanting access to material in connection with criminal proceedings in another country for an offence that would be regarded as a serious arrestable offence in this country. The pre-conditions are either that such proceedings have been started in that other country or that an arrest has been made in the course of an investigation carried on there. It requires a direction given by the Home Secretary in response to a request from the proper authorities in the foreign country. If an order has previously been made by the Treasury, the powers of a constable under Pt II can be exercised also by a Customs and Excise officer.

Common law still applies to extradition crimes

2–11   It has been held that Pt II of PACE only applies to domestic offences and that it therefore does not give the police powers of entry and search of premises in connection with extradition crimes. But in relation to extradition crimes the police still had a common law right to enter and search the home of a person arrested on a provisional arrest warrant issued by a magistrate.[23] It is true that s.17(5) of PACE said that, apart from breaches of the peace, "all the rules of common law under which a constable has power to enter premises without a warrant are hereby abolished". But Lord Rodger for the majority of four Law Lords said that s.17 dealt with entry for the purpose of making an arrest and this provision did not apply to searches for evidence when someone had been arrested. (For comment see [2002] Crim.L.R. 501.)

Terrorism cases

2–12   In terrorism cases, a magistrate can issue a search warrant if he is satisfied that it is sought for the purpose of a terrorist investigation[24]; that there are reasonable grounds for believing that the material sought is likely to be of substantial value to such investigation; that it does not include "excepted material" (see below); and that the issue of the warrant is likely to be necessary.[25] If the application

---

[22] In Northern Ireland, Pt III of the 1989 N.I. PACE Order.
[23] *R. (Rottman) v Metropolitan Police Commissioner and the Secretary of State for the Home Office* [2002] UKHL 20; [2002] 2 All E.R. 865, HL. See also *R. (Hewitson) v Chief Constable Dorset Police, The Times*, January 6, 2004, DC. (The common law power to search after an arrest under a provisional warrant in an extradition case does not cover a search of the girl-friend's flat two and a half hours after his arrest more than 100 metres away.)
[24] Previously it had to be the investigation; now it can be any terrorist investigation, not just the one in hand (Terrorism Act 2000, Sch.5, para.1(5)).
[25] Terrorism Act 2000, Sch.5, para.1(5).

relates to non-residential premises, the warrant can be issued even though the magistrate is not satisfied that the issue of the warrant is necessary, providing the application is made by an officer of the rank of superintendent, though in that case the warrant must be executed within 24 hours.[26]

The Terrorism Act 2000 also provides for a police officer of at least the rank of superintendent to authorise a search of specified premises in a cordoned area.[27] An officer not of that rank may do so if he considers it necessary because of the urgency. Such authority does not cover items covered by legal privilege. It cannot be given unless the person giving it has reasonable grounds for believing that there is material on the premises which is likely to be of substantial value in a terrorist investigation which is not excepted material (see below).

Armed Forces

Section 5 of the Armed Forces Act 2001 makes provisions similar to those in s.8   **2–13**
for warrants authorising entry and search of premises used as living accommodation for Service purposes or the homes of persons subject to Service law. (Statutory powers are not required to enter other areas under Service occupation (s.17(7)).)

Search warrants under s.5 have to be issued by "a judicial officer".[28] They must have similar minimum qualifications to a judge advocate. (In the Army and the Air Force a judge advocate is a civilian lawyer appointed by the Judge Advocate General. In the Royal Navy there are uniformed judge advocates who are naval barristers of at least five years standing.)

The judicial officer must be satisfied of broadly the same matters that a magistrate must be satisfied before issuing a search warrant—*e.g.* that a relevant offence has been committed, that there is on the premises material likely to be of substantial value in its investigation, that it does not consist of or include items subject to legal privilege or excluded or special procedure material, etc. (subss.(1), (4), (5)).

The Secretary of State may make regulations permitting applications for a warrant to be made by live television link (subs.(10)). Regulations may also be made for safeguards relating to the issue and execution of warrants equivalent to ss.15 and 16 of PACE.

However, if the time taken in seeking a warrant under s.5 would be likely to frustrate or seriously prejudice the purpose of the search, s.7 gives commanding officers a limited power to authorise the search without a warrant. Such emergency powers can normally only be exercised by Service police (s.7(2)). Where a search has been carried out without a warrant, the seizure and retention of anything taken during the search must, as soon as practicable, be reviewed by a judicial officer[29] (s.8).

Regulations regarding such reviews require the affirmative approval of Parliament (s.35).

---

[26] Terrorism Act 2000, Sch.5, para.2.
[27] Terrorism Act 2000, Sch.5, para.3.
[28] Defined in s.16(1) as a judicial officer appointed under s.75L of the Army Act 1955 or the Air Force Act 1955 or s.47M of the Naval Discipline Act 1957.
[29] *ibid.*

Access to "excluded" and "special procedure" material: s.9 and Sch.1[30]

2–14   Section 9 deals with the question of police access to material held on a confidential basis. Civilian investigating officers authorised under the Police Reform Act 2002 have the same powers as police officers to obtain access to material under Sch.1.[31] Section 9 also applies to the procedures envisaged under the Act to searches for such material under the authority of other legislation.

Subsection (1) states that the police may only seek access to excluded or special procedure material (as defined in ss.11 and 14 respectively) by applying to a circuit judge under Sch.1 to the Act. (Recorders have no jurisdiction to hear special procedure applications.[32]) Application must also be made to the judge where the material sought is partly excluded or special procedure and partly other material (Sch.1, paras 2(a)(ii) and 3(1)). The judge may order the material to be produced or, in exceptional circumstances, may issue a search warrant. But the police can only gain access to "excluded material" if a search warrant could have been obtained under the previous law for such material (*e.g.* stolen medical records for which a search warrant could have been issued under the Theft Act 1981, s.26(1)). (For a full list of all the then existing police powers to enter and search premises under warrant or other written authority see Philips Royal Commission, *Law and Procedure Volume*, Appendix 5.)

Subsection (2) repealed all existing enactments in so far as they empowered judges or magistrates to authorise searches for excluded or special procedure material consisting of documents or records. All applications for searches for such material, whether in connection with a serious arrestable offence (defined in s.116 and Sch.5) or not, must now therefore be made under subs.(1) and Sch.1. Schedule 1 contains the detailed provisions for the making of orders by circuit judges. (By an amendment introduced by the Criminal Justice and Police Act 2001, orders made in respect of special procedure material can be endorsed for execution in Scotland and Northern Ireland—and vice versa.[33]) The judge must be satisfied that one or other of the two sets of access conditions are satisfied.[34] It is not enough that he finds that the police are acting reasonably in making the request.[35]

2–15   The first set of access conditions set out in para.2 of the Schedule relate only to special procedure material. (Nearly all the applications made have been under the first set of access conditions.) The conditions are: (a) that there are reasonable grounds for believing that the material is likely to constitute relevant evidence of a serious arrestable offence or that the material is likely to be of substantial value to the investigation; (b) that other methods of getting the material have been tried and failed or have not been tried because it appeared that they would be bound to

---

[30] See 1989 N.I. PACE Order, Art.11 and Sch.1.

[31] Sch.4, Pt 2, para.1. See Ch.12 below.

[32] *R. v Central Criminal Court, Ex p. Francis & Francis* [1989] A.C. 346, HL, *per* Lord Bridge at 368 and Lord Griffiths at 382.

[33] New s.9(2A) of PACE inserted by s.86 of the 2001 Act.

[34] There is no requirement, however, to state on the face of the warrant which access condition was satisfied—*R. (on the application of Paul da Costa) v Thames Magistrates' Court and another* (2002) 152 N.L.J. 141.

[35] *R. v Central Criminal Court, Ex p. Bright, Alton, Rusbridger* [2001] 2 All E.R. 244, 259.

fail; and (c) that the public interest would be served by an order requiring access to the material. In weighing the public interest the judge is required to balance the benefit to the investigation of gaining access to the material and "the circumstances under which the person in possession of the material holds it" (para.2(c)).

In *Re Moloney's Application for Judicial Review*[36] a judge's production order in respect of a journalist's notebook was quashed on the ground that the police had not made out the case that the material was likely to be of substantial value to the investigation into solicitor Patrick Finucane's murder. In *R. v Central Criminal Court, Ex p. Bright, Alton, Rusbridger*,[37] the police sought from two newspapers, *inter alia*, the email address of David Shayler, a former employee of MI6, suspected of breaches of the Official Secrets Act. Judge L.J. said there was no evidence to explain why the email address should be treated as relevant and admissible evidence. Gibbs J. concurred. Kay J. dissented. He would have given the police access broadly to "any other documentation provided to 'B' by 'S'". In *R. v Bristol Crown Court, Ex p. Bristol Press and Press and Picture Agency*[38] the applicants argued that the material must be identified as likely to be valuable to an investigation into a specific offence or offences and that the police could not embark on a "fishing expedition". The Divisional Court rejected this view. It held that the judge was entitled to work on the basis that, once obtained, the material would be likely to reveal the commission of offences.

The public interest considerations that are relevant here are therefore relatively narrow but the judge retains an overall discretion as to whether to exercise his discretion to grant the remedy.[39] Those wider public interest considerations were taken into account in the Bristol Press case.[40] In that case, which arose out of riots in St Pauls, Bristol, the Divisional Court ruled that the police were entitled to an order for the production of press photographs of the riot. The public interest in the impartiality of the press would not, it thought, be undermined since the production would be in response to a court order, nor would it create special additional risks for press photographers. In *R. v Central Criminal Court, Ex p. Carr*,[41] Glidewell L.J. took the view that once it is shown that the documents are on the premises and that they are likely to be of substantial value to the investigation and relevant evidence, it followed that it was in the public interest that they be produced. ("If documents of the kinds referred to in the information are on any of the applicant's premises, it is obvious that they are likely to be of substantial value to the investigation, that some or all of them will be relevant evidence, and therefore that it is in the public interest that such documents be produced.") See to the same effect *R. v Crown Court at Northampton, Ex p. DPP*.[42] The High Court judge had held that it was not in the public interest that a firm of solicitors holding material for a client should have to produce the material. Reversing the decision, the Divisional Court found the judge's decision "Wednesbury unreasonable". Taylor L.J. said that once a judge concluded that a serious arrestable

2–16

---

[36] [2000] N.I.J.B. 195, DC.
[37] [2001] 2 All E.R. 244; [2002] Crim.L.R. 64, DC.
[38] (1987) 85 Cr.App.R. 190.
[39] *R. v Central Criminal Court, Ex p. Bright, Alton, Rusbridger,* n.35 above, at 260.
[40] n.38 above.
[41] *The Independent*, March 5, 1987.
[42] (1991) 93 Cr.App.R. 376, DC.

offence had been committed he should not refuse an order for a production order as it was "hardly consistent to find anything other than that it was an offence for which there was a public interest in bringing the matter to justice".[43]

2–17   The case law shows that it is difficult to establish that it would not be in the public interest for the material to be produced to the police. The considerations to be taken into account include such matters as the principle of freedom of expression, the privilege against self-incrimination, the effect of the order on third parties, the antiquity of the matters under investigation and the overall value of requiring production of the material. Whilst being alert to the need to safeguard basic freedoms, the judge should also be alert to the need to discourage and to detect criminal acts.[44]

The second set of access conditions (para.3) applies to both excluded and special procedure material. The effect of this paragraph in Sch.1 and s.9 is that a judge can order the production of the material (rather than issue a warrant) if a warrant could have been issued pre-PACE to search for it and the issue of such a warrant would have been appropriate. The material need not relate to a serious arrestable offence.

Paragraph 4 states that an order made by the judge is an order to produce the material to the police or to give the police access to it within seven days or such other time as it specifies. Paragraph 5 parallels provisions in s.19(4) (below) regarding access to information in a computer and para.6 applies provisions of ss.21 and 22 regarding access and copying and retention of articles seized to items seized under Sch.1.

2–18   When the first PACE Bill was published it provided for special procedure applications to be made *ex parte* (*i.e.* with only the police represented)—as recommended by the Philips Royal Commission. But this was changed. Paragraph 7 provides that an application for such an order must be made *inter partes*. As has been seen, this represented a major climb-down by the Government, though not one that has had much effect since, in practice, special procedure applications are only rarely contested.

Paragraphs 8 to 10 deal with the service of notice of the application on the person concerned.[45] Paragraph 11 provides that a person served with such a notice must not "conceal, destroy, alter or dispose of the material", save with the leave of a judge or the written consent of a police officer until the application is either dismissed or abandoned or the order under para.4 is complied with.

An order to produce material under para.4 can only be enforced by proceedings for contempt (para.15). This again was an important concession by the Government which originally proposed that disobedience of any order for production by the circuit judge should be followed by an application for a search warrant.

---

[43] (1991) 93 Cr.App.R. 376 at 381.
[44] *R. v Central Criminal Court, Ex p. Bright, Alton, Rusbridger*, n.35 above, 260–261, 263, 272. See further Costigan, "Fleet Street Blues: Police Seizure of Journalists' Material" [1996] Crim.L.R. 231, 236; Zuckerman, "The Weakness of the P.A.C.E. Special Procedure for Protecting Confidential Material" [1990] Crim.L.R. 472.
[45] The equivalent in Northern Ireland is in the Interpretation (Northern Ireland) Act 1954.

Search warrants

In certain circumstances (set out in para.12 of Sch.1) the judge can be asked to   **2–19**
issue a search warrant instead of an order to produce. For obvious reasons, an
application for a search warrant would be made *ex parte* (s.15(3) of the Act).

Before issuing a search warrant the judge must be satisfied, first, that one or
other of the two sets of access conditions (see above) is satisfied and, further, that
any of the conditions in para.14 are fulfilled. The conditions set out in para.14
are:

(a) that it is not practicable to communicate with anyone able to authorise
     entry to the premises; or

(b) that it is not practicable to communicate with someone able to give
     access to the material in question; or

(c) that it is excluded material subject to a restriction or obligation of
     secrecy under any enactment as mentioned in s.11(2)(b) and that the
     material is likely to be disclosed in breach of such restriction if a
     warrant is not issued; or

(d) that service of a notice of an application for an order of production
     might seriously prejudice the investigation—or in Northern Ireland
     also "other investigations"[46] introduced to give additional protection
     for sensitive information.

The judge may also issue a warrant if an order for production has been disobeyed,
but only if the order related to material for which a warrant could have been
issued under the previous law. If an order for the production of special procedure
material issued under the first set of access conditions is disobeyed, no search
warrant can be issued.

In a case of any difficulty a judge issuing a search warrant is well advised to   **2–20**
give reasons. This is not a statutory requirement but the absence of reasons has
been criticised. In *R. v Southwark Crown Court and H.M.Customs, Ex p. Sorsky
Defries*,[47] the Divisional Court said that whether the judge should give reasons
depended on what had gone before. If the applicant for the warrant had taken the
judge through the relevant statutory provisions and analysed the evidence in relation to them, it might suffice to say "in the light of the matters put before me I
am satisfied . . .". But where, as in that case, the proceedings took only a couple
of minutes and he was referred to virtually nothing, there was a need for a short
statement of the judge's reasons so that it could be apparent that he had taken
the appropriate matters into account. See to like effect *Gross, Gross and Gross v*

---

[46] See 1989 N.I. PACE Order, Sch.1, para.11(d).
[47] [1996] Crim.L.R. 195.

Southwark Crown Court.[48] The absence of adequate reasons for the judge's decision was one reason for quashing the search warrant.

Most of the provisions of PACE extend only to England and Wales. The House of Lords held in 1999 that a search warrant issued by a sheriff in Scotland and indorsed by a stipendiary magistrate in Manchester authorising search for material held in confidence by Granada Television was valid in England even though Scotland lacked the protection given to special or excluded material under PACE.[49]

Terrorism cases

2–21   Special rules apply in terrorism cases. These are now to be found in the Terrorism Act 2000, s.37 and Sch.5, para.5.[50] Under these rules the application to the circuit judge (or in Northern Ireland, a county court judge) can be made not only for "special procedure material"[51] but also for "excluded material",[52] though it cannot cover items subject to legal privilege.

The application can be for an order that the material be produced for seizure and retention or to give access to the material.[53] Whereas a special procedure application under PACE is normally made *inter partes*, under the Terrorism Act it is made *ex parte*.

The judge needs only to be satisfied (a) that a terrorist investigation (as defined in the Act) is being carried out and that there are reasonable grounds for believing that the material is likely to be of substantial value to the investigation; and (b) that there are reasonable grounds for believing that it is in the public interest that the material should be produced or that access to it should be given.[54] If the material is not in the person's possession, custody or power, the judge may order that person to state to the best of his knowledge and belief where it is (sub-para.5(2)(c)).

Where an order under para.5 to produce the material has not been complied with, the police can ask the judge for a search warrant.[55] A search warrant can also be issued by the judge where it is not appropriate to make an order to produce or to give access because it is not practicable to communicate with a person entitled to produce or to grant access to the material or where a terrorist investigation "may be seriously prejudiced unless a constable can secure immediate access to the material".[56]

2–22   There are further exceptional provisions in Sch.5. One is the possibility of asking the judge to order anyone to provide an explanation of any material seized or

---

[48] [1998] C.O.D. 445, QBD.

[49] *R. v Manchester Stipendiary Magistrate, Ex p. Granada Television* [2000] 1 All E.R. 135, HL.

[50] Replacing the Prevention of Terrorism (Temporary Provisions) Act 1989, s.17 and Sch.7, para.3—as amended by the Criminal Justice Act 1993, s.50 and the Criminal Justice and Public Order Act 1994, s.83(10).

[51] As defined in s.14 of PACE.

[52] As defined in s.11 of PACE.

[53] Terrorism Act 2000, Sch.5, para.5.

[54] Sch.5, para.6. See *R. v Middlesex Guildhall Crown Court, Ex p. Salinger* (1993) 2 All E.R. 310 and *DPP v Channel 4 Television Co. Ltd* [1992] N.L.J. 1412, and comments at 1417.

[55] Sch.5, para.12(1).

[56] Sch.5, para.12(4).

produced (para.13). Legal professional privilege cannot be invaded by such a requirement, except that a lawyer can be required to reveal the name of his client (para.13(3)). Moreover, any answers cannot be used in evidence against the maker of the statement—save in proceedings for refusal to answer such questions.

Where an officer of the rank of superintendent or above has reasonable grounds for believing that the case is one of great emergency and that immediate action is necessary, he may, by written order, authorise a search which would normally require a search warrant (para.15(1)).

There is a remarkable further provision by which the Secretary of State himself can replace the magistrates' court or the judge and himself give orders or issue search warrants in respect of premises in Northern Ireland. The power exists only in relation to certain offences under the Terrorism Act 2000.[57] He must be satisfied of the same matters of which the magistrates or the judge must be satisfied and that disclosure to a court of the information required by the application could place someone in danger or prejudice the capability of police officers to investigate an offence under ss.15 to 18 or 56 of the Terrorism Act 2000 (para.19).

Armed Forces

The Armed Forces Act 2001, s.6 gives the Secretary of State the power to make regulations for procedures for Service police to gain access to excluded or special procedure material held in residential premises for which a search warrant is needed.   **2–23**

Application has to be made to a "judicial officer".[58] The procedures are the Service equivalent of s.9 and Sch.1 of PACE. As in the case of search warrants, the regulations may provide for applications to be made by live television link.

The procedure under Sch.1

Schedule 1 of PACE does not specify what must be the contents of a notice of intention to make an application for access to special procedure material. It is not surprising therefore that a number of reported cases have concerned the requirement of notice.   **2–24**

The notice must be given to the person holding the material not to the person under investigation.[59] As Watkins L.J. said: "It seems to me to be beyond doubt that ... the only parties referred to in the 1984 Act and the Schedule are the police who make the application and the person or institution in whose custody the special procedure material is thought to be".[60] An application does not require that there be a suspect, let alone someone charged. Where the material is held by someone other than the person under investigation, there is no question of giving that person a right to have notice of the application. Moreover, there is nothing

---

[57] Fund-raising (s.15); using and possession of money or property for the purposes of terrorism (s.16); funding (s.17); money laundering (s.18); and directing a terrorist organisation (s.56).
[58] See para.2–13 above.
[59] *R. v Crown Court at Leicester, Ex p. DPP* [1988] 86 Cr.App.R. 254; [1987] 3 All E.R. 654, DC.
[60] *ibid.*, at 656.

wrong with the police indicating in strong terms that they do not wish the persons under suspicion to be informed of the fact of the application.[61]

In a later case[62] the Court of Appeal held that a bank is not under a duty to inform its customer when it receives notice under s.9 of, and Sch.1 to, the Act that the police are applying for access to special procedure material. Its relationship of confidentiality with the customer gave rise to no implied contractual obligation that it would either oppose the police application or inform the customer. The normal duty of confidence owed to the customer could be displaced in four situations: (a) under compulsion of law; (b) where there is a public duty to disclose; (c) where the interests of the bank require it; and (d) where it is done with the express or implied consent of the customer. Here the exception was compulsion of law. The decision did not deal quite so clearly with the converse question of whether banks are under a duty *not* to inform their clients of the fact of police attempts to gain access to special procedure material. Lord Donaldson thought[63] that banks "were no doubt free to ignore a request [by the police] that [the client] not be informed of the application". But he went on to say that he would have been "surprised and disappointed if they had done so in the context of a criminal investigation unless they were under a legal duty to do so".

2–25   The notice must set out a description of all the material sought—even if that would create a risk that it might be destroyed.[64] (If the application would seriously prejudice the investigation, the police should apply for a search warrant under para.14(d).) In *Ex p. Adegbesan* the notice initially only said that an application would be made for an order under Sch.1. On being asked for further information, the police supplemented the original notice by stating that the application would be "on the first set of access conditions". As Watkins L.J. said, "That told the applicants very little more than they already knew".[65] The police had in fact prepared a detailed information to be used on the hearing of the application setting out what they wanted. Counsel for the applicants argued that his clients should have been served with this detailed information. The Divisional Court rejected this argument but it accepted that they should be supplied with some information as to what was sought. Where the information is sensitive the amount of information supplied to the recipient of the order may, however, be restricted.[66] "The overall objective should be to provide the recipient of the order with as much information, preferably in writing, as early as possible provided this is consistent with the security of the operation."[67]

---

[61] *R. v Manchester Crown Court, Ex p. Taylor* (1988) 87 Cr.App.R. 358; [1988] 1 W.L.R. 705 at 716, DC.

[62] *Barclay's Bank plc (trading as Barclaycard) v Taylor and another; Trustee Savings Bank of Wales and Border Counties v Taylor* [1989] 1 W.L.R. 1066; [1989] 3 All E.R. 563, CA.

[63] *ibid.*, [1989] 1 W.L.R. 1066 at 1074; [1989] 3 All E.R. 563 at 569.

[64] *R. v Central Criminal Court at Manchester, Ex p. Adegbesan* (1987) 84 Cr.App.R. 219; [1986] 1 W.L.R. 1292, DC.

[65] *ibid.*, at 1297.

[66] *R. v Middlesex Guildhall Crown Court, Ex p. Salinger* [1993] 2 All E.R. 310, DC, involving material regarding the Lockerbie bombing sought from ABC News International. The application was made under Sch.7 of the Prevention of Terrorism (Temporary Provisions) Act 1989, the terms of which are similar to the equivalent provisions of PACE.

[67] *ibid.*, at 320.

How specific must the notice be? It must specify the nature of the offence but it is sufficient if it indicates this in general terms ("theft", "fraud", "blackmail", etc.).[68] It must also show the address where the material is supposedly held.[69]

The notice itself should be in writing but in exceptional circumstances the detailed information about the material sought can be communicated orally rather than in writing.[70]

Must the prosecution give advance disclosure of the evidence on which the **2–26** application is based? In *Ex p. Baines & Baines*[71] the Divisional Court held that the police were not required to provide in advance the evidence they intended to rely on at the hearing lest advance notice lead to destruction of the material. The decision whether to disclose in advance the evidence to be relied on at the application was "best left to the judgment of the police". But anything given to the judge should also be given to the party against whom the order was sought, at the latest on the day of the hearing. If the police chose not to give that party copies of the evidence they intended to rely on prior to the date of the hearing, the judge should be prepared to grant an adjournment if evidence was given which could not be responded to adequately there and then. The court quashed the order made because neither the solicitors against whom the order was sought nor counsel acting for them had been given a copy of the police proof of evidence.

The officer making the application must satisfy the judge that the relevant set of access conditions have been established. The Divisional Court recently said that this requires grounds for belief, not merely grounds for suspicion, and that the material sought "is not merely general information which might be helpful to police inquiries, but evidence in the sense in which that term is applied in the Crown Court, 'relevant and admissible' at trial".[72]

In *Ex p. Baines & Baines* (above) the court said that the evidence produced in support of the application should equally not contain inadmissible and prejudicial material. ("It has, of course, to be recognised that in an application such as this, compliance with strict rules of evidence is not to be expected but statements which have no substance to the prejudice of the party who is the subject of the order sought are impermissible. They ought not to be made and if made should be ruled out by the judge."[73]) Disclosure must give the court the material it needs to make the decision, including anything that might weigh against making such an order.[74] This is especially so since, as already noted, many of these applications are effectively made *ex parte* because the bank or other party holding the material usually does not contest the application and indeed commonly is not even there at the hearing.[75]

---

[68] *R. v Central Criminal Court, Ex p. Ellis Carr, The Independent*, March 5, 1987, and on Lexis.
[69] *ibid.*
[70] *R. v Manchester Crown Court, Ex p. Taylor* [1988] 1 W.L.R. 705, DC. The police suspected that employees of the bank against whom the order was sought were implicated in the offence.
[71] *R. v Inner London Sessions Crown Court, Ex p. Baines & Baines* [1988] 1 Q.B. 579; [1987] 3 All E.R. 1025, DC.
[72] *R. v Central Criminal Court, Ex p. Bright, Alton, Rusbridger* [2001] 2 All E.R. 244 at 260, *per* Judge L.J.
[73] *op.cit.*, n.71 above, at 584 *per* Watkins L.J.
[74] *R. v Lewes Crown Court, Ex p. Hill* (1990) 93 Cr.App.R. 60; [1991] Crim.L.R. 376, DC.
[75] *ibid.*

2–27   The judge should be very careful before granting a special procedure application. It should never be a matter of common form.[76] As the Divisional Court said
in *Ex p. Waitt*, satisfaction as to fulfillment of the pre-conditions is an important
matter of substance. The special procedure was a serious inroad upon the liberty
of the subject. The responsibility for ensuring that the procedure was not abused
lay with the circuit judges. It was of cardinal importance that they should be
scrupulous in discharging that responsibility and especially when the police were
seeking a search warrant. It was always preferable that applications for special
procedure material should be made *inter partes*.[77]

The judge should state his reasons for finding that the access conditions have
been satisfied. But failure to do so is not fatal if the person concerned is not
prejudiced by the failure. The reasons need not be very full.[78]

Can the order be appealed? An order made by a judge under Sch.1 to produce
or give access to special procedure material is an order made in a "criminal cause
or matter" within s.18(1)(a) of the Supreme Court Act 1981, even though criminal proceedings have not yet been instituted. It follows that the Court of Appeal
has no jurisdiction in the matter. Challenge by way of an application for judicial
review must go from the Divisional Court direct to the House of Lords.[79] If the
police lose a judicial review case, it does not prevent them starting afresh in
seeking an order for production or search warrant under the Schedule.[80]

Although the courts occasionally reject special procedure applications, usually
on procedural grounds, such applications are normally successful and they have
been used a great deal. In the first three years of PACE alone, over 2,000 applications for access to special procedure material were granted. The police have
found the procedure especially useful in investigation of mortgage frauds in relation to records held by banks, building societies, estate agents and solicitors.[81]

"Items subject to legal privilege": s.10[82]

2–28   Material covered by legal professional privilege cannot be the subject of a search
warrant issued by the magistrates nor can it be searched for by the police. What

---

[76] *R. v Maidstone Crown Court, Ex p. Waitt* [1988] Crim.L.R. 384, DC; *cf. R. v Leeds Crown Court, Ex p. Switalski* [1992] Crim.L.R. 559, DC.
[77] See to like effect *R. v Lewes Crown Court, Ex p. Hill* (1991) 93 Cr.App.R. 60; [1991] Crim.L.R. 559, DC; *R. v Southampton Crown Court, Ex p. J and P* [1993] Crim.L.R. 962, DC; *R. v Southwark Crown Court and H.M.Customs and Excise, Ex p. Sorsky Defries* [1996] Crim.L.R. 195, DC; *Gross, Gross and Gross v Southwark Crown Court* [1998] C.O.D. 445, QBD; *R. v Central Criminal Court, Ex p. The Guardian, The Observer and Bright* [2001] 2 All E.R. 244; [2002] Crim.L.R. 64.
[78] *Ex p. Ellis Carr, op.cit.*, n.68 above.
[79] *Carr v Atkins* [1987] 1 Q.B. 963, CA.
[80] For an example of a highly technical decision see *R. v Manchester Crown Court, Ex p. Rogers* [1999] 2 Cr.App.R. 267; [1999] Crim.L.R. 743, DC. The judge's order was quashed even though it might well have been validly made if it had been properly applied for. The Divisional Court in effect sent the prosecution away to apply again properly.
[81] Lidstone, "The Police and Criminal Evidence (Northern Ireland) Order 1989: Powers of Entry, Search and Seizure" (1989) 40 *Northern Ireland Law Qtrly* 333, 344.
[82] See 1989 N.I. PACE Order, Art.12. The same definition of legally privileged material is incorpo-
rated in the Drug Trafficking Offences Act 1986, s.27 and the Terrorism Act 2000, Sch.5, para.4.

is covered by this term? In the first PACE Bill, legal privilege was to be confined to communications between a professional legal adviser and his client made in connection with the giving of legal advice to the client. This was then extended by amendment in Committee to include also communications between a professional legal adviser and his client or between such an adviser or his client and any other person made in connection with or in contemplation of legal proceedings and for the purpose of such proceedings.

Subsequently, by further amendment, the Government changed the definition again. The final version which was adopted in the second Bill and which became law in s.10(1) described the categories covered as: (a) communications made in connection with the giving of legal advice between the professional legal adviser and his client "or any person representing his client"; and (b) communications made[83] in connection with or in contemplation of legal proceedings and for the purposes of such proceedings made between the professional legal adviser and his client or any person representing his client or between such a legal adviser or his client or any such representative and any other person.

Documents or other items mentioned or enclosed with such communications are also covered by legal privilege if the communication is made[84] either in connection with the giving of legal advice or in connection with or contemplation of legal proceedings and for the purpose of such proceedings and if they are in the possession of someone entitled to possession of them (s.10(1)(c)). But documents or articles held with the intention of furthering a criminal purpose are stated not to be items subject to legal privilege (see below).

What does the privilege cover? In *Ex p. Baines & Baines*[85] the police were **2–29** seeking information concerning the purchase of various properties following the £26 million Brink's-Mat Ltd robbery at Heathrow Airport. A judge granted the police a production order against a firm of solicitors, requiring them to make available for inspection "all client account records including ledgers, day books, cash books, account books and other records used in the ordinary business of the [firm]" in whatever form, in connection with the purchase of a named property. As has been seen above para.2–26 the Divisional Court quashed the order on the ground that the formalities had not been properly observed. The court also briefly considered the argument for the solicitors that the material sought was covered by legal professional privilege. It held that an item was covered by legal privilege if it was a communication made in connection with the giving of advice. Records of conveyancing transactions were not privileged since they were not connected with advice. It was held in *R. v Guildhall Magistrates' Court, Ex p. Primlaks Holding Co. (Panama) Inc*[86] that clients' documents sent to solicitors together with correspondence for the purpose of obtaining legal advice are not covered by legal professional privilege if they are pre-existing documents, unless they were made in connection with the giving of legal advice or in connection with or in

---

[83] *R. v Leeds Magistrates' Court, Ex p. Dumbleton* [1993] Crim.L.R. 866, DC—"made" means lawfully made and does not extend to forged documents. See further *Ex p. Francis and Francis* below.

[84] "Made" here means brought into existence—see *R* [1995] 1 Cr.App.R. 183; [1994] 4 All E.R. 260, CA, where it was held that a DNA test obtained by the defence was protected by legal professional privilege and the prosecution were not entitled to ask for its production or for the production of a scientist's opinion based on the test.

[85] *R. v Inner London Sessions Crown Court, Ex p. Baines & Baines* [1988] 1 Q.B. 579, CA.

[86] [1989] 2 W.L.R. 841, HL.

contemplation of legal proceedings and for the purpose of such proceedings.[87] Correspondence between the client and his solicitor seeking or giving advice would be privileged. As has been seen, privilege applies to a blood sample taken for the purpose of legal proceedings—*R.*[88] See also *Davies.*[89] D was charged with murder. He had two medical defence witnesses regarding his diminished responsibility. The defence did not disclose the report of a third doctor who had seen D in prison. The prosecution asked that it be disclosed. The trial judge ruled that although her report was privileged, the third doctor's opinion was not and ordered that it be divulged. Holding the conviction to be unsafe, the Court of Appeal ruled that the instructions sent to the doctor, what D had said to the doctor and her opinion were all equally privileged.

2–30   Commenting on the decision in *Ex p. Baines & Baines*, the head of the Law Society's Legal Practice Directorate, legal adviser's branch, recommended[90] that a practitioner faced with a production order should go through his relevant files and make lists of any communications falling within s.10(1)(a). "He should also make a note of each document or other item which was enclosed with or referred to in any such communication if it is at least arguable that it was made in connection with the giving of legal advice."[91] The list should be served on the police with a copy to the judge. The solicitor should also, of course, seek instructions from the client since the privilege is that of the client. Also, opposing a production order may be a costly business and the solicitor will require his client's or the Legal Service Commission's approval to incur the necessary expense.

"In furtherance of a criminal purpose"

2–31   As has been seen, the privilege does not apply if the material in question is held "with the intention of furthering a criminal purpose". A critical question is, whose intention? In *Ex p. Francis & Francis,*[92] the House of Lords gave this a very wide interpretation. The police sought an order under the Drug Trafficking Offences Act 1986 for access to correspondence and attendance notes held by a firm of solicitors concerning property transactions entered into by a client. (The 1986 Act set out a scheme regarding access to special procedure and excluded material similar to that in PACE and the phrase "legal privilege" was given the

---

[87] See, similarly, *R. v Manchester Crown Court, Ex p. Rogers* [1999] 2 Cr.App.R. 267; [1999] Crim.L.R. 743, DC—a solicitor's appointment diary was not covered by legal professional privilege because no legal advice was involved. See also *R. v Minshull Crown Court, Ex p. Miller Gardner Solicitors* [2002] EWHC 3077 Admin. Likewise in *King (David)* (1983) 77 Cr.App.R. 1, a communication between a solicitor and a handwriting expert was privileged but the documents on which he based his expert opinion were not.

[88] *op. cit.*, n.84, above.

[89] [2002] EWCA Crim 85; (2002) 166 J.P. 243, decision of January 23, 2002.

[90] Eric Hiley, "Production orders under the Police and Criminal Evidence Act: two important cases" Law Soc. Gaz., October 28, 1987, p.3088.

[91] *ibid.*, p.3090.

[92] *R. v Central Criminal Court, Ex p. Francis and Francis* [1989] A.C. 346, HL, overruling, *inter alia*, *R. v Snaresbrook Crown Court, Ex p. DPP* [1988] Q.B. 532, DC.

same definition.[93]) The police suspected that an innocent client had been put in funds by a relative who was thought to be involved in drug trafficking. They obtained a production order from a judge requiring the solicitors to produce all their files relating to a particular transaction. A judge gave leave to have the order quashed in so far as it concerned some privileged documents but on the substantive hearing the Divisional Court refused the application for judicial review on the ground that the documents were held with the intention of furthering a criminal purpose within s.10(2).[94] The criminal intention was not that of either the solicitor or his client but of a third party. The House of Lords (Lords Bridge and Oliver dissenting) upheld the Divisional Court. Since the documents held by the solicitors were intended by the third person to further the purpose of laundering the proceeds of drug trafficking, s.10(2) deprived the documents of privilege. The fact that the solicitor and even the client were innocent of any such intention was irrelevant.

Moreover, it seems that the "criminal purpose" does not have to be a specific one of committing a particular crime. It is enough if the purpose is simply to "salt away" the proceeds of crime through the purchase of property.[95]

On the question as to when the criminal purpose must arise or exist, Lord Goff **2–32** said the critical moment is when the communication is made: did the client or some third person have a criminal purpose at the moment when the communication in question came into the solicitor's possession? That is the point in time at which legal privilege would be negatived under s.10(2). Lord Goff said, *obiter*, however, that he was inclined to think that the common law principle of legal professional privilege could not be excluded on the grounds of a criminal purpose where a communication was made by a client regarding the conduct of his case in criminal or civil proceedings merely because it is untrue and would, if acted upon, lead to perjury.[96]

The House of Lords' decision caused much concern to the professions generally and to the solicitors' branch of the legal profession in particular. Its impact affected barristers and accountants, as well as solicitors.[97] The Law Society's view, expressed in the *Gazette*, was that *Ex p. Francis and Francis* did not go so far as to say that the criminal intention of a third party would, in all cases, deprive an innocent client of privilege. Examination of the speeches of Lords Brandon and Goff suggested that the client's privilege would only be lost if the third party was using the client as an intermediary or innocent tool.[98] But even if this is correct it does not solve the practical problem that where the police allege a criminal intention on the part of a third person, it is difficult for the professional

---

[93] See s.29(2). These provisions were subsequently replaced by the Drug Trafficking Act 1994, s.55. See also the similar but not identical provisions of the Proceeds of Crime Act 1995, s.11 inserting s.93H into the Criminal Justice Act 1988 and the decision of the House of Lords in *R. v Crown Court at Southwark, Ex p. Bowles* [1998] 2 All E.R. 193.

[94] *Ex p. Francis and Francis* [1988] 1 All E.R. 677, DC.

[95] *op. cit.*, n.92 above, at 393–394.

[96] *ibid.*, at 397.

[97] For a severely critical assessment of the House of Lords' decision see Newbold, "The Crime/Fraud Exception to Legal Professional Privilege" (1990) 53 Mod.L.Rev. 472.

[98] Peter Stevenson, "Privilege: Francis & Francis and other recent cases", Law Soc. Gaz., February 1, 1989, p.26.

adviser to establish the nature of the relationship between his client and the third party.[99]

The fact that a document held by a solicitor does not enjoy legal privilege because it is held with the purpose of furthering a criminal purpose does not necessarily mean that it ceases to be special procedure material. In *Ex p. Dumbleton*[1] the Divisional Court held that it would not enjoy the status of special procedure material since a dishonest solicitor could not be said to hold a forged document subject to an express or implied undertaking to hold it in confidence. In that case the solicitor was accused of being involved in the conspiracy. But if the solicitor was innocent of any involvement in the criminal conduct, special procedure status should still apply.

It has been held that material obtained by the police under Pt II of PACE which is subject to legal professional privilege cannot be passed by the police to private individuals for the purposes of civil litigation.[2]

"Excluded material": s.11[3]

2–33   Section 11 defines "excluded material". Anything which is in this category is totally exempt from any order or warrant under Sch.1 unless the police could have obtained a search warrant to look for it pre-PACE, for instance, because it is a stolen or forged article for which a search warrant could have been obtained under pre-PACE legislation such as the Theft Act 1968. (The fact that something is excluded material does not, however, prevent the person holding it from handing it over voluntarily to the police.[4])

Subsection (1) provides that "excluded material" consists of three categories of material held on a confidential basis: (a) personal records (defined in s.12); (b) samples of human tissue or tissue fluid taken for the purpose of diagnosis or medical treatment and which are held in confidence; and (c) journalistic material (defined in s.13) consisting of documents or records if held in confidence. Subsections (2) and (3) define what is meant by the concept of "held in confidence" respectively for excluded material other than journalistic material and for journalistic material.

Excluded material other than journalistic material is held in confidence if it is held subject to an express or implied undertaking to hold it in confidence or it is held subject to a restriction on disclosure or obligation of secrecy contained in any statute. Journalistic material is held in confidence if held subject to such an undertaking, restriction or obligation and it has been continuously so held,

---

[99] See also Alt, "Raids: against the law?" (1991) 135 S.J. 1248.

[1] *R. v Leeds Magistrates' Court, Ex p. Dumbleton* [1993] Crim. L.R. 866.

[2] *Marcel v Metropolitan Police Comr* [1992] 1 All E.R. 72, CA (Civ Div), rejecting an appeal on that point from a decision by the Vice-Chancellor [1991] 1 W.L.R. 1118; [1991] 1 All E.R. 845.

[3] See 1989 N.I. PACE Order, Art.13.

[4] *Singleton* (1995) 1 Cr.App.R. 431; [1995] Crim.L.R. 236, CA. A dentist voluntarily handed over to the police dental records of a patient. The record was part of the prosecution's case. The patient was convicted. He failed to persuade the Court of Appeal to quash the conviction. The confidentiality was that of the dentist not that of the defendant and it could therefore be waived without reference to the suspect.

whether by one or more than one person, since it was first acquired or created for the purposes of journalism. This last requirement does not apply to other categories of excluded material, apparently because of a sense that they are intrinsically more sensitive.

Meaning of "personal records": s.12[5]

"Personal records" for this purpose are defined to mean documents and other   **2–34**
records concerning an individual (whether living or dead) who can be identified from them which relate: (a) to his physical or mental health[6]; or (b) to spiritual counselling or assistance given or to be given to him; or (c) to counselling or assistance given or to be given to him for the purposes of his personal welfare and involving counselling given or to be given to him by any voluntary organisation or by any individual who by reason of his office or occupation has responsibility for his personal welfare or by reason of a court order has responsibility for his supervision.

The exemption of personal records, as defined, from any access by the police is absolute. This was in response to the fierce campaign waged during the passage of the Bill, in particular by the British Medical Association, the bishops and the Citizens' Advice Bureaux. The definition is very wide. It would cover not simply the records of probation officers, social workers and advisory agencies but school and university personal files and records. It does not, however, cover "things" such as the bullet taken from a wound, or bloodstained clothing. The contents of a stomach pumped out by the doctors would probably be excluded material as human tissue or tissue fluids. So too would be any form of medical record. But the records of accountants or other professional advisers do not qualify—save in so far as they gained exemption through legal privilege. An accountant is not an individual who through his office or occupation has responsibility for the client's "personal welfare" within the meaning of the phrase. There is no definition of this phrase in the Act, but the section is plainly intended to cover the caring professions and their voluntary counterparts.

Meaning of "journalistic material": s.13[7]

Mr William Whitelaw, the Home Secretary on the first Bill, was persuaded to   **2–35**
grant an exemption from police action also to the journalists' lobby. Subsequently

---

[5] See 1989 N.I. PACE Order, Art.14.
[6] An attempt to get access to hospital out-patient records failed where the record sought was that of a man suspected of murder who had been injured during the killing. The argument that the records were "administrative" rather than "personal" was rejected by the circuit judge (Lidstone, "Powers of Entry, Search and Seizure" (1989), N.I.L.Q. 333 at 338, n.18). See also *R. v Cardiff Crown Court, Ex p. Kellam, The Times*, May 3, 1993, DC where the court held that records detailing the movements into and out of a hospital for mentally ill people were within the definition of excluded material and quashed a production order made by the judge.
[7] See 1989 N.I. PACE Order, Art.15.

some journalists and newspaper editors expressed disquiet about the desirability of this special status but Mr Leon Brittan, Home Secretary on the second Bill, decided not to respond to their fears. He maintained the concession agreed by his predecessor. (Note however, that if the police can gain access to the material under other legislation—such as the Theft Act or the Official Secrets Act 1989[8]—the "excluded material" category does not give protection. Nor is it protected if the material in question is sought in connection with an inquiry into terrorist offences—see Terrorism Act 2000, Sch.5, paras 4–6.)

As has been seen, excluded material is defined (in s.11(1)(c)) to include journalistic material which consists of documents or other records, held in confidence. Journalistic material is only deemed to be held in confidence in this context if it is both held subject to an undertaking, restriction or obligation to hold it in confidence and if it has been continuously held by one or more persons subject to such an undertaking, restriction or obligation since it was first acquired or created for the purposes of journalism (s.11(2) and (3)). Most material sent to journalists is sent for the purposes of publication and is therefore unlikely to qualify as excluded material, though it could still qualify as special procedure material. The fact that the person who passes the information does not wish to be identified as the source does not in itself make the information excluded material.

2–36   Journalistic material is defined as material "acquired or created for the purposes of journalism" (s.13(1)). Journalism is not defined but it includes any form of publication. It is not confined to publication for reward nor to full-time or even professional journalists. Material is only journalistic material, however, if it is in the possession of someone who either acquired or created it for the purposes of journalism (s.13(2)). This would protect material passed by a journalist to his superiors or to the organisation for which he worked. But it would not cover material that was held by someone not involved in journalism. The Act states that a person who receives unsolicited material from someone who intends that he should use it for the purposes of journalism is taken to have acquired it for that purpose (s.13(3)). Journalistic material that does not qualify as "excluded material" could still be "special procedure material".

Meaning of "special procedure material": s.14[9]

2–37   Section 14 defines "special procedure material" for the purposes of s.9 of the Act. In essence, it comprises material held on a confidential basis which does not qualify as excluded material or material subject to legal privilege.

Subsection (2) states that material is special procedure material if (not being excluded material or subject to legal privilege) it is held subject to an express or implied undertaking of confidentiality or a statutory restriction on disclosure or obligation of secrecy (for instance under the Official Secrets Act) by someone who acquired it or created it in the course of a trade, business, profession or other occupation or for the purpose of any office whether paid or unpaid. This would include, say, company accounts or stock records held on behalf of

---

[8] Which replaced the Official Secrets Act 1911.
[9] See 1989 N.I. PACE Order, Art.16.

a client by a bank, solicitor or accountant. The question of whether there is an implied confidential relationship will be determined by the nature of the relationship, the kind of information imparted together with any relevant custom, usage or understanding.[10]

Subsection (3) provides that material acquired by employees from their employer or by a company from an associated company is only special procedure material if it was such material immediately before it was acquired. This means that company records cannot be special procedure material simply by virtue of an instruction by an employer to an employee that they should be held in confidence. The special procedure is intended primarily for material held in confidence by a third party. But if it is special procedure material it remains special procedure material even though it may be passed by an employer to an employee—say in an accountants' firm or a bank.

Subsections (4) and (5) make similar provision for special procedure material created by an employee in the course of employment or by a company on behalf of an associated company.

Safeguards for obtaining search warrants: ss.15 and 16 and PACE Code B, s.2[11]

The Philips Royal Commission recommended that new safeguards should be laid down to apply to the issue of all search warrants.[12] These proposals were incorporated in s.15.   **2–38**

Subsection (1) states that this section and s.16 apply to search warrants issued under any enactment whether passed before or after PACE and that entry on or search of premises under a warrant is unlawful unless it complies with ss.15 and 16.

An application for a search warrant must state the enactment under which the application is made, the premises to be searched, the object of the search in as much detail as possible and the grounds for making the application. It must also state that the material sought does not include items subject to legal privilege or special procedure or excluded material. If persons other than police officers are to accompany the officers, authority for them to do so should also be included (Code B, para.3.6(f) and Note 3C). The Police Reform Act 2002 provides that s.15 applies as much to the issue of a warrant to authorised civilian investigating officers as to police officers.[13]

A search warrant must relate to premises; it can never authorise a search for material wherever it may be found.[14] But it is not necessary that the items sought

---

[10] See *Gilbert v Star Newspapers Ltd* (1984) 11 T.L.R. 4; *Talbot v General Television Corpn Pty Ltd* [1981] R.P.C. 1; *Fraser v Thames Television Ltd* [1984] Q.B. 44; *Coco v A. N. Clark (Engineers) Ltd* [1969] R.P.C. 41 at 47.

[11] See 1989 N.I. PACE Order, Arts 17 and 18.

[12] Philips Report, paras 3.46 and 3.47.

[13] Sch.4, Pt 2, para.16(d).

[14] *R. v Chief Constable of the Warwickshire Constabulary, Ex p. Fitzpatrick* [1998] 1 All E.R. 65, 71.

should belong to or be in possession of a named person. The person who holds the material may be entirely innocent of any connection with the matter.

2–39   The previously mentioned survey by Lidstone showed a tendency in informations and warrants to use generic terms such as "electrical goods", which he suggested was not good enough.[15] The application, which is invariably made *ex parte* (*i.e.* without the person affected being present), must be supported by an information in writing (s.15(3)). The constable must answer on oath any questions put by the justice of the peace (s.15(4)). (Lidstone's pre-PACE study showed a reliance on the formula "As a result of information received from a previously reliable source" and a lack of questioning as to reliability by magistrates. A post-PACE study by the same writer suggested that this formula continued to be used, though somewhat less frequently, and that magistrates were no more questioning than they were before the Act![16])

The application for the warrant should also state that there are no grounds to believe that the material sought consists of or includes items subject to legal privilege, or special procedure or excluded material.

If it is intended to take civilian support personnel the application for the warrant should ask for their presence to be authorised in the warrant

The warrant must specify[17] the name of the person applying for it; the date of issue; the statutory power under which it is issued; the premises to be searched[18]; and, so far as practicable, the articles or persons sought[19]; and when the search is to take place (s.15(6)).

2–40   Before applying for a search warrant the police should consider very carefully what material they hope the search will reveal. In complex special procedure applications it might be appropriate to ask in the first instance for production of documents appearing to relate to the matter under investigation. Also, on such applications a note should be taken of what was said by the police and the judge.[20] There should be careful briefing of the officers who execute the warrant and both the extent and the limits of the search should be fully understood. Also, the articles identified must be those in the information.[21]

---

[15] See Lidstone, *op.cit.*, para.2–27 n.81 above, p.351, n.54.

[16] *ibid.*, n.55

[17] s.15(6)(a)(i). In *Hunt* (1995) 16 Cr.App.R.(S.) 87; [1994] Crim.L.R. 747 the Court of Appeal held that a warrant that named the officer in charge and specified that no more than 55 officers could enter the premises complied with the requirements of the Act. It rejected the view that the names of all the officers had to be stated.

[18] Where the police wish to search only a part of premises divided into separate dwellings and the common parts of those premises, they must make that clear to the justices in the information when applying for the warrant—*R. v South Western Magistrates' Court, Ex p. Cofie*, *The Times*, August 15, 1996, DC.

[19] But the courts do not require great specificity—see *IRC v Rossminster* [1980] A.C. 952, HL. The requirement as to the specificity of the warrant in the Taxes Management Act 1970 is still less onerous—see *R. v Crown Court at Middlesex Guildhall, Ex p. Tamosius & Partners* [2000] 1 W.L.R. 453, DC.

[20] The value of a note in complex search warrant cases even in the magistrates' court was mentioned by the Divisional Court in *R. v Marylebone Magistrates' Court, Ex p. Amdrell Ltd (trading as Get Stuffed)* (1998) 162 J.P. 719; 148 New L.J. 1230.

[21] *R. v Central Criminal Court, Ex p. AJD Holdings* [1992] Crim.L.R. 669, DC.

The justices are not required to give their reasons for granting the application for a warrant. Providing the material presented by the police in the information is sufficiently detailed they need not even make a note.[22]

Two copies of the warrant must be made (s.15(7)), and certified as copies (s.15(8)) by the court itself, though both functions can be delegated to the court staff.[23] The warrant, of which copies must be made, includes any schedule setting out the particulars of documents and other material sought.[24] One copy is for the occupier of the premises to keep (s.16(5)) and one is to be retained by the police. The original goes back to the issuing court (s.16(10)). The judge or magistrate who issues the warrant should sign the authorisation and ideally should also initial all other pages attached to it.[25] Each warrant can authorise entry on only one occasion (s.15(5)). If nothing is found, the police can therefore only return to have another attempt after they have obtained a second warrant. (But see para. 2–43 below.)

There is one ambiguity in s.15. Subsection (1) states that "an entry on or search of premises under a warrant is unlawful unless it complies with this section and section 16 below". The ambiguity relates to the word "it". Is compliance required only of the warrant or of the whole entry and search? In *Longman*[26] Lord Lane C.J. said, *obiter*, "With some hesitation we are inclined to think it probably refers to the warrant, but the real probability is that the intention of the framers of the Act was to provide that the warrant should comply with the terms of section 15 and the entry and search should comply with section 16. But, that is not what it says. So we leave that problem unresolved."[27] In *R. v Chief Constable of Lancashire, Ex p. Parker and Magrath* the Divisional Court said it read "it" as referring to the entire process so that in order for the process to be lawful the application for and issue of the warrant has to be in compliance with s.15 and its execution has to comply with s.16.[28] This seems the better view. It was adopted by the Divisional Court in *Ex p. Fitzpatrick*[29] and again in *Ex p. Bramley*.[30]

2–41

The Joint Home Office/Cabinet Office Review of PACE reported that the police wanted to see some relaxation of the restraints on search warrants. Problems arose, for instance, from the fact that a warrant authorised only one entry:

"In cases where there is a lot of material or extensive premises to search, this may result in an officer having to 'camp out' in order to fulfil the terms of the warrant. A particular problem was caused by items being moved from one property to another or money from one bank account to another so that additional warrants have to be obtained. The Review's attention was also drawn to restrictions on expanding the scope of a search beyond what is specified in a warrant. For example, if the target of a search is a shotgun there may be legal

---

[22] *R. (Cronin) v Sheffield Justices* [2002] EWHC 2568 Admin; [2003] 1 W.L.R.752.
[23] *R. v Chief Constable of Lancashire, Ex p. Parker and Magrath* [1993] 2 All E.R. 56 at 61, DC.
[24] *ibid.,* at 59.
[25] *ibid.,* at 63.
[26] (1988) 88 Cr.App.R. 148; [1988] 1 W.L.R. 619; [1988] Crim.L.R. 534, CA.
[27] [1988] 1 W.L.R. 619 at 623.
[28] *op.cit.,* n.23 above, at 60–61.
[29] [1998] 1 All E.R. 65 at 75.
[30] *R. v Chesterfield Justices and another, Ex p. Bramley* [2000] 1 All E.R. 411 at 422, *per* Kennedy L.J.

difficulties with searching a small cupboard that could not physically contain the gun. Problems could also arise if the search for the gun actually discovered illegal drugs and officers immediately wanted to re-focus their attention on searching for other drugs which might be on the premises."[31]

2–42   The "Options Proposed" were allowing entry on more than one occasion; having warrants shaped in respect of a person rather than a property or bank account; allowing more generalised searching of premises; and extending the target of a search if circumstances justified it. The "Preferred Action" stated that revising the warrant system to allow more flexibility as proposed in the "Options Proposed" was "attractive" but "more consultation would be needed before producing definite proposals". It suggested (p.19) that a consultation paper be issued.

In August 2004 the Home Office issued a Consultation Paper, *Policing: Modernising Police Powers to Meet Community Needs*, which proposed for consideration:

- that search warrants be capable of covering any premises occupied or controlled or accessible by a named individual;

- that the person granting a warrant be given a discretion to fix its duration so that the one month restriction would be abolished;

- that the rule limiting entry to one occasion also be abolished, so as to permit repeated entry providing each could be justified;

- that applications for a search warrant by telephone or electronic means be permitted.

2–43   The Serious Organised Crime and Police Bill introduced in November 2004 adopted almost all the recommendations of the Consultation Paper.

— In s.8, new (1C) and (1D) allow that a warrant may authorise entry on more than one occasion (or for an unlimited number of occasions) if the magistrate issuing the warrant is satisfied that this is necessary to achieve the purpose for which the warrant is issued (cl.105(2)).

- The officer applying for the warrant must state whether he is asking for unlimited entries or, if not, the maximum number of entries desired (new s.15(2)(a)(iii)—see cl.105(4) of the Bill).

- If the warrant authorises multiple entries, it must specify whether the number is unlimited, or limited to a specified maximum (new s.15(5A)—see cl.105(6) of the Bill).

---

[31] Joint Review, 2002, para.19, p.19.

- Two copies must be made of a specific premises warrant specifiying only one entry and as many as are reasonably required of any other kind of warrant (replacement s.15(7)—see cl.105(7) of the Bill).

- Warrants can be executed within three months instead of within one month as before (amendment of s.16(3)—see cl.105(8)(a) of the Bill).

- No premises may be entered for the second or any subsequent time under a warrant authorising multiple entry unless an officer of the rank of inspector or above has authorised it in writing (new s.16(3B)—see cl.105(8)(b) of the Bill).

- A warrant must be returned to the appropriate person (a) when it has been executed; or (b) in the case of a specific premises warrant, or an all premises warrant, or any warrant authorising multiple entries, upon the expiry of the three months or sooner. If the warrant is issued by a justice of the peace the appropriate person is the designated officer for the local justice area. If it is issued by a judge, it is the appropriate officer of the issuing court (replacement s.16(10) and new (subs.10A)—see cl.105(8)(c) of the Bill).

— *New "all premises warrants"* Clause 105(1) of the Bill makes various amendments to allow a magistrate to authorise searches of premises that cannot be identified at the time of the issue of the warrant.

- A new subs.(1A) of s.8 provides that a search warrant can relate (a) to one or more sets of premises—"specific premises warrant"; or (b) to "any premises occupied or controlled by a person specified in the application"—an "all premises warrant".

- New subs.(1B) adds that if it is an "all premises warrant", the magistrate must also be satisfied (a) that because of the particulars of the offence there are reasonable grounds for believing that in order to find the material sought it is necessary to search premises occupied or controlled by the person in question that are not specified in the application; and (b) that it is not reasonably practicable to specify all the premises which he occupies or controls and which might need to be searched.

- In s.15, a new subs.(2A)(b) states that if the application is for an "all premises warrant" the application must specify (i) as many of the premises to be searched as can be specified; (ii) the person who is in occupation or control of those premises; (iii) why it is necessary to search premises other than those that can be specified under (i); and (iv) why it is not practicable to specify all the premises which it is desired to search.

- Replacement s.15(6)(a)(iv), as to what must be said in the warrant regarding the premises, requires that it must identify each set of premises to be searched (or in the case of an all premises warrant), the person in occupation or control of premises to be searched, including any premises to be searched that can be identified.

- In s.16, new subs.(3A) states that under an all premises warrant, premises that are not specified in the warrant cannot be entered or searched unless an officer of the rank of inspector has authorised such entry in writing.

- New words added to s.16(9)(b) as to what must be endorsed on the warrant regarding anything found during the search, require that this must identify the premises in question.

- In Sch.1, new para.12A states that the judge may not issue an all premises warrant unless he is satisfied (a) that there are reasonable grounds for believing that it is necessary to search premises occupied or controlled by the person in question which are not specified in the application; and (b) that it is not reasonably practicable to specify all such premises.

Execution of warrants: s.16 and Code B[32]

2–44   Section 16 contains provisions to ensure that warrants are executed in a proper and reasonable manner. The provisions are supplemented by Code B for the searching of premises (see paras 2–50—2–57 below). Section 16 applies to all warrants executed by the police. The Police Reform Act 2002 extended the provisions of s.16 to authorised civilian investigating officers whether the warrant was issued to them or to someone else.[33] In so far as other statutes lay down different conditions they were repealed by s.15(1).

The courts have held that a search is a draconian though necessary power and there should be a careful briefing of the officers who are to execute it so as to ensure that they understand the extent and limits of the search and seizure operation.[34]

Until 2004 it was required that an officer of the rank of inspector be the officer in charge of a search under warrant (Code B, paras 2.10 and 6.14). But the requirement that an officer of the rank of inspector be in charge was dropped in the 2004 revision of the Codes.

2–45   Subsection (1) provides that any constable may execute any warrant. This overrides provisions in a number of statutes which specify that only the constable named in the warrant may execute it.

---

[32] See 1989 N.I. PACE Order, Art.18.
[33] Sch.4, Pt 2, para.16(e).
[34] *R. v Central Criminal Court, Ex p. AJD Holdings* [1992] Crim.L.R. 669, DC.

Subsection (2) states that a warrant may authorise persons to accompany the officer executing it. A new Note for Guidance in the 2003 revision of Code B said that this would cover any suitably qualified or skilled person or expert in a particular field whose presence is needed to help in the accurate identification of the material sought or to advise where certain forms of evidence are most likely to be found and how they should be dealt with (Note 3C). This does not give such civilian support personnel a right to force entry but it does give them a right to be there in support and to search for and seize items (Code C, Note 3C as amended in 2004).

As has been seen, the Police Reform Act 2002, Sch.4, Pt 2 gives civilians accredited as "investigating officers" basically the same powers of entry, search and seizure as a police officer.[35] Also, the Criminal Justice Act 2003 included a new subs.(2A) for s.16 stating that a person so authorised "has the same powers as the constable whom he accompanies in respect of (a) the execution of the warrant; and (b) the seizure of anything to which the warrant relates". New subs.(2B) added, however, that the authorised civilian could exercise such powers "only in the company, and under the supervision of a constable".[36] (See also para.2–56 below.)

If unauthorised persons take part, their presence must be revealed to the occupier and his permission sought for their entry. Failure to get such consent makes the entry of an unauthorised person unlawful and the unlawfulness taints the entire procedure.[37]

Section 16(3) provides that the entry and search under a warrant must be **2–46** within one month from the date of its issue.[38] Entry must be at a "reasonable hour" unless "it appears to the constable executing it that the purpose of a search may be frustrated on an entry at a reasonable hour" (subs.(4)). The test is subjective—qualified only by the condition that his belief must be honest. Where the occupier of the premises is present, the constable must produce a copy of the warrant and must give a copy to him (subs.(5)). Failure to do so has been held to be ground for making the search and seizure unlawful which required return by the police of everything seized.[39] If he is not present, a copy must be left there in a prominent place on the premises (subs.(7)). An officer executing a warrant must identify himself and if he is not in uniform he must produce documentary evidence that he is a constable even without being asked (subs.(5) and Code B, para.6.5[40]). If the occupier is not there but someone else is who appears to be in charge, the police should treat him as the occupier for the purposes of this section (subs.(6)).

---

[35] For the text of Pt 2 see the end of Ch.12 below.

[36] Criminal Justice Act, s.2, based on the proposal in the Joint Review, para.20, p.20. See to like effect Code B, para.2.11(c).

[37] *R. v Southwark Crown Court, Ex p. Gross, Gross and Gross*, unreported, Case No.CO 3920–96, March 18, 1997, DC. The unauthorised presence there was that of a US official at the execution of a search warrant pursuant to a request under the Criminal Justice (International Co-operation) Act 1990. The Divisional Court quashed the warrants and issued a declaration that the search and seizure were unlawful.

[38] Provisions for shorter periods in other acts were presumably intended to be repealed by s.15(1)—though the Criminal Justice and Public Order Act 1994, Sch.9, para.23 specifically changed 14 days to a month in s.4(2) of the Protection of Children Act 1978 and s.17(1) of the Video Recording Act 1984. As noted above, the Serious Organised Crime and Police Bill 2004–2005 would extend a month to three months.

[39] *op.cit.*, n.34 above.

[40] Formerly 5.5.

However, the courts recognise that sometimes these rules do not have to be complied with. In *R. v Longman*[41] the police came to the premises with a search warrant for drugs. But in order to gain entry without alerting the occupants to their impending arrival a plain clothes officer posed as a delivery girl from Interflora. When the door was opened a number of officers burst in. They therefore had not identified themselves as required by s.16(5), nor had they shown the householder their search warrant as required by Code B. The Court of Appeal held that force or subterfuge could legitimately be used for the purposes of gaining entry with a search warrant. The warrant was "produced" within the meaning of s.16(5)(a) and (b) when the occupier was given a chance of inspecting it. It was not enough simply to show him the warrant. But in this particular case the occupier had not tried to look at it. Instead he had shouted a warning to others in the building and had then attacked the officers with a knife. In those circumstances the strict terms of s.16(5) and Code B did not have to be complied with.

2–47   Moreover, the Court of Appeal made it clear in that case that it would be prepared to overlook failure to comply with ss.15 and 16 as regards producing the warrant whenever the circumstances made it inappropriate, as, for example, a search for drugs or in a terrorism case.[42] But *Linehan v DPP*[43] is a striking illustration of the importance attached by the courts to the duty to give a proper explanation. The officers, having arrested the defendant's son, came to search his home under s.18. They identified themselves and requested entry. The defendant asked them to slide the warrant under the door. They refused but offered to show it at a window. The defendant did not come to the window. He was warned that they would force the door which they then did. The defendant threw liquid in the officers' faces and was convicted of assaulting a constable in the execution of his duty. The Divisional Court allowed the defendant's appeal on the ground that it was not clear that the officers had properly explained the reasons for their intention to enter the premises.

The warrant must be executed by the police. Even if they have civilian support staff they must be effectively in charge. This was shown dramatically in *R. v Reading Justices, Ex p. South West Meat Ltd.*[44] The warrant there was for the search of a food company's premises. The police conducted the search in conjunction with officials from the Board of Agricultural Produce, who decided what documents should be seized and where they should be taken. The Divisional Court held that the police had gone too far in delegating their functions. It quashed the warrant, declared that its issue was a nullity and that the search and seizure were unlawful. The court awarded general damages of £3,000 and exemplary damages of £22,000 against the chief constable and the Board jointly.

2–48   To have the media in attendance during the execution of a search warrant, even if they do not enter the premises, could be a breach of Code B, para.6.10[45] which states that "Searches must be conducted with due consideration for the property

---

[41] *op.cit.*, n.26 above. For comment see Robert Stevens, "Search Warrants—Entering Uninvited and Unintroduced". J.P., August 27, 1988, p.551.

[42] For commentary on the decision see Kodowo Bentil, "Power of Police Officers to Enter Premises to Search for Drugs", J.P., August 26, 1989, p.542. For another example see for instance, *Thomas* [2004] EWCA Crim 590.

[43] [2000] Crim.L.R. 861, QBD.

[44] [1992] Crim.L.R. 672, DC.

[45] Formerly 5.10.

and privacy of the occupier . . .". In *R. v Marylebone Magistrates' Court, Ex p. Amdrell Ltd, trading as "Get Stuffed", and Robert and Pauline Sclare?*[46] the applicants sought judicial review of the magistrates' decision to issue search warrants, *inter alia*, on the ground that the police had invited unauthorised persons, namely the press, to attend. The application failed but Rose L.J. for the Divisional Court said that save in exceptional circumstances "it does not seem to me to be in the public interest that legitimate investigative procedures by the police, such as the execution of search warrants, or, for that matter, the interviewing of suspects, which may involve the innocent and may not lead to prosecution and trial should be accompanied by representatives of the media encouraged immediately to publish what they have seen". Such publication might lead to new witnesses coming forward but it was far more likely "to impede proper investigation and cause unjustifiable distress or harassment to those being investigated".

A search under a warrant "may only be a search to the extent required for the purpose for which the warrant was issued" (subs.(8))—"Premises may be searched only to the extent necessary to achieve the object of the search, having regard to the size and nature of whatever is sought."[47] In other words, if the search is for large items it would not be legitimate to tear up the floor boards, whereas if it were for prohibited drugs such a search might be lawful. This is an important provision. (As will be seen below (para.2–70), in *R. v Chief Constable of Warwickshire, Ex p. Fitzpatrick*[48] the Divisional Court held that s.16(8) went beyond the method of search and applied also to seizure. If this were correct it would mean that the subsection would invalidate seizures that were not authorised by the warrant, which would be very far-reaching. However, the Divisional Court subsequently held that *Ex p. Fitzpatrick* had been wrongly decided (see para.2–71 below).)

A warrant authorising a search of premises does not in itself entitle the police to search persons on the premises. As the original Home Office Circular on PACE (para.1–11, n.23 above) stated: "Such persons may only be searched if arrested or if there is a specific power to search in the warrant (*e.g.* warrants issued under s.23 of the Misuse of Drugs Act 1971 and s.46 of the Firearms Act 1968)".[49] **2–49**

Subsection (9) requires the police to endorse a warrant stating whether the articles or persons sought were found and whether any other articles were seized. This is intended to enable the courts to monitor the success or otherwise of search warrants. Under subs.(10) the police are subject to a duty to return an executed warrant or one which has expired to the court which issued it. This is intended to give the court basic information as to how the powers are used by the police—though there is no evidence that magistrates are kept informed by their clerks of the results.

---

[46] para.2–40, n.20 above.
[47] See similarly Code B, para.6.9, formerly 5.9.
[48] [1998] 1 All E.R. 65, DC.
[49] See *Hepburn v Chief Constable of Thames Valley* [2002] EWCA Civ 1841, *The Times*, December 19, 2002—damages awarded for arrest and search of H at pub when warrant only covered power to search the premises. No reasonable ground to suspect H when arrested. *cf. DPP v Meaden* [2003] EWHC 3005 (Admin); [2004] 1 W.L.R. 904; [2004] Crim.L.R.587—where the warrant covers search of persons as well as premises the police can detain an individual in one room whilst searching other rooms.

Under subs.(11) warrants must be retained by the courts for 12 months. The occupier has the right to inspect the endorsed warrant at any time within the 12 months. Subsection (12) gives the householder the right to inspect the warrant at any time during the 12–month period during which it has to be retained. But the original Home Office Circular on PACE stated that, in the opinion of the Secretary of State, such a request "should relate to a specific warrant of which the occupier is aware, issued in respect of his premises. There is no requirement under the subsection to respond to non-specific enquiries about warrants which the occupier claims may have been issued" (para.7).

The form of a search warrant is prescribed in the Schedule to the Magistrates' Courts (Forms) (Amendment) Rules 1985, which amended the Magistrates' Courts (Forms) Rules 1981.

Code B on entry, search and seizure

2–50   Further requirements concerning the obtaining and execution of search warrants are laid down in Code of Practice B for the searching of premises and the seizure of property in the context of the investigation of alleged offences. Code B applies to most lawful entries upon and search of premises. But it does not apply to routine scene of crime searches, unless that turns into something different. (This exception is not intended to cover circumstances where a prolonged occupation of premises is required.[50]) Searches following the activation of fire or burglar alarms or calls to a fire or a burglary made by the occupier or bomb threat calls are also excepted (Code B, para.2.3[51]). Code B also does not apply to searches by inspectors under a statutory power to enter or to inspect goods, equipment or procedures where there is no requirement of reasonable grounds to suspect that an offence has been committed (Code B, para.2.5[52]). It applies to searches under a search warrant under PACE or other enactments or under ss.17, 18 and 32 of PACE—see below—and to searches under s.1 of and Sch.1 to PACE or s.42 of or Sch.5 to the Terrorism Act 2000. Code B is intended to apply equally to searches of premises of victims of crime and of suspects.[53] The 2003 revision of Code B (Note 2B) set out a variety of other statutory provisions covered.

The 2003 revision also had a new Introduction. This states that the right to privacy and respect for personal property are key principles of the Human Rights Act 1998. Powers of entry, search and seizure may involve significant interference with privacy of those whose premises are searched and therefore need to be fully and clearly justified before they are used (para.1.3).

Inspector's authority

2–51   The Code requires, first, that police officers check their information carefully before applying for a search warrant to ensure that the information is accurate,

---

[50] *Sanghera* (2001) 1 Cr.App.R. 20.
[51] Formerly 1.3.
[52] Formerly 1.3B.
[53] *Sanghera, op.cit.*, n.50 above.

recent and has not been provided maliciously or irresponsibly. The identity of the informer need not be revealed but an application may not be made on the basis of information from an anonymous source where corroboration has not been sought. The Act (s.8(1)) says that an application for a search warrant can be made by any constable and Sch.1 para.1 says the same in regard to special procedure applications to a circuit judge. However, Code B makes it clear that, apart from in urgent cases, this is not good enough. Paragraph 3.4[54] says that no application to a justice of the peace for a search warrant or to a circuit judge under Sch.1 should be made without the written and signed authority at least of an inspector or, under the terrorism legislation,[55] a superintendent. In urgent cases the next most senior officer may give the authority.

The Notice of Powers and Rights (see below) provides for the indication of authority for the search on the Notice. If that is not practicable, it should be indicated elsewhere. Thus, if the search is of an arrested person's premises under s.18, it could be indicated on the custody record form.[56] The details of the authorisation should, however, be given verbally to the officer in charge of the search and a proper record be made of the fact.[57]

If there is reason to believe that a search "might have an adverse effect on relations between the police and the community", the local police community liaison officer should be consulted, save in urgent cases where he ought to be informed as soon as practicable (Code B, para.3.5[58]).

If the application is refused, no further applications may be made for a warrant to search those premises unless there are fresh grounds (para.3.8[59]).

Superintendent's authority for a search of premises

Schedule 7 of PACE repealed s.26(2) of the Theft Act 1968 which gave a superintendent the power to grant written authority for a search for stolen goods. But the power of a superintendent to issue written orders of search under s.73 of the Explosives Act 1875 (to search for explosives in cases of emergency) and under s.9(2) of the Official Secrets Act 1911 (to search for evidence of breaches of s.1 of the Act in cases of great emergency that in the interests of the State make immediate action necessary) were not affected and therefore remain.

2–52

Occupier's consent

Where it is proposed to search with the consent of the owner or occupier of the premises in question (there being no search warrant or arrest) the police are required, if it is practicable, to get consent in writing on a Notice of Powers and Rights (see para.2–54 below) before the search takes place. If the premises are

2–53

---

[54] Formerly 2.4. The indication that the application should be written and signed was introduced in the 2003 version.
[55] In the case of an application to a circuit judge under Sch.5 to the Terrorism Act 2000 for a production order or warrant or for an order requiring an explanation of material seized or produced under a Sch.5 warrant or production order.
[56] Home Office Circular 15/1991, para.7.
[57] *ibid.,* para.8.
[58] Formerly 2.5.
[59] Formerly 2.8.

occupied, the officer must identify himself and, if not in uniform, show his warrant card (para.6.5). In terrorism cases or in other cases where revealing his identity would put him at risk he can give his warrant number and the name of the police station to which he is attached (para.2.9).[60] The officer must satisfy himself that the person who gives consent has power to do so (Code B, para.5.1). An important addition to Code B first made in the 1991 revision was that an officer does not have a power to search premises "with consent" if the consent has been given under duress or "is withdrawn before the search is completed" (para.5.3). Consent, in other words, can be first granted and later validly withdrawn.

The person who is the occupier need not have entire control over the premises. He could, for instance, be a statutory tenant,[61] a student in a university hall,[62] or even possibly someone who had no right to be on the premises at all, such as a squatter.[63] But in the case of a lodging house or similar accommodation every reasonable effort should be made to obtain the consent of the tenant, lodger or occupier (Note 5A[64]).

Before getting written consent the police officer has to explain the purpose and the extent[65] of the proposed search.[65a]

The 2003 revised Code said this information must be as specific as possible, particularly in relation to the articles or persons to be sought and the parts of the premises it is proposed to search (para.5.2). He must inform the person concerned that he is not obliged to consent and that anything seized may be produced in evidence. If the person is not suspected of an offence, the officer should say so (*ibid.*[66]). There is, however, no necessity to seek consent where to do so would "cause disproportionate inconvenience to the person concerned" (para.5.4[67]). This is intended to apply to situations where innocent occupiers would agree and indeed expect the police to act—for instance to make a quick check of gardens in the pursuit of a thief at night to see whether he is hiding there or has discarded stolen articles as he ran away (Note 5C[68]).

Notice of powers and rights

2–54   A provision introduced in 1991 was for a notice to be given to the occupier whenever a search is to be made under Code B. The notice is in a standard format

---

[60] A new Note 2E says the purpose is to protect "those involved in serious organised crime investigations or arrests of particularly violent suspects when there is reliable information that those arrested or their associates may threaten or cause harm to the officers". In cases of doubt an inspector or above should be consulted (*ibid.*).

[61] *Brown v Minister of Housing and Local Government* [1953] 1 W.L.R. 1370, DC.

[62] *R. v Tao* [1976] 3 W.L.R. 25, CA.

[63] *R. v Josephs and Christie* (1977) 65 Cr.App.R. 253.

[64] The former version of this provision (Note 4A) said that a search should not be made on the basis solely of the landlord's consent unless the tenant, lodger or occupier was unavailable and the matter was urgent.

[65] The words "and the extent" were added in the 2003 revision.

[65a] On the reality of such consent see Mead, "Informed Consent to Police Searches in England and Wales—A Critical (Re-) Appraisal in Light of the Human Rights Act" [2002] Crim.L.R. 791; and Dixon, Bottomly and Coleman, "Consent and the Legal Regulation of Policing" (1990) 17 J.L.S. 345.

[66] Formerly 4.2.

[67] Formerly 4.4.

[68] Formerly Note 4C.

(Code B, para.6.7[69]). It (i) specifies whether the search is made under warrant or with consent or under ss.17, 18 or 32 of the Act; (ii) summarises the powers of search and seizure in the Act; (iii) explains the rights of the occupier and of anyone whose property is taken as a result of search; (iv) explains that compensation may be payable in appropriate cases for damage caused in entering and searching premises and giving the address to which an application for compensation should be sent; and (v) states that a copy of Code B can be consulted at any police station.

The notice is not itself an authority to search, nor does it replace the search warrant where one is required. If the occupier is present, the notice, together with the warrant if the search is under warrant, should be given to him before the search, unless the officer in charge reasonably believes that to do so would frustrate the object of the search or endanger police officers. If the occupier is not there, the notice and a copy of the warrant should be left in a prominent place on the premises (Code B, para.6.8[70]).

Conduct of searches

A caution is not required when a person is asked questions that are solely neces-   **2–55**
sary for the purpose of furthering the proper and effective conduct of a search (Code B, para.6.12 and Code C, para.10.1(c)). That would include questions to discover who is the owner of the premises, to find the key to a locked drawer or cupboard or to establish whether something is subject to seizure. If questions go further in the direction of investigating the person's involvement in an offence the exchange is likely to be an interview as defined in para.11.1A of Code C (see para.6–51 below) which would bring in train the caution and other safeguards dealt with in para.10 of Code C (see Code B, para.6.12).

Paragraph 6.9 of Code B[71] states the general proposition already referred to, that premises may be searched only to the extent necessary to achieve the object of the search "having regard to the size and nature of whatever is sought". A search under warrant may not continue under the authority of the warrant once the items specified in the warrant have been found (paras 6.9A, 6.9B).

Where premises are entered by force, no more than the reasonably necessary   **2–56**
and proportionate degree of force should be used (Code B, para.6.10[72]). The power to use force extends to civilians authorised under the Police Reform Act 2002—called "designated persons" in Code B, para.2.11. But, apart from saving life or limb or preventing serious damage to property, it can only be exercised in the company, and under the supervision of, a police officer (para.2.12). Searches must be conducted "with due consideration for the property and privacy of the occupier searched, and with no more disturbance than necessary" (para.6.12). The occupier should be allowed to have a friend, neighbour or other person to witness the search[73] unless the officer in charge reasonably believes that this

---

[69] Formerly 5.7.
[70] Formerly 5.8.
[71] Formerly 5.9.
[72] Formerly 5.10.
[73] Formerly para.5.11. The 2002 consultation draft said he must be asked whether he wanted such a person to attend.

would seriously hinder the investigation or endanger the officers or other people (para.6.11). If the request is refused, the grounds for refusal must be stated on the search record (*ibid.*)

If premises have been entered by force, the officer in charge is required to satisfy himself before leaving them that they are secure (para.6.13[74]). If the wrong premises are searched by mistake, pre-2003 the Code simply said "everything possible should be done at the earliest opportunity to allay any sense of grievance" and that "in appropriate circumstances assistance should be given to obtain compensation".[75] The 2003 revision of Code B was stronger. Note 6A starts by stating that whether compensation is appropriate depends on the circumstances. It is unlikely to be appropriate if the search was lawful and the force used was reasonable, proportionate and necessary. However, if the wrong premises have been searched by mistake, not only should everything possible be done at the earliest possible time "to allay any sense of grievance", but "there should normally be a strong presumption in favour of paying compensation".

Special procedure material

2–57   A search under warrant for "special procedure" material (*i.e.* one for confidential material authorised by a circuit judge after an application under Sch.1 to the Act[76]), must be under the authority of an inspector or above, who must be there at the time. The officer would be responsible to ensure that the search is conducted with discretion and in such a manner as to cause the least possible disruption to any business or other activities carried on in the premises (para.6.14).

The officer should ask the person in charge of the premises to produce the special procedure material in question. He may also ask to see any index to files and may inspect any files which according to the index appear to contain any of the material sought. But a more extensive search of the premises can only be made if access to the material sought is refused or if it appears that the index is inaccurate or incomplete, or if "for any other reason the officer in charge has reasonable grounds to believe that such a search is necessary in order to find the material sought" (para.6.15).

Records

2–58   Full records must be made of the details of the search and of what is taken (para.8.1). If a search is under warrant, it must be returned to the court that issued it, endorsed to show whether any of the articles specified in the warrant were found, whether any other articles were seized, the date, duration and time of execution and the names of the officers who executed it (para.8.2). (Under the 1989 Northern Ireland PACE Order, Art.18(9) the return must be made to the clerk of the petty sessions for the district in which the premises are situated.)

---

[74] Formerly 5.12.
[75] Formerly Note 5C.
[76] The same applies to searches for excluded or special procedure material authorised under the Terrorism Act 2000, Sch.5.

Self-incrimination

A search warrant under s.8 of PACE does not create any duty on the part of the   **2–59**
occupier of the premises being searched to produce anything. It is simply authority for the police to search. Section 9 regarding special procedure material is different since the order requires that the person to whom it is directed gives the
police access to the material specified. But what if that material would incriminate either the occupier or someone else? In *R. v Central Criminal Court, Ex p.
Bright, Alton, Rusbridger*[77] Gibbs J. said, "I conclude that section 9 by necessary
implication includes the power to make production orders which actually or
potentially infringe a person's right against self-incrimination".[78] Maurice Kay J.
agreed.[79] Judge L.J. dissented on this point.[80]

Is the position now affected by the Human Rights Act 1998? It seems not. In
the Scottish case *Birse v HM Advocate*[81] it was argued that the granting of a
search warrant to look for drugs was a breach of the complainant's rights under
Art.8 of the ECHR which was incorporated into Scottish law by the Scotland Act
1998. The High Court of Justiciary rejected the argument. The justice who
granted the warrant had required the deposing police officer to explain what
information had been relied on. Having done that, he was entitled to issue the
warrant. (It was also held not to be a breach of the Convention that no record had
been kept of what was said at the hearing.)

Entry for purpose of arrest, etc.: s.17[82]

Section 17 makes provision for the circumstances in which the police may exer-   **2–60**
cise statutory authority, if necessary using force, to enter premises in order to
effect an arrest. (Where the entry is by consent these powers do not apply.[83])
There is no power to enter premises forcibly in order simply to question someone.[84] Although the section gives a power of entry for the purposes of making an
arrest, it does not itself create powers of arrest (see Code B, para.4.1).

Premises for these purposes include vehicles. It does not, however, affect statutory provisions giving the police the power to enter premises without a warrant
other than to make an arrest.[85]

Subsection (1) gives the police the power to enter and to search for any of the   **2–61**
following purposes:

---

[77] *op. cit.*, para.2–26, n.72 above.
[78] *ibid.*, at 277.
[79] *ibid.*, see 273–274.
[80] *ibid.*, at 266.
[81] *The Times*, June 28, 2000.
[82] See 1989 N.I. PACE Order, Art.19.
[83] *Hobson and Hobson v Chief Constable of Cheshire Constabulary* [2003] EWHC 3011 (Admin).
This is a problematic concept in the same way that consent to be searched in the street is problematic.
As was seen above (para.1–12), the concept of consensual searching in the street has now in effect
been banned.
[84] *O'Loughlin v Chief Constable of Essex, The Times*, 12 December,1997, CA.
[85] *e.g.* under the Gaming Act 1968, s.43(2) or the Misuse of Drugs Act 1971, s.23(1).

(a) (i) To execute a warrant of arrest in connection with or arising out of criminal proceedings. This follows the common law. The original Home Office Circular on PACE said of this subsection that it was "deliberately widely drawn". It would, for instance, enable entry to be made to search for someone wanted under a warrant for non-payment of a fine (*op.cit.*, para.1–11, n.23, p.8 above at para.8).

(ii) To execute a warrant committing a fine defaulter to prison when magistrates have issued a warrant under s.76 of the Magistrates' Court Act 1980. This removes the doubt as to whether an entry was lawful to execute a warrant of commitment for failure to pay a fine or maintenance order.

(b) To arrest a person for an arrestable offence. The category of arrestable offence (defined in s.24(1) and (2)) is slightly wider than under the previous law.

(c) To arrest for some offences under the Public Order Act 1936 or the Criminal Law Act 1977. These powers follow the provisions of s.26(2) (which with Sch.2, *inter alia*, preserves an unqualified power of arrest without warrant of anyone reasonably suspected of being in the act of committing an offence under ss.1, 4 or 5 of the Public Order Act 1986) and s.11 of the Criminal Law Act 1977. The Criminal Law Act powers (which relate to the offences of entering or remaining on property) can only be exercised by a constable in uniform (subs.3). The power of arrest now extends also to a person who fails to comply with an interim possession order made against squatters under the Criminal Justice and Public Order Act 1994, Sch.10, para.53(a) and to a person who fails to stop in a vehicle when required to do so by a constable in uniform (added by Police Reform Act 2002, s.49(2)).

(d) To recapture someone who is or who is deemed to be unlawfully at large while liable to be detained in a prison, remand centre, young offender institution or secure training centre or in the case of children or young persons guilty of grave crimes, in any other place (Prisoners (Return to Custody) Act 1995, s.2(1)). At common law this power only applied to cases of "hot", or at least warm, pursuit.[86] But in light of the terms of the 1995 Act, the requirement of pursuit no longer seems to exist.

(e) To save life or limb or prevent serious damage to property. This restates the common law in relation to the premises entered. Strictly construed, the subsection would seem to permit entry of premises because of risks to persons or property on other premises or elsewhere not on premises

---

[86] *D'Souza v DPP* [1992] 1 W.L.R. 1073, HL, which concerned entry of premises to recapture someone who had discharged herself from a mental hospital where she had been taken under a warrant issued under s.135 of the Mental Health Act 1983. It was held that forcible entry to recapture her was not lawful even though she was "unlawfully at large" because there was no evidence that she was someone who was being pursued.

at all but this interpretation is probably unsound. It has been held that the subsection does not cover entry to search for the address of the next of kin of someone seriously injured in a road accident who was unconscious in hospital. Evidence of drugs offences found during the entry was held inadmissible. There had been a breach of the right of privacy enshrined in Art.8 of the ECHR.[87]

Subsection (2) states that, save when the entry is under (e) above, a constable can only exercise these powers if he has reasonable grounds for believing that the person sought is on those premises.[88] In the case of a block of flats the power to enter and search only applies to the actual flat in which he is suspected to be, and any common parts. There would be no power without a warrant to search all the flats or a number of them. **2–62**

Subsection (4) states that the search must be consistent with the purpose of the entry to make an arrest. A general search of the premises would therefore be unlawful. But once an arrest has been made, a search under ss.18 or 32 for evidence of the offence for which the person was arrested would presumably be lawful. The only common law power of entry without a warrant that remains now is that to deal with or to prevent a breach of the peace; all the others are abolished (subss.(5) and (6)). But before exercising the power, the police must have a genuine belief that there was a real and imminent risk of a breach of the peace occurring and must act with great care and discretion.[89] There is no requirement that the breach of the peace be serious. On the right of the police to enter private premises against the wishes of the owner when they have reasonable grounds for believing that a breach of the peace is imminent or is likely to be committed see *Thomas v Sawkins*.[90] On the criteria for a breach of the peace see *Albert v Lavin*.[91]

[87] *Veneroso* [2002] Crim.L.R. 306, Crown Ct. The officers acted in good faith but the entry was unlawful as there was no evidence they were entering to save life or limb or prevent serious damage to property. (Courts not infrequently do admit evidence obtained as a result of an unlawful search but not in this instance.)

[88] For cases on what is meant by reasonable grounds for suspicion see *Kynaston v DPP*; *Heron (Joseph) v DPP*; *Heron (Tracey) v DPP* (1988) 87 Cr.App.R. 200; *Castorina v Chief Constable of Surrey, The Times*, June 15, 1988. In *Keegan v Chief Constable of Merseyside* [2003] EWCA Civ 936 Lord Phillips M.R. reserved for future decision whether it could be sufficient for the officer to have reasonable grounds for believing that the person sought *might be* on the premises.

[89] *McLeod v Commissioner of Police of the Metropolis* [1994] 4 All E.R. 553, CA. The police entered in support of the husband who claimed to be entitled to remove property from the matrimonial home. When sued by the wife, the Court of Appeal held that on the facts the police had sufficient justification for the entry. The case subsequently went to the European Court of Human Rights which held that on the facts the police had not had sufficient justification for the entry and that there had been a breach of Art.8 of the Convention. The entry was a disproportionate response to the objective of preventing disorder or crime since (1) the officers had taken no steps to check the court order in favour of the husband; and (2) since the wife was not there it should have been clear that there was little or no risk of a breach of the peace. (*McLeod v UK* (1998) 27 E.H.R.R. 493; [1999] Crim.L.R. 155.)

[90] [1935] 2 K.B. 249, DC.

[91] [1981] 3 All E.R. 878, HL.

Entry and search after arrest: s.18[92]

2–63   For some time prior to PACE it had been assumed that the police had power to search the home of an arrested person at least for evidence connected with the crime for which he was arrested—see especially dicta in *Jeffrey v Black*.[93] But in *McLorie v Oxford*,[94] the Divisional Court, somewhat surprisingly, held that the police had no right to enter the premises of a person arrested for attempted murder to search for the motorcar which it was alleged had been the weapon used. (The decision was especially striking since the accused had actually been arrested on those same premises, but the police had taken him away and then later wanted to come back to pursue their inquiries.)

The 1929 Royal Commission on the police said that the police commonly searched the home of an arrested person and that the position should be regularised by law. The Philips Royal Commission took the same view, subject to the proviso that a search of the arrested person's premises (or vehicle) should only be permitted where there were reasonable grounds for suspicion that relevant evidence might be found there. Search of any other premises should require a warrant. Also, in order to reduce the risk of "fishing expeditions" the decision to search and the reasons should be recorded prior to the search.[95]

2–64   This broadly was the scheme adopted in PACE. It gives a police officer power to enter and search "any premises occupied or controlled by a person who is under arrest for an arrestable offence, if he has reasonable grounds for suspecting that there is on the premises evidence (other than items subject to legal privilege) that relates (a) to that offence; or (b) to some other arrestable offence which is connected with or similar to that offence" (subs.(1)). This reversed the decision in *McLorie v Oxford*. The same power is given to authorised civilian investigating officers under the Police Reform Act 2002.[96]

If the police suspect that evidence of other unconnected offences may be found on the premises, their only recourse is to get a search warrant or to get the householder's consent to a search. This would apply equally if the arrest was not for an arrestable offence (as defined in s.24).

A search of a person's home after an arrest normally requires the written authority of an inspector or above (subs.(4)). In *Badham*[97] it was held that this meant that the inspector must create an independent document setting out his authorisation. The Crown Court quashed a conviction by magistrates because the inspector had merely written down a confirmation of his oral authorisation in his notebook. This was not sufficient. (It seems, however, that this authorisation need not necessarily be produced in court.[98])

2–65   It has been suggested[99] that the authorisation should state: (1) the name of the arrested person; (2) the nature of the offence for which he was arrested; (3) the

---

[92] See 1989 N.I. PACE Order, Art.20.
[93] [1978] 1 Q.B. 490, DC.
[94] [1982] Q.B. 1290.
[95] Philips Report, para.3.12.
[96] Sch.4, Pt 2, para.18(a).
[97] [1987] Crim.L.R. 202, Crown Ct.
[98] *Linehan v DPP* [2000] Crim.L.R. 861, QBD.
[99] Feldman, *The Law Relating to Entry, Search and Seizure* (Butterworths, 1986), p.18.

grounds for suspecting that the evidence is on the premises; (4) the nature of the offence to which the evidence is thought to relate; (5) the address of the premises; (6) the fact that the premises are occupied or controlled by the arrested person; and (7) the name and rank of the authorising officer. There is some uncertainty as to whether the inspector's authorisation must be in, or at least be attached to, the custody record or whether it is sufficient for it to be in the inspector's notebook.

Paragraph 4.3[1] of Code B specifically says that the record required by subs.(7) must be made in the custody record where there is one and otherwise in the officer's pocket book or in the search record. Code B, as revised in 2003, also says that the inspector should only give his written authority if he is satisfied that the necessary grounds exist (*ibid.*).

Subsections (5) and (5A) make an exception to the requirement of prior authorisation when the arrested person is taken to his home rather than to the police station (see s.30 below) or is given street bail (ss.30A–D). If this is not obtained in advance, a report must be made after the event to an officer of that rank (subs.(6)). In either case the inspector must make a written record of the grounds for the search and the nature of the evidence sought (subss.(7)–(8)).[2]

As already noted, a search must not go beyond what is reasonably required to discover the evidence in question. No general search is permitted (subs.(3)). As will be seen below (para.3–34), s.32 gives the police a power to enter premises after an arrest but that power is only available more or less at the time of arrest. In *Badham* the entry was made three hours later. It was held that s.32 could not apply. The power under s.32 is, however, only to search for evidence relating to the offence for which he was arrested (subs.(2)(b)). It seems that the police use s.18 far more frequently than s.32.[3]

The Armed Forces

The Armed Forces Act 2001, s.11(1) gives the Home Secretary the power to make regulations equivalent to those in PACE, s.18 for the search of the arrested person's own premises.   **2–66**

Seizure of articles: s.19[4]; Code B, s.6

One of the most troublesome problems regarding police powers is the extent of the power to seize articles found in the course of a search. At common law, prior   **2–67**

---

[1] Formerly 3.3.
[2] But this requirement is directory not mandatory and, if no record is made, the search can still be lawful—*Krohn v DPP* [1997] C.O.D. 345, QBD.
[3] Ken Lidstone, *op. cit.*, para.2–28, n.81 above, p.355, n.67 reported that in a survey of two city forces s.18 accounted for some 75%, compared with 2% under s.32 and 6% under s.17. Another study, carried out by Professor Keith Bottomley and colleagues found that searches after arrest under s.18 constituted about two-thirds of all recorded searches and that they had increased significantly since PACE. In fact s.18 searches had become almost routine in certain types of cases. Only 15% of recorded searches were with consent. Searches under warrant were one in eight of those recorded. See Bottomley *et al.* (1991).
[4] See 1989 N.I. PACE Order, Art.21.

to PACE, where the search was under warrant the police could seize anything they found which was or which they reasonably believed to be covered by the warrant.[5] If the search was not under warrant, the common law had developed to the point of permitting seizure of evidence where:

(i) it implicated the owner or occupier of the premises searched in the offence for which the search was conducted[6]; or

(ii) it implicated the owner or occupier in some other offence[7]; or

(iii) it implicated third persons in the same offence for which the search was conducted[8]; or

(iv) it was taken from someone innocent of involvement in the crime where his refusal to hand it over was wholly unreasonable.[9]

The Philips Royal Commission said that "it defies common sense to expect the police not to seize items incidentally found during the course of a search".[10] At the same time, it said, "the risk that premises may be ransacked as soon as a warrant is granted for any offence must be minimised".[11] The former law was "uncertain and of little help in this respect".[12]

2–68   The Commission said it wished to avoid legitimising general searches. So the police should only be permitted to seize items found incidentally if there was evidence of a grave offence and then only if the search was carried out lawfully—in accordance with the terms of the warrant and in a manner appropriate to the items being searched for. Items seized otherwise could not be used in evidence.

The Act, however, defined the power of seizure very much more broadly. It provided that, where a constable is searching premises under statutory powers or by consent, he may seize anything which is on the premises (s.19(2)). This applies equally to authorised civilian investigating officers under the Police Reform Act 2002.[13] He may seize it if he reasonably believes that it is evidence in relation to an offence which he is investigating or any other offence and that it is necessary to seize it in order to prevent it being concealed, lost, altered or destroyed (s.19(3)(b)) or that it has been obtained in consequence of the commission of an offence; in which case the reasons for seizure also include the

---

[5] *Chic Fashions (West Wales) Ltd v Jones* [1968] 2 Q.B. 299, CA.
[6] *Ghani v Jones* [1968] 2 Q.B. 299, CA; *Garfinkel v Metropolitan Police Commissioner* [1972] Crim.L.R. 44; *Frank Truman Export Ltd v Metropolitan Police Commissioner* [1977] Q.B. 952.
[7] *ibid.*
[8] *Ghani v Jones* [1968] 2 Q.B. 299, CA.
[9] *ibid.*
[10] Philips Report, para.3.48.
[11] *ibid.*
[12] *ibid.*
[13] Sch.4, Pt 2, para.19(a). "Anything which is on the premises" has been held to include the premises themselves in the form of a vehicle—*Cowan v Commissioner of Police of the Metropolis* [2000] 1 All E.R. 504, CA. In that case sexual offences were alleged to have taken place in the seized car which was taken for forensic examination.

possible damage of the material seized. (This minor difference between s.19(2)(b) and (3)(b) looks like a drafting oversight.) Items exempted from seizure are those reasonably believed to be subject to legal professional privilege (subs.(6)). (The exemption applies equally to seizure by authorised civilian investigating officers.[14]) Excluded material could therefore be seized even though it is usually exempt from a search warrant. When seizable material is stored in a computer the police officer may require it to be produced in a form in which it is visible and legible (subs.(4)). The section differs from the recommendation of the Philips Royal Commission in not being limited to grave offences. Indeed, it is not even limited to serious arrestable offences.

As will be seen below, the Act also did not give effect to the Philips Royal Commission's view that evidence seized in the course of an unlawfully conducted search should be inadmissible. On the other hand, the section went beyond what the Commission recommended in permitting seizure only if the evidence would otherwise be concealed, lost or destroyed—though this is not likely to prove much of a safeguard since, presumably, the police would almost always be able to claim that this condition was fulfilled. This condition does not apply, however, if the item to be seized is the very one for which a search under warrant was authorised. Sections 8(2), 18(2), 32(8) and Sch.1, para.13 give the police an unqualified right to seize anything for which a search was authorised. The condition in s.19 as to what can be seized only applies to other items found in the course of the search.   **2–69**

The section extends the common law by permitting seizure of the fruits of crime and the evidence of crime regardless of the crime and of who is implicated. It applies to seizure from suspects and non-suspects alike.

Because of the broad scope of the seizure power it appears that the power of search has also been broadened.[15] The insistence since *Entick v Carrington*[16] in 1765 that general warrants are unlawful must therefore be qualified by the knowledge that once the police have entered premises lawfully it is difficult to hold them to a search restricted to the specific purpose of the search.

Until recently it seemed that the only restraint was the requirement in s.16(8) that a search under warrant must be carried out in a manner consistent with the items being looked for and in Code B, para.6.9[17] which states that "premises may be searched only to the extent necessary to achieve the object of the search having regard to the size and nature of whatever is sought". Two decisions of the Divisional Court threw this important issue into a state of uncertainty. In *R. v Chief Constable of Warwickshire, Ex p. Fitzpatrick*[18] the court held that where the search went clearly beyond the terms of the warrant, there could be no lawful seizure. The same view had been taken obiter by the court in the earlier decision of *R. v Southwark Crown Court and H.M. Customs and Excise, Ex p. Sorsky Defries*.[19] But in a third decision by the Divisional Court, *R. v Chesterfield*   **2–70**

---

[14] Police Reform Act 2002, Sch.4, Pt 2, para.16(f), para.18(c), para.19(c).
[15] On the former common law see for instance *Chic Fashions (West Wales) Ltd v Jones* [1968] 2 Q.B. 299, CA; *Ghani v Jones* [1970] 1 Q.B. 693, CA.
[16] (1765) 19 St. Tr. 1030.
[17] Formerly 5.9.
[18] [1998] 1 All E.R. 65, *per* Rose L.J. and Jowitt J.
[19] [1996] Crim.L.R. 195.

Justices, Ex p. Bramley,[20] in separate judgments, all three judges (Kennedy L.J., Turner and Jowitt JJ.[21]) agreed that if items were seized unlawfully, that did not make the search itself unlawful, though the items improperly seized had to be returned immediately and damages might have to be paid. Section 16(8) dealt only with the search and did not touch the question of seizure. However, *Ex p. Bramley* confirmed that the police could not lawfully take away material that included items covered by legal privilege in order to sift and sort them at leisure at police premises. If items were removed which on examination were found to be outside the scope of the warrant, PACE gave no protection against an action for damages even if the officer acted in good faith. Such a removal constituted seizure and the right to seize was restricted by s.8(2) to items for which a search had been authorised by the warrant. The court recognised that the practical effect of this view was highly inconvenient and might require legislative attention— which it very soon got in the form of the Criminal Justice and Police Act 2001 (see below).

2–71   The court in *Ex p. Bramley* said that if a claim of legal professional privilege were made, normally a police officer would have to examine the material being seized to test the claim. The officer was not required to accept a claim for privilege made by the owner or a lawyer. But, contrary to what the Divisional Court had held in *Ex p. Sorsky Defries* and *Ex p. Fitzpatrick*, the officer did not have to be satisfied that the items being seized were covered by the requirements of s.8(1). Section 8(1) indicated what the magistrate had to be satisfied of before issuing the warrant. The only inhibition on the officer's power of seizure was if he had reasonable grounds for believing that the material being seized was covered by legal professional privilege (s.19(6)). The court in *Bramley* set out guidelines for such situations:

> If it is thought possible that privileged material may be encountered on execution of a warrant, it is wise to exclude from the searching party any officer engaged to any significant extent in any inquiry to which the material may relate.
>
> If the warrant authorises other persons to accompany the officer executing the warrant, it is wise to take along an independent lawyer.
>
> There should be an attempt to get agreement on the spot as to what material is covered by privilege.
>
> If that cannot be achieved, it is desirable that items that it is thought may be subject to privilege are packaged separately for later examination.

New power to "seize and sift" (Criminal Justice and Police Act 2001, Pt 2, ss.50–66 and Schs 1 and 2 and Code B, paras 7.7–7.12)

2–72   The troublesome effects of the *Bramley* decision were removed by the Criminal Justice and Police Act 2001 (CJPA) which gives the police a power to remove material for the purpose of sifting it elsewhere where it is not practicable to

---

[20] [2000] 1 All E.R. 411, DC.

[21] Jowitt J. dissented but referring to what he had said in *Ex p. Fitzpatrick* he said: "I now believe that that went too far and that I was wrong. The seizure of a document which falls outside a search warrant does not of itself make the search unlawful" (at 428).

examine it on the spot. The power applies not just to the power to seize under PACE but to powers under other legislation enjoyed by other law enforcement agencies.[22] The Police Reform Act 2002 also gave the same powers to authorised civilian investigating officers.[23] Having sifted the material, they can retain only what they are permitted to seize under their existing powers—subject to a new right to retain "inextricably linked material". (In its examination of the Bill, the Joint Parliamentary Committee on Human Rights expressed the view that these provisions "have been drafted carefully in the light of the requirements of the ECHR".[24])

The basic provision is s.50 of the CJPA

Where a person lawfully on any premises finds something that he has reasonable grounds for believing may be or may contain something for which he is authorised to search, and it is not reasonably practicable to ascertain whether and to what extent it is such material, he can remove it in order for that to be determined (subs.(1)) The same power is given where the constable cannot separate the material he is able to seize from that he is not—where, for instance, the material is on a computer (subs.(2)).   **2–73**

What is meant by "reasonably practicable" is to be judged by reference only to the following factors: (a) how long the process would take; (b) how many people would be needed to do the job; (c) whether, if carried out then and there, it would involve damage to property; (d) the equipment needed; and (e), in the case of separation of material, whether the process of separation would risk prejudicing the use of any of the material, for instance, by damaging material on a computer (subs.(3)).

Code B, para.7.7 says:

"Officers must be careful they only exercise these powers when it is essential and they do not remove any more material than necessary. The removal of large volumes of material, much of which may not ultimately be retainable, may have serious implications for the owners, particularly when they are involved in business or activities such as journalism or the provision of medical services. Officers must carefully consider if removing copies or images of relevant material or data would be a satisfactory alternative to removing originals."

The rule that material covered by legal professional privilege is exempt from seizure[25] does not apply to removal of material under s.50—(subs.(4)).

Section 51 of the CJPA creates a virtually identical power to that given by s.50   **2–74** to permit seizure of material from an individual where there is a power to search

[22] Pt I of Sch.1 to the 2001 Act lists over 70 existing powers of seizure to which the new provisions apply. They include powers available to the Serious Fraud Office, the Financial Services Authority, the Inland Revenue, Customs and Excise, the Department of Trade and Industry and the Office of Fair Trading. It also applies in Northern Ireland—Sch.1, para.2.
[23] Sch.4, Pt 2, para.24.
[24] First Report, Criminal Justice and Police Bill, Session 2000–2001, HL Paper 69, HC 427, 2001, para.70.
[25] PACE, s.19(6); and the equivalent in Northern Ireland—Art.21(6) of the 1989 Northern Ireland Order.

him and it is not reasonably practicable to determine whether what has been found can be seized. This might be used, for instance, if a person has a portable computer or computer discs or a mass of papers which cannot be examined in the street. But, as under s.50, the items cannot be taken unless the officer has reasonable grounds for believing that they may be or may contain material he is entitled to search for, and if so, that there is a power to seize them. The factors for judging whether it is reasonably practicable to determine whether the material can be seized are the same as under s.50.

The CJPA provides for safeguards aimed at preventing abuse and to give a power of challenge to a judge.

A detailed record regarding the search and seizure must be made. (Code B, para.8.1 sets out a long list of the items that must be covered in the record.) Section 52 provides that the occupier of premises from which material has been seized under ss.50 or 51 (failing whom, a person in charge of the premises) must be given a written notice specifying what has been seized and the grounds on which it was seized.[26] The notice must set out the gist of ss.59–61 which provide for the right to apply to a judge, a right to attend the examination of the material and a duty on the part of those holding the material to secure the material and to refrain from examining it pending the decision of the judge (Code B, para.7.12).

2–75   Section 53 creates a duty for the person in possession of the seized material to carry out an initial examination "as soon as practicable" and to return anything retention of which is not permitted. (See also Code B, para.7.8.) In deciding what is the earliest practicable time for conducting this initial examination, regard should be had to the desirability of the person from whom it was seized or someone else with an interest in the material or a representative being present (subs.(4)). Code B says that if possible the person from whom it has been seized should be present at the examination in person or by a representative (para.7.8 and Note 7D). Until this initial examination has taken place the material must be kept securely and separate from other seized material. Keeping it securely will normally mean "bagging up" in sealed bags or containers subject to strict control of access (Code B, Note 7F). Inextricably linked material can be retained so that, for instance, the police could hold the whole computer hard drive containing a document that is evidence of an offence if the rest of the hard drive is needed to prove when that document was created, amended or deleted (Code B, Note 7H).

Section 54 deals with material covered by legal privilege that has been seized whether under s.50 or 51 or under any other power of seizure, including powers under later statutes.[27] Section 54 provides that such material must be returned as soon as practicable (subs.(1)) unless it is inextricably linked with material that can be retained and it is not reasonably practicable to separate them (subs.(2)).

Section 55 has similar provisions to require the return of special procedure or excluded material (as defined in PACE) unless retention is permitted under s.56 or it is inextricably linked to other material that can be retained and it is not reasonably practicable to separate them.

---

[26] If there is no one to whom the notice can be given it should be fixed to the premises—s.52(3).
[27] Under PACE a constable is not permitted knowingly to seize material covered by legal privilege but he may have seized it believing that it was not covered by such privilege.

It is the responsibility of the officer in charge of the investigation to ensure that   **2–76**
property is returned as soon as practicable. Delay is only warranted if very clear
and compelling reasons exist (Code B, para.7.9A).

Section 56 mirrors the powers given by s.19 of PACE to permit retention of
seized material if it is reasonably believed to be the proceeds of a crime or
evidence of any offence and there are reasonable grounds for believing that it is
necessary to retain it lest it be concealed, lost, damaged, altered or destroyed.

Section 57 states that material seized by virtue of s.50 or 51 under any of 16
listed statutory provisions can be retained unless it is supposed to be returned.

Section 58 specifies the person to whom seized property should be returned—
normally the person from whom it was taken, unless someone else has a better
claim to it.

Section 59 gives anyone with a sufficient interest the right to apply to an
"appropriate judicial authority"—which in England, Wales and Northern Ireland
means a High Court judge (s.64)[28]—for its return.

Section 60 sets out the circumstances where those holding material seized
under ss.50 or 51 are under a duty to secure it pending the hearing before the
judge. This applies to a claim that the material seized includes legally privileged
material and in some circumstances it may also apply to a claim that the material
includes special procedure or excluded material.

Section 61 deals with the duty to secure. It provides, for instance, that pending   **2–77**
the hearing before the judge, the material may not be examined or copied without the consent of the applicant or a court order. Code B (para.7.10) states that
where an officer involved in the investigation has reasonable grounds for believing that someone with a relevant interest in property seized under s.50 or 51
intends to make an application under s.59 for legally privileged, special procedure or excluded material, the officer in charge of the case must be informed and
the material must be kept secure.

Section 62 confines examination, copying, or use of inextricably linked material to the investigation for which it was seized.

Section 63 makes it clear that Pt 2 applies to copies as well as to originals.

Section 65 refers to the relevant provisions which define the meaning of the
phrase "legal privilege" in different statutes.

Section 66 is the Interpretation and Definitions section. Section 67 applies Pt
2 to customs officers. Part 2 applies to Scotland save in respect to certain powers
specified in s.68. Section 69 allows the Secretary of State to add additional powers of seizure to the list set out in Sch.2. Section 70 introduces Sch.2 which
mainly deals with minor and consequential amendments. The phrase in PACE
and other statutes "contained in a computer" is, for instance, replaced with
"stored in any electronic form" to take account of developments in technology.

The Law Society predicted that if material covered by legal professional priv-   **2–78**
ilege was seized under the Act, good practice would dictate that there was an
immediate application to the court to trigger the securing provisions. If such
action was taken swiftly, such material would be more adequately protected than
previously.[29]

---

[28] The bill originally provided for it to be done by a Crown Court judge.
[29] *Criminal Practitioners Newsletter*, April 2001, p.1.

A challenge to unlawful seizure should normally be made by an action for damages in trespass—not by way of judicial review. For a valuable analysis of the privilege issue arising in cases involving searches under PACE, and by the Revenue under the Taxes Management Act 1970 and by Customs and Excise, see Passmore, "Search warrants and privilege" *New Law Journal*, February 11, 2000, p.161 and February 18, p.219.

Where an officer decides not to seize an item because of an appropriate explanation given by the person holding it (but he has reasonable grounds for believing that it has been obtained in consequence of the commission of an offence by someone) he should inform the holder of his suspicions and explain that if he disposes of the property he may be liable to civil or criminal proceedings (Code B, para.7.4[30]).

Armed Forces

2–79   The Armed Forces Act 2001, s.11 gives the Home Secretary the power to make regulations providing for seizure and retention of material found during a search equivalent to PACE, ss.19–22.

Extension of powers of seizure to computerised information: s.20[31]; Code B, para.7.5[32]

2–80   Section 20 of PACE extends the powers of seizure available in any act (including any passed after the 1984 Act) to enable the police (or an authorised civilian investigating officer[33]) to require that information contained in a computer be produced in a form in which it can be taken away and in which it is visible and legible. The police, in other words, can legitimately object if they are simply handed a floppy disc. In some situations it might be appropriate to secure the computer in order to make sure that a print-out is produced before it can be destroyed or tampered with.

Seized articles: access and copying: s.21[34]; Code B, s.7[35]

2–81   Section 21 makes provision for access to property held by the police. (The same applies to property seized by authorised civilian investigating officers under the Police Reform Act 2002.[36]) There were no previous statutory rules on the subject.

---

[30] Formerly 6.3.
[31] See 1989 N.I. PACE Order, Art.22.
[32] Formerly 6.5.
[33] Police Reform Act 2002, Sch.4, Pt 2, para.16(g)).
[34] See 1989 N.I. PACE Order, Art.23. See also Drug Trafficking Offences Act 1986, s.29.
[35] Formerly 6.
[36] Sch.4, Pt 2, para.19(d)(e).

The provisions of s.21 apply not only to property seized under s.19 but also to that seized under all other provisions in the Act or any other Act.

Subsection (1) states that a person who can show that he was the occupier of premises from which items have been seized by the police (or authorised civilian investigating officer[37]) or that he had custody or control immediately before the seizure, may request that he be given a record of what was taken and such a request shall be complied with. The record must be supplied within a reasonable time (subs.(2) and Code B, para.7.16[38]). Subject to subs.(8), if requested to do so, the investigating officer shall grant that person, or someone acting on his behalf, access to such items under the supervision of a police officer (subs.(3) and Code B, para.7.17[39]). Similarly, and again subject to subs.(8), the investigating officer should either allow that person or someone acting on his behalf access under supervision for the purpose of photographing or copying the items or should have the items photographed or copied for him (subs.(4)).

Photographs or copies made under subs.(4) should then be supplied to the person who made the request within a reasonable time (subss.(6) and (7)).

The caveat in subs.(8) is that there is no duty to grant access to the material or to allow its copying where the officer in charge of the investigation has reasonable grounds for believing that to do so would prejudice the investigation of that offence or of other offences or any criminal proceedings. A challenge against an allegedly wrongful refusal of access under these provisions should be by way of judicial review.[40] The same is the case where the applicant seeks to correct an error by the Crown Court judge.[41]

Retention of seized articles: s.22[42]; Code B, s.7.14

At common law the police could retain items seized for such time as was reasonable in all the circumstances. The Act provides the same power with somewhat more detail.   **2–82**

Subject to subs.(4), anything which has been seized by a police officer in a lawful search and seizure (see below) may be retained[43] so long as is necessary in all the circumstances. In particular, anything seized for the purposes of a criminal investigation may be held by the police for use as evidence at the trial or for forensic examination or for investigation in connection with any offence (subs.(2)(a)). Where the material being held by the police relates to ongoing criminal investigations involving the owner of the material the police will

---

[37] Police Reform Act 2002, Sch.4, Pt 2, para.16(h).

[38] Formerly 6.8.

[39] Formerly 6.9.

[40] *Allen v Chief Constable of Cheshire, The Times,* July 16, 1988, CA

[41] *R. v Liverpool Crown Court, Ex p. Wimpey plc* [1991] Crim.L.R. 635, DC.

[42] See 1989 N.I. PACE Order, Art.24. See also Drug Trafficking Offences Act 1986, s.29.

[43] The word "retained" permits a customs officer to retain material as long as is permitted by the Drug Trafficking Act 1986. The material can also be made available to foreign law enforcement agencies by copying, but the seized material itself must be retained by the officer. (*R. v Southwark Crown Court, Ex p. Customs and Excise Comrs; R. v Same, Ex p. Bank of Credit and Commerce International SA* [1990] 1 Q.B. 650, DC.)

normally succeed in establishing a claim to retain it. But where the owner is not suspected of any criminal conduct the balance would tip in favour of handing it back. The court so held in ordering the Metropolitan Police to hand back to the film-makers confidential videos of Diana Princess of Wales that had been found in the possession of her butler Paul Burrell. They were legitimately seized by the police under PACE s.19 in connection with their investigation of alleged theft of Princess Diana's effects by Burrell. After Burrell's acquittal, the police claimed a right to continue to hold the tapes in connection with their inquiry into the cause of Diana's death but the court rejected this claim.[44]

Seized material may be retained in order to establish its true owner where there are reasonable grounds for believing that it has been obtained as the result of the commission of a criminal offence (subs.(2)(b)). However, even if there are such grounds, the items cannot be retained on that basis if there is no realistic possibility of establishing the identity of the true owner—*Gough v Chief Constable of West Midlands.*[45]

2–83   If the police seize something on the ground that it may be used to cause physical injury or damage to property or to interfere with evidence, or to assist an escape, it cannot be kept by the police once the person from whom it was taken has been released from custody (subs.(3)). The police must equally return the items seized after they have fulfilled their function as exhibits or material used in the investigation. This is so even if the items were stolen! In *Costello*[46] the Court of Appeal held[47] that, in the absence of the true owner, a "highly suspect" driver arrested in possession of a stolen car was entitled to have it returned to him, plus damages for its wrongful detention since 1997. The court held that s.22 gave the police only a temporary right to retain goods for the purposes of criminal investigation. ("Even a thief is entitled to the protection of the criminal law against the theft from him of that which he has stolen.")

No article may be retained by the police if a photograph or a copy would suffice for their purposes (subs.(4)). Subsection (5) preserves the provisions of s.1 of the Police (Property) Act 1897. If someone from whom the police have seized something thinks that it has been retained too long he may make an application to the courts under the 1897 Act, which empowers a magistrates' court to ". . . make an order for the delivery of the property [held by the police] to the person appearing to the magistrate or court to be the owner thereof". Such applications can be made "by an officer of police or by a claimant of the property". If the search or seizure was unlawful, the documents or other material seized must be returned—*R. v Chief Constable of Lancashire, Ex p. Parker and Magrath.*[48] By contrast, it has been held that that is not so where customs officers seize unlawfully held material after a search that is invalid.[49]

2–84   Note that s.22(5) does not apply to Customs and Excise. Most of PACE was applied to Customs and Excise by the Police and Criminal Evidence Act 1984

[44] *Settelen v Commissioner of the Metropolitan Police* [2004] EWHC 2171, Ch D.
[45] [2004] EWCA Crim 206, March 2, 2004.
[46] Unreported, Case No.B2/2000/0416, March 23, 2001, CA.
[47] Following *Webb v Chief Constable of Merseyside* [2000] 2 W.L.R. 546, CA.
[48] (1993) 97 Cr.App.R. 90; [1993] 2 All E.R. 56, DC.
[49] *R. (Hoverspeed Ltd) v Customs and Excise Commissioners* [2002] EWCA Civ 1804; [2003] 2 All E.R. 553.

(Application to Customs and Excise) Order 1985 (SI 1985/1800) but s.22(5) was one of the exceptions. Nor can someone whose property has been seized by Customs and Excise use for aid s.1 of the Police (Property) Act 1897, since that Act only applies to property in the possession of the police.

Section 48 of the Magistrates' Courts Act 1980 relates to the return of property taken from an accused person on his arrest, or after an arrest warrant or summons has been issued. It requires the police to report to the court what property has been seized. The court is then given a discretion as to whether the property, or any part of it, should be returned to the accused. But again this does not apply to seizures by Customs and Excise. In *R. v Southampton Magistrates' Court, Ex p. Newman*[50] the Divisional Court said that this was an anomaly which should be "speedily disposed of" by the legislature. There was so much activity these days by Customs and Excise in the investigation of drugs offences that a magistrates' court should have power to deal effectively at any time with applications for restoration of seized property. (In that case Customs and Excise were retaining eight address books.)

The only recourse in this situation, the Divisional Court said, was the inherent jurisdiction of the magistrates who could, to some extent, control their own procedure. So, if an accused person could not prepare his defence without access to certain documents, the court could adjourn or refuse to go ahead unless the police or Customs and Excise handed over the material. Alternatively, a civil action could be brought.

Interpretation: s.23[51]

Section 23 defines "premises", a definition which is very broad. It includes "any **2–85** place" and, in particular, any vehicle, vessel, aircraft or hovercraft, any offshore installation and any tent or movable structure. The original Home Office Circular on PACE (para.1–11, n.23 above) stated, however, that although theoretically "any place" could mean any open-air site, it ought to be restricted to something that is capable of being premises in the ordinary sense of the word ("That is, it should be a distinct piece of land in single occupation or ownership" (para.10).)

Note however that the meaning of the word "premises" as used in the Codes of Practice is determined not by s.23 but by s.66 which requires that the Home Secretary issue Codes of Practice in regard to "(c) searches of premises by police officers; and (d) the seizure of property found by police officers on persons or premises". The word "premises" there is seemingly governed by s.23, but the word "premises" as used in the Codes is technically not so tied. The Home Office Circular (*ibid.*, para.53) suggested that the word "premises" in Code C should be given a meaning which "conforms to common usage". But the 1991 revised Code B stated that "premises" for the purposes of the Code was defined in s.23 of PACE and "includes any place" (para.2.3[52]).

---

[50] (1988) 152 J.P. 664.
[51] See 1989 N.I. PACE Order, Art.25.
[52] Formerly 1.3.

QUESTIONS AND ANSWERS

ENTRY AND SEARCH OF PREMISES, SEIZURE OF PROPERTY

2–86 **In what circumstances can police enter upon premises without a search warrant?**

Normally a search warrant is needed for the police to get into private premises. But there are some exceptions, namely:

(1) Where the occupier consents to entry. This justification of entry was in fact a very common one,[53] but the reality of the consent must sometimes be a matter of some doubt. Code of Practice B, on the searching of premises and the seizure of property, laid down strict new rules in regard to the obtaining of consent which are directed to this precise point. The Code states that consent must be in writing and the occupier must be told that he is not obliged to consent and that anything seized may be used in evidence. If the person in question is not himself suspected of any complicity in the alleged crime he must be told so. There is no current information as to the extent of the use made by the police of search of premises by consent post-PACE.

(2) To prevent or to stop a breach of the peace which is imminent or taking place, or to save life or limb or to prevent serious damage to property.

(3) To effect an arrest of someone for whom a warrant of arrest has been issued. The police do not need a separate search warrant.

(4) To arrest someone for an arrestable offence.

(5) Where the police enter to search premises of someone who has been arrested for an arrestable offence, where they have reasonable grounds for believing that they will find evidence of that offence or of some similar or connected offence.

(6) To search the premises in which an arrested person was immediately before his arrest, for evidence relating to that offence but only if the officer has reasonable grounds for believing that such evidence is there.

(7) To recapture an escaped prisoner.

---

[53] The first study to produce empirical data about police use of powers of entry and search was published by the Royal Commission on Criminal Procedure in its *Law and Procedure Volume* (Cmnd. 8092–1 (1981)). Ten police forces kept figures for a four-week period in September 1979.

In what circumstances can an officer get a search warrant?   2–87

There are a variety of statutes, including the Police and Criminal Evidence Act, which allow an application to be made to the justices for a search warrant. A magistrate can, under the Act, grant a search warrant if he is satisfied that there are reasonable grounds to believe that:

(1) a "serious arrestable offence" (see paras 11–09—11–12 below) has been committed (under the Serious Organised Crime and Police Bill 2004–2005 it would be an "indictable offence");

(2) what is sought is likely to be relevant admissible evidence; and

(3) any one of the following conditions applies:

    (i)   that there is no practicable way of contacting someone able to grant entry or to grant access to the evidence; or

    (ii) that entry will only be granted if a warrant is produced; or

    (iii) that the purpose of the search may be frustrated or seriously prejudiced if the officers arrive and are then unable to get in immediately (in which case the occupiers would be alerted and could take steps to make the evidence unavailable).

But there are two exceptional categories of items for which no search warrant can normally be obtained:

(1) items subject to legal professional privilege; and

(2) material given special immunity under the 1984 Act—"excluded material".

There is also a category created by the 1984 Act where the material is not immune but where because of its sensitivity a special procedure is required to get a search warrant—"special procedure material". (As will be seen below, to complicate matters, in some circumstances "excluded material" does not qualify for full immunity but does have the status of "special procedure material" (see para.2–94 below).)

2–88   What is meant by legal professional privilege?

Legal professional privilege covers:

(1) Communications between a professional legal adviser and his client (or anyone representing the client) in connection with the giving of legal advice. This need not be in connection with any pending legal proceedings.

(2) Communications between the lawyer and his client (or anyone representing the client) or between the lawyer or the client or the representative and anyone else in connection with actual or pending legal proceedings.

When legal proceedings are in contemplation or are actually in being, the privilege is therefore broader since it then includes communications to third parties. So documents sent to an accountant, a handwriting expert or even just to a witness would be covered by the privilege if the communication was made "in connection with or in contemplation of legal proceedings and for the purposes of such proceedings".

(3) Anything enclosed with communications under (1) above for the purposes of getting advice or with communications under (2) above in connection with actual or pending legal proceedings is also privileged if it is in the hands of someone entitled to possession.

2–89   Whose privilege is it?

The privilege is that of the client not the lawyer. This means that if the material is not privileged it cannot become privileged by the simple expedient of being sent to the lawyer. On the other hand, the client can release the privilege even if the lawyer does not agree.

2–90   Does the privilege apply if the documents are evidence of a crime?

The law does not prevent the police from getting a search warrant to seek evidence of a conspiracy between lawyer and client. The 1984 Act states that "items held with the intention of furthering a criminal purpose are not items subject to legal privilege". Nor would there be any privilege if the client, or a third person who is "using" the client, has a criminal purpose in seeking advice.

**What about if the client has a criminal purpose of which the lawyer knows   2–91
nothing?**

The privilege is lost by virtue of the fact that the client has sent the documents to
the lawyer in order to further a criminal purpose even though the lawyer knows
nothing about it.

What is included in the category of "excluded material"?   2–92

There are three types of "excluded material":

(1) personal records;

(2) journalistic material;

(3) human tissue or tissue fluid taken for the purpose of diagnosis or
    medical treatment.

What do they cover?   2–93

(1) "Personal records" are those acquired in the course of a trade, business,
    profession or other occupation and held in confidence. They must be
    documents or records that make it possible to identify individuals and
    which relate to their physical or mental health (*e.g.* medical or psychi-
    atric records); or to spiritual counselling or help (*e.g.* the files of priests
    or clergymen); or to counselling or help given for the purposes of the
    individual's personal welfare by any voluntary agency or by an indi-
    vidual who has responsibility for the person's personal welfare (such
    as a university or school careers adviser, social worker, or volunteer
    advisory agency such as a Citizens' Advice Bureau).

(2) "Journalistic material" covers anything which comes into existence or
    is acquired for the purposes of journalism providing it is in the hands
    of a person who either acquired or created it for that purpose. This
    would cover, for instance, the contents of the journalist's notebook, or
    documents sent to a journalist with a view to their being considered for
    publication. Once it passes out of the possession of someone who
    acquired it or created it for the purposes of journalism it ceases to be
    "excluded material" though, as will be seen, it can still be "special
    procedure material".
        There is no need for the journalism to be of any very exalted kind to
    attract the total immunity. The Act does not define what is meant by
    journalism but it covers any form of the activity, however humble, paid

or unpaid. It is not clear to what extent it would be held to cover the writers of books.

(3) "Human tissue or tissue fluid" are not further defined and seem to be reasonably unproblematic.

2–94   In what circumstances must access to material be sought from a judge rather than from a magistrate?

The 1984 Act establishes two basic types of "special procedure material", access to which can only be sought from a judge. If and in so far as the previous law already permitted the police to get a search warrant for anything that is now defined as "excluded material", it becomes "special procedure material" and application for access must be made to a circuit judge. In other words the term "excluded material" covers two different categories of material. One is material covered by any of the definitions of excluded material for which the police could search prior to 1984 under, say, the Theft Act or the Official Secrets Act. The Act does not give such material immunity but it does require the special procedure of an application to the judge. However, anything covered by the definition of excluded material for which the police had no legal right to seek access prior to the 1984 Act now has complete immunity from a production order (unless it is sought as part of an inquiry into a terrorism offence). Secondly, the Act requires an application to a circuit judge for material held on a confidential basis, for instance by a bank. It is special procedure material if it is held in confidence by someone who acquired or created it in the course of a trade, business, profession or other occupation or for the purpose of any paid or unpaid office.

2–95   What form does the application to the judge take?

An application to the judge is made under Sch.1 to the Act. The person against whom the order is sought must be given advance notice of the hearing and is entitled to attend—though commonly he does not do so. But this does not apply where advance notice of the application might "seriously prejudice the investigation". Another exception to the principle is where it proves impossible to find anyone to grant access to the premises or to the material sought.

The normal application under Sch.1 is for an order requiring the person concerned to produce the material in question to the police within seven days so that they can take it away or to give them access to it. It is not an application for a search warrant. But a search warrant can be obtained in two situations. One is where the material could have been the subject of a search warrant before the 1984 Act and an order to give the police access to the material has been disobeyed. The other is where the application by the police was for a search warrant in the first place because advance notice of the hearing would have seriously prejudiced the investigation. This would be the case where the police were able to satisfy the judge that there was good reason to suspect that the person who had the material was himself implicated in the crime.

When the material could have been the subject of a search warrant under the previous law the judge must grant the application for an "order to produce", providing he is satisfied that the issue of the warrant under the former law would have been appropriate. It does not appear what tests the judges should apply to determine this question. But such cases will be very rare since there were hardly any statutes that authorised search warrants for what is now termed "excluded material". If the police want access to "excluded material" it will almost always come under the rules which require the judge to be satisfied that there are reasonable grounds for believing that:

(1)   a serious arrestable offence (see paras 11–09—11–12 below) (or, under the Serious Organised Crime and Police Bill 2004–2005, an indictable offence) has been committed;

(2)   material of the kind sought is on the premises;

(3)   it would be likely to be of substantial value to the investigation of the offence in question and would be likely to be relevant admissible evidence;

(4)   other means of getting the material have failed or were not tried because it seemed they were bound to fail;

(5)   it is in the public interest that the material should be produced having regard both to its value to the investigation and to the circumstances in which it is held.

If a person fails to comply with an order to produce the material or to make it available to the police, the sanction is for the police to return to the judge to ask him to punish the person concerned for contempt. As has been seen, they can only get a search warrant as a remedy for disobedience in the rare case where such a warrant could have been sought before the 1984 Act.

What happens if the police want material from premises, some of which   **2–96**
requires a warrant from the magistrates and some of which requires an
order or a warrant from a judge?

The application must be made to the judge who will then deal with it as a whole.

2–97   What is the procedure for search warrants?

The 1984 Act established a uniform procedure for applying for and executing a search warrant under any past or future Act:

(1) This requires a written application stating the grounds on which it is made; the Act under which the warrant would issue; details of the premises in question; and identification "so far as is practicable" of the articles or persons sought.

(2) The application is heard "*ex parte*", *i.e.* with only the police present.

(3) Answers to questions put by the justice of the peace must be given on oath.

(4) The warrant can only be used once. If the police wish to return to the premises they must get another warrant, unless the occupier is prepared to give consent.

(5) There must be two copies of the warrant, one for the person whose premises are to be searched.

(6) The warrant must be executed within a month. If it is not, and the police wish to try again, another warrant must be obtained.

(7) Entry and search under a warrant should be at a reasonable hour unless it appears to the constable executing it that the purpose of a search may be frustrated on an entry at a reasonable hour. (This seems to leave sufficient scope for the dawn raid in cases where it is thought to be necessary. It is left to the judgment of the officer concerned. Providing he reaches his decision honestly it could not be unlawful even if it was unreasonable.) The Code of Practice on the searching of premises and the seizure of property (Code B) lays down further rules in regard to the obtaining of a search warrant.

The Serious Organised Crime and Police Bill 2004–2005 would make important changes: a warrant could cover multiple entries over three months; and an "all-premises warrant" could be obtained in respect of other unnamed premises occupied or controlled by the person named.

2–98   What rules govern the process of getting into the premises to be searched?

The rules derive partly from the Act and partly from Code B.

The 1984 Act states that if the person whose premises are to be searched under warrant is there, the officer must identify himself. If he is not in uniform he must produce documentary evidence that he is a police officer. He must produce the search warrant and give the occupier a copy. If the person named is not there but someone else who appears to be in charge is present, then he should be told instead. (If entry is gained by force or subterfuge, the officer must identify himself and show the occupier his warrant as soon as practicably possible.) If there is no one there at all, the search may be carried out but a copy of the warrant must be left in a prominent place on the premises. Code B requires the police to give the occupier a Notice of Powers and Rights explaining what powers have been exercised and why. This is in addition to showing him the warrant. He must be asked whether he wants a friend, neighbour or other person to witness the search.

If the search is one to which the Code applies the police must supply the occupier with a notice specifying whether the search is made under warrant or with consent or in the exercise of other statutory powers. If the entry and search are with consent, the consent must, if possible, be given in writing on the Notice of Powers and Rights. The Notice must summarise the powers of search and seizure under the Act, must explain the rights of the occupier and of the owner of property seized and it must state that a copy of the Code is available to be consulted at any police station.

Can the occupier's consent be withdrawn after it has been given? 2–99

Consent can be withdrawn at any time. Code B (para.5.3[54]) states that an officer does not have a power to search premises with consent if the consent is given under duress or is withdrawn before the search is completed.

Once in the premises, what can the police search for? 2–100

If the search is under warrant, they must stick to the terms of the warrant and search only for what it authorises. This means that the manner of the search must be determined by what is being sought. A search for large items will obviously be restricted in a way that a search for something very small is not.

If the entry is without a warrant the search will normally be for a person and must be limited to what is reasonable in such a search. Where the search is of the premises after an arrest, it can only be for evidence of the offence or a similar or connected offence. Code B states that a search may not continue after the police have found what they came to find. It must also cease when it is clear that the items for which the police are looking are not there.

---

[54] Formerly 4.3.

2–101   How should a search be made?

The Code states, "Searches must be conducted with due consideration for the property and privacy of the occupier and with no more disturbance than is necessary. Reasonable force may only be used when necessary and proportionate" (para.6.10[55]). If the occupier wishes to have a friend with him to witness the search this should be allowed unless the officer in charge has reasonable grounds for believing that this would seriously hinder the search. But a search need not be delayed for the purpose.

At the end of the search the premises should be left secure. Where the search is under Sch.1 for special procedure material the police are required to exercise particular circumspection (see Code B, paras 6.14–6.15[56]). An officer of the rank of inspector should take over the search and be present. He is responsible for seeing that the search is carried out with discretion. He should ask for the documents which he is seeking. He can also ask for the index to files held on the premises. A more extensive search is only permitted if the person responsible for the premises refuses to produce the material sought or to allow access to the index of files, or if for some other reason the officer in charge has reasonable grounds for believing that such a search is necessary to find the material sought.

2–102   To what kinds of searches does Code B apply?

The Code applies to the following searches:

(1)   any search of premises for the purpose of an investigation of an alleged offence, with the occupier's consent, other than routine searches at the scene of the crime or searches following the activation of fire or burglar alarms;

(2)   searches of premises under the power conferred by ss.17, 18 and 32 of PACE;

(3)   searches of premises under a search warrant granted under s.15 of or Sch.1 to PACE. Section 15 applies to search warrants under any legislation.

The Code of Practice also applies to searches of premises under a search warrant issued under s.42 of or Sch.5 to the Terrorism Act 2000.

---

[55] Formerly 5.10.
[56] Formerly 5.13–5.14.

What can be seized during a search?   2–103

The police can seize anything (including "excluded" material and "special procedure" material) they come across in the course of a lawful search which is covered by any warrant or which they have reasonable grounds for believing is either evidence of any offence or has been obtained in consequence of the commission of an offence (such as the proceeds of a robbery). The only exception is anything covered by legal professional privilege, which is generally immune from seizure. However, the Criminal Justice and Police Act 2001 gave the police the right to "seize and sift"—to take away material in order to sift it elsewhere if it is not practicable to determine immediately whether it can lawfully be seized or which is "inextricably linked" to material that is not protected (see Code B, paras 7.7–7.17). This can include things covered by legal professional privilege.

What access must be given to the person from whom the material has been seized?   2–104

The person from whom material has been taken should, if he asks for it, be given a record of what has been seized within a reasonable time. If he requests access to the material or permission to copy or photograph it, this should be allowed (or he should be given police-made copies or photographs) unless the officer in charge of the case reasonably considers that it would prejudice the investigation of any offence or any criminal proceedings.

Where the material was taken away by virtue of the "seize and sift" power under the Criminal Justice and Police Act 2001, a person with a relevant interest in the seized property has the right to apply to a judge for its return.

How long can material seized in a search be held?   2–105

Items may be held by the police as long as is necessary—for instance for forensic examination or for use as evidence at a trial or for return to the true owner.

Must the police make any reports or returns about the success or otherwise of a search of premises?   2–106

PACE requires that where a search is conducted under a warrant the officer to whom it was issued must endorse on it a statement as to whether it was executed within the one-month time limit and, if so, whether the articles sought or any other articles were found. The warrant must then be returned to the court which issued it.

PART III

ARREST

The Philips Royal Commission, dealing with arrest, said "there is a lack of clarity and an uneasy and confused mixture of common law and statutory powers of arrest, the latter having grown piecemeal and without any consistent rationale".[1] The Philips Royal Commission said it had two main objectives in its proposals:

3–01

> "to restrict the circumstances in which the police can exercise the power to deprive a person of his liberty to those in which it is genuinely necessary . . . and to simplify, clarify and rationalise the existing statutory powers of arrest."[2]

The Philips Royal Commission recommended that there should be a statutory definition of the criteria justifying an arrest ("the necessity principle"[3]). It proposed that the definition of arrestable offences should be expanded, in particular to include all offences carrying any sentence of imprisonment.[4] It also recommended that there be a new power given to the police for when an officer saw someone committing a non-arrestable offence and he did not know that person's name and address. He should be able to arrest and detain him whilst he discovered his identity.[5] The Commission also favoured a new power to detain temporarily anyone found at the scene of a grave incident such as a murder so as to prevent possible suspects or witnesses from leaving. The power would allow persons to be held whilst names and addresses were obtained, a suspect was identified or the matter was otherwise resolved.[6]

The Government did not, however, accept all the Philips Royal Commission's recommendations. In particular, it thought the definition of arrestable offences proposed by the Philips Royal Commission was too wide but that the definition of the power to arrest for non-arrestable offences was too narrow.

The Human Rights Act 1998

Arrest principally involves Art.5 of the ECHR. Article 5(1) provides that, "Everyone has the right to liberty and security of the person". It goes on to state

3–02

---

[1] Philips Report, para.3.68.
[2] Philips Report, para.3.75.
[3] Philips Report, para.3.76.
[4] Philips Report, para.3.83.
[5] Philips Report, para.3.86.
[6] Philips Report, para.3.86.

that no one may be deprived of his liberty save as provided in the subsequent six cases (enumerated (a) to (f)) "and in accordance with a procedure prescribed by law". The relevant case is (c)—"the lawful arrest or detention of a person effected for the purpose of bringing him before the competent legal authority on reasonable suspicion of having committed an offence or when it is reasonably considered necessary to prevent his committing an offence or fleeing after having done so". Article 5(2) states that an arrested person must be informed promptly, in a language which he understands, of the reasons for his arrest and of any charge against him. Article 5(3) requires that a person who has been arrested or detained under Art.5(1)(c) "shall be brought promptly before a judge or other officer authorised by law to exercise judicial power and shall be entitled to trial within a reasonable time or to release pending trial". Release may be conditioned by guarantees to appear for trial. Article 5(4) requires that persons who have been arrested or detained must have a means of speedily challenging the lawfulness of their detention in a court. Anyone who has been held unlawfully "shall have an enforceable right to compensation" (Art.5(5)).

Armed Forces

3–03   The Armed Forces Act 2001, s.9 gives Service police a power without a warrant to enter and search residential premises occupied by persons subject to Service law to exercise a power of arrest under the Service Discipline Acts or to save life or limb or prevent serious damage to property. The power is based on PACE, s.17. The power of search is only a power to search for the person to be arrested (subs.(6)). It does not extend therefore to searching for evidence.

     Section 9 also allows a commanding officer to authorise a member of the armed forces who is not a Service policeman to enter and search without a warrant the living accomodation of a person under his command in order to arrest the person. The offence must be one for which a search warrant could be issued. The commanding officer must have reasonable grounds for believing that waiting to get the assistance of a Service or civilian policeman might result in the person evading capture, concealing or destroying evidence, being a danger to himself or to others or result in discipline being undermined (subs.(8)). If regulations so provide the commanding officer's powers may be delegated.

Arrest without warrant for arrestable and other offences: s.24[7]

3–04   The basic provision is s.24. (As will be seen, s.24 will be significantly changed on implementation of the Serious Organised Crime and Police Bill introduced in November 2004 (see paras 3–42—3–47 below).)

     The scheme of the section is that subss.(1) and (2) define the term "arrestable offence", subs.(3) applies to the inchoate offences and subss.(4) to (7) describe the conditions under which arrest powers may be exercised. All these provisions cover arrest without warrant and are called "powers of summary arrest".

---

[7] See 1989 N.I. PACE Order, Art.26.

Subsection (1) refers to three categories of arrestable offence. The first is offences for which the sentence is fixed by law (subs.(1)(a)). Murder is now the only example. The second is offences for which someone over 18[8] who has not previously been convicted could be given five or more years of imprisonment[9] (subs.(1)(b)). This includes a large number of offences such as theft, all forms of burglary, assault occasioning actual bodily harm, wounding, causing grievous bodily harm, wounding or causing grievous bodily harm with intent, robbery, assault with intent to rob, indecent assault and many others. It also includes certain common law offences carrying more than five years imprisonment such as kidnapping, attempting to pervert the course of justice, conspiring to defraud and false imprisonment.

The third category (subs.(1)(c)) was offences to which subs.(2) applied. But **3–05** this was changed by the Police Reform Act 2002, Sch.6 which put the ever-growing list of these cases into a new Sch.1A to PACE. These are "arrestable offences" even though they do not carry a five-year prison penalty. Some do not even carry any prison sentence. Schedule 1A lists over 20 such statutory offences or categories of offences, most of which have been added since PACE. There were three additions in the 2002 Act: assaulting a police officer in the execution of his duty, making off without payment, and driving while disqualified.[10] The Criminal Justice Act 2003, s.3 added three more—making an untrue statement for procuring a passport, having possession of cannabis or cannabis resin,[11] and making a false statement or withholding material information under s.174 of the Road Traffic Act 1988.

It should be noted that making offences "arrestable offences" is not the same as simply conferring a power of arrest without warrant. There are many offences where the police have a power of arrest without warrant that are not "arrestable offences". One difference is that "arrestable offences" attract additional powers such as that of entry to premises to effect the arrest (s.17(1)(b)), or to enter and search premises without a warrant following arrest (s.18), or to search the premises where the arrested person was immediately before the arrest (s.32). ("Serious arrestable offences"—on which see para.11–09 below—attract further powers.) Another difference is that in so far as ordinary citizens have the power to arrest someone (on which, see below) it applies to "arrestable offences" but obviously not to offences where only the police are given the power to make an arrest.

To say that the list in s.1 and in Sch.1A creates problems for the police is an understatement. There are well over 100 arrestable and serious arrestable offences.[12]

---

[8] It was originally 21 but this was reduced to 18 by the Criminal Justice and Court Services Act 2000, Sch.7, para.77.

[9] Or for which a five-year sentence might have been given if an either way offence were tried by the Crown Court where it could not be given if tried before magistrates.

[10] Sch.6, para.22. For a sharp critique of both the length and the contents of the list see Jason-Lloyd, "Section 24(2) of the Police and Criminal Evidence Act of 1984—Codification or Complication?" (1999) 163 J.P. 944, November 27, and by the same author, "Arrestable offences—an update" (2002) 166 J.P. 736, September 21.

[11] Resulting from the reclassification of cannabis as a Class C drug. For the Northern Ireland equivalent see Criminal Justice (No.2) (N.I.) Order 2003, SI 2003/3194. See also Aviation (Offences) Act 2003, s.1(2).

[12] For a list as at that date see Cape and Luqmani, *Defending Suspects at Police Stations* (Legal Action Group, 1999), App.4. The list was dropped from the latest edition.

Worse, subss.(4) and (5) of s.24 extend the power of summary arrest to ordinary citizens!

3–06   Moreover, subject to the provisions of the Criminal Attempts Act 1981, s.2,[13] subs.(3) extends the power of summary arrest to inchoate offences of conspiring or attempting to commit any such offence or inciting, aiding, abetting, counselling or procuring the commission of such an offence. As was pointed out,[14] there was a problem in regard to the cases in the list that were summary only offences because, according to s.1(4) of the Criminal Attempts Act 1981, there is no offence of attempting to commit a crime which is triable summarily only! This problem has now been cured by an amendment in s.24(3)(b) of PACE inserted by the Police Reform Act 2002, s.48(4)(b) which makes it clear that any arrestable offence that is triable summarily only is excluded from the power to arrest for an attempt to commit such an offence.

Section 24(4)–(7) goes on to reproduce s.2(2)–(5) of the Criminal Law Act 1967, as to circumstances in which arrest without a warrant may be effected on reasonable suspicion that an arrestable offence has been committed, is being committed or is about to be committed.

Powers of arrest are divided into two categories: those which anyone (including a constable) may exercise and those that can be used only by a constable.

Anyone may arrest without a warrant:

(a)   a person who is in the act of committing an arrestable offence; or

(b)   anyone whom he has reasonable grounds for suspecting to be committing such an offence (s.24(4)).

Where an arrestable offence has been committed, any person may arrest without a warrant:

(a)   anyone guilty of the offence; or

(b)   anyone whom he has reasonable grounds for suspecting of having committed the offence (s.24(5)).

3–07   Note however that this power operates only if an arrestable offence has in fact been committed. In *R. v Self*[15] D ran away after being accused of shoplifting by a store detective. After a chase he was arrested by a passer-by. He was charged with theft and assault with intent to resist arrest. The jury acquitted him of theft. The Court of Appeal held that he therefore could not be found guilty of assault with intent to resist arrest because the precondition for the application of s.24(5)

---

[13] This provides that any provision in any enactment (whenever passed) conferring a power of arrest in respect of the offence shall have effect with respect to attempting to commit that offence.
[14] See Jason-Lloyd, "New Arrest Powers under the Criminal Justice and Police Act" (2001) 165 J.P. 536 at 537.
[15] (1992) 95 Cr.App.R. 42, CA.

was not fulfilled. It follows that a citizen should be exceedingly careful before exercising the powers under s.24(5). (But see para.3–44 below)

Where a constable has reasonable grounds for suspecting that an arrestable offence has been committed, he may arrest without a warrant anyone whom he has reasonable grounds for suspecting to be guilty of the offence (s.24(6)). A police officer may also arrest without warrant:

    (a) anyone who is about to commit an arrestable offence;

    (b) anyone whom he has reasonable grounds for suspecting to be about to commit an arrestable offence (s.24(7)).

The Criminal Law Act 1967, s.2 used the formula "may arrest without a warrant anyone whom he with reasonable cause suspects . . .". There was a requirement of actual suspicion [16] Now in s.24 there is only a requirement that reasonable grounds exist, which raises the question whether the person making the arrest must himself have such suspicion. He may, for instance, not have directed his mind to the issue of whether an arrestable offence has been committed.

In *Siddiqui v Swain*[17] the Divisional Court held that the words "has reasonable grounds to suspect" in s.8(5) of the Road Traffic Act 1972 (now s.7 of the Road Traffic Act 1988) "import the further requirement that the constable in fact suspects".[18]   **3–08**

In *Chapman v DPP*[19] the Divisional Court adopted the same approach without argument. It quashed a conviction for assaulting a police officer in the execution of his duty on the ground that the justices had not found as a fact that the officer reasonably suspected that an arrestable offence had occurred.

Bingham L.J. said that reasonable suspicion was "the source from which all a police constable's powers of arrest flow". This was so not least because otherwise how could the officer inform the suspect of the offence in question (previously required at common law by *Christie v Leachinsky* (below) and now codified in s.28)? (*cf. Kynaston v DPP; Heron (Joseph) v DPP; Heron (Tracey) v DPP.*[20])

Since in s.24(4)(a), (5)(a) and (7)(a) there is no requirement of reasonable grounds, it appears that under those subsections the arrester need have no reasonable grounds for his belief providing that an arrestable offence is being or was being or is about to be committed.

[16] The House of Lords held in 1984 that where a police officer reasonably suspects an individual of having committed an arrestable offence, he may arrest that person with a view to questioning her in a police station; *Holgate-Mohammed v Duke* [1984] A.C. 437.

[17] [1979] R.T.R. 454.

[18] [1979] R.T.R. 457.

[19] (1988) 89 Cr.App.R. 190, CA; [1988] Crim.L.R. 843.

[20] (1988) 87 Cr.App.R. 200, CA. Although the prosecution had not proved that the officers had reasonable grounds for suspecting X of robbery, the court inferred it. See also *Cummings and others v Chief Constable of Northumbria* [2003] EWCA Civ 1844—opportunity can provide basis for reasonable suspicion; and *Al Fayed v Commissioner of the Metropolitan Police* [2004] EWCA Civ 1579—police held to have had reasonable suspicion justifying arrest of Mr Al Fayed, the owner of Harrods, and several of his employees, for theft from, and/or criminal damage to a Harrods safe deposit box belonging to his arch rival Mr "Tiny" Rowland.

3–09   An important practical question is what prior inquiries does the arresting officer have to make if he is given only minimal information about the reasons for
arrest? This was the question for the Court of Appeal in *Castorina v Chief
Constable of Surrey*.[21] A burglary at the plaintiff's former workplace appeared to
have been an "inside job". The managing director told the police that the plaintiff had recently been sacked and might have a grudge. The police went to the
plaintiff's home, having been told that she was of previous good character, and
without further inquiry arrested her. She was held for just under four hours. The
trial judge awarded her damages of £4,500 on the ground that the police lacked
reasonable cause for the arrest. He took the definition of "reasonable cause" to be
an "honest belief founded on a reasonable suspicion leading an ordinary cautious
man to the conclusion that the person arrested was guilty of the offence". He took
the view that an ordinary man would have sought more information from the suspect before arresting her. (He relied on dicta of Scott L.J. in *Dumbell v Roberts*[22]
that the principle that every man was presumed innocent until proved guilty
applied also to the arrest situation.)

The Court of Appeal held that the judge had applied too severe a test in asking
whether the officers had an honest belief as opposed to a suspicion or conjecture.
Purchas L.J. said that "reasonable cause" was an objective issue and had nothing
to do with the officer's subjective state of mind. The judge had therefore misdi-
rected himself in making honest belief the test. Also the fact that the officer might
have made further inquiries did not mean that the arrest was unlawful. The question was whether the officer had had reasonable grounds to suspect her of the
offence. In the circumstances of this case the officer had had sufficient reason to
suspect the woman.

3–10   Woolf L.J. suggested that when it is alleged that an arrest is unlawful there are
three questions to be considered:

(a) Did the arresting officer suspect that the person who was arrested was
guilty of the offence? This depended on the finding of fact as to the
officer's subjective state of mind.

(b) Assuming the officer had the necessary suspicion, was there reasonable
proof of that suspicion? This was an objective requirement to be determined by the judge.

(c) If the answer to both these questions was affirmative then the officer
had a discretion to arrest. In *Holgate-Mohammed v Duke*[23] the House
of Lords said that discretion to arrest was justified in order to prevent a
suspect escaping or to dispel or confirm reasonable suspicion by questioning him or seeking further evidence. The question then was whether
a reasonable police officer would have thought it reasonable to make an

---

[21] [1979] R.T.R. 454; [1988] New L.J. 180, CA.
[22] [1944] 1 All E.R. 326 at 329.
[23] See n.16 above.

arrest in those circumstances. This is the test of so-called "Wednesbury unreasonableness".[24]

Sir Frederick Lawton said that the facts upon which a reasonable cause was said to have been founded did not have to be such as to lead an ordinary cautious man to conclude that the person arrested was guilty of the offence. It was enough if they could lead a reasonable person to suspect that he was guilty.

This is not a very exacting standard. Moreover, as the House of Lords' decision in *Holgate-Mohammed*[25] makes clear, once the police officer objectively has reasonable cause to make an arrest the decision can only be challenged successfully if he acted unreasonably within the *Wednesbury* principle by not exercising the discretion (*i.e.* not weighing up the considerations relevant to the particular case) or by taking something irrelevant into account.   **3–11**

It has been argued that sometimes a failure to make inquiries before making an arrest could show that there were insufficient grounds.[26] In *Hussein v Chong Fook Kam*[27] it was accepted that a failure to ask relevant questions could mean that the officer did not have reasonable grounds to suspect. As Lord Devlin said: "It was . . . a premature arrest rather than one which was unjustified from first to last. The police made the mistake of arresting before questioning; if they had questioned first and arrested afterwards, there would have been no case against them." But Lord Devlin also said that in formulating reasonable suspicion, the police can take account of evidence which could not be put in evidence in court. "Suspicion in its ordinary meaning is a state of conjecture or surmise where proof is lacking: 'I suspect but I cannot prove.' Suspicion arises at or near the starting point of an investigation of which the obtaining of prima facie proof is the end."[28]

Purchas L.J. in *Castorina* suggested that if they had enough to go on it was irrelevant to consider what further inquiries the police might have made. They had been told that it was an "inside job" and the plaintiff seemed to be the only person with the relevant inside knowledge. But it would be remarkable if this were right. As Clayton and Tomlinson have said: "If the police are justified in arresting a middle aged woman of good character on such flimsy grounds, without even questioning her as to her alibi or possible motives, the law provides very scant protection for those suspected of crime."[29] The officers should have

---

[24] Laid down by Greene M.R. in *Associated Provincial Picture Houses Ltd v Wednesbury Corpn* [1948] 1 K.B. 223. See *Cummings* n.20 above at [42]–[44] and *Paul v Chief Constable of Humberside Police* [2004] EWCA Civ 358 at [34]–[37]. In *Al Fayed v Commissioner of the Metropolitan Police* [2004] EWCA Civ 1579 the decision to arrest was held to have been reasonable notwithstanding that the suspects had been willing to come to the police station voluntarily, had been willing to be fingerprinted and agreed to allow their premises to be searched. The Court rejected the submission that an arrest was only justifiable if it was necessary.

[25] n.16 above.

[26] Clayton and Tomlinson, "Arrest and reasonable grounds for suspicion", *Law Society Gazette*, September 7, 1988, p.22. They are co-authors also of *Civil Actions Against the Police* (3rd ed., Sweet & Maxwell Ltd, 2003). The writer is indebted to the authors for several of the points made here.

[27] [1970] A.C. 942, HL.

[28] *ibid.*, at 948.

[29] Clayton and Tomlinson, *op.cit.*, p.26.

inquired into what she said. "Any other approach would mean that the law would be encouraging an arrest-first, ask-questions-later policy which would be both sloppy police work and a serious interference with civil liberties."[30] (See also *Ward v Chief Constable of Avon & Somerset Constabulary.*[31])

3–12   It has been recognised that an officer's reasonable grounds to suspect can be based on information received from another officer but such information must go beyond a mere instruction to arrest. This was the gist of the unanimous decision of the House of Lords in *O'Hara v Chief Constable of the Royal Ulster Constabulary.*[32] The case concerned an arrest under the Prevention of Terrorism Act rather than PACE but the decision turned on what was meant by the phrase, common to both statutes, "reasonable grounds to suspect". The officer had attended a police briefing given by a superior officer at which he was told that O had been involved in a terrorist murder and to arrest him. If he had simply been instructed to arrest O, the arrest would have been unlawful as the arresting officer would have had no basis for personally suspecting. But although the information given at the briefing had been scanty it was held to be sufficient to constitute the required state of mind of an arresting officer. Under English law even a low-ranking police officer is independent and accountable. If he is required to have a state of mind it cannot be based on superior orders. The requirement that the arresting officer himself have the necessary suspicion turned on the word reasonable suspicion. The Law Lords distinguished the House of Lords' decision of *McKee v Chief Constable for Northern Ireland*[33] where again the issue had been the lawfulness of the arrest of a suspected terrorist. The relevant statute provided that, "Any constable may arrest without warrant any person whom he suspects of being a terrorist".[34] Interpreting those words, Lord Roskill, speaking for the House, said that the arresting officer's state of mind could be derived from an instruction given by a superior officer. He was not bound—and indeed might well not be entitled—to question those instructions or to ask on what information they were founded.[35] But in that case there was no requirement of reasonable grounds to suspect. It follows that where the statute requires reasonable grounds to suspect, officers who give briefings with instructions to arrest a named person must be careful to ensure that enough information is communicated to provide a basis of reasonable suspicion for the arresting officer. The case then went to the European Court of Human Rights which agreed that the suspicion against the suspect reached the required level for compliance with Art.5(1)(c) of the ECHR as it was based on specific information of his involvement in the murder.[36]

3–13   *O'Hara* was applied in *Hough v Chief Constable of the Staffordshire Constabulary.*[37] The Court of Appeal held there that although the question was what was in the mind of the arresting officer, reasonable suspicion could be based

---

[30] Clayton and Tomlinson, *op.cit.,* p.26.
[31] *The Times,* June 26, 1986.
[32] [1997] 2 W.L.R. 1; [1997] 1 All E.R. 129.
[33] [1984] 1 W.L.R. 1358; [1985] 1 All E.R. 1.
[34] Northern Ireland (Emergency Provisions) Act 1978, s.11(1).
[35] [1984] 1 W.L.R. 1358 at 1361; [1985] 1 All E.R. 1 at 4.
[36] *O'Hara v United Kingdom* [2002] Crim.L.R. 493, decision of October 16, 2001.
[37] [2001] EWCA Civ 39; *The Times,* February 15, 2001, CA.

on an entry in the Police National Computer ("PNC")—in that case, that the driver of the vehicle might be armed. It reversed the finding of the trial judge awarding the person arrested damages of £10,000 for wrongful arrest. But the court made it clear that an entry in the PNC would not always be a sufficient basis for the necessary reasonable suspicion. If, for instance, there was no urgency and some further inquiry seemed indicated, the PNC entry would be insufficient.

Such suspicion need not be based on solid evidence. The courts recognise that at the early stage of an investigation the police may be operating on the basis of a tip-off from a member of the public or information from an informer—though information from an informer should be treated with caution.[38] Hearsay information can be enough. It is not required that there be a *prima facie* case.[39]

In summary, it is sensible to assume that reasonable cause will only be present if a reasonable man in the position of the officer at the time of the arrest would have thought that the plaintiff was probably guilty of the offence.[40] The police officer need not prove every possible explanation or follow up every lead, but it would be surprising if the law were such as not to require that he make at least obvious inquiries before making an arrest.

If the prosecution evidence does not establish that the police had reasonable grounds for suspicion, the arrest will be unlawful—see *Riley v DPP*.[41]

Powers of arrest for cross-border enforcement

New powers of arrest for cross-border enforcement were conferred on the police   **3–14** in England and Wales, Scotland and Northern Ireland by the Criminal Justice and Public Order Act 1994 (CJPOA), Pt X.

Until then police officers in one country had no power or authority in the others. Likewise, the courts had no jurisdiction over offences committed in the other country. The CJPOA addressed the problem of a lack of police powers. The new arrangements came into effect in February 1995 supported by a protocol agreed by chief officers in all United Kingdom countries under which officers can work in each others' countries. The basic concept is that investigators take with them their own law and powers with regard to arrest and detention of suspects and that those rules take precedence over the local rules.

Under the protocol agreed by chief officers, cross-border actions should not be undertaken unless the commander of the local area concerned has been informed of the circumstances and what is planned and guidance or even directions from

---

[38] *James v Chief Constable of South Wales, Independent*, April 29, 1991, CA.
[39] *Shaaban Bin Hussein v Choong Fook Kam* [1970] A.C. 942 at 949; [1969] 3 All E.R. 1626 at 1631; *O'Hara v Chief Constable of RUC* [1997] 1 All E.R. 129 at 134; and *Al Fayed v Commissioner of the Metropolitan Police* [2004] EWCA Civ 1579 at [50]–[52].
[40] *Dallison v Caffery* [1965] 1 Q.B. 348 at 371; *Wiltshire v Barrett* [1966] 1 Q.B. 312 at 322.
[41] (1991) 91 Cr.App.R. 14; [1990] Crim.L.R. 422, DC—the case stated did not show that the justices had been told the reasons for the arrest. See also *R. v DPP, Ex p. Odewale*, unreported, Case No.CO/1381/00, November 28, 2000, DC—no evidence as to the offence for which the defendant was arrested. But *cf. Kynaston v DPP* (1988) 87 Cr.App.R. 200, DC.

the local force have been sought. Subject to that, the investigating team are supposed, so far as possible, to be self-sufficient in terms of staff, vehicles, documentation and equipment to preserve evidence, to manage an arrest and detention and to take the suspect back to their own country.

3–15   Section 137 of the CJPOA provided that if an officer in England and Wales has reasonable grounds for suspecting that someone has committed an arrestable offence in England or Wales and that that person is in Scotland or Northern Ireland, he can arrest him there. The same power of arrest applies equally to the circumstances permitting arrest under s.25 below, and to arrest warrants. Equivalent reciprocal powers are given to the police in Scotland and Northern Ireland.[42]

When arrested, the person should then be taken as soon as practicable to the nearest convenient police station in the jurisdiction where the offence is being investigated.[43] The Act makes appropriate supplementary provisions for power to search the arrested person (for evidence of an offence) and the premises where he was when or immediately before he was arrested (for evidence relating to the offence for which he was arrested).[44] Anything found in the course of such a search that appears to be evidence of an offence may be seized.[45] A police officer in one jurisdiction in the United Kingdom who is in another part of the United Kingdom may use the powers of arrest applicable to the jurisdiction where he is.[46]

General arrest conditions: s.25[47]

3–16   Section 25 gave the police a new general power of arrest in respect of a variety of situations. It is important to appreciate, however, that s.25 did not create arrestable offences. The Act at various points gives the police special powers that relate to arrestable offences, or serious arrestable offences. The only offences which are arrestable offences are those defined in s.24. For offences in that category the power of arrest is unqualified. All other offences now carry a limited power of arrest under s.25 if a constable has reasonable grounds for suspecting that any offence has been committed or attempted or is being committed or attempted and it appears to him that service of a summons is impracticable or inappropriate because "any of the general arrest conditions is satisfied".

The thinking behind the section is that a police officer should be able to make an arrest for an offence normally not arrestable where either he does not know the person's name or address or it is necessary to prevent or stop one of a list of particular social evils. It is in effect either for the purpose of enabling the police to prosecute for a non-arrestable offence or it is preventative.

The first general arrest condition is that the officer does not know and cannot readily ascertain the name and address of the suspect or he reasonably believes

---

[42] CJPOA, ss.136, 137(1)–(6) and 138.
[43] CJPOA, s.137(7).
[44] CJPOA, s.139.
[45] CJPOA, s.10.
[46] CJPOA, s.140.
[47] See 1989 N.I. PACE Order, Art.26.

that the name and address he has been given are false, or he doubts whether the suspect has given a satisfactory address for service of a summons, either because he has given no address at all or because it is doubtful whether he will be there long enough to accept service and there is no one else who can do so (subss.(3)(a), (b), (c)). This is wider than the power proposed by the Philips Royal Commission which was confined to cases where the officer actually saw the offence being committed.

It is sufficient if the officer asks for the name and address of someone sus- **3–17** pected of having committed a non-arrestable offence who refuses to give it. He need not specifically explain that he wants the name and address in order to be able to serve a summons.[48] But the ground for the arrest given by the police must be a valid ground. It has been held that it is not valid, for instance, to say, "You're nicked for obstruction" after trying unsuccessfully to get the person to spit out something suspected of being cannabis which he had seen the suspect put into his mouth. The offence under s.23(4)(a) of the Misuse of Drugs Act 1971 was obstruction but the power of arrest for that offence had been repealed by s.26 of PACE. There was therefore no right to arrest for obstruction and s.25 could not apply because the ground was invalid.[49] (The officer should have said "You're nicked for suspected possession of cannabis".)

The other general arrest condition (subs.(3)(d)) is where there are reasonable grounds for believing that the arrest is necessary to prevent the suspect causing: (i) physical harm to himself or to someone else; (ii) loss of or damage to property; (iii) an unlawful obstruction of the highway[50]; or (iv) an offence against public decency in circumstances "where members of the public going about their normal business cannot readily avoid the person to be arrested" (subs.5). (This last category is seemingly intended to deal, for instance, with the case of a "flasher".) It is also permissible to arrest someone to protect a child or other vulnerable person from the person to be arrested (subs.(3)(e)). This broad power was not recommended by the Philips Royal Commission at all.

The Bill originally included a power for an officer to detain anyone while he **3–18** verified the name and address given to him, exercisable if it appeared that verification could be carried out quickly. This in essence is the power the police in Scotland have under s.2(2) of the Criminal Justice (Scotland) Act 1980. However, the power was deleted by the Government at the Report stage in the House of Commons. No such power exists therefore. Another change made in the course of the Bill's passage was the elimination of the definition of "physical harm" as including serious disease.

Detention under s.25 is normally for a short time but if, for any reason, it becomes protracted, the various provisions in PACE that regulate police detention (ss.34, 37, 38 and 40) apply equally to arrests under this section.

---

[48] *Nicholas v DPP* [1987] R.T.R. 199; [1987] Crim.L.R. 474, DC.
[49] *Edwards v DPP* (1993) 97 Cr.App.R. 301, DC. See also *G. v DPP* [1989] Crim.L.R. 150, DC. But see Professor Birch's comments on this case, following the report, and Lawson, "Whither the 'General Arrest Conditions'?" [1993] Crim.L.R. 568.
[50] This replaces s.137(2) of the Highways Act 1980.

Repeal of statutory powers of arrest without warrant: s.26[51]

3–19 This section provided for the repeal of virtually all statutory powers of arrest by constables without a warrant. With the enactment of the general power of arrest in s.25 these were no longer needed. The Act did not, however, repeal all other statutory powers of arrest. Those preserved are listed in Sch.2. They include, for instance, powers of arrest in connection with drink driving offences and terrorism legislation. Also, Sch.6, para.21(b) of PACE specifically preserves the power to arrest a person for disorderly behaviour while drunk—under s.91(1) of the Criminal Justice Act 1967.[52] The repeal does not affect powers of arrest at common law to prevent or deal with a breach of the peace,[53] nor those dependent on a warrant or order of a court, nor those available to persons other than constables (*e.g.* to gamekeepers under s.2 of the Poaching Act 1828).

There are some powers of arrest given by statute to "any person".[54] These powers were not repealed by s.26 but can they still be exercised by constables on the ground that they come within the concept of "any person", even though statutory powers of arrest for constables were generally abolished by s.26? The better view seems to be that these powers of arrest remain.[55] The original Home Office Circular on PACE suggested that to avoid uncertainty and accusations of arbitrariness, police forces might consider it prudent to use these powers only where the general arrest conditions in s.25 were also met.[56]

Arrest without warrant for fingerprinting: s.27[57]

3–20 Prior to PACE, the compulsory taking of fingerprints in the investigation stage of crime was only possible in certain limited circumstances and on the authority of a magistrate. PACE changed the rules by putting the power essentially in the hands of the police. As will be seen, the main provision is in s.61 which is principally concerned with the investigation stage.

Section 61(6) gives the police power to take a person's fingerprints without his consent if he has been convicted of a recordable offence (s.117 and Code D, para.4.6[58] legitimise the use of reasonable force for the taking of such fingerprints).

---

[51] See 1989 N.I. PACE Order, Art.28.
[52] See *DPP v Kitching* [1990] Crim.L.R. 394, DC.
[53] For discussion by the Court of Appeal of the scope of this power see *DPP v Orum* [1989] 1 W.L.R. 88. See also Sampson, "Breach of the Peace—a Breach in PACE?", J.P., May 4, 1991, p.281.
[54] See *e.g.* Prevention of Offences Act 1851, s.11; Vagrancy Act 1824, s.6 (as amended by Criminal Justice Act 1948, s.68); Sexual Offences Act 1956, ss.32, 41; Licensing Act 1872, s.12; Criminal Justice Act 1967, s.91; Licensing Act 1902, s.1; Sexual Offences Act 1967, s.5(3); Theft Act 1978, s.3(4).
[55] See *e.g.* Home Office Circular No.88/1985 on the 1984 Act, para.11; Birch, "Powers of Arrest and Detention" [1985] Crim.L.R. 545 at 550.
[56] See *e.g.* instance Home Office Circular No.88/1985 on the 1984 Act, para.11; Birch, "Powers of Arrest and Detention" [1985] Crim.L.R. 545 at 550.
[57] See 1989 N.I. PACE Order, Art.29.
[58] Formerly para.3.2.

A conviction for this purpose now includes a caution, a reprimand or a warning as provided for by the Crime and Disorder Act 1998.[59]

Where a person has been convicted of a recordable offence but he has never been in police detention, the question of fingerprinting is dealt with by s.27. This section is therefore limited to the situation of someone who has been convicted of a recordable offence but has been neither fingerprinted nor detained by the police.

Within one month of the conviction (providing at least seven days' notice is given) a constable may require such a person to attend a police station at a specified time in order to obtain his fingerprints (subs.(1)). The same power is given to authorised civilian detention officers under the Police Reform Act 2002.[60]   **3–21**

The Criminal Justice and Police Act 2001, s.78 added a power to retake fingerprints when the initial set of prints taken prove to be incomplete or of poor quality or there were errors in the data capture process.

The power is backed not only by the power to use reasonable force but also by a power of arrest if the person concerned has failed to comply with a request to attend within seven days at a police station (s.27(3)). (There is no equivalent power of arrest under s.61.) Civilian detention officers do not have this (or any other) power of arrest.

Section 27 grants the Home Secretary power to make regulations by statutory instrument specifying the offences constituting recordable offences, and making provision for such offences to be recorded in national police records (subss.(4)–(5)). The regulations specify as recordable offences (and therefore fingerprintable without consent) any conviction, caution, reprimand or warning in respect of an offence punishable with imprisonment or for any offence specified in the regulations. (Some 50 or so offences are specified in the regulations.)[61]

The offences which have to be reported to the National Identification Bureau were listed in Appendix F to the 1985 Home Office Circular on PACE (see para.1–11, n.23 above).

Information to be given on arrest: s.28[62]

The Philips Royal Commission recommended[63] that the common law rule, established by the great case of *Christie v Leachinsky*[64] requiring that an arrested person be told that he is under arrest and the grounds of his arrest should be put into statutory form. Section 28 implements that proposal and adds for good measure that when the arrest is by a police officer (but not otherwise), the requirement to inform the suspect that he is under arrest and the grounds for arrest, applies regardless of whether the fact of the arrest or the grounds for it is obvious. A new   **3–22**

---

[59] Sch.8, para.61.
[60] Sch.4, Pt 3, para.19.
[61] National Police Records (Recordable Offences) Regulations 2000 (SI 2000/1139), as amended by National Police Records (Recordable Offences) (Amendment) Regulations 2003 (SI 2003/2823).
[62] See 1989 N.I. PACE Order, Art.30.
[63] Philips Report, para.3.87.
[64] [1947] A.C. 573, HL.

para.10.3 in Code C introduced in the 2003 revision states that in addition to being cautioned, a person who is arrested (or further arrested) must as soon as is practicable be informed (i) that they are under arrest and (ii) of the grounds for their arrest with sufficient information to enable them to understand that they have been deprived of their liberty and the reason. Vague or technical language should be avoided.

In *Taylor v Chief Constable of Thames Valley Police*[65] the person arrested was ten years old. On being arrested on May 31, he was told that the arrest was for violent disorder at Hillgrove Farm on April 18—the venue for a violent animal rights demonstration involving over a thousand people. The Court held this was sufficient information. Citing *Fox v United Kingdom*[66] Clarke L.J. said the question was whether having regard to the circumstances of the particular case, the person arrested was told in simple, non-technical language that he could understand, the essential legal and factual grounds for his arrest. In *Wilson v Chief Constable of Lancashire*[67] the Court of Appeal said that one of the reasons for requiring that the arrested person be informed why he is under arrest is so that if he is in fact innocent he can convincingly deny the allegation. In that case the Court held that the information given was insufficient. It was unfair to arrest someone for an unidentified offence that took place at an unspecified time and place. It allowed the appeal and ordered damages for false imprisonment to be assessed.

3–23   But there is no need for technical words to indicate the fact of arrest. *Brosch*,[68] decided by the Court of Appeal, makes it clear that it is not necessary for the arrest to be accompanied by words such as "I arrest you" for it to be valid. (See to like effect *Abbassey v Newman*.[69]) Even very informal language will suffice. As Sedley L.J. said: "Although no constable ever admits to saying 'You're nicked for handling this gear' or 'I'm having you for nicking this motor', either will do and, I have no doubt, frequently does."[70]

If several officers are involved, it does not matter which of them tells the arrested person the reasons for the arrest.[71]

Subsection (3) makes the lawfulness of the arrest dependent on the arrested person having been informed at the time of arrest, or as soon as practicable thereafter, of the fact of and the grounds for arrest.[72]

The duty to inform the suspect that he is under arrest obviously does not apply if he escapes before the information can be communicated to him (subs.(5)). In *Hawkins*[73] the Divisional Court held that there is equally an exception where the defendant makes it impossible by his violent conduct for the officer to communicate the reasons to him. In that situation the arrest is lawful and remains lawful until such time as the reasons should have been given. The fact that the reasons

---

[65] [2004] EWCA Civ 858; [2004] 3 All E.R. 503.
[66] (1991) 13 E.H.R.R. 157 at 170, para.40.
[67] *Daily Telegraph*, December 5, 2000.
[68] [1988] Crim.L.R. 743. See also *Nicholas v Parsonage* [1987] R.T.R. 199.
[69] [1990] 1 All E.R. 193, CA.
[70] *Clarke v Chief Constable of North Wales Police* [2000] All E.R. (D) 477, CA.
[71] *Dhesi v Chief Constable of the West Midlands Police, The Times*, May 9, 2000, CA.
[72] On "at the time of . . . arrest" see *Nicholas v DPP* (or *Parsonage*) [1987] R.T.R. 199; [1987] Crim.L.R. 474, DC. The case stands also for the proposition that when the arrest is under s.25 there should be mention of the offence as well as of the grounds for arrest.
[73] [1988] 1 W.L.R. 1166.

were not then given does not retrospectively invalidate the original arrest and does not therefore mean that the officer was not acting in the execution of his office when assaulted. Similarly, where the arrest was initially unlawful, when it becomes lawful by the officer conveying the grounds, that does not alter the original unlawfulness of the arrest.[74]

No reference need be made as to the power of arrest nor to whether the arrest **3–24** was under statute or common law. However, the reason given must be the correct reason. If an incorrect reason is given, the arrest is unlawful and so is the arrest of someone else who intervenes to prevent it—even if there could in fact have been some other valid basis for the arrest.[75]

The rule that the arrested person must be given sufficient information about his situation applies equally in the police station. The Court of Appeal in *Kirk*[76] quashed a conviction for robbery because the police questioned the suspect for quite a while without telling him that the victim of the robbery had died the next day and that the charge might therefore become manslaughter. The Court ruled that the suspect must be told the level of offence in respect of which he is suspected. If he does not know and as a result does not seek legal advice and gives answers which he otherwise might not have given, the evidence would normally have to be excluded.

However, an arrest can be lawful if the reason given is valid, even if it is not the real reason for the arrest. In *R. v Chalkley, R. v Jeffries*[77] the defendants were arrested on reasonable suspicion of involvement in credit card frauds in order to get them out of the house for long enough for a listening device to be installed in connection with an investigation into major robberies. The Court of Appeal held that a collateral motive for an arrest which was otherwise made on good grounds did not necessarily make it unlawful. Auld L.J. said that that "well-known and respectable aid to justice, a 'holding charge'" was an example of the police arresting someone in connection with one matter in order to investigate another.

For consideration of whether in different sections of PACE the word arrest means "lawful arrest" see Marston, "The Reasons for an Arrest", J.P., March 2, 1991, p.131. See also Glanville Williams, "What is an arrest?" (1991) 54 *Modern Law Review* 408.

Voluntary attendance at police station: s.29[78]

The police frequently find it convenient to blur the line between freedom and **3–25** arrest. The newspaper phrase "a man is helping the police with their inquiries" has become a polite euphemism to describe this shadowy area. But in law the position has not been in doubt. A person is either under arrest or he is not. If he

---

[74] *Lewis v Chief Constable of South Wales Constabulary* [1991] 1 All E.R. 206, CA, applying the principle established pre-PACE in *Kulynycz* [1970] 3 All E.R. 881. See also *DPP v L and S* [1999] Crim.L.R. 752, DC.
[75] *Edwards v DPP* (1993) 97 Cr.App.R. 301, DC.
[76] [1999] 4 All E.R. 698, CA.
[77] [1998] Q.B. 848; [1998] 3 W.L.R. 146.
[78] See 1989 N.I. PACE Order, Art.31.

is not under arrest, he is free to go. (However, under the Police Reform Act 2002 civilian community support officers can detain someone suspected of committing a "relevant offence" for up to 30 minutes if they fail to provide their name and address—see paras 12–03, 12–09 below.)

The Philips Royal Commission recommended that this be made clear in the statute[79] and s.29 represents a partial attempt by the Home Office to spell out the details. It specifies, first, that where a person attends voluntarily at a police station or anywhere else "for the purpose of assisting with an investigation", "he shall be entitled to leave at will unless he is placed under arrest" and "he shall be informed at once that he is under arrest if a decision is taken by a constable to prevent him from leaving at will".

The object of this section no doubt is to ensure that the suspect should always know that if he has not been told that he is under arrest he is free to go. But in practice, the suspect will often wrongly assume that he is under arrest and will therefore fail to take advantage of his right to leave. By the time he is told that he is under arrest, it will of course be too late. He will then be unable to leave. The only way to avoid this dilemma would be to give a suspect who is asked whether he would mind coming down to the police station to answer a few questions a warning that this does not mean that he is under arrest and that he is free to come or not to come as he pleases. This would logically complement the later warning that the suspect need not say anything if he does not want to do so.

3–26　The Philips Royal Commission's Report did not discuss this issue and made no recommendation that such a warning should be given and there is nothing about it in the Act. The undoubted value of s.29 is therefore considerably qualified by the fact that the information about his status will usually be communicated to the suspect only at the moment of being cautioned or arrested. If he is cautioned away from the police station and is not then under arrest, the same paragraph of the Code requires that he be told so. This would draw his attention to the fact that he is not under any compulsion to come with the police officer.

The problem of proper accountability for those attending voluntarily at the police station arises not only in regard to those who are genuinely volunteers but also to those defined as volunteers by the police who might reasonably be regarded as there under some degree of compulsion. Research has shown that some forces use the category of voluntary attendance much more than others, indicating a radically different approach.[80] This is less than satisfactory.

Arrest elsewhere than at police station: s.30[81]

3–27　The Philips Royal Commission recommended that persons who have been arrested should normally be taken straight to a police station so that their detention could become subject to the general supervisory measures which the Philips Commission proposed for detained persons.[82] Both the Act and Code C contain

---

[79] Philips Report, para.3.97.
[80] McKenzie *et al.* (1990), pp.23, 27–33.
[81] See 1989 N.I. PACE Order, Art.32.
[82] Philips Report, para.3.102.

various rights for suspects and duties for the police which start to operate from the time of arrival at a police station. It is therefore important that these controls and safeguards take effect from the earliest practicable time. In particular, the time-limit clock only starts to run on arrival at the police station. (There is in any event some value in discouraging the police from "taking the scenic route to the police station" as a way of providing additional time and opportunity for questioning away from the scrutiny of station colleagues.)

The Act implemented the Philips Royal Commission's proposal by stating that where a person is arrested away from a police station he shall be taken to a police station "as soon as practicable" (subs.(1)). Subsection (1) says that the arrested person must be taken by a constable but the Police Reform Act 2002 states that an authorised civilian escort officer can perform the same function. The prisoner is in his lawful custody and he can use reasonable force to prevent his escape.[83]

The effect of the provision in subs.(1) is somewhat weakened by subs.(10) which allows the police to delay taking the prisoner to a police station if the presence of that person elsewhere is necessary to carry out investigations of an offence. But that does not give the police carte blanche to undertake an interrogation of the suspect which ought to be carried out in the police station.[84] Save in exceptional circumstances,[85] interviews of suspects have to be carried out at the police station or other authorised place of detention (Code C, para.11.1).

If there is such a delay the reasons for it must be recorded on first arrival at the police station (subs.(11)). **3–28**

The section does not, however, affect the special powers of the police to hold persons elsewhere than in a police station in immigration and terrorism cases nor the right of the police (under the Criminal Justice Act 1972, s.34) to take a drunk to a detoxification centre (subss.(11) and (12)). Normally, according to s.30(1), a person who has been arrested must be taken to a "designated police station" (defined in s.35). But he may be taken to a non-designated station if any of three alternative conditions is satisfied. The first is where the officer is working in the area of a non-designated police station—unless it appears that the suspect will have to be held for longer than six hours (subss.(3) and (4)). If he is being held in a non-designated station he must be moved to a designated station if he is to be held for more than six hours (subs.(6)). The second (s.30(5)(a)) is where the person is arrested by a police officer acting on his own, no other officer is available to help him and it appears to the arresting officer that he will not be able to take him to a designated station without the detained person injuring someone (himself, the officer or another person). (In Northern Ireland he may be taken to any police station if there is any physical danger: 1989 N.I. PACE Order, Art.32(6), (7) and (8).) The third situation in which he may be taken to a non-designated station (s.30(5)(ii)) is where the officer has taken the person into custody from someone other than a police officer (*e.g.* after a citizen's arrest or from

---

[83] Sch.4, Pt 4, para.34(1).
[84] *R. v Khan* [1993] Crim.L.R. 54, CA; *Raphaie* [1996] Crim.L.R. 812, CA.
[85] For an example of such circumstances see *R. v Kerawalla* [1991] Crim.L.R. 451, CA. The CA approved a fair and properly tape recorded interview of the suspect in a hotel room. There was a reasonable basis for the view that the investigation might be prejudiced if others saw the suspect leave the hotel. See also *R. v Keane* [1992] Crim.L.R. 306, CA, where the breach of s.30(10) was disregarded because of the suspect's "admitted, indeed almost boastful prior experience of being arrested".

a civilian escort officer) and again there is no other officer to help him, and taking him to a designated station creates a risk of the suspect causing someone injury.

3–29   If the officer is satisfied before the arrested person has reached a police station that there are no grounds for keeping him under arrest, he must release him (subs.(7)). He need not take him to the police station in order to book him before allowing him to go. Fearing the danger of corruption, the Police Federation spokesman in the House of Commons argued during the Committee stage that there ought to be a duty for the arresting officer always to take the suspect to the station. But the Government rejected this view, preferring to trust officers and to give the citizen the advantage of immediate release if preliminary inquiries show that no arrest is necessary.[86] The safeguard, for what it is worth, is that where someone is released in this way a record of the fact must be made (subs.(8)).

The provisions of subss.(5) to (9) do not apply to authorised civilian escort officers but subss.(3), (4)(a) and (10) do.[87]

Street bail

3–30   The Joint Home Office/Cabinet Office Review of PACE (2002, p.23) proposed that instead of requiring that arrested persons, unless released, be taken to the police station, police officers should have the option of giving the arrested person "street bail" on condition that he attend at a police station at a later time. This recommendation was given effect in the Criminal Justice Act 2003.[88]

The new provisions state that a person may be released on bail "at any time before he arrives at a police station", that he "must be required to attend a police station" and that, "No other requirement may be imposed on the person as a condition of bail."[89] The person must be given a notice stating the offence for which he was arrested and the ground on which he was arrested. It may but need not specify to which police station he must go and the time when he is required to go. If it does not do so, he must be sent a written notification with that information.[90]

A person who is required to attend a non-designated police station cannot be held there for more than six hours and must therefore either be released or transferred to a designated police station. A person who has been granted "street bail" can be re-arrested without a warrant if new evidence justifying arrest comes to light since his release.[91]

A person who fails to attend at the named time and place can be arrested without a warrant and must then be taken to any police station and such an arrest is to be treated as an arrest for an offence.[92]

---

[86] See House of Commons, *Hansard*, Standing Committee E, February 2, 1984, cols 912–928.
[87] Police Reform Act 2002, Sch.4, Pt 4, para.30(b).
[88] s.4 of the Act amends or replaces s.30, subss.(1), (2), (7), (10), (11), (12) and introduces new subss.(1A), (1B), (7A), (10A) and new ss.30A, 30B, 30C, 30D.
[89] PACE, new s.30A inserted by s.3(7) of the Act.
[90] PACE, new s.30B inserted by s.3(7) of the Act.
[91] PACE, new s.30C inserted by s.4 of the Act.
[92] PACE, new s.30D inserted by s.3(7) of the Act.

Arrest for further offence: s.31[93]

Section 31 addresses the situation of someone at a police station in connection   **3–31**
with several offences, and provides that he must be told afresh if there are
grounds to arrest him for any second or later offence. Each time that he is notionally arrested again he must be so informed.

The Court of Appeal has suggested that the reason for this rule is to prevent the
release and immediate re-arrest of an alleged offender.[94] But, it said, the section
does not impose any duty on the police officer to arrest immediately. ("We see
nothing in the section which would prevent the constable delaying arresting him
until the time (if it ever arrived) when his release was imminent.")

If he is under arrest for one offence but there is not enough evidence to arrest
him in regard to another offence he can nevertheless be questioned about the second offence providing he is cautioned and advised about his right to have a solicitor present.[95] The time limits on detention in the police station under the Act are
not affected. As will he seen, they are normally measured as from his arrival at
the first police station after his arrest (s.41(4)).

Once a person has been charged with one offence, questioning on other mat-   **3–32**
ters can continue subject to the requirement (under s.46 see para.4–79 below) to
bring the suspect before the court as soon as practicable. If there is not enough
time to inquire into all the offences under consideration, the magistrates can be
asked to authorise a remand to police cells ("a three-day lie down")—see s.48
amending s.128 of the Magistrates' Courts Act 1980 (see para.4–89 below).

It should be noted that s.31 has no application where someone is arrested for
breach of bail conditions unless it is for failure to surrender to custody. The reason is that being in breach of bail conditions is not an offence and the arrested
person is therefore not in detention within the meaning of s.118(2) of PACE. The
arrest (which is under the Bail Act 1976, s.7) is simply in order to permit a court
to review the issue of bail and conditions of bail. The arrested person must be
brought before a magistrates' court within 24 hours (Bail Act, s.7(3)).

Section 31 also has no application where a suspect in custody as a result of
an arrest without a warrant is found also to be subject to an arrest warrant.
The police have a discretion as to when to execute the arrest warrant—see
the Court of Appeal's decision in *Henderson v Chief Constable of Cleveland
Constabulary.*[96]

Equally, s.31 is not relevant if the suspect is arrested first under a warrant and   **3–33**
whilst at the police station it is decided that he should also be arrested without a
warrant. His detention under a warrant is not "police detention" for the purposes
of PACE (s.118(2)).

---

[93] See 1989 N.I. PACE Order, Art.33.
[94] *R. v Samuel* [1988] Q.B. 615 at 622.
[95] *R. v Mason and Stephens*, unreported, Case Nos 90/03978/44, 91/561/44, CA.
[96] [2001] EWCA Civ 335—execution of an arrest warrant in respect of fine default could be delayed
until the criminal investigation was completed.

However, the power to make a further arrest of someone in the police station does apply to duly authorised civilians acting as investigating officers under the authority of the Police Reform Act 2002.[97]

Search upon arrest: s.32[98]

3–34 Section 32 deals with search after an arrest somewhere other than at a police station and gives the police a power to search that is somewhat broader than that previously enjoyed at common law. The common law allowed the police to search an arrested person for a weapon or for evidence material to the offence for which he was arrested.[99]

The Philips Royal Commission said it had not received any proposals for alteration of these rules and it recommended that they be confirmed in statute.[1]

Subsection (1) allows the police to search someone arrested where there are reasonable grounds for believing that he may present a danger to himself or to others. For this power to be validly exercised it would be necessary to show that the officer actually had this belief and that it was based on some reasonable grounds. It would not be enough to show that it was believed that he had on him some article normally carried in one's pocket such as a pen which might in theory be used as a weapon unless it was reasonable to believe that it was going to be used in that way.

3–35 Subsection (2)(a) permits a search of the arrested person for anything that might be used to effect an escape or which might be evidence relating to any offence. In addition, subs.(2)(b) gives the police the power to enter and search the premises in which he was when arrested, or immediately before he was arrested, for evidence relating to the offence for which he was arrested.[2] Presumably this includes a power to secure the scene of the crime for the purpose of investigation.

Unlike the power to search under s.18, it is not limited to arrestable offences. Nor need the premises be occupied or controlled by the arrested person. But the power to search under subs.(2)(a) may only be exercised if the officer has reasonable grounds for believing that the person searched may have "concealed on him" a potential weapon or evidence of an offence, and the power of search under subs.(2)(b) only exists if there are reasonable grounds for believing that evidence of the offence for which the person was arrested will be found at the premises (subss.(5) and (6)). In *R. v Churchill*,[3] C was arrested on suspicion of burglary and placed in a police car. The police asked him for the car keys—to lock the car and so prevent vandalism or theft and to preserve it for a later search at the police station. C refused to hand over the keys and during a struggle he hit a police officer. C was convicted of assault. On appeal he argued that the police had had no

---

[97] Sch.4, Pt 2, para.21.
[98] See 1989 N.I. PACE Order, Art.34.
[99] *Dillon v O'Brien and David* (1887) 16 Cox C.C. 245.
[1] Philips Report, para.115.
[2] The question whether the police genuinely entered for that reason is one for the jury—*Beckford* (1991) 94 Cr.App.R. 43; [1991] Crim.L.R. 918.
[3] [1989] Crim.L.R. 226, CA.

power to take the keys since they were not evidence of any crime. The Court of Appeal allowed the appeal and quashed his conviction. The Court said that the case could have been dealt with on the basis of the officer's duty to preserve property. But this was not how it had been argued. Section 32 confers a power to search, either for evidence or a weapon, not only the arrested person but also any premises he was in at the time or immediately before his arrest. This would have included the car since the definition of "premises" in s.23(a) specifically covers any vehicle. But, as the comment in the *Criminal Law Review* points out, the seizing of the car was not for the purposes of a search, because the car was unlocked. (See to like effect *Clinton v Zdenkovic*.[4])

Random or automatic searching is not lawful, as was already determined pre-PACE by the courts.[5] Also a person searched in public cannot be required to take off anything other than his coat, jacket or gloves (subs.(4)),[6] though since 1995 his mouth can also be searched.[7] But he could be required to take off more elsewhere than in public—such as the police van or in a nearby police station—provided reasonable grounds for a more extensive search exist. Also, a person could offer to remove other items even in public if he did so voluntarily, but such consent must be genuine. **3–36**

Where the person is arrested in a block of flats or other premises consisting of two or more separate dwellings, only the premises in which he was when arrested or immediately beforehand and any common parts (such as landings, stairways, yards, etc.) shared with other occupiers may be searched (subs.(7)).

The power under this section to search the premises where an arrest takes place is narrower than that under s.18 to enter and search premises of an arrested person. Under s.18 the police may come in and look for evidence relating to the offence for which he was arrested or "to some other offence which is connected with or similar to that offence". Under this section they may look only for evidence relating to the actual offence for which the arrest was made. On the other hand, under s.32 they can search the arrested person himself for evidence of any offence which enlarges the common law power and goes beyond what the Philips Royal Commission recommended. **3–37**

In *Badham*,[8] as has been seen, it was held that s.32 only applies to a search made at the time of the arrest. It does not apply to permit the police to return to the premises several hours after the arrest (in that case three hours later).

Section 32 itself does not require that a record be made of the search but the duty arises under the Criminal Procedure and Investigations Act 1996. The Code of Practice under the 1996 Act (para.4.1) requires that information which may be relevant to an investigation must be recorded in durable and retrievable form. Material is defined as being "relevant" for this purpose if "it appears to the investigator that it has some bearing on any offence under investigation or any

---

[4] [1997] N.I. 234, CA.
[5] *Lindley v Rutter* [1981] Q.B. 128 and *Brazil v Chief Constable of Surrey* (1983) 77 Cr.App.R. 37. See also *Mann-Cairns v Ministry of Defence, Legal Action*, September 21, 1988—this resulted in damages of £2,001 being awarded to a Greenham Common demonstrator; evidence by a policewoman in a previous trial was to the effect that she had searched some 750 women from the camp.
[6] The 1989 N.I. PACE Order, Art.34(4) also added headgear.
[7] A new provision expressly added by the CJPOA, s.59(2) and in Northern Ireland by the Police (Amendment) (Northern Ireland) Order 1995, art.5.
[8] [1987] Crim.L.R. 202, Crown Ct.

person being investigated or on the surrounding circumstances of the case" (para.2.1).

Armed Forces

3–38   The Armed Forces Act 2001, s.10 allows a Service policeman making an arrest under the Service Discipline Acts to search the arrested person if he has reasonable grounds for believing that he is a danger to himself or others (subs.(1)) or that he has concealed on him something "subject to search"—namely something that could be used to escape or which might be evidence relating to an offence (subs.(2)). Such a search must not go beyond what is reasonably necessary. The section corresponds with s.32(1) and 32(2)(a) of PACE. It does not authorise the removal in public of clothing other than an outer coat, jacket or gloves but it does permit a search of the mouth (subs.(9)).

The same power of search can be exercised by a person making an arrest who is not a Service policeman if authorised by the commanding officer—whether specifically ordered in regard to that arrest or authorised generally (subs.(5)). In the former case the commanding officer, and in the latter case the person searching must have reasonable grounds for believing that the person has something "subject to search" concealed on him (subss.(5)(a), (7)). But such an order or authorisation can only be given if there are reasonable grounds for believing that it is likely that the person arrested would escape or would conceal or destroy evidence before a Service or civilian policeman arrived (subs.6)).

Anything found in the course of a search (unless subject to legal privilege) may be seized and retained if the person conducting the search has reasonable grounds for believing that it may be used to cause injury or to assist an escape or that it is evidence of an offence or has been obtained as a result of committing an offence (subss.(10), (11)).

The Armed Forces Act 2001, s.10(13), (14) gives the Home Secretary the power to make regulations equivalent to those in PACE, s.32 for the search of premises where someone was immediately before he was arrested. (See The Police and Criminal Evidence Act 1984 (Codes of Practice) (Armed Forces) Order 2003, SI 2003/2315.)

Execution of warrant not in possession of constable: s.33[9]

3–39   The common law was that the constable had to have the warrant with him when he came to execute it. This rule was changed for warrants of arrest by the Magistrates' Courts Act 1980, s.125(3). Section 33 extended the same rule to the various kinds of warrants referred to in the section, including even a warrant to arrest a person for breach of community service order.[10]

---

[9] No equivalent exists in the 1989 N.I. PACE Order because this became the law there under Art.156 of the Magistrates' Courts (Northern Ireland) Order (SI 1981/1675).
[10] See *Jones v Kelsey* (1987) 85 Cr.App.R. 226, DC.

The section was repealed by the Access to Justice Act 1999, s.106 and Sch. 15, Pt V, Table (8).[11]

Home Office/Cabinet Office Review of PACE proposals on arrest

In its November 2002 report the Joint Review said that police and lawyers com- **3–40** mented that the current structure of powers of arrest was over-complicated and could and should be simplified. The Association of Chief Police Officers ("ACPO") pointed to the need to simplify ss.24 and 25 of PACE to "remove the myriad different qualifiers". Some police consultees wanted stronger, more generalised powers. The "Options Proposed" were: create a definitive list of arrestable offences and other powers to arrest; give police officers a general power of arrest for any criminal offence; remove the distinction between serious arrestable offences and arrestable offences; and extend provisions for "serious" to all arrestable offences. The Review's "Preferred Actions" were to create a definitive list of powers to arrest, complemented by information on how they could and should be applied. This it suggested could be included in its proposed restructuring of the Codes of Practice (see paras 6–09—6–11 below) by early 2004.[12]

Home Office Consultation Paper

The Home Office Consultation Paper, *Policing: Modernising Police Powers to* **3–41** *Meet Community Needs* (*www.homeoffice.gov.uk*), issued in August 2004, made important proposals concerning arrest:

- Seriousness of the offence should no longer be the basis for the power of arrest. The police should have the power of arrest in respect of *any* offence where it was necessary: (a) to enable communication with the person; (b) to prevent the person evading justice; (c) to confirm the person's name and address; (d) to facilitate immediate inquiries/interviewing at a police station; (e) to prevent loss of, interference with or harm to evidence; (f) to prevent harm to the person concerned; (g) to prevent interference with or harm to other persons; (h) to prevent the alerting of other suspects; (i) to prevent interference with the recovery of stolen property or the proceeds of crime; (j) to prevent loss of or harm to property; (k) to prevent an offence against public decency; (l) to prevent an unlawful obstruction of the highway (para.2.6).

- The common law power to arrest for a breach of the peace should be abolished since it would be covered by the general power of arrest proposed in para.2.6.

- Citizen's arrest should be confined to cases where an arrest appears necessary to prevent the person evading justice, or interference with or harm to other persons or the loss of or harm to property and it is not reasonably

[11] SI 2001/168, arts 2(b), 3.
[12] Joint Review, p.21.

practicable for a police officer to make the arrest. The arrested person should be handed over to a constable as soon as practicable (paras 2.8–2.9).

- At present, exercise of the power of arrest triggers other powers such as entry and search for the purpose of making an arrest; powers of entry, search and seizure of premises controlled by the arrested person. It was not proposed that arrest for any offence should trigger these powers. (That "would be a step too far from where we are currently"). But they should be triggered where the arrest was for any offence triable either way or on indictment (paras 2.11–2.14).

- The extra powers available for serious arrestable offence (in respect of road checks, search warrants, detention without charge beyond 24 hours, delayed access to legal advice, access to confidential material), should apply to all offences triable either way or on indictment (paras 2.15–2.19).

The Serious Organised Crime and Police Bill 2004–2005

3–42 The Serious Organised Crime and Police Bill introduced in November 2004 adopted the changes proposed in the Consultation Paper.

Arrest by constables Clause 101, replacing s.24 of PACE, applies the powers of arrest available to constables under PACE and in other enactments to any offence. Thus under subs.(1) a constable would be able to arrest without a warrant:

(a) anyone about to commit an offence;

(b) anyone who is in the act of committing an offence;

(c) anyone whom he has reasonable grounds for suspecting to be about to commit an offence;

(d) anyone whom he has reasonable grounds for suspecting to be committing an offence.

If a constable has reasonable grounds for suspecting that an offence has been committed, he may arrest without a warrant anyone whom he has reasonable grounds to suspect of being guilty of it (subs.(2)). If an offence has been committed, a constable may arrest without warrant (a) anyone who is guilty of the offence; (b) anyone whom he has reasonable grounds for suspecting to be guilty of it.

3–43 But the power of summary arrest under subss.(1), (2) or (3) would be exercisable only if the constable has reasonable grounds for believing that for any of the reasons in subs.(5) it is necessary to arrest the person. The reasons in subs.(5) are:

(a) to enable the name of the person to be ascertained;

(b) to enable his address to be ascertained;

(c) to prevent the person

    (i) causing physical injury to himself or someone else;
    (ii) suffering physical injury;
    (iii) causing loss of or damage to property;
    (iv) committing an offence against public decency (where members of the public going about their normal business cannot reasonably be expected to avoid the person (subs.(6)); or
    (v) causing an unlawful obstruction of the highway; and

(d) to protect a child or other vulnerable person from the person in question.

These reasons are basically the same as the "general arrest conditions" in s.25(3). New s.24 adds two further concepts justifying an arrest:

(e) "to allow the prompt and effective investigation of the offence or of the conduct of the person in question"; and

(f) "to prevent any prosecution for the offence from being hindered by the disappearance of the person in question".

Arrest by other persons New s.24A of PACE introduced by cl.101 of the Bill **3–44** states the law of arrest by persons other than constables. Under subs.(1) a person other than a constable may arrest without warrant (a) anyone in the act of committing an offence; or (b) anyone whom he has reasonable grounds for suspecting to be committing an offence. Under subs.(2), where an offence has been committed , a person other than a constable may arrest (a) anyone guilty of the offence; (b) anyone whom he has reasonable grounds for suspecting that he is guilty of it. But according to subs.(3), the power of summary arrest under subss.(1) and (2) is exercisable only (a) if the person making the arrest has reasonable grounds for believing that for any of the grounds in subs.(4) an arrest is necessary; and (b) it appears to the person making the arrest that it is not reasonably practicable for a constable to make it instead. The reasons in subs.(4) are to prevent the person in question:

(i) causing injury to himself or any other person;

(ii) suffering physical injury;

(iii) causing loss of or damage to property; or

(iv) making off before a constable can assume responsibility for him.

3–45 *Abolition of common law powers of arrest* Clause 101(4) of the Bill provides for the repeal of all common law powers to arrest without warrant.

3–46 *Repeals* Schedule 7 of the Bill repeals:

- Schedule 1A of PACE (setting out specific offences that are arrestable);

- Section 116 of PACE (defining the meaning of "serious arrestable offences"); and

- Schedule 5 of PACE (other serious arrestable offences).

3–47 *"Indictable offences" to replace "serious arrestable offences"* In places where PACE provides special powers in relation to "serious arrestable offences" or "arrestable" offences, Sch.7 applies them instead to "indictable offences". The relevant provisions are ss.4 (road checks); 8 (power to authorise entry and search); 17 (1)(b) (entry for purpose of arrest etc); 18 (1) (entry and search after arrest); 42(1)(b) (authorisation of continued detention); 43 (4)(b) (warrants of further detention); 56 (2)(a) and (5)(a) and (5A)(a) (right to have someone informed when arrested); 58 (6)(a) and (8)(a) and (8A)(a) (access to legal advice); 114A(2)(c) (power to apply Act to other officers); Sch.1(2)(a)(i) (special procedure material).

Section 32(2)(b) is changed so that it applies only if the offence for which the person was arrested was an indictable offence.

Empirical evidence regarding arrest

3–48 The number arrested nationally currently is 1.3 million.[13] About one quarter of those arrested are aged 17 or under and some two-fifths (39 per cent) are under 21.[14]

In 2003, overall under half (45 per cent) of those directed to appear at magistrates' courts had been arrested[15] but the proportion varied considerably by type of case. (It also varies considerably from force to force.[16]) In indictable offences it was over 90 per cent (91 per cent), in summary offences other than motoring it was two-fifths (40 per cent) and in motoring offences it was just under one-fifth

---

[13] Home Office Statistical Bulletin, *Arrests for Notifiable Offences and the Operation of Certain Police Powers under PACE, 2003–2004*, para.4, p.3.
[14] Home Office Statistical Bulletin, *Arrests for Notifiable Offences and the Operation of Certain Police Powers under PACE, 2003–2004*, Table AB, p.5.
[15] *Criminal Statistics 2003*, Cm.6361, 2004, Table 4.1, p.76.
[16] The Philips Report (para.3.72) indicated huge variations as between forces in the percentage of persons dealt with for indictable offences who were arrested and summonsed. In Cambridgeshire, Cleveland and the Metropolitan District only 1% of adults accused of indictable offences were brought to court by way of summons, compared with over 40% in Thames Valley, West Yorkshire, Wiltshire and North Wales.

(19 per cent). Overall, of those arrested, 86 per cent were bailed from the police station. Even in indictable offences the proportion held in custody between arrest and first court appearance was only 18 per cent.[17]

For the characteristics of those arrested (sex, age, ethnic background, employment, previous convictions, mental disorder, etc.), details of the arrest (reasons for the arrest, circumstances surrounding the arrest, main grounds for suspicion, etc.), and subsequent developments (arrival at the police station, legal advice, the outcome of custody, etc.), see Phillips and Brown, *Entry into the criminal justice system: a survey of police arrests and their outcomes* (Home Office Research Study 185, 1998).

There are no regularly published statistics as to what proportion of those **3–49** arrested are proceeded against. Brown *et al.* (1992) had figures on this derived from large 1990 and 1991 samples.[18] This showed (at p.108) that 41 per cent of those arrested were charged, 12 per cent were cautioned, 10 per cent were summonsed, 10 per cent were bailed to return, 16 per cent were released and 11 per cent were dealt with by a variety of other means or the information was not available—based on 10,167 custody record forms. The 1998 Home Office study by Phillips and Brown showed that 52 per cent of 3,682 arrested suspects were charged, 17 per cent were cautioned and 20 per cent resulted in no further action. Only 2 per cent were summonsed.[19]

See also: Gemmill and Morgan-Giles (1980), a study conducted for the Philips Royal Commission, showing variations in arrest/summons policy as between forces; Bottomley *et al.* (1991); Irving and McKenzie (1989); Dixon *et al.* (1989a); McConville *et al.* (1991), a study of 1,000 non-Road Traffic arrests and summonses in three forces which found that almost all had been arrested; and Brown (1991), a study of household burglary cases.

[17] *op.cit.*, n.15 above, Table 4.1, p.76.
[18] For details of the different samples in this study see para.5–70 below.
[19] The remainder were "transferred", "held on a warrant", "released", "other" or "not known"—Philips and Brown (1998), Table 6.1, p.83.

QUESTIONS AND ANSWERS

ARREST

3–50   What is the difference between "helping the police with their inquiries" and being under arrest?

Being under arrest means being subject to restraint as to one's movements. One is either under arrest or one is not; there is no half-way stage. A person who is "helping the police with their inquiries" is therefore free to go if he pleases. Note however that under the Police Reform Act 2002, authorised civilian Community Support Officers are given a power to detain a person in the street for up to 30 minutes pending the arrival of a police officer. Making off whilst so detained is an offence. But Ministers claimed that this was not the same as arrest. (See further para.12–09 below.)

3–51   Are the police obliged to inform someone being questioned that he is not under arrest?

In general the answer is no. When the police ask someone to come down to the police station to answer a few questions, they are not obliged to caution him that he is under no compulsion to do so. Nor are they obliged to advise him on arrival at the police station of his rights including his right to legal advice, the right to have someone informed of where he is and the right to leave. If he happens to know of these rights he is free to exercise them.

The first point at which the police must inform him that he is not under arrest is when he is cautioned, whether or not in the police station. If he is arrested he must be so informed, but by then it is obviously too late for him to leave.

What procedures follow when someone is arrested?

3–52   The only strict rule on arrest is that the person concerned must as soon as practicable be told that he is under arrest and why he has been arrested, even, the Act says, if it is obvious. (However, this does not apply while he is struggling or trying to run away.) In principle he should then be taken to a police station as soon as possible, though an exception is allowed where his presence is needed elsewhere in the interests of the investigation. Under the Criminal Justice Act 2003 there is now also the possibility that the person arrested will be given "street bail"—meaning that he is sent on his way subject to an obligation to attend a police station at a time and place either specified there and then or sent to him later in a written notification.

To what police station should someone who is arrested be taken?   **3–53**

If it is clear that the suspect will have to be detained for longer than several hours, he should be taken to one of the police stations in the area named by the chief constable as "designated stations" for the receipt of persons in custody. (see s.35 below.) If the police station to which he is taken is not a designated one, the suspect cannot be held there for longer than six hours. At that point he must be transferred to a designated police station.

On what grounds can someone be arrested?   **3–54**

Under PACE there were two main categories of situations where someone could be arrested. One was on reasonable suspicion that the person had committed, was about to commit or was actually committing an arrestable offence. The second was where the officer believed that an arrest was necessary for a non-arrestable offence because of the particular circumstances of the case. One such ground was that the culprit refused to supply his name and address, or gave a "Mickey Mouse" name and address. But the broader ground was that the arrest was thought to be necessary to prevent the person concerned from causing physical injury to himself or others; or suffering physical injury; or causing loss of or damage to property; or committing an offence against public decency; or causing an unlawful obstruction of the highway. There was also a common law power to arrest someone for a breach of the peace.

The Serious Organised Crime and Police Bill introduced in November 2004 changes the position by giving a constable the power to make an arrest for *any* offence providing it is reasonably thought to be necessary for any of the same reasons as above plus two new reasons—"to allow the prompt and effective investigation of the offence or of the conduct of the person in question" or "to prevent any prosecution for the offence from being hindered by the disappearance of the person in question". The Bill also proposed the abolition of all common law powers of arrest.

What amounts to reasonable grounds?   **3–55**

Reasonable grounds for the purposes of making an arrest means such grounds as would lead an ordinary cautious person to suspect that the arrested person was probably guilty of the offence. Such suspicion can be based on information given by another person—be it a police officer, a member of the public or informant. It can also be based on information received from a police computer.

3–56 **Can an arrested person be questioned about other offences than the one for which he was arrested?**

An arrested person can be questioned about any matter. The only restriction is that once he has been charged he cannot normally be asked further questions about that offence.

3–57 **Can a person who has been arrested be searched and, if so, for what reason?**

A person who has been arrested can be searched if there are reasonable grounds to think:

> (1)   that he may present a danger to himself or others; or

> (2)   that he might have on him evidence of a crime or something which he could use to escape.

The police may also enter and search any premises in which he was when arrested or immediately before he was arrested but only to look for evidence of that offence.

   As will be seen, on arrival at a police station the custody officer has a discretion as to whether he itemise what property the detainee has. He may search him for that purpose if it is necessary. Searches may not however take place on a routine basis, without regard to the circumstances. See also below on intimate searches (para.5–08) and the taking of intimate (para.5–108) and non-intimate (para.5–115) body samples.

Part IV

DETENTION

PACE has 19 sections on detention. It established a new framework for the **4–01** regime of detention and, in particular, in relation to time limits, supervision by a custody officer and record keeping.

Human Rights Act 1998

The most directly relevant provision of the ECHR is Art.5—see para.3–02 above **4–02** for details. If the conditions of detention amounted to inhuman or degrading treatment there could also be a breach of Art.3.[1]

Limitations on police detention: s.34[2]

Section 34(1) provides that detention of arrested persons in a police station must **4–03** be in conformity with the provisions of the Act. Subsection (2) states that the custody officer (see s.36 below) must order the release of anyone whose continued detention by the police cannot be justified under the Act. Subsection (3) says that only the custody officer has the authority to release a person from police detention. Subsection (5) requires that release in such a case be unconditional unless further investigation in the matter is needed or further proceedings may be taken against him—which includes a reprimand or warning under the Crime and Disorder Act 1998—in which case the release may be subject to bail. Subsection (6) states that a person arrested under s.6(5) of the Road Traffic Act 1988 or under s.30(2) of the Transport and Works Act 1992[3] is to be treated under PACE as if he has been arrested for an offence. The two sections deal with the processing of drunken drivers and drunken train or tram drivers. That means that all the normal PACE provisions in regard to treatment in custody apply. It also ensures that where a positive breath test is given, the person can then be charged and detained or bailed under PACE. Subsection (7) added by the Criminal Justice and Public Order Act 1994, s.29(3) states that someone who returns to the police station to

---

[1] Applied in *Ireland v United Kingdom* (1979–80) 2 E.H.R.R. 25—UK found in breach of Art.3 in regard to treatment of IRA prisoners in Northern Ireland.
[2] See 1989 N.I. PACE Order, Art.35.
[3] The latter was added by the Police Reform Act 2002, s.53(1).

answer to bail or is arrested under subs.46A (for failure to answer to police bail; see para.4–80 below) is treated as arrested for an offence, and the offence in connection with which he was granted bail is deemed to be that offence. It is therefore not necessary to go through the formalities of arrest. The suspect is deemed to be arrested by the mere act of surrendering to custody.

4–04   "Police detention" is defined in s.118(2) as where someone has been taken to a police station after being arrested or is arrested at a police station after attending there voluntarily. A person is also in police detention where he is in the lawful custody of an investigating officer or an escort officer under the Police Reform Act 2002.[4] A person at court after being charged is no longer in police detention for these purposes.

Strictly speaking, the concept of police detention only applies to those in detention in connection with an offence. But para.1.10 of Code C states that subject to para.1.12, the Code applies to people who are in custody at police stations in England and Wales *whether or not they have been arrested* (emphasis supplied) and to those who have been removed to a police station as a place of safety under ss.135 and 136 of the Mental Health Act 1983. (Reviews and extensions of detention (see below) apply, however, only to persons under police detention.)

Code C, para.1.12 specifies those who are not covered by the Code. They are
4–05 people arrested on warrants issued in Scotland under the Criminal Justice and Public Order Act 1994, s.136(2) or without warrant under s.137(2) (cross-border power of arrest); people arrested under the Immigration and Asylum Act 1999, s.142(3) for the purpose of having their fingerprints taken; people who have been served a notice of detention under the Immigration Act 1971; convicted or remanded prisoners held in police cells on behalf of the Prison Service under the Imprisonment (Temporary Provisions) Act 1980; persons detained under the Terrorism Act 2000 who are covered by the Code of Practice issued under Sch.14, para.6; and persons detained for the purpose of stop and search except as required by Code A. But the provisions on conditions and treatment of prisoners in ss.8 and 9 of Code C "must be considered as the minimum standards of treatment for such detainees" (para.1.21). The 1985 Home Office Circular on PACE (see para.1–11, n.23 above) stated that accordingly "the Code of Practice on detention etc. will apply so far as in common sense it is applicable including, possibly, the opening of a custody record as an administrative convenience" (para.33). The Circular stated that similar considerations apply to persons in police custody in connection with extradition proceedings. The role of the police in such proceedings is not investigative. Interviews of suspects take place not in order to obtain evidence to justify holding the prisoner, but to try to find information which could help the authorities in the requesting state. The Home Office Circular (para.36) stated that although Pt IV of the Act does not apply, "a fugitive offender should be properly treated as far as practicable" and that he should "continue to be treated in many respects like any other person suspected of a serious offence".

Code C, Note 1A adds that those who are at a police station voluntarily "should be treated with no less consideration (*e.g.* offered refreshments at

---

[4] subs.(2A) of s.118 inserted by Sch.7, para.9(9) to the 2002 Act. The lawful custody in question is that in Pt 2, para.22 and Pt 4, paras 34(1) or 35(3) of Sch.4.

appropriate times)", as well as enjoying an absolute right to obtain legal advice or communicate with anyone outside the police station.

Designated police stations: s.35[5]

Until a late stage the PACE Bill drew no distinction between busy police stations **4–06** with large numbers of officers available and small rural stations with slight manpower resources. When the Bill was before the House of Lords, however, the Government introduced amendments to take account of these differences in terms of the functions and duties of the custody officer.

The Government's scheme was to make the full range of custody officer duties and functions available from "designated police stations", whilst other stations would be restricted as to the time for which they could hold suspects. As has already been seen, s.30 provides that a person may not be held in a non-designated police station for longer than six hours. The distinction between designated and non-designated police stations is spelled out in ss.35 and 36.

The chief officer in each area must designate which "are to be the stations in that area to be used for the purpose of detaining arrested persons" (s.35(1)). If a police force maintained by a statutory undertaker (such as the British Transport Police) wants one of its stations to be "designated" it must still be done by the chief officer of the police force in that area. Enough must be designated to meet the needs of that area (subs.(2)). Each designated police station must have one or more custody officers appointed (s.36(1)). A station cannot be designated for parts of a day, though it can be designated for brief periods of one day, one week or one month.

It is increasingly the practice for forces to have special centralised custody centres.

Custody officers at police station: s.36[6]

One of the important developments introduced by PACE was the formal position **4–07** of the custody officer. The custody officer has a multitude of responsibilities.[7] The central nature of the custody officer's role was emphasised in the 2004 revision of the Codes in new para.2.1A of Code C which states that when a person is brought to a police station under arrest or is arrested at the police station having attended there voluntarily or attends a police station to answer bail, "they should be brought before the custody officer as soon as practicable". This applies equally to designated and non-designated police stations.

[5] See 1989 N.I. PACE Order, Art.36.
[6] See 1989 N.I. PACE Order, Art.37.
[7] Specific training for the job is essential but a survey reported in *Police Review*, November 27, 1998, p.5, showed that half of a sample of custody officers in the Metropolitan force had had no training.

Section 36(1) states that "One or more custody officers shall be appointed for each designated police station".[8] In non-designated police stations there must simply be someone able to take on the job if the need arises.

In *Vince v Chief Constable of Dorset Police*[9] the Court of Appeal reversed the ruling that there had to be enough appointed custody officers at designated stations to ensure that there was always one on duty. It held that the chief constable's duty under s.36(1) was to appoint one custody officer for each designated police station and that he had a discretion to appoint more than one. That discretion had to be exercised reasonably—but the courts have repeatedly held that they will not lightly interfere with the daily operation of a police force. The effect of the ruling is that there is no requirement to have an appointed custody officer on duty at all times.

4–08
The appointment of the custody officer must either be by the chief constable himself or by someone acting under powers delegated by the chief constable (s.36(2)). Section 36(3) states that no one may be appointed as a custody officer unless he is of the rank of sergeant but subs.(4) allows an officer who is not a sergeant to perform the functions of a custody officer at a designated station "if a custody officer is not readily available to perform them". In *Vince* the Court of Appeal held that an officer who was not a sergeant could only perform the duties of custody officer if an appointed custody officer was not at the station and could not, without much difficulty, be brought there.

4–09
There is nothing in the Act to require that a custody officer perform his functions over any particular period of time. In some forces officers are detailed to be custody officer over a period of weeks or months so that they are playing that role every day. In others, an officer may not know until he comes on duty on the day whether he is performing the function of custody officer.

Section 36(5) makes it plain that at designated police stations the investigative and custodial functions should be basically distinct. Subject to the provisions of s.39(2), "none of the functions of a custody officer . . . shall be performed by an officer who at the time when the functions falls to be performed is involved in the investigation of an offence for which that person is in police detention at that time". But the prohibition on the custody officer undertaking investigative functions is not total. So the custody officer can do anything authorised by the Act or the Codes—such as searching a suspect or his clothing. He can undertake duties in connection with the identification of the suspect or his clothing, such as taking fingerprints, and he can do anything required by s.7 of the Road Traffic Act 1988 (driving with excess alcohol), such as administering a breath test (subs.(6)). Equally, a person who has previously been the arresting or investigating officer could, in the absence of anyone else appropriate, act later as custody officer. Obviously, the intention and expectation is that the roles should be kept wholly apart. But if this is not possible, subs.(5) prevents one person playing both roles at the same time.

4–10
What if the suspect is taken to a non-designated police station? In that case s.36(7)(a) states that the functions which would be those of the custody officer in a designated police station must be carried out by someone not involved in the investigation, "if such officer is readily available". This clearly leaves scope for the

---

[8] This gave effect to the Philips Royal Commission's recommendation, para.3.112.
[9] [1993] 1 W.L.R. 415; [1993] 2 All E.R. 321, CA.

police to plead that no such officer was readily available. In that case the functions may be carried out by the officer who took the person concerned to the station "or any other officer" (s.36(7)(b)). When this occurs, such an "acting custody officer" must as soon as practicable notify an officer of the rank of inspector or above at a designated police station that this is the case (subss.(9) and (10)). There is no requirement that the notification has to be in writing and normally it will be by telephone or radio. The fact that the notification must be as soon as practicable shows that it is intended to operate before any action is taken, so that the inspector at the larger station can consider whether to have the suspect brought there instead.

Subsection (6), as amended, provides that a person arrested on suspicion of driving with excess alcohol under s.6(5) of the Road Traffic Act 1988 is arrested for an offence for the purposes of subs.(1). This settled the doubt about the matter raised by *R. v Mackenzie*.[10]

Delegation by custody officers to civilian support staff

Civilians are playing an ever-growing role in the police station. As will be seen (para.12–13 below), the Police Reform Act 2002 allows for the appointment, *inter alia*, of civilian "detention officers" with extensive powers that previously could only be exercised by police officers. So far as concerns detention in the police station, these include fingerprinting, searches to ascertain identity, intimate searches, taking intimate and non-intimate samples, taking photographs, etc.[11] **4–11**

Code C distinguishes between civilians who are "designated persons" and others. "Designated person" is defined as "a person other than a police officer designated under the Police Reform Act 2002, Pt 4 who has specified powers and duties of police conferred or imposed on them" (para.1.13(a)). Reference to a police officer, it states, "includes a designated person acting in the exercise or performance of the powers and duties conferred or imposed on them by their designation" (para.1.13(b)).

In addition, the custody officer or other officer given custody of the detainee can allow "police staff [*i.e.* civilians] who are not designated persons to carry out individual procedures or tasks at the police station if the law allows" —though the officer remains responsible for ensuring that they are carried out correctly and in accordance with the Codes of Practice (para.1.15). Any such person must either be employed by a police authority and under the control and direction of the chief officer or be employed by a someone having a contract with a police authority for the provision of services to detainees (*ibid.*).

The Joint Home Office/Cabinet Office Review of PACE (November 2002) considered whether custody officers might be civilian employees. The conclusion was negative. ("Civilianisation of the custody officer role is not supported at this stage. There is real value in retaining the specific skills and experience of a police officer in that role." (p.23).) The Runciman Royal Commission on Criminal Justice (1993) took the same view (Runciman Report, p.31[11a]). However, the Home Office Consultation Paper *Policing: Modernising Police Powers to Meet* **4–12**

[10] [1971] 1 All E.R. 729.
[11] For further details and the text of Sch.4 see Ch.12 below.
[11a] The Report of the Runciman Royal Commission on Criminal Justice (Cmnd.2263, 1993) is referred to throughout in the footnotes as "Runciman Report".

Community Needs, issued in August 2004, seemed to take a different view. In a section on the potential expansion of the role of civilian staff it canvassed the idea of civilian custody officers. ("Experienced police sergeants with frontline supervisory abilities currently invariably undertake this. The custody officer is a crucial role and the need for resourced and co-ordinated transition would be essential. But the benefits of releasing experienced supervisory officers to frontline duties from what is a complex but largely administrative and process driven role would be considerable." (para.4.3(b)(ii)). The Consultation Paper approach was adopted in the Serious Organised Crime and Police Bill published in November 2004. Clauses 111 and 112 would provide chief officers with the ability to designate civilian staff as custody officers under s.38 of the Police Reform Act 2002.

Duties of custody officer before charge: s.37[12]

4–13   Section 37 is extremely important. Its chief purpose is to ensure that a person brought to the police station is charged if there is enough evidence to charge him, but that, if there is not sufficient evidence, he should be released unless the custody officer has reasonable grounds for believing that his detention is needed to preserve or obtain evidence of the offence for which he was arrested. Section 37 therefore deals with (1) the decision whether to detain the suspect for questioning, (2) the decision whether to release him on bail, and (3) the decision whether to charge. In regard to the last of these, a major change was made by the Criminal Justice Act 2003. Previously the decision to charge was made by the custody officer subject to later review by the CPS. The 2003 Act aimed to transfer the decision in a large proportion of cases from the custody officer to the CPS. The basic concept is that the specifying of the initial charges becomes the responsibility of the CPS. If the charge cannot be determined rapidly, the suspect is normally released on bail and (when it is in force) will subsequently receive a written charge and a written requirement (called a "requisition") for him to appear before a magistrates' court to answer the charge.[13]

     The custody officer, however, retains a crucial role in having to make the preliminary determination as to whether there is enough evidence to charge and therefore to send the case through to the CPS for a decision by the Crown Prosecutor. Also, under Guidance issued by the DPP, the custody officer has delegated power in minor cases to formulate and lay the charges and in more serious cases where bail is inappropriate, the custody officer, with or without the advice of the CPS, will lay a holding charge. Even where the decision to charge is made by the CPS, it is the custody officer who actually charges the suspect and under the charging by post system, the charge will be sent out by the police.

4–14   The new arrangements are set out in Sch.2 to the Criminal Justice Act 2003 which amends s.37 and inserts into PACE new ss.37A, 37B, 37C and 37D. These

---

[12] See 1989 N.I. PACE Order, Art.38.
[13] See generally on the new scheme Brownlee, "The Statutory Charging Scheme in England and Wales: Towards a Unified Prosecution System?" [2004] Crim.L.R. 896–907. (Brownlee wrote as a Senior Crown Prosecutor.)

changes are in force[14] but they are being activated gradually. The new system was first piloted in one police station in Greater Manchester. By November 2004 the new system was in place in 14 force areas.[15] It is to be rolled out in the remaining 28 areas between 2005 and 2007.

Subsection (1) of s.37 states that where someone is arrested without a warrant or on a warrant not endorsed for bail[16] the custody officer at any police station to which he is taken must first consider whether there is sufficient evidence to justify a charge for the offence for which he was arrested. (The subsection goes on to state that the custody officer may detain the suspect at the police station "for such period as is necessary to enable him to do so". This "detention" aspect of the subsection is considered below—see para.4–33.)

The duty laid on the custody officer by subs.(1) to consider whether there is enough evidence to justify a charge must be carried out as soon as practicable after the suspect's arrival at the police station or, where he was arrested at the police station, after the arrest (subs.(10)). In practice, despite the clear language of subs.(1), it is very rare for the question of charging to be addressed immediately on arrival at the police station.[17] It also seems to be rare at that first stage for the question of the strength of the evidence to be considered in much, if any, detail.[18] The custody officer, after booking the suspect in, normally authorises detention for questioning regardless of the strength of the evidence[19]—though another option is to report the person for summons and release him without bail.

An initial duty, laid on the custody officer by the 2003 revision of Code C, is an assessment of the risks posed by the suspect. Code C has five paragraphs on the topic (paras 3.6–3.10). The basic thrust is to require the custody officer, by following a structured process, to consider whether the detainee falls into any of the defined categories of risk (whether as a danger to others or himself, or medically or in any other way). The custody officer is then responsible for implementing a response to the risk assessment by, for instance, reducing opportunities for self harm, calling a health care professional or increasing the levels of monitoring or observation. (Code C refers to Home Office Circular 23/2000 for more detailed guidance (Note 3E).)   **4–15**

[14] Criminal Justice Act 2003 (Commencement No.2 and Saving Provisions) Order 2004 (SI 2004/81) and Criminal Justice Act 2003 (Commencement No.4 and Saving Provisions) Order 2004) (SI 2004/1629). The only part of Sch.2 that was not in force at the time of writing was s.37B(8)—relating to the new system of charging by post under s.29 of the 2003 Act.
[15] Avon & Somerset, Cleveland, Greater Manchester, Humberside, Kent, Lancashire, London, Merseyside, Northumbria, Nottinghamshire, South Yorkshire, Thames Valley, West Midlands and West Yorkshire.
[16] This includes someone who returns to the police station to answer to bail—by virtue of the Criminal Justice and Public Order Act, s.29(3) which added a new subs.(7) to s.34 of PACE, to the effect that such a person is treated as having been arrested for an offence.
[17] See McKenzie *et al.* (1990), pp.23–24, and Brown, *PACE Ten Years On: a review of the research* (Home Office, Research Study 155, 1997), p.70.
[18] Phillips and Brown, *Entry into the criminal justice system: a survey of police arrests and their outcomes* (Home Office, Research Study 185, 1998), p.43 ("arresting officers were not typically asked to provide much information about the offence").
[19] Phillips and Brown found that whilst in 60% of cases examined the arresting officer believed that there was sufficient evidence to charge at the time of arrest, in only one case did the custody officer refuse to authorise detention (Phillips and Brown, *Entry into the criminal justice system: a survey of police arrests and their outcomes* (Home Office, Research Study 185, 1998), pp.44 and 49).

Under subs.(2) of s.37, if the custody officer determines that he does not have enough evidence to charge the person detained, he must be released on bail or unconditionally, unless the custody officer "has reasonable grounds for believing that his detention without being charged is necessary to secure or preserve evidence relating to an offence for which he is under arrest or to obtain such evidence by questioning him". If so, further detention may be authorised (subs.(3)) In other words, detention is permitted for the purpose of questioning. When the PACE Bill was going through Parliament, Mr Douglas Hurd, the then Home Office Minister, emphasised in the House of Commons that detention had to be *necessary* for that purpose—not merely desirable or convenient.[20] But practice is not consistent with either the spirit or the letter of this statement since, as noted, it is very rare for an arrested person to be released forthwith. Instead, having been booked, typically he is held in a cell to await questioning.

4–16　　Subsection (4) requires that, as soon as practicable, the custody officer makes a written record of the grounds of detention. The requirement is commonly met by rubber-stamping the custody record: "Detention authorised because of reasonable grounds for believing that detention necessary to secure/preserve evidence relating to offence or to obtain such evidence by questioning". The courts have not ruled whether subs.(4) requires more than this. Certainly it does not require the police to put down a detailed statement as to the evidence in the case but it may be that, if the matter were tested, the court would require something more than a recitation of the statutory formula. Subsection (5) supports this view since it states that the recording of the grounds should normally be done in the presence of the suspect who must be told the grounds by the custody officer. There is not much point in merely telling him that the custody officer is satisfied that the requirements of s.37(2) are fulfilled without giving a clue as to the reasons.

But there is no requirement to tell the detainee if he is not in a fit state to be told (subs.(6)) or if he is asleep at the time (added by the Police Reform Act 2002, s.52). Under para.1.8 of Code C the explanation must then be given as soon as practicable.

If the custody officer considers that there is enough evidence to charge the arrested person, s.37(7) formerly provided that the person should either (a) be charged, or (b) be released without charge on bail, or (c) be released without bail. Now, to take account of the charging system introduced by the Criminal Justice Act 2003, the amended s.37(7) provides that the suspect should either (a) be released without charge and on bail for the purpose of enabling the DPP to make a decision as to charging, or (b) be released without charge and on bail but not for that purpose, or (c) be released without charge and without bail, or (d) be charged.[21] The statute adds that the decision is one for the custody officer.[22]

4–17　　The 2003 Act provided that the DPP could issue guidance for the purpose of enabling custody officers to decide how persons should be dealt with under s.37(7) or under s.37C(2).[23] The first edition of such Guidance was issued in

---

[20] House of Commons, *Hansard*, Standing Committee E, February 16, 1984, col.1229.

[21] Inserted by Criminal Justice Act 2003, Sch.2, para.2(2).

[22] PACE, s.37(7A) inserted by Sch.2, para.2(3) to the 2003 Act.

[23] PACE, s.37C(2), inserted by Sch.2, para.3 to the 2003 Act, deals with a person arrested whilst on bail who has not yet been informed by the DPP whether he is to be charged. In that situation the person must either be charged or released without charge either on bail or without bail.

May 2004. The Guidance was revised in light of experience. The second version took effect as from January 4, 2005. (It is included here as Appendix 1.[24]) The Guidance states, "Custody Officers must comply with this Guidance in deciding how a person is to be dealt with in accordance with s.37(7) PACE, as amended by Sch.2 to the Criminal Justice Act 2003." (sect.2).

Under the heading "Responsibility for determining charges", the Guidance states: "Crown Prosecutors will be responsible for the decision to charge and the specifying or drafting of the charges in all indictable only, either way or summary offences where a custody officer determines that the Threshold Test [as to which see below] is met in any case, except for those offences specified in this Guidance which may be charged or cautioned by the police without reference to a Crown Prosecutor" (para.3.1). Where the CPS decision in a case is to charge, caution, obtain additional evidence or take no action, the police "will not proceed in any other way without first referring the matter back to a Crown Prosecutor" (Guidance, para.11.1).

In areas where the new charging system is in force, the Guidance states that the police may continue to charge in any either way or summary offences where it appears to the custody officer that a guilty plea is likely and that the case is suitable for sentencing in the magistrates' court—other than offences specified in Annex A to the Guidance (Guidance, para.3.2(iii)). Annex A gives a list of offences which under the new system must always be referred to a Crown Prosecutor for early consultation and charging decision whether admitted or not. They include any offence triable only on indictment and any either way offence triable only on indictment due to either the surrounding circumstances of the offence or the previous convictions of the offender.[25] Where the custody officer is unsure whether the case is within para 3.2(iii), "early consultation with a Duty Prosecutor should be undertaken" (*ibid.*, para.3.2(iv)). **4–18**

Paragraph 3.3 of the Guidance sets out the cases where under the new arrangements the police may normally determine the charges under delegated powers: **4–19**

(i) The police can generally charge without reference to the CPS in Road Traffic Act cases. The exceptions are cases involving: a death; an allegation of dangerous driving; an allegation of driving whilst disqualified where there is no admission to both the driving and the disqualification; a statutory defence to being in charge of a motor vehicle (unfit through drink or drugs or excess alcohol (*sic*)); unlawful taking or the aggravated unlawful taking of a motor vehicle (unless the case is suitable for disposal as an early guilty plea in the magistrates' court) (*ibid.*, para.3.3(i)).

---

[24] The Guidance is accessible on the CPS website. See *www.cps.gov.uk*.
[25] If not covered by the above, other offences listed in Annex A are: wounding or inflicting grievous bodily harm contrary to s.20 of the Offences Against the Person Act 1861; assault occasioning actual bodily harm contrary to s.47 of the 1861 Act; violent disorder contrary to s.2 of the Public Order Act 1986; affray contrary to s.3 of the same act; offences involving deception contrary to the Theft Acts 1968 and 1978; and handling stolen goods contrary to s.22 of the Theft Act 1968.

(ii) Other cases where the police can charge are: any offence of absconding under the Bail Act 1976; any offence contrary to s.5 of the Public Order Act 1986; any offence under the Town Police Clauses Act 1847, the Metropolitan Police Act 1839, the Vagrancy Act 1824, the Street Offences Act 1959, under s.91 of the Criminal Justice Act 1967, s.12 of the Licensing Act 1872; offences under any by-law; and any summary-only offence carrying a penalty of three months or less unless the DPP publishes other arrangements (*ibid.*, para.3.3(ii)).

4–20 Cases involving charges against one or more persons some of which can be charged by the police and some of which must be referred to the CPS, must be referred to the CPS (*ibid.*, para.3.5).

If the case is one where bail is not appropriate and it has not been possible to consult with a Crown Prosecutor before the expiry of PACE custody time limits, the police can charge the suspect provided a Duty Inspector authorises a holding charge. (Obviously, the same applies where it has been possible to consult with a Crown Prosecutor but the consultation has not yet resulted in an indication as to what charges should be preferred.) The Duty Inspector must note the custody record and the Report to Crown Prosecutor for Charging Decision (form MG3) and the case must be referred to a Crown Prosecutor as soon as practicable for authority to proceed with the prosecution (*ibid.*, para.3.12).

Note 16AB in the August 2004 revision of Code C states that the custody officer is entitled to take reasonable time to apply the DPP's Guidance in deciding how a detainee is to be dealt with under s.37(7)(a)—including where appropriate consultation with a Duty Prosecutor. This acknowledges the reality that the new charging scheme will often involve more time in the police station for the suspect. But it should be noted that there is no extension of any of the statutory time limits under PACE. (The problem created by the conflict between these facts is considered below at para.4–33.) The DPP's Guidance, in the section headed Key Provisions and Principles (sect.2), states, "Crown Prosecutors will be deployed as Duty Prosecutors for such hours as shall be agreed locally to provide guidance and make charging decisions. This service will be complemented by a centrally managed out-of-hours duty prosecutor arrangement to ensure a continuous 24-hour service". This new service is called CPS Direct. (See also para.5.1 of the Guidance headed "Deployment".)

4–21 Code C, new para.16.1B, provides that where in compliance with the DPP's Guidance the custody officer decides that the case should be immediately referred to the CPS to make the charging decision, consultation should take place with a Crown Prosecutor as soon as reasonably practicable. Where the Crown Prosecutor is unable to make the charging decision on the information available at that time, the detainee may be released without charge and on bail (with conditions if necessary) under s.37(7)(a). He should be informed that he is being released to enable the DPP to make a decision under new s.37B.[26]

New s.37B[27] states that where someone is released under new s.37(7)(a), the police should, as soon as practicable, send the DPP such information as is speci-

---

[26] PACE, s.37(7B) inserted by Sch.2, para.2(3) to the 2003 Act.
[27] Inserted by Sch.2, para.3 to the 2003 Act.

fied in the DPP's Guidance (subs.(1)). The DPP, acting through the CPS, must then decide whether the suspect should be charged and if so, with what offence, or should be cautioned (or warned or reprimanded under s.65 of the Crime and Disorder Act 1998), or should neither be charged nor cautioned (subss.(2) and (3)).[28] The DPP must then give written notice of his decision to a police officer involved in the case (using form MG3) (subs.(4) and DPP's Guidance para.5.5). If the decision is not to charge or to caution, the person must be so informed by the custody officer (s.37B(5)). If the CPS decision is to charge or to caution, "the person shall be charged or cautioned accordingly" by the custody officer (subs.(6)). The charging is to be done either in the police station or under the new "charging by post" system introduced by s.29 of the 2003 Act which at the time of writing was not yet in force. But under this new system it is the police not the CPS that send out the charge. (The DPP's Guidance states that pending the introduction of the charging by post system, the traditional summons procedure may be used in the meanwhile.)

New s.37D of PACE[29] deals with miscellaneous issues that arise where someone has been released on bail under s.37(7)(a): **4–22**

- the custody officer can change the time at which the person must answer bail (subs.(1));

- such change of time must be notified in writing (subs.(2));

- the change of time does not affect any conditions on bail (subs.(3));

- a person in police detention, whether answering bail or otherwise, may be kept there while the question of charging is addressed––subject, though, to the normal rules about time-limits (subs.(4));

- if the person is not in a fit state for the matter to be dealt with, he can be kept in police detention until he is (subs.5));

- where a person is kept in police detention by virtue of subss.(4) or (5)of 37D, s.37(1) to (3) and (7) do not apply (subs.(6)).

When someone is released on bail under s.37(7)(a) for the CPS to consider the charges, conditions may be imposed.[30] Conditions imposed can be varied by a magistrates' court.[31] This is therefore different from the situation where a person is released on bail under s.34(5) to grant bail pending further investigation where conditions cannot be imposed. Nor can conditions be imposed if release is under new s.37(7)(b)—where the custody officer has concluded that although there is

[28] If the decision is that he should be cautioned but it proves impossible to caution him, he must instead be charged (s.37B(7)).
[29] Inserted by Sch.2, para.3 to the 2003 Act.
[30] s.47(1A) of PACE as amended by Criminal Justice Act 2003, Sch.2, para.6(3).
[31] s.47(1E)of PACE inserted by Criminal Justice Act 2003, Sch.2, para.6(4).

sufficient evidence to charge it is not appropriate at that stage either to charge or to seek a charging decision from the CPS.

If a person is released on bail under s.37(7)(a) subject to conditions and the CPS then asks for further investigation, the suspect would have to be re-bailed for that purpose. The new bail could however be subject to conditions as it would still be under s.37(7)(a) rather than under s.34(5).

The test to be applied

4–23 What test is to apply to the decision whether there is sufficient evidence to charge the suspect and, if so, whether he should be charged? These are two separate issues. The 1995 version of Code C, para.16.1 said that when the investigating officer considered that there was sufficient evidence to prosecute and sufficient evidence for a prosecution to succeed he should without delay bring the suspect before the custody officer who would then consider whether or not he should be charged. Did "sufficient evidence to prosecute" mean merely a *prima facie* case or did it mean the higher standard applied by the CPS of a realistic prospect of conviction?[32] The police training manual *A Practical Guide to Investigative Interviewing*[33] stated that the standard required was whether there was a realistic prospect of conviction and this prevailed in the 2003 revision of Code C which was repeated in the 2004 version.[34] Paragraph 16.1 now reads:"When the officer in charge of the investigation reasonably believes there is sufficient evidence to provide a realistic prospect of conviction (see para.11.6), they shall without delay . . . inform the custody officer who will be responsible for considering whether or not the detainee should be charged."

4–24 There is nothing further in Code C on this issue. But the matter is addressed in the DPP's Guidance on charging. Under the heading "The application of the Code for Crown Prosecutors to Charging Decisions", para.3.6 of the Guidance states: "When determining charges, Crown Prosecutors *and Custody Officers* will apply the principles contained in the latest edition of the Code for Crown Prosecutors" (emphasis supplied). This is new in requiring the custody officer to have regard not only to the evidential question but also to the public interest considerations that have always had to be taken into consideration by Crown Prosecutors. (They are set out in the Code for Crown Prosecutors—see *www.cps.gov.uk*—paras 5.6–5.13.)

The DPP's Guidance states that where all the relevant information is available, the standard to be applied in reaching the charging decision is the Full Test under the Code for Crown Prosecutors—namely that there is enough evidence to provide a realistic prospect of conviction and that it is in the public interest to proceed (para.3.8). Where the case is one in which under the Guidance the custody

---

[32] Cape, "Detention without Charge: What does 'Sufficient Evidence to Charge' Mean?" [1999] Crim.L.R. 875 argued for the former which he said was the test under the Judges' Rules and at common law.

[33] National Crime Faculty, 1998.

[34] A draft of the proposed revision of Code C in April 2004 dropped the phrase "realistic prospect of conviction" in paras 11.6 and 16.1 but by the time the proposal was laid before Parliament the phrase had been restored.

officer can charge the suspect without reference to the CPS, the custody officer is equally supposed to apply the Full Code Test (*ibid.*, para.3.11).

Where, however, the evidence gathering is not complete and it is not appropri-   **4–25**
ate for the suspect to be released on bail, a two-stage approach applies. As the DPP has explained,[35] a strict and full application of the Code for Crown Prosecutors at that stage might cause a case to fail the evidential test although there might be enough to satisfy the PACE "sufficient evidence to charge" test. It was appropriate in that situation to assess the case against the "Threshold Test". The Threshold Test is set out in para.3.10 of the DPP's Guidance:

"Application of the Threshold Test will require an overall assessment of whether in all the circumstances of the case there is at least a reasonable suspicion against the suspect of having committed an offence(in accordance with Art.5 of the European Convention on Human Rights[36] and that at the stage it is in the public interest to proceed.

The evidential decision in each case will require consideration of a number of factors including: the evidence available at the time and the likelihood and nature of further evidence being obtained; the reasonableness for believing that evidence will become available; the time that will take and the steps being taken to gather it; the impact of the expected evidence on the case and the charges the totality of the evidence will support.

The public interest means the same as the Full Code test, but will be based on the information available at the time of charge, which will often be limited."

The last sentence of para.3.1 was added in the January 2005 version of the   **4–26**
Guidance. There was no equivalent in the first, May 2004 version. It does not inform the custody officer what are the matters that need to be taken into account in applying the public interest test and may therefore not advance matters greatly. A custody officer who was having difficulty in applying the public interest test would be able to consult with a Duty Prosecutor or, out of hours, with the telephone advice service, CPS Direct.

In cases where the Threshold Test is applied, the second stage is the full review of the evidential material and the public interest under the Code for Crown Prosecutors. This must take place as soon as reasonably practicable—the length of which will depend on the circumstances of each case and which will be agreed with the police (Guidance, para.3.9).

If the custody officer considers that the Threshold Test is not met because of a lack of evidence, he need not refer to the case to the CPS before releasing the person on bail or otherwise (*ibid.*, para.8.4).

The Guidance states that a decision to charge and withhold bail must be kept under review. The evidence gathered must be regularly assessed to ensure that the charge is still appropriate and that continued objection to bail is still appropriate (*ibid.*, para.3.9).

---

[35] A speech by the DPP which was published on the CPS website (*www.cps.gov.uk*) as "Addendum issued by the DPP—'Application of the Code for Crown Prosecutors to Charging Decisions where Suspects are to be detained in custody after charge: the Threshold Test'". The Threshold Test is also set out in the Code for Crown Prosecutors 2004, sect.6.

[36] Art.5 requires that detention be based on "reasonable suspicion of having committed an offence".

4–27   The CPS are responsible for decisions involving Persistent Young Offenders unless the charge is one specified in para.3.3 of the Guidance. Whenever a suspect is, or appears to be under 18, the custody officer must undertake an immediate check to discover whether he is a Persistent Young Offender. Where either the Investigating or the Custody Officer thinks that the person in custody may be a Persistent Youth Offender, "early consultation will be undertaken with the Duty Prosecutor to confirm the likely charges and the evidential requirements in the case". Where it appears that the case will be contested, the Duty Prosecutor and the Investigating Officer will agree, as soon as practicable and in any case within three days from arrest on the evidential requirements to progress the case and on a date for the completion of the agreed work, taking into account the national 71–day target from arrest to sentence for concluding such cases (Guidance, para.4.3).

4–28   The DPP's Guidance (sect.7) sets out the material that must be sent to the Crown Prosecutor depending on the nature of the case. In cases going to the Crown Court or that are expected to be contested the Report to the CPS (form MG3) should be accompanied by an Evidential Report containing the key evidence on which the prosecution will rely together with any unused material which may undermine the prosecution case or assist the defence (including crime reports, initial descriptions and any prior convictions of key witnesses). The Evidential Report should be accompanied also by suggested charge(s), a record of convictions and cautions of the suspect, and any observations of the reporting or supervising officer (*ibid.*, para.7.2(i)). In other cases referred to the CPS for a charging decision, the Report must be accompanied by an Expedited Report containing key witness statements, any other compelling evidence and a summary of an interview with the suspect. The Expedited Report must be accompanied by any other information that may have a bearing on the evidential or public interest test, a record of convictions and cautions and any observations of the reporting or supervising officer (*ibid.*, para.7.2(ii)). Where the Threshold Test is to be applied in a case where bail is inappropriate, the Report to the CPS must be accompanied by an Expedited Report containing sufficient material then available and brief details of any convictions or cautions (para.7.3). There should be early consultation with a Duty Prosecutor to identify cases where an evidential file will be required. An officer involved in the investigation must submit the completed Report to Crown Prosecutor for a Charging Decision (form MG3) within the agreed timescale together with the evidential material (para.7.4).

4–29   Where it appears likely that the charges will be determined by the CPS, custody officers "must direct investigating officers to consult a Duty Prosecutor as soon as is practicable after a person is taken into custody" so that they can agree on the evidential requirements and, where appropriate, on the period of bail to be granted (*ibid.*, para.8.1). Early consultation will also allow the identification of weak cases and of those where the charging decision can be made on the basis of limited information (para.8.2). A great deal of emphasis is placed on the importance of this early consultation.

In indictable only cases where the police decide that they do not wish to proceed even though the Threshold Test is met, the case must be referred to a Duty Prosecutor to confirm whether or not the case is to proceed (*ibid.*, para.8.3).

The police can administer a caution (other than a conditional caution), or a reprimand or final warning in the case of youth, without further reference to the CPS but consultation with a Crown Prosecutor may be desirable—and in the case of conditional cautions is required (*ibid.*, paras 9.1–9.3).

Where someone is arrested for breach of pre-charge bail conditions or for failing to surrender to bail and the custody officer considers he should be detained pending an application to the court for a remand in custody, he must consult a Crown Prosecutor as to whether the person should be charged or released without charges (*ibid.*, para.10.1).

If an investigating officer or custody officer does not agree with the CPS charging decision, the case can be referred for attempted resolution to the Basic Command Unit ("BCU") Crime Manager (normally a Detective Chief Inspector) for consultation with the CPS Unit Head. If further escalation is required, the involvement of the Divisional Commander and the Level E Unit Head or Chief Crown Prosecutor should be obtained (*ibid.*, sect.11).

Questioning when there is already some evidence

If the police do not have enough evidence to justify a charge, the suspect can be detained for questioning under s.37(2). But what if they do have enough evidence to charge from the outset of detention in the police station? Is any questioning then permissible and when must such questioning stop? And what, if any, distinction is to be drawn between questioning by the custody officer and questioning by the interviewing officer? There are several judicial decisions that have touched on these issues.   **4–30**

The basic scheme is that interviews in the police station should be conducted in the interview room with the tape recorder on. Questioning by the custody officer is not part of that scenario. So it is not expected that the custody officer should conduct interviews. (For consideration of what under PACE is "an interview", see para.6–59 below.) On the other hand, as the Runciman Royal Commission on Criminal Justice recognised, it is unsatisfactory if a suspect is not given an opportunity to say something that could influence the custody officer's decisions under s.37 as to charge and as to detention for questioning.[37]

Moreover, Code C, para.16.1 states that the custody officer is responsible "for considering whether or not the detainee should be charged" which requires consideration not only of the strength of the evidence but also of whether a caution (or in the case of young offenders, a reprimand or warning[38]) would be more appropriate than a charge—which in turn requires knowledge of whether the suspect admits the offence. This again points in the direction of there being a possibility of some exchange between the suspect and the custody officer.

Previously, both paras 16.1 and 11.4[39] of Code C referred to the need for the investigating officer to satisfy himself that the suspect has said "all he wishes to say" before terminating questioning. But this was dropped in the 2003 revision.   **4–31**

---

[37] Report of the Royal Commission on Criminal Justice, 1993, p.29, para.16.

[38] Despite the transfer of charging responsibility to the CPS, para.16.1 still refers to Note 16A which requires that the custody officer consider alternatives to prosecution under the Crime and Disorder Act 1998.

[39] Now para.11.6. Former para.11.4 said that as soon as the investigating officer believes that a prosecution should be brought against the suspect "and that there is sufficient evidence for it to succeed" he should ask the person if he has anything further to say. If the person indicates that he has nothing more to say the officer "shall without delay cease to question him about that offence".

In *Coleman, Knight and Hochenburg*[40] the interviewing officers read the suspect a formula prepared on the advice of counsel, saying that they considered that there was sufficient evidence to prosecute for fraudulent trading but that they wanted to give him an opportunity to say whatever he wanted about the allegation. They then proceeded to question him. The Court of Appeal said this was not permissible. Since the officers were satisfied that there was sufficient evidence to prosecute, their function was confined to simply satisfying themselves that the suspect had said all he wished to say. It ruled that evidence of the interview should have been excluded under s.78.

In *Pointer*[41] the defendant had been interviewed at the police station but said nothing. The interviewing officer admitted that before he interviewed P he believed that there was sufficient evidence for a successful prosecution. (This was not surprising considering that several officers gave evidence that whilst working undercover they had purchased drugs from P on various occasions.) The main question on appeal was whether the judge should have allowed the jury to draw an adverse inference from silence. But in the course of dismissing the appeal,[42] the Court of Appeal said that although giving the suspect an opportunity to say something was an interview within the meaning of para.11.1A, this was permissible providing it stopped when the suspect indicated that he did not wish to answer questions.[43]

4–32   In *McGuiness*[44] the Court of Appeal went further. Again, it was argued that M should not have been interviewed, and that therefore the jury should not have been permitted to draw adverse inferences from his silence, because the police had sufficient evidence to prosecute before the interview. The Court of Appeal said if that was right "it would mean that in every case where the police had got together a *prima facie* case against a suspect they would be bound to charge and the opportunity would be lost not only for the police to question the suspect but for the suspect to put forward an explanation which might immediately dispose of any suspicion held against him". Consideration of "sufficient evidence to prosecute" and "sufficient evidence for a prosecution to succeed", the Court said, involved consideration of any explanation or lack of explanation from the suspect. The Court therefore condoned questions not merely to find out if the suspect wanted to say anything, but to discover whether the threshold for charging had been met.[45] In each of these cases the questioning in issue was conducted by the interviewing officer not by the custody officer, but in principle the issue is the same.

The net result of these cases is considerable uncertainty as to whether any and, if so, what kind of questioning of the suspect is permitted where the police start

---

[40] Unreported, Case No.94/4814/X4, October 20, 1995, CA.
[41] [1997] Crim.L.R. 676, CA. See also commentary by Professor Birch at 677.
[42] The Court held that no adverse inferences could be drawn from silence since the interviewing officer was not seeking to discover whether or by whom an offence had been committed within the meaning of s.34. Moreover, the trial judge had specifically told the jury not to draw adverse inferences from silence.
[43] See also *Gayle* [1999] Crim.L.R. 502, CA and Professor Birch's commentary at 502–504.
[44] [1999] Crim.L.R. 318, CA. Again, see also the commentary by Professor Birch at 319.
[45] See also *Ioannou* [1999] Crim.L.R. 586, CA and *Odeyemi* [1999] Crim.L.R. 828, CA.

with sufficient evidence to prosecute.[46] As has been said, "[P]olice officers are faced with contradictory obligations under PACE and the Codes of Practice. The resulting confusion may provide one explanation for why s.37 appears to be ignored by the police."[47] The position, in other words, is unsatisfactory. At all events it appears that in that situation the courts will not countenance extensive questioning of the suspect whether by the interviewing officer or by the custody officer, but, providing the officer has an open mind as to whether to charge, some questioning is permissible—and adverse inferences will be capable of being drawn from a "no comment" interview even though the police already had significant evidence at the outset of the interview.

A further problem arises from an apparent disjunction between the detention **4–33** provisions in the statute and the new charging system. As noted above, s.37(1) states that the custody officer must determine whether there is sufficient evidence to charge the suspect with the offence for which he was arrested "*and may detain him at the police station for such period as is necessary to enable him to do so*"(emphasis supplied). The italicised words are critical because, once the custody officer has reached that decision, there is no longer any legal basis for detaining the suspect without charging him. Yet under the new charging system the suspect is in effect put "on hold" whilst the custody officer seeks the decision of the CPS as to whether any, and if so what, charge should be preferred. If it can sensibly be argued that the custody officer was *subjectively* in doubt, time in custody spent waiting to be informed by the CPS about the charging decision could be said to be within a broad interpretation of s.37(1). There was always some latitude in that regard. But what if it is obvious that there is sufficient evidence to charge the suspect in regard to the offence for which he was arrested and the question for the CPS is whether other or additional charges are indicated, or whether, in the light of the public interest test, he should be charged at all? Can the suspect legitimately be held at all waiting for the CPS' response? If the case is one in which bail is a realistic possibility, and the CPS decision is not forthcoming, the suspect's solicitor would be entitled to pressure the custody officer to cut the Gordian knot and make the decision without delay on the basis that s.37(1) requires it.

The August 2004 revision of Code C states that where the DPP's Guidance on charging is in force, "custody officers are entitled (notwithstanding s.37(1)) to take reasonable time to apply that Guidance in deciding how a detained person is to be dealt with in accordance with s.37(7), as amended by Sch.2 to the Criminal Justice Act 2003, including where appropriate consultation with a Duty Prosecutor" (Note 16AB). The difficulty is that there is no statutory basis for setting aside s.37(1) in this way, nor for introducing the new concept of a reasonable time to allow for the making of the charging decision.

The concept of "a reasonable time" in this context is anyway completely **4–34** uncertain. Reasonable as measured from whose standpoint? What is reasonable

[46] In *Van Bokkum*, unreported, Case No.9900333 Z3 March 7, 2000, CA the court said that if it had to choose between *Gayle* [1999] Crim.L.R. 502, CA on the one hand, and *McGuinness* [1999] Crim.L.R. 318, CA and *Ioannou* [1999] Crim.L.R. 586, CA on the other, it preferred the latter. This was confirmed again in *Elliot* [2002] EWCA Crim 931, CMAC.
[47] Cape, "Detention without Charge: What does 'Sufficient Evidence to Charge' Mean?" [1999] Crim.L.R. 875 at 885.

from the point of view of the prosecution process may be unreasonable from the perspective of the suspect. Does it mean one hour, two hours, four hours, six hours, more than six hours?

Quite apart from the question as to what here is a reasonable time, the Code cannot amend the statute—and 16AB is a Note for Guidance not even a provision of the Code. In the case of a clash, 16AB would be held to be *ultra vires*. It would be surprising if this issue were not soon brought to the attention of the courts. Almost certainly it will require statutory amendment.

Once the custody officer decides that there is sufficient evidence to charge and refers the matter to the CPS for a decision, extra time for holding the suspect in custody cannot be obtained by the superintendent's authority to extend detention from 24 to 36 hours under s.42 nor by a magistrates' court extending detention beyond 36 hours under ss.43 and 44 (as to which see below). Those powers relate solely to the question whether further detention is necessary "to secure or preserve evidence" or "to obtain such evidence by questioning". That does not cover extra time for consideration of the charging decision after the custody officer has determined that there is sufficient evidence to charge. If a statutory time limit is due to expire or if "a reasonable time" has elapsed the suspect must therefore either be released on bail under s.37(7)(a) for the decision to be made by the CPS, or he must be charged with a holding charge.

4–35   A further problem occurs in regard to questioning. According to Code C, para.16.5, questioning must basically cease when a person is charged (para.6–76 below). But what if he has been charged by application of the Threshold Test? Can he be further questioned about that offence either if he is in custody or if he returns to answer bail? The Threshold Test is to be used, by definition, when there is more evidence gathering to be done. But the position seems clear. After the suspect has been charged, para.16.5 applies and he cannot be questioned about that offence unless such questions are necessary to "prevent or minimise harm or loss to some other person, or the public", "to clear up an ambiguity in a previous answer or statement", or where it is "in the interests of justice for the detainee to have put to them, and have an opportunity to comment on, information concerning the offence which has come to light since they were charged or informed they might be prosecuted". Unless those exceptions apply questioning is not permitted.

Paragraph 16.1 has yet another problematic provision—that, "When a person is detained in respect of more than one offence it is permissible to delay informing the custody officer until [the police had decided that there is a realistic prospect of conviction] in respect of all the offences". This has consequences, for instance in terms of permitting further delay in access to a solicitor.[48]

If no decision has been made as to whether the suspect will be prosecuted, he should be so informed (subs.(8)). If he is not in a fit state to be charged, he may be detained until he is in a fit state (subs.(9)). Such detention, however, cannot be for more than 24 hours and must cease when he is in a fit state if that is earlier. This follows from the general prohibition on detention for more than 24 hours in s.41, subject to exceptions which do not apply in such a case.

---

[48] The Court of Appeal held in *Samuel* [1988] Q.B. 615 that when a suspect had been charged with one offence he could no longer be denied access to a solicitor under Annex B of Code C, even though he was still being questioned in connection with other offences.

Subsections (11) to (14) dealt with arrested juveniles. They were not brought **4–36** into effect and were repealed by the Criminal Justice Act 1991, s.72.

Subsection (15) defines "arrested juvenile" and "endorsed for bail".

It has been held that the duties performed by custody officers under s.37 (and s.38) cannot be performed on behalf of a private prosecutor, even when it is intended that the prosecution be carried forward by the private prosecutor. In *R. v Ealing Justices, Ex p. Dixon*[49] the Divisional Court held that under the Prosecution of Offences Act 1985, s.3 all prosecutions had to be taken over by the DPP or the Crown Prosecution Service. If charges were preferred by the police they could not be conducted by a private prosecutor. But in *R. v Stafford Justices, Ex p. Commissioners of Customs and Excise*[50] this decision was rejected by the Divisional Court itself, at least as concerns offences conducted by Customs and Excise. A customs officer investigating an offence had all relevant powers except that of charging an arrested person. He therefore had to take the arrested person to the police for charging. But, the court said, it should not be thought that this meant that Customs and Excise surrendered the prosecution of the offence to the DPP. Section 6 of the 1985 Act envisaged that persons other than the DPP might institute proceedings and prosecute. The right under s.6 of other persons to conduct a prosecution would be nugatory if the prosecution had to be taken over by the police from the moment of charging. It followed, Watkins L.J. said, that *Ex p. Dixon* was wrongly decided.

The custody officer is entitled to assume that the arrest was lawful and he is therefore not under a duty to review the question of the legality of the arrest. Moreover, a defective arrest can be cured at any stage post arrest—notably by the custody officer. But an uncured defective arrest cannot be the basis for a properly authorised detention.[51]

Duties of custody officer after charge: s.38[52]

Section 38 establishes the principles on which the custody officer must decide **4–37** whether to keep someone in custody after he has been charged. It is implicit in the section that the original arrest was lawful so, if this is not the case and the suspect is detained, an action for damages will lie against the police.[53] The custody officer must decide whether the accused person is a good risk for bail with or without conditions. The power to grant bail subject to conditions was granted by the Criminal Justice and Public Order Act 1994 (CJPOA), s.27. But (at the time) this power only applied to persons who had been charged. It therefore did not

---

[49] [1989] 3 W.L.R. 1098; [1989] 2 All E.R. 1050, DC.
[50] [1991] 2 Q.B. 339, DC.
[51] *DPP v L and S, The Times*, February 1, 1994, DC, No.CO/3682/98, December 14, 1998. The Divisional Court agreed with the justices that the arrest was unlawful because the arrested person was not informed that she was under arrest but held that, in the absence of evidence to the contrary, the justices should have assumed that the custody record was correct in stating that the custody officer had told the suspect why she had been arrested.
[52] See 1989 N.I. PACE Order, Art.39 as amended by Criminal Justice (N.I.) Order 2003 (SI 2003/1247), Art.7.
[53] *Hutt v Commissioner of Police of the Metropolis* [2003] EWCA Civ 1911.

apply to someone who had been released on bail without charges to return to a police station at a later date. The Government's White Paper *Justice for All* (July 2002, Cm.5536, para.3.37) said that legislation would be introduced to give the police power to impose conditions on persons granted bail before being charged. The Criminal Justice Act 2003, Sch.2, para.6(3) gave effect to this commitment.

Bail from the police station

4–38   Subsection (1)(a) of s.38 sets out the detention provisions after charge in respect of adults. Where someone who has been arrested without warrant or under a warrant not endorsed for bail is charged, the custody officer must release him with or without bail unless it is decided that one or more of the following conditions apply:

(i)   It appears that he has not provided a satisfactory address for service of a summons.

(ii)   There are reasonable grounds for believing he will fail to appear at court to answer to bail.[54]

(iii) Where someone is arrested for an imprisonable offence, where there are reasonable grounds for believing that detention is necessary to prevent him from committing an offence.

(iiia) If the suspect is over 18,[55] where the custody officer has reasonable grounds for believing that his detention is necessary to enable a sample to be taken to test whether he has a Class A drug in his body. (Such detention may not be for more than six hours.)[56]

(iv)   Where someone is arrested for an offence that is not imprisonable, and there are reasonable grounds for believing that detention is necessary to prevent him from causing physical injury to anyone (*e.g.* assault) or from causing loss of or damage to property (*e.g.* theft or criminal damage).

(v)   If there are reasonable grounds for believing that detention is necessary to prevent him from interfering with the administration of justice or with the investigation of offences.

(vi)   If there are reasonable grounds for thinking that detention is needed for his own protection.[57]

---

[54] In that case a surety or sureties can be required and security from the suspect can be required in the form either of a promise to pay (called "a recognisance") or of actual cash. And other conditions can be imposed to ensure that he attends court.
[55] The Criminal Justice Act 2003, s.5(3) provided for the age to be to be lowered to 14 on condition that in the case of someone under the age of 17 the testing is done in the presence of an appropriate adult.
[56] Added by the Criminal Justice and Court Services Act 2000, s.57(3). Such testing is authorised by s.63B of PACE which was introduced by s.57(2) of the same 2000 Act.
[57] The above circumstances set out in s.38(1) are stated as amended by the Criminal Justice and Public Order Act 1994, s.28(2).

In deciding whether such conditions apply (except for those referred to in (i) and **4–39** (vi)) the custody officer is supposed to have in mind the same considerations that the magistrates are required to bear in mind when considering whether to grant bail to persons arrested for or convicted of imprisonable offences.[58] They are:

(a) the nature and seriousness of the offence and the probable penalty;

(b) the defendant's character, antecedents, associations and community ties;

(c) his record in regard to any previous grant of bail; and

(d) the strength of the evidence; together with any other relevant consideration.

Home Office Circular 111/92 gave guidance on the matters that custody officers should take into account. They include:

(1) the suspect's intentions as expressed, for instance, in any threats;

(2) his disposition as expressed in violent behaviour; and

(3) his prior record.

A criminal record would not in itself justify detention but the custody officer **4–40** must consider that further detention is necessary to prevent injury, loss or damage. It would be legitimate to conclude that such injury, loss or damage exists where there is evidence of persistent and repetitive offending. The grounds for detention would be significantly strengthened if the suspect had previously offended whilst on bail. However, the police should have in mind the nature of the breach of bail. An arrest for burglary in breach of bail for burglary was more of an indication for detention than where he was on bail for some unrelated offence. Each case must be considered on its individual merits.

The procedure for releasing a person on bail from the police station is dealt with in Sch.3 to the CJPOA. If bail is given subject to conditions, the reasons must be stated by the custody officer on the custody record. The accused can ask the custody officer or another custody officer to vary the conditions of bail. Such a request could result in more, as well as less, onerous conditions being imposed. When the matter reaches the magistrates they are free to impose whatever conditions seem right to them. The magistrates can deal with the matter not simply when the matter reaches the court in the ordinary way. Sch.3 to the CJPOA gives the accused the right to go to the magistrates simply for the purpose of seeking a

---

[58] The Criminal Justice and Public Order Act 1994, s.28(3) states that they are as set out in the Bail Act 1976, Sch.1, Pt I, para.9.

variation of the conditions imposed by the police (new s.43B of the Magistrates' Courts Act 1980). See also s.47 below (bail after arrest).

Note that if a person breaches court bail by failing without reasonable cause to surrender to custody, that is an offence under the Bail Act 1976, s.6(1) which should be charged. PACE, s.38 is then brought into operation. But a breach of any other condition is not an offence, so if a person is arrested for breach of such other condition he cannot be charged and s.38 has no application. An information is laid instead and he has to be brought before a court as specified in s.7(4) of the Bail Act "as soon as practicable and in any event within 24 hours".

Detention of juveniles

4–41 The release of juveniles on bail is covered by exactly the same rules as apply to adults, except that a juvenile may also be denied bail if it is in his own interests.[59] An example of this might be the youngster picked up for an offence after he has run away from home. If it is not in practice possible to send him home on overnight bail he could be held in custody "in his own interests".

There are special rules in regard to juveniles who are not released on bail. The basic rule is that juveniles under the age of 17 must be transferred to local authority accommodation. There are, however, two exceptions. (The Criminal Justice and Police Act 2001, s.130 added another exception, namely where the young person has a recent history of repeatedly committing imprisonable offences while remanded on bail or in local authority accommodation—but this exception can only be utilised by a court.[60]) The first exception is where the custody officer certifies that it is impracticable to make the transfer to local authority accommodation.[61] These circumstances must be specified in the certificate. The Home Office Circular to the police issued in August 1992 (78/1992) stated (para.9):

"The construction of the statutory provision makes it clear that the type of accommodation in which the local authority propose to place the juvenile is not a factor which the custody officer may take into account in considering whether the transfer is impracticable. In particular, the unavailability of local authority secure accommodation does not make the transfer impracticable. The circumstances in which a transfer would be impracticable are those, and only those, in which it is physically impossible to place the juvenile in local authority accommodation. These might include extreme weather conditions (*e.g.* floods or blizzards) or the impossibility, despite repeated efforts, of contacting the local authority."

The Circular drew attention to the fact that Code C, Note 16D specifically states that neither a juvenile's behaviour nor the nature of the offence with which he is

---

[59] PACE, s.38(1)(b)(ii).
[60] This section was brought into force on April 22, 2002 in 10 areas and in the rest of the country on September 16, 2002.
[61] This exception was originally in s.38(6) of PACE. The Criminal Justice Act 1991, s.59 replaced subs. (6) by a new (6) and (6A). The test of whether it is "impracticable" was however not altered. For the background see Leng, "Children in police cells—no change", S.J., December 6, 1991, p.1312.

charged provides grounds for the custody officer to hold him in police custody on the ground of impracticability.

Some police forces have interpreted the word "impracticable" to cover cases **4–42** where they considered the juvenile needed to be kept in secure accommodation which the local authority could not or would not provide. This interpretation was in effect approved by the Divisional Court in *R. v Chief Constable of the Cambridgeshire Constabulary, Ex p. Michel*.[62] The police had certified that it was impracticable to transfer a boy of 16 to local authority care because they feared he might commit further offences or interfere with the course of justice. The Divisional Court held that the police could legitimately hold the boy in police cells if the custody officer believed that the local authority's accommodation would be insufficient to prevent the very consequences which led to the original decision to refuse bail. As has been seen, a juvenile arrested for an imprisonable offence can, for instance, like an adult, be refused bail to prevent him committing other offences. Paragraph 9 of the Home Office Circular quoted above as to the meaning of "impracticability" has to be read in light of the Divisional Court's decision.

The second exception to the general rule is that the custody officer does not have to transfer to the local authority a juvenile where no secure accommodation is available and keeping him in other accommodation would "not be adequate to protect the public from serious harm".[63] Originally, this applied only if the juvenile was over 15 but the Criminal Justice and Public Order Act 1994 (s.12) lowered the age from 15 to 12. This means that any juvenile between the ages 12 and 17 can now be held in police cells if the custody officer thinks it necessary to protect the public from serious harm. "Serious harm" is defined in the statute in relation to charges of sexual or violent offences quite narrowly as referring to "death or serious personal injury, whether physical or psychological, occasioned by further such offences".[64] "Serious harm" is not defined in relation to other offences but the Home Office Circular was presumably correct in suggesting that the statutory definition for sexual and violent offences indicated the gravity of risk of harm before the test would be satisfied.

Could children also be held in police cells because of the absence of secure accommodation even if there is no reason to fear serious harm to the public? There is obviously an argument that by making specific provision for detention of children in police cells where the police fear that the public would otherwise suffer serious harm, Parliament intended to indicate that detention for less reason would be illegitimate. But given the Divisional Court's broad interpretation of the word "impracticable" in *Ex p. Michel*, this view cannot be advanced with confidence. The matter remains to be decided.

A child under the age of 12 not released on bail must be transferred to local authority accommodation. Technically this does not apply to the case of a child under the age of 12 who is held by virtue of the Bail Act, s.7(4) for breach of a condition of bail—because there is nothing specific to that effect. But the better view is that the same policy should be applied.

---

[62] (1990) 91 Cr.App.R. 325; [1991] 2 All E.R. 777, DC.
[63] Criminal Justice Act 1991, s.59.
[64] subs.(6A) in s.38 of PACE.

Responsibilities in relation to detained persons: s.39[65]

4-43   Section 39 concerns the responsibility of the custody officer for the proper treatment of detained persons as recommended by the Philips Royal Commission.[66] Subsection (1) requires the custody officer to ensure that anyone detained at his police station is treated in accordance with the requirements of the Act and of any Code of Practice made under it.[67] Code C states that the duties of the custody officer include responsibility also for seeing that everything required to be recorded in the custody record is in fact recorded. Code C spells this duty out further by the provision that the custody officer is "responsible for the accuracy and completeness of the custody record" (para.2.3).

If the custody officer transfers custody of the suspect to the investigating officer, his duties in this regard are taken over by the person who has custody of the suspect (subs.(2)).[68] The Police Reform Act 2002 provides that this now also applies where the custody officer hands over to an authorised civilian investigating officer[69] or to an escort officer.[70] When he returns the suspect to the custody officer's custody the officer is supposed to report "as to the manner in which this section and the Codes of Practice have been complied with" (subs.(3)). This requirement applies equally to the authorised civilian investigating or escort officer.

If an arrested juvenile is handed over to the local authority under s.38(7), the custody officer's responsibility ceases (subs.(4)). The Philips Royal Commission recommended[71] that even where the investigating officer outranks the custody officer it should be the latter not the former who has the decisive responsibility. Subsection (6) gives effect to this view, by requiring that if there is any conflict between the two, the custody officer must refer the issue at once to a superintendent or more senior officer in charge of the police station. This makes it clear that the custody officer is directly responsible to the Divisional or Sub-Divisional Commander.

4-44   Evidence from the police to the Runciman Royal Commission expressed concern that the Code did not acknowledge the difficulty that, for reasons beyond their control, custody officers sometimes faced in complying strictly with the Code's rules. The Runciman Royal Commission supported the police's concern.[72] A new provision in the 1995 revised Code dealt with the point. It states (Code C, para.1.1A) that a custody officer shall not be in breach of the Code for delay in processing a suspect "if the delay is justifiable and reasonable steps are taken to prevent unnecessary delay". The custody record should indicate where such delay has occurred and why. Note for Guidance 1H states that excusable delay may occur, for instance, where a large number of suspects are brought into the police station simultaneously or the interview rooms are all being used or where difficulties are experienced in contacting an appropriate adult or solicitor.

[65] See 1989 N.I. PACE Order, Art.40.
[66] Philips Report, para.3.112.
[67] It is, however, not the custody officer's duty personally to escort a prisoner to the cells!—*DPP v McLean*, unreported, Case No.CO 2217–94, January 30, 1995, DC.
[68] *R. v Ismail* [1990] Crim.L.R. 109, CA.
[69] Sch.4, Pt 2, para.22(3).
[70] Sch.4, Pt 4, para.35(5).
[71] Philips Report, para.3.112.
[72] Recommendation 48, based on para.34, Runciman Report, pp.33–34.

Once the decision is made to release the suspect he should be released without delay. If it is proposed that he should be given a medical examination prior to release, this risks detention beyond what is permitted since there is no provision for this in the rules. (In *Nellins v Chief Constable of the Royal Ulster Constabulary*,[73] the court awarded damages of £45 for the unlawful detention for five minutes involved in such an examination.)

Reviews of police detention: ss.40 and 40A[74]

The Philips Royal Commission recommended[75] that the need for detention **4–45** should be reviewed periodically: on arrival at the police station, after six hours and then after 24 hours. The Government adopted the basic idea but made it somewhat more onerous in requiring that such reviews must be carried out within the first six hours and then at not more than nine hour intervals from the previous review.

The requirement of a s.40 review applies to "each person in police detention"[76]—a technical term defined in s.118(2) (see para.11–15 below). It does not apply to someone arrested in respect of an actual or anticipated breach of bail conditions (under s.7(3) of the Bail Act 1976), who is then detained pending appearance before a magistrate (under s.7(4) of the Bail Act). Arrest in respect of bail conditions is not arrest for an offence. Technically, s.40 reviews also do not apply to someone produced to the police from prison (now covered by the Crime (Sentences) Act 1997, Sch.1, para.3). However, it is sensible to conduct such reviews as if the prisoner were within the definition since he should be returned to prison as soon as the reasons for his production no longer apply.[77] Some police forces adopt the practice of arresting the person produced from prison. This is unnecessary unless it is contemplated that there is need for the taking of an intimate (s.62) or non-intimate (s.63) sample since such samples can only be taken without consent from someone in police detention as defined. If he is arrested, then technically he is in police detention and s.40 applies as a matter of law. A person remanded by magistrates to a police station after charge under s.48 ("a three-day lie-down", see para.4–89 below) is specifically made subject to the s.40 review process by the express terms of s.48(d). Although detention for breach of the peace is not specifically covered by PACE, the police practice of treating a person so detained as subject to PACE requirements of reviews has been held to be correct—*Chief Constable of Cleveland v McGrogan*.[78]

---

[73] [1998] N.I. 1, QBD.
[74] See 1989 N.I. PACE Order, Art.41.
[75] Philips Report, para.3.105.
[76] s.40(1).
[77] A memorandum of understanding between the police and the prison service provides that the transferred prisoner should be detained in a designated police station in accordance with the provisions of Pt IV of PACE. The right to legal advice and reminders about the right to silence are other rights that should be made available.
[78] [2002] EWCA Civ 86; [2002] 1 F.L.R. 707.

4–46   Note 15B in Code C states that the detention of these various categories of persons not subject to the statutory review requirement should still be reviewed periodically "as a matter of good practice". The purpose of such review "is to check the particular power under which a detainee is held continues to apply, any associated conditions are complied with and to make sure appropriate action is taken to deal with any changes. This includes the detainee's prompt release when the power no longer applies, or their transfer if the power requires the detainee be taken elsewhere as soon as the necessary arrangements are made" (*ibid.*).

Time in regard to reviews is measured from the time that detention was first authorised, not, as is the case for detention limits, from first arrival at the police station (subs.(3)(a)). Where the person concerned has already been charged, the review would be by the custody officer; if not, it would be by an officer not involved in the investigation of the rank of inspector or above. (However, if the person charged is remanded to the police station by a magistrates' court for investigation of other offences, the review would be by an inspector rather than by the custody officer—see para.4–89 below.) The person performing the function is known as the review officer. His review is separate from and in addition to the first assessment by the custody officer on the suspect's arrival at the police station under s.37(2) and (3). These reviews must take place even though continued detention under s.42 has been authorised or a warrant of further detention under s.43 has been issued. The purpose of the reviews is to ensure that the detainee is being properly treated and that he is released as soon as possible. Any conflict between the review officer and a more senior officer involved in the case must be referred at once by the review officer to a superintendent or above (subs.(11)).

4–47   The failure to conduct the review at the proper time can be actionable. In the civil case of *Roberts v Chief Constable of the Cheshire Constabulary*[79] the Court of Appeal upheld an award of £500 damages to R whose detention should have been reviewed by 5.25 am but the review was not carried out until 7.45 am. The basis of such a claim is that failure to conduct the review at the proper time—at least if it was due to oversight or neglect—means that any subsequent detention is unlawful. It also follows that any confession or admission that emerges during that period of unlawful detention may be held to be inadmissible under s.78.

A review may be postponed if, having regard to the circumstances, "it is not practicable" to have it at the specified time, or the suspect is actually being questioned at the time and the review officer is satisfied that interruption would prejudice the investigation or if no review officer is readily available (subs.(4)). It must, however, be conducted as soon as practicable. When the delay is because the suspect is being questioned, the review would take place normally in the next break in questioning. The grounds of any delay must be recorded in the custody record. Moreover, when there has been delay, the next review must take place within the time limit as measured from the time when the prior review should have taken place, not when it did in fact take place. Otherwise the suspect would be penalised by the fact of the delay (subs.(6)).

The grounds for keeping the suspect in detention must normally be given to the detainee in his presence if practicable and the written record must similarly be made in his presence.[80] The statute recognises exceptions when the detainee is

---

[79] [1999] 2 All E.R. 326, CA.
[80] s.37(5) incorporated by s.40(8).

incapable of understanding what is said to him, when he is asleep,[81] when he is violent or likely to become violent, or when in urgent need of medical attention.[82] The information must then be given as soon as practicable and in any case before he is first questioned (Code C, para.3.4). The grounds must be recorded in the custody record.

But before authorising continued detention, the review officer must give the suspect (unless he is asleep at the time) or any solicitor representing him who is available at the time, the opportunity of making representations (subs.(12)). On the other hand, as has just been seen, s.40(12) specifically refers to the possibility of the review taking place whilst the suspect is asleep. It follows that a lawful review could take place whilst the prisoner is asleep even if there is no solicitor available to make representations on his behalf. For a review of detention under s.40 the prisoner does not necessarily have to be woken up for the purpose of making representations but he must of course be informed as soon as possible after the making of any decision authorising continued detention (para.15.7). By contrast, for an extension of detention under s.42 he should be awake for that purpose. The suspect also needs to be awake when the review officer records the grounds of further detention because, as just noted, he must inform the suspect of those grounds. Because that should not be done when the suspect is drowsy Code C as redrafted in 2003 said that the review officer should therefore consider postponing the review until the person is fully awake (Note 15C). **4–48**

The review officer can refuse to hear oral representations by the suspect himself "if he considers that he is unfit to make such representations by reason of his condition or behaviour" (subs.(14)). In that case he cannot however refuse to hear representations from a solicitor. At the custody officer's discretion, "other people having an interest in the detainee's welfare" may also be allowed to make representations on his behalf (Code C, para.15.3A[83]).

Guidance Note 15C states that if the detainee is likely to be asleep at the time when the review needs to take place, it should be brought forward (if the time constraints permit) so that he can make representations without being woken up.

Terrorism cases

There are separate rules for terrorism cases. They are now to be found in the Terrorism Act 2000, Sch.8, Pt II. The first review has to be carried out "as soon as is reasonably practicable" after the suspect's arrest. Thereafter, reviews should be carried out at intervals of not more than 12 hours—subject to the possibility of postponement if the suspect is being questioned at that time and an officer is satisfied that interruption would prejudice the investigation, or no review officer is readily available, or "it is not practicable for any other reason to carry it out at that time".[84] The review officer has to be someone who is not involved in the investigation. For the first 24 hours reviews must be done by an officer of at least the rank of inspector; thereafter it must be an officer of at least **4–49**

---

[81] Added by Police Reform Act 2002, s.52.
[82] s.37(6).
[83] Formerly 15.1.
[84] Sch.8, paras 21–22.

the rank of superintendent.[85] The provisions for taking representations,[86] informing the suspect of his rights,[87] and making a record[88] are basically the same as those under PACE.

Telephone or video review

4–50   The third edition of this work stated, "If in the circumstances the only practicable way of conducting a review is over the telephone, then this is permissible". This was the gist of Note 15C of Code C as it then stood. But, in *R. v Chief Constable of Kent, Ex p. Kent Police Federation*[89] the Divisional Court decided that it was not permissible to conduct s.40 reviews by video link. The court held that the officer conducting the review and the prisoner had to be physically present in the same place and in each other's company. Lord Bingham C.J. said, *obiter*, that he had difficulty in seeing how a review conducted over the telephone could ever comply with the requirements of s.40.

This decision was, however, reversed by legislation. The Criminal Justice and Police Act 2001, s.73 inserted into PACE new ss.40A and 45A which, in certain circumstances, allow telephone and video reviews of detention and video links for other custody decisions regarding charging, detention and bail where the review officer is at a different station from the person detained. The Government said that it would pilot the use of video conferencing facilities for s.40 reviews of detention and such other custody decisions. The Act provided for regulations to be drawn up specifying which police stations and which functions were to be piloted. (See equally Code C, Note 15G. These powers have not yet been extended to Northern Ireland.) The pilot took place at two police stations in Hampshire.[90] In June 2004 a further statutory instrument terminated reviews by video conferencing pending the evaluation of the pilot.[91]

Section 40A(1) stated that pre-charge reviews under s.40(1)(b) could lawfully be carried out by telephone (a) if it was not reasonably practicable for an officer of the rank of inspector to conduct it in person and (b) provided that it was not one that could be conducted by video link under s.45A or it was not reasonably practicable to do it by video link. So review by video link was to be preferred to one by telephone, but, failing that, the telephone could be used.

4–51   A critical question was whether the words "not reasonably practicable" used here were to be given a wide or a narrow interpretation. Did they cover the normal exigencies and problems of personnel deployment? It seemed clear that the Home Office's intention was that they should be given a narrow interpretation. The Explanatory Notes accompanying the Act said (para.199): "It is not envisaged that the duties of the review officer should be performed by video link as a

---

[85] Sch.8, paras 21–22.
[86] Sch.8, para.26.
[87] Sch.8, para.27.
[88] Sch.8, para.28.
[89] [2000] 2 Cr.App.R. 196, DC.
[90] Police and Criminal Evidence Act 1984 (Remote Review of Detention) (Specified Police Stations) Regulations 2003 (SI 2003/2397).
[91] Police and Criminal Evidence Act 1984 (Remote Review of Detention) (Specified Police Stations) (Revocation) Regulations 2003 (SI 2004/1503).

matter of course. It is envisaged that a review by telephone might be used, for example, where a review officer is unable to travel to the police station to carry out a review because the road is flooded." That made it sound as if it was intended to be highly exceptional. Code C, Note 15F gave the same impression—"where severe weather conditions or an unforeseen operational emergency prevent the review officer from attending". (The provisions of s.40A did not apply to reviews of detention after charge nor to reviews under Pt II of Sch.8 to the Terrorism Act 2000 (*ibid.*).)

However, the Criminal Justice Act 2003 included a provision for removing the restrictions on telephone reviews under s.40A. Section 6 substituted a new s.40A(1) and (2). Subsection (1) stated that a review "may be carried out by means of a discussion, conducted by telephone, with one or more persons at the police station where the arrested person is held". Subsection (2) stated that subs.(1) did not apply if the review was of the kind authorised by regulations under s.45A for using video-conferencing facilities (see para.4–77 below) and it was reasonably practicable to carry it out in that way.

The provision was the result of a recommendation by the Joint Home Office/Cabinet Office Review of PACE. The Joint Review considered various proposals for relaxing controls on reviews of detention: greater use of reviews by telephone; allowing custody officers to conduct such reviews; amending the review times; removing the need for any review other than spot checks. The only one of these "Options proposed" that it supported was the first. ("The Review recommends an extension of the circumstances under which inspectors can carry out reviews of detention by telephone. Such telephone reviews would effectively become a straightforward alternative to reviews in person"(p. 27). However, it said that it acknowledged the Youth Justice Board's concerns about such arrangements being extended to juveniles and their view that reviews of juvenile detention should, whenever practicable, be carried out in person by an inspector.

The 2004 revision of the Codes reflects the change of approach. Paragraphs 15.9 **4–52** and 15.9A state baldly that the officer reviewing detention under s.40 "need not attend the police station holding the detainee and may carry out the review by telephone". A telephone review is not permitted, however, where facilities for video conferencing exist and it is practicable to use them (para.15.9B). When considering whether a review should be conducted in person or by telephone or by video conference the review officer should consider the benefits of a review in person especially where the person is a juvenile, is mentally vulnerable, has received medical attention other than for something minor or where there are "presentational or community issues around the person's detention" (para.15.3C). No guidance is given as to the meaning of these final words but they probably mean issues that are liable to provoke media or other public concern.

The obligation to make a record of a s.40A review becomes a duty to cause another officer to make it and the record by that officer must be made in the presence of the suspect (s.40A(3)(a) and (b) and Code C, para.15.10). However, representations by the suspect or his solicitor must be made to the person conducting the review either by telephone or, where facilities exist for immediate transmission of written representations—*e.g.* by fax or email—in writing to that officer (s.40A(4) and Code C, para.15.11).

A provision in the 1995 revision of Code C stated that the officer conducting the review should not ask the suspect any specific questions about his involvement in any offence or in respect of any comments made by the suspect—any such questions would turn the review into an interview (para.15.6[92]).

Time limits on detention without charge: s.41[93]

4–53   Under the pre-PACE law the time limit on pre-charge police detention depended on whether the offence was regarded by the police as "serious". Section 43 of the Magistrates' Court Act 1980 required that where the offence was not serious and the suspect could not be brought before a magistrates' court within 24 hours he had to be released on bail. But where the offence was serious (and there was no definition of this in the Act) he had to be brought before a court "as soon as practicable" (s.43(4)).

The police tended to interpret the phrase "as soon as practicable" to mean "as soon as we have decided whether to charge him", rather than "as soon as a court can be found that is sitting". The result was that some suspects were held for long periods without charge. The only safeguard against this was the rare intervention of an application for habeas corpus which usually had the effect of forcing the police either to charge or release the suspect.[94]

The Philips Royal Commission took the view that this problem required drastic change and recommended that a proper system of time limits be imposed. The police, they recommended,[95] should not be permitted to hold a suspect without charge for more than 24 hours unless they had sought and obtained permission from a magistrates' court at a full hearing held in private at which the suspect would be entitled to be both present and legally represented. Moreover, there should be no power to hold anyone for more than 24 hours unless he was suspected of having committed a grave offence.

4–54   Under the Philips Royal Commission's proposed scheme the magistrates' court would have been able to authorise further detention for periods of not more than 24 hours at a time—with no overall limit. After 48 hours, however, there would have been a right of appeal to a judge. When the first Bill was first published it showed that the Government had made certain important modifications to the Philips Royal Commission's proposed scheme. Its basic provision was that holding a suspect without charge for more than 24 hours would require a magistrate's permission. In the first instance an application would be made *ex parte* to a single magistrate. The hearing could be in the magistrate's own home. The suspect would only have the right to appear before the magistrates after 48 hours. On the other hand, the magistrates could not authorise more than a total of 96 hours detention without charge. The provisions for holding a suspect beyond 24 hours only applied to serious arrestable offences.

---

[92] Formerly para.15.2A.
[93] See 1989 N.I. PACE Order, Art.42.
[94] See generally Munro, "Detention after arrest" [1981] Crim.L.R. 802, and Wolchover, "The Police Bill and the scope of existing powers of detention for questioning" (1983) 80 *Law Society Gazette* 2978. The most important cases were: *Houghton and Franciosy* (1978) 68 Cr.App.R. 197; *Hudson* (1980) 72 Cr.App.R. 163; *Sherman and Apps* (1981) 72 Cr.App.R. 266; and *Nycander, The Times,* December 9, 1982.
[95] Philips Report, para.3.106.

These provisions were criticised from different vantage points. Some argued that it was wrong to delay the suspect's right to a full hearing to review further detention by as much as 48 hours. Others contended that the application after 24 hours to a single magistrate possibly in his home and without requiring him to be attended by his clerk would tempt the police to shop around for a compliant magistrate. Also, it was seen by some as undesirable to have matters of such moment determined by a magistrate at his home.

The Government eventually decided to amend the scheme by abolishing the *ex parte* application to the magistrates and by advancing the time of the full hearing before the magistrates' court from the 48-hour point to the 36-hour stage. It resisted the argument that it should be brought forward even further to the 24-hour point mainly on the ground of the burden this would throw on all concerned.[96] Lengthy detention in a police station is relatively rare. The Philips Royal Commission said that about three-quarters of suspects were dealt with within six hours and about 95 per cent within 24 hours. The number of persons held for more than 24 hours was some 22,000 compared with only a few hundred held for over 36 hours. A survey done for the Philips Commission by the Metropolitan Police for three months in 1979 showed that only 0.4 per cent of 48,343 persons had been held for over 72 hours before being charged or released without charge.[97]

The Philips Commission recommended that for the first 24 hours, therefore, **4–55** detention would be authorised by the review officer. At the end of 24 hours it would have to be authorised by an officer of the rank of superintendent or above and from 36 hours onwards for the remaining time up to the maximum of 96 hours it could only be authorised by a magistrates' court after a full hearing at which the suspect could be present and legally represented. This scheme is that adopted in the Act.

As will be seen below, a somewhat different regime applies to terrorism investigations. The periods of time are different—48 hours instead of 36 hours for the period of initial detention, 14 (formerly seven) days instead of 96 hours for the maximum period of detention, and authority for detention beyond the initial period given as from 2001 by a designated judicial person rather than by any two magistrates under PACE or by the Home Secretary as formerly under the Prevention of Terrorism Act. Otherwise, the detention regime for terrorism cases is either the same or similar to that under PACE.

The PACE provisions

Subsection (1) of s.41 provides that, subject to later provisions of the section and **4–56** to ss.42 and 43, a person may not be detained without charge in police detention[98] for more than 24 hours. This is the basic rule. Unless his further detention is authorised, he must be released with or without bail and cannot be re-arrested for the same offence unless new evidence comes to light (subss.(7) and (9)). As noted

---

[96] House of Commons, *Hansard*, Standing Committee E, February 16, 1984, col.1218.
[97] Philips Report, para.3.96.
[98] As has been seen, the phrase "police detention" as defined in s.118(2) covers a person who is taken to a police station under arrest or who is arrested there after coming voluntarily to the police station. It therefore does not cover the time that a suspect is at court.

above, detention can be authorised in some cases for up to an overall maximum of 96 hours, but after 36 hours it requires the permission of the magistrates' court. Detention under the Terrorism Act 2000 is separate from detention under PACE and very occasionally it has happened that a suspect has been held consecutively under the two regimes for a total in excess of the maximum detention time allowed under the "terrorism regime".[99] It has not been determined whether this is lawful.

Subsection (2) defines the time from which the period of detention is to be calculated (the "relevant time"). The normal case, in para.(d), is where the arrest takes place locally for an offence committed in the same area. In such a case time starts to run from the moment that the arrested person arrives at the first police station after his arrest. This applies even if he has to be taken to another, possibly quite distant, police station in the same force area for questioning.

When the person is arrested outside England and Wales, time starts to run from the moment that he arrives at the first police station to which he is taken in the area in which the offence for which he was arrested is being investigated, or 24 hours after his arrival in England and Wales, whichever is the earlier. In the unlikely event that he has not arrived at his destination within 24 hours of entering England and Wales, time therefore starts to run at that point (s.41(2)(b)).

4–57   If, at any stage of being in police detention, the detainee is taken to a hospital for medical treatment, time involved in travel there or back or at the hospital counts if he is actually being questioned about any offence but not otherwise (subs.(6)). Code C, para.14.2 states that a person in police detention in hospital "may not be questioned without the agreement of a responsible doctor". If a person who has been arrested is in a hospital for many hours under police guard the duty of periodic review of the need for further detention under s.40 applies even though the detention clock is not running.

In the case of somebody already under arrest who is then arrested for further offences under s.31, time runs from the first offence for which he was brought into custody (subs.(4)). Otherwise time could be extended by the simple expedient of adding more and more arrests. Nor can extra time be obtained for investigating the further offences by "notionally" giving the suspect bail in respect of such offences. That would be a stratagem to evade the PACE provision. Subject to what is said below, there can be only one relevant time for all offences for which a suspect is under arrest. The solution to the problem, if there is not sufficient time to investigate the further offences, is to charge for the first offence, to bring the suspect before the magistrates and to apply for a remand in custody to police cells ("three-day lie down") to permit further investigation into the other matters—see further below.[1]

For someone who comes to the police station voluntarily, time starts to run from the moment of his arrest (subs.2(c)).

---

[99] In Brown (1993), out of 253 terrorism detainees there were 10 who had previously been held for non-terrorist offences under PACE. In seven of these cases the period of PACE detention was under six hours. In two, PACE detention was for over 30 hours and in one it was over 40 hours. There were four cases in which overall detention was for more than seven days. The longest in the sample was eight days and three hours (p.53).

[1] As has been seen, a person who is at court after being charged is not in police detention (s.118(2)), so the detention clock stops.

But what if the arrested person is actually wanted by police in some other area?[2] According to para.(a) of subs.(2), if the arrested person is arrested in one police area in England and Wales but is wanted in another, time starts to run when he comes into the custody of the second police force or after 24 hours, whichever is the earlier.[3]

This is stated to be on the assumption that the force which has first arrested **4–58** him make no inquiries into the alleged offence. If they in fact do start to question him after he has been arrested about the offence for which they arrested him, then time starts to run under para.(c) from the time that he first comes to a police station in the first area (subs.(3)(c)).

Code C states, however, that if a person has been arrested by one police force on behalf of another and lawful detention under s.37 has not yet commenced, he may not be questioned whilst in transit except to clarify a voluntary statement (para.14.1).

If the suspect is wanted for questioning both where he is and in another area, there would in effect be two relevant times. In relation to the second area, again providing the suspect is not questioned in the first area or en route, the relevant time would be 24 hours after leaving the first area or the moment of arriving at any police station in the second area, whichever was the earlier (subs.(5)).

Taking an intimate or non-intimate sample in force area A from a suspect being transferred to force area B is not "questioning" causing the detention clock to start.[4]

The time-limit provisions of PACE do not apply to a suspect who is at the police station after arrest on a warrant since he is not "in police detention" as defined (s.118(2)). Such a person must be brought before a court as soon as practicable. But if a decision is taken to also arrest him for an offence whilst he is at the police station, the relevant time would be from the time of that arrest.

Authorisation of continued detention: s.42[5]

Section 42 permits an officer of the rank of superintendent or above to authorise **4–59** the detention of a person without charge beyond 24 hours and up to 36 hours if this is necessary for the effective investigation of a serious arrestable offence (defined in Sch.5 and s.116). (But see para.4–62 below for its extension to all arrestable offences by the Criminal Justice Act 2003.) No one may be detained beyond 24 hours without such authorisation. Authorisation requires an overt act. It cannot take place silently in a decision by the officer which is not communicated.[6]

[2] This problem does not occur in Northern Ireland since the whole province is one police force area.
[3] It seems that the numbers transferred from one force to another are very low. In a sample of 5,500 prisoners in 10 force areas 1.5% had been transferred from custody in one area to another: Brown (1989), p.16, n.13.
[4] *DPP v Davis* [1992] Crim.L.R. 911 is applicable by analogy. In that case it was held that the contemporaneous recording of procedures under ss.7 and 8 of the Road Traffic Act 1988 involving taking of specimens did not constitute an interview.
[5] See 1989 N.I. PACE Order, Art.43.
[6] *Maughan's Application, Re* [1998] N.I. 293, QBD (NI), Crown Side.

The preconditions are that the senior officer must be satisfied that the investigation is being conducted diligently and expeditiously and that the detention of the suspect is still necessary to secure or preserve evidence relating to the offence or to obtain such evidence by questioning him (subs.(1)). The review must be conducted in person rather than on the telephone or by video link (Code C, Note 15F).

Such an authorisation may not be given more than 24 hours after time has started to run in regard to detention nor before the second review of detention under s.40 has taken place (subs.(4)). The purpose of the latter limitation is to ensure that continued detention is not authorised prematurely. If detention is authorised for less than the full 36 hours it may later be extended up to the 36 hours providing the conditions set out in subs.(1) still apply (subs.(2)). It does not follow that if the superintendent authorises detention for the full 36 hours, unexpired time cannot be utilised in the same way. That would be a possible interpretation of subs.(2) but it would make no sense. (On utilising the unexpired time see further paras 4–85—4–86 below.)

4–60 When authorisation for continued detention has been given, the suspect must be told the grounds of the decision and they must be recorded in the custody record (subs.(5)).

The section also requires the police again to give the suspect (or his solicitor or, in the discretion of the custody officer, other persons interested in his welfare) an opportunity to make oral or written representations (subs.(6)). The requirement to allow representations to be made is mandatory. Failure to comply with it can be fatal to any application by the police to magistrates for extra time to question the suspect. In a 1998 case in Northern Ireland the Divisional Court granted a habeas corpus application by a suspect whose further detention had been approved by the chief inspector at 8.20 pm but the suspect and his solicitor had not been informed of this until 9.45 pm. They had had no opportunity to make any representations.[7]

The right of the suspect himself to make oral representations can be withheld if the police officer concerned considers that he is unfit by reason of his condition or behaviour (subs.(8)). If the suspect has not yet exercised his rights under ss.56 or 58 (to have someone informed of his whereabouts and to have legal advice) the officer must remind him of those rights (including the fact that legal advice is free—Code C, para.15.3) and decide whether he should be allowed to exercise them.

His decision must be recorded in the custody record, as must the reasons if he is refused permission (subs.(9)). The record should show the number of hours and minutes by which the period of detention without charge is extended (Code C, para.15.16).

A person who has not been charged must be released within 36 hours after the detention clock has started to run unless further detention has been authorised by magistrates under s.43 (s.42(10)). If he has been charged, s.46 applies (see para.4–79 below).

4–61 A person who has been released may not be re-arrested for the same offence unless new evidence justifying a further arrest has come to light since his release

---

[7] *Maughan's Application, Re* [1998] N.I. 293, QBD (NI). See also "In the matter of an application for a warrant of further detention" [1988] Crim.L.R. 296.

(subs.(11)). (But he can be re-arrested for failing to answer to police bail.[8]) As has been seen, a person who has been released on bail pending further inquiries and who answers to his bail is treated as having been arrested for that offence.[9] It does not follow that unexpired time on the detention clock can automatically be utilised. The suspect has been released because there were no longer grounds to hold him in police detention. When he answers to his bail the question of whether there are grounds for his further detention must be considered afresh. But if such grounds do exist, the maximum time available for such further detention is the unexpired time.

Note that s.42 has nothing to do with the question of the moment in time that a suspect has to be charged. In *Samuel* the superintendent delayed charging a suspect in the belief that she was exercising a power granted by s.42. The Court of Appeal held that this was mistaken. ("We cannot accept this argument. In our judgment s.42 is dealing, and dealing only, with authorisation of continued detention and does not give the police any power to delay charging someone where the police have sufficient evidence to charge."[10])

The Act specifically states that the duty to authorise continued detention requires the authority of a superintendent "who is responsible for the police station at which a person is detained" (s.42(1)). This requirement has not been diluted in light of recent changes in command areas and rank structures, which have resulted in reductions in the numbers of superintendents. It should be noted, however, that under s.107(1) (see para.10–02 below), a chief inspector may act as a superintendent if properly authorised to do so. There is no judicial authority as to what is meant here by being "responsible" for the police station in question and, in particular, whether it is lawful to have an "on call" superintendent for PACE matters for several police stations or covering more than one division. It may be that the courts would recognise a distinction between "on call" just for PACE matters and "on call" for a range of operational matters going beyond mere PACE matters.

Authorisation extended to all arrestable offences

The Criminal Justice Act 2003 provided that the superintendent's authorisation applies to all arrestable offences—not just, as before, to serious arrestable offences.[11] The provision derived from a recommendation of the Joint Home Office/Cabinet Office Review of PACE. The Joint Review's report (p.25) said: **4–62**

> "The police, in particular ACPO, argue that the initial detention period of twenty-four hours can provide insufficient time in which to conclude the investigative process and charge a detained person because of delays elsewhere in the custody process. For example, obtaining the services of an appropriate adult, police surgeon or interpreter or where a suspect is initially unfit for

---

[8] Amendment to subs.(11) of s.42 made by CJPOA, s.29(4)(b). On the power of the police to arrest for failure to answer bail see para.4–80 below.

[9] PACE, s.34(7).

[10] [1988] Q.B. 615 at 623, CA.

[11] s.7 of the Act replaced s.42(1)(b) with "(b) an offence for which he is under arrest is an arrestable offence".

interview because of alcohol or drugs intoxication. Delays linked to the provision of legal advice can also put pressure on the custody clock."

The "Options Proposed" were to extend the maximum time for which someone may potentially be detained without charge from 24 to 36 hours for any arrestable offence; to stop the custody clock as/when prescribed delays occur; and to seek to extend the detention clock at the end of 24 hours to make up for hours lost to delay during the initial period of detention.

The Joint Review adopted the first but rejected the second and third of these options. In regard to the two stopping of the detention clock proposals it said (p.26) that they could increase the administrative burdens in the custody suite to an unworkable level. Also, "stopping the clock" could lead to further delay through challenges by suspects and legal advisers. Extending the time for which someone could be detained was the more open and transparent option. It would require little additional recording of information. It recognised, however, concerns expressed by the Youth Justice Board about such an extension for juveniles and suggested that consideration be given to providing additional safeguards for them. New para.15.2A inserted in the 2004 revision of Code C said that detaining a juvenile or a mentally vulnerable person for longer than 24 hours will be dependent on the circumstances of the case and with regard to the person's (a) special vulnerability, (b) the legal obligation to provide an opportunity for representations to be made prior to the decision to extend detention, (c) the need to consult the views of any appropriate adult, and (d) any alternatives to police custody.

Reduce authorisation level to inspector?

4–63   The Joint Review considered but rejected the proposal that authorisation of detention from 24 hours to 36 hours could be given by an inspector. ACPO had suggested that fixing authority levels nationally was not sensitive to the variation in access to ranked officers across the country and that guidance on authority levels should be set internally to take account of local factors. The Joint Review said (p.27), "The view of the Review team is that authority levels are now pitched appropriately . . . Certain key decisions impinging on a detainee's basic rights should be taken on the basis of sufficient seniority and independence."

Terrorism investigations

4–64   Under the Prevention of Terrorism Acts (PTA) the initial period of detention that could be authorised by the police was 48 hours, and thereafter the Secretary of State could authorise further detention for up to a further five days, making an overall maximum of seven days. (It is now 14 days, see para.4–74 below.) In 1988 the European Court of Human Rights in *Brogan v United Kingdom*[12] held that detention for four days and six hours without judicial authorisation breached Art.5(3) of the ECHR. The then Conservative Government thereupon entered a derogation to the Convention on the ground that terrorism investigations required more time.

---

[12] (1989) 11 E.H.R.R. 117.

In its 1998 Consultation Paper *Legislation Against Terrorism* (Cm.4178), the Labour Government said that the Government agreed with the view expressed by Lord Lloyd of Berwick in his 1996 *Inquiry into Legislation Against Terrorism* (Cm.3420) that it was not practicable to reduce the initial period of police detention from 48 hours to the 36 hours allowed under PACE. Lord Lloyd had rejected such reduction as impracticable in view of the time needed to transfer terrorism suspects to high security facilities for questioning and to carry out the necessary reception and identification procedures following arrest. This view was reflected in the Terrorism Act 2000 which preserved the period of initial police detention of 48 hours—measured from the time of arrest.[13]

Detention during that 48-hour period is subject to the PACE rules requiring **4–65** periodic review and the release of the suspect if there are no longer valid reasons to hold him. But review periods are somewhat different. The first review must be carried out "as soon as is reasonably practicable after the time of the person's arrest"[14] (where under PACE, s.40 it must be within six hours). Thereafter, reviews must be carried out not less than every 12 hours—compared with nine hours under PACE. There is the same provision for postponement of the review as under PACE (s.40(4)).[15] A review in the first 24 hours must be carried out by an officer at least of the rank of inspector. Thereafter, reviews must be carried out by an officer at least of the rank of superintendent.[16]

Before reaching a decision the review officer must give the suspect or a solicitor "representing him who is available at the time of the review" the opportunity of making either oral or written representations—though representations from the detainee can be denied if the review officer considers that he is unfit to make them "because of his condition or behaviour".[17]

A written record must be made of the outcome of the review, including, if applicable, the grounds upon which continued detention is authorised, in which case the suspect must be told of the reason why.[18]

Under PACE a review officer may only authorise continued detention if the provisions of s.37(2) still apply. Under the Terrorism Act, a review officer may authorise continued detention also pending a decision by the Secretary of State regarding deportation or pending a decision whether the suspect is to be charged. As under PACE, before approving continued detention the review officer must be satisfied that the matter is being dealt with "diligently and expeditously".[19]

Warrants of further detention: s.43[20]

Section 43 deals with the hearing before a magistrates' court to decide whether **4–66** the police can hold the suspect for longer after the initial 36 hours without charge.

---

[13] Terrorism Act 2000, s.41(3).
[14] Terrorism Act 2000, Sch.8, para.21.
[15] Terrorism Act 2000, Sch.8, para.21.
[16] Terrorism Act 2000, Sch.8, para.24.
[17] Terrorism Act 2000, Sch.8, para.26(3).
[18] Terrorism Act 2000, Sch.8, para.28.
[19] Terrorism Act 2000, Sch.8, para.23(2).
[20] See 1989 N.I. PACE Order, Art.44.

If so, the magistrates grant a warrant of further detention (and later perhaps an extension of the warrant: see s.44 below). By contrast, the authority of a superintendent to continue holding a suspect for longer than 24 hours in the police station is called, as has been seen, authorisation of continued detention.

An application for permission to hold the suspect beyond 36 hours must be made on oath, and *inter partes*, to a magistrates' court. It must be supported by an information from the police officer, a copy of which must have been supplied in advance to the detainee. The court cannot start the hearing unless the suspect has a copy and he is physically present (subs.(2)). If he does not have a lawyer and wishes to have one, the hearing has to be adjourned. The lawyer at the hearing is free, regardless of whether the detainee uses his own or the Duty Solicitor—just like legal advice at the police station. He can be kept in police custody during such an adjournment (subs.(3)). If satisfied that there are sufficient grounds, the court may issue a warrant of further detention (subs.(1)). The tests for the magistrates are exactly the same as those for the superintendent considering further detention under s.42(1)[21]: that detention is necessary to secure or preserve evidence relating to a serious arrestable offence for which he is under arrest or to obtain such evidence by questioning him and that the investigation is being conducted diligently and expeditiously.

The court would clearly be entitled to take into account the suspect's response to police questioning. If, therefore, the evidence was that he had refused to answer all or most questions and if the court took the view that the real purpose of prolonging his detention was to break down his silence it would presumably refuse to grant the police application for further time. (This should still be so even now that the so-called right to silence has been abolished—see below.) At the Committee stage of the Bill in the House of Commons the Opposition tried to persuade the Government to accept an amendment which would have required the magistrates, when considering an application for a warrant of further detention, to have regard specifically to whether the detainee was answering questions willingly. The Government refused to accept the amendment.

4–67 But the then Home Office Minister, Mr Douglas Hurd, made it clear that the principle was accepted:

> "I do not doubt that in practice when interpreting the Bill the court would ask questions and want to hear evidence on how fruitful interviews had been if the application for further detention were based on this ground. That would clearly be an important consideration, and evidence on this subject—because we are talking of an *inter partes* hearing—would be given by the detained person who would be present and would be legally represented."[22]

Mr Hurd then referred to the fact (already mentioned above) that the phrase in the Act was that detention for questioning must be "*necessary* to secure or preserve evidence relating to an offence . . . or to obtain such evidence by questioning him" (italics supplied), not that such questioning would be "desirable, convenient or a good idea".[23] He also drew the attention of the Opposition spokesman to the

---

[21] See para.4–59 above.
[22] House of Commons, *Hansard*, Standing Committee E, February 16, 1984, cols 1228–1229.
[23] House of Commons, *Hansard*, Standing Committee E, February 16, 1984, col.1229.

provision in the Bill (now s.43(14)) which laid down what the police officer had to specify in the way of information in support of an application. Sub-paragraph (d) said the police must give "the reasons for believing the continued detention of that person to be necessary"—"again not convenient, desirable or a good idea but necessary"—for the purposes of such further inquiries. A court, he said, would need to be satisfied on those points.[24] However, whether these tests are stringently applied is uncertain. As will be seen, it is very rare for such applications to be refused. (In *Magennis v Chief Constable of the Royal Ulster Constabulary*[25] Shiel J. referred to a statement by a police witness that one suspect had started answering questions after maintaining silence for no less than six days!)

Timing of applications

An application for a warrant of further detention may be made at any time before the detention clock has run for 36 hours, or, if it is not practicable for a court to sit when the 36 hours expires but it can sit within six hours of that time, up to six hours after the expiry of the 36 hours (subs.(5)). In other words, where the 36-hour limit would expire, say, at 5 am, the police can exceed the 36-hour limit by up to six hours. If the suspect is held in police custody for more than 36 hours, the fact and the reason must be recorded in the custody record (subs.(6)).   **4–68**

But this extra time has to be regarded as available only in special circumstances. If the court thinks that the police could and should have brought the application within the 36-hour period, they must dismiss the application—and as a result the suspect would have to be released (subs.(7)).

In *R. v Slough JJ., Ex p. Stirling*[26] the application was made two hours after the expiry of the 36 hour period. The 36 hours expired at 12.53 pm. The clerk of the magistrates asked them to hear it a few minutes before this. At that time the court was sitting but it postponed hearing the application until after lunch and actually heard the case at 2.45 pm. They granted the police extra time. The Divisional Court allowed an application for judicial review on the ground that the police could have made their application for extra time between 10.30 am and 11.30 am.

The commentary in the *Criminal Law Review* suggested that the decision "throws the whole system into unpredictable chaos" by saying that a court can legitimately postpone the hearing into the six-hour period of extra time beyond the 36-hour period and then refuse it because it could have been made earlier. The simple solution it was suggested would be to regard the application as made when the officer asked the court to consider it. But that is not the position under s.43. This was made clear by *R. v Sedgefield Justices, Ex p. Milne*.[27] In that case the police contacted the court for a hearing at around 9 am. The 36-hour period was due to expire at 10.48 am. The court sat at noon but the hearing only took place at 12.54 pm. The court thought it was legitimately within the extra six-hour period. The Divisional Court said that the application was made when the police actually gave evidence. In this instance the police had acted reasonably but the   **4–69**

---

[24] House of Commons, *Hansard*, Standing Committee E, February 16, 1984, col.1229.
[25] Unreported, April 30, 1998, QBD.
[26] [1987] Crim.L.R. 576, DC.
[27] Unreported, Lexis, November 5, 1987, DC.

court criticised the magistrates for not hearing the application sooner ("magistrates should perhaps be more open than the magistrates were on this occasion to the possibility of dealing with an application such as this at the first available opportunity"). The Police and Criminal Evidence Act 1984 laid down a precise timescale. The court had received the information about the need for a hearing at around 9 am. There was a court due to sit at 10 am. There was no sufficient reason to postpone the hearing until the end of the morning. So there is considerable pressure on the courts to have the hearing as soon as possible.

These hearings may require the court to sit at unsociable hours. But the Note for Guidance in Code C states that applications for a warrant of further detention (or its extension) should be made between 10 am and 9 pm and, if possible, during court hours (Note 15D).

The court's decision

4–70 Under subs.(8), if the court is not satisfied that the further detention of the suspect is justified, it must either dismiss the application and thereby require the release of the suspect or, if time permits, adjourn the hearing until some later stage in the 36-hour period. (Obviously the latter would only be possible if the application has been made well prior to the expiry of the 36-hour period.)

The warrant of further detention must state the time at which it is issued and shall authorise the further detention of the suspect for whatever period the magistrates think—up to a maximum of 36 hours (subss.(10), (11) and (12)). The court can take into account the fact that the police intend to move the suspect to a different police area (subs.(13)).

Any information for the purpose of this section must be on oath in writing and must state the nature of the offence, the general nature of the evidence on which the suspect was arrested, what inquiries have already and are still to be made, and the reasons why further detention is necessary for the purpose of such further inquiries (subs.(14)). When an application is refused, the suspect must then immediately be either charged or released, on bail or unconditionally, unless subs.(16) applies (subs.(15)). Subsection (16) permits the police to continue to hold the suspect for the full initial 36-hour period notwithstanding that permission to hold him longer than 36 hours from the relevant time has not been granted by the magistrates. This would obviously only apply where application had been made to the magistrate well before the expiry of the 36 hours and where a superintendent had authorised continued detention from the 24-hour to the 36-hour point. The right to hold him for the whole of the 36-hour period is so that the police are not penalised for making an early application. The court is asked whether he can be held beyond 36 hours from the relevant time. A refusal does not mean that detention up to 36 hours is improper.

4–71 A form of warrant of further detention and the endorsement to be used where a magistrates' court extends a warrant further are provided in the Schedule to the Magistrates' Courts (Forms) (Amendment) Rules 1985 which amended the Magistrates' Courts (Forms) Rules 1981.

It is important for a solicitor acting in an application for a warrant of further detention to insist that he be given reasonable time to take instructions and to prepare his argument. It seems that sometimes the solicitor is expected to be ready within minutes of seeing his client.[28] The solicitor should ask to have a sight of the custody record form. (The notice given to suspects on arrival at the police station states that the custody record form will be available if the suspect is taken before a court.)

There is no valid reason why the magistrates on such a hearing should be informed of the suspect's previous convictions. His record is not relevant to the issue before the court: namely, whether further detention is still necessary to secure or preserve evidence relating to an offence for which he is under arrest or to obtain such evidence by questioning him; whether the offence is a serious arrestable offence; and whether the inquiry is being conducted diligently and expeditiously.[29]

Obviously, the solicitor acting for the suspect will need to check the custody record form to see that the requirements of the Code have been strictly adhered to. If he cannot persuade the court to refuse the application, he may at least succeed in getting a warrant that extends the period of detention by something less than the maximum of 36 hours.

The right to continue to hold the suspect is of course subject to the overriding principles stated in s.34(2) that the suspect must always be released if there do not appear to be any sufficient grounds to hold him any longer and in s.40 that the need for further detention must be reviewed periodically.

Where an application has been refused by the court, the police cannot make a **4–72** further application unless further evidence has come to light (subs.(17)). There is no right of appeal.

If a warrant of further detention is issued, the person concerned must be released on or before its expiry unless he has previously been charged (in which case ss.38, 40 and 46 apply) or an extension has been obtained (subs.(18)). Someone who has been released on or before the expiry of a warrant of further detention cannot be re-arrested without a warrant for the same offence unless new evidence has come to light (subs.(19) paralleling s.41(9)).

Terrorism cases

As has been seen, the authority for extending detention in terrorist investigations **4–73** under the Prevention of Terrorism legislation was the Home Secretary and the period of time for which such detention could be authorised was five days in addition to the initial period of 48 hours—making seven days in all.

Lord Lloyd, in his 1996 *Inquiry into Legislation Against Terrorism*[30] recommended that in terrorism cases applications for extensions of detention should instead be heard by the Chief Metropolitan Stipendiary Magistrate, and his equivalent in Scotland and Northern Ireland, or a nominated deputy. The Labour Government in its 1998 Consultation Paper *Legislation Against Terrorism*[31] suggested that it was doubtful whether one person, even with a deputy, could deal with the caseload. (It also suggested that wholly *ex parte* proceedings might not conform to the requirement in Art.5(3) of the ECHR that a detained person

[28] John Clegg, "Warrants of further detention" (1988) 132 S.J. 278 at 280.
[29] John Clegg, "Warrants of further detention" (1988) 132 S.J. 278 at 280.
[30] 1996, Cm.3420.
[31] 1998, Cm.4178.

should be brought promptly before a judicial authority.) An alternative, the Consultation Paper suggested, would be to create an independent Commission to hear applications for extensions of detention in terrorist cases. The members would be legally qualified. If they were serving on the bench, practical difficulties would be caused by the fact that they would not be able to take part in any subsequent proceedings against that individual. The problem of numbers, a factor especially in Northern Ireland, could be addressed by utilising retired lawyers, judges and magistrates. There could be one Commission for England, Scotland and Northern Ireland. A third option would be to have a different model for each jurisdiction.

4–74   In the event, however, despite its initial reservations, the Government adopted Lord Lloyd's suggestion. The Terrorism Act 2000 provides that after the period of initial police detention of up to 48 hours, detention for up to seven days can be authorised by what the Act calls "a judicial authority".[32] A judicial authority means in England and Wales the Senior District Judge (Chief Magistrate)[33] or his deputy designated for this purpose by the Lord Chancellor.[34] In Scotland it means a sheriff and in Northern Ireland a county court judge or resident magistrate designated for the purpose by the Lord Chancellor.[35]

As to the length of detention, Lord Lloyd thought that once lasting peace had been established in Northern Ireland it should be possible to reduce the overall maximum period of detention to four days, which was the maximum period in practice observed in international terrorism cases. Initially the Government decided to stick with seven days as the maximum period but as noted, it extended this to 14 days in the Criminal Justice Act 2003, s.306.[36] Fourteen days are measured from the time of arrest. If the suspect had previously been detained at a port or airport under Sch.7 to the Terrorism Act 2000, the 14 days are measured from the commencement of the examining officer's examination of the suspect at the port or airport.[37]

An application for a warrant of further detention beyond 48 hours can only be made by an officer of the rank of superintendent or above. It must be made within the 48-hour period allowed for initial detention—though, as under PACE, an extra six hours is allowed unless the judicial authority considers that it was reasonably practicable to make the application within the 48-hour period.

Extension of warrants of further detention: s.44[38]

4–75   The police can apply to the magistrates for one or more further extensions of the time period up to the limit of 96 hours. The length of any such extension is at the

---

[32] Terrorism Act 2000, Sch.8, para.29(3).
[33] Formerly the Chief Metropolitan Stipendiary Magistrate. Stipendiary Magistrates became District Judges (Magistrates' Courts) by virtue of the Access to Justice Act 1999, s.78.
[34] Terrorism Act 2000, Sch.8, para.29(4).
[35] Terrorism Act 2000, Sch.8, para.29(4).
[36] Inserting a new subss.(3A) and (3B) in para.36 of Sch.8 to the Terrorism Act 2000.
[37] Sch.7, para.2 gives the examining officer the power to question a person for the purpose of determining whether he appears to be someone who is or has been concerned in the commission, preparation or instigation of acts of terrorism.
[38] See 1989 N.I. PACE Order, Art.45.

discretion of the magistrates, save that no single extension can be for more than 36 hours. Such an application must again be made at an *inter partes* hearing and the suspect is entitled to be legally represented. There must again be an information under oath. Subsections (2), (3) and (14) of s.43 apply to such a hearing. If the application is refused the suspect must be either charged or released (subs.(7)), save that he can be held for the full period allowed by the previous application to the court (subs.(8)).

Detention before charge supplementary: s.45[39]

This section makes it clear that a magistrates' court for the purposes of this Part   **4–76**
of the Act means a court sitting with two or more justices in private.

It also states that references to periods of time or times of day shall be treated as approximate only. Police officers therefore do not have to worry if they slightly exceed any specified time limit. It is for the courts to determine what degree of slippage will be regarded as venial. The Home Office Minister assured the House of Commons that there was no suggestion that this would be abused:

> "The Hon. Lady . . . will accept that in some matters that we have discussed where time limits are contained in the Bill, it is difficult to operate by a stop-watch. It should not be a matter of seconds or minutes either way. There will be circumstances when it would not be entirely reasonable to expect absolute and complete exactitude. That is why the word 'approximate' is in the clause. I do not believe that a court will give much leeway because of that word. . . . We do not intend that the word should be used to undermine the important safeguards in the Bill. Equally, I hope that she will accept that some policing matters cannot be conducted with an exact regard for seconds or a few minutes."[40]

Video links and video conferencing for detention decisions: s.45A

As was seen above (para.4–50), this new section was inserted into PACE by the   **4–77**
Criminal Justice and Police Act 2001, s.73. It authorises the Home Secretary to promulgate regulations permitting certain functions relating to arrested persons in police stations to be performed by an officer at a different police station through video-conferencing facilities. In relation to an arrested person taken to a non-designated police station the functions in questions are all the duties of the custody officer under ss.37, 38 or 40. In relation to arrested persons at designated police stations the function in question is the review of detention under s.40(1)(b). As noted above, reviews of detention by video were terminated in 2004 pending evaluation of the pilot study.

---

[39] See 1989 N.I. PACE Order, Art.46.
[40] House of Commons, *Hansard*, Standing Committee E, February 21, 1984, cols 1260–1261.

The function of making the necessary record falls to an officer who is at the police station where the arrested person is held at the instance of the officer at the other end of the video link (s.45A(5)).

Any representations by the arrested person or his solicitor under ss.40(12) and (13) are to be made either by way of the video link or by fax or email (s.45A(7)).

Terrorism cases

4–78   The Criminal Justice and Police Act 2001, s.75 also permits judicial extensions of detention proceedings in terrorism cases to be conducted by video link. Previously, such decisions were taken by the Home Secretary but, as has been seen (para.4–74 above), under the Terrorism Act 2000 they are now taken by a judicial authority. The provisions in s.75 of the CJPA insert new sub-paras (4) to (9) in para.33 of Sch.8 to the Terrorism Act 2000. The provisions only apply, however, where the Secretary of State has notified the judicial authority that the requisite facilities are in place. Also, the judicial authority has a discretion as to whether a video link should be used, having heard representations as to venue from the detainee and the applicant. He must be satisfied that the detainee can see and hear proceedings and can be seen and heard.

Detention after charge: s.46[41]

4–79   Section 46 clarifies the law as to when a person must be brought before a court after he has been charged. Broadly, it provides that he must be brought before a court within 36 hours.

The basic provision is subs.(2) which states that he must be brought before a court "as soon as is practicable" but this hallowed phrase is amplified by the additional provision "and in any event not later than the first sitting after he is charged with the offence". If there is no sitting arranged for the day when he is charged or the next day the custody officer must inform the clerk to the justices so that a special sitting can be arranged (subs.(3)).

If the suspect is to appear at a court in a different part of the country, he must be taken there as soon as is practicable and must similarly be brought before a court there as soon as is practicable—and in any event not later than the first sitting in that area after his arrival (subs.(4)). Subsection (5) requires the police to inform the justices' clerk if there is no sitting scheduled for that day or the next day. When the clerk to the justices has received information under subs.(3) or (5), he is under a duty to arrange a special sitting of the court for the day after the charge (or in the case of the person brought from a different part of the country, the day after his arrival in the area where he is to come before the court).[42] Sundays, Good Friday and Christmas Day can be ignored in this context

---

[41] See 1989 N.I. PACE Order, Art.47.
[42] For administrative problems created by the provisions see *R. v Avon Magistrates' Courts Committee, Ex p. Bath Law Society* [1988] Q.B. 409, DC; *R. v Avon Magistrates' Courts Committee, Ex p. Broome* [1988] 1 W.L.R. 1246, DC.

(subss.(6), (7) and (8)). A person in hospital need not be brought to court if he is not well enough (subs.(9)).

Arrest for failure to answer police bail: s.46A

The Criminal Justice and Public Order Act 1994 added a new section to PACE **4–80** giving the police a power they previously did not have to arrest a person who fails to answer police bail.[43] The Criminal Justice Act 2003 extended this to a person released on bail pending a decision by the CPS on charging where a police officer has reasonable grounds for suspecting that the person has broken any of the conditions of bail.[44] (As will be seen below (para.4–83) there is no general power to arrest for breach of conditions of bail imposed by the police. For the purposes of ss.30 and 31 of PACE such an arrest is to be treated as an arrest for an offence. The arrested person should be taken as soon as practicable to the police station appointed as the place where he was supposed to surrender to custody.[45])

For the purposes of the provisions in Pt IV of PACE regarding police detention, a person arrested for failing to answer police bail is to be treated as arrested for the offence in connection with which he was granted bail.[46] He must as soon as practicable be taken to the police station at which he was supposed to attend.

If it transpires that he is wanted in connection with failure to answer bail at more than one police station he would be deemed to have been arrested for the different offences. But the arrest for each such offence could be staged *seriatim* so that each further arrest takes place immediately before release on the earlier arrest.[47] There is, however, only the original detention clock running.

Bail after arrest: s.47[48]

Release on bail by the police under this part of PACE is stated to be under the **4–81** ordinary provisions of the Bail Act 1976 (s.47(1)). The purpose of police bail is to permit release of the suspect pending inquiries into the matter including inquiries as to whether any and, if so, what offence(s) should be charged.

There is nothing wrong with a person being arrested for one offence, bailed and then charged later with a different offence arising out of those same facts.

---

[43] s.46A added to PACE by s.29(2) of the CJPOA. In Northern Ireland not only do the police have the same power but it is an offence to abscond whilst on bail—Criminal Justice (N.I.) Order, 2003, Arts 5 and 6.
[44] s.46A(1A) added by Criminal Justice Act 2003, Sch.2, para.5.
[45] s.46A(1) and (2) of PACE added by CJPOA, s.29(2). For the equivalent change in Northern Ireland see Police (Amendment) (Northern Ireland) Order 1995, Art.7.
[46] New s.34(7) of PACE added by the CJPOA, s.29(3).
[47] See *Samuel* [1988] Q.B. 615, CA.
[48] See 1989 N.I. PACE Order, Art.48. As amended by Criminal Justice (N.I.) Order 2003 (SI 2003/1247), Art.8.

Police bail on conditions

4–82   Prior to 1994 the police had no power to release someone on bail subject to conditions. The Criminal Justice and Public Order Act 1994, s.27 gave the police that power for persons who have been charged.[49] The Criminal Justice Act 2003 extended it also to persons released on bail pending a decision by the CPS as to what, if any, charges should be laid.[50] Bail subject to conditions can now be granted by a custody officer for any offence whether imprisonable or not. The conditions available are broadly the same as those that can be imposed by a court under the Bail Act 1976[51] but the police cannot require a person to reside at a bail hostel nor to attend anywhere for the preparation of psychiatric or other reports.[52] Nor can a police officer impose a condition, as can a court, for the defendant to attend an interview with a lawyer for the purposes of seeking legal advice.[53] Conditions should not be imposed unless it is necessary to secure:

     (i)   that the person surrenders to custody;

     (ii)   that he does not commit an offence while on bail; or

     (iii)   that he does not interfere with witnesses or otherwise obstruct the course of justice.[54]

Examples of normal conditions imposed would be to report to the police station, to surrender a passport, to reside at a particular address, to comply with curfew requirements, or not to go to a particular place or to see particular people, such as the apparent victim. If it is believed that the person will abscond, a surety or sureties and/or financial security can be required. The previous restriction that financial security could be required from the accused only if it appeared likely that he would leave the country has now gone.[55] The security can be in the form of money or whatever other money's worth is considered appropriate—though the money does not actually have to be produced; a promise to pay is usually sufficient. In juvenile cases, the parent or guardian who consents to be a surety cannot be bound for a sum greater than £50.[56]

The conditions can be varied by the same or a different custody officer—as well as by a court. But the variation may consist in imposing more as well as less onerous conditions.[57]

---

[49] CJPOA, s.27(1) which added a new subs.(1A) to s.47 of PACE giving the "normal powers to impose conditions of bail" where the custody officer releases a person under s.38 (*i.e.* after charge). The normal powers are those given by s.3(6) of the Bail Act 1976.
[50] Criminal Justice Act 2003, Sch.2, para.6(3) amending s.47(1A).
[51] The change was proposed by the Runciman Royal Commission—see Runciman Report, p.73, para.33.
[52] CJPOA 1994, s.27(3).
[53] Magistrates can now impose such a condition under the Crime and Disorder Act 1998, s.54(2).
[54] Bail Act 1976, s.3A(5) added by the CJPOA, s.27(3).
[55] Crime and Disorder Act 1998, s.54(1).
[56] Bail Act 1976, s.3(7).
[57] Bail Act 1976, s.3A(4) added by the CJPOA, s.27(3).

Bucke and Brown (1997) found that 80 per cent of those charged were given bail by the police and 17 per cent got bail subject to conditions (p.64). But, they said, "the use of bail with conditions has not substantially reduced the proportion of suspects detained after charge" (*ibid.*). In other words it seems that bail with conditions is used primarily for people who previously would have been released unconditionally—which is not what was intended.

No arrest for breach of conditions

There are no penalties for breach of conditions of bail nor can the person be   **4–83** arrested for actual or imminent breach of conditions imposed by the police. The police do have the power to arrest someone on bail if they have reasonable grounds for believing that he has broken or is likely to break conditions of bail (Bail Act 1976, s.7(3)) but that power only applies where he is under a duty to surrender into the custody of a court. It therefore does not apply to someone bailed under a duty to surrender to the custody of the police. The only exception is where a person has been released on bail subject to conditions pending a decision by the CPS as to charging. In that case the police can arrest if the officer has reasonable grounds for suspecting that the suspect has broken any of the conditions of bail.[58]

As has been seen, however, the police do now have the power (under s.46A) to arrest someone for failure to answer police bail. A person given police bail can also be arrested if new evidence justifying a further arrest comes to light after his release (subs.(2)). This would constitute a new period of detention with the detention clock starting afresh. "New evidence" here means new relevant evidence and, probably, evidence that is admissible. If the police take fingerprints or other genetic material from the scene of the crime which have not been analysed when the suspect is bailed, it is arguable that there is "new evidence" when later analysis shows the prints or DNA to identify the bailed suspect, thus justifying his immediate arrest and the detention clock starting afresh. But the concept of re-arrest on new evidence which restarts the detention clock is obviously open to abuse. Surprisingly, the point has not yet come before the courts.

A person who comes back to the police station to answer to bail or is arrested there is "detained at a police station".

Continuing police bail

If the custody officer wishes at that point to reconsider whether or not to continue   **4–84** police bail, the only power to do so is under s.37(2). In other words, he can only detain in custody a suspect who has not been charged if he has reasonable grounds for believing that his detention "is necessary to secure or preserve evidence relating to an offence for which he is under arrest or to obtain such evidence by questioning him". If he was previously on police bail, it is unlikely that either condition will be met unless the release on bail was to permit the pursuit of other inquiries before having the suspect come back for further questioning.

---

[58] Criminal Justice Act 2003, Sch.2, para.5 inserting a new subs.(1A) into s.46A of PACE.

Unexpired time on detention clock

4–85 Can the police use unexpired time on the detention clock? The writer does not share the view held by some that if the release on bail occurs after the suspect has been held without charge for more than 24 hours—*i.e.* after the superintendent has authorised continued detention (under s.42) or a court has granted or extended a warrant of further detention (under ss.43 or 44)—any unexpired time on the detention clock is lost. He believes rather that the suspect who returns to the police station to answer to police bail, or after being arrested for failure to do so, can in principle be held for any unexpired time. This seems to be the clear implication of s.47(6) which states that any time in police detention prior to release on bail shall be counted in calculating time limits for detention. That necessarily implies a calculation of unexpired time. Of course, whether the unexpired time can be used also depends on a decision on the separate question as to the necessity for further detention which has to be made by the custody officer under s.37(2). (But see para.4–59 above.)

Does use of unexpired time require fresh authorisation and, if so, from whom?

4–86 The question of unexpired time on the detention clock can arise at different stages. One is where the suspect has been released on bail during the initial period of 24 hours—say, after eight hours of police detention. When he answers to bail (or is arrested for failure to answer bail), the unexpired time is the balance of time up to 24 hours—in that case, 16 hours. There is no need for authorisation for use of any part of that 16 hours other than the decision of the custody officer under s.37(2) and subsequent review by the review officer under s.40.

If the suspect who has been released on bail during the period of a superintendent's authorisation of continued detention beyond the 24 hours, answers to bail, the unexpired time is the balance of time between his release and the time period authorised. So, if the authority was for six hours beyond the 24 hours and he was released on bail four hours beyond the 24 hours, there would be two hours remaining on the clock. Use of that two hours would not require fresh authority of a superintendent. It could be authorised by the custody officer provided he is satisfied that the requirements of s.37(2) are fulfilled. But any extension from the 30-hour point to the 36-hour point would require a fresh authorisation from a superintendent.

Similarly, if the suspect is released on bail prior to the expiry of a warrant of further detention issued by a magistrates' court, he can (again subject to the custody officer being satisfied as to s.37(2)) be held for any unexpired time on the warrant without going back to the magistrates. But, again, any additional time up to the maximum of 96 hours would require the authorisation of a magistrates' court.

4–87 Subsection (8)(a) of s.47 substituted a new section for s.43 of the Magistrates' Courts Act 1980. This deals with the court fixing a later date for a bail hearing and the enforcement of a recognisance of sureties.

Subsection (8)(b) slightly amends the procedure where someone is arrested on a warrant of commitment for fine default under s.117(2)(b) of the 1980 Act. Instead of his having to be taken to a police station to have his recognisance taken, it can be taken on the spot and he can then be released on bail. The purpose is to save the journey to the police station where this is unnecessary. The person who takes the recognisance and gives the release must be qualified to do so. Outside the police station that means the police officer (or civilian enforcement officer) executing the warrant. If the case is dealt with at a police station it would be the custody officer.

Early administrative hearings rank as a court hearing: s.47A

A requirement under this part of PACE that a person appear or be brought before   **4–88** a magistrates' court is satisfied if the person appears at an early administrative hearing[59] conducted by a clerk to the justices.[60]

Remands to police custody: s.48[61]

Magistrates have the power to remand a person who has been charged with   **4–89** offences to police custody for up to three days.[62] This is for the purpose of allowing questioning about other offences. The section provides that in relation to such detention the "necessity principle" applies and when there is no longer any need to detain the suspect to question him about other offences he must be brought back to the magistrates' court. Whilst detained, the custody officer is responsible for him and, as has been seen, the ordinary rules about periodic reviews under s.40(1) apply (para.4–45 above). Contrary to the view expressed in earlier editions of this book, it now seems to this writer that the reviews should be conducted by an officer of the rank of inspector, rather than by the custody officer. There are arguments to support either view. The view of the Home Office is that they should be conducted by an inspector.[63] The reason is that police detention after charge ordered by the magistrates (commonly referred to as a "three-day lie-down") is specifically stated to be solely for the purpose of inquiry into other offences[64] for which, by definition, the suspect has not yet been charged. On this view, it is therefore right that the reviews should be conducted in the manner appropriate to the situation where the suspect has not been charged (s.40(b)) rather than where he has been charged (s.40(1)(a))—even though he has been charged with a different offence or offences. The writer is persuaded that this is the better view.

---

[59] Dealt with by s.50 of the Crime and Disorder Act 1998.
[60] Crime and Disorder Act 1998, Sch.8, para.62. There is no Northern Ireland equivalent.
[61] There was no equivalent in the 1989 N.I. PACE Order. The RUC said they did not want the power.
[62] Under s.128(7) of the Magistrates' Courts Act 1980.
[63] See opinion dated August 7, 1991, quoted in *Police Review*, October 18, 1991, p.2109. The view is shared by Ken Sloan, the then Legal Editor of *Police Review*—see *Police Review*, December 27, 1991, p.2637.
[64] "He shall not be kept in such detention unless there is a need for him to be so detained for the purposes of inquiries into other offences" (new s.128(8)(a) of the Magistrates' Courts Act 1980 added by s.48 of PACE).

The problem of detention time limits under ss.41–44 does not arise because the maximum length of the period of detention is determined in the case of s.48 (remands to police custody) by the authority of the court. The same is the case where the prisoner has been "produced" to the police under the Crime (Sentences) Act 1997 by the authority delegated to the prison authorities by the Home Secretary. In either case the prisoner has no choice as to whether he is remanded or transferred though he, of course, retains his freedom to decide whether he will answer questions or agree to take part in an identification parade. The rules regarding cautions, length of interviews, breaks, access to legal advice and the like must be observed. It is also desirable that a custody record form be maintained to record all relevant events.

The person who is remanded to police custody by the authority of a court or under a production order from a prison is not in "police detention" within the meaning of s.118(2) since he has not been placed under arrest. Even if he is charged with further offences there would seem to be no reason to place him under arrest since he is already lawfully in custody and the custody officer is not at liberty to release him.

Police detention to count towards custodial sentence: s.49[65]

4–90   Section 49 amends s.67 of the Criminal Justice Act 1967 so as to provide that any period spent in police detention (defined in s.118(2)) or under the terrorism legislation shall count towards any subsequent custodial penalty. But this only applies if the custody was in respect of the same offence.[66]

In order to ensure that the prison service has the necessary information to enable it to make the computations, the police are supposed to pass to the prosecution the details of times and dates of any police custody in connection with the offence. The prosecution should then hand the information to the clerk so that it can be linked to the warrant of commitment and passed on to the prison. In the instance of cases dealt with summarily the police should endorse the warrant of commitment themselves with the details, including the name of the police station where the detainee was held and the name of the prison to which he is sent.

Records of detention: s.50[67]

4–91   The section requires each police force to keep records of the numbers of cases where persons are detained for longer than 24 hours and then released without charge, the numbers of applications for warrants of further detention, and the results of such applications and the periods of further detention authorised by the courts and the periods actually spent in custody in such cases. The record must

---

[65] See 1989 N.I. PACE Order, Art.49.
[66] *R. v Towers* (1988) 86 Cr.App.R. 335, CA; *R. v Secretary of State for Home Affairs, Ex p. Read* (1987) 9 Cr.App.R.(S.) 206.
[67] See 1989 N.I. PACE Order, Art.50.

also show whether persons detained under such warrants were eventually released without charge. Every annual report of a chief constable and of the Metropolitan Police Commissioner must likewise include such information.

Unfortunately, the records resulting from the provisions of s.50 which are published as an annual Home Office Statistical Bulletin[68] have proved unsatisfactory. Part of the problem has been the different methods of collecting the data used by different forces. Another has been confusion in the way the categories are defined. But the main problem is that the data the police have been asked to collect is not very informative. The figures show the numbers released without charges after being detained for more than 24 and 36 hours and under a warrant of further detention.[69] They also show the number of warrants of further detention, how many were granted and extended, and the periods of time under such warrants. (Between 1988 and 2004, the number of warrants of further detention applied for annually ranged from a low of 220 in 1995 to a high of 446 in 1988.) Such applications are virtually always granted.[70] The proportion of those detained on warrants of further detention who are ultimately charged varies somewhat from year to year but during the same period it was never less than two-thirds and in many years it was close to 80 per cent or even more. In the three years from 2001 to 2004 it was respectively 83 per cent, 75 per cent and 69 per cent.[71]

Even if these figures were produced in a clear and consistent way, they would tell us little of interest without figures as to the overall numbers arrested and the periods for which they are held prior to application for further time to the magistrates. The Runciman Royal Commission recommended that s.50 be amended so as to require the collection of figures that would show the numbers arrested, the numbers arrested subsequently charged and the numbers charged and not charged held for varying periods of time—under six hours, 6–12 hours, 12–24 hours, 24–36 hours, 36–72 hours and over 72 hours.[72] The recommendation has not been implemented.

A sounder basis for evaluation of the PACE detention provisions are studies of **4–92** large samples conducted by the Home Office. Brown (1989) was based on police custody records of 5,500 prisoners held in March 1987 in 10 force areas. The salient facts relating to detention that emerge from this study are the following:

- Detention without charge for more than 24 hours occurred in less than 1 per cent of the sample (p.61).

- Warrants for further detention (beyond 36 hours) were issued in only 11 out of 5,519 cases (0.2 per cent) (pp.50–51).

---

[68] Previously called *The Operation of Certain Police Powers under PACE*. In October 2001 it was re-titled *Arrest for Notifiable Offences and the Operation of Certain Police Powers under PACE*.
[69] In 2002–2003 there were 633, of whom 559 (88%) were released within 36 hours. The figures for 2003–2004 were 621 of whom 527 (85%) were released within 36 hours (*op.cit.*, Table PE, p.16). From January 2004 superintendents have been able to authorise detention for up to 36 hours for all arrestable offences. First indications were that this would have little effect on the numbers—see Tables P5A and P5B, pp.29 and 30.
[70] In 2003–2004, of the 304 recorded applications, none was refused (*op.cit.*, Table PF, p.17).
[71] *op.cit.*, Table PF, p.17.
[72] Recommendation 42 based on para.21, Runciman Report, p.30.

- Just over half of those detained (56 per cent) were charged (p.56).

- Only 12 per cent of those detained were released unconditionally—half with charges refused and half with no further action taken (p.56).

- The mean period of detention for the sample, irrespective of outcome, was five hours and 10 minutes (the report states "this figure may seem high but . . . this was because a minority of prisoners were held for much longer periods: 11 per cent were held for more than 12 hours" (p.61)). The median length of detention was three hours and 19 minutes. By the six-hour mark, just over three-quarters (76 per cent) of detainees had been dealt with. By the 12-hour point, 89 per cent had been dealt with and by 24 hours, as has already been seen, 99 per cent (see Table 6.5, p.62). These figures suggested that, overall, suspects were being processed somewhat more quickly than pre-PACE (pp.62–63).[73]

- Excluding those detained very briefly after charges (for instance to check an address), 18 per cent of those charged were held in custody prior to court appearance, usually on the ground that they were likely to default on bail or that it was necessary to protect property, the prisoner or others (pp.65–66).

- The mean length of detention after charge was nearly 16 hours (p.67).

4–93 A later study by David Brown and colleagues, based on similarly large samples drawn in 1990 and 1991, showed that the length of detention had not changed. The mean period of detention in the 1990 sample was five hours one minute, and in 1991, five hours 18 minutes. The median period in 1990 was three hours 13 minutes and in 1991 it was three hours 20 minutes. (See Brown *et al.* (1992), pp.104–105.)

In the study of over 3,000 arrests by Phillips and Brown (1998), suspects were held for an average of six hours and 40 minutes—somewhat longer than in the previous studies. Those who obtained legal advice spent longer in custody than those not legally advised—just over nine hours as compared with five and a half hours. Juveniles who came to the police station with an appropriate adult spent an average of five hours in custody compared with over seven hours where the appropriate adult had to be summoned (p.110).

In terrorism cases, not surprisingly, periods of detention are distinctly longer. In Brown (1993), a study of 253 persons detained in 1989–1990 under the PTA showed an average period of detention of nearly 29 hours with a median of 16 hours 24 minutes. However, just under 40 per cent of detainees had been released within 12 hours and nearly two-thirds within 24 hours (p.50).

---

[73] See also the before-and-after research carried out in the Brighton police station by Irving and McKenzie (1989), pp.81–84, 151–155.

Savings: s.51[74]

Section 51 makes an exception from the provisions of Pt IV of the Act for immi-   **4–94**
gration officers in relation to controls of entry, police officers in relation to arrest
and detention under the Terrorism Act 2000 or police officers detaining military
deserters, absentees or persons under escort.

Paragraph (d) of the section also preserves the right of persons detained by the
police to apply for a writ of habeas corpus or any other prerogative remedy.

Children: s.52[75]

Section 52 dealt with the detention of children under the age of 10 in community   **4–95**
or other suitable places. It was repealed by the Children Act 1989, s.108(7),
Sch.15. The Northern Ireland equivalent Art.52 is still in force as amended by the
Criminal Justice (Children) (Northern Ireland) Order 1998, Arts 56 and 57.

---

[74] See 1989 N.I. PACE Order, Art.51.
[75] See 1989 N.I. PACE Order, Art.52.

QUESTIONS AND ANSWERS

DETENTION

4–96   Who is responsible for the well-being of persons in custody?

The custody officer is required to ensure that persons in custody are treated in accordance with the Act and the Codes of Practice. Custody officers of the rank of sergeant or above must be appointed for all designated police stations. But an officer of any rank can perform the functions of the custody officer if none is readily available. At non-designated police stations the role of custody officer should always be played if possible by someone other than the investigation officer, but this is not an absolute requirement.

4–97   What happens if the custody officer and the investigating officer disagree as to how the suspect should be treated?

The custody officer is supposed to be separate from the investigating officer. It is the custody officer who is basically in charge. If the investigating officer is senior in rank and there is some disagreement between them as to the handling of the detainee, the custody officer is required to refer the matter at once to an officer of the rank of superintendent or above responsible for that police station. (The same applies to review officers; see below.)

4–98   What are the custody officer's duties before charge?

He must oversee all aspects of the detainee's treatment. He must ensure that the custody record form is properly maintained with all details of what transpires during the period of the suspect's detention. It is the custody officer's duty, *inter alia*, to decide initially whether the detention of the suspect is warranted.

4–99   On what grounds can someone be detained without charge?

There is only one ground of police detention prior to a charge—namely, that the custody officer reasonably thinks that such detention is "necessary to secure or preserve evidence relating to an offence for which he [the detainee] is under arrest or to obtain such evidence by questioning him" (s.37(2)).

When the suspect first arrives at the police station, it is the custody officer's duty to decide whether there is sufficient evidence to justify charging him. If not, the question arises as to whether he should be detained. The question of the suspect's detention must then be kept under periodic review.

How often must there be reviews of the need for further detention? 4–100

The need for further detention has to be reviewed periodically after the initial consideration of the question by the custody officer. In the case of someone who has not been charged, the review should be by a "review officer" of at least the rank of inspector who has not been directly involved in the investigation. The first review is supposed to be not more than six hours after the initial authorisation of detention by the custody officer. Thereafter the review should be at nine-hour intervals.

Before deciding whether to authorise continued detention the review officer must give the person concerned or any solicitor representing him who is available at that time the chance to make representations either orally or in writing.

What happens if the time limits cannot be adhered to because the suspect is asleep or ill, is being questioned or for some other reason? 4–101

The Act allows for the review to be postponed "if . . . it is not practicable to carry out the review at that time" (s.40(4)(a)).

How long can a suspect be held in the police station without charge? 4–102

The basic rule is that if the police wish to hold the suspect for more than 24 hours such extended detention must be authorised by a superintendent or above after inviting representations from the suspect or his solicitor. Hitherto it has only applied where the matter being investigated is "a serious arrestable offence" but the Serious Organised Crime and Police Bill 2004–2005 will extend it to any indictable offence. If the police wish to hold the suspect beyond the 36-hour point, approval must be obtained from a magistrates' court. The magistrates cannot authorise detention for longer than a total of 96 hours. There are successive stages:

(1) Initial review of detention by the custody officer as soon as possible after arrival at the police station.

(2) Review of the necessity for further detention after the first six hours by an inspector (the review officer) and then at nine-hour intervals.

(3) Review of the necessity for further detention after 24 hours by a superintendent; approval can be given for further detention up to the 36-hour point.

(4) Review of the necessity for further detention after 36 hours by a magistrates' court—the court is permitted to authorise detention for a maximum of 36 hours at one hearing. There must therefore be at least two hearings if the suspect is to be held for the full 96 hours.

If the suspect is being held under the Terrorism Act 2000 he can be detained for up to a total of 14 days. For the first 48 hours detention is authorised by the police. Thereafter, under the Terrorism Act 2000, further detention has to be approved by "a judicial authority". Formerly that gave an overall maximum period of detention of seven days but the Criminal Justice Act 2003 extended this to 14 days.

The Anti-Terrorism, Crime and Security Act 2001 allows for the *indefinite* detention without charges of persons whom the Home Secretary reasonably believes to be suspected international terrorists whose presence in the UK is a risk to national security, but in December 2004 the House of Lords held such detention to be incompatible with the European Convention on Human Rights.

4–103   Who decides as to what charges are laid and who actually charges the suspect?

The rule was that the custody officer both formulated the charge(s) and actually charged the suspect. However, the Criminal Justice Act 2003 provided for a new system. Under this new system the CPS decide on the charges—usually whilst the suspect is on bail. When the new system is fully in place he will then receive a written communication sent by the police informing him either of the charge(s) or that he is not to be charged. But under the new system the custody officer will still formulate the charges in minor routine cases. Also, if bail is inappropriate and if the CPS cannot decide on the charges in time before the PACE time-limits on detention without charge expire, the custody officer retains the power to lay holding charges providing he has the approval of a Duty Inspector. The new system is being brought in gradually but at the time of writing it was in operation in 14 police force areas.

4–104   Must the time limits be strictly adhered to?

The answer is both yes and no. There is a provision in the Act that "Any reference . . . to a period of time or a time of day is to be treated as approximate only" (s.45(2)). This reflects the view that officers are not expected to walk around with stopwatches. Also, the actual rules in the Act and Code make some allowance for the variety of problems that may come up. Thus, as has been seen, the review within the police station may be postponed if it is not practicable to conduct it at the right time. Though when this happens the next review is to be held at the time it should have been held if the first review had been at the correct time.

The hearing in the magistrates' court can be at any stage up to the 36-hour point. But the Act goes further and gives another six hours leeway, thus making a total of 42 hours. So if the 36 hour period would expire at, say, 6 am, the police have a further six hours and can lawfully bring the suspect to the court during the ordinary morning hearing. But if the court takes the view that the application for approval of further detention could and should have been brought within the 36-hour period it must dismiss the application. Although there is therefore some flexibility in the time limits they are certainly not to be treated lightly.

From when is time counted?   4–105

In the ordinary case time starts to run from the moment that the suspect arrives at the first police station to which he is taken. But there are some special cases where the rules are different.

If he is arrested in one police force area but is wanted elsewhere, time starts to run from the time that he arrives at the first police station to which he is taken in the area where he is wanted for questioning—or after 24 hours, whichever is the earlier This is on the assumption, however, that he is not questioned in the area where he was arrested nor on the way to the second area. If he is in fact questioned, time starts to run from that time. If he is wanted in two areas, time starts to run in the second area 24 hours after leaving the first area or the moment when he reaches any police station in the second area—whichever is the earlier.

If he is arrested outside England and Wales, the detention clock starts from the time that he comes to a police station in the area where the case against him is being investigated or after 24 hours, whichever is the earlier. If at any stage he is taken to hospital whilst in police detention, time during which he is actually being questioned, whether en route or at the hospital, counts but the rest of the time involved does not count.

What is the time limit for questioning without charge if the suspect is   4–106
arrested for other offences?

The time limit is unaffected. The time from which detention is measured is on the basis of the offence for which he was first arrested. The same is true where the police are investigating other offences for which he has not yet been arrested.

Once a person has been charged can the police investigate and question the   4–107
suspect about other offences?

Yes. That then becomes a holding charge. If he is lawfully in custody after being charged, inquiries about other offences are not affected by the pre-charge detention limits. The length and place of detention will be determined by the court's decisions on the matter on which he has already been charged.

4–108 **What sort of hearing on continued detention is there before the magistrates?**

The application for continuation of pre-charge detention on a warrant of further detention must be heard by a magistrates' court with at least two magistrates and a court clerk sitting in private. The hearing cannot start unless the suspect is present and unless he has received a copy of the police application for the warrant of further detention. The suspect is entitled to be legally represented and if he has no lawyer and wishes to have one, the case must be adjourned while a lawyer is found. The costs of such representation are borne by public funds. There is no means-test and no contribution from the suspect.

The police usually make their application through the Crown Prosecution Service (CPS). The suspect or his lawyer, or both, can reply. The onus or burden of proof is on the prosecution to show why further detention is necessary.

4–109 **On what grounds can the magistrates approve further detention?**

The grounds on which further detention can be approved by the court are the same as those already applied by the superintendent at the 24-hour point:

(1) whether detention is necessary "to secure or preserve evidence relating to an offence for which he is under arrest or to obtain such evidence by questioning him";

(2) that the offence is a serious arrestable one; and

(3) that the investigation is being conducted diligently and expeditiously.

4–110 **If the suspect has not been answering police questions can the court grant a warrant for further detention in the hope that that will enable the police to break him down by further questioning?**

The answer to this question will require a decision by the courts. But it would seem that the better view is that if that were indeed the main reason for granting a warrant of further detention it would be unlawful. If the police have failed to get the suspect to co-operate with them after 36 hours their only hope of changing his attitude would probably be through conduct that would run the risk of being oppressive.

The justification for the 96-hour period of detention given in Parliament by Home Office Ministers was that it would be necessary in a few very complex and important cases. There was never any suggestion that it was needed in order to "break" the hard detainee. On the contrary, this was repeatedly denied.

On what grounds can the suspect be held after he has been charged? 4–111

Once a person has been charged, the grounds for further detention change. In principle, at that point he should not be questioned further about that offence—though the Code does now allow slightly more scope for questioning after charge (see Code C, para.16.5).

The sole permitted grounds for detention after charge (under s.38(1)) are:

(1) that the detainee's name or address have not been satisfactorily established; or

(2) that the custody officer has reasonable grounds for believing:

– that he will fail to appear in court to answer to bail;
– where he is charged with an imprisonable offence, that detention is necessary to prevent him committing an offence;
– where he is charged with a non-imprisonable offence, that detention is necessary to prevent him from causing physical injury to any other person or from causing loss of or damage to property;
– that detention is necessary to prevent him from interfering with the administration of justice or with the investigation of offences or a particular offence;
– that detention is necessary for his own protection or, in the case of a juvenile, in his own interest;
– if the suspect is over the age of 18, that his detention is necessary to enable a sample to be taken to test whether he has a Class A drug in his body (such detention may not be for more than six hours).

How long can the suspect who has been charged be held in custody without 4–112 being brought before a court?

The former law was that he had to be brought before a court "as soon as practicable". This formula is also that adopted in PACE (s.46(2)). But it is strengthened by further provisions in the same section. These state that if there is no sitting of a local magistrates' court on the day on which he is charged or the next day (not counting Sundays, Christmas Day or Good Friday), the custody officer must inform the clerk to the justices that there is a person in custody for whom a special hearing will have to be held.

The Act then lays upon the clerk to the justices the duty of arranging a hearing not later than the day after he has been charged (or in the case of someone brought from another police district, the day after he arrives in the area).

4–113   **Can the police impose conditions on a person granted bail from the police station?**

Yes—under the provisions of the Criminal Justice and Public Order Act 1994. The police can impose many of the same sort of conditions as can be imposed by the courts—to hand in a passport, to report to the police, not to go to a particular place, not to talk to particular individuals, to reside at a particular address and the like. They cannot, however, make residence at a bail hostel a condition of getting bail nor getting a psychiatric report nor attending for a lawyer's interview. Failure to comply with the conditions imposed by the police does not give the police the right to arrest the person concerned—though he can be arrested if the conditions were imposed by a court.

4–114   **Can the police demand sureties as a condition of granting bail?**

Yes.

4–115   **If a person objects to the conditions imposed by the police, where can he go to have them changed?**

He or his representatives can return to the police station to see whether the custody officer (or a different custody officer) is willing to alter the conditions. Alternatively, he can ask the magistrates' court.

PART V

QUESTIONING AND TREATMENT OF PERSONS BY POLICE

Abolition of certain powers of constables to search persons: s.53[1]

Section 53 abolished all common law and statutory powers to search persons at a police station including the power to conduct intimate searches. The present powers to carry out such searches are now to be found in ss.54 and 55 of PACE.

5–01

Searches of detained persons: s.54[2] and Code C, s.4

Prior to PACE there was no statutory basis for searching someone who had been arrested. The common law recognised the right of the police to do what was necessary to prevent the arrested person escaping, injuring himself or others or destroying evidence, and the Philips Royal Commission recommended[3] that the power should be put onto a proper statutory basis and that it should include the power of making a full inventory. On the other hand, it said the process could be "humiliating and disturbing" and it should not be done routinely and, save in exceptional circumstances, a suspect should not be deprived of his watch.[4]

5–02

Section 54 and Code C, para.4.1 requires the custody officer to take charge of this process. There are two separate aspects to the question—searching, and making a record of the suspect's property. Prior to August 2004 the custody officer had a duty under s.54(1) "to ascertain and record or cause to be recorded" everything which the detainee had with him. As will be seen (para.5–05), as from August 2004, the duty to make a record of the effects was abolished under the Criminal Justice Act 2003, but the custody officer's duty to ascertain everything which the detainee has with him remains. The custody officer can authorise a search of the person if he considers that to be necessary for that purpose (subs.(6)). The duty to ascertain what property a detainee has when they come to the police station applies not only to arrested persons. It applies equally to

---

[1] See 1989 N.I. PACE Order, Art.54.
[2] See 1989 N.I. PACE Order, Art.55 and Code C, s.4.
[3] Philips Report, para.3.116.
[4] Philips Report, para.3.117.

persons committed to prison custody on the order or sentence of a court, to any-one lodged at a police station with a view to their production in court from prison custody, to persons transferred from another police station or a hospital and to persons detained under the Mental Health Act 1983. (Code C, para.4.1.) However, there is no right to search all detainees as a matter of course or routine.[5] Note 4A of Code C states that s.54(1) and para.4.1 require a detainee to be searched "when it is clear that the custody officer will have continuing duties in relation to that detainee or when that detainee's behaviour or offence makes an inventory appropriate". However, it continues, "They do not require every detainee to be searched, *e.g.* if it is clear a person will only be detained for a short period and is not to be placed in a cell".

5–03   In fact searches are very common; virtually routine. Furthermore, by virtue of an amendment to s.54 made by s.147 of the Criminal Justice Act 1988, the police can search anyone in police custody whether at a police station or elsewhere to ascertain whether he has with him anything which he could use to cause physical injury, damage property, interfere with evidence or assist him to escape (subs.(6A)). This amendment was designed to deal with items passed to the suspect by fellow detainees or visitors and also with searches outside the police station.

Subsection (8) says that a search under the section shall be carried out by a con-stable—who must be the same sex as the person being searched (subs.(9)). The Police Reform Act 2002 gives the same power to authorised civilian detention officers.[6]

The 2002 Act also gives the power to authorised civilian escort officers who have lawful custody of arrested persons outside the police station.[7]

The custody officer may at his discretion retain anything which the arrested person has (subs.(3)), except for things subject to legal professional privilege and clothes and personal effects. (The same applies to authorised civilian detention officers[8] and to escort officers.[9])

5–04   According to subs.(4), the custody officer may only retain clothes and personal effects if the custody officer believes that they might be used by the arrested per-son to cause physical injury to himself or anyone else, to damage property, to interfere with evidence or to assist him to escape. He may also retain such items if he has reasonable grounds for believing that they may be evidence relating to an offence. Note the difference between the two halves of this provision. The seizure of items that might be used to do harm does not have to be based on rea-sonable grounds, since police officers cannot be expected to anticipate what exactly the suspect might do. Seizure of evidence does, however, need to be on reasonable grounds. (There is no mention in either the Act or the Code of the Philips Royal Commission's recommendation that a suspect should always be allowed to keep his watch.)

---

[5] *Lindley v Rutter* [1981] Q.B. 128, DC and *Brazil v Chief Constable of Surrey* [1983] 3 All E.R. 537, DC. But see also *Middleweek v Chief Constable of Merseyside, The Times*, August 1, 1985.
[6] Police Reform Act 2002, Sch.4, Pt 3, para.26(1)(a).
[7] Police Reform Act 2002, Sch.4, Pt 4, para.35(4)(a)(i).
[8] Police Reform Act 2002, Sch.4, Pt 3, para.26(1)(b).
[9] Police Reform Act 2002, Sch.4, Pt 4, para.35(4)(a)(ii).

Where property is seized, the person from whom it is taken must (under subs.(5)) be told of the reason why (unless he is or is likely to become violent or is incapable of understanding what is said to him) and the reason must be recorded (Code C, para.4.5). Section 22(2)(a) provides for the retention by the police of items seized.

Abolition of duty to record effects

As has been seen, s.54(1) originally required a full record of the detainee's effects. But this requirement was abolished as from August 2004 by the Criminal Justice Act 2003, s.8(1). This resulted from a recommendation of the Joint Home Office/Cabinet Office Review of PACE. The Joint Review (2002, p.24, para.24) said, that the police claimed the duty to make a full list of the suspect's property was "time-consuming and not always necessary". The "Options Proposed" (p.25) included, "Modify the requirement so that the custody officer must secure all a detained person's property in that person's presence and make whatever supporting records he considers necessary". Reporting on the Bill, the Joint Parliamentary Human Rights Select Committee expressed misgivings about this change. It recommended that "at the least a record be kept of any property taken from a detainee by the police, that it should form part of the custody record, and that the record should be signed by the detainee". (Second Report, January 31, 2003, HL 40, HC 374, para.10.) **5–05**

Section 54 as amended by the Criminal Justice Act 2003, s.8(2) has two new subsections regarding recording. Section 54(2) states that the custody officer "may record or cause to be recorded all or any of the things which he ascertains under subsection (1)". It is entirely up to the custody officer to decide whether any and, if so, what record he makes. (It would not be surprising if many custody officers continued to make a full record much as before.) A new subs.(2A) adds that in the case of an arrested person, any such record *may* (not, as before, *shall*) be made as part of the custody record. Code C, para.4.4 says that where the record is not made as part of the custody record, the custody record should show where such a record exists. It also requires that whenever a record is made, the detainee shall be allowed to check and sign it as correct. A refusal to sign has to be recorded.

Searches and examinations to ascertain identity: s.54A[10]

This section provides additional powers to carry out searches and examinations of persons detained in police stations for identification purposes and to take fingerprints. The Police Reform Act 2002 applied the same powers to authorised civilian detention officers.[11] **5–06**

---

[10] This section was added by the Anti-terrorism, Crime and Security Act 2001, s.90(1). The same provisions were applied to Northern Ireland by s.91(1) inserting a new Art.55A into the 1989 N.I. PACE Order. Both became effective as from Royal Assent.

[11] Sch.4, Pt 3, para.22.

So far as concerns searches, the police have powers to search an arrested person for a weapon, for evidence or where it is necessary in order to perform the custody officer's duty to itemise and record what he has with him. The new provisions in s.54A give the power to search or examine the suspect simply in order to identify him. An officer of the rank of inspector or above can authorise a search (other than an intimate search) or examination of a suspect in order to discover whether he has "any mark" (such as an injury, a birthmark or tattoo) that would either help to identify him as a person involved in the commission of an offence or would establish his true identity (s.54A(1)).

If the purpose is to try to link him to a particular offence, the inspector's authorisation can only be given if the detainee has refused consent or it is not practicable to get such consent—for instance, because he is under the influence of drink or drugs (subs.(2)). If the purpose is to establish his true identity, the inspector's authorisation can only be given if the suspect has refused to identify himself or the officer has reasonable grounds for suspecting that he is not who he claims to be (subs.(3)). If the authorisation is given orally, it must be confirmed in writing as soon as is practicable (subs.(4)).

5–07   Any identifying mark found may be photographed, whether the suspect consents or not (subs.(5)). Taking such photographs without consent does not require separate authorisation by an inspector. The photographs can only be taken by a police officer or by persons specifically designated for the work by the chief officer of police for the area (subs.(6)). Such a non-police officer photographer has the same power as a police officer to use reasonable force for the purpose (*ibid.*). But a search may only be carried out or a photograph taken by someone of the same sex as the suspect (subs.(7)).

A photograph taken under this section may not be used except for a purpose related to the prevention or detection of crime, the investigation of an offence or the prosecution of a case (subs.(8)) whether here or abroad (subs.(9)).

Intimate searches and strip searches: s.55 and Code C, Annex A[12]

5–08   The subject of intimate searches of body orifices is dealt with separately in s.55. The Philips Royal Commission recommended[13] that if the search was of intimate parts of the body it should be carried out only by a doctor and only where the offence in question was a grave one. It should require the authorisation of a sub-divisional commander.

The Government did not agree with the Philips Royal Commission's safeguards. When the first Bill was published, an intimate search required the approval only of a superintendent. Such authorisation could be given if the offence in question was a serious arrestable one and there were reasonable grounds for believing that such a search would produce relevant evidence or that such a search was necessary to establish that the detainee had nothing that could be used to injure himself or

---

[12] See 1989 N.I. PACE Order, Art.56 and Code C, Annex A. Amended by Police (Northern Ireland) Act 2003, Art.41.
[13] Philips Report, para.3.118.

others. The second Bill at first qualified this by limiting the ground for an intimate search to a search for something that could be used as a weapon or to injure oneself or others. Searches for evidence (of drugs offences, for instance) were not permitted. The decision was largely based on the view of the doctors who, according to the then Home Office Minister, Lord Elton, said that they would not be willing to conduct searches without consent to obtain evidence of crime but would do so to protect life.[14] Needless to say the police regarded this alteration as thoroughly unhelpful. They also criticised the logic of denying the police the right to conduct intimate searches for evidence but retaining the power for Customs and Excise officers at airports and ports. The then Home Office Minister, Mr Douglas Hurd, conceded that the powers available to Customs and Excise under the Customs and Excise Management Act 1979, s.164 were "valuable" and should be retained. For reasons that he did not explain, that, however, was a different issue.[15]

During the summer recess, between the Report stage and the Third Reading in the House of Lords, the Government changed its mind again on this controversial issue. It introduced an amendment to the Bill designed, after all, to permit an intimate search for drugs. The rules for searches for weapons and searches for drugs are, however, different in certain important respects.   **5–09**

The rules apply to an "intimate search" which is defined in s.65[16] of PACE (and in Code C, Annex A, para.1) as a search which "consists of the physical examination of a person's body orifices other than the mouth". This would mean anus, vagina, nostrils and probably ears. The original Home Office Circular on PACE (para.1–11, n.23 above, paras 43–44) said that a physical insertion into a body orifice would constitute an intimate search as would "any application of force to a body orifice or its immediate surroundings". The circular also suggested that even a mere visual inspection of intimate parts of a body should be regarded as an intimate search "even though physical contact may be absent". But in *Hughes*[17] the Court of Appeal held that making a suspect spit something out (in that case a plastic wrapper containing cannabis) that he had just put into his mouth was not an intimate search. It was not a search so much as action taken to prevent destruction of evidence. A search required some physical intrusion into a body orifice, some physical examination rather than mere visual examination or an attempt to get the person to extrude what was contained in a body orifice. Equally it would presumably not extend to an X-ray or scan.

All intimate searches are subject to the following rules: **5–10**

    (1)   the search must be authorised by an officer of the rank of an inspector (formerly a superintendent[18]) or above on the basis of reasonable belief

---

[14] House of Lords, *Hansard*, July 19, 1984, col.710.

[15] House of Commons, *Hansard*, Standing Committee E, February 23, 1984, col.3059.

[16] Intimate searches were previously defined in s.118 of PACE. The Criminal Justice and Public Order Act 1994, s.59 moved the definition to s.65 and excluded searches of the mouth.

[17] [1994] 1 W.L.R. 876, CA.

[18] The change was made by the Criminal Justice and Police Act 2001, s.79, despite protest from the Parliamentary Joint Committee on Human Rights—First Report, Session 2000–2001, HL Paper 69, (2001) HC 427 ("[W]e are particularly disturbed by anything which even slightly erodes the protection for a person's interests in physical integrity, and bodily privacy, or gives the impression that an interference with them is being taken less seriously than it was" (para.75)).

(as opposed to mere suspicion) that the arrested person in police detention has concealed on him either something that could be used to cause
physical injury to himself or to others and that he might so use it or a
class A drug which they intended to supply to another or to export
(subs.(1) and Code C, Annex A, para.2);

(2) authorisation may be oral or written, but if oral it must be confirmed in
writing (subs.(3));

(3) authorisation may not be given unless there are reasonable grounds for
believing that the item in question cannot be found without such a
search (subs.(2), Annex A, para.2). If, therefore, it could be expected to
pass through the natural bodily functions and there is time to wait for
this to happen, this should be preferred; and

(4) the suspect must be told the reasons for the intimate search (Annex A,
para.2A).

5–11 The rules diverge, however, in regard to who may carry out such a search.
Searches for weapons can in the last analysis be carried out by police officers—
or, under the authority of the Police Reform Act 2002, authorised civilian detention officers.[19] The former Home Secretary, Mr Douglas Hurd, said on this issue
that all were agreed that, if possible, intimate searches should be carried out by a
doctor both because it was safer and because "it provides a degree of human dig-
nity and reassurance". But it might be that no doctor could be found who could
carry out the search within a reasonable time or the doctor might not be willing
to carry out such a search.[20] Swift action might be necessary. Guidelines issued
by the British Medical Association (BMA) and the Association of Police
Surgeons (APS) state that "The BMA and APS do not consider it appropriate for
doctors to be involved in forced intimate searches and believe that doctors should
only agree to participate where the individual has given consent or where the
situation is life-threatening".[21] There was no way of guaranteeing that the particular doctor approached would agree to carry out such a search without the consent of the suspect. It was therefore necessary to have the reserve power that
permitted such a search to be conducted by a police officer.[22]
    The Joint Home Office/Cabinet Office Review of PACE (2002, pp.31–32) rec-
ommended that efforts should be made to discover whether it was the perceived
threat of civil legal action that prevented Force medical examiners from undertaking intimate searches without consent. If so, a statutory defence should be
devised to cover them. If it was ethical reasons, "attempts should be made to
negotiate search guidelines with the BMA".

---

[19] Sch.4, Pt 3, para.28.
[20] House of Commons, *Hansard*, Standing Committee E, February 23, 1984, col.3039.
[21] See Marston, "Intimate searches" (1999) 163 J.P. 646 at 647. The Guidelines, first issued in 1994,
were revised in 1999.
[22] House of Commons, *Hansard*, Standing Committee E, February 23, 1984, col.3040.

Such a search must be made by a "suitably qualified person" unless an officer   **5–12**
of at least the rank of inspector (again, formerly superintendent[23]) considers that
this is not practicable (subs.(5), Annex A, para.3). The use of the word *practicable*
in this context is not entirely clear. Presumably it is intended to cover the situation where a doctor is asked but refuses to carry out the search without the
consent of the suspect. But does it also cover the rather different case where no
effort is made to contact a doctor because the police believe there is none likely
to be available at that hour of the day or night, or because the police know that
any doctor asked would be likely to refuse? A "suitably qualified person" is either
a registered doctor or a registered nurse (subs.(17), Code C, Annex A, para.3).
There is no stated requirement on the police to make any attempt to get such a
person to carry out the search, nor even to ask the suspect whether he wishes the
search to be carried out by a qualified person—though this duty was in an earlier
version of the Code.

An intimate search may only be carried out by someone other than a doctor or
nurse "as a last resort" (Annex A, para.3A). Where such a search is not carried
out by a doctor or nurse it must be carried out by a police officer of the same sex
as the suspect and not more than two persons, neither of whom may be of the
opposite sex, can be present (Annex A, para.6). An intimate search of a juvenile
or a mentally disturbed or mentally vulnerable suspect can only be conducted in
the presence of an appropriate adult of the same sex unless the detainee specifically requests a particular adult of the opposite sex "who is readily available"
(Annex A, para.5). The custody record must show as soon as practicable which
parts of the body were searched and why (subss.(10) and (11)). The Code (Annex
A, para.7) requires that the record must also show who carried out the search,
who was present, the reason for the search and the result. If the search was by a
police officer, the reason must be explained (Annex A, para.8). Intimate searches
(like strip searches, see below) should be conducted "with proper regard to the
sensitivity and vulnerability of the detainee" (Annex A, paras 6 and 11(d)). Force
can be used by a police officer—but not by a medical practitioner—provided it is
no more than is reasonable in the circumstances (s.117).

If the search is for drugs, it can only be carried out by a doctor or registered   **5–13**
nurse and it cannot be carried out in a police station (subss.(4) and (9)). Intimate
searches for drugs are limited to those for hard drugs defined as Class A drugs in
Sch.2 to the Misuse of Drugs Act 1971. (There are over 80 drugs listed in the
Schedule. They do not include cannabis.) But the officer who authorises the intimate search must reasonably believe not only that the suspect has such drugs concealed in a body orifice but that he was in possession of them at the time of his
arrest with intent either to supply or export them (subss.(1)(b)(ii) and (17)).
Someone suspected merely of being a user could therefore not be subjected to an
intimate search. Anything found in the course of an intimate search may be seized
by the police if it could be used to cause physical injury, or damage to property,
interfere with evidence or to assist an escape or if there are reasonable grounds
for thinking that it could be evidence relating to an offence (subs.(12)). The
power of seizure is therefore broader (in covering evidence) than the power of
intimate search.

---

[23] Changed by the Criminal Justice and Police Act 2001, s.79 over the even stronger protest of the
Parliamentary Joint Committee on Human Rights—see *op.cit.*, n.18 above, paras 76–80.

The chief constable's annual report must include information about the total number of intimate searches, the number carried out by doctors or nurses, the number carried out by someone else in the presence of such a person, and the result of the searches (subss.(14), (15) and (16)). The Home Office gives annual figures for the number of intimate searches. The highest number recorded (in 1997–1998) was 224; the lowest (in 1993) was 41. Almost all these searches are made by or in the presence of "suitably qualified persons".[24] The great majority are for Class A drugs but only a small proportion result in drugs being found. (In 2003–2004, there were a total of 81 intimate searches, of which 73 (88 per cent) were for Class A drugs. Such drugs were found in 11 cases (15 per cent) of intimate searches for drugs.[25])

5–14   The Joint Parliamentary Committee on Human Rights has suggested that intimate searches under PACE may contravene Art.3 of the ECHR which prohibits "inhuman or degrading treatment". ("Intimate searches may include the physical investigation of a person's vagina or anus without his or her consent, using reasonable force to conduct it if necessary. It is hard to imagine a more intrusive or humiliating procedure which could be lawful."[26]) Article 3 is absolute and permits no justification. Such searches certainly engage the right to respect for private life under Art.8.1 of the Convention. The Government told the Joint Committee that it did not accept that there was any potential violation of Art.3 and that any interference with Art.8.1 rights could be justified under Art.8.2 as being necessary in the interests of the prevention of disorder or crime or the protection of health.[27]

Annex A of the 2003 revised Code C had a number of additions designed to emphasise the importance of only undertaking an intimate search in exceptional circumstances. The intrusive nature of such searches means that the actual and potential risks must never be underestimated (Annex A, para.1). Before authorising such a search the authorising officer must make every reasonable effort to persuade the person to hand the item over without the need for a search (Note A1). If that fails, the authorising officer must consider carefully whether the grounds for believing that such an article is hidden are reasonable (Note A2).

5–15   The Joint Home Office/Cabinet Office Review of PACE considered a variety of suggestions for changing the rules on intimate searches in relation to drugs. The police said they lacked effective powers. It was not easy for them to x-ray swallowers or to detain them for sufficient time for nature to take its course. This was a loophole exploited by dealers. The "Options proposed" included: further clarification of what constituted an intimate search; to give the police the same power to undertake intimate searches for drugs as they had for dangerous articles; to improve x-ray facilities; to allow adverse inferences to be drawn from failure

---

[24] In 2003–2004 this was true of all but six of the 81 such searches carried out. (Home Office Statistical Bulletin, *Arrests for Notifiable Offences and the Operation of Certain Police Powers Under PACE, 2003–2004*, Table PG, p.18.) In Brown (1989), intimate searches were found in only seven out of 5,519 cases, 0.1% (p.53).

[25] Home Office Statistical Bulletin, *Arrests for Notifiable Offences and the Operation of Certain Police Powers under PACE, 2003–2004*, Table PG, p.18.

[26] Parliamentary Joint Committee on Human Rights—First Report, Criminal Justice and Police Bill, Session 2000–2001, HL Paper 69, (2001) HC 427, para.75.

[27] Parliamentary Joint Committee on Human Rights—First Report, Criminal Justice and Police Bill, Session 2000–2001, HL Paper 69, (2001) HC 427, para.75.

to agree to be x-rayed or to submit to an intimate search; and increased powers of detention like those enjoyed by Customs and Excise. The Review (p.32) recommended that these issues should be canvassed in a consultation paper.

The Home Office Consultation Paper *Policing: Modernising Police Powers to Meet Community Needs* issued in August 2004 addressed the issue (pp.15–16). It said that, subject to the views of consultees, the Government favoured two changes. One was to give the courts power to remand a person to police detention following charge in order to address the problem of those who have swallowed drugs. HM Customs and Excise had such a power. Detainees were kept in specially equipped facilities. (The average time it took for the drugs to pass through was 12 days!) The second proposal was to enable a judge to direct a jury to draw adverse inferences from a refusal to submit to an intimate search.

Strip searches

Code C, Annex A, as revised in April 1995, for the first time separated the regime for intimate searches[28] from that for strip searches.[29] A strip search is defined as one involving the removal of more than outer clothing which includes socks and shoes (Annex A, para.9). One may take place only "if it is considered necessary to remove an article which a detainee would not be allowed to keep, and the officer reasonably considers the detainee might have concealed such an article" (Annex A, para.10). Previously, authorisation of a strip search had to be by the custody officer. Under the 1995 revised Code this requirement was dropped. The regime for strip searches (Annex A) includes provision:

5–16

   (a)   that the officer should be of the same sex (para.11(a));

   (b)   that the search should take place where it cannot be observed by persons who do not need to be present nor by a person of the opposite sex save for an appropriate adult requested by the suspect (para.11(b));

   (c)   that, except in cases of urgency, where there is a risk of serious harm to the detainee or to others, whenever a strip search involves exposure of intimate body parts, there must be at least two people present. If the search is of a juvenile or a mentally disordered or otherwise mentally vulnerable person, one must be the appropriate adult—unless the juvenile, in the presence of the appropriate adult, says he does not want that adult there and the adult agrees. (para.11(c));

   (d)   that suspects should not be required to remove all their clothes at the same time—so that a man should be allowed to put his shirt back on before removing his trousers or a woman to put on her upper garments before removing other clothing (para.11(d)); and

[28] "An intimate search is a search which consists of the physical examination of a person's body orifices other than the mouth" (Annex A, Pt A, para.1).
[29] "A strip search is a search involving the removal of more than outer clothing" (Annex A, Pt B, para.9).

(e) that a person may be required to hold his or her arms in the air or to stand with legs apart and to bend forward so as to permit examination of the genital and anal areas—provided that no physical contact is made with any body orifice (para.11(e)). Removal of any article from a body orifice by someone other than the detainee constitutes an intimate search (para.11(f)).

5–17 Code C (Annex A, para.12) requires that a record of a strip search be made on the custody record including the reason why it was considered necessary, those present and any result. If there is no custody record form because the person being searched is not under arrest—see Code C, para.2.1—a record should nevertheless be made in the officer's notebook or on the record of search form. Even if authority is not given by the custody officer, he should if possible always be consulted in advance, failing which he should be informed after the event.

The right to have someone informed when arrested: s.56 and Code C, s.5 and Annex B[30]

5–18 Section 56 states that a suspect has a right to have someone informed of the fact of his arrest. It replaced s.62 of the Criminal Law Act 1967. (It is to be distinguished from the quite separate right created by Code C, para.5.6 to make a telephone call "for a reasonable time to one person". This cannot only be delayed it can be denied altogether.) A decision to delay or deny can be taken by an inspector and it can be made if the offence is merely an arrestable one.

The Philips Royal Commission recommended[31] that this right be retained but that the details be spelled out even more fully. This recommendation was reflected in the Act and Code C.

Section 56 states that when a suspect is under arrest and is being held in custody in a police station or elsewhere he is entitled, if he so requests, to have "one friend or relative or other person known to them or who is likely to take an interest in their welfare" to be told at public expense as soon as practicable of their whereabouts (subs.(1) and Code C, para.5.1). Terrorism suspects have similar rights.[32] The right to have someone informed as to one's whereabouts is not specifically applied to persons attending a police station as volunteers, though they can, of course, ask for this to be done.

If such a person cannot be contacted, Code C says that two alternates may be nominated. If they too cannot be contacted, the custody officer has the discretion to allow further attempts until the information has been conveyed (para.5.1). If the suspect knows no one to contact, the custody officer should consider contacting any local agency that might be able to help him (Note 5C).

---

[30] See 1989 N.I. PACE Order, Art.57; Code C, s.5 and Annex B.
[31] Philips Report, para.4.80.
[32] See now the Terrorism Act 2000, Sch.8, para.6 *et seq.*

Delay

Delay has only been permissible in the case of serious arrestable offences[33] and only if authorised by an officer of the rank at least of inspector (subs.(2)). Formerly it required a superintendent's authority; this was changed by the Criminal Justice and Police Act 2001 (s.74) but it was not changed in terrorism cases. There is no requirement that the authorising officer be independent of the investigation. An attempt to persuade the Government to accept this requirement failed.[34] Equally, it is not required that the serious arrestable offence necessarily be the one for which the suspect was arrested.[35] Under Code C (paras 3.1–3.2) this right is one of which the suspect must be told both orally and in writing "when a person is brought to a police station under arrest or arrested at the station having gone there voluntarily". A person who is still voluntarily at the police station is not covered by this requirement since he is deemed to be free to go if he pleases. But there is no doubt that he has a right to have someone informed of his whereabouts and this right is not subject to the provisions for delay.   **5–19**

The grounds for delaying are set out in Annex B, which is dealt with more fully at para.5–51 below. Broadly, they are that there are reasonable grounds for believing that telling the named person of the arrest will lead to interference with or harm to evidence or witnesses or the alerting of others involved in such an offence, or the recovery of any property (subs.(5) and Code C, Annex B). These are the identical grounds for delaying access to legal advice under s.58 below. As will be seen, the courts have interpreted that power to delay very strictly against the police. Presumably the same approach applies to this power to delay. The courts have held that s.56 is quite separate and independent of s.58—as is indeed specifically stated to be the case by Code C.[36] Delay under s.56 therefore has to be separately approved.[37]   **5–20**

If delay is authorised, the suspect must be told of the fact and of the reasons for it and the reasons must be noted on his custody sheet (subs.(6)). When the grounds for delay cease to apply the suspect must be permitted to exercise his right to have someone informed of his whereabouts (subs.(9)). If the suspect is moved from one police station to another, the right to have someone informed of his whereabouts arises again (subs.(8)).

Research data

Brown (1989) found that 18 per cent of the 5,500 or so suspects in the sample requested that someone interested in their welfare be told of their detention (p.34). The take-up varied considerably between police stations. Some of the variation was explicable but some was not. The author suggested that variations both in this regard and in regard to take-up of legal advice (see below) could have   **5–21**

---

[33] Under the Serious Organised Crime and Police Bill 2004–2005 it will apply to any indictable offence.

[34] House of Commons, *Hansard*, Standing Committee E, February 23, 1984, col.1385.

[35] House of Commons, *Hansard*, Standing Committee E, February 23, 1984, col.1387.

[36] "The fact the grounds for delaying notification of arrest may be satisfied does not automatically mean the grounds for delaying access to legal advice will also be satisfied" (Code C, Annex B, para.5).

[37] *R. v Parris* (1989) Cr.App.R. 68, CA; *Lifely, The Times*, July 16, 1990, CA.

been affected "by the way in which custody officers outline detainees' rights to them and levels of awareness among the criminal community of their rights" (p.35). It appeared from the custody record that the police managed to contact the designated person in two-thirds of cases where notification was sought. Usually, this was a parent or other relative (65 per cent of cases) but in a minority of cases it was either a friend (16 per cent) or a social worker (4 per cent). Contact was generally made quickly. In half the cases it was done within 15 minutes, in 60 per cent within half an hour and in 75 per cent within one hour (p.35). Authority to delay notification was given by a superintendent in 53 cases (just under 1 per cent; p.35).

5–22   Brown *et al.* (1992) found that delays were being imposed even less frequently—in only 0.1 per cent of cases (p.68). Bottomley *et al.* (1991a) found that sometimes the police resort to informal means to achieve delay, for instance, by carrying out the duty to inform only when they come to search the suspect's home. This obviously does not comply with the duty to carry out intimation "as soon as practicable" as required by PACE, s.56(1).

Brown (1993) found that far higher proportions of those detained under the terrorism provisions request that someone be informed of their detention. One reason may be that they can be detained for longer. Another may be that they are often arrested at ports and airports and would want to notify those expecting them. Of those detained over an 18 month period, 43 per cent asked to exercise this right. The power to delay was used extensively—in over 70 per cent of cases where requests were made (p.25). In about half (48 per cent) the delay had not been lifted by the time the detention ended (p.27).

Inquiries by relatives or friends

5–23   Where an inquiry as to the whereabouts of a detained person is made by his friends or relatives, or a person with an interest in his welfare, they should be told where he is, unless the exceptions permitting delay in Annex B apply or unless the suspect himself does not consent to this (Code C, para.5.5). Action taken under this paragraph must be recorded on the custody record. No one may be prevented from notifying the outside world of the fact of his arrest under s.56 for more than 36 hours (subs.(3)) from "the relevant time" as defined in s.41 (see above). The time limit applies even to terrorism cases (subs.(11)).[38] However, in regard to terrorism cases, there are additional grounds on which a delay of the exercise of the right for up to a total of 48 hours can be approved, as was recommended by Lord Jellicoe's report[39]—namely where otherwise there would be interference with the gathering of information about acts of terrorism or it would make it more difficult to prevent an act of terrorism or to secure the arrest, prosecution or conviction of anyone in connection with terrorism charges (subs.(11) and Code C, Annex B, para.8).

---

[38] The 1989 N.I. PACE Order, Art.57(10) disapplies subs.(11).
[39] *Review of the Operation of the Prevention of Terrorism (Temporary Provisions) Act* (Cmnd.8803, 1983), para.112.

The permitted telephone call

Code C, para.5.6 provides that, subject to some conditions, the suspect should be   **5–24**
supplied with writing materials on request and should be allowed to speak on the
telephone for a reasonable time to one person. This is specifically stated (in Note
5E) to be separate from the right to have someone informed about the fact of his
arrest under para.5.1 and the right to seek legal advice in person or on the
telephone under para.6.1.

Whether the call is at public expense is in the discretion of the custody officer.
Any officer may listen to what is being said, unless the call is to a solicitor, and may
terminate the call if it is being abused (para.5.7). The detainee must be cautioned
that what he says in any letter, call or message (other than in communication to his
solicitor) may be read or listened to and may be given in evidence (*ibid.*).

There is no obligation to inform the suspect of the right to make a telephone
call—though the Notice of Entitlements does contain this information. Few suspects request to make a telephone call. Brown (1989, pp.35–36) found that only
6 per cent did so. Brown *et al.* (1992, p.58) found that requests were made by 12
per cent of the sample drawn after the 1991 revision of the Codes.

Also, as has been seen, whereas if it is a serious arrestable offence the rights   **5–25**
under paras 5.1 and 6.1 could previously be delayed only on the authority of a
superintendent, these rights could be delayed or denied[40] on the authority of an
inspector if para.1, 2 or 8 of Annex B applied[41] and the suspect was in detention
in connection with a serious arrestable offence. But, according to police records,
they are in practice very rarely either delayed or denied. Brown (1989) found that
4 per cent of requests were delayed; Brown *et al.* (1992) found 2 per cent delayed
or denied (p.58). The latter study does suggest, however, that there is under-
recording both of requests and of the outcome of the request. Their observational
data suggested that 12 per cent of suspects request telephone calls and their interviews with suspects suggested that up to a quarter of requests are delayed or
refused (p.58). Also, the decision was sometimes taken without reference to the
inspector as is required by the Code.

In terrorism cases, Brown (1993) found a higher level of requests for telephone
calls (49 out of 253, or 19 per cent) and a higher level of delays (17 out of 49, or
35 per cent). Nevertheless, calls were eventually made in 12 out of the 17 cases
(or 71 per cent) in which delay was authorised. In two of these cases the call was,
however, only made after the suspect had been charged (pp.27–28).

Foreigners

The previous, somewhat muddling rules relating to foreigners and Commonwealth   **5–26**
citizens in Code C, s.7 were simplified in the 1991 revision of the Code. Instead of
making distinctions between categories of overseas persons they are now all
treated alike. Paragraph 7.1 states that a citizen of an independent Commonwealth
country or a foreign national, including one from Eire, "may communicate at any
time with the appropriate High Commission, Embassy or Consulate". He must be
informed of this right as soon as practicable (Code C, para.3.3). He must also be

---

[40] This power was added by the April 1991 revision of Code C.
[41] Broadly, these provisions cover interference with the investigation.

told as soon as practicable of his right to have the High Commission, Embassy or Consulate told of his whereabouts and the grounds for his detention (para.7.1). In the case of Commonwealth citizens or foreigners from a country with which a bilateral consular Convention is in force,[42] his High Commission, Embassy or Consulate must be informed as soon as practicable (para.7.2) unless he is a political refugee (para.7.4). It is therefore surprising that at least in terrorism cases the rules seem quite often to be flouted. Brown (1993) found 70 terrorism cases in which the suspect came from a country with which there was no consular Convention in force. Most (64 cases) were from the Irish Republic. Embassies were informed in only 17 of the 70 cases. All 17 were Irish cases. In a further 15 cases the suspect was told of his right to inform his Embassy but declined to exercise it (pp.37–38).

Consular officials are stated to be free to visit one of their nationals "to talk to them and if required, to arrange for legal advice" (para.7.3). Such visits "shall take place out of the hearing of a police officer" (*ibid.*).

The rights of Commonwealth citizens and foreign nationals to inform someone of their whereabouts after arrest cannot be interfered with even when it is a case covered by Annex B (Code C, Note 7A).

Juveniles

5–27   The custody officer must inform the parents of a person under the age of 17 or another "appropriate adult" of his detention (Code C, para.3.13). This is a duty laid upon the custody officer which the juvenile cannot veto. It is technically distinct from the right of notification under s.56 (*ibid.*). A juvenile could therefore request that someone in addition to the appropriate adult be informed.

Visitors

5–28   Suspects have no absolute right to visitors while in custody but they are entitled to receive visitors at the custody officer's discretion, which he is encouraged to exercise (Code C, para.5.4, and Note 5B). This is referred to in the Notice of Rights and Entitlements but it is very rarely exercised. Brown (1989, p.36) found that only 5 per cent of suspects had a visitor, usually a parent or other relative (50 per cent) or a friend (24 per cent). In terrorism cases Brown (1993, p.28) found 8 per cent of suspects had visitors.

Additional rights of children and young persons: s.57[43]

5–29   Section 57 replaced s.34(2) of the Children and Young Persons Act 1933 which provided that where a child or young person has been arrested, reasonable steps must be taken to inform his parent or guardian. The Philips Royal Commission recommended[44] that this provision should be reaffirmed and s.57 gave effect to

---

[42] A list of such countries appears in Code C, Annex F.
[43] See also the text of the Act, set out below.
[44] Philips Report, para.4.80.

the recommendation. It requires that when a child or young person is in police detention such steps as are practicable must be taken to ascertain the identity of a person "responsible for their welfare" (Code C, para.3.13). That person should, if possible, be informed as soon as practicable that the child or young person has been arrested and why and where he is being held (subss.(3) and (4) and para.3.13). This rule applies even if the child or young person is held in connection with a terrorism investigation (subs.(10)).

The person responsible for his welfare, in addition to the parent or guardian, is "any other person who has for the time being assumed responsibility for his welfare" (subs.(5)). For a child in care this means the local authority or voluntary organisation which has him in care. For someone in respect of whom there is a supervision order it means the person responsible for his supervision. If no one else can be located, the social services of the local authority or any other responsible adult should be notified. Code C, as will be seen (see paras 5–152, 6–54—6–57 below), has various provisions regarding the interviewing of juveniles. The relevant one regarding notification of the fact of arrest is para.3.9 which requires that if the arrested person is a juvenile, the custody officer must as soon as practicable inform the "appropriate adult" (see paras 6–56—6–64 below) of the grounds for his detention and his whereabouts and ask the adult to come to the police station to see the juvenile.

The custody officer's duty to inform an appropriate adult of the juvenile's arrest and to get him to the police station is quite separate from the juvenile's right to have someone informed of his arrest under s.56 (subs.(9)). Section 57 is headed "Additional rights of children and young persons" but it deals in fact with the duties of the police.

Access to legal advice: s.58 and Code C, s.6[45]

Pre-PACE, the position regarding access to legal advice for suspects in the police station was to be found in the Preamble to the Judges' Rules and in the dicta of judges in a number of cases.[46] The Judges' Rules on the matter sounded very reasonable[47] but in fact the reality was otherwise. It was generally agreed that few suspects knew of the right, few asked to see a solicitor and that, of those who did, the majority were refused such access.[48] Also, there was no system for providing such advice.

5–30

---

[45] See 1989 N.I. PACE Order, Art.59 and Code C, s.6.
[46] See especially *Allen* [1977] Crim.L.R. 63; *Lemsatef* [1977] 2 All E.R. 835; *Elliott* [1977] Crim.L.R. 551; *Reid* [1982] Crim.L.R. 514.
[47] They stated that the rules did not affect certain established principles including the principle that "every person at any stage of an investigation should be able to communicate and to consult privately with a solicitor . . . provided that in such a case no unreasonable delay or hindrance is caused to the processes of investigation".
[48] See, for instance, Zander, "Access to a Solicitor in the Police Station" [1972] Crim.L.R. 342; Baldwin and McConville, "Police Interrogation and the Right to See a Solicitor" [1979] Crim.L.R. 145; Softley, "An Observation Study in Four Police Stations", (Royal Commission on Criminal Procedure, Research Study 4 (1981)), p.68.

The Philips Royal Commission recommended[49] that a suspect should be informed that generally he had a right to see a solicitor privately. The right to see a solicitor, it said, should be withheld only in exceptional circumstances which it listed and which should be confined to grave offences.[50] Refusal of access to a solicitor, it said,[51] should require the authority of a sub-divisional commander and the grounds should be specified on the custody sheet. If for any reason a suspect could not be brought before a magistrate within 24 hours, he should be seen by a solicitor whose duty it would be to ensure that he was being properly cared for.[52]

The 1984 Act broadly adopted the Philips Royal Commission's approach, granting the suspect an absolute right to legal advice (s.58(1)) subject to a strictly defined power to delay such advice in exceptional circumstances (s.58(8)) (see below para.5–51).

The right to legal advice

5–31   The basic provision is s.58(1) which states, "A person arrested and held in custody in a police station[53] or other premises[54] shall be entitled, if he so requests, to consult a solicitor *privately* at any time" (emphasis added). Code C, para.6.1 states:

> "Unless Annex B applies, all detainees must be informed that they may at any time consult and communicate privately, with a solicitor, whether in person, in writing or by telephone and that free independent legal advice is available from the duty solicitor."

The 2003 revision of Code C added in Note 6J, "This right to consult or communicate in private is fundamental".

5–32   The right to consult privately with one's legal adviser has been expressly recognised by the European Court of Human Rights. In *S v Switzerland*[55] the Court insisted on "an accused's right to communicate with his advocate out of the hearing of a third person", saying that legal advice would lose its effectiveness if it were subject to state surveillance. More recently in *Brennan v United Kingdom*[56] the Court held that a suspect's right to communicate confidentially with a lawyer "is part of the basic requirement of a fair trial". The Court found that there had been a breach of Art.6(3)(c) because a police officer had been

[49] Philips Report, para.4.87.
[50] Philips Report, para.4.91.
[51] Philips Report, para.4.91.
[52] Philips Report, para.3.107.
[53] A person on remand in custody at a magistrates' court is technically not within this phrase but it was held that such a person has a common law right to consult a solicitor "as soon as practicable". The police were therefore not justified in having a rule refusing a person in custody at court access to a solicitor if the request was made after 10 am. See *R. v Chief Constable of South Wales, Ex p. Merrick* [1994] 1 W.L.R. 663; [1994] Crim.L.R. 852, DC.
[54] This does not apply therefore where the suspect is questioned at his home—*Stilgoe v Eager, The Times*, January 27, 1994, DC.
[55] (1992) 14 E.H.R.R. 670.
[56] (2001) 34 E.H.R.R. 507, para.58; [2002] Crim.L.R. 216.

present during the suspect's first interview with his lawyer. In *R. (on the application of La Rose) v Commissioner of the Police of the Metropolis*[57] the Divisional Court held that the suspect's Convention rights had not been breached when his first interview with the solicitor took place over a telephone on the custody officer's desk with the officer present throughout. The Court said there was no evidence that the officer had eavesdropped, or attempted to, on his conversation and there was therefore no evidence of prejudice. Commenting, Professor Andrew Ashworth suggested that this decision cannot stand with that of the ECHR in *Brennan* and that the idea that the defendant must establish prejudice is not in line with the Strasbourg decisions.[58]

The right to consult a solicitor privately also generally applies to suspects held under the Terrorism Act[59] though in certain circumstances a very senior officer[60] can direct that the consultation be in the sight and hearing of an inspector in the uniform branch[61] who is not involved in the investigation.[62]

A person who is at a police station voluntarily has the same right to free legal **5–33** advice as a person who is there under arrest (Code C, Note 1A) but he need not be specifically so informed until he is cautioned. At that point he must be told that he is not under arrest, that he is not obliged to remain at the police station, but that, if he does remain there, he has a right to free legal advice, including the right to speak to a solicitor on the telephone (Code C, para.3.21). (It has been held that free legal advice under the scheme is only available to a volunteer being interviewed at a police station and therefore does not apply to a volunteer being interviewed by a social security visitor at a benefit agency building.[63])

Where the suspect being detained by the police is a juvenile or someone who is mentally disordered or mentally vulnerable, either the detainee or the appropriate adult (see para.6–56 below) may exercise the right to ask for legal advice (Code C, para.3.19). That means it could be exercised by the appropriate adult even though the person for whom it is exercised does not agree. A new para.6.5A, added in the 2004 revision of Code C, stated that the appropriate adult has the right to call for a solicitor even though the juvenile does not want legal advice, but that the juvenile cannot be forced to see the solicitor.

Previously, Note 3G stated that if such a person wished to exercise the right to **5–34** legal advice, action should be taken straightaway and not be delayed until the appropriate adult arrives. Presumably as a result of a drafting lapse, Note 3G does not appear in the 2003 revised version of Code C. In respect of the mentally disordered and the mentally vulnerable, the matter is dealt with by Annex E, Note E1. Juveniles are not covered by Annex E. However, para.3.19 says that if the

---

[57] [2002] Crim.L.R. 215, DC.

[58] [2002] Crim.L.R. 215 at 216.

[59] See now the Terrorism Act 2000, Sch.8, para.7(1).

[60] In England and Wales a Commander or Assistant Chief Constable, and in Northern Ireland an Assistant Chief Constable (Sch.8, para.9(2)).

[61] Sch.8, para.9(1), (3). Research has shown that this power is used very rarely. Out of 384 police station consultations between suspects held under the PTA, there were only nine directions, involving two cases, that consultations should take place within the sight and hearing of a police officer (Brown (1993), p.16).

[62] Sch.8, para.9(4)(c).

[63] *R. (on the application of the Secretary of State for Social Security) v South Croydon Central Division Magistrates' Court*, unreported, Case No.CO/248/2000, October 24, 2000, DC.

detainee, or appropriate adult on the detainee's behalf, asks for a solicitor to be called to give legal advice, the provisions of s.6 apply and para.6.5 says, "Whenever legal advice is requested, and unless Annex B applies, the custody officer must act without delay to secure the provision of such advice." The duty to act "without delay" applies regardless of whether the request is made by the detainee or the appropriate adult. The point is therefore still covered, albeit indirectly.

The right is that of the client not of the lawyer—see *Rixon v Chief Constable of Kent*[64] where the Court of Appeal held that the fact that the client has a right to consult the solicitor does not mean that the solicitor's firm can sue for damages for negligence if one of its members is refused access to the client. The court said, *obiter*, that different considerations might apply if the solicitor were removed by force from a police station which he had entered in right of his client. The claimants had placed no reliance on any interference with a client's right. The action was basically about the attitude of the police towards the firm of solicitors. In *Coyle v Reid*[65] the Northern Ireland Court of Appeal held that a solicitor who was forcibly ejected when she tried to insist on her right to remain with the client while a non-intimate sample was taken for DNA testing had no claim for damages. The court ruled that a solicitor had no common law or statutory right to be present during the interview, and therefore, *a fortiori*, there was no right to be present whilst a sample was taken. The court cited *R. v Chief Constable of the Royal Ulster Constabulary, Ex p. Begley* and *Ex p. McWilliams*[66] for the proposition that there was no common law right to have a solicitor present during police interviews. Lord Browne-Wilkinson in that case said that it had never before been argued that there was such a right.

5–35   Code C provides that a suspect who has been permitted to consult a solicitor shall be entitled on request to have the lawyer present during the interview (para.6.8[67]). This now applies in terrorism cases too.[68] In *Coyle v Reid* (para.5–34) the Northern Ireland Court of Appeal held that the solicitor had what it called a statutory licence—rather than a right—and a licence can be revoked. The court said it reserved for another day the question whether the licence could only be revoked on reasonable grounds. In that case there were reasonable grounds because the police anticipated the possibility of a fracas since the suspect had made it clear that he would resist the taking of the sample. But excluding a solicitor would rarely be justifiable.

The consultation can be either in person, on the telephone, or in writing (Code C, para.6.1). Requests to see a solicitor must be recorded on the custody record (subs.(2)). (This requirement does not apply, however, if the request is made "at a time while he [the detainee] is at court after being charged with an offence" (subs.(3)). The Government's reasoning was that he would then be in the custody of the court rather than of the police.[69]) Normally the request must be allowed as

---

[64] *The Times*, April 11, 2000, CA.
[65] [2000] N.I. 7, CA.
[66] [1997] 4 All E.R. 833, HL.
[67] Pre-2003, para.6.8 said "must be allowed to be present".
[68] The Northern Ireland Code of Practice under the Terrorism Act 2000, para.6.7 is in the same terms as the pre-2003 version.
[69] But see *R. v Chief Constable of South Wales, Ex p. Merrick* [1994] 1 W.L.R. 663; [1994] Crim.L.R. 852, DC.

soon as practicable (subs.(4)). In any event, it must be allowed within 36 hours (subs.(5)) or, in terrorism cases, within 48 hours—from the time of arrest, rather than the time of arrival at the police station (subs.(13)(a)).

Code C (para.3.5) requires that when the custody officer authorises a person's detention in the police station (see below) he must be asked to sign on the custody record to signify whether he wants legal advice at that point.

Informing the suspect of his right to free legal advice

Under the US Supreme Court's famous decision in *Miranda v Arizona*[70] the **5–36** American police are required to inform a suspect of his right to legal advice at the point of arrest. The basic English approach, by contrast, is that the suspect should be told of his right to have a lawyer on arrival at the police station. Section 58 itself does not deal with the point directly but it states that a person is entitled to exercise the right if he has been arrested and is held in custody. Code C deals with the point in the same way by requiring that all persons in police detention must be informed about the right to consult a solicitor. In *Kirkup v DPP* the Divisional Court held that the right arose when the custody officer formally detains the suspect by booking him in.[71]

The English rule is based on the theory that, since the suspect must be taken to the police station as soon as practicable (s.30), and interviewing should basically be conducted only at the police station (Code C, para.11.1[72]), there is no need to inform him of his right to consult a solicitor prior to arrival at the police station. Whether that view is sensible is debatable. But what if he is in fact interviewed elsewhere? There is conflicting Court of Appeal authority as to whether in those circumstances he must be informed of his right to have legal advice.[73] It is submitted that the better view is that if the suspect is in fact interviewed at a place other than a police station he must be informed of this important right[74]—whether or not it is practicable to make the necessary arrangements for the solicitor to arrive before the interview takes place. Otherwise the right to be told about the availability of legal advice may come too late to be of any use.[75]

---

[70] (1966) 384 U.S. 436.

[71] [2003] EWHC Admin 2354; [2004] Crim.L.R. 230. See also *Whitley v DPP* [2003] EWHC Admin 2512; [2004] Crim.L.R. 585.

[72] Following a decision to arrest a suspect he must not be interviewed about the relevant offence except at a police station or other authorised place of detention unless delay would cause certain unacceptable consequences, set out in para.11.1(a)–(c).

[73] See *Kerawalla* [1991] Crim.L.R. 451, CA—interview of drugs suspect by customs officers in a hotel; *cf. Sanusi* [1992] Crim.L.R. 43, CA—interview of drugs suspect by customs officers in customs area at Gatwick. In the former case the court held that there was no duty to inform the suspect of his right of access to legal advice. In the latter, the court, which included Lord Taylor C.J., took the contrary view.

[74] The Court of Appeal in *Samuel* said: "Perhaps the most important right given (or rather renewed) to a person detained by the police is his right to obtain legal advice" (1988) 87 Cr.App.R. 232 at p.241, *per* Hodgson J. A person who has been arrested is plainly a person detained by the police.

[75] In *Sanusi*, above n.73, the suspect made admissions when first interviewed. At a later point he was told he could have a solicitor. From then on he declined to answer questions until the solicitor arrived. The Court of Appeal drew attention to this fact when holding that the first interview should have been excluded.

5–37   A person must be told of his right to consult privately with a solicitor "when a person is brought to a police station under arrest" or is arrested there after coming voluntarily (Code C, para.3.1). That means forthwith.

The 1995 revision of the Code added new provisions designed to strengthen access to legal advice.[76] The custody officer must act on a request for legal advice "without delay" (para.6.5). If the detainee declines legal advice, the custody officer must now point out that the right to legal advice includes the right to speak with a solicitor on the telephone and ask whether he wants to do so (*ibid.*). If the detainee still declines legal advice, the custody officer should ask his reasons and record them (*ibid.*).[77] There are also provisions requiring that the detainee be reminded of the right to legal advice at different stages. Where someone chooses to speak to a solicitor on the telephone "he must be allowed to do so in private unless this is impractical because of the design and layout of the custody area or the location of the telephones" (Note 6J).

As has been seen, Note 6J, revised in 2003, has a ringing affirmation of the importance of the right:

> "This right to consult or communicate in private is fundamental. Except as allowed by the Terrorism Act 2000, Sch.8, para.9, if the requirement for privacy is compromised because what is said or written by the detainee or solicitor for the purpose of giving and receiving legal advice is overheard, listened to, or read by others without the informed consent of the detainee, the right will effectively have been denied."

Free legal advice in the police station

5–38   Legal advice given to a suspect in the police station is free of charge regardless of the suspect's means and regardless of whether he chooses to have his own solicitor or a duty solicitor. The suspect must be informed of this fact when he is first brought to a police station under arrest or is arrested there (Code C, para.3.1(ii)). It is one of the items of information he must also be given in written form (Code C, para.3.2).

The Code also lays down that police stations advertise the right to legal advice in posters "prominently displayed in the charging area of every police station" (para.6.3). When that would be helpful and it is practicable, the poster should have translations into the main relevant ethnic minority languages and the principal European Community languages (Note 6H).

The Code lays down precise rules as to the point in time at which someone in a police station must be informed of his right to legal advice and whether such notification should be oral, written or both:

(1)   As has been seen, a person who comes to the station under arrest must be told immediately both orally and in writing (Code C, paras 3.1 and 3.2).

---

[76] Along lines proposed by the Runciman Royal Commission Recommendation 59, based on Runciman Report, para.49, p.36.
[77] "Once it is clear a detainee does not wish to speak to a solicitor in person or by telephone they should cease to be asked their reasons" (para.6.5).

(2) A person who comes to the police station voluntarily, if he asks about legal advice, must be given a written notice about legal advice (Code C, para.3.22). (But there is no duty to inform him if he does not ask unless he is cautioned (para.3.21)!)

(3) A person who comes to the station voluntarily and is arrested there must then be told of his right to legal advice both orally and in writing (Code C, paras 3.1 and 3.2).

(4) A person who comes to the station voluntarily and is then cautioned must then be given verbal notice of the right to legal advice (Code C, para.3.21), and he should be given a copy of the notice explaining the arrangements for getting free legal advice (para.3.16). He should be told that free legal advice includes a right to speak with a solicitor on the telephone and asked whether he wants to do so (*ibid.*).

Code C (Note 6B) says that a person who asks for legal advice should be given   **5–39**
an opportunity to consult a specific solicitor (for example, his own solicitor or one known to him or someone else from that firm), or the duty solicitor (see below). Failing this he should be given an opportunity of choosing a solicitor from a list of those willing to provide legal advice. If this solicitor is unavailable, he can choose up to two alternates. If these attempts to secure legal advice are unsuccessful, the custody officer has the discretion to allow further attempts until a solicitor has been contacted who agrees to provide legal advice. But the police officer is not to advise the suspect about any particular firm of solicitors (*ibid.*).

Code C has a provision that no police officer shall at any time do or say anything with the intention of dissuading a person in detention from obtaining legal advice (para.6.4), and that reminders of the right to legal advice must be given in accordance with various provisions of the Code: paras 11.2 (commencement or recommencement of interviews), 15.4 (reviews of further detention), 16.4(b) (inviting comment on someone else's statement after charge), 16.5(b) (questions after charge), and Code D, paras 3.17(ii)[78] (before identity procedure) and 6.3[79] (request to take an intimate sample).

If a solicitor arrives at the police station to see someone, that person must be informed that the solicitor is there and asked whether he wishes to see him—even if he has already declined legal advice (Code C, para.6.15).[80] This will apply especially when the solicitor has been sent by a family member or friend without the suspect's knowledge. (See to like effect Annex B, para.6[81] after access to a solicitor has been delayed.)

Duty solicitor schemes were originally provided for by s.59 of the Act   **5–40**
which enabled the Law Society to establish such schemes. The Law Society ran these schemes from 1985 to 1988. Under the Legal Aid Act 1988 they were taken over by the new Legal Aid Board. Now, under the Access to

[78] Formerly 2.15(ii).
[79] Formerly 5.2.
[80] See *Franklin, The Times*, June 16, 1994, CA.
[81] Formerly 3.

Justice Act 1999, the Legal Services Commission (LSC) runs what was previously known as the legal aid scheme and the function of providing the duty solicitor system is carried out by the LSC's Criminal Defence Service (CDS) which took over as from April 1, 2001. It is permitted to provide the service both through contracts with firms in private practice and through services provided by lawyers employed directly by the LSC. (For further information see the LSC's website: *www.legalservices.gov.uk/cds*—see especially Duty Solicitor Arrangements 2001 as amended in July 2003 and the Duty Solicitor Manual—both accessible on the Legal Services Commission's website.)

The duty solicitor scheme operates throughout the country. Every police station in the country is covered. (The Legal Services Commission's annual report for 2001–2002 stated that as of March 2002 there were 299 local duty solicitor schemes in operation and 5,465 duty solicitors working on them.[82])

In order to be eligible to act as a duty solicitor, the individual solicitor previously had to be vetted and approved by a local committee, but that system was abolished under the Duty Solicitor Arrangements which began in April 2001.[83] As from that date, the task of assessing competence falls to the LSC's accreditation scheme.[84]

5–41   The Duty Solicitor Arrangements provide that in order to be accepted, an applicant must be a qualified solicitor with a practising certificate who has "comprehensive experience of criminal defence work including the provision of advice in the police station and advocacy in the Crown or magistrates' courts throughout the 12 months prior to the application".[85] A person who has been in full-time employment in the prosecution system for 18 months needs to have been in criminal defence work only for the previous six months.[86] The applicant must establish his competence either by showing that he was accepted as a duty solicitor under the previous Legal Aid Board's Duty Solicitor Arrangements or by fulfilling the requirements of the LSC's accreditation scheme.[87] Broadly speaking, the accreditation scheme means he must be competent to do the relevant work, must have a minimum of relevant experience and have attended both an advocacy course and a course for police station advisers. Although the individual rather than the firm is the duty solicitor, the candidate's firm must also have a contract from the LSC to do criminal work. The applicant would then normally be entitled to join the duty solicitor scheme for the area covered by his office. On application to the LSC, he may or may not be allowed also to join other local schemes. For a description of the scheme see *Criminal Litigation Accreditation Scheme Stage 1: Assessment and Accreditation Procedures* (The Law Society, 2001). There are two components—the Police Station Qualification (PSQ) and the Magistrates' Court Qualification (MSQ). To be included in the regional duty solicitor scheme one must pass both the PSQ and the MSQ.

---

[82] At p.47, para.3.24. There are no more recent figures.
[83] The Duty Solicitor Arrangements are made by the Legal Services Commission under the Access to Justice Act 1999, s.3(4). See Criminal Defence Service Duty Solicitor Arrangements 2001.
[84] Duty Solicitor Arrangements 2001, para.4.3.
[85] Duty Solicitor Arrangements 2001, para.4.5.
[86] Duty Solicitor Arrangements 2001, para.4.6.
[87] See the Law Society's *Criminal Practitioners Newsletter*, January 2001, p.5.

The PSQ involves a Portfolio detailing five cases involving advice at the police station and the Critical Incidents Test where a tape of different scenarios is stopped at various points for the candidate to give appropriate advice. The MSQ consists of a Portfolio—short notes on 20 cases and a detailed summary of a further five cases—and the Interview and Advocacy Test where the applicant must interview a client and then conduct advocacy in front of an assessor in three different cases.

Representatives

Solicitors' firms that undertake criminal work commonly employ non-solicitors   **5–42**
to provide part of this service in police stations. In the 1980s and 1990s the quality of their work became the subject of strong criticism, as a result of which the Law Society and the legal aid authorities put in hand a substantial reform programme designed to raises standards.[88] The rule now is that if their work is to be paid by the Legal Services Commission, non-solicitors undertaking police station work have to be registered as probationary representatives on the accreditation register.[89] Following registration, probationers have six months to pass one of the three accreditation tests: the portfolio test,[90] a two-hour written test and a similar tape-recorded critical incidents test to that taken under the PSQ (para.5–41 above). All three tests must be passed within 12 months. There is no power to extend that period. Failure to comply results in the probationer being suspended—though he can re-apply once all the tests have been passed.

On passing the tests a "probationary" representative becomes an "accredited"   **5–43**
representative. The work that can be done depends on the adviser's status. Probationary representatives cannot do duty solicitor work nor can they provide advice or assistance in cases triable only on indictment (other than "bail backs" or identification procedures). Accredited representatives can provide advice and assistance in any own solicitor cases. They can also undertake work delegated by a duty solicitor once he has accepted the case and given initial telephone advice.

See generally *www.legalservicesc.gov.uk/cds*—Police Station Representatives' Scheme Information sheet, issue 2, September 2003. See also the Law Society's guide by Eric Shepherd, *Police Station Skills for Legal Advisers,* (2004); and Ed Cape, *Defending Suspects at Police Stations* (4th ed., Legal Action Group, 2003).

The telephone service

The duty solicitor is contacted through a special telephone service covering the   **5–44**
whole of England and Wales. It is run currently by FirstAssist, part of the Royal

---

[88] See Bridges and Hodgson, "Improving Custodial Advice", [1995] Crim.L.R. 101; and Bridges and Choongh, *Improving Police Station Legal Advice* (Law Society Research and Policy Planning Unit Research Study No.31 and Legal Aid Board, 1998). The latter report led to further revisions in the requirements which were implemented as from January 1, 2000—for details see *Legal Aid Board Annual Report 1998–99*, p.40, para.4.13 and *Annual Report 1999–2000*, p.33, para.4.10.
[89] See Legal Services Commission in Police Stations Register Arrangements 2001.
[90] Showing nine police station attendances involving advice-giving.

and Sun Alliance Group of companies.[91] When a suspect asks for the duty solicitor a call is made to the service (it does not handle calls to a named solicitor or
a solicitor chosen from a list; rather they are contacted by the police). The service then contacts either the rota duty solicitor or duty solicitors on the panel until
one is found who is willing to assist the suspect. The call centre operates subject
to targets. In 1999–2000 it answered 95 per cent of calls from police stations and
duty solicitors within 20 seconds.[92]

In rota schemes an identifiable solicitor is on duty; in panel schemes the service calls the solicitors on the panel in the order in which they appear on the list,
starting with the next one after the last one used. In 1999–2000, the call centre
deployed within 30 minutes 93 per cent of rota cases and 87 per cent of panel
cases.[93]

A duty solicitor on a rota is under an obligation to accept a referral unless
already engaged with another suspect.[94] A panel duty solicitor is not under such
a duty. The advantage of a rota is that the service only has to contact one solicitor and that he is in principle guaranteed to be available—subject obviously to
the duty solicitor work he already has in hand. The disadvantage is that a solicitor has to hold himself available to go to a police station. Among the advantages of the panel arrangements are that it allows the duty solicitors on the panel
to carry on with their normal occupations, but it may lead to delay in actually
finding a solicitor.

Advice on the telephone or attendance in person

5–45 Whether the solicitor attends in person or only advises over the telephone is
dealt with in the General Criminal Contract between the Legal Services
Commission and solicitors who provide the service.[95] As will be seen below, an
important variation of the Contract introduced in 2004 considerably restricts
personal attendance.

Paragraph 8.2.6 of the Contract states that once a case has been accepted the
following services "shall be provided" by the duty solicitor. It lists eight situations, (a) to (h):

> (a) initial advice given to the client on the telephone unless the solicitor is
> at or so close to the police station that he can immediately advise the
> client in person, or the police refuse to allow the client to speak to the
> solicitor in person;

> (b) attendance to provide advice and to attend police interviews with a
> client who has been arrested under s.24 of PACE;

---

[91] The telephone number for the police is 08457 500640; the telephone number for duty solicitors is
08457 500620.
[92] *Legal Aid Board Annual Report 1999–2000*, p.32, para.4.4. More recent figures have not been
published.
[93] *Legal Aid Board Annual Report 1999–2000*, p.32, para.4.4.
[94] Duty Solicitors Arrangements 2001, para.48(1).
[95] The General Criminal Contract can be accessed on *www.legalservices.gov.uk/cds*. The website also
has the Duty Solicitor Manual.

(c)   attendance at any identification parade, group or video identification or confrontation;

(d)   attendance where the client complains of serious maltreatment by the police;

(e)   attendance where the client is a youth or person at risk;

(f)   provision of advice as to the implications of the caution on being charged and whether the client should make a statement at that time;

(g)   representation on any application for a warrant of further detention;

(h)   if a police interview or any identification procedure is postponed to a time when the duty solicitor is no longer on duty (or if on a panel, when it is no longer convenient to act), he must either make arrangements for someone else to act or continue himself to act on an "Own Solicitor" (not Duty Solicitor) basis.

Attendance at the police station is *mandatory* under paras 8.2.6(b) to (e) and (g)   **5–46** above, unless exceptional circumstances exist. The only example of "exceptional circumstances" justifying non-attendance given is where the client changes his mind and expressly instructs the duty solicitor not to attend. They are said to be "less likely to arise" in the case of paras (d) and (e).[96]

After giving initial advice, the duty solicitor must exercise his discretion whether it is in the interests of the client for him (or an Accredited Representative) to attend the police station. In assessing whether attendance is necessary, the duty solicitor must consider whether advice can be given over the telephone with sufficient confidentiality and if he can communicate effectively with the client in that way.[97]

The question of attendance or no is further regulated by the variation in the Contract introduced in 2004.

Significant retrenchment in access to legal advice in the police station aimed at reducing legal aid expenditure had been signalled in the Consultation Papers issued in June 2003 respectively by the Department for Constitutional Affairs and by the Legal Services Commission—both entitled *Delivering Value for Money in the Criminal Defence Service?* The gist of the proposals was that less serious matters and matters where the lawyer cannot in practice achieve anything for the client should either be removed from the scope of the publicly funded police station advice scheme altogether or be restricted to telephone advice only. As a result of the consultation, the latter option (restricting scope in certain circumstances to advice given over the telephone) was the one adopted. Changes were also made in the rules regarding post-charge attendance at the police station.

[96]   para.8.2.8.
[97]   para.8.2.7.

5–47   The changes were implemented in February and May 2004.[98] Under these new rules attendance at the police station is only permitted when the Sufficient Benefit Test is satisfied. The circumstances when this test are satisfied are said to include (and are therefore not limited to) the situations described in para.8.2.6(b) to (f) (para.5–45 above). They also include, when appropriate, advice that "may materially affect the outcome of the investigation and goes significantly beyond initial advice". If any of those factors are present, the attendance will normally be justified. If not, further justification is required.[99]

Any attendance must be for the purposes of providing legal advice that could not be given over the telephone. The solicitor cannot claim for attendance when the advice could have been provided reasonably by way of telephone advice. The file must show "that the attendance was expected to materially progress the case beyond initial advice".[1]

5–48   However, para.8.2.17 provides that only telephone advice can be provided in the following cases unless any of the exceptions listed in para.8.2.18 (see below) apply:

- Where the client is detained in relation to a non-imprisonable offence.

- Where the client has been arrested on a bench warrant for failing to appear and is being held for production before the court—except where the solicitor has clear documentary evidence which is on the file that would result in the client being released from custody, in which case attendance would be justified.

- Where the client has been arrested on suspicion of (i) driving with excess alcohol who is taken to the police station to provide a specimen (Road Traffic Act 1988, s.5); (ii) failure to provide a specimen (RTA 1988, ss.6, 7 and 7A); (iii) driving whilst unfit/drunk in charge of a motor vehicle (RTA 1988, s.4).

- Where the client is detained in relation to breach of police or court bail conditions.

5–49 Paragraph 8.2.18 states that the duty solicitor can attend and advise on any matter covered by para.8.2.17 if one of the following exceptions applies *and* the Sufficient Benefit Test is satisfied, namely where:

(a)   An interview or identification procedure is going to take place.

(b)   The client is eligible for assistance from an appropriate adult.

---

[98] For an overall assessment by the director of the Legal Aid Practitioners Group see *Independent Lawyer*, April 2004, p.17.
[99] para.8.2.14 and 15.
[1] para.8.2.16.

    (c)   The client requires an interpreter or is otherwise unable to communicate over the telephone.

    (d)   The client complains of serious maltreatment by the police.

    (e)   The investigation includes another offence which does not fall under para.17.

If the solicitor is already at the same police station the client may be attended but the solicitor can only claim the Telephone Advice fixed fee.

If the police state that an interview or ID procedure will take place at a specified time, the solicitor should attend in sufficient time to attend the client *i.e.* to take instructions, attending the officer in the case etc.[2]   **5–50**

The solicitor attending a police station is admonished to minimise travel, waiting and attendance time. In assessing whether claims for payment are reasonable, the Contract ominously warns that the LSC "may take into account the average costs incurred by other CDS suppliers" in the region.[3]

Further legal advice immediately following charge may be provided but the Contract states that it will not be reasonable for the solicitor to continue to attend the client thereafter whilst fingerprints, photographs and swabs are taken, except where the client requires further assistance due to his or her particular circumstances such as youth or vulnerability. It could also be reasonable to stay at the police station to make representations about bail.[4]

Delaying access to legal advice

Unless the suspect is being questioned about a serious arrestable offence[5] there is **5–51** no legal right to delay access to legal advice. On the contrary, Code C, para.6.5 states: "Whenever legal advice is requested, and unless Annex B applies, the custody officer must act without delay to secure the provision of such advice" to the person concerned. If, however, the suspect is being held in police detention[6] in connection with a serious arrestable offence, access to legal advice may be delayed if the case comes within the terms of s.58(8) and Annex B (see below). However, as will be seen, because of a ruling of the European Court of Human Rights, one consequence of authorising delay in the suspect getting legal advice, is that neither a court nor a jury can draw adverse inferences from the suspect's silence whilst that delay continues (see para.5–55 below).

If delay is authorised, the detained person must be told of the reason why and the reason must be recorded in the custody record (subs.(9)). There can be no more delay once the reason for authorising delay no longer applies (subs.(11)).

---

[2] para.8.2.20.
[3] para.8.2.21.
[4] para.8.2.22.
[5] Under the Serious Organised Crime and Police Bill 2004–2005 it will be any indictable offence.
[6] Defined in s.118(2).

If the grounds for delay cease to apply the person must, as soon as practicable, be asked if he wishes to exercise the right, the custody record must be noted accordingly, and action must be taken (Annex B, paras 6 and 11[7]). The maximum period of delay is normally 36 hours (Annex B, para.6[8]). At that stage the suspect is entitled as a right to have legal advice in connection with the hearing which must take place to determine whether the police can hold him further. In the case of those held under the Terrorism Act such delay can continue for up to 48 hours (Annex B, para.11).

Grounds for delay: s.58(8); Code C, s.6 and Annex B

5–52   Delay still has to be authorised by an officer of the rank of superintendent—this was not reduced to inspector by the Criminal Justice and Police Act 2001. It can only be authorised where he has reasonable grounds for believing that the exercise of the right:

"(a) will lead to interference with or harm to evidence connected with a serious arrestable [indictable[8a]] offence or interference with or physical injury to other persons; or

(b) will lead to the alerting of other persons suspected of having committed such an offence but not yet arrested for it; or

(c) will hinder the recovery of any property obtained as a result of such an offence."[9]

5–53   There are additional grounds for delaying access to legal advice for terrorism suspects—namely where there are reasonable grounds for believing that it will lead to interference with the gathering of information about the commission, preparation or instigation of acts of terrorism; or where alerting a person will make it more difficult to prevent an act of terrorism or to secure the apprehension or conviction of someone for a terrorist offence.[10] Delay can also be authorised where the offence involves drug trafficking and the officer has reasonable grounds for believing that the suspect has benefited from such trafficking and that the recovery of the value of the proceeds will be hindered (Code C, Annex B, para.2(i)).[11] Delay can also be authorised if the officer has reasonable grounds for believing that the suspect has committed an offence carrying the possibility of the confiscation of proceeds of crime[12] from which he has bene-

---

[7] Formerly 4 and 9.
[8] Formerly 4.
[8a] Serious Organised Crime and Police Bill 2004–2005, Sch.7, Pt 3, para.(10).
[9] s.58(8) and see Annex B, para.A1.
[10] Terrorism Act 2000, Sch.8, para.8(4).
[11] This does not apply, however, in Northern Ireland since there is no equivalent drug-trafficking legislation.
[12] Under the Criminal Justice Act 1988, Pt VI, or the Proceeds of Crime (Scotland) Act 1995, Pt I, or the Proceeds of Crime (Northern Ireland) Order 1996.

fited and that recovery of the benefit would be hindered by access to legal advice (*ibid.*, para.2(ii)).[13]

During the Parliamentary debates on the PACE Bill the Home Secretary, Mr   **5–54**
Douglas Hurd, put the following gloss on the words of s.58(8):

> "The only reason under the Bill for delaying access to a legal adviser relates to the risk that he would either intentionally or inadvertently convey information to confederates still at large that would undercut an investigation in progress. What a suspect's legal adviser says to him can never be a ground for delaying a consultation between them, nor can anxiety about what the legal adviser might say to the suspect. Delay can be authorised only on the basis of what the legal adviser may do once the consultation has been completed."[14]

The Code specifically states that access to a solicitor may not be delayed or denied on the ground that he may advise the person not to answer questions nor on the ground that someone else instructed the solicitor to attend—provided that the detained person then wishes to see the solicitor (Annex B, para.4[15]).

No adverse inference from silence if legal advice is delayed

Section 58 of the Youth Justice and Criminal Evidence Act 1999 amended the law   **5–55**
regarding the adverse inferences that can be drawn from silence by providing that no such inference can be drawn from silence when a suspect is questioned at a police station or other authorised place of detention if he has not been allowed an opportunity to get legal advice. This clearly applies to a person whose access to legal advice has been delayed. Such a person must be given the "old" rather than the "new" caution.[16] This amendment was introduced to bring the law into compliance with the ruling of the European Court of Human Rights in Strasbourg that there had been a breach of the ECHR as a result of denying the applicant access to legal advice whilst being interviewed repeatedly under the terrorism detention provisions.[17]

---

[13] Terrorism Act 2000, Sch.8, para.8(5).

[14] House of Commons, *Hansard*, Standing Committee E, February 2, 1984, col.1417.

[15] Formerly 3.

[16] See Code C as revised in 2003, Annex C, and see especially paras 5–153—5–157 below. The equivalent provision for Northern Ireland is Criminal Evidence (Northern Ireland) Order 1999 (SI 1999/2789), Art.36.

[17] *Murray (John) v United Kingdom* (1996) 22 E.H.R.R. 29; *Magee v United Kingdom* (2000) 8 B.H.R.C. 646; [2000] Crim.L.R. 681; and *Averill v United Kingdom* (2001) 31 E.H.R.R. 36; [2000] Crim.L.R. 682. In *Averill*, however, the Strasbourg court ruled that despite the breach of Art.6(1), the judge's drawing of adverse inferences from silence did not amount to a breach of the defendant's right to a fair trial.

The attitude of the courts towards s.58

5–56   The courts have frequently held that a breach of the main thrust of s.58 is a serious matter—in the jargon used by the courts a significant and/or substantial breach of the Act and the Code. Sometimes this has led to the court penalising such breaches by excluding evidence or, on appeal, quashing the conviction, though in other instances the courts have in effect condoned the breach, usually on the ground that the suspect knew his rights and legal advice would have made no difference to him.

5–57   The leading case is *Samuel*[18] The Court of Appeal quashed a 10 year prison sentence because the police had refused the suspect access to a solicitor under s.58(8). A superintendent had denied the request on the ground that there was a risk that giving the suspect access to a solicitor would result in accomplices being alerted. The Court of Appeal said that access to a solicitor was "a fundamental right of a citizen". It was not enough for the police to believe that giving access to a solicitor might lead to the alerting of other suspects. They had to believe that it very probably would and that the solicitor either would commit the criminal offence of alerting other suspects or would do so inadvertently or unwillingly. Either belief could only rarely be genuinely held by the police officer. Solicitors were intelligent professional people. The expectation that they would alert accomplices "seems to contemplate . . . a naivety and lack of common sense in solicitors, which we doubt often occurs. When and if it does, we think it would have to have reference to the specific person detained. The archetype would, we imagine, be the sophisticated criminal who is known or suspected of being a member of a gang of criminals."[19] The first question was whether the police officer subjectively held the belief. The second question was whether the belief was objectively reasonable. The difficulty of establishing that the grounds for delaying access to a solicitor existed would be especially great where the suspect wanted to consult a duty solicitor. "Duty solicitors will be well known to the police, and we think it will therefore be very difficult to justify consultation with the duty solicitor being delayed."[20] The police suspicion had to relate to the actual adviser who was being called.[21] The decision in *Samuel* made the power to delay given by s.58(8) virtually unusable in relation to solicitors.[22]

---

[18] [1988] Q.B. 615; [1988] 2 All E.R. 135, CA. See to like effect, *inter alia, Absolam* (1989) 88 Cr.App.R. 332, CA and *Walsh* (1989) 91 Cr.App.R. 161, CA.

[19] [1988] Q.B. 615 at 626; [1988] 2 All E.R. 135 at 144.

[20] [1988] Q.B. 615 at 626; [1988] 2 All E.R. 135 at 144.

[21] This is reflected in Code C, Annex B, para.3: "Authority to delay a detained person's right to consult privately with a solicitor may be given only if the authorising officer has reasonable grounds to believe that the solicitor who the detainee wishes to consult will, inadvertently or otherwise, pass on a message from the detained person or act in some other way which will have any of the consequences specified in paras 1 or 2." Note B3 adds that this is likely to be "a rare occurrence and only when it can be shown the suspect is capable of misleading that particular solicitor and there is more than a substantial risk that the suspect will succeed in causing information to be conveyed which will lead to one or more of the specified consequences".

[22] In *Howe* [2003] EWCA 934 the Court of Appeal quashed a convicted dating from 1986 largely because of the way in which H had been denied access to a solicitor on the pretext that it might lead to alerting of suspects. For a rare case where delay was justified by the delicate nature of the investigation see *R. v Governor of Pentonville Prison, Ex p. Walters* [1987] Crim.L.R. 577, DC.

Matters that the court have emphasised have included the following: Would the solicitor have advised silence (*Samuel*,[23] *Parris*,[24] *Silcott*,[25] *Anderson*[26])? Was the defendant able to cope? Was he of low mental capacity or otherwise unable to look after his own interests? Was he knowledgeable about the police station and his rights (*Hughes*,[27] *Chahal*,[28] *Alladice*,[29] *McGovern*,[30] *Gokan and Hassan*[31])? Was the defendant likely to confess anyway (*Oliphant*,[32] *Anderson*[33])?

The presence or absence of good faith on the part of the police officers is sometimes referred to as being a significant matter. Thus, where the police show bad faith it is much more likely that the court will hold the breach to be substantial and significant—see for instance *Canale*.[34] Where there is good faith the court has sometimes referred to that as a factor to be taken into account when deciding that the breach was insufficient to justify excluding the evidence or quashing the conviction.[35] But the fact that the officers acted in good faith does not mean that the court will necessarily overlook or condone the breach. In *Walsh*[36] the Court of Appeal said that although bad faith may make substantial or significant that which might not otherwise have been so, the contrary did not follow. "Breaches which are in themselves significant and substantial are not rendered otherwise by the good faith of the officers." The Court quashed the conviction even though the police had acted in good faith. The trial judge had said that even if the defendant had had a solicitor it would not have made any difference. But he had not heard the defendant and when the defendant eventually saw a solicitor he exercised his right to silence. At most it could be said that it was perhaps uncertain whether the presence of a solicitor would have made a difference.

[23] n.18 above. The solicitor gave evidence that he would probably have advised silence.
[24] (1989) 89 Cr.App.R. 68; [1989] Crim.L.R. 214, CA. Conviction for armed robbery quashed. The suspect was deprived of the solicitor both as adviser and as "umpire" to see that evidence was not fabricated.
[25] *The Times*, December 9, 1991, CA.
[26] [1993] Crim.L.R. 447, CA.
[27] [1988] Crim.L.R. 519, CA. No breach of s.58. H was an educational psychologist.
[28] [1992] Crim.L.R. 124, CA. No breach of s.58. C, a mature businessman, twice said he did not want a solicitor. *cf. Franklin*, *The Times*, June 16, 1994, CA. F, young, unemployed, no experience of police stations, interviews wrongly admitted.
[29] (1988) 87 Cr.App.R. 380, CA. A, who was 18, was arrested for robbery. Asked for a solicitor but request denied. Held there was breach of s.58 but appeal dismissed because A said he was well able to cope and a solicitor would not have added to his knowledge of his rights. See to same effect *Dunford* (1990) 91 Cr.App.R. 150, CA.
[30] (1991) 92 Cr.App.R. 228; (1991) Crim.L.R. 124, CA. Manslaughter. M had an IQ of 73. Wrongfully denied access to solicitor. Conviction quashed even though the confession was true.
[31] sub nom. *Beycan* [1990] Crim.L.R. 185, CA. D, who was a foreigner, was asked: "Are you happy to be interviewed in the normal way we conduct these interviews, without a solicitor, friend or representative?" He said "yes". Conviction quashed. For a similar case involving a foreigner see *Sanusi* [1992] Crim.L.R. 43, CA. See also *Silcott*, n.25, above.
[32] [1992] Crim.L.R. 40, CA. He knew his rights. A solicitor would have made no difference.
[33] [1993] Crim.L.R. 447, CA.
[34] [1990] 2 All E.R. 187, CA. A "flagrant, deliberate and cynical" breach of the Act and the Code by experienced police officers. Conviction quashed.
[35] See for instance *Kerawalla* [1991] Crim.L.R. 451, CA.
[36] (1989) 91 Cr.App.R. 161; [1989] Crim.L.R. 822, CA.

Can damages be claimed where there has been a failure to comply with s.58?

5–59   The principal use made by the defence of breaches of the rules about access to a solicitor is in attempting to establish that evidence should be excluded or that the conviction should be quashed on appeal. (For cases see paras 8–65, 8–66 below.) But is there also the basis for a claim for damages for breach of statutory duty or for breach of some form of constitutional right? In *Cullen v Chief Constable of the Royal Ulster Constabulary*[37] the House of Lords by a majority held that the duty to provide access to a solicitor was a quasi-constitutional right imposed for the benefit of the public at large. Denial of that right in itself could not give rise to an action for damages, at least where there were no significant adverse consequence for the detainee, such as prolonged unlawful detention. The claimant was detained in connection with serious terrorism offences. The statutory rules[38] had been broken in that the decision to delay access to a solicitor had been taken before the claimant had requested such access and because he had not been told the reasons for the decision. The claimant had suffered no loss or damage as a result. (He confessed after getting legal advice and later pleaded guilty.) The majority held that in such a case the remedy was by way of judicial review. The two dissenting judges, Lords Bingham and Steyn, considered that damages could lie—and assessed them in that case at £500. In their view judicial review was useless in dealing with the issue.

Interviewing before the solicitor arrives

5–60   In addition to the power of the police to delay access to a solicitor, there is also a right to start questioning suspects where a solicitor has not yet arrived if the situation is an emergency or the solicitor is likely not to arrive for a considerable period. This power is dealt with in Code C, para.6.6. However, the same restriction on the drawing of adverse inferences from silence applies as when legal advice is delayed on the basis that it comes within the meaning of the statutory phrase "has not been allowed an opportunity to consult a solicitor prior to being questioned" (Youth Justice and Criminal Evidence Act 1999, s.58)—see para.5–55 above.

     There are three situations mentioned in the Code as exceptions to the general rule that a person who asks for legal advice may not be interviewed or continue to be interviewed until he has received it. One is where Annex B applies (*e.g.* the urgent cases mentioned above affecting only serious offences). The second is where an officer of the rank of superintendent or above has reasonable grounds to believe that the consequent delay would be likely to lead to interference with or harm to evidence connected with an offence; interference with or physical harm to other people; serious loss of, or damage to, property; the alerting of other people suspected of having committed an offence but not yet arrested for it; or

---

[37] [2003] UKHL 39, [2004] 2 All E.R. 237.
[38] The Prevention of Terrorism (Temporary Provisions) Act 1984, s.15.

hinder the recovery of property obtained in consequence of the commission of an offence (para.6.6(b)(i). The third is where awaiting the arrival of a solicitor "would cause unreasonable delay to the process of investigation" (para.6.6(b)(ii)).

In all such cases questioning can commence even though the suspect has   **5–61**
exercised his legal right to ask for a solicitor and whether or not the police are entitled to postpone calling him. In all such cases, as has been seen, if questioning takes place, adverse inferences cannot be drawn from silence.

In considering whether any of the above exceptions apply the police should bear in mind the time the solicitor is likely to take in coming to the station, the time for which detention is permitted, the time of day, whether a rest period is imminent and the requirements of other investigations in progress (Code C, Note 6A). If the solicitor says that he is on his way it will not normally be appropriate to begin an interview before he arrives (*ibid.*).

A further category of exception is where the solicitor cannot be contacted or declines to attend and the suspect, having been told about the duty solicitor scheme, declines to ask for the duty solicitor (or the duty solicitor is unavailable) or where the suspect, having first asked for legal advice, changes his mind (para.6.6(c),(d)). In these cases the interview can begin (or continue) if an inspector agrees . In all such cases the suspect must be cautioned in terms of the "new" caution that silence could harm his case because he has been allowed an opportunity to consult a solicitor (*ibid.*, and para.10.5).

Where the suspect has changed his mind about not wanting legal advice the   **5–62**
interview can only start if an officer of the rank of inspector or above, having inquired into the reasons for the suspect's change of mind,[39] agrees and the suspect's change of mind is recorded on tape or in writing (Code C, para.6.6(d)). That leads to complications in regard to the different caution that then has to be administered—see para.5–157 below. Authorisation can be over the telephone if the inspector is able to satisfy himself as to the suspect's change of mind and that it is proper to continue the interview (Code C, Note 6I). The name of the authorising officer and the reason for the suspect's change of mind should be recorded and repeated on tape at the beginning or recommencement of the interview (para.6.6(d)).[40] It seems that about 4 to 5 per cent of all interviews in police stations follow a change of mind by the suspect.[41] Refusal of consent by the inspector is virtually unheard of.[42]

In *R. v Vernon*[43] it was held that the defendant's consent to being interviewed was vitiated by the fact that she had not been informed of the duty solicitor scheme or of the fact that a solicitor was actually on his way; but see also *R. v Hughes*[44] in which consent was held to be valid even though it was based on an error of fact.

---

[39] This requirement was added by the April 1995 revision of the Code.
[40] This sentence was added by the April 1995 revision of the Code.
[41] Brown *et al.* (1992) at p.88. The figure is based on a sample of nearly 7,000 interviews.
[42] "Observers witnessed many instances in which such authorities were sought, and consent was almost always a formality. No case was observed in which an inspector declined to give this permission" (Brown *et al.* (1992) at p.89).
[43] [1988] Crim.L.R. 445, Crown Ct.
[44] [1988] Crim.L.R. 519, CA.

The police do not have to delay taking a breath, blood or urine sample from a motorist until a solicitor arrives at a police station.[45]

Conduct and misconduct by solicitors

5–63 Code C, para.6.8 specifies that, unless one of the exceptions in para.6.6 applies, a person who is permitted to consult a solicitor may have his solicitor present while he is being interviewed. A solicitor may only be required to leave the interview if his conduct is such as to prevent the proper putting of questions to the suspect (para.6.9). This would seem to give the police only the narrowest of grounds for refusing a suspect permission to have his solicitor present during questioning. Moreover, Note 6D says affirmatively: "A detainee has a right to free legal advice and to be represented by a solicitor. *The solicitor's only role in the police station is to protect and advance the legal rights of their client*" (emphasis supplied).[46] Note 6D says that the solicitor may seek to challenge an improper question to his client or the manner in which it is put, or advise his client not to reply to particular questions or if he wishes to give his client further legal advice.[47] He should not be asked to leave unless his approach or conduct "prevents or unreasonably obstructs proper questions being put to the suspect or the suspect's response being recorded" (*ibid.*, and para.6.9).

5–64 Examples of misconduct, it suggests, might include answering questions on the client's behalf, or providing written replies for the client to quote.[48] Advising a client not to reply to questions does not count as misconduct (Annex B, para.4).

If the investigating officer thinks the solicitor is acting in such a way as to justify his removal he must stop the interview and inform an officer of at least the rank of superintendent, failing which an inspector who is unconnected with the investigation. If that officer decides to confirm the decision to ask the solicitor to leave, the suspect must be given a chance to get another solicitor before the interview continues (para.6.10).

The removal of a solicitor is a serious step and an officer of the rank of superintendent should consider whether the matter ought to be reported to the Law Society (para.6.11). Where the solicitor is a duty solicitor, the report should also be to the Legal Services Commission—as the successor to the Legal Aid Board (*ibid.*).

---

[45] *DPP v Billington* [1988] 1 W.L.R. 535, DC. See also *DPP v Ward* [1999] R.T.R. 11, DC.

[46] The Runciman Royal Commission recommended that there should be a more positive reference to the solicitor's role—Recommendation 64, based on Runciman Report, para.53, p.36. The Commission also suggested that police training should include formal instruction in the role that solicitors are properly expected to play in the criminal justice system. (Runciman Report, para.54, pp.36–37).

[47] It seems in fact to be rare for solicitors to play much of a role in police interviews. The Home Office study Brown *et al.* (1992, p.89) stated that suspects were asked if they had been given any advice during police interviews and, if so, the nature of such advice. Suspects could recall such interruption in only 8% of interviews. In less than half was it likely to impede the flow of questioning: *e.g.* "remain silent", "don't be rushed (or bullied) into answering questions", etc. In a quarter it was more likely to help the police: *e.g.* "tell the truth", "admit the offence", etc.

[48] Note 6D.

Refusing access to a solicitor's clerk

The Code C rules regarding the exclusion of persons who come to advise clients   **5–65**
in the police station differentiate between different categories of adviser. The
original basic rule was that whereas a solicitor could only be excluded in the context of a particular interview and if he behaved in such a way as to make continuation of the interview impossible, a solicitor's clerk could be excluded from
even entering the police station if a police officer considered that his visit to the
police station would hinder the investigation of crime. In the April 1995 version
of Code C the position was altered by a significant enlargement of the definition
of "solicitor" for these purposes to include "a trainee solicitor, a duty solicitor
representative or an accredited representative included on the register of representatives maintained by the [Legal Services Commission]" (para.6.12.). The
August 2004 version of the Code changed the position again. The definition of
the "deemed-to-be-a-solicitor" category was narrowed to read: "an accredited or
probationary representative" on the register of representatives maintained by the
Commission (Code C, para.6.12). (Note that in Northern Ireland, by contrast, the
Code there specifies that "a solicitor means a solicitor qualified to practice"
(para.6.12). There is no custom there, yet, of sending clerks.)

The police discretion to exclude someone not within the definition of "solici-   **5–66**
tor" in the 1995 version of Code C applied to any non-accredited or probationary
representative whose visit an officer of the rank of inspector or above considered
would hinder the investigation of crime and directed otherwise (Code C,
para.6.12A). In the August 2004 version of Code C the discretion to exclude a
clerk applies not only, as before, to "non-accredited" and "probationary" representatives but also to "accredited" representatives (*ibid.*) (For explanation of
these categories of representatives see para.5–43 above.)

As to how this discretion to exclude is to be exercised, the Divisional Court in
Ex p. Robinson[49] held that it can be based on the subjective judgment of the
police officer based on his knowledge of the clerk concerned.[50] The police, the
court held, were entitled to refuse access to a clerk who was not a genuine clerk
or whose visit the police knew or believed from his criminal record or associations would hinder the investigation of crime or who the police knew or believed
was not capable of providing legal advice.

The decision in *Robinson* was applied by the Court of Appeal in *R. v Chief*   **5–67**
Constable of Northumbria, Ex p. Thompson.[51] The deputy chief constable had
issued a blanket ban on a probationary solicitors' representative who was a former police officer who had been dismissed from the force. Lord Woolf C.J. held
that the blanket ban was unlawful as the issue had to be decided in each individual case. It was not for the police to decide whether a particular adviser was sufficiently independent to give legal advice or on the quality of his advice. The only
legitimate question for the police was whether the adviser would hinder the

---

[49] *R. v Chief Constable of the Avon and Somerset Constabulary, Ex p. Robinson* [1989] 1 W.L.R. 793,
DC.
[50] For a worrying instance of the exercise of this subjective judgment see Webster, "Judgment
increases danger of miscarriages of justice, say lawyers" (1993) S.J. 1227.
[51] [2001] EWCA Civ 321; [2001] 4 All E.R. 354, CA.

investigation. As to that, the chief constable would be entitled to issue guidance, taking into account the character of the person concerned. The court accepted that where the advice was about the representative's character the result might be much the same as a blanket ban.

Guidelines issued by the Law Society after the *Robinson* case recommended that the clerk should carry a letter signed by a partner confirming his status and giving him authority to attend police stations. The clerk should identify himself and confirm his status at the same time to the client, giving the name of the partner responsible for his actions. Solicitors were also reminded that their clerks must behave politely and properly at all times and that they are responsible for the clerk's conduct. If a clerk is refused admission under para.6.12, the solicitor is advised to ask for written reasons and if the solicitor thinks these are wrong in fact or law or otherwise he should inform the Law Society's Legal Adviser's branch. A copy of the guidelines was sent to all chief constables and the gist was published in *Police Review*.

5–68 Code C, revised after *Robinson*, contains a new provision (para.6.13) giving police officers guidance as to what they should take into account when exercising their discretion under para.6.12. This provision advises that they should take into account whether the identity and status of the non-accredited or probationary representative had been satisfactorily established; whether he is of suitable character to provide legal advice (a person with a criminal record was unlikely to be suitable unless the conviction was for a minor offence and was not of recent date); and any other matters in a written letter of authorisation provided by the solicitor. Note 6F states that if an officer of the rank of inspector thinks that a particular firm of solicitors is persistently sending as clerks or legal executives persons who are unsuited to provide legal advice, he should inform an officer of at least the rank of superintendent, who might wish to take the matter up with the Law Society.

The problems regarding solicitors' clerks are aggravated by the fact that solicitors use all sorts of persons to help out, including some who have had little training or experience in the work. In *Re B*[52] it was held that a person could be regarded as a solicitor's clerk for the purposes of disciplinary proceedings against the solicitor, even though the clerk worked as an independent contractor as an inquiry agent. In that case the clerk was a former police officer with convictions. There was no master–servant relationship. He had worked for the firm on only three occasions. But this was held to be enough to make the solicitor liable for employing him.

Legal advice: official figures and empirical research

(1) Official figures

5–69 Duty solicitor schemes now cover all police stations in England and Wales.[53] In 2003–2004, some 710,000 suspects received advice under the scheme, at a cost

---

[52] *The Times*, May 12, 1989.
[53] *Legal Services Commission Annual Report 2002–2003*, p.49, Table CDS 2.

of £175 million.[54] Roughly two-thirds of the advice under the scheme is given by "own solicitors" and one-third by duty solicitors. The proportion seems constant year on year.

(2) Studies

There have been various studies of access to legal advice in the police station. **5–70**
Two large studies were those by David Brown of the Home Office in 1989 and 1993 respectively. The first, Brown (1989), was based on a sample of over 5,000 cases.[55] The second, Brown *et al.* (1992), was based on samples of around 5,000 taken in 1990 before (Phase 1) and 5,000 taken after (Phase 2) the April 1991 revision of the Code.[56] David Brown also carried out a study of access to legal advice for suspects in terrorism cases (Brown (1993)) based on a study of custody record forms in regard to 253 terrorism detainees held in England and Wales between March 1989 and November 1990. The great majority (85 per cent) of detainees were held in connection with Northern Irish terrorism.

There have been further large Home Office studies by Buckc and Brown (1997),[57] and by Phillips and Brown (1998).[58]

There are also other studies—see especially Maguire (1988), Sanders *et al.* (1989), Dixon *et al.* (1989a), and McConville and Hodgson (1993).

Asking for a solicitor

The proportion of suspects asking for a solicitor has risen steadily. Pre-PACE a **5–71**
number of studies showed proportions ranging from 3 per cent to 20 per cent.[59]
With the introduction of PACE, the figure went up to around 25 per cent,[60] and then after the 1991 revised Code,[61] to 32 per cent. Phillips and Brown (1998)

---

[54] *Legal Services Commission Annual Report 2003–2004*, p.54, Table 4a.
[55] Brown, *Detention at the Police Station under the Police and Criminal Evidence Act 1984* (HMSO, 1989), p.20.
[56] Brown, Ellis and Larcombe, *Changing the Code: Police Detention under the Revised PACE Codes of Practice* (HMSO, 1992). (The study was summarised in Home Office Research and Statistics Department, Research Findings No.5, March 1993.) It was based on a sample of 10,167 custody record forms from 12 police stations in six force areas, 980 cases that were observed by researchers at six of those police stations and interviews with 810 arresting officers and 543 detained persons in the observed cases.
[57] *In police custody: police powers and suspects' rights under the revised PACE codes of practice* (HMSO, 1997). There were three samples—an observed sample of 3,950 detainees in 13 police stations in 1995–1996, a questionnaire administered to the police officers in those cases (returned by 3,537), and a study of 12,500 custody records drawn from 25 police stations from June 1995.
[58] *Entry into the Criminal Justice System: a survey of police arrests and their outcomes* (HMSO, 1998). The fieldwork was carried out at 10 police stations in 1993–1994. There were 4,250 in the sample of whom most were suspects but some were detained for other reasons—under the Mental Health Act, s.136, or on a warrant for failure to appear at court or whilst being transferred between prison and court.
[59] Softley *et al.* (1980); Brown (1991).
[60] See Brown (1989); and Sanders *et al.* (1989).
[61] The crucial changes introduced by the April 1991 revision of the Code were a requirement that (1) the suspect be told that the entitlement to independent legal advice is free of charge regardless of means and is a continuing right; (2) that a poster about the right to free and independent legal advice be displayed in police stations; and (3) that the Code had a new provision expressly warning police officers not to dissuade the suspect from opting for legal advice.

found it was 38 per cent (p.59). Bucke and Brown's 1997 study (which was conducted after Phillips and Brown (1998)) showed it had risen to 40 per cent (Bucke and Brown (1997), p.19). They suggested that the reason for this may be a higher request rate by juveniles (*ibid.*, p.20).

There are considerable variations between police stations in the request rate[62] and many other variables—the kinds of offence, the level of seriousness, gender, ethnic background, local availability of legal services—all affect the take-up rate.[63]

In terrorism cases the proportion of detainees asking for a solicitor is higher than in other cases. Brown (1993) showed that 49 per cent asked for legal advice at some stage (p.9).

Reasons for not asking for a solicitor

5–72   Although a person is not required to give reasons (Code C, Note 6K) according to Code C, para.6.5 the custody officer is supposed to ask the suspect for his reason for not requesting legal advice, research has shown that this requirement is commonly honoured in the breach. Bucke and Brown (1997) said that it was not done in the majority of cases and that in two stations it was not done at all (p.21).

According to interviews with suspects in Brown *et al.* (1992), the two most common reasons given for declining legal advice were "would not assist" (57 per cent in Phase 1 and 63 per cent in Phase 2); and "would delay release" from the police station (9 per cent in Phase 1 and 12 per cent in Phase 2).[64] Bucke and Brown (1997) said that the most common reason given was that suspects did not feel the situation merited a legal adviser or that they would see how things developed. "Because I'm innocent" accounted for 11 per cent; "because I'm guilty" for 4 per cent. The delay involved accounted for another 4 per cent (p.22).

In Brown *et al.* (1992), those who did not request legal advice on arrival at the police station were asked if they would have done so if a solicitor had been available at that stage (p.53). Nearly half said they would have done so. This suggests that between one half and two-thirds of suspects would wish to have solicitors if they were readily available.

In the study by Sanders *et al.* (1989), the researchers found that a major factor in suspects not asking for, or not getting access to, solicitors was the use by the police of a variety of "ploys". (On this see Brown *et al.* (1992), pp.48–49.)

Making contact with the solicitor

5–73   In Brown *et al.* (1992), the police managed to contact a solicitor in 80 per cent of the custody record sample in Phase 1 and 87 per cent in Phase 2 (pp.58–59). (These figures include a considerable number of cases where the suspect first asked for legal advice and later changed his mind.) In Bucke and Brown (1997) the contact rate was 89 per cent (p.23) and in Phillips and Brown (1998), 88 per cent (p.64). In Brown *et al.* (1992) the average time between the request for a

---

[62] See, for instance, Phillips and Brown (1998), p.60.
[63] See Bucke and Brown (1997), pp.20–23; and Phillips and Brown (1998), pp.60–63.
[64] *op.cit.,* n.56 above, Table 3.6, p.51. In the study by Sanders *et al.* (1989) the most common reason given was that seeking legal advice would cause delay.

solicitor and contact made was a little over one hour, in both the Phase 1 and Phase 2 samples. In a little over half the cases contact was made within half an hour. The median figures were 25 minutes and 30 minutes (p.61). The report said that the increase in time taken to make contact was "almost certainly accounted for by the rise in requests for legal advice" (p.63).

According to Phillips and Brown (1998), the main reason given for failing to make contact was that the suspect changed his mind about wanting legal advice (39 per cent of non-contact cases, p.64). But the observers suggested that many suspects changed their mind because of the difficulties in locating their chosen solicitor. (The majority of non-contacts involved arrests between 11 pm and 2 am.) In 28 per cent of non-contact cases the suspect had been charged or released before contact was made.

Delaying access to legal advice

As has been seen, s.58(8) of PACE allows the police to delay access to legal advice in cases of serious arrestable offences providing certain conditions are fulfilled. As has been seen the Court of Appeal has interpreted those conditions very strictly and it is now very rare for delay to be authorised. In Brown *et al.* (1992) only one such case was found (p.69). In Bucke and Brown's study (1997) no such case was found in 12,500 custody records (p.23) and in Phillips and Brown (1998) none was found in a sample of 4,250 (p.65).   **5–74**

In terrorism cases, the power to delay was in the past used much more extensively. In Brown's study (1993) delay of access was authorised in 26 per cent of cases (66 out of 253).[65] However, it seems that the position has since changed. The Government's 1998 Consultation Paper *Legislation Against Terrorism*[66] stated that the Government was not aware of any case in the previous two years in which the power to delay access had been exercised.[67] Even in Northern Ireland where it had in the past been used more frequently, the power was now used "more sparingly".[68] The Consultation Paper noted, however, without giving figures, that it was more common in Northern Ireland to refuse to allow a solicitor to be present during the interview even though the suspect had been allowed initial access to the solicitor.[69]

Actual consultation with legal advisers

Brown (1989, p.26) suggested that some 7 per cent of contacts, for one of a variety of reasons, did not lead to any legal consultation. Brown *et al.* (1992) broadly found much the same. In the later studies, however, this problem seems to have eased: the figure was 1 per cent in Phillips and Brown (1998, p.65) and about the same in Bucke and Brown (1997, p.23).   **5–75**

---

[65] Brown (1993), p.16. However, in the event, legal advice was not requested in 30 of these 66 cases; the ban was introduced as a precautionary measure only (p.19).
[66] Cm.4178.
[67] The figures for 1997 showed that access was denied in 33 cases out of 512 in which it had been requested (6%) and in the first nine months of 1998 in only three out of 445 cases (0.7%). (para.8.31.)
[68] *ibid.*
[69] *ibid.*

Solicitor or clerk?

5–76 Sanders *et al.* (1989) found that over 40 per cent of advice given at the police station was given by non-solicitor representatives. McConville and Hodgson (1993, p.17) found that three-quarters of all police station attendances were by non-solicitors. Brown *et al.* (1992) found that it was much less—14 per cent in Phase 1 and 9 per cent in Phase 2.[70] But Brown admitted that accurate information about the status of the adviser was not always available and that the figure may well be higher. McConville and Hodgson suggested that probably between two-fifths and one half of all attendances at the police station are by persons other than qualified solicitors. But the use of representatives has since reduced, partly due to the accreditation scheme originally introduced in 1995 by the Law Society for non-solicitor police station representatives. Those not accredited or at least registered to become accredited cannot get remunerated. Bucke and Brown (1997), carried out after the introduction of the new scheme, showed that 10 per cent of police station consultations were with an accredited representative, 6 per cent were with an unaccredited representative and 84 per cent were with a solicitor (p.26).

Quality of legal advice in police station

5–77 McConville and Hodgson (1993) severely criticised the quality of work done by advisers in police stations. They stated that few advisers sought significant details of the case from custody officers. In 86 per cent of cases no inquiries were made of the custody officer. A request to see the custody record form was made in only 10 per cent of cases. In half the cases in the sample the adviser spent less than 10 minutes in private conversation with the client. Baldwin, in a study of 182 audio or video tapes, found that in two-thirds of interviews the adviser said nothing during the police interview.[71] There is no more recent study of this issue.

Advice at the police station or only on the telephone?

5–78 Sanders *et al.* (1989) found that 26 per cent of all advice was given by telephone. Brown *et al.* (1992) found in the custody record sample that it was even higher— 36 per cent in Phase 1, reducing to 30 per cent in Phase 2 (Table 4.3). The national figure for 1999–2000 was considerably lower—21 per cent received only telephone advice.[72] But the overall figures conceal huge differences as between different police stations. In Brown *et al.* (1992) the proportion of telephone-only advice ranged from 81 per cent at one station to 6 per cent at another (Table 4.3, p.67).

Length of first consultation

5–79 In Bucke and Brown (1997) nearly half of all consultations took less than 15 minutes and only 2 per cent lasted over an hour (p.27 and Appendix Table A.3). But the length of interviews had increased—perhaps because of the changes in regard

---

[70] Brown *et al.* (1992), pp.65–66.
[71] Baldwin (1992) p.49.
[72] *Legal Services Commission Annual Report 2003–2004*, p.54, Table 4a.

to the right to silence. Thus, whereas McConville and Hodgson (1993) found that 22 per cent of consultations lasted less than 5 minutes, Bucke and Brown (1997) found that this was true of only 7 per cent. Where McConville and Hodgson (1993) found that 42 per cent lasted between 10 and 30 minutes, this figure had increased to 55 per cent (Bucke and Brown (1997, p.28).

Attendance by legal advisers at interviews

Brown (1989) found that legal advisers attended all police interviews in only 12   **5–80**
per cent of cases. In Bucke and Brown (1997) this figure had risen to 37 per cent (p.32). Sanders *et al.* (1989) found that a legal adviser attended at least one inter-view in two-thirds of cases in which advice was provided; in Bucke and Brown (1997) this had risen to 75 per cent (p.33). When Sanders *et al.* (1989) excluded telephone consultations, legal advisers attended police interviews in 81 per cent of cases in which they consulted with their clients at the police station; in Bucke and Brown (1997) that figure was 91 per cent (p.33). Again, this rise may be due to the changes in the rules regarding the right to silence.

Overall, Bucke and Brown (1997) found that in regard to 2,181 suspects inter-viewed, 52 per cent had no legal advice, 37 per cent had a legal adviser present at all interviews, 2 per cent had one present at some but not all interviews, and 9 per cent had legal advice only prior to interview (p.32).

Tape recording of interviews: s.60[73]

The background

Section 60 places upon the Home Secretary a duty to issue a Code of Practice for   **5–81**
the tape recording of police interviews with suspects. A statutory instrument had to be laid before Parliament subject to annulment by resolution in either House.

The Code was initially approved by Parliament in July 1988.[74] The Police and Criminal Evidence Act 1984 (Code of Practice) Order 1988 (SI 1988/1200) appointed July 29, 1988 as the date for the operation of the Code of Practice on Tape Recording (Code E). As has been seen, the revision of Code E was approved by Parliament in February 2003 for implementation from April 1.

The Philips Royal Commission had proposed a very limited experiment with the tape recording of only the final stages of interviews. Starting in 1984, the Government undertook a much broader experiment which, to the surprise of many (especially the police), proved a great success. This led to the gradual intro-duction of tape recording until, in 1992, it became compulsory by virtue of the Police and Criminal Evidence Act (Tape-recording of Interviews) No. 1 Order 1991 (SI 1991/2687) which came into force on January 1, 1992. Guidance to the police was issued by the Home Office in Circulars Nos 76/1988, 39/1991 and 21/1992.

---

[73] See 1989 N.I. PACE Order, Art.60.
[74] House of Commons, *Hansard*, Vol.138, July 27, 1988, cols 444–463; House of Lords, *Hansard*, Vol.500, July 28, 1988, cols 443–453.

What interviews have to be tape recorded?

5–82   Since January 1, 1992 it has been compulsory for all interviews (for the meaning of an interview see para.6–51 below) with persons who have been cautioned in respect of offences triable on indictment (including either way offences) to be tape recorded (Code E, para.3.1(a)). The requirement of tape recording applies equally to the putting of further questions to such a person and when a written statement is brought to the notice of a person charged with or informed that he may be prosecuted for such an offence.

Tape recording is not required for offences triable summarily only, though in practice it is normal for all interviews to be tape recorded regardless of whether it is technically required.

Terrorism

5–83   An experiment with the taping of interviews in terrorism investigations was conducted in England and Wales from 1992–1995 and taping continued then on a voluntary basis. In Northern Ireland, interviews with terrorism suspects were not tape recorded for security reasons—though from 1996 silent video recordings were made of such interviews. Lord Lloyd's *Inquiry into Legislation Against Terrorism*[75] recommended that interviews with terrorist suspects be brought into the existing statutory regime. The Northern Ireland (Emergency Provisions) Act 1998 made audio recording of interviews with those detained under the PTA in Northern Ireland mandatory and this was brought into operation in 1999.

5–84   The Government's December 1998 Consultation Paper *Legislation Against Terrorism*[76] said that it recognised that audio recording of such interviews "may be an important protection for both the detainee and the police".[77] It therefore proposed that audio recording of all interviews of terrorist suspects should be made mandatory in England and Wales and Scotland as was already the case in Northern Ireland.

The Terrorism Act 2000 gave the Secretary of State the power to make an order requiring the audio and also the video recording in police stations of interviews with persons detained under the Act—subject to a Code of Practice.[78] Such a Code of Practice and the new mandatory audio recording system came into force in England and Wales, Scotland and Northern Ireland on February 18, 2001.[79] In Northern Ireland a Code of Practice was introduced also on February 18, 2001 regulating the video recording of interviews.[80] There is as yet no equivalent on the mainland for the video recording of interviews with terrorism suspects. (But see para.5–95 below on video recording of interviews with PACE suspects and new Code of Practice F which came into force in August 2004.)

---

[75]   1996, Cm.3420.
[76]   1998, Cm.4178.
[77]   1998, Cm.4178, para.8.35.
[78]   Sch.8, para.3.
[79]   See Code of Practice for the Audio Recording of Interviews under Sch.8 to the Terrorism Act 2000. There is also a Code of Practice for "authorised officers" and another for "examining officers" under the same Act.
[80]   Code of Practice on Video Recording with Sound under the Terrorism Act 2000, Northern Ireland Office, 2001.

Conduct of interviews

The custody officer can authorise the interviewing officer not to record the inter- **5–85**
view if the equipment is not working, or no suitable room is available and the
interview should not be delayed. He can also authorise not-recording if it is clear
from the outset that no prosecution will result (Code E, para.3.3).

The rules require that the whole interview be recorded, including the taking
and reading back of any statement (Code E, para.3.5).

There are elaborate rules that have to be followed to ensure that the process
is not open to contamination by tampering. Thus, for instance, a master tape has
to be unwrapped, placed in the tape recorder and at the end sealed, all in the
suspect's presence.

The suspect must be cautioned—in terms of the normal caution which warns
him as to the possible adverse effects of silence (see Code E, para.4.5).

The officer must remind the suspect of his right to free and independent legal **5–86**
advice and that he can speak to a solicitor on the telephone (Code E, para.4.5[81]).

The officer should then put to the suspect any previous significant statement or
silence ("*i.e.* failure or refusal to answer a question or to answer it satisfactorily")
which occurred in the presence and hearing of a police officer or approved person before the start of the interview and should ask whether he confirms or denies
that earlier statement or silence or whether he wishes to add anything (Code E,
para.4.6 referring to Code C, para.11.4).[82]

Recording of interviews

After the interview is over, if proceedings are to follow, a written record of the **5–87**
interview must be made. The preparation by the police of summaries of tape-
recorded interviews has been a vexed issue of considerable practical importance
not least because of the immense amount of time they take to prepare. The
Runciman Royal Commission recommended that the Home Office undertake further study of the matter.[83] Instead of the previous detailed rules in Code E, the Code
now simply states: "Any written record of a tape recorded interview shall be made
in accordance with national guidelines approved by the Secretary of State" (Code
E, Note 5A).[84] The national guidelines were previously to be found in Home Office
Circular 26/1995 but they have now been replaced by the relevant passages in the
Home Office's *Manual of Guidance for the preparation, processing and submission of files* and the *Good Practice Guide*. (The Manual and the Guide are both to
be found on the following website—*www.criminal-justice-system.gov.uk*.)

The Manual (para.7.17.6) states that there are two types of written record of **5–88**
taped interview: (1) short descriptive notes (SDNs); and (2) a record of taped
interview (ROTI).

[81] Formerly 4.3A.
[82] The Runciman Royal Commission recommended this procedure in regard to statements—not
silence (see Recommendation 87 based on Runciman Report, para.50, pp.60–61).
[83] For discussion of the problem by the Runciman Royal Commission see Runciman Report,
pp.41–42.
[84] For an account of the history of the changing requirements from 1990 to 1999 see Mackie,
Burrows and Tarling, "Preparing the prosecution case" [1999] Crim.L.R. 460.

SDNs are used in expedited file cases in the magistrates' courts where it is anticipated that there will not be a trial. They consist of a brief account of certain key aspects of the interview and will normally be in reported speech. They are supposed to cover:

(i)   any admissions made regarding the essential elements of the offence(s) charged;

(ii) the defendant's version of what happened;

(iii) any mitigating circumstances (as opposed to lines of defence);

(iv) anything said by the defendant that relates to aggravating factors (*e.g.* that the offence was premeditated, or that no remorse was shown);

(v) anything else that should be brought to the attention of the CPS.

SDNs can be handwritten.

ROTIs are prepared in cases where a full file is required—contested cases in the magistrates' court and for cases going to the Crown Court. ROTIs must include verbatim all admissions and the questions and answers leading up to them. They should also include ambiguous admissions and qualified admissions. ROTIs must be typed.

5–89   Where the police believe that the material is "sensitive", within the meaning of the disclosure rules (under the Criminal Procedure and Investigations Act 1996 and the Code of Practice) or that it contains prejudicial or inadmissible material, the police should draw the fact to the attention of the CPS. Any editing of the tapes is supposed to be done under the direction of the crown prosecutor.

A police officer has no authority to break the seal on the master tape. If it needs to be done, it should be done in the presence of a representative of the CPS and, if they wish to attend, the defence (Code E, para.6.2).

A suspect retains his right to make a written statement under caution. Such statements should be taken whilst the tape is running.

The prosecutor normally expects to rely on the written record of the interview, so keeping to a minimum the occasions when the CPS have to listen to a tape or read a transcript.

Experience shows that transcripts are only rarely necessary, save in complex cases. If the police needs a transcript they provide it to the CPS who make it available to the defence.

5–90   If the defence wish to have a transcript of a tape which is still in the possession of the police, the police should provide them with a copy of the tape so that they can make their own arrangements for the transcript to be made. The solicitor whose client is legally aided should apply to the Legal Services Commission in advance for approval of the cost of having a transcript prepared.

In order to save costs and time, each side is supposed to hand any transcript it may have had made to the other. The Divisional Court has held that the police have a duty to supply the suspect's solicitor with details of an interview so that he can advise as to whether the suspect should consent to a formal caution. Failure to make such disclosure led to a stay of the case as an abuse of process.[85]

Any disagreements as to the accuracy of the tape which cannot be resolved pre-trial are normally settled by playing the tape at the trial.

The Home Office Circular 76/1988 stated (para.38) that, "It is in the spirit of   **5–91** the tape recording arrangements that the content of the record of the taped interview should be agreed between the prosecution and the defence before the case comes to court". The tapes are physically kept by the police. If the defence wants access to a tape, they should either be given copies or allowed to listen to them at the police station. The Home Office 1988 Circular stated (*ibid.*, para.40): "Unadmitted employees of defence solicitors should normally be given the same right of access but should have the prior authority of an admitted solicitor".

If the suspect is not legally represented, he should be allowed access to the tapes, either in the prison where he is held or in police cells, or, if he is on bail, at a police station or at home. But applications for the defence to have access to the tapes should be made normally to the CPS.

If the defence requires an officer to come to court to prove the tape according to the guidelines laid down by the Court of Appeal in *Rampling*,[86] this should be brought to the attention of the crown prosecutor.

Court guidelines

In *Rampling* the court laid down the following guidelines: **5–92**

(1) The tape can be produced and proved by the interviewing officer or any other officer present when it was taken. There is no need to call the audio typist.

(2) The officer should have listened to the tape before the trial so that he can deal with any objections to authenticity that may be made.

(3) As regards authenticity, he can prove who spoke on the tape.

(4) On accuracy, he can deal with any challenge such as, for instance, that the tape has been falsified by alteration.

(5) The transcript can be produced by the interviewing officer who should have checked it previously for accuracy. The tape is the evidence. The transcript is like a schedule and available for convenience.

(6) The use made of the tape is an administrative matter for the discretion of the judge. In many cases the defendant will agree for the transcript to be used with no need to play the tape. The transcript can then be read

---

[85] *DPP v Ara* [2001] EWHC Admin 493; [2001] 4 All E.R. 559.
[86] [1987] Crim.L.R. 823, CA.

by the officer who produces it, like a contemporaneous note. But the defendant can have the tape played if he wishes.

(7) If the tape is played, it is for the judge to decide whether the jury should have the transcript whilst the tape is being played.

(8) The defendant's consent is not necessary. The court said that "in the collective experience of this court, a transcript is usually of very considerable value to the jury to follow the evidence and to take to the jury room when they retire".

The mechanics for dealing with tape recordings in court were the subject of a Practice Direction issued in May 1989.[87] On the adducing of tape recorded evidence see also Mirfield, *Silence, Confessions and Improperly Obtained Evidence* (Clarendon, 1997), pp.166–173.

Tape recording: the empirical evidence

5–93 For early research on tape recording see Willis *et al.* (1988). Broadly speaking, this showed that the experiment was a success in that interviews tended to be shorter, the rate of confessions and suspects' talk about others involved in crime did not go down, the rate of guilty pleas went up and there were fewer disputes at court as to what was said in the police station.

For research identifying problems associated with tape recording and making summaries of tapes see especially Baldwin and Bedward (1991) and Baldwin (1992a).

When should the defence solicitor listen to the tape?

5–94 The Law Society has laid down guidelines as to the situations in which solicitors acting for the defence should listen to the tape recording of the interview in the police station.[88] Each case must be judged on its merits. The written police record of interview was intended to be a balanced account of the interview but solicitors "should use their own experience of recent written records in deciding to what extent reliance should be placed on them".

If the solicitor doubts the reliability of the written record he should listen to the tape in three situations:

(1) When the client instructs him to do so, or when the client cannot confirm the accuracy of the record of interview.

---

[87] Practice Direction (Crime: Tape Recording of Police Interviews) (1989) 1 W.L.R. 631. For consideration of the special problems of taping interviews with interpreters see Brown, "Tape Recording Interviews with Foreigners" [1989] Crim.L.R. 643. For detailed guidance as to the needs of defence solicitors and operation of the system see Snook, "Getting your clients taped", 133 S.J. 1366.
[88] *Law Society Gazette*, April 20, 1994, p.29.

(2) If the client intends to plead not guilty or is unsure how to plead:

   (a) where there is a material dispute about the content of the written record;

   (b) where the client complains that the conduct of the police was such as to make his confession unreliable;

   (c) where the client tells the solicitor that the "tone", "timing" or "intonation" of the interview are significant; and

   (d) where the CPS and/or prosecuting counsel have listened to the tape.

(3) In the case of a guilty plea, where the solicitor has reason to believe that there may be mitigatory factors on the tape which do not appear on the written summary.

Video recording of interviews: s.60A

The Runciman Royal Commission on Criminal Justice recommended that police stations be fitted for continuous, 24-hour video recording of all public parts in the custody area where suspects are likely to be. Suspects, it thought, should be informed of the fact that cameras in custody suites are switched on, but should not have the right to require them to be switched off.[89] The April 1995 revised Code C implemented this proposal which now reads: **5–95**

> "If video cameras are installed in the custody area, notices shall be prominently displayed showing cameras are in use. Any request to have video cameras switched off shall be refused." (Para.3.11.)

The Runciman Royal Commission, considering that there were pros and cons to the issue, made no specific recommendation as to video recording of interviews but it called for further research—see Runciman Report, pp.39–41.

The Home Office issued a circular on the subject in February 1993 (6/1993). This referred to the considerable cost of video recording[90] for which there was no current provision. Chief officers were "strongly discouraged from moving too quickly to the wholesale introduction of video recording interviews". For the immediate future, it was suggested that such recording should be confined to the most serious cases in which there were specified, justifiable reasons for requiring a visual record. These might include cases of serious violence including serious sexual assaults. The decision in individual cases should be made at inspector level or above. Chief officers who decided to use video recording on a wider basis were   **5–96**

---

[89] Recommendation 51, based on Runciman Report paras 36–38, pp.33–34.
[90] Estimated to be £10m capital cost and £25m–£28m annual running cost for the police and the CPS combined if all interviews currently taped were recorded by video. In addition there would be an estimated £59m cost for the Lord Chancellor's Department, mainly in legal aid fees for lawyers' viewing time.

asked to recognise that this would "cause them and all agencies in the criminal justice system to divert resources from other work".

However, matters were taken a stage further by the Criminal Justice and Police Act 2001 (CJPA). Section 76 of the CJPA inserted new s.60A into PACE, authorising video recording of interviews under a new Code of Practice to be issued by the Home Secretary.

5–97 A Code of Practice under these provisions needs Parliamentary approval—though only by the negative resolution procedure, as compared with the affirmative resolution required for the other Codes. The new section was inserted in order to settle the uncertainty as to whether it was lawful to video record an interview with a suspect where the suspect objects. Before rolling out video recording nationally a pilot study was conducted in selected police stations.[91] During the pilot all interviews in those areas had to be video recorded. The draft of Code F issued in September 2001 in preparation for the pilot was excluded from the consultation process for the other Codes which was launched a month later. It was laid before Parliament on April 10, 2002 and came into force in the pilot areas on May 7, 2002. When the pilot was completed, a statutory instrument brought mandatory video recording in the pilot areas to an end as from November 2003.[92] The Code was activated for all forces on a discretionary basis as part of the general revision of the PACE Codes of Practice which came into effect on August 1, 2004. (The Police (Northern Ireland) Act 2000, s.72 inserted the equivalent Art.60A into the 1989 PACE Order but it is not operational and there is as yet no Code of Practice equivalent to Code F.)

5–98 Code F states that the recording of interviews shall be carried out openly "to instil confidence in its reliability as an impartial and accurate record of the interview" (para.2.1). The cameras should be placed so as to ensure coverage of as much of the interview room as possible (para.2.2). The recording medium records the date and time of the recording second by second (para.2.3). The master tape has to be sealed in the presence of the suspect (para.2.4). In terrorism cases or in other cases where an officer believes that recording or disclosing his identity would put him in danger he is permitted to use his identification number and the name of his police station instead of his name and he can have his back to the camera (para.2.5).

If an interviewing officer decides to use video recording, Code F, para.3.1 suggests that it might be appropriate for interviews with suspects in respect of indictable offences, including either way offences, or where further questions are exceptionally put to a suspect after he has been charged,[93] or where an officer wants to put the content of a statement by someone else, to someone who has been charged[94]; and for interviews with or in the presence of anyone who requires an appropriate adult, or if the suspect requires deaf signing, or where the suspect or his representative requests that the interview be recorded visually (para.3.1). The custody officer has the power to authorise that an interview should not be

---

[91] The pilot initially took place in three police stations in each of five forces—Kent, Hampshire, Essex, West Mercia and the Metropolitan force. Three further police stations in Essex were subsequently added to the pilot. (See SI 2002/1069 and SI 2002/2527.)
[92] SI 2003/2463.
[93] As permitted by Code C, para.16.5.
[94] As permitted by Code C, para.16.4.

visually recorded on practical grounds such as the failure of the equipment or non-availability of a suitable room (para.3.3), or where the suspect refuses to go to a suitable interview room and the custody officer considers on reasonable grounds that the interview should not be delayed (*ibid.*).

The rules for the handling of video recording set out in the Code of Practice are similar to those for audio recording.   **5–99**

The Draft Code provided that if the suspect objected to a visual recording being made, the interviewing officer had a discretion as to whether or not to turn the equipment off (Draft Code F, para.4.8). This provision was not in the final version of Code F which merely states that the suspect's objections must be recorded and noted (para.4.8).

If the suspect wishes to tell the officer "off the record" about matters not directly related to the offence of which he was suspected, he should be given a chance to tell the officer after the conclusion of the formal interview (para.4.10.)

An audio tape of the interview has to be provided to the defence in the ordinary way, but receipt of the video requires an undertaking by the legal representative not to give the videotape or a copy to the defendant. (This is because in the Scottish pilots it was found that the videotapes were used by criminal elements to try to identify the police officers involved.[95]) A summary of the interview is provided anyway.

Fingerprinting: s.61 and Identification Code D, s.4[96]

The pre-PACE law on fingerprinting in s.49 of the Magistrates' Courts Act 1980 provided that fingerprints could be taken compulsorily only on the order of a magistrates' court, if the person was 14 years old and if proceedings against him had already begun. The Philips Royal Commission recommended[97] that the minimum age should be reduced to 10 years and that it should be possible to take fingerprints, where it was necessary for purposes of the investigation, before proceedings were started. It also proposed[98] that supervision or control should be transferred from the magistrates to the police on the ground that in an operational matter of this nature the magistrates could not in practice exercise any real supervision. Section 61 gave effect to those proposals.   **5–100**

It states that, except as provided, no one's fingerprints may be taken without consent, as defined in s.65. Under s.65, consent of a person over the age of 17 must be his own and in the case of someone under 14 years old the consent must be that of a parent or guardian. For someone between 14 and 17 years old consent must be his own and that of his parent or guardian.

Consent in a police station (though not elsewhere it seems) must be given in writing (s.61(2); Code D, para.4.2[99]). This therefore does not affect the practice

---

[95] Law Society's *Criminal Practitioners Newsletter*, No.46, October 2001, p.6.
[96] See 1989 N.I. PACE Order, Art.61 and Code D, s.3.
[97] Philips Report, paras 3.128–3.132.
[98] Philips Report, para.3.131.
[99] Formerly 3.1.

of fingerprinting the victims of burglaries in their homes in order to distinguish their prints from any others found there.

5–101 There are, however, a great variety of situations where fingerprints may be taken without consent. (They are helpfully set out in the 2004 revision of Code D, paras 4.3 and 4.4. See also para.5–105 below for the provisions of the Serious Organised Crime and Police Bill on fingerprinting away from the police station.) Prior to the Criminal Justice Act 2003, fingerprints could be taken without consent if an officer at least of the rank of inspector (formerly superintendent[1]) authorised it, and he had reasonable grounds for suspecting the involvement of the person in a criminal offence and that his fingerprints would "tend to confirm or disprove that involvement".[2] Where there were reasonable grounds for suspecting that he was not who he claimed to be, fingerprints could also be taken without consent—on the authority of an inspector—if it would "facilitate the ascertainment of his identity".[3]

Fingerprints could also be taken compulsorily without consent if the person affected was in police detention and he had been charged with or informed that he would be reported for an offence recordable in national police records (a "recordable offence").[4] Reporting takes place either to consider the issue of a summons or where the institution of proceedings requires the consent of the Attorney-General or the Director of Public Prosecutions. It is interpreted to include reporting a juvenile to the Juvenile Bureau or the situation when the suspect is bailed pending consideration of the case by the police or the CPS. Fingerprints may also be taken without consent—and even without an inspector's authorisation—where the suspect has been convicted of a recordable offence or cautioned for such an offence which he admitted, or he has been warned or reprimanded for such an offence under s.65 of the Crime and Disorder Act 1998.[5] Where a person charged with or informed that he will be reported for a recordable offence has previously had his fingerprints taken but they did not constitute a complete set of prints or they were not of sufficient quality, they can be taken compulsorily again.[6]

5–102 The Criminal Justice Act 2003, s.9(2) replaced the existing provisions in s.61(3) and (4) about the taking of fingerprints on the authority of an inspector, with a wider power to take fingerprints without such authorisation from any person detained in consequence of his arrest for a recordable offence. The requirement that the person whose fingerprints are taken without consent must be given reasons which must be recorded, apply to this new power.[7] The Explanatory Notes to the 2003 Act state (at para.132) that this amendment to s.61 could prevent persons who come into police custody and who had previously been finger-

---

[1] The change was made in the Criminal Justice and Police Act 2001, s.78(2).
[2] subs.(3)(a) and (4) and Code D, para.4.3(a). Formerly 3.2(a).
[3] Added by the Anti-terrorism, Crime and Security Act 2001, s.90(2).
[4] s.61(3)(b). National police records of convictions are kept by the National Identification Bureau (NIB) at New Scotland Yard. Only serious offences are recorded by the NIB—broadly those punishable by imprisonment. NIB records consist of convictions and the national fingerprint collection.
[5] CJPA 2001, s.78(6) amending s.61(6) of PACE.
[6] CJPA 2001, s.78(3) inserting new subs.(3A) into s.61 of PACE.
[7] s.9(5) of the 2003 Act extending s.61(8A)of PACE.

printed from avoiding detection by giving a false name and address. It could also reveal whether they were wanted in connection with other offences.

Section 61 does not actually specify that fingerprints must be taken by a police officer. But the Police Reform Act 2002[8] does specify that an authorised civilian detention officer has the power of a constable under s.61 to take fingerprints without consent.

If someone who answers to bail at a court or a police station has previously had his fingerprints taken and there is now doubt as to his identity or whether he is the same person, the magistrates' court or an officer of the rank of inspector respectively can order that his fingerprints be taken compulsorily.[9]   **5–103**

Note that although fingerprints can in some circumstances be taken from a juvenile without either his consent or that of his parent or guardian, Code D, para.2.15[10] would seem to require the presence of an appropriate adult for fingerprinting of a juvenile which precedes the decision whether to charge, to caution or to take no further action.

Under s.27(3), as has been seen,[11] police officers are given a power to require someone who has been convicted of or cautioned, warned or reprimanded in respect of a recordable offence to come to the police station to be fingerprinted and a power of arrest is given if the person fails to comply with that requirement. The power applies if the person convicted has not at any time been in police detention and either he has not previously had his fingerprints taken or they did not constitute a complete set of prints or they were not of sufficient quality. There is no equivalent power of arrest under s.61. If the defendant has received a non-custodial penalty and declines a request to come in to have his fingerprints taken, there is no power to compel him to do so. It is therefore important to ensure that anyone who has been charged with a recordable offence, or told that he will be reported for such an offence, has been fingerprinted before he leaves the police station.

Where a person's fingerprints are taken without his consent, he must be told the reason beforehand and this must be recorded. If he is detained at a police station at the time, the reason must be put into the custody record (subss.(7) and (8)).   **5–104**

The Criminal Justice and Public Order Act 1994 (CJPOA) added a requirement of a new caution for anyone whose fingerprints are taken, with or without consent, telling them that they may be the subject of a "speculative search" against other records, and the fact that they have been told this must be recorded as soon as practicable after the fingerprints have been taken.[12] The requirement can be fulfilled either by a police officer or by an authorised civilian detention officer.[13]

Subsection (9) preserves the power of compulsory fingerprinting contained in the terrorism legislation. It is now to be found unchanged in the Terrorism Act

---

[8] Sch.4, Pt 3, para.29(a).

[9] CJPA 2001, s.78(4) inserting new subss.(4A) and (4B) into s.61 of PACE.

[10] Formerly para.2.14. ("Any procedure in this Code involving the participation of a person (whether as a suspect or a witness) who is . . . a juvenile, must take place in the presence of the appropriate adult").

[11] See para.3–20 above.

[12] CJPOA, Sch.10, para.56 inserting new subs.(7A) in s.61 of PACE—and Code D, para.4.7(c). For the equivalent changes in Northern Ireland see the Police (Amendment) (Northern Ireland) Order 1995 (SI 1995/2993).

[13] Police Reform Act 2002, Sch.4, Pt 3, para.24(b).

2000, Sch.8, para.10. It requires the authorisation of an officer of the rank of superintendent (para.10(4)(a)). The rules regarding the warnings and information to be given to the suspect and the written record to be made are the same as those under PACE.

Serious Organised Crime and Police Bill

5–105   The Home Office Consultation Paper *Modernising Police Powers to Meet Community Needs* (August 2004) recommended that the police be given the power to take fingerprints outside police stations for purposes of identification. (Approximately 60 per cent of disqualified drivers provide false identities when stopped!) This recommendation was adopted in the Serious Organised Crime and Police Bill introduced in November 2004. The Explanatory Notes accompanying the Bill state that mobile digital fingerprint readers can be connected to the National Automated Fingerprint Identification System (NAFIS). Fingerprint impressions of two fingers can be taken and checked against NAFIS in a matter of minutes.

The Bill would amend s.61 so as to give the police the power to take a person's fingerprints prior to an arrest and away from a police station if the constable reasonably suspects that the person is committing, or attempting to commit an offence, or that he has committed or attempted to commit an offence and either the name of the person is unknown to, and cannot be readily ascertained by, the constable or the constable has reasonable grounds for doubting whether the name given by the person is his real name.[14] Amendment of s.63A allows fingerprints taken in this way to be checked against the NAFIS database and speculatively searched against the database of fingerprints recovered from crime scenes.[15] Fingerprints taken prior to arrest must however be destroyed. They may not be retained nor added to the NAFIS database.[16]

[s.61A Impressions of footwear

5–106   The Home Office Consultation Paper *Modernising Police Powers to Meet Community Needs* (August 2004) recommended that the police be given the power to take footwear impressions with or without the suspect's consent. The Serious Organised Crime and Police Bill introduced in November 2004 gave effect to this recommendation. The Bill (cl.109(2)) inserts a new s.61A into PACE. This states that, save as provided by the section, impressions of footwear may not be taken without appropriate consent (subs.(1)) which must be in writing if it is given at a police station (subs.(2)). It goes on to say however that an impression of footwear may be taken without consent from a person detained at a police station if (a) the person has been arrested for, or charged with, a recordable offence or has been informed that he will be reported for such an offence;

---

[14] New PACE s.61(6A), (6B) and (6C) and amendment to subs.(7A)—see cl.108(2) and (4) of the Bill.
[15] New PACE s.63A(1ZA) inserted by cl.108(5) of the Bill.
[16] New PACE s.64(IBA) inserted by cl.108(7) of the Bill.

and (b) he has not previously had such an impression taken (subs.(3)). If a previous impression was incomplete or of poor quality, it can be taken again (subs.(4)). The suspect must be told that the impression may be the subject of a speculative search (subs.(5)) and the reasons—which must be recorded on the custody record (subs.(6)). The rules in s.64 that apply to the non-destruction of fingerprints apply equally to impressions of footwear (s.61A(4)).

The Explanatory Notes to the Bill (para.246) state that the Forensic Science   **5–107** Service (FSS) maintain two databases of footwear impressions. One (the Mark Intelligence Index) contains impressions recovered from crime scenes. Footwear impressions are recovered from around 20–30 per cent of all crime scenes. The other database (the National Footwear Reference Collection) contains impressions from different items of footwear not linked to any individual. Most manufacturers supply the FSS with photographs and footwear impressions from any new product for loading onto the database.]

Intimate samples: s.62 and Identification Code D, s.5[17]

The Act distinguishes between two kinds of body samples. One kind is "intimate   **5–108** samples" which may be taken only with written consent in advance and only by a registered medical person—see para.5–113 below. The other kind is "non-intimate samples" which may exceptionally be taken without consent and by a police officer. Intimate samples are dealt with in s.62, non-intimate samples in s.63. The definition of both kinds of body samples is to be found in s.65.

Certain changes in the powers regarding the taking of intimate and non-intimate samples were made in the CJPOA 1994—mainly on the basis of recommendations of the Runciman Royal Commission on Criminal Justice. The Runciman Royal Commission wanted to see a considerable extension of the taking of samples, especially in view of advances in the technology of DNA evidence.[18]

Intimate samples may only be taken if an officer of the rank of at least inspector (not, as formerly, superintendent[19]) gives permission and written consent is given by the suspect or an appropriate adult.

Intimate samples were defined originally in PACE as samples of blood, semen,   **5–109** other tissue fluid, urine, saliva, pubic hair or a swab taken from a person's body orifice. Neither swab nor sample is defined in the Act. In Northern Ireland a sample of saliva and a swab taken from someone's mouth were treated as non-intimate samples and could therefore be taken without consent.[20] The Runciman Royal Commission recommended that the police should be permitted to pluck a sample of hair (other than pubic hair) without consent, that saliva be reclassified as a non-intimate sample to enable mouth swabs to be taken forcibly if necessary, and that intimate samples be permitted to be taken not just for serious arrestable

---

[17] See 1989 N.I. PACE Order, Art.62 and Code D, s.5. Amended by Police (Nothern Ireland) Act 2003, Art.42(2).
[18] See Runciman Report, pp.14–16.
[19] The change was made in the Criminal Justice and Police Act 2001, s.80(1) despite concerns expressed by the Parliamentary Joint Committee on Human Rights—First Report, Session 2000–2001, HL Paper 69, (2001) HC 427, para.81.
[20] Criminal Justice Act 1988, s.149 and Sch.14, para.6.

offences but for less serious offences. The Runciman Royal Commission also accepted the police suggestion that dental impressions should be classified as intimate samples.[21] The Government acted on these recommendations in the CJPOA, s.54(5).

The Serious Organised Crime and Police Bill introduced in November 2004 amends the definition of both intimate and non-intimate samples to make it clear that swabs taken from the genital area are intimate samples.[22] The Explanatory Notes to the Bill state that in a case of suspected sexual assault the police may wish to take swabs of the coronal sulcus, shaft or glans of the penis from a male suspect, and also perineum or vulval swabs and swabs from matted pubic hair from a victim or female suspect. Making it clear that such swabs are intimate samples requiring consent avoids the possibility of an allegation of assault.

5–110   In regard to intimate samples, s.54(3)(b) of the 1994 Act[23] permits such samples to be taken in regard to any recordable offence.[24] Saliva was removed from the definition of intimate samples and dental impressions were added to the definition (subs.(5)(a) and Code D, para.6.1). A dental impression can only be taken by a registered dentist (subs.(5)(b) and Code D, para.6.4[25]).[26]

The 1994 Act also added a new situation where an intimate sample may be taken.[27] This is where the accused is not in police detention and in the course of investigation two or more non-intimate samples suitable for the same means of analysis have been taken from him which have proved insufficient.[28] The procedure must have the authorisation of an officer of the rank of at least inspector (not, as formerly, a superintendent[29]) and the person concerned (or an appropriate adult on his behalf) must give written consent.

5–111   The detailed guidelines regarding DNA samples and the National DNA Database were set out in Home Office Circular No.16/95. (For the text see the third edition of this work at pp.536–541.) It is clear that the police believe that DNA evidence is of very great importance. They anticipate that the database will eventually hold some 5 million records. (For further elaboration of the issues involved see Redmayne, "The DNA Database: Civil Liberty and Evidentiary Issues" [1998] Crim.L.R. 437 and the literature cited in the article.)

There is no legal requirement that the inspector who gives the authority for a sample to be taken must be independent of the investigation, though if he is much involved in the case it might be wise to seek authority from another officer who is less involved. (The same is true in regard to the need for authorisation under ss.56, 58 and 61 of the Act.) The officer can only give authority if he has reason-

---

[21] Runciman Report, pp.14–15. Dental impressions were not defined as either intimate or non-intimate samples under PACE.

[22] cl.110 of the Bill amending s.65.

[23] See also Code D, paras 6.2–6.4.

[24] For the equivalent change in Northern Ireland see Police (Amendment) (Northern Ireland) Order 1995, Art.10(3)(b).

[25] Formerly 5.3.

[26] For the equivalent change in Northern Ireland see Police (Amendment) (Northern Ireland) Order 1995, Art.10(7)(b).

[27] CJPOA, s.54(2) adding new subs.(1A) to s.62 of PACE. See also Code D, para.6.2(b). For the equivalent change in Northern Ireland see Police (Amendment) (Northern Ireland) Order 1995, Art.10(2).

[28] For definition of an insufficient sample see Code D, Note 6B.

[29] The change was made by the Criminal Justice and Police Act 2001, s.80(1).

able grounds for believing that the sample will tend to confirm or disprove the suspect's involvement in the offence (subs.(2)(b)). The authorisation, if given orally in advance, must be confirmed in writing as soon as practicable (subs.(3)).

The question asking the suspect whether he is prepared to consent to provide   **5–112** an intimate sample can be put by any officer.[30] If he agrees, it then requires the authority of the inspector to carry out the procedure. The suspect must be told that the authorisation has been given and the grounds for it and also the nature of the offence in which it is suspected that he is involved (subss.(5) and (6)). He must be warned that a refusal to provide an intimate sample may harm his case in any proceedings brought against him (Code D, para.6.3[31]); Note 6D[32] suggests that the appropriate words for this might be: "You do not have to [provide this sample] but I must warn you that if you refuse without good cause, your refusal may harm your case if it comes to trial". He must also be reminded of his right to free legal advice and this reminder must be recorded in the custody record form (para.6.3[33]).

PACE originally provided that refusal to provide an intimate sample could also be taken as corroboration of other evidence against that person (subs.(10)). That provision was, however, repealed by the CJPOA 1994.[34] A record must be made as soon as possible of the authorisation, the grounds and the fact of consent. If the sample is taken at a police station, this must be put into the custody record (subss.(7) and (8)).

Save in the case of urine, only a doctor, registered nurse,[35] registered para-   **5–113** medic[36] registered health care professional, or, in the case of dental impressions, a registered dentist, may take an intimate sample (subs.(9) and (9A)).[37]

The CJPOA 1994 added a new requirement that if an intimate sample is taken at a police station, the suspect must be informed that it may be the subject of a "speculative search" against other records (see s.65) and the fact that he has been so informed must be recorded as soon as practicable after the sample has been taken.[38] (These functions can also be discharged by an authorised civilian

---

[30] In earlier editions of this book I suggested otherwise. I am indebted to Mr Martyn Levett, of counsel, for drawing my attention to this error.

[31] Formerly 5.2.

[32] Formerly 5A.

[33] Formerly 5.2.

[34] See Sch.11. So far the corroboration provision has remained in the Northern Ireland law.

[35] Added by the Criminal Justice and Police Act 2001, s.80(2).

[36] Added by the August 2004 revision of Code D, para.6.4. Paramedics were designated as registered health care professionals by the Registered Health Care Profession (Designation) Order 2003 (SI 2003/2461), on the basis of the Health Professions Order 2001 (SI 2002/254).

[37] Replacing previous subs.(9). Inserted by Police Reform Act 2002, s.54 which replaced "registered nurse" by registered health care professionals defined in s.65 as being members of a health care profession designated by order made by the Home Secretary for this purpose. The health care professions which may be designated are those specified in s.60(2) of the Health Act 1999—namely: those regulated by the Pharmacy Act 1954, the Medical Act 1983, the Dentists Act 1984, the Opticians Act 1989, the Osteopaths Act 1993 and the Chiropractors Act 1994; those regulated by the Nurses, Midwives and Health Visitors Act 1997; those regulated by an Order in Council under s.60 of the Health Act 1999. (The Police Reform Act 2002, s.55 also gave health care professionals the power to take intimate blood samples under the Road Traffic Act which could previously be taken only by medical practitioners.)

[38] CJPOA, Sch.10, para.57 inserting new subs.(7A) in s.62 of PACE. For the equivalent change in Northern Ireland see the Police (Amendment) (Northern Ireland) Order 1995, Art.10(5).

detention officer.[39]) A sample taken in the course of one investigation can be compared with a sample taken in another investigation relating to a completely different offence.[40]

Subsection (11) (as amended) makes it clear that the taking of samples of blood and urine in connection with offences of drink and driving under the Road Traffic Act 1988, ss.4 to 11 are exempt from the requirement to obtain a senior officer's authorisation. This exemption formerly did not cover train or tram drivers arrested for drunken driving under the Transport and Works Act 1992. Requiring a blood or urine sample from them without having the senior officer's authorisation was therefore technically unlawful—which might render the sample inadmissible in evidence. But this loophole was closed by the Police Reform Act 2002, s.53(2).

Terrorism cases

5–114 The taking of intimate samples in terrorism investigations is on virtually the same basis as under PACE. The relevant provisions are now to be found in the Terrorism Act 2000, Sch.8. A superintendent[41] can give his authorisation for the procedure if he is satisfied that it is necessary to determine whether the suspect is or has been concerned in the commission, preparation or instigation of terrorism[42] or to discover whether he has been involved in various related offences including fund-raising, financial support, money laundering or weapons training in connection with terrorism.[43]

Taking non-intimate samples: s.63 and Identification Code D, s.5[44]

5–115 Section 63 deals with non-intimate samples. A non-intimate sample (defined in s.65)[45] means (a) a sample of hair[46] other than pubic hair[47]; (b) a sample taken from a nail or from under a nail; (c) a swab from any part of the body including

---

[39] Police Reform Act 2002, Sch.4, Pt 3, para.30.

[40] *Kelt* [1997] 1 W.L.R. 1365; [1997] 3 All E.R. 1099, CA.

[41] No change has been made in the requirement of a superintendent's authorisation.

[42] Terrorism Act 2000, Sch.8, para.10(6)(b), referring to s.40(1)(b).

[43] Sch.8, para.10(6)(a), referring to s.40(1)(a). The offences in question are those in the Terrorism Act 2000, ss.11, 12, 15–18, 54, 56–63.

[44] See 1989 N.I. PACE Order, Art.63 and Code D, s.5.

[45] As amended by s.55 of the Criminal Justice and Public Order Act 1994. For the equivalent change in Northern Ireland see the Police (Amendment) (Northern Ireland) Order 1995, Art.11(2).

[46] See *Cooke* [1995] 1 Cr.App.R. 318, CA. (A sample of hair plucked from the suspect's head without his consent was held to be validly admitted in evidence.)

[47] Where hair samples are taken for the purpose of DNA analysis the suspect should be allowed "a reasonable choice as to what part of the body the hairs are taken from". When hairs are plucked they should be plucked individually unless the suspect prefers otherwise and no more should be plucked than is reasonably necessary. (Code D, Note 6A.) The Northern Ireland PACE Order, Art.63 states that a non-intimate sample of hair may be taken by cutting or plucking hairs with their roots so long as no more are taken than is necessary for analysis. (CJPOA 1994, Sch.9, para.39—which became Art.63A(2) by virtue of the 1995 Police (Amendment) (Northern Ireland) Order, Art.12.)

the mouth but not from a body orifice; (d) saliva; and (e) a footprint or similar impression of a part of the body other than hands.

As with the taking of fingerprints, the basic rule is said to be that consent is required (subs.(1)) and that such consent must be in writing (subs.(2)). However the basic rule is now almost completely swallowed by statutory exceptions. Thus, an officer of the rank of inspector (formerly superintendent[48]) or above can authorise the compulsory taking of a non-intimate sample where the offence in question is "a recordable one"[49] and there are reasonable grounds for believing that the sample will tend to confirm or disprove the suspect's involvement (subss.(3) and (4)). In such a situation an officer must inform the suspect that authorisation for taking the sample compulsorily has been given, and the grounds and the nature of the offence in which it is suspected that he is involved (subss.(6) and (7)). The reason for taking the sample without consent must be recorded as soon as practicable.[50]

The Criminal Justice Act 2003 significantly extended the provision for compulsorily taking a non-intimate sample by giving the police a power to take such a sample from anyone in police detention who has been arrested for a recordable offence who has not had a sample of the same type and from the same part of the body taken already in the course of the investigation or if one has been taken that it proved insufficient.[51] It does not require authorisation from an inspector rank officer. Also the power is available whether or not the sample is required for investigation of the offence for which he was arrested. It can therefore be used simply to build up the DNA database. The requirement to give the person the reason for taking the sample applies equally to the new power,[52] but specifying the nature of the offence in question does not.[53]

5–116

Section 63 does not require that a non-intimate sample be taken from the suspect by a police officer. The Police Reform Act 2002 specifies that it can be done by an authorised civilian detention officer.[54]

The CJPOA added a similar new requirement to that for intimate samples, that if a non-intimate sample is taken, with or without consent, the person must be informed that it may be the subject of a "speculative search" against other records

---

[48] Changed by the Criminal Justice and Police Act 2001, s.80(1).

[49] PACE originally required it to be a serious arrestable offence but this was changed to a recordable offence by the CJPOA, s.55(3) and Code D, para.5.5—now para.6.6(b). For the equivalent change in Northern Ireland see the 1995 Police (Amendment) (Northern Ireland) Order, Art.11(3).

[50] CJPOA, s.55(4) adding new subs.(8A) to s.63 of PACE. See also Code D, paras 6.8 and 6.10. For the equivalent change in Northern Ireland see the Police (Amendment) Northern Ireland Order 1995, Art.11(4). Failure to comply with such procedural requirements does not necessarily mean that the evidence will be held to be inadmissible—*Duffy*, unreported, N.I. CA, Lexis, September 15, 1997.

[51] New subss.(2A), (2B), and (2C) of s.63 of PACE inserted by s.10(2) of the Criminal Justice Act 2003 and Code D, para.6.6(aa)(i).

[52] s.63(8A); Code D, para.6.8.

[53] There was an error in the drafting of Code D, para.6.8 as revised in August 2004. The revised version of para.6.8 removed the requirement that the nature of the offence be indicated whenever an intimate or non-intimate sample is taken with or without consent. This is not correct since s.62(6) requires it in regard to the taking of any intimate sample and s.63(7) requires it in regard to the taking of any non-intimate sample that has been authorised under subs.(3). The Home Office informed the writer that this would be put right when the Codes were next amended.

[54] Sch.4, Pt 3, para.31(a).

(see below) and the fact that he has been so informed must be recorded as soon as practicable.[55] This too can be done by an authorised civilian detention officer.[56]

5–117   Originally, a non-intimate sample, like an intimate sample, could only be taken from someone in police detention or who was in police custody on the authority of a court. No distinction is made in the Act between pre-charge and post-charge. As has been seen the CJPOA provided for the taking of samples from persons not in custody. This applies to non-intimate samples as well. Section 63 of PACE was amended in 1994 to include two new cases[57] and in 1997 to include a third. The first (subs.(3A)) is where someone has been charged with a recordable offence, whether or not he is in police custody, and either no non-intimate sample has been taken from him or a sample was taken but it proved not suitable for the same means of analysis or insufficient[58] for such analysis. The second (subs.(3B)) is someone who has been convicted after April 10, 1995 of a recordable offence—except that under subs.(3C) some persons are covered who were convicted before that date. The third (subs.(3C)[59]) is a person who has been convicted before April 10, 1995 of a sex or violence offence listed in Sch.1 to the Criminal Evidence (Amendment) Act 1997 who is still serving a term of imprisonment[60] for that offence at the date when the sample is taken. The third category was added to enable the police to get DNA samples from a group of serious offenders in prison. Home Office Circular No.27/1997 said that there were an estimated 5,900 people in prison and another 2,000 mentally disordered offenders in psychiatric hospitals to whom subs.(3C) applied. (For implementation see *The Times*, January 17, 2003.)

Reasonable force may be used to take a non-intimate sample.[61]

Terrorism cases

5–118   The taking of a non-intimate sample in terrorist investigations under the Terrorism Act 2000[62] is on the same basis as under PACE—and is available for the same terrorism offences as for intimate samples (see para.5–114 above).

Fingerprints and samples: miscellaneous supplementary provisions: s.63A

5–119   The CJPOA, s.56 added a substantial new section (s.63A) to PACE. This first of all clarified the power to check fingerprints and samples against existing records

---

[55] CJPOA, Sch.10, para.58 inserting new subs.(8B) in s.63 of PACE, and Code D, Note 6E. For the equivalent change in Northern Ireland see the Police (Amendment) (Northern Ireland) Order 1995, Art.11(4).

[56] Police Reform Act 2002, Sch.4, Pt 3, para.26(c).

[57] By CJPOA, s.55(2). For the equivalent change in Northern Ireland see the Police (Amendment) (Northern Ireland) Order 1995, Art.11(2).

[58] For definition see Code D, Note 6B.

[59] Added by the Criminal Evidence (Amendment) Act 1997. At the time of writing, it had not yet been extended to Northern Ireland.

[60] Or is detained under Pt III of the Mental Health Act 1983 for such an offence, including persons acquitted on grounds of insanity or a finding of unfitness to plead—Criminal Evidence (Amendment) Act 1997, ss.1(4) and 2.

[61] Code D, para.6.7.

[62] Sch.8, para.10.

(subs.(1)). Such a search is defined as a "speculative search".[63] The records that can be searched are extremely wide and now include those of police forces throughout the United Kingdom, foreign police forces and the military.[64] The new section then provided that hairs, other than pubic hairs, may be plucked as well as cut, so long as no more is taken than is reasonably considered to be necessary for a sufficient sample (subs.(2) and see also Code D, para.6.1(b)(i)[65]). It permitted the exercise of powers to take samples in prisons (subs.(3)). (For the equivalent changes in Northern Ireland see the 1995 Police (Amendment) Order, Art.12.)

A constable can require someone who is not in police custody to attend a police station to have his fingerprints taken where he has been charged with or convicted of a recordable offence and either has not previously had his fingerprints taken or they were taken but proved unsuitable or an insufficient sample (subs.(4)).

The Criminal Evidence (Amendment) Act 1997, s.3 extended the power to take non-intimate samples to persons detained in psychiatric hospitals as permitted by s.63(3C) of PACE (above).[66]

Power to require someone to attend a police station to give a sample

Section 63A also creates a power for a person not in police detention to be   **5–120**
required to attend at a police station for the purpose of providing a sample. The pre-condition is that either (a) he must have been charged with a recordable offence or informed that he will be reported for such an offence, or (b) he has been convicted of a recordable offence and either he has not had a sample taken or one was taken but it was found not to be suitable for the same means of analysis, or the sample proved insufficient (s.63A(4)). An authorised civilian detention officer has the same power.[67] The attendance deadline for those in category (a) is one month from the date of charge, or of being told that he will be reported for such an offence,[68] or one month from the date when the officer is informed that the sample is not suitable or not sufficient. The deadline for those in category (b) is one month from the date of conviction or one month from the date when the officer is told that the sample is unsuitable or insufficient (s.63A(5)). The person must be given at least seven days' notice but the police can direct the time at which or between what times he should attend (s.63A(6)). A person who fails to attend can be arrested for this fact (s.63A(7)).

As has been seen, the Serious Organised Crime and Police Bill introduced in November 2004 would authorise fingerprints taken away from the police station prior to arrest to be checked against the database.[69]

---

[63] CJPOA, s.58 amending s.65 of PACE.
[64] subs.(1A) of s.63—introduced by the Criminal Justice and Police Act 2001, s.81(1), (2) which came into force on December 14, 2001.
[65] Formerly 5.11(b)(i) and Note 6A formerly 5C.
[66] This has not yet been extended to Northern Ireland.
[67] Police Reform Act 2002, Sch.4, Pt 3, para.32.
[68] These words were added by the Criminal Evidence (Amendment) Act 1997, s.4.
[69] New s.63A(1ZA) inserted by cl.108(5) of the Bill.

Taking a non-intimate sample for a drug test: ss.63B and 63C

5–121   The Criminal Justice and Court Services Act 2000 (CJCSA), s.57 added a power under a new s.63B of PACE to take a urine sample or a non-intimate sample such as a saliva swab from a person in police detention in order to test for drugs. The main purposes of this new power are to assist in the monitoring of drug misuse and to provide assistance to the courts when they make bail decisions. It can also help in referring suspects to drug counselling agencies. A two-year pilot study of this new power in three areas began in spring 2001.[70] The pilot was later extended to six other areas. This required modification of the Code.[71] These changes were therefore not included in the revised Codes implemented in April 2003. However, they were included in the revision of the Codes in August 2004, in a new s.17.

The pre-conditions are that the person must be over 14 years old[72] and that he must have been charged[73] with a "trigger offence"[74] or with any other offence where an officer of the rank of inspector or above has authorised the taking of the sample on the basis of reasonable grounds to suspect that misuse of specified Class A drugs[75] has caused or contributed to the offence (CJCSA, s.63B(2)).

5–122   Failure to provide a sample when requested to do so is an offence carrying a penalty of up to three months' imprisonment or a level 4 fine[76] or both (ss.63B(8), 63C(1)). (There is no power of arrest in respect of this offence.) When the request is made, the person must be warned that failure to comply without good cause may be the basis for prosecution (Code C, Note 17A). Where the suspect is under 17 an appropriate adult must be present when the request is made, when the warning is given and when the sample is taken (Criminal Justice Act 2003, s.5(3)). The taking of the sample must be in accordance with regulations approved by both

---

[70] Preliminary research on these pilots by an independent research organisation showed that the testing in all three areas had become successfully embedded into normal working procedures—see Mallender, Roberts and Seddon, "Evaluation of drug testing in the criminal justice system in three pilot areas", Research Findings No.176 (Home Office, 2002).

[71] See the Police and Criminal Evidence Act 1984 (Codes of Practice) (Modification) Order 2001 (SI 2001/2254) and Codes of Practice (Temporary Modification of Code D) Order 2002 (SI 2002/615). And see also the Police and Criminal Evidence Act 1984 (Codes of Practice) (Modification to Codes C and D) (Certain Police Areas) Order 2003 (SI 2003/704) and the Police and Criminal Evidence Act 1984 (Codes of Practice) (Modification to Codes C and D) (Certain Police Areas) (Amendment) Order (SI 2004/78).

[72] Originally, under the CJCSA 2000 the minimum age was 18 but the Criminal Justice Act 2003, s.5(3) lowered this to 14. Note 17F of the 2004 revision of Code C states that drug testing under s.17 of Code C only applies in police areas where it has been brought into force. Those in which testing of persons over 18 have been brought into force were listed in a new Annex I. Testing of persons aged 14 to 17 is only permitted in force areas where the necessary provisions have been brought into force (listed in a new Annex J) and where the Home Secretary has notified the Chief Constable that the necessary arrangements have been made.

[73] The Act gives the Secretary of State the power to extend the power to those merely arrested but not yet charged with those offences (s.63C(5)).

[74] Defined in Sch.6 to the CJCSA as theft, robbery, burglary, aggravated burglary, taking a conveyance without consent, aggravated vehicle-taking, obtaining property by deception, going equipped for stealing, and various offences under the Misuse of Drugs Act 1971 such as the production or supply of controlled drugs, possession of such drugs or possession with intent to supply. (Code C, Note 16E gives some but not all of the above.)

[75] Initially defined as heroin, cocaine or "crack" cocaine but the list can be extended to other drugs.

[76] Currently £2,500.

Houses of Parliament. Detention for this purpose cannot be longer than six hours after charge.[77]

The inspector's authorisation must be reduced to writing as soon as is practicable (subs.(2)). A record must be made also of the grounds for the authorisation (subs.(3)). If the sample is taken from someone detained at a police station it must be entered into the custody record (subs.(4)).

Force may not be used to take a sample for the purpose of drug testing **5–123** (para.17.11). A sample taken under these provisions may not be used for any purpose other than to ascertain whether the person has a specified Class A drug in their body (Code C, para.17.14(a)). They must be retained until the person concerned has made his first appearance in court so that, if the detainee disputes the test, the sample can be sent for confirmatory testing and analysis. But such samples, and the information derived from them, cannot be used in the investigation of any offence or in evidence against the person from whom they were taken (Code C, para.17.14(b) and Note 17D. See to like effect Code D, Note 6F). Information derived from the sample may be disclosed, however, for the purposes of a bail or a sentencing decision by a court, or in connection with his supervision in police detention (PACE, s.63B(7)). There is no equivalent as yet in Northern Ireland.

Photographing of suspects: s.64A and Identification Code D, s.5[78]

At common law it was unclear whether the taking of photographs of suspects by **5–124** the police without consent was lawful. The Philips Royal Commission recommended[79] that the photographing of suspects should be on the same basis as fingerprinting both in regard to the means for getting written consent and in regard to the rules regarding authorisation and safeguards where no written consent was forthcoming.

PACE, as passed, did not say anything on the subject. However, Code D did make some provision for photographs. It provided that the photographing of suspects normally required written consent but went on to list a number of particular circumstances in which photographs could be taken without consent (former para.4.2). A more general basis for photographs was introduced in the 1995 revision of Code D—where an officer or superintendent or above authorised it, "having reasonable grounds for suspecting the involvement of the person in a criminal offence and where there is identification evidence in relation to that offence" (para.4.2(iv)). The Northern Ireland Divisional Court (Crown Side) held in 1997 that the taking of photographs permitted by Code D was not *ultra vires* and was not a breach of the ECHR—*Re McCullough's Application* [1997] N.I. 423.

All these provisions have now been overtaken by the Anti-terrorism, Crime and **5–125** Security Act 2001 which for the first time gave general statutory authority for the photographing of detainees—with or without consent. It inserted a new s.64A into PACE. (The section came into force on December 14, 2001.) Subsection (1)

---

[77] CJCSA, s.63C(3).
[78] Formerly s.4. See N.I. PACE Order, Code D, s.4.
[79] Philips Report, para.3.133.

says simply, "A person who is detained at a police station may be photographed (a) with the appropriate consent; or (b) if the appropriate consent is withheld or it is not practicable to obtain it, without it".[80]

The Serious Organised Crime and Police Bill 2004–2005 would make it lawful for a person to be photographed without his consent elsewhere than at a police station provided that one of the following conditions is met[81]: the suspect has been arrested by a constable; or he has been taken into custody by a constable after being arrested for an offence by someone who is not a constable; or he has been made subject to a requirement to wait with a Community Service Officer (CSO)[82]; or issued with a fixed penalty notice by a constable,[83] a CSO[84] or an accredited person.[85] A photograph includes a moving image, as in a video film.[86]

5–126   The power to take a photograph of a detained person is not restricted to any particular situation or purpose. The power can be exercised by an authorised civilian detention officer.[87]

The use to which a photograph may be put is restricted, but the restriction is very broad. A photograph may be "used by, or disclosed to, any person for any purpose related to the prevention or detection of crime, the investigation of an offence or the conduct of a prosecution",[88] including offences, investigations or prosecutions abroad[89] and once so used may be retained. A photograph may be taken covertly at any time on a camera system installed in the custody area or elsewhere in the police station but after a photograph is obtained in this way the person must be informed as soon as practicable (Code D, paras 5.15–5.16).

There is power to require the removal of anything covering or obscuring the face such as masks, coverings or face paint (s.64A(2) and Code D, para.5.13). If necessary, force may be used to secure their removal (s.64A(2)(b) and Code D, para.5.14).

5–127   The police have been held to have been entitled to send "mug shot" photographs to local shops to assist them to identify troublemakers. The judge ruled that police who made reasonable use of suspects' photographs for the purpose of the prevention and detection of crime had a public interest defence to any action brought against them by the persons whose photographs had been circulated in that way.[90]

Note that under s.41 of the Criminal Justice Act 1925 it is an offence to take a photograph in any court, which includes not only the courtroom itself but also the building and the precincts of the building. In *Loveridge (William), Lee (Charles*

---

[80] See Anti-terrorism, Crime and Security Act 2001, s.92 and Code D, para.5.12. The Act (s.93) applies the same provisions to Northern Ireland—by inserting new Art.64A into the 1989 N.I. PACE Order.

[81] New s.64A(1A) and (1B) of PACE inserted by cl.107(2) of the Bill.

[82] Under Police Reform Act 2002, Sch.4, Pt 1, para.2(3) or (3A).

[83] Under Criminal Justice and Police Act 2001, Ch.1 of Pt.1; the Education Act 1996, s.444A; or the Road Traffic Offenders Act 1988, s.54.

[84] Under Police Reform Act 2002, Sch.4, Pt 1, para.1.

[85] Under Police Reform Act 2002, Sch.5, para.1.

[86] cl.107(3) of the Bill inserting new s.64A(6A) in PACE.

[87] Police Reform Act 2002, Sch.4, Pt 3, para.33.

[88] subs.(4).

[89] subs.(5).

[90] *Hellewell v Chief Constable of Derbyshire* [1995] 1 W.L.R. 804 (*per* Laws J.).

Sonny) and Loveridge (Christine),[91] the Court of Appeal held that the covert video filming of the Loveridges in the cell area of the local magistrates' court for identification purposes by comparison with CCTV footage at the scene of the crime was a breach of s.41. Also, the prosecution had not been able properly to establish that authority to take the photographs without consent had been given in terms of former para.4.2 of Code D. Nevertheless, the accused had not been prejudiced and there had been no unfairness within the terms of s.78 of PACE. The Court accepted that there had, in addition, been a breach of the right of privacy enshrined in Art.8(1) of the ECHR but it held that the breach of Art.8(1) did not render the trial unfair within the meaning of Art.8(2). It therefore upheld the convictions.

Destruction of fingerprints, samples and photographs: s.64/Criminal Justice and Police Act 2001, s.82 and Code D, Annex F

The Philips Royal Commission recommended[92] that fingerprints and samples   **5–128**
taken must be destroyed if the person concerned was cleared. Section 64 gave effect to that recommendation. At that time DNA testing had not been developed. By 1993 when the Runciman Royal Commission on Criminal Justice reported, DNA testing had been invented. However, Runciman took the same view of the policy issue as the Philips Royal Commission.[93]

Section 64 provided that fingerprints and samples, whether taken with consent or under compulsion, had to be destroyed as soon as practicable after the suspect had been cleared of the offence (subs.(1), (2)). He was to be treated as having been cleared if it was decided neither to prosecute nor formally to caution him; or if the offence was indictable and he was not sent for trial; or if he was tried for the offence and was acquitted.

If fingerprints were destroyed, any copies that had been made also had to be destroyed (subs.(5)) and if the data were held on computer, access to the data had to be made impossible.[94] A person who asked to be allowed to be present to witness the destruction had a right to do so (subs.(6))[95] if he asked within five days[96] of being cleared (Code D, former para.3.1). The rules regarding destruction of fingerprints and body samples did not, however, apply to terrorism cases (see pre-2003 Code D, para.1.16).

Under Code D (former para.4.4) the same destruction rule applied to photo-   **5–129**
graphs. But there was one important difference between the provisions for the destruction of fingerprints and those for the destruction of photographs. According to the 1995 revised Code D, para.4.4(a), photographs did not have to

---

[91] [2001] EWCA Crim 973; [2001] 2 Cr.App.R. 29.
[92] Philips Report, para.3.131.
[93] Runciman Report, p.16, para.36.
[94] Criminal Justice Act 1988, s.149. The equivalent provision for Northern Ireland is in the 1989 N.I. PACE Order, Art.64(5), (6).
[95] As amended by the Criminal Justice Act 1988, s.148.
[96] Under the original Code D it was a period of two months.

be destroyed, even though the suspect was cleared, or charged but not prosecuted, where he had a previous conviction for a recordable offence.

Where someone was entitled to have samples destroyed, information derived from them could not be used "(a) in evidence against the person so entitled; or (b) for the purposes of any investigation of an offence" (PACE, s.64(3B)[97]).

On May 26, 2000, in two decisions given on the same day, the Court of Appeal held that this provision meant exactly what it said. In *Weir*,[98] a case of murder, the police were led to the defendant by a sample of saliva taken from him the previous year after arrest in a drugs case which was subsequently dropped. The sample should therefore have been destroyed. In *Re Attorney General's Reference (No.3 of 1999)*[99] a woman aged 66 had been brutally raped and assaulted in her home in January 1997. The police eventually arrested the accused 18 months later on the basis of a match between samples taken from the victim of the rape and a mouth swab saliva sample taken from the accused after he was arrested for burglary in January 1998—a charge on which he was acquitted. (Unfortunately, the accused gave a false name as a result of which the police did not at that stage realise that he had a previous recordable offence. If that had been known, information from the sample could legitimately have been used for the purpose of a speculative search (under s.63(3B)) which would have avoided the whole problem.) In both cases, therefore, there was a sample that should have been destroyed which led the police to the suspect. In both cases, too, the prosecution relied not on the sample that ought to have been destroyed but on samples taken after the arrest for, respectively, the murder and the rape. But in the view of the Court of Appeal, that made no difference. The judges said that (a) and (b) of s.64(3B) had to be treated alike. The decisions provoked widespread criticism of the requirement to destroy.

5–130   In December 2000, the House of Lords, hearing the Attorney-General's appeal in the second case, took a different view.[1] It agreed that a sample which ought to have been destroyed could not be used in evidence against the person who supplied it because of the plain language of s.64(3B)(a). But it did not agree that the same was true where the sample that ought to have been destroyed had been the basis of further investigation (s.64(3B)(b)). It was in the interests of everyone that serious crime should be effectively investigated and prosecuted. There had to be fairness to all sides. In a criminal case this required the court to take into account the position of the accused, the victim and his or her family, and the public. The Court of Appeal's austere interpretation produced results that were contrary to good sense. The interests of the accused, the House of Lords held, were sufficiently safeguarded by the discretion vested in the judge by s.78 of PACE.

The effect of the House of Lords' decision was to encourage the police to continue their practice of holding fingerprint and DNA samples unlawfully in the hope of producing a result which the courts would condone.

---

[97] New s.64(3B) of PACE added by CJPOA, s.57(3). For the equivalent change in Northern Ireland see the 1995 Police (Amendment) (Northern Ireland) Order, Art.13(3), (3B).
[98] *The Times*, June 16, 2000, Case No.99/4829/W2.
[99] [2000] 4 All E.R. 360.
[1] *R. v B., Re Attorney General's Reference (No.3 of 1999)* [2001] 2 W.L.R. 56, HL.

Samples need no longer be destroyed

This concern was immediately addressed by legislation. Stimulated by the two   **5–131**
Court of Appeal decisions, and not satisfied that the House of Lords' decision
dealt sufficiently with the matter, the Home Office included a provision in the
Criminal Justice and Police Act 2001 in effect cancelling the rule requiring
destruction of fingerprints and samples. The CJPA 2001, s.82 provides that
where fingerprints or samples are taken from a person in connection with an
investigation of an offence, they need no longer be destroyed. The obligation to
destroy them is replaced by the rule that they can only be used for purposes
related to the prevention and detection of crime, the investigation of any offence
or the conduct of any prosecution. The term "use" includes the retaining of fingerprints or samples on databases that will allow speculative searches.[2] "Crime"
for these purposes includes acts committed abroad. The references to
"investigation" and "prosecution" include investigations or prosecutions abroad.[3]

Where someone who is not a suspect provides a sample voluntarily—say, for   **5–132**
the purposes of elimination in a mass testing exercise after a major crime—there
is no obligation for him to allow his samples to be retained or used other than for
that purpose. He will be asked if he consents to their retention and use. (Annex F
in Code D, added in the 2003 revision, gives examples of different kinds of consent form.) Once given in writing, that consent permits use of the sample as if it
had been taken from a suspect—and it makes no difference when the consent was
given. Also, the consent, once given, cannot be withdrawn.[4] But if consent is not
given, the fingerprints and samples and the information obtained from them cannot be used in evidence against the person concerned or for the purposes of investigation of any offence.[5] (Though, if they are so used, the evidence might still be
admitted under s.78 as in the House of Lords' decision in *Attorney General's
Reference (No.3 of 1999)* above.)

When the Criminal Justice and Police Bill was introduced it provided that the   **5–133**
new rules would apply only prospectively from the date they came into force.
However, the Government was persuaded to make the provision retrospective, so
cases such as *Weir* and *Attorney General's Reference (No.3 of 1999)* would not
be repeated.[6] The Parliamentary Joint Committee on Human Rights said that an
argument could be made that the retrospective application of these changes could
be incompatible with the ECHR but that such an argument was, on balance, not
likely to be successful.[7] The Joint Committee expressed reservations, however,
about the provision in the CJPA regarding fingerprints and samples given voluntarily for elimination purposes. It stressed the importance of continuous monitoring of the use made of these extended powers to ensure that the right of privacy
under Art.8 of the ECHR was being protected.[8]

---

[2] PACE, s.64(1B)(a), (b) introduced by CJPA 2001, s.82(2). The equivalent for Northern Ireland was
s.83(2).
[3] PACE, s.64(1B)(c), (d) introduced by CJPA 2001, s.82(2) and s.83(2).
[4] PACE, s.64(3AC), (3AD) introduced by CJPA 2001, s.82(4) and Code D, Annex F, 1, 2. The equivalent for Northern Ireland was s.83(4).
[5] PACE, s.64(3AC), (3AD) introduced by CJPA 2001, s.82(4).
[6] CJPA 2001, s.82(6) and the equivalent s.83(6) for Northern Ireland.
[7] First Report, Session 2000–2001, HL Paper 69, (2001) HC 427, paras 91–92.
[8] First Report, Session 2000–2001, HL Paper 69, (2001) HC 427, para.85.

5–134   The fingerprint and DNA sample destruction and speculative search provisions made by ss.81 and 82 of the Criminal Justice and Police Act 2001 came into force on December 14, 2001.[9] A subsequent challenge to the new powers to retain fingerprints and DNA samples brought under the Human Rights Act was unsuccessful. The challenge was brought under the privacy provisions of Art.8.1 of the ECHR. The two applicants sought judicial review of the police decision to retain their fingerprints and DNA samples after one had been acquitted of the charge of attempted robbery and proceedings for harassment had been dropped against the other. The Divisional Court in March 2002 rejected the application. It was not clear that Art.8 applied at all, but if it did, any interference with the right to privacy under Art.8.1 was justified under Art.8.2. The interference was necessary in a democratic society for the prevention of disorder or crime "as there was a pressing social need for the restriction, the restriction corresponded to that need and was proportionate". Accordingly, s.64(1A) as amended by s.82 of the Criminal Justice and Police Act 2001 was compatible with Art.8.[10] The decision was upheld by the Court of Appeal[11] and in July 2004 by a unanimous House of Lords.[12]

Under the provisions of the Serious Organised Crime and Police Bill fingerprints taken prior to arrest away from the police station do have to be destroyed—"as soon as they have fulfilled the purpose for which they were taken".[13]

Terrorism cases

5–135   As has been seen, the rules requiring fingerprints and samples to be destroyed did not apply in terrorism cases though they could only be used for the purposes of a terrorist investigation.[14] The CJPA modified this restriction by permitting their use for the same purposes as under PACE (the prevention and detection of any crime, the investigation of any offence or the conduct of any prosecution).[15]

Definitions relating to fingerprints and samples: s.65[16]

5–136   Section 65 of PACE defined "appropriate consent", "fingerprints",[17] "intimate sample", "non-intimate sample" and "the terrorism provisions". As has been seen, the CJPOA 1994 slightly changed the definitions of "intimate" and "non-intimate"

---

[9] The changes to s.64 affecting the retention and use of samples in ss.81–82 of the CJPA, which mirror those for fingerprints, came into force on May 11, 2001.

[10] *R. (S) v Chief Constable of South Yorkshire* and *R. (Marper) v Same* [2002] EWHC Admin 478.

[11] [2002] EWCA Civ 1275; [2002] 1 W.L.R. 3223; [2003] 1 All E.R. 148; [2003] Crim.L.R. 39.

[12] [2004] UKHL 39; [2004] 4 All E.R.193.

[13] New s.64(1BA) inserted by cl.108(7) of the Bill.

[14] PACE, s.64(7); Code D, former para.1.16.

[15] CJPA 2001, s.84(2), Code D, Annex F, para.4.

[16] See 1989 N.I. PACE Order, Art.53. Amended by Police (Northern Ireland) Act 2003, Art.42(3),(4).

[17] The definition of fingerprints was broadened by the Criminal Justice and Police Act 2001, s.78(8) to include records in any form, and produced by any methods, of fingers, palms and other parts of the hand where there are characteristic skin patterns.

samples partly to reflect the redefinition of saliva and mouth swabs (now both non-intimate samples) and dental impressions (now intimate samples), and partly to improve the drafting. As has been seen, the Serious Organised Crime and Police Bill introduced in November 2004 (cl.110) redefines intimate and non-intimate samples by making it clear that any swab taken from the genital area is an intimate sample.

The words and phrases defined in s.65 were enlarged by CJPOA, s.58(4) to include "registered dentist", "speculative search" and "sufficient" and "insufficient" in relation to the quantity or quality of samples. Section 59(1) of the CJPOA added a further new definition to s.65—of "intimate search" which is defined as a physical examination of a person's body orifices other than his mouth. Subsection (2) stated that in s.32, which gives the police power to search a person on arrest, the police are permitted to search a person's mouth. (For the equivalent change in Northern Ireland see Police (Amendment) (Northern Ireland) Order 1995, Arts 5 and 8.)   **5–137**

Further definitional changes were made by the Criminal Justice and Police Act 2001. Thus "footprints or similar impressions" has been replaced by a new definition of "skin impressions" covering impressions made by any means or parts of the body other than the hand.[18] The definition section now spells out what makes samples insufficient, thus allowing them to be retaken. This includes where scientific failure inhibits the production of a DNA profile or where the sample is damaged or destroyed prior to analysis.[19]

---

[18] CJPA 2001, s.80(5).
[19] CJPA 2001, s.80(6)

QUESTIONS AND ANSWERS

THE SUSPECT'S RIGHTS IN THE POLICE STATION

5–138   **For how long can the police keep someone incommunicado in the police station?**

Where someone is in custody in a police station he has the right "to have one friend or relative or other person who is known to him or who is likely to take an interest in his welfare told, without delay—except to the extent that delay is permitted" (s.56(1)).

The Code states that if that person cannot be contacted, the suspect may choose up to two alternates. If they too cannot be contacted, the custody officer has discretion to allow further attempts until the information has been conveyed. The right not to be held incommunicado applies every time one is taken to a new police station.

5–139   **In what circumstances can the police delay the suspect's right to have someone informed as to his whereabouts?**

Both the Act and Code C specify the circumstances in which delay is permitted. The Code sets these out in Annex B. Annex B is based on the identical provisions in the Act itself. Delay is permissible for a limited period if:

(1)   the suspect is detained in connection with a serious arrestable offence (indictable offence under the Serious Organised Crime and Police Bill 2004–2005); and

(2)   an officer of the rank of inspector (formerly superintendent) or above reasonably believes that exercise of the right

(a)   would lead to interference with or harm to witnesses or interference with or physical harm to other persons; or

(b)   would lead to the alerting of others suspected of involvement; or

(c)   would hinder the recovery of the proceeds of the crime.

But if these grounds cease to apply, the person must be asked as soon as practicable if he wishes to exercise the right and action must then be taken on any affirmative response. The maximum period of delay is 36 hours.

If someone rings the police station asking about the detainee must he be told where he is?   5–140

Code C, para.5.5 provides that when an inquiry is made as to the whereabouts of a detained person by his friends or relatives, the information "shall be given, if he agrees and if Annex B does not apply". But Note 5D says that "in some circumstances it may not be appropriate to use the telephone to disclose information". The meaning of this caveat is unclear.

Does the right not to be held incommunicado apply also to persons held as suspects under the anti-terrorism legislation?   5–141

Under the previous law, suspects held under the Prevention of Terrorism (Temporary Provisions) Act had no right to make contact with the outside world while they were held, for anything up to one week. But as a result of Lord Jellicoe's 1983 Report into the working of the Act, this was changed by PACE. A suspect held under the terrorism provisions cannot be denied the right to have someone informed of his arrest for longer than 48 hours. The grounds for delaying the exercise of this right are the same as those set out in Annex B (para.5–139 above), but there are in addition two further grounds on which delay may be authorised: if there are reasonable grounds for believing that the notification will lead to interference with the gathering of information relating to acts of terrorism; or that it will, by alerting any person, make it more difficult to prevent an act of terrorism; or to secure the arrest, prosecution or conviction of someone involved in terrorism. Whereas the Criminal Justice and Police Act 2001 legitimised authorisation by an inspector for delay in making a phone call, in terrorism cases this still requires a superintendent's authority.

Can detained persons demand to have visits or to make phone calls, send letters or cables?   5–142

Code C has provisions on all these matters. It states that detained persons may receive visits at the custody officer's discretion and that he should exercise his discretion as to visits in the light of the availability of sufficient manpower to supervise a visit and any possible hindrance to the investigation (Note 5B). The detained person may also speak on the telephone to one person—unless an officer of the rank of inspector or above delays or denies such a call by applying the provisions of Annex B. This can be done not only in serious arrestable offence cases but also when the offence being investigated is merely an arrestable one. Whether or not the call is at public expense is at the discretion of the custody officer. A police officer may listen to what is said unless the call is to a solicitor. He may terminate the call if it is being abused. If the person does not speak English, an interpreter may make a call for him. The person should be cautioned that what he says in any letter, call or message may be listened to and given in evidence.

A detained person should be supplied, on request, with writing materials. Any letter or other message should be sent at his expense as soon as practicable unless Annex B applies. All letters except those to solicitors may be read by the police. The only suspects who have an absolute and unqualified right to make a call and to have visits are those from abroad. The Code says that a foreign national or a citizen of a Commonwealth country may communicate "at any time" with his High Commission, Embassy or Consulate" (para.7.1). In regard to visits, the Code states that "consular officers may visit one of their nationals in police detention to talk to them and, if required, to arrange for legal advice". Such visits should take place out of hearing of a police officer (para.7.3). Note 7A states that the rules regarding foreign and Commonwealth detainees cannot be suspended even though Annex B applies.

5–143   In what circumstances can a suspect get a lawyer in the police station?

The Philips Royal Commission hoped to see a dramatic improvement in the suspect's access to legal advice in the police station. The Government broadly implemented its recommendations.

A suspect under arrest at a police station has a right to ask to see a solicitor privately. This is an absolute right, though if the crime being investigated is a serious arrestable (or, under the Serious Organised Crime and Police Bill 2004–2005, an indictable) offence, the police can sometimes delay giving access to the lawyer. This is only permitted, however, in the rare situation where an inspector (formerly a superintendent and in terrorism cases still a superintendent) reasonably believes that allowing access to that lawyer could lead to accomplices being alerted or evidence being destroyed. He should then permit access to another lawyer. The maximum period of delay is 36 hours or in terrorism cases 48 hours. If the reasons for delay cease, the suspect should be asked whether he wishes to exercise his right. If the suspect has asked for a solicitor but he has not yet arrived, questioning can begin only if: (1) an inspector (or in terrorism cases a superintendent) reasonably believes that to delay would involve an immediate risk of harm to persons or serious loss of or damage to property; or (2) a superintendent reasonably believes that to wait for the solicitor to arrive would unreasonably delay the inquiry; or (3) the suspect indicates in writing or on tape that he has changed his mind and that the interview may be started without waiting for the solicitor—but an officer of the rank of inspector, having inquired into the matter, must assent.

Code C, Annex B, para.4 specifically makes it clear that access to a solicitor cannot be denied or delayed on the ground that the solicitor might advise the suspect to say nothing.

How in practice does a suspect go about trying to find the name of a local solicitor?   **5–144**

If the suspect does not know the name of a solicitor to contact, the detainee should (1) be told of the availability of the local duty solicitor scheme, and (2) be provided with a list of local solicitors who have indicated their willingness to act in such situations (Code C, Note 6B).

There are two basic duty solicitor systems—the rota system where an identifiable solicitor is on duty, and a panel arrangement where the national telephone service can telephone the duty solicitors in the order in which they appear on the panel until one willing to advise the suspect is found. The advantage of the rota system is that the central telephone service only has to contact one solicitor; the disadvantage is that that solicitor has to hold himself available to go to the police station for the whole period for which he is on duty. The advantage of the panel system is that the solicitors can carry on with their ordinary routine and it is economical since it does not involve the payment of stand-by fees. On the other hand it often involves a delay in finding a solicitor who is available. The police are now required initially to contact the duty solicitor via FirstAssist which is part of the Royal and Sun Alliance Group which runs the system.

How could suspects in the police station expect to pay for the help of lawyers?   **5–145**

Advice and assistance by solicitors in police stations are exempted from the normal requirement of a means test and a graduated contribution. The service, in other words, is free of charge at public expense. The same is true of the services of solicitors at hearings before magistrates on applications by the police for warrants of further detention.

If the detained person wants a lawyer and one has been called, can the police start questioning him before the lawyer arrives?   **5–146**

A person who has asked for legal advice "may not be interviewed or continue to be interviewed until they have received such advice". But there are three exceptions. The first is where Annex B (to prevent the alerting of accomplices, etc.) applies. The second is where an officer of the rank of superintendent or above has reasonable grounds to believe that there is an immediate risk of harm to persons or serious loss of or damage to the property, or that waiting for the arrival of the solicitor would cause unreasonable delay to the investigation (but when the danger has passed, questioning may not continue until the person has received the legal advice he asked for). The third is where the suspect, having first asked for legal advice, changes his mind. The interview can then start provided an officer of the rank of inspector or above agrees and the suspect's change of mind is recorded on tape or in writing (Code C, para.6.6).

5–147   Can the solicitor remain during the interview with the detained person?

The Code states that the solicitor can be asked to withdraw if an officer of the rank of superintendent or above considers that by his misconduct he is preventing the proper putting of questions to his client (Code C, paras 6.9–6.11 and Note 6E). The superintendent should consider whether a report to the Law Society is appropriate.

5–148   If the solicitor sends his clerk or legal executive does he count as a solicitor for these purposes?

Someone who is not a solicitor counts as a solicitor for the purposes of the Code of Practice if he is "an accredited or probationary representative included on the register of representatives maintained by the Legal Services Commission" (Code C, para.6.12). Someone who qualifies under these heads should be admitted to the police station to provide advice on behalf of his firm unless an officer of the rank of inspector or above "considers that such a visit will hinder the investigation and directs otherwise" (Code C, para.6.12A). The Divisional Court held in the *Robinson* case that it is up to the inspector on the spot to decide whether any individual clerk should be admitted and that it is his subjective judgment which is decisive.

5–149   What is the position if a solicitor sent by a friend or relative arrives at the police station but the suspect has not asked for a solicitor?

The general provision (in Code C, para.6.15) is that unless Annex B applies (even if he previously declined legal advice), the suspect must be informed if a solicitor comes to see him and he must be asked if he wants to see the solicitor.

5–150   At what point must the person in the police station be told of his rights?

The answer depends on whether he is there voluntarily or under arrest. If he is not under arrest he must be told of his rights only when he is cautioned. If he is under arrest he must be told of his rights when he first comes to the police station or, if he comes voluntarily but is then arrested, at that time. (It is the custody officer's duty to consider whether he ought to be detained as soon as practicable after he arrives at the police station, or, if he has been arrested at the station, as soon as practicable after his arrest.)

Of what rights must he be informed?   **5–151**

He must be told: (1) the grounds of his detention; (2) of the right to have someone informed of his detention; (3) of the right to consult a copy of the Codes; (4)
of the right to free legal advice. He must be told of these rights orally and must
also be given a notice setting them out together with a statement that he is entitled to ask for a copy of the custody record form, providing he does so within 12
months. He must also now be given a notice of his entitlements whilst a detainee.

A person who is at the police station voluntarily and who has been cautioned
must be told of the same rights but he must also be told that he has a right to leave
if he wishes.

To what extent do the rules make special provision for the needs of the   **5–152**
young, those with mental handicaps, the deaf, those who cannot speak
English, etc.?

There are special rules in Code C for each of these groups.

(1) *The young.* Code C (para.3.13; Note 3C) provides that when a child or
young person has been arrested an "appropriate adult" must be informed and
asked to come to the police station. This means his parent or guardian, or, if he is
in care, the care authority or the voluntary organisation he is with. Failing contact
with the parent or guardian the information should be communicated to a social
worker, a member of a youth offending team (YOT) or to another responsible
adult who is not a police officer.

The custody officer has a specific duty (under Code C, para.3.13) to discover
the person responsible for the juvenile's welfare. It may be his parent or guardian
(or, if he is in care, the care authority or organisation). It may be anyone who has
assumed responsibility for his welfare. That person must be informed as soon as
practicable that the juvenile has been arrested, why he was arrested and where he
is detained. The concept of the person responsible for the juvenile's welfare (who
may or may not be the appropriate adult) was introduced in the 1991 revision of
the Codes. The custody officer should as soon as possible inform the appropriate
adult of the grounds of detention and of the detainee's whereabouts and should
ask the adult to come to the police station (para.3.15). The information about the
suspect's right to legal advice and to inform someone else of his arrest and to consult the Codes must be given to the juvenile in the adult's presence, or, if not,
must be given to him when he arrives at the police station (para.3.17). If the
appropriate adult is already at the police station when information about his
rights is given to the juvenile as required in paras 3.1 to 3.4 of the Code, then it
must be given in the appropriate adult's presence. If the adult comes later it must
be given to the juvenile again in his presence. (The same applies to other
categories of persons for whom an appropriate adult has to be called.)

When the appropriate adult arrives at the police station the juvenile must be
informed that he is there and that he has the right to consult privately with the
adult *at any time* (para.3.18, emphasis supplied).

The Code (para.11.15) states categorically that "A juvenile ... must not be interviewed regarding their involvement or suspected involvement in a criminal offence or offences or asked to provide or sign a written statement under caution or record of interview in the absence of the appropriate adult unless para.11.1 or paras 11.18 to 11.20 apply".[20] The previous version of this rule said "whether suspected or not"—in other words it applied to witnesses and victims of crime as well as suspects. This is no longer the case.

Paragraph 11.18 lists categories of persons who may not be interviewed at all unless an officer of the rank of superintendent or above considers that delay will lead to the consequences set out in para.11.1(a) to (c)—such as interference or harm to evidence, harm to persons, the alerting of accomplices, or the hindering of the recovery of property—and even then only if he is satisfied that interviewing them would not significantly harm their physical or mental state. The categories are: (a) a juvenile or someone who is mentally disordered or otherwise mentally vulnerable without an appropriate adult; (b) anyone else who at the time of the interview because of the effects of drink or drugs or any illness or ailment or condition appears unable to appreciate the significance of the questions put and their answers or to understand what is happening; and (c) a person who has difficulty in understanding English or who has a hearing disability if there is no interpreter. If an interview does take place, questioning in these circumstances may not continue once sufficient information to avert the feared consequences has been obtained (para.11.19[21]).

If the adult thinks that the juvenile needs legal advice the police are required to treat this as a request for a lawyer by the juvenile himself (para.3.19).

Juveniles may only be interviewed at school "in exceptional circumstances" and then only when the principal or his nominee agree (para.11.16[22]). Every effort should be made to notify both the parent(s) or other person responsible for the juvenile's welfare and the appropriate adult if this is someone different. If waiting for the appropriate adult would cause unreasonable delay, the principal or his nominee can act as appropriate adult (*ibid.*) unless the offence is against the educational institution. But the head teacher or his nominee should agree and be present (*ibid.*). Note 1C states that a person, including a parent or guardian, should not be an appropriate adult if he is suspected of involvement in the offence, or is the victim, or a witness, or is involved in the investigation, or has "received admissions". (An estranged parent should not be the appropriate adult if the juvenile "expressly and specifically" objects (Note 1B).) Police are warned that juveniles (like the mentally disordered or otherwise mentally vulnerable) are "particularly prone in certain circumstances to provide information that may be unreliable, misleading or self-incriminating" and that it is important to obtain corroboration of any facts admitted whenever possible (Note 11C[23]). A juvenile should not be arrested at school unless this is unavoidable, in which case the head teacher or his nominee must be informed (Note 11D[24]).

---

[20] A redraft of what was formerly 11.14. In the 2003 revision of Code C, paras 11.18–11.20 replaced Annex C.

[21] Formerly Annex C, para.2.

[22] Formerly 11.15.

[23] Formerly 11B.

[24] Formerly 11C.

A juvenile should not be placed in police cells unless no other secure accommodation is available and the custody officer considers that it is not practicable to supervise him if he is not in a cell. He may not, however, be placed in a cell with an adult (para.8.8). An intimate search of a juvenile may only take place in the presence of an appropriate adult of the same sex, unless the juvenile signifies that he would prefer it to be done in the adult's absence and the adult agrees (Code C, Annex A(a), para.5).

(2) *The suspect who is mentally disordered or otherwise mentally vulnerable.* The rules in the Code for the mentally disordered and the otherwise mentally vulnerable[25] are similar to those for juveniles (Code C, Note 1G). An appropriate adult must be notified that such a person is in the police station (Code C, para.3.15). The "appropriate adult" would be a relative or guardian responsible for his care, someone experienced in dealing with such people not employed by the police, failing whom some other responsible adult not employed by the police (Code C, para.1.7(b)). It may in some circumstances be better if the appropriate adult is someone who has experience or training in regard to the mentally disordered or mentally vulnerable rather than a relative lacking such qualifications. But if the person has a preference that should be respected it practicable (Note 1D).

Just as in the case of the juvenile, the custody officer must call the appropriate adult to the police station and must give the same information. The prohibitions on interviewing a mentally disordered person or mentally vulnerable person on his own are the same as for juveniles—subject to the exceptions set out in paras 11.18–11.20 (see above). The whole lengthy list of provisions affecting the treatment of the mentally disordered and mentally vulnerable is to be found in Annex E to Code C.

(3) *The deaf.* Code C, para.13.5 states that if a person is deaf or there is doubt about his hearing ability he must not be interviewed in the absence of an interpreter unless he agrees in writing or paras 11.1 or 11.18–11.20 apply. The principle relates equally where the appropriate adult is deaf (para.13.6). The interviewing officer shall ensure that the interpreter makes a note of the interview at the time for use in the event of his being called to give evidence. The suspect should be given an opportunity to read and sign it as correct or to indicate any respects in which he considers it to be inaccurate. Such an interpreter is provided free of charge at public expense.

(4) *Those who cannot speak or understand English.* Code C, para.13.2 states that if someone has difficulty in understanding English and either the police officer does not speak the person's own language or the suspect wishes to have an interpreter to be present, "he must not be interviewed in the absence of a person capable of interpreting". The only exception is again where paras 11.1 or 11.18–11.20 apply.

The interviewing officer must ensure that the interpreter makes a note at the time of the interview in the language of the person being interviewed and that he certifies its accuracy. The suspect should be given a chance to read it and to sign it as accurate or to indicate the respects in which he considers it to be inaccurate (para.13.3). If the suspect makes a statement in a language other than English the interpreter should take down the statement in the language in which it is made;

---

[25] The phrase that replaced "mentally handicapped" in the 2003 revision of the Codes.

the person making the statement should be invited to sign the statement; and an official English translation should be made in due course (para.13.4).

Interpreters must be provided at public expense and all reasonable efforts must be made to make this clear to the detainee (para.13.8). If a person is charged, arrangements have to be made as soon as practicable to have the interpreter explain the offence and any other information given by the custody officer.

(5) *The blind.* If a person is blind or visually handicapped or cannot read, the custody officer should ensure that someone appropriate is called to the police station to help him in checking any documentation and to sign any document on his behalf if the blind person so wishes (para.3.20).

5–153   Does the suspect have to answer questions put to him by the police?

A police officer has the right to ask any questions and the Code states that citizens have a civic duty to "help police officers to prevent crime and discover offenders" (Code A, Note 1). But the citizen has no legal duty to answer; a person detained in the police station, like everyone else in the community, has a "right to silence". The purpose of the caution is precisely to remind him of this right.

Until 1995 the ("old") caution told the suspect "You do not have to say anything unless you wish to do so but what you say may be given in evidence". When the case came to court neither the prosecution nor the judge could suggest that silence was evidence of guilt. However, the position was changed by the Criminal Justice and Public Order Act 1994. Both the prosecution and the judge are now allowed to suggest to the jury that silence can be evidence of guilt. So the caution had to be changed. It still tells the suspect that he is entitled to be silent. It has not become a criminal offence to be silent. The right to be silent remains but the suspect must now be warned that silence might be penalised by the jury drawing adverse inferences. The only exception to this (introduced together with the revised Codes in 2003) is when the suspect in a police station has asked for but has not yet been allowed an opportunity to get legal advice. In that case he must be cautioned in terms of the former pre-1995 caution. If later he does get legal advice (or get an opportunity to have it) he must be cautioned in terms of the new caution. (Code C, Annex C, Note C2 suggests how the suspect's likely confusion might be addressed—see further para.5–157.)

5–154   What is the wording of the caution?

The caution introduced as from April 1995 ("the new caution") is: "You do not have to say anything. But it may harm your defence if you do not mention when questioned something which you later rely on in court. Anything you do say may be given in evidence."

Minor variations in the way the caution is put are permitted. If the suspect does not understand the caution, the officer is supposed to try to explain it in his own words.

Adverse inferences can also be drawn from a failure by the suspect to answer specific police questions about objects, marks or substances on or about his person or at the place where he was arrested, or the failure to account for his presence at the scene of the crime. For such an inference to be drawn the officer must first, however, have told the suspect in ordinary language:

(a) what offence he is investigating;

(b) what fact he is asking the suspect to account for;

(c) that he believes this fact may be due to the suspect being involved in the offence; and

(d) that a court may draw a proper inference from his silence.

For more details see the separate Chapter on the right to silence, Ch.13 below.

When does a person have to be cautioned?   **5–155**

The caution has to be given to a person "whom there are grounds to suspect of an offence" before any questions or further questions are put to him if either his answers or his silence (*i.e.* failure or refusal to answer a question or to answer satisfactorily) may be given in evidence to a court in a prosecution (Code C, para.10.1).

The person need not be cautioned if he is being questioned just to establish his identity or his ownership of a vehicle or "in the furtherance of the proper and effective conduct of a search"—providing that it does not consist of questions about his possible involvement in a criminal offence.

When should the former caution rather than the new caution be used?   **5–156**

The former caution (see para.5–153 above) has to be given to a person who:

• is detained in a police station or other authorised place of police detention. (It therefore does not apply to someone who is not detained because he cannot be prevented from seeking legal advice);

• has asked for legal advice (it therefore does not apply to a suspect who, after being told about the availability of free legal advice, does not ask for it);

- has not been allowed an opportunity to consult a solicitor; and

- has not changed his mind about wanting legal advice.[26]

The former caution also applies to a person who has been charged or informed that he may be prosecuted for an offence, who:

- is shown a statement by someone else or the content of an interview with someone else that relates to the offence (see Code C, para.16.4);

- is interviewed about the offence (see Code C, para.16.5); or

- makes a written statement about the offence (see Code C, Annex D, paras 4 and 9).

5–157   What happens if the situation changes regarding access to legal advice?

If the suspect has been cautioned and the situation as regards getting legal advice later changes, he must be cautioned again in different terms. The revised version of Code C (Annex C, para.C2) suggests that this should be explained to the suspect as follows:

(a) *Adverse inferences now cannot be drawn.* If, having previously been cautioned in terms of the "new" caution about the possible adverse inferences that might be drawn from silence, the situation changes because access to legal advice is delayed by the police or it is decided that it is necessary to interview the suspect as a matter of urgency, he should be told: "The caution you were previously given no longer applies. This is because after that caution you asked to speak to a solicitor but have not yet been allowed an opportunity to speak to a solicitor [or you have been charged with/informed that you may be prosecuted] ... This means that from now on, adverse inferences cannot be drawn at court and your defence will not be harmed just because you choose to say nothing. Please listen carefully to the caution I am about to give you because it will apply from now on. You will see that it does not say anything about your defence being harmed." He is then cautioned in terms of the "old caution".

(b) *If adverse inferences can now been drawn.* If, having been previously cautioned in terms of the former caution because he was not allowed an opportunity of seeking legal advice, he now is allowed access to legal advice or, although still now allowed such access, he decides that he does not after all want it, he should be told: "The caution you were previously given no longer applies. This is because after that caution you have been allowed an opportunity to speak to a solicitor. Please listen carefully to the caution I am about to give you because it will apply from now on. It explains how your defence at court

---

[26] See Code C as revised in 2003, Annex C, para.1.

may be affected if you choose to say nothing." He is then cautioned in terms of the "new caution".

The ordinary suspect may find this a bit difficult to follow—and the ordinary police officer may find it difficult to explain.

THE EXERCISE OF POLICE POWERS IN THE POLICE STATION

What rules restrict the police in their questioning of the suspect?   **5–158**

There are rules in the Code about interviews with a suspect:

(1) In any 24-hour period a continuous period of eight hours must be allowed for rest, free from questioning, or travel. If possible, this period should be at night (Code C, para.12.2).

(2) There is no rule as to the maximum length of an interview[27] but there are rules as to meal breaks. Breaks should be made at recognised mealtimes. In addition, there should be short breaks for light refreshment at intervals of approximately two hours (*ibid.*, para.12.8). Meal breaks should normally last at least 45 minutes and shorter breaks every two hours should last at least 15 minutes. If breaks are delayed, they should be longer. But breaks can be delayed at the interviewing officer's discretion if there are reasonable grounds for believing that the break would involve a risk of harm to persons, or serious loss of or damage to property, or would unnecessarily delay the person's release from custody, or would otherwise prejudice the investigation (Note 12B). Two light meals and one main meal should be provided in any 24-hour period.

(3) Persons being questioned should not be required to stand whilst being questioned (para.12.6).

(4) If it is necessary to take a person's clothing for investigatory or health and hygiene reasons, adequate replacement clothing must be provided. A person may not be interviewed unless adequate clothing has been offered to him (*ibid.*, para.8.5).

(5) No officer should try to obtain answers to questions or to elicit a statement "by the use of oppression" (*ibid.*, para.11.5).

---

[27] The Home Office study by Brown *et al.* (1992, pp.89–90) based on nearly 7,000 interviews showed that the average length of an interview is of the order of half an hour—31 minutes in the 1990 sample and 26 minutes in the 1991 sample. Many arrests did not involve questioning at all. Over 40% of those detained were not interviewed. Only 8% of the two samples were questioned more than once.

(6) An officer should not indicate, save in answer to a direct question, what action will be taken by the police if the detainee answers questions, makes a statement or refuses to do so. If the person directly asks the officer such a question, then the officer may inform the person what action the police proposes to take in that event provided that that action is itself proper and warranted (Code C, para.11.5). It would therefore appear to be proper, for instance, for the officer in answer to a question to say to the suspect "If you make a statement I will let you go home, or let you off the more serious charges or not pursue charges against your wife", etc. (This represented a major shift in the rules.)

5–159   In what circumstances can the police fingerprint the detainee?

There are various situations in which a person's fingerprints can be taken:

(1) With consent in writing from the suspect (PACE, s.61(1) and (2)).

(2) Without consent, if authorised by an inspector (formerly a superintendent) if he has reasonable grounds for suspecting the person's involvement in a criminal offence and that the fingerprints will prove or disprove his involvement (s.61(3)(a) and (4)) or if it would "facilitate the ascertainment of his identity" (Anti-Terrorism, Crime and Security Act 2001, s.90(2)).

(3) Without consent, if charged or reported for a recordable offence and fingerprints have not previously been taken in the course of the investigation or they were taken but proved unsatisfactory (PACE, s.61(3)(b)).

(4) Without consent, if convicted of a recordable offence or given a caution in respect of such an offence which he admitted, or if warned or reprimanded for a recordable offence (s.61(6)), or if cautioned for such an offence which he admitted, or if he has been warned or reprimanded for such an offence.[28]

(5) Without consent, where the person has been convicted of a recordable offence, has not been in police detention and has not had his fingerprints taken during the investigation or since the conviction, or where fingerprints have previously been taken but they are not satisfactory and need to be retaken (PACE, s.27). He can be required to attend at a police station for the purposes of being fingerprinted and it is an offence not to comply. But there is no power of arrest for that offence.

---

[28] Inserted by Criminal Justice and Police Act 2001, s.78(6).

(6) Without consent, from someone who has answered to bail at court or police station for someone who had their fingerprints taken previously and there is reason to doubt whether he is that person or he claims not to be that person (PACE, s.61(4A)).[29]

Can a suspect in the police station be photographed?

5–160

Previously, a person who had been arrested but not convicted had to give his consent to be photographed. But that was changed by the Anti-terrorism, Crime and Security Act 2001. This states that "A person who is detained at a police station may be photographed (a) with the appropriate consent; or (b) if the appropriate consent is withheld or it is not practicable to obtain it, without it."

In what circumstances can the suspect's personal clothes and effects be taken from him?

5–161

A detained person may retain clothing and personal effects at his own risk unless the custody officer considers that he may use them to cause harm to himself or others, to interfere with evidence, to damage property, to effect an escape, or if they are needed as evidence. In that event the custody officer can withhold such articles as he considers necessary. He must tell the person why.

In what circumstances can a search take place of body orifices?

5–162

A search of body orifices (an "intimate search") may only take place where an officer of the rank of inspector (formerly superintendent) or above has reasonable grounds for believing that the arrested person has concealed on him something which could be used to cause physical injury to himself or others and that it cannot be found without an intimate search. With one exception, it cannot be a search for evidence of crime. The exception is where an inspector reasonably believes that the suspect has on him hard drugs (Class A drugs) which he intended to supply to others or to export. An inmate search should in principle be carried out by a doctor or nurse but in an urgent case, if an inspector thinks that this is not practicable, it can be done by a police officer providing he is of the same sex as the person being searched and provided that no officer of the opposite sex is present. But this is not so with searches for drugs. They can only be carried out by a doctor or nurse and it cannot be done in a police station. Anything found in the course of an intimate search can be used in evidence.

---

[29] Inserted by Criminal Justice and Police Act 2001, s.78(4).

5–163   Can a doctor or nurse be compelled to carry out a search of body orifices where the suspect refuses to consent?

The answer is no. It is for them to decide whether or not to conduct an intimate search in such circumstances. Most such searches are conducted by police surgeons. Note that consent to such a search by the suspect is not essential and force could therefore be used to carry out the search—presumably even if it is being carried out by a medical practitioner or nurse.

5–164   When can a person be asked to provide a bodily sample?

Previously, an intimate and a non-intimate sample could only be asked for if the offence was a serious arrestable offence. But the Criminal Justice and Public Order Act 1994 gave the police the power to ask for a sample in connection with any recordable (*i.e.* imprisonable) offence. The change was made to provide more opportunities in particular for DNA testing.

5–165   Does taking a sample require consent?

Taking an intimate sample always requires written consent—though failure to give consent can lead to the jury being invited to draw adverse inferences from the refusal. It also requires the authority of an officer at least of the rank, now, of inspector. (Formerly it required a superintendent's authorisation.) Save in the case of urine, an intimate sample must be taken by a doctor, a registered nurse, a member of a recognised health care profession or, in the case of a dental impression, by a registered dentist.

Taking a non-intimate sample should also, if possible, not be done without the suspect's consent. But an officer of the rank of inspector can authorise the taking of a non-intimate sample if there are reasonable grounds for believing that it will tend to confirm or disprove the suspect's involvement in the offence.

Under the Criminal Justice and Courts Service Act, s.57 a urine sample or a non-intimate sample can now also be taken if it would facilitate a test for the presence of Class A drugs. It requires the authorisation of an inspector or above. An officer must ask the person to give the sample but refusal without good cause is an offence.

5–166   What are intimate and non-intimate samples?

An intimate sample is blood, semen or other tissue fluid, urine, pubic hair or a swab taken from a person's body orifice or genital area, and dental impressions. Saliva was at first classified as an intimate sample but as from April 1995 it was re-classified as a non-intimate sample.

A non-intimate sample is a sample of hair other than pubic hair, a sample taken from a nail or under a nail, a swab taken from a part of the body other than a body orifice, saliva, and a footprint.

Do photographs and samples taken of or from a suspect have to be   **5–167**
destroyed if he is acquitted or the case against him does not proceed?

Until recently the answer was yes. Now, under the Criminal Justice and Police Act, s.82, the answer is no.

PART VI

THE CODES OF PRACTICE

Codes of practice: ss.66–67 and the Codes[1]

The Philips Royal Commission on Criminal Procedure said that all aspects of the **6–01** treatment of suspects in custody should be statutory. This would involve the use of primary legislation in some matters. But the rules to regulate the facilities to be provided for, and the treatment to be accorded to, suspects, and the rules to govern the conduct and recording of interviews should, it thought, be contained in subordinate legislation. "This should be made by the Home Secretary with consultation as appropriate, and subject to the approval of Parliament by affirmative resolution."[2]

The actual method adopted in the Act, however, was somewhat different. The Act required the Secretary of State, subject to Parliament's approval, to issue Codes of Practice in relation to:

    (i)   searches of persons and of vehicles without an arrest;

    (ii) the detention, treatment, questioning and identification of persons; and

    (iii) searches of premises and seizure of property found in searches of persons or premises (s.66(1)).

As has been seen above, there is an equivalent duty in respect of the tape record- **6–02** ing of interviews with suspects (s.60). The Criminal Justice and Police Act 2001 gave the Home Secretary the power to issue a Code of Practice regarding the video recording of interviews with suspects.[3]

PACE specified that, having prepared and published drafts of any Codes of Practice, the Home Secretary must consider any representations made on them and must lay a draft of the Code before both Houses of Parliament. He may then

---

[1] See 1989 N.I. PACE Order, Arts 65, 66. Amended by Police (Northern Ireland) Act 2003, Art.43.
[2] Philips Report, para.4.116.
[3] PACE s.60A, inserted by the CJPA, s.76.

bring the Code into operation by order made by statutory instrument (s.67(4)) which must be approved by a resolution of each House of Parliament (subs.(5)).

Until recently, the same procedure had to be followed for any subsequent revision of the whole or any part of the Codes (subs.(7)). However, the Criminal Justice and Police Act 2001, s.77 gave the Home Secretary the power to make limited modifications to the Codes of Practice for trial purposes for up to two years subject only to the negative resolution procedure. This means that such modifications no longer require the affirmative resolution of both Houses. They become effective unless they are negatived by resolution—a much weaker form of Parliamentary control and one that rarely leads even to a debate.

6–03   This new power to amend the Codes on an experimental basis applies to changes that affect particular areas, particular offences or particular classes of offenders. (It was first utilised in March 2002 to change for two years from April 1, 2002 the rules on identification procedures by giving the same weight to video identification as is given to identification parades—see para.6–90 below.)

The normal procedure contemplates two separate stages. The first is publishing the draft Codes. This has proved to be a quite lengthy process of consultation. Each version of the original version of the Codes went through successive drafts as a result of comments from a wide range of organisations and individuals. By the time that Parliament considered them they had been extensively amended and re-amended and this has been the same with each successive revision of the Codes. The preliminary stage of publishing drafts therefore proved very important in practice. (For the latest developments see paras 6–09—6–10 below.)

The second stage is laying them before Parliament and the order bringing them into force.[4] One of the ironies of the process of bringing the Codes into existence is that parliamentarians are the group least able to influence the content of the Codes since the debate on the draft Codes cannot lead to them being amended.[5]

6–04   The reason given by the Home Office for not following the Philips Royal Commission's recommendation that the Codes be in the form of a statutory instrument was that it proved an unworkable proposal in the light of the need to make the Codes self-contained. The object was to produce booklets for police officers that would be used as comprehensive guides to the various aspects of their duties. Some of the material in the Code, it was thought, should come from the statute so as to reduce the need to refer to two documents. It was felt that it would be impossible to have a statutory instrument that repeated parts of the primary legislation in different language.

A second reason given for having a Code rather than a statutory instrument was that the language of a Code could be less formal which would be valuable since it must be intelligible to police officers.

Thirdly, the Home Office considered that the underlying objectives for making the Codes statutory instruments could all be fulfilled by the procedure adopted in the Act. There could be a parliamentary debate on the content of the Codes and there would therefore be parliamentary accountability. True, there would be no

---

[4] For the House of Commons debate on the original Codes see *Hansard*, December 5, 1985, cols 484–521. By a coincidence, Parliament approved the Codes of Practice for Northern Ireland precisely four years later on December 5, 1989.
[5] Parliamentary procedure does not permit amendments to be moved when delegated legislation is being debated.

opportunity to move amendments—but this would be the same with any statutory instrument.

Whether the Codes would have a higher status in the eyes of the police if they   **6–05**
were statutory instruments is impossible to say. The ordinary police officer is not a close student of the niceties of the parliamentary system and is therefore not likely to be aware of the difference between the procedure for passing a statutory instrument as compared with the bringing into force of the Codes of Practice. It is possible that the words "statutory instrument" have more of the ring of law about them than the words "Code of Practice". But again the difference may not be very great.

The crux of the matter is whether the police treat the rules in the Codes of Practice as rules to which they must adhere. Pre-PACE, the Judges' Rules were not law and the judges over the years showed themselves lax in enforcing their provisions. Breaches of the Judges' Rules were generally not regarded by the judges as a reason to exclude evidence or on appeal to quash a conviction.

But the Judges' Rules were undoubtedly regarded by the police as something of which they had to take account. They formed part of the material a police officer had to master. The informal view of police officers tended to be that the Judges' Rules were a bit of a nuisance—which in itself indicated that they did have some real existence. If they had been treated as wholly irrelevant they would have provoked little or no reaction amongst police officers.

What consequences flow from a breach of the Codes of Practice? Section 67   **6–06**
states that a failure on the part of any person to observe any provision of a Code of Practice shall not of itself render him liable to any criminal or civil proceedings[6] (subs.(10)) but in any proceedings the Code of Practice shall be admissible and shall be taken into account if it is thought "by the court" to be relevant to any question arising in those proceedings (subs.(11)).[7] In other words, the extent to which a breach of the Codes results in evidence being excluded is a matter for the judges but they are obliged to take it into account. It will be seen from many of the cases referred to in this book that the courts have frequently used breaches of the Codes as the basis for exclusion of evidence or the quashing of convictions. Commentators (including the writer) were surprised, given the judges' pre-PACE attitudes, at the way they have often been prepared to "punish" police breaches of the Codes in this way.

There is even one Court of Appeal decision holding that the Codes have suffi-   **6–07**
cient status to replace legal rules emerging from case law! The case, *McCay*,[8] raised the question of whether a police officer could tell the court in what way a witness had identified the accused at an identification parade. The witness himself had forgotten that he had said "It is number eight" on the parade. Obviously, the police officer's statement was hearsay. The Court of Appeal upheld the trial judge's decision to allow the evidence in—either because it was original evidence as part of the *res gestae* or, if not, as an admissible exception to the hearsay rule. The Code, the court said, had the full authority of Parliament, having been

---

[6] For an account of a rare successful action for damages for false imprisonment founded on breaches of PACE see, however, MacKenzie "Civil Liability for PACE breaches" (1991) New L.J. 788.
[7] This may include being taken into account by the jury as well as by the judge—see *R. v Kenny* [1992] Crim.L.R. 800, CA.
[8] [1990] 1 W.L.R. 645; [1990] Crim.L.R. 338, CA.

approved by both Houses of Parliament. The provisions of Code D had been complied with. If the words used by the witness were hearsay there was "statutory authority" (*sic*) for the words used to be admissible.

Professor Diane Birch in her commentary on the case[9] was surely correct to argue that the Court of Appeal's view was mistaken. It cannot be the case that the rules of admissibility of evidence were abolished by PACE and that the courts need only look to see whether there has been compliance with the Codes. Nor does a resolution in both Houses of Parliament amount to "statutory authority". But the decision indicates how powerfully the concept of the Codes has influenced the judges.

6–08   So far the discussion has referred to "the Codes". But there are also the "Notes for Guidance". As has been seen, s.67(11) states that the court may take into account "any provision" of any Code that it considers relevant. Each Code includes an express statement that the Notes for Guidance are not provisions of the Code. They are "guidance to police officers and others about its application and interpretation".[10] The Notes for Guidance are therefore technically of a lower status in terms of their authority and it might even be said that the courts should not pay attention to them. But they contain much of importance and in practice the distinction between the rules in the Codes and the principles in the Notes for Guidance is not of much significance.[11]

Section 67(8) originally stated that a police officer "shall be liable to disciplinary proceedings" for any breach of the Codes. This subsection making even trivial breaches automatically a breach of discipline was, however, repealed by the Police and Magistrates' Courts Act 1994, s.37(a) mainly because the Runciman Royal Commission established that breaches of PACE virtually never resulted in disciplinary proceedings.[12]

Proposals of the Home Office/Cabinet Office Joint Review

6–09   One of the most far-reaching proposals of the Home Office/Cabinet Office Joint Review of PACE relates to the Codes. The proposals concerned first, the process for developing and amending the Codes and secondly, their presentation.

The Joint Review said that the process by which the Codes were updated was "long and complicated" and had "resulted in considerable delays in effecting changes and ensuring that the Codes accurately reflect legislation".[13] Amendment required broad public consultation and affirmative approval by Parliament. But the regularity and speed with which police procedures and legislation changed meant that the Codes needed frequent amendment which could not be achieved under the existing arrangements. The result was that the Codes became out of date and increasingly unhelpful to operational officers.

The Joint Review proposed more limited consultation. ("More stringent processes of consultation and debate were appropriate in the 1980s when the con-

---

[9] [1990] Crim.L.R. 338 at 340.
[10] Pre-2003, Code C, para.1.3. Inexplicably, this statement was dropped in the 2003 revision.
[11] See, for instance, *Menard* (1995) 1 Cr.App.R. 306, CA; *Weerdesteyn* (1995) 1 Cr.App.R. 405, CA; or *DPP v Blake* (1988) 89 Cr.App.R. 179, CA.
[12] See Runciman Report, p.48, para.102.
[13] Joint Review, 2002, Ch.2, p.12, para.2(i).

cept of the Codes was new and developing. However, that concept is now well established and new protections for those subject to police procedures are either in place (such as the Human Rights Act) or shortly [then] to be established (such as the Independent Police Complaints Commission)."[14]) The Home Secretary's obligation to consult should be limited to those representing chief constables and police authorities and "anyone else he thought appropriate". The Criminal Justice Bill, when first introduced, in November 2002 adopted precisely this formula.[15] (During the Committee stage in the Commons the Home Office Minister, Mr Hilary Benn, said that proposed changes to the Codes would also be posted in draft on the web.[16]) However, the Government was persuaded to amend the Bill by adding to the list of automatic consultees the Bar Council, the Law Society and the Institute of Legal Executives.[17]

The Joint Review proposed secondly, that the requirement of Parliamentary **6–10** approval be entirely removed. ("The detailed Parliamentary procedure would be removed and replaced with a straightforward requirement to lay new or changed Codes before Parliament."[18]) This too was included in the Criminal Justice Bill but the Government was forced to retreat on this provision. It eventually accepted that where changes to the Codes were significant or where a new Code was to be introduced the old procedure of express approval by both Houses would continue to apply. The procedure of simply laying the proposed changes before Parliament would only apply to minor changes. The Government also agreed to consult the House of Commons Home Affairs Committee as to whether proposed changes were minor or significant—and to accept its advice. (These concessions were only partly reflected in the statutory amendments made to s.67 of PACE by s.11 of the Criminal Justice Act 2003. The new statutory provisions s.67(7) and (7A) have to be read together with the statement by Baroness Scotland, a Home Office Minister—see House of Lords, *Hansard,* July 7, 2003, cols 44–45.) These arrangements were tested almost immediately. The Home Office hoped that the 2004 revision of the Codes could be simply laid before Parliament under the new provisions. They were laid before Parliament at the end of April for implementation a few days later on May 1. But on April 27 the Home Affairs Select Committee informed the Home Office that the proposed changes were too substantial for the new expedited procedure. They had to be withdrawn and relaid. They were approved in the Commons on June 28 and in the Lords on July 2 for implementation on August 1, 2004—the Police and Criminal Evidence Act (Codes of Practice) Order 2004 (SI 2004/1887).

The Joint Review also made an important recommendation under the heading **6–11** "Improving the functionality and transparency of the Codes". Many police officers, it said, "view the Codes as lacking in clarity".[19] The Codes were meant to be used by the public, as well as the police. "Police and solicitors questioned whether the Codes are sufficiently comprehensible to those who are not expert

---

[14] *ibid.*, p.13.
[15] New PACE s.67(4) substituted by cl.7 of the Bill.
[16] House of Commons, Standing Committee B, January 7, 2003, col.117.
[17] PACE s.67(4) substituted by s.11 of the Criminal Justice Act 2003.
[18] Joint Review, p.13.
[19] Joint Review, p.13, para.5.

practitioners."[20] The solution, it suggested, was to produce the Codes in a new way:

- "The Codes should be simplified and reduced in bulk by being reworked into a framework of key principles with the more detailed guidance moving to National Standards. To aid decision-making, guidance could be augmented by examples and explanations of the intention of the provision. The Review recommends that flow diagrams should be included in future versions of the Codes in order to make processes more transparent, because they are often easier to understand than large amounts of text."[21]

- Efforts should be made to simplify the language.

- The Codes should be issued in ring-binder format to ease revision. They should also be on a website.

- "Finally, the Codes could be given a different thematic structure (for example advice on how to treat juveniles could be contained in a separate section rather than repeated) or alternatively a structure focussed on outcome rather than process, leaving police with more scope to use their professional judgement. Further consultation is needed to establish the best approach."[22]

6–12 These recommendations, it suggested, should be incorporated into "a thorough and structured revision of the Codes" which would be completed by the early part of 2004.

It has to be said that the writer was both baffled and concerned by the recommendation that the format of the Codes should be reduced in bulk "by being reworked into a framework of key principles with the more detailed guidance moving to National Standards". What would be a key principle? What are National Standards? Where are they to be found? How would anyone benefit from having to consult two sources instead of one? Equally, what would a structure "focussed on outcome rather than process" look like? It was a nice irony that a proposal to make the Codes more comprehensible should itself be incomprehensible.

Other forces

6–13 "Police force" for the purpose of s.67 is defined as "any body of constables". The journal *Police Review* in 1988 published a letter from the Home Office explaining the meaning of this phrase:

---

[20] *ibid.*, para.6
[21] *ibid.*, p.14.
[22] *ibid.*

"The term constable in the 1984 Act includes any sworn constable. It is not restricted to officers of forces established under the 1964 Police Act but includes any member of a body of constables maintained by an authority other than a police authority. It will be the case, of course, that the constabulary powers of these bodies are limited to the specific activities for which the officers are employed and outside these activities they will cease to have constabulary powers. This will be the case with, for example, the British Transport Police and the Mersey Tunnels Police (who are both maintained by statutory undertakers), as well as with those such as the Ministry of Defence Police (who are not) . . . On a final point, I do not believe that the Royal Military Police officers are constables."[23]

The Philips Royal Commission took the view that the Codes should also apply to persons who are not constables but who do a similar job.[24] The Act gave effect to this objective in s.67(9) which provides that "persons other than police officers who are charged with the duty of investigating offences or charging offenders shall in the discharge of that duty have regard to any relevant provision of such a code". The 2003 revised Code C states that persons designated under the Police Reform Act 2002, Pt 4 who have specified powers and duties of police officers conferred or imposed on them and other civilians support staff "must have regard to any relevant provisions of the Codes of Practice" (paras 1.13,1.16). **6–14**

Again, the same piece in the *Police Review* quoted the Home Office view on the meaning of this phrase: "Our view is that in using the words of the Judges Rules, s.67(9) of the Act does not change the position hitherto that charged with the duty means charged by law with the duty. This refers, for example, to local authority officials such as trading standards officers,[25] Post Office investigation officers, or central government officers such as DTI inspectors."[26] Customs and Excise officers are also covered.[27] The Home Office opinion continued:

"Our advice in the case of people such as store detectives and security officers who take it upon themselves to investigate offences, is that they should have regard to the standards set out in the Codes so far as in common sense they are applicable to the work they do. These people, however, have no special powers of arrest, search, entry, or seizure. If they make an arrest under their citizen's powers, or question a suspect in order to obtain evidence, they should observe the provisions of the Codes as far as they are applicable to ensure that,

---

[23] Alan Harding, *Police Review*, January 22, 1988, p.185. Mr Harding was at the time the senior Home Office official dealing with PACE.

[24] Philips Report, para.4.135.

[25] This was confirmed in *Dudley Metropolitan Council v Debenhams plc, The Times*, August 16, 1994, DC. When trading standards officers attended at premises to see whether an offence under the Consumer Protection Act 1987 had been committed they were under a duty to enforce compliance and intended, if appropriate, to prosecute. The Divisional Court held that they had a power of entry under the 1987 Act if there were at that time reasonable grounds to suspect that an offence had been committed. But absent such grounds, the employee should have been told, as under Code B of PACE, that he was not obliged to comply with a request to hand over the relevant documents.

[26] But see *R. v Seelig and Spens* (1991) 94 Cr.App.R. 17 in which the Court of Appeal held that DTI inspectors inquiring into the so-called Guiness affair under ss.432 and 442 of the Companies Act 1985 were not investigating offences within the meaning of s.67(9) and that the Codes therefore did not apply.

[27] See s.114, para.11–05 below and *Sanusi* [1992] Crim.L.R. 43, CA.

in any subsequent trial, a court will regard their behaviour as fair and reasonable. What we are talking about is essentially a matter of common sense. If a civilian (like a store detective) oversteps the mark in regard to a suspect and obtains evidence by means that would not be open to a police officer, then he must expect his evidence to be at risk in subsequent proceedings."[28]

6–15   It was held in *R. v Director of Serious Fraud, Ex p. Saunders*[29] that the Codes apply to the officers of the Serious Fraud Office.[30] The PACE Codes have been held to apply not only to store detectives[31] but also to commercial investigators—in this case employed by Ladbroke's betting shops.[32] The Court of Appeal held there that the Codes applied to commercial investigators in so far as they were charged with the duty of investigating offences.[33] Another example of persons who must have regard to the Codes of Practice by virtue of subs.67(9) are customs officers.[34]

But each case has to be decided on its particular facts. A head teacher inquiring into an alleged case of assault by a teacher on a pupil was held not to be a person charged with investigating offences.[35] Similarly, a child's social worker to whom the father admitted sex acts with his daughter was held not to be a person charged with investigating an offence. The father had gone uninvited to see the social worker and the conversation had essentially been a monologue by him.[36] Any danger of unfairness in such cases can be avoided by s.78.

In *Smith*[37] the Court of Appeal accepted that because the Bank of England had a special department dedicated to the investigation of offences, other officers of the Bank were not covered by s.67. However, it also held that the PACE Codes "enshrine principles of fairness which in our judgment may have a wider application"[38] and that confessions obtained by the bank official in interviews should have been excluded under s.78.

6–16   Investigations by the Inland Revenue are "investigations" within the meaning of s.67. In a written parliamentary answer soon after PACE came into force the Financial Secretary to the Treasury stated that copies of the 1984 Act and of the Codes had been made available to Revenue officials "involved in interviewing those who may be charged with a criminal offence" and that departmental

---

[28] *op.cit.*, n.23 above.
[29] [1988] Crim.L.R. 837, DC.
[30] In *R. v Director of Serious Fraud Office, Ex p. Smith* [1993] A.C. 1, HL it was held that the general provisions of the Codes regarding questioning and cautioning of suspects gave way, however, to the explicit provisions of the Criminal Justice Act 1987 which established an inquisitorial regime for serious fraud investigations.
[31] See *R. v Bayliss* (1993) 98 Cr.App.R. 235; [1994] Crim.L.R. 687, CA. The Court of Appeal said it was possible for a store detective to be a person "charged with the duty of investigating offences" within the meaning of s.67(9). It was a question of fact in each case.
[32] *R. v Twaites and Brown* (1991) 92 Cr.App.R. 106; [1990] Crim.L.R. 863, CA.
[33] See also *Joy v Federation Against Copyright Theft Ltd* [1993] Crim.L.R. 588, DC where an investigator for FACT operating with a warrant under the Copyright, Designs and Patents Act 1988, s.107(c) was considered to be someone "charged with the duty of investigating offences".
[34] *R. (Hoverspeed Ltd) v Customs and Excise Commissioners* [2002] EWCA Civ 1804; [2003] 2 All E.R. 553 at [37].
[35] *DPP v G, The Times*, November 24, 1997, DC; *Solicitor's Journal*, December 12, 1997, p.1180.
[36] *Dennison*, unreported, Case No.97/4643/X5, February 2, 1998, CA.
[37] [1994] 1 W.L.R. 1396, CA.
[38] *ibid.*, at 1405, *per* Neill L.J.

instructions had been issued "to ensure that Inland Revenue procedures comply with the provisions of that Act and the Codes of Practice".[39] This applies to so-called "*Hansard* interviews" in which Inland Revenue inspectors interview tax payers with a view usually to accepting a money settlement, but which can end in criminal proceedings.[40]

The relevant provisions of the Code have been held not to apply to the circumstances of the motorist being processed under the drink–drive provisions of the Road Traffic Act.[41] Thus it has been held that a motorist cannot delay the processes of testing by claims of wanting legal advice[42] or wanting to study the Codes of Practice.[43] The courts insist that the public interest requires that samples be taken and the tests be done without unnecessary delay. The only concession the courts have made is to allow that if a solicitor happens actually to be there in the police station and the motorist says he just wants to consult him for a couple of minutes, or he wishes to speak on the telephone to his own solicitor or to the duty solicitor "and the solicitor in question is immediately available" that that should be permitted.[44] Equally, in the motoring context, a juvenile can have a breath or blood sample taken without the consent of an appropriate adult, though s.78 of PACE does apply.[45]

Where the police operate undercover, or by means of bugging or other such tricks and stratagems, the courts have sometimes held that the PACE Codes apply and sometimes that they do not apply (see para.8–68 below).

The 1989 Northern Ireland PACE Order (Art.66(22)) stated that the Codes of **6–17** Practice do not apply to persons arrested or detained under the emergency powers or terrorism legislation. However, separate guidance for terrorism cases was issued. (The latest version is the Code of Practice under the Terrorism Act 2000 issued by the Northern Ireland Office which came into force on February 19, 2001.) There is no equivalent general exclusion of terrorism cases from the effect of the Codes of Practice in England and Wales. On the contrary, Code C specifically states (para.1.11) that people in police custody for the purposes of the Code include persons taken to a police station after being arrested under terrorism legislation. There is also no separate Code of Practice under the Terrorism Act in respect of England and Wales. (There is one for Northern Ireland but it is mystifying why unfortunate police officers there should have to cope with two virtually identical codes.)

[39] House of Commons, *Hansard*, Vol.100, June 23, 1986, col.51.
[40] *Gill and Gill* [2003] EWCA Crim 2256; [2003] 4 All E.R. 681; [2004] Crim.L.R. 883. See also Ormerod, "*Hansard* invitations and confessions in the criminal trial" (2000) 4 Int'l Jrnl. of Ev. and Proof 147 at 155–60; and "Caution with Tax Investigations" [2001] *British Tax Review* 194.
[41] See generally Tucker, "Drink-Drivers' PACE Rights: A cause for concern" [1990] Crim.L.R. 177.
[42] *DPP v Billington* [1988] R.T.R. 231; [1988] 1 All E.R. 454, CA; *Campbell v DPP* [2002] EWHC Admin 1314; [2003] Crim.L.R.118; *Kennedy v DPP* [2002] EWHC Admin 2297; [2003] Crim.L.R.120; *Miles* [2004] EWHC 5494; *R (Forde) v DPP* [2004] EWHC 1156 (Admin); *Kirkup v DPP* [2003] EWHC Admin 2354; [2004] Crim.L.R. 230.
[43] *DPP v Whalley* [1991] R.T.R.161; [1991] Crim.L.R. 211, DC; *DPP v Cornell* [1990] R.T.R. 254, DC.
[44] *Kennedy*, n.42 above, *per* Kennedy L.J. at [31].
[45] *DPP v Rouse and Davis* (1992) 94 Cr.App.R. 185; [1991] Crim.L.R. 911, DC; *Kennedy v DPP*, n.42 above.

The Codes

6–18   The Codes are drafted by the Home Office. There are now six PACE Codes of Practice: Code A on Stop and Search, Code B on Search of Premises, Code C on Detention and Questioning of Suspects, Code D on Identification, Code E on Tape Recording and Code F on Video Recording of Interviews with Suspects.

    The first edition of Codes A to D came into force together on January 1, 1986. Code E was added in 1988. A second, revised edition of Codes A to D came into force on April 1, 1991. The third revision, affecting all five Codes, came into force on April 10, 1995. Code F came into operation on a provisional basis on December 2, 2001 and was confirmed by Parliament as from April 10, 2002. A consultation draft of a revised Code A was circulated in March 2002 with the consultation period ending on April 19. The final revised text was approved after debates in both Houses of Parliament in December 2002 to come into force on April 1, 2003.[46] A revised version of s.2 of Code D was brought into force without consultation as from April 1, 2002.[47] The fourth major revision of Codes B to E started with consultation drafts issued by the Home Office in June 2002 with a deadline for the consultation period of August 16. They were approved in both Houses of Parliament (with slight hitches[48]) in March 2003 to come into force on April 1, 2003. As has been seen (para.6–10 above), the fifth major revision of the Codes was originally laid before Parliament in April 2004 but it had to be withdrawn for procedural reasons. It was relaid on May 27 and was approved in the Commons on June 28 and in the Lords on July 2 for implementation on August 1, 2004.[49]

6–19   As has been noted, the Codes make a distinction between the actual rules and "Notes for Guidance". There are also "Annexes" which collect in one place provisions that recur at various points in the main text and would otherwise have to be repeated several times. The Annexes, by contrast with the Notes for Guidance, are stated to be part of the Codes (Code C, para.1.3).

    The Codes, which are sold as a booklet by the Stationery Office priced £12.50,[50] are distributed by the Home Office to the police free of charge. (They are accessible on the internet at *www.homeoffice.gov.uk/crimpol/police/system/pacecodes.html.*) They state that the document containing the Codes "must be readily available at all police stations for consultation by police officers, detained persons and members of the public".[51] Research since the Act suggests, however, that it is very rare for suspects to ask for a copy of the Codes.

---

[46] See Police and Criminal Evidence Act 1984 (Code of Practice) (Statutory Powers of Stop and Search) Order 2002 (SI 2002/3075).

[47] Under the provisions for expedited promulgation in the Criminal Justice and Police Act 2001, s.77 amending s.67 of PACE.

[48] The Codes were approved by the House of Lords on February 24, 2003 (after a debate lasting 25 minutes). The same Order was due to be approved by the Commons two days later but at that stage some typographical and other minor slips were noticed and they had to be withdrawn. They were relaid and approval was obtained from both Houses of Parliament in time for them to become operational as intended on April 1, 2003.

[49] Police and Criminal Evidence Act (Codes of Practice) Order 2004 (SI 2004/1887).

[50] The publication comes with a CD-ROM.

[51] See for instance Code C, para.1.2.

The content of Codes A (Stop and Search), B (Search of Premises), E (Tape Recording) and F (Video Recording) has already been dealt with above. Codes C (on Detention) and D (on Identification), in so far as they have not previously been treated, are dealt with in this Chapter.

Code C: the Code for the detention, treatment and questioning of persons suspected of crime[52] (the Detention Code)

Code C starts with the statement that "all persons in custody must be dealt with   **6–20** expeditiously, and released as soon as the need for detention no longer applies" (para.1.1). A new provision in the 1995 version of the Code (para.1.1A) added that the custody officer is required to perform his functions "as soon as is practicable" but that he will not be in breach of the Code if there is justifiable delay and every reasonable step has been taken to prevent delay. Note 1H specifies that this is intended to cover the situation where a large number of persons are brought into the police station at the same time, or the interview rooms are all being used, or there are delays in contacting an appropriate adult, solicitor or interpreter. Those who are at the police station voluntarily should be treated "with no less consideration" than those in custody (Note 1A).

The custody record: s.2[53]

Code C requires that a separate custody record be opened as soon as practicable   **6–21** for every person brought into the police station under arrest or who is arrested there having attended voluntarily or who attends a police station in order to answer "street bail" (para.2.1).[54] One can be in police custody without being under arrest but para.2.1 makes it clear that a custody record is only required in respect of someone who has been arrested. But the statement that the record must be opened as soon as practicable after someone is brought to the station under arrest means that it must be done before any decision has been taken as to whether detention is authorised. Paragraph 2.1 then continues by stating that all information that has to be recorded must be recorded "as soon as practicable, in the custody record unless otherwise specified". In the case of any action requiring the authority of an officer of a specified rank, his name and rank must normally be noted in the custody record (para.2.2). In the case of terrorism, the warrant or other identification number and duty station can be noted instead and, by virtue of an addition made in 2003 to the Codes, the same applies to any other situation where an officer reasonably believes that recording names might endanger them (para.2.6A).

---

[52] See also the Code itself.
[53] The section and paragraph numbers of the N.I. Codes are not necessarily the same as those of the Codes for England and Wales.
[54] Any documentation linked to the arrest should be linked to the custody record (Code C, para.3.25).

6–22   The custody officer is responsible for the accuracy and completeness of the record and for ensuring that the record or a copy accompanies a detained person if he is transferred to another station. The record should show the time and the reason for the transfer and the time a person is released from detention (para.2.3).

A provision introduced in the 1995 revision of the Code states that a solicitor or appropriate adult must be allowed to consult the custody record of a detainee "as soon as practicable after their arrival at the police station" (para.2.4). The detainee, the appropriate adult or legal representative should, on request, be supplied with a copy of the custody record as soon as practicable. This right was significantly further strengthened by the 2003 revised version of para.2.4 which added that they must be permitted to consult the custody record "as soon as practicable *after their arrival at the station and at any other time whilst the person is detained*". (Emphasis supplied) Arrangements for this access, it continues, "must be agreed with the custody officer and may not unreasonably interfere with the custody officer's duties" (*ibid.*). The right lasts for 12 months after release (para.2.4A). After the person has left police detention there is a separate right to inspect the custody record on giving reasonable notice (para.2.5).

6–23   All entries in custody records must be timed and signed by the maker (para.2.6). In the case of a record entered on a computer this has to be timed and must identify the operator (*ibid.*). Neither the Act nor the Code deals specifically with whether the custody officer may delegate the function of "making a record" to someone else, including a civilian computer operative, but common sense suggests that this increasingly normal practice would be held to be lawful. Obviously, however, the custody officer rather than the civilian employee would be accountable for any errors or deficiencies in the record.

Any refusal by a person to sign a custody record when asked to do so in accordance with the provisions of the Code must itself be recorded (para.2.7).

What must be recorded?

6–24   The long list of matters that must be stated in the custody record include: the grounds of detention (Code C, para.3.23); the suspect's signature acknowledging receipt of a notice of his rights, or the custody officer's note that he refused to sign (para.3.2); the suspect's signature as to whether he wants to have legal advice (para.3.5); any list made of the suspect's effects, signed by him as correct or, if he refuses, with a note to that effect (para.4.4); details of any intimate search or strip search, including the reason for it and its result (Code C, Annex A, para.7); a statement of reasons for withholding articles of clothing from the suspect (Code C, para.4.5); requests to inform a relative or friend of the fact of the arrest and any action taken on such a request, and details of any letters, messages or telephone calls made or received and of visits (para.5.8)[55]; the ground for delaying notification by the suspect of a friend or relative of the fact of detention and his whereabouts (para.5.8 and Annex B, paras 6 and 13); the time of any later grant of this right (para.5.8); action taken on any request for legal advice (para.6.16); the

---

[55] Brown *et al.* (1992, pp.56–57) stated that in around a quarter of cases where a request was made the action taken was not recorded. They note that the outcome of requests is often lost when the task of carrying them out falls to beat officers or those conducting searches of premises or where initial attempts fail and further attempts are left to the next shift.

grounds for delaying access to legal advice (Annex B, para.13); when a foreigner or Commonwealth citizen is told of his right to inform his Embassy or High Commission and details of any call made on his behalf regarding the fact of his detention (para.7.5); details of the times at which meals are served to the suspect (para.8.9); the grounds for why a child or young person is placed in police cells (para.8.10); details of any complaint by a suspect regarding his treatment (para.9.7); details of any medical treatment or action taken regarding a condition requiring medical attention (para.9.15); the medication the suspect claims he needs which he does not have with him (para.9.17); the time of any caution[56] (para.10.13); the record of any interview and of any comments made outside the context of an interview and the refusal of the person to sign the record (paras 11.7–11.14[57]); the time at which the suspect is handed over by the custody officer for questioning (para.12.10[58]); the grounds for delay of a required break in interviews (para.12.12[59]); action taken to call an interpreter and any waiver of the right not to be interviewed without one (para.13.11); the grounds for and extent of any delay in conducting a review of detention (para.15.13[60]); the details of any such review including the method by which representations (oral or written) were made (paras 15.10–15.16[61]); any decision to interview a mentally disordered person or one who is mentally vulnerable or a juvenile without waiting for a responsible person who has been asked to come to be with him (para.11.20[62]); and the details of anything the suspect said on being charged (para.16.8[63]).

It has already been seen that the Home Office Circular on PACE advised that   **6–25**
although strictly a custody record form was not required for some categories of detainees it might nevertheless be wise to keep such a record for administrative reasons. Categories of persons for whom this could be true would be those held awaiting a court appearance on the authority of a production order, following a remand to prison custody, or during examination under the Terrorism Act where the person has not been arrested.

Initial action: information to the person in detention: s.3

When a person is brought to a police station under arrest or is arrested at the   **6–26**
police station having attended there voluntarily, Code C requires that the custody officer must inform him of the following rights and that they are continuing rights which need not be exercised immediately. The rights of which he must be told forthwith (para.3.1) are:

(i) the right to have someone informed of his arrest in accordance with s.5 of the Code;

---

[56] This should be made in the officer's notebook or in the interview record as appropriate.
[57] Formerly paras 11.12, 11.13.
[58] Formerly para.12.9.
[59] Formerly para.12.11.
[60] Formerly para.15.4.
[61] Amended form of what was previously para.15.6.
[62] Formerly Annex C.
[63] Formerly para.16.7.

    (ii) the right to consult privately with a solicitor and that independent legal advice is available free of charge; and

    (iii) the right to consult the Codes of Practice.

6–27   Note 3D states that the right to consult the Codes does not entitle the person concerned unreasonably to delay any necessary investigative or administrative action while he is doing so.[64] Code C, para.1.8 states, however, that if the Code requires a person to be given information, "they do not have to be given it if at the time they are incapable of understanding what is said, are violent or may become violent or in urgent need of medical attention, but they must be given it as soon as practicable".

    The custody officer must give the person a written notice setting out the above three rights, the right to a copy of the custody record and the caution in the terms prescribed in s.10 of the Code (para.3.2). He must also give the person a copy of a notice explaining the arrangements for obtaining legal advice (*ibid.*).[65]

    The custody officer must also give the suspect a notice setting out "his entitlements" while in custody (para.3.2). The "Notice of Entitlements" is intended to give detainees brief details of matters over and above the statutory rights set out in the "notice of rights". It covers such matters as visits and contact with outside parties, standards of physical comfort, food and drink, access to toilet and writing facilities, clothing, medical treatment, and exercise. It also mentions the provisions relating to the conduct of interviews, when the appropriate adult should be available and the right to make representations on reviews of detention. It should be available in relevant languages and, the 2004 revision of the Codes added, audio versions should also be available (Notes 3A and 3B).

6–28   The custody officer should then ask the person to sign the custody record to acknowledge receipt of these notices. The person should be asked to sign on the custody record to signify whether he wants legal advice at that point (para.3.5). The custody officer must ensure that he signs in the right place.

    If the custody officer authorises the person's detention he must inform him of the grounds as soon as practicable and in any event before he is questioned about any offence (para.3.4). He must also note on the custody record any comments made by the suspect in relation to the arresting officer's account and in relation to the decision to detain him (*ibid.*).

    A study of the implementation of these rights by Brown *et al.* (1992)[66] suggested that, generally, the information was communicated to suspects both in

---

[64] See to same effect *DPP v Cornell* [1990] R.T.R. 254, holding that a motorist cannot prevent the police doing a breath, blood or urine test on the ground that he wants time to study the Codes. For critical comment see Tucker, "Drink-Drivers' PACE Rights: A cause for concern" [1990] Crim.L.R. 177.

[65] These notices are supposed to be available in a variety of languages. The original Home Office Circular on PACE stated that National Form 7, providing the information that a custody officer had to give a detained person under this part of the Code, was to be translated into Arabic, Punjabi, Urdu, Hindi, Gujerati and Bengali with the Welsh Office translating it into Welsh. The 1995 revision of the Code added a requirement that it be available in "the principal European languages" (Note 3B).

[66] Brown *et al.* (1992) summarised in Home Office Research and Statistics Department, Research Findings No. 5, March 1993.

written and oral form—though when orally, not always as clearly as it might be[67]—but that most suspects did not avail themselves of these rights.[68]

Special groups

If the person does not understand English or appears to be deaf or to have diffi-   **6–29**
culty in understanding English, the custody officer should as soon as practicable call an interpreter and ask him to communicate to the detained person the information required (para.3.12—on interpreters see generally Code C, s.13).

If the person is a juvenile, mentally disordered or otherwise mentally vulnera-ble[69] the custody officer must, as soon as practicable, inform an appropriate adult of the grounds for his detention and his whereabouts, and ask the adult to come to the police station to see the person (Code C, para.3.15). The information required to be given to the detained person under paras 3.1 to 3.4 should be given in the presence of the appropriate adult (para.3.17). If the juvenile is a ward of court the police can interview him without getting permission from the court, providing they follow the rules for interviewing juveniles.[70]

If, having been informed of the right to legal advice either the appropriate adult or the detained person considers that legal advice should be taken, the provisions of s.6 of the Code apply (para.3.19). Note E1 of Annex A says that if a mentally disordered or mentally vulnerable suspect wants legal advice, action should be taken immediately without waiting for the appropriate adult to arrive. (As noted above, in the pre-2003 Code, Note 3G said the same also for juveniles but, as a result of what presumably was oversight, this Note was dropped in the 2003 revision. But there is no doubt that the same does apply to juveniles—see the expla-nation at para.5–34 above.) Again, if the person is blind or "seriously visually impaired or unable to read", the custody officer should ensure that his solicitor, relative, the appropriate adult or some other suitable person is available to help check any documentation (para.3.20).

Note E1 (like former Note 3G which however included juveniles) says that the   **6–30**
purpose of para.3.19 is to protect the rights of a juvenile, mentally disordered or otherwise mentally vulnerable detained person who may not understand the sig-nificance of what is being said to him. If the detainee says that he does not want legal advice, the appropriate adult can override his view on the basis that there is

---

[67] The researchers considered that information about rights was given too quickly, incompletely or incomprehensibly in about a quarter of the cases of adults and in one-third of the cases where the detainee was a juvenile (Brown *et al.* (1992, pp.22–35)).

[68] Thus, according to Brown *et al.* (1992), after the April 1991 revisions in the Codes the proportion of suspects who: (1) asked for legal advice was 32% for adults and 26% for juveniles; (2) asked for someone to be informed of the fact of their detention was 17% for adults and 7% for juveniles; (3) asked for a telephone call was 8%; and (4) asked for a copy of the Codes was 4%. However, of those who did not want someone informed, 40% said that the relevant parties knew already (*ibid.*, p.55). It should be remembered in this context that about 70% of suspects have previous experience of arrest. "Many of this group clearly indicated that they were not interested in hearing about their rights; they knew what they were entitled to and could make a decision unaided" (*ibid.*, p.37).

[69] The phrase was altered in 2003. Formerly it was "mentally disordered or mentally handicapped or mentally incapable of understanding the significance of questions put to him"—Code C, para.1.4.

[70] *Re R; Re G, The Times,* March 29, 1990.

reason to think that he does not understand the significance of what he has been told about legal advice. But the right to legal advice is ultimately that of the detainee not that of the appropriate adult. A lawyer who arrives at the police station at the request of the appropriate adult to advise a detainee who maintains that he does not want legal advice may decide that he cannot usefully give advice. But he might decide nevertheless to offer his advice for what it is worth.

On the position of specially vulnerable groups see further para.5–152 above and paras 6–54—6–57 below.

Conditions of detention: s.8

6–31   The Judges' Rules and Administrative Directions annexed to the Judges' Rules made only a few rather general references to the conditions of detention. Code C provides many very detailed rules.

So far as practicable, there should be no more than one person per cell (para.8.1). Cells should be adequately heated, lit and reasonably clean (para.8.2). Code C, as revised in 2003, warns that no additional restraints may be used in a locked cell unless absolutely necessary and then only equipment approved by the Chief Constable, which is reasonable and necessary in the circumstances having regard to the detainee's behaviour and his safety and the safety of others (*ibid.*). Bedding should be in a clean and sanitary condition (para.8.3). There should be access to toilet and washing facilities (para.8.4). Replacement clothing should be of reasonable standard and no questioning can take place unless the suspect has been offered adequate clothing (para.8.5). There should be at least two light meals and one main meal per 24 hours and any dietary requirements should be met so far as possible (para.8.6). If necessary, the advice of health care professionals should be sought (*ibid.*, and Note 9A). Drinks should be provided at mealtimes and on reasonable request between mealtimes (para.8.6). The prisoner may have meals supplied by family or friends at his or their expense (*ibid.*). The Joint Home Office/Cabinet Office Review of PACE recommended (p.32) that the police should have a discretion to ban outside provision of food to specific detainees if there is a suspicion that drugs and other illicit items are being smuggled in. Brief outdoor exercise should be permitted daily if possible (para.8.7).

6–32   A juvenile should not be placed in police cells unless there is no other secure accommodation available and the custody officer thinks that it is not practicable to supervise him if he is not put in a cell (para.8.8).[71]

Pre-2003, the Code stated that reasonable force could be used by a police officer to secure compliance with reasonable instructions, to prevent the suspect's escape or to restrain him from causing injury to persons or damage to property or evidence (former para.8.9). There is no equivalent to para.8.9 in Code C as revised in 2003. In fact, the subject of the use of reasonable force by police officers is not mentioned anywhere in Code C—though it is mentioned in several places in Codes A, B and D, and in Code C there is mention of the use of reasonable force by civilian support staff (para.1.14). This omission is certainly

---

[71] Dixon (1990) reported that in the force in which he conducted research this requirement was "fulfilled" by simply designating ordinary cells as "juvenile detention rooms".

odd,[72] and may be unfortunate, but it does not mean that police officers are unable to use reasonable force in exercising their powers under Code C. The power to use force does not derive from the Codes, it derives from statute and the common law.[73] The power to use force under PACE is enshrined in s.117—see para.11–13 below. So the power continues unaffected.

Persons detained are supposed to be visited every hour (para.9.3). Juveniles and persons at risk should, if possible, be visited more often (Note 9B). Those who are suspected of being intoxicated through drink or drugs should be visited and roused at least every half an hour.[74] Such visits or rousing of intoxicated persons do not constitute an interruption in the suspect's rest period for the purposes of the rules regarding rest periods (para.12.2).   **6–33**

If any ill-treatment or unlawful force has been used, any officer who has notice of it should draw it to the attention of the custody officer who in turn must inform an officer of at least the rank of inspector not connected with the investigation. If it involves an assault or the use of force he in turn must summon an appropriate health care professional to examine the suspect (para.9.2). A complaint from the suspect or someone on his behalf to this effect must similarly be reported to an inspector or above *(ibid.)*

Medical treatment: s.9

The Code requires that appropriate action be taken by the custody officer to deal with any medical condition—whether or not the person in custody asks for it (para.9.5).[75] The 2004 revision of Code C added a new para.9.5B requiring the custody officer to consider the need for clinical attention in relation to those suffering the effects of alcohol or drugs. The police surgeon should be called immediately if the suspect is injured or appears to be suffering from any physical or mental illness or does not show awareness or fails to respond normally to conversation (other than through being drunk). The section warns that a person who appears to be drunk may in fact be suffering from illness or the effects of drugs or some injury (Note 9C). The police should therefore always call an appropriate health care professional when in any doubt, and act urgently *(ibid.)*. But Code C (Note 9C) makes it clear that the need to call a health care professional need not apply to minor ailments or injuries nor when a Mental Health Act assessment under s.136 of the Mental Health Act 1983 can be made without delay. The 2003 revision of Code C urges that whenever practicable such assessments be made in hospital (Note 9D).   **6–34**

If the suspect says he needs medication for a serious condition such as heart disease, diabetes or epilepsy, the advice of an appropriate health care professional   **6–35**

---

[72] The equivalent of para.8.9 was in the 2002 Consultation Draft of Code C.

[73] See *R. v Jones (Derek); R. v Nelson (Gary), The Times*, April 21 1999, CA.

[74] The requirement that drunks be roused on each visit was added in the April 1995 revision.

[75] It seems that this admonition is taken to heart at least in terrorism cases. Brown (1993, pp.35–36) found that although only 19 detainees asked for medical attention the police called a doctor in 105 cases. In Paddington Green it was standard practice to call the doctor every morning to monitor the detainee's fitness for detention and questioning *(ibid.,* p.36). Three-quarters of the terrorism suspects held for more than 24 hours were examined by a doctor at least once *(ibid.)*.

must be obtained (para.9.12). As regards administration of drugs, a distinction is made in the 2003 revision between controlled drugs listed in the Misuse of Drugs Regulations 1985. Those listed in Sch.1, 2 or 3 can be self-administered by the detainee only under the personal supervision of the registered medical practitioner authorising their use. Those listed in Sch.4 or 5 may be distributed to the custody officer for self-administration if the registered medical practitioner authorising their use has been consulted (by telephone or otherwise) and both are satisfied that self-administration will not expose the detainee or anyone else to the risk of harm or injury (para.9.10).

New provisions in the 2003 revision of the Code include the admonition that it is important to respect a person's right to privacy. Information about their health must be kept confidential and only disclosed with their consent or in accordance with clinical advice when it is necessary to protect their health or the health of others (Note 9E). The duty to maintain records does not require any information about the cause of injury or a condition to be recorded if it appears capable of providing evidence of an offence (Note 9F).

Cautions and inferences from silence: s.10

6–36   Pre-PACE, the questioning of suspects was subject to the Judges' Rules. These were rules formulated by a committee of the judges of the Queen's Bench Division for the guidance of the police. Their origin was a letter from the Lord Chief Justice to the Chief Constable of Birmingham in October 1906 responding to a request for such guidance. The Judges' Rules were reformulated in 1964[76] and again in 1978. They provided that "as soon as a police officer has evidence which affords him reasonable grounds for suspecting that a person has committed an offence" the suspect should be cautioned: "You are not obliged to say anything unless you wish to do so but what you say may be put into writing and given in evidence".

This traditional caution[77] was carried into the PACE system. As has been seen above, however, the rules regarding the caution were significantly altered by the so-called abolition of the right to silence by the Criminal Justice and Public Order Act 1994 (CJPOA), s.33 (see Chapter 13 below). As has been seen, the suspect does still have to be cautioned about his right to silence but he must now be warned that silence may be the subject of adverse comment by both the prosecution and the judge either of whom may invite the jury to draw adverse inferences from silence.

6–37   The basic caution now is: "You do not have to say anything. But it may harm your defence if you do not mention when questioned something which you later rely on in court. Anything you do say may be given in evidence" (para.10.5). A new provision in Code C as revised in 2003 states that minor deviations from the words of the caution are not a breach of the Code provided that the sense of the

---

[76] [1964] 1 All E.R. 237.
[77] Modified only by the removal of the words "be put into writing and" to take account of tape recording.

relevant caution is conveyed (para.10.7). If the person does not understand the caution it should be restated in the officer's own words (Note 10D).

Where this is relevant, the suspect must also be cautioned about the adverse inferences that may be drawn from his failure to account for objects, marks, or substances found on or about his person or his presence at the place where he was arrested at or about the time the crime was allegedly committed. (This flows from ss.36 and 37 of the CJPOA.) In order for an adverse inference to be drawn in regard to marks, etc., the officer must first have told the person being questioned: what offence he is investigating; what facts he is asking the suspect to account for; that he believes the suspect has taken part in the commission of the offence; that the court can draw a proper inference if he fails or refuses to account for that fact; and that a record is being made (para.10.11[78]). Sections 36 and 37 of the CJPOA only apply if the suspect has been arrested by a police officer or Customs and Excise officer (Note 10F).

However, as has also been seen, in order to comply with the European   **6–38**
Convention on Human Rights, in some situations the suspect now has to be cautioned in terms of the "old caution", rather than the "new caution". This is where, being detained in a police station, he has not had the opportunity of access to legal advice. (Code C, Annex C, see paras 5–153—5–157 above.) The duty to caution the suspect does not apply where the interview is conducted by the Serious Fraud Office exercising its special inquisitorial powers under s.2 of the Criminal Justice Act 1987. Moreover, this continues to be the case even after charge—*R. v Director of Serious Fraud Office, Ex p. Smith*.[79]

Who must be cautioned and when?

Where there are grounds to suspect a person of having committed an offence, he   **6–39**
must be cautioned before any questions (or further questions) about it are put if either the person's answers or silence may be given in evidence to a court in a prosecution (para.10.1[80]). As has been seen above, a person must also be cautioned on arrest (or further arrest).[81] A person need not be cautioned unless questions are put to him to obtain evidence that may be given in court. There are a variety of other situations where questioning takes place "for other necessary purposes" but no caution is required (see para.10.1(a)–(e)[82]), *e.g.*:

    (a)   if the questions are solely to establish a person's identity or ownership of a vehicle though if questioning is both for the purpose of establishing the person's identity and partly because of suspicion about the person's involvement in the crime, he should be cautioned[83];

---

[78] Formerly para.10.5B.
[79] [1993] A.C. 1; (1992) 95 Cr.App.R. 191; [1992] 3 W.L.R. 66; [1992] 3 All E.R. 456, HL.
[80] A slight redraft in 2003.
[81] Code C, para.10.4(b).
[82] Slightly redrafted in the 2003 version of the Code.
[83] *Nelson and Rose* [1998] 2 Cr.App.R.399; [1998] Crim.L.R. 814, CA.

    (b) when obtaining information in accordance with a statutory require-
ment[84];

    (c) in furtherance of the proper and effective conduct of a search of the
person or of premises; or

    (d) when asking the suspect to verify a written record made by an officer
as required by the Codes.

6–40   The requirement that there be grounds for suspicion is less than a requirement
that there be a *prima facie* case. But "grounds" means objective grounds, as distinct from a mere hunch or sixth sense.[85] Note 10A introduced in 2003 says,
"There must be some reasonable, objective grounds for the suspicion, based on
known facts or information which are relevant to the likelihood the offence has
been committed and the person being questioned committed it".

    A caution may not be necessary if the inquiries are at an early stage. The
court's ruling as to whether sufficient grounds existed on the particular facts is
sometimes difficult to comprehend. For an extreme example see, for instance,
James[86] where J was interviewed on four of the eight days following the report
that his business partner had gone missing. He was later convicted of the partner's
murder. The Court of Appeal held that there had been no requirement to caution
him even on the third or fourth occasion despite the fact that by then the police
had evidence that he had lied in his previous statements.[87] The grounds are not
even required to be reasonable.[88]

    If questioning is interrupted and restarted the officer must ensure that the sus-
pect knows that he is still under caution and, if there is any doubt, he should be
cautioned again in full (para.10.8[89]). A new Note for Guidance added in 2003
says that officers should bear in mind that they may have to show a court that
nothing occurred during a break that influenced the suspect's recorded evidence. They should consider after a break or at the beginning of a subsequent
interview summarising the reason for the break and confirming this with the
suspect (Note 10E).

6–41   If a person cautioned at the police station is not under arrest the officer should
tell him that that is the position, that he is free to leave if he pleases and that he
may get free legal advice if he wishes (paras 3.21 and 10.2). (The fact that he is
not under arrest means that he cannot be prevented from seeking legal advice

---

[84] See, for instance, *Mawdesley v DPP* [2003] EWHC 1586 (Admin); [2004] 1 W.L.R. 1035; *Francis v DPP* [2004] EWHC 591 (Admin), both of which concerned forms sent under the Road Traffic Act 1988, s.172.

[85] *op.cit.*, n.83 above.

[86] [1996] Crim.L.R. 650, CA.

[87] See to like effect *Mellor* [1996] 2 Cr.App.R. 245, CA. For two contrasting cases concerning whether a caution should have been administered by Customs and Excise officers prior to a field test for drugs see *Shah* [1994] Crim.L.R. 125, CA—no need to caution before field test for cocaine; and *Nelson and Rose*, n.83 above—caution required from the outset of questioning because the Customs and Excise officer had suspicions aroused by the thickness of the suitcase.

[88] For case law on failure to give a caution see paras 8–65, 8–68 below.

[89] Formerly para.10.5.

which in turn means that the "new" caution should be used, which warns that silence could result in adverse inferences being drawn, rather than the former caution.)

A person who is under arrest should be cautioned: before being asked questions or further questions for the purpose of obtaining evidence for use in court; when being arrested for any further offence; when being charged; and when being told about someone else's written statement or answers to questions.

If a juvenile or a person who is mentally disordered or vulnerable is cautioned in the absence of the appropriate adult, the caution should be repeated in the adult's presence (para.10.12[90]).

Interviews: general: para.11(a)

Code C (para.11.1) makes it clear that interviews with arrested persons are basi-   **6–42**
cally to be conducted at a police station (or other authorised place of detention).[91] Interviews may only be conducted somewhere other than at a police station where the same risks (of interference with evidence, of the alerting of accomplices, etc.) exist as justify delay of access to legal advice under s.58(8)—as to which see paras 5–51—5–54 above—and questioning outside the police station should cease once that risk has been averted. Despite this rule, studies have shown that suspects are sometimes questioned prior to arrival at the police station.[92]

The Code states that after both reminding the suspect of his right to free legal advice (para.11.2) and cautioning him (para.11.4), the interviewing officer shall put to him "any significant statement or silence which occurred in the presence and hearing of a police officer or civilian interviewer before the start of the interview" and shall ask him whether he confirms or denies that earlier statement or silence and whether he wishes to add anything (para.11.4[93]). A significant statement is defined as one which "appears capable of being used in evidence against the suspect, in particular a direct admission of guilt" (para.11.4A). A significant silence is "a failure or refusal to answer a question or to answer it satisfactorily when under caution which might . . .[94] give rise to an inference under the Criminal Justice and Public Order Act 1994, Part III" (*ibid.*).

---

[90] Formerly para.10.6.

[91] In *Goddard*, unreported, Case No.91/5291/Z2, May 18, 1993, CA, the Court of Appeal said that to interview a suspect after he has been arrested and prior to his arrival at the police station was improper. The conviction for possessing heroin was quashed.

[92] Brown *et al.* (1992), based on replies from police officers, showed that in 1991 questioning of the suspect by the police outside the police station occurred in 10% of cases, that the suspect made unsolicited comments in 16% of cases and that there was questioning and/or unsolicited comments in 24% of cases. The comparable figures for the 1990 sample were 19%, 19% and 35% (Table 6.1, p.81). See also Moston and Stephenson (1993, p.22) which show that 8% of the sample taken were questioned before arrival at the police station.

[93] A revised version of what until 2003 was para.11.2A. The revision was important as the previous rule only related to what had occurred before arrival at the police station. This includes anything that happened before the interview.

[94] The words omitted here for clarity are "allowing for the restriction on drawing adverse inferences from silence".

Code C confirms the traditional common law rule that no police officer may try to obtain answers to questions by the use of oppression (para.11.5[95]). Nor may an officer indicate, save in response to a direct question, what action would be taken by the police if the suspect answered questions, made a statement or refused to do either. If asked a direct question, as has been seen, the officer may answer—provided the action he refers to is "proper and warranted" (*ibid.*).

6–43   But it is important to be careful not to offer improper inducements. For a case raising difficult issues see *de Silva*[96] in which the Court of Appeal held that there was nothing wrong with Customs officers seeking the appellant's co-operation in a drugs smuggling investigation but to say that the invitation to co-operate and the inducement in mentioning that a judge would potentially take it into account were proper was not to say that the evidence obtained as a result was admissible against him. The inducement had persuaded the appellant to supply evidence against himself. A normal caution was not sufficient warning. The Court said that he should have been specifically told that anything he said in the recorded telephone calls he agreed to make to others involved in the offence might be held against him, which might have resulted in the appellant not participating. In that instance there was enough other evidence for the Court of Appeal to uphold the conviction, but if the suggestion of a stricter caution becomes a requirement in such situations, it would make the task of the police or customs officers more difficult. (For critical commentary on the decision—which cited no authorities— see [2003] Crim.L.R. 476.)

6–44   A basic principle of the English system is that, subject to some exceptions, when a person has been charged, questioning about that offence should cease. This principle, which pre-dated PACE, is now reflected in Code C, paras 11.6 and 16.5. Paragraph 11.6 now provides that the interview must cease when the officer in charge of the investigation, taking into account any other available evidence, is satisfied that all the questions relevant to obtaining accurate and reliable information about the offence being investigated have been put to the suspect— and that the suspect has been allowed an opportunity to give an innocent explanation and that questions to test whether such an explanation is accurate and reliable have been put.[97] A caveat dating from the 1991 revision of the Code states that this should not, however, be read as preventing officers from inviting suspects in revenue cases or in confiscation proceedings under the Criminal Justice Act 1988 or the Drug Trafficking Act 1994 to complete a formal question and answer record after the interview is concluded.[98] Code C, para.16.1 (para.6–74 below) requires a person to be charged when the officer in the case reasonably believes that there is enough evidence for a successful prosecution, and para.16.5 still provides that, subject to some caveats, after being charged, questioning about that offence must basically cease.

---

[95] Formerly para.11.3.
[96] [2002] EWCA Crim 2673; [2003] Crim.L.R.474.
[97] A significant redraft of what until 2003 was para.11.4 which required that questioning cease when the officer believed that there was enough evidence for a successful prosecution and the suspect, having been asked, indicated that he had nothing further to say. For a critical assessment of the new version of para.11.6 see Wolchover and Heaton-Armstrong, "A new encroachment on the right to silence?", 5 *Archbold News*, June 2004, p.4.
[98] Code C, para.11.6.

The previous admonition that the interviewer should ask the suspect if he has anything else to say was dropped in the 2003 redraft. Note 11B[99] reminds interviewers that the Code of Practice under the Criminal Procedure and Investigations Act 1996 states (para.3.4), "In conducting an investigation, the investigator should pursue all reasonable lines of enquiry, whether these point towards or away from the suspect".

For consideration of Code C, para.16, which deals with questioning after charge, see para.6–76 below.

Interview records: para.11(b)

The provisions for the recording of interviews have given rise to considerable difficulty, controversy and case law. Paragraph 11.13 states "a written record shall be made of any comments made by a suspect [*in the presence and hearing of a police officer or approved person*][1] including unsolicited comments, which are outside the context of an interview but which might be relevant to the offence".   **6–45**

Curiously, the written record required by para.11.13 does not, it seems, have to be in the custody record—though, if the suspect refuses to sign the record, that does have to be in the custody record (para.11.14).[2] Any such record must be timed and signed by the maker (para.11.9). Where the person has been arrested he must be given the opportunity of reading the record and of signing it as correct or of indicating the respects in which he considers it inaccurate (para.11.11).

In regard to interviews properly so called, the first and basic provision, as set out in Code C, para.11.7(a),[3] is that, "An accurate record must be made of each interview, whether or not the interview takes place at a police station". The record must state the place of the interview, the time it starts and ends, details of any breaks, and the names of those present (para.11.7(b)). (The requirement to record the names of all those present does not apply to interviews under the terrorism legislation or where the officer or approved person reasonably believes that giving the name might put him in danger in which case the record must state the warrant number or other identification number (para.2.6A).) The record must be made on forms provided or in the officer's pocket book or be tape recorded or videoed (para.11.7(b)[4]). The record has to be made during the course of the interview "unless this would not be practicable or would interfere with the conduct of the interview"[5] (para.11.7(c)[6]). It must be either a verbatim record or, failing that, an account which adequately and accurately summarises it (*ibid.*).   **6–46**

---

[99] Added in 2003.
[1] The italicised words were in the 2002 consultation draft but were not in the final version.
[2] *Heslop* [1996] Crim.L.R. 730, CA. But query—see Code C, para.2.1.
[3] Formerly para.11.5(a).
[4] Formerly para.11.5(b).
[5] See *Langiert* [1991] Crim.L.R. 777, CA; *Chung* (1991) 92 Cr.App.R. 314, CA; *Park, The Times*, July 30, 1992, CA; *Davis*, unreported, Case No.90/0816/Y3, November 10, 1992, CA.
[6] Formerly 11.5.(c).

An accurate record must be made, as has been seen whether or not the interview takes place in a police station. The questions therefore are, first, whether the exchange amounts to "an interview" (on which see para.6–51 below) and, secondly, whether it is practicable to make a contemporaneous record.

6–47   If a record is not made during the course of the interview, it must be made as soon as practicable afterwards (para.11.8[7]). Written records must be timed and signed by the maker (para.11.9[8]). If a record is not completed during the interview the reason for this must be recorded in the officer's interview record (para.11.10[9]). As has been noted, the police are equally under a duty to make a written record of any comments made by a suspected person, including unsolicited comments, which are outside of an interview but which might be relevant to the offence (Code C, para.11.13).[10] Any such record must equally be timed and signed by the maker.

Unless it is not practicable, the person interviewed must be given the opportunity to read the interview record and to sign it as correct or to indicate in what respects he considers it inaccurate (para.11.11[11]). The defendant's simple signature is therefore not sufficient.[12] If the suspect cannot read or refuses to read the record or to sign it, the senior police officer present must read it to him and ask whether he wishes to sign it as correct or to state in what way it is not accurate. He must then record what happens as a result (*ibid.*). The same rule applies equally to written records made (under para.11.13) of anything said by the suspect which is not technically part of an interview. Failure to comply with this requirement has frequently led to evidence of admissions and confessions being excluded and even to convictions being quashed. The courts have treated it as a very important provision safeguarding the suspect. Curiously, considering how important the rule has become, it is not required that the suspect must be shown the record immediately or even as soon as practicable. If the appropriate adult or the person's solicitor is present during the interview he should also be given an opportunity to read and sign the interview record or any written statement taken down by the police (para.11.12[13]). Any refusal by a person to sign an interview record, or a record of other comments required by para.11.13, when asked to do so must itself be recorded (para.11.14[14]).[15]

6–48   The police fail to keep proper records of interviews at the risk of having the fruits of the interview held inadmissible or, even worse, of having the conviction quashed on appeal. The decision in the case of *Canale*[16] in November 1989 given in the Court of Appeal by Lord Lane, the Lord Chief Justice, stands as a classic warning. C had been sentenced to six years imprisonment for conspiracy to rob.

[7] Formerly para.11.7. Strangely there is no duty to state when the record is made.
[8] Formerly para.11.8.
[9] Formerly para.11.9 which said "in the officer's pocketbook".
[10] In *R. v DPP, Ex p. Khan*, unreported, Case No.CO 657/00, March 21, 2000, DC, the court allowed the appeal because there had been a failure to show the accused an inculpatory remark made on arrest either for his agreement contrary to para.11.13 or at the start of the later interview contrary to para.11.2A (now para.11.4).
[11] Formerly para.11.10
[12] *Heslop*, n.2 above.
[13] Formerly para.11.11.
[14] Formerly para.11.12.
[15] See *Heslop*, n.2 above.
[16] [1990] 2 All E.R. 187, CA

The court quashed his conviction because of what the Lord Chief Justice described as "flagrant, deliberate and cynical" breaches of the rules regarding the keeping of records of interviews. He had allegedly made admissions during two separate interviews, neither of which had been contemporaneously recorded. Each was followed by another interview which was recorded, in which he repeated his earlier admissions. At the trial he claimed that he had made false admissions as a result of a trick by the police.

The reasons given by the police officers for not having recorded the interviews were stated in each of their notebooks as "B.W." which they explained meant "best way". In their view it was best not to record contemporaneously. This, Lord Lane said, was not a valid reason. It "demonstrated a lamentable attitude towards the 1984 Act and the rules" and a "cynical disregard of the rules". It was argued for the police that the real reason for not recording the interviews was that they wanted to get the suspect's stories "into apple pie order" before making the contemporaneously recorded interviews "so that it would be easier for the jury to follow the eventual statements". The court doubted whether this was the truth. The police had also failed to show the record they eventually made to the suspect for him to initial as required by the rules.

The importance of the rules relating to the contemporaneous noting of interviews "could scarcely be over-emphasized". The object, Lord Lane said, was twofold: "to ensure as far as possible that the suspect's remarks were accurately recorded and that he had an opportunity, when he went through the contemporaneous record afterwards, of checking and initialling each answer; likewise, it was a vital protection for the police to ensure that it could not be suggested that they had induced the suspect to confess by improper approaches or improper promises". If the contemporaneous note was not made, each of those laudable objects "was apt to be stultified". Its absence deprived the trial judge of vital evidence as to the circumstances of the admissions. Since there was no evidence against the defendant other than the admissions made in the various interviews and since they should have been excluded the court said it had no option but to quash the conviction.[17]   **6–49**

What if the police officer is acting undercover? An undercover officer obviously cannot make a contemporaneous note of things said by a suspect, nor can he show any note made to the suspect to get him to sign it. Does that mean that questions cannot be put for fear that they would be treated as an interview subject to the rules for the recording of interviews in Code C? The courts have grappled with that problem in several cases. In *Christou*[18] the Court of Appeal dismissed appeals from victims of a police "sting" operation set up to catch burglars wishing to dispose of the proceeds of their crimes. Conversations with customers of the phoney fencing operation were found to have been on equal terms. The Court said that the Code was not intended to apply in such a context. But evidence would be excluded if the court took the view that officers had adopted an undercover disguise in order to ask questions with the effect of circumventing the Code. Such a case was *Bryce*[19] where an undercover officer phoned the defendant about a car for sale. Asked by the officer how warm the car was, B replied "a couple of days". At a second conversation in person, B allegedly said the car   **6–50**

---

[17] See, to similar effect, the Court of Appeal's decision in *Keenan* [1989] 3 All E.R. 598, CA.
[18] (1992) Cr.App.R. 264, CA.
[19] (1992) 95 Cr.App.R. 320, CA

had been nicked for two or three days. The Court of Appeal said the questions put by the undercover officer offended the rules laid down in *Christou*. Much turns on whether the officers played an active or a passive role in obtaining the evidence, and whether the court thinks that they went beyond their undercover role by asking questions rather than simply observing and listening.

What is an interview?

6–51   The question of what constitutes "an interview" for the purposes of the rules about interviewing and the recording of interviews has caused considerable difficulty. The 1991 revision of Code C produced a confusing definition of "interview"[20] which was criticised both by the courts[21] and by the Runciman Royal Commission on Criminal Justice.[22] The Commission recommended that this confusion be cleared up when Code C was next revised.

The April 1995 revised Code attempted to deal with the problem in para.11.1A by employing a shorter and simpler definition: "An interview is the questioning of a person regarding his involvement or suspected involvement in a criminal offence or offences which, by virtue of para.10.1 of Code C, is required to be carried out under caution".[23] This redraft was a considerable improvement on the previous formula and it remains the definition.[24] The cases appear to establish the following propositions:

  (1) The word "interview" is to be given a wide rather than a narrow interpretation.[25] The Court of Appeal said in *Matthews, Voss and Dennison* that "normally any discussion or talk between a suspect or prisoner and a police officer would amount to an interview, whether instigated by the suspect, a prisoner or a police officer".

  (2) The fact that the exchange consisted merely of a "quick chat" does not prevent it being an interview.[26] One word or one question can constitute an interview.[27]

---

[20] Note 11A in 1991 stated: "An interview is the questioning of a person regarding his involvement or suspected involvement in a criminal offence or offences. Questioning a person only to obtain information or his explanation of the facts or in the ordinary course of the officer's duties, does not constitute an interview for the purposes of this Code. Neither does questioning which is confined to the proper and effective conduct of a search."

[21] *Cox* (1999) 96 Cr.App.R.464; [1993] Crim.L.R. 382.

[22] See Runciman Report, p.27, para.10. Both pointed out that the second part of the definition conflicted with the first.

[23] The statutory breathalyser procedure under ss.7 and 8 of the Road Traffic Act 1988 does not constitute an interview—Code C, para.11.1A; *DPP v Billington* [1988] 1 All E.R. 434, DC; *DPP v Rouse*; *DPP v Davis* [1991] Crim.L.R. 911, DC.

[24] Except that the 2003 redraft substituted "their" for "his" and "of this Code" for "Code C".

[25] *R. v Matthews, Voss and Dennison* (1990) 91 Cr.App.R. 43; [1990] Crim.L.R. 190, CA.

[26] *R. v Foster* [1987] Crim.L.R. 821, Crown Ct. What mattered, the court said, was not the length of the exchange but its content. See also *Younis and Ahmed* [1990] Crim.L.R. 425, CA.

[27] *Ward* (1993) 98 Cr.App.R. 337, CA; *Miller* [1998] Crim.L.R. 209, CA; *Batley* [1998] T.L.R. 137, DC.

(3) Where an officer asks a question which produces an incriminating response, the exchange can be an interview even though the officer had no real grounds for suspicion when he put the question.[28]

(4) The fact that the exchange takes place in the street or at the scene of the crime does not prevent it being an interview.[29]

(5) The fact that the questions put by the officer are designed to give the arrested person or suspect an opportunity to give an innocent explanation (as opposed to eliciting admissions) does not prevent the exchange being an interview. In *Maguire*[30] the Court of Appeal distinguished *Absolam* on the ground that the purpose of the questions there was to get an admission to a more serious offence, whereas in *Maguire* the questions were to give the arrested person the opportunity to give an innocent explanation of the facts. This basis of distinction seems unreal. The officer said: "Look, you've been caught. Now tell us the truth . . . It's for your own good. Don't be stupid." As Professor Diane Birch, commenting on the decision, said,[31] it is highly unlikely that the officer was not trying to get a confession from Maguire. But in any event the definition of an interview in the 1991 revised Code covers this precise situation. (The point should have been clear even under the previous Code since Note 12A stated, in terms, that "The purpose of any interview is to obtain from the person concerned his explanation of the facts, and not necessarily to obtain an admission".)

(6) Questioning during the course of a search can be an interview—which must, if practicable, be recorded—even though Code C, para.10.1 says that a person need not be cautioned, *inter alia*, if questions are put "in furtherance of the proper and effective conduct of a search".[32]

(7) The fact that the suspect has asked for the interview to be "off the record" does not prevent it being an interview.[33] The Code does not allow for "off the record" conversations—even in the form of a "general chat"—though if the suspect is not warned of this, a resulting

---

[28] *R. v Absolam* (1989) 88 Cr.App.R. 332, CA. A, who had been arrested for threatening behaviour, was asked by the custody officer to empty his pockets. He did so. The officer, knowing that he had previous convictions for possession of cannabis, then said "Put the drugs on the table", whereupon A produced a bag containing cannabis from the inside of his trousers and admitted selling the drug. It was held that this exchange was an interview which should have been recorded contemporaneously. The conviction was quashed.

[29] *R. v Maloney and Doherty* [1988] Crim.L.R. 523 Crown Ct: 16 questions asked at the scene of the crime were held to be an interview which should have been recorded contemporaneously. See also *Fogah* [1989] Crim.L.R. 141.

[30] (1989) 90 Cr.App.R.115; [1989] Crim.L.R. 815, CA.

[31] [1989] Crim.L.R. 815 at 816.

[32] See, for instance, *Manji* [1990] Crim.L.R. 512, CA; *Langiert* [1991] Crim.L.R. 777, CA; *Raphaie* [1996] Crim.L.R. 812, CA—*cf. Marsh* [1991] Crim.L.R. 455, CA; *Hanchard*, unreported, Case No.99/1822/X4, December 6, 1999, CA.

[33] *R. v Saunders (Rosemary)* [1988] Crim.L.R. 521, Crown Ct.

admission may be excluded on the ground that its admission would be unfair.[34]

(8) The fact that it is difficult in the particular circumstances to make a record does not prevent the exchange from being an interview. In *Fogah*,[35] a juvenile was questioned in the street a quarter of a mile from the scene of a robbery. The resulting admissions were excluded on the ground that no appropriate adult had been present at the interview—which, by definition, meant that the exchange was counted as an interview even though it took place in the street.[36]

(9) If the meeting between the police officers and the suspect is wholly at his request, without any suggestion or inducement from them and the officers ask no questions but simply record what he tells them, it is not an interview.[37] But this situation is probably very rare and should not be regarded as a basis for ignoring the rules for interviews. Certainly it is clear that there is a fine line between a "social visit" and an "interview".[38] In *de Silva*[39] the Court of Appeal held that a cooperation conversation was not an interview for the purposes of gathering evidence against the suspect, it was a conversation to encourage him to give evidence, information and to assist law enforcement authorities, by informing him of the benefits to him if he should do so. The commentary in the *Criminal Law Review* rightly observes that this is a very narrow interpretation of para.11.1A—and in this writer's view it is of doubtful authority.

6–52   In view of the provisions of para.11.13, the only safe course for the police is always to make a record of every significant exchange with an actual or potential suspect in regard to a criminal offence. However, taking a statement from a victim or other potential witness is not an interview for these purposes.[40]

Informing the suspect about a drug referral scheme is not an interview

6–53   In most force areas there are now drug referral programmes available not only to suspects arrested on drugs-related charges but also to arrested suspects gener-

---

[34] *Woodall* [1989] Crim.L.R. 288, Crown Ct. See also *Trussler (Barry)* [1988] Crim.L.R. 446, Crown Ct.
[35] [1989] Crim.L.R. 141.
[36] See to like effect *Brezeanu and Francis* [1989] Crim.L.R. 650, CA. But see also *Vivian Parchment* [1989] Crim.L.R. 290, Crown Ct, where the court held that it had not been practicable to record exchanges with the suspect, first after he emerged naked from a cupboard at his house during a police search, then while he was getting dressed and then, thirdly, in a moving police car on the way back to the police station.
[37] *Menard* (1995) 1 Cr.App.R. 306, CA.
[38] See *Williams (Mark Alexander)*, *The Times*, February 6, 1992. The police had visited the defendant in the cells after he had been charged and remanded by the magistrates. The trial judge allowed in the record of the conversation.
[39] [2002] EWCA Crim 2673; [2003] Crim.L.R. 474.
[40] *Dixon* [2001] EWCA Crim 2020.

ally.[41] Where such a scheme exists it is important that the suspect be told about it in such a way that the communication of the information does not turn into an exchange which can be defined as an interview. Also, Code C, para.3.4 specifically prohibits the custody officer from asking questions or engaging in exchanges about anything to do with the suspect's involvement with the offence.

The Home Office Guidance Manual[42] recommends that the information be communicated by the custody officer and that the following words be used: "A drug referral scheme operates at this police station. If you are interested, I can arrange for you to see an independent drugs worker in due course. Are you interested?" If possible, such words should be accompanied by a leaflet which explains the scheme.[43]

Questioning of mentally disordered or mentally vulnerable persons, children and young persons: ss.1 and 11

Persons at risk

As has been seen, the Code makes detailed provision for special safeguards for persons at risk and notably for juveniles and persons who have some form of mental disability or vulnerability. (The 2003 redraft of the Codes deleted the term "mentally handicapped" in favour of "mentally vulnerable".[44]) Juveniles are around one-fifth of all persons arrested. The mentally disordered or vulnerable represent around 1 per cent of those arrested.[45]   **6–54**

The provisions in the Code for the questioning of persons with the handicap of mental disorder or of youth more generally were a much fuller and greatly improved version of the equivalent provisions in the former Judges' Rules and Administrative Directions. Paragraph 1.4[46] states that if an officer has any suspicion or is told in good faith that a person of any age may be mentally disordered or otherwise mentally vulnerable, in the absence of clear evidence to the contrary, he must treat him as such a person and an appropriate adult must be called. Similarly, in the absence of evidence to the contrary, he must treat someone as a juvenile if he appears to be under 17 years old (para.1.5). In all such cases an "appropriate adult" (see below) must be informed and asked to come to be with the person in question unless an urgent interview (as defined in para.11.1) is required.

---

[41] The Government's anti-drugs strategy is to have such schemes in every custody suite—see Home Office Circular, HOC 41/1999, para.3.

[42] *Drugs Interventions in the Criminal Justice System, Guidance Manual* (Home Office Drugs Prevention Advisory Service, 1999), p.18.

[43] For criticism of a decision in which the judge held that this information should have been preceded by a caution, see Zander, "Is arrest referral to a drugs scheme a PACE interview?", New L.J., June 1, 2001, p.822.

[44] Note 1G states that "mentally vulnerable" applies to anyone who, because of that person's mental state or incapacity, "may not understand the significance of what is said, of questions or of their replies". The definition of "mental disorder" in Note 1G has not been changed.

[45] See Brown *et al.* (1992), p.70.

[46] As redrafted in 2003.

6–55   The Code also provides that other persons at risk may only be interviewed if the interview is urgent (as defined in para.11.1(a) to (c)). This applies to anyone unable to appreciate the significance of questions put to them and their answers or to understand what is happening because of the effects of drink or drugs or any illness, ailment or condition, or to anyone who has difficulty in understanding English or who has a hearing disability if there is no interpreter present. A further qualification is that even an urgent interview in such cases is only permitted if the authorising officer is satisfied that the interview would not significantly harm the person's physical or mental state (Code C, para.11.18[47]).

Note 11C[48] states that although persons at risk are capable of providing reliable evidence they may "without knowing or wishing to do so, be particularly prone in certain circumstances to provide information that may be unreliable, misleading or self-incriminating. Special care should always be taken when questioning such a person and the appropriate adult should be involved, if there is any doubt about a person's age, mental state or capacity. Because of the risk of unreliable evidence it is also important to obtain corroboration of any facts admitted whenever possible."

Juveniles can only be interviewed at school in "exceptional circumstances" and then only when the head or his nominee agree (para.11.16[49]). It is stated to be preferable that a juvenile should not be arrested at his school unless this is unavoidable. The head or his nominee should be informed (Note 11D[50]).

"The appropriate adult"

6–56   In the case of a juvenile, appropriate adult means a parent or guardian, or, if he is in care, the care authority or voluntary organisation, or a social worker or member of a Youth Offending Team (YOT), failing which another responsible adult who is not a police officer or employed by the police (paras 1.7(a), 3.14). It is now rare for a juvenile not to have an appropriate adult.[51]

Note 1C in the 1991 revised Code addressed the problem of the parent who, for one reason or another, might not be suitable as an appropriate adult. It said that, if the parent was involved in the offence either as victim or perpetrator or witness, he or she should not be the "appropriate adult". In the 1995 revision of the Code this provision was made even stronger and broader. Note 1B now states categorically:

> "A person, including a parent or guardian, should not be an appropriate adult if he is suspected of involvement in the offence in question, is the victim, is a witness, is involved in the investigation or has received admissions prior to attending to act as the appropriate adult."

---

[47] Based on previous Annex C which is no longer part of the Code.
[48] Formerly Note 11B.
[49] Formerly para.11.15.
[50] Formerly Note 11C.
[51] In Bucke and Brown's (1997) study, 91% of the juveniles had an appropriate adult. In Phillips and Brown's (1998) study, 97% of 599 juveniles had an appropriate adult (p.53).

The estranged parent of a juvenile should equally not be asked to act as appro-   **6–57**
priate adult if the juvenile specifically objects to his presence (*ibid.*[52]). Also, if a
child in care admits an offence to a social worker (other than during the time that
the social worker is acting as appropriate adult), another social worker should act
as appropriate adult (Note 1D).

If he is subject to a supervision order, action plan order, reparation order, curfew order, or community part of a detention and training order, his supervisor
("the responsible officer") should, if possible, be told (para.3.14, as amended in
2003). The responsible officer will normally be a member of a YOT, unless the
curfew order involves electronic monitoring ("tagging") in which case the contractor providing the monitoring will normally be the responsible officer (*ibid.*).
Where the juvenile is a ward of court an application to interview him or her must
be made to the court but if the interview is urgent the parent, foster parent or
"appropriate adult" should be informed and invited to attend or to nominate
someone to be present.[53] In Phillips and Brown (1998), in almost two-thirds of
cases (63 per cent) the juvenile's appropriate adult was a parent or guardian and
in a further 10 per cent it was another relative. Social workers attended in 20 per
cent of cases, mainly because the juvenile was in care.[54]

In the case of someone who is mentally disordered or mentally vulnerable, an   **6–58**
appropriate adult means a relative, guardian or other person responsible for his
care, or someone experienced in dealing with such cases not employed by the
police, failing whom some other responsible adult who is not a police officer or
employed by the police (para.1.7(b)). Note 1D suggests that it may, in some circumstances, be better if the appropriate adult is someone who has training or
experience in care of the mentally disordered or mentally vulnerable rather than
a relative who lacks such qualifications. But the note says that if the person
himself "prefers a relative to a better qualified stranger or objects to a particular
person their wishes should if practicable be respected".[55]

In England and Wales a solicitor, an independent custody visitor (formerly
known as lay visitor), cannot act as the appropriate adult if he is present in a
professional capacity (Code C, Note 1F).[56]

---

[52] In *DPP v B., The Times*, January 2, 1990, the Divisional Court rejected a prosecution appeal after
the magistrates had held a confession to be inadmissible, partly because the appropriate adult was an
estranged father. Therefore there had not been an appropriate adult present. This was affirmed by the
Court of Appeal: sub nom. *DPP v Blake* [1989] 1 W.L.R. 432.

[53] Practice Direction [1988] 2 All E.R. 1015.

[54] The figures in Brown *et al.* (1992, Table 5.1, p.71) were very similar—the appropriate adult for
juveniles was a parent in 59% of cases, some other relative in 7%, a social worker, children's home
worker or the like in 28%, and miscellaneous others or identity not known in the remaining 6%.

[55] Phillips and Brown (1998) found that an appropriate adult had been called in half of the 67 cases
diagnosed as mentally disordered or mentally handicapped. The prisoners saw one or more of the following: an approved social worker (in 20 cases); a psychiatrist (10); or someone else, usually a parent or guardian (14). Many were seen first by a doctor. There were 11 who saw neither a doctor nor
an appropriate adult (p.56). In Bucke and Brown (1997) an appropriate adult attended in two-thirds
of the cases involving mentally disordered detainees. In many of the other cases a doctor had advised
that it was unnecessary to call an appropriate adult (p.8).

[56] But see *Lewis (Martin)* [1996] Crim.L.R. 260, CA where it was held that although the solicitor was
not an appropriate adult he was "an independent person" for the purposes of s.77 (on which see
para.8–49 below). Application was made on appeal to call fresh evidence showing that L had an IQ
of 69 and should have had an appropriate adult present. The CA dismissed the appeal.

6–59   It should be recalled, however, that under Code C, para.6.1 a person in police detention must be told that he may at any time consult and communicate privately with a solicitor and that accordingly, at the request of the young person, the appropriate adult could be excluded from such consultation. Note 1E states that when an appropriate adult is called to the police station, the suspect should always be given an opportunity to consult privately with the solicitor in the absence of the appropriate adult if they wish to do so. In one case the suspect's own probation officer was held not to be an appropriate adult as she was in a position of authority over her client and she was not his preferred choice.[57] The suspect had an IQ of just over 50. The probation officer had mainly assisted the police in questioning the suspect.

Paragraph 11.17[58] states that the appropriate adult should be informed (presumably, though this is not stated, by the police) that he is not expected to act simply as an observer and that the purposes of his presence are, first, to advise the person being questioned, to observe whether the interview is being conducted properly and fairly, and to facilitate communication with the person being interviewed.[59] The person performing the role must have the requisite mental capacity to do so.[60]

The Code requires that the suspect be informed that the appropriate adult is there to assist and advise him and that he can consult privately with the appropriate adult at any time (para.3.18). This requirement does not seem to be much honoured.[61] (The pre-2003 version of this provision (former para.3.12) laid the duty to inform the suspect on the custody officer but, for whatever reason, that has been removed.)

6–60   Experience shows that it is difficult to make the concept of the appropriate adult effective. As has been seen, in the majority of cases the appropriate adult is a parent, guardian or relative. He or she is by no means always favourably disposed towards the person being interviewed; quite commonly the appropriate adult sides with the police against the suspect.[62] Nor does a parent necessarily understand what his role is supposed to be, even if the police act on the above

---

[57] Cited in Sheppard, *The Appropriate Adult: A review of the case law 1988–95* (Institute of Mental Health Law, Norfolk, 1996).

[58] Formerly para.11.16.

[59] In Bucke and Brown's (1997) study, 29% of family members, as compared with only 4% of social worker appropriate adults, got some form of explanation of the role of the appropriate adult from the custody officer (p.10).

[60] In *Morse* [1995] Crim.L.R. 195 the father was held not to be an appropriate adult because he was of low intelligence, almost illiterate and probably unable to grasp the gravity of the situation his son was in. *cf. W* [1994] Crim.L.R. 130 where the Court of Appeal upheld the trial judge's view that a mother who was herself mentally ill was nevertheless fit to act as the appropriate adult. In *H and M v DPP* [1998] Crim.L.R. 653 the Court of Appeal accepted that an appropriate adult was present even though the parent could not speak English because there was another adult there who actually performed the role—even though it had not been explained to him as required by Code C, para.11.17.

[61] See Brown *et al.* (1992), p.72.

[62] In *Jefferson, Skerritt, Readman and Keogh* (1994) 99 Cr.App.R.13; [1993] Crim.L.R. 881, CA the court upheld a conviction even though the suspect's father had intervened repeatedly on the side of the police. Encouragement by an appropriate adult to tell the truth, it said, should not normally be stigmatised as a failure by the adult to perform his function. See also Bucke and Brown (1997), pp.11–15.

admonition. What seems to be required is a form of notice that could be handed to the appropriate adult to specify concretely both his role and his rights.

As has been seen, generally[63] no interview is supposed to take place with a juvenile or a mentally disordered or mentally vulnerable person (whether suspected of crime or not) in the absence of an appropriate adult (para.11.15[64]). For a striking example see, for instance, *Aspinall.*[65] The Court of Appeal held that it is an absolute requirement for an appropriate adult to be present if a suspect who is known to suffer from mental illness is being interviewed. This is so even if there are no acute symptoms, there is a fitness certificate from a doctor and the suspect seems to be able to understand and to answer questions. Where there has been a breach of Code C, para.11.15, analysis of which parts of an interview are reliable and which are not may be possible and appropriate.[66]

An interview may, however, take place in the absence of the appropriate adult   **6–61**
or lawyer if an officer of the rank of superintendent or above reasonably believes that the delay in waiting for such a person will lead to interference with evidence or physical injury, serious loss of or damage to property, or to the alerting of accomplices or the hindering of recovery of the proceeds of crime (paras 11.1 and 11.18).[67]

Where a person who is mentally ill or mentally vulnerable or a juvenile is interviewed in the absence of a responsible adult because of a risk of harm to persons or serious loss or damage to property, the interview may not continue in the absence of an accompanying adult once the risk of such harm has been averted (para.11.19[68]). All the provisions relating to the mentally disordered and mentally vulnerable are conveniently set out in Annex E to Code C.

The attitude of the courts regarding the absence of an appropriate adult where one is required under the Code has varied. For the relevant cases see paras 8–65, 8–66 below.

The Runciman Royal Commission on Criminal Justice recommended the   **6–62**
establishment of a Home Office Working Party to undertake a comprehensive review of the role and functions of the appropriate adult.[69] In 1994 the Home Office set up a Review Group on appropriate adults with wide membership. It published its report in June 1995.[70] Its 13 recommendations included:

---

[63] That is to say unless paras 11.1 or 11.18–11.20 regarding urgent interviews apply.
[64] Formerly para.11.14.
[65] (1999) 2 Cr.App.R. 115; [1999] Crim.L.R. 741, CA.
[66] *Haroon Ali*, unreported, Case No.98/04160/X2, November 24, 1998, CA—18-year-old defendant interviewed for nine minutes without solicitor or appropriate adult during which he made admissions regarding drugs offences. The judge accepted medical evidence that he was mentally handicapped and that there had been a breach of para.11.15 (at that time still para.11.14) but held that some parts of the admissions were reliable. The Court of Appeal allowed the defendant's appeal on the ground that within two minutes the defendant had made unreliable admissions.
[67] In Brown (1992, p.73) the average time before the appropriate adult for juveniles came to the police station was 2 hours 23 minutes with a median of 84 minutes. Where the appropriate adult was a social worker it took longer.
[68] Formerly Annex C, para.2.
[69] Recommendation 72 based on Runciman Report, paras 81–86, pp.42–44.
[70] Originally available from the Home Office.

- That appropriate adults should be entitled to confidential interviews with suspects and that the relationship with the suspect should therefore be covered by legal privilege.[71]

- That the Codes should reflect guidance on which persons are suitable to play the role of appropriate adult in respect of particular suspects.

- That a clear definition of the role of appropriate adult be included in the Codes.

- The provision of guidance through leaflets, posters in police stations, incorporation into police training and guidance for professionals and others likely to act in this role.

- The establishment of local appropriate adult panels.

6–63   The Joint Home Office/Cabinet Office Review of PACE in its report published in November 2002 echoed the Runciman proposals. The problem, it said (p.28), was that neither PACE nor the Codes established a consistent scheme for recruitment and use of appropriate adults. ("They are often in very limited supply and may not be appropriately informed or trained."(*ibid.*).) Delay in getting an appropriate adult led to delays in interviewing detained persons and the whole custody process. Serious attention needed to be given to the issue. The "Options proposed" were to establish a national policy for securing of an effective service including guidance on roles and competencies and devising a notice for appropriate adults to read on arrival at the police station explaining their role and responsibility. The Review supported both proposals. A consistent approach based on local good practice should be extended nationally by 2004. A notice covering roles and responsibilities was already under development and was expected to be in use before the end of 2002.

6–64   The task of being an appropriate adult can, on occasion, be mentally or psychologically very difficult. It has been held that the police owe no duty toward an appropriate adult to take care to protect him or her from mental trauma in performing the role—see *Leach v Chief Constable of Gloucestershire Constabulary*.[72] Leach was the appropriate adult for Fred West who had been charged with horrific multiple murders.

See generally see Littlechild, "Reassessing the Role of the Appropriate Adult" [1995] Crim.L.R. 540; Palmer, "Still vulnerable after all these years" [1996] Crim.L.R. 633 at 639–644; Palmer, "The appropriate adult", *Legal Action*, May 1996, p.6; Hodgson, "Vulnerable suspects and the Appropriate Adult" [1997] Crim.L.R. 785–795. For a consideration of the implications for the role of appro-

---

[71] What is said to an appropriate adult can at present be used in evidence against the suspect unless the court excludes the evidence under s.78. In *Brown*, unreported, Case No.9807320/Y2, May 21, 1999 the Court of Appeal held that the confession was admissible even though the defendant had confessed to the social worker acting as appropriate adult thinking that it was a "protected" situation after the conclusion of the formal interview by the police.
[72] [1999] 1 All E.R. 215, CA.

priate adult of cautions under the Crime and Disorder Act see Williams, "The Crime and Disorder Act 1998: Conflicting Roles for the Appropriate Adult" [2000] Crim.L.R. 911.

Interviews in police stations: s.12

Code C, s.12 makes detailed provisions for the physical circumstances in which suspects must be questioned.[73]   **6–65**

In any period of 24 hours the suspect is supposed to be given eight hours of rest, free from questioning, travel or other interruptions (para.12.2). This should normally be at night[74] or other appropriate time which takes account of when the suspect last slept or rested.[75] For someone who comes to the police station as a volunteer, the period of time is measured from their arrival there, not from the time of arrest.

Code C, para.12.2[76] specifies three kinds of reasons justifying interruption or delay of the rest period. The first is where there are reasonable grounds for believing that there would otherwise be a risk of harm to persons or serious loss of or damage to, property or delay in the release of the individual or that it would "otherwise prejudice the outcome of the investigation" (para.12.2(a)). The second is where such interruption or delay is at the request of the suspect, the appropriate adult or a legal representative. The third is to comply with the duty to carry out reviews of the need for further detention or to give the suspect medical treatment (para.12.2(b), (c)).

The custody officer, in consultation with the officer in charge of the case and appropriate health care professionals as necessary, must assess whether a detained person is fit to be interviewed. Paragraph 12.3 as redrafted in 2003 says that this means considering the risks to the suspect's phsyical and mental state if the interview takes place and determining what safeguards need to be put in place. As has been seen, a new Annex G headed Fitness to be Interviewed was added to Code C in the 2003 revision. The custody officer should not allow a person to be interviewed at a time when he considers that it would cause significant harm to the suspect's physical or mental state (para.12.3).   **6–66**

Interviews in a police station are supposed to take place in an interview room (which must be adequately heated, lit and ventilated (para.12.4)), although in *Dures*[77] the Court of Appeal allowed an interview conducted in the cells to be admitted in evidence even though the rules about the tape recording of interviews and contemporaneous notes had been broken. The suspect should not be required to stand (para.12.6[78]). The interviewing officers should identify themselves and

---

[73] For comments on the scheme of the Code and a suggestion that the Code's interview safeguards do not sufficiently address the problem of unreliability see Fenwick, "Confessions, Recording Rules and Miscarriages of Justice: A Mistaken Emphasis?" [1993] Crim.L.R. 174.

[74] For a case in which breach of this provision resulted in a conviction being quashed see *R. v Trussler (Barry)* [1988] Crim.L.R. 446, Crown Ct.

[75] para.12.2 sets out the various circumstances in which sleep may be interrupted or delayed.

[76] Redrafted in 2003.

[77] (1997) 2 Cr.App.R. 247, CA.

[78] Formerly para.12.5.

anyone else present—save that in terrorism cases or other cases potentially creating danger, each officer should identify himself by warrant or other identification number rather than by name (paras 12.7 and 2.6A[79]). In addition to meal breaks there should also be short breaks for refreshment approximately every two hours unless this would prejudice the investigation (para.12.8[80]).

Taking a statement: s.12 and Annex D

6–67   Traditionally, at the end of the process of relatively informal questioning, police officers prepare, or help the person being interviewed to prepare, a "statement". This is a summary of the salient features of the interview. Code C sets out in Annex D the procedure for the taking of such "written statements under caution" but the Notes for Guidance do also say that if the interview has been contemporaneously recorded and the record has been signed by the person interviewed or the interview has been tape recorded, there is normally no need also for a statement under caution. In those circumstances such a statement should only be taken at the request of the person concerned (Code C, Note 12A). This would normally be the case, but if Annex D applies, the suspect should always be invited to write down himself what he wants to say (Annex D, para.1). The terms of the initial statement the suspect will be asked to write depends on which caution is applicable—the former or the new one depending on whether he has been allowed an opportunity to receive legal advice. Thus, normally before writing the statement, he should be asked to write down and sign the following: "I make this statement of my own free will. I understand that I need not say anything but that it may harm my defence if I do not mention when questioned something which I later rely on in court. This statement may be given in evidence." If, however, he has asked for but has not yet been allowed an opportunity to receive legal advice, the statement would be: "I make this statement of my own free will. I understand that I do not have to say anything. This statement may be given in evidence." (Annex D, paras 2–4.)

6–68   He should be allowed to write his statement without any prompting except that a police officer or interviewer may indicate to him which matters are material or question any ambiguity in the statement (Annex D, para.5). If the suspect wishes the officer to write it for him he must so signify in written form ("I . . . wish to make a statement. I want someone to write down what I say . . .") and that he has been cautioned in one or other form as above (Annex D(b) paras 7–9).

The rules in Annex D state specifically that if a police officer writes the statement, he "must take down the exact words spoken by the person making [the statement]" and "must not edit or paraphrase it" (para.10[81]). Faithful compliance with this admonition plainly prohibits the traditional practice of police officers of putting suspects' statements into a coherent, tidy form.

When the writing of the statement is finished, the person whose statement it is must be asked to read it and to make any corrections he wishes. He should then

---

[79] Formerly para.12.6.
[80] Formerly para.12.7.
[81] Formerly para.5.

be asked to sign that he has read the statement, that he has been allowed to make corrections, that the statement is true and that he has made it of his own free will. If he cannot read or refuses to do so, the senior officer present should read it to him and ask whether he wishes to make any corrections and to sign. He should then certify on the statement that this is what has occurred (paras 11 and 12[82]).

Interpreters: s.13

The Administrative Directions accompanying the former Judges' Rules referred   **6–69**
to statements made by those who could not speak English being translated by an interpreter. But they did not positively require an interpreter to be called. Code C remedied this deficiency. It states (para.13.2) that where (a) someone has difficulty in understanding English, (b) the interviewing officer does not speak the relevant language and (c) the person wants an interpreter, a person may only be interviewed without one if the matter is urgent (as defined in paras 11.1 or 11.18–20).

An interpreter called to assist a person with the obtaining of legal advice should not be a police officer. In other situations he can be if the person being questioned, and the appropriate adult, agrees in writing or the interview is tape recorded or visually recorded in accordance with Codes E or F (para.13.9).

Interpreters are to be provided at public expense (and all reasonable steps must be made so to inform the person concerned) (para.13.8).

Interpreting is not easy and the Home Office has accepted that the responsibil-   **6–70**
ity for finding competent interpreters basically lies with the police. The original Home Office Circular on PACE (para.1–11, n.23 above, paras 61–62) stated that chief officers should ensure that the police have access to persons whose proficiency in interpretation is sufficiently high to enable them to carry out the task efficiently. A new introductory sentence to the section on interpreters in Code C, as revised in 2003, says, "Chief officers are responsible for making sure appropriate arrangements are in place for provision of suitably qualified interpreters for people who are deaf or do not understand English" (para.13.1). The interpreter must be able to understand, speak, read and write both English and the other language to a standard that includes the specialised terms and procedures encountered in police interviews (such as "caution", "bail", etc.). He must be familiar with both cultural backgrounds and be able to translate and interpret accurately. He must also act in an impartial professional manner and respect confidentiality. Local Community Relations Councils may be able to provide lists of suitable interpreters.

The Joint Home Office/Cabinet Office Review of PACE said (p.33) that the qualifications required of interpreters by the police were quite extensive: "to be included on the projected ACPO centrally approved national register of interpreters, interpreters must hold a diploma in Public Service Interpreting, be approved by ACPO and be security vetted". The Review said it supported the ACPO initiative of creating a national register of interpreters. The 2004 revision

---

[82] Formerly paras 6 and 7.

of Code C added to para.13.1 that whenever possible they should be drawn from the National Register of Public Service Interpreters (NRPSI).

6–71   The interpreter should take down a note of the interview in the language of the suspect and should certify its accuracy. Enough time must be allowed by the interviewing officer for a note to be made of each question and answer. The person interviewed should be given a chance of reading it or having it read to him and sign it as accurate or to indicate in what respects he considers it to be inaccurate (Code C, para.13.3). If the suspect makes a statement to a police officer or other police staff in a language other than English, the interpreter should take it down in that language, the person who made it should sign the statement and it should be translated into English in due course (para.13.4).

For a case in which the failure to comply with this requirement led to the exclusion of interviews admitting involvement in importation of £2.5 million worth of cannabis see *Bassil and Mouffareg*.[83] See also the decision of the Strasbourg Court in *Cuscani v UK*.[84]

Questioning of deaf persons: s.13

6–72   The Code also provides that where there is a doubt as to a person's hearing, he should be treated as deaf (para.1.6). No interview should take place without an interpreter save in urgent cases or where paras 11.18–11.20 apply or if he agrees in writing (para.13.5). If the appropriate adult is deaf, an interpreter should be called, unless he agrees in writing that the interview should proceed without one or it is a case for an urgent interview (para.13.6).

The original Home Office Circular on PACE (para.1–11, n.23 above, para.65) said that, except where legal advice is given, a police officer may act as an interpreter for a deaf person—providing he is sufficiently proficient to have reached a recognised standard in interpreting. A police officer should obviously not act as interpreter if the deaf person has expressed a wish for an independent interpreter. The local authority's Social Services Department may be able to supply lists of interpreters who have the necessary skills and experience to act as interpreters for the deaf.

6–73   In *Clarke (Raymond Maurice)*[85] the Court of Appeal declined to grant leave to appeal to a defendant who turned out to have a severe hearing defect, although this had not been appreciated by the officer who questioned him. The police evidence was that he had in effect admitted the charge of attempted theft. The defence case was that no such conversation had taken place. The defence tried to have the conversation excluded on the ground that there had been a breach of the rule that a deaf person must not be interviewed without an interpreter being present. The trial judge had admitted the evidence. The Court of Appeal said that it could not be shown that there was a breach of the Code provision if the police officers were not aware of the fact that the person was deaf. A breach could only

---

[83] *Legal Action*, December 1990, p.23, Crown Ct.
[84] [2003] Crim.L.R. 50.
[85] [1989] Crim.L.R. 892, CA.

occur if the officers continued to interview a person after they realised that he was deaf or at least had doubts on the matter.

But it might still be possible to exclude the evidence under s.78 (see below) if it was established that there was in fact a serious impairment of hearing, which made it unfair to admit the evidence, or, possibly, that it was unfair to admit the evidence even though the police officer had been unaware of the dangers.

Charging of persons in custody: s.16

The suspect must be charged as soon as there is enough evidence to charge him   **6–74**
(s.37(7)). Code C, para.16.1 says that when the officer in charge of the case reasonably believes that there is sufficient evidence to provide a realistic prospect of the detained person's conviction he should, without delay, inform the custody officer.[86] It was then the responsibility of the custody officer to decide whether the suspect should be charged—or given a reprimand or warning under the Crime and Disorder Act 1998 or a caution (*ibid.,* and Note 16A). However, as has been seen, under the Criminal Justice Act 2003, charging becomes the responsibility instead of the CPS. Under this new system, to be rolled out gradually between 2004 and 2007, the decision whether to charge, and if so, to specify the charge is made by the CPS—save in minor routine cases where it is delegated to the custody officer. Also, in cases where bail is inappropriate the custody officer has the power to lay a holding charge. (The new provisions are in Sch.2 to the 2003 Act and in Guidance issued by the DPP—see Appendix 1 below and, generally, paras 4–17—4–21, 4–24—4–29 above.)

When the new system is fully operational, if the matter of the charge is referred   **6–75**
to the CPS and the suspect has been bailed from the police station, he will generally receive the charge in the form of a written communication from the police. Section 29 of the Criminal Justice Act 2003 provides for "a public prosecutor"[87] to institute criminal proceedings by issuing a written charge accompanied by a second document ("a requisition") which requires the person to appear before a magistrates' court to answer the written charge. The written charge and the requisition must be served on the person named. (Rules under the Magistrates' Courts Act 1980, s.144 will govern the form, content, recording, authentication and service of written charges or requisitions.[88])

There will still be many cases however when the suspect is charged in person in the police station. The procedure for charging is dealt with in s.16 of the Code. The suspect must be cautioned (in terms of either the new or the former caution, depending on whether he has asked for and been allowed an opportunity to receive legal advice—see Code C, para.16.2 and Annex C) and given a written

---

[86] The reference to a realistic prospect of conviction was introduced in the 2003 revision.

[87] "Public prosecutor" is defined in the Act to include not only the DPP and anyone authorised by him, but a police force, the Commissioners of Inland Revenue, the Commissioners of Customs and Excise and anyone authorised by any of them or by order made by any Secretary of State to institute criminal proceedings—s.29(5). At the time of writing s.29 was not in force even in the police force areas where the DPP's Guidance on charging had been introduced.

[88] Criminal Justice Act 2003, s.30(1). At the time of writing these rules had not been made.

statement of the particulars of the charge, the name of the officer in the case,[89] of the police station and the police reference number. If the person is a juvenile or is mentally disordered or otherwise mentally vulnerable, the notice should be given to the appropriate adult (para.16.3).

6–76   As seen above, if an officer or an approved civilian investigating officer wants to tell a suspect who has been charged about someone else's statement, he must simply show him a copy of the statement or of the record of the interview. Nothing shall be done or said to invite any reply or comment, save that he should be cautioned, "You do not have to say anything unless you wish to do so, but what you say may be given in evidence", and be reminded of the right to legal advice (para.16.4).

Questions about the offence that is the subject of charges may not normally be put after the suspect has been charged with that offence—though questioning about other offences can be put. And questions about the offence itself may be put exceptionally where it "is necessary to prevent or minimise harm or loss to some other person, or the public, to clear up an ambiguity" or where it is "in the interests of justice for the detainee to have put to them, and have an opportunity to comment on, information concerning the offence which has come to light since they were charged" (para.16.5).

Before being asked "exceptional" questions under para.16.5 he must be cautioned again in the same way as under para.16.4. A record must be made of anything the detained person says on being charged (para.16.8[90]). Questions and answers after charge must be recorded contemporaneously in full and the record signed by the person. If the person charged refuses, the officer and any third person present should sign (para.16.9[91]). If the questions are tape recorded the provisions of Code E apply. If they are recorded visually the equivalent provisions of Code F apply.

6–77   Where the person charged is a juvenile whose continued detention is authorised by the custody officer, arrangements should be made for him to be taken into care by the local authority unless he certifies that this is impracticable or, where the juvenile is 12 years old or over, no secure accommodation is available and there is a risk of serious harm from that juvenile (para.4–41 above). If it is not practicable to make such arrangements the custody officer must record the reasons and make out a certificate to be produced before the court together with the juvenile (Code C, para.16.10).

Note 16D[92] states that neither a juvenile's behaviour nor the nature of the offence with which he is charged provides grounds for the custody officer to retain him in police custody rather than to arrange for his transfer to the care of the local authority. Nor does the lack of secure accommodation make it impracticable to transfer the juvenile. "The availability of secure accommodation is only a factor in relation to a juvenile aged 12 or over when the local authority accommodation would not be adequate to protect the public from serious harm from them" (*ibid.*).

---

[89] Or in terrorism cases or other cases where to give the name would put the officer at risk, his warrant number (Code C, para.2.6A).
[90] Formerly para.16.7.
[91] Formerly para.16.8.
[92] Formerly Note 16B.

Code D: Identification

There is nothing in the Act itself about identification procedures. These rules are wholly the creature of Code D and case law. Code D does not, however, apply to all identification evidence. Thus, for instance, a witness who recognises a suspect when he meets him accidentally is not prevented from giving evidence to that effect on the ground that Code D procedures were not followed. Code D does not apply to the situation.[93] Similarly, the courts do not require Code D procedures when the witness recognises the suspect from prior knowledge of the person.[94] Also, Code D may not apply where the victim or witness identifies the suspect immediately after the crime.[95]

    6–78

    Code D (the Code of Practice on Identification of Persons) replaced a previous instruction to police (Home Office Circular No.109/1978 entitled *Identification parades and the use of photographs for identification*). Partly it repeated previous rules, partly it added to and expanded on them and partly it introduced new procedures.

    The revised versions of Code D in 1991, 1995 and 2003 added further new elements. The 2003 revision was especially important in providing that video identification should be used in preference to an identification parade if it can be arranged sooner than a parade and requiring that an identification parade must be held as soon as practicable. A letter to police forces informing them of the changes said, "It has become increasingly apparent that problems in identification parades within a reasonable time have contributed significantly to delays in processing cases and such delays can impact on the quality of evidence and compromise the whole process of justice".[96] (The Government's White Paper *Justice for All*[97] said that use of this new facility had in some instances reduced the average time taken to hold identification parades from around 10 weeks to within a week (and often faster). (The cancellation rate for video ID parades was around 5 per cent compared with 52 per cent for live ID parades.) The 2003 revision combined with the provisions of the Police Reform Act also makes it possible for

    6–79

---

[93] *Miah* [2001] EWCA Crim 2281; [2001] All E.R. (D/453 Oct.); *Thomas*, unreported, Case No.9806853/X2, November 22, 1999, CA—a police officer who had studied video pictures of robberies in progress, all apparently committed by the same person, was allowed to give evidence of recognising that person whom he had happened to see when visiting the cells in connection with a different case. Similarly, in *D v DPP*, unreported, Case No.CO/3096/96, November 18, 1996, DC, the complainant in an indecent assault case happened to see the defendant in a group of youths and shouted out "That's him". The police were called and arrested him. The victim saw him being escorted by the police and, without being prompted, said, "That's definitely him". Dismissing the appeal, the court said that the identification procedures of Code D only applied once a suspect says "It's not me".

[94] See *Ryan* [1992] Crim.L.R. 50, CA—no identification parade necessary where the witness said she recognised the defendant as the brother of a classmate she had seen at the school gates two or three times. *cf. Conway* (1991) 91 Cr.App.R. 143, CA—there should have been an identification parade where the defendant denied knowing two witnesses who claimed to know him. D had asked for a parade. The two witnesses made only a dock identification. In *Fergus* [1992] Crim.L.R. 363, CA the court said it was an "identification" not a "recognition" case.

[95] *Oscar* [1991] Crim.L.R. 778, CA. See also *Kelly* [1992] Crim.L.R. 181, CA; *Rogers* [1993] Crim.L.R. 386, CA; *Anastasiou* [1998] Crim.L.R. 67, CA; *Malashev* [1997] Crim.L.R. 587, CA.

[96] Home Office letter dated March 25, 2002.

[97] July 2002, Cm.5563, para.3.14.

civilian staff to be used in identification procedures. ("The aim is to facilitate the use of civilian staff in appropriate circumstances and maximise police resources."[98])

6–80   The first tranche of the changes made in 2002 were announced at the end of March and came into effect a few days later on April 1, 2002 under the new power in s.77 of the Criminal Justice and Police Act 2001 (see para.6–02 above). They affected only what was then s.2 (and is now s.3) of Code D—Identification by Witnesses. This was swiftly followed in June 2002 by the whole of Code D circulated as a consultation draft. This, as further amended, was approved by Parliament (with Codes B, C and E) in March 2003 to come into effect on April 1, 2003.[99] The 2004 revision of Code D made no further changes to identification procedures other than in regard to the taking of fingerprints and of non-intimate samples.

The revised Code D had several new features. One was an Introduction.[1] It states at the outset that identification procedures are designed to test the ability of the witness to identify the person they saw on the previous occasion and to provide safeguards against mistaken identification (para.1.2). It adds, "to make sure fingerprints, samples, impressions and photographs are taken, used and retained, and identification procedures carried out, only when justified and necessary for preventing, detecting or investigating crime" (para.1.7). Having explained the different methods of identification (witnesses, fingerprints, body samples, searching for bodily marks such as tatoos, etc.), the consultation draft version of the Introduction stated that it was the custody officer's responsibility to ensure that the requirements of the Act and the Codes were respected and for keeping the custody record. However, this desirable and seemingly uncontroversial, passage was dropped in the final version laid before Parliament.

6–81   The general preliminaries to Code D (s.2[2]) are broadly similar to those in Code C.

The substantive provisions of Code D begin with s.3 which in its recast form has 33 subsections, six Notes for Guidance and six annexes—Annex A on Video Identification (18 paragraphs), Annex B on Identification Parades (28 paragraphs), Annex C on Group Identification (44 paragraphs), Annex D on Confrontation by a Witness (7 paragraphs), Annex E on Showing Photographs (12 paragraphs) and Annex F on Fingerprints and Samples—Destruction and Speculative Searches (5 paragraphs).

6–82   Section 3 begins with an important rule recommended by the Runciman Royal Commission[3]: "A record shall be made of the suspect's description as first given by a potential witness" (para.3.1[4]). The record must be made before the witness takes part in any identification procedure. In *Vaughan*,[5] in quashing a conviction because there had been no note of the witness' prior description, the Court of Appeal said that this requirement was not mere bureaucracy. ("It affords the best

---

[98] Code D, March 2002, Foreword.
[99] For a critical review of the new provisions see Roberts and Clover, "Managerialism and Myopia—The Government's Consultation Draft on PACE—Code D" [2002] Crim.L.R. 873.
[1]   s.1—with the consequential result that the succeeding sections all had to be renumbered.
[2]   Formerly s.1
[3]   Recommendation 4, based on Runciman Report, para.10, p.11.
[4]   Formerly para.2.
[5]   Case No.96/6431/Y3, *Independent*, May 12, 1997 (C.S.), CA (Crim Div).

safeguard so far devised against the possibility of auto-suggestion.") But there is no requirement to make a note if it is impracticable do so.[6] It can be made in any form providing that the details can accurately be produced from it in a written form which can be provided to the suspect or his solicitor. Copies of the details given by the witness have to be made and given to the suspect or his solicitor before any identification procedure takes place (*ibid.*).

The Code provides for different ways of proceeding depending on whether the suspect (a) is known to the police and available, (b) is known to the police but not available, or (c) is not known to the police. The distinction between being known or not known to the police is not an easy one to grasp since, unless he is seen actually committing the offence, every suspect starts off by being unknown to the police and, on the other hand, at some stage every suspect who is being dealt with by the police becomes known to them. Paragraph 3.4[7] says that being "known" means "there is sufficient information known to the police to justify the arrest of a particular person for suspected involvement in the offence".[8] Being "available" means being immediately available to take part in the procedure or that they will be available within a reasonably short time and that they are willing to take part (*ibid.*). A known suspect who fails or refuses to take part in any identification procedure or who takes steps to prevent himself from being seen by a witness in such a procedure can therefore be treated as not being available.

The courts have disagreed as to whether identification procedures apply where the suspect admits he was present at the scene of the crime but denies that he was a participant. In *Chen*[9] the Court of Appeal held that Code D did not apply since the issue was not identification. In *K v DPP*[10] the Divisional Court took the opposite view. For discussion see Andy Roberts, "Questions of 'Who was there?' and 'Who did what?': The application of Code D in cases of dispute as to participation but not presence" [2003] Crim.L.R. 708–716. Roberts argues that the question "Who did what?" in relation to various persons present may indeed involve an issue as to identification but that Code D is not relevant because its procedures are directed towards circumstances in which an arrested person claims not to have been there. If the identity of the others present was known, what could be relevant, however, would be to have some other procedure enabling the witness to compare their characteristics—whether by identification parade, showing of photographic images or other means.

6–83

(a) Where the suspect is known to the police and available

The alternative procedures

The Code (paras 3.4–3.9) sets out four alternative methods to be used in cases involving disputed identification where the suspect is known to the police and available: "video identification" where the witness is shown moving images of

6–84

---

[6] *El Hannachi, Conney, Ward and Tanswell* [1998] 2 Cr.App.R.266; [1998] Crim.L.R. 881, CA. (Witness taken by the police in haste after an affray to see if she could identify any of the culprits.)
[7] Formerly Note 2E.
[8] For discussion see *Popat* (1998) 2 Cr.App.R. 208; [1998] Crim.L.R. 825, CA, *per* Hobhhouse L.J.
[9] [2001] EWCA 885; (2001) 5 *Archbold News* 3.
[10] [2003] EWHC Admin 351.

the known suspect with images of other people who resemble the suspect; an "identification parade", where the witness is shown a line-up consisting of the suspect and others who resemble him; a "group identification" where the witness sees the suspect in an informal group of people. There is also "confrontation" where the suspect is directly confronted by the witness (para.3.23).

Responsibility for the procedure

6–85   The arrangements for and the conduct of any of these identification procedures is normally the responsibility of an officer not below the rank of inspector (para.3.11). The exception is when the custody officer or some other officer performs the function (under para.3.19) because it is proposed to hold an identification procedure later and an inspector is not available to act as the "identification officer" (I.O.). The I.O. must be someone who is not involved in the investigation (para.3.11). But the I.O. may now allow another officer or civilian support staff (para.2.21) *i.e.* a civilian, "to make arrangements for, and to conduct" any of the above-mentioned identification procedures (para.3.11). The Code (paras 2.20–2.21) distinguishes between "designated persons", designated under the Police Reform Act 2002, Pt 4 with specified powers and duties of police officers and "civilian support staff who are not designated persons" but who either are employed by a police authority and are under the control and direction of the Chief Constable or are employed by a contractor with whom the police have contracted for services in regard to persons in custody. In regard to both categories of civilian support staff the I.O. remains responsible "for making sure that the procedure and tasks are carried out correctly" (para.2.21). The courts may have to decide at what point delegation to civilian support staff has gone too far.

Which procedure?

6–86   Prior to 1995, Code D provided that an identification parade had to be held "if the suspect asks for one and it is practicable to hold one".[11] A parade could also be held if the officer in charge thought it would be useful. In the 1995 revised Code, the first part of para.2.3 was changed to the following: "Whenever a suspect disputes an identification, an identification parade *shall be held*[12] if the suspect consents[13] unless paras 2.4 or 2.7 or 2.10 apply". (Paragraph 2.4 dealt with impracticability because of the suspect's unusual appearance; para.2.7 permitted a group identification in certain circumstances; para.2.10 permitted the witness to be shown a video film of the suspect in certain circumstances.)

The significant difference in the 1995 rule was that the criterion was no longer whether the suspect asked for a parade. Read literally the 1995 rule said that, pro-

[11] Previously para.2.3.
[12] Emphasis supplied.
[13] If consent is required it must be real—see *Harley*, unreported, Case No.99/4468/W4, February 22, 2000, CA. The suspect's lawyer asked for a postponement of the parade to allow his client's facial injuries to heal. The inspector in charge of the parade said that if the suspect did not consent to a parade right away he would organise a confrontation, if necessary by force. The suspect then agreed. Allowing the appeal, the Court held that the consent had not been valid.

viding he consented, a parade had to be held in cases of disputed identification if it was practicable unless a group identification or video film were thought in the circumstances to be more appropriate.

The courts vacillated on the question of whether a literal reading was the cor-   **6–87**
rect one. At first the Court of Appeal held that it was.[14] Then in *Popat* the Court of Appeal said it was not. The court preferred a purposive to a literal interpretation of para.2.3.[15] An identification parade was not required if it would serve no useful purpose. However, in *Forbes*[16] a differently constituted Court of Appeal said that *Popat* was inconsistent with *Brown* and that it preferred *Brown* ("The Code is plainly mandatory. The judgment in *Popat* amounts to a rewriting of the Code."). The court said that in *Popat* there was confusion of two issues. One was whether there had been a breach of para.2.3. The other was whether the evidence should be excluded under s.78.[17] The issue was referred back to the Court of Appeal by the Criminal Cases Review Commission and in July 1999 in *Popat (No.2)*[18] the Court of Appeal said that it preferred *Popat* to *Forbes*.

In December 2000 the House of Lords overruled the Court of Appeal. Deciding   **6–88**
the appeal in *Forbes*, the Law Lords unanimously held that the Court of Appeal in *Popat* and *Popat (No.2)* was wrong and that the original view that the requirement of an identification parade was mandatory was correct.[19] Giving judgment on behalf of the five law lords, Lord Bingham said that Code D was a practical document giving police officers clear instructions. It was not old-fashioned literalism but sound interpretation to read the Code as meaning what it said. To replace an apparently hard-edged mandatory obligation by an obviously difficult judgmental decision was bound to produce challenges in the courts and resulting appeals. Neither the language of Code D nor the decided cases supported the distinction drawn in *Popat* between a suspect being produced by the police to a witness rather than by a witness to the police. (In regard to the actual case, the House of Lords held that although there should have been an identification parade, the identification evidence in the case had been properly admitted in evidence.)

It was felt in some quarters that the mandatory requirement of an identification parade put unreasonable burdens on the police.[20] The view began to be expressed that identification parades were not as useful as the rule suggested and that video libraries could do the job better.[21] The suspect is photographed in front of a neutral background. The photograph is then transferred into the computer system which holds a vast and growing database of digital photos taken in the same way. The suspect and his solicitor are shown a range of photographs similar to the

---

[14] *Brown* [1991] Crim.L.R. 212, CA; *Conway* (1990) 91 Cr.App.R. 143, CA; *Graham* [1994] Crim.L.R. 212, CA; *McMath* [1997] Crim.L.R. 586, CA; *Wait* [1998] Crim.L.R. 68, CA.

[15] *Popat*, n.8 above. For decisions to like effect see *Hickin* [1996] Crim.L.R. 584, CA; *Anastasiou* [1998] Crim.L.R. 67, CA; *El-Hannachi* [1998] 2 Cr.App.R.266, CA; *Bell* [1998] Crim.L.R. 879, CA.

[16] (1999) 2 Cr.App.R. 501, CA.

[17] For identification evidence cases on s.78 see paras 8–65 and 8–66 below.

[18] (2000) 1 Cr.App.R. 387; [2000] Crim.L.R. 54, CA.

[19] [2001] 1 A.C. 473; [2001] 1 All E.R. 686, HL.

[20] See Roberts, "Does Code D Impose an Unrealistic Burden on the System of Summary Justice?" (2001) 165 J.P. 756 and Conner, "*Forbes*: Have all the issues been properly identified?" (2001) 165 J.P. 839.

[21] See, for instance, Tinsley, "Even better than the real thing? The case for reform of identification procedures" [2001] 5 Jrnl.of Ev. and Proof 99–110.

suspect and are asked to agree on eight or nine to be used in the video film. The suspect decides where he wishes to be in the film. A composite video is then made. Each photograph is shown to the witness for the same period of time.

6–89   The view that video identification is preferable to identity parades has now prevailed. In the 2003 revision, para.3.12 says that whenever a suspect disputes being the person the witness claims to have seen, an identification *procedure*[22] (not, as before, "identification parade") shall be held unless it is not practicable or it would secure no useful purpose. The courts have been quite strict as regards what "not practical" means in this context. It does not mean merely "inconvenient".[23] An identification procedure can also be held if the I.O. "considers that it would be useful" (para.3.13). When an identification procedure is required to be held, "in the interests of fairness to suspects and witnesses, it must be held as soon as practicable" (para.3.11).

New para.3.12 made a major change. Former para.2.4 said that a parade need not be held if the I.O. thought that, whether because of his unusual appearance or for some other reason, it would not be practicable to assemble sufficient persons who resembled the suspect to make a parade fair. Paragraph 3.12 expands this concept considerably. It provides that an identification procedure need not be held if "it would serve no useful purpose in proving or disproving whether the suspect was involved in committing the offence". An example given is where it is not in dispute that the suspect is already well known to the witness.[24] Another would be where there is no reasonable possibility that a witness would be able to make an identification. No doubt a body of case law will develop over the years as to what other circumstances are covered by the phrase "it would serve no useful purpose".[25]

6–90   The Consultation draft of Code D issued in June 2002 (para.3.15) said that if it was proposed to hold an identification procedure the suspect had to be offered either a video identification or a parade unless the officer in charge of the case considered that in the particular circumstances a group identification would be more satisfactory. In the equivalent provision in the 2003 revised version, however, this was changed significantly to, "the suspect shall *initially* be offered a video identification unless: (a) a video identification is not practicable; or (b) an identification parade is both practicable and more suitable than a video identification; or (c) para.3.16 [group identification] applies" (para.3.14, emphasis supplied). The decision as to which method to use is made by the officer in charge of the case after consulting with the I.O. as to which is "the most suitable and practicable in the particular case" (para.3.14). Thus a parade may not be practi-

---

[22] Emphasis supplied.

[23] See *Gaynor* [1988] Crim.L.R. 242; *Britton and Richards* [1989] Crim.L.R. 144; *Ladlow, Moss, Green and Jackson* [1989] Crim.L.R. 219, DC; *Conway* (1990) Cr.App.R. 143, CA; [1990] Crim.L.R. 402, CA; *Brown* [1991] Crim.L.R. 368, CA; *Graham* [1994] Crim.L.R. 212, CA; *Rutherford and Palmer* (1994) 98 Cr.App.R. 191, CA; *Tomkinson v DPP* [1995] Crim.L.R. 60, DC.

[24] For exchanges in *Archbold News* disputing the meaning of the new provisions see Wolchover and Heaton-Armstrong, "Farewell to *Forbes*", Issue 7, 2003, p.4; Bogan, "*Forbes* Alive and Well", Issue 9, 2003, p.5; Wolchover and Heaton-Armstrong, "A reply to *Forbes* Alive and Well", Issue 9, 2003, p.6; and English, "Letter to Editor", Issue 1, 2004, p.9.

[25] Code D, para.3.12.

cable because of factors relating to the witnesses—such as their number, state of health, availability and travelling requirements. A video identification would normally be more suitable if it could be completed sooner than a parade (*ibid.*).

A suspect who refuses the procedure first offered must be asked for his reasons **6–91** for so doing. He can seek advice from a solicitor and/or an appropriate adult. The suspect, the solicitor or the appropriate adult can make representations as to why another procedure should be used instead. A record should be made of the reasons for refusal and of any such representations. After considering the reasons and any representations, the I.O. makes his decision as to whether to accept the alternative suggestion. If he decides that it is not suitable and practicable to offer an alternative identification procedure, he must record the reasons for the decision (para.3.15).

If the suspect refuses or fails to take part in a video identification, parade or group identification, the I.O. has discretion to arrange for a covert video using moving or still pictures or covert group identification (para.3.21). Failing any other alternative, he can arrange for a confrontation (para.3.23). This means that the suspect must be prepared to take part in an identification procedure or face the alternative of an inferior method of identification,

Notice to the suspect

Before a video identification, an identification parade or a group identification is **6–92** arranged, the suspect must be given certain basic information orally including: the purpose of the procedure in question; his entitlement to free legal advice; the relevant procedure including the right to have a solicitor present; that he does not have to take part; whether for the purposes of video identification, images of the suspect have already been taken and, if so, that they may help by providing further images which can be used instead; any special arrangements for juveniles or mentally disordered or vulnerable people; that refusal to take part in an identification procedure can be brought to the court's attention at a trial and that the police can then proceed covertly to try to get an identification; that any attempt significantly to alter one's appearance before an identification procedure can be brought to the court's attention; whether the witness has been shown a photograph or identikit likeness of the suspect before the identity of the suspect became known; and that the suspect or his solicitor will be given details of the witness' first description of the suspect (para.3.17[26]). He must also be given a written notice with this information and be asked to sign a copy indicating whether he is willing to co-operate in the making of a video film, or to take part in a parade or group identification (para.3.18[27]).

If the I.O. and the officer in charge of the case have reasonable grounds to sus- **6–93** pect that the provision of such information in advance might lead the suspect to "take steps to avoid being seen by a witness in any identification procedure", the I.O. can arrange for images of the suspect to be obtained for use in a video film before the information and notice is given (para.3.20). It was suggested that this

---

[26] Formerly para.2.15.
[27] Formerly para.2.16.

provision could be open to challenge under Art.6 of the ECHR.[28] The suggestion proved prescient as in July 2003 the European Court of Human Rights held that taking video film of the suspect without his knowledge or consent could amount to a breach of the Convention—though of Art.8 (right to privacy) rather than Art.6 (right to a fair trial). The applicant P had been arrested in connection with armed robberies. He was released on bail pending the holding of an identification parade. But he failed to show up for that and for further appointments for an ID parade. The police then obtained authority under the then prevailing Home Office Guidelines (1984) to take video film of him covertly. He was taken to the police station where he again refused to take part in a parade. But he was covertly filmed by a video camera that had been adjusted so that it pointed at the custody suite. P was not told about the filming, he therefore did not give his consent, did not have an opportunity to view and comment on the film, nor could he have a solicitor do so. The PACE rules had not been complied with. Even though P had had a fair trial his right to protection of his privacy had been infringed.[29]

If the identity of the suspect is known to the police and the suspect is available to take part in an identification procedure, a witness must not be shown photographs or photofit or identikit likenesses (para.3.3).

(b) Where the suspect is known but is not available

6–94 Where a known suspect is not available for any reason, para.3.21 states that the I.O. has the discretion to organise a video identification in accordance with the provisions for covert identification (Annex A), group identification (Note 3D) and showing photographs to the public (para.3.28 and Note 3D).

(c) Where the identity of the suspect is not known

6–95 Where the suspect is not known to the police, the witness can be taken to a particular neighbourhood or place to see whether he can identify the person he said he saw (para.3.2[30]). However, if practicable, a record should first be made of any description of the suspect given by the witness (para.3.2(a)[31]).

Care must be taken "not to direct the witness' attention to anyone unless . . . this cannot be avoided" (para.3.2(b)[32]). But the 2003 version added that this does not prevent a witness being asked to look carefully or to look towards a group or in a particular direction if this appears to be necessary (*ibid.*, see also Note 3F). If there is more than one witness, they should, if possible, not be taken there together (para.3.2(c)). Once there is sufficient information to justify an arrest,

---

[28] "The 2002 Order, in short, authorises the police, if they have the requisite belief, to withhold the notice of the suspect's rights for an unspecified amount of time, in order to obtain images that a suspect has not consented to give, to carry out a procedure that the suspect has no information about, in the absence of legal advice and other support that the suspect has not been told he is entitled to. This must be wide open to numerous challenges under our domestic law of evidence and under Art.6 of the European Convention on Human Rights." (Clover and Roberts, "Short-sighted or forward looking?", (2002) New L.J. 870 at 871).
[29] *Perry v United Kingdom* (2004) 39 E.H.R.R. 3.
[30] Formerly para.2.17.
[31] Formerly para.2.17.
[32] Formerly para.2.17 which did not have the caveat "unless . . . this cannot be avoided".

formal identification procedures must be used for any other witnesses (para.3.2(d)). A proper record must be made of the event—*i.e.* date, time and place, the nature of any identification made, the circumstances and conditions, and anything said by the witness or the suspect about the identification or the conduct of the procedure (para.3.2(e)).[33]

Photographs, photofits, identikits or similar pictures can only be shown to the witness if the identity of the suspect is not known to the police or he is not available to take part in an identification procedure (para.3.3). If that is the case the showing of such pictures to the witness must follow the procedure set out in Annex E[34] to Code D.

6–96

The witness must be shown not less than 12 photographs at a time (Annex E, para.4). So far as practicable they should be of a similar type (*ibid.*). He should not be prompted in any way (para.5).

If the witness makes a positive identification from photographs, unless that person is otherwise eliminated from enquiries or is not available or there is no dispute about the identification of the suspect, that witness and any other witnesses should be asked to attend a video identification or identification parade or group identification (para.6). At any such subsequent procedure the suspect or his solicitor must be told that the witness(es) have previously been shown photographs or identikit pictures (para.9).

The photographs used should be numbered and a separate photograph should be made of the frame or part of the album from which the witness made the identification (para.10).

(d) Documentation

A record must be made on the relevant form of the identification procedure used (para.3.25[35]). If the I.O. considers that it is not practicable to hold a video identification or identification parade when either are requested by the suspect, the reasons must be recorded and explained to the suspect (para.3.26[36]). A record also has to be made of a suspect's failure or refusal to co-operate in an identification procedure.

6–97

(e) Showing films and photographs of incidents and information released to the media

New provisions in the 1995 revision of Code D permitted the showing of video films or photographs to police officers and to the public at large through the national or local media (now para.3.28[37]). But when such material is shown to potential witnesses (including police officers), it should be shown individually[38]

6–98

---

[33] This new rule responds to Mitchell J.'s plea in *Hickin* [1996] Crim.L.R. 584, CA, echoed in Professor Diane Birch's commentary on the case at 586, that further attention should be given in the Code to informal identification procedures. For criticism of this form of identification evidence see Wolchover, "Ending the farce of staged street-identification" (2004) 3 *Archbold News* 5.

[34] Formerly Annex D.

[35] Formerly para.2.19.

[36] Formerly para.2.20.

[37] Formerly para.2.21A.

[38] See *Caldwell and Dixon* (1994) 99 Cr.App.R. 73; [1993] Crim.L.R. 863, CA.

and, so far as possible, in accordance with the rules for video identification if the suspect is known (Annex A) or identification by photographs if the suspect is not known (Annex E). Where there is a broadcast or publication of such material, a copy of the material released to the media should be made and retained and the suspect or his solicitor should be allowed to view such material before any identification procedure is carried out providing this is practicable and would not unreasonably delay the investigation. Any witness must be asked whether he has seen any broadcast or published film or photograph and any reply must be recorded (para.3.29[39]).

(f) Destruction and retention of photographs and images taken or used in identification procedures

6–99   Photographs and images of suspects detained at police stations may be retained provided they are only used or disclosed for purposes related to the prevention or detection of crime, the investigation of offences or the conduct of prosecutions whether inside or outside the UK (s.64A of PACE inserted by the Anti-terrorism, Crime and Security Act 2001, s.92; see para.5–124 above).

But s.64A does not apply to photographs and images of suspects who were not detained at police stations nor to moving images of suspects whether or not they have been detained which are taken for the purposes of, or in connection with, the identification procedures. Paragraph 3.31 of revised Code D provides that such photographs and images (and the negatives and all copies) taken for the purposes of, or in connection with, the identification procedures must be destroyed unless the suspect (a) is charged with (or informed that they may be prosecuted for) a recordable offence; (b) is prosecuted for a recordable offence; (c) is cautioned for a recordable offence or given a warning or reprimand for a recordable offence under the Crime and Disorder Act 1998; or (d) gives informed consent in writing for the photograph or image to be retained. The suspect must be given an opportunity to witness the destruction or to have a certificate confirming such destruction providing that a request for one or the other is made within five days of being informed that the destruction is required (para.3.32).

THE FOUR BASIC IDENTIFICATION PROCEDURES

Video identification (Code D, Annex A)

6–100   Code D (para.3.6) states that "video identifications must be carried out in accordance with Annex A". Annex A relates to a video made after the offence.

The video film must include the suspect and at least 8 other people who so far as possible resemble him, or 12 if there are 2 suspects of roughly similar appearance in the film (para.2). The suspect and other persons should, so far as possible, be

---

[39] Formerly para.2.21B.

filmed in the same positions or carrying out the same activity (para.3). They should show the suspect and others under identical conditions unless the I.O. reasonably believes that, because of the suspect's failure or refusal to co-operate or other reasons, it is not practicable for the conditions to be identical or that any difference in the conditions is immaterial (*ibid.*[40]). In that case the reasons why identical conditions are not practicable must be recorded (para.4). The suspect and his solicitor, friend or appropriate adult must be given a chance to see the film before it is shown to witnesses, to make any objections (para.7). If practicable, steps should be taken to remove the ground for any reasonable objections. This is so even when the video has been made covertly because the suspect refused to take part in any ID procedure. Before the images are shown, the suspect or his solicitor must be provided with details of the first description of the suspect by any witness attending the showing (para.8). The suspect cannot be present when the film is shown to witnesses but his solicitor can and he (or, if he is unrepresented, the suspect) must be given notice of the time and place of such showings (para.9). If there is no representative of the suspect present the viewing should be recorded on video (*ibid.*).

Where a broadcast or publication is made, the suspect or his solicitor must be allowed to view any material released to the media by the police, unless this is impracticable or it would unreasonably delay the investigation (para.8).　　**6–101**

Witnesses may not communicate with each other before viewing the film nor may they discuss the matter with the I.O. (para.10). Only one witness may see the film at a time (para.11). He should not be asked to make an identification until he has seen the film at least twice (para.12).

The I.O. must be careful not to direct the witness' attention to any one individual on the film or to give any other indication of the suspect's identity (para.13).

A record must be made of the names (if known) of all those participating in or seeing the set of images (para.17). The record should also include anything said by the witness about any identification or the conduct of the procedure (para.18).　　**6 102**

Video films will increasingly be available that were made before or during the offence by CCTV cameras placed on buildings, in shops and pubs and other premises. This form of video was the subject of the Court of Appeal's decision in the case of *Jones, Dowling, Jones and Brown*.[41] The offence involved an attack by a group of assailants in a pub. The victim was at first unable to name any of the attackers. The doorman said that one of the attackers was known to him by sight. Some weeks later, video equipment was installed in the pub. As a result, the doorman picked out from the video film the person known to him who was then named by the police. The police also recognised three other persons. The video was then shown to the victim who picked out the same four persons. These four were convicted of the offence. The Court of Appeal rejected the argument that once the police had a name they should have employed one of the methods of identification listed in Code D. The prosecution argued that Code D only came into play when there was a dispute over identification and no such dispute could arise until the evidence had been challenged, or not accepted by the suspect. Until then the police were free to obtain other forms of identification evidence. The

[40] This was first added in 2002.
[41] *The Times*, January 13, 1994, CA.

court said that this submission was correct. There was no element of unfairness. The video film was equivalent to a street identification or to an informal group identification. The appeal showed that the modern practice of installing video cameras which routinely filmed places was a tool available to investigating police officers—and that their use was not governed by the express terms of Code D. But where the film was made after the offence the process involved three stages. First, did the witness identify a person present when the film was made? Secondly, did the witness identify that person as having been present at the time of the offence? Thirdly, did the witness identify that person as having taken part in the crime itself?

6–103   Where the incident itself was recorded on video tape and it is shown to police and other witnesses, care must be taken to maximise the prospect of any recognition evidence being truly spontaneous and independent.

In *Attorney-General's Reference (No.2 of 2002)*[42] the Court of Appeal held that on the authorities there were at least four situations in which the jury can be asked to conclude that the defendant committed the offence on the basis of a photographic image from the scene of the crime:

(1)   where the photographic image is sufficiently clear the jury can compare it with the defendant sitting in the dock;

(2)   where a witness knew the defendant sufficiently well to recognise him as the offender shown in the photographic image the witness could give evidence of this—even if the image was no longer available for the jury;

(3)   where a witness who did not know the defendant had spent time viewing and analysing the photographic images from the scene, thereby acquiring special knowledge that the jury did not have, the witness could give evidence of identification based on a comparison between those images and a reasonably contemporary photograph of the defendant, provided the images and the photograph were available to the jury;

(4)   similarly, where the witness was qualified in facial mapping.

The decision confirms the role of the ad hoc expert whose expertise is based on repeated viewing of CCTV or other photographic material. (Research evidence suggests that repeated replays of images do not significantly increase the accuracy of identification but do create false levels of confidence.[43])

---

[42] [2002] EWCA 2373; [2003] Crim.L.R.192. See the valuable commentary at 193–95 and generally Elliott, "Video-Tape Evidence: The Risk of Over-Persuasion" [1998] Crim.L.R. 159.
[43] Bruce *et al*, "Face Recognition in Poor Quality Video: Evidence from Security Surveillance" (1999) 10 *Psychological Science* 243.

Identification parades (Code D, Annex B)

The detailed procedures for running an identification parade are set out in Annex   **6–104**
B to Code D. The procedure should be strictly followed. Where the judge admits
identification evidence despite breaches of the rules, he should ensure that he
deals with the breaches in his summing up.[44]

An important new rule about identification parades added to the 1995 revision
of the Code was that "a colour photograph or video film of the parade shall be
taken" (now Annex B, para.23[45]).[46] (Before that a video or photo of the parade
had to be made only where it was held without a solicitor or friend of the suspect
being present.) In the 2003 version this rule was tightened. The rule now is that
a video film of the parade must be made unless that is impracticable, in which
case a colour photograph must be taken (*ibid.*). A copy must be supplied on
request to the suspect or his solicitor.

Before the parade the suspect and his solicitor must be given copies of any
material released to the media for the purposes of identification of a suspect
unless this would not be practicable or would unduly delay the investigation
(para.3[47]). Where material has been released to the media, each witness must be
asked after the parade whether he saw any broadcast or published film or photographs relating to the offence (para.21[48]). This is in addition to the rule noted
above in relation to video identification that before the parade, the suspect and his
solicitor must be told about the first description of the suspect given by the
witness (*ibid.*, para.3[49]).

A rule introduced in 2003 is that where the suspect has unusual physical fea-   **6–105**
tures—a facial scar, tattoo, unusual hair colour—which cannot be replicated on
other members of the parade, providing the suspect and his solicitor or appropriate adult agree, steps can be taken to hide that feature—for instance by use of a
plaster or a hat (Annex B, para.10).[50] If the witness asks for the person to remove
that item he can be asked to remove it (para.19).

Under another provision introduced in 2003, if the witness makes an identification after the parade is over, the suspect and his solicitor, interpreter or friend
should be informed. Consideration should be given to whether the witness should
be given a second opportunity to identify the suspect, though it is not clear by
what procedure—presumably at a second identification parade (*ibid.*, para.20).

For an assessment of ID parades see Ian McKenzie, "Psychology and Legal
Practice: Fairness and Accuracy in Identification Parades" [1995] Crim.L.R. at
200–208.

---

[44] *Payne and Quinn* [1995] Crim.L.R. 56, CA.
[45] Formerly Annex A, para.19
[46] This was one of the recommendations of the Runciman Royal Commission—Recommendation 6
based on Runciman Report, para.10, p.11.
[47] Formerly para.2A.
[48] Formerly para.17A.
[49] Formerly para.2A.
[50] In *Marrin* [2002] EWCA Crim 251 the Court of Appeal held that it was acceptable to apply
make-up to other persons on the parade to make them look like the suspect who had distinctive
facial stubble.

Group identification (Code D, Annex C)

6–106   A group identification is where the witness sees the suspect in an informal group of people (Code D, para.3.9).

The 1995 revision included a new Annex (E) with 43 paragraphs setting out the detailed procedure for group identifications. The latest version of this Annex (now Annex C) has 44 paragraphs and is virtually identical.

A group identification can take place either with the suspect's consent and co-operation or covertly where the suspect has refused to co-operate with a parade or group identification or has failed to appear (Annex C, para.2). The previous version of Code D stated that a group identification could also be arranged where the officer in charge considers that it would be better than a parade—for instance, because of a witness' fear (1995, Code D, para.2.7). In Code D, as revised in 2003, it is still stated (para.3.16) that a group identification may initially be offered if the officer in charge of the case considers it to be more satisfactory than other procedures, but there is no longer a mention of an example of why that might be the case.

The place where it is held is a matter for the I.O. though he may take into account representations made by or on behalf of the suspect (Annex C, para.3). The place should be somewhere where people are passing by or waiting around informally—such as an escalator, a shopping centre, queues on railway or bus stations, etc. The foyer of a magistrates' court could be such a place.[51] A record by photograph or video film should be taken of the place and, if possible, of the actual identification procedure (paras 8–9).

6–107   The witness must not be told whether anyone else has made an identification (para.15). Anything said to or by the witness regarding the identification should be said in the presence and hearing of everyone present (para.15).

Witnesses must not be able to communicate with each other. They should be brought to the place one at a time. They should not see or be reminded of any photographs or description of the suspect (paras 17, 18). If two or more suspects are involved, each should be the subject of separate identification procedures though they can take place consecutively on the same occasion (para.20). Slightly different rules apply depending on whether the group being observed is moving (paras 19–24) or stationary (paras 25–29).

If the group identification is held covertly, the suspect obviously has no right to have a solicitor or friend there but the procedure adopted should so far as possible be the same as when it is done with the suspect's consent (paras 34, 35).

Group identifications should only take place in a police station for reasons of safety, security or because it is impracticable to hold them elsewhere (para.37). It can be done behind a one-way mirror or other means where the witness can see without being seen (para.38).

---

[51] *Tiplady* [1995] Crim.L.R. 651, CA.

Confrontation by a witness (Code D, Annex D[52])

If it is not possible to arrange a parade, a group identification or a video identifi-   **6–108**
cation, the suspect may simply be confronted by a witness. The Code says that a
confrontation can be used "if none of the options referred to in paras 3.5 to 3.10
or 3.21 are practicable" (Code D, para.3.23).[53] A confrontation "must be carried
out in accordance with Annex D" (*ibid.*). Such a confrontation does not require
the suspect's consent.

The confrontation should take place in the presence of the suspect's solicitor,
friend or appropriate adult unless that would cause unreasonable delay (Annex D,
para.4). The suspect should be confronted independently by each witness who
should be asked, "Is this the person?" (para.5). The confrontation should normally take place in the police station, either in a normal room or in one equipped
with a screen allowing the witness to see without being seen. But such a screen
may only be used if the suspect's solicitor, friend or appropriate adult is present
or the confrontation is recorded on video (para.6).

Voice identification

Code D, para.1.2 says of voice identification, "While this Code concentrates on   **6–109**
visual identification procedures, it does not preclude the police making use of
aural identification procedures such as a 'voice identification parade', where they
judge that appropriate." That is the only mention of the topic. In *Hersey*[54] the
Court of Appeal considered a voice identification parade. Two men had robbed a
shop in balaclava helmets. The robbery lasted some 15 minutes. The shopkeeper
W was convinced that he recognised H's voice as that of one of his long-standing
customers. At the voice identification parade 11 volunteers and H read a text. W
picked out H's voice. Another witness picked out a volunteer and a third witness
picked out no one. On appeal it was argued that the identification evidence should
have been excluded and that the trial judge had been wrong to disallow expert
evidence. The Court of Appeal held that the judge had been right to allow the evidence in and to disallow expert evidence on matters that, in this case at least, were
within the competence of the jury. The commentary in the *Criminal Law Review*
suggested (at p.283) that voice identification should be the subject of a detailed
inquiry. In the earlier case of *Deenik*[55] the Court of Appeal doubted the propriety
of applying visual identification parade safeguards to voice identification. In
Gummerson and Steadman[56] the Court of Appeal held that there was no duty to
hold a voice identification parade under Code D since the Code had no application since it related only to visual identification. The matter, it suggested, should
be dealt with by the careful application of suitably adapted *Turnbull* guidelines.[57]

---

[52] Formerly Annex C.
[53] The previous version of the Code was slightly more categorical, saying that it "may not take place
unless none of the other pocedures are practicable" (para.2.13).
[54] [1998] Crim.L.R. 281, CA.
[55] [1992] Crim.L.R. 578, CA.
[56] [1999] Crim.L.R. 680, CA.
[57] [1977] Q.B. 224, CA.

6–110   In *Roberts*[58] the Court of Appeal emphasised that the warning given to jurors in cases involving voice identification should be even more stringent than that given in cases of visual identification. The victim had been attacked by someone with a knife who had grabbed her from behind and who, when disturbed, had run away. It emerged during her evidence that she had identified him by his voice. The defence request for an adjournment to deal with this had been denied. The Court of Appeal held that the adjournment should have been allowed and that the conviction was unsafe. Identification of a stranger's voice was particularly difficult.

For more detailed comment on the scientific evidence in this area see Bull and Clifford, "Earwitness Testimony" in Heaton-Armstrong, Shepherd and Wolchover (eds.), *Analysing Witness Testimony* (Blackstone, 1999).

Dock identification[59]

6–111   Where identification is an issue, a dock identification on its own will not normally be acceptable unless the witness knows the accused.[60]

Conclusion

6–112   Identification is complicated by the ambivalence of both the police and the courts as regards identification processes which, given the conflicting values they embody, is unsurprising. On the one hand, identification procedures can be seen as a valuable tool for the police. A positive identification of the suspect by the witness strengthens the prosecution's case. On the other hand, the rules, which are far from straightforward, are there to ensure that identification evidence is as reliable as possible which means that they are there as a safeguard against miscarriages of justice. The decisions of the courts reflect this ambivalence. Sometimes they emphasise "crime control", sometimes "due process". It is not always easy to reconcile the decisions.[61]

The cases show that the police must make genuine (and, if necessary, considerable) efforts to organise the best possible method of identification. (For a case

---

[58] [2000] Crim.L.R. 183, CA.

[59] See generally, Watkin, "In the Dock—an Overview of the Decisions of the High Court on Dock Identifications in the Magistrates' Court" [2003] Crim.L.R. 463–67.

[60] *Reid* [1994] Crim.L.R. 442, CA. In *North Yorkshire Trading Standards Department v Williams, The Times*, November 22, 1994, the Divisional Court said that dock identification was generally undesirable even where the prosecution had no power to require a defendant to attend an identification parade. The principles applicable to more serious cases should apply equally to trivial cases. If this created unacceptable difficulties for the prosecution it was a matter for Parliament. The prosecution's appeal was dismissed.

[61] The point was made by Sharpe, "Identification Parades: Continuing Doubts about When and Why", *Archbold News*, March 13, 1998, p.4—contrasting *Allen* [1995] Crim.L.R. 643; *Johnson* [1996] Crim.L.R. 504; *Ryan* [1992] Crim.L.R. 187; *Rutherford and Palmer* (1994) 98 Cr.App.R. 191, CA; *Hickin* [1996] Crim.L.R. 534, CA; *Anastasiou* [1998] Crim.L.R. 67, CA; and *Wait* [1998] Crim.L.R. 68, CA. See also *Bell* [1998] Crim.L.R. 879, CA.

where the conviction was quashed because the court held that an identity parade should have been held rather than a street identification see *Nagah*.[62])

Also, the rules must be followed carefully. In *Gall*[63] the Court of Appeal **6–113** quashed a conviction because the I.O. had come into the room, looked at the parade and then spoken to a witness before he came to the parade. The judge at the first trial had excluded the witness' identification evidence but at a retrial it had been allowed in on the ground that in the view of the judge there had been no breach of the rules. The Court of Appeal disagreed. The court thought it was obvious that there had been a breach of the rule that the I.O. must have nothing to do with the parade. In *Quinn*[64] the Court of Appeal allowed an appeal and quashed a count carrying six years' imprisonment[65] on the ground that the witnesses were not asked to walk down the parade at least twice as required by para.14 of Annex A of Code D. (For more cases on failures in identification procedures see paras 8–65, 8–66 below.)

The cases show that the courts are capable of being very particular about compliance with the rules. On the other hand, sometimes they will overlook breaches of the Code rules. As the Court of Appeal said in *Grannell*,[66] "It is important that the Code be followed but what is equally important is to see whether any unfairness arose from the failure to do so" (at p.153).

In *Perry*[67] it was submitted that alleged breaches of the identification rules were violations of Arts 5, 6 and 8 of the ECHR. Dismissing the appeal, the Court of Appeal gave a warning that if the Convention was utilised by lawyers to jump on a bandwagon in suggesting that there had been violations when there had not or when the violations were amply covered by domestic law, then both the lawyers and the Human Rights Act would be brought into disrepute. In the later case of *Loveridge*[68] the Court of Appeal said that although the filming of the suspects in the precincts of a court had been a breach of Art.8 of the Convention (as well as a breach of Code D), it had not affected the fairness of the trial.

See generally, Paul Bogan, *Identification: Investigation, trial and scientific evidence* (Legal Action Group, 2004).

---

[62] (1991) 92 Cr.App.R. 344, CA. *cf. Penny* (1992) 94 Cr.App.R. 345 where in similar circumstances the Court of Appeal dismissed the appeal.
[63] (1990) 90 Cr.App.R. 64; [1989] Crim.L.R. 745, CA.
[64] [1995]] 1 Cr.App.R.480; [1995] Crim.L.R.56, CA.
[65] Other counts involving consecutive 6-year sentences were not appealed so that the sentence was in effect cut from 12 years to 6 years.
[66] (1989) 90 Cr.App.R. 149.
[67] Unreported, Case No.99/2968Y2, April 3, 2000, CA.
[68] [2001] EWCA Crim 973; [2001] 2 Cr.App.R. 29.

QUESTIONS AND ANSWERS

CODES OF PRACTICE

6–114   **What is the status of the PACE Codes of Practice?**

The Codes of Practice replaced the Judges' Rules. They are far more detailed than the Judges' Rules. They cover a far wider area. Whereas the Judges' Rules were promulgated by a committee of judges, the Codes of Practice are put out by the Home Office under the authority of the 1984 Act which requires the Home Secretary to issue them and to bring them into force by a statutory instrument approved by affirmative resolution in both Houses of Parliament. Before that occurs they must have been debated in both Houses.

The judges consulted no one before promulgating the Judges' Rules. The PACE Codes of Practice, by contrast, are exposed to a long period of prior public consultation.

6–115   **Can a breach of the Codes lead to criminal or civil proceedings?**

Only if the breach is also a breach of the criminal or the civil law.

6–116   **What effect therefore does a breach of the rules have on the criminal proceedings against the person himself?**

The Act states that "in all criminal and civil proceedings, any [such] Code shall be admissible in evidence, and if any provision of such a Code appears to the court or tribunal conducting the proceedings to be relevant to any question arising in the proceedings it shall be taken into account in determining that question".

This means that the court may take such account of the breach of the Codes as it thinks fit. In particular it can exclude evidence obtained in breach of the Codes or on appeal it can quash a conviction because evidence that ought for that reason to have been ruled inadmissible was allowed in at the trial. Both have happened quite often (see paras 8–65 and 8–66 below).

PART VII

DOCUMENTARY EVIDENCE IN CRIMINAL PROCEEDINGS

Evidence from documentary records: ss.68–70

[Section 68 of PACE as originally passed into law made admissible certain cate-   **7–01**
gories of documentary evidence. It had to be read in conjunction with Sch.3 to the
Act. Section 68 and Sch.3 were replaced by Pt II of, and Sch.2 to, the Criminal Justice Act 1988 which were in turn repealed and replaced by the Criminal Justice Act
2003. The 2003 Act deals with the law on hearsay in Pt 11, Ch.2. (For the Northern Ireland equivalent see Criminal Justice (Evidence) (Northern Ireland) Order
2004, SI 2004/1501, Art.21.) Section 69 which provided for the admissibility of
computer records was repealed by the Youth Justice and Criminal Evidence Act
1999, s.60. (The Northern Ireland equivalent Art.68 was repealed by the Criminal
Evidence (Northern Ireland) Order 1999, SI 1999/2789.) Section 70 merely
explained the application of Sch.3. It was repealed by the same provisions of the
Youth Justice and Criminal Evidence Act 1999 that repealed s.69. Since the law on
hearsay evidence no longer has any connection with a book on PACE, the subject
has been removed from the book.

The only surviving sections of the original Pt VII of PACE therefore are ss.71
and 72.]

Microfilm copies: s.71[1]

Under the pre-PACE law microfilm copies of certain categories of documents   **7–02**
were admissible under certain statutory provisions.[2] It seemed unclear whether
other microfilm copies were admissible.

Section 71 was intended to put the matter beyond doubt. It provides that the
contents of a document may be proved by the production of an enlargement of a
microfilm copy of that document or part of it. The copy must be authenticated "in
such manner as the court may approve". The microfilm copy is admissible
whether or not the original document is still in existence.

---

[1] See 1989 N.I. PACE Order, Art.69.
[2] Banking Act 1979, Sch.6; Finance Act 1972, ss.34 and 39.

Definitions: s.72[3]

7–03   Section 72(1) defines "copy", "statement" and "proceedings". The first two have the same meanings as in Pt I of the Civil Evidence Act 1968. The expression "proceedings" if not further defined means criminal proceedings.

Subsection (2) saves any power of a court to exclude evidence at its discretion. It is similar to s.18(5)(a) of the Civil Evidence Act 1968. It includes exclusion of evidence by preventing questions from being put or by excusing the witness from answering questions already put or by directing the jury to disregard evidence.

---

[3] See 1989 N.I. PACE Order, Art.67.

PART VIII

EVIDENCE IN CRIMINAL PROCEEDINGS—GENERAL

Convictions and acquittals: ss.73–75[1]

The Criminal Law Revision Committee (CLRC) in its 11th Report recommended **8–01** that the law on proof of convictions and acquittals in criminal cases should be tidied up, and ss.73–75 broadly followed the recommendations of the Committee.[2] But the reforms have produced serious problems which seem not to have been anticipated by the CLRC.

Section 73 replaced statutory provisions which contained references to court procedures that were outdated.[3] It provides for proof of both a conviction or an acquittal in a court in the UK (or a Service court outside the UK) by a certificate signed by the appropriate officer of the court, together with evidence identifying the person named in the certificate.[4]

There is a saving (in subs.(4)) for any other authorised manner of providing evidence of a conviction or acquittal—such as by a person present in court, or by means of fingerprints under s.39 of the Criminal Justice Act 1948, or by written statements under ss.2 or 9 of the Criminal Justice Act 1967 or by an admission under s.10 of the 1967 Act.

In *R. v Derwent Magistrates' Court, Ex p. Heaviside*[5] where H was convicted for driving whilst disqualified, the Divisional Court, granting judicial review, ruled that strict proof of the previous conviction was required. The certificate of conviction was supported by a police officer who had not been in court at the time and by the court register. That was held to be insufficient.[6] But in *Olakanori v DPP*[7] the Divisional Court upheld the convictions despite discrepancies in identifying details between the certificate of conviction and the birth certificate

---

[1] See 1989 N.I. PACE Order, Arts 71–73.

[2] *Evidence (General)*, 1972, paras 217–220.

[3] Evidence Act 1851, s.13; Criminal Procedure Act 1865, s.6; and the Prevention of Crimes Act 1871, s.18.

[4] In *Hacker* [1994] 1 W.L.R. 1659; [1995] 1 All E.R. 45, the House of Lords held that the whole certificate is admissible even if it gives details of the defendant's previous conviction—subject to the judge's overriding discretion to exclude evidence if the prejudicial effect would outweigh the probative value. For commentary see Munday (1995) 159 J.P. 22.

[5] [1996] R.T.R. 384.

[6] See to same effect *Bailey v DPP* (1999) 163 J.P. 518, DC.

[7] Unreported, Case No.CO/1814/98, July 8, 1998, DC.

because the name was unusual, that there was a case to answer and the court could draw adverse inferences from the accused's failure to give evidence.

8–02   Section 74 amended the law on admissibility of convictions as evidence of the commission of an offence. In accordance with *Hollington v Hewthorn*,[8] evidence that a person other than the accused had been convicted of an offence was not admissible for the purpose of proving that that person committed the offence. Thus, in a trial for handling it could not be shown that the goods were stolen by introducing the conviction of the thief.

The rule was abolished for civil proceedings by the Civil Evidence Act 1968, s.11. The difficulties that the rule gave rise to were illustrated in *Spinks*.[9] S had been convicted of acting with intent to impede the arrest of F, having hidden the knife used by F in a stabbing. S's conviction was quashed on appeal because the only evidence at his trial that F had committed the offence was inadmissible and F's conviction for the stabbing was inadmissible because of the rule in *Hollington v Hewthorn*.

The Criminal Law Revision Committee recommended in its 11th Report[10] that the rule in *Hollington v Hewthorn* should be abolished for criminal cases as well. Section 74 follows the CLRC's proposals in regard to convictions of persons other than the accused. In regard to the accused himself, the section made no change in the rules regarding the admissibility of his past misconduct. But it did alter the rules regarding his commission of a previous offence by allowing it to be proved by evidence of his conviction. The consequences of this have been surprising and unfortunate.

8–03   Subsection (1) states that the conviction[11] of someone other than the accused is admissible as proof that he committed that offence whether or not any other evidence of the fact is given. So, if A is charged with handling goods stolen by B, evidence that B was convicted of stealing the goods is admissible to prove that they were stolen.

Subsection (2) provides that the person convicted shall be taken to have committed that offence unless the contrary is proved.[12]

Subsection (3) deals with the position of the accused. Where evidence is admissible of the fact that he has committed an offence, in so far as that is relevant to a matter in issue other than a tendency to show a disposition to commit the kind of offence with which he is charged, the conviction shall be taken as proof that he committed that offence unless the contrary is proved. The section also specifically preserves the operation of any statute making a conviction or finding of fact conclusive for the purpose of other proceedings. It is also provided that the admissibility of any conviction which would be admissible apart from the clause, is not prejudiced. (For a similar provision in regard to civil cases, see Civil Evidence Act 1968, s.11(3).)

---

[8] [1943] K.B. 587.
[9] [1982] 1 All E.R. 587.
[10] *op. cit.*, para.8–01, n.2 above, para.218.
[11] In the UK or in a service court outside the UK.
[12] Even though a co-defendant pleaded guilty, the defendant can argue that the offence did not take place—see *Dixon, The Times*, November 2, 2000, CA in which the conviction was quashed because of the trial judge's error.

The case law on s.74 has, however, given it an unexpectedly broad interpreta- **8–04**
tion, especially through the application of the power to exclude "unfair" evidence
under s.78. As has been seen, the main thrust of the CLRC's recommendation
was to help the prosecution where the guilt of the accused depends on a third
party's guilt. But s.74 is not limited in this way. It simply provides that the conviction is admissible in evidence where it is "relevant to any issue" in the
proceedings to establish the guilt of the convicted person.

The courts have found two meanings of the word "issue". The narrow meaning is an issue which is an essential ingredient in the offence charged. An example of the use of this meaning would be to establish against an alleged accessory
that the principal committed the offence—see *Turner*[13] or *Fredrick*.[14] The
extended meaning is other matters that are less important, such as evidential matters that come up in the course of the case.[15] So, in *Golder*[16] D was charged with
robbery. Convictions of two other men in respect of the same offence were said
to be relevant for the purpose, first, of showing that a robbery had occurred (the
narrow meaning of issue) and, secondly, to show that facts allegedly narrated by
D in a disputed confession which were consistent with the guilt of the other two
were likely to be true.[17]

Given that his out-of-court admission would not be admissible against the **8–05**
accused, it is plainly unfair, at least in some circumstances, to allow a third person's conviction to be introduced as evidence against the accused. It is this unfairness which has led the courts to try to restrict the use of the section by use of
s.78.[18] So, where D and E are charged with conspiring together and E pleads
guilty to conspiring with D, his conviction becomes admissible evidence from
which the jury may infer that D must have conspired with E. Indeed, unless the
contrary be proved, the facts on which the conviction was based, namely that D
and E conspired together, are established. This in effect reverses the burden of
proof which, as the late Professor Sir John Smith said, "was surely never intended
and is contrary to all principle".[19] In *Robertson*, Lord Lane warned that "Section
74 is a provision which should be sparingly used".[20] But the courts have used s.78
to exclude the evidence where its impact would be too damning.[21]

Note that s.78 has no application, however, to evidence tendered by a co-
defendant. A judge therefore has no discretion either under that section or at

[13] [1991] Crim.L.R. 57, CA.
[14] [1990] Crim.L.R. 403.
[15] *R. v Robertson* [1987] 1 Q.B. 920 at 927, CA.
[16] *Heard* and reported with *Robertson* above.
[17] See also *Grey* (1989) 88 Cr.App.R. 375, CA; *Castle* [1989] Crim.L.R. 567, CA; *Steers*, unreported,
Case No.91/2551/X3, January 12, 1993, CA.
[18] *O'Connor* (1987) 85 Cr.App.R. 298, CA; *Curry* [1988] Crim.L.R. 527, CA; *Kempster* [1989] 1
W.L.R. 1125, CA. *cf. Robertson and Golder* [1987] 1 Q.B. 920; *Lunnon* (1988) 88 Cr.App.R. 71, CA;
Bennett [1988] Crim.L.R. 686, CA; *Mattison* [1990] Crim.L.R. 117, CA; and *Skinner, Pick, Skinner
and Mercer* [1995] Crim.L.R. 805, CA.
[19] [1988] Crim.L.R. 456 commenting on the Court of Appeal's decision in *Lunnon*. See also
Professor's Smith's comment on *Curry* [1988] Crim.L.R. 527 at 528. See also *Humphreys and Tully*
[1993] Crim.L.R. 288, CA.
[20] *op.cit.*, n.15 above at 928.
[21] For further commentary see, for instance, Munday, "Proof of Guilt by Association and section 74
of the Police and Criminal Evidence Act 1984" [1990] Crim.L.R. 236.

common law to prevent one defendant from adducing the previous conviction of a third party, however prejudicial its effect on a co-defendant.[22]

8–06   In *Boyson*[23] the defendant had been convicted of importing a drug. Her three co-defendants pleaded guilty. A fourth, her co-habitee and, later, husband, was separately convicted of importing a different drug. All the pleas and convictions were admitted in the trial of the defendant under s.74. The Court of Appeal held that the trial judge had been wrong to admit the evidence under s.74 without having regard to fairness under s.78. In order to admit evidence of a co-accused's conviction or plea it was necessary to observe the following principles:

(1)   the conviction must be clearly relevant to an issue in the case;

(2)   s.74 should be sparingly used;

(3)   the judge should consider the question of fairness under s.78 of the Act and whether the probative value of the conviction outweighs its prejudicial value; and

(4)   the judge must direct the jury clearly as to the issues to which the conviction is and is not relevant.

Here the accused's conviction was both irrelevant and prejudicial. The Court of Appeal said that it did not approve of the growing practice of allowing evidence to go before the jury which was irrelevant, inadmissible, prejudicial or unfair simply because it was convenient for the jury to have "the whole picture".[24] On the combined effect of ss.74 and 78 see also *Lee*.[25] On the effect of s.74 where the conviction in question is that of a co-accused who was tried separately see *Hayter*.[26]

8–07   In *Warner and Jones*[27] the Court of Appeal in effect appeared to condone proof of guilt by association. The defendants were convicted of conspiracy to supply heroin. The prosecution led evidence that a great number of persons briefly visited the second defendant's premises—and that eight of these had convictions for possession of or supplying heroin. Rejecting the appeal, the Court of Appeal said the judge should have told the jury that the appellants were not to be convicted simply because of their association with such people but it held that it could not be said that the earlier convictions were irrelevant to the question of what was taking place. But in *Hasson and Davey*[28] this doctrine was rejected where it was

---

[22] See *Bedo and Otto*, unreported, Case No.91/1643/Y4, October 15, 1992, CA.

[23] [1991] Crim.L.R. 274, CA.

[24] See to like effect *Mattison* [1990] Crim.L.R. 117, CA; *Humphreys and Tully*, n.19 above; *Hall* [1993] Crim.L.R. 527, CA; *Manzur and Mahmood* [1997] 1 Cr.App.R. 414; [1997] Crim L.R. 447; *Marlow* [1997] Crim.L.R. 457, CA. In this respect *cf. Bennett* [1988] Crim.L.R. 686, CA; and *Turpin* [1990] Crim.L.R. 514, CA. It is suggested that *Boyson* represents the better view.

[25] [1996] Crim.L.R. 825, CA.

[26] [2003] EWCA Crim 1048; [2003] 1 W.L.R. 1910; [2003] Crim.L.R. 887.

[27] (1993) 96 Cr.App.R. 324, CA.

[28] [1997] Crim.L.R. 579, CA.

not part of the prosecution's case that the drugs were actually being supplied to the associates who had previous drug-related convictions. The Court of Appeal allowed the appeal on the ground that there was no sufficient nexus between the convictions and an issue or allegation in the case.

In *Potamitis*[29] the Court of Appeal said that evidence of antecedent offending by a stranger to the indictment was not relevant or admissible, but this proposition is too broad.[30] If the evidence is relevant and there is no rule of exclusion, the court will admit it unless it would be unfair.[31]

Section 75 has supplementary provisions making admissible duly certified   **8–08**
copies of documents to prove the facts of the offence—including the information, complaint, indictment or charge sheet. Without such factual details it may be difficult to determine whether a previous conviction is or is not relevant. In *O'Connor*[32] the Court of Appeal held that where the conviction is admitted it comes in with all the detail contained in the relevant count of the indictment. In that case the first defendant was charged with conspiracy to obtain property by deception with the second defendant. The second defendant pleaded guilty to count one. The court said that it would be difficult to contend from that admission and the details that not only had the second defendant conspired with the first defendant but that the converse had also taken place. Moreover, it was not open to the defence to challenge what the second defendant had said in the first defendant's absence since he had not given evidence. This was most unfair and the evidence should have been excluded under s.78. (But the court nevertheless dismissed the appeal on the ground that there was no substantial miscarriage of justice—known under the then current law as "applying the proviso".)

Oral evidence is also admissible. Subsection (3) provides that certain enactments under which a conviction leading to probation or discharge is to be disregarded shall not affect the admissibility of the conviction for evidentiary reasons. The enactments in question prevent the conviction from counting as part of the criminal record for the purpose of sentencing.

Confessions: s.76[33]

The common law background and the CLRC

One of the most important sections in PACE is s.76 which made a major change   **8–09**
in the law on confessions.[34] Under the classic common law a confession was only admissible if the prosecution could show that it was voluntary, in the sense that

---

[29] [1994] Crim.L.R. 434, CA.

[30] For criticism of the proposition see Professor John Smith's commentary on the case, *ibid.*, at 435.

[31] See, for instance, *Roberts (Brian)* [1995] Crim.L.R. 638, CA.

[32] (1986) 85 Cr.App.R. 298, CA.

[33] See to same effect N.I. 1989 PACE Order, Art.74. Article 74(a) excluded trials on indictment for scheduled cases under the Northern Ireland (Emergency Provisions) Act 1978, s.8. Section 8 has now been replaced by s.76 of the Terrorism Act 2000.

[34] For two major texts on confessions see Wolchover and Heaton-Armstrong, *Confession Evidence* (Sweet & Maxwell, 1996); and Mirfield, *Silence, Confessions and Improperly Obtained Evidence* (Clarendon, Oxford, 1997).

it had not been induced "by fear of prejudice or hope of advantage exercised or held out by a person in authority".[35] Also, a confession must not have been obtained by oppression.[36]

In the past, the courts took this principle very seriously and interpreted it strictly against the police. Even the mildest threat or inducement had been held to make a resulting confession inadmissible. Thus in *Northam*,[37] a person charged with housebreaking was being questioned about his part in other offences. Before confessing he asked whether the other offences might be taken into consideration at his trial rather than being the subject of a separate trial. The Court of Appeal quashed the conviction because of the police officer's acceptance of this suggestion. In *Zaveckas*[38] the Court of Appeal quashed a conviction because the trial judge had admitted a confession made after the defendant asked the police officer whether he could have bail if he made a statement.

8–10   In its 1972 11th Report, the CLRC said that two reasons had been given for the rule. One was that a confession not made voluntarily might not be reliable (the "reliability principle"); and, secondly, that the police should be discouraged from using improper methods to obtain a confession (the "disciplinary principle"). It thought that historically the reliability principle underlay the law. This was shown by the authorities and also by the fact that if the police discovered something such as a body or a gun as a result of an involuntary confession, the evidence of that fact was admissible.

After reviewing the case law, the CLRC said that it was unsatisfactory.[39] It recommended that only threats or inducements likely to produce an unreliable confession or oppression should cause a confession to be inadmissible. It would be for the judge to imagine that he was present at the interrogation and to consider whether at that point the threat or inducement would have been likely to make a confession unreliable.

After the report of the CLRC in 1972, the case law on confessions moved somewhat in the direction of the Committee's proposals. In *DPP v Ping Lin*[40] the suspect, a drugs dealer, asked: "If I help the police, will you help me?". The officer replied: "I can make no deal with you but if you show the judge that you have helped the police to trace bigger people I am sure he will bear it in mind when he sentences you." The House of Lords said that the prosecution had to show as a matter of fact that the threat or promise had not induced the confession. The judge had been entitled to hold the statement admissible.

8–11   In the later case of *Rennie*[41] this ruling was applied to a confession which the police officer actually admitted had been prompted by the suspect's fear that the police would otherwise interview and perhaps arrest other members of his family. The Lord Chief Justice said that the speculation of the police officer as to what prompted the confession was irrelevant and inadmissible. But he went on (at 388): "Even if the appellant had decided to admit his guilt because he hoped

---

[35] *R. v Ibrahim* [1914] A.C. 599, PC.
[36] See especially *R. v Prager* [1972] 1 All E.R. 1114, CA; *R. v Priestley* (1966) 50 Cr.App.R. 183, CA.
[37] (1967) 52 Cr.App.R. 97, CA.
[38] (1970) 54 Cr.App.R. 202, CA.
[39] *op.cit.*, para.8–01, n.2 above, paras 53–69.
[40] [1976] A.C. 574, HL.
[41] [1982] 1 All E.R. 385, CA.

that if he did so the police would cease their inquiries into the part played by his mother, it does not follow that the confession should have been excluded."

Lord Lane said that the law did not require that every confession should be excluded simply because it was prompted in part by some hope of advantage. The question was whether on a common sense view the statement had been made voluntarily, which in ordinary parlance meant "of one's own free will". This was a question of fact which should be approached by the judge much in the way that a jury would. The confession was held to be admissible.

Plainly the definition of voluntariness in *Rennie* was very different from that in cases like *Northam and Zaveckas*. Much of the bite in the rule had been removed.

The Philips Royal Commission

The Philips Royal Commission[42] criticised the voluntariness test as unrealistic.   **8–12**
Even a trained psychologist present during questioning, it suggested, could not determine to what extent any particular confession was truly voluntary.[43] In the Commission's view it would be better to abandon the vain attempt to distinguish between voluntary and involuntary confessions and concentrate instead on the behaviour of the police officer. If the suspect was subjected to torture, violence, the threat of violence or inhuman or degrading treatment any subsequent confession should be inadmissible. This would mark society's "abhorrence of such conduct".[44] But any lesser breach of the rules of questioning should merely lead to the judge warning the jury of the danger of relying on the resulting confession if there was no independent evidence.[45] As will be seen, this advice was partly followed and partly not followed.

Section 76(1)

Section 76(1) states that in any proceedings a confession made by an accused   **8–13**
person may be given in evidence against him "so far as it is relevant to any matter in the proceedings and is not excluded by the court in pursuance of this section".

Section 76(2)

The Act imposes two tests on the admissibility of confessions which are in addi-   **8–14**
tion to the general tests on the admissibility of all evidence contained in s.78 and s.82(3). The first is that the confession should not be the result of oppression (s.76(2)(a)) and the second is that it should not be the result of conduct likely to

---

[42] Philips Report, para.4.73.
[43] The Commission based its view largely on the research of Dr Barrie Irving, "Police Interrogation: A Case Study of Current Practice", *Royal Commission Research Study No.2* (1980).
[44] Philips Report, para.4.132.
[45] Philips Report, para.4.133.

render a confession unreliable (s.76(2)(b)). In other words, the Philips Royal Commission's proposal that the voluntariness test be abandoned altogether was rejected—on the ground that the Philips Royal Commission's approach did not provide adequate protection against the danger of an unreliable confession.

If it is represented to the court[46] that the confession was, or may have been, obtained either by oppression or in a way likely to make it unreliable, the court is directed by subs.(2) not to allow it to be given in evidence "except in so far as the prosecution proves to the court beyond reasonable doubt that the confession (notwithstanding that it may be true)[47] was not obtained as aforesaid".

8–15 In regard to both subss.(2)(a) and (2)(b), the burden of proof is squarely on the prosecution. So, in the case of *Paris, Abdullai and Miller* where murder convictions were quashed, the Lord Chief Justice said: "It is sufficient to say that in our judgment, the Crown did not and could not discharge the burden upon them to prove beyond reasonable doubt that the confessions were not obtained by oppression or by interviews which were likely to render them unreliable."[48] It would therefore be wrong for the judge to say that he was unable to make up his mind as to the matter. If he could not make up his mind the prosecution had failed to discharge the burden of proof.[49]

The section specifically says that the prosecution must affirmatively prove that the confession was not so obtained—"notwithstanding that it may be true". This means that the court cannot take into consideration the fact that the confession appears to be true.[50] In fact, it seems that during the *voire dire* the defendant should not be asked any questions as to the truth of the confession.[51] If the truth of the confession is not to be taken into account, it is difficult to see any justification for asking such questions. Indeed, the asking of such questions must create a danger that the apparent truth of the confession will affect the judge's decision on admissibility.

---

[46] A mere suggestion in cross-examination is not enough: *R. v Liverpool Juvenile Court, Ex p. R.* [1988] Q.B. 1, DC.

[47] When the Bill was first published it contained a provision that evidence could be admitted to prove the truth or falsity of the confession if the court thought that such evidence would assist in determining the issue of admissibility. This rejected the view of the majority of the Judicial Committee of the Privy Council in *Wong Kam-Ming v The Queen* [1980] A.C. 247 in which it was held that on a *voire dire* as to the admissibility of an extra-judicial statement by an accused the prosecution could not cross-examine him as to the truth of the statement. The sole issue on the *voire dire*, the majority held, was whether the statement had been made voluntarily, and whether it was true was not relevant to that issue. The subsection adopted the minority view expressed by Lord Hailsham which reflected the decision in *Hammond* (1941) 28 Cr.App.R. 84, CCA. However, the Government was persuaded to drop this provision with the result that the majority view in *Wong Kam-Ming* stood after all.

[48] (1993) 97 Cr.App.R. 99 at 105, CA.

[49] *Baker*, unreported, Case No.92/3437/Z3, August 18, 1992, CA. See also *Jerome*, unreported, Case No.91/3384/W3, February 1, 1994, CA; and *Taylor*, unreported, Case No.99/1413/Y4, March 16, 2000, CA.

[50] *Cox* [1991] Crim.L.R. 276, CA. The court said: "It is perfectly true that the judge must have regard to all the circumstances. But one of the matters to which he plainly cannot have regard is the truth of the statement." See also *Jones* [2003] EWCA Crim 3309. The Court of Appeal quashed the conviction of a mentally subnormal defendant for manslaughter on the ground that even though his confession appeared true the prosecution had not disclosed a police note made at the time describing him to be "mental".

[51] *Davis* [1990] Crim.L.R. 860 in which the Court of Appeal indicated that it approved of the view of the Privy Council in *Wong Kam-Ming* [1980] A.C. 247 that the defendant could not be questioned on the *voire dire* regarding the truth of the confession. See also *Tyrer* (1990) 90 Cr.App.R. 446, CA.

Where the prosecution proposes to give a confession in evidence, the court **8–16** may of its own motion require the prosecution to prove that the confession was not so obtained (subs.(3)).

The fact that the confession itself is held to be inadmissible does not affect the admissibility of (a) facts discovered as a result of the confession (such as the gun with the fingerprints on it)[52]; or (b) so much of the confession as is necessary to show that the accused speaks, writes or expresses himself in a particular way where this is relevant (subs.(4)).[53]

But if the real evidence is only another form of an improperly obtained confession it is not admissible—*Lam Chi-Ming*[54] in which the Judicial Committee of the Privy Council held that a video re-enactment by the defendant of where he had thrown the murder weapon into Hong Kong harbour was another version of the confession obtained by oppression. Also, evidence that a fact was discovered as a result of an inadmissible confession is only admissible if given by or on behalf of the accused (subss.(5) and (6)). It cannot be produced by the prosecution.

What is a confession?

Section 82(1) defines "confession" thus: "'confession' includes any statement **8–17** wholly or partly adverse to the person who made it, whether made to a person in authority or not and whether made in words or otherwise".[55] A statement in which a person admits matters that are relevant and that are adverse to the maker is a confession even though it does not amount to a confession in the ordinary sense.[56]

Where admissions are "mixed" in that they contain self-serving parts, they count as confessions and therefore s.76 must be satisfied. (In *Sharp*[57] the House of Lords held that such statements are evidence of the truth of the self-serving as well as the incriminating parts.)

In *Sat-Bhambra*[58] the Court of Appeal held that the statutory definition of **8–18** "confession" did not include a statement which when made was purely self-serving but which becomes adverse to the defendant at trial, for example because it is inconsistent with his defence. Such statements therefore did not need to satisfy the conditions of s.76—though they might still be excluded under s.78 or at common law. But in *Z*[59] the Court of Appeal held that under s.3(1) of the Human Rights Act 1998 they had to reconsider the concept of "adverse" and "self incriminating".

---

[52] Preserving the common law rule in *Warwickshall* (1783) 1 *Leach* 263.

[53] As in the old case of *R. v Voisin* [1918] 1 K.B. 531.

[54] [1991] A.C. 212.

[55] In *Mawdesley v DPP* [2003] EWHC Admin 1586; [2004] Crim. L.R.232, the Divisional Court referred back to the magistrates the question whether a form returned by a motorist which included some of the information required by the Road Traffic Act 1988, s.172 but which was not signed could amount to a confession.

[56] *Theobald v Nottingham Magistratres' Court* [2003] EWHC 1720 (Admin).

[57] [1988] 1 W.L.R. 7.

[58] (1988) 88 Cr.App.R. 55; [1988] Crim.L.R. 453, CA; see further Birch, "The PACE Hots Up: Confessions and Confusions under the 1984 Act" [1989] Crim.L.R. 95 at 115 and Kodowo Bentil, "Issues Concerning the Admissibility of Confession Evidence in a Criminal Trial," J.P.N., November 25, 1989, 750 at 752.

[59] [2003] EWCA Crim 191; [2003] 1 W.L.R. 1489; [2003] Crim.L.R. 627. For discussion approving the decision in *K* see Munday, "Adverse Denial and Purposive Confession" [2003] Crim.L.R. 850–64.

They preferred the interpretation of the European Court of Human Rights in *Saunders v UK* (1997) 23 E.H.R.R. 313 to that in *Sat-Bhambra.* Whether the defendant's statement ("I did it but under duress") was a confession had to be judged at the time it was made—not, as determined in *Sat-Bhambra,* at the time of the trial.

In *Doolan*[60] it was held that the defendant's admission that he had been drinking with the victim on the evening of the robbery did amount to a confession.[61]

It should be noted that even after the "abolition of the right to silence" silence presumably cannot be brought within the concept of a "statement"—and therefore could not count as a confession that is subject to s.76.

The importance of confessions

8–19   Confessions and admissions are a very important factor in criminal investigation. Pre-PACE studies estimated that over 60 per cent of interviews with suspects led to confessions. (Softley *et al.* (1980); Irving (1980)). Post-PACE, the proportion has remained high: Irving and McKenzie (1989) showed a confession rate of 65 per cent in their 1986 sample and 46 per cent in the 1987 sample; Sanders *et al.* (1989), in a study of 250 cases in 10 police stations, had an admission rate of 54 per cent overall—with 60 per cent where no legal advice was given and 44 per cent where legal advice was given; Moston and Stephenson (1993), based on 558 cases, had an overall admission rate of 59 per cent—with 51 per cent in legal advice cases compared with 63 per cent in other cases; Moston *et al.* (1990), based on 1,067 CID cases in the Metropolitan Police District, had a 41 per cent overall admission rate—with only 29 per cent in legal advice cases compared with 50 per cent in others. See also Evans (1993) in regard to confessions by juveniles.

The danger of false confessions

8–20   It has been recognised in recent years that the problem of false confessions is serious and more widespread than had formerly been appreciated. There is now an extensive literature on the subject. One of the leading experts has identified four different types of false confessions: (1) those borne from a desire to attract publicity or notoriety, or to relieve guilt about real or imagined misdeeds, or from an inability to distinguish between reality and fantasy; (2) confessions to protect others; (3) confessions to obtain a short-term advantage such as respite from questioning or bail; and (4) the false confession that the suspect is persuaded by the interrogator is true. (Gudjonnson, *The Psychology of Interrogations, Confessions and Testimony* (Wiley, 1992). For a summary see Gudjonnson, "The Psychology of False Confessions", *New Law Journal*, September 18, 1992, 1277. See also Lowenstein, "Aspects of Confessions: What the Legal Profession Should Know" (1999) 163 *Justice of the Peace* at 586–591, which has a substantial bibliography.)

---

[60] [1998] Crim.L.R. 747.
[61] See further Mirfield, *Silence, Confessions and Improperly Obtained Evidence* (Clarendon, Oxford, 1997), pp.52–68.

"Oppression": s.76(2)(a)

The word "oppression" was defined by the Court of Appeal very and perhaps too widely in *Prager*[62] as: "questioning which by its nature, duration, or other attendant circumstances (including the fact of custody) excites hope (such as the hope of release) or fears, or so affects the mind of the subject that his will crumbles and he speaks when otherwise he would have stayed silent". **8–21**

"Oppression", according to subs.(8), "includes torture, inhuman or degrading treatment[63] and the use or threat of violence." The use of the word "includes" means that this list is not intended to be exhaustive.

The concept of "oppression" has been considered in several cases since the Act became law. In the first three cases the courts found that there had not been oppression.

In *Miller*[64] the Court of Appeal had to consider a confession by a paranoid schizophrenic who confessed to killing his girlfriend. When first interviewed he consistently denied the allegation. The next day however, he admitted it in a statement which contained both reliable and unreliable matter. Then he tried to retract the confession. At the trial it was argued on his behalf that the confession should be excluded under s.76(2)(a) because it had been obtained as a result of protracted and oppressive interviews which had caused him to suffer an episode of schizophrenic terror. Medical evidence was given that the style and length of questioning had produced a state of involuntary insanity in which his language reflected hallucinations and delusion. The judge refused to exclude the evidence. The defendant was found guilty of manslaughter.

On appeal it was contended for the defendant that oppression meant conduct which in fact produced the effects of oppression regardless of the police officer's intention or state of mind. The Court of Appeal rejected this view. The court held that although questions which were asked deliberately with the intention of producing a disordered state of mind would amount to oppression, the mere fact that questions addressed to the defendant triggered off hallucinations was not evidence of oppression. Here there had been no evidence of oppression "within the ordinary meaning of that word".[65] **8–22**

In *Fulling*[66] the Court of Appeal held that it was not oppression for the police to tell the defendant that her lover had been having an affair with another woman which so affected her that she made a confession. The court held that the word "oppression" should be given its ordinary dictionary meaning as stated in the Oxford English Dictionary: "The exercise of authority or power in a burdensome, harsh or wrongful manner; unjust or cruel treatment of subjects, inferiors, etc.;

---

[62] [1972] 1 W.L.R. 260, CA.
[63] The phrase comes from the ECHR. It was considered by the European Court in *Tyrer v UK* 2 E.H.R.R. 1 at 9–12; and *Ireland v UK* 2 E.H.R.R. 25 at 75–85. For a Northern Ireland view see *R. v McCormick* [1977] N.I. 105.
[64] [1986] 1 W.L.R. 1191, CA. For a valuable discussion of the case see Beaumont, "Confessions and the Mentally Ill", *Law Society Gazette*, September 3, 1986, 256.
[65] *ibid.*, at 1201.
[66] [1987] Q.B. 426, CA.

the imposition of unreasonable or unjust burdens." The court cited a quotation from the OED: "There is not a word in our language which expresses more detestable wickedness than oppression".

8–23   It was argued for the appellant that the trial judge had been wrong to hold that "oppression" necessarily involved some impropriety on the part of the police, but Lord Lane C.J. for the court said: "We find it hard to envisage any circumstances in which such oppression would not entail impropriety on the part of the interrogator". The judge had therefore not erred.

In *Emmerson*[67] shouting and swearing at the suspect were held not to amount to oppressive conduct.

An early post-PACE case in which oppression was held to have occurred was *Davison*,[68] a decision at the Central Criminal Court. D had been arrested at home at 6.30 am for handling a stolen ring, the proceeds of an armed robbery. He was questioned at various stages during the course of the day both about that offence and about a bullion robbery. Eventually he confessed. There were a whole series of breaches of the rules in the Act and the Code. The judge considered the Court of Appeal's ruling in Fulling that oppression "is the exercise of authority or power in . . . a wrongful manner". Here there had been various wrongs including, in particular, unlawful detention.[69] The authority of the police was being exercised in a wrongful manner and it was therefore capable of amounting to oppression. The burden was on the Crown to prove that it had not amounted to oppression and this they had failed to do. Accordingly, all the evidence after the first interview had to be excluded under s.76(2)(a).

8–24   Commenting on the decision in the *Criminal Law Review*,[70] Professor Diane Birch suggested that the decision showed the significance of the word "wrongful" in the phrase "burdensome, harsh or wrongful" used by the Court of Appeal in *Fulling*. She suggested that it would be "unfortunate", however, if every breach of the detention rules, even mandatory rules, were to be regarded as oppression. It would be more than unfortunate.[71] She was surely right to suggest that "wrongful" in the context of the phrase used in *Fulling* must mean some flagrant or deliberate breach of the rules. No doubt, as she suggests, a court would take into account the number and extent of breaches of the rules and whether they indicate incompetence or design. In *Davison* there might have been enough evidence of serious police misconduct to have justified a finding of oppression even if the narrower interpretation of the term was implied.

There are, however, now several decisions which give the police clearer guidance as to what will amount to oppression.[72] In the case of *Timothy John West* in

---

[67] (1991) 92 Cr.App.R. 284, CA.

[68] [1988] Crim.L.R. 442.

[69] The police failed to release D after the first interview at which stage there was no evidence against him (breach of s.34). Also, he had never been arrested in connection with the bullion robbery (breach of s.31).

[70] [1988] Crim.L.R. 444–445.

[71] See also *Parker* [1995] Crim.L.R. 233, CA and Professor Birch's commentary.

[72] In addition to those dealt with here in some detail see also *Madeley*, unreported, March 18, 1992, CA (confession in interview excluded where officers insulted and bullied M and said that by remaining silent he was making matters worse for himself); and *Beales* [1991] Crim.L.R. 118, Crown Ct (deliberate misstatement of the evidence in order to mislead B "stepped into the realm" of oppression).

1988 the trial judge held the following to have been oppressive: (1) The police officer had interrupted the defendant on a large number of occasions before he had finished his replies. The officer interrupted the defendant vigorously and with a raised voice sometimes shouting rudely. (2) The officer used obscenity to interrupt the defendant to indicate that he was lying. It was also used to show that the officer had a clear view that the defendant had committed the offences and would continue to question him until he admitted them.[73]

In *Paris, Abdullai and Miller*,[74] where the Court of Appeal quashed the defendants' convictions for murder, the defendant, Miller, who it turned out was on the borderline of mental handicap, made admissions after having denied the offence more than 300 times. Lord Taylor C.J. said the court had been horrified by the hectoring and bullying manner of the questioning on Tape No.7, much of which had been conducted in the form of shouting at the accused and repeating accusations over and over again. ("The officers . . . were not questioning him so much as shouting at him what they wanted him to say. Short of physical violence, it is hard to conceive a more hostile and intimidating approach to a suspect. It is impossible to convey on the printed page the pace, force and menace of the officer's delivery.") Miller had stood his ground and had made no admissions until the next interview an hour later, but the Lord Chief Justice said the court had no doubt that there had been oppression. He drew attention also to other matters that supported counsel's argument that the conviction should be quashed on the ground that questioning had been oppressive. The officers had made it clear to Miller on many occasions that they would go on questioning him until "they got it right"—meaning until he agreed with the version they were putting. Additional pressure was applied by telling Miller that he was talking drivel and rubbish and that his alibi had been blown away. ("The alibi had never been totally water-tight, but so far as it went, it was not, on the police information, blown away.") The prosecution's version of events was said to be supported by a number of witnesses which was not the case. Miller had more than once been threatened with the prospect of a life sentence. The officers persistently suggested to Miller that he was "stoned" due to the effects of cocaine so as to persuade him that he might have been present at the scene of the crime even though he had no recollection of it. Counsel for Miller submitted that he had in effect been brainwashed over the 13 hours of questioning into repeating back to the officers facts they had asserted many times to him. For extended periods Miller had been crying and sobbing but he had been given no respite. Lord Taylor said that having considered the tenor and length of these interviews taken as a whole, "we are of opinion that they would have been oppressive and confessions obtained in consequence of them would have been unreliable even with a suspect of normal mental capacity".[75] In saying that the oppressive methods of conducting the interview would have made the confession unreliable the Court of Appeal indicated that when the oppression is bad enough there is overlap between s.76(2)(a) and 76(2)(b).

8–25

---

[73] Transcript of decision of His Honour Judge Hutton at Gloucester Crown Court, April 22, 1988.

[74] n.48 above.

[75] *R.v. L* (1994) Cr.App.R. 839; [1994] Crim.L.R. 839, CA—aggressive and hostile questioning held not to be either oppression or sufficient to render the confession unreliable. *Emmerson*, n.60 above, is a similar case. It is always a question of the degree of pressure.

8–26   In the *George Heron* case in November 1993 the defendant was charged with the murder of a 7-year-old child. Mitchell J. at Leeds Crown Court ruled on the *voire dire* that confessions and admissions obtained from the defendant could not be admitted in evidence because they had been obtained through oppression. As a result the prosecution's case collapsed. Unlike the previous case, there had been no hectoring or shouting or aggressive language. Mitchell J. said[76]:

> "But oppression may take more insidious forms. The hallmark of such forms contains, in my judgment, two elements, continuity and injustice . . . Where these elements are combined and are systematically visited upon a suspect there is prima facie evidence of oppression . . . The police, of course, are not prohibited from putting questions to a suspect merely because he chooses not to answer them. They are not required to accept any answer or answers a suspect chooses to give. Nor are they prohibited from being persistent, searching and robust in their questioning. If they do not believe what they are being told they are entitled to say so. Persistence must not, however, develop into bullying; robustness must not develop into insulting or gratuitously demeaning questions, nor must robustness be regarded as an acceptable label for what, in truth, is no more than a repetitive verbal pounding alleging the certainty of a suspect's guilt. The balance between questions and comment should be appropriate and comment should be kept to a minimum. Where the line is to be drawn between proper and robust persistence and oppressive interrogation, can only be identified in general terms."

8–27   There was no suggestion that Heron had been especially vulnerable or subject to any mental incapacity. He had had a legal executive with him throughout each of the 12 tapes of interviews. The PACE rules had been complied with. The judge allowed the first four tapes in as evidence. But he excluded the subsequent tapes on which Heron had made admissions and then confessed. A crucial factor the judge seems to have taken into account in ruling that the confessions were inadmissible on the grounds of oppression was the fact that the police repeatedly misrepresented the evidence as to identification by stating that there were witnesses who had seen him with the girl at critical times when there was in fact no clear identification. The judge said:

> "I have no hesitation in concluding that there came a time in that interview when the police began to act oppressively . . . I regard it as oppressive to misrepresent repeatedly the evidence and/or the strength of the evidence in relation to a fact which, if true, would be a most compelling indicator of the defendant's responsibility for the child's death . . . It was wrong, in the teeth of his constant denials to pound him with accusations of being a killer, pound him with sexual motives for taking her . . . It was wrong, quite wrong, to tell him that it was in his interest to tell them the truth when they had made it all too clear that they regarded the truth that he was the killer. It was wrong, in the teeth of his denials about being the killer, to pound him with questions about

---

[76] The quotations from the *Heron* judgment are taken from the transcript of the judgment of Mitchell J. at Leeds Crown Court on November 1, 1993.

why he had done it. This interview, in short, was a continuing injustice and at an early stage, in my judgment, it did become oppressive."

He ruled that tapes five to eight recorded "a tale of continual injustice, such that it is, in my judgment, a tale of an insidious form of oppression". It amounted to an exercise in breaking the defendant's resolve to make no admissions. "The means adopted to achieve that end meant, in effect, that regardless of the fact that his eventual confession may very well have been true, the prosecution were prevented from discharging the burden imposed upon them by the two limbs of Section 76(2)." See also the Privy Council decision in *Burut v Public Prosecutor*[77] where suspects who had been interviewed whilst manacled and hooded later confessed. It was held that the confessions obtained in later interviews where that did not occur were improperly admitted. The aura of oppression continued.[78]

8–28

The cases, together with answers to specific questions put to and answered by the trial judge in the case of *Timothy West*,[79] permit the following general propositions about oppression. It would be oppressive to repeat a question dozens of times in order to gain an admission. It would be oppressive repeatedly to use abusive language, to shout at or bully the suspect, constantly to interrupt the suspect, or to pound him with allegations of guilt, with accusations that he is lying. It is legitimate to go over the same ground more than once but to do so for the umpteenth time becomes oppressive. It can also be oppressive to seek to break down the suspect's denials by false assertions as to the strength of the evidence held by the police.

Section 76(2)(b): unreliability

The second category of confession evidence that is wholly excluded is where it has been obtained "in consequence of anything said or done which was likely in the circumstances existing at the time, to render unreliable any confession which might be made by [the accused] in consequence thereof" (subs.(2)(b)).

8–29

This adopts the approach recommended by the Criminal Law Revision Committee that reliability should be the test. The fact that the section abandons the former approach of cases like *Northam* and *Zaveckas* (see para.8–09) is explicitly recognised in Code C. As has been seen, this states that no police officer shall seek to obtain answers to questions by the use of oppression or "shall indicate, except in answer to a direct question, what action will be taken on the part of the police if the person being interviewed answers questions, makes a statement or refuses to do either" (para.11.3). However, if the suspect directly asks the officer "what action will be taken in the event of his answering questions, making a statement or refusing to do either, the officer may inform him what

---

[77] [1995] 2 AC 579.
[78] See also *Samuel* [1988] Q.B. 615 at 629, in which the Court of Appeal accepted that denial of access to a solicitor might be oppression—though not in that particular case.
[79] See para.8–24 above.

action he proposes to take in that event provided that the action is itself proper and warranted" (*ibid.*).

8–30   In other words, indications of threats or promises within the limits of what is lawful and proper will not render a confession inadmissible if they emerge as a result of questions from the suspect. This is a far cry from the traditional common law approach to these matters. But, as has been seen, *Ping Lin* and *Rennie* (see paras 8–10, 8–11 above) could be said to have paved the way.

The proper interpretation of s.76(2)(b) has been considered in several reported cases.

"In consequence of anything said or done"

8–31   The section seems to require that the unreliability must arise as a result of the breaches of the law or the Codes and that there must be some causal connection. But neither is the case. Subsection (2)(b) can apply even though there was no impropriety on the part of the police and equally where there was some breach of the law or the Codes but no causal link between that impropriety and the confession. In *Fulling*, Lord Lane C.J. said: "what, however, is abundantly clear is that a confession may be invalidated under s.76(2)(b) where there is no suspicion of impropriety".[80] In *DPP v Blake* there was a breach of the Code in that the juvenile had not had an appropriate adult with him within the meaning of the concept but no misconduct in that the police had called the suspect's estranged father. Excluding the confession, Auld L.J. said: "the Code of Practice and [its] provisions . . . are simply matters to be taken into account, albeit important matters; but they are not necessarily conclusive either way in the particular circumstances of a case, and they are not the only matters to be taken into account."[81]

In *Doolan*[82] the Court of Appeal held that the confession had been wrongly admitted after the police had failed to caution the suspect, failed to keep a contemporaneous record of the interview, failed to show him a subsequent note of the interview and failed to record the times of the interview. Only the first of these could logically have had any impact on the reliability of the confession (and that was something not done rather than something done) but the court cited subs.(2)(b) as the reason for holding that the evidence should have been excluded. (See, however, *Matthews, Voss and Dennison*.[83])

8–32   In *Goldenberg*[84] the Court of Appeal[85] took the view that there had to be a causal link between what was said and done and the resulting confession. The court also held that the words "in consequence of anything said or done" meant said or done by someone other than the suspect. The court could not look at what the suspect himself had said or done. This seems too restrictive—and not required by the words of the subsection, especially as in other cases (see below) the courts have applied the subsection where the matter complained was something not said

[80] [1987] Q.B. 426 at 432.
[81] (1988) 89 Cr.App.R. 179 at 186, CA.
[82] [1988] Crim.L.R. 747, CA.
[83] (1990) 91 Cr.App.R. 43; [1990] Crim.L.R. 190, CA.
[84] (1989) Cr.App.R. 285; [1988] Crim.L.R. 678, CA.
[85] As in *Matthews, Voss and Dennison*, n.83 above.

or done—omission rather than commission. The crucial issue is not whether the police have misbehaved but whether the confession was likely to be unreliable because of what occurred.[86] However, it may be that such a case could be dealt with adequately under the discretion to exclude evidence under s.78. In *Harvey*[87] the trial judge excluded a confession to a murder under s.76(2)(b) on the ground that it might have been made to protect the defendant's lesbian lover. The defendant was a woman of low IQ, suffering from a psychopathic disorder aggravated by alcohol abuse. Nothing was "said or done" by the police to induce the confession.[88]

Under s.76(2)(b) it is no longer necessary, as it was at common law, to confine   **8–33**
the inquiry to what was done by persons in authority. (The definition of "confession" in s.82(1) explicitly states that a confession includes an adverse statement "whether made to a person in authority or not".) In *M*[89] the Court of Appeal allowed an appeal by a defendant convicted of four counts of rape on the ground of his own solicitor's hostility towards him during police questioning. The solicitor's sarcastic interventions were such as may have rendered any resulting confession unreliable.

Further examples

Other examples of things said or done which have been held to constitute grounds   **8–34**
for holding a confession to be unreliable include: an offer of bail[90]; minimising the significance of a serious sex offence and suggesting that psychiatric help might be appropriate[91]; saying to a defendant who has previously denied the offence, "Do I gather that you are now admitting the offence?"[92]; falsely telling the suspect that his voice has been recognised on tape[93]; falsely telling the suspect that he has been identified by a witness[94]; and indicating that the suspect will have to stay in the police station until the matter is cleared up.[95]

Examples of things not said or done which have been held to be grounds for holding a confession to be unreliable include: failure to obtain a solicitor[96]; breaches of the provisions of Code C[97]; and failure to see that the suspect has an

---

[86] See, for instance, *Walker* [1998] Crim.L.R. 211, CA and cases cited in para.8–37 below where the suspect's mental state is a "circumstance" within the meaning of the subsection.

[87] [1988] Crim.L.R. 241.

[88] See also *Crampton* (1991) 92 Cr.App.R. 369; [1991] Crim.L.R. 277, CA, and commentary by Professor Diane Birch at 279, on the effect of withdrawal from heroin during an interview.

[89] Unreported, Case No.99/4259/X4, June 12, 2000, CA.

[90] *Barry* (1992) 95 Cr.App.R. 384, CA.

[91] *Delaney* (1989) 88 Cr.App.R. 338, CA.

[92] *Waters* [1989] Crim.L.R. 62, CA.

[93] *Blake* [1989] 1 W.L.R. 432.

[94] *Heron*, see text paras 8–26—8–28 above.

[95] *Jasper*, unreported Case No.93/6043/X5, April 25, 1994, CA. *cf. Weeks* [1995] Crim.L.R. 52, CA.

[96] *Trussler* [1988] Crim.L.R. 446, Crown Ct; *McGovern* (1990) 92 Cr.App.R. 228, CA; *Chung* (1991) 92 Cr.App.R. 314, CA.

[97] *Delaney* (1989) 88 Cr.App.R. 338, CA—"flagrant" breaches in regard to making a contemporaneous note; *Doolan* [1988] Crim.L.R. 747, CA—failure to caution as well as failure to make a record. See also *Menard* [1995] 1 Cr.App.R. 306, CA.

appropriate adult present.[98] But such grounds will not necessarily result in the confession being held to be inadmissible.[99]

"Which was likely, in the circumsances existing at the time, to render unreliable any confession which might be made by him in consequence thereof"

8–35 This test is objective in the sense that it is assessing not what the police officers thought about the suspect's mental state but what it actually was, whether or not that state was known to the police.[1] But the test is subjective in the sense that, as has been seen, it relates to the actual accused with all his personal characteristics. At the same time it is hypothetical so that the court has to consider whether any confession which D might have made would be likely to be unreliable without taking into account whether in fact it was true.[2] In *Barry*[3] the Court of Appeal described the test as in a sense hypothetical since it relates not to the confession but to any confession. However, in *R. v Bow Street Magistrates' Court, Ex p. Proulx*,[4] the Divisional Court said that this does not mean that the subject matter or nature of the actual confession can be disregarded. The word "any" must be understood as indicating "any such" or "such a" confession as the applicant in fact made.

8–36 The formula in the subsection was that proposed by the CLRC. Its essential feature, the Committee thought:

"is that it applies not to the confession which the accused in fact made but to any confession which he might have made in consequence of the threat or inducement. On this scheme the judge should imagine that he was present at the interrogation and heard the threat or inducement. In the light of all the evidence given he will consider whether, at the point when the threat was uttered or the inducement offered, any confession which the accused might make as a result of it would be likely to be unreliable. If so, the confession would be inadmissible. For example, if the threat was to charge the suspect's wife jointly with him, the judge might think that a confession even of a serious offence would be likely to be unreliable.[5] If there was a promise to release the accused on bail to visit a sick member of his family, the judge might think that this

---

[98] See, for instance, *Everett* [1988] Crim.L.R. 826, CA; *Moss* (1990) 91 Cr.App.R. 371, CA; *Cox* [1991] Crim.L.R. 276, CA; *Morse* [1991] Crim.L.R. 195, Crown Ct; *Glaves* [1993] Crim.L.R. 685, CA—in that case the evidence was excluded even though a solicitor had been present.

[99] See, for instance, *Waters* [1989] Crim.L.R. 62, CA where the Court of Appeal held that various breaches of Code did not render the confession unreliable. See to like effect *Maguire* (1990) 90 Cr.App.R. 115, CA. In *Heath*, unreported, Case No.1757/A3/88, the Court of Appeal held that wrongfully denying access to a solicitor and wrongly delaying making notes did not render the admissions unreliable since they were made to a co-defendant. See also *Tyrer* (1990) 90 Cr.App.R. 446, CA.

[1] *R. v Everett* [1988] Crim.L.R. 826, CA.

[2] See *Cox* [1991] Crim.L.R. 276, CA; and *McGovern* (1991) 92 Cr.App.R. 228, CA.

[3] (1992) 95 Cr.App.R. 384, CA.

[4] [2001] 1 All E.R. 57 at 76–77.

[5] See, however, *Howden-Simpson* [1991] Crim.L.R. 49 in which the Court of Appeal upheld the trial judge's decision that the confession was admissible despite the fact that the police had told the accused that, if he did not confess, they would bring a variety of charges against him instead of merely two specimen charges.

would be unlikely to render a confession of a serious offence unreliable but likely to do so in the case of a minor offence."[6]

When the question was debated in Parliament, the Opposition moved an amend- **8–37** ment that no one should be convicted on the basis of a confession obtained as a result of detention in which there had been any breach of Pts IV and V of the Act (dealing with Detention and the Questioning and Treatment of Persons by the Police), or from a juvenile or someone suffering from a mental disorder in response to police questioning without a responsible adult being present unless there was corroboration of the confession. The Government resisted the amendment, but the Home Office Minister, Mr Mellor, said that in his view "most, if not all the circumstances set out in the amendment render the confession unreliable".[7]

In several cases the "circumstances existing at the time" have been held to be the fact that the suspect was highly suggestible or vulnerable by virtue of low IQ or mental incapacity.[8] In *Silcott, Braithwaite and Raghip* the Court of Appeal held that medical or psychiatric evidence as to the defendant's likely mental state at the time of the interview could be taken into account. (See to the same effect also *McKenzie*,[9]) But *cf. Heaton*[10] where the Court of Appeal (with Lord Taylor L.C.J., presiding[11]) approved the decision of the trial judge not to permit evidence of a psychiatrist to the effect that H was not bright and was abnormally suggestible. Unless the evidence was based on scientific data or expert analysis outside the experience of the judge and jury a mere impression, even of a highly qualified doctor, was not admissible.

It could be argued that the courts have failed to focus sufficiently on the ques- **8–38** tion of reliability. Professor Birch has suggested that the fact that Code provisions have been broken does not necessarily mean that a resultant confession is likely to be unreliable ("were the Criminal Law Revision Committee to report on developments to date they would surely repeat their criticisms, with breaches of the Code taking the place of threats or inducements as the obstacles to the proper consideration of reliability").[12] (Thus, for instance, there are quite a number of decisions where failure to follow the rules regarding recording of questioning has led to the confession being excluded even though it might be thought that there is no necessary connection between such failure and the confession being unreliable.[13])

Confessions can of course be challenged not only under s.76 but also under s.78 and s.82(3).

---

[6] *op.cit.*, para.8–01, n.2 above, pp.43–44.
[7] House of Commons, *Hansard*, Standing Committee, March 8, 1984, col.1657.
[8] See, for instance, *Everett* [1988] Crim.L.R. 826, CA; *Dutton, The Independent*, December 5, 1988, CA; *Moss* (1989) 91 Cr.App.R. 371, CA; *Delaney* (1988) Cr.App.R. 338, CA; *Silcott, Braithwaite and Raghip, The Times*, December 9, 1991.
[9] (1993) 96 Cr.App.R. 98, CA.
[10] [1993] Crim.L.R. 593, CA.
[11] Lord Taylor had presided also in *McKenzie* and in *Miller, Paris and Abdullai*.
[12] Birch, "The Evidence Provisions" (1989) N.I.L.Q. 411 at 419.
[13] *Doolan*, n.97 above; *Delaney*, n.8 above; *Chung*, n.96 above; *Barry*, n.90 above.

Co-accused running "cut-throat" defences

8–39　　It has been held that if two co-accused are running "cut-throat" defences in which each seeks to blame the other, one can use a hearsay admission or confession made by the other even though it could not be adduced on behalf of the prosecution. The co-accused can use the confession against its maker—as evidence of guilt as well as evidence going to credibility as a witness.[14] The Law Commission in its report on hearsay in criminal proceedings recommended that the admissibility of a confession by one co-accused at the instance of another should be governed by provisions similar to s.76 of PACE, but that whereas the standard of proof for the prosecution is beyond a reasonable doubt, for the co-accused it should be only on the balance of probabilities.[15]

Procedure

8–40　　In *Barry*[16] the Court of Appeal said the first step under s.76(2)(b) was to identify everything that had been said and done. The second stage was for the judge to consider whether anything said or done was likely to render unreliable anything said or done in consequence. The third stage was for the judge to ask himself whether the prosecution had proved beyond reasonable doubt that the confession had not been made as a consequence of anything said or done.

　　If the prosecution case depends entirely on confession evidence and the defendant suffers from a significant degree of mental handicap, the trial judge should withdraw the case from the jury if the confessions are unconvincing to a point where a properly directed jury could not convict on them—see the Court of Appeal's important decision in *McKenzie*.[17]

　　Section 76 read literally requires that the issue of admissibility be determined before the evidence is given. The court must not allow the evidence to be given until its admissibility is established if it is represented by the defendant that the confession is inadmissible (subs.(2)); and the same applies where the court of its own motion requires proof of admissibility (subs.(3)). Subsections (2) and (3) both specify that this applies to "any proceedings".

8–41　　In 1982 the Divisional Court said that a trial within a trial was not an appropriate procedure in a magistrates' court.[18] But whether it was intended by Parliament or not, PACE changed this. The requirement of a trial within a trial has been held to apply not only to trials in the Crown Court but equally to those in magistrates' courts: *R. v Liverpool Juvenile Court, Ex p. R.*[19] The Divisional Court granted an application for judicial review after the justices had declined an application by the prosecution (supported by the defence) for the court to hold a trial within a trial to consider the admissibility of a confession. The Divisional

---

[14] *Myers* [1996] 2 Cr.App.R. 335; [1996] Crim.L.R. 735, CA. The decision resolved the conflict in the authorities between *Beckford and Daley* [1991] Crim.L.R. 833, CA and *Campbell and Williams* [1993] Crim.L.R. 448, CA in favour of the latter.
[15] *Law Commission Final Report*, No.245, Cm.3670 (1997), p.118.
[16] (1992) 95 Cr.App.R. 384, CA.
[17] (1993) 96 Cr.App.R. 98, CA.
[18] *F. v Kent Chief Constable* [1982] Crim.L.R. 682, Crown Ct.
[19] [1988] Q.B. 1; Crim.L.R. 572, DC. For comment see Robert Stevens, "Trials within Trials in the Magistrates' Courts: A Panoramic View", J.P.N., August 22, 1988, 531.

Court ruled that a *voire dire* must be held if it was "represented" that a confession was inadmissible. The defendant's evidence could be confined to the issue of admissibility without prejudice to his right to be silent at the trial proper. The court was not concerned at that stage with the truth or otherwise of the confession. The defendant was entitled to a ruling on admissibility before or at the end of the prosecution's case. It should not be necessary to call the prosecution's evidence relating to the obtaining of a confession twice.

As to timing, until recently it seemed that the defendant had both a discretion **8–42** as to whether to raise the issue of admissibility as a preliminary matter and, if so, a second opportunity of attacking the admissibility of the evidence when it came to making his own case. Thus in *Ex p. R.*[20] the Divisional Court ruled that a trial within a trial would only take place before the close of the prosecution case if the defence made representations (or, presumably, if the court took the point under subs.(3)). If no such representation was made, the defence could raise the question of admissibility as much as that of weight at any subsequent stage of the trial. This was the position recognised pre-PACE in the decision of the Judicial Committee of the Privy Council of *Ajodha v The State*.[21]

In the pre-PACE decision of *Watson*[22] the Court of Appeal held that a judge was not prevented from reconsidering a decision on admissibility taken at a trial within a trial. He retained control over the evidence to be submitted to the jury throughout the trial. So if at a later stage further evidence emerged relevant to the voluntariness of the confessions it could be the basis of a ruling to exclude the evidence. But such occasions would obviously be rare.

Both these principles were rejected by the Court of Appeal in *Sat-Bhambra*.[23] **8–43** The trial judge had ruled that 6 of 10 tapes of recorded conversations between the accused and Customs and Excise officers were inadmissible because of the possible effects of medication given to the defendant who was a diabetic. Four other tapes were admitted. Before the jury the doctor put his view about the accused's medical condition even more strongly than on the *voire dire* and the defence submitted that the evidence of the four tapes should also be excluded. The judge said that he was precluded from doing so by the terms of s.76. The Court of Appeal agreed. If a defendant wished to exclude a confession under s.76 he had to raise the issue before the confession was given in evidence. He could not do so afterwards. Once the judge had ruled on s.76, the section ceased to have effect—and (*obiter*) the same applied to s.78. *Watson*, the Court of Appeal ruled, had not survived PACE. The judge could, however, avoid injustice either by applying s.82(3) (see para.8–95 below) or by directing the jury either to disregard the evidence or on weight. He could even discharge the jury and order a retrial.

It seems very unsatisfactory that the court should lose its right to reconsider the issue of admissibility after an initial ruling on the *voire dire*. It is to be hoped that the Court of Appeal will decide that its obiter dictum in *Sat-Bhambra* on the effect of s.78 was wrong and that *Watson* did survive PACE in the sense that a judge can still withdraw evidence from a jury (or in the case of the bench, treat it

---

[20] *R. v Liverpool Juvenile Court, Ex p. R.* [1988] Q.B. 1, DC.
[21] [1982] A.C. 202, PC.
[22] [1980] 1 W.L.R. 991, CA.
[23] (1988) 88 Cr.App.R. 55; [1988] Crim.L.R. 453, CA.

as inadmissible) even after first admitting it.[24] Professor Diane Birch has suggested that "in these enlightened times when s.3 of the Human Rights Act 1998 invites us to look afresh at matters of construction, that if the best way to achieve fairness is to hold a belated voir dire then the judge should not be shy about doing so".[25]

Committal proceedings

8–44 Prior to PACE, magistrates in committal proceedings had no discretion to refuse to admit evidence and the Divisional Court would not interfere with a committal on the ground that inadmissible evidence had been admitted.[26] After PACE was enacted the courts ruled that s.76—and s.78—of PACE could apply to committal proceedings but that in practice it would be rare for them to be applied since it was the trial judge who had to determine questions of the admissibility of evidence.[27] However, the Criminal Procedure and Investigations Act 1996 provided that neither s.76 nor 78 should apply to the attenuated form of committal proceedings that survived that statute.[28] Committal proceedings were further attenuated by the Crime and Disorder Act 1998, s.51 which provided that indictable-only cases should be sent direct to the Crown Court. The Criminal Justice Act 2003, s.41 and Sch.3, when in force, will build on this development by applying the allocation process to either way cases.

Extradition cases

8–45 The Criminal Justice and Public Order Act 1994, s.158(1),(5) provided that the powers of magistrates in extradition committal proceedings should be the same as in a summary trial. In extradition cases, provided the magistrate correctly directs himself on the law, the Divisional Court will only interfere with a magistrates' findings of fact and assessment of their significance when ruling on the admissibility of evidence if they are outside the range of conclusions open to a reasonable magistrate.[29] The issue of the admissibility of evidence eventually has to be considered by the trial judge if extradition takes place.

---

[24] A similar view was expressed forcibly by Professor Smith in a comment on the case: [1988] Crim.L.R. 454–455. Professor Smith argued that it was difficult to see why s.76 should be thought to have had this effect or why the common law position should be thought to have been changed. See to like effect Professor Birch commenting on *Millard* [1987] Crim.L.R. 196 at 198 and Bentil, *op.cit.*, n.58 above. But see *Davis* [1990] Crim.L.R. 860. In *Marshall (Mark)*, *The Times*, December 28, 1992, the Court of Appeal quashed the conviction on the ground of problems with the confession despite the fact that the defence failed to object to the confession evidence being given until the end of the prosecution's case. In *Sayer*, unreported, Case No.72223/F3/86 the Court of Appeal said that the trial had taken place before the decision in *Sat-Bhambra*. However, where evidence was heard and then a submission was made the judge was not powerless. He had powers under s.82(3) "to take such decision as he thinks fit to ensure fairness both to the prosecution . . . and to the defendant".
[25] [2001] Crim.L.R. 653 commenting on the Court of Appeal's decision in *Langley* at 651.
[26] *R. v Norfolk Quarter Sessions, Ex p. Brunson* [1953] 1 Q.B. 503; *R. v Highbury Magistrates' Court, Ex p. Boyce* (1984) 79 Cr.App.R. 132.
[27] On s.76 see, for instance, *R. v Oxford City Justices, Ex p. Berry* [1987] 1 All E.R. 1244.
[28] CPIA 1996, Sch.1, paras 25 and 26.
[29] *R. v Bow Street Magistrates' Court, Ex p. Proulx* [2001] 1 All E.R. 57, DC.

Confessions may be given in evidence for co-accused: s.76A

The Criminal Justice Act 2003 inserted into PACE as from a date to be appointed **8–46** new s.76A headed "Confessions may be given in evidence for co-accused".[30] The position had been that while the prosecution could not make use of a confession which was in breach of ss.76 or 76, a co-defendant could use it to undermine another co-defendant's account or to strengthen his own case. The new subsection when it comes into force applies the same rules to both. Subsection (1) provides that a confession made by an accused person may be given in evidence for another person charged in the same proceedings in so far as it is relevant to any matter in issue and is not excluded under the section. Confession evidence would be excluded under s.76A for the same reasons that it is excluded under s.76 (oppression or unreliability). But whereas the prosecution have to establish beyond reasonable doubt that the confession was not obtained as a result of oppression or in circumstances likely to render it unreliable, a co-defendant need do so only on a balance of probabilities (76A(2)).

Confessions by mentally handicapped persons: s.77[31]

This section requires a judge, in cases brought against persons who are mentally **8–47** handicapped, to warn the jury of the need for special caution before convicting such an accused in reliance on his confession. The judge has to give this warning where the case against the accused depends wholly or mainly on his confession where he is satisfied that the confession was not made in the presence of an independent person. It seems that this applies even to confessions made to friends.[32]

In *Walker*[33] the Court of Appeal said that in cases where the defendant was significantly mentally handicapped and the prosecution would not have a case in the absence of the defendant's confession, the judge was required not only to give a full account of the defence case and of the medical evidence regarding the defendant's mental state, but also to give the jury a general warning that the experience of the courts was that people with significant mental handicaps made false confessions for a variety of reasons. On the other hand, the warning need not be given if the confession was obtained in the presence of a solicitor since he is an independent person.[34]

If the case is a summary one in a magistrates' court, the bench are required to treat it in the same way "as one in which there is a special need for caution before convicting the accused on his confession" (subs.(2)). There is no need for a s.77

---

[30] Criminal Justice Act 2003, s.128.

[31] See 1989 N.I. PACE Order, Art.75.

[32] *Bailey* [1995] Crim.L.R. 723, CA. Conviction for murder and arson was quashed and a retrial ordered because the judge did not give the s.77 warning where the defendant had confessed first to friends and then later to the police. The court gave detailed guidance as to the contents of the warning that should have been given to the jury.

[33] para.8–32, n.86 above.

[34] *Lewis (Martin)* [1996] Crim.L.R. 260, CA.

warning, however, if the prosecution's case is equally strong without the confession or if there is another confession in the presence of an independent person.[35]

8–48   A person is mentally handicapped for the purposes of this section if the court is satisfied that he "is in a state of arrested or incomplete development of mind which includes significant impairment of intelligence and social functioning" (subs.(3)). The decision should be taken on medical evidence rather than on the trial judge's own assessment.[36]

Whereas the Codes of Practice generally treat the mentally handicapped, the mentally disordered and the mentally vulnerable[37] in the same way, the section does not mention the mentally disordered at all. (This may have been simply due to oversight. The section was the result of a last minute amendment to the Bill.)

There have been very few cases on the interpretation of s.77—partly perhaps because cases that might have raised the issue of a s.77 warning have instead been dealt with as issues of admissibility under ss.76 or 78. In *Lamont*,[38] however, the Court of Appeal quashed a conviction for attempted murder and assault occasioning bodily harm where the judge had failed to give the warning. The defendant was mentally sub-normal with the reading age of a child of 8 and an IQ of 73. There was little evidence of the offence other than his confession. The Court of Appeal said that giving the s.77 warning was "an essential part of a fair summing up". It substituted a verdict of assault occasioning bodily harm.

Exclusion of "unfair evidence": s.78[39]

The common law

8–49   The English common law tradition in regard to the exclusion of improperly obtained evidence, other than confessions, was that such evidence was basically admissible subject to a rarely exercised judicial discretion to exclude it. This approach was in marked contrast to that of the common law in regard to confession evidence where, as has been seen, the judges adopted a much more rigorous approach.

The leading authority was *Kuruma, Son of Kaniu v R.*[40] in which, on an appeal from Kenya, the Judicial Committee of the Privy Council held that, if evidence was relevant, it mattered not how it was obtained. The accused in that case had been convicted of being in unlawful possession of ammunition discovered during the course of a search by an officer of a lower rank than the rules required for such searches. But the Board recognised that a judge always had a discretion to

---

[35] *Campbell* (1995) 1 Cr.App.R. 522; [1995] Crim.L.R. 157, CA.
[36] *Everett* and *Silcott, Braithwaite and Raghip, op.cit.*, para.8–37, n.8 above.
[37] As has been seen, this phrase replaced "mentally handicapped" in the 2003 revision of the Codes of Practice but that change has not been reflected in the statute.
[38] [1989] Crim.L.R. 813, CA.
[39] 1989 N.I. PACE Order, Art.76(2)(b) excluded trials on indictment for scheduled offences under the Northern Ireland (Emergency Provisions) Act 1978, s.8. But the tests under Art.76 and s.8 were very similar: see *Mullan* [1988] N.I.J.B. 36 and Birch, "The Evidence Provisions" (1989) N.I.L.Q. 411 at 427–429. See further paras 8–84—8–86 below.
[40] [1955] A.C. 197.

exclude evidence in a criminal case if the rules of admissibility would operate unfairly against the accused. Lord Goddard C.J. said that if evidence was admissible "the court is not concerned with how the evidence was obtained", but he went on to say: "no doubt in a criminal case the judge always has a discretion to disallow evidence if the strict rules of admissibility would operate unfairly against the accused . . . If, for instance, some admission of some piece of evidence, *e.g.* a document, had been obtained from a defendant by a trick, no doubt the judge might properly rule it out."[41]

The continuing existence of the judicial discretion to exclude improperly obtained evidence was confirmed by the Divisional Court in *Jeffrey v Black* in 1978.[42] The accused was arrested for the suspected theft of a sandwich in a pub. The police then went to his home where they discovered drugs. The court held that this search had been unlawful since it was not for the offence for which he was arrested. But it went on to consider whether the evidence should nevertheless have been admitted. Lord Widgery, the Lord Chief Justice, said: ". . . the justices sitting in this case, like any other criminal tribunal in England sitting under the English law, have a general discretion to decline to allow any evidence to be called by the prosecution if they think it would be unfair or oppressive to allow that to be done . . . It is a discretion which every criminal judge has all the time in respect of all the evidence which is tendered by the prosecution."[43] The discretion, he went on, would be rarely used. "But if the case is exceptional, if the case is such that not only have the police officers entered without authority, but they have been guilty of trickery or they have misled someone, or they have been oppressive or they have been unfair, or in other respects they have behaved in a manner which is morally reprehensible, then it is open to the justices to apply their discretion and decline to allow the particular evidence to be let in as part of the trial."[44]

But the following year in *Sang*[45] the House of Lords drastically reduced the scope of the common law discretion to exclude improperly obtained evidence. Lord Diplock in the leading judgment said that there were dicta suggesting that the courts had a general discretion to exclude evidence. There were in fact no decisions that supported such dicta. The fountainhead for all subsequent dicta on the subject was Lord Goddard's statement in *Kuruma* (cited in para.8–49 above). But properly understood this was an example of evidence obtained unfairly from the accused which came within the category of protecting his right not to incriminate himself. *Payne*[46] was a similar case. The court there excluded the evidence of a doctor who said the accused had been drunk while driving, on the ground that the motorist had been told that the doctor would only be looking to see whether he was ill or injured. He was specifically assured by the police that the doctor would not be asked to give an opinion about his sobriety. Lord Parker C.J. said the doctor's evidence should be excluded as a matter of discretion on the basis that, if the motorist had known the true position, he might have refused to subject

8–50

8–51

---

[41] *ibid.*, at 204.
[42] [1978] 1 Q.B. 490, DC.
[43] *ibid.*, at 497–498.
[44] *ibid.*
[45] [1980] A.C. 402; [1979] 2 All E.R. 1222, HC.
[46] [1963] 1 W.L.R. 637.

himself to examination. But apart from *Payne*, Lord Diplock said: "there never has been a case in which these courts have come across conduct so unfair, so tricky or so oppressive as to justify them in holding that the discretion ought to have been exercised in favour of exclusion."[47] The fact was that the common law discretion was very narrow. The courts were not concerned with how evidence was obtained, but merely with how it was used by the prosecution at the trial. Save in regard to confessions or admissions or evidence obtained directly from the accused himself, a judge had no discretion to exclude evidence simply on the ground that it had been improperly obtained. The only broad principle of exclusion was where the prejudicial effect of the evidence greatly outweighed its probative effect. It followed that if, as in *Sang*, evidence had been improperly obtained by use of an agent provocateur, that was not a basis for discretionary exclusion.

The Philips Royal Commission and PACE

8–52 The Philips Royal Commission considered whether the courts ought to be given a broad exclusionary rule. It was invited by some witnesses to recommend some form of exclusionary rule of evidence. In the United States, illegally obtained evidence was generally inadmissible and various bodies giving evidence to the Commission argued for the adoption of such a ("fruit of the poisoned tree") rule. But the Philips Royal Commission was not persuaded. It said that experience in the United States did not suggest that such a rule significantly deterred improper police conduct. It could only affect the small numbers of cases in which the defendant ultimately pleaded not guilty. It operated many months after the event. The proper way to check police misconduct was through actions for damages or disciplinary action by the police themselves.[48] The Commission's views on this issue were much criticised in some quarters.[49]

Neither Mr Whitelaw's nor Mr Brittan's version of the Police and Criminal Evidence Bill initially addressed the problem. But at a very late stage the question suddenly surfaced as one of importance and the Government decided after all to react to the pressure that was developing. The initiative was taken by Lord Scarman who moved an amendment at the Committee stage of the second PACE Bill in the House of Lords to give the courts a discretion to exclude evidence that had arguably been unlawfully obtained—unless the prosecution could prove beyond reasonable doubt that it had been lawfully obtained or that the illegality was of no material significance or that the overriding interests of justice required that it be allowed in as evidence notwithstanding that it was obtained unlawfully.

8–53 The Lord Chancellor, Lord Hailsham, said that he was against the amendment but that there was a case for some form of discretion to be exercised by the judge

---

[47] [1980] A.C. 402 at 435; [1979] All E.R. 1222 at 1229.

[48] Philips Report, paras 4.123–4.128.

[49] See, for instance, Driscoll, "Excluding Illegally Obtained Evidence—Can we learn from the United States?", *Legal Action Group Bulletin*, June 1981, p.131. See also generally Heydon, "Illegally Obtained Evidence" [1973] Crim.L.R. 690; Ashworth, "Excluding Evidence as Protecting Rights" [1977] Crim.L.R. 723. For a comparison with the US see Hartman, "Admissibility of Evidence Obtained by Illegal Search and Seizure under the U.S. Constitution" (1965) 28 M.L.R. 298. See also William J. Stuntz, "The American Exclusionary Rule and Defendants' Changing Rights" [1989] Crim.L.R. 117.

as to when admitting evidence would be unfair to the accused. On that basis Lord Scarman withdrew his amendment.[50]

On the Report stage in the House of Lords, Lord Scarman returned to the point with a similar, though slightly redrafted, amendment. But this time the Lord Chancellor himself proffered his own amendment which would have given the courts a discretion to exclude evidence but only where it was obtained from the accused himself. The court would have a discretion to exclude any evidence obtained from the accused if it appeared to the court "that, having regard to all circumstances, including the circumstances in which the evidence was obtained, the admission of the evidence would be so prejudicial to the fairness of those proceedings that the court ought not to allow it to be given".

The House of Lords debated Lord Scarman's amendment first. Against the advice of the Lord Chancellor, it was approved by 125 votes to 118. In the light of that result, Lord Hailsham's amendment was not debated.[51]

But the Government decided not to accept Lord Scarman's amendment. Mr **8–54** Leon Brittan, the then Home Secretary, told the House of Commons that the reason for this was partly that it would lead to the acquittal of guilty persons for reasons that were insufficiently related to the fairness of the case and partly to avoid excessive burdens on the courts of "trials within trials".[52] Instead he brought forward a new government amendment. This was broadly the same as the clause originally introduced by Lord Hailsham, with the difference that the evidence covered by the clause was no longer limited to that obtained from the accused himself. The new clause became s.78 which provides:

"In any proceedings the court may refuse to allow evidence on which the prosecution proposes to rely to be given if it appears to the court that, having regard to all the circumstances, including the circumstances in which the evidence was obtained, the admission of the evidence would have such an adverse effect on the fairness of the proceedings that the court ought not to admit it."

It is an irony that this last-minute addition to the Bill became the most used and arguably the most important section of the Act.[53]

In *Mason*[54] the Court of Appeal said that s.78 "in our opinion, does no more **8–55** than to restate the power which judges had at common law before the 1984 Act was passed". That view was manifestly wrong. The legislative history clearly indicates an intention to broaden the court's approach to the exclusion of evidence. Moreover, as Professor Dennis has argued, the wording of s.78 gives

---

[50] House of Lords, *Hansard*, July 11, 1984, cols 931–948.
[51] House of Lords, *Hansard*, July 31, 1984, cols 635–675.
[52] House of Commons, *Hansard*, October 29, 1984, cols 1012–1013.
[53] For a critical view however, see Carter, "Evidence Obtained by Use of a Covert Listening Device" (1997) 113 L.Q.R. 468 ("In the course of the past 20 years s.78 would appear to have given rise to many unmeritorious appeals and to the unnecessary prolongation of many meritorious appeals. Its interpretation has been a source of uncertainty and difficulty. It is hard to detect anything of value that it has added to the common law; indeed its existence may in fact have impeded the development of the common law. It is submitted that the time has come for at least consideration to be given to the case for its repeal." (at 479).)
[54] [1988] 1 W.L.R. 139 at 144; [1987] 3 All E.R. 481 at 484, CA.

additional indications.[55] First, the "fairness" discretion in s.78 is not restricted to evidence obtained from the accused. Secondly, whereas *Sang* rejected the idea that the court should be concerned how the evidence was obtained, s.78 specifically refers to "the circumstances in which the evidence was obtained" as one of the factors to be taken into account. Thirdly, s.78 is not limited to evidence obtained by means which violate the accused's privilege against self-incrimination. Fourthly, the court is required to consider the fairness of "the proceedings" not the fairness of "the trial".[56]

8–56   There have been cases, other than *Mason*, in which it was said that the s.78 discretion to exclude evidence is no different from the common law discretion. In *Christou*[57] Lord Taylor said that although the discretion under s.78 was wider in the sense that it was not restricted to evidence obtained from the defendant, the criteria for judging unfairness were the same as under the common law.[58] In *Chalkley and Jeffries*[59] the Court of Appeal denied that s.78 widened the common law rule ("[W]e consider that the inclusion in s.78 of the words 'the circumstances in which the evidence was obtained' was not intended to widen the common law rule in this respect as stated by Lord Diplock in *R. v Sang*"[60]). (The judgment distinguished the exercise of the discretion under s.78 from the discretion as to whether to stay a case for abuse of process which involved broader considerations.)

But the courts have rejected this narrow reading of s.78. In *Looseley* and *Attorney General's Reference (No.3 of 2000)*,[61] two decisions given on the same day, the law lords made it clear that they consider that the judicial discretion under s.78 is a broad one.[62]

8–57   Lord Nicholls of Birkenhead said that the law had "undergone substantial development over the comparatively short period of 20 years since *Sang* was decided" (para.11):

> "The decision in *Sang* on the admissibility of evidence obtained unfairly has been reversed by Parliament, by s.78 of the Police and Criminal Evidence Act 1984. Under s.78 the court now has power to exclude evidence on which the prosecution proposes to rely if, having regard to all the circumstances, the court considers the admission of the evidence would have such an adverse effect on the fairness of the proceedings that the court ought not to admit it. The circumstances to which the court is to have regard include, expressly, the circumstances in which the evidence was obtained. The phrase 'fairness of the proceedings' in s.78 is directed primarily at matters going to fairness in the

---

[55] Dennis, *The Law of Evidence* (2nd ed., Sweet and Maxwell, 2002), p.77.
[56] *cf.* ss.77 and 79 which refer to a duty and a discretion of the court "at trial".
[57] (1992) 95 Cr.App.R. 264, CA.
[58] *ibid.*, at 269.
[59] (1998) 2 Cr.App.R. 79, CA. The decision in *Chalkley* also stands for the separate proposition that the word "unsafe" in s.2 of the Criminal Appeal 1995 should be given a narrow rather than a broad interpretation.
[60] *ibid.*, at 105, *per* Auld L.J. For a critique of *Chalkley* see, for instance, Dennis, *op.cit.*, n.55. above, at pp.80–84.
[61] [2001] UKHL 53; [2001] 4 All E.R. 897, HL.
[62] For another leading case disapproving the narrow view in *Chalkley* see the Court of Appeal's decision in *Togher* [2001] 3 All E.R. 463, *per* Woolf C.J. See to like effect *Cooke* [1995] 1 Cr.App.R. 318, CA, *per* Glidewell L.J.

actual conduct of the trial; for instance, the reliability of the evidence and the defendant's ability to test its reliability. But, rightly, the courts have been unwilling to limit the scope of this wide and comprehensive expression strictly to procedural fairness" (paras.11–12).

Secondly, there had been important developments in the common law: **8–58**

"In *R. v Horseferry Road Magistrates' Court, Ex p. Bennett* [1994] 1 AC 42 your Lordships' House held that the court has jurisdiction to stay proceedings and order the release of the accused when the court becomes aware there has been a serious abuse of power by the executive. The court can refuse to allow the police or prosecuting authorities to take advantage of such an abuse of power by regarding it as an abuse of the court's process. Lord Griffiths, at p 62, echoed the words of Lord Devlin that the courts 'cannot contemplate for a moment the transference to the executive of the responsibility for seeing that the process of law is not abused': see *Connelly v Director of Public Prosecutions* [1964] AC 1254, 1354. The judiciary should accept a responsibility for the maintenance of the rule of law that embraces a willingness to overrule executive action and to refuse to countenance behaviour that 'threatens either basic human rights or the rule of law'. In *Bennett* the defendant claimed he had been forcibly abducted and brought to this country to face trial in disregard of extradition laws. It was not an entrapment case. But in *R. v Latif* [1996] 1 WLR 104 the House confirmed that the same principle is applicable in entrapment cases: see Lord Steyn, at pp 112–113" (paras 13,14).

A third new development identified by Lord Nicholls was the Human Rights Act **8–59**
1998:

"These statutory and common law developments have been reinforced by the Human Rights Act 1998. It is unlawful for the court, as a public authority, to act in a way which is incompatible with a Convention right . . . the court may stay the relevant criminal proceedings, and the court may exclude evidence pursuant to s.78. In these respects *Sang* has been overtaken" (paras 15,16).

The jurisdiction to stay a case for abuse of process and that to exclude evidence under s.78 are distinct but they overlap. In *Loosely* and *Attorney General's Reference (No.3 of 2000)* the House of Lords indicated that in entrapment cases the defence should first ask the court to halt the proceedings for abuse of process and only seek to use s.78 if that failed. But the Law Lords agreed that s.78 could be used to deal with the same kind of issues that would be appropriate matters for an application to stay the case for abuse of process.

In *Sang* Lord Diplock said that there was not a single recorded case in which **8–60**
the Court of Criminal Appeal or the Court of Appeal, Criminal Division had allowed an appeal on the ground that magistrates or the trial judge ought to have excluded evidence because the evidence had been obtained "unfairly or by trickery or in some other way that is morally reprehensible".[63] In the years since

---

[63] [1980] A.C. 402 at 435; [1979] 2 All E.R. 1222 at 1229.

January 1, 1986 there have been numbers of such cases—some based on the application of s.78 and some using the newly developed doctrine of abuse of process.[64] The cases show that English courts have abandoned the amoral common law tradition of receiving non-confession evidence regardless of how it was obtained. As has already been seen, there have, for instance, been numbers of cases in which the courts have rejected identification evidence because the police failed to comply with the PACE procedures—see para.8–65. Thus in *Gall*[65] a conviction for affray was quashed by the Court of Appeal because the investigating officer spoke to the identification officer at the identification parade, contrary to the rules of Code D.[66] Perhaps even stronger are the drink-driving cases where the courts have rejected the scientific (*i.e.* even more "real") evidence of intoxication because of the way the evidence was obtained.[67] In *Sharpe*, for instance, there was dangerous driving, a police car chase and the defendant was found to be way over the alcohol limit. In spite of those strong facts, the Divisional Court quashed the conviction of driving with excess alcohol because the police, having followed him home, had dragged the motorist from his own driveway onto the road where he was required to undergo a breath test. Buckley J. said he put his decision "on the grounds of oppression by the police officers in their general conduct, in particular in his driveway".[68]

8–61   Not that the courts have articulated a consistent and all-embracing theory for the application of s.78. Various principles explaining the exercise of the discretion to exclude evidence have been suggested by academic commentators. These include the "reliability" principle (to promote the reliability of evidence), the "disciplinary" principle (to penalise the police for breaches of the rules as a way of promoting adherence to the rules), and the "protective" principle (to protect the accused).[69] Many cases could be said to fall within those broad approaches— though there is little or no sign that the judges themselves deal with the problems in that way. Indeed, the evidence from the cases is to the contrary.[70]

---

[64] In *Loosely*, Lord Hoffman said that the jurisdiction to stay a case for abuse of process was a recently developed concept. It had not even been mentioned in *Sang*. Moreover, he opined, "if anyone had suggested such a jurisdiction, it would have been emphatically rejected" [*op.cit.*, para.38].

[65] (1990) 90 Cr.App.R. 64, CA.

[66] See also, for instance, *Conway* (1990) 91 Cr.App.R. 143; [1990] Crim.L.R. 402, CA; *Nagah* (1991) 92 Cr.App.R. 344; [1991] Crim.L.R. 55, CA; *Finley* [1993] Crim.L.R. 50, CA; *Kensett* (1993) 157 J.P. 1116, DC; *Knowles* [1994] Crim.L.R. 217, CA; *Ladlow, Moss, Green and Jackson* [1989] Crim.L.R. 219, Crown Ct.

[67] Compare the House of Lords' decision in *Fox* [1986] A.C. 281, given before PACE, with *DPP v McGladrigan* (1991) R.T.R. 297; (1991) 155 J.P. 785, DC; *DPP v Godwin* [1991] R.T.R. 303, DC; and *Sharpe (George Hugo) v DPP* [1993] R.T.R.392, DC. It seems clear that *Thomas* [1990] Crim.L.R. 269, DC was wrongly decided in holding that s.78 could only be applied where there were *mala fides*. But there must be more than merely procedural error. For later drink driving cases see, for instance, *DPP v Kay* [1999] R.T.R.109 and *DPP v Kennedy* [2003] EWHC 2583 (Admin).

[68] *op.cit.*, n.67 above, at 597. See to like effect the earlier case of *Matto v DPP* [1987] R.T.R. 337, DC. But see also two "real" evidence cases: *Cooke* [1995] Crim.L.R. 497, CA and *Stewart* [1995] Crim.L.R. 500, CA.

[69] See especially Ashworth, "Excluding Evidence as Protecting Rights" [1977] Crim.L.R. 723.

[70] See also Hunter, "Judicial Discretion: Section 78 in Practice" [1994] Crim.L.R. 558 reporting on an empirical study in Leeds Crown Court. The judges she interviewed were unanimous in rejecting the idea that they considered any of these theoretical principles when deciding whether to exclude disputed evidence. In this writer's view the same would probably be equally true of most judges in the Court of Appeal.

The writer believes rather that s.78 has become both established and accepted as a means for the courts to determine what breaches of the rules or improper conduct are unacceptable on a case-by-case basis, without any clearly articulated theory. Usually, even when there has been some breach or impropriety, the trial judge allows the evidence in and, even when it finds there to have been impropriety, the Court of Appeal usually ends by dismissing the appeal. But there have been many cases, including non-confession cases, in which the appeal court has quashed a conviction because of such improprieties. In the great majority of such cases the court's chief concern seems to be that the verdict should be based on reliable evidence. But sometimes the court is expressing a more fundamental concern directed not so much to the result in the particular case as to a view that the system demands a minimum of procedural correctness and moral integrity.[71]

To some extent the decisions of the courts applying s.78 can be systematised.   **8–62** Certain basic distinctions have emerged. But there remains—and will always remain—a significant and irreducible degree of pure discretion left to the court, which, by definition, means that its decision could go either way. Professor Diane Birch, writing about the entrapment cases, has suggested that "The more principled the discretion can be said to be, and the more its underlying aims can be articulated, the more consistent will be the decisions made under it".[72] She cites another academic view of the need to avoid the "mushiness and unpredictability of a general doctrine of exclusion for 'unfairness'".[73] In this writer's view consistency in the application of a discretion to exclude evidence on the grounds of unfairness may be desirable but it is unattainable.

In his *Review of the Criminal Courts*[74] published in October 2001, Lord Justice Auld recommended (at pp.562–563) that as part of an overall reform of the law of criminal evidence, the rules regarding the exclusion of evidence because of its unfairness and the staying of a prosecution on account of improperly obtained evidence should be rationalised. He said there was a confusing overlap between the various provisions and uncertainty as to the ambit of s.78(1) and the common law power to exclude and as to their relationship one with another. The central problem he suggested was whether the courts could exclude evidence (other than confessions or admissions) because of the way it had been obtained or only if its reliability was questionable. But this question has now been answered and it is difficult to see that there is need for statutory "rationalisation" unless it is felt that the broad approach adopted by the courts is wrong. In that case, a possible model for statutory "rationalisation" could be the formula proposed by P.B. Carter in his critique of s.78, *op.cit.*, n.53 above. He proposed (at p.478) that apart from admissions, confessions and other evidence obtained from the accused or from his premises, the court's discretion to exclude evidence on the ground that it has been

---

[71] See further Dennis, "Reconstructing the Law of Criminal Evidence" [1989] 42 *Current Legal Problems* 21; Zuckerman, "Illegally Obtained Evidence: Discretion as a Guardian of Legitimacy" [1987] 40 *Current Legal Problems* 55; and Sharpe, "Search warrants: Process protection or process validation" (1999) 3 Int'l Jrnl. of Ev. and Proof 101.

[72] "Excluding evidence from entrapment: what is a 'fair cop'?" [1994] 47 *Current Legal Problems* 73 at 89.

[73] Heydon, "Entrapment and unfairly obtained evidence in the House of Lords" [1980] Crim.L.R. 129 at 134.

[74] The *Review* is available from HMSO and on the internet at *www.criminalcourts-review.org.uk* and also at *www.lcd.gov.uk*.

obtained by improper or unfair means should exist only "where the public interest in the fair administration of the criminal law undoubtedly requires that the court should have the power to exclude the evidence".

8–63   Carter's proposal is not dissimilar to the rule in Scotland where the courts decide whether to admit improperly obtained real evidence by balancing the need to preserve civil liberties and the need to ensure that justice is done.[75] But it has proved that this is not a recipe for a principled or consistent line. According to Professor Peter Duffy of Aberdeen University, the factors taken into account by the judges include the gravity of the crime, the seriousness of the irregularity, the urgency of the investigation, the likelihood that the evidence would disappear if not seized immediately; the authority of those obtaining the evidence, the good faith of the investigators and fairness to the accused. In Duffy's view, it was not clear from the jurisprudence why each factor was relevant nor in what circumstances it should be taken into account. On examining the case law, he said, it was difficult to avoid the conclusion that the decision whether to admit improperly obtained real evidence is made by the courts on the basis mainly of a "'gut reaction" which is then rationalised with whatever factor or factors from the list above best justifies the decision". As yet "no principled, logical and coherent regime [had] emerged in Scotland to guide the courts in the use of their power to admit or exclude irregularly obtained real evidence".[76]

8–64   Mr David Ormerod and Professor Diane Birch proposed some structuring of s.78 to identify for the judiciary and magistrates the significant factors to which they should attach importance in exercising their discretion: "This," they argued, "should ease the burden on the trier of law by unpacking the concept of unfairness. In addition, the cataloguing of significant factors would have an important value in providing clarity and transparency in the decision making process . . . Arguably, nearly twenty years of unstructured discretion should yield more specific guidelines for its future exercise."[77] Professor Duffy's picture of what has happened in Scotland gives little reason to believe that any such hope is well founded.

By far the most common basis for the Court of Appeal to apply s.78 has been "significant and substantial" breaches of the PACE rules. There are now a very great number of such decisions—too many to include here. What follows is an indication of the case law under the different main headings.

Breaches of PACE and/or the Codes not condoned

8–65   **D not told his rights or not given required information**—*Beycan,*[78] *Sanusi,*[79] *Absolam,*[80] *Oransaye,*[81] *Fennelley.*[82]

---

[75] Ross, *Walker and Walker The Law of Evidence in Scotland* (Edinburgh, 2000), p.7.
[76] Duffy, "Irregularly obtained real evidence: The Scottish solution?" (2004) 8 *International Journal of Evidence and Proof* 77 at 98–99.
[77] Ormerod and Birch, "50th Anniversary Article: The Evolution of the Discretionary Exclusion of Evidence" [2004] Crim.L.R. 767 at 786–77.
[78] [1990] Crim.L.R. 185, CA.
[79] [1992] Crim.L.R. 43, CA.
[80] (1988) Cr.App.R. 332, CA—*cf. Iroegbu, The Times,* August 2, 1988, CA.
[81] [1993] Crim.L.R. 722, CA.
[82] [1989] Crim.L.R.142, Crown Ct—*cf. McCarthy* [1996] Crim.L.R. 818, CA.

D not given access to a solicitor—*Samuel,*[83] *Parris,*[84] *Walsh,*[85] *Chung,*[86] *Silcott,*[87] *Sanusi,*[88] *Wadman.*[89]

D not cautioned—*Doolan,*[90] *Sparks,*[91] *Hunt,*[92] *Okafor,*[93] *Bryce,*[94] *Weerdesteyn,*[95] *Batley v DPP,*[96] *Miller,*[97] *Kirk,*[98] *Allen.*[99]

D not provided with an appropriate adult—*Fogah,*[1] *Dutton,*[2] *Coker and Marshall,*[3] *Weekes,*[4] *Glaves,*[5] *Aspinall,*[6] *Haroon Ali,*[7] *Kenny.*[8]

Interview formalities not complied with—*Doolan,*[9] *Manji,*[10] *Chung,*[11] *Hunt,*[12] *Scott,*[13] *Townend,*[14] *Keenan,*[15] *Rowe,*[16] *Joseph,*[17] *Gizzi,*[18] *Bassil and*

[83] [1988] Q.B. 615; [1988] 2 W.L.R. 920, CA.
[84] (1989) 89 Cr.App.R. 68; [1989] Crim.L.R. 214, CA.
[85] (1989) 91 Cr.App.R. 161; [1989] Crim.L.R. 822, CA.
[86] (1991) 92 Cr.App.R. 314; [1991] Crim.L.R. 622, CA.
[87] *The Times,* December 9, 1991, CA.
[88] [1992] Crim.L.R. 43, CA; *Maynard,* unreported, Case No.97132551W3, April 2, 1998, CA.
[89] Unreported, Case No.9607211/Z4, August 22, 1997, CA.
[90] [1988] Crim.L.R. 747, CA. But the court applied the proviso.
[91] [1991] Crim.L.R. 128, CA. But the court applied the proviso.
[92] [1992] Crim.L.R. 582, CA. The court allowed the appeal
[93] (1994) 99 Cr.App.R. 97; [1994] Crim.L.R. 221, CA. But the court applied the proviso.
[94] (1992) 95 Cr.App.R. 230; [1992] 4 All E.R. 567; [1992] Crim.L.R. 728, CA. Undercover police officer. The conviction was quashed for failure to caution.
[95] [1995] 1 Cr.App.R. 405; [1995] Crim.L.R. 239.
[96] [1998] T.L.R. 137, DC.
[97] [1998] Crim.L.R. 209, CA.
[98] [1999] 4 All E.R. 698, CA (*cf.* *MJ,* unreported, Case No.9902830/Z2).
[99] [2001] EWCA Crim 1607.
[1] (1989) 90 Cr.App.R. 115, CA.
[2] *The Independent,* December 5, 1988, CA.
[3] Unreported, Case No.T900616, August 6, 1990, CCC. The police had no reason to suppose that the suspect was in the bottom 1% of the intellectual range of the population. He gave long and coherent replies to proper and unoppressive questioning in regard to a rape charge. But the judge excluded his confession on the ground that the Code proceeds on the basis that without an appropriate adult, confessions "are or maybe inherently unreliable". The judge said "Whatever . . . the practical advantages may in reality [be] derive[d] from the presence of such adults, it is the intention and spirit of the legislation of Parliament which the courts must loyally observe".
[4] (1993) 97 Cr.App.R. 222; [1993] Crim.L.R. 211, CA.
[5] [1993] Crim.L.R. 685, CA.
[6] [1999] 2 Cr.App.R. 115; [1999] Crim.L.R. 741, CA.
[7] Unreported, Case No.98/04160/X2, November 24, 1998, CA.
[8] [1994] Crim.L.R. 284, CA.
[9] n.90 above.
[10] [1990] Crim.L.R. 512, CA.
[11] (1991) 92 Cr.App.R. 314, CA. The Court of Appeal found it "quite astonishing" that four officers had not between them managed to make a contemporaneous note of an interview with the defendant whilst his home was being searched. Held: that this (together with unlawful delay of access to a solicitor) could have made the confession unreliable (which could not have been the case) or the record unreliable (which is not relevant under s.76(2)(b)).
[12] n.92 above.
[13] [1991] Crim.L.R. 56, CA.
[14] Unreported, Case No.5860/X2/88, CA.
[15] (1990) 90 Cr.App.R. 1; [1989] Crim.L.R. 720, CA. The court said that breaches must be "significant and substantial" to justify exclusion under ss.76 or 78. If the defendant intended not to give evidence if the officer's evidence was excluded, admitting it unfairly robbed him of his right to remain silent. Also by attacking the police evidence he put his character in evidence.
[16] [1994] Crim.L.R. 837, CA—but the court applied the proviso.
[17] [1993] Crim.L.R. 206, CA.
[18] Unreported, Case No.92/5227/Y5, July 15, 1993, CA.

Mouffareg,[19]   *Kenny,*[20]   *Conway,*[21]   *Thompson,*[22]   *Coleman, Knight and Hochenburg,*[23] *Raphaie,*[24] *C,*[25] *Haroon Ali,*[26] *Aspinall,*[27] *Gayle,*[28] *Allen.*[29]

Initial breach contaminates later interviews—*Canale,*[30] *Wilkinson,*[31] *Bryce,*[32] *McGovern,*[33] *Wood,*[34] *Ismail,*[35] *Neil,*[36] *Glaves,*[37] *Burut,*[38] *Conway,*[39] (*cf. Y v DPP,*[40] *Gillard,*[41] *Madeley,*[42] *Doran,*[43] *Barrell, Cooke and Cooke*[44]), *Cross.*[45] (For discussion of this problem see Mirfield, "Successive Confessions and the Poisonous Tree" [1996] Crim.L.R. 554–67.)

[19] *Legal Action*, December 1990, p.23, Crown Ct.
[20] [1994] Crim.L.R. 284, CA.
[21] [1994] Crim.L.R. 838, CA.
[22] Unreported, Case No.94/7253/X4, May 9, 1995, CA.
[23] Unreported, Case No.94/4814/X4, October 20, 1995, CA.
[24] [1996] Crim.L.R. 812, CA.
[25] [1997] N.I.J.B. 37.
[26] Unreported, Case No.98/04160/X2, November 24, 1998, CA.
[27] [1999] 2 Cr.App.R. 115; [1999] Crim.L.R. 741, CA.
[28] [1999] Crim.L.R. 502, CA
[29] [2001] EWCA Crim 1607, CA.
[30] (1989) 91 Cr.App.R. 1; [1990] Crim.L.R. 329, CA. The court said the importance of the rules relating to contemporaneous noting of interviews could scarcely be over-emphasised. The object was twofold: "not merely to ensure, so far as possible that the suspect's remarks are accurately recorded and that he has an opportunity when he goes through the contemporaneous note afterwards of checking each answer and initialling each answer, but likewise it is protection for the police, to ensure, so far as is possible, that it cannot be suggested that they induced the suspect to confess by improper approaches or improper promises".
[31] Unreported, Case No.91/4143/WA, CA.
[32] n.94 above.
[33] (1991) 92 Cr.App.R. 228, CA.
[34] [1996] 1 Cr.App.R. 207; [1994] Crim.L.R. 222, CA. The court said that where there had been oppression or an inducement in an earlier interview, it may be more difficult for the prosecution to prove that it has not carried through to a later interview. But in the case of a person of normal intellect who has had the opportunity of a full discussion with his solicitor before the later interview, the crown may be able to discharge the burden.
[35] [1990] Crim.L.R. 109, CA.
[36] [1994] Crim.L.R. 441, CA. Fatal stabbing. The court held that the question whether later unobjectionable interviews are contaminated by breaches in earlier interviews is a question of fact and degree. Were the breaches of a fundamental and continuing character, and, if so, was the accused given a sufficient opportunity to make an informed decision whether to retract what he had previously said?
[37] n.5 above.
[38] [1995] 2 A.C. 579, PC.
[39] [1994] Crim.L.R. 838, CA.
[40] [1991] Crim.L.R. 917, CA.
[41] (1991) 92 Cr.App.R. 61; [1991] Crim.L.R. 280, CA.
[42] Unreported, March 18, 1992, CA.
[43] Unreported, Case No.88/7185/Y2, February 6, 1990, CA.
[44] Unreported, Case No.89/3403/S, February 21, 1992, CA. There is no hard and fast rule that because earlier tapes are held inadmissible, the same will apply to later ones.
[45] Unreported, February 26, 1997, Lexis, Belfast Crown Ct.

Identification procedures not complied with—*Conway,*[46] *Payne and Quinn,*[47] *Brown,*[48] *Graham,*[49] *Rutherford and Palmer,*[50] *Ventour,*[51] *Coleman,*[52] *Gall,*[53] *Martin and Nicholls,*[54] *Finley,*[55] *Walker,*[56] *Allen,*[57] *Payne and Quinn,*[58] *Hickin,*[59] *Johnson,*[60] *McMath,*[61] *Vaughan,*[62] *Wait,*[63] *Jones and Nelson,*[64] *Fuller,*[65] *Sangarie,*[66] *Miah.*[67]

[46] (1990) 91 Cr.App.R. 143; [1990] Crim.L.R. 402, CA. Conviction quashed because there was a dock identification rather than an identity parade. No reference was made either by counsel or the court to s.78. In *North Yorkshire Trading Standards Department v Williams*, November 22, 1994 the Divisional Court said that dock identification was generally undesirable even where the prosecution had no power to require a defendant to attend an identification parade. The principles applicable to more serious cases should apply equally to trivial cases. The prosecution's appeal was dismissed.

[47] *The Times*, March 15, 1995, CA. Conviction quashed because of defects in identification procedure. The court said the judge could have admitted the evidence but he should have pointed out the breaches to the jury in his summing up. See, however, *Middlebrook*, n.12 below, where the Court of Appeal said that it was not the function of the jury to supervise the Codes. It is not easy to see how these two positions regarding the role of the jury can be reconciled.

[48] [1991] Crim.L.R. 368, CA. Failure to hold identification parade was a breach of Code D. But appeal dismissed because of the cumulative strength of the evidence.

[49] [1994] Crim.L.R. 212, CA. Failure to hold a parade was fatal. Conviction quashed.

[50] (1994) Cr.App.R. 141, CA. Breach of Code D in not holding a parade. But appeal dismissed because of the strength of the evidence.

[51] Unreported, Case No.418/C1/88, December 16, 1988, CA. Failure to hold parade and showing photograph before a confrontation resulted in conviction being quashed.

[52] Unreported, Case No.729/A2/88 March 30, 1990, CA. A variety of breaches of Code D. Conviction quashed.

[53] (1990) 90 Cr.App.R. 64; [1989] Crim.L.R. 745, CA. An officer concerned with the ID parade brought the witness to the parade, looked in and spoke to the identification officer. At first trial this breach of Code D2.2 resulted in the identification evidence being excluded. At the second trial it was allowed in. Held: should have been excluded.

[54] [1994] Crim.L.R. 218, CA. Two black defendants identified by schoolboy victims of theft from the person in the court building where there were very few non-White youths. Held: identifications were made in highly unsatisfactory conditions and a long time after the incidents.

[55] [1993] Crim.L.R. 50, CA. Many breaches of the Code. Difficult to believe it was mere inefficiency as opposed to deliberate flouting of the Code. It was bound to appear that justice did not seem to have been done.

[56] Unreported, Case No.94/1733/Y2, November 14, 1994, CA.

[57] [1995] Crim.L.R. 643, CA.

[58] [1995] Crim.L.R. 56, CA.

[59] [1996] Crim.L.R. 584, CA.

[60] [1996] Crim.L.R. 504, CA.

[61] [1997] Crim.L.R. 586, CA.

[62] Unreported, Case No.96/6431/Y3, April 30, 1997, CA.

[63] [1998] Crim.L.R. 68, CA.

[64] *The Times*, April 21, 1999, CA.

[65] Unreported, Case No.1999/06023/WA, May 22, 2000, CA.

[66] [2001] EWCA Crim 1734 CA.

[67] [2001] EWCA Crim 2281, CA.

Sometimes, however, the courts are prepared in effect to condone or overlook breaches of the PACE rules:

Breaches of PACE and/or the Codes condoned

8–66   **No caution where one is required**—*O'Shea*,[68] *Weekes*,[69] *de Sayrah*,[70] *Allison and Murray*,[71] *Pall*,[72] *Nelson and Rose*[73] (*cf.* no caution where one is not required—*Konscol*,[74] *Shah*,[75] *Park*,[76] *Nesbeth*,[77] *Oni*,[78] *Purcell*,[79] *Scholfield*[80]). (See also *Slater and Douglas*.[81])

Access to legal advice wrongly refused—*Alladice*,[82] *Dunford*,[83] *McGovern*,[84] *Oliphant*.[85]

Interview or other procedural formalities not complied with—*Langiert*,[86] *White*,[87] *Hoyte*,[88] *Walsh*,[89] *Dunn*,[90] *Bedford*,[91] *Wright*,[92] *Duffy*,[93] *Dures, Dures and Williams*.[94]

D not provided with appropriate adult—*Ham*,[95] *Law-Thompson*.[96]

---

[68] [1993] Crim.L.R. 951, CA.

[69] Unreported, Case No.90/859/Y4, January 11, 1991, CA.

[70] Unreported, Case No.89/5270/Y3, June 25, 1990, CA.

[71] Unreported, Case No.1731/A1/88, October 25, 1988, CA. Both appellants knew they did not have to answer questions.

[72] [1992] Crim.L.R. 126, CA.

[73] [1998] 2 Cr.App.R. 399; [1998] Crim.L.R. 814, CA.

[74] Unreported, Case No.92/1352/Z2, May 18, 1993, CA. The interview took place abroad.

[75] [1994] Crim.L.R. 128, CA. Insufficient reason to suspect at that stage.

[76] (1994) 99 Cr.App.R. 270, CA. Insufficient reason to suspect at that stage.

[77] Unreported, Case No.336/Y3/90, February 12, 1991. Insufficient reason to suspect at that stage.

[78] [1992] Crim.L.R. 183, CA. Just cautioned in respect of a different offence.

[79] [1992] Crim.L.R. 806, CA.

[80] Unreported, Case No.97/08475 Y3, February 3, 1998, CA.

[81] [2001] EWCA Crim 2869.

[82] (1988) 87 Cr.App.R. 380; [1988] Crim.L.R. 608, CA.

[83] (1990) 91 Cr.App.R. 150; [1991] Crim.L.R. 370, CA.

[84] (1991) 92 Cr.App.R. 228; [1991] Crim.L.R. 124, CA.

[85] [1992] Crim.L.R. 40, CA.

[86] [1991] Crim.L.R. 777, CA.

[87] [1991] Crim.L.R. 779, CA.

[88] [1994] Crim.L.R. 215, CA.

[89] (1989) 91 Cr.App.R. 161, CA. The court said that not every significant or substantial breach of the Code will result in the evidence being excluded under s.78. The court must always consider whether there would be such an adverse effect on the fairness of the proceedings that justice required the evidence to be excluded.

[90] (1990) 91 Cr.App.R. 237, CA. The court found that there had been "serious and inexcusable breaches" but refused to apply s.78 because a solicitors' clerk had been present.

[91] (1991) 93 Cr.App.R. 113, CA

[92] [1994] Crim.L.R. 55, CA.

[93] [1997] N.I.J.B. 228.

[94] [1997] 2 Cr.App.R. 247, CA; *Roberts (Stephen)* [1997] Crim.L.R. 222, CA.

[95] Unreported, Case No.95/2020/W3, December 1, 1995, CA.

[96] [1997] Crim.L.R. 674, CA

Identification evidence allowed in, despite breach of PACE or Code— *Quinn,*[97] *McClay,*[98] *Ryan,*[99] *Grannell,*[1] *Tiplady,*[2] *Cooke,*[3] *Montgomery,*[4] *McEvoy,*[5] *Khan,*[6] *Bell,*[7] *Forbes,*[8] *Loveridge (William), Lee (Charles Sonny) and Loveridge (Christine),*[9] *Davis v DPP.*[10]

The crucial question for the trial court and the Court of Appeal is always **8–67** whether the effect of the way in which the evidence was obtained is such as to make the proceedings so unfair as to require it to be excluded. This, unavoidably, is a matter of judgment (discretion) on which reasonable people and reasonable judges may disagree. The Court of Appeal has indicated that generally it will leave the matter to trial judges and will not interfere with the view they have taken unless no trial judge could reasonably have reached that view.[11] In *Middlebrook*[12] the Court of Appeal said that if a reasonable judge must have concluded that the evidence would produce unfairness, the Court of Appeal would set aside a ruling going the other way.[13]

It is not necessary to establish that there has been a breach of PACE or other police misconduct. In *Brine,*[14] for instance, the Court of Appeal allowed the appeal because the trial judge had not taken into account the defendant's psychological pre-disposition to stress even though the police were unaware of this condition. But police misconduct does commonly come into the question.

---

[97] [1990] Crim.L.R. 581, CA. The charge was an IRA murder of a police officer in 1975. The identification was 11 weeks later, in court when the defendant was being tried on other charges. The murder trial was in 1988 after the defendant had been extradited from the United States. The Court of Appeal said there were five relevant circumstances that the court should take into account when deciding whether to exclude identification evidence: (1) the possibility of difficulty for the defence in cross-examining; (2) the court should insist on the best possible identification evidence, (3) the denial of a parade was capable of being unfair but here the defendant had himself refused a parade; (4) the reasons for delay—here the delay was caused by the long fight over extradition; and (5) the nature of other evidence. *Mala fides* and breaches of the Codes were relevant but not necessarily decisive.
[98] Unreported, Case No.91/3142/W3, December 15, 1992, CA. No ID parade, therefore a breach of Code D, but less important where the witness who identified D knew him previously.
[99] [1992] Crim.L.R. 187, CA. Major breach of Code para.2.2 in investigating officer being involved in setting up the parade but evidence allowed in because the defendant's interests had been sufficiently protected by his solicitor.
[1] (1989) 90 Cr.App.R. 149, CA. The breach, consisting of an informal group identification in the foyer of the court, held not to be unfair.
[2] [1995] Crim.L.R. 651, CA
[3] [1995] 1 Cr.App.R. 318, CA.
[4] [1996] Crim.L.R. 507, CA.
[5] [1997] Crim.L.R. 887, CA.
[6] [1997] Crim.L.R. 584, CA.
[7] [1998] Crim.L.R. 879, CA.
[8] [2001] 1 Cr.App.R. 31; [2001] 1 All E.R. 686, HL.
[9] [2001] EWCA Crim 973; [2001] 2 Cr.App.R. 29.
[10] [2001] EWHC Admin 1129.
[11] *Quinn* [1995] 1 Cr.App.R. 480 at 489 *per* Lord Taylor C.J.
[12] Unreported, Case No.92/6701/Z2, February 18, 1994, CA.
[13] In *Dures, Dures and Williams* [1997] 2 Cr.App.R. 247, CA, the Court of Appeal said (at 261–262) that if there was any difference between *Quinn* and *Middlebrook*, what was said by Lord Taylor in the former case should be followed.
[14] [1992] Crim.L.R. 122, CA.

8–68   Where the police have used deception in the process of investigation, again sometimes the court allow the evidence in, whilst sometimes they will apply s.78 to exclude it.[15]

Evidence obtained by deception, tricks, stratagems or undercover police work held inadmissible—*Mason*,[16] *H*,[17] *Gary Blake*,[18] *Bryce*,[19] *George Heron*,[20] *Keith Hall*,[21] *Colin Stagg*,[22] *Tonnessen*,[23] *Sargent*.[24] See also *Allan v United Kingdom*[24a] *and Lewis v United Kingdom*.[24b]

However, there are many more cases when the courts have allowed in evidence obtained as a result of police tricks and stratagems, even sometimes where there was an element of entrapment.

---

[15] There is considerable literature on this subject: Ashworth, "Re-drawing the Boundaries of Entrapment" [2002] Crim.L.R. 161; Ormerod and Roberts, "The trouble with *Teixeira*: Developing a principled approach to entrapment" (2000) 6(1) Int'l Jrnl. of Ev. and Proof 38; Ashworth, "Testing Fidelity to Legal Values: Official Involvement and Criminal Justice" (2000) 63 *Modern Law Review* 633; Jennings, "The future of covert policing: will it rest in peace?" (2000) *Archbold News*, No.8 at 6, No.9 at 6; Chalmers, "Test purchasing, entrapment and human rights" [2000] New L.J. 1444; Bronit and Roche, "Between rhetoric and reality: socio-legal and republican perspectives on entrapment" [2000] Int'l Jrnl. of Ev. and Proof 77; Davies, "The Fruit of the Poisoned Tree—Entrapment and the Human Rights Act 1998" (1999) 163 J.P. 84; Uglow, "Court Surveillance and the European Convention on Human Rights" [1999] Crim.L.R. 287; Ashworth, "Defending the entrapped" (1999) 9 *Archbold News* 5; Ashworth, "The Exclusion of Evidence Obtained by Entrapment and the Use of Agents Provocateurs" (1999) 9 *Archbold News* 5; Ashworth, "Should the police be allowed to use deceptive practices" (1998) 114 L.Q.R. 108; Sharpe, "Judicial Discretion and Investigative Impropriety" (1997) 1(2) Int'l Jrnl. of Ev. and Proof 149; Grevling, "Undercover operations: Balancing the Public Interest?" (1996) 112 L.Q.R. 401; Sharpe, "Covert Police Operations and the Discretionary Exclusion of Evidence" [1994] Crim.L.R. 793; Robertson. "Entrapment Evidence: Manna from Heaven, or Fruit of the Poisoned Tree" *ibid.*, at 805; Birch, "Excluding evidence from entrapment: when is it a fair cop?" (1994) *Current Legal Problems* 73.
[16] [1988] 1 W.L.R. 139; [1987] 3 All E.R. 481; (1988) 86 Cr.App.R. 349, CA. Police falsely told D and his solicitor that D's fingerprints had been found at scene of crime. Held: subsequent confession not admissible especially it seems because of the deceit on the solicitor.
[17] [1987] Crim.L.R. 47, Crown Ct. Police arranged for rape victim to lure alleged rapist into a taped telephone conversation. She specifically told him it was not being taped. Held: the conversation had to be excluded as an unfair trap.
[18] [1991] Crim.L.R. 119, Crown Ct. Falsely told that his voice had been identified. Held: inadmissible.
[19] See para.8–66, n.94.
[20] See para.8–26 above.
[21] National newspapers, March 11, 1994. Waterhouse J. at Leeds Crown Court held inadmissible taped admissions regarding murder of accused's first wife made to undercover WPC who had befriended him.
[22] See similarly the view of Ognall J. on the evidence of the undercover WPC who befriended Colin Stagg accused of the Wimbledon Common murder. She tried to get him to confess by sending him lurid sex material. Described by the judge as an attempt to incriminate him "by deceptive conduct of the grossest kind". See national newspapers, September 15, 1994.
[23] (1998) 2 Cr.App.R.(S) 328 where the appeal resulted not in exclusion of the evidence but in a reduction of sentence because of entrapment. The accused was set up by two journalists to supply them with heroin for a sheikh for whom they said they worked. They then published the story with a picture.
[24] [2001] 3 W.L.R. 992, HL—defendant confessed after he was confronted with an illegally recorded telephone transcript. The Law Lords held that the transcript of the telephone interview should not have been admitted, that the judge was right nevertheless to admit the confession in evidence but that the conviction was unsafe under s.78—*cf. P* [2001] 2 W.L.R. 463; [2001] 2 All E.R. 58, HL.
[24a] (2003) 36 E.H.R.R. 12. The European Court of Human Rights held covert recording of suspect questioned by a police informant in a police cell infringed his rights under Art.8 of the Convention.
[24b] (2004) 39 E.H.R.R. 9. Covert listening device installed by the police in L's home before the statutory procedure established by the Police Act 1997 was in place. Breach of Art.8 of the ECHR.

Evidence obtained by deception, tricks, stratagems or undercover police work held admissible—*DPP v Marshall and Downes*,[25] *Jelen and Katz*,[26] *Shaukat Ali*,[27] *Bailey and Smith*,[28] *Edwards*,[29] *Effik, Mitchell*,[30] *Christou, Wright*,[31] *Maclean and Kosten*,[32] *Smurthwaite, Gill*,[33] *Gill and Ranuana*,[34] *Gibbons and Winterburn*,[35] *Cadette*,[36] *Morley and Hutton*,[37] *Farooq and Ramzan*,[38] *Lin, Hung and Tsui*,[39] *Latif and Shahzad*,[40] *Khan*,[41] *Chalkley and*

[25] [1988] 3 All E.R. 683; [1988] Crim.L.R. 750, CA. Out-of-hours test purchases by plain-clothes officer of liquor from licensed premises. See to like effect *London Borough of Ealing v Woolworths plc* [1995] Crim.L.R. 58, DC.

[26] (1990) 90 Cr.App.R. 456, CA. Surreptitious tape recording of a conversation between the defendant and a co-defendant allowed in. *H*, n.17 above, distinguished on the ground that here the inquiries were at an early stage.

[27] *The Times*, February 19, 1991, CA. Police bugged interview room in police station after the defendant had been charged with murder and recorded an incriminatory conversation between D and his family.

[28] [1993] Crim.L.R. 681, CA. Defendants in robbery cases tricked into believing that the cell in which they had been placed was not bugged. Evidence of their conversation held to have been correctly admitted. The court said such stratagems should only be used in grave cases and nothing should be done oppressively or so as to render the admission unreliable.

[29] [1991] Crim.L.R. 45, CA. Undercover drugs squad officers offered to buy drugs from drugs dealer. Ample evidence that he was involved in the conspiracy before the police came on the scene. (The charge was conspiracy to supply to persons unknown—not to the police officers.)

[30] (1992) 95 Cr.App.R. 427, CA. Court of Appeal upheld trial judge's decision to allow in evidence of overheard incriminatory phone conversation on a cordless telephone between the defendant and a third person. Even if the interception was illegal under the Interception of Communications Act 1985, it was not unfair to admit it.

[31] (1992) 95 Cr.App.R. 264; [1992] Crim.L.R. 729, CA. Police set up phoney jewellery business as a "sting fencing operation" and recorded transactions on film and tape. Held: evidence admissible. They did not incite the crime, nor did they question the suspects. The judge could exclude the evidence where an undercover disguise was adopted in order to question the suspect without complying with the Code.

[32] [1993] Crim.L.R. 687, CA. Importing cannabis. Defendant tricked into coming to this country and tricked into revealing his involvement in the offence. Held: he had applied himself to the ruse as in *Christou*.

[33] [1994] 1 All E.R. 898, CA. Two wives solicited undercover police officers as "hitmen" to murder their husbands. The conversations, which were tape-recorded, were held to have been rightly admitted. There had been no incitement by the officer.

[34] [1989] Crim.L.R. 358, CA. Conspiracy to murder Rajiv Gandhi. Conversations with undercover officers posing as IRA members held admissible.

[35] *The Times*, July 19, 1993. Conspiracy to supply drugs. Conversation with undercover officers admitted in evidence even though not all were not taped. But the defence did not deny the content of the conversations—only their import.

[36] [1995] Crim.L.R. 229, CA.

[37] [1994] Crim.L.R. 919, CA.

[38] [1995] Crim.L.R. 169, CA.

[39] [1995] Crim.L.R. 817, CA.

[40] [1996] 1 W.L.R. 104; [1996] 1 All E.R. 353, HL. Defendant was lured to come to the UK by trickery but he was not a vulnerable unwilling person but a willing heroin dealer.

[41] [1997] A.C. 558; [1996] 3 W.L.R. 162; [1996] Cr.App.R. 440; [1996] 3 All E.R. 289, HL. Bug fixed to the outside walls of home in heroin investigation. Evidence from the bugging admissible even if the result of trespass or of a breach of the ECHR. (In May 2000 the bugging was held by the Strasbourg court to be a breach of Art.8 of the ECHR because of the absence at that time of any statutory framework for such surveillance. But the court went on to hold that the breach of Art.8 did not mean that the admission of the evidence had been unfair such as to be a breach of Art.6.) (*Khan v United Kingdom* (2001) 31 E.H.R.R. 822; [2000] Crim.L.R. 684. See commentary by Professor Ashworth at 684–86 and to like effect Nash, "Secretly recorded conversations and the European Convention on Human Rights" [2000] 4 Int'l Jrnl.of Ev. and Proof 268–74. Note that the Police Act 1997 and the Regulation of Investigatory Powers Act 2000, both of which are in force, are designed to ensure that surveillance of the kind in issue in *Khan* is on a statutory basis.)

Jeffries,[42] *Brown*,[43] *Nottingham City Council v Amin*,[44] *Loosely*,[45] *Shannon*.[46-47] For two cases in which foreign intercepts were admitted in evidence under s.78 see *Aujla*[48] and *P*.[49]

8–69   In *Smurthwaite* the Court of Appeal said: "the fact that the evidence had been obtained by entrapment, or by an agent provocateur, or by a trick does not of itself require the judge to exclude it". Everything will depend on the particular circumstances. In a case involving an undercover operation the judge would take into account various factors: "Was the officer acting as an agent provocateur in the sense that he was enticing the defendant to commit an offence he would not otherwise have committed? What was the nature of any entrapment? Does the evidence consist of admissions to a completed offence? How active or passive was the officer's role in obtaining the evidence? Is there an unassailable record of what occurred or is it strongly corroborated?"[50]

8–70   In *Teixeira de Castro v Portugal*[51] the European Court of Human Rights adopted a similar approach. There, undercover police officers had approached a suspected drug dealer, VS, to supply them with drugs. VS mentioned T and, after an approach to him, a heroin deal was done which resulted in his conviction. The Strasbourg Court ruled that the officers had acted as agents provocateurs. The Court was influenced by various considerations including that the officers were not conducting a supervised drugs operation, T had no previous convictions and was not known to the police, he had got the drugs from someone else, and he had no more than the agreed quantity in his possession. The officers had exercised an influence such as to incite the commission of the offence. In *Edwards and Lewis*

---

[42] [1998] Q.B. 848; [1998] 2 All E.R. 155, CA listening device installed by police after phoney arrest. Evidence from the tape recordings held admissible in conspiracy to rob case.

[43] Unreported, Case No.9807320/Y2, May 21, 1999, CA. Defendant, aged 17, admitted the crime to his appropriate adult thinking it was a confidential communication. She told the police. Dismissing the appeal, the Court of Appeal said the trial judge had addressed the question that the defendant had been lulled into a false sense of security. Insufficient reasons for going behind the judge's ruling.

[44] [2001] Cr.App.R. 426; [2000] 2 All E.R. 946; [2000] Crim.L.R. 174, CA. Unlicensed taxi-driver flagged down by plain clothes police officers.

[45] [2001] 4 All E.R. 897, HL. Drugs supplied to undercover officer. Note that *Attorney General's Reference (No.3 of 2000)* reported together with *Loosely* went the other way on the facts.

[46-47] [2001] 1 Cr.App.R. 12; [2000] Crim.L.R. 1001, CA—drugs supplied to a journalist pretending to be an Arab sheikh. *McLeod* [2002] EWCA Crim 989—covert recording of two suspects talking on the way to the police station in the police van held admissible under s.78 even though the recording should be treated as a breach of Art.8 of the ECHR. The real issue was whether M's admission was reliable and whether it was fair to admit the recorded conversation. *Mason* [2002] EWCA Crim 385; [2002] All E.R.(D) 161—police bugged cells in order to get evidence of robberies against three defendants. Held to be a breach of Art.8 of the ECHR in that it was not conducted according to law. But it was not contrary to the spirit of PACE or of the Codes and the remedy was not to exclude the evidence. For consideration of whether it makes any difference that the agent of the trap is a police officer or private person such as a journalist see Ashworth, "Private Entrapment as Commercial Lawlessness", *Criminal Bar Association Newsletter*, June 2001, p.9.

[48] [1998] 2 Cr.App.R. 16, CA.

[49] [2001] 1 A.C.146; [2001] 2 All E.R. 58, HL.

[50] n.33 above, at 902–903.

[51] (1998) 28 E.H.R.R. 101; (1998) 4 B.H.R.C.C. 533.

v United Kingdom[52] the Strasbourg court held that it was unable to determine whether the applicants had been victims of entrapment because the relevant evidence had been withheld on the grounds of public interest immunity. The court therefore examined the procedure whereby the plea of entrapment was determined to ensure that the rights of the defendants had been adequately protected. It found that the procedure employed to determine the issues of disclosure of evidence and entrapment did not comply with the requirement "to provide adversarial proceedings and equality of arms.

In *Looseley* and *Attorney General's Reference (No.3 of 2000)*[53] the Law Lords said that police conduct which brings about state-created crime is unacceptable and to prosecute in such circumstances is an affront to the public conscience. The question in both cases was whether the police conduct was so seriously improper as to bring the administration of justice into disrepute. Considerations that were of particular relevance included the nature of the offence and the difficulty of investigating it by other means and the nature and extent of police participation in the crime. The more forceful and persistent the police overtures, the more readily the court might hold that the police had overstepped the boundary. If the police officer achieved his aim whilst acting in the way that an ordinary member of the public could have acted, that would normally be acceptable. (Ordering a drink in a pub after hours or flagging down an unlicensed cab would be examples.) The defendant's criminal record was only relevant if there were grounds for suspicion that he was currently involved in criminal activity. Whether the police conduct was being properly supervised was another relevant factor. (An appeal was taken to Strasbourg, arguably with some prospect of success,[54] but in the end the appeal was not pursued.)

8–71

The courts have stated that there is a need to strike a balance between fairness to the defendant and fairness to the prosecution and the needs of law enforcement—especially in serious cases. A classic instance was the Court of Appeal's decision in *Khan (Sultan)* delivered by Lord Taylor C.J.,[55] in which he referred to the public interest, that investigation of criminal conduct of great gravity be aided by sophisticated bugging devices. ("There are, as Art.8 [of the ECHR] recognises, circumstances in which such intrusion is necessary and therefore justifiable in a democratic society."[56]) The trial judge had therefore been right to conclude that the invasion of privacy involved in placing the bug, with the attendant trespass and damage, was outweighed by other considerations "and should plainly not be regarded as having such an adverse effect on the fairness of the

8–72

---

[52] (2003) E.H.R.R.; unreported, July 22, 2003. The Court distinguished its own decision in *Jasper and Fitt v UK* (2000) 30 E.H.R.R. 480 in which the evidence subject to PII was not part of the prosecution case and was not put to the jury. In *Edwards and Lewis* the trial judge was the tribunal of fact on the issue of entrapment having seen the undisclosed evidence. That failed to provide "adequate safeguards to protect the interests of the accused" [59].

[53] [2001] UKHL 53; [2001] 1 W.L.R. 2060; [2001] 4 All E.R. 897.

[54] "The conduct of the undercover officer in this case, as in *Texeira*, was active and directly responsible for the three offences of which he was convicted. It is difficult to see how the European Court could conclude that such conduct did not likewise amount to incitement." Cousens, "Ignoring Amber Signals", *Criminal.Bar Association Newsletter*, June 2002, p.11 at p.13. (Mr Cousens was counsel in the case.)

[55] [1994] 4 All E.R. 426.

[56] *ibid.*, at 437–438.

proceedings that the court ought to exclude the evidence".[57] Similarly, in *Brown v Stott*,[58] Lord Bingham, referring to the ECHR, Art.6 right to a fair trial, said that its constituent elements were not themselves absolute: "Limited qualification of these rights is acceptable if reasonably directed by national authorities towards a clear and proper public objective and if representing no greater qualification than the situation calls for".[59] The general language of the Convention, Lord Bingham said:

> "could have led to the formulation of hard-edged and inflexible statements of principle from which no departure could be sanctioned whatever the background or the circumstances. But this approach has been consistently eschewed by the court throughout its history. The case law shows that the court has paid very close attention to the facts of particular cases . . . The court has also recognised the need for a fair balance between the general interests of the community and the personal rights of the individual, the search for which balance has been described as inherent in the whole of the convention."[60]

8–73   The cases on s.78 seem to permit some general propositions:

(1) *There are no general guidelines*. The courts have declined to lay down guidelines for the application of the section—each case has to be taken on its own facts. Thus in *Samuel*[61] Hodgson J. said: "It is undesirable to attempt any general guidance as to the way in which a judge's discretion under s.78 or his inherent powers should be exercised. Circumstances vary infinitely." In *Parris*[62] Lord Lane C.J. said that a breach of the Act or Codes does not mean that any statement made by a defendant after such a breach would necessarily be ruled inadmissible. "Every case has to be determined on its own facts."[63] In *Jelen and Katz*[64] Auld J. said: "The circumstances of each case are almost always different, and judges may well take different views in the proper exercise of their discretion even where the circumstances are similar." Despite this, the courts will look at, and do cite, previous cases—especially decisions of the Court of Appeal.[65]

8–74   (2) *Wednesbury unreasonableness*. If the trial judge has found there to have been a breach of the rules or some other impropriety and has gone on to exercise his discretion under s.78, the Court of Appeal says that it will only interfere on the well-known *Wednesbury* principle,[66] *i.e.* if the discretion was exercised on

---

[57] *ibid.*, at 438.
[58] [2001] 2 W.L.R. 817; [2001] 2 All E.R. 97, HL.
[59] [2001] 2 W.L.R. 817 at 836; [2001] 2 All E.R. 97 at 115.
[60] [2001] 2 W.L.R. at 836; [2001] 2 All E.R. at 115 citing *Sporrong v Sweden* (1982) 5 E.H.R.R. 35 at 52–53, para.69 and *Sheffield v UK* (1998) 5 B.H.R.C. 83 at 94, para.52. For criticism of this "balancing" exercise see Ashworth, "Criminal Proceedings after the Human Rights Act: The First Year" [2001] Crim.L.R. 855 at 863–868 and 871–872.
[61] [1988] Q.B. 615 at 630; (1988) Cr.App.R. 232 at 245, CA.
[62] (1989) 89 Cr.App.R. 68 at 72, CA.
[63] *ibid.*, at 72.
[64] (1990) 90 Cr.App.R. 456 at 465, CA.
[65] The Court of Appeal is less impressed with citation of first instance authorities—see *Grannell* (1990) 90 Cr.App.R. 149, CA in which Tucker J. said of such decisions: "We do not find them of any assistance in deciding whether the trial judge . . . exercised his discretion wrongly".
[66] *Associated Provincial Picture Houses Ltd v Wednesbury Corporation* [1948] 1 K.B. 223.

wholly wrong grounds.[67] As a matter of impression, it may be said, however, that the Court of Appeal does seem somewhat readier to take a different view from that adopted by the trial judge in this area than in some others where the principle of *Wednesbury* unreasonableness comes into issue.

(3) *No discretion exercised by trial judge.* Different considerations apply where **8–75** the judge has not exercised his discretion, or has directed his mind to the wrong issue. Thus, if the trial judge wrongly decides that there has been no breach, he has, by definition, failed to apply his mind to the matter. In that situation the appeal court may exercise the discretion.[68]

(4) *Voire dire.* Whereas under s.76 there has to be a trial within a trial (*voire dire*) **8–76** in both Crown courts and magistrates' courts, this does not apply to challenges under s.78.[69] Where the challenge is under both sections, there has to be a *voire dire*. Where it is only under s.78 the Crown Court has a discretion,[70] though in the magistrates' court there is no need to hold a *voire dire* on a s.78 application.[71]

(5) *Committal proceedings.* As has been seen (see para.8–44 above) the basic **8–77** approach of the courts was that questions of the admissibility of evidence should be determined by the trial judge. In *R. v King's Lynn Magistrates' Court, Ex p. Holland*[72] the Divisional Court held that magistrates should only exclude evidence on the grounds of unfairness under s.78 in the clearest case and in exceptional circumstances where they were satisfied that to admit the evidence at trial would be so obviously unfair that no judge properly directing himself could admit it. But the Criminal Procedure and Investigations Act 1996 went further. It included a provision adding a new para.(3) to s.78 stating baldly that "This section shall not apply in the case of proceedings before a magistrates' court inquiring into an offence as examining justices".[73]

(6) *Extradition proceedings.* The Extradition Act 1989, s.9(2) provided that **8–78** extradition proceedings were akin to a committal but this was amended by the Criminal Justice and Public Order Act 1994, s.158(1)(5) which provided instead that they should be treated like a summary trial. So s.78 does apply. (In *R. v Governor of Pentonville Prison, Ex p. Chinoy*[74] it was common ground between the parties that s.78 applied to extradition proceedings and the court so held.) But the attitude of the courts to exclusion of evidence in extradition cases is restrictive

---

[67] See, for instance, *Penny* (1992) 94 Cr.App.R. 345; [1992] Crim.L.R. 184, CA. Failure to hold an identification parade. Even if there had been a breach of the Code it had to be shown that the judge was wholly wrong in the exercise of the s.78 discretion. See also *O'Leary* (1988) 87 Cr.App.R. 387 at 391; and *Christou* [1992] Q.B. 979.

[68] *Samuel*, CA, para.8–65, n.83 above, *Alladice*, CA, para.8–66, n.82 above and *Absolam*, CA, para.8–65, n.80 above were all examples. See also *Parris*, CA, para.8–65, n.84 above, *Keenan*, CA, para.8–65, n.15 above and *Howden-Simpson* [1991] Crim.L.R. 49, CA.

[69] For Crown court, see *Beveridge* (1987) 85 Cr.App.R. 255, CA; for magistrates' courts see *Vel v Owen* [1987] Crim.L.R. 496; *Liverpool Juvenile Court, Ex p. R.* [1988] Q.B. 1, DC. See further Stevens, "Trials within trials in the magistrates' court: a panoramic view", J.P.N., August 22, 1987, 531.

[70] In *Manji* [1990] Crim.L.R. 512, CA it was held that the judge had been wrong to refuse an application for a trial within a trial as to whether the defendant had or had not been cautioned.

[71] *Vel v Owen*, n.69 above. See now also *Halawa v Federation Against Copyright Theft* [1995] Crim.L.R. 409.

[72] (1993) 96 Cr.App.R.74; [1993] 2 All E.R. 377.

[73] CPIA 1996, Sch.1, para.26.

[74] [1992] 1 All E.R. 317, DC.

on the ground, again, that it is for the trial judge in the foreign country to consider the admissibility of the evidence in question. In *Ex p. Levin* Lord Hoffmann (having cited *Ex p. Holland*) said that there was even less scope for the exercise of the discretion than for examining magistrates:

> "[E]xtradition procedure is founded on concepts of comity and reciprocity. It would undermine the effectiveness of international treaty obligations if the courts were to superimpose discretions based on local notions of fairness upon the ordinary rules of admissibility. I do not wish to exclude the possibility that the discretion may be used in extradition proceedings founded upon evidence which though technically admissible, has been obtained in a way which outrages civilised values. But such cases are also likely to be very rare."[75]

8–79   (7) *Previous convictions admissible.* When deciding whether a confession is admissible under s.78, the court can take into account the defendant's previous similar convictions—even though they would otherwise be inadmissible and even though under s.76(2) the court cannot consider whether a confession is true.[76]

8–80   (8) *Not penalising the police.* The courts have made it clear that a decision to exclude evidence should not be made to penalise or to discipline the police.[77]

8–81   (9) *Burden of proof.* It is not entirely clear where the burden of proof lies in regard to points raised under s.78.[78] There is nothing in s.78 equivalent to the provision in s.76 which requires the prosecution to establish that a confession was not obtained in breach of s.76(2)(a) or (b). The prosecution need not disprove unfairness.[79] On the other hand, the defence have to persuade the court that there is a serious issue as to unfairness in regard to the admissibility of the evidence in question. The prosecution will seek to persuade the court either that there was no breach of the rules or other impropriety, or, if there was, that it was not "significant and substantial", or that even so, there was not sufficient reason for the evidence to be excluded.[80] As has been seen, the court takes into account fairness to the prosecution as well as to the defence.[81]

In summary, the court generally will uphold the defence position under s.78 only where it is persuaded, (a) that there was a breach of the rules or other impropriety, (b) that it was significant and substantial, (c) that it affects the proceedings unfairly from the defence standpoint, and (d) that the unfairness is so great as to

---

[75] *R. v Governor of Brixton Prison, Ex p. Levin* [1997] A.C. 741 at 748, HL. Cited and applied in *R. v Bow Street Magistrates' Court, Ex p. Proulx* [2001] 1 All E.R. 57 at 75, DC. For critical comment on *Proulx* see [2000] Crim.L.R. at 998–1001.

[76] *Bailey* [1995] 2 Cr.App.R. 262, CA. See also Doherty, "Judicial discretion: victimising the villains?" (1999) 3 Int'l Jrnl. of Ev. and Proof, 44–56. The author argues that the fact that a case involves professional criminals influences the courts' use of discretion, including the discretion under s.78.

[77] *Mason* [1988] 1 W.L.R. 139, CA; *Delaney* (1989) 88 Cr.App.R. 338, CA.

[78] In previous editions the writer's view (cited in *Archbold 1994*, para.15–366) was that the burden fell on the defence. In *Anderson* [1993] Crim.L.R. 447, CA the court said it was not entirely clear where the burden of proof lay.

[79] *Vel v Owen* [1987] Crim.L.R. 496, DC.

[80] See *Ryan* [1992] Crim.L.R. 187, CA—major breach of Code D in regard to identification evidence. The court said that even quite serious breaches might not result in the evidence being excluded if they did not cause unjust prejudice to the accused.

[81] See for instance *McDonald* [1991] Crim.L.R. 122, CA.

require that the evidence be excluded.[82] If this does not amount to the burden of proof being on the defence, it is remarkably close.

(10) *Breach of the ECHR does not necessarily mean the trial is unfair.* As has   **8–82** been seen (see para.8–68 n.41 above), in *Khan (Sultan) v United Kingdom*[83] the European Court of Human Rights held that although there had been violations of Arts 8 and 13 of the Convention, the defendant had not been deprived of his right to a fair trial under Art.6(1) of the Convention. That case concerned reception of evidence from a listening device installed in his home by the police. The European Court reached the same decision in *P.G. and J.H. v United Kingdom*[84] which concerned covert listening devices both at the suspects' home and at the police station. The House of Lords adopted the same approach in *Sultan Khan*[85] and in *P.*[86] In both it held that the question of whether the trial was fair should be judged by application of s.78.

There is a considerable literature on s.78. See for instance: Stone, "Exclusion   **8–83** of Evidence under section 78 of the Police and Criminal Evidence Act: Practice and Principles" [1995] 3 Web Jrnl. of Current Legal Issues— *www.webjcli.ncl.ac.uk/index*; Wolchover and Heaton-Armstrong, *Confession Evidence* (Sweet and Maxwell, 1996), pp.555–583; Mirfield, *Silence, Confessions and Improperly Obtained Evidence* (Clarendon, Oxford, 1997); Grevling, "Fairness and Exclusion of Evidence under section 78(1) of the Police and Criminal Evidence Act" (1997) 113 L.Q.R. 667; Choo and Nash, "What's the Matter with section 78?" [1999] Crim.L.R. 929; Dennis, *The Law of Evidence* (2nd ed., Sweet and Maxwell, 2002), pp.76–85, 261–83; and, more recently, Roberts and Zuckerman, *Criminal Evidence* (Oxford University Press, 2004), Chs 4 and 9.

See also Ormerod, "ECHR and the Exclusion of Evidence: Trial Remedies for Article 8 Breaches" [2003] Crim.L.R. 61–80 and Cape, "Incompetent Police Station Advice and the Exclusion of Evidence" [2002] Crim.L.R. 471–484.

Exclusion of confession and other evidence in Northern Ireland

Until 1973 Northern Ireland had the same rules on the exclusion of confession   **8–84** and other evidence for ordinary cases and for terrorism cases. The rules were, first, that a confession had to be voluntary in the classic common law sense[87] and beyond that, the court had a discretion to exclude evidence if its prejudicial effect outweighed its probative value. There was further an ultimate discretion of

---

[82] In *Walsh* (1990) 91 Cr.App.R. 161 at 163, the Court of Appeal said: "The task of the court is not merely to consider whether there would be an adverse effect on the fairness of the proceedings, but such an adverse effect that justice requires the evidence to be excluded".
[83] [2001] 31 E.H.R.R. 1016; [2000] Crim.L.R. 684. For critical comment see Professor Ashworth's commentary, *ibid.*, at 684–686.
[84] [2002] Crim.L.R. 308.
[85] [1997] A.C. 558.
[86] [2001] 2 W.L.R. 463, HL.
[87] See *Corr* [1968] N.I. 193, CA.

uncertain scope to exclude (at least confession) evidence in the interests of justice or to ensure that the trial was fair.[88]

In 1973 the Northern Ireland (Emergency Provisions) Act of that year introduced a narrower rule for terrorism ("scheduled") offences triable by judge alone in "Diplock courts". Section 6 stated that relevant statements by the accused would be excluded if they had been induced by torture or inhuman or degrading treatment. This formula cancelled the common law rule that a confession had to be voluntary and set a lower threshold of admissibility. But the judges held that they still had their common law discretion to exclude evidence where the prejudicial effect outweighed the probative value and generally in the interests of justice—see *Corey* and *Cowan*. This was given statutory effect in the 1987 Emergency Provisions Act which stated that the court had an additional discretion to exclude a statement made by the accused which was not excluded as being induced by torture, etc., "if it appears to the court that it is appropriate to do so in order to avoid unfairness to the accused or otherwise in the interests of justice". The provisions of s.6 of the 1973 Emergency Provisions Act were continued in the Emergency Provisions Act of 1978 (s.8), of 1987 (s.5), of 1991 (s.11) and of 1996 (s.12).

8–85   The definition of confessions that would be excluded was extended in the 1987 Act to ones induced by "any violence or threat of violence" and this was the same in all the subsequent Acts.[89]

In the meanwhile, the Northern Ireland PACE Order of 1989 in Arts 74, 75 and 76 introduced provisions identical to ss.76, 77 and 78 of PACE for ordinary trials.

The latest legislation applicable to the admissibility of evidence in trials of scheduled offences in Northern Ireland is the Terrorism Act 2000. Section 76 of that Act again has the same formula. It provides that if *prima facie* evidence is adduced that the accused was subjected to "torture, inhuman or degrading treatment, violence or the threat of violence[90] in order to induce him to make the statement" (subs.(3)(b)) then, unless the prosecution satisfies the court that the statement was not so obtained, the court has three alternatives—to exclude the statement, or, if the statement has already been received in evidence, to ignore it, or in either case to restart the case before a different judge (subss.(4), (5)).

8–86   In addition there remains the broader general discretion expressed in s.76(6) which states: "This section is without prejudice to any discretion of a court to (a) exclude or ignore a statement, or (b) direct a trial to be restarted, where the court considers it appropriate in order to avoid unfairness to the accused or otherwise in the interests of justice".

The discretion in s.76(6) is restricted to statements and admissions and does not apply to real evidence. The question of the exclusion of real evidence in Northern Ireland terrorism cases is dealt with under the common law and the PACE Order.

---

[88] See *Corey* reported as a note in *O'Halloran* [1979] N.I. 45 at 49, CA; *Cowan* [1987] N.I. 338 at 352, CA; *Brennan*, unreported, Lexis, ref. MACE 1907, September 24, 1996, CA.
[89] s.8(2)(b) of the 1978 Act inserted by s.5 of the 1987 Act. For a discussion of the significance of the broader test see Jackson, "The Northern Ireland (Emergency Provisions) Act 1987" (1988) 39 N.I.L.Q. 235 at 249.
[90] The same formula as that in Art.3 of the ECHR.

The different and lower threshhold for the admissibility of confessions in trials in non-jury Diplock courts than in the ordinary courts has been the subject of criticism. The Diplock Review Group established by the Home Secretary in 1999 as part of the Peace Process recommended that the Government consider repealing Art.76. Lord Carlisle of Berriew in his *Report on the Operation in 2001 of Part VII of the Terrorism Act 2000* agreed. He said that there was "an overwhelming case for applying the PACE standard uniformly" to terrorism cases (2002, para.6.7, p.18). The Government accepted this recommendation which was implemented in July 2002—see the Terrorism Act 2000 (Cessation of Effect of Section 76) Order 2002 (SI 2002/2141). So the test is now the same for all cases.

See generally Dermot Walsh, *Criminal Procedure* (Dublin Round Hale, 2002), pp.433–490.

Time for taking accused's evidence: s.79[91]

Under the previous law, the accused had to give evidence before hearing the evidence and cross-examination of any witnesses he intended to call.[92] The Criminal Law Revision Committee in its 11th Report recommended[93] that the court should have a discretion—for instance to allow a witness to be called before the accused. Section 79 implemented this proposal. The accused gives evidence first "unless the court in its discretion otherwise directs".   **8–87**

Competence and compellability of accused's spouse: s.80[94]

Section 80 originally dealt with the rules of the incompetence of the accused's spouse to give evidence (when she could not give evidence even when willing to do so), and of the spouse's compellability (when she can be required to give evidence even though unwilling to do so). The Criminal Law Revision Committee in its 11th Report proposed changes to these rules and s.80 broadly adopted these recommendations—but, as will be seen, the rules have since been somewhat modified by the Youth Justice and Criminal Evidence Act 1999.   **8–88**

Under the pre-PACE law the accused's spouse was generally not competent for the prosecution[95] (save when the charge was one of personal violence against her) but was always competent as a defence witness for the accused[96] and was competent as a defence witness for the spouse's co-accused but normally only with the spouse's consent.[97] The CLRC said that it had no doubt that a wife should

---

[91] See 1989 N.I. PACE Order, Art.77.
[92] *R. v Morrison* (1911) 6 Cr.App.R. 159; *R. v Smith* (1968) 52 Cr.App.R. 224.
[93] *op.cit.*, para. 8–01, n.2 above, para.107.
[94] See 1989 N.I. PACE Order, Art.79.
[95] There were certain statutory exceptions including the Evidence Act 1898, s.4(1); Sexual Offences Act 1956, s.39; Theft Act 1968, s.30.
[96] By virtue of the Criminal Evidence Act 1898, s.1.
[97] Also by virtue of the Criminal Evidence Act 1898, s.1.

always be competent as a witness for the prosecution in all cases. "If she is willing to give evidence, we think that the law would be showing excessive concern for the preservation of marital harmony if it were to say that she must not do so."[98] Subsection (1) adopted this view, subject to an exception in subs.(4) where the spouse was jointly charged with the same offence—though the exception did not apply where he or she was no longer liable to be convicted for that offence by virtue of having pleaded guilty or otherwise. But subs.(1) has now been repealed by the Youth Justice and Criminal Evidence Act 1999[99] which provided in s.53(1) that subject to subss.(3) and (4), "At every stage in criminal proceedings all persons are (whatever their age) competent to give evidence".[1] So competence is now dealt with by the 1999 Act, s.53.

8–89   Compellability is dealt with in subss.(2) to (4A) of s.80 of PACE (as amended by the Youth Justice and Criminal Evidence Act 1999, Sch.4, para.13). Pre-PACE, a spouse was not compellable for the accused. The CLRC recommended[2] that the spouse should always be compellable as well as competent as a witness for the accused. Subsection (2) of s.80 gave effect to this recommendation save for an exception in subs.(4) where they are jointly charged. The 1999 Act made a slight further modification of the rule. The spouse is compellable to give evidence for a co-accused only in respect of the specific offence for which he is charged (s.2A).

There were few cases where the spouse was compellable for the prosecution. For some time it was thought that at common law a spouse was compellable against the marriage partner if the case involved violence against her (or him). But the House of Lords rejected this view in *Hoskyn v Metropolitan Police Commissioner*.[3] However, the exemption from being compellable only applies to persons who are married; it does not extend to long-term partners.[4]

8–90   The CLRC proposed[5] that a wife should be compellable for the prosecution not only where the case involved violence against her but also in cases of violence towards children under the age of 16 belonging to the same household as the accused. Often in such cases the wife was in fear of her husband but wanted to give evidence against him. To make her compellable as a witness would make her position easier rather than more difficult. The Committee did not however go so far as to recommend compellability where the child was not from the same household.

The Act went beyond what the CLRC recommended. Subsection (3): (a) makes the spouse compellable for the prosecution where the case involves violence against him or her or against anyone who was under 16 years old at the

---

[98] *op.cit.*, para.8–01, n.2 above, para.148.

[99] Sch.6.

[1] subs.(3) excludes persons not competent by virtue of lack of understanding; subs.(4) excludes as a witness for the prosecution the defendant himself or a co-accused.

[2] *op.cit.*, para.8–01, n.2 above, para.153.

[3] [1979] A.C. 474. There is no power to prevent on grounds of public policy, the marriage between a prisoner on remand and his long-term partner, even though the marriage would make her a non-compellable witness for the prosecution in his forthcoming trial for murder—*R.(CPS) v Registrar-General of Births, Deaths and Marriages* [2002] EWCA 1661; [2003] 1 F.C.R. CA.

[4] *Pearce* [2001] E.W.C.A. 2834; [2002] 1 W.L.R. 1553.

[5] *op.cit.*, para.8–01, n.2 above, para.150.

time; (b) where the offence is a sexual one against a person aged under 16; or (c) where it consists of attempting or conspiring to commit an offence within (a) or (b).[6] Again, the same exception under subs.(4) applies for the case where the spouses are charged jointly.[7]

The CLRC also dealt with the problem of one spouse as witness for the co-accused of the other spouse.

At common law a spouse was competent for the defence with the consent of **8–91** the accused but was not generally compellable. In the view of the CLRC[8] a defendant's spouse should always be competent to give evidence for a co-accused regardless of the accused's consent. Subsection (1)(b) gave effect to this proposal—although, as has been seen, it has now been superceded by the repeal of subs.(1) by the Youth Justice and Criminal Evidence Act 1999 which made all persons competent to give evidence for the defence. It is therefore now unnecessary to have a specific provision making a spouse a competent witness for the co-accused.

Pre-PACE it seemed that a divorced wife was not competent to give evidence about something that occurred during the marriage.[9] The CLRC proposed[10] that, after the marriage had been dissolved, former spouses should be both competent and compellable as if they had never been married. The Act accepted this proposal (subs.(5)). It applies to anything that occurred whilst they were married.[11] Following the views of the CLRC it does not apply, however, unless the marriage has been ended by divorce or annulment. Judicial separation is not enough.

The CLRC proposed[12] that the prohibition in s.1(b) of the Criminal Evidence **8–92** Act 1898 of comment by the prosecution on the failure by the accused's spouse to give evidence should be abolished. At the time the Government rejected this recommendation and s.1(b) of the 1898 Act was expressly confirmed in subs.(8) of s.80. However, subs.(8) was repealed by the Youth Justice and Criminal Evidence Act 1999[13] so such comment is now permissible.

The final subsection of s.80 dealt with the privilege of a witness not to answer questions about a communication made to the witness by his or her spouse during the marriage and the right to decline to say whether marital intercourse did or did not take place. The Law Reform Committee recommended in its 16th Report in 1967 that these privileges should be abolished for civil cases.[14] This was achieved by ss.16(3) and (4) of the Civil Evidence Act 1968 and the CLRC made

---

[6] For comment on the slight difference of meaning between "involves" and "consists of" see Creighton, "Spouse Competence and Compellability" [1990] Crim.L.R. 34 at 38–39.
[7] For a critique of this extension of the law of compellability as either being too wide or too narrow see Creighton, *ibid.*, at 35–36.
[8] *op.cit.*, para.8–01, n.2 above, para.155.
[9] See *Algar* [1955] 1 Q.B. 279; *Lapworth* [1931] 1 K.B. 117.
[10] *op.cit.*, para.156.
[11] In *Mathias* [1989] Crim.L.R. 64 the trial judge applied s.80(5) to a confession made by a co-defendant to his then wife before the Act came into force. Subsequently they were divorced. A month later in April 1988 she made a statement to the police in which she gave the details of the confession which also implicated two other co-defendants. The court allowed in the statement, subject to the replacement of the names of the other co-defendants by letters of the alphabet so that the jury would not be prejudiced by having their names included.
[12] *op.cit.*, para.8–01, n.2 above, pp.43–44.
[13] Sch.6.
[14] "Privilege in Civil Proceedings", Cmnd.3472 (1967).

the same recommendation in regard to criminal cases.[15] The Act gave effect to the recommendation in subs.(9).

Rule where accused's spouse not compellable: s.80A

8–93   The Youth Justice and Criminal Evidence Act 1999, Sch. 4, para.14 added a new section providing that the failure of a defendant's spouse to give evidence "shall not be made the subject of any comment by the prosecution". It is therefore an exception to the general rule that the prosecution may make such comment if the defendant decides not to go into the witness box. The importance of the marriage relationship is given priority over the needs of the prosecution.

Advance notice of the defence case: s.81[16]

8–94   Under the pre-PACE law the only requirement that the defendant reveal any part of his case in advance of the trial concerned an alibi defence. The Philips Royal Commission recommended[17] that the defence should be required to give advance notice also of expert evidence so as to reduce the danger of surprise causing adjournments. The Philips Royal Commission said that obvious examples were defences depending on medical evidence or expert forensic evidence which the prosecution needs an opportunity to evaluate or on which it may wish to call its own expert witnesses.

    The Act adopted this suggestion by granting powers for Crown Court Rules to be made to require either party to disclose to the other any expert evidence he proposes to adduce in the proceedings and to prohibit a party who fails to comply with such rules to adduce such evidence, save with leave of the court. The Rules may specify the kinds of expert evidence covered.

    The Crown Court (Advance Notice of Expert Evidence) Rules (SI 1987/716) came into effect in July 1987.[18] The rules provided for the disclosure, as soon as practicable after committal, of a statement in writing of any finding or opinion of an expert upon which a party proposes to rely. Rule 4 allows non-disclosure if there are reasonable grounds to believe that compliance with the rules might lead to the intimidation of a potential witness. Subject to Rule 4, a party who fails to comply with the requirement of disclosure cannot adduce expert evidence without leave of the court.

---

[15] *op.cit.*, para.8–01, n.2 above, para.173.
[16] See 1989 N.I. PACE Order, Art.80.
[17] Philips Report, para.8.22.
[18] The Northern Ireland equivalent was SI 1989/394.

Exclusion of evidence: s.82[19]

At the end of the interpretation section for Pt VIII of the Act is the sentence: **8–95**
"Nothing in this part of this Act shall prejudice any power of a court to exclude
evidence (whether by preventing questions from being put or otherwise) at its
discretion" (s.82(3)).

The meaning of subs.(3) is far from clear. At the time of the passage of the Act
it was generally thought to have a rather narrow scope. This certainly is the clear
implication of the reference to the power of the judge to protect a witness from
objectionable questions. But what is the import of the phrase "or otherwise",
which taken literally could be said to be open-ended. Certainly it covers the
court's power to instruct the jury to disregard evidence it has heard.

The general view now is that s.82(3) preserved the whole of the common law
on the exclusion of evidence. On this view the admissibility of a confession can
be challenged under s.76, or under s.78, or under this section; evidence other than
a confession can be challenged under either s.78 or this section.

The main thrust of s.82(3) therefore is to retain the power allowed by the   **8–96**
House of Lords in *Sang*[20] to exclude evidence if the prejudicial effect outweighs
its probative value.[21] The late Judge Richard May suggested[22] that another example would be in cases arising out of cross-examination of the accused under s.1(f)
of the Criminal Evidence Act 1898. Another example is where evidence has
already been given and where it therefore cannot be challenged under ss.76 or 78.
This was specifically referred to by the Court of Appeal in *Sat-Bhambra*[23] in
which Lord Lane C.J. said that a judge who could not exclude evidence under
s.78 could still do so under his common law power preserved by s.82(3) "to prevent injustice". In the trial of Colin Stagg for the murder of Rachel Nickell on
Wimbledon Common the judge referred to his discretion under s.82(3) as the
basis for excluding evidence obtained by the questioning carried out by an undercover policewoman who befriended Stagg. (The officer had engaged in "a skilful
and sustained enterprise to manipulate the accused. Sometimes subtle, sometimes
blatant in its technique, it was designed to manoevre and seduce him to reveal
fantasies of a suggested incriminating character . . .".[24])

---

[19] See 1989 N.I. PACE Order, Art.70.
[20] [1980] A.C. 402.
[21] See, for instance, *O'Leary* (1988) 87 Cr.App.R. 387, CA; *Eatough (J)* [1989] Crim.L.R. 289,
Crown Ct.
[22] Richard May, "Fair Play at Trial: an Interim Assessment of section 78 of the Police and Criminal
Evidence Act 1984" [1988] Crim.L.R. 722 at 726.
[23] (1989) 88 Cr.App.R. 55; [1988] Crim.L.R. 453, CA and see para.8–43 above.
[24] Transcript of Ognall J.'s ruling, September 15, 1994.

QUESTIONS AND ANSWERS

CONFESSIONS

8–97   How did PACE alter the law regarding the admissibility of confessions?

The common law excluded confessions that (1) were obtained as a result of oppression; and (2) that could not be shown by the prosecution to have been voluntary.

"Oppression" was defined by the courts to have two aspects. First, that the presence or absence of oppression was a function of both the circumstances of the questioning and the characteristics of the defendant. Secondly, that oppressive questioning was questioning which by its nature or duration or other circumstances so affected the accused that his will crumbled.

The 1984 Act retained the rule that confessions which result from oppressive questioning must be excluded. The judge has no discretion. Oppression is defined in the Act as including "torture, inhuman or degrading treatment, and the use or threat of violence (whether or not amounting to torture)".

But the Act did alter the law as regards the "voluntariness" test. The former test was whether the confession had been obtained from the accused "by fear of prejudice or hope of advantage exercised or held out by a person in authority". The test under PACE is whether the confession was or may have been obtained "in consequence of anything said or done which was likely, in the circumstances existing at the time, to render unreliable any confession which might be made by him in consequence thereof".

Under the former test the judges were supposed to consider primarily whether there had been any threat or promise. Under PACE they have to consider the likely impact on the mind of the accused of all the circumstances at the time of his confession and evaluate whether they would be likely to have made the confession unreliable.

When a case poses this problem the burden of proof is firmly on the prosecution. The statute says, if the question of the admissibility of the confession is raised, "the court shall not allow the confession to be given in evidence against him except in so far as the prosecution proves to the court beyond reasonable doubt that the confession (notwithstanding that it may be true) was not obtained as aforesaid" (*i.e.* by oppression or in circumstances likely to make it unreliable). Indeed the Act has an unusual additional provision that, even if the defence fail to make representations about the admissibility of the confession, the court can require the prosecution to prove that the confession was not obtained in ways that would make it inadmissible.

What is the rule about the admissibility of real evidence (fingerprints, bloodstains, stolen goods, etc.) found as a direct result of an inadmissible confession?   8–98

The Act continued the common law rule that such real evidence was admissible even though the confession which led to its discovery was inadmissible. But no evidence can be given by the prosecution about how the inadmissible confession led to the discovery of the real evidence unless the defence state that that was what had happened.

In what circumstances will the court exclude evidence (other than confessions) obtained by improper means?   8–99

Under s.78 a court has the power in its absolute discretion to exclude any evidence where, having regard to the circumstances (including the way the evidence in question was obtained), it considers that its admission would have an unduly adverse effect on the fairness of the proceedings. So, if the court takes serious exception to the way in which the prosecution have obtained any evidence, it can rule that the evidence should not be admitted. It can also exclude evidence on the ground that the police have broken the rules of the Codes—sometimes even if there was no causal relationship between those breaches and the evidence obtained. The courts have used s.78 in this way in a very large number of cases.

THE EVIDENCE OF SPOUSES

In what circumstances can a spouse be compelled to give evidence against her spouse?   8–100

Under the previous law, one spouse could not be compelled to give evidence against the other spouse, even in a case where the charge arose from a violent attack by one on the other.

This rule was changed by PACE which provides that one spouse can be compelled to give evidence against the other spouse where the offence charged involves an assault on, injury or threat of injury to, the first spouse or against a person under 16 years old or a sexual offence against a person under 16 years old.

When else is a spouse permitted to give evidence against her husband?   8–101

Under the pre-PACE law, subject to a few exceptions, one spouse was generally not allowed to testify against the other. The only important exception was where the charge arose out of personal violence by the accused on the other spouse. The

Act changed the rule by making each spouse eligible ("competent") though not required ("compellable") to give evidence against the other.

8–102   Is one spouse compellable to give evidence for the other?

The former law generally did not treat one spouse as a compellable witness for the other. But this rule was changed by the Act which made husband and wife each compellable to give evidence for each other.

8–103   What happens if one spouse is charged together with the other?

The Act made this an exception to the new rules. In other words a wife charged jointly with her husband is neither competent nor compellable to give evidence against him unless she is no longer liable to conviction because she pleaded guilty or for any other reason.

8–104   How are these rules affected by the fact that the spouses are divorced?

The former law took no notice of divorce. A spouse who had been divorced was in exactly the same position in regard to the question of competence and compellability as beforehand.

The Act changed this by providing that once spouses have been divorced they must be treated as if they had never been married. In other words, they are free to give evidence even as to what occurred during the marriage—and can be compelled to do so for the prosecution where the case arises out of physical injury by one spouse on the other or on someone under 16 years old.

POLICE COMPLAINTS AND DISCIPLINE: SECTIONS 83–105

Part IX of PACE (comprising ss.83 to 105) established the Police Complaints   **9–01**
Authority and instituted a new system for dealing with complaints against the
police and with discipline. The whole of Pt IX of PACE (as amended by the Police
and Magistrates' Courts Act 1994) was then re-enacted in Pt IV of the Police Act
1996, a consolidation act which incorporated and reconstituted the then existing
system. These provisions were brought into operation as from 1999.[1]

In 1997, the House of Commons Home Affairs Committee called for radical
reform of the system, notably by the introduction of the independent investigation of complaints,[2] a call echoed by the Macpherson report into the Stephen
Lawrence case.[3]

In May 2000, the Home Office published a Consultation Paper[4] in which it
rehearsed proposals put forward, respectively, in a report it commissioned from
KPMG[5] and by Liberty.[6]

In December 2000 the Home Office published its own proposals.[7] The
Government's intentions were translated into reality in Pt 2 of, and Schs 2 and 3
to, the Police Reform Act 2002 and by the subsequent statutory instruments.[8]

The Act established the Independent Police Complaints Commission (IPCC)   **9–02**
to replace the Police Complaints Authority which became operational as from
April 1, 2004. (The IPCC's website address is *www.ipcc.gov.uk*.) The IPCC has
referred to it all serious cases falling into specified categories *whether or not a
complaint has been made*. It has its own powers of investigation and a substantial body of independent investigators at its disposal. It has the power to supervise police investigations of complaints and to call-in any case to investigate or

---

[1] See SI 1999/533, Art.2(a).
[2] Home Affairs Committee, First Report, *Police Complaints and Disciplinary Procedure* (1997).
[3] Sir William Macpherson of Cluny, *The Stephen Lawrence Report* (1999).
[4] *Complaints Against the Police: A Consultation Paper* (May 2000) (available on the Home Office
website at *www.homeoffice.gov.uk*).
[5] KPMG, *Feasibility of an Independent System for Investigating Complaints Against the Police* (May
2000), ISBN 1–84082–453–0.
[6] Harrison and Cunneen, *An Independent Police Complaints Commission* (Liberty, May 2000) (available on Liberty's website at *www.liberty-human-rights.org.uk*).
[7] *Complaints Against the Police: Framework for a new system* (available on the Home Office website at *www.homeoffice.gov.uk*). For a brief assessment of the KPMG, Liberty and Home Office proposals written by the authors of the Liberty report, see *Legal Action*, August 2001, pp.6–8.
[8] Police (Complaints and Misconduct) Regulations 2004 (SI 2004/643) and the Police (Conduct)
Regulations 2004 (SI 2004/645).

to supervise. Chief officers have to co-operate with IPCC investigations. They have a legal obligation to provide the IPCC with access to documentation or other material, to allow the IPCC to copy such documentation and to allow the IPCC access to police premises.

Also, access to the complaints system has been broadened. Persons other than the victim are able to make a complaint against the police. Complainants can make their complaints via a third party or through independent organisations such as the Citizens' Advice Bureau. Complainants have the right to appeal to the IPCC against a refusal by the appropriate authority to record a complaint.

9–03   Subject to a test relating to potential harm that might be risked by disclosure of the information, complainants must be provided with an account of how the complaint investigation has been conducted, a summary of the evidence and an explanation of why the conclusions to an investigation were reached. Complainants have a right of appeal to the IPCC if they feel that the written account does not provide a satisfactory explanation of the investigation.

The Explanatory Notes to the Act conclude (para.22): "These provisions are intended to provide a more robust system for dealing with complaints against the police and to increase public confidence in the complaints system as a whole".

For description of the new provisions see Ormerod and Roberts, "The Police Reform Act 2002—Increasing Centralisation, Maintaining Confidence and Contracting out Crime Control" [2003] Crim.L.R. 141 at 147–54. For further information about the IPCC see also its website—*www.ipcc.gov.uk.*

Since the subject is no longer part of the Police and Criminal Evidence Act, it has been dropped from this book.

Northern Ireland

9–04   The Police (Northern Ireland) Order 1977 established the Police Complaints Board to provide independent oversight of complaints against police officers. Following the recommendations of the Philips Royal Commission on Criminal Procedure, changes were made to the system by the Police (Northern Ireland) Order 1987. This established the Independent Commission for Police Complaints as from February 1988. The provisions of the 1987 Order relating to complaints against the police were re-enacted with amendments in the Police (Amendment) (Northern Ireland) Order 1995 (SI 1995/2993) (N.I. 17). The 1987 Order and those provisions of the 1995 Order were repealed by the Police (Northern Ireland) Act 1998 (c.32)—Pt VII of which established the Office of the Police Ombudsman of Northern Ireland. For the latest amendments see Police (Northern Ireland) Act 2000, Pt VIII establishing the Police Service of Northern Ireland and Police (Northern Ireland) Act 2003, ss.30 and 31 and Sch.3.

Part X

POLICE—GENERAL: SECTIONS 106–112

Arrangements for obtaining the views of the community on policing: s.106

This section was repealed by the Police Act 1996, Sch.9, Pt I and re-enacted as s.96 of that Act.

10–01

Police officers performing duties of higher rank: s.107

Many sections in the Act require that an action or decision be made or taken by an officer of a specified rank. Section 107 provided for the situation where an officer of that rank may not be available and permits an officer of a lower rank to be "made up".

10–02

The section originally provided that a chief inspector could act as a superintendent if properly authorised to do so by a chief superintendent and that a sergeant could act as an inspector, again, if authorised to do so by a chief superintendent. In 1994 the rank of chief superintendent was abolished by the Police and Magistrates' Courts Act 1994, s.7(c).[1] (The rank of chief superintendent was, however, subsequently restored by the Criminal Justice and Police Act 2001, s.125.) The 1994 Act amended PACE, s.107 by providing that a chief inspector can be "made up" on the authority of an officer above superintendent in rank. It also said that a chief inspector can act in place of a superintendent who has authorised him to do so during his absence.[2] (Code C as revised in 2003 reflects the position in para.1.9A.)

There is no reference in the Act for any special procedure to be followed for such "making up", nor for the authorisation to be in writing.

The Home Office Circular on PACE (para.1–11, n.23 above, para.41) stated that the power in this section was supposed to be used only in specific situations to meet the particular needs of a situation and did not "provide for a blanket authority to be issued". According to the Circular, it would, for instance, be within the terms of the section for authority to be given to those chief inspectors who were Deputy Sub-Divisional Commanders to carry out the full duties

10–03

---

[1] Later translated into the consolidating Police Act 1996, s.13(1).
[2] Police and Magistrates Court Act 1994, Sch.5, Pt II, para.35.

of the Sub-Divisional Commander in the superintendent's absence. Other chief inspectors could not be so authorised.

In *Alladice*[3] the Court of Appeal dismissed an appeal brought, *inter alia*, on the ground that the officer who had denied him access to a solicitor was not qualified by rank to make that decision. Lord Lane C.J. for the court held that the officer was a chief inspector who had been given authority to exercise the necessary power by an acting chief superintendent. The holder of an acting rank was to be treated, so far as authority and powers were concerned, as if he were the holder of the substantive rank—"unless his appointment was a colourable pretence".

Deputy chief constables: s.108

10–04   Section 108 of PACE established the separate rank of deputy chief constable. The Sheehy Report (*Inquiry into Police Responsibilties & Rewards*, Cm.2280 (1993)) recommended the abolition of the rank. This was effected by the Police and Magistrates' Courts Act 1994, Sch.9.

However, the change was short-lived. The rank of deputy chief constable was re-established by the Criminal Justice and Police Act 2001, s.123 which baldly stated: "Every police force maintained under section 2 shall have a deputy chief constable".[4] The Act also re-introduced the equivalent rank of deputy assistant commissioner in the Metropolitan Police.[5]

Amendments relating to the Police Federations: s.109

10–05   This section was repealed by the Police Act 1996, Sch.9, Pt I.

Functions of special constables in Scotland: s.110

10–06   Section 110 consisted of only two and a half lines. They repealed s.17(6) of the Police (Scotland) Act 1967 (restriction on functions of special constables).

---

[3] (1988) 87 Cr.App.R. 380; [1988] Crim.L.R. 608, CA.
[4] s.11A of the Police Act 1996.
[5] s.9FA of the Police Act 1996 inserted by s.122 of the 2001 Act.

Regulations for police forces and police cadets—Scotland: s.111

Section 111 provided for powers of delegation in regard to regulations affecting   **10–07** the government and administration of police forces in Scotland.

Metropolitan police officers: s.112

Section 112 was repealed by the Police Act 1996, Sch.9, Pt I.   **10–08**

PART XI

MISCELLANEOUS AND SUPPLEMENTARY

Application of Act to Armed Forces: s.113

Section 113 provided for some parts of the Act to apply to the Armed Forces. **11–01**
Subsection (1) permitted the Secretary of State for Defence to apply any of the provisions of the Act relating to the investigation of offences (subject to any qualifications he may specify) to the investigation of offences under the Army Act 1955, the Air Force Act 1955 and the Naval Discipline Act 1957 (collectively known as the "Service Discipline Acts" or "SDAs") and to persons under arrest under any of those Acts.

Subsections (3), (4) and (5) stated that the Home Secretary should issue suitably adapted Codes of Practice for persons other than police officers concerned with investigations in the Armed Services. They must be laid before Parliament, subject to the negative resolution procedure, rather than the affirmative procedure applicable to the Codes for the police.[1]

Subsection (12) provides that the Secretary of State may modify the applica- **11–02** tion of Pts VII (Documentary Evidence in Criminal Proceedings) and VIII (Evidence in Criminal Proceedings—General) in regard to courts martial or a Standing Civilian Court which tries civilian personnel for offences against military law overseas. In December 1985 the Secretary of State for Defence laid before Parliament the Police and Criminal Evidence Act 1984 (Application to Armed Forces) Order 1985 which became SI 1985/1882. The Order applied PACE, ss.58, 59 (legal advice), 61 (fingerprinting), 62 (intimate samples), 63 (non-intimate samples), 64 (destruction of fingerprints and samples) and 117 (use of reasonable force) to the investigation of offences conducted by the Service police, subject to modifications.

In 1990, the 1985 Order was amended by the Police and Criminal Evidence Act 1984 (Application to Armed Forces) (Amendment) Order 1990 (SI

---

[1] For the most recent version see Police and Criminal Evidence Act 1984 (Codes of Practice) (Armed Forces) Order 2003 (SI 2003/2315). The Codes were: Code A—the exercise by the Service Police of statutory powers of stop and search; Code B—the exercise by the Services Police of statutory powers for the entry and search of premises and the seizure of property found on persons and premises by the Services Police; and the Commanding Officer's Code of Practice.

1990/1488). In 1997, both the 1985 and the 1990 Orders were revoked and replaced by a new Order (SI 1997/15).

11–03   The 1997 Order substantially re-enacted the 1985 Order, as amended in 1990, and extended its effect to ss.54 (searches of detained persons), 55 (intimate searches), 56 (right to have someone informed when arrested) and 63A (speculative searches of fingerprints or samples). Apart from these extensions, the main change from the 1985/1995 Orders was to require that, if possible, authorisation of the procedures should be by a senior officer—in the Navy, a lieutenant, in the Army, a captain, and in the Air Force, a flight lieutenant—who is not the investigating Service policeman. But if it is not practicable to have authorisation at that level, it can be provided by anyone holding a rank senior to that of the person asking for authorisation.[2]

The equivalent of a serious arrestable offence in Service terms is "a serious service offence", defined as a Service offence that cannot be dealt with summarily or which appears to a Service policeman to be serious.[3]

11–04   *The Armed Forces Act 2001* The Armed Forces Act 2001 made major changes. The SDAs did not set out the powers which might need to be exercised in the investigation of offences allegedly committed by members of the armed forces or other persons subject to the SDAs. The principal powers in question were those of stop and search and of entry and search of living accommodation. Instead, those powers were exercised on the authority of the commanding officers under his inherent powers. As was stated in the preface, in order to put these matters onto a proper footing, especially in light of the requirements of the European Convention on Human Rights, the 2001 Act, Pt 2 gave statutory authority for these powers. The powers, which are exercisable by the Service police of each of the armed forces, are broadly equivalent to those available to the civilian police with appropriate modification. However, under the Act, commanding officers retain more limited versions of the powers of investigation given to the Service police.

The PACE power in s.113 for the Secretary of State to use subordinate legislation in this context was not broad enough to cover these changes—thus the need for primary legislation. Conversely, the power given by s.113 to make regulations in regard to any provision of PACE was now too broad, since the new provisions in Pt 2 of the 2001 Act themselves provide for subordinate legislation. It was therefore necessary to amend s.113(1) by narrowing the scope of the order-making power.[4] The 2001 Act also amended subs.(3) by requiring additional codes of practice to be issued covering the existence of the new powers under Pt 2.[5]

---

[2] subss.(2), (3) and (4) inserted into s.65 of PACE by the 1997 Order.
[3] Definition inserted into s.65 of PACE by the 1997 Order.
[4] See s.13(2) of the 2001 Act.
[5] See s.13(3) of the 2001 Act.

Application of Act to Customs and Excise: s.114

Many of the activities of the Customs and Excise are similar to those of the   **11–05**
police. Section 114 was broadly intended to apply the same regime to Customs
officials as applied under the Act to the police, where and to the extent that this
has been decreed by Treasury Order.

The Treasury made such an Order in 1985[6] which came into force on January
1, 1986. Article 3 of the Order applied to officers of Customs and Excise provisions of PACE relating to the investigation of offences and detention of persons
by the police subject to appropriate modifications. In *Sanusi* [1992] Crim.L.R.
43, CA it was held that quite apart from s.114, under s.67(9) of PACE, Customs
officers have a duty to observe the provisions of Code C. Questioning by
Customs officers of a person arriving at the airport can therefore be a PACE interview and accordingly be subject to the provisions of Code C. See to like effect
Weerdestyn [1995] Crim.L.R. 239, CA. Schedule 2 to the 1985 Order substituted
for words and phrases in PACE equivalent terms for Customs and, for police
ranks, the equivalent Customs and Excise ranks.

Article 4 stated that Customs officers do not have the power to charge a person   **11–06**
with an offence, to release a person on bail or to detain him after he has been
charged. Article 5 gave Customs officers the power to retain articles they have
seized which are evidence of an offence and to retain articles seized by others. It
also distinguished articles seized under PACE from goods seized and liable to
forfeiture under Customs and Excise Acts and provided that the PACE sections
on access and copying did not apply to goods seized under Customs laws. Article
6 retained the previous power of Customs officers to obtain search warrants
where the material sought is acquired or created in the course of a trade, business
or profession. So the rules under PACE regarding excluded material and special
procedure material do not apply. It was not felt appropriate to require application
to be made to a circuit judge in such cases. It follows that s.9 of PACE replacing
existing powers to obtain a search warrant with Sch.1 to PACE does not affect
legislation for Customs and Excise.

Article 7 limited the right of a Customs officer to enter and search premises
under s.18(1) of PACE to premises occupied or controlled by someone under
arrest for a Customs offence which is also an arrestable offence.

Article 8 provided for the keeping and publication of records regarding persons
held in Customs detention. Article 9 extended existing powers of intimate search
to include searches by Customs officers for items which the detainee might use
to cause physical injury to himself or others. Article 11 gave Customs officers,
like police officers, the power to use reasonable force in exercising their power
under the Act.

---

[6] The Police and Criminal Evidence Act 1984 (Application to Customs and Excise) Order 1985 (SI
1985/1800).

Power to apply Act to officers of the Secretary of State, etc; s.114A

11–07   A new s.114A of PACE introduced by the Criminal Justice and Police Act 2001 gives the Home Secretary the power to direct by order that the "special procedure" provisions of PACE Sch.1 shall apply to investigations conducted by persons who are not police officers. The section specifies that this power shall apply only to investigations of serious arrestable offences conducted by an officer of the Department for Trade and Industry or someone authorised to act on its behalf (subs.(2)). The order can apply to offences committed before it comes into force (subs.(3)). The order has to be made by statutory instrument subject to negative resolution of either House of Parliament (subs.(4)). (See Police and Criminal Evidence Act 1984 (Department of Trade and Industry Investigations) Order 2002, SI 2002/2326.)

Expenses: s.115

11–08   Section 115 made financial provision out of central funds for expenditure incurred under PACE.

Meaning of "serious arrestable offence": s.116

11–09   The Philips Royal Commission recommended that the police should have additional powers to deal with what it termed "grave offences". It said that it thought that this category should cover the following broad categories of offences: serious offences against the person or serious sexual offences (murder, manslaughter, causing grievous bodily harm, armed robbery, kidnapping, rape); serious offences of damaging property (arson, causing explosions); serious dishonesty offences (counterfeiting, corruption, and burglary, theft and fraud where major amounts are involved); and a miscellaneous group (the supply, importation or exportation of controlled drugs, perversion of the course of justice and blackmail).[7]

The Government did not, however, accept the recommendation that special powers should be so narrowly confined. Instead, it defined a category of "serious arrestable offences".

Various sections in the Act give the police special powers when a "serious arrestable offence" is under consideration. This arises in s.4 (road checks); s.8 (search warrants); s.9 (orders and warrants issued by judges under Sch.1); s.42 (authority to detain without charge for up to 36 hours); ss.43 and 44 (magistrates' warrants of further detention); s.56 (delay in allowing notification of a person's arrest); and s.58 (delay in allowing access to legal advice). (In August 2004 the Home Office Consultation Paper *Policing: Modernising Police Powers to Meet Community Needs* proposed that the special powers attaching to serious

---

[7] Philips Report, para.3.5.

arrestable offences should be available in respect of all offences triable either way or on indictment when they are relevant and necessary, and proportionate having regard to the rights of the individual (para.2.18). The Serious Organised Crime and Police Bill 2004–2005, Sch.7, Pt 3 gave effect to this proposal (1) by substituting "indictable offence" for "serious arrestable offence" in ss.4, 8, 17, 18, 32, 42, 43, 56, 58, 114A and Sch.1, para.2(a)(i); and (2) by repealing s.116 and Sch.5.)

When the first PACE Bill was published, the definition of a "serious arrestable **11–10** offence" was simply that the person exercising a power under the Act considered the offence to be sufficiently serious to justify his exercising that power. This wholly circular definition was criticised from all sides and the Home Office made several attempts to find a more acceptable definition.

The eventual definition divided offences into two categories. One is that of offences that are so serious that they are always serious arrestable offences. These are listed in Sch.5, Pts I and II (see below). (For the Northern Ireland equivalent see the 1989 Order Sch.5.) Part I is quite short. It lists: treason; murder; manslaughter; rape; kidnapping; incest or intercourse with a girl under 13 years old; buggery with a person under 16 years old[8], indecent assault which amounts to an act of indecency; and importing indecent or obscene articles. Part II is longer. It includes possession of firearms with intent to injure; carrying firearms with criminal intent; use of firearms or imitation firearms to resist arrest; causing explosions likely to endanger life or property; hostage taking; hijacking; and torture. Attempts or conspiracies are treated as if they were completed. Causing death by dangerous driving and causing death by careless driving when under the influence of drink are both serious arrestable offences under s.116. Other offences specifically listed are endangering safety at aerodromes; hijacking of ships; seizing or exercising control of oil platforms at sea; and hijacking of Channel Tunnel trains or seizing control of the tunnel itself. As has already been seen, making, having or distributing indecent photographs of children[9] and publication of obscene matter[10] also became serious arrestable offences.

The sexual offences in the list were added by the House of Commons at Report **11–11** stage. Fears were expressed about the inclusion in the list of offences of indecent assault amounting to acts of gross indecency. The effect, it was said, could be to give the police the means of harassment of the homosexual community. The offence of committing an act of gross indecency with another man under s.13 of the Sexual Offences Act 1956 is only an arrestable offence if one is over 21 years old and the other is under 21 years old. But if one is over 21 and the other is under 21, it could be a serious arrestable offence if there is an assault—and the fact of the assault would result from the incapacity of the person under 21 to give valid consent to what takes place. Any other arrestable offence is serious only if its commission has led or is intended or is likely to lead to any of the consequences specified in subs.(6)—namely:

---

[8] Originally it was "buggery with a boy under 16 or someone who has not consented". This was altered to the formula stated in the text by the Criminal Justice and Public Order Act 1994 (CJPOA), Sch.10, para.59.

[9] See PACE, Sch.5, para.14 added by CJPOA, s.85(3). Section 85(3) of the CJPOA also makes the equivalent alteration to the Northern Ireland PACE Order. See also Criminal Justice (No.2) (Northern Ireland) Order 2004 (SI 2004/1991) adding aggravated vehicle taking.

[10] See PACE, Sch.5, para.15 added by CJPOA s.85(3).

    (a)   serious harm to the security of the State or public order;

    (b)   serious interference with the administration of justice or with the investigation of offences;

    (c)   the death of anyone;

    (d)   serious injury to anyone;

    (e)   substantial financial gain to anyone; and

    (f)   serious financial loss to anyone in the sense that having regard to all the circumstances, it is serious for the person suffering the loss.

The words "or is intended" would cover the situation of the burglar who goes intending to steal a major haul but who is disturbed and leaves with little or nothing. The definition of "loss" in (f) takes into account the particular circumstances of the person in question. The application of this definition obliged the police officer to consider the matter from the point of view of the person who has suffered the loss—an exercise obviously fraught with difficulty. But the test was whether the loss is serious not whether it is felt to be serious by the person concerned. His feeling that the loss is serious is only evidence of whether it is in fact serious. Nevertheless, the definition could result in the theft of £20 from an old age pensioner being a serious arrestable offence! But the converse was also true. In *McIvor (Neil)*[11] Lawton L.J., sitting as a Deputy High Court judge, held that the theft of beagles worth £880 from a hunt was not a serious arrestable offence because that amount shared amongst the members was not serious. Similarly, in *Smith (Eric)*[12] a robbery from Woolworths involving two video recorders valued at some £800, plus cash of £116, was thought by the trial judge probably not to be a serious arrestable offence because the financial gain to the robbers was not necessarily substantial and the store was large and might not regard the loss as serious.

11–12   Subsection (8) defines injury in such a way as to make it clear that it includes disease and impairment of a person's mental as well as physical condition. This is very imprecise but it would include at least severe mental distress even though the physical abuse was minor (as in some sexual offences). However, if the judges were to hold that "impairment of a person's mental condition" also covered "upset", it would drive the proverbial coach-and-four through the definition.

    According to research, the police categorise about 2 per cent of all suspects in the police station as being involved in serious arrestable offences.[13]

---

[11] [1987] Crim.L.R. 409.
[12] [1987] Crim.L.R. 579, Crown Ct.
[13] Brown (1989), pp.48–49; and Brown *et al.* (1992), p.68.

Power of constables to use reasonable force: s.117

The Criminal Law Act 1967, s.3 provided that such force as is reasonable in the circumstances may be used in the prevention of crime or in effecting or assisting in the lawful arrest of offenders or suspected persons or of persons unlawfully at large. Section 117 of PACE is a much wider provision in that it permits the use of reasonable force in exercising any power under the Act unless it specifically requires the consent of a person who is not a police officer. (Holding an identification parade depends on the consent of the suspect, so this is an example of a situation where the police do not have the power to use reasonable force.[14]) **11–13**

The sections of PACE affected are: **11–14**

- powers of search and detention for the purposes of a search (ss.1 and 2);

- entry and search of premises to execute a search warrant (s.16);

- entry and search of premises to make an arrest (s.17);

- entry and search of premises following arrest for an arrestable offence (s.18);

- seizure of evidence (s.19);

- arrest (ss.24, 25, 27, 31);

- search of the person on arrest (s.32);

- detention of a person at a station (ss.36 and 37);

- search of a detained person at a police station (s.54);

- intimate searches of detained persons (s.55);

- fingerprinting without consent (s.61);

- taking a non-intimate sample without consent (s.63).

What is reasonable force is a question of fact to be judged by the particular situation. The same is true of the level of force permitted by way of self-defence. Sometimes the use of force in exercising a power may overlap with the right of self-defence. The right of self-defence may include the right to strike the first

---

[14] *Jones and Nelson, The Times*, April 21, 1999, CA.

blow. In *Chisam*[15] it was held that a person can use force to ward off an anticipated attack, provided it is anticipated as being "imminent".

As will be seen, civilian police staff basically have the same power to use reasonable force—see para.12–07 below.

General interpretation: s.118

11–15   Section 118 defines or indicates the source of the definition for the following terms: "arrestable offence"; "designated police station"; "document"; "item subject to legal privilege"; "parent or guardian"; "premises"; "recordable offence"; "vessel". (The Serious Organised Crime and Police Bill introduced in November 2004 eliminates the definition of "arrestable offence".[16])

Section 114 also defines the term "police detention" as (a) where a person has been taken to a police station after being arrested and is detained there; or (b) where he is arrested at a police station after attending voluntarily or accompanying a constable to it and is detained there or elsewhere in the charge of a constable. It is specifically stated that a person who is at court after being charged is not in police detention. The case of someone who, after being arrested, because of his injuries is taken directly to a hospital is not covered. This would seem to be a gap in the legislation. Various powers, such as the power under s.63 to take an intimate sample only apply, for instance, to someone in police detention. There are categories of persons at the police station who therefore seem to be outside the definition of "police detention". They include: someone attending voluntarily at the police station; persons arrested under s.136 of the Mental Health Act 1983; and persons in custody awaiting extradition or deportation. Also, someone detained after an unlawful arrest which has not yet been cured is probably not within the definition of being in police detention. Another category of person who is not in police detention is someone arrested for breach of bail conditions under the Bail Act 1976, s.7.[17]

11–16   However, as has been seen, Code C, para.1.10 states:

". . . this code applies to persons who are in custody at police stations whether or not they have been arrested for an offence and to those who have been removed to a police station as a place of safety under sections 135 and 136 of the Mental Health Act 1983. Section 15 of Code C[18] applies however solely to persons in police detention."

In Northern Ireland, the definition of police detention was expanded in 1995 to include persons produced to a police station from a custodial establishment—see The Police (Amendment) (Northern Ireland) Order 1995, Art.3.

---

[15] (1963) 47 Cr.App.R. 130.
[16] Sch.7, Pt 1, para.2(2) of the Bill.
[17] See *R. v Havering Magistrates Court, Ex p. the DPP* and *R. v Wirral Borough Magistrates' Court, Ex p. McKeown* [2001] 1 W.L.R. 805; [2001] 2 Cr.App.R. 2.
[18] Reviews and extensions of detention.

Amendments and repeals: s.119

Section 119 provided for consequential amendments in Sch.6 and for the repeal   **11–17**
of enactments mentioned in Sch.7.

Extent: s.120

Section 120 detailed the sections which apply to the different parts of the United   **11–18**
Kingdom.

Commencement: s.121

Section 121 dealt with commencement.   **11–19**

Short title: s.122

The short title of the Act is the Police and Criminal Evidence Act 1984.   **11–20**

POLICE POWERS FOR CIVILIANS

CHAPTER 12

THE POLICE REFORM ACT 2002

The Police Reform Act 2002 gives unprecedented powers to civilians acting in **12–01**
support of the police. As the Home Office Minister told the House of Commons,
"The reality is that the Government . . . are embarking on a new development in
British policing".[1]

The proposals were initially outlined in December 2001 in the White Paper
Policing a New Century: A Blueprint for Reform (Cm.5326—available at
www.policereform.gov.uk).

The Explanatory Notes attached to the Act (para.25) say that the purpose was
threefold:

- First, it is intended to free up police time for their core functions by
  making more effective use of support staff including "detention officers", "escort officers", and "investigating officers" acting as scene of
  crime officers (SOCOS).

- Secondly, as part of the drive to tackle crime more effectively, the
  Government intended that police forces could employ specialist investigating officers to combat specialist crime in areas such as finance and
  Information Technology. The Act enables such investigators to be given
  the powers they need to do their job effectively.

- Thirdly, it is designed to provide additional capacity to combat low-
  level disorder, and thereby help reduce the public's fear of crime. The
  Act will enable chief officers to appoint suitable support staff ("community support officers", or CSOs) to roles providing a visible presence in the community with powers sufficient to deal with minor
  issues. Such staff would be under the direction and control of the chief
  officer.

---

[1] Standing Committee A, *Hansard*, June 25, 2002, col.347. See also Jason-Lloyd, *Quasi-Policing*
(Cavendish, 2003); Morris, "Extending the police family: issues and anomalies" [2002] *Public Law*
670; and Ormerod and Roberts, "The Police Reform Act 2002" [2003] Crim.L.R. 141 at 154–60.

12–02   The Government also wanted to harness others already involved in crime reduction activities such as traffic wardens, neighbourhood and street wardens and security staff "through an extended police family". The Act also makes provision for "community safety accreditation schemes" (and a railway accreditation scheme) and the granting of limited powers to accredited members of those schemes.

According to the House of Commons Home Affairs Select Committee, the idea for giving police powers to a new type of semi-trained civilian came mainly from the Metropolitan Police.[2] ("The Metropolitan Police Service wants community support officers because, they say, policing central London does not need all the skills of police officers who would be better deployed in the boroughs."[3])

The Select Committee, however, cited the concerns of the Police Federation which strongly opposed the Bill. ("We see this as adding an unnecessary and unwieldy additional tier to policing, with the potential both to confuse the public and to provoke breaches of the peace. Many of the functions envisaged for the deployment of CSOs are potentially some of the most dangerous and difficult faced by police officers." (para.55).) The Police Superintendents' Association had been equally worried. ("There is a real danger that police officers will be left to clear up the mess created by mistakes rather than being supported, and that officers will be called upon to deal with low level offences rather than concentrating on other issues [as] the Government expects." (*ibid.*).)

12–03   On the basis that the extent (if any) of the use of such civilians was entirely at the discretion of the police, the Home Affairs Committee said that, while recognising that there were genuine concerns, "the only way of finding out whether this proposal will work is to try it" (para.67).

The Bill was introduced in the House of Lords in January 2002. Some of its provisions attracted particular criticism—and the Government was defeated on several issues including in particular the proposed power of community support officers and of accredited persons to detain people in the street for up to 30 minutes.[4]

When the Bill went to the Commons the Government compromised on this issue. It moved amendments to restore, *inter alia*, the power of detention for community support officers.[5] But although it restored the power of accredited persons to ask for name and address, it did not seek to restore their power to detain someone who refused to comply with the request.[6] On the Bill's Third Reading, the Government also intimated that the power to detain for up to 30 minutes with reasonable force would not be implemented nationally until, first, it had been piloted in a maximum of six force areas over a two-year period and, secondly, there had been a report on the pilot by the Chief Inspector of Constabulary.[7] When the Bill came back to the Lords this compromise proved acceptable and the matter went through without a vote.[8] The report on the pilot carried out over 15 months in six

---

[2] 2001–2002 session, Second Report, 2002, HC 612, para.52.
[3] 2001–2002 session, Second Report, 2002, HC 612, para.52.
[4] Respectively by 168 to 121 (House of Lords, *Hansard*, April 25, 2002, cols 403–411) and by 158 to 101 (*ibid.*, cols 415–421).
[5] Standing Committee A, *Hansard*, June 20, 2002, cols 266–273.
[6] Standing Committee A, *Hansard*, June 20, 2002, cols 324–329.
[7] House of Commons, *Hansard*, July 10, 2002, cols 980–981.
[8] House of Lords, *Hansard*, July 22, 2002, cols 94–98.

force areas stated that it had proved "very positive with no indication of there being a significant risk to either the CSO or the detainee".[9] In half the cases studied the detainee was arrested by a police officer. In just over a fifth he was released by the CSO after giving a satisfactory name and address and in just over another fifth he was released after the arrival of a police officer. In the overwhelming majority of cases the matter was disposed of well within the 30 minutes time frame. The power to detain for up to 30 minutes was activated as from December 22, 2004.

CSOs were introduced in London in September 2002 and in 26 other forces early in 2003. By September 2004 most forces had some CSOs. At that stage there were some 4,000 nationally—of whom over two-fifths (1,809 out of 4,199, or 43 per cent) were in London. The Government envisaged further significant development of the concept (Home Office Press Release 397/2004, December 22, 2004).

The powers under discussion are in Pt 4 of the Act and Schs 4 and 5. They are printed in full at the end of this Chapter. **12–04**

The Bill originally had a clause giving the Home Secretary the power to alter the provisions of Schs 4 or 5 by order confirmed by affirmative resolution of both Houses. This power was removed as unacceptable by the House of Lords.[10] It was then restored by the Commons.[11] But in a surprise and highly unusual move, the Government brought forward an amendment on Third Reading in the Commons to remove the clause which it had itself included in the Bill only two weeks earlier.[12] This was plainly to avoid the embarrassment of a further defeat on the issue in the Lords.

Part 4 begins with s.38.

Police powers for police authority employees: s.38

This section enables chief constables to designate suitably skilled and trained civilians employed by their police authority who are under the chief constable's direction and control to exercise powers and to undertake duties in carrying out specified functions (subs.(1)). Lord Condon, former Commissioner of the Metropolitan Police, told the House of Lords on the Report stage of the Bill that about one-third of the police services in the country were keen to explore the notion of community support officers.[13] Did this include employees of companies like Group 4? The Home Minister, Lord Rooker, told the House of Lords that in this context, "[A]n employee is an employee, not a contractor or sub-contractor. **12–05**

---

[9] Singer, "Community Support Officers (Detention Power) Pilot: Evaluation" (Home Office, October 2004), p.1 (*www.homeoffice.gov.uk/rds/pdfs04/csos.pdf*). See also the later Home Office report, *National Evaluation of Community Support Officers*, December 2004 (*www.policereform.gov.uk/publications/publications/index.html*).

[10] *Hansard*, April 25, 2002, cols 382–394.

[11] Standing Committee A, *Hansard*, June 25, 2002, cols 345–356.

[12] House of Commons, *Hansard*, July 9, 2002, col.813.

[13] House of Lords, *Hansard*, April 16, 2002, col.834.

People working for contractors would be the employees of someone else, not the police authority. Part of the whole reassurance in [Clause 35[14]] is that the people concerned are employees of the police authority under the direct, specific employer control of the chief constable."[15]

However, despite these categorical assurances, the Government subsequently introduced a new clause which became s.39 to permit employees of contractors like Group 4 to act as detention officers or escort officers.[16]

12–06   The civilians can be designated to perform functions in four categories—community support officer, investigating officer, detention officer or escort officer (subs.(2)). The Director General of the National Criminal Intelligence Service and of the National Crime Squad is given the power to designate investigating officers (subs.(3)).

A person cannot be so designated unless the chief officer or Director General is satisfied that he (a) is a suitable person to carry out the functions for which he is designated, (b) is capable of effectively carrying out those functions, and (c) has received adequate training (subs.(4)). ("They will not be vigilantes or 'have a go' characters in uniform; they will be properly trained and equipped professionals. They will be quality people."[17]) No details were given as to the expected level of training. Obviously it would be far less than for police officers. Training varies from force to force, the norm being three weeks. At the time of writing a national training package for CSOs being prepared by the National Centre for Policing Excellence (Centrex) envisaged a course of some six weeks.

The person only has the powers granted by the designation granted by the chief officer (subs.(5), (7)). These could vary from force area to force area and even within a force area as between different individuals. But the powers that can be conferred are restricted to those that are applicable under the relevant Parts of Sch.4 (subs.(6)).

12–07   The Act does not specifically state but the Minister made clear that designated civilians would have to "have regard to the relevant Police and Criminal Evidence Act codes of practice, which will also form a necessary part of their training" and this was made good (see Code B, para.2.13, Code C, para.1.16 and Code D, para.2.22).[18]

Subsection (8) provides that where a power exercised by a community service officer, an investigating officer, a detention officer or an escort officer allows for the use of reasonable force when exercised by a constable, a person operating such a power under a designation can equally use reasonable force (Code C, para.1.14). However, where the designation includes the power to force entry to premises, it can only be exercised by the person on his own for the purpose of saving life or limb or to prevent serious damage to property. Apart from such emergency situations, the power to force entry to premises can only be exercised in the company of and under the supervision of a constable (subs.(9)).

[14] Now s.38.
[15] House of Lords, *Hansard*, March 7, 2002, col.484.
[16] The Government had been urged to do so by the Home Affairs Select Committee in its May 2002 Report, 2001–2002 session, Second Report, 2002, HC 612, para.70.
[17] Lord Rooker, Home Office Minister, House of Lords, *Hansard*, April 16, 2002, col.840.
[18] House of Lords, *Hansard*, March 7, 2002, col.459. For Northern Ireland see Police (Northern Ireland) Act 2003, Sch. 3, para.7 inserting new para.(8A) into Art.66 of the 1989 PACE Order.

The available applicable powers for each category are set out in Sch.4. (For the text, including the extensive new powers under the Serious Organised Crime and Police Bill 2004–2005, see below). For similar provisions for Northern Ireland see Police (Northern Ireland) Act 2003, ss.30 and 31 and Sch.2.

Community support officers: Sch.4, Pt 1

The range of powers that can be given to CSOs under Pt 1 are linked to dealing with minor misconduct. They include issuing a range of fixed penalty notices relating to anti-social behaviour. (The offences in question (set out in Pt 1 above) include being drunk in a public place, cycling on a footway, dog fouling, littering and a range of minor public disorder offences triggering fixed penalty notices set out in s.1 of the Criminal Justice and Police Act 2001.[19])   **12–08**

A person reasonably believed to have acted or to be acting in an anti-social manner (within the meaning of the Crime and Disorder Act 1998, s.1) in the police area covered by the designation can be requested to give his name and address (para.3 (2)). The same applies in respect of offences that appear to have caused injury, alarm or distress to any other person, or the loss of or damage to any other person's property (para.(6)).

A power to detain for 30 minutes

If the person refuses to give his name and address or gives what appears to be a false one, the CSO has the power to detain him for up to 30 minutes pending the arrival of a constable (para.2(3)). The person may instead elect to accompany the CSO to a police station in that area (para.2(4)). Refusing to give one's name and address or making off whilst so detained or whilst accompanying the CSO to a police station is an offence punishable on summary conviction to a level 3 fine (currently £1,000) (para.2(5)). Reasonable force may be used to prevent someone making off (para.4). (The Serious Organised Crime and Police Bill 2004–2005 would extend this to keeping him under control.[20])   **12–09**

Ministers were at pains to make it clear that this power to detain was not a power of arrest. ("If the person makes off, the support officers will not have the power to go after him, as it were to 'search and rescue'. I make it clear that the officers do not have a power of arrest."[21] A CSO would be exercising "a power of enforcement not a power of arrest".[22])

Precisely how detention backed by force differs from temporary arrest is not clear—save that this form of detention is restricted to 30 minutes. Also, a CSO

---

[19] Being drunk in a highway, or other place or licensed premises; throwing fireworks in a thoroughfare; knowingly giving a false alarm to a fire brigade; trespassing on a railway; throwing stones, etc., at trains or other things on railways; someone under the age of 18 buying or attempting to buy alcohol for consumption in a bar or licensed premises; disorderly behaviour while drunk in a public place; wasting police time or giving a false report; using a public telecommunication system for sending a message known to be false in order to cause annoyance; consumption of alcohol in a designated public place.

[20] Sch.9, para.3 of the Bill.

[21] House of Lords, *Hansard*, April 16, 2002, col.852.

[22] House of Commons, Standing Committee A, *Hansard*, June 20, 2002, col.266.

would technically at the very least have the citizen's power to make an arrest—though Ministers seemed to be saying that it was not expected that they would exercise any power of arrest. (We could "have simply relied on the citizen's power of arrest. The Government chose not to do that, because there would have been a general feeling of discomfort at the idea of employing full-time professionals who were trained with the general citizen's power of arrest."[23])

12–10   If detention is limited to 30 minutes, it follows that detention beyond 30 minutes is unlawful and therefore, if he troubled to bring a claim, entitles the detainee to damages. If a police officer has not arrived within 30 minutes the CSO must therefore let the detainee go. Can the detainee then be detained again and, if so, immediately or only after a period of time? When the Home Office Minister was asked in the Commons what was the minimum time for redetention he was obviously at a loss to know what to answer—"That would be a matter of judgment in the circumstances".[24] The Act does not specifically prohibit immediate further detention for another 30 minutes, but the courts are unlikely to countenance such a blatant device to extend the power of detention. Since arrival of a police officer within 30 minutes cannot be guaranteed, this could turn out to be a significant practical problem.

There is nothing in the Act that addresses the responsibility of the police officer when he does arrive. Presumably his main task is to consider whether there is a case to justify an arrest under PACE, s.25(3)(a), (b) or (c) for the offence of not giving name and address to the CSO—or otherwise. (The Serious Organised Crime and Police Bill introduced in November 2004 provides that the CSO is under a duty to remain with the constable until the control of the detainee has been transferred to the constable and that the same applies where he takes the detainee to a police station.[25])

The Bill would also give a CSO who has been given this power the same power to search the person detained, and to seize items found, as a constable has under s.32 of PACE. If such a search results in any item being seized, the CSO must inform the detainee where inquiries about its recovery can be made and must also comply with a constable's instruction about what to do with it.[26]

Other powers

12–11   CSOs under Pt I are given a variety of other powers. These include the power under s.17 of PACE to enter premises for the purpose of saving life or limb or preventing serious damage to property (para.8); the power under s.4 of PACE to carry out road checks (para.13); the power under the Terrorism Act 2000, s.36 to enforce cordoned areas, for instance by requiring a person to leave the area or arranging for the removal of a vehicle (para.12); and the powers under s.44(1)(a), 44(1)(d) and 45(2) of the Terrorism Act to stop and search persons and vehicles (para.14). But whereas the power under s.17 can be exercised by a CSO on his own, the other powers of stop, search or seizure can only be exercised by a CSO in the company of and under the supervision of a constable (para.15(2)).

---

[23] Denham, House of Commons, Standing Committee A, *Hansard*, June 20, 2002, col.251.
[24] *ibid.*
[25] Sch.9, para.2 of the Bill.
[26] New para.2A of Sch.4, Pt 1 to the 2002 Act, inserted by Sch.8, para.3 to the Bill.

The Serious Organised Crime and Police Bill introduced in November 2004 would give CSOs various new powers: to direct traffic and pedestrians; to require a driver or pedestrian who fails to follow such directions to give their name and address and to detain anyone who fails to do so for up to 30 minutes; to enter and search licensed premises if he believes that an offence relating to the sale or consumption of alcohol by and to young people and to persons who are already drunk has been or is being committed; to place temporary traffic signs on a road; to photograph a person who has been arrested, detained or given a fixed penalty notice elsewhere than at a police station; and to take footwear impressions.[27]

Investigating officers: Sch.4, Pt 2

The Explanatory Notes accompanying the Act (para.208) state that this Part   **12–12**
includes a range of powers needed to support the work of civilian investigating officers in specialist areas such as financial and information technology crime and to the work of Scenes of Crime Officers. They could also have a role in interviewing. Investigating officers may be given a variety of police powers which can be exercised without any constable being present:

- Under PACE, ss.8, 15, 16, 19, 20, 21 and 22, to apply for a search warrant, to execute such a warrant and when lawfully on any premises to seize and retain things for which a search has been authorised (paras.16, 20).

- To apply for and to obtain access to special procedure material under s.9 of and Sch.1 to PACE (para.17).

- To have lawful custody of persons in police detention (para.22).

- Under s.31 of PACE, to make a further arrest of someone already under arrest at the police station—and the provisions of CJPOA 1994, s.36 (adverse inferences drawn from failure to account for objects or marks) apply (para.21).

- Under s.18 of PACE, to enter and search premises of a person who has been arrested (para.18)—including a constable's power to conduct such a search before the arrested person is taken to a police station and without the authority of an inspector if the presence of the arrested person is "necessary for the effective investigation of the offence" (PACE, s.18(5)).

- Under Pt 2 of the Criminal Justice and Police Act 2001, to "seize and sift" material that cannot conveniently be sorted on site (para.24).

---

[27] Sch.8, paras 4, 5, 6, 7 and 8 to the Bill.

- Under the Criminal Justice and Public Order Act 1994, ss.36 and 37, to question someone about his presence at the scene of the crime or about marks or objects on him or his clothing—and to give the person the necessary warnings about the possible adverse consequences of exercising a right to silence (para.23).

Detention officers: Sch.4, Pt 3

12–13   The powers of detention officers to be exercised at police stations are:

- Under s.27(1) of PACE, to require a person to attend a police station to have his fingerprints taken (para.25).

- Under s.61 of PACE, to take fingerprints without consent (para.29).

- Under s.54 of PACE, to carry out non-intimate searches and to seize items found in such searches (paras.26, 28).

- Under s.54A of PACE, to carry out searches and examinations in order to determine the identity of persons detained at police stations. Identifying marks found during such searches may be photographed (para.27).

- Under s.55 of PACE, to carry out intimate searches (para.28).

- To give the required warnings under s.62(7) of PACE regarding intimate samples (para.30) and the power under s.63 of PACE to take non-intimate samples (para.31). (There is no power for detention officers to take intimate samples.)

- Under s.63A(4) of PACE, to require someone who has been charged with or convicted of a recordable offence to attend a police station to have a sample taken (para.32).

- Under s.64A of PACE, to photograph detained suspects (para.33).

Escort officers: Sch.4, Pt 4

12–14   The powers that can be given to escort officers are:

- The power to transport arrested persons to police stations and to escort detained persons between police stations and between police stations and other locations specified by the custody officer.

- Under s.30 of PACE, to take an arrested person to a police station (para.34). This must be a designated police station unless the escort officer is working in an area not covered by one and it appears that it will not be necessary to hold the arrested person for more than six hours. A designated escort officer is regarded as having the arrested person in lawful custody. He has a duty to prevent escape, and he is entitled to use reasonable force and to carry out non-intimate searches (para.34).

- A power, with the authority of the custody officer, to escort detainees between police stations within the police area or between a police station and some other place in the police area. The escort officer then becomes responsible for seeing that the arrested person is treated in accordance with PACE as required by PACE, s.39(2)—(para.35).

Police powers for contracted-out staff: s.39

Police authorities are empowered to enter into contracts with contractors "for the provision of services relating to the detention or escort of persons who have been arrested or are otherwise in custody" (subs.(1)). The chief officer of police for that area may designate any employee of such a contractor as either or both a detention officer or an escort officer with such powers and duties derived from Pts 3 and 4 of Sch.4 as are set out in the designation (subss.(2), (3), (6)). Where the power when exercised by a constable includes the use of reasonable force the same applies to the employee of the contractor (subs.(8)). **12–15**

He must be satisfied that the individual is a suitable person capable of carrying out those functions and that he has had adequate training (subs.(4)). He must also be satisfied that the contractor is a fit and proper person to supervise the carrying out of the functions (subs.(5))

The Secretary of State is given power to make regulations covering the handling of complaints or allegations of misconduct against designated persons when carrying out the relevant functions (subs.(9)). Such regulations may apply to any provision of Pt 2 of the Act in respect of complaints against police officers to complaints against designated persons. Part 2 of the 2002 Act establishes the new machinery for dealing with complaints against the police. The Explanatory Notes to the Act stated (para.237), "The intention is to bring contracted-out persons within the remit of the Independent Police Complaints Commission."

Community safety accreditation schemes: s.40

The chief constable can "if he considers it appropriate" establish and maintain a community safety accreditation scheme that accredits suitably skilled and trained civilian employees with powers to undertake specified functions in support of the police (subs.(1)). Before establishing such a scheme the chief officer must consult with his police authority and every local authority any part of whose area lies within the police area (subs.(4)). In the case of London he must consult with the **12–16**

Metropolitan Police Authority, the Mayor and every local authority any part of whose area lies within the metropolitan police district (subs.(5)). Annual policing plans must detail proposals to establish such a scheme and its nature (subs.(7)). Lord Rooker told the House of Lords that the Government planned that accreditation schemes would be piloted before they would be available for implementation nationally.[28]

A scheme under s.36 has to have arrangements with employers for the supervision of employees who have had conferred on them any police powers by way of community safety functions (subs.(8)). It is the chief officer's responsibility to see that such employers have satisfactory arrangements for handling complaints relating to the carrying out of these functions by their employees (subs.(9)).

The Home Office Minister expressed the view in the House of Commons debates on the Bill that employers under community safety accreditation schemes would be regarded as public authorities for the purposes of the Human Rights Act 1998.[29]

Accreditation under community safety accreditation schemes: s.41 and Sch.5

12–17   This section only applies where the chief officer has made arrangements with an employer for the carrying out of community safety functions by employees (subs.(1)). The chief officer can accredit an employee of an employer who has entered into arrangements for the purposes of a community safety accreditation scheme to permit the exercise of powers under Sch.5. Such accreditation may not be given unless the chief officer is satisfied that the employer is a fit and proper person to supervise the carrying out of the functions in question by the employee, that the employee himself is a suitable person capable of exercising his functions effectively and that he has had adequate training (subs.(4)). The functions to be performed cannot go beyond what is permitted by the accreditation (subs.(6)).

The powers that can be exercised by an accredited person are set out in Sch.5. They are not as great as those that can be exercised by CSOs under Pt 1. Thus they cannot issue fixed penalty notices under the Criminal Justice and Police Act 2001. But they can be given the same power as CSOs to require the names and address of someone acting in an anti-social manner and it is an offence not to comply with the request. As has been seen, unlike CSOs, they cannot detain a person for up to 30 minutes nor can they use reasonable force when exercising their powers. Nor can they be given the power to enter premises to save life or limb or to prevent serious damage to property. They have no power to carry out PACE road checks nor any powers under the Terrorism Act 2000 nor any of the PACE powers exercised in the police station or in regard to arrested persons outside the police station. The powers they can be given include the removal of abandoned vehicles, the stopping of vehicles for testing and the the escorting of abnormal loads.

12–18   The Serious Organised Crime and Police Bill introduced in November 2004 lists new powers that can be conferred on persons accredited under a community

---

[28] House of Lords, *Hansard*, March 7, 2002, cols 494–495.
[29] Standing Committee A, *Hansard*, June 25, 2002, col.317.

safety accreditation scheme. They include: the power to direct traffic and to require the name and address of a person who fails to follow directions; the power to deal with begging and to require the name and address of a person who he believes has committed an offence under ss.3 and 4 of the Vagrancy Act 1824 (begging in a public place or encouraging a child to beg, sleeping in unoccupied premises or in the open air without a valid reason); the power to photograph a person to whom they have issued a fixed penalty notice.[30]

Supplementary provisions relating to designations and accreditations: s.42

Where a designated or accredited person relies on any power or duty in relation **12–19** to a member of the public, they must show that person their designation or accreditation if asked to do so (subs.(1)). They can only exercise their powers if they are wearing a uniform endorsed by the chief officer. They must also wear an approved badge (subs.(2)). (The Serious Organised Crime and Police Bill introduced in November 2004 provides that an investigating officer designated under s.38 of the 2002 Act shall, on the authority of an inspector or above, be allowed not to wear a uniform for specific and individual operations.[31])

Railway safety accreditation schemes: s.43

Section 43 allows the Secretary of State to make regulations to enable the chief **12–20** constable of the British Transport Police to establish and maintain a railway safety accreditation scheme. The regulations would specify the powers that could be conferred on accredited persons under such a scheme but such powers could not exceed those available to an accredited person under a community safety accreditation scheme. The powers could also include the giving of fixed penalty notices in respect of trespassing on the railway or of throwing stones and similar missiles at trains.

Offences against designated and accredited persons: s.46

Assaulting a designated person or an accredited person or anyone assisting them **12–21** in the execution of their duty is an offence punishable with up to six month's imprisonment or a level 5 fine (£5,000) (subs.(1)). Resisting or wilfully obstructing them is an offence carrying a penalty of up to one month's imprisonment and a level 3 fine (£1,000). Impersonating a designated or accredited person is an offence carrying a penalty of up to six month's imprisonment and a level 5 fine (subs.(3)).

---

[30] Sch.8, Pt 2 to the Bill.
[31] New s.42(2A) inserted by cl.113(2) of the Bill.

POLICE REFORM ACT 2002

POLICE REFORM ACT 2002

PART 4

POLICE POWERS ETC.

CHAPTER 1

EXERCISE OF POLICE POWERS ETC. BY CIVILIANS

Police powers for police authority employees

38.—(1) The chief officer of police of any police force may designate any person who—

    (a) is employed by the police authority maintaining that force, and

    (b) is under the direction and control of that chief officer,

as an officer of one or more of the descriptions specified in subsection (2).

    (2) The description of officers are as follows—

    (a) community support officer;

    (b) investigating officer;

    (c) detention officer;

    (d) escort officer.

[*The Serious Organised Crime and Police Bill 2004–05, cl.111(2) adds "(e) staff custody officer."*]

    (3) A Director General may designate any person who—

    (a) is an employee of his Service Authority, and

    (b) is under the direction and control of that Director General,

as an investigating officer. [1]

    (4) A chief officer of police or a Director General[2] shall not designate a person under this section unless he is satisfied that that person—

    (a) is a suitable person to carry out the functions for the purposes of which he is designated;

    (b) is capable of effectively carrying out those functions; and

    (c) has received adequate training in the carrying out of those functions and in the exercise and performance of the powers and duties to be conferred on him by virtue of the designation.

---

[1] The Serious Organised Crime and Police Bill 2004–05, Sch.4, para.182(2) repeals subs.(3).

[2] The words "or a Director General" are omitted by the Serious Organised Crime and Police Bill 2004–05, Sch.4, para.182(3).

(5) A person designated under this section shall have the powers and duties conferred or imposed on him by the designation.

(6) Powers and duties may be conferred or imposed on a designated person by means only of the application to him by his designation of provisions of the applicable Part of Schedule 4 that are to apply to the designated person; and for this purpose the applicable Part of that Schedule is—

    (a)   in the case of a person designated as a community support officer, Part 1;

    (b)   in the case of a person designated as an investigating officer, Part 2;

    (c)   in the case of a person designated as a detention officer, Part 3; and

    (d) in the case of a person designated as an escort officer, Part 4.

[*The Serious Organised Crime and Police Bill 2004–05, cl.111(3) adds "(e) in the case of a person designated as a staff custody officer, Part 4A."*]

(7) An employee of a police authority or of a Service Authority[3] authorised or required to do anything by virtue of a designation under this section—

    (a)   shall not be authorised or required by virtue of that designation to engage in any conduct otherwise than in the course of that employment; and

    (b)   shall be so authorised or required subject to such restrictions and conditions (if any) as may be specified in his designation.

(8) Where any power exercisable by any person in reliance on his designation under this section is a power which, in the case of its exercise by a constable, includes or is supplemented by a power to use reasonable force, any person exercising that power in reliance on that designation shall have the same entitlement as a constable to use reasonable force.

(9) Where any power exercisable by any person in reliance on his designation under this section includes power to use force to enter any premises, that power shall not be exercisable by that person except—

    (a)   in the company, and under the supervision, of a constable; or

    (b)   for the purpose of saving life or limb or preventing serious damage to property.

[*The Serious Organised Crime and Police Bill 2004–05, cl.111(4) adds new subs.(10):*

"(10) References in this section, section 42 or section 46(4) to powers and duties conferred or imposed on a designated person, or to a designated person's being authorised or required to do anything by virtue of a designation under this section, or to a power or duty exercisable by a designated person in reliance on or by virtue of a designation under this section are, in the case of a staff custody officer at a police station designated under section 35(1) of the 1984 Act, references to those things in relation to him after his appointment as a custody officer for that police station under section 36(2) of that Act."]

---

[3] The words "or of a Service Authority" are omitted by the Serious Organised Crime and Police Bill 2004–05, Sch.4, para.182(4).

Police powers for contracted-out staff

39.—(1) This section applies if a police authority has entered into a contract with a person ("the contractor") for the provision of services relating to the detention or escort of persons who have been arrested or are otherwise in custody.

(2) The chief officer of police of the police force maintained by that police authority may designate any person who is an employee of the contractor as either or both of the following—

    (a)   a detention officer; or

    (b)   an escort officer.

(3) A person designated under this section shall have the powers and duties conferred or imposed on him by the designation.

(4) A chief officer of police shall not designate a person under this section unless he is satisfied that that person—

    (a)   is a suitable person to carry out the functions for the purposes of which he is designated;

    (b)   is capable of effectively carrying out those functions; and

    (c)   has received adequate training in the carrying out of those functions and in the exercise and performance of the powers and duties to be conferred on him by virtue of the designation.

(5) A chief officer of police shall not designate a person under this section unless he is satisfied that the contractor is a fit and proper person to supervise the carrying out of the functions for the purposes of which that person is designated.

(6) Powers and duties may be conferred or imposed on a designated person by means only of the application to him by his designation of provisions of the applicable Part of Schedule 4 that are to apply to the designated person; and for this purpose the applicable Part of that Schedule is—

    (a)   in the case of a person designated as a detention officer, Part 3; and

    (b)   in the case of a person designated as an escort officer, Part 4.

(7) An employee of the contractor authorised or required to do anything by virtue of a designation under this section—

    (a)   shall not be authorised or required by virtue of that designation to engage in any conduct otherwise than in the course of that employment; and

    (b)   shall be so authorised or required subject to such restrictions and conditions (if any) as may be specified in his designation.

(8) Where any power exercisable by any person in reliance on his designation under this section is a power which, in the case of its exercise by a constable, includes or is supplemented by a power to use reasonable force, any person exercising that power in reliance on that designation shall have the same entitlement as a constable to use reasonable force.

(9) The Secretary of State may by regulations make provision for the handling of complaints relating to, or other instances of misconduct involving, the carrying out by any person designated under this section of the functions for the purposes of which any power or duty is conferred or imposed by his designation.

(10) Regulations under subsection (9) may, in particular, provide that any provision made by Part 2 of this Act with respect to complaints against persons serving with the police is to apply, with such modifications as may be prescribed by them, with respect to complaints against persons designated under this section.

(11) Before making regulations under this section, the Secretary of State shall consult with—

    (a) persons whom he considers to represent the interests of police authorities;

    (b) persons whom he considers to represent the interests of chief officers of police;

    (c) the Independent Police Complaints Commission; and

    (d) such other persons as he thinks fit.

(12) A designation under this section, unless it is previously withdrawn or ceases to have effect in accordance with subsection (13), shall remain in force for such period as may be specified in the designation; but it may be renewed at any time with effect from the time when it would otherwise expire.

(13) A designation under this section shall cease to have effect—

    (a) if the designated person ceases to be an employee of the contractor; or

    (b) if the contract between the police authority and the contractor is terminated or expires.

Community safety accreditation schemes

40.—(1) The chief officer of police of any police force may, if he considers that it is appropriate to do so for the purposes specified in subsection (3), establish and maintain a scheme ("a community safety accreditation scheme").

(2) A community safety accreditation scheme is a scheme for the exercise in the chief officer's police area by persons accredited by him under section 41 of the powers conferred by their accreditations under that section.

(3) Those purposes are—

    (a) contributing to community safety and security; and

    (b) in co-operation with the police force for the area, combatting crime and disorder, public nuisance and other forms of anti-social behaviour.

(4) Before establishing a community safety accreditation scheme for his police area, a chief officer of any police force (other than the Commissioner of Police of the Metropolis) must consult with—

    (a) the police authority maintaining that force, and

    (b) every local authority any part of whose area lies within the police area.

(5) Before establishing a community safety accreditation scheme for the metropolitan police district, the Commissioner of Police of the Metropolis must consult with—

    (a) the Metropolitan Police Authority;

    (b) the Mayor of London; and

    (c) every local authority any part of whose area lies within the metropolitan police district.

(6) In subsections (4)(b) and (5)(c) "local authority" means—

    (a) in relation to England, a district council, a London borough council, the Common Council of the City of London or the Council of the Isles of Scilly; and

    (b) in relation to Wales, a county council or a county borough council.

(7) Every police plan under section 8 of the 1996 Act which is issued after the commencement of this section, and every draft of such a plan which is submitted by a chief officer of police to a police authority after the commencement of this section, must set out—

    (a) whether a community safety accreditation scheme is maintained for the police area in question;

    (b) if not, whether there is any proposal to establish such a scheme for that area during the period to which the plan relates;

    (c) particulars of any such proposal or of any proposal to modify during that period any community safety accreditation scheme that is already maintained for that area;

    (d) the extent (if any) of any arrangements for provisions specified in Schedule 4 to be applied to designated persons employed by the police authority; and

    (e) the respects in which any community safety accreditation scheme that is maintained or proposed will be supplementing those arrangements during the period to which the plan relates.

(8) A community safety accreditation scheme must contain provision for the making of arrangements with employers who—

    (a) are carrying on business in the police area in question, or

    (b) are carrying on business in relation to the whole or any part of that area or in relation to places situated within it,

for those employers to supervise the carrying out by their employees of the community safety functions for the purposes of which powers are conferred on those employees by means of accreditations under section 41.

(9) It shall be the duty of a chief officer of police who establishes and maintains a community safety accreditation scheme to ensure that the employers of the persons on whom powers are conferred by the grant of accreditations under section 41 have established and maintain satisfactory arrangements for handling complaints relating to the carrying out by those persons of the functions for the purposes of which the powers are conferred.

Accreditation under community safety accreditation schemes

41.—(1) This section applies where a chief officer of police has, for the purposes of a community safety accreditation scheme, entered into any arrangements with any employer for or with respect to the carrying out of community safety functions by employees of that employer.

(2) The chief officer of police may, on the making of an application for the purpose by such person and in such manner as he may require, grant accreditation under this section to any employee of the employer.

(3) Schedule 5 (which sets out the powers that may be conferred on accredited persons) shall have effect.

(4) A chief officer of police shall not grant accreditation to a person under this section unless he is satisfied—

    (a) that that person's employer is a fit and proper person to supervise the carrying out of the functions for the purposes of which the accreditation is to be granted;

    (b)   that the person himself is a suitable person to exercise the powers that will be conferred on him by virtue of the accreditation;

    (c)   that that person is capable of effectively carrying out the functions for the purposes of which those powers are to be conferred on him; and

    (d)   that that person has received adequate training for the exercise of those powers.

(5) A chief officer of police may charge such fee as he considers appropriate for one or both of the following—

    (a)   considering an application for or for the renewal of an accreditation under this section;

    (b)   granting such an accreditation.

(6) A person authorised or required to do anything by virtue of an accreditation under this section—

    (a)   shall not be authorised or required by virtue of that accreditation to engage in any conduct otherwise than in the course of his employment by the employer with whom the chief officer of police has entered into the arrangements mentioned in subsection (1); and

    (b)   shall be so authorised or required subject to such other restrictions and conditions (if any) as may be specified in his accreditation.

(7) An accreditation under this section, unless it is previously withdrawn or ceases to have effect in accordance with subsection (8), shall remain in force for such period as may be specified in the accreditation; but it may be renewed at any time with effect from the time when it would otherwise expire.

(8) An accreditation under this section shall cease to have effect—

    (a)   if the accredited person ceases to be an employee of the person with whom the chief officer of police has entered into the arrangements mentioned in subsection (1); or

    (b)   if those arrangements are terminated or expire.

Supplementary provisions relating to designations and accreditations

42.—(1) A person who exercises or performs any power or duty in relation to any person in reliance on his designation under section 38 or 39 or his accreditation under section 41, or who purports to do so, shall produce that designation or accreditation to that person, if requested to do so.

(2) A power exercisable by any person in reliance on his designation by a chief officer of police under section 38 or 39 or his accreditation under section 41[4] shall be exercisable only by a person wearing such uniform as may be—

    (a)   determined or approved for the purposes of this Chapter by the chief officer of police who granted the designation or accreditation; and

    (b)   identified or described in the designation or accreditation;

and, in the case of an accredited person, such a power shall be exercisable only if he is also wearing such badge as may be specified for the purposes of this subsection by the Secretary of State, and is wearing it in such manner, or in such place, as may be so specified.

---

[4] The Serious Organised Crime and Police Bill 2004–05, cl.113(2)(a) adds here "; subject to subsection (2A),".

[*The Serious Organised Crime and Police Bill, cl.113(2)(b) inserts here new subss.(2A) and (2B):*

"(2A) A police officer of or above the rank of inspector may direct a particular investigating officer not to wear a uniform for the purposes of a particular operation; and if he so directs, subsection (2) shall not apply in relation to that investigating officer for the purposes of that operation.

(2B) In subsection (2A), 'investigating officer' means a person designated as an investigating officer under section 38 by the chief officer of police of the same force as the officer giving the direction."]

(3) A chief officer of police who has granted a designation or accreditation to any person under section 38, 39 or 41 may at any time, by notice to the designated or accredited person, modify or withdraw that designation or accreditation.

(4) A Director General may at any time, by notice to a person he has designated as an investigating officer under section 38, modify or withdraw that designation.[5]

(5) Where any person's designation under section 39 is modified or withdrawn, the chief officer giving notice of the modification or withdrawal shall send a copy of the notice to the contractor responsible for supervising that person in the carrying out of the functions for the purposes of which the designation was granted.

(6) Where any person's accreditation under section 41 is modified or withdrawn, the chief officer giving notice of the modification or withdrawal shall send a copy of the notice to the employer responsible for supervising that person in the carrying out of the functions for the purposes of which the accreditation was granted.

(7) For the purposes of determining liability for the unlawful conduct of employees of a police authority, conduct by such an employee in reliance or purported reliance on a designation under section 38 shall be taken to be conduct in the course of his employment by the police authority; and, in the case of a tort, that authority shall fall to be treated as a joint tortfeasor accordingly.

(8) For the purposes of determining liability for the unlawful conduct of employees of a Service Authority, conduct by such an employee in reliance or purported reliance on a designation under section 38 shall be taken to be conduct in the course of his employment; and, in the case of a tort, the Service Authority shall fall to be treated as a joint tortfeasor accordingly.[6]

(9) For the purposes of determining liability for the unlawful conduct of employees of a contractor (within the meaning of section 39), conduct by such an employee in reliance or purported reliance on a designation under that section shall be taken to be conduct in the course of his employment by that contractor; and, in the case of a tort, that contractor shall fall to be treated as a joint tortfeasor accordingly.

(10) For the purposes of determining liability for the unlawful conduct of employees of a person with whom a chief officer of police has entered into any arrangements for the purposes of a community safety accreditation scheme, conduct by such an employee in reliance or purported reliance on an accreditation under section 41 shall be taken to be conduct in the course of his employment by that employer; and, in the case of a tort, that employer shall fall to be treated as a joint tortfeasor accordingly.

---

[5] subs.(4) is repealed by the Serious Organised Crime and Police Bill 2004–05, Sch.4, para.183.
[6] subs.(8) is omitted by the Serious Organised Crime and Police Bill 2004–05, Sch.4, para.183.

Railway safety accreditation scheme

43.—(1) The Secretary of State may make regulations for the purpose of enabling the chief constable of the British Transport Police Force to establish and maintain a scheme ("a railway safety accreditation scheme").

(2) A railway safety accreditation scheme is a scheme for the exercise in, on or in the vicinity of policed premises in England and Wales, by persons accredited by the chief constable of the British Transport Police Force under the scheme, of the powers conferred on those persons by their accreditation under that scheme.

(3) The regulations may make provision—

   (a) as to the purposes for which a railway safety accreditation scheme may be established;

   (b) as to the procedure to be followed in the establishment of such a scheme; and

   (c) as to matters for which such a scheme must contain provision.

(4) The regulations may make provision as to the descriptions of persons who may be accredited under a railway safety accreditation scheme and as to the procedure and criteria to be applied for the grant of any accreditation under such a scheme.

(5) The regulations may make provision as to the powers which may be conferred on a person by an accreditation under such a scheme.

(6) Subject to subsection (7), no regulations made by virtue of subsection (5) shall permit a power to be conferred on a person accredited under a railway safety accreditation scheme which could not be conferred on an accredited person under a community safety accreditation scheme.

(7) The regulations may provide that the powers which may be conferred on a person by an accreditation under a railway safety accreditation scheme include the powers of a constable in uniform and of an authorised constable to give a penalty notice under Chapter 1 of Part 1 of the Criminal Justice and Police Act 2001 (fixed penalty notices) in respect of the following offences—

   (a) an offence under section 55 of the British Transport Commission Act 1949 (c.xxix) (trespassing on a railway);

   (b) an offence under section 56 of that Act (throwing stones etc. at trains or other things on railways).

(8) In relation to a person accredited under a railway safety accreditation scheme, the regulations may apply, with such modifications as may be prescribed by them, any provision of this Chapter which applies in relation to an accredited person.

(9) Before making regulations under this section the Secretary of State shall consult with—

   (a) persons whom he considers to represent the interests of chief officers of police;

   (b) the chief constable of the British Transport Police Force;

   (c) persons whom he considers to represent the interests of police authorities;

   (d) the British Transport Police Committee;

   (e) persons whom he considers to represent the interests of local authorities;

    (f)   the Mayor of London; and

    (g)   such other persons as he thinks fit.

  (10) In this section—

"local authorities" means district councils, London borough councils, county councils in Wales, county borough councils and the Common Council of the City of London; and

"policed premises" has the meaning given by section 53(3) of the British Transport Commission Act 1949.

Removal of restriction on powers conferred on traffic wardens

44.—(1) Section 96 of the Road Traffic Regulation Act 1984 (c.27) (additional powers of traffic wardens) shall be amended as follows.

(2) In subsection (2)(c) (powers under the Road Traffic Act 1988 (c.52) which may be conferred on traffic wardens), after sub-paragraph (i) there shall be inserted—

"(ia) section 67(3) (which relates to the power of a constable in uniform to stop vehicles for testing);".

(3) In subsection (3) (traffic wardens not to be given the powers of a constable under sections 163, 164(1), (2) and (6) and 165 of the Road Traffic Act 1988 except for the purposes of exercising them in the circumstances specified in that subsection)—

    (a)   in the words before paragraph (a), the words "163" (which refer to the power to stop a vehicle) shall be omitted; and

    (b)   paragraph (c) and the word "or" immediately preceding it shall cease to have effect.

Code of practice relating to chief officers' powers under Chapter 1

45.—(1) The Secretary of State shall issue a code of practice about the exercise and performance by chief officers of police and by Directors General[7] of their powers and duties under this Chapter.

(2) The Secretary of State may from time to time revise the whole or any part of a code of practice issued under this section.

(3) Before issuing or revising a code of practice under this section, the Secretary of State shall consult with—

    (a)   the Service Authority for the National Criminal Intelligence Service[8];

    (b)   the Service Authority for the National Crime Squad;

    (c)   persons whom he considers to represent the interests of police authorities;

    (d)   the Director General of the National Criminal Intelligence Service;

    (e)   the Director General of the National Crime Squad;

    (f)   persons whom he considers to represent the interests of chief officers of police;

[7] The words "and by Directors General" are omitted by the Serious Organised Crime and Police Bill 2004–05, Sch.4, para.184(2).

[8] sub-paras (a), (b), (d) and (e) of s.45(3) are omitted by the Serious Organised Crime and Police Bill 2004–05, Sch.4, para.184(3).

    (g)   persons whom he considers to represent the interests of local authorities;

    (h)   the Mayor of London; and

    (i)   such other persons as he thinks fit.

(4) The Secretary of State shall lay any code of practice issued by him under this section, and any revisions of any such code, before Parliament.

(5) In discharging any function to which a code of practice under this section relates, a chief officer of police or a Director General[9] shall have regard to the code.

(6) For the purposes of subsection (3)(g), "local authorities" means district councils, London borough councils, county councils in Wales, county borough councils, the Common Council of the City of London and the Council of the Isles of Scilly.

Offences against designated and accredited persons etc.

46.—(1) Any person who assaults—

    (a)   a designated person in the execution of his duty,

    (b)   an accredited person in the execution of his duty, or

    (c)   a person assisting a designated or accredited person in the execution of his duty,

is guilty of an offence and shall be liable, on summary conviction, to imprisonment for a term not exceeding six months or to a fine not exceeding level 5 on the standard scale, or to both.

(2) Any person who resists or wilfully obstructs—

    (a)   a designated person in the execution of his duty,

    (b)   an accredited person in the execution of his duty, or

    (c)   a person assisting a designated or accredited person in the execution of his duty,

is guilty of an offence and shall be liable, on summary conviction, to imprisonment for a term not exceeding one month or to a fine not exceeding level 3 on the standard scale, or to both.

(3) Any person who, with intent to deceive—

    (a)   impersonates a designated person or an accredited person,

    (b)   makes any statement or does any act calculated falsely to suggest that he is a designated person or that he is an accredited person, or

    (c)   makes any statement or does any act calculated falsely to suggest that he has powers as a designated or accredited person that exceed the powers he actually has,

is guilty of an offence and shall be liable, on summary conviction, to imprisonment for a term not exceeding six months or to a fine not exceeding level 5 on the standard scale, or to both.

(4) In this section references to the execution by a designated person or accredited person of his duty are references to his exercising any power or performing any duty which is his by virtue of his designation or accreditation.

[9] The words "or a Director General" are omitted by the Serious Organised Crime and Police Bill 2004–05, Sch.4, para.184(4).

Interpretation of Chapter 1

47.—(1) In this Chapter—
"accredited person" means a person in relation to whom an accreditation under section 41 is for the time being in force;
"community safety functions" means any functions the carrying out of which would be facilitated by the ability to exercise one or more of the powers mentioned in Schedule 5;
"conduct" includes omissions and statements;
"designated person" means a person in relation to whom a designation under section 38 or 39 is for the time being in force;
"Director General"[10] means—
(a) the Director General of the National Criminal Intelligence Service; or
(b) the Director General of the National Crime Squad;
"Service Authority"[11] means—
(a) in relation to employment with the National Criminal Intelligence Service or to its Director General, the Service Authority for the National Criminal Intelligence Service; and
(b) in relation to employment with the National Crime Squad or to its Director General, the Service Authority for the National Crime Squad.

(2) In this Chapter—
(a) references to carrying on business include references to carrying out functions under any enactment; and
(b) references to the employees of a person carrying on business include references to persons holding office under a person, and references to employers shall be construed accordingly.

Section 38 **SCHEDULE 4**

Powers Exercisable By Police Civilians

Part 1

Community Support Officers

Powers to issue fixed penalty notices

1.—(1) Where a designation applies this paragraph to any person, that person shall have the powers specified in sub-paragraph (2) in relation to any individual who he has reason to believe has committed a relevant fixed penalty offence at a place within the relevant police area.

---

[10] The definition of "Director General" is omitted by the Serious Organised Crime and Police Bill 2004–05, Sch.4, para.185.
[11] The definition of "Service Authority" is omitted by the Serious Organised Crime and Police Bill 2004–05, Sch.4, para.185.

(2) Those powers are the following powers so far as exercisable in respect of a relevant fixed penalty offence—

    (a) the powers of a constable in uniform and of an authorised constable to give a penalty notice under Chapter 1 of Part 1 of the Criminal Justice and Police Act 2001 (c.16) (fixed penalty notices in respect of offences of disorder[12]);

    [(aa)the power of a constable to give a penalty notice under section 444A of the Education Act 1996 (penalty notice in respect of failure to secure regular attendance at school of registered pupil)][13]

    (b) the power of a constable in uniform to give a person a fixed penalty notice under section 54 of the Road Traffic Offenders Act 1988 (c.53) (fixed penalty notices) in respect of an offence under section 72 of the Highway Act 1835 (c.50) (riding on a footway) committed by cycling;

    (c) the power of an authorised officer of a local authority to give a notice under section 4 of the Dogs (Fouling of Land) Act 1996 (c.20) (fixed penalty notices in respect of dog fouling); and

    (d) the power of an authorised officer of a litter authority to give a notice under section 88 of the Environmental Protection Act 1990 (c.43) (fixed penalty notices in respect of litter).

[*The Serious Organised Crime and Police Bill 2004–05, cl.113(3) (a) inserts here new sub-para.(2A) stating that the reference to the powers mentioned in sub-para.(2)(a) does not include those powers under s.1 of the Theft Act 1968 or s.87 of the Environmental Protection Act 1990.*]

(3) In this paragraph "relevant fixed penalty offence", in relation to a designated person, means an offence which—

    (a) is an offence by reference to which a notice may be given to a person in exercise of any of the powers mentioned in sub-paragraph 1(2)(a) to (d); and

    (b) is specified or described in that person's designation as an offence he has been designated to enforce under this paragraph.

[(4) In its application to an offence which is an offence by reference to which a notice may be given to a person in exercise of the power mentioned in sub-paragraph (2)(aa), sub-paragraph (1) shall have effect as if for the words from "who he has reason to believe" to the end there were substituted "in the relevant police area who he has reason to believe has committed a relevant fixed penalty offence".][14]

---

[12] This power does not include powers under s.1 of the Theft Act 1968 or s.87 of the Environmental Protection Act 1990—see the Criminal Justice and Police Act 2001 (Amendment) and the Police Reform Act 2002 (Modification) Order 2004, SI 2004/2540, Art.4.
[13] sub-para.(aa) inserted by the Anti-social Behaviour Act 2003, s.23(3).
[14] sub-para.(4) inserted by the Anti-social Behaviour Act 2003, s.23(4).

Power to detain etc.

2.—(1) This paragraph applies if a designation applies it to any person.[15]

(2) Where that person has reason to believe that another person has committed a relevant offence in the relevant police area,[16] he may require that other person to give him his name and address.

(3) Where, in a case in which a requirement under sub-paragraph (2) has been imposed on another person—

> (a) that other person fails to comply with the requirement, or
> (b) the person who imposed the requirement has reasonable grounds for suspecting that the other person has given him a name or address that is false or inaccurate,

the person who imposed the requirement may require the other person to wait with him, for a period not exceeding thirty minutes, for the arrival of a constable.

[*The Serious Organised Crime and Police Bill 2004–05, Sch.8, para.2(4) inserts here: "This sub-paragraph does not apply if the requirement was imposed in connection with a relevant licensing offence mentioned in paragraph (a), (c) or (f) of sub-paragraph (6A) believed to have been committed on licensed premises (within the meaning of the Licensing Act 2003),"*]

[*The Serious Organised Crime and Police Bill 2004–05, Sch.8, para.2(5) inserts new sub-para.(3A) here:*

"(3A) Where a person to whom this paragraph applies ('the CSO') has reason to believe that another person is committing an offence under section 3 or 4 of the Vagrancy Act 1824, and requires him to stop doing whatever gives rise to that belief, the CSO may, if the other person fails to stop as required, require him to wait with the CSO, for a period not exceeding thirty minutes, for the arrival of a constable."]

(4) A person who has been required under sub-paragraph (3)[17] to wait with a person to whom this Part of this Schedule applies may, if requested to do so, elect that (instead of waiting) he will accompany the person imposing the requirement to a police station in the relevant police area.

[*The Serious Organised Crime and Police Bill 2004–05, Sch.9, para.2 inserts here new sub-paras.(4A) and (4B):*

"(4A) If a person has imposed a requirement under sub-paragraph (3) or (3A) on another person ('P'), and P does not make an election under sub-paragraph (4), the person imposing the requirement shall, if a constable arrives within the thirty-minute period, be under a duty to remain with the constable and P until he has transferred control of P to the constable.

(4B) If, following an election under sub-paragraph (4), the person imposing the requirement under sub-paragraph (3) or (3A) ('the CSO') takes the person upon whom it is imposed ('P') to a police station, the CSO—

---

[15] The Serious Organised Crime and Police Bill 2004–05, Sch.8, para.2(2) adds at the end of sub-para.(1): ", but such a designation may specify that, in relation to that person, the application of sub-paragraph (2) of this paragraph is confined to one or more only (and not to all) of the relevant offences set out in sub-paragraph (6) and the relevant licensing offences set out in sub-paragraph (6A)."

[16] The Serious Organised Crime and Police Bill 2004–05, Sch.8, para.2(3) inserts here "or a relevant licensing offence (whether or not in the relevant police area),".

[17] The Serious Organised Crime and Police Bill 2004–05, Sch.8, para.2(6) inserts "or (3A)" here.

(a) shall be under a duty to remain at the police station until he has transferred control of P to the custody officer there;

(b) until he has so transferred control of P, shall be treated for all purposes as having P in his lawful custody; and

(c) for so long as he is at the police station, or in its immediate vicinity, in compliance with, or having complied with, his duty under paragraph (a), shall be under a duty to prevent P's escape and to assist in keeping P under control."]

(5) A person who—

(a) fails to comply with a requirement under sub-paragraph (2),

(b) makes off while subject to a requirement under sub-paragraph (3),[18] or

(c) makes off while accompanying a person to a police station in accordance with an election under sub-paragraph (4),

is guilty of an offence and shall be liable, on summary conviction, to a fine not exceeding level 3 on the standard scale.

(6) In this paragraph "relevant offence", in relation to a person to whom this paragraph applies, means any offence which is—

(a) a relevant fixed penalty offence for the purposes of the application of paragraph 1 to that person;

[(aa) an offence under section 32(2) of the Anti-social Behaviour Act 2003; or][19]

[*The Serious Organised Crime and Police Bill 2004–05, Sch.13, Pt 2, para.12(2) inserts here:*

"*(ab) an offence committed in a specified park which by virtue of section 2 of the Parks Regulation (Amendment)Act 1926 is an offence against the Parks Regulation Act 1872; or*"]

[*Sch.8, para.2(8) of the same Bill inserts here:*

"*(ac) an offence under section 3 or 4 of the Vagrancy Act 1824; or*"]

(b) an offence the commission of which appears to that person to have caused—

(i) injury, alarm or distress to any other person; or

(ii) the loss of, or any damage to, any other person's property;

but a designation applying this paragraph to any person may provide that an offence is not to be treated as a relevant offence by virtue of paragraph (b) unless it satisfies such other conditions as may be specified in the designation.

[*The Serious Organised Crime and Police Bill 2004–05, Sch.8, para.2(9) inserts new sub-para.(6A) here stating that "In this paragraph 'relevant licensing offence' means an offence under the Licensing Act 2003 s.141 (otherwise than by virtue of subs.(2)(c) or (3)); s.142; s.146(1); s.149(1)(a), (3)(a) or (4)(a); s.150(1); s.150(2)(otherwise than by virtue of subs.(3)(b)); s.152(1) (excluding para.(b))."*]

[(7) In its application to an offence which is an offence by reference to which a notice may be given to a person in exercise of the power mentioned in paragraph 1(2)(aa), sub-paragraph (2) of this paragraph shall have effect as if for the

---

[18] The Serious Organised Crime and Police Bill 2004–05, Sch.8, para.2(7) inserts "or (3A)" here.

[19] sub-para.(aa) inserted by the Anti-social Behaviour Act 2003, s.33(2).

words "has committed a relevant offence in the relevant police area" there were substituted "in the relevant police area has committed a relevant offence".][20]

[*The Serious Organised Crime and Police Bill 2004–05, Sch.8, para.3 inserts new para.2A:*

"*Powers to search individuals and to seize and retain items*

2A.—*(1) Where a designation applies this paragraph to any person, that person shall (subject to sub-paragraph (3)) have the powers mentioned in sub-paragraph (2) in relation to a person upon whom he has imposed a requirement to wait under paragraph 2(3) or (3A) (whether or not that person makes an election under paragraph 2(4)).*

(2) Those powers are the same powers as a constable has under section 32 of the 1984 Act in relation to a person arrested at a place other than a police station—

    (a) *to search the arrested person if the constable has reasonable grounds for believing that the arrested person may present a danger to himself or others; and to seize and retain anything he finds on exercising that power, if the constable has reasonable grounds for believing that the person being searched might use it to cause physical injury to himself or to any other person;*

    (b) *to search the arrested person for anything which he might use to assist him to escape from lawful custody; and to seize and retain anything he finds on exercising that power (other than an item subject to legal privilege) if the constable has reasonable grounds for believing that the person being searched might use it to assist him to escape from lawful custody.*

(3) If in exercise of the power conferred by sub-paragraph (1) the person to whom this paragraph applies seizes and retains anything by virtue of sub-paragraph (2), he must—

    (a) *tell the person from whom it was seized where inquiries about its recovery may be made; and*

    (b) *comply with a constable's instructions about what to do with it.*"]

Power to require name and address of person acting in an anti-social manner

3.—(1) Where a designation applies this paragraph to any person, that person shall, in the relevant police area, have the powers of a constable in uniform under section 50 to require a person whom he has reason to believe to have been acting, or to be acting, in an anti-social manner (within the meaning of section 1 of the Crime and Disorder Act 1998 (c.37) (anti-social behaviour orders)) to give his name and address.

(2) Sub-paragraphs (3) to (5) of paragraph 2 apply in the case of a requirement imposed by virtue of sub-paragraph (1) as they apply in the case of a requirement under sub-paragraph (2) of that paragraph.

[*The Serious Organised Crime and Police Bill 2004–05, Sch.8, para.4 inserts new para.3A:*

---

[20] sub-para.(7) inserted by the Anti-social Behaviour Act 2003, s.23(5).

"Power to require name and address: road traffic offences

3A.—*(1) Where a designation applies this paragraph to any person, that person shall, in the relevant police area, have the powers of a constable—*

(a) *under subsection (1) of section 165 of the Road Traffic Act 1988 to require a person mentioned in paragraph (c) of that subsection whom he has reasonable cause to believe has committed, in the relevant police area, an offence under subsection (1) or (2) of section 35 of that Act (including that section as extended by paragraphs 11B(4) and 12(2) of this Schedule) to give his name and address; and*

(b) *under section 169 of that Act to require a person committing an offence under section 37 of that Act (including that section as extended by paragraphs 11B(4) and 12(2) of this Schedule) to give his name and address.*

(2) Sub-paragraphs (3) to (5) of paragraph 2 apply in the case of a requirement imposed by virtue of sub-paragraph (1) as they apply in the case of a requirement under sub-paragraph (2) of that paragraph.

(3) The reference in section 169 of the Road Traffic Act 1988 to section 37 of that Act is to be taken to include a reference to that section as extended by paragraphs 11B(4) and 12(2) of this Schedule."]

Power to use reasonable force to detain person

4.—(1) This paragraph applies where a designation—

(a) applies this paragraph to a person to whom any or all of paragraphs 1 to 3 are also applied; and

(b) sets out the matters in respect of which that person has the power conferred by this paragraph.

(2) The matters that may be set out in a designation as the matters in respect of which a person has the power conferred by this paragraph shall be confined to—

(a) offences that are relevant penalty notice offences for the purposes of the application of paragraph 1 to the designated person;

(b) offences that are relevant offences for the purposes of the application of paragraph 2 to the designated person; and

(c) behaviour that constitutes acting in an anti-social manner (within the meaning of section 1 of the Crime and Disorder Act 1998 (c.37) (anti-social behaviour orders)).

(3) In any case in which a person to whom this paragraph applies has imposed a requirement on any other person under paragraph 2(2) or 3(1) in respect of anything appearing to him to be a matter set out in the designation, he may use reasonable force to prevent that other person from making off[21] while he is either—

(a) subject to a requirement imposed in that case by the designated person under sub-paragraph (3) of paragraph 2; or

---

[21] The Serious Organised Crime and Police Bill 2004–05, Sch.9, para.3 adds "and to keep him under control" here.

    (b)   accompanying the designated person to a police station in accordance with an election made in that case under sub-paragraph (4) of that paragraph.

[*The Serious Organised Crime and Police Bill 2004–05, Sch.9, para.4 inserts new paras 4ZA and 4ZB:*

"*4ZA. Where a designation applies this paragraph to any person, that person may, if he has imposed a requirement on any person under sub-paragraph (3A) of paragraph 2, use reasonable force to prevent that other person from making off and to keep him under control while he is either—*

    (a)   *subject to that requirement; or*

    (b)   *accompanying the designated person to a police station in accordance with an election made under sub-paragraph (4) of paragraph 2.*

4ZB. Where a designation applies this paragraph to any person, that person, if he is complying with any duty under sub-paragraph (4A) or (4B) of paragraph 2, may use reasonable force to prevent P (as identified in those sub-paragraphs) from making off (or escaping) and to keep him under control."]

[*Power to disperse groups and remove young persons to their place of residence*

4A. Where a designation applies this paragraph to any person, that person shall, within the relevant police area, have the powers which, by virtue of an authorisation under section 30 of the Anti-social Behaviour Act 2003, are conferred on a constable in uniform by section 30(3) to (6) of that Act (power to disperse groups and remove persons under 16 to their place of residence).

4B.—(1) Where a designation applies this paragraph to any person, that person shall, within the relevant police area, have the power of a constable under section 15(3) of the Crime and Disorder Act 1998 (power to remove child to their place of residence).

(2) Section 15(1) of that Act shall have effect in relation to the exercise of that power by that person as if the reference to a constable in that section were a reference to that person.

(3) Where that person exercises that power, the duty in section 15(2) of that Act (duty to inform local authority of contravention of curfew notice) is to apply to him as it applies to a constable.][22]

Alcohol consumption in designated public places

5. Where a designation applies this paragraph to any person, that person shall, within the relevant police area, have the powers of a constable under section 12 of the Criminal Justice and Police Act 2001 (c.16) (alcohol consumption in public places)—

    (a)   to impose a requirement under subsection (2) of that section; and

    (b)   to dispose under subsection (3) of that section of anything surrendered to him;

---

[22] paras 4A and 4B inserted by the Anti-social Behaviour Act 2003, s.33(3).

and that section shall have effect in relation to the exercise of those powers by that person as if the references to a constable in subsections (1) and (5) were references to that person.

Confiscation of alcohol

6. Where a designation applies this paragraph to any person, that person shall, within the relevant police area, have the powers of a constable under section 1 of the Confiscation of Alcohol (Young Persons) Act 1997 (c.33) (confiscation of intoxicating liquor)—
>   (a)   to impose a requirement under subsection (1) of that section; and
>   (b)   to dispose under subsection (2) of that section of anything surrendered to him;

and that section shall have effect in relation to the exercise of those powers by that person as if the references to a constable in subsections (1) and (4) (but not the reference in subsection (5) (arrest)) were references to that person.

Confiscation of tobacco etc.

7. Where a designation applies this paragraph to any person, that person shall, within the relevant police area, have—
>   (a)   the power to seize anything that a constable in uniform has a duty to seize under subsection (3) of section 7 of the Children and Young Persons Act 1933 (c.12) (seizure of tobacco etc. from young persons); and
>   (b)   the power to dispose of anything that a constable may dispose of under that subsection;

and the power to dispose of anything shall be a power to dispose of it in such manner as the police authority may direct.

[*The Serious Organised Crime and Police Bill 2004–05, Sch.13, Pt 2, para.12(3) inserts new para.7A:*

"Park Trading offences

7A.—(1) *This paragraph applies if—*
>   (a)   *a designation applies it to any person ('the CSO'), and*
>   (b)   *the CSO has under paragraph 2(3) required another person('P') to wait with him for the arrival of a constable.*

(2) *If the CSO reasonably suspects that P has committed a park trading offence, the CSO may take possession of anything of a non-perishable nature which—*
>   (a)   *P has in his possession or under his control, and*
>   (b)   *the CSO reasonably believes to have been used in the commission of the offence.*

(3) *The CSO may retain possession of the thing in question for a period not exceeding 30 minutes unless P makes an election under paragraph 2(4), in which case the CSO may retain possession of the thing in question until he is able to transfer control of it to a constable.*

(4) In this paragraph 'park trading offence' means an offence committed in a specified park which is a park trading offence for the purposes of the Royal Parks (Trading) Act 2000."]

Entry to save life or limb or prevent serious damage to property

8. Where a designation applies this paragraph to any person, that person shall have the powers of a constable under section 17 of the 1984 Act to enter and search any premises in the relevant police area for the purpose of saving life or limb or preventing serious damage to property.

[*The Serious Organised Crime and Police Bill 2004–05, Sch.8, para.5 inserts new para.8A:*

"Entry to investigate licensing offences

8A.—(1) Where a designation applies this paragraph to any person, that person shall have the powers of a constable under section 180 of the Licensing Act 2003 to enter and search premises other than clubs in the relevant police area, but only in respect of a relevant licensing offence (as defined for the purposes of paragraph 2 above).

(2) Except as mentioned in sub-paragraph (3), a person to whom this paragraph applies shall not, in exercise of the power conferred by sub-paragraph (1), enter any premises except in the company, and under the supervision, of a constable.

(3) The prohibition in sub-paragraph (2) does not apply in relation to premises in respect of which the person to whom this paragraph applies reasonably believes that a premises licence under Part 3 of the Licensing Act 2003 authorises the sale of alcohol for consumption off the premises."]

Seizure of vehicles used to cause alarm etc.

9. (1) Where a designation applies this paragraph to any person—
    (a) that person shall, within the relevant police area, have all the powers of a constable in uniform under section 59 of this Act which are set out in subsection (3) of that section; and
    (b) references in that section to a constable, in relation to the exercise of any of those powers by that person, are references to that person.

(2) A person to whom this paragraph applies shall not enter any premises in exercise of the power conferred by section 59(3)(c) except in the company, and under the supervision, of a constable.

Abandoned vehicles

10. Where a designation applies this paragraph to any person, that person shall have any such powers in the relevant police area as are conferred on persons designated under that section by regulations under section 99 of the Road Traffic Regulation Act 1984 (c.27) (removal of abandoned vehicles).

Power to stop vehicle for testing

11. Where a designation applies this paragraph to any person, that person shall, within the relevant police area, have the power of a constable in uniform to stop

a vehicle under subsection (3) of section 67 of the Road Traffic Act 1988 (c.52) for the purposes of a test under subsection (1) of that section.

[*Power to stop bicycles*

11A.—(1) Subject to sub-paragraph (2), where a designation applies this paragraph to any person, that person shall, within the relevant police area, have the power of a constable in uniform under section 163(2) of the Road Traffic Act 1988 to stop a cycle.

(2) The power mentioned in sub-paragraph (1) may only be exercised by that person in relation to a person who he has reason to believe has committed an offence under section 72 of the Highway Act 1835 (riding on a footway) by cycling.][23]

[*The Serious Organised Crime and Police Bill 2004–05, Sch.8, para.6 inserts new para.11B:*

"*Power to control traffic for purposes other than escorting a load of exceptional dimensions*

11B.—(1) Where a designation applies this paragraph to any person, that person shall have, in the relevant police area—
   (a) *the power of a constable engaged in the regulation of traffic in a road to direct a person driving or propelling a vehicle to stop the vehicle or to make it proceed in, or keep to, a particular line of traffic;*
   (b) *the power of a constable in uniform engaged in the regulation of vehicular traffic in a road to direct a person on foot to stop proceeding along or across the carriageway.*

(2) The purposes for which those powers may be exercised do not include the purpose mentioned in paragraph 12(1).

(3) Where a designation applies this paragraph to any person, that person shall also have, in the relevant police area, the power of a constable, for the purposes of a traffic survey, to direct a person driving or propelling a vehicle to stop the vehicle, to make it proceed in, or keep to, a particular line of traffic, or to proceed to a particular point on or near the road.

(4) Sections 35 and 37 of the Road Traffic Act 1988 (offences of failing to comply with directions of constable engaged in regulation of traffic in a road) shall have effect in relation to the exercise of the powers mentioned in sub-paragraphs (1) and (3), for the purposes for which they may be exercised and by a person whose designation applies this paragraph to him, as if the references to a constable were references to him.

(5) A designation may not apply this paragraph to any person unless a designation also applies paragraph 3A to him."]

Power to control traffic for purposes of escorting a load of exceptional dimensions

12.—(1) Where a designation applies this paragraph to any person, that person shall have, for the purpose of escorting a vehicle or trailer carrying a load of

---

[23] para.11A inserted by the Anti-social Behaviour Act 2003, s.89(3).

exceptional dimensions either to or from the relevant police area, the power of a constable engaged in the regulation of traffic in a road—

    (a)   to direct a vehicle to stop;

    (b)   to make a vehicle proceed in, or keep to, a particular line of traffic; and

    (c)   to direct pedestrians to stop.

(2) Sections 35 and 37 of the Road Traffic Act 1988 (offences of failing to comply with directions of constable engaged in regulation of traffic in a road) shall have effect in relation to the exercise of those powers for the purpose mentioned in sub-paragraph (1) by a person whose designation applies this paragraph to him as if the references to a constable engaged in regulation of traffic in a road were references to that person.

(3) The powers conferred by virtue of this paragraph may be exercised in any police area in England and Wales.

(4) In this paragraph "vehicle or trailer carrying a load of exceptional dimensions" means a vehicle or trailer the use of which is authorised by an order made by the Secretary of State under section 44(1)(d) of the Road Traffic Act 1988.

Carrying out of road checks

13. Where a designation applies this paragraph to any person, that person shall have the following powers in the relevant police area—

    (a)   the power to carry out any road check the carrying out of which by a police officer is authorised under section 4 of the 1984 Act (road checks); and

    (b)   for the purpose of exercising that power, the power conferred by section 163 of the Road Traffic Act 1988 (c.52) (power of police to stop vehicles) on a constable in uniform to stop a vehicle.

[*The Serious Organised Crime and Police Bill 2004–05, Sch.8, para.7 inserts new para.13A:*

"Power to place traffic signs

13A.—(1) Where a designation applies this paragraph to any person, that person shall have, in the relevant police area, the powers of a constable under section 67 of the Road Traffic Regulation Act 1984 to place and maintain traffic signs.

(2) Section 36 of the Road Traffic Act 1988 (drivers to comply with traffic directions) shall apply to signs placed in the exercise of the powers conferred by virtue of sub-paragraph (1)."]

Cordoned areas

14. Where a designation applies this paragraph to any person, that person shall, in relation to any cordoned area in the relevant police area, have all the powers of a constable in uniform under section 36 of the Terrorism Act 2000 (c.11) (enforcement of cordoned area) to give orders, make arrangements or impose prohibitions or restrictions.

Power to stop and search vehicles etc. in authorised areas

15.—(1) Where a designation applies this paragraph to any person—

    (a) that person shall, in any authorised area within the relevant police area, have all the powers of a constable in uniform by virtue of section 44(1)(a) and (d) and (2)(b) and 45(2) of the Terrorism Act 2000 (powers of stop and search)—

        (i) to stop and search vehicles;

       (ii) to search anything in or on a vehicle or anything carried by the driver of a vehicle or any passenger in a vehicle;

      (iii) to search anything carried by a pedestrian; and

      (iv) to seize and retain any article discovered in the course of a search carried out by him or by a constable by virtue of any provision of section 44(1) or (2) of that Act;

  and

    (b) the references to a constable in subsections (1) and (4) of section 45 of that Act (which relate to the exercise of those powers) shall have effect in relation to the exercise of any of those powers by that person as references to that person.

(2) A person shall not exercise any power of stop, search or seizure by virtue of this paragraph except in the company, and under the supervision, of a constable.

[*The Serious Organised Crime and Police Bill 2004–05, Sch.8, para.8 inserts new para.15ZA:*

"Photographing of persons arrested, detained or given fixed penalty notices

15ZA. Where a designation applies this paragraph to any person, that person shall, within the relevant police area, have the power of a constable under section 64A(1A) of the Police and Criminal Evidence Act 1984 (photographing of suspects etc.) to take a photograph of a person elsewhere than at a police station."]

[*Power to modify paragraph 1(2)(a)*

15A.—(1) The Secretary of State may by order provide that paragraph 1(2)(a) is to have effect as if the reference to the powers there mentioned did not include those powers so far as they relate to an offence under any provision for the time being mentioned in the first column of the Table in section 1(1) of the Criminal Justice and Police Act 2001 which is specified in the order.

[*The Serious Organised Crime and Police Bill 2004–05, cl.113(3)(b) substitutes a new sub-para.(1) providing that the Secretary of State may amend para.1(2A)—Note not 1(2)(a)— by adding to or removing a provision.*]

(2) The Secretary of State shall not make an order containing (with or without any other provision) any provision authorised by this paragraph unless a draft of that order has been laid before Parliament and approved by a resolution of each House.][24]

---

[24] para.15A inserted by the Anti-social Behaviour Act 2003, s.89(4).

PART 2

INVESTIGATING OFFICERS

Search warrants

16. Where a designation applies this paragraph to any person—

(a)   he may apply as if he were a constable for a warrant under section 8 of the 1984 Act (warrants for entry and search) in respect of any premises in the relevant police area[25];

(b)   the persons to whom a warrant to enter and search any such premises may be issued under that section shall include that person;

(c)   that person shall have the power of a constable under section 8(2) of that Act in any premises in the relevant police area to seize and retain things for which a search has been authorised under subsection (1) of that section;

(d)   section 15 of that Act (safeguards) shall have effect in relation to the issue of such a warrant to that person as it has effect in relation to the issue of a warrant under section 8 of that Act to a constable;

(e)   section 16 of that Act (execution of warrants) shall have effect in relation to any warrant to enter and search premises that is issued (whether to that person or to any other person) in respect of premises in the relevant police area[26] as if references in that section to a constable included references to that person;

(f)   section 19(6) of that Act (protection for legally privileged material from seizure) shall have effect in relation to the seizure of anything by that person by virtue of sub-paragraph (c) as it has effect in relation to the seizure of anything by a constable;

(g)   section 20 of that Act (extension of powers of seizure to computerised information) shall have effect in relation to the power of seizure conferred on that person by virtue of sub-paragraph (c) as it applies in relation to the power of seizure conferred on a constable by section 8(2) of that Act;

(h)   section 21(1) and (2) of that Act (provision of record of seizure) shall have effect in relation to the seizure of anything by that person in exercise of the power conferred on him by virtue of sub-paragraph (c) as if the references to a constable and to an officer included references to that person; and

(i)   sections 21(3) to (8) and 22 of that Act (access, copying and retention) shall have effect in relation to anything seized by that person in exercise of that power, or taken away by him following the imposition of a requirement by virtue of sub-paragraph (g)—

[25] The Serious Organised Crime and Police Bill 2004–05, Sch.8, para.9(a) substitutes "whether in the relevant police area or not" for "in the relevant police area".

[26] The Serious Organised Crime and Police Bill 2004–05, Sch.8, para.9(b) substitutes ",but in respect of premises in the relevant area only" for "in respect of premises in the relevant police area".

     (i)   as they have effect in relation to anything seized in exercise of the power conferred on a constable by section 8(2) of that Act or taken away by a constable following the imposition of a requirement by virtue of section 20 of that Act; and

    (ii) as if the references to a constable in subsections (3), (4) and (5) of section 21 included references to a person to whom this paragraph applies.

[*The Serious Organised Crime and Police Bill 2004–05, Sch.8, para.10 inserts new paras 16A and 16B:*

"16A. Where a designation applies this paragraph to any person—

    (a) *the persons to whom a warrant may be addressed under section 26 of the Theft Act 1968 (search for stolen goods) shall, in relation to persons or premises in the relevant police area, include that person; and*

    (b) *in relation to such a warrant addressed to him, that person shall have the powers under subsection (3) of that section.*

16B. Where a designation applies this paragraph to any person, subsection (3), and (to the extent that it applies subsection (3))subsection (3A), of section 23 of the Misuse of Drugs Act 1971 (powers to search and obtain evidence) shall have effect as if, in relation to premises in the relevant police area, the reference to a constable included a reference to that person."]

Access to excluded and special procedure material

17. Where a designation applies this paragraph to any person—

    (a) he shall have the powers of a constable under section 9(1) of the 1984 Act (special provisions for access) to obtain access, in accordance with Schedule 1 to that Act and the following provisions of this paragraph, to excluded material and special procedure material;

    (b) that Schedule shall have effect for the purpose of conferring those powers on that person as if—

      (i)   the references in paragraphs 1, 4, 5, 12 and 13 of that Schedule to a constable were references to that person; and

      (ii) the references in paragraphs 12 and 14 of that Schedule to premises were references to premises in the relevant police area[27].

   [(bb) section 15 of that Act (safeguards) shall have effect in relation to the issue of any warrant under paragraph 12 of that Schedule to that person as it has effect in relation to the issue of a warrant under that paragraph to a constable;

   (bc) section 16 of that Act (execution of warrants) shall have effect in relation to any warrant to enter and search premises that is issued under paragraph 12 of that Schedule (whether to that person or to any other person) in respect of premises in the relevant police area[28]

---

[27] The Serious Organised Crime and Police Bill 2004–05, Sch.8, para.11(a) adds at the end of (b) (ii): "(in the case of a specific premises warrant) or any premises, whether in the relevant police area or not (in the case of an all-premises warrant);"

[28] The Serious Organised Crime and Police Bill 2004–05, Sch.8, para.11(b) adds the word "but" before "in respect of" and "only" after "police area".

as if references in that section to a constable included references to that person;]²⁹

(c) section 19(6) of that Act (protection for legally privileged material from seizure) shall have effect in relation to the seizure of anything by that person in exercise of the power conferred on him by paragraph 13 of Schedule 1 to that Act as it has effect in relation to the seizure of anything under that paragraph by a constable;

(d) section 20 of that Act (extension of powers of seizure to computerised information) shall have effect in relation to the power of seizure conferred on that person by paragraph 13 of Schedule 1 to that Act as it applies in relation to the power of seizure conferred on a constable by that paragraph;

(e) section 21(1) and (2) of that Act (provision of record of seizure) shall have effect in relation to the seizure of anything by that person in exercise of the power conferred on him by paragraph 13 of Schedule 1 to that Act as if the references to a constable and to an officer included references to that person; and

(f) sections 21(3) to (8) and 22 of that Act (access, copying and retention) shall have effect in relation to anything seized by that person in exercise of that power or taken away by him following the imposition of a requirement by virtue of sub-paragraph (d), and to anything produced to him under paragraph 4(a) of Schedule 1 to that Act—

   (i) as they have effect in relation to anything seized in exercise of the power conferred on a constable by paragraph 13 of that Schedule or taken away by a constable following the imposition of a requirement by virtue of section 20 of that Act or, as the case may be, to anything produced to a constable under paragraph 4(a) of that Schedule; and

   (ii) as if the references to a constable in subsections (3), (4) and (5) of section 21 included references to a person to whom this paragraph applies.

Entry and search after arrest

18. Where a designation applies this paragraph to any person—

(a) he shall have the powers of a constable under section 18 of the 1984 Act (entry and search after arrest) to enter and search any premises in the relevant police area and to seize and retain anything for which he may search under that section;

(b) subsections (5) and (6) of that section (power to carry out search before arrested person taken to police station and duty to inform senior officer) shall have effect in relation to any exercise by that person of those powers as if the references in those subsections to a constable were references to that person;

(c) section 19(6) of that Act (protection for legally privileged material from seizure) shall have effect in relation to the seizure of anything

---

²⁹ sub-paras (bb) and (bc) inserted by Criminal Justice Act 2003, Sch.1, para.17.

by that person by virtue of sub-paragraph (a) as it has effect in relation to the seizure of anything by a constable;

(d) section 20 of that Act (extension of powers of seizure to computerised information) shall have effect in relation to the power of seizure conferred on that person by virtue of sub-paragraph (a) as it applies in relation to the power of seizure conferred on a constable by section 18(2) of that Act;

(e) section 21(1) and (2) of that Act (provision of record of seizure) shall have effect in relation to the seizure of anything by that person in exercise of the power conferred on him by virtue of sub-paragraph (a) as if the references to a constable and to an officer included references to that person; and

(f) sections 21(3) to (8) and 22 of that Act (access, copying and retention) shall have effect in relation to anything seized by that person in exercise of that power or taken away by him following the imposition of a requirement by virtue of sub-paragraph (d)—

    (i) as they have effect in relation to anything seized in exercise of the power conferred on a constable by section 18(2) of that Act or taken away by a constable following the imposition of a requirement by virtue of section 20 of that Act; and

    (ii) as if the references to a constable in subsections (3), (4) and (5) of section 21 included references to a person to whom this paragraph applies.

General power of seizure

19. Where a designation applies this paragraph to any person—

(a) he shall, when lawfully on any premises in the relevant police area, have the same powers as a constable under section 19 of the 1984 Act (general powers of seizure) to seize things;

(b) he shall also have the powers of a constable to impose a requirement by virtue of subsection (4) of that section in relation to information accessible from such premises;

(c) subsection (6) of that section (protection for legally privileged material from seizure) shall have effect in relation to the seizure of anything by that person by virtue of sub-paragraph (a) as it has effect in relation to the seizure of anything by a constable;

(d) section 21(1) and (2) of that Act (provision of record of seizure) shall have effect in relation to the seizure of anything by that person in exercise of the power conferred on him by virtue of sub-paragraph (a) as if the references to a constable and to an officer included references to that person; and

(e) sections 21(3) to (8) and 22 of that Act (access, copying and retention) shall have effect in relation to anything seized by that person in exercise of that power or taken away by him following the imposition of a requirement by virtue of sub-paragraph (b)—

    (i) as they have effect in relation to anything seized in exercise of the power conferred on a constable by section 19(2) or (3) of that Act or taken away by a constable following the imposition of a requirement by virtue of section 19(4) of that Act; and

(ii)   as if the references to a constable in subsections (3), (4) and (5) of section 21 included references to a person to whom this paragraph applies.

Access and copying in the case of things seized by constables

20. Where a designation applies this paragraph to any person, section 21 of the 1984 Act (access and copying) shall have effect in relation to anything seized in the relevant police area by a constable [or by a person authorised to accompany him under 16(2) of that Act][30] as if the references to a constable in subsections (3), (4) and (5) of section 21 (supervision of access and photographing of seized items) included references to a person to whom this paragraph applies.

Arrest at a police station for another offence

21.—(1) Where a designation applies this paragraph to any person, he shall have the power to make an arrest at any police station in the relevant police area in any case where an arrest—

(a)   is required to be made under section 31 of the 1984 Act (arrest for a further offence of a person already at a police station); or

(b)   would be so required if the reference in that section to a constable included a reference to a person to whom this paragraph applies.

(2) Section 36 of the Criminal Justice and Public Order Act 1994 (c.33) (consequences of failure by arrested person to account for objects etc.) shall apply (without prejudice to the effect of any designation applying paragraph 23) in the case of a person arrested in exercise of the power exercisable by virtue of this paragraph as it applies in the case of a person arrested by a constable.

Power to transfer persons into custody of investigating officers

22.—(1) Where a designation applies this paragraph to any person, the custody officer for a designated police station in the relevant police area may transfer or permit the transfer to him of a person in police detention for an offence which is being investigated by the person to whom this paragraph applies.

(2) A person into whose custody another person is transferred under subparagraph (1)—

(a)   shall be treated for all purposes as having that person in his lawful custody;

(b)   shall be under a duty[31] to prevent his escape; and

(c)   shall be entitled to use reasonable force to keep that person in his custody[32].

---

[30] Text in square brackets inserted by Criminal Justice Act 2003, Sch.1, para.18.

[31] The Serious Organised Crime and Police Bill 2004–05, Sch.9, para.5(a) adds here "to keep that person under control and".

[32] The Serious Organised Crime and Police Bill 2004–05, Sch.9, para.5(b) adds here "and under his control".

(3) Where a person is transferred into the custody of a person to whom this paragraph applies, in accordance with sub-paragraph (1), subsections (2) and (3) of section 39 of the 1984 Act shall have effect as if—

    (a)   references to the transfer of a person in police detention into the custody of a police officer investigating an offence for which that person is in police detention were references to that person's transfer into the custody of the person to whom this paragraph applies; and

    (b)   references to the officer to whom the transfer is made and to the officer investigating the offence were references to the person to whom this paragraph applies.

[*The Serious Organised Crime and Police Bill 2004–05, Sch.9, para.5 inserts new para.22A:*

"Powers in respect of detained persons

22A. Where a designation applies this paragraph to any person, he shall be under a duty, when in the course of his employment he is present at a police station—

    (a)   to assist any officer or other designated person to keep any person detained at the police station under control; and

    (b)   to prevent the escape of any such person,

and for those purposes shall be entitled to use reasonable force."]

Power to require arrested person to account for certain matters

23. Where a designation applies this paragraph to any person—

    (a)   he shall have the powers of a constable under sections 36(1)(c) and 37(1)(c) of the Criminal Justice and Public Order Act 1994 (c.33) to request a person who—

        (i)   has been arrested by a constable, or by any person to whom paragraph 21 applies, and

        (ii)   is detained at any place in the relevant police area,

    to account for the presence of an object, substance or mark or for the presence of the arrested person at a particular place; and

    (b)   the references to a constable in sections 36(1)(b) and (c) and (4) and 37(1)(b) and (c) and (3) of that Act shall have effect accordingly as including references to the person to whom this paragraph is applied.

Extended powers of seizure

24. Where a designation applies this paragraph to any person—

    (a)   the powers of a constable under Part 2 of the Criminal Justice and Police Act 2001 (c.16) (extension of powers of seizure) that are exercisable in the case of a constable by reference to a power of a constable that is conferred on that person by virtue of the provisions of this Part of this Schedule shall be exercisable by that person by reference to that power to the same extent as in the case of a constable but in relation only to premises in the relevant police area and things found on any such premises; and

(b) section 56 of that Act (retention of property seized by a constable) shall have effect as if the property referred to in subsection (1) of that section included property seized by that person at any time when he was lawfully on any premises in the relevant police area.

Persons accompanying investigating officers

[24A.—(1) This paragraph applies where a person ("an authorised person") is authorised by virtue of section 16(2) of the 1984 Act to accompany an investigating officer designated for the purposes of paragraph 16 (or 17) in the execution of a warrant.

(2) The reference in paragraph 16(h) (or 17(e)) to the seizure of anything by a designated person in exercise of a particular power includes a reference to the seizure of anything by the authorised person in exercise of that power by virtue of section 16(2A) of the 1984 Act.

(3) In relation to any such seizure, paragraph 16(h) (or 17(e)) is to be read as if it provided for the references to a constable and to an officer in section 21(1) and (2) of the 1984 Act to include references to the authorised person.

(4) The reference in paragraph 16(i) (or 17(f)) to anything seized by a designated person in exercise of a particular power includes a reference to anything seized by the authorised person in exercise of that power by virtue of section 16(2A) of the 1984 Act.

(5) In relation to anything so seized, paragraph 16(i)(ii) (or 17(f)(ii)) is to be read as if it provided for-

(a) the references to the supervision of a constable in subsections (3) and (4) of section 21 of the 1984 Act to include references to the supervision of a person designated for the purposes of paragraph 16 (or paragraph 17), and

(b) the reference to a constable in subsection (5) of that section to include a reference to such a person or an authorised person accompanying him.

(6) Where an authorised person accompanies an investigating officer who is also designated for the purposes of paragraph 24, the references in sub-paragraphs (a) and (b) of that paragraph to the designated person include references to the authorised person.][33]

PART 3

DETENTION OFFICERS

Attendance at police station for fingerprinting

25. Where a designation applies this paragraph to any person, he shall, in respect of police stations in the relevant police area, have the power of a constable under section 27(1) of the 1984 Act (fingerprinting of suspects) to require a person to attend a police station in order to have his fingerprints taken.

---

[33] para.24A inserted by Criminal Justice Act 2003, Sch.1, para.19.

Non-intimate searches of detained persons

26.—(1) Where a designation applies this paragraph to any person, he shall have the powers of a constable under section 54 of the 1984 Act (non-intimate searches of detained persons)—

    (a)   to carry out a search under that section of any person at a police station in the relevant police area or of any other person otherwise in police detention in that area; and

    (b)   to seize or retain, or cause to be seized or retained, anything found on such a search.

(2) Subsections (6C) and (9) of section 54 of that Act (restrictions on power to seize personal effects and searches to be carried out by a member of the same sex) shall apply to the exercise by a person to whom this paragraph is applied of any power exercisable by virtue of this paragraph as they apply to the exercise of the power in question by a constable.

Searches and examinations to ascertain identity

27. Where a designation applies this paragraph to any person, he shall have the powers of a constable under section 54A of the 1984 Act (searches and examinations to ascertain identity)—

    (a)   to carry out a search or examination at any police station in the relevant police area; and

    (b)   to take a photograph at any such police station of an identifying mark.

Intimate searches of detained persons

28.—(1) Where a designation applies this paragraph to any person, he shall have the powers of a constable by virtue of section 55(6) of the 1984 Act (intimate searches) to carry out an intimate search of a person at any police station in the relevant police area.

(2) Subsection (7) of section 55 of that Act (no intimate search to be carried out by a constable of the opposite sex) shall apply to the exercise by a person to whom this paragraph applies of any power exercisable by virtue of this paragraph as it applies to the exercise of the power in question by a constable.

Fingerprinting without consent

29. Where a designation applies this paragraph to any person—

    (a)   he shall have, at any police station in the relevant police area, the power of a constable under section 61 of the 1984 Act (fingerprinting) to take fingerprints without the appropriate consent; and

    (b)   the requirement by virtue of subsection (7A)(a) of that section that a person must be informed by an officer that his fingerprints may be the subject of a speculative search shall be capable of being discharged, in the case of a person at such a station, by his being so informed by the person to whom this paragraph applies.

Warnings about intimate samples

30. Where a designation applies this paragraph to any person, the requirement by virtue of section 62(7A)(a) of the 1984 Act (intimate samples) that a person must be informed by an officer that a sample taken from him may be the subject of a speculative search shall be capable of being discharged, in the case of a person in a police station in the relevant police area, by his being so informed by the person to whom this paragraph applies.

Non-intimate samples

31. Where a designation applies this paragraph to any person—
    (a)   he shall have the power of a constable under section 63 of the 1984 Act (non-intimate samples), in the case of a person in a police station in the relevant police area, to take a non-intimate sample without the appropriate consent;
    (b)   the requirement by virtue of subsection (6) of that section (information about authorisation) that a person must be informed by an officer of the matters mentioned in that subsection shall be capable of being discharged, in the case of an authorisation in relation to a person in a police station in the relevant police area, by his being so informed by the person to whom this paragraph applies; and
    (c)   the requirement by virtue of subsection (8B)(a) of that section that a person must be informed by an officer that a sample taken from him may be the subject of a speculative search shall be capable of being discharged, in the case of a person in such a police station, by his being so informed by the person to whom this paragraph applies.

Attendance at police station for the taking of a sample

32. Where a designation applies this paragraph to any person, he shall, as respects any police station in the relevant police area, have the power of a constable under subsection (4) of section 63A of the 1984 Act (supplementary provisions relating to fingerprints and samples) to require a person to attend a police station in order to have a sample taken.

Photographing persons in police detention

33. Where a designation applies this paragraph to any person, he shall, at police stations in the relevant police area, have the power of a constable under section 64A of the 1984 Act (photographing of suspects etc.) to take a photograph of a person detained at a police station.

[*The Serious Organised Crime and Police Bill 2004–05, Sch.8, para.12 inserts new para.33A:*

"Taking of impressions of footwear

33A. Where a designation applies this paragraph to any person—
    (a)   he shall, at any police station in the relevant police area, have the powers of a constable under section 61A of the 1984 Act (impressions

of footwear) to take impressions of a person's footwear without the appropriate consent; and

(b) *the requirement by virtue of section 61A(5)(a) of the 1984 Act that a person must be informed by an officer that an impression of his footwear may be the subject of a speculative search shall be capable of being discharged, in the case of a person at such a station, by his being so informed by the person to whom this paragraph applies."*]

[*The Serious Organised Crime and Police Bill 2004–05, Sch.9, para.7 inserts new paras 33B and 33C:*

"Powers in respect of detained persons

33B. Where a designation applies this paragraph to any person, he shall be under a duty, when in the course of his employment he is present at a police station—

(a) *to keep under control any person detained at the police station and for whom he is for the time being responsible;*

(b) *to assist any officer or other designated person to keep any other person detained at the police station under control; and*

(c) *to prevent the escape of any such person as is mentioned in paragraph (a) or (b),*

and for those purposes shall be entitled to use reasonable force.

33C. Where a designation applies this paragraph to any person, he shall be entitled to use reasonable force when—

(a) *securing, or assisting an officer or another designated person to secure, the detention of a person detained at a police station in the relevant police area, or*

(b) *escorting within a police station in the relevant police area, or assisting an officer or another designated person to escort within such a police station, a person detained there."*]

PART 4

ESCORT OFFICERS

Power to take an arrested person to a police station

34.—(1) Where a designation applies this paragraph to any person—

(a) the persons who, in the case of a person arrested by a constable in the relevant police area, are authorised for the purposes of [subsection (1A) of section 30][34] of the 1984 Act (procedure on arrest of person elsewhere than at a police station) to take the person arrested to a police station in that area shall include that person;

(b) that section shall have effect in relation to the exercise by that person of the power conferred by virtue of paragraph (a) as if the references

---

[34] Amended by the Criminal Justice Act 2003, Sch.1, para.20.

to a constable in subsections (3), (4)(a) and (10) (but not the references in subsections (5) to (9)) included references to that person; and

(c) a person who is taking another person to a police station in exercise of the power conferred by virtue of paragraph (a)—

    (i) shall be treated for all purposes as having that person in his lawful custody;

    (ii) shall be under a duty[35] to prevent his escape; and

    (iii) shall be entitled to use reasonable force to keep that person in his charge[36].

[The Serious Organised Crime and Police Bill 2004–05, Sch.9, para.8(3) inserts here new (d):

    "(d) a person who has taken another person to a police station in exercise of the power conferred by virtue of paragraph (a)—

    (i)   shall be under a duty to remain at the police station until he has transferred control of the other person to the custody officer at the police station;

    (ii) until he has so transferred control of the other person, shall be treated for all purposes as having that person in his lawful custody;

    (iii) for so long as he is at the police station or in its immediate vicinity in compliance with, or having complied with, his duty under sub-paragraph (i), shall be under a duty to prevent the escape of the other person and to assist in keeping him under control; and

    (iv) shall be entitled to use reasonable force for the purpose of complying with his duty under subparagraph (iii)."]

(2) Without prejudice to any designation under paragraph 26, where a person has another in his lawful custody by virtue of sub-paragraph (1) of this paragraph—

(a) he shall have the same powers under subsections (6A) and (6B) of section 54 of the 1984 Act (non-intimate searches) as a constable has in the case of a person in police detention—

    (i) to carry out a search of the other person; and

    (ii) to seize or retain, or cause to be seized or retained, anything found on such a search;

(b) subsections (6C) and (9) of that section (restrictions on power to seize personal effects and searches to be carried out by a member of the same sex) shall apply to the exercise by a person to whom this paragraph is applied of any power exercisable by virtue of this sub-paragraph as they apply to the exercise of the power in question by a constable.

---

[35] The Serious Organised Crime and Police Bill 2004–05, Sch.9, para.8(2)(a) adds here "to keep the person under control and".

[36] The Serious Organised Crime and Police Bill 2004–05, Sch.9, para.8(2)(b) adds here "and under his control".

Escort of persons in police detention

35.—(1) Where a designation applies this paragraph to any person, that person may be authorised by the custody officer for any designated police station in the relevant police area to escort a person in police detention—

(a) from that police station to another police station in that or any other police area; or

(b) from that police station to any other place specified by the custody officer and then either back to that police station or on to another police station in that area or in another police area.

(2) Where a designation applies this paragraph to any person, that person may be authorised by the custody officer for any designated police station outside the relevant police area to escort a person in police detention—

(a) from that police station to a designated police station in that area; or

(b) from that police station to any place in that area specified by the custody officer and either back to that police station or on to another police station (whether in that area or elsewhere).

(3) A person who is escorting another in accordance with an authorisation under sub-paragraph (1) or (2)—

(a) shall be treated for all purposes as having that person in his lawful custody;

(b) shall be under a duty[37] to prevent his escape; and

(c) shall be entitled to use reasonable force to keep that person in his charge[38].

[*The Serious Organised Crime and Police Bill 2004–05, Sch.9, para.9(3) inserts here new sub-para.(3A):*

"(3A). A person who has escorted another person to a police station or other place in accordance with an authorisation under subparagraph (1) or (2)—

(a) shall be under a duty to remain at the police station or other place until he has transferred control of the other person to a custody officer or other responsible person there;

(b) until he has so transferred control of the other person, shall be treated for all purposes as having that person in his lawful custody;

(c) for so long as he is at the police station or other place, or in its immediate vicinity, in compliance with, or having complied with, his duty under paragraph (a), shall be under a duty to prevent the escape of the other person and to assist in keeping him under control; and

(d) shall be entitled to use reasonable force for the purpose of complying with his duty under paragraph (c)."]

(4) Without prejudice to any designation under paragraph 26, where a person has another in his lawful custody by virtue of sub-paragraph (3) of this paragraph—

(a) he shall have the same powers under subsections (6A) and (6B) of section 54 the 1984 Act (non-intimate searches) as a constable has in the case of a person in police detention—

---

[37] The Serious Organised Crime and Police Bill 2004–05, Sch.9, para.9(2)(a) adds here "to keep the person under control and".

[38] The Serious Organised Crime and Police Bill 2004–05, Sch.9, para.9(2)(b) adds here "and under his control".

      (i)   to carry out a search of the other person; and

      (ii) to seize or retain, or cause to be seized or retained, anything found on such a search;

  (b) subsections (6C) and (9) of that section (restrictions on power to seize personal effects and searches to be carried out by a member of the same sex) shall apply to the exercise by a person to whom this paragraph is applied of any power exercisable by virtue of this sub-paragraph as they apply to the exercise of the power in question by a constable.

(5) Section 39(2) of that Act (responsibilities of custody officer transferred to escort) shall have effect where the custody officer for any police station transfers or permits the transfer of any person to the custody of a person who by virtue of this paragraph has lawful custody outside the police station of the person transferred as it would apply if the person to whom this paragraph applies were a police officer.

[*The Serious Organised Crime and Police Bill 2004–05, cl.111(5) inserts new para.35A:*

"PART 4A

STAFF CUSTODY OFFICERS

Exercise of functions of custody officers

35A.—(1) Where a designation applies this paragraph to any person, he may (subject to sub-paragraph (2)) perform all the functions of a custody officer under the 1984 Act (except those under section 45A(4) of that Act) and under any other enactment which confers functions on such a custody officer.

(2) But in relation to a police station designated under section 35(1) of the 1984 Act, the person must first also be appointed a custody officer for that police station under section 36(2) of that Act.

(3) A person performing the functions of a custody officer by virtue of a designation under this paragraph (together with, if appropriate, an appointment as such) shall have all the powers and duties of a

    custody officer.

(4) Except in sections 36 and 45A(4) of the 1984 Act, references in any enactment to a custody officer within the meaning of that Act include references to a person performing the functions of a custody officer by virtue of a designation under this paragraph."]

[*The Serious Organised Crime and Police Bill 2004–05, Sch.9, para.10 inserts new para.35B:*

"Powers in respect of detained persons

35B. Where a designation applies this paragraph to any person, he shall be under a duty, when in the course of his employment he is present at a police station—

(a) to keep under control any person detained at the police station and for whom he is for the time being responsible;

(b) to assist any officer or other designated person to keep any other person detained at the police station under control;and

(c) to prevent the escape of any such person as is mentioned in paragraph (a) or (b),

and for those purposes shall be entitled to use reasonable force."]

PART 5

INTERPRETATION OF SCHEDULE

36.—(1) In this Schedule "the relevant police area"—

(a) in relation to a designation under section 38 or 39 by the chief officer of any police force, means the police area for which that force is maintained; and

(b) in relation to a designation under section 38 by a Director General, means England and Wales.[39]

(2) In this Schedule "a designation" means a designation under section 38.

(3) In Parts 3 and 4 of this Schedule "a designation" also includes a designation under section 39.[40]

(4) Expressions used in this Schedule and in the 1984 Act have the same meanings in this Schedule as in that Act.

Section 41   **SCHEDULE 5**

POWERS EXERCISABLE BY ACCREDITED PERSONS

Power to issue fixed penalty notices

1.—(1) An accredited person whose accreditation specifies that this paragraph applies to him shall have the powers specified in sub-paragraph (2) in relation to any individual who he has reason to believe has committed or is committing a relevant fixed penalty offence at a place within the relevant police area.

(2) Those powers are the following powers so far as exercisable in respect of a relevant offence—

(a) the power of a constable in uniform to give a person a fixed penalty notice under section 54 of the Road Traffic Offenders Act 1988 (c.53) (fixed penalty notices) in respect of an offence under section 72 of the Highway Act 1835 (c.50) (riding on a footway) committed by cycling;

---

[39] The Serious Organised Crime and Police Bill 2004–05, Sch.4, para.191 omits (b) and the word "and" before it.

[40] The Serious Organised Crime and Police Bill 2004–05, Sch.13, para.12(4) inserts here new sub-para.(3A): "In this Schedule 'specified park' has the same meaning as in section 139 of the Serious Organised Crime and Police Act 2005."

[(aa) the powers of a constable in uniform to give a penalty notice under Chapter 1 of Part 1 of the Criminal Justice and Police Act 2001 (fixed penalty notices in respect of offences of disorder) except in respect of an offence under section 12 of the Licensing Act 1872 or section 91 of the Criminal Justice Act 1967;][41]

[(ab) the power of a constable to give a penalty notice under section 444A of the Education Act 1996 (penalty notice in respect of failure to secure regular attendance at school of registered pupil);][42]

(b) the power of an authorised officer of a local authority to give a notice under section 4 of the Dogs (Fouling of Land) Act 1996 (c.20) (fixed penalty notices in respect of dog fouling); and

(c) the power of an authorised officer of a litter authority to give a notice under section 88 of the Environmental Protection Act 1990 (c.43) (fixed penalty notices in respect of litter).

(3) In this paragraph "relevant fixed penalty offence", in relation to an accredited person, means an offence which—

(a) is an offence by reference to which a notice may be given to a person in exercise of any of the powers mentioned in sub-paragraph (2)(a) to (c), and

(b) is specified or described in that person's accreditation as an offence he has been accredited to enforce.

[(4) In its application to an offence which is an offence by reference to which a notice may be given to a person in exercise of the power mentioned in sub-paragraph (2)(ab), sub-paragraph (1) shall have effect as if for the words from "who he has reason to believe" to the end there were substituted "in the relevant police area who he has reason to believe has committed or is committing a relevant fixed penalty offence".][43]

Power to require giving of name and address

2.—(1) Where an accredited person whose accreditation specifies that this paragraph applies to him has reason to believe that another person has committed a relevant offence in the relevant police area, he may require that other person to give him his name and address.

(2) A person who fails to comply with a requirement under sub-paragraph (1) is guilty of an offence and shall be liable, on summary conviction, to a fine not exceeding level 3 on the standard scale.

(3) In this paragraph "relevant offence", in relation to any accredited person, means any offence which is—

(a) a relevant fixed penalty offence for the purposes of any powers

---

[41] sub-para.(aa) was inserted by the Anti-social Behaviour Act 2003, s.89(5). But this power does not apply to offences under s.1 of the Theft Act 1968, s.1(1) of the Criminal Damage Act 1971 or s.87 of the Environmental Protection Act 1990—see Criminal Justice and Police Act (Amendment) and Police Reform Act 2002 (Modification) Order 2004, SI 2004/2540, para.5. The Serious Organised Crime and Police Bill, cl.113(5)(a) provides that the last words of the sub-para.—from "except in respect of" to the end of (aa)—are omitted. Clause 113(5)(b) also excludes from the operation of (2)(aa) s.12 of the Licensing Act 1872, s.91 of the Criminal Justice Act 1967 and s.1(1) of the Criminal Damage Act 1971.

[42] sub-para.(ab) inserted by the Anti-social Behaviour Act 2003, s.23(6).

[43] sub-para.(4) inserted by the Anti-social Behaviour Act 2003, s.23(7).

exercisable by the accredited person by virtue of paragraph 1;

[*The Serious Organised Crime and Police Bill 2004–05, Sch.8, Pt 1, para.14 inserts here "(aa) an offence under section 3 or 4 of the Vagrancy Act 1824; or"*]

    (b)   an offence the commission of which appears to the accredited person to have caused—

        (i)   injury, alarm or distress to any other person; or

        (ii)   the loss of, or any damage to, any other person's property;

but the accreditation of an accredited person may provide that an offence is not to be treated as a relevant offence by virtue of paragraph (b) unless it satisfies such other conditions as may be specified in the accreditation.

[(4) In its application to an offence which is an offence by reference to which a notice may be given to a person in exercise of the power mentioned in paragraph 1(2)(ab), sub-paragraph (1) of this paragraph shall have effect as if for the words "has committed a relevant offence in the relevant police area" there were substituted "in the relevant police area has committed a relevant offence"][44]

Power to require name and address of person acting in an anti-social manner

3. An accredited person whose accreditation specifies that this paragraph applies to him shall, in the relevant police area, have the powers of a constable in uniform under section 50 to require a person whom he has reason to believe to have been acting, or to be acting, in an anti-social manner (within the meaning of section 1 of the Crime and Disorder Act 1998 (c.37) (anti-social behaviour orders)) to give his name and address.

[*The Serious Organised Crime and Police Bill 2004–05, Sch.8, Pt 1, para.15 inserts here new para.3A:*

"Power to require name and address: road traffic offences

3A.—(1) An accredited person whose accreditation specifies that this paragraph applies to him shall, in the relevant police area, have the powers of a constable—

    (a)   *under subsection (1) of section 165 of the Road Traffic Act 1988 to require a person mentioned in paragraph (c) of that subsection whom he has reasonable cause to believe has committed, in the relevant police area, an offence under subsection (1) or (2) of section 35 of that Act (including that section as extended by paragraphs 8B(4) and 9(2) of this Schedule) to give his name and address; and*

    (b)   *under section 169 of that Act to require a person committing an offence under section 37 of that Act (including that section as extended by paragraphs 8B(4) and 9(2) of this Schedule) to give his name and address.*

(2) The reference in section 169 of the Road Traffic Act 1988 to section 37 of that Act is to be taken to include a reference to that section as extended by paragraphs 8B(4) and 9(2) of this Schedule."]

---

[44] sub-para.(4) inserted by the Anti-social Behaviour Act 2003, s.23(8).

Alcohol consumption in designated public places

4. An accredited person whose accreditation specifies that this paragraph applies to him shall, within the relevant police area, have the powers of a constable under section 12 of the Criminal Justice and Police Act 2001 (c.16) (alcohol consumption in public places)—

    (a) to impose a requirement under subsection (2) of that section; and

    (b) to dispose under subsection (3) of that section of anything surrendered to him;

and that section shall have effect in relation to the exercise of those powers by that person as if the references to a constable in subsections (1) and (5) were references to the accredited person.

Confiscation of alcohol

5. An accredited person whose accreditation specifies that this paragraph applies to him shall, within the relevant police area, have the powers of a constable under section 1 of the Confiscation of Alcohol (Young Persons) Act 1997 (c.33) (confiscation of intoxicating liquor)—

    (a) to impose a requirement under subsection (1) of that section; and

    (b) to dispose under subsection (2) of that section of anything surrendered to him;

and that section shall have effect in relation to the exercise of those powers by that person as if the references to a constable in subsections (1) and (4) (but not the reference in subsection (5) (arrest)) were references to the accredited person.

Confiscation of tobacco etc.

6.—(1) An accredited person whose accreditation specifies that this paragraph applies to him shall, within the relevant police area, have—

    (a) the power to seize anything that a constable in uniform has a duty to seize under subsection (3) of section 7 of the Children and Young Persons Act 1933 (c.12) (seizure of tobacco etc. from young persons); and

    (b) the power to dispose of anything that a constable may dispose of under that subsection;

and the power to dispose of anything shall be a power to dispose of it in such manner as the relevant employer of the accredited person may direct.

(2) In this paragraph "relevant employer", in relation to an accredited person, means the person with whom the chief officer of police for the relevant police area has entered into arrangements under section 40.

Abandoned vehicles

7. An accredited person whose accreditation specifies that this paragraph applies to him shall have all such powers in the relevant police area as are conferred on accredited persons by regulations under section 99 of the Road Traffic Regulation Act 1984 (c.27) (removal of abandoned vehicles).

Power to stop vehicle for testing

8. A person whose accreditation specifies that this paragraph applies to him shall, within the relevant police area, have the power of a constable in uniform to stop a vehicle under subsection (3) of section 67 of the Road Traffic Act 1988 (c.52) for the purposes of a test under subsection (1) of that section.

Power to stop cycles

8A.—(1) Subject to sub-paragraph (2), a person whose accreditation specifies that this paragraph applies to him shall, within the relevant police area, have the power of a constable in uniform under section 163(2) of the Road Traffic Act 1988 to stop a cycle.

(2) The power mentioned in sub-paragraph (1) may only be exercised by that person in relation to a person who he has reason to believe has committed an offence under section 72 of the Highway Act 1835 (riding on a footway) by cycling.][45]

[*The Serious Organised Crime and Police Bill 2004–05, Sch.8, Pt 1, para.16 inserts here new para.8B:*

"Power to control traffic for purposes other than escorting a load of exceptional diimensions

8B.—(1) A person whose accreditation specifies that this paragraph applies to him shall have, in the relevant police area—

(a) *the power of a constable engaged in the regulation of traffic in a road to direct a person driving or propelling a vehicle to stop the vehicle or to make it proceed in, or keep to, a particular line of traffic;*

(b) *the power of a constable in uniform engaged in the regulation of vehicular traffic in a road to direct a person on foot to stop proceeding along or across the carriageway.*

(2) The purposes for which those powers may be exercised do not include the purpose mentioned in paragraph 9(1).

(3) A person whose accreditation specifies that this paragraph applies to him shall also have, in the relevant police area, the power of a constable, for the purposes of a traffic survey, to direct a person driving or propelling a vehicle to stop the vehicle, to make it proceed in, or keep to, a particular line of traffic, or to proceed to a particular point on or near the road.

(4) Sections 35 and 37 of the Road Traffic Act 1988 (offences of failing to comply with directions of constable engaged in regulation of traffic in a road) shall have effect in relation to the exercise of the powers mentioned in sub-paragraphs (1) and (3), for the purposes for which they may be exercised and by a person whose accreditation specifies that this paragraph applies to him, as if the references to a constable were references to him.

(5) A person's accreditation may not specify that this paragraph applies to him unless it also specifies that paragraph 3A applies to him."]

---

[45] para.8A inserted by the Anti-social Behaviour Act 2003, s.89(6).

Power to control traffic for purposes of escorting a load of exceptional dimensions

9.—(1) A person whose accreditation specifies that this paragraph applies to him shall have, for the purpose of escorting a vehicle or trailer carrying a load of exceptional dimensions either to or from the relevant police area, the power of a constable engaged in the regulation of traffic in a road-

    (a)   to direct a vehicle to stop;

    (b)   to make a vehicle proceed in, or keep to, a particular line of traffic; and

    (c)   to direct pedestrians to stop.

(2) Sections 35 and 37 of the Road Traffic Act 1988 (offences of failing to comply with directions of constable engaged in regulation of traffic in a road) shall have effect in relation to the exercise of those powers for the purpose mentioned in sub-paragraph (1) by a person whose accreditation specifies that this paragraph applies to him as if the references to a constable engaged in regulation of traffic in a road were references to that person

(3) The powers conferred by virtue of this paragraph may be exercised in any police area in England and Wales.

(4) In this paragraph "vehicle or trailer carrying a load of exceptional dimensions" means a vehicle or trailer the use of which is authorised by an order made by the Secretary of State under section 44(1)(d) of the Road Traffic Act 1988.

[The Serious Organised Crime and Police Bill 2004–05, Sch.8, Pt 1, para.17 inserts here new para.9ZA:

"Photographing of persons given fixed penalty notices

9ZA. An accredited person whose accreditation specifies that this paragraph applies to him shall, within the relevant police area, have the power of a constable under section 64A(1A) of the Police and Criminal Evidence Act 1984 (photographing of suspects etc.) to take a photograph, elsewhere than at a police station, of a person to whom the accredited person has given a penalty notice (or as the case may be a fixed penalty notice) in exercise of any power mentioned in paragraph 1(2)."]

Power to modify paragraph 1(2)(aa)

9A.—(1) The Secretary of State may by order provide that paragraph 1(2)(aa) is to have effect as if the reference to the powers there mentioned did not include those powers so far as they relate to an offence under any provision for the time being mentioned in the first column of the Table in section 1(1) of the Criminal Justice and Police Act 2001 which is specified in the order.

[The Serious Organised Crime and Police Bill, cl.113(6) substitutes a new sub-para.(1) providing that the Secretary of State may amend para.1(2A)— Note not 1(2)(a)—by adding to or removing a provision.]

(2) The Secretary of State shall not make an order containing (with or without any other provision) any provision authorised by this paragraph unless a draft of

that order has been laid before Parliament and approved by a resolution of each House.][46]

Meaning of "relevant police area"

10. In this Schedule "the relevant police area", in relation to an accredited person, means the police area for which the police force whose chief officer granted his accreditation is maintained.

---

[46] para.9A inserted by the Anti-social Behaviour Act 2003, s.89(7).

THE RIGHT TO SILENCE

CHAPTER 13

THE RIGHT TO SILENCE

Giving judgment in the House of Lords, Lord Mustill distinguished six separate **13–01** meanings for the phrase "right to silence"[1]:

> "This expression arouses strong but unfocused feelings. In truth it does not denote any single right, but rather refers to a disparate group of immunities, which differ in nature, origin, incidence and importance, and also as to the extent to which they have already been encroached upon by statute. Amongst these may be identified:
>
> (1) a general immunity, possessed by all persons and bodies, from being compelled on pain of punishment to answer questions posed by other persons or bodies;
> (2) a general immunity, possessed by all persons and bodies, from being compelled on pain of punishment to answer questions the answers to which may incriminate them;
> (3) a specific immunity, possessed by all persons under suspicion of criminal responsibility whilst being interviewed by police officers and others in similar positions of authority, from being compelled on pain of punishment to answer questions of any kind;
> (4) a specific immunity, possessed by accused persons undergoing trial, from being compelled to give evidence, and from being compelled to answer questions put to them in the dock;
> (5) a specific immunity, possessed by persons who have been charged with a criminal offence, from having questions material to the offence addressed to them by police officers or persons in a similar position of authority;
> (6) a specific immunity (at least in certain circumstances, which it is unnecessary to explore) possessed by accused persons undergoing trial, from having adverse comment made on any failure (a) to answer questions before the trial, or (b) to give evidence at the trial."

The "right to silence" mainly considered here is the sixth in Lord Mustill's list. It **13–02** was this that was said to have been "abolished" by the Criminal Justice and

[1] *Smith v Director of Serious Fraud Office* [1992] 3 All E.R. 456 at 463–464. Lord Mustill also briefly identified the very different policy reasons underlying the different concepts implicit in the phrase—at 464–465.

Public Order Act 1994—and in Northern Ireland by the 1988 Criminal Evidence Order. In fact the new law did not abolish the right to silence. It is not an offence for a suspect to decline to answer questions put by a police officer nor for a defendant to refuse to go into the witness box. The right to silence remains. But the new law changed the traditional common law rule that protected the accused from adverse comment at his trial in respect of silence when being questioned by the police and in respect of a refusal to go into the witness box.[2]

The background

13–03   The Police and Criminal Evidence Act itself said nothing regarding the right to silence. The Philips Royal Commission had recommended by a majority that the right to silence be preserved. Philips rejected the view of the Criminal Law Revision Committee (CLRC) in its 11th Report in 1972[3] that the right to silence be abolished. The Commission gave two distinct reasons. One was the fear that additional pressure on suspects to say something might cause some innocent persons to make a false confession. The other was that such pressure was contrary to the principle that it was for the prosecution to prove its case and that it was, therefore, wrong to put the defendant under pressure to participate in the process by saying something in his own defence.[4] The Government accepted the Philips Royal Commission's recommendation and this was reflected in the provisions in Code C, paras 10.1–10.4 regarding the caution as it then was ("You do not have to say anything unless you wish to do so but what you say may be given in evidence.").

13–04   But 18 months after PACE came into force, in July 1987, the then Home Secretary, Mr Douglas Hurd, signalled that he took a different view. Giving the annual Police Foundation lecture he asked:

> "Is it really in the interests of justice, for example, that experienced criminals should be able to refuse to answer all police questions secure in the knowledge that a jury will never hear of it?[5] Does the present law really protect the innocent whose interests will generally lie in answering questions frankly? Is it really unthinkable that the jury should be allowed to know about the defendant's silence and, in the light of other facts brought to light during a trial, be able to draw its own conclusions?"

---

[2] For an early bibliography regarding the right to silence see Leng, "The Right-to-Silence Debate" in Morgan and Stephenson (eds), *Suspicion and Silence* (Blackstone, 1994), pp.35–38. There is a post-1994 bibliography at the end of this Chapter.

[3] *Evidence (General)*, Cmnd.491 (1972).

[4] "To use a suspect's silence as evidence against him seems to run counter to a central element in the accusatorial system." There was an inconsistency of principle "in requiring the onus of proof at trial to be upon the prosecution and to be discharged without any assistance from the accused, and yet in enabling the prosecution to use the accused's silence in the face of police questioning under caution as any part of the case against him at trial" (Philips Report, paras 4.50–4.51).

[5] This was a factual error. The jury normally did learn of the fact that the suspect was silent—see Zander and Henderson, *The Crown Court Study*, Royal Commission on Criminal Justice, Research Study No.19 (HMSO, 1993) p.7, para.1.2.5. Both prosecution and defence barristers agreed that in the overwhelming majority of cases where the defendant had been silent in response to police questions the jury learnt of it.

He called for a public debate.

Less than a year later Mr Hurd seemed virtually to have made up his mind. He announced the setting up of a Home Office Working Group to consider not whether the right to silence should be abolished but "the precise form of the change in the law which would best achieve our purpose". But before the Working Group produced its report, the Government moved to abolish the right to silence in Northern Ireland not merely in relation to terrorist offences but for all offences.

Northern Ireland

In October 1988 the Secretary of State for Northern Ireland laid before **13–05** Parliament a draft order which after being approved[6] and then made on November 14 became the Criminal Evidence (Northern Ireland) Order 1988 which came into force one month later.[7]

The Order permits such inferences as appear proper from an accused's silence in the following circumstances:

- When an accused person fails to mention a fact relied on in his defence on being questioned by a police officer trying to discover whether or by whom an offence was committed, or on being charged, if the fact was one which in the circumstances existing at the time the accused could reasonably have been expected to mention when questioned or charged (Art.3).

- When an accused person at his trial refuses to be sworn, or having been sworn, refuses without just cause to answer any questions under oath (Art.4). This does not apply to persons under 14 years old or to persons whose physical or mental condition makes it undesirable for them to give evidence.

- When an accused persons fails or refuses to account for the presence of objects, substances or marks on his person, clothing or possession or in any place in which he was at the time of his arrest and a constable reasonably believes that these are attributable to his participation in an offence (Art.5).

- When an accused person fails or refuses to account for his presence in a place at or about the time an offence for which he has been arrested is alleged to have been committed and a constable reasonably believes that his presence is attributable to his participation in the offence (Art.6).

[6] House of Commons, *Hansard*, Vol.140, November 8, 1988, cols 184–253; House of Lords, *Hansard*, Vol.501, November 10, 1989, cols 774–803.
[7] SI 1988/1987 (N.I. 20).

In the case of Arts 3, 5 and 6, the Order permitted inferences to be drawn at the committal stage, or when deciding whether there was a case to answer at trial, or when determining guilt. Originally, all the Articles permitted silence also to amount to corroboration but this was removed by the Criminal Justice (N.I.) Order 1996.

Home Office Working Group and the Runciman Royal Commission

13–06 The Report of the Home Office Working Group on the Right of Silence was published a few months later in July 1989.[8] It recommended changes that were similar but not identical to those already introduced for Northern Ireland.

However, no action was taken on the matter, no doubt because of the mounting concern relating to a series of notorious miscarriage of justice cases—the Guildford Four, the Maguires and the Birmingham Six. This culminated in 1991 in the announcement by the Prime Minister, Mr John Major, of the establishment of the Runciman Royal Commission on Criminal Justice on the day the Court of Appeal quashed the convictions of the Birmingham Six. The terms of reference of the Commission asked it to consider, *inter alia*: "(v) the opportunities available for an accused person to state his position on the matters charged and the extent to which the courts might draw adverse inferences from primary facts, the conduct of the accused, and any failure on his part to take advantage of an opportunity to state his position".

The Runciman Royal Commission, like the Philips Royal Commission, recommended by a majority (of 8 to 3) that the right to silence be preserved. The chief reason they gave was concern that abolition of the right to silence would increase the risk of miscarriages of justice: "The majority of us, however, believe that the possibility of an increase in the convictions of the guilty is outweighed by the risk that the extra pressure on suspects to talk in the police station and the adverse inferences invited if they do not, may result in more convictions of the innocent".[9]

The Criminal Justice and Public Order Act 1994

13–07 The Government, however, rejected the Runciman Royal Commission's recommendation and preferred the view of the minority. Mr Michael Howard Q.C., the Home Secretary, announced his decision at the Conservative Party's annual conference on October 6, 1993. The decision was translated into legislative action in the Criminal Justice and Public Order Bill which received the Royal Assent in November 1994 (CJPOA). The right to silence provisions became effective on April 10, 1995 together with the revised Codes.

The choice faced by the Government was whether to follow the Northern Ireland legislation or the variant proposed by the Home Office Working Group.[10] It opted essentially for the Northern Ireland model—with the important exception

---

[8] The report was obtainable from the Home Office Library, 50 Queen Anne's Gate, London SW1A 9AT; ISBN 0–862–52424–5.

[9] Runciman Report, p.54, para.22.

[10] For a consideration of the differences between the two see Zander, "How will the right to silence be abolished?", New L.J., December 3, 1993, p.1710.

that it did not adopt the then Northern Ireland rule that silence can be taken not merely as an indication of guilt but also as corroboration of other evidence.[11]

On the other hand, the 1994 legislation which enacted the new right to silence provisions for England and Wales also changed the equivalent Northern Ireland provisions in a variety of ways to bring them into line with the English rules.[12] The most important change made was to provide that adverse inferences can be drawn from silence under police questioning only if the suspect has first been cautioned.[13] The 1994 Act also abolished the Northern Ireland procedure for calling the defendant into the witness box and replaced it with the less intrusive procedure applicable in England.[14]

The CJPOA provisions regarding silence in the face of questioning by the police are ss.34, 36 and 37 of the 1994 Act. The drawing of adverse inferences from a refusal to testify at the trial is dealt with in s.35. (The text below deals first with ss.34, 36 and 37 and then with s.35.) Section 38 deals with "Interpretation and savings". Section 39 gives the Secretary of State the power to apply any or all of the provisions of ss.34 to 38 (subject to whatever modifications he may specify) to disciplinary or other proceedings in the Armed Forces—"wherever the proceedings take place". This includes both summary proceedings and courts martial. It also includes proceedings before a Standing Civilian Court. Section 39 requires an order to be made by statutory instrument. A Commencement Order brought the provisions into effect as from April 10, 1995. **13–08**

These provisions have generated a great deal of case law and literature. The provisions are first described and there is then a section considering the implications of the case law. The full text of ss.34 to 39 follows at the end of this Chapter. **13–09**

For an evaluation of the practical effect of the change see Bucke, Street, Brown, *The right of silence: the impact of the Criminal Justice and Public Order Act 1994*, Home Office Research Study (2000). For an assessment of the Northern Ireland experience see Jackson, Wolfe, Quinn, *Legislating Against Silence: The Northern Ireland Experience* (Northern Ireland Office, 2000). For separate, caustic, overall assessments of the new law by two leading scholars see Birch, "Suffering in Silence: A Cost-Benefit Analysis of Section 34 of the Criminal Justice and Public Order Act 1994" [1999] Crim.L.R. 769–88 and Dennis, "Silence in the Police Station: the Marginalisation of Section 34" [2002] Crim.L.R. 25–38. (See also the select bibliography on the right to silence issues at the end of this Chapter (para.13–63).)

---

[11] The corroboration provisions in the 1988 Northern Ireland Order, were Art.3(2)(ii), Art.4(4)(b), Art.5(2)(ii) and Art.6(2)(ii).

[12] See Criminal Justice and Public Order Act, Sch.10, para.61 amending the Criminal Evidence (Northern Ireland) Order 1988.

[13] CJPOA, Sch.10, para.61(2).

[14] CJPOA, Sch.10, para.61(3)(b).

Failure to mention facts when questioned or charged: CJPOA, s.34

13–10　　Section 34 applies to silence while being questioned under caution (s.34(1)(a)).[15] It also applies to silence on being charged (s.34(1)(b)).[16] The questioning must be by a constable trying to discover whether or by whom the offence has been committed (s.34(1)(a)). The silence consists of failure to mention a fact relied on in his defence which "in the circumstances existing at the time the accused could reasonably have been expected to mention when so questioned [or] charged".

　　Section 34(2) states that, where the subsection applies, such inferences may be drawn from the failure as appear proper. The subsection applies to a court or jury determining whether the accused is guilty of the offence charged (s.34(2)(d)). It also applies to applications by the defendant to dismiss charges that are to be transferred to the crown court and considering whether there is a case to answer (s.34(2)(a), (b), (c)). As has been seen, the "new" caution to take account of the 1994 change in the law is in the following terms:

　　"You do not have to say anything. But it may harm your defence if you do not mention when questioned something which you later rely on in court. Anything you do say may be given in evidence."[17]

13–11　　(As has also been seen, as a result of rulings by the European Court of Human Rights, if the suspect has asked for but has not yet been allowed an opportunity to get legal advice, no adverse inferences may be drawn from silence.[18] In that case the caution remains the same as it was before the CJPOA—"You do not have to say anything but anything you do say may be given in evidence". The different circumstances in which this is so under the 2003 revision of Code C were rehearsed above (see paras 5–153—5–157) and are not repeated in this Chapter which is concerned with the changes made by the 1994 Act.)

　　To what extent the "new" caution introduced by the CJPOA is understood by suspects is uncertain.[19] In the JUSTICE report, "Right of Silence Debate: The Northern Ireland experience" (May 1994), the authors interviewed 12 experienced solicitors. They were unanimous "that suspects do not understand the

---

[15] As to when a caution is required see Code C, para.10.1, 10.3, 10.5 and 10.6. The requirement that the defendant must first have been cautioned was introduced into the Bill by a Government amendment largely because of an intervention by the Lord Chief Justice—see House of Lords, *Hansard*, Vol.555, May 23, 1994, col.523.

[16] They are separate. The fact that no adverse inference can be drawn from silence during questioning does not mean that no adverse inference can be drawn from silence when being charged. *Dervish and Anori* [2001] EWCA Crim 2789.

[17] The caution in Northern Ireland was amended to bring it into line with the new caution in England and Wales. In fact it was slightly neater: "You do not have to say anything, but I must caution you that if you do not mention when questioned something which you later rely on in court, it may harm your defence. If you do say anything it may be given in evidence." (Code C, para.10.5).

[18] Youth Justice and Criminal Evidence Act 1999, s.58 and Code C, para.10.4.

[19] For evidence that many suspects could not understand the former "Notice to Detained Persons" which included the caution, see Gudjonsson, "Understanding the notice to detained persons", *Law Society Gazette*, November 28, 1990, pp.24, 27; Gudjonsson *et al.*, *Persons at Risk during Interviews in Police Custody: The Identification of Vulnerabilities*, Royal Commission on Criminal Justice Research Study No.12 (HMSO, London, 1993); and Gudjonsson, "Psychological Vulnerability: Suspects at Risk" in Morgan and Stephenson (eds), *Suspicion & Silence* (Blackstone, 1994). On the

caution under the Order when it is read to them by the police and that only a small minority, estimated at around 5 per cent, actually appreciate its significance". This was despite the fact "that clients will usually claim that they have understood it when asked".[20] This is consistent with the research conducted for the Runciman Royal Commission by Dr Ghisli Gudjonsson.[21]

As has been seen, adverse inferences can only be drawn if the silence was **13–12** while "being questioned under caution by a constable trying to discover whether or by whom the offence had been committed" (s.34(1)(a)). So if the officer conducting the questioning already has sufficient information to make him believe that the person being questioned is the culprit, no adverse inferences can be drawn.[22]

From a police point of view it is obviously desirable to caution the suspect at the earliest possible time—so that any subsequent silence can be taken into account by the court. The parliamentary history of the CJPOA shows that the Government resisted an amendment seeking to limit the right of silence provisions to questioning in the police station.[23] So can adverse inferences be drawn from silence prior to arrival at the police station? The answer should be no. Code C, para.11.1 makes it clear that, save in exceptional circumstances, a suspect must not be interviewed except at a police station. More importantly, as has been seen, an arrested person does not have to be informed of his right to free legal advice until he gets to the police station. Since the opportunity to get legal advice is now a critical factor as to whether adverse inferences can be drawn, it would be grossly unfair if silence before the suspect has been informed of the right should be capable of being penalised in that way.

Section 58 of the Youth Justice and Criminal Evidence Act 1999,[24] which pro- **13–13** vided that no adverse inferences can be drawn from silence if the suspect has not yet been allowed an opportunity to get legal advice, states that it applies "where the accused was at an authorised place of detention".[25] The revised Code C, refers repeatedly to "a detainee at a police station" and Annex C, Note C1 states, "The restriction on drawing inferences from silence does not apply to a person who has not been detained and who therefore cannot be prevented from seeking legal advice if they want to". This is consistent with the policy of s.58.[26]

Section 34(3) says that "subject to any directions by the court, evidence tending to establish the failure [to mention facts] may be given before or after

new caution see Tully and Morgan, "Fair warning?" (1997) *Police Review*, 24–35; Jackson *et al.*, *Legislating Against Silence: The Northern Ireland Experience* (Northern Ireland Office, 2000), pp.119–20.

[20] At p.14.

[21] See n.19 above. The research found that only about half the suspects (52%) understood the right to remain silent.

[22] *Pointer* [1997] Crim.L.R. 676, CA. But see cases cited at paras 4–31—4–32 above.

[23] See House of Lords, *Hansard*, Vol.555, May 23, 1994, cols 495–506. In fact, the amendment moved by Lord Ackner would have required both prior legal advice and tape recording before silence could be taken as evidence of guilt. The amendment was however not pressed to a vote.

[24] s.58 became effective as from April 1, 2003—SI 2003/707.

[25] s.34(2A), s.36(4A) and s.37(3A) of the CJPOA inserted by the 1999 Act, s.58. "Authorised place of detention is defined as either a police station or 'any other place prescribed for the purpose'" by the Home Secretary—s.38(2A) of the CJPOA inserted by the 1999 Act, s.58(5).

[26] This section is related to the situation where legal advice is potentially available—namely at the police station.

evidence tending to establish the fact which the accused is alleged to have failed to mention". In other words, the silence as to a relevant fact may emerge from prosecution witnesses or from cross-examination of the accused.

Section 34(5) states that the section does not prejudice the admissibility in evidence of the silence of the accused or of any other reaction to what is said in his presence about the matter under investigation. The arresting or investigating officer can therefore still state in evidence that the defendant was silent or replied "No comment" to questions put, whether before or after he had been cautioned.

13–14 The rules apply to questioning not only by police officers but also by "persons (other than constables) charged with the duty of investigating offences or charging offenders as it applies in relation to questioning by constables" (s.34(4)). This is the same wording as is used in s.67(9) of PACE regarding the applicability of the Codes to persons other than police officers.[27]

Revised Code C, para.114 states that at the beginning of an interview at the police station, the interviewing officer after cautioning the suspect shall put to him any significant statement or silence (*i.e.* a failure or refusal to answer a question or refusal to answer it satisfactorily) which occurred before the start of the interview and shall ask him whether he confirms or denies that earlier statement or silence and whether he wishes to add anything.

Section 34 has generated an enormous amount of case law. The implications of the cases are analysed below but there is one case in particular which deserves mention here because it is referred to so frequently. In *Argent*[28] Lord Bingham C.J. set out six formal conditions that must be satisfied before adverse inferences can be drawn:

(1) There must be proceedings against a person for an offence.

(2) The alleged failure to mention a fact at trial must have occurred before charge (s.34(1)(a)), or on charge (s.34(1)(b)).

(3) The alleged failure must have occurred during questioning under caution (s.34(1)(a)).

(4) The questioning must have been directed to trying to discover whether or by whom the alleged offence was committed.

(5) The alleged failure of the accused must have been to mention any fact relied on in his defence in those proceedings.

(6) The alleged failure must have been to mention a fact which in the circumstances existing at the time the accused could reasonably have been expected to mention when so questioned.

---

[27] For the Northern Ireland equivalent see Criminal Evidence (Northern Ireland) Order 1988, Art.3(4).
[28] [1997] 2 Cr.App.R. 27 at 32–33, CA.

Statistics

Home Office research conducted before and after the CJPOA suggests that the **13–15** proportion of "no comment" interviews in police stations has gone down. In a study in eight police stations a year before the new "right to silence" provisions were introduced, 10 per cent of suspects answered no questions and 13 per cent answered some questions. In a study including the same police stations after the changes had been introduced, 6 per cent answered no questions and 10 per cent answered some questions.[29]

Failure or refusal to account for objects, substances or marks: CJPOA, s.36

Section 36 deals with the failure or refusal of the accused to answer police ques- **13–16** tions about objects, substances or marks on his person, clothing or footwear, or in his possession, or at the place where he is arrested. Where a police officer rea sonably believes that the presence of the object, substance or mark may be attrib utable to the person's participation in the commission of an offence actually specified by the officer and he tells the person and asks him to account for the object, substance or mark, failure to do so may result in adverse inferences being drawn by the court or the jury (s.36(1)(2)). The same is true in regard to the con dition of clothing or footwear (s.36(3)). But the person must first be warned in ordinary language what may be the consequences of a failure or refusal to answer such questions (s.36(4)). The revised Code C for England and Wales does not prescribe a set form of words but it states (para.10.12[30]) that for an inference to be drawn in this regard the interviewing officer must first tell the suspect "in ordi nary language" (a) what offence he is investigating; (b) what fact he is asking the suspect to account for; (c) that he believes this fact may be due to the suspect's involvement in the offence in question; (d) that a court may draw proper infer ence from his silence; and (e) that a record is being made of the interview and that it may be given in evidence.[31]

Section 36 does not apply unless the accused was under arrest at the time **13–17** when he failed to explain the object, substance or mark (s.36(1)(a)). Whether adverse inferences will be drawn depends on the same considerations as in regard to failure to mention facts later relied on by the defendant in his

---

[29] Bucke *et al.* (2000), p.31.
[30] Formerly para.10.5B.
[31] In Northern Ireland there is a set form of words set in stages: "(a) When you were arrested on (date) at (time) at (place) there was (i) on your person (ii) in or on your clothing/footwear (iii) in your pos session (iv) in the place where you were at the time of your arrest a (state the object/substance or mark). (b) I believe this (state the object/substance/mark) may be due to your involvement in the offence of (state the offence). (c) You do not have to say anything about (object, substance or mark), but I must caution you that if you fail or refuse to account for (object/substance/mark) then a court may treat your failure or refusal as supporting any relevant evidence against you. If you do say any thing it may be given in evidence. (d) I now ask you to account for (state the object/substance/mark). Have you anything you wish to say?" (Code C, para.10.7). Paragraph 10.9 is similar in regard to explaining one's presence at the scene of the crime.

defence—including whether he has asked for and had an opportunity to get legal advice (see above).[32]

By what may have been a slip in the drafting of this section (and the next), the questions to, and cautioning of the suspect must have been by the officer who made the arrest. Section 34(1)(a), (b) and (c) specifically draw a distinction between the arresting officer and any other officer (s.37).

The Police Reform Act 2002 provides that civilian "Investigating Officers" (see para.12–12 above) have the same power as constables to require someone to account for the presence of an object, substance or mark under s.36(1)(c) of the CJPOA.[33] The power was originally given in the Bill to Detention Officers but was moved by Government amendment to Investigating Officers as being more relevant and appropriate to them.[34]

Failure or refusal to account for presence at a particular place: CJPOA, s.37

13–18   Section 37 deals in terms similar to those of s.36 with the suspect's failure or refusal to answer police questions regarding his presence "at a place at or about the time the offence for which he was arrested is alleged to have been committed". The investigating officer must reasonably believe that his presence at that place and at that time may be attributable to his having participated in the commission of the offence. Otherwise the requirements—and the restriction on adverse inferences until the suspect has had an opportunity to get legal advice— are the same as under s.36.[35]

Investigating officers under the Police Reform Act 2002 can be given this power; Detention officers cannot.

Effect of accused's silence at trial: CJPOA, s.35

13–19   The defendant has the right not to give evidence. Previously, if he exercised that right, the Criminal Evidence Act 1898, s.1 provided that "the failure of any person charged with an offence . . . to give evidence shall not be made the subject of any comment by the prosecution". But no such prohibition was imposed on the judge. The extent of the judge's right to comment was considered in 1994 by the Court of Appeal in *Martinez-Tobon*. Giving judgment, the Lord Chief Justice cited the standard direction approved at the time by the Judicial Studies Board[36]:

---

[32] The revised Code (para.10.11) says that when the restriction on drawing adverse inferences from silence applies, the suspect may still be asked to account for objects, marks or substances on their clothing but the special warning required by para.10.12 will not apply and should not be given.
[33] Police Reform Act 2002, Sch.4, para.23.
[34] House of Commons, Standing Committee A, *Hansard*, June 20, 2002, cols 281 and 287.
[35] For the Northern Ireland equivalent see Criminal Evidence (Northern Ireland) Order 1988, Art.6.
[36] [1994] 1 W.L.R. 388 at 394.

"The defendant does not have to give evidence. He is entitled to sit in the dock and require the prosecution to prove its case. You must not assume that he is guilty because he has not given evidence. The fact that he has not given evidence proves nothing one way or the other. It does nothing to establish his guilt. On the other hand, it means that there is no evidence from the defendant to undermine, contradict, or explain the evidence put before you by the prosecution."

13–20

The Court of Appeal had on occasion approved comments going beyond the conventional direction. The court said that provided the essentials of the conventional direction were given, the judge might go beyond that where the defence case alleged facts that (a) were at variance with the prosecution's evidence or additional to it and exculpatory, and (b) must, if true, be within the defendant's knowledge. The court approved the particular comment to which the defence had taken exception.

In its 1972 Report, as has been seen, the CLRC recommended that the defendant should be put under pressure to give evidence:

"In our opinion the present law and practice are much too favourable to the defence. We are convinced that, when a *prima facie* case has been made against the accused, it should be regarded as incumbent on him to give evidence in all ordinary cases. We have no doubt that the prosecution should be entitled, like the judge, to comment on his failure to do so. The present prohibition of comment seems to us wrong in principle and entirely illogical."[37]

The CJPOA, s.35 implemented this recommendation.

13–21

When the Bill was first introduced it included a provision following the CLRC's suggestion that the accused should actually be called by the court to give evidence—as was then the rule in Northern Ireland.[38] However, the judges, led by Lord Taylor, the Lord Chief Justice, made it clear that they were not happy with this procedure which they argued would have the effect of bringing the judge too much into the arena. The Government eventually introduced an amendment which provided that at the close of the prosecution's evidence the court shall "satisfy itself (in the case of proceedings on indictment, in the presence of the jury) that the accused is aware that the stage has been reached at which evidence can be given for the defence and that he can, if he wishes, give evidence and that, if he chooses not to give evidence, or, having been sworn, without good cause refuses to answer any question, it will be permissible for the court or jury to draw such inferences as appear proper from his failure to give evidence or his refusal, without good cause, to answer any question" (CJPOA, s.35(2)). (The Court of Appeal has held that if the accused absconds during the trial so that he does not receive the mandatory warning as to the effect of the failure to give evidence, the jury cannot be invited to draw adverse inferences from his failure to do so![39])

---

[37] Criminal Law Revision Committee 11th Report in 1972, *Evidence (General)*, para.110.
[38] Criminal Evidence (Northern Ireland) Order 1988, Art.4. However, the Northern Ireland procedure was brought into line with that in England and Wales—see CJPOA, Sch.10, para.61(3)(b).
[39] *Gough (Stephen)* [2001] EWCA 2545; [2002] 2 Cr.App.R. 8.

Good cause for refusal to answer questions may exist under statute or by virtue of privilege or if the court, exercising its discretion, excuses it (subs.(5)).

13–22   The court may draw such inferences from a refusal to go into the witness box as appear proper (s.35(3)). The procedure does not apply if the defendant's legal representative informs the court that the accused will give evidence or, where he is unrepresented, he says so himself. Originally, the procedure did not apply if the defendant was under 14 years old but this exception was removed by the Crime and Disorder Act 1998.[40] The procedure does not apply however where it appears to the court that "the physical or mental condition of the accused makes it undesirable for him to give evidence" (s.35(1)(b)).

Failure to give evidence does not, however, render the accused liable to proceedings for contempt of court (s.35(4)).

The implications of the case law on ss.34–38 are considered below. A *locus classicus* on s.35 is the Court of Appeal's decision in *Cowan*[41] in which Lord Taylor C.J. listed five essentials:

(1)   The judge must tell the jury that the burden of proof remains upon the prosecution throughout and what the required standard is.

(2)   The judge must make clear to the jury that the defendant has the right to remain silent.

(3)   An inference from failure to give evidence cannot on its own prove guilt.

(4)   Therefore the jury must be satisfied that the prosecution have established a case to answer before drawing any inferences from silence. The jury may not believe witnesses whose evidence the judge thought raised a *prima facie* case.

(5)   If, having considered the defence case, the jury concludes that the silence can only sensibly be attributed to the defendant's having no answer or none that would stand up to cross-examination, they may draw an adverse inference.

The procedure under s.35

13–23   The actual mechanics of the procedure as regards s.35 were laid down in Practice Direction (Crown Court: Evidence: Advice to Defendant) [1995] 1 W.L.R. 657; [1995] 2 All E.R. 499 issued on the day the new provisions came into force. Issuing the Practice Direction, the Lord Chief Justice said that if the defendant was legally represented and chose to give evidence, his legal representative should indicate this intention in open court. The case then proceeds in the normal way.

---

[40]   Crime and Disorder Act 1998, s.35(a).
[41]   [1996] Q.B. 373; [1995] 3 W.L.R. 818; [1995] 4 All E.R. 939; [1996] 1 Cr.App.R. 1, CA.

If the court is not informed that the defendant intends to give evidence or it is informed that the accused does not intend to give evidence, the judge should in the presence of the jury inquire of the lawyer in the following terms: "Have you advised your client that the stage has now been reached at which he may give evidence and if he chooses not to do so or, having been sworn, without good cause refuses to answer any questions, the jury may draw such inferences as appear proper from his failure to do so?" If the legal representative replies to the judge that the accused has been so advised, the case proceeds. If he or she says that the accused has not been so advised, the judge should briefly adjourn the case for that to be done.

If the accused is unrepresented,[42] the judge should at the conclusion of the **13–24** prosecution's case and in the presence of the jury say to the defendant:

"You have heard the evidence against you. Now is the time for you to make your defence. You may give evidence on oath, and be cross-examined like any other witness. If you do not give evidence, or having been sworn, without good cause refuse to answer any question the jury may draw such inferences as appear proper. That means they may hold it against you. You may also call any witness or witnesses whom you have arranged to attend court. Afterwards you may also, if you wish, address the jury by arguing your case from the dock. But you cannot at that stage give evidence. Do you now intend to give evidence?"

Statistics

The Crown Court Study carried out by the writer in 1992 for the Runciman Royal **13–25** Commission suggested that about one quarter of defendants in contested cases in the Crown Court did not give evidence.[43] There are no statistics as to the impact of s.35 in England and Wales since 1995 but in Northern Ireland the proportion of defendants not testifying went down after the 1988 Order, both in terrorist and in ordinary cases.[44]

Interpretation and savings for ss.34, 35, 36 and 37: s.38

Section 38 first defines "legal representative" and "place". It then makes it clear **13–26** that reference to an offence in ss.34(2), 35(3) and 37(2) includes any other offence of which the accused could be convicted on that charge.

Subsection (3) establishes the fundamental point that a person cannot be convicted solely on the basis of inferences drawn from silence (*i.e.* a failure or refusal such as is mentioned in ss.34(2), 35(3), 36(2) or 37(2)). There must always be

---

[42] Around 1% of defendants in the Crown Court are unrepresented.

[43] Zander and Henderson, *The Crown Court Study*, Royal Commission on Criminal Justice Research Study No.19 (HMSO, 1993) p.114, para.4.5.1.

[44] In terrorism cases the proportion of defendants pleading not guilty who did not testify dropped from 64% in 1987 to 46% in 1991 and in ordinary Crown Court cases it dropped from 23% in 1987 to 15% in 1991. In 1995, the proportion of defendants pleading not guilty who did not testify was 25% in terrorist cases and 3% in other Crown Court cases (Jackson *et al.* (2000), Ch.8).

some positive prosecution evidence. The same applies equally to transfer of proceedings to the Crown Court (subs.(3) and (4)).[45] But, as will be seen below, the Strasbourg Court has established a stricter test in stating that a conviction must not be based "wholly or mainly" on inferences from silence.

13–27   Subsection (5) makes it clear that the new provisions do not affect the operation of any enactment which provides that any answer or evidence[46] given by a person in certain circumstances is not admissible in evidence against him or someone else in civil or criminal proceedings. An obvious example is the provision in s.2 of the Criminal Justice Act 1987 regarding statements made to the Serious Fraud Office.

Subsection (6) states that "nothing in ss.34, 35, 36 or 37 prejudices any power of a court, in any proceedings, to exclude evidence (whether by preventing questions being put or otherwise) at its discretion". This appears to be the same reservation of the judge's overall discretion to exclude evidence as is the subject of s.82(3) of PACE—discussed at para.8–96 above.

THE CASE LAW ON THE RIGHT TO SILENCE AND THE RIGHT NOT TO INCRIMINATE ONESELF

13–28   The "right to silence" provisions in the Criminal Justice and Public Order Act 1994 have generated a huge body of case law. (Indeed, in *Brizzalari*[47] the Court of Appeal expressed its dissatisfaction with the complexities generated by the case law when it urged prosecutors not to complicate trials and summings up by invoking the 1994 Act "unless the merits of the individual case required that that should be done".)The great majority of the decisions have concerned ss.34 or 35. There have also been a number of decisions on the related but distinct issue of the right (or privilege) not to incriminate oneself. The European Court of Human Rights has given significant decisions on both the right to silence and on the right not to incriminate oneself.

13–29   The following are the main propositions that have emerged from the case law as regards adverse inferences (or "conclusions"[48]) from silence:

- *The right to silence is protected by the European Convention.* Although the European Convention does not expressly refer to the right to silence (or to the privilege against self-incrimination), the Strasbourg Court has

---

[45] Including the decision whether to dismiss charges of serious fraud under ss.4 and 6 of the Criminal Justice Act 1987 and charges of violent or sexual offences involving a child under s.53 and Sch.6, para.5 of the Criminal Justice Act 1991.

[46] This is stated to mean giving evidence in any manner "whether by furnishing information, making discovery, producing documents or otherwise" (subs.(5)).

[47] [2004] EWCA Crim 310; *The Times*, March 3, 2004.

[48] The Judicial Studies Board suggests that juries are likely to find the word "conclusions" easier to follow than "inferences".

said that both are part of the generally recognised international standards of justice and are part of the system established by the ECHR.[49]

- *The CJPOA right to silence rules are not in themselves a breach of the Convention.* The Strasbourg Court has held that permitting adverse inferences from silence is not necessarily a breach of Article 6 of the Convention.[50] In a situation which clearly calls for an explanation, silence is relevant in assessing the persuasiveness of the evidence adduced by the prosecution.[51]

- *The CJPOA aims to strike the balance.* The Strasbourg Court has held that English law and practice attempt to strike "an appropriate balance" between the right to silence and the drawing of adverse inferences.[52]

- *Strict interpretation.* Proper effect must be given to the adverse inference provisions, but because "they restrict rights recognised at common law as appropriate to protect defendants against the risk of injustice they should not be construed more widely than the statutory language requires".[53]

- "Particular caution" is required before an adverse inference can be drawn from silence during questioning.[54]

- If the defence simply put the prosecution to its proof and does not rely **13–30** on any fact—not calling witnesses or giving evidence—there is no basis for drawing adverse inferences.[55]

- *Defendant must have known the undisclosed fact.* No adverse inferences can be drawn under s.34 if the facts in question were not known to the defendant at the time when he "failed to disclose them".[56]

- *No adverse inferences if the police have made up their mind to charge.* If the officer doing the questioning already believes there is enough evidence to charge, according to Code C, para.11.4 no adverse inferences can be drawn because the interview should not have taken place.[57] But if the officer still has an open mind, an interview can proceed even if there is clear evidence of guilt.[58]

---

[49] *Murray (John) v UK* (1996) 22 E.H.R.R. 29 at para.45; *Saunders v UK* (1997) 23 E.H.R.R. 313 at para.61.
[50] *Murray (John) v UK* (1996) 22 E.H.R.R. 29 at paras 47, 51.
[51] *Condron v UK* (2001) 31 E.H.R.R. 1; 8 B.H.R.C. 290 at para.56.
[52] *Condron v UK* (2001) 31 E.H.R.R. 1; 8 B.H.R.C. 290 at para.58; *Averill v UK* (2001) 31 E.H.R.R. 36 at paras 57–58; *Magee v UK* (2001) 31 E.H.R.R. 35 at para.39.
[53] *Bowden* [1999] 2 Cr.App.R. 176 at 181, *per* Lord Bingham, CA.
[54] *Condron v UK* (2001) 31 E.H.R.R. 1; 8 B.H.R.C. 290 at para.60.
[55] *Moshaid* [1998] Crim.L.R. 420, CA.
[56] *Nickolson* [1999] Crim.L.R. 61; *Barrett*, J.P., November 20, 1999, p.922.
[57] *Pointer* [1997] Crim.L.R. 676, CA.
[58] *Gayle* [1999] Crim.L.R. 502, CA; *McGuinness* [1999] Crim.L.R. 318, CA; *Ioannou* [1999] Crim.L.R. 586, CA.

- *Reliance on a fact need not be in defendant's own evidence.* The defendant's reliance on a fact does not have to be in the form of his testimony. It can be through the evidence of other witnesses or even through cross-examination of prosecution witnesses[59] and maybe cross-examination of D or his witnesses.[60] But mere suggestion or hypothesis cannot be a foundation for adverse inferences.[61]

13–31
- Adverse inferences can be drawn from failure to mention facts even though the police did not ask questions about all the charges eventually laid—especially where the suspect could have made a note for his legal advisers.[62]

- The failure to mention a fact could relate to something said at interview no.2 which was not mentioned at interview no.1, or to something said on being charged which was not mentioned whilst being questioned or the contents of a written statement.[63] It could also relate to failure to mention something on being charged even though no adverse inferences could be drawn from earlier silence.[64]

- Adverse inferences can be drawn even though the details of the fact relied on and not mentioned to the police had been communicated to some third party.[65]

- Adverse inferences can be drawn from failure to mention a fact later relied on even though it causes no surprise to the prosecution.[66]

13–32
- Adverse inferences can be drawn (it seems) even when the truth or otherwise of the defendant's explanation for failure to mention the fact is the very question the jury has to decide in determining guilt.[67]

- A bare admission of facts in the prosecution's case are not facts relied on by the defence for the purposes of s.34.[68]

---

[59] *Bowers* [1998] Crim.L.R. 817, CA; *McLernon* [1992] N.I. 168 at 179, CA; *Chenia* [2002] EWCA Crim 2345; [2004] 1 All E.R. 543; and *Webber* [2004] UKHL 1; [2004] 1 All E.R. 770. In *Webber* the House of Lords said that "fact" should be given a broad meaning (at [33]).
[60] *Bowers* [1998] Crim.L.R. 817, CA; *Fox and Sullivan*, unreported, July 2, 1996, N.I.
[61] *Nickolson* [1999] Crim.L.R. 61; *B(MT)* [2000] Crim.L.R. 181, CA.
[62] *Napper* [1996] Crim.L.R. 591, CA.
[63] *McLernon* [1992] N.I. 168 at 179. As to written statements see *Ali* [2001] 6 *Archbold News* 2.
[64] *Dervish and Anori* [2001] EWCA Crim 2789; [2002] Cr.App.R. 6.
[65] *Taylor* [1999] Crim.L.R. 77, CA.
[66] *Fox and Sullivan*, unreported, July 2, 1996, N.I.
[67] *Hearne and Coleman* [2000] 6 *Archbold News* 2, May 4 (transcript nos 99/4240/Z4 and 99/5060/Z4), CA; *Milford*, Lexis transcript, December 20, 2000, CA; and *Gowland-Wynn* [2001] EWCA Crim 2715; [2002] 1 Cr.App.R. 41; [2002] Crim.L.R. 211 disapproving *Mountford* [1999] Crim.L.R. 575, CA and *Gill* [2001] 1 Cr.App.R. 160, CA. In *Hearne* the Court of Appeal said that *Mountford* would drive a coach-and-four through the legislation. In *Gowland-Wynn* Lord Woolf said that *Mountford* and *Gill* should be "consigned to oblivion". For helpful (and critical) commentary on this series of cases see Munday, "Inferences and Explanations" [2002] 2 *Archbold News* 6, March 26.
[68] *Betts and Hall* [2001] 2 Cr.App.R. 16; [2001] Crim.L.R. 754, CA.

- The language of ss.34, 36 and 37 indicates that adverse inferences cannot be drawn if the defendant is charged with a different offence from that with which he was charged or given warning of prosecution (s.34) or which was originally specified when he was cautioned (s.36) or arrested (s.37).

- Sections 36 and 37 do not require there to be reliance on a fact not disclosed earlier. Provided the special caution has been given, mere failure to respond to questions can result in adverse inferences.

- *Suspect must have been cautioned.* For ss.34, 36 and 37, adverse inferences can only be drawn if (a) the accused has been properly cautioned and (b) the restriction on the drawing of adverse inferences regarding an opportunity to get legal advice does not apply. For s.35, adverse inferences can only be drawn if the defendant has been made aware of the risk attached to not giving evidence.

- *There must be a prima facie case.* No adverse inference can be drawn at the trial under ss.34 or 35 unless there is a *prima facie* case against the accused.[69]

This does not mean that the police are required to present a *prima facie* case **13–33** before questioning the accused in order for silence to be the basis of adverse inferences. Certainly there is no duty to give the defence solicitor a full briefing before questioning the suspect.[70] On the other hand, failure to inform the suspect (and/or his legal adviser) of the gist of the case may be used by the defence to justify legal advice to give a no comment interview.

- *What is a prima facie case?* A *prima facie* case means one strong enough to go to the jury ("*i.e.* a case consisting of direct evidence which, if believed, could lead a properly directed jury to be satisfied beyond reasonable doubt . . . that each of the essential elements of the offence is proved").[71]

- *What is meant by "in the circumstances"?* Failure to mention a fact which "in the circumstances. . ." is not to be construed restrictively. Matters such as the time of day, the defendant's age, experience, mental capacity, state of health, sobriety, tiredness, knowledge, personality and legal advice might all be relevant.[72]

---

[69] *Cowan* [1996] Q.B. 373 at 379, CA; *Murray (Kevin)* [1994] 1 W.L.R. 1 at 4, 11; *Murray (John) v UK* (1996) 22 E.H.R.R. 29 at paras 47, 51; *Birchall* [1999] Crim.L.R. 311, CA; *cf. Doldur* [2000] Crim.L.R. 178. But see now *Gill* [2001] 1 Cr.App.R. 11, CA and *Milford* [2001] Crim.L.R. 330, CA.
[70] *Imran and Hussain* [1997] Crim.L.R. 754, CA; *Farrell* [2004] EWCA Crim 597.
[71] *Murray (Kevin)* [1994] 1 W.L.R. 1 at 4, *per* Lord Mustill.
[72] *Argent* [1997] 2 Cr.App.R. 27 at 33.

- *The actual accused.* References to the accused means the actual accused. ("When reference is made to the 'accused' attention is drawn not to some hypothetical, reasonable accused of ordinary phlegm and fortitude but to the actual accused with such qualities, apprehensions, knowledge and advice as he is shown to have had."[73]) (In the House of Lords' debates on the provisions Lord Taylor C.J. emphasised that the courts would be vigilant to protect the vulnerable from adverse inferences that it would be unfair to draw from silence.[74])

13–34
- *Is the defendant in condition to give evidence?* If the defence want to argue that the defendant's physical or mental state make it undesirable that he give evidence (s.35(1)(b)) they must establish that that is the case by evidence—usually of experts. It is not for the court to take the point of its own motion.[75] By definition, the incapacity will be something less than what makes a defendant unfit to plead. The judge must first decide, in a *voir dire*, whether it is "undesirable" for the defendant to give evidence. There is no test; it is up to the judge. If he declines to make such a ruling and the defendant does not give evidence, the jury, having heard the evidence, will then decide whether or not to draw adverse inferences.[76]

- *Once in the witness box the defendant risks adverse inferences for failing to answer questions.* The defendant must answer questions or have adverse inferences drawn unless he has a statutory right not to answer or he can raise a ground of privilege or the court exercises its general discretion.[77]

- *No adverse inference unless legal advice available.* The Strasbourg Court has ruled that even in terrorism cases the accused must be given the opportunity of legal advice from the initial stages of interrogation.[78]

- The requirement that legal advice must be offered before questioning is not affected by whether the suspect is silent after he has received advice and is irrespective of whether overall the suspect is denied a fair trial.[79]

13–35
- *The effect of legal advice to be silent.* The initial approach of the English courts was that legal advice to exercise the right to silence was not a magic wand to give protection against adverse inferences. The jury was to be directed that they had to decide whether the defendant's

---

[73] *Argent* [1997] 2 Cr.App.R. 27 at 33.
[74] House of Lords, *Hansard,* Vol.555, May 23, 1994, col.520.
[75] *Anderson* [1997] Crim.L.R. 883, CA.
[76] *Friend* [1997] 1 W.L.R. 1433; [1997] 2 All E.R. 1011, CA.
[77] *Ackinclose* [1996] Crim.L.R. 747, CA.
[78] *Murray (John) v UK* (1996) 22 E.H.R.R. 29 at para.66; *Averill v UK* (2001) 31 E.H.R.R. 36 at para.57. These decisions were reflected in the Youth Justice and Criminal Evidence Act 1999, s.58 and Code C, Annex C. See further paras 5–153—5–157 above.
[79] *Murray (John) v UK* (1996) 22 E.H.R.R. 29; *Averill v UK* (2001) 31 E.H.R.R. 36; *Magee v UK* (2001) 31 E.H.R.R. 35.

conduct in acting on the advice was reasonable in all the circumstances. It was not the correctness of the advice or whether it complied with the Law Society's guidelines but the reasonableness of relying on it that was critical.[80] But this approach has had to be revised in light of the Strasbourg Court's decision in *Condron v UK* (see below). As Professor Ian Dennis has said in regard to the Strasbourg Court's insistence that the suspect must have been offered legal advice, "What is the point of insisting that a person should have access to legal advice before being interviewed if the jury is to be given the opportunity to say that although he relied on the advice to remain silent he should not have done so?".[81]

- *What are good reasons for a lawyer advising silence?* One way for the defendant to hope to persuade the jury that he was silent on legal advice is simply to state this without embellishment. The defendant then cannot be pressed in cross-examination to give the reasons for the advice. (See Wolchover, "An obituary for inferences on police station silence" [2002] 6 *Archbold News* 3.) The alternative is to give an explanation. Good reasons for advising silence might be, for instance, that the suspect is of low intelligence,[82] that the interviewing officer has disclosed little or nothing of the case against the suspect,[83] or where the nature of the offence or the material in the hands of the police is so complex or relates to matters so long ago that no sensible immediate response is feasible.[84] Drug withdrawal may not be a good reason—at least without solid medical evidence.[85] (See further paras 13–41 and 13–51— 13–58 below.)

- *Is mention of the solicitor's advice to be silent inadmissible hearsay?* **13–36** The defendant's statement that he was silent on legal advice is not inadmissible as hearsay provided that the purpose is limited to explaining why D decided to remain silent. It would be hearsay to rely on the solicitor's words as evidence of their truth.[86]

- *When is legal privilege waived?* The inquiry into the reasonableness or otherwise of relying on legal advice may lead to the privilege arising from the lawyer-client relationship to be deemed to have been waived with the result that the lawyer may have to give evidence about the advice given. Evidence from the defendant that he was advised to be silent does not waive the privilege but if he goes into the matter by

---

[80] *Argent* [1997] 2 Cr.App.R. 27 at 35–36; *Roble* [1997] Crim.L.R. 449, CA.
[81] Dennis, "Silence in the Police Station" [2002] Crim.L.R. 25 at 34.
[82] *R. v Condron and Condron* [1997] 1 W.L.R. 827 at 837.
[83] *Roble* [1997] Crim.L.R. 449, CA—but see *Imran and Hussain* [1997] Crim.L.R. 754, CA.
[84] *Roble* [1997] Crim.L.R. 449, CA.
[85] *Kavanagh*, unreported, Case No.9503897, February 7, 1997, CA.
[86] *Daniel* [1998] 2 Cr.App.R. 373, CA; *Davis (Desmond)* [1998] Crim.L.R. 659, CA.

explaining the reasons for the advice or the circumstances that could be a waiver of the privilege.[87]

- *The pressure to waive legal privilege to explain silence is not a breach of Article 6 of the ECHR.* In *Condron v UK* the Strasbourg Court said that the defendants had been under no compulsion to disclose the advice given by their solicitor other than the indirect compulsion to avoid the reason for their silence remaining at the level of a bare explanation. "The applicants chose to make the content of their solicitor's advice a live issue as part of their defence. For that reason they cannot complain that the scheme of s.34 is such as to override the confidentiality of their discussions with their solicitors."[88]

- Calling the solicitor to rebut an inference of subsequent fabrication by evidence that the fact was communicated to him by the defendant at or about the time of the interview is not a waiver of privilege.[89]

- *Effect of prepared statement.* Where the defendant hands the police a full pre-prepared statement which covers all the facts later relied on at his trial and then refuses to answer any questions, adverse inferences cannot be drawn from failure to answer police questions.[90]

PROCEDURE

13–37
- *Should the prosecution initially go into details of silence?* Evidence of the failure to mention the fact in question can be given either before or after evidence tending to establish the fact.[91] In dealing with the matter initially, the prosecution should normally just state that the defendant, after being cautioned, did not answer questions. If and when he gives evidence and mentions facts which in the view of prosecution counsel he could reasonably have been expected to mention in interview, he can then be questioned as to why he did not mention them and his answers can be tested in cross-examination.[92]

- *Submissions made in absence of the jury.* In the Crown Court the issue is normally put to the judge in the absence of the jury at the conclusion of the evidence.[93]

---

[87] *R. v Condron and Condron* [1997] 1 W.L.R. 827 at 837; *Bowden,* n.53 above, at 183–184; *Roble,* n.80 above. See generally Wright, "The Solicitor in the Witness Box" [1998] Crim.L.R. 44.
[88] *Condron v UK* (2001) 31 E.H.R.R. 1; 8 B.H.R.C. 290 at para.60.
[89] *R. v Condron and Condron* [1997] 1 W.L.R. 827 at 837; *Bowden* [1999] 2 Cr.App.R. 176 at 182–183.
[90] *Knight* [2003] EWCA 1977; [2004] 1 W.L.R. 340; [2004] 1 Cr.App.R. 9. See also *Turner* [2003] EWCA Crim 3108; [2004] 1 Cr.App.R. 24; [2004] 1 All E.R. 1025.
[91] *R. v Condron and Condron* [1997] 1 W.L.R. 827 at 836;
[92] *ibid.; Griffin* [1998] Crim.L.R. 418, CA.
[93] *ibid.,* at 837.

- *Timing of submissions on right to silence issues*. Though the issue can be raised earlier, submissions should normally be made in the absence of the jury at the conclusion of all the evidence. If the judge rules that no adverse inferences can be drawn the jury will have to do their best to expunge from their collective memory the effect of any cross-examination regarding the defendant's silence.[94]

THE JUDGE'S DIRECTIONS TO THE JURY

- The judge should give the jury the standard direction issued from time to time by the Judicial Studies Board.[95] ("Standard directions are devised to serve the ends of justice and the court must be astute to ensure that these ends are not jeopardised by failure to give directions where they are called for."[96])   **13–38**

- The judge should discuss any proposed direction with counsel before closing speeches.[97]

- It is exceptional for the judge to withdraw the case from the jury.[98] If it is decided that no direction is to be given, the jury should be specifically told that they should not draw adverse inferences from silence[99]— although if this does not happen it does not necessarily render the conviction unsafe.[1]

- Although the judge should normally direct the jury regarding the drawing of inferences, he should ordinarily leave the issue to the jury to decide. ("Only rarely would it be right for the judge to direct the jury that they should, or should not, draw the appropriate inference".[2])

- The judge must tell the jury that the burden of proof remains throughout on the prosecution.[3]

---

[94] *Griffin* [1998] Crim.L.R. 418, CA.
[95] The Specimen Directions on ss.34–37 with valuable accompanying footnotes are now extensive (and are accessible on the Judicial Studies Board (JSB) website—*www.jsboard.co.uk*). The revised version, issued in July 2001, ran to seven A4 pages for s.34 and nearly five pages for s.35. There are equivalent Specimen Directions for ss.36 and 37.
[96] *Birchall* [1999] Crim.L.R. 311, CA. See also *Cowan* [1996] Q.B. 373 at 380–381; *Price* [1996] Crim.L.R. 738, CA; *Byrne*, unreported, November 21, 1995, CA. In *Pektar and Farquhar* [2003] EWCA Crim 2668; [2004] 1 Cr.App.R. 22; [2004] Crim.L.R. 157, Rix L.J. identified no fewer than eight matters which should be dealt with in a "well crafted and careful direction on s.34".
[97] This is specifically stated in the JSB's Specimen Directions, Pt IV, Directions 39, 40. See also *Chenia* [2002] EWCA Crim 2345; [2004] 1 All E.R. 543 at [36].
[98] *Argent* [1997] 2 Cr.App.R. 27 at 33.
[99] *McGarry* [1999] 1 Cr.App.R. 377, CA.
[1] *Bowers* [1998] Crim.L.R. 817, CA; *Taylor* [1999] Crim.L.R. 77, CA; *Francom* [2001] 1 Cr.App.R. 17; [2000] Crim.L.R. 1018, CA.
[2] *Argent* [1997] 2 Cr.App.R. 27 at 33.
[3] *Cowan* [1996] Q.B. 373 at 381.

13–39 • The judge must tell the jury that the defendant is entitled to remain silent.[4] Thus, the Specimen Direction on s.34 says: "Before his interview(s) the defendant was cautioned. He was first told that he need not say anything. It was therefore his right to remain silent." The Specimen Direction on s.35 says: "The defendant has not given evidence. That is his right. He is entitled to remain silent and to require the prosecution to make you sure of his guilt. You must not assume he is guilty because he has not given evidence."

• Under s.34 the judge will tell the jury that the suspect was warned by the police officer that it might harm his defence if he did not mention when questioned something which he later relied on in court. As part of his defence the defendant did rely on certain facts [and the judge will then enumerate the facts to which the direction applies]. The prosecution say that he failed to mention those facts when he was questioned by the police. "If you are sure that is so, his failure to do so may count against him. This is because you may draw the conclusion from his failure that he [had no answer then/had no answer that he then believed would stand up to scrutiny/has since invented his account/has since tailored his account to fit the prosecution's case/or whatever other reasonable inference is contended for]. If you do draw that conclusion, you must not convict him wholly or mainly on the strength of it but you may take it into account as some additional support for the prosecution's case."[5]

• Under s.35, having told the jury that they must try the case on the evidence and that the defendant has not given evidence, the judge will tell them that silence at the trial may count against the defendant. The Specimen Direction says: "This is because you may draw the conclusion that he has not given evidence because he has no answer to the prosecution's case, or none that would bear examination. If you do draw that conclusion, you must not convict him wholly or mainly on the strength of it, but you may treat it as some additional support for the prosecution's case."

13–40 • The Specimen Directions regarding ss.34–37 each state that the jury must be told that they may only draw such a conclusion against the defendant "if you think it is a fair and proper conclusion".

• They should be told that they may do so only if they are satisfied that there is a case to answer before any question of an adverse inference

---

[4] *Cowan* [1996] Q.B. 373 at 378, 381.
[5] In *Cowan* [1996] Q.B. 373 at para.12–42, Lord Taylor said: "The effect of section 35 is that the ... jury may regard the inference from failure to testify as, in effect, a further evidential factor in support of the prosecution's case". In *Murray (John) v UK* (1996) 22 E.H.R.R. 29 at para.47, the ECHR spoke of the accused's silence being ". . . taken into account in assessing the persuasiveness of the evidence adduced by the prosecution" and when deciding whether his [evidence/case] about these facts is true".

can arise.[6] The Specimen Directions on ss.34–37 each say that the jury should be told that they must be satisfied that "the prosecution's case against him is so strong that it clearly calls for an answer by him".

- The judge must remind the jury what, if any, explanation the defence gave for silence and the evidence[7] adduced in that regard. He must direct them as follows "If you (accept the evidence) and think this amounts to a reason why you should not draw any conclusion from his silence, do not do so. Otherwise, subject to what I have said, you may do so."

- *Function of s.78 of PACE.* Section 78 has little function in this context. Ordinarily the proper course is for a trial judge to allow evidence as to the defendant's silence to be given and to direct a jury carefully concerning the drawing of inferences.[8]

- *Legal advice.* If there is evidence that the defendant declined to answer questions or to give evidence on legal advice, the judge must direct the jury on that matter. The Strasbourg Court in *Condron* ruled that the jury must give appropriate weight to the fact that the accused was advised to be silent by his legal adviser. The court held that the judge's direction to the jury in that instance did not reflect the required balance between the right to silence and the drawing of adverse inferences because although the judge did remind the jury of the Condrons' explanation that they had been silent on legal advice that they were unfit to be interviewed, "he did so in terms which left the jury at liberty to draw an adverse inference notwithstanding that it may have been satisfied as to the plausibility of the explanation".[9] In *Betts and Hall*[10] Kay L.J. stated: "If it is a plausible explanation that the reason for not mentioning facts is that the [defendant] acted on the advice of his solicitor and not because he had no, or no satisfactory, answer to give then no inference can be drawn".[11] The court went on to give a model direction emphasising that the jury's task is to make a decision of fact and causation. If the jury thinks that the defendant was hiding behind the legal advice because he had no story to give, adverse inferences would be legitimate. But if the jury concludes that legal advice was genuinely the reason for failure to mention facts, no adverse inferences can be drawn.

13–41

---

[6] *Cowan* [1996] Q.B. 373 at 381; *Birchall* [1999] Crim.L.R. 311 at 312; *Gill* [2001] 1 Cr.App.R. 11, CA. The need for such a passage in s.34 cases was challenged by Auld L.J. in *Doldur* [2000] Crim.L.R. 178, but the weight of authority is to the contrary.

[7] It must be evidence. In *Cowan* Lord Taylor C.J. said: "We wish to make it clear that the rule against advocates giving evidence dressed up as a submission applies in this context. It cannot be proper for a defence advocate to give the jury reasons for his client's silence at trial in the absence of evidence to support such reasons" ([1996] Q.B. 373 at 383; [1995] 3 W.L.R. 818 at 826; [1995] 4 All E.R. 939 at 996–947). The JSB's Specimen Direction No.40 on s.34, n.17, says "These remarks apply equally to section 34 and 35 cases".

[8] *Argent* [1997] 2 Cr.App.R. 27 at 31; *Kavanagh*, unreported, Case No.9503897, February 7, 1997, CA.

[9] *Condron v UK* (2001) 31 E.H.R.R. 1; 8 B.H.R.C. 290 at [61]. See also *Averill v UK* (2001) 31 E.H.R.R. 36 at [33].

[10] [2001] 2 Cr.App.R. 257.

[11] [2001] 2 Cr.App.R. 257 at 270.

See also the Strasbourg Court's decision in *Beckles v UK* (2003) 36 E.H.R.R. 13 in which the court unanimously held that there had been a breach of the applicant's right to a fair trial because of shortcomings in the judge's summing up. Quoting *Betts v Hall*, the Court noted at [64] that the Court of Appeal had recently emphasised the importance of giving due weight to an accused's reliance on legal advice to explain his failure to respond to police questioning. A more disparaging view however, was expressed by Laws L.J. in *Howell*: "the public interest that inheres in reasonable disclosure by a suspected person of what he has to say when faced with a set of facts which accuse him, is thwarted if currency is given to the belief that if a suspect remains silent on legal advice he may systematically avoid adverse comment at his trial. And it may encourage solicitors to advise silence for other than good objective reasons."[12]

13–42   The Specimen Direction issued by the Judicial Studies Board says that the fact that the defendant was advised not to answer questions by his legal adviser is important but it does not automatically prevent the jury from drawing a conclusion about his silence. Having taken into account all the circumstances, including the age of the defendant, the advice given, and the complexity of the facts:

"decide whether the defendant could reasonably have been expected to mention the facts on which he now relies. If, for example, you considered that he had or may have had an answer to give, but genuinely relied on the legal advice to remain silent, you should not draw any conclusion against him. But if, for example, you were sure that the defendant had no answer, and merely latched onto the legal advice as a convenient shield behind which to hide, you would be entitled to draw a conclusion against him. . ." (Specimen Direction No.40).

In *Hoare and Pierce* [2004] EWCA Crim 784, the Court of Appeal held that when the defendant remains silent on legal advice, the test for the jury of whether it was reasonable is objective not subjective. So it is not enough that the jury believes that the accused genuinely relied on legal advice as a reason for silence. They must also believe that it was reasonable for him to have done so. In *Beckles* [2004] EWCA Crim 2766 the Court of Appeal said that a revised Judicial Studies Board direction was in draft "which would direct the jury to consider whether the defendant genuinely *and reasonably* relied on the legal advice to remain silent" (emphasis supplied). "Genuinely and reasonably" seems likely to be the new governing formula. (See further paras 13–52—13–58 below.)

- The procedural niceties must be scrupulously observed.[13]

---

[12] [2003] EWCA Crim 1; [2003] Crim.L.R. 405. The Court of Appeal held that the judge had been entitled to withdraw from the jury the question whether the defendant had reasonably relied on legal advice when giving a no comment interview. For critical discussion see Choo and Jennings, "Silence on legal advice revisited: *R v Howell*", (2003) 7 *International Journal of Evidence and Proof* at 185–190.
[13] *Birchall* [1999] Crim.L.R. 311, CA; *Price* [1996] Crim.L.R. 738, CA; *Byrne*, unreported, November 21, 1995, CA (95/4159/W4); *Allan* [2004] EWCA 2236—conviction for murder quashed.

THE JURY'S DECISION

- Having a jury decide whether adverse inferences should be drawn is not a breach of the ECHR.[14]   **13–43**

- *What inferences can be drawn?* The jury may draw whatever inferences they think proper.[15]

- *The test is common sense.* The common sense of the jury is the key factor.[16]

- The jury can draw adverse inferences not only if they consider that there is no explanation for silence or none that will stand up to cross-examination (recent fabrication) but also if they take the view that the defendant is simply reluctant to have his story be the subject of questioning and investigation [17–18] The Specimen Direction under s.34 says they must be satisfied that the "only sensible explanation" for the defendant's failure to mention the facts in question is "that he had no answer at the time or none that would stand up to scrutiny". The equivalent under s.35 is "that the only sensible explanation for his silence is that he has no answer, or none that would bear examination".

- *Reasons for not drawing adverse inferences.* There are "a host of reasons" why the jury may decide that the accused's silence was reasonable—"such as that he was tired, ill, frightened, drunk, drugged, unable to understand what was going on, suspicious of the police, afraid that his answer would not be fairly recorded, worried at committing himself without legal advice, acting on legal advice or some other reason accepted by the jury".[19] The Strasbourg Court has said that legal advice is "a powerful justification for maintaining silence" but there may be other reasons why an innocent person would not answer questions.[20]   **13–44**

---

[14] "The fact that the issue of the applicant's silence was left to a jury cannot of itself be considered incompatible with the requirements of a fair trial" though it was "another relevant consideration to be weighed in the balance" in deciding whether there had been a fair trial (*Condron v UK* (2001) 31 E.H.R.R. 1; 8 B.H.R.C. 290 at para.57).

[15] *Cowan* [1996] Q.B. 373 at 381–382; *Beckles and Montague* [1999] Crim.L.R. 148, CA; *Argent* [1997] 2 Cr.App.R. 27 at 32.

[16] *Murray (Kevin)* [1994] 1 W.L.R. 1 at 12, *per* Lord Slynn; Argent [1997] 2 Cr.App.R. 27 at 33.

[17–18] *Roble* [1997] Crim.L.R. 449, CA; *Daniel* [1998] 2 Cr.App.R. 373, CA; *Taylor* [1999] Crim.L.R. 77, CA; *Beckles and Montague* [1999] Crim.L.R. 148, CA.

[19] *Argent* [1997] 2 Cr.App.R. 27 at 33.

[20] *Averill v UK* (2001) 31 E.H.R.R. 36 at para.47.

• The crux of the matter is whether the reason given for not mentioning the fact was genuine. Adverse inferences should only be drawn where the jury decides that the real reason why the defendant failed to mention a fact relied on is that he had no answer to the allegation or none that would stand up to questioning and investigation.[21]

ROLE OF COURT OF APPEAL AND OF THE STRASBOURG COURT

13–45
• The Court of Appeal is very reluctant to interfere with the trial judge's discretion as to the drawing of inferences from silence.[22]

• The Strasbourg Court may find that there was a breach of the Art.6 of the European Convention requirement of a fair trial even though in the view of the Court of Appeal the verdict was safe. The two tests are somewhat different.[23]

The right not to incriminate oneself
13–46

The privilege against self-incrimination means that it is not permissible to use in evidence in a criminal case answers given to questions put under the threat of prosecution for refusing to answer. Until recently there were many statutory exceptions to the rule, in particular in relation to company investigations conducted by the Department of Trade and Industry, the Inland Revenue, HM Customs, the Office of Fair Trading and others. Another exception was the powers enjoyed by the Serious Fraud Office. The compulsory powers available to each of the relevant authorities differed somewhat but typically they included the power to put questions orally and in writing, to seek the production of documents and in some instances to seek explanations regarding the documents produced. A refusal to comply with such requests without reasonable excuse was treated either as a contempt of court or as the commission of a separate criminal offence. Refusal to answer such questions or to produce such documents resulted in prosecution. If answers were given or documents were produced they could be used in evidence in subsequent criminal proceedings against the person who had supplied them.

But in 1997 in *Saunders*[24] the European Court of Human Rights held that use by the prosecution in a criminal trial of answers given to DTI inspectors during their investigations violated the Convention, Art.6(1) rights of the defendant to a fair trial. This far-reaching decision was given effect by the Youth Justice and

---

[21] *Betts and Hall* [2001] 2 Cr.App.R. 257; [2001] Crim.L.R. 754, CA.
[22] *Cowan* [1996] Q.B. 373 at 382, CA.
[23] *Condron v UK* (2001) 31 E.H.R.R. 1; 8 B.H.R.C. 290 at para.65; *Gill* [2001] 1 Cr.App.R. 11 at [29]; [2000] Crim.L.R. 922, CA.
[24] *Saunders v UK* (1997) 23 E.H.R.R. 313.

Criminal Evidence Act 1999, s.59 and Sch.3 repealing a variety of statutory powers to use such information in evidence in criminal proceedings.[25]

What is not yet clear is how far the principle extends. In *R. v Hertfordshire County Council, Ex p. Green Environmental Industries*[26] the House of Lords unanimously held that the rule established in *Saunders* did not apply to questions put by a local authority under the Environmental Protection Act 1990, s.71(2) because the request for responses did not form even a preliminary part of any criminal proceedings and accordingly Art.6 was not relevant. The European jurisprudence was firmly anchored to the fairness of the trial and was not concerned with extra-judicial activities. Although the local authority had power to prosecute in criminal proceedings, its request for responses under s.71(2) could not be described as an adjudication, either in form or substance. Nor had the request invited any admission of wrongdoing. Therefore the questions had to be answered.

13–47

In September 2000 the Strasbourg Court seemed to approve the distinction drawn by Lord Hoffmann in *Ex p. Green* (above). It gave judgment in a case brought by three defendants convicted with Ernest Saunders in the case arising out of the takeover of the Distillers company by Guinness.[27] Like Saunders, they had been questioned by inspectors appointed by the DTI under powers of compulsion and the transcripts had then been used by the prosecution in the subsequent trial. Applying its ruling in *Saunders* the Court held that this was a breach of Art.6(1). But it did not agree with the applicants' contention that the DTI's compulsory powers of questioning infringed Art.6: "The applicants are not correct in their assertion that a legal requirement for an individual to give information demanded by an administrative body necessarily infringes Article 6 of the Convention. The Court considers that whether or not information obtained under compulsory powers by such a body violates the right to a fair hearing must be seen from the standpoint of the use made of that information at trial."[28]

In some circumstances, despite *Saunders*, the fruits of compulsory questioning may be usable in a prosecution. This was the conclusion in December 2000 of the Judicial Committee of the Privy Council in *Brown v Stott (Procurator Fiscal, Dunfermline)*.[29] The five Law Lords unanimously held that s.172(2)(a) of the Road Traffic Act 1988, which requires a vehicle's keeper who is suspected of being guilty of an offence to provide information as to the identity of the driver, is not a breach of a defendant's right to a fair trial under Art.6 of the Convention. The High Court of Justiciary in Scotland had held that when a police officer who suspected someone of driving while drunk asked that person whether he had driven the car and the reply was used in evidence in a drink-driving case the Art.6 right to a fair trial was infringed. The court applied the Strasbourg Court's ruling

13–48

---

[25] For critical comment on the *Saunders* decision see Andrews, "Hiding Behind the Veil: Financial Delinquency and the Law" (1997) 22 Eur.L.Rev. 369; Davies, "Self Incrimination, Fair Trials, and the Pursuit of Corporate and Financial Wrongdoing", in *The Impact of the Human Rights Bill of English Law* (Oxford University Press, 1998); and Lord Justice Sedley, "Wringing out the Fault: Self Incrimination in the 21st Century" (2001) 52 *Northern Ireland Legal Quarterly* 108–206.

[26] [2000] 2 A.C. 412; [2002] 2 W.L.R. 373; [2000] 1 All E.R. 773.

[27] *IJL, GMR, AKP v UK* (2001) 33 E.H.R.R. 12; [2001] Crim.L.R. 133.

[28] para.100.

[29] [2001] 2 W.L.R. 817; [2001] 2 All E.R. 97, PC.

in *Saunders*. The Privy Council, which heard the appeal said that the rule protecting self-incrimination was not expressly mentioned in the Convention anymore than was the right to silence. Both were implied in the right to a fair trial. Neither was absolute. Qualification of the privilege was permissible if such qualification was directed towards a clear and legitimate objective and was proportionate to that objective. Inherent in the whole of the Convention was the need for a fair balance between the general interests of the community and the personal rights of the individual. Danger caused by motor vehicles was a serious social problem that had to be addressed in an effective way by regulatory systems that provided for enforcement by identifying, prosecuting and punishing offending drivers. Section 172 properly applied did not represent a disproportionate response to this serious problem nor did it undermine the defendant's right to a fair trial. There was no prolonged questioning as there had been in *Saunders*. The section provided for the putting of a simple question, the answer to which did not in itself incriminate the suspect since it is not an offence to drive. The penalty for not answering was moderate. Everyone who drives knowingly subjects himself to a regulatory regime because of the potential to cause grave injury.[30]

13–49   It remains to be seen whether the kind of balancing exercise favoured by the Privy Council in the *Brown* case is upheld by the Strasbourg Court. In *Saunders* the court said: "The general requirements of fairness contained in Article 6, including the right not to incriminate oneself, apply to criminal proceedings in respect of all types of criminal offence without distinction from the most simple to the most complex. The public interest cannot be invoked to justify the use of answers compulsorily obtained in a non-judicial investigation to incriminate the accused during the trial proceedings."[31] These words are difficult to reconcile with the Privy Council's decision in *Brown*.[32] The Strasbourg Court held unanimously that making it a criminal offence[33] punishable by six months imprisonment, for a person detained on suspicion of a terrorist offence to refuse to give a full account to the police of, *inter alia*, his movements and actions during a specified period, violated the privilege against self-incrimination under Art.6 of the Convention.[34]

     The emerging jurisprudence of the Strasbourg Court raises a doubt whether the Privy Council in *Brown v Stott* was right to apply a balancing or proportionality test.[35]

---

[30] In *DPP v Wilson* [2001] EWHC Admin 198; [2002] R.T.R. 6 the Divisional Court applied the decision in *Brown* to the wider requirement in s.172(2)(b) that "any other person" give any information which it is in his power to give and which may lead to the identification of the driver. In *Mawdesley and Yorke v Chief Constable of Cheshire* [2003] EWHC 1586 (Admin); [2004] 1 All E.R. 58; [2004] Crim.L.R. 232 the decision in *Brown v Stott* was applied to speeding.

[31] *Saunders v UK* (1997) 23 E.H.R.R. 313 at para.74.

[32] See also *Heaney and McGuiness v Ireland* (2000) 33 E.H.R.R. 264 and *Quinn v Ireland*, December 2000, ECHR. The two decisions were in similar terms. Both were decided by the Strasbourg Court on December 21, 2000. For *Heaney and McGuiness* and commentary by Professor Andrew Ashworth see also [2001] Crim.L.R. 481; and by Judith Seddon, New L.J., January 18, 2002, p.50.

[33] Under Offences Against the State Act 1939, s.52.

[34] Similarly, in *J.B. v Switzerland* [2001] Crim.L.R. 748, the Strasbourg Court held that the imposition of fines by tax authorities for refusal to furnish documents was a breach of Art.6.

[35] For discussion see Professor Andrew Ashworth's very full note on the case, *op.cit.*, n.32, at 482–485, his "The Self-Incrimination Saga" (2001) 5 *Archbold News* 5, and "Criminal proceedings after the Human Rights Act: the first year" [2001] Crim.L.R. 855 at 866–868. See also Pillay, "Self-incrimination and Article 6: the decision of the Privy Council in *Procurator v Brown*" [2001] E.H.R.L.R. 78 at 78–84.

The Court of Appeal held in 1998 that answers produced under compulsion **13–50** can be used in proceedings for the disqualification of directors—*R. v Secretary of State for Trade and Industry, Ex p. McCormick*.[36] In *Kearns*[37] in March 2002 the Court of Appeal rejected an argument that s.354(3)(a) of the Insolvency Act 1986 which made it an offence to fail without reasonable excuse to account for the loss of property was incompatible with the right against self-incrimination protected by Art.6(1) of the ECHR.

In *Saunders* the Strasbourg Court said that compulsorily taking real evidence which has an existence independent of the will of the accused—such as a blood or urine specimen, DNA sample, breath test or even documents taken under a warrant—is not subject to the rule against self-incrimination.[38] This was applied by the Court of Appeal in respect of books and papers handed over under compulsion in connection with bankruptcy proceedings[39] and by the Strasbourg Court itself in regard to recorded voice samples taken from suspects in the police station by trickery.[40] For discussion see the comment on the case, [2001] Crim.L.R. at 737, and Henderson, "Defining the limits" (2001) 145 Sol.J. 432.

Lord Mustill's six meanings of the right to silence in *Smith v Director of* **13–51** *Serious Fraud Office* (see para.13–01 above) dealt only with immunities concerned with being questioned whereas the underlying principle is that no one should be obliged to provide evidence against themselves—which extends beyond being questioned. The exception for real evidence is therefore illogical— explicable perhaps in terms of crime control.

The right to silence provisions pose serious problems for lawyers advising their clients. The Law Society has issued guidance to solicitors as to how they should deal with the issue.[41] In the original version of this advice, issued before the law came into effect, the Law Society sounded a bold almost defiant note: "You should not be panicked into thinking that these changes mean that you have to adopt a completely different approach to formulating your advice to a client. In practical terms, the change makes little difference to the actual advice you

---

[36] *The Times*, February 10, 1998, CA.

[37] [2002] EWCA Crim 748; (2002) 4 *Archbold News* 1: "A law will not be likely to infringe the right to silence or not to incriminate oneself if it demands the production of information for an administrative purpose or in the course of an extra-judicial inquiry. However, if the information so produced is or could be used in subsequent judicial proceedings, whether criminal or civil, then the use of the information in such proceedings could breach those rights and so make the trial unfair. Whether that is the case will depend on all the circumstances of the case but in particular: (a) whether the information demanded is factual or an admission of guilt; and (b) whether the demand for the information and its subsequent use in proceedings is proportionate to the particular social or economic problem that the relevant law is intended to address." Here the demand for information was made in the course of an extra-judicial procedure and was not made to prove a case against the appellant by coercion or oppression; the demand was not made to prove another charge; there was no possibility that the information would be used in subsequent criminal proceedings; and, finally, if s.354(3)(a) did infringe the right to silence, this was amply justified in the field of bankruptcy where there is an obvious need to impose a duty of co-operation on the bankrupt person.

[38] *Saunders v UK* (1997) 23 E.H.R.R. 313 at para.69.

[39] *Attorney-General's Reference (No.7 of 2000)* [2001] 1 W.L.R. 1879; [2001] 2 Cr.App.R. 19; [2001] Crim.L.R. 736.

[40] *PG and JH v UK* [2002] Crim.L.R. 308.

[41] Originally published in the Law Society's *Criminal Practitioners Newsletter* in October 1994. The latest version, by Professor Ed Cape, was issued with Issue 54 of the *Newsletter* in October 2003. Professor Cape updated the advice in Issue 55, January 2004 and Issue 58, October 2004.

give." But in the October 2003 version, the tone was markedly different: "Solicitors should approach the issue of advising clients on silence with extreme caution and should explain to clients that the fact that they are advising them to remain silent will not necessarily prevent inferences being drawn." (p.7)

13–52   The Law Society's 2003 advice started by rehearsing the basic features of the law:

- The failure to mention facts later relied on must occur before charge or on being charged.

- The suspect must have been cautioned.

- The questioning must be directed to trying to discover whether or by whom the alleged offence was committed.

- The accused's failure must be to mention any fact relied on in his defence.

- The accused could reasonably have been expected in the circumstances existing at the time to have mentioned those facts.

13–53   It then considered the effect of legal advice, especially in light of the decisions in *Betts and Hall* and *Howell*. It concluded that the position was unclear since, according to *Howell,* inferences could be drawn even if the jury was satisfied that legal advice was a genuine reason for silence. There was no way of knowing what the courts would accept as "soundly based objective reasons for silence". (As has been seen, the test is objective.[42] In *Beckles*[43] the Court of Appeal said that even if the jury considered that the defendant genuinely relied on the advice that was not necessarily the end of the matter. If for instance he acted on the advice but did so because it suited his purpose that might mean he was not acting reasonably. It was for the jury to decide whether acting on the advice was reasonable.)

13–54   In advising the client the solicitor had to balance the risks. The following were among the relevant factors:

- *How much information have the police disclosed?* A record should be kept of what has been disclosed prior to interview. If the police make disclosure gradually, the advice to the client should be reconsidered at each stage.

- *The nature of the case.* Silence would be justifiable where the material in the hands of the police was so complex or related to matters so long ago, that no sensible immediate response was appropriate.

---

[42] *Hoare and Pierce* [2004] EWCA Crim 784.
[43] [2004] EWCA Crim 2766.

- *The circumstances of the suspect.* Relevant factors would be ill-health, mental disorder or vulnerability, confusion, intoxication, shock etc. If possible, evidence of the suspect's condition should be obtained from an appropriate doctor or other health care professional. The solicitor should make a careful record of the condition.

- *The apparent strength of the police case.* The stronger the case, the more likely that the court (and the jury) would expect an explanation from the suspect.

- *The client's instructions.* If, on the basis of his instructions, the solici-   **13–55**
tor concluded that the client was guilty of the offence charged and if the police evidence was strong, he should consider the potential pros and cons of making admissions—including the likely effect on sentence or on alternatives to prosecution *e.g.* caution, final warning or reprimand. But if the police evidence was weak, or the solicitor did not know the strength of the police case, the solicitor should consider the pros and cons of remaining silent at that stage. If the client had a defence, the solicitor should consider the dangers of not putting it forward in interview and the best tactical approach to adopt—answering questions or making a written statement. The advice concluded this section by reminding solicitors that it was their duty to advise and to act in the client's best interests which might mean "advising silence even in the absence of reasons recognised by the courts as 'good' reasons" (p.10).

- *Waiver of privilege.* The advice then considered waiver of privilege. Citing *Bowden*[44] it warned that, "If the accused or his or her lawyer, tells the police of the reasons for the advice, or gives evidence of the basis or reasons for the advice, this is likely to amount to waiver of privilege. . . Normally therefore the solicitor should not tell the police nor state in the police interview the reason(s) for advice given to the client." (pp.10–11). An exception would be if the reason did not require reference to information obtained or advice given in priviliged circumstances—for example that the detention or the interview were considered to be unlawful.

- *Keeping a record.* The advice urged the importance of the solicitor   **13–56**
keeping a full record of all relevant matters: the physical and mental state of the suspect; the conduct of the police; what the police allege was said by the suspect before the arrival of the lawyer; what information was disclosed by the police; what requests for information and disclosure were made by the solicitor; what instructions were given by the client; the suspect's apparent understanding regarding the allegation and the significance of his replies or failure to respond; what advice was given by the solicitor, and the reasons for the advice; what was said during the interview and at the time of charge.

---

[44] [1999] 4 All E.R. 43.

- *Appropriate strategies.* Where the client was not answering police questions, the Law Society's advice suggested that the solicitor should consider and advise on the appropriate strategy to adopt. At the start of the interview he should normally make an opening statement informing the police that he had advised the client not to answer questions but (as mentioned above) not give the reasons. He should refer to disclosure made or not made by the police.

13–57   If the police officer told the suspect that he was not obliged to accept the lawyer's advice to remain silent, the lawyer should intervene immediately to the effect that it would be for the court to decide on the merits of the legal advice and the client's decision.

Handing in a written statement, it suggested, should be considered "where there are good reasons for informing the police of facts that are likely to be relied on by the defence at trial [or for providing an account], whilst not wanting to place the client at risk of 'cross-examination' by the police (*e.g.* because they are nervous or because the police disclosure has been limited)". (p.14). Handing in a written statement will not avoid inferences being drawn if the defendant later relies on facts not mentioned in the statement. The written statement should therefore cover the essential features of the defence in as much detail as possible, taking care to anticipate the facts that are likely to be relied on at trial.

In a straightforward case it might be appropriate to hand such a statement to the police at the start of the interview. But in a more complex case it could be wiser to hand it in after the interview had ended.[45]

13–58   The client who is advised to be silent under police questioning may still be advised to make a statement when being charged. As has been seen, s.34 distinguishes between inferences from silence when being questioned (s.34(1)(a)) and inferences from silence on being charged or officially informed that one might be prosecuted (s.34(1)(b)). If the suspect makes a full statement on being charged he does not expose himself to questioning and he can be presented to the jury as someone who was prepared at an early stage to set out his position—though it is not impossible that the jury may nevertheless be invited to draw adverse inferences from the fact that he did not mention relevant facts earlier.

See further: Keogh, "No Comment interviews—a lawyer's survival kit", *New Law Journal*, December 13, 2002, p.1882; and "The right to silence—revisited again", *New Law Journal*, September 12, 2003, p.1352; and Emanuel, "Legal Advice to Remain Silent", (2004) 5 *Archbold News* 6–9. Emanuel ends his article:

"The current position is again confused. Conflicting decisions from the Court of Appeal on specific areas of s.34 once again abound. Jurors continue to appear confused by the lengthy direction and convictions continue to be challenged because of judicial errors on that direction. Until the Court of Appeal reviews further the apparent inconsistencies that exist in its decisions on s.34, juries and practitioners alike will have to continue to tread their way through the minefield with bated breath."

---

[45] See Cape, *op.cit.* n.41 above, January 2004, p.7 and October 2004, p.1.

Empirical evidence on the right to silence

A study of the impact of the new provisions was published by the Home Office **13–59** in 2000. The study included observation of the processing of suspects in 13 police stations. In total there were some 4,100 hours of observation involving 3,950 suspects. The fieldwork was carried out from August 1995 to February 1996. There were also semi-structured interviews with some police officers, legal advisers, CPS lawyers and barristers.[46] The main findings were as follows:

Silence at the police station

- About 40 per cent of suspects consulted a legal adviser—much the **13–60** same as before the introduction of the CJPOA (p.21).[47]

- Legal advisers were increasingly asking for, and generally being given, more information about the case against their clients (p.23).

- Legal advisers reported that they had to be very careful about advising the client to be silent. They might still do so if there was insufficient police disclosure, the evidence was weak or the client was vulnerable. Otherwise they would advise clients to give an account to the police when being interviewed (pp.24–27).

- Both police officers and legal advisers felt that many suspects, especially those who had not been arrested before, did not understand the caution (pp.27–30).

- The proportion of suspects who refused to answer some or all questions dropped from 23 per cent to 16 per cent. The proportion who gave complete "no comment" interviews dropped from 10 per cent to 6 per cent (Table 3.2, p.31).

- The largest drop in the use of silence was in groups who had previously exercised the right most frequently—those held by the Metropolitan Police, suspects who had legal advice, black suspects and those held for more serious offences (pp.31–34).

- Despite decreased reliance on silence, there was no change in the proportion of suspects providing admissions: this remained at 55 per cent (p.34).

---

[46] Bucke, Street and Brown, *The right of silence: the impact of the Criminal Justice and Public Order Act 1994*, Home Office Research Study No.199 (2000).
[47] The comparison was with results reported in Phillips and Brown, *Entry into the Criminal Justices System: a survey of police arrests and their outcomes*, Home Office Research Study No.185 (1998), the fieldwork for which was carried out in 1993–1994.

- Police officers were sceptical about the impact of the CJPOA on "professional" criminals who were thought still to give "no comment" interviews or to use a variety of tactics to circumvent the new provisions. This included the provision of a written statement at the start of an interview and a refusal to expand on it when questioned (pp.36–37).

- Nearly 40 per cent of suspects exercising their right to silence had been given "special warnings" under ss.36 or 37. Few gave a satisfactory account in response (pp.38–39).

- The proportion of silent suspects charged had fallen. The authors speculate that this may be because those who now exercise the right to silence do so where the evidence against them is weak (pp.40–41).

Prosecution and trial

13–61

- CPS interviewees thought that silence would generally only play a marginal role in the decision to prosecute (p.43).

- Defence solicitors did not think that the provisions had had much impact at magistrates' courts because most defendants used to testify and still did (p.46).

- Most CPS respondents, barristers and defence solicitors agreed that fewer defendants were declining to testify, especially in the Crown Court (p.52).

- Official statistics provide no evidence of an increase in convictions. In the Crown Court, the guilty plea rate has fallen slightly—probably due to other factors. But since the provisions affect only a small proportion of cases it was unlikely that any changes would show up in aggregate national figures (pp.64–68).

13–62 Similar research was carried out in Northern Ireland and reached somewhat similar conclusions—see Jackson, Wolfe and Quinn, *Legislating against silence: the Northern Ireland experience* (Northern Ireland office, 2000). For a brief report on this research see Zander, "Silence in Northern Ireland", *New Law Journal*, February 2, 2001, p.138.

For an assessment of both studies see Jackson, "Silence and proof: extending the boundaries of criminal proceedings in the United Kingdom" (2001) 5 *International Journal of Evidence and Proof* 145–173.

Further reading on the right to silence

A. Ashworth, "Article 6 and the Fairness of Trials" [1999] Crim.L.R. 261.   **13–63**

Di Birch, "Suffering in Silence: A Cost-Benefit Analysis of Section 34 of the Criminal Justice and Public Order Act 1994" [1999] Crim.L.R. 769–788.

T. Bucke, R. Street and D. Brown, *The right of silence: the impact of the Criminal Justice and Public Order Act 1994*, Home Office Research Study No.199 (2000).

Ed Cape, "Mentally disordered suspects and the right to silence", *New Law Journal*, January 26, 1996, p.80.

Ed Cape, "Police station advice: defence strategies after Condron", *Legal Action*, October 1997, pp.17–19.

Ed Cape, "Sidelining defence lawyers: Police station advice after Condron" (1997) *International Journal of Evidence and Proof* 386–402.

Ed Cape, "Advising on Silence: new cases new strategies", *Legal Action*, June 1999, p.14.

Ian Dennis, "Instrumental Protection, Human Right or Functional Necessity? Re-assessing the Privilege against Self-incrimination" (1995) 54(2) *Cambridge Law Journal* 342–376.

Ian Dennis, "The Criminal Justice and Public Order Act 1994: The Evidence Provisions" [1995] Crim.L.R. 1–18.

Ian Dennis, "Silence in the police station: the Marginalisation of Section 34" [2002] Crim.L.R. 25–38.

Haydn Davies and Beverley Hopkins, "Environmental crime and the privilege against self-incrimination" (2000) *International Journal of Evidence and Proof* 177–193.

S. Easton, "Legal advice, common sense and the right to silence" (1998) *International Journal of Evidence and Proof* 109–122.

D.J. Galligan, "The Right to Silence Reconsidered" [1988] C.L.P. 80.

J. Jackson, "Interpreting the Silence Provisions: The Northern Ireland Cases" [1995] Crim.L.R. 587–601.

J. Jackson, "Silence and proof: extending the boundaries of criminal proceedings in the United Kingdom" (2001) 5 *International Journal of Evidence and Proof* 145–173.

J. Jackson, M. Wolfe and K. Quinn, *Legislating Against Silence: The Northern Ireland Experience*, Northern Ireland Office Research and Statistical Series, Report No.1 (2000).

Anthony F. Jennings, "Resounding silence", *New Law Journal*, May 17, 1996, p.725, May 24, 1996, p.764, May 31, 1996, p.821 and "More resounding silence", *New Law Journal*, July 30, 1999, p.1180.

Anthony Jennings, Andrew Ashworth and Ben Emmerson, "Silence and Safety: The Impact of Human Rights Law" [2000] Crim.L.R. 879.

Roger Leng, "Silence pre-trial, reasonable expectations and the normative distortion of fact-finding" (2001) *International Journal of Evidence and Proof* 240–256.

James Michael and Ben Emmerson, "The right to silence" (1995) E.H.R.L.R. 4–19.

Peter Mirfield, *Silence, Confessions and Improperly Obtained Evidence* (Clarendon, Oxford, 1997).

Roderick Munday, "Inferences from Silence and European Human Rights Law" [1996] Crim.L.R. 370–385.

Rosemary Pattenden, "Inferences from Silence" [1995] Crim.L.R. 602–611.

Rosemary Pattenden, "Silence: Lord Taylor's legacy" (1998) *International Journal of Evidence and Proof* 141–165.

Paul Roberts and Adrian Zuckerman, *Criminal Evidence* (Oxford University Press, 2004), Ch.9.

Stephen Seabrooke, "More caution needed on s.34 of the Criminal Justice and Public Order Act 1994" (1999) 3 *International Journal of Evidence and Proof* 209–216.

S. Sedley, "Wringing out the Fault: Self-incrimination in the 21st Century" (2001) 52 N.I.L.Q 107.

Sybil Sharpe, "The Privilege against Self-Incrimination: Do we need a Preservation Order? (1998) 27(4) *Anglo-American L.R.* 494–524.

A.J. Turner, "Inferences under section 34 of the Criminal Justice and Public Order Act 1994" (1999) 163 *Justice of the Peace* 243 at 323, 924.

D. Wolchover, *Silence and Guilt* (Lion Court Lawyers, 2001).

Adrian Zuckerman, *see* Paul Roberts.

CRIMINAL JUSTICE AND PUBLIC ORDER ACT 1994

CRIMINAL JUSTICE AND PUBLIC ORDER ACT 1994

Effect of accused's failure to mention facts when questioned or charged.

34.—(1) Where, in any proceedings against a person for an offence, evidence is given that the accused—

    (a) at any time before he was charged with the offence, on being questioned under caution by a constable trying to discover whether or by whom the offence had been committed, failed to mention any fact relied on in his defence in those proceedings; or

    (b) on being charged with the offence or officially informed that he might be prosecuted for it, failed to mention any such fact,

being a fact which in the circumstances existing at the time the accused could reasonably have been expected to mention when so questioned, charged or informed, as the case may be, subsection (2) below applies.

(2) Where this subsection applies—

    (a) a magistrates' court, in deciding whether to grant an application for dismissal made by the accused under section 6 of the Magistrates' Courts Act 1980 (application for dismissal of charge in course of proceedings with a view to transfer for trial);

    (b) a judge, in deciding whether to grant an application made by the accused under—

        (i)   section 6 of the Criminal Justice Act 1987 (application for dismissal of charge of serious fraud in respect of which notice of transfer has been given under section 4 of that Act); or

        (ii) paragraph 5 of Schedule 6 to the Criminal Justice Act 1991 (application for dismissal of charge of violent or sexual offence involving child in respect of which notice of transfer has been given under section 53 of that Act);

    (c) the court, in determining whether there is a case to answer; and

    (d) the court or jury, in determining whether the accused is guilty of the offence charged,

may draw such inferences from the failure as appear proper.

[(2A) Where the accused was at an authorised place of detention at the time of the failure, subsections (1) and (2) above do not apply if he had not been allowed an opportunity to consult a solicitor prior to being questioned, charged or informed as mentioned in subsection (1) above.][1]

---

[1] subs.(2A) was inserted by the Youth Justice and Criminal Evidence Act 1999, s.58(2).

(3) Subject to any directions by the court, evidence tending to establish the failure may be given before or after evidence tending to establish the fact which the accused is alleged to have failed to mention.

(4) This section applies in relation to questioning by persons (other than constables) charged with the duty of investigating offences or charging offenders as it applies in relation to questioning by constables; and in subsection (1) above "officially informed" means informed by a constable or any such person.

(5) This section does not—

    (a) prejudice the admissibility in evidence of the silence or other reaction of the accused in the face of anything said in his presence relating to the conduct in respect of which he is charged, in so far as evidence thereof would be admissible apart from this section; or

    (b) preclude the drawing of any inference from any such silence or other reaction of the accused which could properly be drawn apart from this section.

(6) This section does not apply in relation to a failure to mention a fact if the failure occurred before the commencement of this section.

(7) In relation to any time before the commencement of section 44 of this Act, this section shall have effect as if the reference in subsection (2)(a) to the grant of an application for dismissal was a reference to the committal of the accused for trial.

Effect of accused's silence at trial

35.—(1) At the trial of any person . . .[2] for an offence, subsections (2) and (3) below apply unless—

    (a) the accused's guilt is not in issue; or

    (b) it appears to the court that the physical or mental condition of the accused makes it undesirable for him to give evidence;

but subsection (2) below does not apply if, at the conclusion of the evidence for the prosecution, his legal representative informs the court that the accused will give evidence or, where he is unrepresented, the court ascertains from him that he will give evidence.

(2) Where this subsection applies, the court shall, at the conclusion of the evidence for the prosecution, satisfy itself (in the case of proceedings on indictment, in the presence of the jury) that the accused is aware that the stage has been reached at which evidence can be given for the defence and that he can, if he wishes, give evidence and that, if he chooses not to give evidence, or having been sworn, without good cause refuses to answer any question, it will be permissible for the court or jury to draw such inferences as appear proper from his failure to give evidence or his refusal, without good cause, to answer any question.

(3) Where this subsection applies, the court or jury, in determining whether the accused is guilty of the offence charged, may draw such inferences as appear proper from the failure of the accused to give evidence or his refusal, without good cause, to answer any question.

---

[2] The words "who has attained the age of fourteen years" were removed by the Crime and Disorder Act 1998, s.35(a).

(4) This section does not render the accused compellable to give evidence on his own behalf, and he shall accordingly not be guilty of contempt of court by reason of a failure to do so.

(5) For the purposes of this section a person who, having been sworn, refuses to answer any question shall be taken to do so without good cause unless—

(a) he is entitled to refuse to answer the question by virtue of any enactment, whenever passed or made, or on the ground of privilege; or

(b) the court in the exercise of its general discretion excuses him from answering it.

(6) . . .[3]

(7) This section applies—

(a) in relation to proceedings on indictment for an offence, only if the person charged with the offence is arraigned on or after the commencement of this section;

(b) in relation to proceedings in a magistrates' court, only if the time when the court begins to receive evidence in the proceedings falls after the commencement of this section.

Effect of accused's failure or refusal to account for objects, substances or marks

36.—(1) Where—

(a) a person is arrested by a constable, and there is—

(i) on his person; or

(ii) in or on his clothing or footwear; or

(iii) otherwise in his possession; or

(iv) in any place in which he is at the time of his arrest, any object, substance or mark, or there is any mark on any such object; and

(b) that or another constable investigating the case reasonably believes that the presence of the object, substance or mark may be attributable to the participation of the person arrested in the commission of an offence specified by the constable; and

(c) the constable informs the person arrested that he so believes, and requests him to account for the presence of the object, substance or mark; and

(d) the person fails or refuses to do so,

then if, in any proceedings against the person for the offence so specified, evidence of those matters is given, subsection (2) below applies.

(2) Where this subsection applies—

(a) a magistrates' court, in deciding whether to grant an application for dismissal made by the accused under section 6 of the Magistrates' Courts Act 1980 (application for dismissal of charge in course of proceedings with a view to transfer for trial);

(b) a judge, in deciding whether to grant an application made by the accused under—

---

[3] Repealed by the Crime and Disorder Act 1998, s.35(b).

     (i)   section 6 of the Criminal Justice Act 1987 (application for dismissal of charge of serious fraud in respect of which notice of transfer has been given under section 4 of that Act); or

     (ii)   paragraph 5 of Schedule 6 to the Criminal Justice Act 1991 (application for dismissal of charge of violent or sexual offence involving child in respect of which notice of transfer has been given under section 53 of that Act);

   (c)   the court, in determining whether there is a case to answer; and

   (d)   the court or jury, in determining whether the accused is guilty of the offence charged,

may draw such inferences from the failure or refusal as appear proper.

(3) Subsections (1) and (2) above apply to the condition of clothing or footwear as they apply to a substance or mark thereon.

(4) Subsections (1) and (2) above do not apply unless the accused was told in ordinary language by the constable when making the request mentioned in subsection (1)(c) above what the effect of this section would be if he failed or refused to comply with the request.

[(4a) Where the accused was at an authorised place of detention at the time of the failure or refusal, subsections (1) and (2) above do not apply if he had not been allowed an opportunity to consult a solicitor prior to the request being made.][4]

(5) This section applies in relation to officers of customs and excise as it applies in relation to constables.

(6) This section does not preclude the drawing of any inference from a failure or refusal of the accused to account for the presence of an object, substance or mark or from the condition of clothing or footwear which could properly be drawn apart from this section.

(7) This section does not apply in relation to a failure or refusal which occurred before the commencement of this section.

(8) In relation to any time before the commencement of section 44 of this Act, this section shall have effect as if the reference in subsection (2)(a) to the grant of an application for dismissal was a reference to the committal of the accused for trial.

Effect of accused's failure or refusal to account for presence at a particular place

37.—(1) Where—

   (a)   a person arrested by a constable was found by him at a place at or about the time the offence for which he was arrested is alleged to have been committed; and

   (b)   that or another constable investigating the offence reasonably believes that the presence of the person at that place and at that time may be attributable to his participation in the commission of the offence; and

---

[4] subs.(4A) was inserted by the Youth Justice and Criminal Evidence Act 1999, s.58 (3).

(c) the constable informs the person that he so believes, and requests him to account for that presence; and

(d) the person fails or refuses to do so,

then if, in any proceedings against the person for the offence, evidence of those matters is given, subsection (2) below applies.

(2) Where this subsection applies—

(a) a magistrates' court, in deciding whether to grant an application for dismissal made by the accused under section 6 of the Magistrates' Courts Act 1980 (application for dismissal of charge in course of proceedings with a view to transfer for trial);

(b) a judge, in deciding whether to grant an application made by the accused under—

(i) section 6 of the Criminal Justice Act 1987 (application for dismissal of charge of serious fraud in respect of which notice of transfer has been given under section 4 of that Act);

(ii) paragraph 5 of Schedule 6 to the Criminal Justice Act 1991 (application for dismissal of charge of violent or sexual offence involving child in respect of which notice of transfer has been given under section 53 of that Act);

(c) the court, in determining whether there is a case to answer; and

(d) the court or jury, in determining whether the accused is guilty of the offence charged,

may draw such inferences from the failure or refusal as appear proper.

(3) Subsections (1) and (2) do not apply unless the accused was told in ordinary language by the constable when making the request mentioned in subsection (1)(c) above what the effect of this section would be if he failed or refused to comply with the request.

[(3A) Where the accused was at an authorised place of detention at the time of the failure or refusal, subsections (1) and (2) do not apply if he had not been allowed an opportunity to consult a solicitor prior to the request being made.][5]

(4) This section applies in relation to officers of customs and excise as it applies in relation to constables.

(5) This section does not preclude the drawing of any inference from a failure or refusal of the accused to account for his presence at a place which could properly be drawn apart from this section.

(6) This section does not apply in relation to a failure or refusal which occurred before the commencement of this section.

(7) In relation to any time before the commencement of section 44 of this Act, this section shall have effect as if the reference in subsection (2)(a) to the grant of an application for dismissal was a reference to the committal of the accused for trial.

[5] subs.(3A) was inserted by the Youth Justice and Criminal Evidence Act 1999, s.58(4).

Interpretation and savings for sections 34, 35, 36 and 37

38.—(1) In sections 34, 35, 36 and 37 of this Act—

"legal representative" means an authorised advocate or authorised litigator, as defined by section 119(1) of the Courts and Legal Services Act 1990; and

"place" includes any building or part of a building, any vehicle, vessel, aircraft or hovercraft and any other place whatsoever.

(2) In sections 34(2), 35(3), 36(2) and 37(2), references to an offence charged include references to any other offence of which the accused could lawfully be convicted on that charge.

[(2A) In each of sections 34(2A), 36(4A) and 37(3A) "authorised place of detention" means—

(a) a police station; or

(b) any other place prescribed for the purpose of that provision by order made by the Secretary of State;

and the power to make an order under this subsection shall be exercisable by statutory instrument which shall be subject to annulment in pursuance of a resolution of either House of Parliament.][6]

(3) A person shall not have the proceedings against him transferred to the Crown Court for trial, have a case to answer or be convicted of an offence solely on an inference drawn from such a failure or refusal as is mentioned in section 34(2), 35(3), 36(2) or 37(2).

(4) A judge shall not refuse to grant such an application as is mentioned in section 34(2)(b), 36(2)(b) and 37(2)(b) solely on an inference drawn from such a failure as is mentioned in section 34(2), 36(2) or 37(2).

(5) Nothing in sections 34, 35, 36 or 37 prejudices the operation of a provision of any enactment which provides (in whatever words) that any answer or evidence given by a person in specified circumstances shall not be admissible in, evidence against him or some other person in any proceedings or class of proceedings (however described, and whether civil or criminal). In this subsection, the reference to giving evidence is a reference to giving evidence in any manner, whether by furnishing information, making discovery, producing documents or otherwise.

(6) Nothing in sections 34, 35, 36 or 37 prejudices any power of a court, in any proceedings, to exclude evidence (whether by preventing questions being put or otherwise) at its discretion.

Power to apply sections 34 to 38 to armed forces

39.—(1) The Secretary of State may by order direct that any provision of sections 34 to 38 of this Act shall apply, subject to such modifications as he may specify, to any proceedings to which this section applies.

(2) This section applies—

(a) to proceedings whereby a charge is dealt with summarily under Part II of the Army Act 1955;

---

[6] subs.(2A) was inserted by the Youth Justice and Criminal Evidence Act 1999, s.58(5).

(b) to proceedings whereby a charge is dealt with summarily under Part II of the Air Force Act 1955;

(c) to proceedings whereby a charge is summarily tried under Part II of the Naval Discipline Act 1957;

(d) to proceedings before a court martial constituted under the Army Act 1955;

(e) to proceedings before a court martial constituted under the Air Force Act 1955;

(f) to proceedings before a court martial constituted under the Naval Discipline Act 1957;

(g) to proceedings before a disciplinary court constituted under section 50 of the Naval Discipline Act 1957;

(h) to proceedings before the Courts-Martial Appeal Court;

(i) to proceedings before a Standing Civilian Court;

and it applies wherever the proceedings take place.

(3) An order under this section shall be made by statutory instrument and shall be subject to annulment in pursuance of a resolution of either House of Parliament.

THE HUMAN RIGHTS ACT 1998 AND THE
EUROPEAN CONVENTION ON HUMAN RIGHTS

CHAPTER 14

THE HUMAN RIGHTS ACT 1998 AND THE EUROPEAN CONVENTION ON HUMAN RIGHTS

The Human Rights Act 1998 became operative as from October 2, 2000. The **14–01** effect of the Act was to make the European Convention on Human Rights (ECHR) greatly more accessible to anyone in the UK who believes that he or she is the victim of a breach of the Convention.

The United Kingdom was the first country to ratify the ECHR in 1951 and it has accorded the right of individual petition to Strasbourg since 1966. There are now some 40 countries that have ratified the Convention.

Until 1998, the Strasbourg ECHR system consisted of the Commission, the Committee of Ministers and the Court. Under the more streamlined system introduced in November 1998, the Commission was abolished and the Committee of Ministers was stripped of its role in regard to decisions on cases. Complainants now have direct access to the Court.[1]

From the initiation of a case to judgment by the Strasbourg Court normally takes several years. There have been a considerable number of cases involving the UK in which the Court has found a violation of the Convention. Quite a few have required the UK to change the law or the system to take account of the Court's judgment.

There is a system for the early weeding-out of cases that are inadmissible. One **14–02** reason for holding a complaint to be inadmissible is that local remedies have not been exhausted. In other words, a complainant from the UK must first try to get a remedy under the system available from our law, which now includes the Human Rights Act 1998 (HRA).

The HRA did not incorporate the ECHR into UK law. Nor did it give the judges the power to strike down legislation found to conflict with the Convention. The Act therefore preserved the constitutional dominance of Parliament. But at the same time it changed the situation in various important respects.

First, the Act says that when considering a question of the Convention rights the courts must take account of the jurisprudence developed in Strasbourg (s.2).[2]

---

[1] For a brief account of the new system and of how to bring a case in Strasbourg see Leach, "European Convention on Human Rights: System and procedure", *Legal Action*, March 2001, p.17. See also Luke Clements, *European Human Rights—Taking a Case under the Convention* (Sweet & Maxwell, 2nd ed., 1998).

[2] The case law of the Strasbourg Court can be accessed via *www.echr.coe.int.Eng/judgments.html* or via Google at HUDOC.

Secondly, it established a new principle of statutory interpretation according to which the courts must read legislation "so far as possible" in a way that is consistent with the Convention rights (s.3(1)). The effect of this is that a court may feel able (or obliged) to give a statutory provision a meaning that Parliament did not intend—because it is a possible interpretation of the statutory language.[3] If the court finds that it cannot reconcile the statute and the Convention, it must give effect to the statute, but it can make a "declaration of incompatibility" which then enables the Government, if it so decides, to use a special "fast-track" procedure[4] for amending the legislation by statutory instrument so as to bring the statute into line with the Convention (s.4).[5] A declaration of incompatibility can equally be made in respect of a provision in subordinate legislation, such as a statutory instrument, where the primary legislation prevents removal of the incompatibility (s.4(4)).

14–03 Thirdly, the HRA makes it unlawful for a public authority to act in a way that is inconsistent with a Convention right (s.6(1)) unless required to do so by inconsistent legislation (s.6(2)). A public authority includes a court or tribunal (s.6(3)(a)).

Anyone who claims that he is the victim of an act by a public authority that is made unlawful by s.6(1) can bring legal proceedings to establish the fact and to ask for a remedy which may include damages (s.7(1)(a)). Alternatively, such a person can use the power defensively as a shield in proceedings, for instance in a criminal prosecution that is being brought against him (s.7(1)(b)). Actively taking proceedings under s.7(1)(a) applies only to acts that occurred after October 1, 2000. Using the Convention defensively as a shield applies to acts whenever they occurred in respect of proceedings brought by a public authority (s.22(4)). But the House of Lords has held that a person convicted prior to October 2, 2000 cannot use the HRA to reopen his conviction.[6]

The provisions of PACE and of the PACE Codes have figured only rarely in cases brought to Strasbourg, and in the nearly twenty years since 1986 when the Act came into force none of the provisions of PACE were found to be in breach of the Convention.

14–04 It is important to appreciate that even if a breach of the Convention is held to have occurred it does not follow that the evidence in question is necessarily inadmissible or that a conviction based on such evidence has to be quashed. Thus, for instance, in *P.G. and J.H. v United Kingdom*[7] the Strasbourg Court held that covert listening devices at a suspect's home and at a police station in 1995 vio-

---

[3] For a clear example see *A* [2001] UKHL 25; [2001] 3 All E.R. 1, HL in which the Law Lords rewrote the statutory provision regarding cross-examination of the complainant in a rape case regarding her sexual relationship with the accused. This issue now has an extensive literature.

[4] Called in the Act, "remedial action" (s.10).

[5] The power to make a declaration of incompatibility is only given to the higher courts—the House of Lords, the Court of Appeal, the High Court (including the Divisional Court), the Judicial Committee of the Privy Council and the Courts-Martial Appeal Court (s.4(5)). A dramatic example was the decision of the Law Lords on December 16 2004 by 8 to 1 that the provisions of the Anti-terrorism, Crime and Security Act 2001 permitting the detention without trial of international terrorism suspects were incompatible with the ECHR—*A and others v Secretary of State for the Home Department* [2004] UKHL 56. The Home Secretary announced on January 26, 2005 that as a result the system would be changed.

[6] *Lambert* [2001] UKHL 37; [2001] 3 All E.R. 577, HL.

[7] [2002] Crim.L.R. 308.

lated Arts 8 and 13 of the Convention which respectively guarantee the right to respect for private life and the right to an effective remedy. (The Police Act 1997 and the Regulation of Investigatory Powers Act 2000 now provide the authority for such covert surveillance but neither existed in 1995.) However, the Court held that although the surveillance had been in breach of the Convention, the use of the resulting tapes in evidence at the trial was not a violation of the Art.6 right to a fair trial. There had been other evidence against the two applicants. The domestic courts could have excluded the evidence under s.78 of PACE but exercised their discretion not to do so. There was no unfairness in leaving it to the jury on the basis of a careful and thorough summing-up by the judge to decide where the weight of the evidence lay.

The English courts, similarly, have held that the crux of the matter is whether the defendant had a fair trial. If the trial was not fair the Court of Appeal will hold the conviction to be unsafe.[8] But conversely, if the trial overall was fair, the court will normally not intervene even if it finds that there has been a breach of the Convention.

Articles of the Convention most relevant to criminal proceedings

The Articles mainly in issue are 3, 5, 6 and 8:   **14–05**

Article 3: "No one shall be subjected to torture or to inhuman or degrading treatment or punishment."

Article 5: "Everyone has the right to liberty and security of person." No one may be deprived of his liberty save in the circumstances specified in Art.5(a) to (f), which include conviction by a competent court, and lawful arrest on reasonable suspicion of having committed an offence.

Article 5 also sets out basic procedural safeguards for the suspect such as the right to be told the reasons for his arrest and the duty to bring him promptly before a court and the right to be tried within a reasonable period or to be released pending trial.

Article 6: "In the determination . . . of any criminal charge against him everyone is entitled to a fair and public hearing within a reasonable time by an independent and impartial tribunal established by law" (Art.6(1)). The defendant is "presumed innocent until proved guilty according to law" (Art.6(2)). The defendant's rights include: the right to be told the nature and cause of the accusation against him; adequate time and facilities to prepare his defence; the right to defend himself in person or through legal assistance, paid for by the state where he has inadequate resources and the interests of justice require it; the right to examine witnesses; and, if required, the right to an interpreter (Art.6(3)).

Article 8 is also relevant—especially in regard to surveillance, interception of communications and the seizure and retention of personal items:

---

[8] *Togher* [2001] 3 All E.R. 463, CA; *Forbes* [2001] 1 All E.R. 686, HL.

Article 8: "Everyone has the right to respect for his private and family life, his home and his correspondence." No interference with the exercise of this right by a public authority is permitted unless it is in accordance with the law and is necessary in a democratic society in the interests of "national security, public safety or the economic well-being of the country, for the prevention of disorder or crime, for the protection of health or morals, or for the protection of the rights and freedoms of others".

14–06   *Parliamentary Joint Committee on Human Rights.* The Joint Committee monitors pending legislation for compliance with the ECHR and issues reports on these and other aspects of human rights. The reports can be found on its website—*www.parliament.uk/commons/selcom/hrhome.htm*

Select Bibliography

14–07   R. Clayton and H. Tomlinson, *The Law of Human Rights* (2nd ed., Oxford, forthcoming 2005).
Ben Emmerson and Andrew Ashworth, *Human Rights and Criminal Justice* (2nd ed., Sweet & Maxwell, forthcoming 2005).
D. Feldman, *Civil Liberties and Human Rights in England and Wales* (Oxford University Press, 2002).
Keith Starmer, Michelle Strange and Quincy Whitaker with Anthony Jennings and Tim Owen, *Criminal Justice, Police Powers and Human Rights* (Blackstone, 2001).

POLICE AND CRIMINAL EVIDENCE ACT 1984

POLICE AND CRIMINAL EVIDENCE ACT 1984

[Amended as at January 2005. For a list of the provisions that were not yet in force at that date see Appendix 2[1]]

---

[1] Some sections included in the Table of Contents have been repealed.
[2] Unless otherwise indicated, the numbers in this column refer to the equivalent provisions in the Police and Criminal Evidence (Northern Ireland) Order 1989, SI 1989/1341 (N.I. 12).

[3] Art.47A was inserted into the 1989 N.I. PACE Order by the Police (Amendment) (Northern Ireland) Order 1995, SI 1995/2993 (N.I. 17), Art.7.

PART V VI

QUESTIONING AND TREATMENT OF PERSONS BY POLICE

PART VI

CODES OF PRACTICE—GENERAL

Part VII VIII

DOCUMENTARY EVIDENCE IN CRIMINAL PROCEEDINGS

[4] Art.55A was inserted into the 1989 N.I. PACE Order by the Anti-Terrorism, Crime and Security Act 2001, s.91(1).
[5] Art.60A was inserted into the 1989 N.I. PACE Order by the Police (Northern Ireland) Act 2000, s.72.
[6] Art.63A was inserted into the 1989 N.I. PACE Order by the Police (Amendment) (Northern Ireland) Order 1995, SI 1995/2993 (N.I.17), Art.12.
[7] Repealed by the Criminal Evidence (Northern Ireland) Order 1999.

EVIDENCE IN CRIMINAL PROCEEDINGS—GENERAL

Convictions and acquittals

Confessions

Part VIII—Supplementary

PART IX

POLICE COMPLAINTS AND DISCIPLINE

The Police Complaints Authority

Handling of complaints etc.

---

[8] Inserted by the Youth Justice and Criminal Evidence Act 1999, Sch.4, para.14.

[9] Police complaints and discipline never appeared in the Northern Ireland PACE Order. The Police (Northern Ireland) Order 1977 introduced such arrangements. They were amended by the 1987 Order of the same title and again by the Police (Amendment) (Northern Ireland) Order 1995. They were repealed by the Police (Northern Ireland) Act 1998 establishing the Police Ombudsman. For latest amendments see Police (Northern Ireland) Act 2000, Pt VIII.

PART X

POLICE–GENERAL

PART XI

MISCELLANEOUS AND SUPPLEMENTARY

SCHEDULES

PART I[1]

POWERS TO STOP AND SEARCH

Power of constable to stop and search persons, vehicles etc.

1.—(1) A constable may exercise any power conferred by this section—

    (a) in any place to which at the time when he proposes to exercise the power the public or any section of the public has access, on payment or otherwise, as of right or by virtue of express or implied permission; or

    (b) in any other place to which people have ready access at the time when he proposes to exercise the power but which is not a dwelling.

  (2) Subject to subsection (3) to (5) below, a constable—

    (a) may search—

      (i) any person or vehicle;

     (ii) anything which is in or on a vehicle,

    for stolen or prohibited articles [or any article to which subsection (8A) below applies][2]; and

    (b) may detain a person or vehicle for the purpose of such a search.

  (3) This section does not give a constable power to search a person or vehicle or anything in or on a vehicle unless he has reasonable grounds for suspecting that he will find stolen or prohibited articles [or any article to which subsection (8A) below applies].[3]

  (4) If a person is in a garden or yard occupied with and used for the purposes of a dwelling or on other land so occupied and used, a constable may not search him in the exercise of the power conferred by this section unless the constable has reasonable grounds for believing—

    (a) that he does not reside in the dwelling; and

    (b) that he is not in the place in question with the express or implied permission of a person who resides in the dwelling.

  (5) If a vehicle is in a garden or yard or other place occupied with and used for the purposes of a dwelling or on other land so occupied and used a constable may not search the vehicle or anything in it or on it in the exercise of the power conferred by this section unless he has reasonable grounds for believing—

    (a) that the person in charge of the vehicle does not reside in the dwelling; and

    (b) that the vehicle is not in the place in question with the express or implied permission of a person who resides in the dwelling.

  (6) If in the course of such a search a constable discovers an article which he has reasonable grounds for suspecting to be a stolen or prohibited article [or an article to which subsection (8A) below applies],[4] he may seize it.

---

[1] The 1989 Northern Ireland Order has a Pt I consisting of two Articles. Article 1 deals with Title and commencement; Art.2 deals with General Interpretation of PACE, s.118.

[2] Words in square brackets inserted by the Criminal Justice Act 1988, s.140(1). The Serious Organised Crime and Police Bill 2004–05, cl.106(2) adds here: "or any firework to which subsection (8B) below applies".

[3] Words in square brackets inserted by the Criminal Justice Act 1988, s.140(1). The Serious Organised Crime and Police Bill 2004–05, cl.106(2) adds here: "or any firework to which subsection (8B) below applies".

[4] Words in square brackets inserted by the Criminal Justice Act 1988, s.140(1). The Serious Organised Crime and Police Bill 2004–05, cl.106(2) adds here: "or any firework to which subsection (8B) below applies".

(7) An article is prohibited for the purposes of this Part of this Act if it is—
    (a) an offensive weapon; or
    (b) an article—
        (i) made or adapted for use in the course of or in connection with an offence to which this sub-paragraph applies; or
        (ii) intended by the person having it with him for such use by him or by some other person.

(8) The offences to which subsection (7)(b)(i) above applies are—
    (a) burglary;
    (b) theft;
    (c) offences under section 12 of the Theft Act 1968 (taking motor vehicle or other conveyance without authority);
    (d) offences under section 15 of that Act (obtaining property by deception); [and
    (e) offences under section 1 of the Criminal Damage Act 1971 (destroying or damaging property).][5]

[(8A) This subsection applies to any article in relation to which a person has committed, or is committing or is going to commit an offence under section 139 of the Criminal Justice Act 1988.][6]

[*The Serious Organised Crime and Police Bill 2004–05, cl.106(5) adds new subss.(8B) and (8C):*

"(8B) This subsection applies to any firework which a person possesses in contravention of a prohibition imposed by fireworks regulations.

(8C) In this section—
    (a) 'firework' shall be construed in accordance with the definition of 'fireworks' in section 1(1) of the Fireworks Act 2003; and
    (b) 'fireworks regulations' has the same meaning as in that Act."]

(9) In this Part of this Act—
    "offensive weapon" means any article—
    (a) made or adapted for use for causing injury to persons; or
    (b) intended by the person having it with him for such use by him or by some other person.

Provisions relating to search under section 1 and other powers

2.—(1) A constable who detains a person or vehicle in the exercise—
    (a) of the power conferred by section 1 above; or
    (b) of any other power—
        (i) to search a person without first arresting him; or
        (ii) to search a vehicle without making an arrest,
    need not conduct a search if it appears to him subsequently—
        (i) that no search is required; or
        (ii) that a search is impracticable.

(2) If a constable contemplates a search, other than a search of an unattended vehicle, in the exercise—
    (a) of the power conferred by section 1 above; or

---

[5] Inserted by Criminal Justice Act 2003, s.1(2). For the Northern Ireland equivalent see Criminal Justice (Northern Ireland) Order 2004, SI 2004/1500, Art.3.
[6] subs.(8A) was inserted by the Criminal Justice Act 1988, s.140(1). Section 139 of that Act created a new offence of carrying an article with a blade in a public place.

    (b)   of any other power, except the power conferred by section 6 below and the power conferred by section 27(2) of the Aviation Security Act 1982[7]—

        (i) to search a person without first arresting him; or

        (ii) to search a vehicle without making an arrest,

it shall be his duty, subject to subsection (4) below, to take reasonable steps before he commences the search to bring to the attention of the appropriate person—

        (i) if the constable is not in uniform, documentary evidence that he is a constable; and

        (ii) whether he is in uniform or not, the matters specified in subsection (3) below,

and the constable shall not commence the search until he has performed that duty.

    (3) The matters referred to in subsection (2)(ii) above are—

    (a)   the constable's name and the name of the police station to which he is attached[8];

    (b)   the object of the proposed search;

    (c)   the constable's grounds for proposing to make it; and

    (d)   the effect of section 3(7) or (8) below, as may be appropriate.

    (4) A constable need not bring the effect of section 3(7) or (8) below to the attention of the appropriate person if it appears to the constable that it will not be practicable to make the record in section 3(1) below.

    (5) In this section "the appropriate person" means—

    (a)   if the constable proposes to search a person, that person; and

    (b)   if he proposes to search a vehicle, or anything in or on a vehicle, the person in charge of the vehicle.

    (6) On completing a search of an unattended vehicle or anything in or on such a vehicle in the exercise of any such power as is mentioned in subsection (2) above a constable shall leave a notice—

    (a)   stating that he has searched it;

    (b)   giving the name of the police station to which he is attached;

    (c)   stating that an application for compensation for any damage caused by the search may be made to that police station; and

    (d)   stating the effect of section 3(8) below.

    (7) The constable shall leave the notice inside the vehicle unless it is not reasonably practicable to do so without damaging the vehicle.

    (8) The time for which a person or vehicle may be detained for the purposes of such a search is such time as is reasonably required to permit a search to be carried out either at the place where the person or vehicle was first detained or nearby.

    (9) Neither the power conferred by section 1 above nor any other power to detain and search a person without first arresting him or to detain and search a vehicle without making an arrest is to be construed—

    (a)   as authorising a constable to require a person to remove any of his clothing in public other than an outer coat, jacket or gloves[9]; or

    (b)   as authorising a constable not in uniform to stop a vehicle.

---

[7] The equivalent 1989 Northern Ireland PACE Order, Art.4(3)(b) excluded searches under ss.15, 16 and 20 of the Northern Ireland (Emergency Provisions) Act 1978 which was repealed by the Northern Ireland (Emergency Provisions) Act 1991 but which substituted ss.19, 20 and 26 of the 1991 Act.
[8] The 1989 Northern Ireland PACE Order, Art.4(4)(a) substituted the constable's number for his name.
[9] The 1989 Northern Ireland PACE Order, Art.4(10)(a) inserted headgear.

(10) This section and section 1 above apply to vessels, aircraft and hovercraft as they apply to vehicles.

Duty to make records concerning searches

3.—(1) Where a constable has carried out a search in the exercise of any such power as is mentioned in section 2(1) above, other than a search—

    (a)   under section 6 below; or

    (b)   under section 27(2) of the Aviation Security Act 1982,

he shall make a record of it in writing unless it is not practicable to do so.

    (2) If—

    (a)   a constable is required by subsection (1) above to make a record of a search; but

    (b)   it is not practicable to make the record on the spot,

he shall make it as soon as practicable after the completion of the search.

    (3) The record of a search of a person shall include a note of his name, if the constable knows it, but a constable may not detain a person to find out his name.

    (4) If a constable does not know the name of a person whom he has searched, the record of the search shall include a note otherwise describing that person.

    (5) The record of a search of a vehicle shall include a note describing the vehicle.

    (6) The record of a search—

    (a)   shall state—

       (i)   the object of the search;

       (ii)   the grounds for making it;

       (iii)   the date and time when it was made;

       (iv)   the place where it was made;

       (v)   whether anything, and if so what, was found;

       (vi)   whether any, and if so what, injury to a person or damage to property appears to the constable to have resulted from the search; and

    (b)   shall identify the constable making it.

    (7) If a constable who conducted a search of a person made a record of it, the person who was searched shall be entitled to a copy of the record if he asks for one before the end of the period specified in subsection (9) below.

    (8) If—

    (a)   the owner of a vehicle which has been searched or the person who was in charge of the vehicle at the time when it was searched asks for a copy of the record of the search before the end of the period specified in subsection (9) below; and

    (b)   the constable who conducted the search made a record of it,

the person who made the request shall be entitled to a copy.

    (9) The period mentioned in subsections (7) and (8) above is the period of 12 months beginning with the date on which the search was made.

    (10) The requirements imposed by this section with regard to records of searches of vehicles shall apply also to records of searches of vessels, aircraft and hovercraft.

Road checks

4.—(1) This section shall have effect in relation to the conduct of road checks by police officers for the purpose of ascertaining whether a vehicle is carrying—

(a) a person who has committed an offence other than a road traffic offence or a [vehicle][10] excise offence;

(b) a person who is a witness to such an offence;

(c) a person intending to commit such an offence; or

(d) a person who is unlawfully at large.

(2) For the purposes of this section a road check consists of the exercise in a locality of the power conferred by [section 163 of the Road Traffic Act 1987][11] in such a way as to stop during the period for which its exercise in that way in that locality continues all vehicles or vehicles selected by any criterion.

(3) Subject to subsection (5) below, there may only be such a road check if a police officer of the rank of superintendent or above authorises it in writing.

(4) An officer may only authorise a road check under subsection (3) above—

(a) for the purpose specified in subsection (1)(a) above, if he has reasonable grounds—

(i) for believing that the offence is a serious arrestable offence[12] and

(ii) for suspecting that the person is, or is about to be, in the locality in which vehicles would be stopped if the road check were authorised;

(b) for the purpose specified in subsection (1)(b) above, if he has reasonable grounds for believing that the offence is a [serious arrestable offence];

(c) for the purpose specified in subsection (1)(c) above, if he has reasonable grounds—

(i) for believing that the offence would be a [serious arrestable offence]; and

(ii) for suspecting that the person is, or is about to be in the locality in which vehicles would be stopped if the road check were authorised;

(d) for the purpose specified in subsection (1)(d) above, if he has reasonable grounds for suspecting that the person is, or is about to be, in that locality.

(5) An officer below the rank of superintendent may authorise such a road check if it appears to him that it is required as a matter of urgency for one of the purposes specified in subsection (1) above.

(6) If an authorisation is given under subsection (5) above, it shall be the duty of the officer who gives it—

(a) to make a written record of the time at which he gives it; and

(b) to cause an officer of the rank of superintendent or above to be informed that it has been given.

(7) The duties imposed by subsection (6) above shall be performed as soon as it is practicable to do so.

(8) An officer to whom a report is made under subsection (6) above may, in writing, authorise the road check to continue.

---

[10] As amended by the Vehicle Excise and Registration Act 1994, Sch.3, para.19.

[11] As amended by the Road Traffic (Consequential Provisions) Act 1988, Sch.3, para.27.

[12] The Serious Organised Crime and Police Bill 2004–05, Sch.7, Pt 3, para.8, replaces "a serious arrestable offence" in each place where it occurs in s.4 with "indictable offence". (It occurs in ss.4(4)(b) and (c)(i), and subs.(14).)

(9) If such an officer considers that the road check should not continue, he shall record in writing—

    (a)   the fact that it took place; and

    (b)   the purpose for which it took place.

(10) An officer giving an authorisation under this section shall specify the locality in which vehicles are to be stopped.

(11) An officer giving an authorisation under this section, other than an authorisation under subsection (5) above—

    (a)   shall specify a period, not exceeding seven days, during which the road check may continue; and

    (b)   may direct that the road check—

        (i)   shall be continuous; or

        (ii)   shall be conducted at specified times, during that period.

(12) If it appears to an officer of the rank of superintendent or above that a road check ought to continue beyond the period for which it has been authorised he may, from time to time, in writing specify a further period, not exceeding seven days, during which it may continue.

(13) Every written authorisation shall specify—

    (a)   the name of the officer giving it;

    (b)   the purpose of the road check; and

    (c)   the locality in which vehicles are to be stopped.

(14) The duties to specify the purposes of a road check imposed by subsections (9) and (13) above include duties to specify any relevant [serious arrestable offence].

(15) Where a vehicle is stopped in a road check, the person in charge of the vehicle at the time when it is stopped shall be entitled to obtain a written statement of the purpose of the road check, if he applies for such a statement not later than the end of the period of twelve months from the day on which the vehicle was stopped.

(16) Nothing in this section affects the exercise by police officers of any power to stop vehicles for purposes other than those specified in subsection (1) above.

Reports of recorded searches and of road checks

5.—(1) Every annual report—

    [(a)   under section 22 of the Police Act 1996; or][13]

    (b)   made by the Commissioner of Police of the Metropolis,

shall contain information—

        (i)   about searches recorded under section 3 above which have been carried out in the area to which the report relates during the period to which it relates; and

        (ii)   about road checks authorised in that area during that period under section 4 above.

[(1A) Every annual report under section 57 of the Police Act 1997 (reports by Director General of the National Crime Squad) shall contain information—

    (a)   about searches recorded under section 3 above which have been carried out by members of the National Crime Squad during the period to which the report relates; and

---

[13] As amended by the Police Act 1996, s.103, Sch.7, para.34.

(b) about road checks authorised by members of the National Crime
Squad during that period under section 4 above.][14]

(2) The information about searches shall not include information about specific
searches but shall include—

(a) the total numbers of searches in each month during the period to
which the report relates—
   (i) for stolen articles;
   (ii) for offensive weapons [or articles to which section 1(8A) above
   applies],[15] and
   (iii) for other prohibited articles;

(b) the total number of persons arrested in each such month in consequence of searches of each of the descriptions specified in paragraph
(a)(i) to (iii) above.

(3) The information about road checks shall include information—

(a) about the reason for authorising each road check; and

(b) about the result of each of them.

Statutory undertakers etc.

6.—(1) A constable employed by statutory undertakers may stop, detain and
search any vehicle before it leaves a goods area included in the premises of the
statutory undertakers.

[(1A) Without prejudice to any powers under subsection (1) above, a constable employed by the [Strategic Rail Authority][16] may stop, detain and search
any vehicle before it leave a goods area which is included in the premises of
any successor of the British Railways Board and is used wholly or mainly for
the purposes of a relevant undertaking.][17]

(2) In this section—

"goods area" means any area used wholly or mainly for the storage or
handling of goods[; and

"successor of the British Railways Board" and "relevant undertaking" have
the same meaning as in the Railways Act 1993 (Consequential Modifications) Order 1999.][18]

(3) For the purposes of section 6 of the Public Stores Act 1875, any person
appointed under the Special Constables Act 1923 to be a special constable within
any premises which are in the possession or under the control of British Nuclear
Fuels Limited shall be deemed to be a constable deputed by a public department
and any goods and chattels belonging to or in the possession of British Nuclear
Fuels Limited shall be deemed to be Her Majesty's Stores.

(4) In the application of subsection (3) above to Northern Ireland, for the
reference to the Special Constables Act 1923 there shall be substituted a reference to paragraph 1(2) of Schedule 2 to the Emergency Laws (Miscellaneous
Provisions) Act 1947.

---

[14] subs.(1A) was inserted by Police Act 1997, s.134, Sch.9, para.46. The Serious Organised Crime
and Police Bill 2004–05, Sch.4, para.44, repeals the subsection.
[15] Words in square brackets inserted by Criminal Justice Act 1988, s.140(2).
[16] Substituted by the Transport Act 2000, Sch.18, Pt 1, para.5.
[17] subs.(1A) inserted by SI 1999/1998, Art.5(1).
[18] Words in square brackets inserted by SI 1999/1998, Art.5(2).

Part I—Supplementary[19]

7.—(1) The following enactments shall cease to have effect—
   (a)   section 8 of the Vagrancy Act 1824;
   (b)   section 66 of the Metropolitan Police Act 1839;
   (c)   section 11 of the Canals (Offences) Act 1840;
   (d)   section 19 of the Pedlars Act 1871;
   (e)   section 33 of the County of Merseyside Act 1980; and
   (f)   section 42 of the West Midlands County Council Act 1980.
  (2) There shall also cease to have effect—
   (a)   so much of any enactment contained in an Act passed before 1974, other than—
     (i) an enactment contained in a public general Act; or
     (ii) an enactment relating to statutory undertakers, as confers power on a constable to search for stolen or unlawfully obtained goods; and
   (b)   so much of any enactment relating to statutory undertakers as provides that such a power shall not be exercisable after the end of a specified period.
  (3) In this Part of this Act "statutory undertakers" means persons authorised by any enactment to carry on any railway, light railway, road transport, water transport, canal, inland navigation, dock or harbour undertaking.

PART II

POWERS OF ENTRY, SEARCH AND SEIZURE

Search warrants

Power of the justice of the peace to authorise entry and search of premises

8.—(1) If on an application made by a constable a justice of the peace is satisfied that there are reasonable grounds for believing—
   (a)   that a [serious arrestable offence][20] has been committed; and
   (b)   that there is material on premises [specified in the application][21] which is likely to be of substantial value (whether by itself or together with other material) to the investigation of the offence; and
   (c)   that the material is likely to be relevant evidence; and
   (d)   that it does not consist of or include items subject to legal privilege, excluded material or special procedure material; and
   (e)   that any of the conditions specified in subsection (3) below applies,[22]
he may issue a warrant authorising a constable to enter and search the premises.
  [*The Serious Organised Crime and Police Bill 2004–05, cl.104(4) inserts new subss.(1A) and (1B) and cl.105(2) of the Bill insert new subss.(1C) and (1D):*

---

[19] Note drafting differences in the 1989 Northern Ireland PACE Order, Art.9(2).
[20] The Serious Organised Crime and Police Bill 2004–05, Sch.7, Pt 3, para.8(3) replaces "a serious arrestable offence" here and in s.8(6) with "indictable offence".
[21] The Serious Organised Crime and Police Bill 2004–05, cl.104(3)(a) replaces the words in square brackets with "mentioned in subsection 1A below".
[22] The Serious Organised Crime and Police Bill 2004–05, cl.104(3)(b) adds at the end of (e), "in relation to each set of premises specified in the application".

"*(1A) The premises referred to in subsection (1)(b) above are—*

    (a) one or more sets of premises specified in the application (in which case the application is for a 'specific premises warrant');or

    (b) any premises occupied or controlled by a person specified in the application, including such sets of premises as are so specified (in which case the application is for an 'all premises warrant').

(1B) If the application is for an all premises warrant, the justice of the peace must also be satisfied—

    (a) that because of the particulars of the offence referred to in paragraph (a) of subsection (1) above, there are reasonable grounds for believing that it is necessary to search premises occupied or controlled by the person in question which are not specified in the application in order to find the material referred to in paragraph (b) of that subsection; and

    (b) that it is not reasonably practicable to specify in the application all the premises which he occupies or controls and which might need to be searched.

(1C) The warrant may authorise entry to and search of premises on more than one occasion if, on the application, the justice of the peace is satisfied that it is necessary to authorise multiple entries in order to achieve the purpose for which he issues the warrant.

(1D) If it authorises multiple entries, the number of entries authorised may be unlimited, or limited to a maximum."]

(2) A constable may seize and retain anything for which a search has been authorised under subsection (1) above.

(3) The conditions mentioned in subsection (1)(e) above are—

    (a) that it is not practicable to communicate with any person entitled to grant entry to the premises;

    (b) that it is practicable to communicate with a person entitled to grant entry to the premises but it is not practicable to communicate with any person entitled to grant access to the evidence;

    (c) that entry to the premises will not be granted unless a warrant is produced;

    (d) that the purpose of a search may be frustrated or seriously prejudiced unless a constable arriving at the premises can secure immediate entry to them.

(4) In this Act "relevant evidence", in relation to an offence, means anything that would be admissible in evidence at a trial for the offence.

(5) The power to issue a warrant conferred by this section is in addition to any such power otherwise conferred.

[(6) This section applies in relation to a relevant offence (as defined in section 28D(4) of the Immigration Act 1971) as it applies to a [serious arrestable offence].][23]

Special provisions as to access[24]

9.—(1) A constable may obtain access to excluded material or special procedure material for the purposes of a criminal investigation by making an application under Schedule 1 below and in accordance with that Schedule.

---

[23] subs.(6) inserted by the Immigration and Asylum Act 1999, s.169(1), Sch.14, para.80(1), (2); words in square brackets within subs.(6), see n.20 above.

[24] Note drafting differences in the 1989 Northern Ireland PACE Order, Art.11(2) and (3).

(2) Any Act (including a local Act) passed before this Act under which a search of premises for the purposes of a criminal investigation could be authorised by the issue of a warrant to a constable shall cease to have effect so far as it relates to the authorisation of searches—

    (a)   for items subject to legal privilege; or

    (b)   for excluded material; or

    (c)   for special procedure material consisting of documents or records other than documents.

[(2A) Section 4 of the Summary Jurisdiction (Process) Act 1881 (c. 24) (which includes provision for the execution of process of English courts in Scotland) and section 29 of the Petty Sessions (Ireland) Act 1851 (c. 93) (which makes equivalent provision for execution in Northern Ireland) shall each apply to any process issued by a [judge][25] under Schedule 1 to this Act as it applies to process issued by a magistrates' court under the Magistrates' Courts Act 1980 (c. 43).][26]

Meaning of "items subject to legal privilege"

10.—(1) Subject to subsection (2) below, in this Act "items subject to legal privilege" means—

    (a)   communications between a professional legal adviser and his client or any person representing his client made in connection with the giving of legal advice to the client;

    (b)   communications between a professional legal adviser and his client or any person representing his client or between such an adviser or his client or any such representative and any other person made in connection with or in contemplation of legal proceedings and for the purposes of such proceedings; and

    (c)   items enclosed with or referred to in such communications and made—

        (i) in connection with the giving of legal advice; or

        (ii) in connection with or in contemplation of legal proceedings and for the purposes of such procedings, when they are in the possession of a person who is entitled to possession of them.

(2) Items held with the intention of furthering a criminal purpose are not items subject to legal privilege.

Meaning of "excluded material"

11.—(1) Subject to the following provisions of this section, in this Act "excluded material" means—

    (a)   personal records which a person has acquired or created in the course of any trade, business, profession or other occupation or for the purposes of any paid or unpaid office and which he holds in confidence;

    (b)   human tissue or tissue fluid which has been taken for the purposes of diagnosis or medical treatment and which a person holds in confidence;

---

[25] Changed from "circuit judge" by the Courts Act 2003, Sch.4, para.5—not yet in force.

[26] subs.(2A) inserted by the Criminal Justice and Police Act 2001, s.86(1).

    (c) journalistic material which a person holds in confidence and which consists—

        (i) of documents; or

        (ii) of records other than documents.

(2) A person holds material other than journalistic material in confidence for the purposes of this section if he holds it subject—

    (a) to an express or implied undertaking to hold it in confidence; or

    (b) to a restriction on disclosure or an obligation of secrecy contained in any enactment, including an enactment contained in an Act passed after this Act.

(3) A person holds journalistic material in confidence for the purposes of this section if—

    (a) he holds it subject to such an undertaking, restriction or obligation; and

    (b) it has been continuously held (by one or more persons) subject to such an undertaking, restriction or obligation since it was first acquired or created for the purposes of journalism.

Meaning of "personal records"

12.—In this Part of this Act "personal records" means documentary and other records concerning an individual (whether living or dead) who can be identified from them, and relating—

    (a) to his physical or mental health;

    (b) to spiritual counselling or assistance given or to be given to him;

    (c) to counselling or assistance given or to be given to him, for the purposes of his personal welfare, by any voluntary organisation or by any individual who—

        (i) by reason of his office or occupation has responsibilities for his personal welfare; or

        (ii) by reason of an order of a court, has responsibilities for his supervision.

Meaning of "journalistic material"

13.—(1) Subject to subsection (2) below, in this Act "journalistic material" means material acquired or created for the purposes of journalism.

(2) Material is only journalistic material for the purposes of this Act if it is in the possession of a person who acquired or created it for the purposes of journalism.

(3) A person who receives material from someone who intends that the recipient shall use it for the purposes of journalism is to be taken to have acquired it for those purposes.

Meaning of "special procedure material"

14.—(1) In this Act "special procedure material" means—

    (a) material to which subsection (2) below applies; and

    (b) journalistic material, other than excluded material.

(2) Subject to the following provisions of this section, this subsection applies to material, other than items subject to legal privilege and excluded material, in the possession of a person who—

    (a) acquired or created it in the course of any trade, business, profession or other occupation or for the purpose of any paid or unpaid office and

(b) holds it subject—
    (i) to an express or implied undertaking to hold it in confidence; or
    (ii) to a restriction or obligation such as is mentioned in section 11(2)(b) above.

(3) Where material is acquired—
    (a) by an employee from his employer and in the course of his employment; or
    (b) by a company from an associated company,

it is only special procedure material if it was special procedure material immediately before the acquisition.

(4) Where material is created by an employee in the course of his employment, it is only special procedure material if it would have been special procedure material had his employer created it.

(5) Where material is created by a company on behalf of an associated company, it is only special procedure material if it would have been special procedure material had the associated company created it.

(6) A company is to be treated as another's associated company for the purposes of this section if it would be so treated under section 302 of the Income and Corporation Taxes Act 1970.

Search warrants—safeguards[27]

15.—(1) This section and section 16 below have effect in relation to the issue to constables under any enactment, including an enactment contained in an Act passed after this Act, of warrants to enter and search premises, and an entry on or search of premises under a warrant is unlawful unless it complies with this section and section 16 below.

(2) Where a constable applies for any such warrant, it shall be his duty—
    (a) to state—
      (i) the ground on which he makes the application; and
      (ii) the enactment under which the warrant would be issued;
    [The Serious Organised Crime and Police Bill 2004–05, cl.105(4) inserts a new subs.(iii):
    "(iii) if the application is for a warrant authorising entry and search on more than one occasion, the ground on which he applies for such a warrant, and whether he seeks a warrant authorising an unlimited number of entries, or (if not) the maximum number of entries desired;"]
    (b) [to specify the premises which it is desired to enter and search; and][28]
    (c) to identify, so far as is practicable, the articles or persons to be sought.

[The Serious Organised Crime and Police Bill 2004–05, cl.104(7) inserts a new subs.(2A):

"(2A) The matters which must be specified pursuant to subsection (2)(b) above are—

    (a) if the application is for a specific premises warrant made by virtue of section 8(1A)(a) above or paragraph 12 of Schedule 1 below, each set of premises which it is desired to enter and search;

---

[27] Note drafting changes in the 1989 Northern Ireland PACE Order, Art.17(1), (3), (4) and (8).
[28] The Serious Organised Crime and Police Bill 2004–05, cl.104(6) substitutes: "to specify the matters set out in subsection (2A) below; and".

(b) if the application is for an all premises warrant made by virtue of
section 8(1A)(b) above or paragraph 12 of Schedule 1 below—
   (i) as many sets of premises which it is desired to enter and search
        as it is reasonably practicable to specify;
   (ii) the person who is in occupation or control of those premises
         and any others which it is desired to enter and search;
   (iii) why it is necessary to search more premises than those specified
          under sub-paragraph (i); and
   (iv) why it is not reasonably practicable to specify all the premises
         which it is desired to enter and search."]

(3) An application for such a warrant shall be made ex parte and supported by
an information in writing.

(4) The constable shall answer on oath any question that the justice of the
peace or judge hearing the application asks him.

(5) A warrant shall authorise an entry on one occasion only.[29]

[*The Serious Organised Crime and Police Bill 2004–05, cl.105(6) inserts new
subs.(5A):*

"*(5A) If it specifies that it authorises multiple entries, it must also specify
whether the number of entries authorised is unlimited, or limited to a specified
maximum.*"]

(6) A warrant—
   (a) shall specify—
      (i) the name of the person who applies for it;
      (ii) the date on which it is issued;
      (iii) the enactment under which it is issued; and
      (iv) the premises to be searched; and
      [*The Serious Organised Crime and Police Bill 2004–05, cl.104(8)
      substitutes a new subs.(iv):*
      "*(iv) each set of premises to be searched, or (in the case of an all
             premises warrant) the person who is in occupation or control of
             premises to be searched, together with any premises under his
             occupation or control which can be specified and which are to
             be searched; and*"]
   (b) shall identify, so far as is practicable, the articles or person to be
        sought.

(7) Two copies shall be made of a warrant.

[*The Serious Organised Crime and Police Bill 2004–05, cl.105(7) substitutes
a new subs.(7):*

"*(7) Two copies shall be made of a specific premises warrant (see section
8(1A)(a) above) which specifies only one set of premises and does not authorise
multiple entries; and as many copies as are reasonably required may be made of
any other kind of warrant.*"]

(8) The copies shall be clearly certified as copies.

Execution of warrants[30]

16.—(1) A warrant to enter and search premises may be executed by any
constable.

---

[29] The Serious Organised Crime and Police Bill 2004–05, cl.105(5) adds: "unless it specifies that it
authorises multiple entries".

[30] Note drafting changes in the 1989 Northern Ireland PACE Order, Art.18(5)(c), (7), (10) and (11).

(2) Such a warrant may authorise persons to accompany any constable who is executing it.

[(2A) A person so authorised has the same powers as the constable whom he accompanies in respect of—

    (a) the execution of the warrant, and

    (b) the seizure of anything to which the warrant relates.

(2B) But he may exercise those powers only in the company, and under the supervision, of a constable.][31]

(3) Entry and search under a warrant must be within one month from the date of its issue.

[*The Serious Organised Crime and Police Bill 2004–05, cl.105(8)(a) substitutes three months for one month. Clause 104(9)(a) inserts new subs.(3A) and cl.105(8)(b) inserts new subs.(3B):*

"(3A) If the warrant is an all premises warrant, no premises which are not specified in it may be entered or searched unless a police officer of at least the rank of inspector has in writing authorised them to be entered.

(3B) No premises may be entered or searched for the second or any subsequent time under a warrant which authorises multiple entries unless a police officer of at least the rank of inspector has in writing authorised that entry to those premises."]

(4) Entry and search under a warrant must be at a reasonable hour unless it appears to the constable executing it that the purposes of a search may be frustrated on an entry at a reasonable hour.

(5) Where the occupier of premises which are to be entered and searched is present at the time when a constable seeks to execute a warrant to enter and search them, the constable—

    (a) shall identify himself to the occupier and, if not in uniform, shall produce to him documentary evidence that he is a constable;

    (b) shall produce the warrant to him; and

    (c) shall supply him with a copy of it.

(6) Where—

    (a) the occupier of such premises is not present at the time when a constable seeks to execute such a warrant; but

    (b) some other person who appears to the constable to be in charge of the premises is present,

subsection (5) above shall have effect as if any reference to the occupier were a reference to that other person.

(7) If there is no person present who appears to the constable to be in charge of the premises, he shall leave a copy of the warrant in a prominent place on the premises.

(8) A search under a warrant may only be a search to the extent required for the purpose for which the warrant was issued.

(9) A constable executing a warrant shall make an endorsement on it stating—

    (a) whether the articles or persons sought were found; and

    (b) whether any articles were seized, other than articles which were sought.[32]

---

[31] Inserted by Criminal Justice Act 2003, s.2.

[32] The Serious Organised Crime and Police Bill 2004–05, cl.104(9)(b) adds the requirement that if the warrant is for more than one set of premises he shall do so separately in respect of each set of premises.

(10) A warrant which—
  (a) has been executed; or
  (b) has not been executed within the time authorised for its execution, shall be returned—
    (i) if it was issued by a justice of the peace, to the [designated officer for the local justice area in which the justice was acting when he issued the warrant][33]; and
    (ii) if it was issued by a judge, to the appropriate officer of the court from which he issued it.

[*The Serious Organised Crime and Police Bill 2004–05, cl.105(8) replaces subs.(10) and inserts new subs.(10A):*

"(10) A warrant shall be returned to the appropriate person mentioned in subsection (10A) below—
  (a) when it has been executed; or
  (b) in the case of a specific premises warrant which has not been executed, or an all premises warrant, or any warrant authorising multiple entries, upon the expiry of the period of three months referred to in subsection (5) above or sooner.

(10A) The appropriate person is—
  (a) if the warrant was issued by a justice of the peace, the designated officer for the local justice area in which the justice was acting when he issued the warrant;
  (b) if it was issued by a judge, the appropriate officer of the court from which he issued it."]

(11) A warrant which is returned under subsection (10) above shall be retained for 12 months from its return—
  (a) by the [designated officer for the local justice area][34] if it was returned under paragraph (i) of that subsection; and
  (b) by the appropriate officer, if it was returned under paragraph (ii).

(12) If during the period for which a warrant is to be retained the occupier of the premises to which it relates asks to inspect it, he shall be allowed to do so.

Entry and search without search warrant

Entry for purpose of arrest etc.[35]

17.—(1) Subject to the following provisions of this section, and without prejudice to any other enactment, a constable may enter and search any premises for the purpose—
  (a) of executing—
    (i) a warrant of arrest issued in connection with or arising out of criminal proceedings; or
    (ii) a warrant of commitment issued under section 76 of the Magistrates' Courts Act 1980;
  (b) of arresting a person for an [arrestable][36] offence;

---

[33] The Access to Justice Act 1999, Sch.13, para.126 inserted "chief executive". The Courts Act 2003, Sch.8, para.281(2)—not yet in force—changed this to the words in the square bracket.
[34] The Access to Justice Act 1999, Sch.13, para.126 inserted "chief executive". The Courts Act 2003, Sch.8, para.281(3)—not yet in force—changed this to the words in the square bracket.
[35] Note drafting change in the 1989 Northern Ireland PACE Order, Art.19(1)(c).
[36] The Serious Organised Crime and Police Bill 2004–05, Sch.7, Pt 3, para.8(4) changes "arrestable" to "indictable".

   (c) of arresting a person for an offence under—
      (i) section 1 (prohibition of uniforms in connection with political objects) . . .[37] of the Public Order Act 1936;
      (ii) any enactment contained in sections 6 to 8 or 10 of the Criminal Law Act 1977 (offences relating to entering and remaining on property);
     [(iii) s.4 of the Public Order Act 1986 (fear or provocation of violence);][38]
    [(iiia) section 163 of the Road Traffic Act 1988 (c.52) (failure to stop when required to do so by a constable in uniform);][39]
     [(iv) section 76 of the Criminal Justice and Public Order Act 1994 (failure to comply with interim possession order);][40]
  [(ca) of arresting, in pursuance of section 32(1A) of the Children and Young Persons Act 1969, any child or young person who has been remanded or committed to local authority accommodation under section 23(1) of that Act;
  (cb) of recapturing any person who is, or is deemed for any purpose to be, unlawfully at large while liable to be detained—
      (i) in a prison, remand centre, young offender institution or secure training centre; or
      (ii) in pursuance of [section 92 of the Powers of Criminal Courts (Sentencing) Act 2000][41] (dealing with children and young persons guilty of grave crimes), in any other place;][42]
   (d) of recapturing [any person whatsoever][43] who is unlawfully at large and whom he is pursuing[44]; or
   (e) of saving life or limb or preventing serious damage to property.

(2) Except for the purpose specified in paragraph (e) of subsection (1) above, the powers of entry and search conferred by this section—
   (a) are only exercisable if the constable has reasonable grounds for believing that the person whom he is seeking is on the premises; and
   (b) are limited, in relation to premises consisting of two or more separate dwellings, to powers to enter and search—
      (i) any parts of the premises which the occupiers of any dwelling comprised in the premises use in common with the occupiers of any other such dwelling; and
      (ii) any such dwelling in which the constable has reasonable grounds for believing that the person whom he is seeking may be.

(3) The powers of entry and search conferred by this section are only exercisable for the purposes specified in subsection (1)(c)(ii) [or (iv)][45] above by a constable in uniform.

---

[37] Words deleted by Public Order Act 1986, s.40(2), Sch.2, para.7.
[38] subs.(iii) inserted by Public Order Act 1986, s.40(2), Sch.2, para.7.
[39] subs.(iiia) inserted by the Police Reform Act 2002, s.49(2).
[40] subs.(iv) inserted by the Criminal Justice and Public Order Act 1994, Sch.10, para.53(a).
[41] Words in square brackets substituted by the Powers of Criminal Courts (Sentencing) Act 2000, s.165(1), Sch.9, para.95.
[42] subss.(ca), (cb) inserted by the Prisoners (Return to Custody) Act 1995, s.2(1).
[43] Words in square brackets substituted by the Prisoners (Return to Custody) Act 1995, s.2(1).
[44] As amended for Northern Ireland by Police (Amendment) (Northern Ireland) Order 1995, Art.7.
[45] Inserted by the Criminal Justice and Public Order Act 1994, Sch.10, para.53(b).

(4) The power of search conferred by this section is only a power to search to the extent that is reasonably required for the purpose for which the power of entry is exercised.

(5) Subject to subsection (6) below, all the rules of common law under which a constable has power to enter premises without a warrant are hereby abolished.

(6) Nothing in subsection (5) above affects any power of entry to deal with or prevent a breach of the peace.

Entry and search after arrest

18.—(1) Subject to the following provisions of this section, a constable may enter and search, any premises occupied or controlled by a person who is under arrest for an [arrestable][46] offence, if he has reasonable grounds for suspecting that there is on the premises evidence other than items subject to legal privilege, that relates—

(a) to that offence; or

(b) to some other [arrestable] offence which is connected with or similar to that offence.

(2) A constable may seize and retain anything for which he may search under subsection (1) above.

(3) The power to search conferred by subsection (1) above is only a power to search to the extent that is reasonably required for the purpose of discovering such evidence.

(4) Subject to subsection (5) below, the powers conferred by this section may not be exercised unless an officer of the rank of inspector or above has authorised them in writing.

[(5) A constable may conduct a search under subsection (1)—

(a) before [the person is taken][46a] to a police station or released on bail under section 30A, and

(b) without obtaining an authorisation under subsection (4),

if the condition in subsection (5A) is satisfied.

(5A) The condition is that the presence of the person at a place (other than a police station) is necessary for the effective investigation of the offence.][47]

(6) If a constable conducts a search by virtue of subsection (5) above, he shall inform an officer of the rank of inspector or above that he has made the search as soon as practicable after he has made it.

(7) An officer who—

(a) authorises a search; or

(b) is informed of a search under subsection (6) above, shall make a record in writing—

(i) of the grounds for the search; and

(ii) of the nature of the evidence that was sought.

(8) If the person who was in occupation or control of the premises at the time of the search is in police detention at the time the record is to be made, the officer shall make the record as part of his custody record.[48]

---

[46] The Serious Organised Crime and Police Bill 2004–05, Sch.7, Pt 3, para.8(5) changes "arrestable" to "indictable" in both places where it occurs in subs.(1).

[46a] Substituted by Police Reform Act 2002, Sch.7, para.9(1).

[47] subs.(5) was substituted and subs.(5A) was inserted by the Criminal Justice Act 2003, Sch.1, para.2. For the Northern Ireland equivalent see Criminal Justice (Northern Ireland)Order 2004, SI 2004/1500, Sch.1, para.1.

[48] The 1989 Northern Ireland PACE Order, Art.20 had an extra para.(9) to take account of the fact that Ministry of Defence police in the province have no rank two above constable.

Seizure etc.

General power of seizure etc.

19.—(1) The powers conferred by subsections (2), (3), and (4) below are exercisable by a constable who is lawfully on any premises.

(2) The constable may seize anything which is on the premises if he has reasonable grounds for believing—

    (a) that it has been obtained in consequence of the commission of an offence; and

    (b) that it is necessary to seize it in order to prevent it being concealed, lost, damaged, altered or destroyed.

(3) The constable may seize anything which is on the premises if he has reasonable grounds for believing—

    (a) that it is evidence in relation to an offence which he is investigating or any other offence; and

    (b) that it is necessary to seize it in order to prevent the evidence being concealed, lost, altered or destroyed.

(4) The constable may require any information which is [stored in any electronic form][49] and is accessible from the premises to be produced in a form in which it can be taken away and in which it is visible and legible [or from which it can readily be produced in a visible and legible form][50] if he has reasonable grounds for believing—

    (a) that—

        (i) it is evidence in relation to an offence which he is investigating or any other offence; or

        (ii) it has been obtained in consequence of the commission of an offence; and

    (b) that it is necessary to do so in order to prevent it being concealed, lost, tampered with or destroyed.

(5) The powers conferred by this section are in addition to any power otherwise conferred.

(6) No power of seizure conferred on a constable under any enactment (including an enactment contained in an Act passed after this Act) is to be taken to authorise the seizure of an item which the constable exercising the power has reasonable grounds for believing to be subject to legal privilege.[51]

Extension of powers of seizure to computerised information

20.—(1) Every power of seizure which is conferred by an enactment to which this section applies on a constable who has entered premises in the exercise of a power conferred by an enactment shall be construed as including a power to require any information [stored in any electronic form][52] and accessible from the

---

[49] Words in square brackets substituted for "contained in a computer" by Criminal Justice and Police Act 2001, Sch.2, Pt 2, para.13(1)(a), (2)(a).

[50] Words in square brackets substituted by the Criminal Justice and Police Act 2001, Sch.2, Pt 2, para.13(1)(b), (2)(a).

[51] This rule is now qualified by the power to seize material where it is not practicable to establish on the spot whether it is or is not covered by legal privilege—see the Criminal Justice and Police Act 2001, s.50(4) which affects subs.(6) and its equivalent in Northern Ireland, The Police and Criminal Evidence (Northern Ireland) Order 1989, Art.21(6).

[52] Words in square brackets substituted for "contained in a computer" by Criminal Justice and Police Act 2001, Sch.2, Pt 2, para.13(1)(a), (2)(a).

premises to be produced in a form in which it can be taken away and in which it is visible and legible [or from which it can readily be produced in a visible and legible form].[53]

(2) This section applies—

    (a)   to any enactment contained in an Act passed before this Act;

    (b)   to sections 8 and 18 above;

    (c)   to paragraph 13 of Schedule 1 to this Act; and

    (d)   to any enactment contained in an Act passed after this Act.

Access and copying

21.—(1) A constable who seizes anything in the exercise of a power conferred by any enactment, including an enactment contained in an Act passed after this Act, shall, if so requested by a person showing himself—

    (a)   to be the occupier of premises on which it was seized; or

    (b)   to have had custody or control of it immediately before the seizure,

provide that person with a record of what he seized.

(2) The officer shall provide the record within a reasonable time from the making of the request for it.

(3) Subject to subsection (8) below, if a request for permission to be granted access to anything which—

    (a)   has been seized by a constable; and

    (b)   is retained by the police for the purpose of investigating an offence,

is made to the officer in charge of the investigation by a person who had custody or control of the thing immediately before it was so seized or by someone acting on behalf of such a person the officer shall allow the person who made the request access to it under the supervision of a constable.

(4) Subject to subsection (8) below, if a request for a photograph or copy of any such thing is made to the officer in charge of the investigation by a person who had custody or control of the thing immediately before it was so seized, or by someone acting on behalf of such a person, the officer shall—

    (a)   allow the person who made the request access to it under the supervision of a constable for the purpose of photographing or copying it; or

    (b)   photograph or copy it, or cause it to be photographed or copied.

(5) A constable may also photograph or copy, or have photographed or copied, anything which he has power to seize, without a request being made under subsection (4) above.

(6) Where anything is photographed or copied under subsection (4)(b) above, the photograph or copy shall be supplied to the person who made the request.

(7) The photograph or copy shall be so supplied within a reasonable time from the making of the request.

(8) There is no duty under this section to grant access to, or to supply a photograph or copy of, anything if the officer in charge of the investigation for the purposes of which it was seized has reasonable grounds for believing that to do so would prejudice—

    (a)   that investigation;

    (b)   the investigation of an offence other than the offence for the purposes of investigating which the thing was seized; or

---

[53] Words in square brackets substituted by the Criminal Justice and Police Act 2001, Sch.2, Pt 2, para.13(1)(b), (2)(a).

(c) any criminal proceedings which may be brought as a result of—
    (i) the investigation of which he is in charge; or
    (ii) any such investigation as is mentioned in paragraph (b) above.
[(9) The references to a constable in subsections (1), (2), (3)(a) and (5) include a person authorised under section 16(2) to accompany a constable executing a warrant.][54]

Retention

22.—(1) Subject to subsection (4) below, anything which has been seized by a constable or taken away by a constable following a requirement made by virtue of section 19 or 20 may be retained so long as is necessary in all the circumstances.

(2) Without prejudice to the generality of subsection (1) above—
    (a) anything seized for the purposes of a criminal investigation may be retained, except as provided by subsection (4) below,—
        (i) for use as evidence at a trial for an offence; or
        (ii) for forensic examination or for investigation in connection with an offence; and
    (b) anything may be retained in order to establish its lawful owner, where there are reasonable grounds for believing that it has been obtained in consequence of the commission of an offence.

(3) Nothing seized on the ground that it may be used—
    (a) to cause physical injury to any person;
    (b) to damage property;
    (c) to interfere with evidence; or
    (d) to assist in escape from police detention or lawful custody,
may be retained when the person from whom it was seized is no longer in police detention or the custody of a court or is in the custody of a court but has been released on bail.

(4) Nothing may be retained for either of the purposes mentioned in subsection (2)(a) above if a photograph or copy would be sufficient for that purpose.

(5) Nothing in this section affects any power of a court to make an order under section 1 of the Police (Property) Act 1897.

[(6) This section also applies to anything retained by the police under section 28H(5) of the Immigration Act 1971.][55]

[(7) The reference in subsection (1) to anything seized by a constable includes anything seized by a person authorised under section 16(2) to accompany a constable executing a warrant.][56]

Part II—Supplementary

Meaning of "premises" etc.

23.—In this Act—
    "premises" includes any place and, in particular, includes—
    (a) any vehicle, vessel, aircraft or hovercraft;
    (b) any offshore installation; and

---

[54] Inserted by Criminal Justice Act 2003, Sch.1, paras 1,3.
[55] subs.(6) was inserted by the Immigration and Asylum Act 1999, s.169(1), Sch.14, para.80(1), (3).
[56] subs.(7) was inserted by Criminal Justice Act 2003, Sch.1, paras 1,4.

(c)   any tent or movable structure; and

"offshore installation" has the meaning given to it by section 1 of the Mineral Workings (Offshore Installations) Act 1971.

PART III

ARREST

Arrest without warrant for arrestable and other offences

24.—(1) The powers of summary arrest conferred by the following subsections shall apply—

(a)   to offences for which the sentence is fixed by law;

(b)   to offences for which a person of [18][57] years of age or over (not previously convicted) may be sentenced to imprisonment for a term of five years (or might be so sentenced but for the restrictions imposed by section 33 of the Magistrates' Courts Act 1980); and

(c)   to the offences [listed in Schedule 1A][58]

and in this Act "arrestable offence" means any such offence.

(2) [Schedule 1A (which lists the offences referred to in subsection (1)(c) shall have effect.][59]

(3) Without prejudice to section 2 of the Criminal Attempts Act 1981, the powers of summary arrest conferred by the following subsections shall also apply to the offences of—

(a)   conspiring to commit any of the offences [listed in Schedule 1A][60];

(b)   attempting to commit any such offence [other than [one which is a summary offence]][61];

(c)   inciting, aiding, abetting, counselling or procuring the commission of any such offence,

and such offences are also arrestable offences for the purposes of this Act.

(4) Any person may arrest without a warrant—

(a)   anyone who is in the act of committing an arrestable offence;

(b)   anyone whom he has reasonable grounds for suspecting to be committing such an offence.

(5) Where an arrestable offence has been committed, any person may arrest without a warrant—

(a)   anyone who is guilty of the offence;

(b)   anyone whom he has reasonable grounds for suspecting to be guilty of it.

(6) Where a constable has reasonable grounds for suspecting that an arrestable offence has been committed, he may arrest without a warrant anyone whom he has reasonable grounds for suspecting to be guilty of the offence.

---

[57] 18 was substituted for 21 by the Criminal Justice and Courts Services Act 2000, Sch.7, Pt II, para.77—not yet in force.
[58] Words in square brackets substituted by the Police Reform Act 2002, s.48(2).
[59] subs.(2) substituted by the Police Reform Act 2002, s.48(3).
[60] Words in square brackets substituted by the Police Reform Act 2002, s.48(4)(a).
[61] "Other than" survives from an earlier amendment made by the Criminal Justice Act 1988, Sch.15, para.98. That amendment was itself amended by the Police Reform Act 2002, s.48(4)(b) which substituted the other words in the square brackets.

(7) A constable may arrest without a warrant—
  (a) anyone who is about to commit an arrestable offence;
  (b) anyone whom he has reasonable grounds for suspecting to be about to commit an arrestable offence.

[*The Serious Organised Crime and Police Bill 2004–05, cl.101(1) replaces s.24 and adds a new s.24A. Clause 101(5) states that they are to have effect in relation to any offence whenever committed. Clause 101(4) abolishes any common law power of arrest.*]

"Arrest without warrant: constables

24.—*(1) A constable may arrest without a warrant—*
  (a) anyone who is about to commit an offence;
  (b) anyone who is in the act of committing an offence;
  (c) anyone whom he has reasonable grounds for suspecting to be about to commit an offence;
  (d) anyone whom he has reasonable grounds for suspecting to be committing an offence.

(2) If a constable has reasonable grounds for suspecting that an offence has been committed, he may arrest without a warrant anyone whom he has reasonable grounds to suspect of being guilty of it.

(3) If an offence has been committed, a constable may arrest without a warrant—
  (a) anyone who is guilty of the offence;
  (b) anyone whom he has reasonable grounds for suspecting to be guilty of it.

(4) But the power of summary arrest conferred by subsection (1), (2) or (3) is exercisable only if the constable has reasonable grounds for believing that for any of the reasons mentioned in subsection (5) it is necessary to arrest the person in question.

(5) The reasons are—
  (a) to enable the name of the person in question to be ascertained (in the case where the constable does not know, and cannot readily ascertain, the person's name, or has reasonable grounds for doubting whether a name given by the person as his name is his real name);
  (b) correspondingly as regards the person's address;
  (c) to prevent the person in question—
    (i) causing physical injury to himself or any other person;
    (ii) suffering physical injury;
    (iii) causing loss of or damage to property;
    (iv) committing an offence against public decency (subject to subsection (6)); or
    (v) causing an unlawful obstruction of the highway;
  (d) to protect a child or other vulnerable person from the person in question;
  (e) to allow the prompt and effective investigation of the offence or of the conduct of the person in question;
  (f) to prevent any prosecution for the offence from being hindered by the disappearance of the person in question.

(6) Subsection (5)(c)(iv) applies only where members of the public going about their normal business cannot reasonably be expected to avoid the person in question.

Arrest without warrant: other persons

24A.—*(1) A person other than a constable may arrest without a warrant—*

   (a)   anyone who is in the act of committing an offence;

   (b)   anyone whom he has reasonable grounds for suspecting to be committing an offence.

(2) Where an offence has been committed, a person other than a constable may arrest without a warrant—

   (a)   anyone who is guilty of the offence;

   (b)   anyone whom he has reasonable grounds for suspecting to be guilty of it.

(3) But the power of summary arrest conferred by subsection (1) or (2) is exercisable only if—

   (a)   the person making the arrest has reasonable grounds for believing that for any of the reasons mentioned in subsection (4) it is necessary to arrest the person in question; and

   (b)   it appears to the person making the arrest that it is not reasonably practicable for a constable to make it instead.

(4) The reasons are to prevent the person in question—

   (a)   causing physical injury to himself or any other person;

   (b)   suffering physical injury;

   (c)   causing loss of or damage to property; or

   (d)   making off before a constable can assume responsibility for him."]

General arrest conditions

25.—(1) Where a constable has reasonable grounds for suspecting that any offence which is not an arrestable offence has been committed or attempted, or is being committed or attempted, he may arrest the relevant person if it appears to him that service of a summons is impracticable or inappropriate because any of the general arrest conditions is satisfied.

(2) In this section, "the relevant person" means any person whom the constable has reasonable grounds to suspect of having committed or having attempted to commit the offence or of being in the course of committing or attempting to commit it.

(3) The general arrest conditions are—

   (a)   that the name of the relevant person is unknown to, and cannot be readily ascertained by, the constable;

   (b)   that the constable has reasonable grounds for doubting whether a name furnished by the relevant person as his name is his real name;

   (c)   that—

      (i) the relevant person has failed to furnish a satisfactory address for service; or

      (ii) the constable has reasonable grounds for doubting whether an address furnished by the relevant person is a satisfactory address for service;

   (d)   that the constable has reasonable grounds for believing that arrest is necessary to prevent the relevant person—

      (i) causing physical harm to himself or any other person;

      (ii) suffering physical injury;

      (iii) causing loss of or damage to property;

  (iv) committing an offence against public decency; or

  (v) causing an unlawful obstruction of the highway;

(e) that the constable has reasonable grounds for believing that arrest is necessary to protect a child or other vulnerable person from the relevant person.

(4) For the purposes of subsection (3) above an address is a satisfactory address for service if it appears to the constable—

(a) that the relevant person will be at it for a sufficiently long period for it to be possible to serve him with a summons; or

(b) that some other person specified by the relevant person will accept service of a summons for the relevant person at it.

(5) Nothing in subsection (3)(d) above authorises the arrest of a person under sub-paragraph (iv) of that paragraph except where members of the public going about their normal business cannot reasonably be expected to avoid the person to be arrested.

(6) This section shall not prejudice any power of arrest conferred apart from this section.

[*The Serious Organised Crime and Police Bill 2004–05, cl.101(2) repeals s.25.*]

Repeal of statutory powers of arrest without warrant or order

26.—(1) Subject to subsection (2) below, so much of any Act (including a local Act) passed before this Act as enables a constable—

(a) to arrest a person for an offence without a warrant; or

(b) to arrest a person otherwise than for an offence without a warrant or an order of a court,

shall cease to have effect.

(2) Nothing in subsection (1) above affects the enactments specified in Schedule 2 to this Act.

Fingerprinting of certain offenders

27.—(1) If a person—

(a) has been convicted of a recordable offence;

(b) has not at any time been in police detention for the offence; and

(c) has not had his fingerprints taken—

  (i) in the course of the investigation of the offence by the police; or

  (ii) since the conviction;

any constable may at any time not later than one month after the date of the conviction require him to attend a police station in order that his fingerprints may be taken.

[(1A) Where a person convicted of a recordable offence has already had his fingerprints taken as mentioned in paragraph (c) of subsection (1) above, that fact (together with any time when he has been in police detention for the offence) shall be disregarded for the purposes of that subsection if—

(a) the fingerprints taken on the previous occasion do not constitute a complete set of his fingerprints; or

(b) some or all of the fingerprints taken on the previous occasion are not of sufficient quality to allow satisfactory analysis, comparison or matching.

(1B) Subsections (1) and (1A) above apply—

> (a)   where a person has been given a caution in respect of a recordable offence which, at the time of the caution, he has admitted, or
>
> (b)   where a person has been warned or reprimanded under section 65 of the Crime and Disorder Act 1998 (c. 37) for a recordable offence,

as they apply where a person has been convicted of an offence, and references in this section to a conviction shall be construed accordingly.][62]

(2) A requirement under subsection (1) above—

> (a)   shall give the person a period of at least 7 days within which he must so attend; and
>
> (b)   may direct him to so attend at a specified time of day or between specified times of day.

(3) Any constable may arrest without warrant a person who has failed to comply with a requirement under subsection (1) above.

(4) The Secretary of State may by regulations make provision for recording in national police records convictions for such offences as are specified in the regulations.

(4A) . . .[63]

(5) Regulations under this section shall be made by statutory instrument and shall be subject to annulment in pursuance of a resolution of either House of Parliament.

Information to be given on arrest

28.—(1) Subject to subsection (5) below, when a person is arrested otherwise than by being informed that he is under arrest, the arrest is not lawful unless the person arrested is informed that he is under arrest as soon as is practicable after his arrest.

(2) Where a person is arrested by a constable subsection (1) above applies regardless of whether the fact of the arrest is obvious.

(3) Subject to subsection (5) below, no arrest is lawful unless the person arrested is informed of the ground for the arrest at the time of, or as soon as is practicable after, the arrest.[64]

(4) Where a person is arrested by a constable, subsection (3) above applies regardless of whether the ground for the arrest is obvious.

(5) Nothing in this section is to be taken to require a person to be informed—

> (a)   that he is under arrest; or
>
> (b)   of the ground for the arrest,

if it was not reasonably practicable for him to be so informed by reason of his having escaped from arrest before the information could be given.

Voluntary attendance at police station etc.

29.—Where for the purpose of assisting with an investigation a person attends voluntarily at a police station or at any other place where a constable is present or accompanies a constable to a police station or any such other place without having been arrested—

> (a)   he shall be entitled to leave at will unless he is placed under arrest;

---

[62] subss.(1A) and (1B) inserted by Criminal Justice and Police Act 2001, s.78(1).

[63] subs.(4A) was inserted by the Crime and Disorder Act 1998, s.119, Sch.8, para.61 but was repealed by the Criminal Justice and Police Act 2001, Sch.7, Pt 2(1).

[64] The 1989 Northern Ireland PACE Order, Art.30(3) excluded arrests by the Army under s.14(2) of the Northern Ireland (Emergency Provisions) Act 1978. See now s.18(2) of the 1991 Northern Ireland (Emergency Provisions) Act.

    (b)   he shall be informed at once that he is under arrest if a decision is taken by a constable to prevent him from leaving at will.

Arrest elsewhere than at police station

30.—[(1) Subsection (1A) applies where a person is, at any place other than a police station—
    (a)   arrested by a constable for an offence, or
    (b)   taken into custody by a constable after being arrested for an offence by a person other than a constable.

(1A) The person must be taken by a constable to a police station as soon as practicable after the arrest.

(1B) Subsection (1A) has effect subject to section 30A (release on bail) and subsection (7) (release without bail).][65]

(2) Subject to subsections (3) and (4) below, the police station to which an arrested person is taken under subsection [(1A)][66] above shall be a designated police station.

(3) A constable to whom this subsection applies may take an arrested person to any police station unless it appears to the constable that it may be necessary to keep the arrested person in police detention for more than six hours.

(4) Subsection (3) above applies—
    (a)   to a constable who is working in a locality covered by a police station which is not a designated police station; and
    (b)   to a constable belonging to a body of constables maintained by an authority other than a police authority.

(5) Any constable may take an arrested person to any police station if—[67]
    (a)   either of the following conditions is satisfied—
        (i)   the constable has arrested him without the assistance of any other constable and no other constable is available to assist him;
        (ii)   the constable has taken him into custody from a person other than a constable without the assistance of any other constable and no other constable is available to assist him; and
    (b)   it appears to the constable that he will be unable to take the arrested person to a designated police station without the arrested person injuring himself, the constable or some other person.

(6) If the first police station to which an arrested person is taken after his arrest is not a designated police station he shall be taken to a designated police station not more than six hours after his arrival at the first police station unless he is released previously.

[(7) A person arrested by a constable at any place other than a police station must be released without bail if the condition in subsection (7A) is satisfied.

(7A) The condition is that, at any time before the person arrested reaches a police station, a constable is satisfied that there are no grounds for keeping him under arrest or releasing him on bail under section 30A.][68]

---

[65] subs.(1) was substituted and subss.(1A) and (1B) were inserted by Criminal Justice Act 2003, s.4(2). For the Northern Ireland equivalent see Criminal Justice (Northern Ireland) Order 2004, SI 2004/1500, Art.4 amending Art.32 and adding new Arts 32A–32D.
[66] Changed from "subs.(1)" by Criminal Justice Act 2003, s.4(3).
[67] The 1989 Northern Ireland PACE Order, Art.32(6), (7) and (8), added the danger to the suspect or officer of an unacceptable risk of injury. He can be held on a superintendent's authority.
[68] subs.(7) was substituted and subs.(7A) was inserted by the Criminal Justice Act 2003, s.4(4).

(8) A constable who releases a person under subsection (7) above shall record the fact that he has done so.

(9) The constable shall make the record as soon as is practicable after the release.

[(10) Nothing in subsection (1A) or in section 30A prevents a constable delaying taking a person to a police station or releasing him on bail if the condition in subsection (10A) is satisfied.

(10A) The condition is that the presence of the person at a place (other than a police station) is necessary in order to carry out such investigations as it is reasonable to carry out immediately.

(11) Where there is any such delay the reasons for the delay must be recorded when the person first arrives at the police station or (as the case may be) is released on bail.][69]

(12) Nothing in subsection [(1A)][70] above shall be taken to affect—

    (a)   paragraphs 16(3) or 18(1) of Schedule 2 to the Immigration Act 1971;

    (b)   section 34(1) of the Criminal Justice Act 1972; or

    (c)   [any provision of the Terrorism Act 2000.][71]

(13) Nothing in subsection (9) above shall be taken to affect paragraph 18(3) of Schedule 2 to the Immigration Act 1971.

[Bail elsewhere than at police station[72]

30A.— (1) A constable may release on bail a person who is arrested or taken into custody in the circumstances mentioned in section 30(1).

(2) A person may be released on bail under subsection (1) at any time before he arrives at a police station.

(3) A person released on bail under subsection (1) must be required to attend a police station.

(4) No other requirement may be imposed on the person as a condition of bail.

(5) The police station which the person is required to attend may be any police station.

Bail under section 30A: notices

30B.—(1) Where a constable grants bail to a person under section 30A, he must give that person a notice in writing before he is released.

(2) The notice must state—

    (a)   the offence for which he was arrested, and

    (b)   the ground on which he was arrested.

(3) The notice must inform him that he is required to attend a police station.

(4) It may also specify the police station which he is required to attend and the time when he is required to attend.

(5) If the notice does not include the information mentioned in subsection (4), the person must subsequently be given a further notice in writing which contains that information.

(6) The person may be required to attend a different police station from that specified in the notice under subsection (1) or (5) or to attend at a different time.

[69] subss.(10) and (11) were substituted and subs.(10A) was inserted by the Criminal Justice Act 2003, s.4(5).

[70] Substituted for (1) by the Criminal Justice Act 2003, s.4(6).

[71] The new text of para.12(c) was substituted by the Terrorism Act 2000, Sch.15, para.5(2).

[72] ss.30A, 30B, 30C and 30D were inserted by the Criminal Justice Act 2003, s.4(7).

(7) He must be given notice in writing of any such change as is mentioned in subsection (6) but more than one such notice may be given to him.

Bail under section 30A: supplemental

30C.—(1) A person who has been required to attend a police station is not required to do so if he is given notice in writing that his attendance is no longer required.

(2) If a person is required to attend a police station which is not a designated police station he must be—

    (a)   released, or

    (b)   taken to a designated police station,

not more than six hours after his arrival.

(3) Nothing in the Bail Act 1976 applies in relation to bail under section 30A.

(4) Nothing in section 30A or 30B or in this section prevents the re-arrest without a warrant of a person released on bail under section 30A if new evidence justifying a further arrest has come to light since his release.

Failure to answer to bail under section 30A

30D.—(1) A constable may arrest without a warrant a person who—

    (a)   has been released on bail under section 30A subject to a requirement to attend a specified police station, but

    (b)   fails to attend the police station at the specified time.

(2) A person arrested under subsection (1) must be taken to a police station (which may be the specified police station or any other police station) as soon as practicable after the arrest.

(3) In subsection (1), "specified" means specified in a notice under subsection (1) or (5) of section 30B or, if notice of change has been given under subsection (7) of that section, in that notice.

(4) For the purposes of—

    (a)   section 30 (subject to the obligation in subsection (2)), and

    (b)   section 31,

an arrest under this section is to be treated as an arrest for an offence.]

Arrest for further offence

31.—Where—

    (a)   a person—

       (i) has been arrested for an offence; and

      (ii) is at a police station in consequence of that arrest; and

    (b)   it appears to a constable that, if he were released from that arrest, he would be liable to arrest for some other offence,

he shall be arrested for that offence.

Search upon arrest

32.—(1) A constable may search an arrested person, in any case where the person to be searched has been arrested at a place other than a police station, if the constable has reasonable grounds for believing that the arrested person may present a danger to himself or others.

(2) Subject to subsections (3) to (5) below, a constable shall also have power in any such case—

   (a) to search the arrested person for anything—
      (i) which he might use to assist him to escape from lawful custody; or
      (ii) which might be evidence relating to an offence; and
   (b) to enter and search any premises in which he was when arrested or immediately before he was arrested for evidence relating to the offence for which he has been arrested.

[*The Serious Organised Crime and Police Bill 2004–05, Sch.7, Pt 3, para.8(6) substitutes a new (b) in the same terms permitting entry and search after an arrest for an indictable offence.*]

(3) The power to search conferred by subsection (2) above is only a power to search to the extent that is reasonably required for the purpose of discovering any such thing or any such evidence.

(4) The powers conferred by this section to search a person are not to be construed as authorising a constable to require a person to remove any of his clothing in public other than an outer coat, jacket or gloves,[73] [but they do authorise a search of a person's mouth].[74]

(5) A constable may not search a person in the exercise of the power conferred by subsection (2)(a) above unless he has reasonable grounds for believing that the person to be searched may have concealed on him anything for which a search is permitted under that paragraph.

(6) A constable may not search premises in the exercise of the power conferred by subsection (2)(b) above unless he has reasonable grounds for believing that there is evidence for which a search is permitted under that paragraph on the premises.

(7) In so far as the power of search conferred by subsection (2)(b) above relates to premises consisting of two or more separate dwellings, it is limited to a power to search—
   (a) any dwelling in which the arrest took place or in which the person arrested was immediately before his arrest; and
   (b) any parts of the premises which the occupier of any such dwelling uses in common with the occupiers of any other dwellings comprised in the premises.

(8) A constable searching a person in the exercise of the power conferred by subsection (1) above may seize and retain anything he finds, if he has reasonable grounds for believing that the person searched might use it to cause physical injury to himself or to any other person.

(9) A constable searching a person in the exercise of the power conferred by subsection (2)(a) above may seize and retain anything he finds, other than an item subject to legal privilege, if he has reasonable grounds for believing—
   (a) that he might use it to assist him to escape from lawful custody; or
   (b) that it is evidence of an offence or has been obtained in consequence of the commission of an offence.

(10) Nothing in this section shall be taken to affect the power conferred by [section 43 of the Terrorism Act 2000].[75]

---

[73] The 1989 Northern Ireland PACE Order, Art.34(4) added headgear.
[74] Inserted by the Criminal Justice and Public Order Act 1994, s.59(2).
[75] The new text of subs.(10) was substituted by the Terrorism Act 2000, Sch.15, para.5(3).

Execution of warrant not in possession of constable

33. . . .[76]

PART IV

DETENTION

Detention—conditions and duration

Limitations on police detention

34.—(1) A person arrested for an offence shall not be kept in police detention except in accordance with the provisions of this Part of this Act.

(2) Subject to subsection (3) below, if at any time a custody officer—

    (a)   becomes aware, in relation to any person in police detention, that the grounds for the detention of that person have ceased to apply; and

    (b)   is not aware of any other grounds on which the continued detention of that person could be justified under the provisions of this Part of this Act,

it shall be the duty of the custody officer, subject to subsection (4) below, to order his immediate release from custody.

(3) No person in police detention shall be released except on the authority of a custody officer at the police station where his detention was authorised or, if it was authorised at more than one station, a custody officer at the station where it was last authorised.

(4) A person who appears to the custody officer to have been unlawfully at large when he was arrested is not to be released under subsection (2) above.

(5) A person whose release is ordered under subsection (2) above shall be released without bail unless it appears to the custody officer—[77]

    (a)   that there is need for further investigation of any matter in connection with which he was detained at any time during the period of his detention; or

    (b)   [that, in respect of any such matter, proceedings may be taken against him or he may be reprimanded or warned under section 65 of the Crime and Disorder Act 1998,][78]

and if it so appears, he shall be released on bail.

(6) For the purposes of this Part of this Act a person arrested under [section 6(D) of the Road Traffic Act 1988][79] [or section 30(2) of the Transport and Works Act 1992 c.42)][80] is arrested for an offence.

[(7) For the purposes of this Part a person who—

    (a)   attends a police station to answer to bail granted under section 30A,

---

[76] Repealed by Access to Justice Act 1999, Sch.15, Pt V(8), para.1.

[77] Note drafting changes in the 1989 Northern Ireland PACE Order, Art.35(5), (6) and (7).

[78] The new text of subs.(5)(b) was substituted by the Criminal Justice and Court Services Act 2000, s.56(2).

[79] As amended by the Road Traffic (Consequential Provisions) Act 1988, Sch.3, para.27.

[80] Words in square brackets inserted by the Police Reform Act 2002, s.53(1). The reference earlier in the subsection to s.6(D) of the 1988 Act was substituted by the Railways and Transport Safety Act 2003, Sch.7, para.12—replacing 6(5).

    (b)   returns to a police station to answer to bail granted under this Part, or

    (c)   is arrested under section 30D or 46A,

is to be treated as arrested for an offence and that offence is the offence in connection with which he was granted bail.][81]

Designated police stations

35.—(1) The chief officer of police for each police area shall designate the police stations in his area which, subject to [sections 30(3) and (5), 30A(5) and 30D(2)][82] above, are to be the stations in that area to be used for the purpose of detaining arrested persons.

(2) A chief officer's duty under subsection (1) above is to designate police stations appearing to him to provide enough accommodation for that purpose.

[(2A) The Chief Constable of the British Transport Police Force may designate police stations which (in addition to those designated under subsection (1) above) may be used for the purpose of detaining arrested persons.][83]

(3) Without prejudice to section 12 of the Interpretation Act 1978 (continuity of duties) a chief officer—

    (a)   may designate a station which was not previously designated; and

    (b)   may direct that a designation of a station previously made shall cease to operate.

(4) In this Act "designated police station" means a police station for the time being designated under this section.

Custody officers at police stations

36.—(1) One or more custody officers shall be appointed for each designated police station.

(2) A custody officer for a [police station designated under section 35(1) above][84] shall be appointed—

    (a)   by the chief officer of police for the area in which the designated police station is situated; or

    (b)   by such other police officer as the chief officer of police for that area may direct.

[(2A) A custody officer for a police station designated under section 35(2A) above shall be appointed—

    (a)   by the Chief Constable of the British Transport Police Force; or

    (b)   by such other member of that Force as that Chief Constable may direct.][85]

(3) No officer may be appointed a custody officer unless he is of at least the rank of sergeant.

---

[81] subs.(7) was originally inserted by the Criminal Justice and Public Order Act 1994, s.29(3). (For the equivalent change in Northern Ireland see Police (Amendment) (Northern Ireland) Order 1995, Art.7.) It was substituted by the Criminal Justice Act 2003, Sch.1, para.5 primarily to take account of street bail. (For the Northern Ireland equivalent see Criminal Justice (Northern Ireland) Order 2004, SI 2004/1500, Sch.1, para.2.)

[82] Inserted by Criminal Justice Act 2003, Sch.1, para.6.

[83] subs.(2A) inserted by Anti-Terrorism, Crime and Security Act 2001, Sch.7, para.12

[84] Amendment made by Anti-Terrorism, Crime and Security Act 2001, Sch.7, para.13(2).

[85] subs.(2A) was inserted by the Anti-Terrorism, Crime and Security Act 2001, Sch.7, para.13(3).

[*The Serious Organised Crime and Police Bill, cl.112(2) replaces subs.(3) with: "(3) No person may be appointed a custody officer unless—(a) he is a police officer of at least the rank of sergeant; or (b) he is a staff custody officer."*]

(4) An officer of any rank may perform the functions of a custody officer at a designated police station if a custody officer is not readily available to perform them.

(5) Subject to the following provisions of this section and to section 39(2) below, none of the functions of a custody officer in relation to a person shall be performed by [an officer][86] who at the time when the function falls to be performed is involved in the investigation of an offence for which that person is in police detention at that time.

(6) Nothing in subsection (5) above is to be taken to prevent a custody officer—
    (a) performing any function assigned to custody officers—
        (i) by this Act; or
        (ii) by a code of practice issued under this Act;
    (b) carrying out the duty imposed on custody officers by section 39 below;
    (c) doing anything in connection with the identification of a suspect; or
    (d) doing anything under [sections 7 and 8][87] of the Road Traffic Act 1988.[88]

(7) Where an arrested person is taken to a police station which is not a designated police station, the functions in relation to him which at a designated police station would be the functions of a custody officer shall be performed—
    (a) by an officer[89] who is not involved in the investigation of an offence for which he is in police detention, if such an officer is readily available; and
    (b) if no such officer is readily available, by the officer who took him to the station or any other officer.

[(7A) Subject to subsection (7B), subsection (7) applies where a person attends a police station which is not a designated station to answer to bail granted under section 30A as it applies where a person is taken to such a station.

(7B) Where subsection (7) applies because of subsection (7A), the reference in subsection (7)(b) to the officer who took him to the station is to be read as a reference to the officer who granted him bail.][90]

(8) References to a custody officer in[91] the following provisions of this Act include references to an officer other than a custody officer who is performing the functions of a custody officer by virtue of subsection (4) or (7) above.

(9) Where by virtue of subsection (7) above an officer of a force maintained by a police authority who took an arrested person to a police station is to perform the functions of a custody officer in relation to him, the officer shall inform an officer who—
    (a) is attached to a designated police station; and
    (b) is of at least the rank of inspector,
that he is to do so.

[86] The Serious Organised Crime and Police Bill, cl.112(3) replaces "an officer" with "an individual".
[87] As amended by the Road Traffic (Consequential Provisions) Act 1988, Sch.3, para.27.
[88] Words in square brackets substituted by the Road Traffic (Consequential Provisions) Act 1988, Sch.3, para.27. In the 1989 Northern Ireland PACE Order, Art.37(6)(d) the equivalent reference is to Arts 144, 146 and 147 of the Road Traffic (Northern Ireland) Order 1981.
[89] The Serious Organised Crime and Police Bill, cl.112(4) inserts here "or a staff custody officer"; and here and in para.(b) for "such an officer" substitutes "such a person".
[90] subss.(7A) and (7B) were inserted by the Criminal Justice Act 2003, Sch.1, para.7.
[91] The Serious Organised Crime and Police Bill, cl.112(5) inserts here "section 34 above or in" and for "an officer" substitutes "a person".

(10) The duty imposed by subsection (9) above shall be performed as soon as it is practicable to perform it.

[*The Serious Organised Crime and Police Bill,2004–05, cl.112(6) inserts here:*
"(11) In this section, 'staff custody officer' means a person who has been designated as such under section 38 of the Police Reform Act 2002."]

Duties of custody officer before charge

37.—(1) Where—
    (a) a person is arrested for an offence—
        (i) without a warrant; or
        (ii) under a warrant not endorsed for bail,
    (b) . . .[92]
the custody officer at each police station where he is detained after his arrest shall determine whether he has before him sufficient evidence to charge that person with the offence for which he was arrested and may detain him at the police station for such period as is necessary to enable him to do so.

(2) If the custody officer determines that he does not have such evidence before him, the person arrested shall be released either on bail or without bail, unless the custody officer has reasonable grounds for believing that his detention without being charged is necessary to secure or preserve evidence relating to an offence for which he is under arrest or to obtain such evidence by questioning him.

(3) If the custody officer has reasonable grounds for so believing, he may authorise the person arrested to be kept in police detention.

(4) Where a custody officer authorises a person who has not been charged to be kept in police detention, he shall, as soon as is practicable, make a written record of the grounds for the detention.

(5) Subject to subsection (6) below, the written record shall be made in the presence of the person arrested who shall at that time be informed by the custody officer of the grounds for his detention.

(6) Subsection (5) above shall not apply where the person arrested is, at the time when the written record is made—
    (a) incapable of understanding what is said to him;
    [(aa) asleep][93]
    (b) violent or likely to become violent; or
    (c) in urgent need of medical attention.

(7) Subject to section 41(7) below, if the custody officer determines that he has before him sufficient evidence to charge the person arrested with the offence for which he was arrested, the person arrested—
    [(a) shall be released without charge and on bail for the purpose of enabling the Director of Public Prosecutions to make a decision under section 37B below;
    (b) shall be released without charge and on bail but not for that purpose;
    (c) shall be released without charge and without bail, or
    (d) shall be charged.][94]

[(7A) The decision as to how a person is to be dealt with under subsection (7) above shall be that of the custody officer.

---

[92] Repealed by the Criminal Justice and Public Order Act 1994, s.29(4)(a), s.168(3), and Sch.11.
[93] Inserted by Police Reform Act 2002, s.52(2).
[94] Words in square brackets substituted by the Criminal Justice Act 2003, Sch.2, para.2(2).

(7B) Where a person is released under subsection (7)(a) above, it shall be the duty of the custody officer to inform him that he is being released to enable the Director of Public Prosecutions to make a decision under section 37B below.][95]

(8) Where—

    (a) a person is released under subsection (7)(b) [or (c)][96] above; and

    (b) at the time of his release a decision whether he should be prosecuted for the offence for which he was arrested has not been taken,

it shall be the duty of the custody officer so to inform him.

(9) If the person arrested is not in a fit state to be dealt with under subsection (7) above, he may be kept in police detention until he is.

(10)The duty imposed on the custody officer under subsection (1) above shall be carried out by him as soon as practicable after the person arrested arrives at the police station or, in the case of a person arrested at the police station, as soon as practicable after the arrest.

(11) . . .[97]

(12) . . .[98]

(13) . . .[99]

(14) . . .[1]

(15) In this Part of this Act—

"arrested juvenile" means a person arrested with or without a warrant who appears to be under the age of 17 . . .,[2]

"endorsed for bail" means endorsed with a direction for bail in accordance with section 117(2) of the Magistrates' Courts Act 1980.

[Guidance[3]

37A.—(1) The Director of Public Prosecutions may issue guidance—

    (a) for the purpose of enabling custody officers to decide how persons should be dealt with under section 37(7) above or 37C(2) below, and

    (b) as to the information to be sent to the Director of Public Prosecutions under section 37B(1) below.

(2) The Director of Public Prosecutions may from time to time revise guidance issued under this section.

(3) Custody officers are to have regard to guidance under this section in deciding how persons should be dealt with under section 37(7) above or 37C(2) below.

(4) A report under section 9 of the Prosecution of Offences Act 1985 (report by DPP to Attorney General) must set out the provisions of any guidance issued, and any revisions to guidance made, in the year to which the report relates.

(5) The Director of Public Prosecutions must publish in such manner as he thinks fit—

    (a) any guidance issued under this section, and

    (b) any revisions made to such guidance.

---

[95] Inserted by the Criminal Justice Act 2003, Sch.2, para.2(3).
[96] Inserted by the Criminal Justice Act 2003, Sch.2, para.2(4).
[97] Repealed by the Criminal Justice Act 1991, s.72 and Sch.13.
[98] Repealed by the Criminal Justice Act 1991, s.72 and Sch.13.
[99] Repealed by the Criminal Justice Act 1991, s.72 and Sch.13.
[1] Repealed by the Criminal Justice Act 1991, s.72 and Sch.13.
[2] Words repealed by the Children Act 1989, s.108(7), Sch.15.
[3] New ss.37A, 37B, 37C and 37D were inserted by the Criminal Justice Act 2003, Sch.2, para.3. Note that pending activation of s.29 of the Criminal Justice Act 2003 (charging by post), s.37B(8) of PACE was not yet in force.

(6) Guidance under this section may make different provision for different cases, circumstances or areas.

Consultation with the Director of Public Prosecutions

37B.—(1) Where a person is released on bail under section 37(7)(a) above, an officer involved in the investigation of the offence shall, as soon as is practicable, send to the Director of Public Prosecutions such information as may be specified in guidance under section 37A above.

(2) The Director of Public Prosecutions shall decide whether there is sufficient evidence to charge the person with an offence.

(3) If he decides that there is sufficient evidence to charge the person with an offence, he shall decide—

    (a)   whether or not the person should be charged and, if so, the offence with which he should be charged, and

    (b)   whether or not the person should be given a caution and, if so, the offence in respect of which he should be given a caution.

(4) The Director of Public Prosecutions shall give written notice of his decision to an officer involved in the investigation of the offence.

(5) If his decision is—

    (a)   that there is not sufficient evidence to charge the person with an offence, or

    (b)   that there is sufficient evidence to charge the person with an offence but that the person should not be charged with an offence or given a caution in respect of an offence,

a custody officer shall give the person notice in writing that he is not to be prosecuted.

(6) If the decision of the Director of Public Prosecutions is that the person should be charged with an offence, or given a caution in respect of an offence, the person shall be charged or cautioned accordingly.

(7) But if his decision is that the person should be given a caution in respect of the offence and it proves not to be possible to give the person such a caution, he shall instead be charged with the offence.

(8) For the purposes of this section, a person is to be charged with an offence either—

    (a)   when he is in police detention after returning to a police station to answer bail or is otherwise in police detention at a police station, or

    (b)   in accordance with section 29 of the Criminal Justice Act 2003.

(9) In this section "caution" includes—

    (a)   a conditional caution within the meaning of Part 3 of the Criminal Justice Act 2003, and

    (b)   a warning or reprimand under section 65 of the Crime and Disorder Act 1998.

Breach of bail following release under section 37(7)(a)

37C.—(1) This section applies where—

    (a)   a person released on bail under section 37(7)(a) above or subsection (2)(b) below is arrested under section 46A below in respect of that bail, and

    (b)   at the time of his detention following that arrest at the police station

561

mentioned in section 46A(2) below, notice under section 37B(4) above has not been given.

(2) The person arrested—

    (a)   shall be charged, or

    (b)   shall be released without charge, either on bail or without bail.

(3) The decision as to how a person is to be dealt with under subsection (2) above shall be that of a custody officer.

(4) A person released on bail under subsection (2)(b) above shall be released on bail subject to the same conditions (if any) which applied immediately before his arrest.

Release under section 37(7)(a): further provision

37D.—(1) Where a person is released on bail under section 37(7)(a) or section 37C(2)(b) above, a custody officer may subsequently appoint a different time, or an additional time, at which the person is to attend at the police station to answer bail.

(2) The custody officer shall give the person notice in writing of the exercise of the power under subsection (1).

(3) The exercise of the power under subsection (1) shall not affect the conditions (if any) to which bail is subject.

(4) Where a person released on bail under section 37(7)(a) or 37C(2)(b) above returns to a police station to answer bail or is otherwise in police detention at a police station, he may be kept in police detention to enable him to be dealt with in accordance with section 37B or 37C above or to enable the power under subsection (1) above to be exercised.

(5) If the person is not in a fit state to enable him to be so dealt with or to enable that power to be exercised, he may be kept in police detention until he is.

(6) Where a person is kept in police detention by virtue of subsection (4) or (5) above, section 37(1) to (3) and (7) above (and section 40(8) below so far as it relates to section 37(1) to (3)) shall not apply to the offence in connection with which he was released on bail under section 37(7)(a) or 37C(2)(b) above.]

Duties of custody officer after charge

38.—(1) Where a person arrested for an offence otherwise than under a warrant endorsed for bail is charged with an offence, the custody officer shall, [subject to section 25 of the Criminal Justice and Public Order Act 1994][4] order his release from police detention, either on bail or without bail, unless—

    (a)   if the person arrested is not an arrested juvenile—

        (i) his name or address cannot be ascertained or the custody officer has reasonable grounds for doubting whether a name or address furnished by him as his name or address is his real name or address;

      [(ii) the custody officer has reasonable grounds for believing that the person arrested will fail to appear in court to answer bail;

      (iii) in the case of a person arrested for an imprisonable offence, the custody officer has reasonable grounds for believing that the

---

[4] Words in square brackets inserted by the Criminal Justice and Public Order Act 1994, s.168(2), Sch.10, para.54.

detention of the person arrested is necessary to prevent him from committing an offence;

[(iiia) except in a case where (by virtue of subsection (9) of section 63B below) that section does not apply, the custody officer has reasonable grounds for believing that the detention of the person is necessary to enable a sample to be taken from him under that section;][5]

(iv) in the case of a person arrested for an offence which is not an imprisonable offence, the custody officer has reasonable grounds for believing that the detention of the person arrested is necessary to prevent him from causing physical injury to any other person or from causing loss of or damage to property;

(v) the custody officer has reasonable grounds for believing that the detention of the person arrested is necessary to prevent him from interfering with the administration of justice or with the investigation of offences of a particular offence; or

(vi) the custody officer has reasonable grounds for believing that the detention of the person arrested is necessary for his own protection][6];

(b) if he is an arrested juvenile—

(i) any of the requirements of paragraph (a) above is satisfied [(but, in the case of paragraph (a)(iiia) above, only if the arrested juvenile has attained the minimum age)][7]; or

(ii) the custody officer has reasonable grounds for believing that he ought to be detained in his own interests.

(2) If the release of a person arrested is not required by subsection (1) above, the custody officer may authorise him to be kept in police detention [but may not authorise a person to be kept in police detention by virtue of subsection (1)(a)(iiia) after the end of the period of six hours beginning when he was charged with the offence.][8]

[(2A) The custody officer, in taking the decisions required by subsection (1)(a) and (b) above (except (a)(i) and (vi) and b(ii)), shall have regard to the same considerations as those which a court is required to have regard to in taking the corresponding decisions under paragraph [2(1)] of Part I of Schedule 1 to the Bail Act 1976 [(disregarding paragraph 2(2) of that Part)].[9]]

(3) Where a custody officer authorises a person who has been charged to be kept in police detention he shall, as soon as practicable, make a written record of the grounds for the detention.

(4) Subject to subsection (5) below the written record shall be made in the presence of the person charged who shall at that time be informed by the custody officer of the grounds for his detention.

(5) Subsection (4) above shall not apply where the person charged is, at the time when the written record is made—

5 Initially inserted by the Criminal Justice and Court Services Act 2000, s.57(3)(a). Replaced by the Criminal Justice Act 2003, s.5(2).
6 paras (a)(ii), (iii), (iv), (v), (vi) substituted for paras (a)(ii), (iii) as originally enacted, by the Criminal Justice and Public Order Act 1994, s.28(2).
7 Inserted by Criminal Justice Act 2003, s.5(2)(a)(ii).
8 Words in square brackets inserted by Criminal Justice and Court Services Act 2000, s.57(3)(b).
9 subs.(2A) inserted by the Criminal Justice and Public Order Act 1994, s.28(3), (4). The words in square brackets within subs.(2A) were inserted by the Criminal Justice Act 2003, Sch.36, para.5.

   (a)   incapable of understanding what is said to him;

   (b)   violent or likely to become violent; or

   (c)   in urgent need of medical attention.

[(6) Where a custody officer authorises an arrested juvenile to be kept in police detention under subsection (1) above, the custody officer shall, unless he certifies—

   (a)   that, by reason of such circumstances as are specified in the certificate, it is impracticable for him to do so; or

   (b)   in the case of an arrested juvenile who has attained [the age of 12 years][10] that no secure accommodation is available and that keeping him in other local authority accommodation would not be adequate to protect the public from serious harm from him,

secure that the arrested juvenile is moved to local authority accommodation.][11–12]

(6A) In this section—

   "local authority accommodation" means accommodation provided by or on behalf of a local authority (within the meaning of the Children Act 1989);

   ["minimum age" means the age specified in section 63B(3) below;][13]

   "secure accommodation" means accommodation provided for the purpose of restricting liberty;

   ["sexual offence" means an offence specified in Part 2 of Schedule 15 to the Criminal Justice Act 2003;

   "violent offence" means murder or an offence specified in Part I of that Schedule;][14–15]

and any reference, in relation to an arrested juvenile charged with a violent or sexual offence, to protecting the public from serious harm from him shall be construed as a reference to protecting members of the public from death or serious personal injury, whether physical or psychological, occasioned by further such offences committed by him.

[(6B) Where an arrested juvenile is moved to local authority accommodation under subsection (b) above, it shall be lawful for any person acting on behalf of the authority to detain him.][16]

(7) A certificate made under subsection (6) above in respect of an arrested juvenile shall be produced to the court before which he is first brought thereafter.

[(7A) In this section "imprisonable offence" has the same meaning as in Schedule 1 to the Bail Act 1976.][17]

(8) In this Part of this Act "local authority" has the same meaning as in the [Children Act 1989].[18]

---

[10]   Words in square brackets substituted by Criminal Justice and Public Order Act 1994, s.24.

[11–12] subs.(6), (6A) substituted for previous subss.(6), (6A) by Criminal Justice Act 1991, s.59.

[13]   Inserted by the Criminal Justice Act 2003, s.5(2)(b).

[14–15] Replaced by Criminal Justice Act 2003, Sch.32, para.44.

[16]   subs.(6B) inserted by the Children Act 1989, s.108(5), Sch.13, para.53(2).

[17]   Inserted by the Criminal Justice and Public Order Act 1994, s.28(4).

[18]   Words in square brackets substituted by the Children Act 1989, s.108(5), Sch.13, para.53(3).

Responsibilities in relation to persons detained

39.—(1) Subject to subsections (2) and (4) below, it shall be the duty of the custody officer at a police station to ensure—

    (a) that all persons in police detention at that station are treated in accordance with this Act and any code of practice issued under it and relating to the treatment of persons in police detention; and

    (b) that all matters relating to such persons which are required by this Act or by such codes of practice to be recorded are recorded in the custody records relating to such persons.

(2) If the custody officer, in accordance with any code of practice issued under this Act, transfers or permits the transfer of a person in police detention—

    (a) to the custody of a police officer investigating an offence for which that person is in police detention;

    (b) to the custody of an officer who has charge of that person outside the police station,

the custody officer shall cease in relation to that person to be subject to the duty imposed on him by subsection (1)(a) above; and it shall be the duty of the officer to whom the transfer is made to ensure that he is treated in accordance with the provisions of this Act and of any such codes of practice as are mentioned in subsection (1) above.

(3) If the person detained is subsequently returned to the custody of the custody officer, it shall be the duty of the officer investigating the offence to report to the custody officer as to the manner in which this section and the codes of practice have been complied with while that person was in his custody.

(4) If an arrested juvenile is [moved to local authority accommodation][19] under section 38(6) above, the custody officer shall cease in relation to that person to be subject to the duty imposed on him by subsection (1) above.

(5) . . .[20]

(6) Where—

    (a) an officer of higher rank than the custody officer[21] gives directions relating to a person in police detention; and

    (b) the directions are at variance—

        (i) with any decision made or action taken by the custody officer in the performance of a duty imposed on him under this Part of this Act; or

        (ii) with any decision or action which would but for the directions have been made or taken by him in the performance of such a duty,

the custody officer shall refer the matter at once to an officer of the rank of superintendent or above who is responsible for the police station for which the custody officer is acting as custody officer.

[*The Serious Organised Crime and Police Bill 2004–05, cl.112(7)(b) inserts here new subs.(7):*

"(7) In subsection (6) above—

---

[19] Words in square brackets substituted by the Children Act 1989, s.108(5), Sch.13, para.54.

[20] Repealed by the Children Act 1989, s.108(7), Sch.15.

[21] The Serious Organised Crime and Police Bill, cl.112(7) inserts here "(or, if the custody officer is a staff custody officer, any police officer or any police employee)".

'*police employee' means a person employed under section 15 of the Police Act 1996;*

'*staff custody officers' has the same meaning as in the Police Reform Act 2002.*"]

Review of police detention

40.—(1) Reviews of the detention of each person in police detention in connection with the investigation of an offence shall be carried out periodically in accordance with the following provisions of this section—

    (a)   in the case of a person who has been arrested and charged, by the custody officer; and

    (b)   in the case of a person who has been arrested but not charged, by an officer of at least the rank of inspector who has not been directly involved in the investigation.

(2) The officer to whom it falls to carry out a review is referred to in this section as a "review officer".

(3) Subject to subsection (4) below—

    (a)   the first review shall be not later than six hours after the detention was first authorised;

    (b)   the second review shall be not later than nine hours after the first;

    (c)   subsequent reviews shall be at intervals of not more than nine hours.

(4) A review may be postponed—

    (a)   if, having regard to all the circumstances prevailing at the latest time for it specified in subsection (3) above, it is not practicable to carry out the review at that time;

    (b)   without prejudice to the generality of paragraph (a) above—

        (i)   if at that time the person in detention is being questioned by a police officer and the review officer is satisfied that an interruption of the questioning for the purpose of carrying out the review would prejudice the investigation in connection with which he is being questioned; or

        (ii)   if at that time no review officer is readily available.

(5) If a review is postponed under subsection (4) above it shall be carried out as soon as practicable after the latest time specified for it in subsection (3) above.

(6) If a review is carried out after postponement under subsection (4) above, the fact that it was so carried out shall not affect any requirement of this section as to the time at which any subsequent review is to be carried out.

(7) The review officer shall record the reasons for any postponement of a review in the custody record.

(8) Subject to subsection (9) below, where the person whose detention is under review has not been charged before the time of the review, section 37(1) to (6) above shall have effect in relation to him, but with [the modifications specified in subsection (8A)].[22]

[(8A) The modifications are—

    (a)   the substitution of references to the person whose detention is under review for references to the person arrested;

    (b)   the substitution of references to the review officer for references to the custody officer; and

---

[22] Words in square brackets substituted by Police Reform Act 2002, s.52(1).

  (c) in subsection (6), the insertion of the following paragraph after paragraph (a)—"(aa) asleep;".][23]

(9) Where a person has been kept in police detention by virtue of section 37(9) [or 37D(5)][24] above, section 37(1) to (6) shall not have effect in relation to him but it shall be the duty of the review officer to determine whether he is yet in a fit state.

(10) Where the person whose detention is under review has been charged before the time of the review, section 38(1) to [(6B)] above shall have effect in relation to him, but with [the modifications specified in subsection (10A)].[25]

[(10A) The modifications are—

  (a) the substitution of a reference to the person whose detention is under review for any reference to the person arrested or to the person charged; and

  (b) in subsection (5), the insertion of the following paragraph after paragraph (a)—"(aa) asleep;".][26]

(11) Where—

  (a) an officer of higher rank than the custody officer gives directions relating to a person in police detention;

  (b) the directions are at variance—

      (i) with any decision made or action taken by the review officer in the performance of a duty imposed on him under this Part of this Act; or

      (ii) with any decision or action which would but for the directions have been made or taken by him in the performance of such a duty,

the review officer shall refer the matter at once to an officer of the rank of superintendent or above who is responsible for the police station for which the review officer is acting as review officer in connection with the detention.

(12) Before determining whether to authorise a person's continued detention the review officer shall give—

  (a) that person (unless he is asleep); or

  (b) any solicitor representing him who is available at the time of the review,

an opportunity to make representations to him about the detention.

(13) Subject to subsection (14) below, the person whose detention is under review or his solicitor may make representations under subsection (12) above either orally or in writing.

(14) The review officer may refuse to hear oral representations from the person whose detention is under review if he considers that he is unfit to make such representations by reason of his condition or behaviour.

[Use of telephone for review under s.40[27]

40A.—[(1) A review under section 40(1)(b) may be carried out by means of a discussion, conducted by telephone, with one or more persons at the police station where the arrested person is held.

---

[23] subs.(8A) was inserted by the Police Reform Act 2002, s.52(2).

[24] Inserted by Criminal Justice Act 2003, Sch.2, para.4.

[25] Words in square brackets substituted by the Police Reform Act 2002, s.52(3)(a).

[26] subs.(10A) was inserted by the Police Reform Act 2002, s.52(4).

[27] s.40A was originally inserted by the Criminal Justice and Police Act 2001, s.73(2).

(2) But subsection (1) does not apply if—

    (a)   the review is of a kind authorised by regulations under section 45A to be carried out using video-conferencing facilities; and

    (b)   it is reasonably practicable to carry it out in accordance with those regulations.][28]

(3) Where any review is carried out under this section by an officer who is not present at the station where the arrested person is held—

    (a)   any obligation of that officer to make a record in connection with the carrying out of the review shall have effect as an obligation to cause another officer to make the record;

    (b)   any requirement for the record to be made in the presence of the arrested person shall apply to the making of that record by that other officer; and

    (c)   the requirements under section 40(12) and (13) above for—

        (i)   the arrested person, or

        (ii)   a solicitor representing him,

to be given any opportunity to make representations (whether in writing or orally) to that officer shall have effect as a requirement for that person, or such a solicitor, to be given an opportunity to make representations in a manner authorised by subsection (4) below.

(4) Representations are made in a manner authorised by this subsection—

    (a)   in a case where facilities exist for the immediate transmission of written representations to the officer carrying out the review, if they are made either—

        (i)   orally by telephone to that officer; or

        (ii)   in writing to that officer by means of those facilities; and

    (b)   in any other case, if they are made orally by telephone to that officer.

(5) In this section "video-conferencing facilities" has the same meaning as in section 45A below.]

Limits on period of detention without charge

41.—(1) Subject to the following provisions of this section and to sections 42 and 43 below, a person shall not be kept in police detention for more than 24 hours without being charged.

(2) The time from which the period of detention of a person is to be calculated (in this Act referred to as "the relevant time")—

    (a)   in the case of a person to whom this section applies, shall be[29]—

        (i)   the time at which that person arrives at the relevant police station, or

        (ii)   the time 24 hours after the time of that person's arrest, whichever is the earlier;

    (b)   in the case of a person arrested outside England and Wales, shall be—

        (i)   the time at which that person arrives at the first police station to which he is taken in the police area in England or Wales in which the offence for which he was arrested is being investigated; or

---

[28]   subss.(1) and (2) were substituted by the Criminal Justice Act 2003, s.6.

[29]   Not relevant in Northern Ireland where the whole province is treated as one police area.

        (ii) the time 24 hours after the time of that person's entry into England and Wales, whichever is the earlier;

    (c) in the case of a person who—

        (i) attends voluntarily at a police station; or

        (ii) accompanies a constable to a police station without having been arrested, and is arrested at the police station, the time of his arrest;

    [(ca) in the case of a person who attends a police station to answer to bail granted under section 30A, the time when he arrives at the police station;][30]

    (d) in any other case, except when subsection (5) below applies, shall be the time at which the person arrested arrives at the first police station to which he is taken after his arrest.

(3) Subsection (2)(a) above applies to a person if—

    (a) his arrest is sought in one police area in England and Wales;

    (b) he is arrested in another police area; and

    (c) he is not questioned in the area in which he is arrested in order to obtain evidence in relation to an offence for which he is arrested,

and in sub-paragraph (i) of that paragraph "the relevant police station" means the first police station to which he is taken in the police area in which his arrest was sought.

(4) Subsection (2) above shall have effect in relation to a person arrested under section 31 above as if every reference in it to his arrest or his being arrested were a reference to his arrest or his being arrested for the offence for which he was originally arrested.

(5) If—[31]

    (a) a person is in police detention in a police area in England and Wales ("the first area"); and

    (b) his arrest for an offence is sought in some other police area in England and Wales ("the second area"); and

    (c) he is taken to the second area for the purposes of investigating that offence, without being questioned in the first area in order to obtain evidence in relation to it,

the relevant time shall be—

        (i) the time 24 hours after he leaves the place where he is detained in the first area; or

        (ii) the time at which he arrives at the first police station to which he is taken in the second area, whichever is the earlier.

(6) When a person who is in police detention is removed to hospital because he is in need of medical treatment, any time during which he is being questioned in hospital or on the way there or back by a police officer for the purpose of obtaining evidence relating to an offence shall be included in any period which falls to be calculated for the purposes of this Part of this Act, but any other time while he is in hospital or on his way there or back shall not be so included.

(7) Subject to subsection (8) below, a person who at the expiry of 24 hours after the relevant time is in police detention and has not been charged shall be released at that time either on bail or without bail.

[30] Inserted by the Criminal Justice Act 2003, Sch.1, para.8.

[31] Not relevant in Northern Ireland where the whole province is treated as one police area.

(8) Subsection (7) above does not apply to a person whose detention for more than 24 hours after the relevant time has been authorised or is otherwise permitted in accordance with section 42 or 43 below.

(9) A person released under subsection (7) above shall not be re-arrested without a warrant for the offence for which he was previously arrested unless new evidence justifying a further arrest has come to light since his release[; but this subsection does not prevent an arrest under section 46A below.][32]

Authorisation of continued detention

42.—(1) Where a police officer of the rank of superintendent or above who is responsible for the police station at which a person is detained has reasonable grounds for believing that—

   (a)   the detention of that person without charge is necessary to secure or preserve evidence relating to an offence for which he is under arrest or to obtain such evidence by questioning him

   [(b)   an offence for which he is under arrest is an arrestable[33] offence; and][34]

   (c)   the investigation is being conducted diligently and expeditiously,

he may authorise the keeping of that person in police detention for a period expiring at or before 36 hours after the relevant time.

(2) Where an officer such as is mentioned in subsection (1) above has authorised the keeping of a person in police detention for a period expiring less than 36 hours after the relevant time, such an officer may authorise the keeping of that person in police detention for a further period expiring not more than 36 hours after that time if the conditions specified in subsection (1) above are still satisfied when he gives the authorisation.

(3) If it is proposed to transfer a person in police detention to another police area, the officer determining whether or not to authorise keeping him in detention under subsection (1) above shall have regard to the distance and the time the journey would take.[35]

(4) No authorisation under subsection (1) above shall be given in respect of any person—

   (a)   more than 24 hours after the relevant time; or

   (b)   before the second review of his detention under section 40 above has been carried out.

(5) Where an officer authorises the keeping of a person in police detention under subsection (1) above, it shall be his duty—

   (a)   to inform that person of the grounds for his continued detention; and

   (b)   to record the grounds in that person's custody record.

(6) Before determining whether to authorise the keeping of a person in detention under subsection (1) or (2) above, an officer shall give—

   (a)   that person; or

   (b)   any solicitor representing him who is available at the time when it falls to the officer to determine whether to give the authorisation,

an opportunity to make representations to him about the detention.

[32] The words in square brackets were inserted by the Criminal Justice and Public Order Act 1994, s.29(4)(b).

[33] The Serious Organised Crime and Police Bill 2004–05, Sch.7, Pt 3, para.8(7) changes "arrestable" to "indictable".

[34] Inserted by the Criminal Justice Act 2003, s.7. For the Northern Ireland equivalent see Criminal Justice (Northern Ireland) Order 2004, SI 2004/1500, Art.5.

[35] Not relevant in Northern Ireland where the whole province is treated as one police area.

(7) Subject to subsection (8) below, the person in detention or his solicitor may make representations under subsection (6) above either orally or in writing.

(8) The officer to whom it falls to determine whether to give the authorisation may refuse to hear oral representations from the person in detention if he considers that he is unfit to make such representations by reason of his condition or behaviour.

(9) Where—

    (a) an officer authorises the keeping of a person in detention under subsection (1) above; and

    (b) at the time of the authorisation he has not yet exercised a right conferred on him by section 56 or 58 below,

the officer—

        (i) shall inform him of that right;

      (ii) shall decide whether he should be permitted to exercise it;

    (iii) shall record the decision in his custody record; and

    (iv) if the decision is to refuse to permit the exercise of the right, shall also record the grounds for the decision in that record.

(10) Where an officer has authorised the keeping of a person who has not been charged in detention under subsection (1) or (2) above, he shall be released from detention, either on bail or without bail, not later than 36 hours after the relevant time, unless—

    (a) he has been charged with an offence; or

    (b) his continued detention is authorised or otherwise permitted in accordance with section 43 below.

(11) A person released under subsection (10) above shall not be re-arrested without a warrant for the offence for which he was previously arrested unless new evidence justifying a further arrest has come to light since his release[; but this subsection does not prevent an arrest under section 46A below].[36]

Warrants of further detention

43.—(1) Where, on an application on oath made by a constable and supported by an information, a magistrates' court is satisfied that there are reasonable grounds for believing that the further detention of the person to whom the application relates is justified, it may issue a warrant of further detention authorising the keeping of that person in police detention.

(2) A court may not hear an application for a warrant of further detention unless the person to whom the application relates—

    (a) has been furnished with a copy of the information; and

    (b) has been brought before the court for the hearing.

(3) The person to whom the application relates shall be entitled to be legally represented at the hearing and, if he is not so represented, but wishes to be so represented—

    (a) the court shall adjourn the hearing to enable him to obtain representation; and

    (b) he may be kept in police detention during the adjournment.

(4) A person's further detention is only justified for the purposes of this section or section 44 below if—

---

[36] Words in square brackets inserted by the Criminal Justice and Public Order Act 1994, s.29(4)(b).

(a) his detention without charge is necessary to secure or preserve evidence relating to an offence for which he is under arrest or to obtain such evidence by questioning him;

(b) an offence for which he is under arrest is a serious arrestable offence[37]; and

(c) the investigation is being conducted diligently and expeditiously.

(5) Subject to subsection (7) below, an application for a warrant of further detention may be made—

(a) at any time before the expiry of 36 hours after the relevant time; or

(b) in a case where—

(i) it is not practicable for the magistrates' court to which the application will be made to sit at the expiry of 36 hours after the relevant time; but

(ii) the court will sit during the 6 hours following the end of that period,

at any time before the expiry of the said 6 hours.

(6) In a case to which subsection (5)(b) above applies—

(a) the person to whom the application relates may be kept in police detention until the application is heard; and

(b) the custody officer shall make a note in that person's custody record—

(i) of the fact that he was kept in police detention for more than 36 hours after the relevant time; and

(ii) of the reason why he was so kept.

(7) If—

(a) an application for a warrant of further detention is made after the expiry of 36 hours after the relevant time; and

(b) it appears to the magistrates' court that it would have been reasonable for the police to make it before the expiry of that period,

the court shall dismiss the application.

(8) Where on an application such as is mentioned in subsection (1) above a magistrates' court is not satisfied that there are reasonable grounds for believing that the further detention of the person to whom the application relates is justified, it shall be its duty—

(a) to refuse the application; or

(b) to adjourn the hearing of it until a time not later than 36 hours after the relevant time.

(9) The person to whom the application relates may be kept in police detention during the adjournment.

(10) A warrant of further detention shall—

(a) state the time at which it is issued;

(b) authorise the keeping in police detention of the person to whom it relates for the period stated in it.

(11) Subject to subsection (12) below, the period stated in a warrant of further detention shall be such period as the magistrates' court thinks fit, having regard to the evidence before it.

(12) The period shall not be longer than 36 hours.

---

[37] The Serious Organised Crime and Police Bill 2004–05, Sch.7, Pt 3, para.8(8) changes "serious arrestable" to "indictable".

(13) If it is proposed to transfer a person in police detention to a police area other than that in which he is detained when the application for a warrant of further detention is made, the court hearing the application shall have regard to the distance and the time the journey would take.[38]

(14) Any information submitted in support of an application under this section shall state—

    (a) the nature of the offence for which the person to whom the application relates has been arrested;

    (b) the general nature of the evidence on which that person was arrested;

    (c) what inquiries relating to the offence have been made by the police and what further inquiries are proposed by them;

    (d) the reasons for believing the continued detention of that person to be necessary for the purposes of such further inquiries.

(15) Where an application under this section is refused the person to whom the application relates shall forthwith be charged or, subject to subsection (16) below, released, either on bail or without bail.

(16) A person need not be released under subsection (15) above—

    (a) before the expiry of 24 hours after the relevant time; or

    (b) before the expiry of any longer period for which his continued detention is or has been authorised under section 42 above.

(17) Where an application under this section is refused, no further application shall be made under this section in respect of the person to whom the refusal relates, unless supported by evidence which has come to light since the refusal.

(18) Where a warrant of further detention is issued, the person to whom it relates shall be released from police detention, either on bail or without bail, upon or before the expiry of the warrant unless he is charged.

(19) A person released under subsection (18) above shall not be re-arrested without a warrant for the offence for which he was previously arrested unless new evidence justifying a further arrest has come to light since his release[; but this subsection does not prevent an arrest under section 46A below.][39]

Extension of warrants of further detention

44.—(1) On an application on oath made by a constable and supported by an information a magistrates' court may extend a warrant of further detention issued under section 43 above if it is satisfied that there are reasonable grounds for believing that the further detention of the person to whom the application relates is justified.

(2) Subject to subsection (3) below, the period for which a warrant of further detention may be extended shall be such period as the court thinks fit, having regard to the evidence before it.

(3) The period shall not—

    (a) be longer than 36 hours; or

    (b) end later than 96 hours after the relevant time.

(4) Where a warrant of further detention has been extended under subsection (1) above, or further extended under this subsection, for a period ending before 96 hours after the relevant time, on an application such as is mentioned in that subsection a magistrates' court may further extend the warrant if it is satisfied

---

[38] Not relevant in Northern Ireland where the whole province is treated as one police area.

[39] Words in square brackets inserted by the Criminal Justice and Public Order Act 1994, s.29(4)(b).

as there mentioned; and subsections (2) and (3) above apply to such further extensions as they apply to extensions under subsection (1) above.

(5) A warrant of further detention shall, if extended or further extended under this section, be endorsed with a note of the period of the extension.

(6) Subsections (2), (3) and (14) of section 43 above shall apply to an application made under this section as they apply to an application made under that section.

(7) Where an application under this section is refused, the person to whom the application relates shall forthwith be charged or, subject to subsection (8) below, released, either on bail or without bail.

(8) A person need not be released under subsection (7) above before the expiry of any period for which a warrant of further detention issued in relation to him has been extended or further extended on an earlier application made under this section.

Detention before charge—supplementary

45.—(1) In sections 43 and 44 of this Act "magistrates' court" means a court consisting of two or more justices of the peace sitting otherwise than in open court.

(2) Any reference in this Part of this Act to a period of time or a time of day is to be treated as approximate only.

Detention—miscellaneous

[Use of video-conferencing facilities for decisions about detention[40]

45A.—(1) Subject to the following provisions of this section, the Secretary of State may by regulations provide that, in the case of an arrested person who is held in a police station, some or all of the functions mentioned in subsection (2) may be performed (notwithstanding anything in the preceding provisions of this Part) by an officer who—

    (a)   is not present in that police station; but

    (b)   has access to the use of video-conferencing facilities that enable him to communicate with persons in that station.

    (2) Those functions are—

    (a)   the functions in relation to an arrested person taken to[,or answering to bail at,][41] a police station that is not a designated police station which, in the case of an arrested person taken to a station that is a designated police station, are functions of a custody officer under section 37, 38 or 40 above; and

    (b)   the function of carrying out a review under section 40(1)(b) above (review, by an officer of at least the rank of inspector, of the detention of person arrested but not charged).

(3) Regulations under this section shall specify the use to be made in the performance of the functions mentioned in subsection (2) above of the facilities mentioned in subsection (1) above.

(4) Regulations under this section shall not authorise the performance of any of the functions mentioned in subsection (2)(a) above by such an officer as is mentioned in subsection (1) above unless he is a custody officer for a designated police station.

---

[40] s.45A was inserted by the Criminal Justice and Police Act 2001, s.73(3).
[41] Inserted by the Criminal Justice Act 2003, Sch.1, para.9.

(5) Where any functions mentioned in subsection (2) above are performed in a manner authorised by regulations under this section—

    (a)   any obligation of the officer performing those functions to make a record in connection with the performance of those functions shall have effect as an obligation to cause another officer to make the record; and

    (b)   any requirement for the record to be made in the presence of the arrested person shall apply to the making of that record by that other officer.

(6) Where the functions mentioned in subsection (2)(b) are performed in a manner authorised by regulations under this section, the requirements under section 40(12) and (13) above for—

    (a)   the arrested person, or

    (b)   a solicitor representing him,

to be given any opportunity to make representations (whether in writing or orally) to the person performing those functions shall have effect as a requirement for that person, or such a solicitor, to be given an opportunity to make representations in a manner authorised by subsection (7) below.

(7) Representations are made in a manner authorised by this subsection—

    (a)   in a case where facilities exist for the immediate transmission of written representations to the officer performing the functions, if they are made either—

        (i) orally to that officer by means of the video-conferencing facilities used by him for performing those functions; or

       (ii) in writing to that officer by means of the facilities available for the immediate transmission of the representations; and

    (b)   in any other case if they are made orally to that officer by means of the video-conferencing facilities used by him for performing the functions.

(8) Regulations under this section may make different provision for different cases and may be made so as to have effect in relation only to the police stations specified or described in the regulations.

(9) Regulations under this section shall be made by statutory instrument and shall be subject to annulment in pursuance of a resolution of either House of Parliament.

(10) Any reference in this section to video-conferencing facilities, in relation to any functions, is a reference to any facilities (whether a live television link or other facilities) by means of which the functions may be performed with the officer performing them, the person in relation to whom they are performed and any legal representative of that person all able to both see and to hear each other.]

Detention—miscellaneous

Detention after charge[42]

46.—(1) Where a person—

    (a)   is charged with an offence; and

    (b)   after being charged—

        (i) is kept in police detention; or

---

[42] Note the 1989 Northern Ireland PACE Order, Art.47 was slightly redrafted to take account of the fact that there is no "first sitting" of a magistrates' court in Northern Ireland and it is therefore not necessary to specify a period within which magistrates' courts will be held.

(ii) is detained by a local authority in pursuance of arrangements made under section 38(6) above,

he shall be brought before a magistrates' court in accordance with the provisions of this section.

(2) If he is to be brought before a magistrates' court [in the local justice]⁴³ area in which the police station at which he was charged is situated, he shall be brought before such a court as soon as is practicable and in any event not later than the first sitting after he is charged with the offence.

(3) If no magistrates' court [in that area] is due to sit either on the day on which he is charged or on the next day, the custody officer for the police station at which he was charged shall inform the [designated officer] for the area that there is a person in the area to whom subsection (2) above applies.

(4) If the person charged is to be brought before a magistrates' court [in a local justice] area other than that in which the police station at which he was charged is situated, he shall be removed to that area as soon as is practicable and brought before such a court as soon as is practicable after his arrival in the area and in any event not later than the first sitting of a magistrates' court [in] that area after his arrival in the area.

(5) If no magistrates' court [in] that area is due to sit either on the day on which he arrives in the area or on the next day—

    (a) he shall be taken to a police station in the area; and

    (b) the custody officer at that station shall inform [the designated officer] for the area that there is a person in the area to whom subsection (4) applies.

(6) Subject to subsection (8) below, where [the designated officer for a local justice] area has been informed—

    (a) under subsection (3) above that there is a person in the area to whom subsection (2) above applies; or

    (b) under subsection (5) above that there is a person in the area to whom subsection (4) above applies,

the [designated officer] shall arrange for a magistrates' court to sit not later than the day next following the relevant day.

(7) In this section "the relevant day"—

    (a) in relation to a person who is to be brought before a magistrates' court [in the local justice] area in which the police station at which he was charged is situated, means the day on which he was charged; and

    (b) in relation to a person who is to be brought before a magistrates' court [in any other local justice] area, means the day on which he arrives in the area.

(8) Where the day next following the relevant day is Christmas Day, Good Friday or a Sunday, the duty of the [designated officer] under subsection (6) above is a duty to arrange for a magistrates' court to sit not later than the first day after the relevant day which is not one of those days.

---

⁴³ A number of minor amendments (not yet in force) were made to s.46(2) to (8) by the Courts Act 2003, s.109, Sch.8, para.282(2) to (8). The amendments, indicated in square brackets, replaced "petty sessions area" by "the local justice area"; and the "justices' chief executive" by "designated officer". (The words "the justices' chief executive" had been substituted for "clerk to the justices" in subss.(3), (5), (6) and (8) by Access to Justice Act 1999 (Transfer of Justices' Clerks' Functions) Order, SI 2001/618, Art.4(c).)

(9) Nothing in this section requires a person who is in hospital to be brought before a court if he is not well enough.

[Power of arrest for failure to answer to police bail[44]

46A.—(1) A constable may arrest without a warrant any person who, having been released on bail under this Part of this Act subject to a duty to attend at a police station, fails to attend at that police station at the time appointed for him to do so.

[(1A) A person who has been released on bail under section 37(7)(a) or 37C(2)(b) above may be arrested without warrant by a constable if the constable has reasonable grounds for suspecting that the person has broken any of the conditions of bail.][45]

(2) A person who is arrested under this section shall be taken to the police station appointed as the place at which he is to surrender to custody as soon as practicable after the arrest.

(3) For the purpose of—

    (a)   section 30 above (subject to the obligation in subsection (2) above), and

    (b)   section 31 above,

an arrest under this section shall be treated as an arrest for an offence.]

Bail after arrest

47.—(1) [Subject to the following provisions of this section],[46] a release on bail of a person under this Part of this Act shall be a release on bail granted in accordance with [sections 3, 3A, 5 and 5A of the Bail Act 1976 as they apply to bail granted by a constable].[47]

[(1A) The normal powers to impose conditions of bail shall be available to him where a custody officer releases a person on bail under section [37(7)(a) above or section][48] 38(1) above (including that subsection as applied by section 40(10) above) but not in any other cases. In this subsection "the normal powers to impose conditions of bail" has the meaning given in section 3(6) of the Bail Act 1976.][49]

[(1B) No application may be made under section 5B of the Bail Act 1976 if a person is released on bail under section 37(7)(a) or 37C(2)(b) above.

(1C) Subsections (1D) to (1F) below apply where a person released on bail under section 37(7)(a) or 37C(2)(b) above is on bail subject to conditions.

(1D) The person shall not be entitled to make an application under section 43B of the Magistrates' Courts Act 1980.

(1E) A magistrates' court may, on an application by or on behalf of the person, vary the conditions of bail; and in this subsection "vary" has the same meaning as in the Bail Act 1976.

---

[44] s.46A was inserted by the Criminal Justice and Public Order Act 1994, s.29(2). (For the equivalent change in Northern Ireland see Police (Amendment) (Northern Ireland) Order 1995, Art.7.) The words in the square bracket in subs.(3A)(b) were substituted by the Courts Act 2003, Sch.8, para.283.
[45] Inserted by Criminal Justice Act 2003, Sch.2, para.5.
[46] Substituted by Criminal Justice Act 2003, Sch.2, para.6(2).
[47] The words in square brackets were substituted by the Criminal Justice and Public Order Act 1994, s.27(1)(a). Note that the 1989 Northern Ireland PACE Order, Art.48 was redrafted to amalgamate the bail provisions of Art.130 of the Magistrates' Courts (Northern Ireland) Order 1981 with those of Art.48.
[48] Inserted by the Criminal Justice Act 2003, Sch.2, para.6(3).
[49] s.1A was inserted by the Criminal Justice and Public Order Act 1994, s.27(1)(b).

(1F) Where a magistrates' court varies the conditions of bail under subsection (1E) above, that bail shall not lapse but shall continue subject to the conditions as so varied.][50]

(2) Nothing in the Bail Act 1976 shall prevent the re-arrest without warrant of a person released on bail subject to a duty to attend at a police station if new evidence justifying a further arrest has come to light since his release.

(3) Subject to [subsections (3A) and (4)][51] below, in this Part of this Act references to "bail" are references to bail subject to a duty—

> (a) to appear before a magistrates' court at such time and such place; or
>
> (b) to attend at such police station at such time,

as the custody officer may appoint.

[(3A) Where a custody officer grants bail to a person subject to a duty to appear before a magistrates' court, he shall appoint for the appearance—

> (a) a date which is not later than the first sitting of the court after the person is charged with the offence; or
>
> (b) where he is informed by the [designated officer for the relevant local justice][52] area that the appearance cannot be accommodated until a later date, that later date.][53]

(4) Where a custody officer has granted bail to a person subject to a duty to appear at a police station, the custody officer may give notice in writing to that person that his attendance at the police station is not required.

(5) . . .[54]

(6) Where a person [who has been granted bail [under this Part][55] and either has attended at the police station in accordance with the grant of bail or has been arrested under section 46A above is detained at a police station],[56] any time during which he was in police detention prior to being granted bail shall be included as part of any period which falls to be calculated under this Part of this Act.

(7) Where a person who was released on bail [under this Part][57] subject to a duty to attend at a police station is re-arrested, the provisions of this Part of this Act shall apply to him as they apply to a person arrested for the first time[; but this subsection does not apply to a person who is arrested under section 46A above or has attended a police station in accordance with the grant of bail (and who accordingly is deemed by section 34(7) above to have been arrested for an offence)].[58]

(8) In the Magistrates' Courts Act 1980—

> (a) the following section shall be substituted for section 43—
>> "Bail on arrest
>>
>> 43.—(1) Where a person has been granted bail under the Police and Criminal Evidence Act 1984 subject to a duty to appear before a magistrates' court, the court before which he is to appear may

[50] subs.(1B)–(1F) inserted by the Criminal Justice Act 2003, Sch.2, para.6(4).
[51] Words in brackets inserted by the Crime and Disorder Act 1998, s.46(1).
[52] Words in square brackets substituted by the Courts Act 2003, Sch.8, para.283 replacing "justices' chief executive for the relevant petty sessions", inserted by the Access to Justice Act 1999, Sch.13, para.127.
[53] subs.(3A) was inserted by the Crime and Disorder Act 1998, s.46(2).
[54] Repealed by the Criminal Justice and Public Order Act 1994, ss.29(4)(c), 168(3) and Sch.11.
[55] Inserted by the Criminal Justice Act 2003, Sch.1, para.10(a).
[56] Words in square brackets substituted by the Criminal Justice and Public Order Act 1994, s.29(4)(d).
[57] Inserted by the Criminal Justice Act 2003, Sch.1, para.10(b).
[58] Words in square brackets inserted by the Criminal Justice and Public Order Act 1994, s.29(4)(e).

appoint a later time as the time at which he is to appear and may enlarge the recognizances of any sureties for him at that time.

(2) The recognizance of any surety for any person granted bail subject to a duty to attend at a police station may be enforced as if it were conditioned for his appearance before a magistrates' court for the petty sessions area in which the police station named in the recognizance is situated." ; and

(b)   the following subsection shall be substituted for section 117(3)—

"(3) Where a warrant has been endorsed for bail under subsection (1) above—

(a) where the person arrested is to be released on bail on his entering into a recognizance without sureties, it shall not be necessary to take him to a police station, but if he is so taken, he shall be released from custody on his entering into the recognizance; and

(b) where he is to be released on his entering into a recognizance with sureties, he shall be taken to a police station on his arrest, and the custody officer there shall (subject to his approving any surety tendered in compliance with the endorsement) release him from custody as directed in the endorsement."

[Early administrative hearings conducted by justices' clerks[59]

47A.—Where a person has been charged with an offence at a police station, any requirement imposed under this Part for the person to appear or be brought before a magistrates' court shall be taken to be satisfied if the person appears or is brought before [a justice's clerk][60] in order for the clerk to conduct a hearing under section 50 of the Crime and Disorder Act 1998 (early administrative hearings).]

Remands to police custody

48.—In section 128 of the Magistrates' Courts Act 1980—

(a)   in subsection (7) for the words "the custody of a constable" there shall be substituted the words "detention at a police station";

(b)   after subsection (7) there shall be inserted the following subsection—

"(8) Where a person is committed to detention at a police station under subsection (7) above—

(a) he shall not be kept in such detention unless there is a need for him to be so detained for the purposes of inquiries into other offences;

(b) if kept in such detention, he shall be brought back before the magistrates' court which committed him as soon as that need ceases;

(c) he shall be treated as a person in police detention to whom the duties under section 39 of the Police and Criminal Evidence Act 1984 (responsibilities in relation to persons detained) relate;

---

[59] s.47A was inserted by the Crime and Disorder Act 1998, s.119, Sch.8, para.62.
[60] Words in square brackets substituted by the Courts Act 2003, Sch.8, para.284.

(d) his detention shall be subject to periodic review at the times set out in section 40 of that Act (review of police detention)."

Police detention to count towards custodial sentence

49.—(1) In subsection (1) of section 67 of the Criminal Justice Act 1967 (computation of custodial sentences) for the words from "period", in the first place where it occurs, to "the offender" there shall be substituted the words "relevant period, but where he".

(2) The following subsection shall be inserted after that subsection—

"(1A) In subsection (1) above "relevant period" means—

(a) any period during which the offender was in police detention in connection with the offence for which the sentence was passed; or

(b) any period during which he was in custody—

(i) by reason only of having been committed to custody by an order of a court made in connection with any proceedings relating to that sentence or the offence for which it was passed or any proceedings from which those proceedings arose; or

(ii) by reason of his having been so committed and having been concurrently detained otherwise than by order of a court."

(3) The following subsections shall be added after subsection (6) of that section—

"(7) A person is in police detention for the purposes of this section—

(a) at an [sic] time when he is in police detention for the purposes of the Police and Criminal Evidence Act 1984; and

(b) at any time when he is detained [under section 41 of the Terrorism Act 2000].[61]

(8) No period of police detention shall be taken into account under this section unless it falls after the coming into force of section 49 of the Police and Criminal Evidence Act 1984."

Records of detention

50.—(1) Each police force shall keep written records showing on an annual basis—

(a) the number of persons kept in police detention for more than 24 hours and subsequently released without charge;

(b) the number of applications for warrants of further detention and the results of the applications; and

(c) in relation to each warrant of further detention—

(i) the period of further detention authorised by it;

(ii) the period which the person named in it spent in police detention on its authority; and

(iii) whether he was charged or released without a charge.

---

[61] Words in square brackets substituted by the Terrorism Act 2000, Sch.13, para.1(2).

(2) Every annual report—
- (a) under section [22 of the Police Act 1996][62]; or
- (b) made by the Commissioner of Police of the Metropolis,

shall contain information about the matters mentioned in subsection (1) above in respect of the period to which the report relates.

Savings

51.—Nothing in this Part of this Act shall affect—
- (a) the powers conferred on immigration officers by section 4 of and Schedule 2 to the Immigration Act 1971 (administrative provisions as to control on entry etc.);
- [(b) the powers conferred by virtue of section 41 of, or Schedule 7 to, the Terrorism Act 2000 (powers of arrest and detention);][63]
- (c) any duty of a police officer under—
  - (i) section 129, 190 or 202 of the Army Act 1955 (duties of governors of prisons and others to receive prisoners, deserters, absentees and persons under escort);
  - (ii) section 129, 190 or 202 of the Air Force Act 1955 (duties of governors of prisons and others to receive prisoners, deserters, absentees and persons under escort); or
  - (iii) section 107 of the Naval Discipline Act 1957 (duties of governors of civil prisons etc.); or
  - (iv) paragraph 5 of Schedule 5 to the Reserve Forces Act 1980 (duties of governors of civil prisons); or
- (d) any right of a person in police detention to apply for a writ of habeas corpus or other prerogative remedy.

Children

52.—. . .[64]

PART V

QUESTIONING AND TREATMENT OF PERSONS BY POLICE

Abolition of certain powers of constables to search persons

53.—(1) Subject to subsection (2) below, there shall cease to have effect any Act (including a local Act) passed before this Act in so far as it authorises—
- (a) any search by a constable of a person in police detention at a police station; or
- (b) an intimate search of a person by a constable,

and any rule of common law which authorises a search such as is mentioned in paragraph (a) or (b) above is abolished.

(2) . . .[65]

---

[62] Words in square brackets substituted by the Police Act 1996, s.103, Sch.7, para.35.
[63] para.(b) substituted by the Terrorism Act 2000, Sch.15, para.5(4).
[64] Repealed by the Children Act 1989, Sch.15, para.1. The 1989 Northern Ireland PACE Order, Art.52 stated that Pt V does not apply to a child "apparently under 14".
[65] subs.(2) was repealed by the Prevention of Terrorism (Temporary Provisions) Act 1989, Sch.9, Pt I.

Searches of detained persons

54.—(1) The custody officer at a police station shall ascertain [. . .]⁶⁶ everything which a person has with him when he is—

    (a) brought to the station after being arrested elsewhere or after being committed to custody by an order or sentence of a court; or

    [(b) arrested at the station or detained there[, as a person falling within section 34(7), under section 37 above].]⁶⁷

[(2) The custody officer may record or cause to be recorded all or any of the things which he ascertains under subsection (1).

(2A) In the case of an arrested person, any such record may be made as part of his custody record.]⁶⁸

(3) Subject to subsection (4) below, a custody officer may seize and retain any such thing or cause any such thing to be seized and retained.

(4) Clothes and personal effects may only be seized if the custody officer—

    (a) believes that the person from whom they are seized may use them—

        (i) to cause physical injury to himself or any other person;

        (ii) to damage property;

        (iii) to interfere with evidence; or

        (iv) to assist him to escape; or

    (b) has reasonable grounds for believing that they may be evidence relating to an offence.

(5) Where anything is seized, the person from whom it is seized shall be told the reason for the seizure unless he is—

    (a) violent or likely to become violent; or

    (b) incapable of understanding what is said to him.

(6) Subject to subsection (7) below, a person may be searched if the custody officer considers it necessary to enable him to carry out his duty under subsection (1) above and to the extent that the custody officer considers necessary for that purpose.

[(6A) A person who is in custody at a police station or is in police detention otherwise than at a police station may at any time be searched in order to ascertain whether he has with him anything which he could use for any of the purposes specified in subsection (4)(a) above.

(6B) Subject to subsection (6C) below, a constable may seize and retain, or cause to be seized and retained, anything found on such a search.

(6C) A constable may only seize clothes and personal effects in the circumstances specified in subsection (4) above.]⁶⁹

(7) An intimate search may not be conducted under this section.

(8) A search under this section shall be carried out by a constable.⁷⁰

(9) The constable carrying out a search shall be of the same sex as the person searched.⁷¹

---

⁶⁶ Words in square brackets removed by the Criminal Justice Act 2003, s.8(1).

⁶⁷ para.(b) substituted by the Criminal Justice and Public Order Act 1994, Sch.10, para.55. Words in square brackets substituted by the Criminal Justice and Public Order Act 1994, s.168(2), Sch.10, para.55.

⁶⁸ The Criminal Justice Act 2003, s.8(2) replaced subs.(2) with a new (2) and (2A). For the Northern Ireland equivalent see Criminal Justice (Northern Ireland) Order 2004, SI 2004/1500, Art.6.

⁶⁹ subss.(6A) to (6C) were inserted by the Criminal Justice Act 1988, s.147(b).

⁷⁰ Save in the case of the Services—see n.71 below.

⁷¹ In the case of the Services, if a Service policeman of the same sex is not readily available, a search may be carried out by an officer, warrant officer, non-commissioned officer or leading rate who is of the same sex as the person searched and is acting under the direction of a Service policeman. (Police and Criminal Evidence Act 1984 (Application to the Armed Forces) Order, SI 1997/15, Sch.1, para.1.)

[Searches and examinations to ascertain identity[72]

54A.—(1) If an officer of at least the rank of inspector authorises it, a person who is detained in a police station may be searched or examined, or both—

   (a) for the purpose of ascertaining whether he has any mark that would tend to identify him as a person involved in the commission of an offence; or

   (b) for the purpose of facilitating the ascertainment of his identity.

(2) An officer may only give an authorisation under subsection (1) for the purpose mentioned in paragraph (a) of that subsection if—

   (a) the appropriate consent to a search or examination that would reveal whether the mark in question exists has been withheld; or

   (b) it is not practicable to obtain such consent.

(3) An officer may only give an authorisation under subsection (1) in a case in which subsection (2) does not apply if—

   (a) the person in question has refused to identify himself; or

   (b) the officer has reasonable grounds for suspecting that that person is not who he claims to be.

(4) An officer may give an authorisation under subsection (1) orally or in writing but, if he gives it orally, he shall confirm it in writing as soon as is practicable.

(5) Any identifying mark found on a search or examination under this section may be photographed—

   (a) with the appropriate consent; or

   (b) if the appropriate consent is withheld or it is not practicable to obtain it, without it.

(6) Where a search or examination may be carried out under this section, or a photograph may be taken under this section, the only persons entitled to carry out the search or examination, or to take the photograph, are [constables.][73]

(7) A person may not under this section carry out a search or examination of a person of the opposite sex or take a photograph of any part of the body of a person of the opposite sex.

(8) An intimate search may not be carried out under this section.

(9) A photograph taken under this section—

   (a) may be used by, or disclosed to, any person for any purpose related to the prevention or detection of crime, the investigation of an offence or the conduct of a prosecution; and

   (b) after being so used or disclosed, may be retained but may not be used or disclosed except for a purpose so related.

(10) In subsection—

   (a) the reference to crime includes a reference to any conduct which—

      (i) constitutes one or more criminal offences (whether under the law of a part of the United Kingdom or of a country or territory outside the United Kingdom); or

      (ii) is, or corresponds to, any conduct which, if it all took place in any one part of the United Kingdom, would constitute one or more criminal offences;

      and

---

[72] s.54A was inserted by the Anti-terrorism, Crime and Security Act 2001, s.90(1).

[73] The word "constables" was substituted by the Police Reform Act 2002, Sch.7, para.9(2).

(b) the references to an investigation and to a prosecution include references, respectively, to any investigation outside the United Kingdom of any crime or suspected crime and to a prosecution brought in respect of any crime in a country or territory outside the United Kingdom.

(11) In this section—

(a) references to ascertaining a person's identity include references to showing that he is not a particular person; and

(b) references to taking a photograph include references to using any process by means of which a visual image may be produced, and references to photographing a person shall be construed accordingly.

(12) In this section "mark" includes features and injuries; and a mark is an identifying mark for the purposes of this section if its existence in any person's case facilitates the ascertainment of his identity or his identification as a person involved in the commission of an offence.]

[(13) Nothing in this section applies to a person arrested under an extradition arrest power.][74]

Intimate searches

55.—(1) Subject to the following provisions of this section if an officer of at least the rank of [inspector][75] has reasonable grounds for believing—

(a) that a person who has been arrested and is in police detention may have concealed on him any thing which

(i) he could use to cause physical injury to himself or others; and

(ii) he might so use while he is in police detention or in the custody of a court; or

(b) that such a person—

(i) may have a Class A drug concealed on him; and

(ii) was in possession of it with the appropriate criminal intent before his arrest,

he may authorise [an intimate][76] search of that person.

(2) An officer may not authorise an intimate search of a person for anything unless he has reasonable grounds for believing that it cannot be found without his being intimately searched.

(3) An officer may give an authorisation under subsection (1) above orally or in writing but, if he gives it orally, he shall confirm it in writing as soon as is practicable.

(4) An intimate search which is only a drug offence search shall be by way of examination by a suitably qualified person.

(5) Except as provided by subsection (4) above, an intimate search shall be by way of examination by a suitably qualified person unless an officer of at least the rank of [inspector][77] considers that this is not practicable.

(6) An intimate search which is not carried out as mentioned in subsection (5) above shall be carried out by a constable.

---

[74] Inserted by Extradition Act 2003, Pt 4, s.169(2).

[75] Changed from superintendent by the Criminal Justice and Police Act 2001, s.79.

[76] "an intimate" replaced "such a" in the original—which was plainly a drafting error; see Criminal Justice Act 1988, Sch.15, para.99.

[77] Changed from superintendent by the Criminal Justice and Police Act 2001, s.79.

(7) A constable may not carry out an intimate search of a person of the opposite sex.

(8) No intimate search may be carried out except—

    (a)   at a police station;

    (b)   at a hospital;

    (c)   at a registered medical practitioner's surgery; or

    (d)   at some other place used for medical purposes.

(9) An intimate search which is only a drug offence search may not be carried out at a police station.

(10) If an intimate search of a person is carried out, the custody record relating to him shall state—

    (a)   which parts of his body were searched; and

    (b)   why they were searched.

(11) The information required to be recorded by subsection (10) above shall be recorded as soon as practicable after the completion of the search.

(12) The custody officer at a police station may seize and retain anything which is found on an intimate search of a person, or cause any such thing to be seized and retained—

    (a)   if he believes that the person from whom it is seized may use it—

        (i) to cause physical injury to himself or any other person;

        (ii) to damage property;

        (iii) to interfere with evidence; or

        (iv) to assist him to escape; or

    (b)   if he has reasonable grounds for believing that it may be evidence relating to an offence.

(13) Where anything is seized under this section, the person from whom it is seized shall be told the reason for the seizure unless he is

    (a)   violent or likely to become violent; or

    (b)   incapable of understanding what is said to him.

(14) Every annual report—

    (a)   under section [22 of the Police Act 1996][78]; or

    (b)   made by the Commissioner of Police of the Metropolis,

shall contain information about searches under this section which have been carried out in the area to which the report relates during the period to which it relates.

[(14A) Every annual report under section 57 of the Police Act 1997 (reports by Director General of the National Crime Squad) shall contain information about searches authorised under this section by members of the National Crime Squad during the period to which the report relates.][79]

(15) The information about such searches shall include—

    (a)   the total number of searches;

    (b)   the number of searches conducted by way of examination by a suitably qualified person;

    (c)   the number of searches not so conducted but conducted in the presence of such a person; and

    (d)   the result of the searches carried out.

---

[78] Words in square brackets substituted by the Police Act 1996, s.103, Sch.7, para.36.

[79] subs.(14A) inserted by the Police Act 1997, s.134(1), Sch.9, para.47. The subsection is repealed by the Serious Organised Crime and Police Bill 2004–05, Sch.4, para.45.

(16) The information shall also include, as separate items—
    (a) the total number of drug offence searches; and
    (b) the result of those searches.

(17) In this section—

"the appropriate criminal intent" means an intent to commit an offence under—

    (a) section 5(3) of the Misuse of Drugs Act 1971 (possession of controlled drug with intent to supply to another); or
    (b) section 68(2) of the Customs and Excise Management Act 1979 (exportation etc. with intent to evade a prohibition or restriction);

"Class A drug" has the meaning assigned to it by section 2(1)(b) of the Misuse of Drugs Act 1971;

"drug offence search" means an intimate search for a Class A drug which an officer has authorised by virtue of subsection (1)(b) above; and

"suitably qualified person" means—

    (a) a registered medical practitioner; or
    (b) a registered nurse.[80]

Right to have someone informed when arrested

56.—(1) Where a person has been arrested and is being held in custody in a police station or other premises, he shall be entitled, if he so requests, to have one friend or relative or other person who is known to him or who is likely to take an interest in his welfare told, as soon as is practicable except to the extent that delay is permitted by this section, that he has been arrested and is being detained there.

(2) Delay is only permitted—

    (a) in the case of a person who is in police detention for [a serious arrestable offence][81]; and
    (b) if an officer of at least the rank of [inspector][82] authorises it.

(3) In any case the person in custody must be permitted to exercise the right conferred by subsection (1) above within 36 hours from the relevant time, as defined in section 41(2) above.

(4) An officer may give an authorisation under subsection (2) above orally or in writing but, if he gives it orally, he shall confirm it in writing as soon as is practicable.

(5) [Subject to subsection (5A)][83] below, an officer may only authorise delay where he has reasonable grounds for believing that telling the named person of the arrest—

    (a) will lead to interference with or harm to evidence connected with [a serious arrestable offence][84] or interference with or physical injury to other persons; or
    (b) will lead to the alerting of other persons suspected of having committed such an offence but not yet arrested for it; or
    (c) will hinder the recovery of any property obtained as a result of such an offence.

[80] The 1989 Northern Ireland PACE Order, Art.56(17)(b) expanded the definition of nurse.
[81] The Serious Organised Crime and Police Bill 2004–05, Sch.7, Pt 3, para.8(9)(a) changes "serious arrestable offence" to "indictable offence".
[82] Changed from "superintendent" by the Criminal Justice and Police Act 2001, s.74.
[83] Words in square brackets inserted by the Drug Trafficking Offences Act 1986, s.32(1).
[84] The Serious Organised Crime and Police Bill 2004–05, Sch.7, Pt 3, para.8(9)(a) changes "serious arrestable offence" to "indictable offence".

[(5A) An officer may also authorise delay where he has reasonable grounds for believing that—

    (a) the person detained for the serious arrestable offence has benefited from his criminal conduct, and

    (b) the recovery of the value of the property constituting the benefit will be hindered by telling the named person of the arrest.][85]

(5B) For the purposes of subsection (5A) above the question whether a person has benefited from his criminal conduct is to be decided in accordance with Part 2 of the Proceeds of Crime Act 2002.

(6) If a delay is authorised—

    (a) the detained person shall be told the reason for it; and

    (b) the reason shall be noted on his custody record.

(7) The duties imposed by subsection (6) above shall be performed as soon as is practicable.

(8) The rights conferred by this section on a person detained at a police station or other premises are exercisable whenever he is transferred from one place to another, and this section applies to each subsequent occasion on which they are exercisable as it applies to the first such occasion.

(9) There may be no further delay in permitting the exercise of the right conferred by subsection (1) above once the reason for authorising delay ceases to subsist.

(10) [Nothing in this section applies to a person arrested or detained under the terrorism provisions].[86]

(11) . . .[87]

Additional rights of children and young persons who are arrested

57.—The following subsections shall be substituted for section 34(2) of the Children and Young Persons Act 1933—

"(2) Where a child or young person is in police detention, such steps as are practicable shall be taken to ascertain the identity of a person responsible for his welfare.

(3) If it is practicable to ascertain the identity of a person responsible for the welfare of the child or young person, that person shall be informed, unless it is not practicable to do so—

    (a) that the child or young person has been arrested;

    (b) why he has been arrested; and

    (c) where he is being detained.

(4) Where information falls to be given under subsection (3) above, it shall be given as soon as it is practicable to do so.

(5) For the purposes of this section the persons who may be responsible for the welfare of a child or young person are—

    (a) his parent or guardian; or

    (b) any other person who has for the time being assumed responsibility for his welfare.

---

[85] subs.(5A) was inserted by the Drug Trafficking Offences Act 1986, s.32. It was amended by the Criminal Justice Act 1988, s.99. subss.(5A) and (5B) were then replaced by the Proceeds of Crime Act 2002, Sch.11, para.14(2). (The Northern Ireland equivalent provision was in Sch.11, para.19(2).) The Serious Organised Crime and Police Bill 2004–05, Sch.8(9)(b) changes "the serious arrestable offence" in subs.(5A)(a) to "the indictable offence".

[86] subs.(10) substituted by the Terrorism Act 2000, Sch.15, para.5(5).

[87] Repealed by the Terrorism Act 2000, Sch.15, para.5(5).

(6) If it is practicable to give a person responsible for the welfare of the child or young person the information required by subsection (3) above, that person shall be given it as soon as it is practicable to do so.

(7) If it appears that at the time of his arrest a supervision order, as defined in section 11 of the Children and Young Persons Act 1969, is in force in respect of him, the person responsible for his supervision shall also be informed as described in subsection (3) above as soon as it is reasonably practicable to do so.[88]

(8) The reference to a parent or guardian in subsection (5) above is—

    (a) in the case of a child in the care of a local authority, a reference to that authority; and

    (b) in the case of a child or young person in the care of a voluntary organisation in which parental rights and duties with respect to him are vested by virtue of a resolution under section 64(1) of the Child Care Act 1980, that organisation.

(9) The rights conferred on a child or young person by subsections (2) to (8) above are in addition to his rights under section 56 of the Police and Criminal Evidence Act 1984.

(10) The reference in subsection (2) above to a child or young person who is in police detention includes a reference to a child or young person who has been detained under the terrorism provisions, and in subsection (3) above "arrest" includes such detention.

(11) In subsection (10) above "the terrorism provisions" has the meaning assigned to it by section 65 of the Police and Criminal Evidence Act 1984."

Access to legal advice

58.—(1) A person arrested and held in custody in a police station or other premises shall be entitled, if he so requests, to consult a solicitor privately at any time.

(2) Subject to subsection (3) below, a request under subsection (1) above and the time at which it was made shall be recorded in the custody record.

(3) Such a request need not be recorded in the custody record of a person who makes it at a time while he is at a court after being charged with an offence.

(4) If a person makes such a request, he must be permitted to consult a solicitor as soon as is practicable except to the extent that delay is permitted by this section.

(5) In any case he must be permitted to consult a solicitor within 36 hours from the relevant time, as defined in section 41(2) above.

(6) Delay in compliance with a request is only permitted—

    (a) in the case of a person who is in police detention for [a serious arrestable offence][89]; and

    (b) if an officer of at least the rank of superintendent authorises it.

(7) An officer may give an authorisation under subsection (6) above orally or in writing but, if he gives it orally, he shall confirm it in writing as soon as is practicable.

(8) [Subject to subsection (8A) below],[90] an officer may only authorise delay where he has reasonable grounds for believing that the exercise of the right con-

---

[88] The 1989 Northern Ireland PACE Order, Art.58(7) added a reference also to a probation order.

[89] The Serious Organised Crime and Police Bill 2004–05, Sch.7, Pt 3, para.8(10)(a) changes "a serious arrestable offence" to "an indictable offence".

[90] Words in square brackets inserted by the Drug Trafficking Offences Act 1986, s.32(2).

ferred by subsection (1) above at the time when the person in police detention desires to exercise it—

    (a)   will lead to interference with or harm to evidence connected with [a serious arrestable offence][91] or interference with or physical injury to other persons; or

    (b)   will lead to the alerting of other persons suspected of having committed such an offence but not yet arrested for it; or

    (c)   will hinder the recovery of any property obtained as a result of such an offence.

[(8A) An officer may also authorise delay where he has reasonable grounds for believing that—

    (a)   the person detained for the serious arrestable offence has benefited from his criminal conduct, and

    (b)   the recovery of the value of the property constituting the benefit will be hindered by the exercise of the right conferred by subsection (1) above.

(8B) For the purposes of subsection (8A) above the question whether a person has benefited from his criminal conduct is to be decided in accordance with Part 2 of the Proceeds of Crime Act 2002.][92]

(9) If delay is authorised—

    (a)   the detained person shall be told the reason for it; and

    (b)   the reason shall be noted on his custody record.

(10) The duties imposed by subsection (9) above shall be performed as soon as is practicable.

(11) There may be no further delay in permitting the exercise of the right conferred by subsection (1) above once the reason for authorising delay ceases to subsist.

(12) Nothing in this section applies to a person arrested or detained under the terrorism provisions.[93]

    (13) . . .[94]

    (14) . . .[95]

    (15) . . .[96]

    (16) . . .[97]

    (17) . . .[98]

    (18) . . .[99]

[91] The Serious Organised Crime and Police Bill 2004–05, Sch.7, Pt 3, para.8(10)(a) changes "a serious arrestable offence" to "an indictable offence".

[92] subs.(8A) was originally inserted by the Drug Trafficking Offences Act 1986, s.32. It was amended by the Criminal Justice Act 1988, s.99. subss.(8A) and (8B) were then replaced by the Proceeds of Crime Act 2002, Sch.11, para.14(3). (The Northern Ireland equivalent provision was in Sch.11, para.19(3).) The Serious Organised Crime and Police Bill 2004–05, Sch.8(10)(b) changes "the serious arrestable offence" in (8A)(a) to "the indictable offence".

[93] The new text of subs.(12) was inserted by the Terrorism Act 2000, Sch.15, para.5(6).

[94] Repealed by the Terrorism Act 2000, Sch.15, para.5(6).

[95] Repealed by the Terrorism Act 2000, Sch.15, para.5(6).

[96] Repealed by the Terrorism Act 2000, Sch.15, para.5(6).

[97] Repealed by the Terrorism Act 2000, Sch.15, para.5(6).

[98] Repealed by the Terrorism Act 2000, Sch.15, para.5(6).

[99] Repealed by the Terrorism Act 2000, Sch.15, para.5(6).

Legal aid for persons in police stations

59.—...[1]

Tape-recording of interviews

60.—(1) It shall be the duty of the Secretary of State—

    (a) to issue a code of practice in connection with the tape-recording of interviews of persons suspected of the commission of criminal offences which are held by police officers at police stations; and

    (b) to make an order requiring the tape-recording of interviews of persons suspected of the commission of criminal offences, or of such descriptions of criminal offences as may be specified in the order, which are so held, in accordance with the code as it has effect for the time being.

(2) An order under subsection (1) above shall be made by statutory instrument and shall be subject to annulment in pursuance of a resolution of either House of Parliament.

[Visual recording of interviews[2]

60A.—(1) The Secretary of State shall have power—

    (a) to issue a code of practice for the visual recording of interviews held by police officers at police stations; and

    (b) to make an order requiring the visual recording of interviews so held, and requiring the visual recording to be in accordance with the code for the time being in force under this section.

(2) A requirement imposed by an order under this section may be imposed in relation to such cases or police stations in such areas, or both, as may be specified or described in the order.

(3) An order under subsection (1) above shall be made by statutory instrument and shall be subject to annulment in pursuance of a resolution of either House of Parliament.

(4) In this section—

    (a) references to any interview are references to an interview of a person suspected of a criminal offence; and

    (b) references to a visual recording include references to a visual recording in which an audio recording is comprised.]

Fingerprinting

61.—(1) Except as provided by this section no person's fingerprints may be taken without the appropriate consent.

(2) Consent to the taking of a person's fingerprints must be in writing if it is given at a time when he is at a police station.

[(3) The fingerprints of a person detained at a police station may be taken without the appropriate consent if—

    (a) he is detained in consequence of his arrest for a recordable offence; and

    (b) he has not had his fingerprints taken in the course of the investigation of the offence by the police.][3]

---

[1] The whole of s.59 was repealed under the Legal Aid Act 1988, s.45, Sch.6.

[2] s.60A was inserted by the Criminal Justice and Police Act 2001, s.76(1).

[3] subs.(3) was substituted by the Criminal Justice Act 2003, s.9(1), (2). For the Northern Ireland equivalent see Criminal Justice (Northern Ireland) Order 2004, SI 2004/1500, Art.6.

[(3A) [Where a person mentioned in paragraph (a) of subsection (3) or (4) has already had his fingerprints taken in the course of the investigation of the offence by the police],[4] that fact shall be disregarded for the purposes of that subsection if—

    (a) the fingerprints taken on the previous occasion do not constitute a complete set of his fingerprints; or

    (b) some or all of the fingerprints taken on the previous occasion are not of sufficient quality to allow satisfactory analysis, comparison or matching (whether in the case in question or generally).][5]

[(4) The fingerprints of a person detained at a police station may be taken without the appropriate consent if—

    (a) he has been charged with a recordable offence or informed that he will be reported for such an offence; and

    (b) he has not had his fingerprints taken in the course of the investigation of the offence by the police.][6]

[(4A) The fingerprints of a person who has answered to bail at a court or police station may be taken without the appropriate consent at the court or station if—

    (a) the court, or

    (b) an officer of at least the rank of inspector,

authorises them to be taken.

(4B) A court or officer may only give an authorisation under subsection (4A) if—

    (a) the person who has answered to bail has answered to it for a person whose fingerprints were taken on a previous occasion and there are reasonable grounds for believing that he is not the same person; or

    (b) the person who has answered to bail claims to be a different person from a person whose fingerprints were taken on a previous occasion.][7]

(5) An officer may give an authorisation under subsection [. . .][8] (4A) above orally or in writing but, if he gives it orally, he shall confirm it in writing as soon as is practicable.

(6) Any person's fingerprints may be taken without the appropriate consent if—

    [(a) he has been convicted of a recordable offence;

    (b) he has been given a caution in respect of a recordable offence which, at the time of the caution, he has admitted; or

    (c) he has been warned or reprimanded under section 65 of the Crime and Disorder Act 1998 (c. 37) for a recordable offence.][9]

[*The Serious Organised Crime and Police Bill 2004–05, cl.108(2) inserts new subss.(6A), (6B) and (6C):*

"*(6A) A constable may take a person's fingerprints without the appropriate consent if—*

---

4 Words in square brackets were rewritten by the Criminal Justice Act 2003, s.9(3).

5 subs.(3A) was inserted by the Criminal Justice and Police Act 2001, s.78(3).

6 subs.(4) which had previously been amended by the Anti-Terrorism, Crime and Security Act 2001, s.90(2), was rewritten by the Criminal Justice Act 2003, s.9(2). For the Northern Ireland equivalent see Criminal Justice (Northern Ireland) Order 2004, SI 2004/1500, Art.6.

7 subss.(4A) and (4B) were inserted by the Criminal Justice and Police Act 2001, s.78 (4).

8 Words in square brackets inserted by the Criminal Justice and Police Act 2001, s.78(5) as amended by the Criminal Justice Act 2003, s.9(4).

9 paras (a)–(c) inserted by the Criminal Justice and Police Act 2001, s.78 (6).

> (a) the constable reasonably suspects that the person is committing or attempting to commit an offence, or has committed or attempted to commit an offence; and
>
> (b) either of the two conditions mentioned in subsection (6B) is met.
>
> (6B) The conditions are that—
>
> (a) the name of the person is unknown to, and cannot be readily ascertained by, the constable;
>
> (b) the constable has reasonable grounds for doubting whether a name furnished by the person as his name is his real name.
>
> (6C) The taking of fingerprints by virtue of subsection (6A) does not count for any of the purposes of this Act as taking them in the course of the investigation of an offence by the police."]

(7) In a case where by virtue of subsection (3)[, (4)] or (6)[10] above a person's fingerprints are taken without the appropriate consent—

> (a) he shall be told the reason before his fingerprints are taken; and
>
> (b) the reason shall be recorded as soon as is practicable after the fingerprints are taken.

[(7A) If a person's fingerprints are taken at a police station,[11] whether with or without the appropriate consent—

> (a) before the fingerprints are taken, an officer[12] shall inform him that they may be the subject of a speculative search; and
>
> (b) the fact that the person has been informed of this possibility shall be recorded as soon as is practicable after the fingerprints have been taken.][13]

(8) If he is detained at a police station when the fingerprints are taken, the reason for taking them [and, in the case falling within subsection (7A) above, the fact referred to in paragraph (b) of that subsection][14] shall be recorded on his custody record.

[(8A) Where a person's fingerprints are taken electronically, they must be taken only in such manner, and using such devices, as the Secretary of State has approved for the purposes of electronic fingerprinting.][15]

[(8B) The power to take the fingerprints of a person detained at a police station without the appropriate consent shall be exercisable by any constable].[16]

(9) Nothing in this section—

> (a) affects any power conferred by paragraph 18(2) of Schedule 2 to the Immigration Act 1971[, section 141 of the Immigration and Asylum Act 1999 or regulations made under section 144 of that Act][17]; or

[10] The Criminal Justice Act 2003, s.9(5) susbstituted for "(3) or (6)" , "(3),(4) or (6)". The Serious Organised Crime and Police Bill 2004–05, cl.108(3) changes "or (6)" to ", (6) or (6A)".

[11] The Serious Organised Crime and Police Bill 2004–05, cl.108(4)(a) adds here "or by virtue of subsection (6A) at a place other than a police station".

[12] The Serious Organised Crime and Police Bill 2004–05, cl.108(4)(b) adds here "(or, in a subsection (6A) case, the constable)".

[13] subs.(7A) was inserted by the Criminal Justice and Public Order Act 1994, s.168(2), Sch.10, para.56(a). For the equivalent change in Northern Ireland see Police (Amendment) (Northern Ireland) Order 1995, Art.9(2).

[14] As amended by the Criminal Justice and Public Order Act 1994, s.168(2), Sch.10, para.56(b). For the equivalent change in Northern Ireland see Police (Amendment) (Northern Ireland) Order 1995, Art.9(3).

[15] subs.(8A)—not yet in force—was inserted by Criminal Justice and Police Act 2001, s.78(7).

[16] Inserted by Police Reform Act 2002, Sch.7, para.9(3).

[17] Words in square brackets—not yet in force—were inserted by the Immigration and Asylum Act 1999, s.169(1), Sch.14, para.80(1), (4).

(b) [applies to a person arrested or detained under the terrorism provisions.][18]

[(10) Nothing in this section applies to a person arrested under an extradition arrest power.][19]

[*The Serious Organised Crime and Police Bill 2004–05, cl.109(2) inserts new s.61A:*

"Impressions of footwear

61A.—(1) Except as provided by this section, no impression of a person's footwear may be taken without the appropriate consent.

(2) Consent to the taking of an impression of a person's footwear must be in writing if it is given at a time when he is at a police station.

(3) Where a person is detained at a police station, an impression of his footwear may be taken without the appropriate consent if—

(a) *he is detained in consequence of his arrest for a recordable offence, or has been charged with a recordable offence, or informed that he will be reported for a recordable offence; and*

(b) *he has not had an impression taken of his footwear in the course of the investigation of the offence by the police.*

(4) Where a person mentioned in paragraph (a) of subsection (3) above has already had an impression taken of his footwear in the course of the investigation of the offence by the police, that fact shall be disregarded for the purposes of that subsection if the impression of his footwear taken previously is –

(a) *incomplete; or*

(b) *is not of sufficient quality to allow satisfactory analysis, comparison or matching (whether in the case in question or generally).*

(5) If an impression of a person's footwear is taken at a police station, whether with or without the appropriate consent—

(a) *before it is taken, an officer shall inform him that it may be the subject of a speculative search; and*

(b) *the fact that the person has been informed of this possibility shall be recorded as soon as is practicable after the impression has been taken, and if he is detained at a police station, the record shall be made on his custody record.*

(6) In a case where by virtue of subsection (3) above, an impression of a person's footwear is taken without the appropriate consent—

(a) *he shall be told the reason before it is taken; and*

(b) *the reason shall be recorded on his custody record as soon as is practicable after the impression is taken.*

(7) The power to take an impression of the footwear of a person detained at a police station without the appropriate consent shall be exercisable by any constable.

(8) Nothing in this section applies to any person—

(a) *arrested or detained under the terrorism provisions,*

(b) *arrested under an extradition arrest power."*]

---

[18] New text for (b) was substituted by the Terrorism Act 2000, Sch.15, para.5(7).
[19] Inserted by the Extradition Act 2003, Pt 4, s.169(3).

Intimate samples[20]

62.—(1) [Subject to section 63B below],[21] an intimate sample may be taken from a person in police detention only—

(a) if a police officer of at least the rank of [inspector][22] authorises it to be taken; and

(b) if the appropriate consent is given.

[(1A) An intimate sample may be taken from a person who is not in police detention but from whom, in the course of the investigation of an offence, two or more non-intimate samples suitable for the same means of analysis have been taken which have proved insufficient—

(a) if a police officer of at least the rank of [inspector][23] authorises it to be taken; and

(b) if the appropriate consent is given.][24]

(2) An officer may only give an authorisation [under subsection (1) or (1A) above][25] if he has reasonable grounds—

(a) for suspecting the involvement of the person from whom the sample is to be taken in a [recordable offence][26]; and

(b) for believing that the sample will tend to confirm or disprove his involvement.

(3) An officer may give an authorisation under subsection (1) [or (1A)][27] above orally or in writing but, if he gives it orally, he shall confirm it in writing as soon as is practicable.

(4) The appropriate consent must be given in writing.

(5) Where—

(a) an authorisation has been given; and

(b) it is proposed that an intimate sample shall be taken in pursuance of the authorisation,

an officer shall inform the person from whom the sample is to be taken—

(i) of the giving of the authorisation; and

(ii) of the grounds for giving it.

(6) The duty imposed by subsection (5)(ii) above includes a duty to state the nature of the offence in which it is suspected that the person from whom the sample is to be taken has been involved.

(7) If an intimate sample is taken from a person—

(a) the authorisation by virtue of which it was taken;

(b) the grounds for giving the authorisation; and

(c) the fact that the appropriate consent was given,

shall be recorded as soon as is practicable after the sample is taken.

---

[20] For the comparable Northern Ireland provisions see Criminal Justice Act 1988, Sch.14 and see also Police (Amendment) (Northern Ireland) Order 1995, Art.10.
[21] Words in square brackets inserted by the Criminal Justice and Courts Services Act 2000, Sch.7, para.78.
[22] Changed from "superintendent" by the Criminal Justice and Police Act 2001, s.80(1).
[23] Changed from "superintendent" by the Criminal Justice and Police Act 2001, s.80(1).
[24] subs.(1A) was inserted by the Criminal Justice and Public Order Act 1994, s.54(2). For the equivalent change in Northern Ireland see Police (Amendment) (Northern Ireland) Order 1995, Art.10(2).
[25] As amended by the Criminal Justice and Public Order Act 1994, s.54(3)(a) and (b). For the equivalent change in Northern Ireland see Police (Amendment) (Northern Ireland) Order 1995, Art.10(3).
[26] As amended by the Criminal Justice and Public Order Act 1994, s.54(3)(a) and (b). For the equivalent change in Northern Ireland see Police (Amendment) (Northern Ireland) Order 1995, Art.10(3).
[27] Inserted by the Criminal Justice and Public Order Act 1994, s.54(4). For the equivalent change in Northern Ireland see Police (Amendment) (Northern Ireland) Order 1995, Art.10(4).

[(7A) If an intimate sample is taken from a person at a police station—

    (a)   before the sample is taken, an officer shall inform him that it may be the subject of a speculative search; and

    (b)   the fact that the person has been informed of this possibility shall be recorded as soon as practicable after the sample has been taken.][28]

(8) If an intimate sample is taken from a person detained at a police station, the matters required to be recorded by subsection (7) [or (7A)][29] above shall be recorded in his custody record.

[(9) In the case of an intimate sample which is a dental impression, the sample may be taken from a person only by a registered dentist.

(9A) In the case of any other form of intimate sample, except in the case of a sample of urine, the sample may be taken from a person only by—

    (a)   a registered medical practitioner; or

    (b)   a registered health care professional.][30]

(10) Where the appropriate consent to the taking of an intimate sample from a person was refused without good cause, in any proceedings against that person for an offence—

    (a)   the court, in determining—

        (i)   [whether to commit that person for trial][31]

        (ii)   whether there is a case to answer; and

   [(aa) a judge, in deciding whether to grant an application made by the accused under—

        (i)   [section 6 of the Criminal Justice Act 1987 (application for dismissal of charge of serious fraud in respect of which notice of transfer has been given under section 4 of that Act); or

        (ii)   paragraph 5 of Schedule 6 to the Criminal Justice Act 1991 (application for dismissal of charge of violent or sexual offence involving child in respect of which notice of transfer has been given under section 53 of that Act); and] [paragraph 2 of Schedule 3 to the Crime and Disorder Act 1998 (applications for dismissal); and]][32]

    (b)   the court or jury, in determining whether that person is guilty of the offence charged,

may draw such inferences from the refusal as appear proper; . . .[33]

---

[28] Inserted by the Criminal Justice and Public Order Act 1994, ss.54(2), 168(2), Sch.10, paras 57(a). For the equivalent change in Northern Ireland see Police (Amendment) (Northern Ireland) Order 1995, Art.10(5).

[29] Words in square brackets inserted by the Criminal Justice and Public Order Act 1994, s.168(2), Sch.10, para.57(b). For the equivalent change in Northern Ireland see Police (Amendment) (Northern Ireland) Order 1995, Art.10(6).

[30] New subss.(9) and (9A) inserted by Police Reform Act 2002, s.54(1). For previous amendments see Criminal Justice and Public Order Act 1994, s.54(5)(a) and (b) and Criminal Justice and Police Act 2001, s.80(2).

[31] The original sub-para.(i) was replaced by the Criminal Justice and Public Order Act 1994, Sch.4, para.58. (The equivalent change was made in Northern Ireland by the Police (Amendment) (Northern Ireland) Order Act 1995, Art.10(7).) Sub-para.(i) in square brackets was repealed by the Criminal Justice Act 2003, Sch.3, para.56(2)—not yet in force.

[32] para.(aa) was inserted by the Criminal Justice and Public Order Act 1994, s.168(1), (3), Sch.9, para.24, Sch.11. The Criminal Justice Act 2003, Sch.3, para.56(2)—not yet in force—substituted the words in the second square brackets for sub-paras (i) and (ii).

[33] Omitted words repealed by the Criminal Justice and Public Order Act 1994, Sch.11.

(11) Nothing in this section [applies to the taking of a specimen for the purposes of any provisions of][34] [sections 4 to 11 of the Road Traffic Act 1988][35] [or of sections 26 to 38 of the Transport and Works Act 1992].[36]

[(12) Nothing in this section applies to a person arrested or detained under the terrorism provisions; and subsection (1A) shall not apply where the non-intimate samples mentioned in that subsection were taken under paragraph 10 of Schedule 8 to the Terrorism Act 2000.][37]

Other samples[38]

63.—(1) Except as provided by this section a non-intimate sample may not be taken from a person without the appropriate consent.

(2) Consent to the taking of a non-intimate sample must be given in writing.

[(2A) A non-intimate sample may be taken from a person without the appropriate consent if two conditions are satisfied.

(2B) The first is that the person is in police detention in consequence of his arrest for a recordable offence.

(2C) The second is that—

(a) he has not had a non-intimate sample of the same type and from the same part of the body taken in the course of the investigation of the offence by the police, or

(b) he has had such a sample taken but it proved insufficient.][39]

(3) A non-intimate sample may be taken from a person without the appropriate consent if—

(a) he [. . ..][40] is being held in custody by the police on the authority of a court[41]; and

(b) an officer of at least the rank of [inspector][42] authorises it to be taken without the appropriate consent.

[(3A) A non-intimate sample may be taken from a person (whether or not he [is in police detention or held in custody by the police on the authority of a court][43]) without the appropriate consent if—

(a) he has been charged with a recordable offence or informed that he will be reported for such an offence; and

(b) either he has not had a non-intimate sample taken from him in the course of the investigation of the offence by the police or he has had a non-intimate sample taken from him but either it was not suitable for the same means of analysis or, though so suitable, the sample proved insufficient.

---

[34] Words in square brackets substituted by the Police Reform Act 2002, s.53(2).

[35] As amended by the Road Traffic (Consequential Provisions) Act 1988, s.4, Sch.3, para.27 and in Northern Ireland by the Road Traffic (Amendment) (Northern Ireland) Order 1991, Arts 143 to 152A.

[36] Words in square brackets inserted by the Police Reform Act 2002, s.53(2)(b).

[37] subs.(12) inserted by the Terrorism Act 2000, Sch.15, para.5(8).

[38] For the Northern Ireland equivalent see Criminal Justice (Northern Ireland) Order 2004, SI 2004/1500, Art.6.

[39] subss.(2A), (2B) and (2C) were inserted by the Criminal Justice Act 2003, s.10(2). For the Northern Ireland equivalent see Criminal Justice (Northern Ireland) Order 2004, SI 2004/1500, Art.8.

[40] The words "is in police detention" were deleted by the Criminal Justice Act 2003, s.10(3).

[41] The words "is being held in custody by the police on the authority of a court" were not in the 1989 Northern Ireland PACE Order, Art.63(3)(a) as there is no provision in Northern Ireland for a person charged with an offence to be remanded by a court into police custody.

[42] Changed from "superintendent" by the Criminal Justice and Police Act 2001, s.80(1).

[43] As amended by the Criminal Justice Act 2003, s.10(4).

(3B) A non-intimate sample may be taken from a person without the appropriate consent if he has been convicted of a recordable offence.][44]

[(3C) A non-intimate sample may also be taken from a person without the appropriate consent if he is a person to whom section 2 of the Criminal Evidence (Amendment) Act 1997 applies (persons detained following acquittal on grounds of insanity or finding of unfitness to plead).][45]

(4) An officer may only give an authorisation under subsection (3) above if he has reasonable grounds—

    (a) for suspecting the involvement of the person from whom the sample is to be taken in a [recordable offence][46]; and

    (b) for believing that the sample will tend to confirm or disprove his involvement.

(5) An officer may give an authorisation under subsection (3) above orally or in writing but, if he gives it orally, he shall confirm it in writing as soon as is practicable.

[(5A) An officer shall not give an authorisation under subsection (3) above for the taking from any person of a non-intimate sample consisting of a skin impression if—

    (a) a skin impression of the same part of the body has already been taken from that person in the course of the investigation of the offence; and

    (b) the impression previously taken is not one that has proved insufficient.][47]

(6) Where—

    (a) an authorisation has been given; and

    (b) it is proposed that a non-intimate sample shall be taken in pursuance of the authorisation,

an officer shall inform the person from whom the sample is to be taken—

        (i) of the giving of the authorisation; and

        (ii) of the grounds for giving it.

(7) The duty imposed by subsection (6)(ii) above includes a duty to state the nature of the offence in which it is suspected that the person from whom the sample is to be taken has been involved.

(8) If a non-intimate sample is taken from a person by virtue of subsection (3) above—

    (a) the authorisation by virtue of which it was taken; and

    (b) the grounds for giving the authorisation,

shall be recorded as soon as is practicable after the sample is taken.

[(8A) In a case where by virtue of subsection [(2A),][48] (3A)[, (3B) or (3C) above][49] a sample is taken from a person without the appropriate consent—

    (a) he shall be told the reason before the sample is taken; and

    (b) the reason shall be recorded as soon as practicable after the sample is taken.][50]

---

[44] subss.(3A) and (3B) were inserted by the Criminal Justice and Public Order Act 1994, ss.55(2).
[45] subs.(3C) was inserted by the Criminal Evidence (Amendment) Act 1997, s.2(2).
[46] As amended by the Criminal Justice and Public Order Act 1994, s.55(3).
[47] subs.(5A) was inserted by the Criminal Justice and Police Act 2001, s.80(3).
[48] Inserted by the Criminal Justice Act 2003, s.10(5).
[49] Substituted by the Criminal Evidence (Amendment) Act 1997, s.2(2)(b).
[50] subs.(8A) was inserted by the Criminal Justice and Public Order Act 1994, s.55(4).

[(8B) If a non-intimate sample is taken from a person at a police station, whether with or without the appropriate consent—

(a) before the sample is taken, an officer shall inform him that it may be the subject of a speculative search; and

(b) the fact that the person has been informed of this possibility shall be recorded as soon as practicable after the sample has been taken.][51]

(9) If a non-intimate sample is taken from a person detained at a police station, the matters required to be recorded by subsection (8) [or (8A)] [or (8B)][52] above shall be recorded in his custody record.

[(9ZA) The power to take a non-intimate sample from a person without the appropriate consent shall be exercisable by any constable.][53]

[(9A) Subsection (3B) above shall not apply to any person convicted before 10th April 1995 unless he is a person to whom section 1 of the Criminal Evidence (Amendment) Act 1997 applies (persons imprisoned or detained by virtue of pre-existing conviction for sexual offence etc).]

[(9A) Where a non-intimate sample consisting of a skin impression is taken electronically from a person, it must be taken only in such manner, and using such devices, as the Secretary of State has approved for the purpose of the electronic taking of such an impression.][54]

(10) [Nothing in this section applies to a person arrested or detained under the terrorism provisions.][55]

[(11) Nothing in this section applies to a person arrested under an extradition arrest power.][56]

[Fingerprints and samples—supplementary provisions[57]

63A.—[(1) Where a person has been arrested on suspicion of being involved in a recordable offence or has been charged with such an offence or has been informed that he will be reported for such an offence, fingerprints[58] or samples or the information derived from samples taken under any power conferred by this Part of this Act from the person may be checked against—

(a) other fingerprints or samples to which the person seeking to check has access and which are held by or on behalf of [any one or more relevant

---

[51] subs.(8B) was inserted by the Criminal Justice and Public Order Act 1994, s.168(2), Sch.10, para.58(a).
[52] Words in square brackets inserted by the Criminal Justice and Public Order Act 1994, s.168(2), Sch.10, para.58(b).
[53] Inserted by Police Reform Act 2002, Sch.7, para.9(4).
[54] subs.(9A) in the first square brackets was inserted by the Criminal Evidence (Amendment) Act 1997, s.1 to replace subs.(10) which had been introduced by the Criminal Justice and Public Order Act 1994, s.55(6). A new subs.(9A)—in the second square brackets, not yet in force— was substituted by the Criminal Justice and Police Act 2001, s.80(4).
[55] New text substituted by the Terrorism Act 2000, Sch.15, para.5(9), replacing text inserted by the Criminal Justice and Public Order Act 1994, s.168(2), Sch.10, para.62(4)(b).
[56] Inserted by the Extradition Act 2003, Pt 4, s.169(4).
[57] s.63A was originally inserted by the Criminal Justice and Public Order Act 1994, s.56. It applies where a person—(a) is arrested on suspicion of being involved in a recordable offence, (b) is charged with a recordable offence, or (c) is informed that he will be reported for a recordable offence (Criminal Procedure and Investigations Act 1996, s.64(2)). The original text of subs.(1) was replaced by the above in the Criminal Procedure and Investigations Act 1996, s.64. For the Northern Ireland version see Criminal Procedure and Investigations Act 1996, Sch.4, para.27.
[58] The Serious Organised Crime and Police Bill 2004–05, cl.109(3) inserts ", impressions of footwear" after "fingerprints" in both places where it occurs in subs.(1).

law-enforcement authorities or which]⁵⁹ are held in connection with or as a result of an investigation of an offence;

   (b)   information derived from other samples if the information is contained in records to which the person seeking to check has access and which are held as mentioned in paragraph (a) above.]

[The Serious Organised Crime and Police Bill 2004–05, cl.108(5) inserts new subs.(1ZA):

"(1ZA) Fingerprints taken by virtue of section 61(6A) above may be checked against other fingerprints to which the person seeking to check has access and which are held by or on behalf of any one or more relevant law-enforcement authorities or which are held in connection with or as a result of an investigation of an offence."]

   [(1A) In subsection (1)⁶⁰ above "relevant law-enforcement authority" means—

   (a)   a police force;
   (b)   the National Criminal Intelligence Service;
   (c)   the National Crime Squad⁶¹;
   (d)   a public authority (not falling within paragraphs (a) to (c)) with functions in any part of the British Islands which consist of or include the investigation of crimes or the charging of offenders;
   (e)   any person with functions in any country or territory outside the United Kingdom which—
        (i)   correspond to those of a police force; or
        (ii)   otherwise consist of or include the investigation of conduct contrary to the law of that country or territory, or the apprehension of persons guilty of such conduct;
   (f)   any person with functions under any international agreement which consist of or include the investigation of conduct which is—
        (i)   unlawful under the law of one or more places,
        (ii)   prohibited by such an agreement, or
        (iii)   contrary to international law,
        or the apprehension of persons guilty of such conduct.

   (1B) The reference in subsection (1A) above to a police force is a reference to any of the following—

   (a)   any police force maintained under section 2 of the Police Act 1996 (c. 16) (police forces in England and Wales outside London);
   (b)   the metropolitan police force;
   (c)   the City of London police force;
   (d)   any police force maintained under or by virtue of section 1 of the Police (Scotland) Act 1967 (c. 77);
   (e)   the Police Service of Northern Ireland;
   (f)   the Police Service of Northern Ireland Reserve;
   (g)   the Ministry of Defence Police;
   (h)   the Royal Navy Regulating Branch;
   (i)   the Royal Military Police;
   (j)   the Royal Air Force Police;
   (k)   the Royal Marines Police;
   (l)   the British Transport Police;

⁵⁹ Words in square brackets substituted by the Criminal Justice and Police Act 2001, s.81(1).
⁶⁰ The Serious Organised Crime and Police Bill 2004–05, cl.108(5)(b) inserts here "and (IZA)".
⁶¹ The Serious Organised Crime and Police Bill 2004–05, Sch.4, para.46 replaces paras (b) and (c) with "(b) the Serious Organised Crime Agency;".

    (m) the States of Jersey Police Force;

    (n) the salaried police force of the Island of Guernsey;

    (o) the Isle of Man Constabulary.

(1C) Where—

    (a) fingerprints or samples have been taken from any person in connection with the investigation of an offence but otherwise than in circumstances to which subsection (1) above applies, and

    (b) that person has given his consent in writing to the use in a speculative search of the fingerprints or of the samples and of information derived from them,

the fingerprints or, as the case may be, those samples and that information may be checked against any of the fingerprints, samples or information mentioned in paragraph (a) or (b) of that subsection.

(1D) A consent given for the purposes of subsection (1C) above shall not be capable of being withdrawn.][62]

(2) Where a sample of hair other than pubic hair is to be taken the sample may be taken either by cutting hairs or by plucking hairs with their roots so long as no more are plucked than the person taking the sample reasonably considers to be necessary for a sufficient sample.

(3) Where any power to take a sample is exercisable in relation to a person the sample may be taken in a prison or other institution to which the Prison Act 1952 applies.

[(3A) Where—

    (a) the power to take a non-intimate sample under section 63(3B) above is exercisable in relation to any person who is detained under Part III of the Mental Health Act 1983 in pursuance of—

        (i) a hospital order or interim hospital order made following his conviction for the recordable offence in question, or

       (ii) a transfer direction given at a time when he was detained in pursuance of any sentence or order imposed following that conviction, or

    (b) the power to take a non-intimate sample under section 63(3C) above is exercisable in relation to any person,

the sample may be taken in the hospital in which he is detained under that Part of that Act. Expressions used in this subsection and in the Mental Health Act 1983 have the same meaning as in that Act.

(3B) Where the power to take a non-intimate sample under section 63(3B) above is exercisable in relation to a person detained in pursuance of directions of the Secretary of State under [section 92 of the Powers of Criminal Courts (Sentencing) Act 2000] the sample may be taken at the place where he is so detained.][63]

(4) Any constable may, within the allowed period, require a person who is neither in police detention nor held in custody by the police on the authority of a court to attend a police station in order to have a sample taken where—

---

[62] subs.(1A) was first inserted by the Criminal Procedure and Investigations Act 1996, s.64. The Criminal Justice and Police Act 2001, s.81(2) substituted (1A), (1B), (1C) and (1D).

[63] subss.(3A) and (3B) were inserted by the Criminal Evidence (Amendment) Act 1997, s.3. The words in square brackets in (3B) were substituted by the Powers of Criminal Courts (Sentencing) Act 2000, s.165(1), Sch.9, para.97.

> (a) the person has been charged with a recordable offence or informed that he will be reported for such an offence and either he has not had a sample taken from him in the course of the investigation of the offence by the police or he has had a sample so taken from him but either it was not suitable for the same means of analysis or, though so suitable, the sample proved insufficient; or
>
> (b) the person has been convicted of a recordable offence and either he has not had a sample taken from him since the conviction or he has had a sample taken from him (before or after his conviction) but either it was not suitable for the same means of analysis or, though so suitable, the sample proved insufficient.

(5) The period allowed for requiring a person to attend a police station for the purpose specified in subsection (4) above is—

> (a) in the case of a person falling within paragraph (a), one month beginning with the date of the charge [or of his being informed as mentioned in that paragraph][64] or one month beginning with the date on which the appropriate officer is informed of the fact that the sample is not suitable for the same means of analysis or has proved insufficient, as the case may be;
>
> (b) in the case of a person falling within paragraph (b), one month beginning with the date of the conviction or one month beginning with the date on which the appropriate officer is informed of the fact that the sample is not suitable for the same means of analysis or has proved insufficient, as the case may be.

(6) A requirement under subsection (4) above—

> (a) shall give the person at least 7 days within which he must so attend; and
>
> (b) may direct him to attend at a specified time of day or between specified times of day.

(7) Any constable may arrest without a warrant a person who has failed to comply with a requirement under subsection (4) above.

(8) In this section "the appropriate officer" is—

> (a) in the case of a person falling within subsection (4)(a), the officer investigating the offence with which that person has been charged or as to which he was informed that he would be reported;
>
> (b) in the case of a person falling within subsection (4)(b), the officer in charge of the police station from which the investigation of the offence of which he was convicted was conducted.]

[Testing for presence of Class A drugs[65]

63B.—(1) A sample of urine or a non-intimate sample may be taken from a person in police detention for the purpose of ascertaining whether he has any specified Class A drug in his body if the following conditions are met.

(2) The first condition is—

> (a) that the person concerned has been charged with a trigger offence; or
>
> (b) that the person concerned has been charged with an offence and a police officer of at least the rank of inspector, who has reasonable

---

[64] Words in square brackets inserted by the Criminal Evidence (Amendment) Act 1997, s.4.

[65] s.63B was inserted by the Criminal Justice and Court Services Act 2000, s.57(1), (2).

grounds for suspecting that the misuse by that person of any specified Class A drug caused or contributed to the offence, has authorised the sample to be taken.

(3) The second condition is that the person concerned has attained the age of [14].[66]

(4) The third condition is that a police officer has requested the person concerned to give the sample.

(5) Before requesting the person concerned to give a sample, an officer must—

    (a)   warn him that if, when so requested, he fails without good cause to do so he may be liable to prosecution, and

    (b)   in a case within subsection (2)(b) above, inform him of the giving of the authorisation and of the grounds in question.

[(5A) In the case of a person who has not attained the age of 17—

    (a)   the making of the request under subsection (4) above;

    (b)   the giving of the warning and (where applicable) the information under subsection (5) above; and

    (c)   the taking of the sample,

may not take place except in the presence of an appropriate adult.][67]

(6) A sample may be taken under this section only by a person prescribed by regulations made by the Secretary of State by statutory instrument.

No regulations shall be made under this subsection unless a draft has been laid before, and approved by resolution of, each House of Parliament.

[(6A) The Secretary of State may by order made by statutory instrument amend subsection (3) above by substituting for the age for the time being specified a different age specified in the order.

(6B) A statutory instrument containing an order under subsection (6A) above shall not be made unless a draft of the instrument has been laid before, and approved by a resolution of, each House of Parliament.][68]

(7) Information obtained from a sample taken under this section may be disclosed—

    (a)   for the purpose of informing any decision about granting bail in criminal proceedings (within the meaning of the Bail Act 1976) to the person concerned;

    (b)   where the person concerned is in police detention or is remanded in or committed to custody by an order of a court or has been granted such bail, for the purpose of informing any decision about his supervision;

    (c)   where the person concerned is convicted of an offence, for the purpose of informing any decision about the appropriate sentence to be passed by a court and any decision about his supervision or release;

    (d)   for the purpose of ensuring that appropriate advice and treatment is made available to the person concerned.

(8) A person who fails without good cause to give any sample which may be taken from him under this section shall be guilty of an offence.]

[(9) In relation to a person who has not attained the age of 18, this section applies only where—

    (a)   the relevant chief officer has been notified by the Secretary of State that arrangements for the taking of samples under this section from

---

[66] Changed from 18 by the Criminal Justice Act 2003, s.5(3)(a).

[67] subs.(5A) was inserted by the Criminal Justice Act 2003, s.5(3)(b).

[68] subss.(6A), (6B) were inserted by the Criminal Justice Act 2003, s.5(3)(c).

persons who have not attained the age of 18 have been made for the police area as a whole, or for the particular police station, in which the person is in police detention; and

(b) the notice has not been withdrawn.

(10) In this section—

"appropriate adult", in relation to a person who has not attained the age of 17, means—

(a) his parent or guardian or, if he is in the care of a local authority or voluntary organisation, a person representing that authority or organisation; or

(b) a social worker of a local authority social services department; or

(c) if no person falling within paragraph (a) or (b) is available, any responsible person aged 18 or over who is not a police officer or a person employed by the police;

"relevant chief officer" means—

(a) in relation to a police area, the chief officer of police of the police force for that police area; or

(b) in relation to a police station, the chief officer of police of the police force for the police area in which the police station is situated.][69]

[Testing for presence of Class A drugs—supplementary[70]

63C.—(1) A person guilty of an offence under section 63B above shall be liable on summary conviction to imprisonment for a term not exceeding [51 weeks][71], or to a fine not exceeding level 4 on the standard scale, or to both.

(2) A police officer may give an authorisation under section 63B above orally or in writing but, if he gives it orally, he shall confirm it in writing as soon as is practicable.

(3) If a sample is taken under section 63B above by virtue of an authorisation, the authorisation and the grounds for the suspicion shall be recorded as soon as is practicable after the sample is taken.

(4) If the sample is taken from a person detained at a police station, the matters required to be recorded by subsection (3) above shall be recorded in his custody record.

(5) Subsections (11) and (12) of section 62 above apply for the purposes of section 63B above as they do for the purposes of that section; and section 63B above does not prejudice the generality of sections 62 and 63 above.

(6) In section 63B above—

"Class A drug" and "misuse" have the same meanings as in the Misuse of Drugs Act 1971;

"specified" (in relation to a Class A drug) and "trigger offence" have the same meanings as in Part III of the Criminal Justice and Court Services Act 2000.]

---

[69] subss.(9) and (10) were inserted by the Criminal Justice Act 2003, s.5(3)(d).
[70] s.63C was inserted by the Criminal Justice and Court Services Act 2000, s.57(1), (2).
[71] Substituted by the Criminal Justice Act 2003, Sch.26, para.35.

Destruction of fingerprints and samples

64.—[(1A) Where—

 (a) fingerprints[72] or samples are taken from a person in connection with the investigation of an offence, and

 (b) subsection (3) below does not require them to be destroyed,

the fingerprints or samples may be retained after they have fulfilled the purposes for which they were taken but shall not be used by any person except for purposes related to the prevention or detection of crime, the investigation of an offence or the conduct of a prosecution.

 (1B) In subsection (1A) above—

 (a) the reference to using a fingerprint includes a reference to allowing any check to be made against it under section 63A(1) or (1C) above and to disclosing it to any person;

 (b) the reference to using a sample includes a reference to allowing any check to be made under section 63A(1) or (1C) above against it or against information derived from it and to disclosing it or any such information to any person;

 (c) the reference to crime includes a reference to any conduct which—

  (i) constitutes one or more criminal offences (whether under the law of a part of the United Kingdom or of a country or territory outside the United Kingdom); or

  (ii) is, or corresponds to, any conduct which, if it all took place in any one part of the United Kingdom, would constitute one or more criminal offences; and

 (d) the references to an investigation and to a prosecution include references, respectively, to any investigation outside the United Kingdom of any crime or suspected crime and to a prosecution brought in respect of any crime in a country or territory outside the United Kingdom.][73]

[The Serious Organised Crime and Police Bill 2004–05, cl.108(7) inserts new subs.(IBA):

"(1BA) Fingerprints taken from a person by virtue of section 61(6A) above must be destroyed as soon as they have fulfilled the purpose for which they were taken."]

 (3) If—

 (a) fingerprints or samples are taken from a person in connection with the investigation of an offence; and

 (b) that person is not suspected of having committed the offence,

they must, [except as provided in [the following provisions of this section],][74] be destroyed as soon as they have fulfilled the purpose for which they were taken.

---

[72] The Serious Organised Crime and Police Bill 2004–05, cl.109(4) adds "and impressions of footwear" wherever the word "fingerprint" or "fingerprints" appears in this section: *i.e.* in subss.(1A), (1B), (3), (3AA), (3AB), (3AC), (3AD), (5), (6) and (6A).

[73] subss.(1A) and (1B) replaced subss.(1) and (2) by Criminal Justice and Police Act 2001, s.82(2). For the equivalent changes in regard to Northern Ireland see the Criminal Justice and Police Act 2001, s.83(1) and (2) substituting new subss.(1A) and (1B) in place of Art.64(1) and (2) of the Police and Criminal Evidence (Northern Ireland) Order 1989.

[74] Words in square brackets substituted by the Criminal Justice and Public Order Act 1994, s.57(2) and the Criminal Justice and Police Act 2001, s.82(3). For the equivalent change to the Northern Ireland Order see s.83(3) of the Criminal Justice and Police Act 2001.

[(3AA)—Samples and fingerprints
are not required to be destroyed under subsection (3) above if—

  (a)   they were taken for the purposes of the investigation of an offence of
        which a person has been convicted; and

  (b)   a sample or, as the case may be, fingerprint was also taken from the
        convicted person for the purposes of that investigation.

(3AB) Subject to subsection (3AC) below, where a person is entitled under
subsection (3)[75] above to the destruction of any fingerprint or sample taken from
him (or would be but for subsection (3AA) above), neither the fingerprint nor the
sample, nor any information derived from the sample, shall be used—

  (a)   in evidence against the person who is or would be entitled to the
        destruction of that fingerprint or sample; or

  (b)   for the purposes of the investigation of any offence;

and subsection (1B) above applies for the purposes of this subsection as it applies
for the purposes of subsection (1A) above.

(3AC) Where a person from whom a fingerprint or sample has been taken
consents in writing to its retention—

  (a)   that[76] sample need not be destroyed under subsection (3) above;

  (b)   subsection (3AB) above shall not restrict the use that may be made
        of the fingerprint or sample or, in the case of a sample, of any infor-
        mation derived from it; and

  (c)   that consent shall be treated as comprising a consent for the purposes
        of section 63A(1C) above;

and a consent given for the purpose of this subsection shall not be capable of
being withdrawn.[77]

(3AD) For the purposes of subsection (3AC) above it shall be immaterial
whether the consent is given at, before or after the time when the entitlement to
the destruction of the fingerprint or sample arises.][78]

(4) . . .[79]

[(5) If fingerprints are destroyed—

  (a)   any copies of the fingerprints shall also be destroyed; and

  (b)   any chief officer of police controlling access to computer data
        relating to the fingerprints shall make access to the data impossible,
        as soon as it is practicable to do so.][80]

(6) A person who asks to be allowed to witness the destruction of his fingerprints
or copies of them shall have a right to witness it.

[(6A) If—

  (a)   subsection (5)(b) above falls to be complied with; and

  (b)   the person to whose fingerprints the data relate asks for a certificate
        that it has been complied with,

such a certificate shall be issued to him, not later than the end of the period of
three months beginning with the day on which he asks for it, by the responsible

---

[75] The Serious Organised Crime and Police Bill 2004–05, cl.108(8) substitutes "subsection (1BA) or
(3)" for "subsection (3)".

[76] The Serious Organised Crime and Police Bill 2004–05, cl.108(9)(a) inserts here "fingerprint or"

[77] The Serious Organised Crime and Police Bill 2004–05, cl.108(9)(b) inserts here: "This subsection
does not apply to fingerprints taken from a person by virtue of section 61(6A) above."

[78] subss.(3AA) to (3AD) replaced (3A) and (3B) which had been inserted by the Criminal Justice and
Public Order Act 1994, s.57(3)—see Criminal Justice and Police Act 2001, s.82(4). For the equivalent change to the Northern Ireland Order see CJPA, s.83(4).

[79] subs.(4) repealed by the Criminal Justice and Police Act 2001, Sch.7, Pt 2(1).

[80] subs.(5) substituted by the Criminal Justice Act 1988, s.148.

chief officer of police or a person authorised by him or on his behalf for the purposes of this section.

(6B) In this section—[...]

"the responsible chief officer of police" means the chief officer of police in whose [police][81] area the computer data were put on to the computer.][82]

(7) Nothing in this section—

    (a)   affects any power conferred by paragraph 18(2) of Schedule 2 to the Immigration Act 1971 [or section 20 of the Immigration and Asylum Act 1999 (c. 33) (disclosure of police information to the Secretary of State for use for immigration purposes)][83]; or

    (b)   applies to a person arrested or detained under the terrorism provisions.

[NB Retrospective effect—The final subsection of section 82 of the Criminal Justice and Police Act 2000 states—

"(6) The fingerprints, samples and information the retention and use of which is now authorised in accordance with the above amended provisions of section 64 of PACE, include—

    (a)   fingerprints and samples the destruction of which should have taken place before the commencement of this section, but did not; and

    (b)   information deriving from any such samples or from samples the destruction of which did take place, in accordance with that section [s.64], before the commencement of this section."][84]

[Photographing of suspects etc.[85]

64A.—(1) A person who is detained at a police station may be photographed—

    (a)   with the appropriate consent; or

    (b)   if the appropriate consent is withheld or it is not practicable to obtain it, without it.

[*The Serious Organised Crime and Police Bill 2004–05, cl.107(2)inserts new subs.(1A) and (1B):*

"(1A) A person falling within subsection (1B) below may, on the occasion of the relevant event referred to in subsection (1B), be photographed elsewhere than at a police station—

    (a)   *with the appropriate consent; or*

    (b)   *if the appropriate consent is withheld or it is not practicable to obtain it, without it.*

(1B) A person falls within this subsection if he has been—

    (a)   *arrested by a constable for an offence;*

    (b)   *taken into custody by a constable after being arrested for an offence by a person other than a constable;*

    (c)   *made subject to a requirement to wait with a community support officer under paragraph 2(3) or (3A) of Schedule 4 to the Police Reform Act 2002 ('the 2002 Act');*

---

[81] The Police Act 1996, s.103, Sch.7, para.37 repealed the definition of "chief officer" and inserted the word "police".

[82] subss.(6A) and (6B) inserted by the Criminal Justice Act 1988, s.148.

[83] Words in square brackets inserted by the Criminal Justice and Police Act 2001, s.82(5). For the equivalent change in Art.64(8)(a) of the Northern Ireland Order see Criminal Justice and Police Act 2001, s.83(5).

[84] For the equivalent change in Northern Ireland see Criminal Justice and Police Act 2001, s.83(6).

[85] s.64A was inserted by the Anti-Terrorism, Crime and Security Act 2001, s.92. For the Northern Ireland equivalent see Anti-Terrorism, Crime and Security Act 2001, s.93.

    (d)   *given a penalty notice by a constable in uniform under Chapter 1 of Part 1 of the Criminal Justice and Police Act 2001, a penalty notice by a constable under section 444A of the Education Act 1996, or a fixed penalty notice by a constable in uniform under section 54 of the Road Traffic Offenders Act 1988;*

    (e)   *given a notice in relation to a relevant fixed penalty offence (within the meaning of paragraph 1 of Schedule 4 to the 2002 Act) by a community support officer by virtue of a designation applying that paragraph to him; or*

    (f)   *given a notice in relation to a relevant fixed penalty offence (within the meaning of paragraph 1 of Schedule 5 to the 2002 Act) by an accredited person by virtue of accreditation specifying that that paragraph applies to him."*]

(2) A person proposing to take a photograph of any person under this section—

    (a)   may, for the purpose of doing so, require the removal of any item or substance worn on or over the whole or any part of the head or face of the person to be photographed; and

    (b)   if the requirement is not complied with, may remove the item or substance himself.

(3) Where a photograph may be taken under this section, the only persons entitled to take the photograph are [constables].[86]

(4) A photograph taken under this section—

    (a)   may be used by, or disclosed to, any person for any purpose related to the prevention or detection of crime, the investigation of an offence or the conduct of a prosecution; and

    (b)   after being so used or disclosed, may be retained but may not be used or disclosed except for a purpose so related.

(5) In subsection (4)—

    (a)   the reference to crime includes a reference to any conduct which —

       (i)   constitutes one or more criminal offences (whether under the law of a part of the United Kingdom or of a country or territory outside the United Kingdom); or

      (ii)   is, or corresponds to, any conduct which, if it all took place in any one part of the United Kingdom, would constitute one or more criminal offences;

      and

    (b)   the references to an investigation and to a prosecution include references, respectively, to any investigation outside the United Kingdom of any crime or suspected crime and to a prosecution brought in respect of any crime in a country or territory outside the United Kingdom.

(6) References in this section to taking a photograph include references to using any process by means of which a visual image may be produced; and references to photographing a person shall be construed accordingly.]

[*The Serious Organised Crime and Police Bill 2004–05, cl.107(3) inserts new subs.(6A):*

"(6A) In this section, a 'photograph' includes a moving image, and corresponding expressions shall be construed accordingly."]

[86] As amended by Police Reform Act 2002, Sch.7, para.9(5).

[(7) Nothing in this section applies to a person arrested under an extradition arrest power.][87]

Fingerprints and samples—supplementary

65.—(1) In this Part of this Act—

["analysis", in relation to a skin impression, includes comparison and matching][88];

"appropriate consent" means—

(a) in relation to a person who has attained the age of 17 years, the consent of that person;

(b) in relation to a person who has not attained that age but has attained the age of 14 years, the consent of that person and his parent or guardian; and

(c) in relation to a person who has not attained the age of 14 years, the consent of his parent or guardian;

["extradition arrest power" means any of the following—

(a) a Part 1 warrant (within the meaning given by the Extradition Act 2003) in respect of which a certificate under section 2 of that Act has been issued;

(b) section 5 of that Act;

(c) a warrant issued under section 71 of that Act;

[. . .][89]

(d) a provisional warrant (within the meaning given by that Act).][90]

["fingerprints", in relation to any person, means a record (in any form and produced by any method) of the skin pattern and other physical characteristics or features of—

(a) any of that person's fingers; or

(b) either of his palms][91];

["intimate sample" means

(a) a sample of blood, semen or any other tissue fluid, urine or pubic hair;

(b) a dental impression;

[*The Serious Organised Crime and Police Bill 2004–05, cl.110(2) substitutes new (c):*

(c) *"a swab taken from any part of a person's genitals (including pubic hair) or from a person's body orifice other than the mouth;"*]

(d) a swab taken from a person's body orifice other than the mouth;][92]

["intimate search" means a search which consists of the physical examination of a person's body orifices other than the mouth;][93]

["non-intimate sample" means—

(a) a sample of hair other than pubic hair;

---

[87] Inserted by the Extradition Act 2003, Pt 4, s.169(5).

[88] Inserted by the Criminal Justice and Police Act 2001, s.80(5)(a).

[89] Definition of "drug trafficking" and "drug trafficking offence" repealed by the Proceeds of Crime Act 2002, s.457, Sch.12.

[90] Inserted by the Extradition Act 2003, Pt 4, s.169(6).

[91] Definition of "fingerprints" substituted by the Criminal Justice and Police Act 2001, s.78(8).

[92] Inserted by the Criminal Justice and Public Order Act 1994, s.58(2) and (3). For the equivalent change in Northern Ireland see Police (Amendment) (Northern Ireland) Order 1995, Art.8(2).

[93] Inserted by the Criminal Justice and Public Order Act 1994, s.59(1). For the equivalent change in Northern Ireland see Police (Amendment) (Northern Ireland) Order 1995, Art.5(2).

(b)   a sample taken from a nail or from under a nail;

(c)   a swab taken from any part of a person's body including the mouth but not any other body orifice;

[*The Serious Organised Crime and Police Bill 2004–05, cl.110(3) substitutes new subs.(c):*

"(c)   a swab taken from any part of a person's body other than a part from which a swab taken would be an intimate sample;"]

(d)   saliva;

[(e)   a skin impression;][94][94a]

["registered dentist" has the same meaning as in the Dentists Act 1984][95];

["registered health care professional" means a person (other than a medical practitioner) who is—

(a)   a registered nurse; or

(b)   a registered member of a health care profession which is designated for the purposes of this paragraph by an order made by the Secretary of State;][96]

["skin impression", in relation to any person, means any record (other than a fingerprint) which is a record (in any form and produced by any method) of the skin pattern and other physical characteristics or features of the whole or any part of his foot or of any other part of his body;][97]

["speculative search", in relation to a person's fingerprints or samples, means such a check against other fingerprints or samples or against information derived from other samples as is referred to in section 63A(1) above;][98]

["sufficient" and "insufficient", in relation to a sample, means [(subject to subsection (2) below)][99] sufficient or insufficient (in point of quantity or quality) for the purpose of enabling information to be produced by the means of analysis used or to be used in relation to the sample.][1]

["the terrorism provisions" means section 41 of the Terrorism Act 2000, and any provision of Schedule 7 to that Act conferring a power of detention; and

"terrorism" has the meaning given in section 1 of that Act.][2]

[. . .][2a]

[(1A) A health care profession is any profession mentioned in section 60(2) of the Health Act 1999 other than the profession of practising medicine and the profession of nursing.

(1B) An order under subsection (1) shall be made by statutory instrument and shall be subject to annulment in pursuance of a resolution of either House of Parliament.][3]

[(2) References in this Part of this Act to a sample's proving insufficient include references to where, as a consequence of—

---

94   para.(e) substituted by the Criminal Justice and Police Act 2001, s.80(5)(b).

94a Definition of "non-intimate sample" substituted by Criminal Justice and Public Order Act 1994, s.58(3).

95   Inserted by the Criminal Justice and Public Order Act 1994, s.58(1), (4).

96   Inserted by the Police Reform Act 2002, s.54(2).

97   Inserted by the Criminal Justice and Police Act 2001, s.80(5)(c).

98   Inserted by the Criminal Justice and Public Order Act 1994, s.58(1), (4).

99   Words in square brackets inserted by the Criminal Justice and Police Act 2001, s.80(5)(d).

1   Inserted by the Criminal Justice and Public Order Act 1994, s.58(1), (4). For the equivalent change in Northern Ireland see Police (Amendment) (Northern Ireland) Order 1995, Art.8(4).

2   Substituted by the Terrorism Act 2000, Sch.15, para.5(10).

2a Words omitted were repealed by the Proceeds of Crime Act 2002, s.457 Sch.12.

3   subss.(1A) and (1B) were inserted by the Police Reform Act 2002, s.54(3).

    (a) the loss, destruction or contamination of the whole or any part of the sample,

    (b) any damage to the whole or a part of the sample, or

    (c) the use of the whole or a part of the sample for an analysis which produced no results or which produced results some or all of which must be regarded, in the circumstances, as unreliable,

the sample has become unavailable or insufficient for the purpose of enabling information, or information of a particular description, to be obtained by means of analysis of the sample.][4]

Part VI

Codes of Practice—General

Codes of practice

66.—(1) The Secretary of State shall issue codes of practice in connection with—

    (a) the exercise by police officers of statutory powers—

       (i) to search a person without first arresting him; or

      (ii) to search a vehicle without making an arrest;

       [*The Serious Organised Crime and Police Bill 2004–05, cl.101(3) adds: "(iii) to arrest a person."*]

    (b) the detention, treatment, questioning and identification of persons by police officers;

    (c) searches of premises by police officers; and

    (d) the seizure of property found by police officers on persons or premises.

  [(2) Codes shall (in particular) include provision in connection with the exercise by police officers of powers under section 63B above.][5]

Codes of practice—supplementary

67.—[(1) In this section, "code" means a code of practice under section 60, [60A][6] or 66.

  (2) The Secretary of State may at any time revise the whole or any part of a code.

  (3) A code may be made, or revised, so as to—

    (a) apply only in relation to one or more specified areas,

    (b) have effect only for a specified period,

    (c) apply only in relation to specified offences or descriptions of offender.

  (4) Before issuing a code, or any revision of a code, the Secretary of State must consult—

    (a) persons whom he considers to represent the interests of police authorities,

    (b) persons whom he considers to represent the interests of chief officers of police,

---

[4] subs.(2) inserted by the Criminal Justice and Police Act 2001, s.80(6).
[5] subs.(2) inserted by the Criminal Justice and Courts Services Act 2000, s.57(4).
[6] Inserted by the Criminal Justice and Police Act 2001, s.76(2).

    (c)   the General Council of the Bar,

    (d)   the Law Society of England and Wales,

    (e)   the Institute of Legal Executives, and

    (f)   such other persons as he thinks fit.

(5) A code, or a revision of a code, does not come into operation until the Secretary of State by order so provides.

(6) The power conferred by subsection (5) is exercisable by statutory instrument.

(7) An order bringing a code into operation may not be made unless a draft of the order has been laid before Parliament and approved by a resolution of each House.

(7A) An order bringing a revision of a code into operation must be laid before Parliament if the order has been made without a draft having been so laid and approved by a resolution of each House.

(7B) When an order or draft of an order is laid, the code or revision of a code to which it relates must also be laid.

(7C) No order or draft of an order may be laid until the consultation required by subsection (4) has taken place.

(7D) An order bringing a code, or a revision of a code, into operation may include transitional or saving provisions.][7]

(8) . . .[8]

(9) Persons other than police officers who are charged with the duty of investigating offences or charging offenders shall in the discharge of that duty have regard to any relevant provision of [such][9] a code.

[(9A) Persons on whom powers are conferred by—

    (a)   any designation under section 38 or 39 of the Police Reform Act 2002 (c.30) (police powers for police authority employees), or

    (b)   any accreditation under section 41 of that Act (accreditation under community safety accreditation schemes),

shall have regard to any relevant provisions of a code [of practice to which this section applies][10] in the exercise or performance of the powers and duties conferred or imposed on them by that designation or accreditation.][11]

(10) A failure on the part—

    (a)   of a police officer to comply with any provision of such a code;

    (b)   of any person other than a police officer who is charged with the duty of investigating offences or charging offenders to have regard to any relevant provision of such a code in the discharge of that duty, or

    [(c)   of a person designated under section 38 or 39 or accredited under section 41 of the Police Reform Act 2002 (c.30) to have regard to any relevant provision of such a code in the exercise or performance of the powers and duties conferred or imposed on him by that designation or accreditation,][12]

shall not of itself render him liable to any criminal or civil proceedings.

---

[7] subss.(1) to (7D), inserted by the Criminal Justice Act 2003, s.11, replace former subss.(1) to (7C)
[8] Repealed by the Police and Magistrates' Courts Act 1994, s.37 and Sch.9. See also Police Act 1996, s.103, Sch.9, Pt II.
[9] The Criminal Justice Act 2003, Sch.37, Pt 1 provides that the word "such" is omitted here and in subss.(9), (10(a), (b) and (c) and in both places where it occurs in subs.(11).
[10] Words in square brackets repealed by the Criminal Justice Act 2003, Sch.37, Pt 1.
[11] subs.(9A) was inserted by the Police Reform Act 2002, Sch.7, para.9(7).
[12] subs.(10)(c) was inserted by the Police Reform Act 2002, Sch.7, para.9(8).

(11) In all criminal and civil proceedings any such code shall be admissible in evidence, and if any provision of such a code appears to the court or tribunal conducting the proceedings to be relevant to any question arising in the procedings it shall be taken into account in determining that question.

(12) In this section "criminal proceedings" includes[13]—

    (a) proceedings in the United Kingdom or elsewhere before a court-martial constituted under the Army Act 1955, or the Air Force Act 1955 or the Naval Discipline Act 1957. . ..[14];

    (b) proceedings before the Courts-Martial Appeal Court; and

    (c) proceedings before a Standing Civilian Court.

PART VII

DOCUMENTARY EVIDENCE IN CRIMINAL PROCEEDINGS

[Evidence from documentary records

68.—s.68 was repealed by the Criminal Justice Act 1988, Sch.16 and was replaced by ss.23–28 of that Act. Part I of Sch.3 to the Police and Criminal Evidence Act, which accompanied the provisions of s.68, was replaced by Sch.2 to the Criminal Justice Act 1988. Previously they were included here but (as noted at para.7–01 above), they were repealed by the Criminal Justice Act 2003, Sch.37, Pt 6. The topic is no longer treated in this book and accordingly the new statutory provisions are not included here. (ed.)]

Evidence from computer records

69.—. . .[15]

Provisions supplementary to sections 68 and 69

70.—. . .[16]

Microfilm copies

71.—In any proceedings the contents of a document may (whether or not the document is still in existence) be proved by the production of an enlargement of a microfilm copy of that document or of the material part of it, authenticated in such manner as the court may approve.

[Where the proceedings concerned are proceedings before a magistrates' court inquiring into an offence as examining justices this section shall have effect with the omission of the words "authenticated in such manner as the court may approve.][17]

---

[13] The equivalent provision in the 1989 Northern Ireland PACE Order, Art.66(11) applies only to Northern Ireland proceedings. Para.(12) of the order stated that these Codes do not apply to terrorism cases

[14] Words at the end of this subsection (and their equivalent in the 1989 NI PACE Order, Art.66(11)(a)) were deleted by the Armed Forces Act 2001, Sch.7, Pt 1.

[15] Repealed by the Youth Justice and Criminal Evidence Act 1999, s.60 and Sch.6. The Northern Ireland equivalent Art.68 of the 1989 PACE Order was repealed by the Criminal Evidence (Northern Ireland) Order 1999.

[16] Repealed by the Youth Justice and Criminal Evidence Act 1999, s.67(3) and Sch.6.

[17] Words in square brackets which were inserted by the Criminal Procedure and Investigations Act 1996, s.47 and Sch.1 para.24 were removed by the Criminal Justice Act 2003, Sch.3, para.56(3)—not yet in force.

Part VII—supplementary

72.—(1) In this Part of this Act—

["copy", in relation to a document means anything onto which information recorded in the document has been copied, by whatever means and whether directly or indirectly, and

"statement" means any representation of fact, however made; and][18]

"proceedings" means criminal proceedings, including—

(a) proceedings in the United Kingdom or elsewhere before a court-martial constituted under the Army Act 1955, [the Air Force Act 1955 or the Naval Discipline Act 1957,]

(b) proceedings in the United Kingdom or elsewhere before the Courts-Martial Appeal Court—

(i) on an appeal from a court-martial so constituted . . .; or

(ii) on a reference under section 34 of the Courts-Martial (Appeals) Act 1968; and

(c) proceedings before a Standing Civilian Court.][19]

(2) Nothing in this Part of this Act shall prejudice any power of any court to exclude evidence (whether by preventing questions from being put or otherwise) at its discretion.

PART VIII

EVIDENCE IN CRIMINAL PROCEEDINGS—GENERAL

Convictions and acquittals

Proof of convictions and acquittals

73.—(1) Where in any proceedings the fact that a person has in the United Kingdom been convicted or acquitted of an offence otherwise than by a Service court is admissible in evidence, it may be proved by producing a certificate of conviction or, as the case may be, of acquittal relating to that offence, and proving that the person named in the certificate as having been convicted or acquitted of the offence is the person whose conviction or acquittal of the offence is to be proved.

(2) For the purposes of this section a certificate of conviction or of acquittal—

(a) shall, as regards a conviction or acquittal on indictment, consist of a certificate, signed by the [proper officer][20] of the court where the conviction or acquittal took place, giving the substance and effect (omitting the formal parts) of the indictment and of the conviction or acquittal; and

(b) shall, as regards a conviction or acquittal on a summary trial, consist of a copy of the conviction or of the dismissal of the information,

---

[18] Definition "copy" substituted for definitions "copy" and "statement" as originally enacted, by the Civil Evidence Act 1995, s.15(1), Sch.1, para.9(2).

[19] Words in square brackets in subs.(1) substituted with savings, and words omitted repealed with savings, by the Armed Forces Act 1996, ss.5, 35(2), and Sch.1, para.106, Sch.7, Pt I. For savings see SI 1997/304, Arts 3(1), (3), 4, Sch.2.

[20] Words in square brackets substituted by the Access to Justice Act 1999, Sch.13, para.128(2).

signed by the [proper officer] of the court where the conviction or acquittal took place or by the [proper officer] of the court, if any, to which a memorandum of the conviction or acquittal was sent;

and a document purporting to be a duly signed certificate of conviction or acquittal under this section shall be taken to be such a certificate unless the contrary is proved.

[(3) In subsection (2) above "proper officer" means—

    (a)   in relation to a magistrates' court in England and Wales, the justices' chief executive [designated officer][21] for the court; and

    (b)   in relation to any other court, the clerk of the court, his deputy or any other person having custody of the court record.][22]

(4) The method of proving a conviction or acquittal authorised by this section shall be in addition to and not to the exclusion of any other authorised manner of proving a conviction or acquittal.

Conviction as evidence of commission of offence

74.—(1) In any proceedings the fact that a person other than the accused has been convicted of an offence by or before any court in the United Kingdom or by a Service court outside the United Kingdom shall be admissible in evidence for the purpose of proving, [that that person committed that offence, where evidence of his having done so is admissible,][23] whether or not any other evidence of his having committed that offence is given.

(2) In any proceedings in which by virtue of this section a person other than the accused is proved to have been convicted of an offence by or before any court in the United Kingdom or by a Service court outside the United Kingdom, he shall be taken to have committed that offence unless the contrary is proved.

(3) In any proceedings where evidence is admissible of the fact that the accused has committed an offence, [. . .],[24] if the accused is proved to have been convicted of the offence—

    (a)   by or before any court in the United Kingdom; or

    (b)   by a Service court outside the United Kingdom,

he shall be taken to have committed that offence unless the contrary is proved.

(4) Nothing in this section shall prejudice—

    (a)   the admissibility in evidence of any conviction which would be admissible apart from this section; or

    (b)   the operation of any enactment whereby a conviction or a finding of fact in any proceedings is for the purposes of any other proceedings made conclusive evidence of any fact.

Provisions supplementary to section 74

75.—(1) Where evidence that a person has been convicted of an offence is admissible by virtue of section 74 above, then without prejudice to the reception of any other admissible evidence for the purpose of identifying the facts on which the conviction was based—

---

[21] Words in square brackets substituted for "justices' chief executive" by the Courts Act 2003, Sch.8, para.285—not yet in force.

[22] The text of subs.(3) was substituted by the Access to Justice Act 1999, Sch.13, para.128(3).

[23] Substituted by Criminal Justice Act 2003, Sch.36, para.85(2).

[24] Words in square brackets removed by the Criminal Justice Act 2003, Sch.36, para.85(3).

    (a)   the contents of any document which is admissible as evidence of the conviction; and

    (b)   the contents of the information, complaint, indictment or charge-sheet on which the person in question was convicted,

shall be admissible in evidence for that purpose.

(2) Where in any proceedings the contents of any document are admissible in evidence by virtue of subsection (1) above, a copy of that document, or of the material part of it, purporting to be certified or otherwise authenticated by or on behalf of the court or authority having custody of that document shall be admissible in evidence and shall be taken to be a true copy of that document or part unless the contrary is shown.

(3) Nothing in any of the following—

    (a)   [section 14 of the Powers of Criminal Courts (sentencing) Act 1995][25] under which a conviction leading to probation or discharge is to be disregarded except as mentioned in that section);

    (b)   [section 247 of the Criminal Procedure (Scotland) Act 1995][26] (which makes similar provision in respect of convictions on indictment in Scotland); and

    (c)   section 8 of the Probation Act (Northern Ireland) 1950 (which corresponds to section 13 of the Powers of Criminal Courts Act 1973) or any legislation which is in force in Northern Ireland for the time being and corresponds to that section,

shall affect the operation of section 74 above; and for the purposes of that section any order made by a court of summary jurisdiction in Scotland under [section 228 or section 246(3) of the said Act of 1995][27] shall be treated as a conviction.

(4) Nothing in section 74 above shall be construed as rendering admissible in any proceedings evidence of any conviction other than a subsisting one.

Confessions

Confessions

76.—(1) In any proceedings a confession made by an accused person may be given in evidence against him in so far as it is relevant to any matter in issue in the proceedings and is not excluded by the court in pursuance of this section.

(2) If, in any proceedings where the prosecution proposes to give in evidence a confession made by an accused person, it is represented to the court that the confession was or may have been obtained—

    (a)   by oppression of the person who made it; or

    (b)   in consequence of anything said or done which was likely, in the circumstances existing at the time, to render unreliable any confession which might be made by him in consequence thereof,

the court shall not allow the confession to be given in evidence against him except in so far as the prosecution proves to the court beyond reasonable doubt that the confession (notwithstanding that it may be true) was not obtained as aforesaid.

[25] Words in square brackets substituted by the Powers of Criminal Courts (Sentencing) Act 2000, s.165(1), Sch.9, para.98.

[26] Words in square brackets substituted by the Criminal Procedure (Consequential Provisions) (Scotland) Act 1995, s.5, Sch.4, para.55(a).

[27] Words in square brackets substituted by the Criminal Procedure (Consequential Provisions) (Scotland) Act 1995, s.5, Sch.4, para.55(b).

(3) In any proceedings where the prosecution proposes to give in evidence a confession made by an accused person, the court may of its own motion require the prosecution, as a condition of allowing it to do so, to prove that the confession was not obtained as mentioned in subsection (2) above.

(4) The fact that a confession is wholly or partly excluded in pursuance of this section shall not affect the admissibility in evidence—

    (a) of any facts discovered as a result of the confession; or

    (b) where the confession is relevant as showing that the accused speaks, writes or expresses himself in a particular way, of so much of the confession as is necessary to show that he does so.

(5) Evidence that a fact to which this subsection applies was discovered as a result of a statement made by an accused person shall not be admissible unless evidence of how it was discovered is given by him or on his behalf.

(6) Subsection (5) above applies—

    (a) to any fact discovered as a result of a confession which is wholly excluded in pursuance of this section; and

    (b) to any fact discovered as a result of a confession which is partly so excluded, if that fact is discovered as a result of the excluded part of the confession.

(7) Nothing in Part VII of this Act shall prejudice the admissibility of a confession made by an accused person.

(8) In this section "oppression" includes torture, inhuman or degrading treatment, and the use or threat of violence (whether or not amounting to torture).

[(9) Where the proceedings mentioned in subsection (1) above are proceedings before a magistrates' court inquiring into an offence as examining justices this section shall have effect with the omission of

    (a) in subsection (1) the words "and is not excluded by the court in pursuance of this section", and

    (b) subsections (2) to (6) and (8).][28]

[Confessions may be given in evidence for co-accused[29]

76A.—(1) In any proceedings a confession made by an accused person may be given in evidence for another person charged in the same proceedings (a co-accused) in so far as it is relevant to any matter in issue in the proceedings and is not excluded by the court in pursuance of this section.

(2) If, in any proceedings where a co-accused proposes to give in evidence a confession made by an accused person, it is represented to the court that the confession was or may have been obtained—

    (a) by oppression of the person who made it; or

    (b) in consequence of anything said or done which was likely, in the circumstances existing at the time, to render unreliable any confession which might be made by him in consequence thereof,

the court shall not allow the confession to be given in evidence for the co-accused except in so far as it is proved to the court on the balance of probabilities that the confession (notwithstanding that it may be true) was not so obtained.

---

[28] subs.(9) was inserted by the Criminal Procedure and Investigations Act 1996, s.47, Sch.1, para.25. The subsection was repealed by the Criminal Justice Act 2003, Sch.3, para.56(4)—not yet in force.
[29] s.76A—not yet in force—was inserted by the Criminal Justice Act 2003, s.128(1).

(3) Before allowing a confession made by an accused person to be given in evidence for a co-accused in any proceedings, the court may of its own motion require the fact that the confession was not obtained as mentioned in subsection (2) above to be proved in the proceedings on the balance of probabilities.

(4) The fact that a confession is wholly or partly excluded in pursuance of this section shall not affect the admissibility in evidence—

    (a)   of any facts discovered as a result of the confession; or

    (b)   where the confession is relevant as showing that the accused speaks, writes or expresses himself in a particular way, of so much of the confession as is necessary to show that he does so.

(5) Evidence that a fact to which this subsection applies was discovered as a result of a statement made by an accused person shall not be admissible unless evidence of how it was discovered is given by him or on his behalf.

(6) Subsection (5) above applies—

    (a)   to any fact discovered as a result of a confession which is wholly excluded in pursuance of this section; and

    (b)   to any fact discovered as a result of a confession which is partly so excluded, if the fact is discovered as a result of the excluded part of the confession.

(7) In this section "oppression" includes torture, inhuman or degrading treatment, and the use or threat of violence (whether or not amounting to torture).]

Confessions by mentally handicapped persons[30]

77.—(1) Without prejudice to the general duty of the court at a trial on indictment [with a jury][31] to direct the jury on any matter on which it appears to the court appropriate to do so, where at such a trial—

    (a)   the case against the accused depends wholly or substantially on a confession by him; and

    (b)   the court is satisfied—

        (i)   that he is mentally handicapped; and

        (ii) that the confession was not made in the presence of an independent person,

the court shall warn the jury that there is special need for caution before convicting the accused in reliance on the confession, and shall explain that the need arises because of the circumstances mentioned in paragraphs (a) and (b) above.

(2) In any case where at the summary trial of a person for an offence it appears to the court that a warning under subsection (1) above would be required if the trial were on indictment [with a jury][32], the court shall treat the case as one in which there is a special need for caution before convicting the accused on his confession.

[(2A) In any case where at the trial on indictment without a jury of a person for an offence it appears to the court that a warning under subsection (1) above would be required if the trial were with a jury, the court shall treat the case as one in which there is a special need for caution before convicting the accused on his confession.][33]

---

[30] s.77 does not apply to appeals under the Naval Discipline Act 1957, s.52FK—see SI 2000/2370, Sch.3, Pt III, para.18(d).

[31] Inserted by the Criminal Justice Act 2003, Sch.36, para.48(2) and (3).

[32] Inserted by the Criminal Justice Act 2003, Sch.36, para.48(2) and (3).

[33] subs.(2A) was inserted by the Criminal Justice Act 2003, Sch.36, para.48(4).

(3) In this section—

"independent person" does not include a police officer or a person employed for, or engaged on police purposes;

"mentally handicapped", in relation to a person, means that he is in a state of arrested or incomplete development of mind which includes significant impairment of intelligence and social functioning; and

"police purposes" has the meaning assigned to it by [section 101(2) of the Police Act 1996].[34]

Miscellaneous

Exclusion of unfair evidence

78.—(1) In any proceedings the court may refuse to allow evidence on which the prosecution proposes to rely to be given if it appears to the court that, having regard to all the circumstances, including the circumstances in which the evidence was obtained, the admission of the evidence would have such an adverse effect on the fairness of the proceedings that the court ought not to admit it.

(2) Nothing in this section shall prejudice any rule of law requiring a court to exclude evidence.[35]

[(3) This section shall not apply in the case of proceedings before a magistrates' court inquiring into an offence as examining justices.][36]

Time for taking accused's evidence

79.—If at the trial of any person for an offence—

(a)   the defence intends to call two or more witnesses to the facts of the case; and

(b)   those witnesses include the accused,

the accused shall be called before the other witness or witnesses unless the court in its discretion otherwise directs.

Competence and compellability of accused's spouse

80.—(1) . . .[37]

[(2) In any proceedings the wife or husband of a person charged in the proceedings shall, subject to subsection (4) below, be compellable to give evidence on behalf of that person.

(2A) In any proceedings the wife or husband of a person charged in the proceedings shall, subject to subsection (4) below, be compellable—

(a) to give evidence on behalf of any other person charged in the proceedings but only in respect of any specified offence with which that other person is charged; or

---

[34] Words in square brackets substituted by the Police Act 1996, s.103, Sch.7, para.38.

[35] The 1989 Northern Ireland PACE Order, Art.76(2)(b) stated that this provision also excluded statements to which s.8(1) of the Northern Ireland (Emergency Provisions) Act 1978 applies. The 1978 Act was repealed by the 1991 Act of the same name. See now s.11 of the 1991 Act.

[36] subs.(3) inserted, in relation to alleged offences into which no criminal procedure has begun before April 1, 1997, by the Criminal Procedure and Investigations Act 1996, s.47, Sch.1, para.26. The subsection was removed by the Criminal Justice Act 2003, Sch.3, para.56(5)—not yet in force.

[37] Repealed by the Youth Justice and Criminal Evidence Act 1996, Sch.4, para.13(2), Sch.6.

  (b) to give evidence for the prosecution but only in respect of any spec-
       ified offence with which any person is charged in the proceedings.

(3) In relation to the wife or husband of a person charged in any proceedings,
an offence is a specified offence for the purposes of subsection (2A) above if—

  (a) it involves an assault on, or injury or a threat of injury to, the wife or
       husband or a person who was at the material time under the age of 16;

  (b) it is a sexual offence alleged to have been committed in respect of a
       person who was at the material time under that age; or

  (c) it consists of attempting or conspiring to commit, or of aiding, abet-
       ting, counselling, procuring or inciting the commission of, an
       offence falling within paragraph (a) or (b) above.

(4) No person who is charged in any proceedings shall be compellable by
virtue of subsection (2) or (2A) above to give evidence in the proceedings.

(4A) References in this section to a person charged in any proceedings do not
include a person who is not, or is no longer, liable to be convicted of any
offence in the proceedings (whether as a result of pleading guilty or for any
other reason).][38]

(5) In any proceedings a person who has been but is no longer married to the
accused shall be . . .[39] compellable to give evidence as if that person and the
accused had never been married.

(6) Where in any proceedings the age of any person at any time is material for
the purposes of subsection (3) above, his age at the material time shall for the purposes of that provision be deemed to be or to have been that which appears to the
court to be or to have been his age at that time.

(7) In subsection (3)(b) above "sexual offence" means an offence under
[. . . . .] the Protection of Children Act 1978 [or Part I of the Sexual Offences
Act 2003.][40]

(8) . . .[41]

(9) Section 1(d) of the Criminal Evidence Act 1898 (communications between
husband and wife) and section 43(1) of the Matrimonial Causes Act 1965 (evidence as to marital intercourse) shall cease to have effect.

[Rule where accused's spouse not compellable[42]

80A.—The failure of the wife or husband of a person charged in any proceedings
to give evidence in the proceedings shall not be made the subject of any comment
by the prosecution.]

Advance notice of expert evidence in Crown Court[43]

81.—(1) [Criminal Procedure Rules][44] may make provision for—

---

[38] subss.(2) to (4A) were substituted by the Youth Justice and Criminal Evidence Act 1999, Sch.4,
para.13(3).
[39] The words "competent and" were repealed by the Youth Justice and Criminal Evidence Act 1999,
Sch.4, para.13(4), Sch.6.
[40] The words in the first square bracket were repealed and the words in the second square bracket
were inserted respectively by the Sexual Offences Act 2003, Sch.7, para.1 and Sch.6, para.28.
[41] Repealed by the Youth Justice and Criminal Evidence Act 1996, Sch.4, para.13(4), Sch.6.
[42] s.80A inserted by Youth Justice and Criminal Evidence Act 1999 Sch.4, para.14.
[43] s.81 does not apply to appeals under the Naval Discipline Act 1957, s.52FK—see SI 2000/2370,
Sch.3, Pt III, para.18(g).
[44] Words in square brackets in subss.(1) and (2) were substituted for "Crown Court Rules" by the
Courts Act 2003, Sch.8, para.286.

(a) requiring any party to proceedings before the Court to disclose to the other party or parties any expert evidence which he proposes to adduce in the proceedings; and

(b) prohibiting a party who fails to comply in respect of any evidence with any requirement imposed by virtue of paragraph (a) above from adducing that evidence without the leave of the court.

(2) [Criminal Procedure Rules] made by virtue of this section may specify the kinds of expert evidence to which they apply and may exempt facts or matters of any description specified in the rules.

Part VIII—Supplementary

Interpretation of Part VIII

82.—(1) In this Part of this Act—

"confession" includes any statement wholly or partly adverse to the person who made it, whether made to a person in authority or not and whether made in words or otherwise;

"court-martial" means a court-martial constituted under the Army Act 1955, the Air Force Act 1955 or the Naval Discipline Act 1957 . . .[45];

"proceedings" means criminal proceedings, including—

(a) proceedings in the United Kingdom or elsewhere before a court-martial [constituted under the Army Act 1955, the Air Force Act 1955 or the Naval Discipline Act 1955][46];

(b) proceedings in the United Kingdom or elsewhere before the Courts-Martial Appeal Court—

(i) on an appeal from a court-martial [so constituted][47]; or

(ii) on a reference under section 34 of the Courts-Martial (Appeals) Act 1968; and

(c) proceedings before a Standing Civilian Court; and

"Service court" means a court-martial or a Standing Civilian Court.

(2) In this Part of this Act references to conviction before a Service court are [references to a finding of guilty which is, or falls to be treated as, the finding of the court; and][48] "convicted" shall be construed accordingly.[49]

(3) Nothing in this Part of this Act shall prejudice any power of a court to exclude evidence (whether by preventing questions from being put or otherwise) at its discretion.

---

[45] Words deleted by the Armed Forces Act 2001, Sch.7, Pt 1.

[46] Words in square brackets repealed by the Youth Justice and Criminal Evidence Act 1996, Sch.6—not yet in force. For previous amendment of para.(a) see Armed Forces Act 1996, s.5, Sch.1, para.107(a).

[47] Words first repealed by the Armed Forces Act 1996, ss.5, 35(2), Sch.1, para.107(b), Sch.7, Pt I and then by the Youth Justice and Criminal Evidence Act 1996, Sch.6—not yet in force.

[48] Words in square brackets substituted with savings by the Armed Forces Act 1996, s.35(1), Sch.6, para.14. For savings see SI 1997/304, Arts 3(1), (3), 4, Sch.2.

[49] The words "and 'convicted' shall be construed accordingly" do not appear in the 1989 Northern Ireland PACE Order, Art.70(2)(b). They are not necessary in light of s.35 of the Interpretation Act (Northern Ireland) 1954.

PART IX

POLICE COMPLAINTS AND DISCIPLNE[50]

[*As has been seen (para.9–01 above), Pt IX (ss. 83–105) and its accompanying Sch.4, were repealed and largely re-enacted by Pt IV of the Police Act 1996 which in turn has been replaced by Pt 2 of the Police Reform Act 2002 establishing a new Independent Police Complaints Commission. (ed.)*].

PART X

POLICE—GENERAL

Arrangements for obtaining the views of the community on policing

106.— . . .[51]

Police officers performing duties of higher rank

107.—(1) For the purpose of any provision of this Act or any other Act under which a power in respect of the investigation of offences or the treatment of persons in police custody is exercisable only by or with the authority of a police officer of at least the rank of superintendent, an officer of the rank of chief inspector shall be treated as holding the rank of superintendent if—

[(a) he has been authorised by an officer holding a rank above the rank of superintendent to exercise the power or, as the case may be, to give his authority for its exercise, or

(b) he is acting during the absence of an officer holding the rank of superintendent who has authorised him, for the duration of that absence, to exercise the power or, as the case may be, to give his authority for its exercise.][52]

(2) For the purpose of any provision of this Act or any other Act under which such a power is exercisable only by or with the authority of an officer of at least the rank of inspector, an officer of the rank of sergeant shall be treated as holding the rank of inspector if he has been authorised by an officer of at least the rank of [superintendent] to exercise the power or, as the case may be, to give his authority for its exercise.

Deputy chief constables

108.—[(1)] . . .[53]

---

[50] Police Act 1996, s.103, Sch.9, Pt II, brought into force in England and Wales as from April 1, 1999—see SI 1999/533, Art.2(a).

[51] Repealed by the Police Act 1996, Sch.9, Pt I and re-enacted as s.96 of that Act.

[52] Words in square brackets in subss.(1) and (2) substituted by the Police and Magistrates' Court Act 1994, s.44, Sch.5, Pt II, para.35.

[53] PACE, s.108(1) stated, "The office of deputy chief constable is hereby abolished". These words were confirmed by the Police Act 1996, s.13(2) which stated that police ranks "shall not include that of deputy chief constable". However they were reversed by the Criminal Justice and Police Act 2001, s.123(1) which inserted into the Police Act 1996, s.11A, subs.(1) which stated "Every police force maintained under section 2 shall have a deputy chief constable".

(2) . . .[54]

(3) . . .[55]

(4) In section 5 of the Police (Scotland) Act 1967—

    (a)   in subsection (1), after the word "a" there shall be inserted the words "person holding the rank of";

    (b)   subsection (3) shall be omitted; and

    (c)   in subsection (5), for the words from the beginning to "of", in the second place where it occurs, there shall be substituted the words "Appointments or promotions to the rank of deputy chief constable or."

(5) The following section shall be inserted after that section—

    "Deputy chief constables—supplementary

       5A.—(1) Any police force may include more than one person holding the rank of deputy chief constable, but only if the additional person or persons holding that rank—

        (a)   was a deputy chief constable before a period—

           (i)   of central service; or

           (ii)   of overseas service, as defined in section 3 of the Police (Overseas Service) Act 1945; or

           (iii)   of service in pursuance of an appointment under section 10 of the Overseas Development and Co-operation Act 1980 as an officer to whom that section applied; or

        (b)   became a deputy chief constable by virtue of section 23(2) of this Act.

       (2) If there is more than one person in a police force who holds the rank of deputy chief constable, one of the persons who hold it shall be designated as the officer having the powers and duties conferred on a deputy chief constable by section 5(1) of this Act.

       (3) A person shall be designated under subsection (2) of this section by the police authority after consultation with the chief constable and subject to the approval of the Secretary of State."

(6) In . . . section 23(2) of the Police (Scotland) Act 1967 (under . . . which a chief constable affected by an amalgamation holds the rank of assistant chief constable) for the word "assistant" there shall be substituted the word "deputy".[56]

Amendments relating to Police Federations

109.— . . .[57]

Functions of special constables in Scotland

110.—Subsection (6) of section 17 of the Police (Scotland) Act 1967 (restriction on functions of special constables) is hereby repealed.

---

[54] Repealed by the Police and Magistrates' Court Act 1994, Sch.9, Pt I.

[55] Repealed by the Police and Magistrates' Court Act 1994, Sch.9, Pt I.

[56] Words omitted from subs.(6) were repealed by Police and Magistrates' Courts Act 1994, Sch.9, Pt I.

[57] Repealed by the Police Act 1996, Sch.9, Pt I.

Regulations for Police Forces and Police Cadets—Scotland

111.—(1) In section 26 of the Police (Scotland) Act 1967 (regulations as to government and administration of police forces)—
- (a) after subsection (1) there shall be inserted the following subsection—
  "(1A) Regulations under this section may authorise the Secretary of State, the police authority or the chief constable to make provision for any purpose specified in the regulations." ; and
- (b) at the end there shall be inserted the following subsection—
  "(10) Any statutory instrument made under this section shall be subject to annulment in pursuance of a resolution of either House of Parliament."

(2) In section 27 of the said Act of 1967 (regulations for police cadets) in subsection (3) for the word "(9)" there shall be substituted the words "(1A), (9) and (10)."

Metropolitan police officers

112.— . . .[58]

PART XI

MISCELLANEOUS AND SUPPLEMENTARY

Application of Act to Armed Forces

113.—(1) The Secretary of State may by order direct that any provision of [Part 5 of this Act (or Part 11 of this Act so far as relating to that Part][59] which relates to the investigation of offences conducted by police officers or to persons detained by the police shall apply, subject to such modifications as he may specify, to investigations of offences conducted under the Army Act 1955, the Air Force Act 1955 or the Naval Discipline Act 1957 or to persons under arrest under any of those Acts.

(2) Section 67(9) above shall not have effect in relation to investigations of an offence under the Army Act 1955, the Air Force Act 1955 or the Naval Discipline Act 1957.

(3) The Secretary of State shall issue a code of practice or a number of such codes, for persons other than police officers who are concerned [with (a) the exercise of the powers conferred by Part 2 of the Armed Forces Act 2001, or (b) enquiries into offences under the Army Act 1955, the Air Force Act 1955 or the Naval Discipline Act 1957.][60]

[(3A) In subsections (4) to (10), "code" means a code of practice under subsection (3).][61]

(4) Without prejudice to the generality of subsection (3) above, a code [. . .][62] may contain provisions, in connection with [the powers mentioned in subsection

---

[58] Repealed by the Police Act 1996, Sch.9, Pt I.
[59] Words in square brackets substituted by the Armed Forces Act 2001, s.13(1), (2).
[60] Words in square brackets inserted by the Armed Forces Act 2001, s.13(3).
[61] Inserted by the Criminal Justice Act 2003, s.11(3).
[62] Words "issued under that subsection" deleted by Criminal Justice Act 2003, Sch.37, Pt I.

(3)(a) above or the enquiries mentioned in subsection (3)(b) above],[63] as to the following matters—

    (a)   the tape-recording of interviews;

    (b)   searches of persons and premises; and

    (c)   the seizure of things found on searches.

[(5) The Secretary of State may at any time revise the whole or any part of the code.

(6) A code may be made, or revised, so as to –

    (a)   apply only in relation to one or more specified areas,

    (b)   have effect only for a specified period,

    (c)   apply only in relation to specified offences or descriptions of offender.

(7) The Secretary of State must lay a code, or any revision of a code, before Parliament.][64]

(8) A failure on the part of any person to comply with any provision of a code [. . .][65] shall not of itself render him liable to any criminal or civil proceedings except those to which this subsection applies.

(9) Subsection (8) applies—

    (a)   to proceedings under any provision of the Army Act 1955 or the Air Force Act 1955 other than section 70; and

    (b)   to proceedings under any provision of the Naval Discipline Act 1957 other than section 42.

(10) In all criminal and civil proceedings any [. . ..][66] code shall be admissible in evidence, and if any provision of [. . .] a code appears to the court or tribunal conducting the proceedings to be relevant to any question arising in the proceedings it shall be taken into account in determining that question.

(11) In subsection (10) above "criminal proceedings" includes—

    (a)   proceedings in the United Kingdom or elsewhere before a court-martial constituted under the Army Act 1955, the Air Force Act 1955 or the Naval Discipline Act 1957 . . . [67];

    (b)   proceedings before the Courts-Martial Appeal Court; and

    (c)   proceedings before a Standing Civilian Court.

(12) Parts VII and VIII of this Act have effect for the purposes of proceedings—

    (a)   before a court-martial constituted under the Army Act 1955 or the Air Force Act 1955

    (b)   before the Courts-Martial Appeal Court; and

    (c)   before a Standing Civilian Court,

subject to any modifications which the Secretary of State may by order specify.

(13) An order under this section shall be made by statutory instrument and shall be subject to annulment in pursuance of a resolution of either House of Parliament.

Application of Act to Customs and Excise

114.—(1) "Arrested", "arresting", "arrest" and "to arrest" shall respectively be substituted for "detained", "detaining", "detention" and "to detain" wherever in

---

[63] Words in square brackets substituted by the Armed Forces Act 2001, s.13(4).

[64] subss.(5)–(7) substituted by the Criminal Justice Act 2003, s.11(4).

[65] Words deleted by Criminal Justice Act 2003, Sch.37, Pt I.

[66] Word "such" in both places where it occurs deleted by Criminal Justice Act 2003, Sch.37, Pt I.

[67] Words deleted by the Armed Forces Act 2001, Sch.7, Pt I.

the customs and excise Acts, as defined in section 1(1) of the Customs and Excise Management Act 1979, those words are used in relation to persons.

(2) The Treasury may by order direct—

    (a)   that any provision of this Act which relates to the investigation of offences by police officers or to persons detained by the police shall apply, subject to such modifications as the order may specify, to investigations by officers of Customs and Excise of offences which relate to assigned matters, as defined in section 1 of the Customs and Excise Management Act 1979, or to persons detained by such officers; and

    (b)   that, in relation to investigations of offences conducted by officers of Customs and Excise,

        (i)   this Act shall have effect as if the following section were inserted after section 14—

           "Exception for customs and excise

           14A. Material in the possession of a person who acquired or created it in the course of any trade, business, profession or other occupation or for the purpose of any paid or unpaid office and which relates to an assigned matter, as defined in section 1 of the Customs and Excise Management Act 1979, is neither excluded material nor special procedure material for the purposes of any enactment such as is mentioned in section 9(2) above."; and

        (ii)   section 55 above shall have effect as if it related only to things such as are mentioned in subsection (1)(a) of that section.

    and

    [(c)   that in relation to customs detention (as defined in any order made under this subsection) the Bail Act 1976 shall have effect as if references in it to a constable were references to an officer of Customs and Excise of such grade as may be specified in the order.][68]

(3) Nothing in any order under subsection (2) above shall be taken to limit any powers exercisable under section 164 of the Customs and Excise Management Act 1979.

(4) In this section "officers of Customs and Excise" means officers commissioned by the Commissioners of Customs and Excise under section 6(3) of the Customs and Excise Management Act 1979.

(5) An order under this section shall be made by statutory instrument and shall be subject to annulment in pursuance of a resolution of either House of Parliament.

[Power to apply Act to officers of the Secretary of State etc.[69]

114A.—(1) The Secretary of State may by order direct that—

    (a)   the provisions of Schedule 1 to this Act so far as they relate to special procedure material, and

    (b)   the other provisions of this Act so far as they relate to the provisions falling within paragraph (a) above,

shall apply, with such modifications as may be specified in the order, for the purposes of investigations falling within subsection (2) as they apply for the purposes of investigations of offences conducted by police officers.

---

[68] subs.(2)(c) was inserted by the Criminal Justice Act 1988, s.150.
[69] s.114A was inserted by the Criminal Justice and Police Act 2001, s.85.

(2) An investigation falls within this subsection if—

    (a) it is conducted by an officer of the department of the Secretary of State for Trade and Industry or by another person acting on that Secretary of State's behalf;

    (b) it is conducted by that officer or other person in the discharge of a duty to investigate offences; and

    (c) the investigation relates to a serious arrestable offence or to anything which there are reasonable grounds for suspecting has involved the commission of a serious arrestable offence.[70]

(3) The investigations for the purposes of which provisions of this Act may be applied with modifications by an order under this section include investigations of offences committed, or suspected of having been committed, before the coming into force of the order or of this section.

(4) An order under this section shall be made by statutory instrument and shall be subject to annulment in pursuance of a resolution of either House of Parliament.]

Expenses

115.—Any expenses of a Minister of the Crown incurred in consequence of the provisions of this Act, including any increase attributable to those provisions in sums payable under any other Act, shall be defrayed out of money provided by Parliament.

Meaning of "serious arrestable offence"

[*The Serious Organised Crime and Police Bill 2004–05, Sch.7, Pt 3, para.8(12) repeals s.116.*]

116.—(1) This section has effect for determining whether an offence is a serious arrestable offence for the purposes of this Act.

(2) The following arrestable offences are always serious—

    (a) an offence (whether at common law or under any enactment) specified in Part I of Schedule 5 to this Act; and

    (aa) . . .[71]

    (b) an offence under an enactment specified in Part II of that Schedule;

    [(c) any offence which is specified in paragraph 1 of Schedule 2 to the Proceeds of Crime Act 2002 (drug trafficking offences),

    (d) any offence under section 327, 328 or 329 of that Act (certain money laundering offences).][72]

(3) Subject to subsection (4) . . .[73] below, any other arrestable offence is serious only if its commission—

    (a) has led to any of the consequences specifed in subsection (6) below; or

    (b) is intended or is likely to lead to any of those consequences.

---

[70] The Serious Organised Crime and Police Bill 2004–05, Sch.7, Pt 3, para.8(11) changes "a serious arrestable offence" to "an indictable offence".

[71] Inserted by the Drug Trafficking Offences Act 1986, s.36; repealed by the Drug Trafficking Act 1994, s.67(i), Sch.3.

[72] Inserted by the Drug Trafficking Act 1994, Sch.1, para.9. Replaced by the Proceeds of Crime Act 2002, Sch.11, para.14(4). (The equivalent Northern Ireland provision was in Sch.11, para.19(4).)

[73] The words "and (5)" were repealed by the Terrorism Act 2000, Sch.15, para.5(11)(a).

(4) An arrestable offence which consists of making a threat is serious if carrying out the threat would be likely to lead to any of the consequences specified in subsection (6) below.

(5) . . .[74]

(6) The consequences mentioned in subsections (3) and (4) above are—

    (a)   serious harm to the security of the State or to public order;

    (b)   serious interference with the administration of justice or with the investigation of offences or of a particular offence;

    (c)   the death of any person;

    (d)   serious injury to any person;

    (e)   substantial financial gain to any person; and

    (f)   serious financial loss to any person.

(7) Loss is serious for the purposes of this section if, having regard to all the circumstances, it is serious for the person who suffers it.

(8) In this section "injury" includes any disease and any impairment of a person's physical or mental condition.

Power of constable to use reasonable force[75]

117. Where any provision of this Act

    (a)   confers a power on a constable; and

    (b)   does not provide that the power may only be exercised with the consent of some person, other than a police officer,

the officer may use reasonable force, if necessary, in the exercise of the power.

General interpretation

118.—(1) In this Act—

    "arrestable offence" has the meaning assigned to it by section 24 above[76];

    [. . ..][77];

    "designated police station" has the meaning assigned to it by section 35 above;

    "document" [means anything in which information of any description is recorded][78];

    ["intimate search" . . .;][79]

    "item subject to legal privilege" has the meaning assigned to it by section 10 above;

    "parent or guardian" means—

        (a)   in the case of a child or young person in the care of a local authority, that authority [. . .;

        (b)   . . .][80];

---

[74] Repealed by the Terrorism Act 2000, Sch.15, para.5(11)(b).

[75] Modified in relation to investigation of offences conducted by a Service policeman under the Army Act 1955, the Air Force Act 1955 or the Naval Discipline Act 1957 by the Police and Criminal Evidence Act 1984 (Application to the Armed Forces) Order 1997, SI 1997/15, Art.2 and Sch.

[76] The Serious Organised Crime and Police Bill 2004–05, Sch.7, Pt 1, para.2(2) removes the definition of "arrestable offence".

[77] The definition of "British Transport Police Force" was inserted by the Anti-Terrorism, Crime and Security Act 2001, Sch.7, para.14. It was repealed by the Railways and Transport Safety Act 2003, Sch.5, para.4(2)(c).

[78] Words in square brackets substituted by the Civil Evidence Act 1995, s.15(1), Sch.1, para.9(3).

[79] Repealed by the Criminal Justice and Public Order Act 1994, Sch.11.

[80] Words omitted repealed by the Children Act 1989, s.108(7), Sch.15.

"premises" has the meaning assigned to it by section 23 above;

"recordable offence" means any offence to which regulations under section 27 above apply;

"vessel" includes any ship, boat, raft or other apparatus constructed or adapted for floating on water.

(2) [Subject to subsection (2A)][81] a person is in police detention for the purposes of this Act if—

[(a) he has been taken to a police station after being arrested for an offence or after being arrested under section 41 of the Terrorism Act 2000][82]; or

(b) he is arrested at a police station after attending voluntarily at the station or accompanying a constable to it; and—

(a) is detained there; or

(b) is detained elsewhere in the charge of a constable,

except that a person who is at a court after being charged is not in police detention for those purposes.

[(2A) Where a person is in another's lawful custody by virtue of paragraph 22, 34(1) or 35(3) of Schedule 4 to the Police Reform Act 2002, he shall be treated as in police detention.][83]

Amendments and repeals

119.—(1) The enactments mentioned in Schedule 6 to this Act shall have effect with the amendments there specified.

(2) The enactments mentioned in Schedule 7 to this Act (which include enactments already obsolete or unnecessary) are repealed to the extent specified in the third column of that Schedule.

(3) The repeals in Parts II and IV of Schedule 7 to this Act have effect only in relation to criminal proceedings.

Extent

120.—(1) Subject to the following provisions of this section, this Act extends to England and Wales only.

(2) The following extend to Scotland only—

section 108(4) and (5);

section 110;

section 111;

section 112(1);

and section 119(2), so far as it relates to the provisions of the Pedlars Act 1871 repealed by Part VI of Schedule 7.

(3) The following extend to Northern Ireland only—

section 6(4); and

section 112(2).

(4) The following extend to England and Wales and Scotland—

section 6(1) and (2);

section 7;

section 83(2), so far as it relates to paragraph 8 of Schedule 4;

---

[81] Inserted by Police Reform Act 2002, Sch.7, para.9(9).
[82] New definition in the Terrorism Act 2000, Sch.15, para.5(12).
[83] subs.(2A) was inserted by Police Reform Act 2002, Sch.7, para.9(9).

section 108(1) and (6);

section 109; and

section 119(2), so far as it relates to section 19 of the Pedlars Act 1871.

(5) The following extend to England and Wales, Scotland and Northern Ireland—

section 6(3); section 9(2A)[84];

section 83(2), so far as it relates to paragraph 7(1) of Schedule 4; and

section 114(1).

(6) So far as they relate to proceedings before courts-martial and Standing Civilian Courts, the relevant provisions extend to any place at which such proceedings may be held.

(7) So far as they relate to proceedings before the Courts-Martial Appeal Court, the relevant provisions extend to any place at which such proceedings may be held.

(8) In this section "the relevant provisions" means—

(a)   subsection (11) of section 67 above;

(b)   subsection (12) of that section so far as it relates to subsection (11);

(c)   Parts VII and VIII of this Act except paragraph 10 of Schedule 3;

(d)   subsections (2), (8) to (12) of section 113 above; and

(e)   subsection (13) of that section, so far as it relates to an order under subsection (12).

(9) Except as provided by the foregoing provisions of this section, section 113 above extends to any place to which the Army Act 1955, the Air Force Act 1955 or the Naval Discipline Act 1957 extends.

(9A) Section 119(1), so far as it relates to any provision amended by Part II of Schedule 6, extends to any place to which that provision extends.[85]

(10) Section 119(2), so far as it relates—

(a)   to any provision contained in—

the Army Act 1955;

the Air Force Act 1955;

the Armed Forces Act 1981; or

the Value Added Tax Act 1983,

(b)   to any provision mentioned in Part VI of Schedule 7, other than section 18 of the Pedlars Act 1871,

extends to any place to which that provision extends.

(11) So far as any of the following—

section 115;

in section 118;

the definition of "document";

this section;

section 121;

and section 122,

has effect in relation to any other provision of this Act, it extends to any place to which that provision extends.

Commencement

121.—(1) This Act, except section 120 above, this section and section 122 below, shall come into operation on such day as the Secretary of State may by order

---

[84]   Inserted by the Criminal Justice and Police Act 2001, s.86(2).

[85]   subs.(9A) renumbered as such by the Criminal Justice Act 1988, s.170(1), Sch.15, para.101.

made by statutory instrument appoint, and different days may be so appointed for different provisions and for different purposes.

(2) Different days may be appointed under this section for the coming into force of section 60 above in different areas.

(3) When an order under this section provides by virtue of subsection (2) above that section 60 above shall come into force in an area specified in the order, the duty imposed on the Secretary of State by that section shall be construed as a duty to make an order under it in relation to interviews in that area.

(4) An order under this section may make such transitional provision as appears to the Secretary of State to be necessary or expedient in connection with the provisions thereby brought into operation.

Short title

122.—This Act may be cited as the Police and Criminal Evidence Act 1984.

SCHEDULES

Section 9 **Schedule 1**

SPECIAL PROCEDURE

Making of orders by circuit [judge][1]

1. If on an application made by a constable a circuit judge [judge] is satisfied that one or other of the sets of access conditions is fulfilled, he may make an order under paragraph 4 below.

2. The first set of access conditions is fulfilled if—
   (a) there are reasonable grounds for believing—
      (i) that a serious arrestable offence[2] has been committed;
      (ii) that there is material which consists of special procedure material or also includes special procedure material and does not also include excluded material on premises specified in the application[2a];
      (iii) that the material is likely to be of substantial value (whether by itself or together with other material) to the investigation in connection with which the application is made; and
      (iv) that the material is likely to be relevant evidence;
   (b) other methods of obtaining the material—
      (i) have been tried without success; or
      (ii) have not been tried because it appeared that they were bound to fail; and
   (c) it is in the public interest, having regard—
      (i) to the benefit likely to accrue to the investigation if the material is obtained; and
      (ii) to the circumstances under which the person in possession of the material holds it,
   that the material should be produced or that access to it should be given.

3. The second set of access conditions is fulfilled if—
   (a) there are reasonable grounds for believing that there is material which consists of or includes excluded material or special procedure material on premises specified in the application[3];
   (b) but for section 9(2) above a search of the premises for that material could have been authorised by the issue of a warrant to a constable under an enactment other than this Schedule; and
   (c) the issue of such a warrant would have been appropriate.

4. An order under this paragraph is an order that the person who appears to the circuit judge [judge] to be in possession of the material to which the application relates shall—

[1] The Courts Act 2003, Sch.4, para.6(1)—not yet in force—replaces references to a "circuit judge" in paras 1, 4, 12 and 15 with "judge".
[2] The Serious Organised Crime and Police Bill 2004–05, Sch.7, Pt 3, para.8(13) changes "a serious arrestable offence" to "an indictable offence".
[2a] The Serious Organised Crime and Police Bill 2004–05, cl.104(11) adds: "or on premises occupied or controlled by a person specified in the application (including all such premises on which there are reasonable grounds for believing that there is such material as it is reasonably practicable so to specify)."
[3] *ibid.*

    (a)   produce it to a constable for him to take it away; or

    (b)   give a constable access to it,

not later than the end of the period of seven days from the date of the order or the end of such longer period as the order may specify.

5. Where the material consists of information [stored in any electronic form][4]—

    (a)   an order under paragraph 4(a) above shall have effect as an order to produce the material in a form in which it can be taken away and in which it is visible and legible [or from which it can readily be produced in a visible and legible form],[5] and

    (b)   an order under paragraph 4(b) above shall have effect as an order to give a constable access to the material in a form in which it is visible and legible.

6. For the purposes of sections 21 and 22 above material produced in pursuance of an order under paragraph 4(a) above shall be treated as if it were material seized by a constable.

Notices of applications for orders

7. An application for an order under paragraph 4 above shall be made inter partes.

8. Notice of an application for such an order may be served on a person either by delivering it to him or by leaving it at his proper address or by sending it by post to him in a registered letter or by the recorded delivery service.

9. Such a notice may be served—

    (a)   on a body corporate, by serving it on the body's secretary or clerk or other similar officer; and

    (b)   on a partnership, by serving it on one of the partners.

10. For the purposes of this Schedule, and of section 7 of the Interpretation Act 1978 in its application to this Schedule, the proper address of a person, in the case of secretary or clerk or other similar officer of a body corporate, shall be that of the registered or principal office of that body, in the case of a partner of a firm shall be that of the principal office of the firm, and in any other case shall be the last known address of the person to be served.

11. Where notice of an application for an order under paragraph 4 above has been served on a person, he shall not conceal, destroy, alter or dispose of the material to which the application relates except—

    (a)   with the leave of a judge; or

    (b)   with the written permission of a constable,

until—

       (i)   the application is dismissed or abandoned; or

      (ii)   he has complied with an order under paragraph 4 above made on the application.

---

[4] These words replaced "contained in a computer"—see Criminal Justice and Police Act 2001, Sch.2, Pt 2, para.14(a).

[5] Words in square brackets were inserted by the Criminal Justice and Police Act 2001, Sch.2, para.14(b).

Issue of warrants by a judge

12. If on an application made by a constable a circuit judge [judge]—
    (a)   is satisfied—
        (i) that either set of access conditions is fulfilled; and
        (ii) that any of the further conditions set out in paragraph 14 below is also fulfilled[6]; or
    (b)   is satisfied—
        (i) that the second set of access conditions is fulfilled; and
        (ii) that an order under paragraph 4 above relating to the material has not been complied with,

he may issue a warrant authorising a constable to enter and search the premises[7].

[*The Serious Organised Crime and Police Bill 2004–05, cl.104(14) inserts new para.12A:*

"*12A. The judge may not issue an all premises warrant unless he is satisfied—*
    (a)   *that there are reasonable grounds for believing that it is necessary to search premises occupied or controlled by the person in question which are not specified in the application, as well as those which are, in order to find the material in question; and*
    (b)   *that it is not reasonably practicable to specify all the premises which he occupies or controls which might need to be searched.*"]

13. A constable may seize and retain anything for which a search has been authorised under paragraph 12 above.

14. The further conditions mentioned in paragraph 12(a)(ii) above are—
    (a)   that it is not practicable to communicate with any person entitled to grant entry to the premises to which the application relates[8];
    (b)   that it is practicable to communicate with a person entitled to grant entry to the premises but it is not practicable to communicate with any person entitled to grant access to the material;
    (c)   that the material contains information which—
        (i) is subject to a restriction or obligation such as is mentioned in section 11(2)(b) above; and
        (ii) is likely to be disclosed in breach of it if a warrant is not issued;
    (d)   that service of a notice of an application for an order under paragraph 4 above may seriously prejudice the investigation.

15.—(1) If a person fails to comply with an order under paragraph 4 above, a circuit judge [judge] may deal with him as if he had committed a contempt of the Crown Court.

(2) Any enactment relating to contempt of the Crown Court shall have effect in relation to such a failure as if it were such a contempt.

---

[6] The Serious Organised Crime and Police Bill 2004–05, cl.104(13(a) inserts here: "in relation to each set of premises specified in the application".

[7] The Serious Organised Crime and Police Bill 2004–05, cl.104(13(b) inserts here: "or (as the case may be) all premises occupied or controlled by the person referred to in paragraph 2(a)(ii) or 3(a), including such sets of premises as are specified in the application (an 'all premises warrant')".

[8] The Serious Organised Crime and Police Bill 2004–05, cl.104(15) removes the words "to which the application relates".

Costs

16. The costs of any application under this Schedule and of anything done or to be done in pursuance of an order made under it shall be in the discretion of the judge.

[17. In this Schedule "judge" means a Circuit judge or a District Judge (Magistrates' Courts).][9]

Schedule 1A[10]

SPECIFIC OFFENCES WHICH ARE ARRESTABLE OFFENCES

Customs and Excise Acts

1. An offence for which a person may be arrested under the customs and excise Acts (within the meaning of the Customs and Excise Management Act 1979 (c.2)).

Official Secrets Act 1920

2. An offence under the Official Secrets Act 1920 (c.75) which is not an arrestable offence by virtue of the term of imprisonment for which a person may be sentenced in respect of them.

[Criminal Justice Act 1925

2ZA. An offence under s.36 of the Criminal Justice Act 1925 (untrue statement for procuring a passport)][11]

[Wireless Telegraphy Act 1949

2A. An offence mentioned in section 14(1) of the Wireless Telegraphy Act 1949 (offences under that Act which are triable either way).Prevention of Crime Act 1953][12]

Prevention of Crime Act 1953

3. An offence under section 1(1) of the Prevention of Crime Act 1953 (c.14) (prohibition of carrying offensive weapons without lawful authority or excuse).
4. . . .[13]

Obscene Publications Act 1959

5. An offence under section 2 of the Obscene Publications Act 1959 (c.66) (publication of obscene matter).

---

[9] para.17 was inserted by the Courts Act 2003, Sch.4, para.6(2). The Serious Organised Crime and Police Bill 2004–05, cl.105(9) replaces "Circuit judge"here by "a judge of the High Court, a Circuit judge, a Recorder".
[10] Sch.1A was inserted by Police Reform Act 2002, s.48(5) and Sch.6. The Serious Organised Crime and Police Bill 2004–05, Sch.7, Pt 1, para.2(3) repeals the whole schedule.
[11] Inserted by Criminal Justice Act 2003, s.3(2).
[12] Inserted by the Communication Act 2003, Pt 2, s.181(1).
[13] Repealed by the Sexual Offences Act 2003, Sch.7, para.1.

[Firearms Act 1968

5A. An offence under section 19 of the Firearms Act 1968 (carrying firearm or imitation firearm in public place) in respect of an air weapon or imitation firearm.][14]

Theft Act 1968

6. An offence under—
   (a) section 12(1) of the Theft Act 1968 (c.60) (taking motor vehicle or other conveyance without authority etc.); or
   (b) section 25(1) of that Act (going equipped for stealing etc.).

[Misuse of Drugs Act 1971

6A. An offence under section 5(2) of the Misuse of Drugs Act 1971 (having possession of a controlled drug) in respect of cannabis or cannabis resin (within the meaning of that Act).][15]

Theft Act 1978

7. An offence under section 3 of the Theft Act 1978 (c.31) (making off without payment).

Protection of Children Act 1978

8. An offence under section 1 of the Protection of Children Act 1978 (c.37) (indecent photographs and pseudo-photographs of children).

Wildlife and Countryside Act 1981

9. An offence under section 1(1) or (2) or 6 of the Wildlife and Countryside Act 1981 (c.69) (taking, possessing, selling etc. of wild birds) in respect of a bird included in Schedule 1 to that Act or any part of, or anything derived from, such a bird.
   10. An offence under—
   (a) section 1(5) of the Wildlife and Countryside Act 1981 (disturbance of wild birds);
   (b) section 9 or 13(1)(a) or (2) of that Act (taking, possessing, selling etc. of wild animals or plants); or
   (c) section 14 of that Act (introduction of new species etc.).

Civil Aviation Act 1982

11. An offence under section 39(1) of the Civil Aviation Act 1982 (c.16) (trespass on aerodrome).
   [11A. An offence of contravening a provision of an Order in Council under section 60 of that Act (air navigation order) where the offence relates to–
   (a) a provision which prohibits specified behaviour by a person in an aircraft towards or in relation to a member of the crew, or

---

[14] Inserted by the Anti-social Behaviour Act, Pt 5, s.37(3).
[15] Inserted by Criminal Justice Act 2003, s.3(3).

(b)   a provision which prohibits a person from being drunk in an aircraft, in so far as it applies to passengers.][16]

Aviation Security Act 1982

12. An offence under section 21C(1) or 21D(1) of the Aviation Security Act 1982 (c.36) (unauthorised presence in a restricted zone or on an aircraft).

Sexual Offences Act 1985

13. An offence under section 1 of the Sexual Offences Act 1985 (c.44) (kerb-crawling).

Public Order Act 1986

14. An offence under section 19 of the Public Order Act 1986 (c.64) (publishing etc. material likely to stir up racial or religious hatred).

[*Domestic Violence, Crime and Victims Act 2004*

14A. An offence under section 10(1) of the Domestic Violence, Crime and Victims Act 2004 (c.28) (common assault).][17]

Criminal Justice Act 1988

15. An offence under—
(a)   section 139(1) of the Criminal Justice Act 1988 (c.33) (offence of having article with a blade or point in public place); or
(b)   section 139A(1) or (2) of that Act (offence of having article with a blade or point or offensive weapon on school premises).

Road Traffic Act 1988

16. An offence under section 103(1)(b) of the Road Traffic Act 1988 (c.52) (driving while disqualified).

17. An offence under subsection (4) of section 170 of the Road Traffic Act 1988 (failure to stop and report an accident) in respect of an accident to which that section applies by virtue of subsection (1)(a) of that section (accidents causing personal injury).

[17A. An offence under section 174 of the Road Traffic Act 1988 (false statements and withholding material information).][18]

Official Secrets Act 1989

18. An offence under any provision of the Official Secrets Act 1989 (c.6) other than subsection (1), (4) or (5) of section 8 of that Act.

---

[16]   Inserted by the Aviation (Offences) Act 2003, s.1(1).
[17]   Inserted by the Domestic Violence, Crime and Victims Act, 2004, s.10(1).
[18]   Inserted by Criminal Justice Act 2003, s.3(4).

Football Spectators Act 1989

19. An offence under section 14J or 21C of the Football Spectators Act 1989 (c.37) (failing to comply with requirements imposed by or under a banning order or a notice under section 21B).

Football (Offences) Act 1991

20. An offence under any provision of the Football (Offences) Act 1991 (c.19).

Criminal Justice and Public Order Act 1994

21. An offence under—
  (a) section 60AA(7) of the Criminal Justice and Public Order Act 1994 (c.33) (failing to comply with requirement to remove disguise);
  (b) section 166 of that Act (sale of tickets by unauthorised persons); or
  (c) section 167 of that Act (touting for car hire services).

Police Act 1996

22. An offence under section 89(1) of the Police Act 1996 (c.16) (assaulting a police officer in the execution of his duty or a person assisting such an officer).

Protection from Harassment Act 1997

23. An offence under section 2 of the Protection from Harassment Act 1997 (c.40) (harassment).

Crime and Disorder Act 1998

24. An offence falling within section 32(1)(a) of the Crime and Disorder Act 1998 (c.37) (racially or religiously aggravated harassment).

Criminal Justice and Police Act 2001

25. An offence under—
  (a) section 12(4) of the Criminal Justice and Police Act 2001 (c.16) (failure to comply with requirements imposed by constable in relation to consumption of alcohol in public place); or
  (b) section 46 of that Act (placing of advertisements in relation to prostitution).

[Licensing Act 2003

26. An offence under section 143(1) of the Licensing Act 2003 (failure to leave licensed premises, etc.)][19]

---

[19] Inserted by the Licensing Act 2003, Sch.6, para.93.

[Sexual Offences Act 2003

27. An offence under—

(a)   section 66 of the Sexual Offences Act 2003 (exposure);

(b)   section 67 of that Act (voyeurism);

(c)   section 69 of that Act (intercourse with an animal);

(d)   section 70 of that Act (sexual penetration of a corpse); or

(e)   section 71 of that Act (sexual activity in public lavatory).][20]

Section 26   **Schedule 2**

PRESERVED POWERS OF ARREST[21]

1892 c.43.	Section 17(2) of the Military Lands Act 1892.
1911 c.27.	Section 12(1) of the Protection of Animals Act 1911.
1920 c.55.	Section 2 of the Emergency Powers Act 1920.
1936 c.6.	Section 7(3) of the Public Order Act 1936.
1952 c.52.	Section 49 of the Prison Act 1952.
1952 c.67.	Section 13 of the Visiting Forces Act 1952.
1955 c.18.	Sections 186 and 190B of the Army Act 1955.
1955 c.19.	Sections 186 and 190B of the Air Force Act 1955.
1957 c.53.	Sections 104 and 105 of the Naval Discipline Act 1957.
1959 c.37.	Section 1(3) of the Street Offences Act 1959.
1969 c.54.	Section 32 of the Children and Young Persons Act 1969.[22]
1971 c.77.	Section 24(2) of the Immigration Act 1971 and paragraphs 17, 24 and 33 of Schedule 2 and paragraph 7 of Schedule 3 to that Act.
. . .[23]	
1976 c.63.	Section 7 of the Bail Act 1976.
1977 c.45.	Sections 6(6), 7(11), 8(4), 9(7) and 10(5) of the Criminal Law Act 1977.
. . .[24]	
. . .[25]	
1981 c.22.	Sections 60(5) and 61(1) of the Animal Health Act 1981.
1983 c.2.	Rule 36 in Schedule 1 to the Representation of the People Act 1983.[26]
1983 c.20.	Sections 18, 35(10), 36(8), 38(7), 136(1) and 138 of the Mental Health Act 1983.
. . .[27]	
1984 c.47.	Section 5(5) of the Repatriation of Prisoners Act 1984.

[20] Inserted by the Sexual Offences Act 2003, Sch.6, para.28(3)—as amended by a corrections slip.
[21] Note a number of additional preserved powers of arrest in Sch.2 to the Northern Ireland PACE Order.
[22] As amended by the Children Act 1989, s.108(5) to (7), Sch.13, para.55.
[23] The entry relating to the Road Traffic Act 1972 was repealed by the Road Traffic (Consequential Provisions) Act 1988, Sch.1.
[24] The previous entry relating to the Child Care Act 1980 s.16 was repealed by the Children Act 1989, Sch.15.
[25] The entry relating to the Reserve Forces Act 1980 was repealed by the Reserve Forces Act 1996, s.131(2), Sch.11.
[26] Inserted by Representation of the People Act 1985, s.25.
[27] The entry relating to the Prevention of Terrorism (Temporary Provisions) Act 1984 was repealed by the Prevention of Terrorism (Temporary Provisions) Act 1989, Sch.9.

Section 68 **Schedule 3**

PROVISIONS SUPPLEMENTARY TO SECTIONS 68 AND 69

PART I

PROVISIONS SUPPLEMENTARY TO SECTION 68

[*Part I and para.13 of Sch.3 were repealed by the Criminal Justice Act 1988, Sch.16. They were replaced by Sch.2 to that Act which accompanied ss.23 to 28 of the 1988 Act. But as was noted above, hearsay evidence is now treated by Ch.2 of Pt 11 of the Criminal Justice Act 2003. Schedule 2 to the 1988 Act was repealed by Sch.37, Pt 6 of the 2003 Act.*]

PART II

PROVISIONS SUPPLEMENTARY TO SECTION 69 . . .[28]

Section 83 **Schedule 4**[29]

Section 116 **Schedule 5**

SERIOUS ARRESTABLE OFFENCES

[*The Serious Organised Crime and Police Bill 2004–05, Sch.7, Pt 3, para.8(14) repeals Sch.5.*]

PART I

OFFENCES MENTIONED IN SECTION 116(2)(A)

1.   Treason.
2.   Murder.
3.   Manslaughter.
4.   . . .[30]
5.   Kidnapping.
6.   . . .[31]
7.   . . .[32]
8.   . . .[33]

[9.   An offence under section 170 of the Customs and Excise Management Act 1979 (c.2) of being knowingly concerned, in relation to any goods, in any fraudulent evasion or attempt at evasion of a prohibition in force with respect to the goods under section 42 of the Customs Consolidation Act 1876 (c.36) (prohibition on importing indecent or obscene articles).][34]

---

[28] What remained of Sch.3 was repealed by the Youth Justice and Criminal Evidence Act 1999, s.67(3), and Sch.6 which, as has been seen, also repealed s.69.
[29] Repealed by the Police Act 1996, s.103, Sch.9, Pt II.
[30] Repealed by the Sexual Offences Act 2003, Sch.7, para.1.
[31] Repealed by the Sexual Offences Act 2003, Sch.7, para.1.
[32] Originally substituted by the Criminal Justice and Public Order Act 1994, s.168(2), Sch.10, para.59. Repealed by the Sexual Offences Act 2003, Sch.7, para.1.
[33] Repealed by the Sexual Offences Act 2003, Sch.7, para.1.
[34] Inserted by the Criminal Justice and Police Act 2001, s.72.

PART II

OFFENCES MENTIONED IN SECTION 116(2)(B)

Explosive Substances Act 1883 (c.3)

1. Section 2 (causing explosion likely to endanger life or property).
2. . . .[35]

Firearms Act 1968 (c.27)

3. Section 16 (possession of firearm with intent to injure).
4. Section 17(1) (use of firearms and imitation firearms to resist arrest).
5. Section 18 (carrying firearms with criminal intent).

Road Traffic Act 1972 (c.20)

6. . . .[36]

Taking of Hostages Act 1982 (c.28)

7. Section 1 (hostage-taking).

Aviation Security Act 1982 (c.36)

8. Section 1 (hijacking).

[Criminal Justice Act 1988 (c.33)

9. Section 134 (torture).][37]

[Road Traffic Act 1988 (c.52)

10. Section 1 (causing death by [dangerous][38] driving).][39]
[Section 3A (causing death by careless driving when under the influence of drink or drugs).][40]

[Aviation and Maritime Security Act 1990 (c.31)

11. Section 1 (endangering safety at aerodromes).
12. Section 9 (hijacking of ships).
13. Section 10 (seizing or exercising control of fixed platforms).][41]

---

[35] Repealed by the Sexual Offences Act 2003, Sch.7, para.1.
[36] Repealed by the Road Traffic (Consequential Provisions) Act 1988, s.3(1), Sch.1, Pt I.
[37] para.9 inserted by the Criminal Justice Act 1988, s.170(2), Sch.15, s.102.
[38] As amended by the Road Traffic Act 1991, s.48, Sch.4, para.39.
[39] Inserted by the Road Traffic (Consequential Provisions) Act 1988, s.4, Sch.3, para.27.
[40] As amended by the Road Traffic Act 1991, s.48, Sch.4, para.39
[41] paras 11–13 inserted by the Aviation and Maritime Security Act 1990, s.53(1), Sch.3, para.8.

[Channel Tunnel (Security) Order 1994 No. 570

14.   Article 4 (hijacking of Channel Tunnel trains).
15.   Article 5 (seizing or exercising control of the tunnel system).][42]

[Protection of Children Act 1978 (c.37)

16.   Section 1 (indecent photographs and pseudo-photographs of children).][43]

[Obscene Publications Act 1959 (c.66)

17.   Section 2 (publication of obscene matter).][44]

[Sexual Offences Act 2003

18.   Section 1 (rape).
19.   Section 2 (assault by penetration).
20.   Section 4 (causing a person to engage in sexual activity without consent), where the activity caused involved penetration within subsection (4)(a) to (d) of that section.
21.   Section 5 (rape of a child under 13).
22.   Section 6 (assault of a child under 13 by penetration).
23.   Section 8 (causing or inciting a child under 13 to engage in sexual activity), where an activity involving penetration within subsection (3)(a) to (d) of that section was caused.
24.   Section 30 (sexual activity with a person with a mental disorder impeding choice), where the touching involved penetration within subsection (3)(a) to (d) of that section.
25.   Section 31 (causing or inciting a person, with a mental disorder impeding choice, to engage in sexual activity), where an activity involving penetration within subsection (3)(a) to (d) of that section was caused.][45]

[Domestic Violence, Crime and Victims Act 2004

26.   Section 5 (causing or allowing the death of a child or vulnerable adult)][46]

---

[42] paras 14,15 inserted by the Channel Tunnel (Security) Order 1994, SI 1994/570, Art.38, Sch.3, para.4.
[43] Inserted by the Criminal Justice and Public Order Act 1994, s.85(3). The equivalent addition to the Northern Ireland PACE Order was made by s.85(6).
[44] Inserted by the Criminal Justice and Public Order Act 1994, s.85(3).
[45] paras 18 to 25 were inserted by the Sexual Offences Act 2003, Sch.6, para.28(4).
[46] para.26 was inserted by the Domestic Violence, Crime and Victims Act 2004, Sch.10, para.24. The numbering of the paragraph as 24 was an error.

Section 119   **Schedule 6**

CONSEQUENTIAL AMENDMENTS

PART I

ENGLAND AND WALES

Game Act 1831 (32)

1. The following section shall be inserted after section 31 of the Game Act 1831—
"Powers of constables in relation to trespassers
    31A. The powers conferred by section 31 above to require a person found on land as mentioned in that section to quit the land and to tell his Christian name, surname, and place of abode shall also be exercisable by a police constable."

Metropolitan Police Act 1839 (c.47)

2. In section 39 of the Metropolitan Police Act 1839 (fairs within the metropolitan police district) after the word "amusement" there shall be inserted the words "shall be guilty of an offence".

Railway Regulation Act 1840 (c.97)

3. In section 16 of the Railway Regulation Act 1840 (persons obstructing officers of railway company or trespassing upon railway) for the words from "and" in the third place where it occurs to "justice," in the third place where it occurs there shall be substituted the words, "upon conviction by a magistrates' court, at the discretion of the court,".

London Hackney Carriages Act 1843 (c.86)

4. In section 27 of the London Hackney Carriages Act 1843 (no person to act as driver of carriage without consent of proprietor) for the words after "constable" there shall be substituted the words "if necessary, to take charge of the carriage and every horse in charge of any person unlawfully acting as a driver and to deposit the same in some place of safe custody until the same can be applied for by the proprietor".

Town Gardens Protection Act 1863 (c.13)

5. In section 5 of the Town Gardens Protection Act 1863 (penalty for injuring garden) for the words from the beginning to "district" there shall be substituted the words "Any person who throws any rubbish into any such garden, or trespasses therein, or gets over the railings or fence, or steals or damages the flowers or plants, or commits any nuisance therein, shall be guilty of an offence and".

Parks Regulation Act 1872 (c.15)

6. The following section shall be substituted for section 5 of the Parks Regulation Act 1872 (apprehension of offender whose name or residence is not known)—

"5. Any person who—

(a) within the view of a park constable acts in contravention of any of the said regulations in the park where the park constable has jurisdiction; and

(b) when required by any park constable or by any police constable to give his name and address gives a false name or false address,

shall be liable on summary conviction to a penalty of an amount not exceeding level 1 on the standard scale, as defined in section 75 of the Criminal Justice Act 1982."

Dogs (Protection of Livestock) Act 1953 (c.28)

7. In the Dogs (Protection of Livestock) Act 1953 the following section shall be inserted after section 2—

"Power of justice of the peace to authorise entry and search

2A. If on an application made by a constable a justice of the peace is satisfied that there are reasonable grounds for believing—

(a) that an offence under this Act has been committed; and

(b) that the dog in respect of which the offence has been committed is on premises specified in the application,

he may issue a warrant authorising a constable to enter and search the premises in order to identify the dog."

Army Act 1955 (c.18)

Air Force Act 1955 (c.19)

8. The following subsection shall be substituted for section 195(3) of the Army Act 1955 and section 195(3) of the Air Force Act 1955—

"(3) A constable may seize any property which he has reasonable grounds for suspecting of having been the subject of an offence against this section."

9. . . .[47]

Game Laws (Amendment) Act 1960 (c.30)

10. In subsection (1) of section 2 of the Game Laws (Amendment) Act 1960 (power of police to enter on land) for the words "purpose of exercising any power conferred on him by the foregoing section" there shall be substituted the words "purpose—

(a) of exercising in relation to him the powers under section 31 of the Game Act 1831 which section 31A of that Act confers on police constables; or

(b) of arresting him in accordance with section 25 of the Police and Criminal Evidence Act 1984."

11. In subsection (1) of section 4 of that Act (enforcement powers) for the words from "under", in the first place where it occurs, to "thirty-one" there shall be substituted the words, "in accordance with section 25 of the Police and Criminal Evidence Act 1984, for an offence under section one or section nine of the Night Poaching Act 1828, or under section thirty".

---

[47] Repealed by the Sexual Offences Act 2003, Sch.7, para.1.

Betting, Gaming and Lotteries Act 1963 (c.2)

12. The following subsection shall be substituted for subsection (2) of section 8 of the Betting, Gaming and Lotteries Act 1963 (prohibition of betting in streets and public places)—

    "(2) Where a person is found committing an offence under this section, any constable may seize and detain any article liable to be forfeited under this section."

Deer Act 1963 (c.36)

13.   ...[48]

Police Act 1964 (c.48)

14.   ...[49]
15.   ...[50]
16.   ...[51]

Criminal Law Act 1967 (c.58)

[*The Serious Organised Crime and Police Bill 2004–05, Sch.16, Pt 2, repeals para.17.*]

17. The following subsection shall be inserted after section 4(1) of the Criminal Law Act 1967—

    "(1A) In this section and section 5 below 'arrestable offence' has the meaning assigned to it by section 24 of the Police and Criminal Evidence Act 1984."

Theatres Act 1968 (c.54)

18. In section 15(1) of the Theatres Act 1968 (powers of entry and inspection) for the words "fourteen days" there shall be substituted the words "one month".

Children and Young Persons Act 1969 (c.54)

19. In the Children and Young Persons Act 1969—

    (a)   ...[52]

    (b)   the following section shall be substituted for section 29—

  "Recognisance on release of arrested child or young person

    29. A child or young person arrested in pursuance of a warrant shall not be released unless he or his parent or guardian (with or without sureties) enters into a recognisance for such amount as the custody officer at the police station where he is detained considers will secure his attendance at the hearing of the charge; and the recognisance entered into in pursuance of this section may, if the custody officer thinks fit, be conditioned for the

---

[48] Repealed by the Deer Act 1991, Sch.4.
[49] Repealed by the Police and Magistrates' Courts Act 1994, Sch.9.
[50] Repealed by the Police and Magistrates' Courts Act 1994, Sch.9.
[51] Repealed by the Police Officers (Central Service) Act 1989, Sch.
[52] Repealed by the Children Act 1989, Sch.15, para.1.

attendance of the parent or guardian at the hearing in addition to the child or young person."

Immigration Act 1971 (c.77)

20. In section 25(3) of the Immigration Act 1971 for the words "A constable or" there shall be substituted the word "An".

Criminal Justice Act 1972 (c.71)

21. In subsection (1) of section 34 of the Criminal Justice Act 1972 (powers of constable to take drunken offender to treatment centre) for the words from the beginning to "section the" there shall be substituted the words "On arresting an offender for an offence under—
  (a)   section 12 of the Licensing Act 1872; or
  (b)   section 91(1) of the Criminal Justice Act 1967,
a".

Child Care Act 1980 (c.5)

22.   . . .[53]

Deer Act 1980 (c.49)

23.   . . .[54]

Animal Health Act 1981 (c.22)

24. In subsection (5) of section 60 of the Animal Health Act 1981 (enforcement powers) for the words "a constable or other officer" there shall be substituted the words "an officer other than a constable".

Wildlife and Countryside Act 1981 (c.69)

25. In subsection (2) of section 19 of the Wildlife and Countryside Act 1981 (enforcement powers) after the words "subsection (1)" there shall be inserted the words "or arresting a person in accordance with section 25 of the Police and Criminal Evidence Act 1984 for such an offence".

Mental Health Act 1983 (c.20)

26. In section 135(4) of the Mental Health Act 1983 for the words "the constable to whom it is addressed", in both places where they occur, there shall be substituted the words "a constable".

Prevention of Terrorism (Temporary Provisions) Act 1984 (c.8)

27.   . . .[55]

---

[53] Repealed by the Children Act 1989, Sch.15, para.1.
[54] Repealed by the Deer Act 1991, Sch.4.
[55] Repealed by the Prevention of Terrorism (Temporary Provisions) Act 1989, s.25(2), Sch.9, Pt I.

PART II

OTHER AMENDMENTS

Army Act 1955 (c.18)

28.—(1) The Army Act 1955 shall be amended as follows.
(2) In section 99—

   (a)   in subsection (1), after the word "below" there shall be inserted the
         words "and to service modifications"; and

   (b)   the following subsections shall be inserted after that subsection—

         "(1A) In this section 'service modifications' means such modifi-
         cations as the Secretary of State may by regulations made by statu-
         tory instrument prescribe, being modifications which appear to him
         to be necessary or proper for the purposes of proceedings before a
         court-martial; and it is hereby declared that in this section—

         'rules' includes rules contained in or made by virtue of an
         enactment; and

         'enactment' includes an enactment contained in an Act passed
         after this Act.

         (1B) Regulations under subsection (1A) above may not modify
         section 99A below.

         (1C) Regulations under subsection (1A) above shall be subject
         to annulment in pursuance of a resolution of either House of
         Parliament."

(3) In section 99A(1) for the word "Section" there shall be substituted the
words "Without prejudice to section 99 above, section".

(4) . . .[56]

Air Force Act 1955 (c.19)

29.—(1) The Air Force Act 1955 shall be amended as follows.
(2) In section 99—

   (a)   in subsection (1), after the word "below" there shall be inserted the
         words "and to service modifications"; and

   (b)   the following subsections shall be inserted after that subsection—

         "(1A) In this section 'service modifications' means such modifi-
         cations as the Secretary of State may by regulations made by statu-
         tory instrument prescribe, being modifications which appear to him
         to be necessary or proper for the purposes of proceedings before a
         court-martial; and it is hereby declared that in this section—

         'rules' includes rules contained in or made by virtue of an
         enactment; and

         'enactment' includes an enactment contained in an Act passed
         after this Act.

         (1B) Regulations under subsection (1A) above may not modify
         section 99A below.

         (1C) Regulations under subsection (1A) above shall be subject to
         annulment in pursuance of a resolution of either House of Parliament."

---

[56] Repealed by the Armed Forces Act 2001, Sch.7, Pt 5.

(3) In section 99A(1) for the word "Section" there shall be substituted the words "Without prejudice to section 99 above, section" .

(4) . . .[57]

Police (Scotland) Act 1967 (c.77)

30. In section 6(2) of the Police (Scotland) Act 1967 (constables below rank of assistant chief constable) for the words "an assistant chief constable or a constable holding the office of deputy chief constable" there shall be substituted the words "a deputy chief constable or an assistant chief constable".

31. In section 7(1) of that Act (ranks) after the words "chief constable," there shall be inserted the words "deputy chief constable".

32. In section 26(7) of that Act (disciplinary authority) immediately before the words "deputy chief constable" there shall be inserted the word "any".

33. In section 31(2) of that Act (compulsory retirement of chief constable etc.) for the words "the deputy or an assistant chief constable" there shall be substituted the words "a deputy or assistant chief constable".

Courts-Martial (Appeals) Act 1968 (c.20)

34. . . .[58]

House of Commons Disqualification Act 1975 (c.24)

Northern Ireland Assembly Disqualification Act 1975 (c.25)

35. In Part II of Schedule 1 to the House of Commons Disqualification Act 1975 and Part II of Schedule 1 to the Northern Ireland Assembly Disqualification Act 1975 (bodies of which all members are disqualified under those Acts) there shall be inserted at the appropriate place in alphabetical order—

"The Police Complaints Authority."

Armed Forces Act 1976 (c.52)

36.   . . .[59]

Customs and Excise Management Act 1979 (c.2)

37. The following subsection shall be substituted for section 138(4) of the Customs and Excise Management Act 1979—

"(4) Where any person has been arrested by a person who is not an officer—

(a)   by virtue of this section; or

(b)   by virtue of section 24 of the Police and Criminal Evidence Act 1984 in its application to the Customs and Excise Acts,

the person arresting him shall give notice of the arrest to an officer at the nearest convenient office of customs and excise."

---

[57] Repealed by the Armed Forces Act 2001, Sch.7, Pt 5.
[58] Repealed by the Armed Forces Act 2001, Sch.7, Pt 5.
[59] Repealed by the Armed Forces Act 2001, Sch.7, Pt 5.

38. In section 161 of that Act—

    (a) in subsection (3), for the words from "that officer" to the end of the subsection there shall be substituted the words "any officer and any person accompanying an officer to enter and search the building or place named in the warrant within one month from that day"; and

    (b) in subsection (4), for the words "person named in a warrant under subsection (3) above" there shall be substituted the words "other person so authorised".

Betting and Gaming Duties Act 1981 (c.63)

39. In the following provisions of the Betting and Gaming Duties Act 1981, namely—

    (a) . . .[60]

    (b) paragraph 16(1) of Schedule 1;

    (c) paragraph 17(1) of Schedule 3; and

    (d) paragraph 17(1) of Schedule 4,

for the words "fourteen days" there shall be substituted the words "one month".

Car Tax Act 1983 (c.53)

40.   . . .[61]

Value Added Tax Act 1983 (c.55)

41.   . . .[62]

Section 119   **Schedule 7**

REPEALS

PART I

ENACTMENTS REPEALED IN CONSEQUENCE OF PARTS I TO V

Chapter	Short title	Extent of repeal
5 Geo. 4. c.83.	Vagrancy Act 1824	Section 8 Section 13
1 & 2 Will. 4. c.32.	Game Act 1831.	In section 31, the words "or for any police constable".
2 & 3 Vict. c.47.	Metropolitan Police Act 1839.	Section 34. In section 38, the words from "it" to "and" in the sixth place where it occurs. In section 39, the words "to take into custody".

[60] Repealed by the Finance Act 1997, s.113, Sch.18, Pt II, para.1.
[61] Repealed by the Statute Law (Repeals) Act 2004, Sch.1, Pt 9, Group 5.
[62] Repealed by the Value Added Tax Act 1994, Sch.15.

Chapter	Short title	Extent of repeal
		In section 47, the words "take into custody" and the words, "and every person so found".
		In section 54, the words from "And" to the end of the section.
		In section 62, the words from "may" in the first place where it occurs to "and" in the second place where it occurs.
		Sections 63 to 67.
3 & 4 Vict. c.50.	Canals (Offences) Act 1840.	The whole Act.
5 & 6 Vict. c.55.	Railway Regulation Act 1842.	In section 17, the words "or for any special constable duly appointed".
8 & 9 Vict. c.20.	Railways Clauses Consolidation Act 1845.	In section 104, the words "and all constables, gaolers, and police officers,".
10 & 11 Vict. c.89.	Town Police Clauses Act 1847.	In section 15, the words "may be taken into custody, without a warrant, by any constable, or" and the words from "Provided" to the end of the section.
		In section 28, the words from "and" in the first place where it occurs to "offence" in the second place where it occurs.
14 & 15 Vict. c.19.	Prevention of Offences Act 1851.	Section 11.
23 & 24 Vict. c.32.	Ecclesiastical Courts Jurisdiction Act 1860.	In section 3, the words "constable or".
24 & 25 Vict. c.100.	Offences against the Person Act 1861.	In section 65, the words "in the daytime".
34 & 35 Vict. c.96.	Pedlars Act 1871.	Sections 18 and 19.
35 & 36 Vict.c.93.	Pawnbrokers Act 1872.	In section 36, the words, "within the hours of business".
38 & 39 Vict. c.17.	Explosives Act 1875.	In section 78, the words "a constable, or".
52 & 53 Vict. c.18.	Indecent Advertisements Act 1889.	Section 6.
52 & 53 Vict. c.57.	Regulation of Railways Act 1889.	In section 5(2), the words "or any constable".

Chapter	Short title	Extent of repeal
8 Edw. 7. c.66.	Public Meeting Act 1908.	In section 1, in subsection (3) the words from "and" in the sixth place where it occurs to the end of the subsection.
1 & 2 Geo. 5. c.28.	Official Secrets Act 1911.	In section 9(1), the words "named therein".
15 & 16 Geo. 5. c.71.	Public Health Act 1925.	Section 74(2) and (3).
23 & 24 Geo. 5. c.12.	Children and Young Persons Act 1933.	Section 10(2). Section 13(1) and (2). In section 40, in subsection (1) the words "named therein" and in subsection (4) the words "addressed to and".
11 & 12 Geo. 6. c.58.	Criminal Justice Act 1948.	Section 68.
1 & 2 Eliz. 2. c.14.	Prevention of Crime Act 1953.	Section 1(3).
3 & 4 Eliz. 2. c.28.	Children and Young Persons (Harmful Publications) Act 1955.	In section 3(1), the words "named therein".
4 & 5 Eliz. 2. c.69.	Sexual Offences Act 1956.	Section 40. In section 43(1), the word "named".
5 & 6 Eliz. 2. c.53.	Naval Discipline Act 1957.	In section 106(1), the words from "may" in the first place where it occurs to "and".
7 & 8 Eliz. 2. c.66.	Obscene Publications Act 1959.	In section 3(1), the words, "within fourteen days from the date of the warrant,".
8 & 9 Eliz. 2. c.36.	Game Laws (Amendment) Act 1960.	Section 1.
1963 c.2.	Betting, Gaming and Lotteries Act 1963.	In section 51(1), the words "at any time within fourteen days from the time of the issue of the warrant" and the words "arrest and".
1963 c.36.	Deer Act 1963.	Section 5(1)(c).
1964 c.26.	Licensing Act 1964.	Section 187(5).
1967 c.58.	Criminal Law Act 1967	Section 2.
1968 c.27.	Firearms Act 1968.	In section 46(1), the words "named therein". Section 50.
1968 c.52.	Caravan Sites Act 1968.	Section 11(5).
1968 c.60.	Theft Act 1968.	Section 12(3). Section 26(2).

Chapter	Short title	Extent of repeal
1968 c.65.	Gaming Act 1968.	Section 5(2). In section 43, in subsection (4), the words "at any time within fourteen days from the time of the issue of the warrant", and in subsection (5)(b), the words "arrest and".
1970 c.30.	Conservation of Seals Act 1970.	Section 4(1)(a).
1971 c.38.	Misuse of Drugs Act 1971.	Section 24.
1971 c.77.	Immigration Act 1971.	In Schedule 2, in paragraph 17(2), the words "acting for the police area in which the premises are situated," and the words "at any time or times within one month from the date of the warrant".
1972 c.20.	Road Traffic Act 1972.	Section 19(3). Section 164(2)
1972 c.27.	Road Traffic (Foreign Vehicles) Act 1972.	Section 3(2).
1972 c.71.	Criminal Justice Act.	Section 34(3).
1973 c.57.	Badgers Act 1973.	Section 10(1)(b).
1974 c.6.	Biological Weapons Act 1974.	In section 4(1), the words "named therein".
1976 c.32.	Lotteries and Amusements Act 1976.	In section 19, the words "at any time within 14 days from the time of the issue of the warrant".
1976 c.58.	International Carriage of Perishable Foodstuffs Act 1976.	Section 11(6).
1977 c.45.	Criminal Law Act 1977.	Section 11. Section 62.
1979 c.2.	Customs and Excise Management Act 1979.	In section 138, in subsections (1) and (2), the words "or constable".
1980 c.43.	Magistrates' Courts Act 1980.	Section 49.
1980 c.49.	Deer Act 1980.	Section 4(1)(c).
1980 c.66.	Highways Act 1980.	Section 137(2).
1980 c.x.	County of Merseyside Act 1980.	Section 33.
1980 c.xi.	West Midlands County Council Act 1980.	Section 42.

Chapter	Short title	Extent of repeal
1981 c.14.	Public Passenger Vehicles Act 1981.	Section 25(2).
1981 c.22.	Animal Health Act 1981.	In section 60, subsection (3), in subsection (4) the words "or apprehending", and in subsection (5) the words "constable or" in the second place when they occur.
1981 c.42.	Indecent Displays (Control) Act 1981.	Section 2(1). In section 2(3), the words "within fourteen days from the date of issue of the warrant".
1981 c.47.	Criminal Attempts Act 1981.	Section 9(4).
1981 c.69.	Wildlife and Countryside Act 1981.	Section 19(1)(c).
1982 c.48.	Criminal Justice Act 1982.	Section 34.
1983 c.2.	Representation of the People Act 1983.	In section 97(3), the words from "and" in the fifth place where it occurs to "him" in the third place where it occurs. . . .[63]
1983 c.20.	Mental Health Act 1983.	In section 135, in subsections (1) and (2), the words "named in the warrant".

PART II

ENACTMENTS REPEALED IN RELATION TO CRIMINAL PROCCEDINGS IN CONSEQUENCE OF PART VII

Chapter	Short title	Extent of repeal
1971 c.liv.	Cornwall County Council Act 1971.	Section 98(4).
1972 c.xlvii.	Hampshire County Council Act 1972.	Section 86(2).

---

[63] Words deleted by Representation of the People Act 1985, s.28, Sch.5.

PART III

ENACTMENTS REPEALED GENERALLY IN CONSEQUENCE OF PART VII

Chapter	Short title	Extent of repeal
3 & 4 Eliz. 2. c.18.	Army Act 1955.	In section 198(1), the words "of this section and of sections 198A and 198B of this Act". Sections 198A and 198B.
3 & 4 Eliz. 2. c.19.	Air Force Act 1955.	In section 198(1), the words "of this section and of sections 198A and 198B of this Act". Sections 198A and 198B.
1965 c.20.	Criminal Evidence Act 1965.	The whole Act.
1969 c.48.	Post Office Act 1969.	In section 93(4), the words "the Criminal Evidence Act 1965 and". In Schedule 4, paragraph 77.
1981 c.55.	Armed Forces Act 1981.	Section 9.
1981 c.xviii.	County of Kent Act 1981.	Section 82.
1983 c.55.	Value Added Tax Act 1983.	In Schedule 7, paragraph 7(7) and (8).

PART IV

ENACTMENTS REPEALED IN RELATION TO CRIMINAL PROCEEDINGS IN CONSEQUENCE OF PART VIII

Chapter	Short title	Extent of repeal
14 & 15 Vict. c.99.	Evidence Act 1851.	Section 13.
28 & 29 Vict. c.18.	Criminal Procedure Act 1865.	In section 6 the words from "and a certificate" onwards.
34 & 35 Vict. c.112.	Prevention of Crimes Act 1871.	Section 18 except the words "A previous conviction in any one part of the United Kingdom may be proved against a prisoner in any other part of the United Kingdom."

PART V

ENACTMENTS REPEALED GENERALLY IN CONSEQUENCE OF PART VIII

Chapter	Short title	Extent of repeal
16 & 17 Vict. c.83.	Evidence (Amendment) Act 1853.	Section 3.
46 & 47 Vict. c.3.	Explosive Substances Act 1883.	Section 4(2).
58 & 59 Vict. c.24.	Law of Distress Amendment Act 1895.	Section 5.
61 & 62 Vict. c.36.	Criminal Evidence Act 1898.	In section 1, the words "and the wife or husband, as the case may be, of the person so charged", the words (in paragraph (b)) "or the wife or husband, as the case may be, of the person so charged" and paragraphs (c) and (d). Section 4. In section 6(1), the words from "notwithstanding" to the end. The Schedule.
4 & 5 Geo. 5. c.58.	Criminal Justice Administration Act 1914.	Section 28(3).
19 & 20 Geo. 5. c.34.	Infant Life (Preservation) Act 1929.	Section 2(5).
23 & 24 Geo. 5. c.12.	Children and Young Persons Act 1933.	Section 15. Section 26(5).
4 & 5 Eliz. 2. c.69.	Sexual Offences Act 1956.	Section 12(2) and (3). Section 15(4) and (5). Section 16(2) and (3). Section 39. In Schedule 3 the entry relating to section 15 of the Children and Young Persons Act 1933.
8 & 9 Eliz. 2. c.33.	Indecency with Children Act 1960.	In section 1, subsection (2) and in subsection (3) the words "except in section 15 (which relates to the competence as a witness of the wife or husband of the accused)".
1965 c.72.	Matrimonial Causes Act 1965.	Section 43(1).

Chapter	Short title	Extent of repeal
1968 c.60.	Theft Act 1968.	Section 30(3).
1970 c.55.	Family Income Supplements Act 1970.	Section 12(5).
1973 c.38.	Social Security Act 1973.	In Schedule 23, paragraph 4.
1975 c.14.	Social Security Act 1975.	Section 147(6).
1975 c.16.	Industrial Injuries and Diseases (Old Cases) Act 1975.	Section 10(4).
1975 c.61.	Child Benefit Act 1975.	Section 11(8).
1976 c.71.	Supplementary Benefits Act 1976.	Section 26(5).
1977 c.45.	Criminal Law Act 1977.	In section 54(3) the words "subsection (2) (competence of spouse of accused to give evidence)"
1978 c.37.	Protection of Children Act 1978.	Section 2(1).
1979 c.18.	Social Security Act 1979.	Section 16.
1980 c.43.	Magistrates' Courts Act 1980.	In Schedule 7, paragraph 4.
1982 c.24.	Social Security and Housing Benefits Act 1982.	Section 21(6).

PART VI

MISCELLANEOUS REPEALS

Chapter	Short title	Extent of repeal
2 & 3 Vict. c.47.	Metropolitan Police Act 1839.	Section 7.
34 & 35 Vict. c.96.	Pedlars Act 1871.	In section 18, the words from "or" where secondly occurring to "Act," and the words from "and forthwith" to the end of the section.
1964 c.48.	Police Act 1964.	Section 49. Section 50.
1967 c.77.	Police (Scotland) Act 1967.	Section 5(3) and section 17(6).
1972 c.11.	Superannuation Act 1972.	In Schedule 1, the reference to the Police Complaints Board.

Chapter	Short title	Extent of repeal
1975 c.24.	House of Commons Disqualification Act 1975.	In Part II of Schedule 1, the entry relating to the Police Complaints Board.
1975 c.25.	Northern Ireland Assembly Disqualification Act 1975.	In Part II of Schedule 1, the entry relating to the Police Complaints Board.
1976 c.46.	Police Act 1976.	Section 1(1) to (4). Sections 2 to 13. Section 14(2). In the Schedule, paragraphs 1 to 3, in paragraph 4, the words "remuneration" and "allowances" and paragraphs 5 to 13.

CODES OF PRACTICE

CODES OF PRACTICE

[The Codes of Practice as approved by Parliament for implementation on August 1, 2004 are printed here in full. Where the text is substantively different from the pre-2003 version of the Codes this is indicated by a single vertical line in the margin. Where the text is substantively different from the 2003 version this is indicated by a double vertical line in the margin. The numbering changed considerably in the 2003 version. This is indicated in the footnotes—as in "pre-2003. . .". Where there is neither a vertical line nor a footnote, both the text and the numbering are the same as before—or the differences in the text are purely of a drafting character. The footnotes, showing the relationship between the text and the pre-2003 version of the codes, have been added by the author. (ed.)]

CODE A

CODE OF PRACTICE FOR THE EXERCISE BY: POLICE OFFICERS OF STATUTORY POWERS OF STOP AND SEARCH AND POLICE OFFICERS AND POLICE STAFF OF REQUIREMENTS TO RECORD PUBLIC ENCOUNTERS

Commencement—Transitional Arrangements

This code applies to any search by a police officer which commences after midnight on 31 July, 2004.

Recording of public encounters must be implemented in all force areas by 1 April 2005. Prior to that date, it is up to individual forces to decide when they implement paragraphs 4.11 to 4.20 of this Code.

General[1]

This code of practice must be readily available at all police stations for consultation by police officers, police staff, detained persons and members of the public.

The notes for guidance included are not provisions of this code, but are guidance to police officers and others about its application and interpretation. Provisions in the annexes to the code are provisions of this code.

This code governs the exercise by police officers of statutory powers to search a person or a vehicle without first making an arrest. The main stop and search powers to which this code applies are set out in Annex A, but that list should not be regarded as definitive. [See Note 1] In addition, it covers requirements on police officers and police staff to record encounters not governed by statutory powers.

This code does not apply to:
    (a) the powers of stop and search under;
         (i) Aviation Security Act 1982, section 27(2);
        (ii) Police and Criminal Evidence Act 1984, section 6(1) (which relates specifically to powers of constables employed by statutory undertakers on the premises of the statutory undertakers).
    (b) searches carried out for the purposes of examination under Schedule 7 to the Terrorism Act 2000 and to which the Code of Practice issued under paragraph 6 of Schedule 14 to the Terrorism Act 2000 applies.

1 Principles governing stop and search

1.1 Powers to stop and search must be used fairly, responsibly, with respect for people being searched and without unlawful discrimination. The Race Relations (Amendment) Act 2000 makes it unlawful for police officers to discriminate on the grounds of race, colour, ethnic origin, nationality or national origin when using their powers.

---

[1] Pre-2003 the paragraphs in this section were in s.1.

1.2   The intrusion on the liberty of the person stopped or searched must be brief and detention for the purposes of a search must take place at or near the location of the stop.

1.3   If these fundamental principles are not observed the use of powers to stop and search may be drawn into question. Failure to use the powers in the proper manner reduces their effectiveness. Stop and search can play an important role in the detection and prevention of crime, and using the powers fairly makes them more effective.

1.4   The primary purpose of stop and search powers is to enable officers to allay or confirm suspicions about individuals without exercising their power of arrest. Officers may be required to justify the use or authorisation of such powers, in relation both to individual searches and the overall pattern of their activity in this regard, to their supervisory officers or in court. Any misuse of the powers is likely to be harmful to policing and lead to mistrust of the police. Officers must also be able to explain their actions to the member of the public searched. The misuse of these powers can lead to disciplinary action.[2]

1.5   An officer must not search a person, even with his or her consent, where no power to search is applicable. Even where a person is prepared to submit to a search voluntarily, the person must not be searched unless the necessary legal power exists, and the search must be in accordance with the relevant power and the provisions of this Code. The only exception, where an officer does not require a specific power, applies to searches of persons entering sports grounds or other premises carried out with their consent given as a condition of entry.

2   Explanation of powers to stop and search

2.1[3]   This code applies to powers of stop and search as follows:

    (a)   powers which require reasonable grounds for suspicion, before they may be exercised, that articles unlawfully obtained or possessed are being carried, or under Section 43 of the Terrorism Act 2000 that a person is a terrorist;

    (b)   authorised under section 60 of the Criminal Justice and Public Order Act 1994, based upon a reasonable belief that incidents involving serious violence may take place or that people are carrying dangerous instruments or offensive weapons within any locality in the police area;

    (c)   authorised under section 44(1) and (2) of the Terrorism Act 2000 based upon a consideration that the exercise of one or both powers is expedient for the prevention of acts of terrorism;

    (d)   powers to search a person who has not been arrested in the exercise of a power to search premises (see Code B paragraph 2.3a).

Searches requiring reasonable grounds for suspicion

2.2[4]   Reasonable grounds for suspicion depend on the circumstances in each case. There must be an objective basis for that suspicion based on facts, information, and/or intelligence which are relevant to the likelihood of finding an

---

[2] Based in part on former Note 1AA.
[3] Based on pre-2003 para.1.5.
[4] Developed from pre-2003 paras 1.6 and 1.7.

article of a certain kind or, in the case of searches under section 43 of the Terrorism Act 2000, to the likelihood that the person is a terrorist. Reasonable suspicion can never be supported on the basis of personal factors alone without reliable supporting intelligence or information or some specific behaviour by the person concerned. For example, a person's race, age, appearance, or the fact that the person is known to have a previous conviction, cannot be used alone or in combination with each other as the reason for searching that person. Reasonable suspicion cannot be based on generalisations or stereotypical images of certain groups or categories of people as more likely to be involved in criminal activity.

2.3[5]   Reasonable suspicion can sometimes exist without specific information or intelligence and on the basis of some level of generalisation stemming from the behaviour of a person. For example, if an officer encounters someone on the street at night who is obviously trying to hide something, the officer may (depending on the other surrounding circumstances) base such suspicion on the fact that this kind of behaviour is often linked to stolen or prohibited articles being carried. Similarly, for the purposes of section 43 of the Terrorism Act 2000, suspicion that a person is a terrorist may arise from the person's behaviour at or near a location which has been identified as a potential target for terrorists.

2.4   However, reasonable suspicion should normally be linked to accurate and current intelligence or information, such as information describing an article being carried, a suspected offender, or a person who has been seen carrying a type of article known to have been stolen recently from premises in the area. Searches based on accurate and current intelligence or information are more likely to be effective. Targeting searches in a particular area at specified crime problems increases their effectiveness and minimises inconvenience to law-abiding members of the public. It also helps in justifying the use of searches both to those who are searched and to the public. This does not however prevent stop and search powers being exercised in other locations where such powers may be exercised and reasonable suspicion exists.

2.5   Searches are more likely to be effective, legitimate, and secure public confidence when reasonable suspicion is based on a range of factors. The overall use of these powers is more likely to be effective when up to date and accurate intelligence or information is communicated to officers and they are well-informed about local crime patterns.

2.6[6]   Where there is reliable information or intelligence that members of a group or gang habitually carry knives unlawfully or weapons or controlled drugs, and wear a distinctive item of clothing or other means of identification to indicate their membership of the group or gang, that distinctive item of clothing or other means of identification may provide reasonable grounds to stop and search a person. [See Note 9]

2.7[7]   A police officer may have reasonable grounds to suspect that a person is in innocent possession of a stolen or prohibited article or other item for which he or she is empowered to search. In that case the officer may stop and search the person even though there would be no power of arrest.

2.8   Under section 43(1) of the Terrorism Act 2000 a constable may stop and search a person whom the officer reasonably suspects to be a terrorist to discover

---

[5] Developed from pre-2003 para.1.6.
[6] Based on former paras 1.6A and 1.7AA.
[7] Based on pre-2003 para.1.7A.

whether the person is in possession of anything which may constitute evidence that the person is a terrorist. These searches may only be carried out by an officer of the same sex as the person searched.

2.9[8]   An officer who has reasonable grounds for suspicion may detain the person concerned in order to carry out a search. Before carrying out a search the officer may ask questions about the person's behaviour or presence in circumstances which gave rise to the suspicion. As a result of questioning the detained person, the reasonable grounds for suspicion necessary to detain that person may be confirmed or, because of a satisfactory explanation, be eliminated. [See Notes 2 and 3] Questioning may also reveal reasonable grounds to suspect the possession of a different kind of unlawful article from that originally suspected. Reasonable grounds for suspicion however cannot be provided retrospectively by such questioning during a person's detention or by refusal to answer any questions put.

2.10[9]   If, as a result of questioning before a search, or other circumstances which come to the attention of the officer, there cease to be reasonable grounds for suspecting that an article is being carried of a kind for which there is a power to stop and search, no search may take place. [See Note 3] In the absence of any other lawful power to detain, the person is free to leave at will and must be so informed.

2.11[10]   There is no power to stop or detain a person in order to find grounds for a search. Police officers have many encounters with members of the public which do not involve detaining people against their will. If reasonable grounds for suspicion emerge during such an encounter, the officer may search the person, even though no grounds existed when the encounter began. If an officer is detaining someone for the purpose of a search, he or she should inform the person as soon as detention begins.

Searches authorised under section 60 of the Criminal Justice and Public Order Act 1994[11]

2.12   Authority for a constable in uniform to stop and search under section 60 of the Criminal Justice and Public Order Act 1994 may be given if the authorising officer reasonably believes:

   (a)   that incidents involving serious violence may take place in any locality in the officer's police area, and it is expedient to use these powers to prevent their occurrence, or

   (b)   that persons are carrying dangerous instruments or offensive weapons without good reason in any locality in the officer's police area.

2.13   An authorisation under section 60 may only be given by an officer of the rank of inspector or above, in writing, specifying the grounds on which it was given, the locality in which the powers may be exercised and the period of time for which they are in force. The period authorised shall be no longer than appears reasonably necessary to prevent, or seek to prevent incidents of serious violence, or to deal with the problem of carrying dangerous instruments or offensive weapons. It may not exceed 24 hours. [See Notes 10–13]

---

[8]   Based on pre-2003 paras 2.1, 2.2, 2.3.
[9]   Based on pre-2003 para.2.2.
[10]   Pre-2003, first sentence was in para.2.1.
[11]   Paras 2.12–2.14 are based on previous para.1.8.

2.14   If an inspector gives an authorisation, he or she must, as soon as practicable, inform an officer of or above the rank of superintendent. This officer may direct that the authorisation shall be extended for a further 24 hours, if violence or the carrying of dangerous instruments or offensive weapons has occurred, or is suspected to have occurred, and the continued use of the powers is considered necessary to prevent or deal with further such activity. That direction must also be given in writing at the time or as soon as practicable afterwards. [See Note 12]

Powers to require removal of face coverings[12]

2.15   Section 60AA of the Criminal Justice and Public Order Act 1994 also provides a power to demand the removal of disguises. The officer exercising the power must reasonably believe that someone is wearing an item wholly or mainly for the purpose of concealing identity. There is also a power to seize such items where the officer believes that a person intends to wear them for this purpose. There is no power to stop and search for disguises. An officer may seize any such item which is discovered when exercising a power of search for something else, or which is being carried, and which the officer reasonably believes is intended to be used for concealing anyone's identity. This power can only be used if an authorisation under section 60 or an authorisation under section 60AA is in force.
2.16   Authority for a constable in uniform to require the removal of face coverings and to seize them under section 60AA may be given if the authorising officer reasonably believes that activities may take place in any locality in the officer's police area that are likely to involve the commission of offences and it is expedient to use these powers to prevent or control these activities.
2.17   An authorisation under section 60AA may only be given by an officer of the rank of inspector or above, in writing, specifying the grounds on which it was given, the locality in which the powers may be exercised and the period of time for which they are in force. The period authorised shall be no longer than appears reasonably necessary to prevent, or seek to prevent the commission of offences. It may not exceed 24 hours. [See Notes 10–13]
2.18   If an inspector gives an authorisation, he or she must, as soon as practicable, inform an officer of or above the rank of superintendent. This officer may direct that the authorisation shall be extended for a further 24 hours, if crimes have been committed, or is suspected to have been committed, and the continued use of the powers is considered necessary to prevent or deal with further such activity. This direction must also be given in writing at the time or as soon as practicable afterwards. [See Note 12]

Searches authorised under section 44 of the Terrorism Act 2000[13]

2.19   An officer of the rank of assistant chief constable (or equivalent) or above, may give authority for the following powers of stop and search under section 44 of the Terrorism Act 2000 to be exercised in the whole or part of his or her police area if the officer considers it is expedient for the prevention of acts of terrorism:
    (a)   under section 44(1) of the Terrorism Act 2000, to give a constable in uniform power to stop and search any vehicle, its driver, any passenger

---

[12] Paras 2.15 to 2.18 were added pursuant to the Anti-Terrorism, Crime and Security Act 2001, s.94(1).
[13] This section brings up-to-date the provisions on terrorism—see especially pre-2003 Code paras 1.8 to 1.16 and accompanying Notes.

in the vehicle and anything in or on the vehicle or carried by the driver or any passenger; and

(b)   under section 44(2) of the Terrorism Act 2000, to give a constable in uniform power to stop and search any pedestrian and anything carried by the pedestrian.

An authorisation under section 44(1) may be combined with one under section 44(2).

2.20   If an authorisation is given orally at first, it must be confirmed in writing by the officer who gave it as soon as reasonably practicable.

2.21   When giving an authorisation, the officer must specify the geographical area in which the power may be used, and the time and date that the authorisation ends (up to a maximum of 28 days from the time the authorisation was given). [See Notes 12 and 13]

2.22   The officer giving an authorisation under section 44(1) or (2) must cause the Secretary of State to be informed, as soon as reasonably practicable, that such an authorisation has been given. An authorisation which is not confirmed by the Secretary of State within 48 hours of its having been given, shall have effect up until the end of that 48 hour period or the end of the period specified in the authorisation (whichever is the earlier). [See Note 14]

2.23   Following notification of the authorisation, the Secretary of State may:

(i)   cancel the authorisation with immediate effect or with effect from such other time as he or she may direct;

(ii)   confirm it but for a shorter period than that specified in the authorisation; or

(iii)   confirm the authorisation as given.

2.24   When an authorisation under section 44 is given, a constable in uniform may exercise the powers:

(a)   only for the purpose of searching for articles of a kind which could be used in connection with terrorism (see paragraph 2.25);

(b)   whether or not there are any grounds for suspecting the presence of such articles.

[2.24A   When a Community Support Officer on duty and in uniform has been conferred powers under Section 44 of the Terrorism Act 2000 by a Chief Officer of their force, the exercise of this power must comply with the requirements of this Code of Practice, including the recording requirements.][14]

2.25   The selection of persons stopped under section 44 of the Terrorism Act 2000 should reflect an objective assessment of the threat posed by the various terrorist groups active in Great Britain. The powers must not be used to stop and search for reasons unconnected with terrorism. Officers must take particular care not to discriminate against members of minority ethnic groups in the exercise of these powers. There may be circumstances, however, where it is appropriate for officers to take account of a person's ethnic origin in selecting persons to be stopped in response to a specific terrorist threat (for example, some international terrorist groups are associated with particular ethnic identities). [See Notes 12 and 13]

2.26   The powers under sections 43 and 44 of the Terrorism Act 2000 allow a constable to search only for articles which could be used for terrorist purposes. However, this would not prevent a search being carried out under other powers if, in the course of exercising these powers, the officer formed reasonable grounds for suspicion.

---

[14]   Para.2.24A was added in 2004.

Powers to search in the exercise of a power to search premises

2.27   The following powers to search premises also authorise the search of a person, not under arrest, who is found on the premises during the course of the search:

    (a)   section 139B of the Criminal Justice Act 1988 under which a constable may enter school premises and search the premises and any person on those premises for any bladed or pointed article or offensive weapon; and

    (b)   under a warrant issued under section s.23(3) of the Misuse of Drugs Act 1971 to search premises for drugs or documents but only if the warrant specifically authorises the search of persons found on the premises.

2.28   Before the power under section 139B of the Criminal Justice Act 1988 may be exercised, the constable must have reasonable grounds to believe that an offence under section 139A of the Criminal Justice Act 1988 (having a bladed or pointed article or offensive weapon on school premises) has been or is being committed. A warrant to search premises and persons found therein may be issued under section s.23(3) of the Misuse of Drugs Act 1971 if there are reasonable grounds to suspect that controlled drugs or certain documents are in the possession of a person on the premises.

2.29   The powers in paragraph 2.27(a) or (b) do not require prior specific grounds to suspect that the person to be searched is in possession of an item for which there is an existing power to search. However, it is still necessary to ensure that the selection and treatment of those searched under these powers is based upon objective factors connected with the search of the premises, and not upon personal prejudice.

3   Conduct of searches[15]

3.1[16]   All stops and searches must be carried out with courtesy, consideration and respect for the person concerned. This has a significant impact on public confidence in the police. Every reasonable effort must be made to minimise the embarrassment that a person being searched may experience. [See Note 4]

3.2   The co-operation of the person to be searched must be sought in every case, even if the person initially objects to the search. A forcible search may be made only if it has been established that the person is unwilling to co-operate or resists. Reasonable force may be used as a last resort if necessary to conduct a search or to detain a person or vehicle for the purposes of a search.

3.3   The length of time for which a person or vehicle may be detained must be reasonable and kept to a minimum. Where the exercise of the power requires reasonable suspicion, the thoroughness and extent of a search must depend on what is suspected of being carried, and by whom. If the suspicion relates to a particular article which is seen to be slipped into a person's pocket, then, in the absence of other grounds for suspicion or an opportunity for the article to be moved elsewhere, the search must be confined to that pocket. In the case of a small article which can readily be concealed, such as a drug, and which might be concealed anywhere on the person, a more extensive search may be necessary. In the case

---

[15] This section develops the provisions in s.3 in the previous version of Code A.
[16] Based on pre-2003 Note 1AA and para.3.1.

of searches mentioned in paragraph 2.1(b), (c), and (d), which do not require reasonable grounds for suspicion, officers may make any reasonable search to look for items for which they are empowered to search. [See Note 5]

3.4 The search must be carried out at or near the place where the person or vehicle was first detained. [See Note 6]

3.5[17] There is no power to require a person to remove any clothing in public other than an outer coat, jacket or gloves except under section 45(3) of the Terrorism Act 2000 (which empowers a constable conducting a search under section 44(1) or 44(2) of that Act to require a person to remove headgear and footwear in public) and under section 60AA of the Criminal Justice and Public Order Act 1994 (which empowers a constable to require a person to remove any item worn to conceal identity). [See Notes 4 and 6] A search in public of a person's clothing which has not been removed must be restricted to superficial examination of outer garments. This does not, however, prevent an officer from placing his or her hand inside the pockets of the outer clothing, or feeling round the inside of collars, socks and shoes if this is reasonably necessary in the circumstances to look for the object of the search or to remove and examine any item reasonably suspected to be the object of the search. For the same reasons, subject to the restrictions on the removal of headgear, a person's hair may also be searched in public (see paragraphs 3.1 and 3.3).

3.6[18] Where on reasonable grounds it is considered necessary to conduct a more thorough search (e.g. by requiring a person to take off a T-shirt), this must be done out of public view, for example, in a police van unless paragraph 3.7 applies, or police station if there is one nearby. [See Note 6] Any search involving the removal of more than an outer coat, jacket, gloves, headgear or footwear, or any other item concealing identity, may only be made by an officer of the same sex as the person searched and may not be made in the presence of anyone of the opposite sex unless the person being searched specifically requests it. [See Notes 4, 7 and 8]

3.7[19] Searches involving exposure of intimate parts of the body must not be conducted as a routine extension of a less thorough search, simply because nothing is found in the course of the initial search. Searches involving exposure of intimate parts of the body may be carried out only at a nearby police station or other nearby location which is out of public view (but not a police vehicle). These searches must be conducted in accordance with paragraph 11 of Annex A to Code C except that an intimate search mentioned in paragraph 11(f) of Annex A to Code C may not be authorised or carried out under any stop and search powers. The other provisions of Code C do not apply to the conduct and recording of searches of persons detained at police stations in the exercise of stop and search powers. [See Note 7]

Steps to be taken prior to a search

3.8[20] Before any search of a detained person or attended vehicle takes place the officer must take reasonable steps to give the person to be searched or in charge of the vehicle the following information:

---

[17] Based on pre-2003 para.3.5 and Note 3C.
[18] Partly based on pre-2003 para.3.5.
[19] Based on pre-2003 para.3.5.
[20] An expanded version of pre-2003 para.2.4.

(a) that they are being detained for the purpose of a search;
(b) the officer's name (except in the case of enquiries linked to the investigation of terrorism, or otherwise where the officer reasonably believes that giving his or her name might put him or her in danger, in which case a warrant or other identification number shall be given) and the name of the police station to which the officer is attached;
(c) the legal search power which is being exercised; and
(d) a clear explanation of:
      (i) the purpose of the search in terms of the article or articles for which there is a power to search; and
      (ii) in the case of powers requiring reasonable suspicion (see paragraph 2.1(a)), the grounds for that suspicion; or
      (iii) in the case of powers which do not require reasonable suspicion (see paragraph 2.1(b), and (c)), the nature of the power and of any necessary authorisation and the fact that it has been given.

3.9[21]   Officers not in uniform must show their warrant cards. Stops and searches under the powers mentioned in paragraphs 2.1(b) and (c) may be undertaken only by a constable in uniform.

3.10[22]   Before the search takes place the officer must inform the person (or the owner or person in charge of the vehicle that is to be searched) of his or her entitlement to a copy of the record of the search, including his entitlement to a record of the search if an application is made within 12 months, if it is wholly impracticable to make a record at the time. If a record is not made at the time the person should also be told how a copy can be obtained (see section 4). The person should also be given information about police powers to stop and search and the individual's rights in these circumstances.

3.11[23]   If the person to be searched, or in charge of a vehicle to be searched, does not appear to understand what is being said, or there is any doubt about the person's ability to understand English, the officer must take reasonable steps to bring information regarding the person's rights and any relevant provisions of this Code to his or her attention. If the person is deaf or cannot understand English and is accompanied by someone, then the officer must try to establish whether that person can interpret or otherwise help the officer to give the required information.

4   Recording requirements[24]

4.1[25]   An officer who has carried out a search in the exercise of any power to which this Code applies, must make a record of it at the time, unless there are exceptional circumstances which would make this wholly impracticable (e.g. in situations involving public disorder or when the officer's presence is urgently required elsewhere). If a record is not made at the time, the officer must do so as soon as practicable afterwards. There may be situations in which it is not practicable to obtain the information necessary to complete a record, but the officer should make every reasonable effort to do so.

---

[21] Based on pre-2003 para.2.5.
[22] Based on pre-2003 para.2.6.
[23] Pre-2003 para.2.7.
[24] Previously entitled "Action after a search is carried out".
[25] Based on pre-2003 para.4.1.

4.2[26]   A copy of a record made at the time must be given immediately to the person who has been searched. The officer must ask for the name, address and date of birth of the person searched, but there is no obligation on a person to provide these details and no power of detention if the person is unwilling to do so.

4.3[27]   The following information must always be included in the record of a search even if the person does not wish to provide any personal details:

   (i)   the name of the person searched, or (if it is withheld) a description;

  (ii)   a note of the person's self-defined ethnic background; [See Note 18]

 (iii)   when a vehicle is searched, its registration number; [See Note 17]

 (iv)   the date, time and place that the person or vehicle was first detained;

  (v)   the date, time and place the person or vehicle was searched (if different from (iv));

 (vi)   the purpose of the search;

 (vii)   the grounds for making it, or in the case of those searches mentioned in paragraph 2.1(b) and (c), the nature of the power and of any necessary authorisation and the fact that it has been given; [See Note 17]

(viii)   its outcome (e.g. arrest or no further action);

 (ix)   a note of any injury or damage to property resulting from it;

  (x)   subject to paragraph 3.8(a), the identity of the officer making the search. [See Note 15]

4.4[28]   Nothing in paragraph 4.3(x) requires the names of police officers to be shown on the search record or any other record required to be made under this code in the case of enquiries linked to the investigation of terrorism or otherwise where an officer reasonably believes that recording names might endanger the officers. In such cases the record must show the officers' warrant or other identification number and duty station.

4.5[29]   A record is required for each person and each vehicle searched. However, if a person is in a vehicle and both are searched, and the object and grounds of the search are the same, only one record need be completed. If more than one person in a vehicle is searched, separate records for each search of a person must be made. If only a vehicle is searched, the name of the driver and his or her self-defined ethnic background must be recorded, unless the vehicle is unattended.

4.6[30]   The record of the grounds for making a search must, briefly but informatively, explain the reason for suspecting the person concerned, by reference to the person's behaviour and/or other circumstances.

4.7   Where officers detain an individual with a view to performing a search, but the search is not carried out due to the grounds for suspicion being eliminated as a result of questioning the person detained, a record must still be made in accordance with the procedure outlined above.

4.8   After searching an unattended vehicle, or anything in or on it, an officer must leave a notice in it (or on it, if things on it have been searched without opening it) recording the fact that it has been searched.

---

[26]   Based on pre-2003 para.4.4.
[27]   Based on pre-2003 para.4.5.
[28]   Based on pre-2003 para.4.5(x).
[29]   An expanded version of pre-2003 para.4.6.
[30]   Based on pre-2003 para.4.7.

4.9   The notice must include the name of the police station to which the officer concerned is attached and state where a copy of the record of the search may be obtained and where any application for compensation should be directed.

4.10   The vehicle must if practicable be left secure.

Recording of encounters not governed by statutory powers[31]

4.11   It is up to individual forces to decide when they implement paragraphs 4.12 to 4.20 of this Code. However, there must be full implementation across every force prior to 1st April 2005. Consequently, if an officer requests a person in a public place to account for themselves prior to 1st April 2005 and in an area where the force has not at that time implemented these provisions, no record will be completed.

4.12   When an officer requests a person in a public place to account for themselves, i.e. their actions, behaviour, presence in an area or possession of anything, a record of the encounter must be completed at the time and a copy given to the person who has been questioned. This does not apply under the exceptional circumstances outlined in 4.1.

4.13   This requirement does not apply to general conversations such as when giving directions to a place, or when seeking witnesses. It also does not include occasions on which an officer is seeking general information or questioning people to establish background to incidents which have required officers to intervene to keep the peace or resolve a dispute.

4.14   When stopping a person in a vehicle, a separate record need not be completed when an HORT/1 form, a Vehicle Defect Rectification Scheme Notice, or an Endorsable Fixed Penalty ticket is issued. It also does not apply when a specimen of breath is required under Section 6 of the Road Traffic Act 1988.

4.15   Officers must inform the person of their entitlement to a copy of a record of the encounter.

4.16   The provisions of paragraph 4.4 apply equally when the encounters described in 4.11 and 4.12 are recorded.

4.17   The following information must be included in the record:
(i)   the date, time and place of the encounter;
(ii)   if the person is in a vehicle, the registration number;
(iii)   the reason why the officer questioned that person; [See Note 18]
(iv)   a note of the person's self-defined ethnic background; [See Note 19]
(v)   the outcome of the encounter.

4.18   There is no power to require the person questioned to provide personal details. If a person refuses to give their self-defined ethnic background, a form must still be completed, which includes a description of the person's ethnic background. [See Note 19]

4.19   A record of an encounter must always be made when a person requests it, regardless of whether the officer considers that the criteria set out in 4.12 have been met. If the form was requested when the officer does not believe the criteria were met, this should be recorded on the form.

4.20   All references to officers in this section include police staff designated as Community Support Officers under section 38 of the Police Reform Act 2002.

---

[31] Paras 4.11 to 4.20 were included in August 2004.

5　Monitoring and supervising the use of stop and search powers

5.1[32]　Supervising officers must monitor the use of stop and search powers and should consider in particular whether there is any evidence that they are being exercised on the basis of stereotyped images or inappropriate generalisations. Supervising officers should satisfy themselves that the practice of officers under their supervision in stopping, searching and recording is fully in accordance with this Code. Supervisors must also examine whether the records reveal any trends or patterns which give cause for concern, and if so take appropriate action to address this. [This should include trends and patterns related to the encounters described in 4.11 and 4.12.]

5.2　Senior officers with area- or force-wide responsibilities must also monitor the broader use of stop and search powers and, where necessary, take action at the relevant level.

5.3　Supervision and monitoring must be supported by the compilation of comprehensive statistical records of stops and searches at force, area and local level. Any apparently disproportionate use of the powers by particular officers or groups of officers or in relation to specific sections of the community should be identified and investigated.

5.4　In order to promote public confidence in the use of the powers, forces in consultation with police authorities must make arrangements for the records to be scrutinised by representatives of the community, and to explain the use of the powers at a local level. [See Note 19]

Notes for guidance

Officers exercising stop and search powers

1[33]　*This code does not affect the ability of an officer to speak to or question a person in the ordinary course of the officer's duties without detaining the person or exercising any element of compulsion . It is not the purpose of the code to prohibit such encounters between the police and the community with the co-operation of the person concerned and neither does it affect the principle that all citizens have a duty to help police officers to prevent crime and discover offenders. This is a civic rather than a legal duty; but when a police officer is trying to discover whether, or by whom, an offence has been committed he or she may question any person from whom useful information might be obtained, subject to the restrictions imposed by Code C. A person's unwillingness to reply does not alter this entitlement, but in the absence of a power to arrest, or to detain in order to search, the person is free to leave at will and cannot be compelled to remain with the officer.*

2[34]　*In some circumstances preparatory questioning may be unnecessary, but in general a brief conversation or exchange will be desirable not only as a means of avoiding unsuccessful searches, but to explain the grounds for the stop/search, to gain co-operation and reduce any tension there might be surrounding the stop/search.*

---

[32] Partly based on pre-2003 Note 4DA.
[33] Partly based on pre-2003 Note 1B.
[34] Pre-2003 Note 2A.

3[35]   *Where a person is lawfully detained for the purpose of a search, but no search in the event takes place, the detention will not thereby have been rendered unlawful.*

4[36]   *Many people customarily cover their heads or faces for religious reasons —for example, Muslim women, Sikh men, Sikh and Hindu women or Rastafarian men and women. A police officer cannot order the removal of a head or face covering except where there is reason to believe that the item is being worn by the individual wholly or mainly for the purpose of disguising identity, not simply because it disguises identity. Where there may be religious sensitivities about ordering the removal of such an item, the officer should permit the item to be removed out of public view. Where practicable, the item should be removed in the presence of an officer of the same sex as the person and out of sight of anyone of the opposite sex.*

5[37]   *A search of a person in public should be completed as soon as possible.*

6   *A person may be detained under a stop and search power at a place other than where the person was first detained, only if that place, be it a police station or elsewhere, is nearby. Such a place should be located within a reasonable travelling distance using whatever mode of travel (on foot or by car) is appropriate. This applies to all searches under stop and search powers, whether or not they involve the removal of clothing or exposure of intimate parts of the body (see paragraphs 3.6 and 3.7) or take place in or out of public view. It means, for example, that a search under the stop and search power in section 23 of the Misuse of Drugs Act 1971 which involves the compulsory removal of more than a person's outer coat, jacket or gloves cannot be carried out unless a place which is both nearby the place they were first detained and out of public view, is available. If a search involves exposure of intimate parts of the body and a police station is not nearby, particular care must be taken to ensure that the location is suitable in that it enables the search to be conducted in accordance with the requirements of paragraph 11 of Annex A to Code C.*

7[38]   *A search in the street itself should be regarded as being in public for the purposes of paragraphs 3.6 and 3.7 above, even though it may be empty at the time a search begins. Although there is no power to require a person to do so, there is nothing to prevent an officer from asking a person voluntarily to remove more than an outer coat, jacket or gloves (and headgear or footwear under section 45(3) of the Terrorism Act 2000) in public.*

8[39]   *Where there may be religious sensitivities about asking someone to remove headgear using a power under section 45(3) of the Terrorism Act 2000, the police officer should offer to carry out the search out of public view (for example, in a police van or police station if there is one nearby).*

9[40]   *Other means of identification might include jewellery, insignias, tattoos or other features which are known to identify members of the particular gang or group.*

---

[35] Pre-2003 Note 2A.
[36] Pre-2003 Note 1AA. This text is the result of a significant redrafting after Code A had received Parliamentary approval, on the basis that notes for guidance are not part of the Codes.
[37] Based on pre-2003 Note 3B.
[38] Previously Note 3A.
[39] Pre-2003 Note 3C.
[40] Pre-2003 Note 1H.

Authorising officers

10   The powers under section 60 are separate from and additional to the
      normal stop and search powers which require reasonable grounds to
      suspect an individual of carrying an offensive weapon (or other article).
      Their overall purpose is to prevent serious violence and the widespread
      carrying of weapons which might lead to persons being seriously
      injured by disarming potential offenders in circumstances where other
      powers would not be sufficient. They should not therefore be used to
      replace or circumvent the normal powers for dealing with routine crime
      problems. The purpose of the powers under section 60AA is to prevent
      those involved in intimidatory or violent protests using face coverings to
      disguise identity.

11   Authorisations under section 60 require a reasonable belief on the part
      of the authorising officer. This must have an objective basis, for exam-
      ple: intelligence or relevant information such as a history of antagonism
      and violence between particular groups; previous incidents of violence
      at, or connected with, particular events or locations; a significant
      increase in knife-point robberies in a limited area; reports that individ-
      uals are regularly carrying weapons in a particular locality; or in the
      case of section 60AA previous incidents of crimes being committed
      while wearing face coverings to conceal identity.

12[41] It is for the authorising officer to determine the period of time during
      which the powers mentioned in paragraph 2.1(b) and (c) may be exer-
      cised. The officer should set the minimum period he or she considers nec-
      essary to deal with the risk of violence, the carrying of knives or offensive
      weapons, or terrorism. A direction to extend the period authorised under
      the powers mentioned in paragraph 2.1(b) may be given only once.
      Thereafter further use of the powers requires a new authorisation. There
      is no provision to extend an authorisation of the powers mentioned in
      paragraph 2.1(c); further use of the powers requires a new authorisation.

13[42] It is for the authorising officer to determine the geographical area in
      which the use of the powers is to be authorised. In doing so the officer
      may wish to take into account factors such as the nature and venue of
      the anticipated incident, the number of people who may be in the imme-
      diate area of any possible incident, their access to surrounding areas
      and the anticipated level of violence. The officer should not set a geo-
      graphical area which is wider than that he or she believes necessary for
      the purpose of preventing anticipated violence, the carrying of knives or
      offensive weapons, acts of terrorism, or, in the case of section 60AA, the
      prevention of commission of offences. It is particularly important to
      ensure that constables exercising such powers are fully aware of where
      they may be used. If the area specified is smaller than the whole force
      area, the officer giving the authorisation should specify either the
      streets which form the boundary of the area or a divisional boundary
      within the force area. If the power is to be used in response to a threat
      or incident that straddles police force areas, an officer from each of the
      forces concerned will need to give an authorisation.

---

[41] Previously Note 1G.
[42] Pre-2003 Note 1G.

14[43]   *An officer who has authorised the use of powers under section 44 of the Terrorism Act 2000 must take immediate steps to send a copy of the authorisation to the National Joint Unit, Metropolitan Police Special Branch, who will forward it to the Secretary of State. The Secretary of State should be informed of the reasons for the authorisation. The National Joint Unit will inform the force concerned, within 48 hours of the authorisation being made, whether the Secretary of State has confirmed or cancelled or altered the authorisation.*

Recording

15[44]   *Where a stop and a search is conducted by more than one officer the identity of all the officers engaged in the stop or search must be recorded on the record. Nothing prevents an officer who is present but not directly involved in searching from completing the record during the course of the encounter.*

16[45]   *Where a vehicle has not been allocated a registration number (e.g. a rally car or a trials motorbike) that part of the requirements under 4.3(iii) [or 4.17(iii)] does not apply.*

17[46]   *It is important for monitoring purposes to specify whether the authority for exercising a stop and search power was given under section 60 of the Criminal Justice and Public Order Act 1994, or under section 44(1) or 44(2) of the Terrorism Act 2000.*

18   *Officers should record the self-defined ethnicity of every person stopped according to the categories used in the 2001 census question listed in Annex B. Respondents should be asked to select one of the five main categories representing broad ethnic groups and then a more specific cultural background from within this group. The ethnic classification should be coded for recording purposes using the coding system in Annex B. An additional "Not stated" box is available but should not be offered to respondents explicitly. Officers should be aware and explain to members of the public, especially where concerns are raised, that this information is required to obtain a true picture of stop and search activity and to help improve ethnic monitoring, tackle discriminatory practice, and promote effective use of the powers. If the person gives what appears to the officer to be an "incorrect" answer (e.g. a person who appears to be white states that they are black), the officer should record the response that has been given. Officers should also record their own perception of the ethnic background of every person stopped and this must be done by using the PNC/Phoenix classification system. If the "Not stated" category is used the reason for this must be recorded on the form.*

19   *Arrangements for public scrutiny of records should take account of the right to confidentiality of those stopped and searched. Anonymised forms and/or statistics generated from records should be the focus of the examinations by members of the public.*

---

[43] Based on pre-2003 Note 1I.
[44] Based on pre-2003 Note 4A.
[45] Pre-2003 Note 4B.
[46] Pre-2003 Note 4C.

ANNEX A

SUMMARY OF MAIN STOP AND SEARCH POWERS

Power	Object of search	Extent of search	Where Exercisable
Unlawful articles general			
1. Public Stores Act 1875, s.6	HM Stores stolen or unlawfully obtained	Persons, vehicles and vessels	Anywhere where the constabulary powers are exercisable
2. Firearms Act 1968, s.47	Firearms	Persons and vehicles	A public place, or anywhere in the case of reasonable suspicion of offences of carrying firearms with criminal intent or trespassing with firearms
3. Misuse of Drugs Act 1971, s.23	Controlled drugs	Persons and vehicles	Anywhere
4. Customs and Excise Management Act 1979, s.163	Goods: (a) on which duty has not been paid; (b) being unlawfully removed, imported or exported; (c) otherwise liable to forfeiture to HM Customs and Excise	Vehicles and vessels only	Anywhere

Power	Object of search	Extent of search	Where Exercisable
5. Aviation Security Act 1982, s.27(1)	Stolen or unlawfully obtained goods	Airport employees and vehicles carrying airport employees or aircraft or any vehicle in a cargo area whether or not carrying an employee	Any designated airport
6. Police and Criminal Evidence Act 1984, s.1	Stolen goods; articles for use in certain Theft Act offences; offensive weapons, including bladed or sharply-pointed articles (except folding pocket knives with a bladed cutting edge not exceeding 3 inches)	Persons and vehicles	Where there is public access
	Criminal Damage: Articles made, adapted or intended for use in destroying or damaging property	Persons and vehicles	Where there is public access
Police and Criminal Evidence Act 1984, s.6(3) (by a constable of the United Kingdom Atomic Energy Authority Constabulary in respect of property owned or controlled by British Nuclear Fuels plc)	HM Stores (in the form of goods and chattels belonging to British Nuclear Fuels plc)	Persons, vehicles and vessels	Anywhere where the constabulary powers are exercisable

Power	Object of search	Extent of search	Where Exercisable
7. Sporting events (Control of Alcohol etc.) Act 1985, s.7	Intoxicating liquor	Persons, coaches and trains	Designated sports grounds or coaches and trains travelling to or from a designated sporting event
8. Crossbows Act 1987, s.4	Crossbows or parts of crossbows (except crossbows with a draw weight of less than 1.4 kilograms)	Persons and vehicles	Anywhere except dwellings
9. Criminal Justice Act 1988, s.139B	Offensive weapons, bladed or sharply-pointed article	Persons	School premises
Evidence of game and wildlife offences			
10. Poaching Prevention Act 1862, s.2	Game or poaching equipment	Persons and vehicles	A public place
11. Deer Act 1991, s.12	Evidence of offences under the Act	Persons and vehicles	Anywhere except dwellings
12. Conservation of Seals Act 1970, s.4	Seals or hunting equipment	Vehicles only	Anywhere
13. Badgers Act 1992, s.11	Evidence of offences under the Act	Persons and vehicles	Anywhere
14. Wildlife and Countryside Act 1981, s.19	Evidence of wildlife offences	Persons and vehicles	Anywhere except dwellings

Power	Object of search	Extent of search	Where Exercisable
Other			
15. Terrorism Act 2000, s.43	Evidence of liability to arrest under section 14 of the Act	Persons	Anywhere
16. Terrorism Act 2000, s.44(1)	Articles which could be used for a purpose connected with the commission, preparation or instigation of acts of terrorism	Vehicles, driver and passengers	Anywhere within the area or locality authorised under subsection (1)
17. Terrorism Act 2000, s.44(2)	Articles which could be used for a purpose connected with the commission, preparation or instigation of acts of terrorism	Pedestrians	Anywhere within the area of locality authorised
18. Paragraphs 7 and 8 of Schedule 7 to the Terrorism Act 2000	Anything relevant to determining if a person being examined falls within paragraph 2(1)(a) to (c) of Schedule 5	Persons, vehicles, vessels etc.	Ports and airports
19. Section 60 Criminal Justice and Public Order Act 1994, as amended by s.8 of the Knives Act 1997	Offensive weapons or dangerous instruments to prevent incidents of serious violence or to deal with the carrying of such items	Persons and vehicles	Anywhere within a locality authorised under subsection (1)

ANNEX B

SELF-DEFINED ETHNIC CLASSIFICATION CATEGORIES

White   **W**
A. White-British   W1
B. White-Irish   W2
C. Any other White background   W9

Mixed   **M**
D. White and Black Caribbean   M1
E. White and Black African   M2
F. White and Asian   M3
G. Any other mixed background   M9

Asian/Asian-British   **A**
H. Asian-Indian   A1
I. Asian-Pakistani   A2
J. Asian-Bangladeshi   A3
K. Any other Asian background   A9

Black/Black-British   **B**
L. Black-Caribbean   B1
M. Black African   B2
N. Any other Black background   B9

Other   **O**
O. Chinese   O1
P. Any other   O9

Not stated   **NS**

CODE B

CODE OF PRACTICE FOR SEARCHES OF PREMISES BY POLICE OFFICERS AND THE SEIZURE OF PROPERTY FOUND BY POLICE OFFICERS ON PERSONS OR PREMISES

Commencement—Transitional Arrangements

This code applies to applications for warrants made after 31 July 2004 and to searches and seizures taking place after midnight on 31 July 2004.

1 Introduction[1]

1.1 This Code of Practice deals with police powers to:
- search premises
- seize and retain property found on premises and persons

1.1A These powers may be used to find:
- property and material relating to a crime
- wanted persons
- children who abscond from local authority accommodation where they have been remanded or committed by a court

1.2 A justice of the peace may issue a search warrant granting powers of entry, search and seizure, e.g. warrants to search for stolen property, drugs, firearms and evidence of serious offences. Police also have powers without a search warrant. The main ones provided by the Police and Criminal Evidence Act 1984 (PACE) include powers to search premises:
- to make an arrest
- after an arrest

1.3 The right to privacy and respect for personal property are key principles of the Human Rights Act 1998. Powers of entry, search and seizure should be fully and clearly justified before use because they may significantly interfere with the occupier's privacy. Officers should consider if the necessary objectives can be met by less intrusive means.

1.4 In all cases, police should:
- exercise their powers courteously and with respect for persons and property
- only use reasonable force when this is considered necessary and proportionate to the circumstances

1.5 If the provisions of PACE and this Code are not observed, evidence obtained from a search may be open to question.

2 General[2]

2.1 This Code must be readily available at all police stations for consultation by:
- police officers
- police staff

---

[1] The Introduction is a new feature as of 2003.
[2] Pre-2003 this was s.1.

- detained persons
- members of the public

2.2   The Notes for Guidance included are not provisions of this Code.

2.3   This Code applies to searches of premises:

(a)   by police for the purposes of an investigation into an alleged offence, with the occupier's consent, other than:
- routine scene of crime searches;
- calls to a fire or burglary made by or on behalf of an occupier or searches following the activation of fire or burglar alarms or discovery of insecure premises;
- searches when paragraph 5.4 applies;
- bomb threat calls;

(b)   under powers conferred on police officers by PACE, sections 17, 18 and 32;

(c)   undertaken in pursuance of search warrants issued to and executed by constables in accordance with PACE, sections 15 and 16. See Note 2A;

(d)   subject to paragraph 2.6, under any other power given to police to enter premises with or without a search warrant for any purpose connected with the investigation into an alleged or suspected offence. See Note 2B.

For the purposes of this Code, 'premises' as defined in PACE, section 23, includes any place, vehicle, vessel, aircraft, hovercraft, tent or movable structure and any offshore installation as defined in the Mineral Workings (Offshore Installations) Act 1971, section 1. See Note 2D

2.4   A person who has not been arrested but is searched during a search of premises should be searched in accordance with Code A. See Note 2C

2.5   This Code does not apply to the exercise of a statutory power to enter premises or to inspect goods, equipment or procedures if the exercise of that power is not dependent on the existence of grounds for suspecting that an offence may have been committed and the person exercising the power has no reasonable grounds for such suspicion.

2.6   This Code does not affect any directions of a search warrant or order, lawfully executed in England or Wales that any item or evidence seized under that warrant or order be handed over to a police force, court, tribunal, or other authority outside England or Wales. For example, warrants and orders issued in Scotland or Northern Ireland, see Note 2B(f) and search warrants issued under the Criminal Justice (International Co-operation) Act 1990, section 7.

2.7   When this Code requires the prior authority or agreement of an officer of at least inspector or superintendent rank, that authority may be given by a sergeant or chief inspector authorised to perform the functions of the higher rank under PACE, section 107.

2.8   Written records required under this Code not made in the search record shall, unless otherwise specified, be made:
- in the recording officer's pocket book ('pocket book' includes any official report book issued to police officers) or
- on forms provided for the purpose

2.9   Nothing in this Code requires the identity of officers (or anyone accompanying them during a search of premises) to be recorded or disclosed:

(a)   in the case of enquiries linked to the investigation of terrorism; or

(b)   if officers reasonably believe recording or disclosing their names might put them in danger.

In these cases officers should use warrant or other identification numbers and the name of their police station. Police staff should use any identification number provided to them by the police force. See Note 2E

2.10 The 'officer in charge of the search' means the officer assigned specific duties and responsibilities under this Code. Whenever there is a search of premises to which this Code applies one officer must act as the officer in charge of the search. See Note 2F

2.11 In this Code:

    (a) 'designated person' means a person other than a police officer, designated under the Police Reform Act 2002, Part 4 who has specified powers and duties of police officers conferred or imposed on them;

    (b) any reference to a police officer includes a designated person acting in the exercise or performance of the powers and duties conferred or imposed on them by their designation

    (c) a person authorised to accompany police officers or designated persons in the execution of a warrant has the same powers as a constable in the execution of the warrant and the search and seizure of anything related to the warrant. These powers must be exercised in the company and under the supervision of a police officer.

2.12   If a power conferred on a designated person:

    (a) allows reasonable force to be used when exercised by a police officer, a designated person exercising that power has the same entitlement to use force;

    (b) includes power to use force to enter any premises, that power is not exercisable by that designated person except:

      (i) in the company and under the supervision of a police officer; or

      (ii) for the purpose of:

          ● saving life or limb; or

          ● preventing serious damage to property.

2.13   Designated persons must have regard to any relevant provisions of the Codes of Practice.

Notes for guidance

2A   PACE sections 15 and 16 apply to all search warrants issued to and executed by constables under any enactment, e.g. search warrants issued by a:

   (a) justice of the peace under the:

       ● *Theft Act 1968, section 26—stolen property;*

       ● *Misuse of Drugs Act 1971, section 23—controlled drugs;*

       ● *PACE, section 8—evidence of serious arrestable offence;*

       ● *Terrorism Act 2000, Schedule 5, paragraph 1;*

   (b) circuit judge under the:

       ● *PACE, Schedule 1;*

       ● *Terrorism Act 2000, Schedule 5, paragraph 11.*

2B   Examples of the other powers in paragraph 2.3(d) include:

(a) *Road Traffic Act 1988 giving police power to enter premises:*
 (i) *under section 4(7) to:*
 - *arrest a person for driving or being in charge of a vehicle when unfit;*
 (ii) *under section 6(6) to:*
 - *require a person to provide a specimen of breath; or*
 - *arrest a person following:*
   ~ a positive breath test;
   ~ failure to provide a specimen of breath;

(b) *Transport and Works Act 1992, sections 30(3) and 30(4) giving police powers to enter premises mirroring the powers in (a) in relation to specified persons working on transport systems to which the Act applies;*

(c) *Criminal Justice Act 1988, section 139B giving police power to enter and search school premises for offensive weapons, bladed or pointed articles;*

(d) *Terrorism Act 2000, Schedule 5, paragraphs 3 and 15 empowering a superintendent in urgent cases to give written authority for police to enter and search premises for the purposes of a terrorist investigation;*

(e) *Explosives Act 1875, section 73(b) empowering a superintendent to give written authority for police to enter premises, examine and search them for explosives;*

(f) *search warrants and production orders or the equivalent issued in Scotland or Northern Ireland endorsed under the Summary Jurisdiction (Process) Act 1881 or the Petty Sessions (Ireland) Act 1851 respectively for execution in England and Wales.*

2C *The Criminal Justice Act 1988, section 139B provides that a constable who has reasonable grounds to believe an offence under the Criminal Justice Act 1988, section 139A has or is being committed may enter school premises and search the premises and any persons on the premises for any bladed or pointed article or offensive weapon. Persons may be searched under a warrant issued under the Misuse of Drugs Act 1971, section 23(3) to search premises for drugs or documents only if the warrant specifically authorises the search of persons on the premises.*

2D *The Immigration Act 1971, Part III and Schedule 2 gives immigration officers powers to enter and search premises, seize and retain property, with and without a search warrant. These are similar to the powers available to police under search warrants issued by a justice of the peace and without a warrant under PACE, sections 17, 18, 19 and 32 except they only apply to specified offences under the Immigration Act 1971 and immigration control powers. For certain types of investigations and enquiries these powers avoid the need for the Immigration Service to rely on police officers becoming directly involved. When exercising these powers, immigration officers are required by the Immigration and Asylum Act 1999, section 145 to have regard to this Code's corresponding provisions. When immigration officers are dealing with persons or property at police stations, police officers should give appropriate assistance to help them discharge their specific duties and responsibilities.*

2E   *The purpose of paragraph 2.9(b) is to protect those involved in serious organised crime investigations or arrests of particularly violent suspects when there is reliable information that those arrested or their associates may threaten or cause harm to the officers or anyone accompanying them during a search of premises. In cases of doubt, an officer of inspector rank or above should be consulted.*

2F   *For the purposes of paragraph 2.10, the officer in charge of the search should normally be the most senior officer present. Some exceptions are:*

    (a)   a supervising officer who attends or assists at the scene of a premises search may appoint an officer of lower rank as officer in charge of the search if that officer is:

- *more conversant with the facts;*
- *a more appropriate officer to be in charge of the search;*

    (b)   when all officers in a premises search are the same rank. The supervising officer if available must make sure one of them is appointed officer in charge of the search, otherwise the officers themselves must nominate one of their number as the officer in charge;

    (c)   a senior officer assisting in a specialist role. This officer need not be regarded as having a general supervisory role over the conduct of the search or be appointed or expected to act as the officer in charge of the search.

Except in (c), nothing in this Note diminishes the role and responsibilities of a supervisory officer who is present at the search or knows of a search taking place.

3   Search warrants and production orders[3]

(a)   Before making an application

3.1   When information appears to justify an application, the officer must take reasonable steps to check the information is accurate, recent and not provided maliciously or irresponsibly. An application may not be made on the basis of information from an anonymous source if corroboration has not been sought. See Note 3A

3.2   The officer shall ascertain as specifically as possible the nature of the articles concerned and their location.

3.3   The officer shall make reasonable enquiries to:

    (i)   establish if:

- anything is known about the likely occupier of the premises and the nature of the premises themselves;
- the premises have been searched previously and how recently;

    (ii)   obtain any other relevant information.

3.4   An application:

    (a)   to a justice of the peace for a search warrant or to a circuit judge for a search warrant or production order under PACE, Schedule 1 must be supported by a signed written authority from an officer of inspector rank or above:

    Note: If the case is an urgent application to a justice of the peace and an inspector or above is not readily available, the next most senior officer on duty can give the written authority.

---

[3] Pre-2003 this was s.2.

(b) to a circuit judge under the Terrorism Act 2000, Schedule 5 for
*   a production order;
*   search warrant; or
*   an order requiring an explanation of material seized or produced under such a warrant or production order

must be supported by a signed written authority from an officer of superintendent rank or above.

3.5   Except in a case of urgency, if there is reason to believe a search might have an adverse effect on relations between the police and the community, the officer in charge shall consult the local police/community liaison officer:

*   before the search; or
*   in urgent cases, as soon as practicable after the search

(b)   Making an application

3.6   A search warrant application must be supported in writing, specifying:
(a)   the enactment under which the application is made, see Note 2A;
(b)   the premises to be searched;
(c)   the object of the search, see Note 3B;
(d)   the grounds for the application, including, when the purpose of the proposed search is to find evidence of an alleged offence, an indication of how the evidence relates to the investigation;
(e)   there are no reasonable grounds to believe the material to be sought, when making application to a:
  (i)   justice of the peace or a circuit judge, consists of or includes items subject to legal privilege;
  (ii)   justice of the peace, consists of or includes excluded material or special procedure material;
  Note: this does not affect the additional powers of seizure in the Criminal Justice and Police Act 2001, Part 2 covered in paragraph 7.7, see Note 3B;
(f)   if applicable, a request for the warrant to authorise a person or persons to accompany the officer who executes the warrant, see Note 3C.

3.7   A search warrant application under PACE, Schedule 1, paragraph 12(a), shall if appropriate indicate why it is believed service of notice of an application for a production order may seriously prejudice the investigation. Applications for search warrants under the Terrorism Act 2000, Schedule 5, paragraph 11 must indicate why a production order would not be appropriate.

3.8   If a search warrant application is refused, a further application may not be made for those premises unless supported by additional grounds.

Notes for guidance

3A[4]   *The identity of an informant need not be disclosed when making an application, but the officer should be prepared to answer any questions the magistrate or judge may have about:*

*   *the accuracy of previous information from that source*
*   *any other related matters*

---

[4] Pre-2003 this was Note 2A.

3B   The information supporting a search warrant application should be as specific as possible, particularly in relation to the articles or persons being sought and where in the premises it is suspected they may be found. The meaning of 'items subject to legal privilege', 'special procedure material' and 'excluded material' are defined by PACE, sections 10, 11 and 14 respectively.

3C   Under PACE, section 16(2), a search warrant may authorise persons other than police officers to accompany the constable who executes the warrant. This includes, e.g. any suitably qualified or skilled person or an expert in a particular field whose presence is needed to help accurately identify the material sought or to advise where certain evidence is most likely to be found and how it should be dealt with. It does not give them any right to force entry, but it gives them the right to be on the premises during the search and to search for or seize property without the occupier's permission.

4   Entry without warrant—particular powers

(a)   Making an arrest etc

4.1   The conditions under which an officer may enter and search premises without a warrant are set out in PACE, section 17. It should be noted that this section does not create or confer any powers of arrest. See other powers in Note 2B(a).

(b)   Search of premises where arrest takes place or the arrested person was immediately before arrest

4.2   The powers of an officer to search premises where that officer arrested a person or where the person was immediately before being arrested are set out in PACE, section 32.

(c)   Search of premises occupied or controlled by the arrested person

4.3   The specific powers to search premises occupied or controlled by an arrested person are set out in PACE, section 18. They may not be exercised, except if section 18 (5) applies, unless an officer of inspector rank or above has given written authority. That authority should only be given when the authorising officer is satisfied the necessary grounds exist. If possible the authorising officer should record the authority on the Notice of Powers and Rights and, subject to paragraph 2.9, sign the Notice. The record of the grounds for the search and the nature of the evidence sought as required by section 18(7) of the Act should be made in:

- the custody record if there is one, otherwise
- the officer's pocket book, or
- the search record

5   Search with consent[5]

5.1   Subject to paragraph 5.4, if it is proposed to search premises with the consent of a person entitled to grant entry the consent must, if practicable, be given in writing on the Notice of Powers and Rights before the search. The officer must make any necessary enquiries to be satisfied the person is in a position to give such consent. See Notes 5A and 5B

5.2   Before seeking consent the officer in charge of the search shall state the purpose of the proposed search and its extent. This information must be as specific as possible, particularly regarding the articles or persons being sought and the parts of the premises to be searched. The person concerned must be clearly informed they are not obliged to consent and anything seized may be produced in evidence. If at the time the person is not suspected of an offence, the officer shall say this when stating the purpose of the search.

5.3   An officer cannot enter and search or continue to search premises under paragraph 5.1 if consent is given under duress or withdrawn before the search is completed.

5.4   It is unnecessary to seek consent under paragraphs 5.1 and 5.2 if this would cause disproportionate inconvenience to the person concerned. See Note 5C

Notes for guidance

5A   *In a lodging house or similar accommodation, every reasonable effort should be made to obtain the consent of the tenant, lodger or occupier. A search should not be made solely on the basis of the landlord's consent unless the tenant, lodger or occupier is unavailable and the matter is urgent.*

5B   *If the intention is to search premises under the authority of a warrant or a power of entry and search without warrant, and the occupier of the premises co-operates in accordance with paragraph 6.4, there is no need to obtain written consent.*

5C   *Paragraph 5.4 is intended to apply when it is reasonable to assume innocent occupiers would agree to, and expect, police to take the proposed action, e.g. if:*

- *a suspect has fled the scene of a crime or to evade arrest and it is necessary quickly to check surrounding gardens and readily accessible places to see if the suspect is hiding*
- *police have arrested someone in the night after a pursuit and it is necessary to make a brief check of gardens along the pursuit route to see if stolen or incriminating articles have been discarded*

6   Searching premises—general considerations[6]

(a)   Time of searches

6.1   Searches made under warrant must be made within one calendar month of the date of the warrant's issue.

---

[5] Pre-2003 this was s.4.
[6] Pre-2003 this was s.5.

6.2 Searches must be made at a reasonable hour unless this might frustrate the purpose of the search.

6.3 A warrant authorises an entry on one occasion only. When the extent or complexity of a search mean it is likely to take a long time, the officer in charge of the search may consider using the seize and sift powers referred to in section 7.

(b) Entry other than with consent

6.4 The officer in charge of the search shall first try to communicate with the occupier, or any other person entitled to grant access to the premises, explain the authority under which entry is sought and ask the occupier to allow entry, unless:

(i) the search premises are unoccupied;

(ii) the occupier and any other person entitled to grant access are absent;

(iii) there are reasonable grounds for believing that alerting the occupier or any other person entitled to grant access would frustrate the object of the search or endanger officers or other people.

6.5 Unless sub-paragraph 6.4(iii) applies, if the premises are occupied the officer, subject to paragraph 2.9, shall, before the search begins:

(i) identify him or herself, show their warrant card (if not in uniform) and state the purpose of and grounds for the search;

(ii) identify and introduce any person accompanying the officer on the search (such persons should carry identification for production on request) and briefly describe that person's role in the process.

6.6 Reasonable and proportionate force may be used if necessary to enter premises if the officer in charge of the search is satisfied the premises are those specified in any warrant, or in exercise of the powers described in paragraphs 4.1 to 4.3, and if:

(i) the occupier or any other person entitled to grant access has refused entry;

(ii) it is impossible to communicate with the occupier or any other person entitled to grant access; or

(iii) any of the provisions of paragraph 6.4 apply.

(c) Notice of Powers and Rights

6.7 If an officer conducts a search to which this Code applies the officer shall, unless it is impracticable to do so, provide the occupier with a copy of a Notice in a standard format:

(i) specifying if the search is made under warrant, with consent, or in the exercise of the powers described in paragraphs 4.1 to 4.3. Note: the notice format shall provide for authority or consent to be indicated, see paragraphs 4.3 and 5.1;

(ii) summarising the extent of the powers of search and seizure conferred by PACE;

(iii) explaining the rights of the occupier, and the owner of the property seized;

(iv) explaining compensation may be payable in appropriate cases for damages caused entering and searching premises, and giving the address to send a compensation application, see Note 6A;

(v) stating this Code is available at any police station.

6.8 If the occupier is:

- present, copies of the Notice and warrant shall, if practicable, be given to them before the search begins, unless the officer in charge of the search reasonably believes this would frustrate the object of the search or endanger officers or other people
- not present, copies of the Notice and warrant shall be left in a prominent place on the premises or appropriate part of the premises and endorsed, subject to paragraph 2.9 with the name of the officer in charge of the search, the date and time of the search

The warrant shall be endorsed to show this has been done.

(d)   Conduct of searches

6.9   Premises may be searched only to the extent necessary to achieve the object of the search, having regard to the size and nature of whatever is sought.

6.9A   A search may not continue under:

- a warrant's authority once all the things specified in that warrant have been found
- any other power once the object of that search has been achieved

6.9B   No search may continue once the officer in charge of the search is satisfied whatever is being sought is not on the premises. See Note 6B. This does not prevent a further search of the same premises if additional grounds come to light supporting a further application for a search warrant or exercise or further exercise of another power. For example, when, as a result of new information, it is believed articles previously not found or additional articles are on the premises.

6.10   Searches must be conducted with due consideration for the property and privacy of the occupier and with no more disturbance than necessary. Reasonable force may be used only when necessary and proportionate because the co-operation of the occupier cannot be obtained or is insufficient for the purpose. See Note 6C

6.11   A friend, neighbour or other person must be allowed to witness the search if the occupier wishes unless the officer in charge of the search has reasonable grounds for believing the presence of the person asked for would seriously hinder the investigation or endanger officers or other people. A search need not be unreasonably delayed for this purpose. A record of the action taken should be made on the premises search record including the grounds for refusing the occupier's request.

6.12   A person is not required to be cautioned prior to being asked questions that are solely necessary for the purpose of furthering the proper and effective conduct of a search, see Code C, paragraph 10.1(c). For example, questions to discover the occupier of specified premises, to find a key to open a locked drawer or cupboard or to otherwise seek co-operation during the search or to determine if a particular item is liable to be seized.

6.12A   If questioning goes beyond what is necessary for the purpose of the exemption in Code C, the exchange is likely to constitute an interview as defined by Code C, paragraph 11.1A and would require the associated safeguards included in Code C, section 10.

(e)   Leaving premises

6.13   If premises have been entered by force, before leaving the officer in charge of the search must make sure they are secure by:

- arranging for the occupier or their agent to be present
- any other appropriate means

(f) Searches under PACE Schedule 1 or the Terrorism Act 2000, Schedule 5

6.14 An officer shall be appointed as the officer in charge of the search, see paragraph 2.10, in respect of any search made under a warrant issued under PACE Act 1984, Schedule 1 or the Terrorism Act 2000, Schedule 5. They are responsible for making sure the search is conducted with discretion and in a manner that causes the least possible disruption to any business or other activities carried out on the premises.

6.15 Once the officer in charge of the search is satisfied material may not be taken from the premises without their knowledge, they shall ask for the documents or other records concerned. The officer in charge of the search may also ask to see the index to files held on the premises, and the officers conducting the search may inspect any files which, according to the index, appear to contain the material sought. A more extensive search of the premises may be made only if:

- the person responsible for them refuses to:
  - ~ produce the material sought, or
  - ~ allow access to the index
- it appears the index is:
  - ~ inaccurate, or
  - ~ incomplete
- for any other reason the officer in charge of the search has reasonable grounds for believing such a search is necessary in order to find the material sought

Notes for guidance

6A *Whether compensation is appropriate depends on the circumstances in each case. Compensation for damage caused when effecting entry is unlikely to be appropriate if the search was lawful, and the force used can be shown to be reasonable, proportionate and necessary to effect entry. If the wrong premises are searched by mistake everything possible should be done at the earliest opportunity to allay any sense of grievance and there should normally be a strong presumption in favour of paying compensation.*

6B *It is important that, when possible, all those involved in a search are fully briefed about any powers to be exercised and the extent and limits within which it should be conducted.*

6C *In all cases the number of officers and other persons involved in executing the warrant should be determined by what is reasonable and necessary according to the particular circumstances.*

7   Seizure and retention of property[7]

(a)   Seizure

7.1   Subject to paragraph 7.2, an officer who is searching any person or premises under any statutory power or with the consent of the occupier may seize anything:

   (a) covered by a warrant

   (b) the officer has reasonable grounds for believing is evidence of an offence or has been obtained in consequence of the commission of an offence but only if seizure is necessary to prevent the items being concealed, lost, disposed of, altered, damaged, destroyed or tampered with

   (c) covered by the powers in the Criminal Justice and Police Act 2001, Part 2 allowing an officer to seize property from persons or premises and retain it for sifting or examination elsewhere

See Note 7B

7.2   No item may be seized which an officer has reasonable grounds for believing to be subject to legal privilege, as defined in PACE, section 10, other than under the Criminal Justice and Police Act 2001, Part 2.

7.3   Officers must be aware of the provisions in the Criminal Justice and Police Act 2001, section 59, allowing for applications to a judicial authority for the return of property seized and the subsequent duty to secure in section 60, see paragraph 7.12(iii).

7.4   An officer may decide it is not appropriate to seize property because of an explanation from the person holding it but may nevertheless have reasonable grounds for believing it was obtained in consequence of an offence by some person. In these circumstances, the officer should identify the property to the holder, inform the holder of their suspicions and explain the holder may be liable to civil or criminal proceedings if they dispose of, alter or destroy the property.

7.5   An officer may arrange to photograph, image or copy, any document or other article they have the power to seize in accordance with paragraph 7.1. This is subject to specific restrictions on the examination, imaging or copying of certain property seized under the Criminal Justice and Police Act 2001, Part 2. An officer must have regard to their statutory obligation to retain an original document or other article only when a photograph or copy is not sufficient.

7.6   If an officer considers information stored in any electronic form and accessible from the premises could be used in evidence, they may require the information to be produced in a form:

   ● which can be taken away and in which it is visible and legible; or

   ● from which it can readily be produced in a visible and legible form

(b)   Criminal Justice and Police Act 2001: Specific procedures for seize and sift powers

7.7   The Criminal Justice and Police Act 2001, Part 2 gives officers limited powers to seize property from premises or persons so they can sift or examine it elsewhere. Officers must be careful they only exercise these powers when it is essential and they do not remove any more material than necessary. The

---

[7]   Pre-2003 this was s.6.

removal of large volumes of material, much of which may not ultimately be retainable, may have serious implications for the owners, particularly when they are involved in business or activities such as journalism or the provision of medical services. Officers must carefully consider if removing copies or images of relevant material or data would be a satisfactory alternative to removing originals. When originals are taken, officers must be prepared to facilitate the provision of copies or images for the owners when reasonably practicable. See Note 7C

7.8   Property seized under the Criminal Justice and Police Act 2001, sections 50 or 51 must be kept securely and separately from any material seized under other powers. An examination under section 53 to determine which elements may be retained must be carried out at the earliest practicable time, having due regard to the desirability of allowing the person from whom the property was seized, or a person with an interest in the property, an opportunity of being present or represented at the examination.

7.8A   All reasonable steps should be taken to accommodate an interested person's request to be present, provided the request is reasonable and subject to the need to prevent harm to, interference with, or unreasonable delay to the investigatory process. If an examination proceeds in the absence of an interested person who asked to attend or their representative, the officer who exercised the relevant seizure power must give that person a written notice of why the examination was carried out in those circumstances. If it is necessary for security reasons or to maintain confidentiality officers may exclude interested persons from decryption or other processes which facilitate the examination but do not form part of it. See Note 7D

7.9   It is the responsibility of the officer in charge of the investigation to make sure property is returned in accordance with sections 53 to 55. Material which there is no power to retain must be:

- separated from the rest of the seized property
- returned as soon as reasonably practicable after examination of all the seized property

7.9A   Delay is only warranted if very clear and compelling reasons exist, e.g. the:

- unavailability of the person to whom the material is to be returned
- need to agree a convenient time to return a large volume of material

7.9B   Legally privileged, excluded or special procedure material which cannot be retained must be returned:

- as soon as reasonably practicable
- without waiting for the whole examination

7.9C   As set out in section 58, material must be returned to the person from whom it was seized, except when it is clear some other person has a better right to it. See Note 7E

7.10   When an officer involved in the investigation has reasonable grounds to believe a person with a relevant interest in property seized under section 50 or 51 intends to make an application under section 59 for the return of any legally privileged, special procedure or excluded material, the officer in charge of the investigation should be informed as soon as practicable and the material seized should be kept secure in accordance with section 61. See Note 7C

7.11   The officer in charge of the investigation is responsible for making sure property is properly secured. Securing involves making sure the property is not examined, copied, imaged or put to any other use except at the request, or with the consent, of the applicant or in accordance with the directions of the appropriate judicial authority. Any request, consent or directions must be recorded in writing and signed by both the initiator and the officer in charge of the investigation. See Notes 7F and 7G

7.12   When an officer exercises a power of seizure conferred by sections 50 or 51 they shall provide the occupier of the premises or the person from whom the property is being seized with a written notice:

    (i)   specifying what has been seized under the powers conferred by that section;

    (ii)   specifying the grounds for those powers;

    (iii)   setting out the effect of sections 59 to 61 covering the grounds for a person with a relevant interest in seized property to apply to a judicial authority for its return and the duty of officers to secure property in certain circumstances when an application is made;

    (iv)   specifying the name and address of the person to whom:

- notice of an application to the appropriate judicial authority in respect of any of the seized property must be given;
- an application may be made to allow attendance at the initial examination of the property.

7.13   If the occupier is not present but there is someone in charge of the premises, the notice shall be given to them. If no suitable person is available, so the notice will easily be found it should either be:

- left in a prominent place on the premises
- attached to the exterior of the premises

(c)   Retention

7.14   Subject to paragraph 7.15, anything seized in accordance with the above provisions may be retained only for as long as is necessary. It may be retained, among other purposes:

    (i)   for use as evidence at a trial for an offence;

    (ii)   to facilitate the use in any investigation or proceedings of anything to which it is inextricably linked, see Note 7H;

    (iii)   for forensic examination or other investigation in connection with an offence;

    (iv)   in order to establish its lawful owner when there are reasonable grounds for believing it has been stolen or obtained by the commission of an offence.

7.15   Property shall not be retained under paragraph 7.14(i), (ii) or (iii) if a copy or image would be sufficient.

(d)   Rights of owners etc

7.16   If property is retained, the person who had custody or control of it immediately before seizure must, on request, be provided with a list or description of the property within a reasonable time.

7.17   That person or their representative must be allowed supervised access to the property to examine it or have it photographed or copied, or must be provided with a photograph or copy, in either case within a reasonable time of any request and at their own expense, unless the officer in charge of an investigation has reasonable grounds for believing this would:

    (i)   prejudice the investigation of any offence or criminal proceedings; or

   (ii)   lead to the commission of an offence by providing access to unlawful material such as pornography.

A record of the grounds shall be made when access is denied.

Notes for guidance

7A   *Any person claiming property seized by the police may apply to a magistrates' court under the Police (Property) Act 1897 for its possession and should, if appropriate, be advised of this procedure.*

7B   *The powers of seizure conferred by PACE, sections 18(2) and 19(3) extend to the seizure of the whole premises when it is physically possible to seize and retain the premises in their totality and practical considerations make seizure desirable. For example, police may remove premises such as tents, vehicles or caravans to a police station for the purpose of preserving evidence.*

7C   *Officers should consider reaching agreement with owners and/or other interested parties on the procedures for examining a specific set of property, rather than awaiting the judicial authority's determination. Agreement can sometimes give a quicker and more satisfactory route for all concerned and minimise costs and legal complexities.*

7D   *What constitutes a relevant interest in specific material may depend on the nature of that material and the circumstances in which it is seized. Anyone with a reasonable claim to ownership of the material and anyone entrusted with its safe keeping by the owner should be considered.*

7E   *Requirements to secure and return property apply equally to all copies, images or other material created because of seizure of the original property.*

7F   *The mechanics of securing property vary according to the circumstances; 'bagging up', i.e. placing material in sealed bags or containers and strict subsequent control of access is the appropriate procedure in many cases.*

7G   *When material is seized under the powers of seizure conferred by PACE, the duty to retain it under the Code of Practice issued under the Criminal Procedure and Investigations Act 1996 is subject to the provisions on retention of seized material in PACE, section 22.*

7H   *Paragraph 7.14 (ii) applies if inextricably linked material is seized under the Criminal Justice and Police Act 2001, sections 50 or 51. Inextricably linked material is material it is not reasonably practicable to separate from other linked material without prejudicing the use of that other material in any investigation or proceedings. For example, it may not be possible to separate items of data held on computer disk without damaging their evidential integrity. Inextricably linked material must not be examined, imaged, copied or used for any purpose other than for proving the source and/or integrity of the linked material.*

8 Action after searches[8]

8.1   If premises are searched in circumstances where this Code applies, unless the exceptions in paragraph 2.3(a) apply, on arrival at a police station the officer in charge of the search shall make or have made a record of the search, to include:

  (i) the address of the searched premises;
  (ii) the date, time and duration of the search;
  (iii) the authority used for the search:
- if the search was made in exercise of a statutory power to search premises without warrant, the power which was used for the search:
- if the search was made under a warrant or with written consent;
  ~ a copy of the warrant and the written authority to apply for it, see paragraph 3.4; or
  ~ the written consent;

  shall be appended to the record or the record shall show the location of the copy warrant or consent.
  (iv) subject to paragraph 2.9, the names of:
- the officer(s) in charge of the search;
- all other officers and authorised persons who conducted the search;
  (v) the names of any people on the premises if they are known;
  (vi) any grounds for refusing the occupier's request to have someone present during the search, see paragraph 6.11;
  (vii) a list of any articles seized or the location of a list and, if not covered by a warrant, the grounds for their seizure;
  (viii) whether force was used, and the reason;
  (ix) details of any damage caused during the search, and the circumstances;
  (x) if applicable, the reason it was not practicable:
    (a) to give the occupier a copy of the Notice of Powers and Rights, see paragraph 6.7;
    (b) before the search to give the occupier a copy of the Notice, see paragraph 6.8;
  (xi) when the occupier was not present, the place where copies of the Notice of Powers and Rights and search warrant were left on the premises, see paragraph 6.8.

8.2   When premises are searched under warrant, the warrant shall be endorsed to show:

  (i) if any articles specified in the warrant were found;
  (ii) if any other articles were seized;
  (iii) the date and time it was executed;
  (iv) subject to paragraph 2.9, the names of the officers who executed it and any authorised persons who accompanied them;
  (v) if a copy, together with a copy of the Notice of Powers and Rights was:
- handed to the occupier; or
- endorsed as required by paragraph 6.8; and left on the premises and where.

---

[8] Pre-2003 this was s.7.

8.3   Any warrant shall be returned within one calendar month of its issue, if it was issued by a:

- justice of the peace, to the clerk to the justices for the petty sessions area concerned
- judge, to the appropriate officer of the court concerned

9   Search registers[9]

9.1   A search register will be maintained at each sub-divisional or equivalent police station. All search records required under paragraph 8.1 shall be made, copied, or referred to in the register. See Note 9A

Note for guidance

9A   Paragraph 9.1 also applies to search records made by immigration officers. In these cases, a search register must also be maintained at an immigration office. See also Note 2D.

---

[9] Pre-2003 this was s.8.

CODE C

CODE OF PRACTICE FOR THE DETENTION, TREATMENT AND QUESTIONING OF PERSONS BY POLICE OFFICERS

Commencement—Transitional Arrangements

This Code applies to people in police detention after midnight on 31 July 2004, notwithstanding that their period of detention may have commenced before that time.

1   General

1.1   All persons in custody must be dealt with expeditiously, and released as soon as the need for detention no longer applies.

1.1A   A custody officer must perform the functions in this Code as soon as practicable. A custody officer will not be in breach of this Code if delay is justifiable and reasonable steps are taken to prevent unnecessary delay. The custody record shall show when a delay has occurred and the reason. See Note 1H

1.2   This Code of Practice must be readily available at all police stations for consultation by:
- police officers
- police staff
- detained persons
- members of the public.

1.3   The provisions of this Code:
- include the Annexes
- do not include the Notes for Guidance.

1.4   If an officer has any suspicion, or is told in good faith, that a person of any age may be mentally disordered or otherwise mentally vulnerable, in the absence of clear evidence to dispel that suspicion, the person shall be treated as such for the purposes of this Code. See Note 1G

1.5   If anyone appears to be under 17, they shall be treated as a juvenile for the purposes of this Code in the absence of clear evidence that they are older.

1.6   If a person appears to be blind, seriously visually impaired, deaf, unable to read or speak or has difficulty orally because of a speech impediment, they shall be treated as such for the purposes of this Code in the absence of clear evidence to the contrary.

1.7   'The appropriate adult' means, in the case of a:
- (a)   juvenile:
  - (i)   the parent, guardian or, if the juvenile is in local authority or voluntary organisation care, or is otherwise being looked after under the Children Act 1989, a person representing that authority or organisation;
  - (ii)   a social worker of a local authority social services department;
  - (iii)   failing these, some other responsible adult aged 18 or over who is not a police officer or employed by the police.

(b) person who is mentally disordered or mentally vulnerable: See Note 1D
　(i) a relative, guardian or other person responsible for their care or custody;
　(ii) someone experienced in dealing with mentally disordered or mentally vulnerable people but who is not a police officer or employed by the police;
　(iii) failing these, some other responsible adult aged 18 or over who is not a police officer or employed by the police.

1.8　If this Code requires a person be given certain information, they do not have to be given it if at the time they are incapable of understanding what is said, are violent or may become violent or in urgent need of medical attention, but they must be given it as soon as practicable.

1.9　References to a custody officer include those performing the functions of a custody officer.

1.9A　When this Code requires the prior authority or agreement of an officer of at least inspector or superintendent rank, that authority may be given by a sergeant or chief inspector authorised to perform the functions of the higher rank under the Police and Criminal Evidence Act 1984 (PACE), section 107.

1.10　Subject to paragraph 1.12, this Code applies to people in custody at police stations in England and Wales, whether or not they have been arrested, and to those removed to a police station as a place of safety under the Mental Health Act 1983, sections 135 and 136. Section 15 applies solely to people in police detention, e.g. those brought to a police station under arrest or arrested at a police station for an offence after going there voluntarily.

1.11　People in police custody include anyone detained under the Terrorism Act 2000, Schedule 8 and section 41, having been taken to a police station after being arrested under the Terrorism Act 2000, section 41. In these cases, reference to an offence in this Code includes the commission, preparation and instigation of acts of terrorism.

1.12　This Code's provisions do not apply to people in custody:
　(i) arrested on warrants issued in Scotland by officers under the Criminal Justice and Public Order Act 1994, section 136(2), or arrested or detained without warrant by officers from a police force in Scotland under section 137(2). In these cases, police powers and duties and the person's rights and entitlements whilst at a police station in England or Wales are the same as those in Scotland;
　(ii) arrested under the Immigration and Asylum Act 1999, section 142(3) in order to have their fingerprints taken;
　(iii) whose detention is authorised by an immigration officer under the Immigration Act 1971;
　(iv) who are convicted or remanded prisoners held in police cells on behalf of the Prison Service under the Imprisonment (Temporary Provisions) Act 1980;
　(v) detained for examination under the Terrorism Act 2000, Schedule 7 and to whom the Code of Practice issued under that Act, Schedule 14, paragraph 6 applies;
　(vi) detained for searches under stop and search powers except as required by Code A.

The provisions on conditions of detention and treatment in sections 8 and 9 must be considered as the minimum standards of treatment for such detainees.

1.13   In this Code:
   (a)   'designated person' means a person other than a police officer, designated under the Police Reform Act 2002, Part 4 who has specified powers and duties of police officers conferred or imposed on them;
   (b)   reference to a police officer includes a designated person acting in the exercise or performance of the powers and duties conferred or imposed on them by their designation.

1.14   If a power conferred on a designated person:
   (a)   allows reasonable force to be used when exercised by a police officer, a person exercising that power has the same entitlement to use force; or
   (b)   includes power to use force to enter any premises, that power is not exercisable by that designated person except:
       (i)   in the company, and under the supervision, of a police officer;
       (ii) for the purpose of:
           ● saving life or limb; or
           ● preventing serious damage to property.

1.15   Nothing in this Code prevents the custody officer, or other officer given custody of the detainee, from allowing police support staff who are not designated persons to carry out individual procedures or tasks at the police station if the law allows. However, the officer remains responsible for making sure the procedures and tasks are carried out correctly in accordance with the Codes of Practice. Any such person must be:
   (a)   a person employed by a police authority maintaining a police force and under the control and direction of the Chief Officer of that force;
   (b)   employed by a person with whom a police authority has a contract for the provision of services relating to persons arrested or otherwise in custody.

1.16   Designated persons and other police support staff must have regard to any relevant provisions of the Codes of Practice.

1.17   References to pocket books include any official report book issued to police officers or police support staff.

Notes for guidance

1A   *Although certain sections of this Code apply specifically to people in custody at police stations, those there voluntarily to assist with an investigation should be treated with no less consideration, e.g. offered refreshments at appropriate times, and enjoy an absolute right to obtain legal advice or communicate with anyone outside the police station.*

1B[1]   *A person, including a parent or guardian, should not be an appropriate adult if they:*
   ● *are*
       ~ suspected of involvement in the offence
       ~ the victim
       ~ a witness
       ~ involved in the investigation
   ● *received admissions prior to attending to act as the appropriate adult.*
   Note: If a juvenile's parent is estranged from the juvenile, they should not be asked to act as the appropriate adult if the juvenile expressly and specifically objects to their presence.

---

[1] Based on pre-2003 Note 1C.

1C²   *If a juvenile admits an offence to, or in the presence of, a social worker or member of a youth offending team other than during the time that person is acting as the juvenile's appropriate adult , another appropriate adult should be appointed in the interest of fairness.*

1D³   *In the case of people who are mentally disordered or otherwise mentally vulnerable, it may be more satisfactory if the appropriate adult is someone experienced or trained in their care rather than a relative lacking such qualifications. But if the detainee prefers a relative to a better qualified stranger or objects to a particular person their wishes should, if practicable, be respected.*

1E⁴   *A detainee should always be given an opportunity, when an appropriate adult is called to the police station, to consult privately with a solicitor in the appropriate adult's absence if they want.*

1F⁵   *A solicitor or independent custody visitor (formerly a lay visitor) present at the police station in that capacity may not be the appropriate adult.*

1G   *'Mentally vulnerable' applies to any detainee who, because of their mental state or capacity, may not understand the significance of what is said, of questions or of their replies. 'Mental disorder' is defined in the Mental Health Act 1983, section 1(2) as 'mental illness, arrested or incomplete development of mind, psychopathic disorder and any other disorder or disability of mind'. When the custody officer has any doubt about the mental state or capacity of a detainee, that detainee should be treated as mentally vulnerable and an appropriate adult called.*

1H   *Paragraph 1.1A is intended to cover delays which may occur in processing detainees e.g. if:*
- *a large number of suspects are brought into the station simultaneously to be placed in custody;*
- *interview rooms are all being used;*
- *there are difficulties contacting an appropriate adult, solicitor or interpreter.*

1I   *The custody officer must remind the appropriate adult and detainee about the right to legal advice and record any reasons for waiving it in accordance with section 6.*

2   Custody records

2.1A   When a person is brought to a police station:
- under arrest
- is arrested at the police station having attended there voluntarily or
- attends a police station to answer bail

they should be brought before the custody officer as soon as practicable after their arrival at the station or, if appropriate, following arrest after attending the police station voluntarily. This applies to designated and non-designated police stations. A person is deemed to be 'at a police station' for these purposes if they are within the boundary of any building or enclosed yard which forms part of that police station.

---

² Pre-2003 Note 1D.
³ Pre-2003 Note 1E.
⁴ Pre-2003 Note 1EE.
⁵ Pre-2003 Note 1F.

2.1   A separate custody record must be opened as soon as practicable for each person brought to a police station under arrest or arrested at the station having gone there voluntarily *or attending a police station in answer to street bail*. All information recorded under this Code must be recorded as soon as practicable in the custody record unless otherwise specified. Any audio or video recording made in the custody area is not part of the custody record.

2.2   If any action requires the authority of an officer of a specified rank, subject to paragraph 2.6A, their name and rank must be noted in the custody record.

2.3   The custody officer is responsible for the custody record's accuracy and completeness and for making sure the record or copy of the record accompanies a detainee if they are transferred to another police station. The record shall show the:

- time and reason for transfer;
- time a person is released from detention.

2.4   A solicitor or appropriate adult must be permitted to consult a detainee's custody record as soon as practicable after their arrival at the station and at any other time whilst the person is detained. Arrangements for this access must be agreed with the custody officer and may not unreasonably interfere with the custody officer's duties.

2.4A   When a detainee leaves police detention or is taken before a court they, their legal representative or appropriate adult shall be given, on request, a copy of the custody record as soon as practicable. This entitlement lasts for 12 months after release.

2.5   The detainee, appropriate adult or legal representative shall be permitted to inspect the original custody record after the detainee has left police detention provided they give reasonable notice of their request. Any such inspection shall be noted in the custody record.

2.6   Subject to paragraph 2.6A, all entries in custody records must be timed and signed by the maker. Records entered on computer shall be timed and contain the operator's identification.

2.6A   Nothing in this Code requires the identity of officers or civilian support staff to be recorded or disclosed:

(a)   in the case of enquiries linked to the investigation of terrorism; or

(b)   if the officer or police staff reasonably believe recording or disclosing their name might put them in danger.

In these cases, they shall use their warrant or other identification numbers and the name of their police station. See Note 2A

2.7   The fact and time of any detainee's refusal to sign a custody record, when asked in accordance with this Code, must be recorded.

Note for guidance

2A   *The purpose of paragraph 2.6A(b) is to protect those involved in serious organised crime investigations or arrests of particularly violent suspects when there is reliable information that those arrested or their associates may threaten or cause harm to those involved. In cases of doubt, an officer of inspector rank or above should be consulted.*

3 Initial action

(a) Detained persons—normal procedure

3.1 When a person is brought to a police station under arrest or arrested at the station having gone there voluntarily, the custody officer must make sure the person is told clearly about the following continuing rights which may be exercised at any stage during the period in custody:

 (i) the right to have someone informed of their arrest as in section 5;

 (ii) the right to consult privately with a solicitor and that free independent legal advice is available;

 (iii) the right to consult these Codes of Practice. See Note 3D

3.2 The detainee must also be given:

- a written notice setting out:
  - ~ the above three rights;
  - ~ the arrangements for obtaining legal advice;
  - ~ the right to a copy of the custody record as in paragraph 2.4A;
  - ~ the caution in the terms prescribed in section 10.
- an additional written notice briefly setting out their entitlements while in custody, see Notes 3A and 3B.

Note: The detainee shall be asked to sign the custody record to acknowledge receipt of these notices. Any refusal must be recorded on the custody record.

3.3 A citizen of an independent Commonwealth country or a national of a foreign country, including the Republic of Ireland, must be informed as soon as practicable about their rights of communication with their High Commission, Embassy or Consulate. See section 7

3.4 The custody officer shall:

- note on the custody record any comment the detainee makes in relation to the arresting officer's account but shall not invite comment. If the arresting officer is not physically present when the detainee is brought to a police station, the arresting officer's account must be made available to the custody officer remotely or by a third party on the arresting officer's behalf. If the custody officer authorises a person's detention the detainee must be informed of the grounds as soon as practicable and before they are questioned about any offence;
- note any comment the detainee makes in respect of the decision to detain them but shall not invite comment;
- not put specific questions to the detainee regarding their involvement in any offence, nor in respect of any comments they may make in response to the arresting officer's account or the decision to place them in detention. Such an exchange is likely to constitute an interview as in paragraph 11.1A and require the associated safeguards in section 11.

See paragraph 11.13 in respect of unsolicited comments.

3.5 The custody officer shall:

 (a) ask the detainee, whether at this time, they:

  (i) would like legal advice, see paragraph 6.5;

  (ii) want someone informed of their detention, see section 5;

 (b) ask the detainee to sign the custody record to confirm their decisions in respect of (a);

(c) determine whether the detainee:
    (i) is, or might be, in need of medical treatment or attention, see section 9;
    (ii) requires:
- an appropriate adult;
- help to check documentation;
- an interpreter;

(d) record the decision in respect of (c).

3.6   When determining these needs the custody officer is responsible for initiating an assessment to consider whether the detainee is likely to present specific risks to custody staff or themselves. Such assessments should always include a check on the Police National Computer, to be carried out as soon as practicable, to identify any risks highlighted in relation to the detainee. Although such assessments are primarily the custody officer's responsibility, it may be necessary for them to consult and involve others, e.g. the arresting officer or an appropriate health care professional, see paragraph 9.13. Reasons for delaying the initiation or completion of the assessment must be recorded.

3.7   Chief Officers should ensure that arrangements for proper and effective risk assessments required by paragraph 3.6 are implemented in respect of all detainees at police stations in their area.

3.8   Risk assessments must follow a structured process which clearly defines the categories of risk to be considered and the results must be incorporated in the detainee's custody record. The custody officer is responsible for making sure those responsible for the detainee's custody are appropriately briefed about the risks. If no specific risks are identified by the assessment, that should be noted in the custody record. See Note 3E and paragraph 9.14

3.9   The custody officer is responsible for implementing the response to any specific risk assessment, e.g.:
- reducing opportunities for self harm;
- calling a health care professional;
- increasing levels of monitoring or observation.

3.10   Risk assessment is an ongoing process and assessments must always be subject to review if circumstances change.

3.11[6]   If video cameras are installed in the custody area, notices shall be prominently displayed showing cameras are in use. Any request to have video cameras switched off shall be refused.

(b) Detained persons—special groups

3.12[7]   If the detainee appears deaf or there is doubt about their hearing or speaking ability or ability to understand English, and the custody officer cannot establish effective communication, the custody officer must, as soon as practicable, call an interpreter for assistance in the action under paragraphs 3.1–3.5. See section 13

3.13[8]   If the detainee is a juvenile, the custody officer must, if it is practicable, ascertain the identity of a person responsible for their welfare. That person:
- may be:
  - ~ the parent or guardian;

---

[6] Pre-2003 para.3.5A.
[7] Pre-2003 para.3.6.
[8] Pre-2003 para.3.7.

~ if the juvenile is in local authority or voluntary organisation care, or is otherwise being looked after under the Children Act 1989, a person appointed by that authority or organisation to have responsibility for the juvenile's welfare;

~ any other person who has, for the time being, assumed responsibility for the juvenile's welfare.

• must be informed as soon as practicable that the juvenile has been arrested, why they have been arrested and where they are detained. This right is in addition to the juvenile's right in section 5 not to be held incommunicado. See Note 3C

3.14[9]   If a juvenile is known to be subject to a court order under which a person or organisation is given any degree of statutory responsibility to supervise or otherwise monitor them, reasonable steps must also be taken to notify that person or organisation (the 'responsible officer'). The responsible officer will normally be a member of a Youth Offending Team, except for a curfew order which involves electronic monitoring when the contractor providing the monitoring will normally be the responsible officer.

3.15[10]   If the detainee is a juvenile, mentally disordered or otherwise mentally vulnerable, the custody officer must, as soon as practicable:

• inform the appropriate adult, who in the case of a juvenile may or may not be a person responsible for their welfare, as in paragraph 3.13, of:

~ the grounds for their detention;

~ their whereabouts.

• ask the adult to come to the police station to see the detainee.

3.16[11]   It is imperative a mentally disordered or otherwise mentally vulnerable person, detained under the Mental Health Act 1983, section 136, be assessed as soon as possible. If that assessment is to take place at the police station, an approved social worker and a registered medical practitioner shall be called to the station as soon as possible in order to interview and examine the detainee. Once the detainee has been interviewed, examined and suitable arrangements made for their treatment or care, they can no longer be detained under section 136. A detainee must be immediately discharged from detention under section 136 if a registered medical practitioner, having examined them, concludes they are not mentally disordered within the meaning of the Act.

3.17[12]   If the appropriate adult is:

• already at the police station, the provisions of paragraphs 3.1 to 3.5 must be complied with in the appropriate adult's presence;

• not at the station when these provisions are complied with, they must be complied with again in the presence of the appropriate adult when they arrive.

3.18[13]   The detainee shall be advised that:

• the duties of the appropriate adult include giving advice and assistance;

• they can consult privately with the appropriate adult at any time.

3.19[14]   If the detainee, or appropriate adult on the detainee's behalf, asks for a solicitor to be called to give legal advice, the provisions of section 6 apply.

[9] Based on pre-2003 para.3.8.
[10] Pre-2003 para.3.9.
[11] Pre-2003 para.3.10.
[12] Pre-2003 para.3.11.
[13] Pre-2003 para.3.12.
[14] Pre-2003 para.3.13.

3.20[15]   If the detainee is blind, seriously visually impaired or unable to read, the custody officer shall make sure their solicitor, relative, appropriate adult or some other person likely to take an interest in them and not involved in the investigation is available to help check any documentation. When this Code requires written consent or signing the person assisting may be asked to sign instead, if the detainee prefers. This paragraph does not require an appropriate adult to be called solely to assist in checking and signing documentation for a person who is not a juvenile, or mentally disordered or otherwise mentally vulnerable (see paragraph 3.15).

(c)   Persons attending a police station voluntarily

3.21[16]   Anybody attending a police station voluntarily to assist with an investigation may leave at will unless arrested. If it is decided they shall not be allowed to leave, they must be informed at once that they are under arrest and brought before the custody officer, who is responsible for making sure they are notified of their rights in the same way as other detainees. If they are not arrested but are cautioned as in section 10, the person who gives the caution must, at the same time, inform them they are not under arrest, they are not obliged to remain at the station but if they remain at the station they may obtain free and independent legal advice if they want. They shall be told the right to legal advice includes the right to speak with a solicitor on the telephone and be asked if they want to do so.
3.22[17]   If a person attending the police station voluntarily asks about their entitlement to legal advice, they shall be given a copy of the notice explaining the arrangements for obtaining legal advice. See paragraph 3.2

(d)   Documentation

3.23[18]   The grounds for a person's detention shall be recorded, in the person's presence if practicable.
3.24[19]   Action taken under paragraphs 3.12 to 3.20 shall be recorded.

(e)   Persons answering street bail

3.25   When a person is answering street bail, the custody officer should link any documentation held in relation to arrest with the custody record. Any further action shall be recorded on the custody record in accordance with paragraphs 3.23 and 3.24 above.

Notes for guidance

3A   *The notice of entitlements should:*
- *list the entitlements in this Code, including:*
  ~ *visits and contact with outside parties, including special provisions for Commonwealth citizens and foreign nationals;*

---

[15]   Pre-2003 para.3.14.
[16]   Pre-2003 para.3.15.
[17]   Pre-2003 para.3.16.
[18]   Pre-2003 para.3.17.
[19]   Pre-2003 para.3.18.

~ *reasonable standards of physical comfort;*

~ *adequate food and drink;*

~ *access to toilets and washing facilities, clothing, medical attention, and exercise when practicable.*

● *mention the:*

~ *provisions relating to the conduct of interviews;*

~ *circumstances in which an appropriate adult should be available to assist the detainee and their statutory rights to make representation whenever the period of their detention is reviewed.*

3B   In addition to notices in English, translations should be available in Welsh, the main minority ethnic languages and the principal European languages, whenever they are likely to be helpful. Audio versions of the notice should also be made available.

3C   If the juvenile is in local authority or voluntary organisation care but living with their parents or other adults responsible for their welfare, although there is no legal obligation to inform them, they should normally be contacted, as well as the authority or organisation unless suspected of involvement in the offence concerned. Even if the juvenile is not living with their parents, consideration should be given to informing them.

3D[20] The right to consult the Codes of Practice does not entitle the person concerned to delay unreasonably any necessary investigative or administrative action whilst they do so. Examples of action which need not be delayed unreasonably include:

● *procedures requiring the provision of breath, blood or urine specimens under the Road Traffic Act 1988 or the Transport and Works Act 1992*

● *searching detainees at the police station*

● *taking fingerprints or non-intimate samples without consent for evidential purposes.*

3E   Home Office Circular 23/2000 provides more detailed guidance on risk assessments and identifies key risk areas which should always be considered.

4 Detainee's property

(a) Action

4.1 The custody officer is responsible for:

(a) ascertaining what property a detainee:

(i) has with them when they come to the police station, whether on:

● arrest or re-detention on answering to bail;

● commitment to prison custody on the order or sentence of a court;

● lodgement at the police station with a view to their production in court from prison custody;

● transfer from detention at another station or hospital;

● detention under the Mental Health Act 1983, section 135 or 136;

---

[20] Pre-2003 Note 3E.

(ii)   might have acquired for an unlawful or harmful purpose while in custody;

(b)   the safekeeping of any property taken from a detainee which remains at the police station.

The custody officer may search the detainee or authorise their being searched to the extent they consider necessary, provided a search of intimate parts of the body or involving the removal of more than outer clothing is only made as in Annex A. A search may only be carried out by an officer of the same sex as the detainee. See Note 4A

4.2   Detainees may retain clothing and personal effects at their own risk unless the custody officer considers they may use them to cause harm to themselves or others, interfere with evidence, damage property, effect an escape or they are needed as evidence. In this event the custody officer may withhold such articles as they consider necessary and must tell the detainee why.

4.3   Personal effects are those items a detainee may lawfully need, use or refer to while in detention but do not include cash and other items of value.

(b)   Documentation

4.4   It is a matter for the custody officer to determine whether a record should be made of the property a detained person has with him or had taken from him on arrest. Any record made is not required to be kept as part of the custody record but the custody record should be noted as to where such a record exists. Whenever a record is made the detainee shall be allowed to check and sign the record of property as correct. Any refusal to sign shall be recorded.

4.5   If a detainee is not allowed to keep any article of clothing or personal effects, the reason must be recorded.

Notes for guidance

4A   *PACE, Section 54(1) and paragraph 4.1 require a detainee to be searched when it is clear the custody officer will have continuing duties in relation to that detainee or when that detainee's behaviour or offence makes an inventory appropriate. They do not require every detainee to be searched, e.g. if it is clear a person will only be detained for a short period and is not to be placed in a cell, the custody officer may decide not to search them. In such a case the custody record will be endorsed 'not searched', paragraph 4.4 will not apply, and the detainee will be invited to sign the entry. If the detainee refuses, the custody officer will be obliged to ascertain what property they have in accordance with paragraph 4.1.*

4B   *Paragraph 4.4 does not require the custody officer to record on the custody record property in the detainee's possession on arrest if, by virtue of its nature, quantity or size, it is not practicable to remove it to the police station.*

4C   *Paragraph 4.4 does not require items of clothing worn by the person be recorded unless withheld by the custody officer as in paragraph 4.2.*

5   Right not to be held incommunicado

(a)   Action

5.1   Any person arrested and held in custody at a police station or other premises may, on request, have one person known to them or likely to take an interest in their welfare informed at public expense of their whereabouts as soon as practicable. If the person cannot be contacted the detainee may choose up to two alternatives. If they cannot be contacted, the person in charge of detention or the investigation has discretion to allow further attempts until the information has been conveyed. See Notes 5C and 5D

5.2   The exercise of the above right in respect of each person nominated may be delayed only in accordance with Annex B.

5.3   The above right may be exercised each time a detainee is taken to another police station.

5.4   The detainee may receive visits at the custody officer's discretion. See Note 5B

5.5   If a friend, relative or person with an interest in the detainee's welfare enquires about their whereabouts, this information shall be given if the suspect agrees and Annex B does not apply. See Note 5D

5.6   The detainee shall be given writing materials, on request, and allowed to telephone one person for a reasonable time, see Notes 5A and 5E. Either or both these privileges may be denied or delayed if an officer of inspector rank or above considers sending a letter or making a telephone call may result in any of the consequences in:

    (a)   Annex B paragraphs 1 and 2 and the person is detained in connection with an arrestable or serious arrestable offence; or

    (b)   Annex B paragraphs 8 and 9 and the person is detained under the Terrorism Act 2000, Schedule 7 or section 41

For the purposes of this paragraph, any reference to a serious arrestable offence in Annex B includes an arrestable offence. However, nothing in this paragraph permits the restriction or denial of the rights in paragraphs 5.1 and 6.1.

5.7   Before any letter or message is sent, or telephone call made, the detainee shall be informed that what they say in any letter, call or message (other than in a communication to a solicitor) may be read or listened to and may be given in evidence. A telephone call may be terminated if it is being abused. The costs can be at public expense at the custody officer's discretion.

(b)   Documentation

5.8   A record must be kept of any:

    (a)   request made under this section and the action taken;

    (b)   letters, messages or telephone calls made or received or visit received;

    (c)   refusal by the detainee to have information about them given to an outside enquirer. The detainee must be asked to countersign the record accordingly and any refusal recorded.

Notes for guidance

5A   A person may request an interpreter to interpret a telephone call or translate a letter.

5B At the custody officer's discretion, visits should be allowed when possible, subject to having sufficient personnel to supervise a visit and any possible hindrance to the investigation.

5C If the detainee does not know anyone to contact for advice or support or cannot contact a friend or relative, the custody officer should bear in mind any local voluntary bodies or other organisations who might be able to help. Paragraph 6.1 applies if legal advice is required.

5D In some circumstances it may not be appropriate to use the telephone to disclose information under paragraphs 5.1 and 5.5.

5E The telephone call at paragraph 5.6 is in addition to any communication under paragraphs 5.1 and 6.1.

6 Right to legal advice

(a) Action

6.1 Unless Annex B applies, all detainees must be informed that they may at any time consult and communicate privately with a solicitor, whether in person, in writing or by telephone, and that free independent legal advice is available from the duty solicitor. See paragraph 3.1, Note 6B and Note 6J

6.2 Not Used

6.3 A poster advertising the right to legal advice must be prominently displayed in the charging area of every police station. See Note 6H

6.4 No police officer should, at any time, do or say anything with the intention of dissuading a detainee from obtaining legal advice.

6.5 The exercise of the right of access to legal advice may be delayed only as in Annex B. Whenever legal advice is requested, and unless Annex B applies, the custody officer must act without delay to secure the provision of such advice. If, on being informed or reminded of this right, the detainee declines to speak to a solicitor in person, the officer should point out that the right includes the right to speak with a solicitor on the telephone. If the detainee continues to waive this right the officer should ask them why and any reasons should be recorded on the custody record or the interview record as appropriate. Reminders of the right to legal advice must be given as in paragraphs 3.5, 11.2, 15.4, 16.4 and 16.5 and Code D, paragraphs 3.17(ii) and 6.3. Once it is clear a detainee does not want to speak to a solicitor in person or by telephone they should cease to be asked their reasons. See Note 6K

6.5A In the case of a juvenile, an appropriate adult should consider whether legal advice from a solicitor is required. If the juvenile indicates that they do not want legal advice, the appropriate adult has the right to ask for a solicitor to attend if this would be in the best interests of the person. However, the detained person cannot be forced to see the solicitor if he is adamant that he does not wish to do so

6.6 A detainee who wants legal advice may not be interviewed or continue to be interviewed until they have received such advice unless:

(a) Annex B applies, when the restriction on drawing adverse inferences from silence in Annex C will apply because the detainee is not allowed an opportunity to consult a solicitor; or

(b) an officer of superintendent rank or above has reasonable grounds for believing that:

    (i) the consequent delay might:
- lead to interference with, or harm to, evidence connected with an offence;
- lead to interference with, or physical harm to, other people;
- lead to serious loss of, or damage to, property;
- lead to alerting other people suspected of having committed an offence but not yet arrested for it;
- hinder the recovery of property obtained in consequence of the commission of an offence.

    (ii) when a solicitor, including a duty solicitor, has been contacted and has agreed to attend, awaiting their arrival would cause unreasonable delay to the process of investigation.

Note: In these cases the restriction on drawing adverse inferences from silence in Annex C will apply because the detainee is not allowed an opportunity to consult a solicitor;

(c) the solicitor the detainee has nominated or selected from a list:

    (i) cannot be contacted;

    (ii) has previously indicated they do not wish to be contacted; or

    (iii) having been contacted, has declined to attend; and

       the detainee has been advised of the Duty Solicitor Scheme but has declined to ask for the duty solicitor. In these circumstances the interview may be started or continued without further delay provided an officer of inspector rank or above has agreed to the interview proceeding.

Note: The restriction on drawing adverse inferences from silence in Annex C will not apply because the detainee is allowed an opportunity to consult the duty solicitor;

(d) the detainee changes their mind, about wanting legal advice.

     In these circumstances the interview may be started or continued without delay provided that:

    (i) the detainee agrees to do so , in writing or on tape; and

    (ii) an officer of inspector rank or above has inquired about the detainee's reasons for their change of mind and gives authority for the interview to proceed.

Confirmation of the detainee's agreement, their change of mind, the reasons for it if given and, subject to paragraph 2.6A, the name of the authorising officer shall be recorded in the taped or written interview record. See Note 6I.

    Note: In these circumstances the restriction on drawing adverse inferences from silence in Annex C will not apply because the detainee is allowed an opportunity to consult a solicitor if they wish.

6.7 If paragraph 6.6(b)(i) applies, once sufficient information has been obtained to avert the risk, questioning must cease until the detainee has received legal advice unless paragraph 6.6(a), (b)(ii), (c) or (d) applies.

6.8 A detainee who has been permitted to consult a solicitor shall be entitled on request to have the solicitor present when they are interviewed unless one of the exceptions in paragraph 6.6 applies.

6.9 The solicitor may only be required to leave the interview if their conduct is such that the interviewer is unable properly to put questions to the suspect. See Notes 6D and 6E

6.10 If the interviewer considers a solicitor is acting in such a way, they will stop the interview and consult an officer not below superintendent rank, if one is readily available, and otherwise an officer not below inspector rank not connected with the investigation. After speaking to the solicitor, the officer consulted will decide if the interview should continue in the presence of that solicitor. If they decide it should not, the suspect will be given the opportunity to consult another solicitor before the interview continues and that solicitor given an opportunity to be present at the interview. See Note 6E

6.11 The removal of a solicitor from an interview is a serious step and, if it occurs, the officer of superintendent rank or above who took the decision will consider if the incident should be reported to the Law Society. If the decision to remove the solicitor has been taken by an officer below superintendent rank, the facts must be reported to an officer of superintendent rank or above who will similarly consider whether a report to the Law Society would be appropriate. When the solicitor concerned is a duty solicitor, the report should be both to the Law Society and to the Legal Services Commission.

6.12 'Solicitor' in this Code means:

- a solicitor who holds a current practising certificate;
- an accredited or probationary representative included on the register of representatives maintained by the Legal Services Commission.

6.12A An accredited or probationary representative sent to provide advice by, and on behalf of, a solicitor shall be admitted to the police station for this purpose unless an officer of inspector rank or above considers such a visit will hinder the investigation and directs otherwise. Hindering the investigation does not include giving proper legal advice to a detainee as in Note 6D. Once admitted to the police station, paragraphs 6.6 to 6.10 apply.

6.13 In exercising their discretion under paragraph 6.12A, the officer should take into account in particular:

- whether:
  - ~ the identity and status of the non-accredited or probationary representative have been satisfactorily established;
  - ~ they are of suitable character to provide legal advice, e.g. a person with a criminal record is unlikely to be suitable unless the conviction was for a minor offence and not recent.
- any other matters in any written letter of authorisation provided by the solicitor on whose behalf the person is attending the police station. See Note 6F

6.14 If the inspector refuses access to an accredited or probationary representative or a decision is taken that such a person should not be permitted to remain at an interview, the inspector must notify the solicitor on whose behalf the representative was acting and give them an opportunity to make alternative arrangements. The detainee must be informed and the custody record noted.

6.15 If a solicitor arrives at the station to see a particular person, that person must, unless Annex B applies, be so informed whether or not they are being interviewed and asked if they would like to see the solicitor. This applies even if the detainee has declined legal advice or, having requested it, subsequently agreed to be interviewed without receiving advice. The solicitor's attendance and the detainee's decision must be noted in the custody record.

(b) Documentation

6.16 Any request for legal advice and the action taken shall be recorded.

6.17 A record shall be made in the interview record if a detainee asks for legal advice and an interview is begun either in the absence of a solicitor or their representative, or they have been required to leave an interview.

Notes for guidance

6A   *In considering if paragraph 6.6(b) applies, the officer should, if practicable, ask the solicitor for an estimate of how long it will take to come to the station and relate this to the time detention is permitted, the time of day (i.e. whether the rest period under paragraph 12.2 is imminent) and the requirements of other investigations. If the solicitor is on their way or is to set off immediately, it will not normally be appropriate to begin an interview before they arrive. If it appears necessary to begin an interview before the solicitor's arrival, they should be given an indication of how long the police would be able to wait before 6.6(b) applies so there is an opportunity to make arrangements for someone else to provide legal advice.*

6B   *A detainee who asks for legal advice should be given an opportunity to consult a specific solicitor or another solicitor from that solicitor's firm or the duty solicitor. If advice is not available by these means, or they do not want to consult the duty solicitor, the detainee should be given an opportunity to choose a solicitor from a list of those willing to provide legal advice. If this solicitor is unavailable, they may choose up to two alternatives. If these attempts are unsuccessful, the custody officer has discretion to allow further attempts until a solicitor has been contacted and agrees to provide legal advice. Apart from carrying out these duties, an officer must not advise the suspect about any particular firm of solicitors.*

6C   *Not Used*

6D   *A detainee has a right to free legal advice and to be represented by a solicitor. The solicitor's only role in the police station is to protect and advance the legal rights of their client. On occasions this may require the solicitor to give advice which has the effect of the client avoiding giving evidence which strengthens a prosecution case. The solicitor may intervene in order to seek clarification, challenge an improper question to their client or the manner in which it is put, advise their client not to reply to particular questions, or if they wish to give their client further legal advice. Paragraph 6.9 only applies if the solicitor's approach or conduct prevents or unreasonably obstructs proper questions being put to the suspect or the suspect's response being recorded. Examples of unacceptable conduct include answering questions on a suspect's behalf or providing written replies for the suspect to quote.*

6E   *An officer who takes the decision to exclude a solicitor must be in a position to satisfy the court the decision was properly made. In order to do this they may need to witness what is happening.*

6F   *If an officer of at least inspector rank considers a particular solicitor or firm of solicitors is persistently sending probationary representatives who are unsuited to provide legal advice, they should inform an officer of at least superintendent rank, who may wish to take the matter up with the Law Society.*

6G   *Subject to the constraints of Annex B, a solicitor may advise more than one client in an investigation if they wish. Any question of a conflict of*

714

interest is for the solicitor under their professional code of conduct. If, however, waiting for a solicitor to give advice to one client may lead to unreasonable delay to the interview with another, the provisions of paragraph 6.6(b) may apply.

6H *In addition to a poster in English, a poster or posters containing translations into Welsh, the main minority ethnic languages and the principal European languages should be displayed wherever they are likely to be helpful and it is practicable to do so.*

6I *Paragraph 6.6(d) requires the authorisation of an officer of inspector rank or above to the continuation of an interview when a detainee who wanted legal advice changes their mind. It is permissible for such authorisation to be given over the telephone, if the authorising officer is able to satisfy themselves about the reason for the detainee's change of mind and is satisfied it is proper to continue the interview in those circumstances.*

6J *Whenever a detainee exercises their right to legal advice by consulting or communicating with a solicitor, they must be allowed to do so in private. This right to consult or communicate in private is fundamental. Except as allowed by the Terrorism Act 2000, Schedule 8, paragraph 9, if the requirement for privacy is compromised because what is said or written by the detainee or solicitor for the purpose of giving and receiving legal advice is overheard, listened to, or read by others without the informed consent of the detainee, the right will effectively have been denied. When a detainee chooses to speak to a solicitor on the telephone, they should be allowed to do so in private unless this is impractical because of the design and layout of the custody area or the location of telephones. However, the normal expectation should be that facilities will be available, unless they are being used, at all police stations to enable detainees to speak in private to a solicitor either face to face or over the telephone.*

6K *A detainee is not obliged to give reasons for declining legal advice and should not be pressed to do so.*

7 Citizens of independent Commonwealth countries or foreign nationals

(a) Action

7.1 Any citizen of an independent Commonwealth country or a national of a foreign country, including the Republic of Ireland, may communicate at any time with the appropriate High Commission, Embassy or Consulate. The detainee must be informed as soon as practicable of:

- this right;
- their right, upon request, to have their High Commission, Embassy or Consulate told of their whereabouts and the grounds for their detention. Such a request should be acted upon as soon as practicable.

7.2 If a detainee is a citizen of a country with which a bilateral consular convention or agreement is in force requiring notification of arrest, the appropriate High Commission, Embassy or Consulate shall be informed as soon as practicable, subject to paragraph 7.4. The countries to which this applies as at 1 April 2003 are listed in Annex F.

7.3 Consular officers may visit one of their nationals in police detention to talk to them and, if required, to arrange for legal advice. Such visits shall take place out of the hearing of a police officer.

7.4   Notwithstanding the provisions of consular conventions, if the detainee is a political refugee whether for reasons of race, nationality, political opinion or religion, or is seeking political asylum, consular officers shall not be informed of the arrest of one of their nationals or given access or information about them except at the detainee's express request.

(b)   Documentation

7.5   A record shall be made when a detainee is informed of their rights under this section and of any communications with a High Commission, Embassy or Consulate.

Note for guidance

7A   *The exercise of the rights in this section may not be interfered with even though Annex B applies.*

8   Conditions of detention

(a)   Action

8.1   So far as it is practicable, not more than one detainee should be detained in each cell.

8.2   Cells in use must be adequately heated, cleaned and ventilated. They must be adequately lit, subject to such dimming as is compatible with safety and security to allow people detained overnight to sleep. No additional restraints shall be used within a locked cell unless absolutely necessary and then only restraint equipment, approved for use in that force by the Chief Officer, which is reasonable and necessary in the circumstances having regard to the detainee's demeanour and with a view to ensuring their safety and the safety of others. If a detainee is deaf, mentally disordered or otherwise mentally vulnerable, particular care must be taken when deciding whether to use any form of approved restraints.

8.3   Blankets, mattresses, pillows and other bedding supplied shall be of a reasonable standard and in a clean and sanitary condition. See Note 8A

8.4   Access to toilet and washing facilities must be provided.

8.5   If it is necessary to remove a detainee's clothes for the purposes of investigation, for hygiene, health reasons or cleaning, replacement clothing of a reasonable standard of comfort and cleanliness shall be provided. A detainee may not be interviewed unless adequate clothing has been offered.

8.6   At least two light meals and one main meal should be offered in any 24 hour period. See Note 8B. Drinks should be provided at meal times and upon reasonable request between meals. Whenever necessary, advice shall be sought from the appropriate health care professional, see Note 9A, on medical and dietary matters. As far as practicable, meals provided shall offer a varied diet and meet any specific dietary needs or religious beliefs the detainee may have. The detainee may, at the custody officer's discretion, have meals supplied by their family or friends at their expense. See Note 8A

8.7   Brief outdoor exercise shall be offered daily if practicable.

8.8   A juvenile shall not be placed in a police cell unless no other secure accommodation is available and the custody officer considers it is not practicable to supervise them if they are not placed in a cell or that a cell provides more comfortable accommodation than other secure accommodation in the station. A juvenile may not be placed in a cell with a detained adult.

(b)   Documentation

8.9[21]   A record must be kept of replacement clothing and meals offered.
8.10[22]   If a juvenile is placed in a cell, the reason must be recorded.
8.11   The use of any restraints on a detainee whilst in a cell, the reasons for it and, if appropriate, the arrangements for enhanced supervision of the detainee whilst so restrained, shall be recorded. See paragraph 3.9

Notes for guidance

8A   *The provisions in paragraph 8.3 and 8.6 respectively are of particular importance in the case of a person detained under the Terrorism Act 2000, immigration detainees and others likely to be detained for an extended period. In deciding whether to allow meals to be supplied by family or friends, the custody officer is entitled to take account of the risk of items being concealed in any food or package and the officer's duties and responsibilities under food handling legislation.*

8B   *Meals should, so far as practicable, be offered at recognised meal times, or at other times that take account of when the detainee last had a meal.*

9   Care and treatment of detained persons

(a)   General

9.1   Nothing in this section prevents the police from calling the police surgeon or, if appropriate, some other health care professional, to examine a detainee for the purposes of obtaining evidence relating to any offence in which the detainee is suspected of being involved. See Note 9A

9.2[23]   If a complaint is made by, or on behalf of, a detainee about their treatment since their arrest, or it comes to notice that a detainee may have been treated improperly, a report must be made as soon as practicable to an officer of inspector rank or above not connected with the investigation. If the matter concerns a possible assault or the possibility of the unnecessary or unreasonable use of force, an appropriate health care professional must also be called as soon as practicable.

9.3[24]   Detainees should be visited at least every hour. If no reasonably foreseeable risk was identified in a risk assessment, see paragraphs 3.6–3.10, there is no need to wake a sleeping detainee. Those suspected of being intoxicated through drink or drugs or whose level of consciousness causes concern must, subject to any clinical directions given by the appropriate health care professional, see paragraph 9.13:

- be visited and roused at least every half hour
- have their condition assessed as in Annex H
- and clinical treatment arranged if appropriate

See Notes 9B, 9C and 9H

---

[21]   Pre-2003 para.8.11.
[22]   Pre-2003 para.8.12.
[23]   Pre-2003 para.9.1.
[24]   Developed from former para.8.10 and Note 8A.

9.4 When arrangements are made to secure clinical attention for a detainee, the custody officer must make sure all relevant information which might assist in the treatment of the detainee's condition is made available to the responsible health care professional. This applies whether or not the health care professional asks for such information. Any officer or police staff with relevant information must inform the custody officer as soon as practicable.

(b) Clinical treatment and attention

9.5[25] The custody officer must make sure a detainee receives appropriate clinical attention as soon as reasonably practicable if the person:
   (a) appears to be suffering from physical illness; or
   (b) is injured; or
   (c) appears to be suffering from a mental disorder; or
   (d) appears to need clinical attention.

9.5A This applies even if the detainee makes no request for clinical attention and whether or not they have already received clinical attention elsewhere. If the need for attention appears urgent, e.g. when indicated as in Annex H, the nearest available health care professional or an ambulance must be called immediately.

9.5B The custody officer must also consider the need for clinical attention as set out in Note for Guidance 9C in relation to those suffering the effects of alcohol or drugs.

9.6[26] Paragraph 9.5 is not meant to prevent or delay the transfer to a hospital if necessary of a person detained under the Mental Health Act 1983, section 136. See Note 9D. When an assessment under that Act takes place at a police station, see paragraph 3.16, the custody officer must consider whether an appropriate health care professional should be called to conduct an initial clinical check on the detainee. This applies particularly when there is likely to be any significant delay in the arrival of a suitably qualified medical practitioner.

9.7[27] If it appears to the custody officer, or they are told, that a person brought to a station under arrest may be suffering from an infectious disease or condition, the custody officer must take reasonable steps to safeguard the health of the detainee and others at the station. In deciding what action to take, advice must be sought from an appropriate health care professional. See Note 9E. The custody officer has discretion to isolate the person and their property until clinical directions have been obtained.

9.8[28] If a detainee requests a clinical examination, an appropriate health care professional must be called as soon as practicable to assess the detainee's clinical needs. If a safe and appropriate care plan cannot be provided, the police surgeon's advice must be sought. The detainee may also be examined by a medical practitioner of their choice at their expense.

9.9[29] If a detainee is required to take or apply any medication in compliance with clinical directions prescribed before their detention, the custody officer must

---

[25] Pre-2003 para.9.2.
[26] Pre-2003 para.9.3.
[27] Pre-2003 para.9.3.
[28] Pre-2003 para.9.4.
[29] Pre-2003 para.9.5.

consult the appropriate health care professional before the use of the medication. Subject to the restrictions in paragraph 9.10, the custody officer is responsible for the safekeeping of any medication and for making sure the detainee is given the opportunity to take or apply prescribed or approved medication. Any such consultation and its outcome shall be noted in the custody record.

9.10[30]   No police officer may administer or supervise the self-administration of controlled drugs of the types and forms listed in the Misuse of Drugs Regulations 2001, Schedule 1, 2 or 3. A detainee may only self-administer such drugs under the personal supervision of the registered medical practitioner authorising their use. Drugs listed in Schedule 4 or 5 may be distributed by the custody officer for self-administration if they have consulted the registered medical practitioner authorising their use, this may be done by telephone, and both parties are satisfied self-administration will not expose the detainee, police officers or anyone else to the risk of harm or injury.

9.11   When appropriate health care professionals administer drugs or other medications, or supervise their self-administration, it must be within current medicines legislation and the scope of practice as determined by their relevant professional body.

9.12[31]   If a detainee has in their possession, or claims to need, medication relating to a heart condition, diabetes, epilepsy or a condition of comparable potential seriousness then, even though paragraph 9.5 may not apply, the advice of the appropriate health care professional must be obtained.

9.13   Whenever the appropriate health care professional is called in accordance with this section to examine or treat a detainee, the custody officer shall ask for their opinion about:

- any risks or problems which police need to take into account when making decisions about the detainee's continued detention;
- when to carry out an interview if applicable; and
- the need for safeguards.

9.14   When clinical directions are given by the appropriate health care professional, whether orally or in writing, and the custody officer has any doubts or is in any way uncertain about any aspect of the directions, the custody officer shall ask for clarification. It is particularly important that directions concerning the frequency of visits are clear, precise and capable of being implemented. See Note 9F.

(c)   Documentation

9.15[32]   A record must be made in the custody record of:

- (a) the arrangements made for an examination by an appropriate health care professional under paragraph 9.2 and of any complaint reported under that paragraph together with any relevant remarks by the custody officer;
- (b) any arrangements made in accordance with paragraph 9.5;
- (c) any request for a clinical examination under paragraph 9.8 and any arrangements made in response;
- (d) the injury, ailment, condition or other reason which made it necessary to make the arrangements in (a) to (c), see Note 9G;

---

[30] Pre-2003 para.9.5.
[31] Pre-2003 para.9.6.
[32] Pre-2003 paras 9.7, 9.8.

(e) any clinical directions and advice, including any further clarifications, given to police by a health care professional concerning the care and treatment of the detainee in connection with any of the arrangements made in (a) to (c), see Note 9F;

(f) if applicable, the responses received when attempting to rouse a person using the procedure in Annex H, see Note 9H.

9.16[33] If a health care professional does not record their clinical findings in the custody record, the record must show where they are recorded. See Note 9G. However, information which is necessary to custody staff to ensure the effective ongoing care and well being of the detainee must be recorded openly in the custody record, see paragraph 3.8 and Annex G, paragraph 7.

9.17[34] Subject to the requirements of Section 4, the custody record shall include:

- a record of all medication a detainee has in their possession on arrival at the police station;
- a note of any such medication they claim to need but do not have with them.

Notes for guidance

9A   A 'health care professional' means a clinically qualified person working within the scope of practice as determined by their relevant professional body. Whether a health care professional is 'appropriate' depends on the circumstances of the duties they carry out at the time.

9B[35]   Whenever possible juveniles and mentally vulnerable detainees should be visited more frequently.

9C[36]   A detainee who appears drunk or behaves abnormally may be suffering from illness, the effects of drugs or may have sustained injury, particularly a head injury which is not apparent. A detainee needing or dependent on certain drugs, including alcohol, may experience harmful effects within a short time of being deprived of their supply. In these circumstances, when there is any doubt, police should always act urgently to call an appropriate health care professional or an ambulance. Paragraph 9.5 does not apply to minor ailments or injuries which do not need attention. However, all such ailments or injuries must be recorded in the custody record and any doubt must be resolved in favour of calling the appropriate health care professional.

9D   Whenever practicable, arrangements should be made for persons detained for assessment under the Mental Health Act 1983, section 136 to be taken to a hospital. There is no power under that Act to transfer a person detained under section 136 from one place of safety to another place of safety for assessment.

9E   It is important to respect a person's right to privacy and information about their health must be kept confidential and only disclosed with their consent or in accordance with clinical advice when it is necessary

[33] Pre-2003 Note 9C.
[34] Pre-2003 para.9.9.
[35] Pre-2003 Note 8A.
[36] Pre-2003 Notes 9A, 9B.

*to protect the detainee's health or that of others who come into contact
with them.*

9F   *The custody officer should always seek to clarify directions that the
detainee requires constant observation or supervision and should ask
the appropriate health care professional to explain precisely what
action needs to be taken to implement such directions.*

9G   *Paragraphs 9.15 and 9.16 do not require any information about the
cause of any injury, ailment or condition to be recorded on the custody
record if it appears capable of providing evidence of an offence.*

9H   *The purpose of recording a person's responses when attempting to rouse
them using the procedure in Annex H is to enable any change in the individual's consciousness level to be noted and clinical treatment arranged
if appropriate.*

10   Cautions

(a)   When a caution must be given

10.1   A person whom there are grounds to suspect of an offence, see Note
10A, must be cautioned before any questions about an offence, or further
questions if the answers provide the grounds for suspicion, are put to them if
either the suspect's answers or silence, (i.e. failure or refusal to answer or
answer satisfactorily) may be given in evidence to a court in a prosecution. A
person need not be cautioned if questions are for other necessary purposes,
e.g.:
   (a)   solely to establish their identity or ownership of any vehicle;
   (b)   to obtain information in accordance with any relevant statutory
         requirement, see paragraph 10.9;
   (c)   in furtherance of the proper and effective conduct of a search,
         e.g. to determine the need to search in the exercise of powers of
         stop and search or to seek co-operation while carrying out a
         search;
   (d)   to seek verification of a written record as in paragraph 11.13;
   (e)   when examining a person in accordance with the Terrorism Act 2000,
         Schedule 7 and the Code of Practice for Examining Officers issued
         under that Act, Schedule 14, paragraph 6.

10.2   Whenever a person not under arrest is initially cautioned, or reminded they
are under caution, that person must at the same time be told they are not under
arrest and are free to leave if they want to. See Note 10C

10.3   A person who is arrested, or further arrested, must be informed at the time,
or as soon as practicable thereafter, that they are under arrest and the grounds for
their arrest, see Note 10B.

10.4   A person who is arrested, or further arrested, must also be cautioned
unless:
   (a)   it is impracticable to do so by reason of their condition or behaviour at
         the time;
   (b)   they have already been cautioned immediately prior to arrest as in
         paragraph 10.1.

(b)   Terms of the cautions

10.5[37]   The caution which must be given on:
    (a)   arrest;
    (b)   all other occasions before a person is charged or informed they may be prosecuted, see section 16,
should, unless the restriction on drawing adverse inferences from silence applies, see Annex C, be in the following terms:

'You do not have to say anything. But it may harm your defence if you do not mention when questioned something which you later rely on in court. Anything you do say may be given in evidence.'

See Note 10G

10.6   Annex C, paragraph 2 sets out the alternative terms of the caution to be used when the restriction on drawing adverse inferences from silence applies.

10.7[38]   Minor deviations from the words of any caution given in accordance with this Code do not constitute a breach of this Code, provided the sense of the relevant caution is preserved. See Note 10D

10.8[39]   After any break in questioning under caution, the person being questioned must be made aware they remain under caution. If there is any doubt the relevant caution should be given again in full when the interview resumes. See Note 10E

10.9[40]   When, despite being cautioned, a person fails to co-operate or to answer particular questions which may affect their immediate treatment, the person should be informed of any relevant consequences and that those consequences are not affected by the caution. Examples are when a person's refusal to provide:

- their name and address when charged may make them liable to detention;
- particulars and information in accordance with a statutory requirement, e.g. under the Road Traffic Act 1988, may amount to an offence or may make the person liable to a further arrest.

(c)   Special warnings under the Criminal Justice and Public Order Act 1994, sections 36 and 37

10.10[41]   When a suspect interviewed at a police station or authorised place of detention after arrest fails or refuses to answer certain questions, or to answer satisfactorily, after due warning, see Note 10F, a court or jury may draw such inferences as appear proper under the Criminal Justice and Public Order Act 1994, sections 36 and 37. Such inferences may only be drawn when:
    (a)   the restriction on drawing adverse inferences from silence, see Annex C, does not apply; and
    (b)   the suspect is arrested by a constable and fails or refuses to account for any objects, marks or substances, or marks on such objects found:
        - on their person;
        - in or on their clothing or footwear;

---

[37] Based on pre-2003 para.10.4.
[38] Pre-2003 para.10.5.
[39] Based on pre-2003 para.10.5C.
[40] Based on pre-2003 para.10.5C.
[41] Pre-2003 para.10.5A.

- otherwise in their possession; or
- in the place they were arrested;

(c) the arrested suspect was found by a constable at a place at or about the time the offence for which that officer has arrested them is alleged to have been committed, and the suspect fails or refuses to account for their presence there.

When the restriction on drawing adverse inferences from silence applies, the suspect may still be asked to account for any of the matters in (b) or (c) but the special warning described in paragraph 10.11 will not apply and must not be given.

10.11[42] For an inference to be drawn when a suspect fails or refuses to answer a question about one of these matters or to answer it satisfactorily, the suspect must first be told in ordinary language:

(a) what offence is being investigated;
(b) what fact they are being asked to account for;
(c) this fact may be due to them taking part in the commission of the offence;
(d) a court may draw a proper inference if they fail or refuse to account for this fact;
(e) a record is being made of the interview and it may be given in evidence if they are brought to trial.

(d) Juveniles and persons who are mentally disordered or otherwise mentally vulnerable

10.12[43] If a juvenile or a person who is mentally disordered or otherwise mentally vulnerable is cautioned in the absence of the appropriate adult, the caution must be repeated in the adult's presence.

(e) Documentation

10.13[44] A record shall be made when a caution is given under this section, either in the interviewer's pocket book or in the interview record.

Notes for guidance

10A There must be some reasonable, objective grounds for the suspicion, based on known facts or information which are relevant to the likelihood the offence has been committed and the person to be questioned committed it.

10B An arrested person must be given sufficient information to enable them to understand they have been deprived of their liberty and the reason they have been arrested, e.g. when a person is arrested on suspicion of committing an offence they must be informed of the suspected offence's nature, when and where it was committed. If the arrest is made under the general arrest conditions in PACE, section 25, the grounds for arrest must include an explanation of the conditions which make the arrest necessary. Vague or technical language should be avoided.

[42] Pre-2003 para.10.5B.
[43] Pre-2003 para.10.6.
[44] Pre-2003 para.10.7.

10C   *The restriction on drawing inferences from silence, see Annex C, para-graph 1, does not apply to a person who has not been detained and who therefore cannot be prevented from seeking legal advice if they want, see paragraph 3.21.*

10D[45] *If it appears a person does not understand the caution, the person giv-ing it should explain it in their own words.*

10E   *It may be necessary to show to the court that nothing occurred during an interview break or between interviews which influenced the suspect's recorded evidence. After a break in an interview or at the beginning of a subsequent interview, the interviewing officer should summarise the reason for the break and confirm this with the suspect.*

10F   *The Criminal Justice and Public Order Act 1994, sections 36 and 37 apply only to suspects who have been arrested by a constable or Cus-toms and Excise officer and are given the relevant warning by the police or customs officer who made the arrest or who is investigating the offence. They do not apply to any interviews with suspects who have not been arrested.*

10G   *Nothing in this Code requires a caution to be given or repeated when informing a person not under arrest they may be prosecuted for an offence. However, a court will not be able to draw any inferences under the Criminal Justice and Public Order Act 1994, section 34, if the person was not cautioned.*

11   Interviews—general

(a)   Action

11.1A   An interview is the questioning of a person regarding their involvement or suspected involvement in a criminal offence or offences which, under para-graph 10.1, must be carried out under caution. Whenever a person is inter-viewed they must be informed of the nature of the offence, or further offence. Procedures under the Road Traffic Act 1988, section 7 or the Transport and Works Act 1992, section 31 do not constitute interviewing for the purpose of this Code.

11.1   Following a decision to arrest a suspect, they must not be interviewed about the relevant offence except at a police station or other authorised place of detention, unless the consequent delay would be likely to:

(a)   lead to:
- interference with, or harm to, evidence connected with an offence;
- interference with, or physical harm to, other people; or
- serious loss of, or damage to, property;

(b)   lead to alerting other people suspected of committing an offence but not yet arrested for it; or

(c)   hinder the recovery of property obtained in consequence of the com-mission of an offence.

Interviewing in any of these circumstances shall cease once the relevant risk has been averted or the necessary questions have been put in order to attempt to avert that risk.

[45] Pre-2003 Note 10C.

11.2 Immediately prior to the commencement or re-commencement of any interview at a police station or other authorised place of detention, the interviewer should remind the suspect of their entitlement to free legal advice and that the interview can be delayed for legal advice to be obtained, unless one of the exceptions in paragraph 6.6 applies. It is the interviewer's responsibility to make sure all reminders are recorded in the interview record.

11.3 Not Used

11.4[46] At the beginning of an interview the interviewer, after cautioning the suspect, see section 10, shall put to them any significant statement or silence which occurred in the presence and hearing of a police officer or other police staff before the start of the interview and which have not been put to the suspect in the course of a previous interview. See Note 11A. The interviewer shall ask the suspect whether they confirm or deny that earlier statement or silence and if they want to add anything.

11.4A[47] A significant statement is one which appears capable of being used in evidence against the suspect, in particular a direct admission of guilt. A significant silence is a failure or refusal to answer a question or answer satisfactorily when under caution, which might, allowing for the restriction on drawing adverse inferences from silence, see Annex C, give rise to an inference under the Criminal Justice and Public Order Act 1994, Part III

11.5[48] No interviewer may try to obtain answers or elicit a statement by the use of oppression. Except as in paragraph 10.9, no interviewer shall indicate, except to answer a direct question, what action will be taken by the police if the person being questioned answers questions, makes a statement or refuses to do either. If the person asks directly what action will be taken if they answer questions, make a statement or refuse to do either, the interviewer may inform them what action the police propose to take provided that action is itself proper and warranted.

11.6[49] The interview or further interview of a person about an offence with which that person has not been charged or for which they have not been informed they may be prosecuted, must cease when:

    (a)   the officer in charge of the investigation is satisfied all the questions they consider relevant to obtaining accurate and reliable information about the offence have been put to the suspect, this includes allowing the suspect an opportunity to give an innocent explanation and asking questions to test if the explanation is accurate and reliable, e.g. to clear up ambiguities or clarify what the suspect said;

    (b)   the officer in charge of the investigation has taken account of any other available evidence; and

    (c)   the officer in charge of the investigation, or in the case of a detained suspect, the custody officer, see paragraph 16.1, reasonably believes there is sufficient evidence to provide a realistic prospect of conviction for that offence. See Note 11B

This paragraph does not prevent officers in revenue cases or acting under the confiscation provisions of the Criminal Justice Act 1988 or the Drug Trafficking Act 1994 from inviting suspects to complete a formal question and answer record after the interview is concluded.

---

[46] Pre-2003 para.11.2A.
[47] Pre-2003 para.11.2A.
[48] Pre-2003 para.11.3.
[49] Pre-2003 para.11.7.

(b)   Interview records

11.7[50] (a) An accurate record must be made of each interview, whether or not the interview takes place at a police station

(b)   The record must state the place of interview, the time it begins and ends, any interview breaks and, subject to paragraph 2.6A, the names of all those present; and must be made on the forms provided for this purpose or in the interviewer's pocket book or in accordance with the Codes of Practice E or F;

(c)   Any written record must be made and completed during the interview, unless this would not be practicable or would interfere with the conduct of the interview, and must constitute either a verbatim record of what has been said or, failing this, an account of the interview which adequately and accurately summarises it.

11.8[51]   If a written record is not made during the interview it must be made as soon as practicable after its completion.

11.9[52]   Written interview records must be timed and signed by the maker.

11.10   If a written record is not completed during the interview the reason must be recorded in the interview record.

11.11[53]   Unless it is impracticable, the person interviewed shall be given the opportunity to read the interview record and to sign it as correct or to indicate how they consider it inaccurate. If the person interviewed cannot read or refuses to read the record or sign it, the senior interviewer present shall read it to them and ask whether they would like to sign it as correct or make their mark or to indicate how they consider it inaccurate. The interviewer shall certify on the interview record itself what has occurred. See Note 11E

11.12[54]   If the appropriate adult or the person's solicitor is present during the interview, they should also be given an opportunity to read and sign the interview record or any written statement taken down during the interview.

11.13[55]   A written record shall be made of any comments made by a suspect, including unsolicited comments, which are outside the context of an interview but which might be relevant to the offence. Any such record must be timed and signed by the maker. When practicable the suspect shall be given the opportunity to read that record and to sign it as correct or to indicate how they consider it inaccurate. See Note 11E

11.14[56]   Any refusal by a person to sign an interview record when asked in accordance with this Code must itself be recorded.

(c)   Juveniles and mentally disordered or otherwise mentally vulnerable people

11.15[57]   A juvenile or person who is mentally disordered or otherwise mentally vulnerable must not be interviewed regarding their involvement or suspected involvement in a criminal offence or offences, or asked to provide or sign a

---

[50] Pre-2003 para.11.7.
[51] Pre-2003 para.11.8.
[52] Pre-2003 para.11.9.
[53] Pre-2003 para.11.10.
[54] Pre-2003 para.11.11.
[55] Pre-2003 para.11.13.
[56] Pre-2003 para.11.12.
[57] Pre-2003 para.11.14.

written statement under caution or record of interview, in the absence of the appropriate adult unless paragraphs 11.1, 11.18 to 11.20 apply. See Note 11C

11.16[58]   Juveniles may only be interviewed at their place of education in exceptional circumstances and only when the principal or their nominee agrees. Every effort should be made to notify the parent(s) or other person responsible for the juvenile's welfare and the appropriate adult, if this is a different person, that the police want to interview the juvenile and reasonable time should be allowed to enable the appropriate adult to be present at the interview. If awaiting the appropriate adult would cause unreasonable delay, and unless the juvenile is suspected of an offence against the educational establishment, the principal or their nominee can act as the appropriate adult for the purposes of the interview.

11.17[59]   If an appropriate adult is present at an interview, they shall be informed:
- they are not expected to act simply as an observer; and
- the purpose of their presence is to:
    - ~ advise the person being interviewed;
    - ~ observe whether the interview is being conducted properly and fairly;
    - ~ facilitate communication with the person being interviewed.

(d)   Vulnerable suspects—urgent interviews at police stations

11.18[60]   The following persons may not be interviewed unless an officer of superintendent rank or above considers delay will lead to the consequences in paragraph 11.1(a) to (c), and is satisfied the interview would not significantly harm the person's physical or mental state (see Annex G):

(a)   a juvenile or person who is mentally disordered or otherwise mentally vulnerable if at the time of the interview the appropriate adult is not present;

(b)   anyone other than in (a) who at the time of the interview appears unable to:
- appreciate the significance of questions and their answers; or
- understand what is happening because of the effects of drink, drugs or any illness, ailment or condition;

(c)   a person who has difficulty understanding English or has a hearing disability, if at the time of the interview an interpreter is not present.

11.19   These interviews may not continue once sufficient information has been obtained to avert the consequences in paragraph 11.1(a) to (c).

11.20   A record shall be made of the grounds for any decision to interview a person under paragraph 11.18.

Notes for guidance

11A   Paragraph 11.4 does not prevent the interviewer from putting significant statements and silences to a suspect again at a later stage or a further interview.

11B   The Criminal Procedure and Investigations Act 1996 Code of Practice, paragraph 3.4 states 'In conducting an investigation, the investigator

---

[58] Pre-2003 para.11.15.
[59] Pre-2003 para.11.16.
[60] Paras 11.18 to 11.20 are based on pre-2003 C Annex C.

should pursue all reasonable lines of enquiry, whether these point towards or away from the suspect. What is reasonable will depend on the particular circumstances.' Interviewers should keep this in mind when deciding what questions to ask in an interview.

11C[61] *Although juveniles or people who are mentally disordered or otherwise mentally vulnerable are often capable of providing reliable evidence, they may, without knowing or wishing to do so, be particularly prone in certain circumstances to provide information that may be unreliable, misleading or self-incriminating. Special care should always be taken when questioning such a person, and the appropriate adult should be involved if there is any doubt about a person's age, mental state or capacity. Because of the risk of unreliable evidence it is also important to obtain corroboration of any facts admitted whenever possible.*

11D[62] *Juveniles should not be arrested at their place of education unless this is unavoidable. When a juvenile is arrested at their place of education, the principal or their nominee must be informed.*

11E   Significant statements described in paragraph 11.4 will always be relevant to the offence and must be recorded. When a suspect agrees to read records of interviews and other comments and sign them as correct, they should be asked to endorse the record with, e.g. 'I agree that this is a correct record of what was said' and add their signature. If the suspect does not agree with the record, the interviewer should record the details of any disagreement and ask the suspect to read these details and sign them to the effect that they accurately reflect their disagreement. Any refusal to sign should be recorded.

12   Interviews in police stations

(a)   Action

12.1   If a police officer wants to interview or conduct enquiries which require the presence of a detainee, the custody officer is responsible for deciding whether to deliver the detainee into the officer's custody.

12.2   Except as below, in any period of 24 hours a detainee must be allowed a continuous period of at least 8 hours for rest, free from questioning, travel or any interruption in connection with the investigation concerned. This period should normally be at night or other appropriate time which takes account of when the detainee last slept or rested. If a detainee is arrested at a police station after going there voluntarily, the period of 24 hours runs from the time of their arrest and not the time of arrival at the police station. The period may not be interrupted or delayed, except:

 (a)   when there are reasonable grounds for believing not delaying or interrupting the period would:

   (i)   involve a risk of harm to people or serious loss of, or damage to, property;

   (ii)   delay unnecessarily the person's release from custody;

   (iii)   otherwise prejudice the outcome of the investigation;

---

[61] Pre-2003 Note 11B.
[62] Pre-2003 Note 11C.

    (b)   at the request of the detainee, their appropriate adult or legal representative;

    (c)   when a delay or interruption is necessary in order to:

        (i)   comply with the legal obligations and duties arising under section 15;

        (ii) to take action required under section 9 or in accordance with medical advice.

If the period is interrupted in accordance with (a), a fresh period must be allowed. Interruptions under (b) and (c), do not require a fresh period to be allowed.

12.3   Before a detainee is interviewed the custody officer, in consultation with the officer in charge of the investigation and appropriate health care professionals as necessary, shall assess whether the detainee is fit enough to be interviewed. This means determining and considering the risks to the detainee's physical and mental state if the interview took place and determining what safeguards are needed to allow the interview to take place. See Annex G. The custody officer shall not allow a detainee to be interviewed if the custody officer considers it would cause significant harm to the detainee's physical or mental state. Vulnerable suspects listed at paragraph 11.18 shall be treated as always being at some risk during an interview and these persons may not be interviewed except in accordance with paragraphs 11.18 to 11.20.

12.4   As far as practicable interviews shall take place in interview rooms which are adequately heated, lit and ventilated.

12.5   A suspect whose detention without charge has been authorised under PACE, because the detention is necessary for an interview to obtain evidence of the offence for which they have been arrested, may choose not to answer questions but police do not require the suspect's consent or agreement to interview them for this purpose. If a suspect takes steps to prevent themselves being questioned or further questioned, e.g. by refusing to leave their cell to go to a suitable interview room or by trying to leave the interview room, they shall be advised their consent or agreement to interview is not required. The suspect shall be cautioned as in section 10, and informed if they fail or refuse to co-operate, the interview may take place in the cell and that their failure or refusal to co-operate may be given in evidence. The suspect shall then be invited to co-operate and go into the interview room.

12.6[63]   People being questioned or making statements shall not be required to stand.

12.7[64]   Before the interview commences each interviewer shall, subject to paragraph 2.6A, identify themselves and any other persons present to the interviewee.

12.8[65]   Breaks from interviewing should be made at recognised meal times or at other times that take account of when an interviewee last had a meal. Short refreshment breaks shall be provided at approximately two hour intervals, subject to the interviewer's discretion to delay a break if there are reasonable grounds for believing it would:

    (i)   involve a:

        ●   risk of harm to people;

        ●   serious loss of, or damage to, property;

---

[63] Pre-2003 para.12.5.

[64] Pre-2003 para.12.6.

[65] Pre-2003 para.12.7.

(ii) unnecessarily delay the detainee's release;

(iii) otherwise prejudice the outcome of the investigation.

See Note 12B

12.9[66]   If during the interview a complaint is made by or on behalf of the interviewee concerning the provisions of this Code, the interviewer should:

(i) record it in the interview record;

(ii) inform the custody officer, who is then responsible for dealing with it as in section 9.

(b)   Documentation

12.10[67]   A record must be made of the:

- time a detainee is not in the custody of the custody officer, and why
- reason for any refusal to deliver the detainee out of that custody

12.11   A record shall be made of:

(a) the reasons it was not practicable to use an interview room; and

(b) any action taken as in paragraph 12.5.

The record shall be made on the custody record or in the interview record for action taken whilst an interview record is being kept, with a brief reference to this effect in the custody record.

12.12[68]   Any decision to delay a break in an interview must be recorded, with reasons, in the interview record.

12.13[69]   All written statements made at police stations under caution shall be written on forms provided for the purpose.

12.14[70]   All written statements made under caution shall be taken in accordance with Annex D. Before a person makes a written statement under caution at a police station they shall be reminded about the right to legal advice. See Note 12A

Notes for guidance

12A   *It is not normally necessary to ask for a written statement if the interview was recorded or taped at the time and the record signed by the interviewee in accordance with paragraph 11.11. Statements under caution should normally be taken in these circumstances only at the person's express wish. A person may however be asked if they want to make such a statement.*

12B[71] *Meal breaks should normally last at least 45 minutes and shorter breaks after two hours should last at least 15 minutes. If the interviewer delays a break in accordance with paragraph 12.8 and prolongs the interview, a longer break should be provided. If there is a short interview, and another short interview is contemplated, the length of the break may be reduced if there are reasonable grounds to believe this is necessary to avoid any of the consequences in paragraph 12.8(i) to (iii).*

[66] Pre-2003 para.12.8.
[67] Pre-2003 para.12.9.
[68] Pre-2003 para.12.11.
[69] Pre-2003 para.12.12.
[70] Pre-2003 para.12.13.
[71] Pre-2003 Note 12C.

13   Interpreters

(a)   General

13.1   Chief officers are responsible for making sure appropriate arrangements are in place for provision of suitably qualified interpreters for people who:
- are deaf;
- do not understand English.

Whenever possible, interpreters should be drawn from the National Register of Public Service Interpreters (NRPSI).

(b)   Foreign languages

13.2   Unless paragraphs 11.1, 11.18 to 11.20 apply, a person must not be interviewed in the absence of a person capable of interpreting if:
- (a)   they have difficulty understanding English;
- (b)   the interviewer cannot speak the person's own language;
- (c)   the person wants an interpreter present.

13.3   The interviewer shall make sure the interpreter makes a note of the interview at the time in the person's language for use in the event of the interpreter being called to give evidence, and certifies its accuracy. The interviewer should allow sufficient time for the interpreter to note each question and answer after each is put, given and interpreted. The person should be allowed to read the record or have it read to them and sign it as correct or indicate the respects in which they consider it inaccurate. If the interview is tape-recorded or visually recorded, the arrangements in Code E or F apply.

13.4   In the case of a person making a statement to a police officer or other police staff other than in English:
- (a)   the interpreter shall record the statement in the language it is made;
- (b)   the person shall be invited to sign it;
- (c)   an official English translation shall be made in due course.

(c)   Deaf people and people with speech difficulties

13.5   If a person appears to be deaf or there is doubt about their hearing or speaking ability, they must not be interviewed in the absence of an interpreter unless they agree in writing to being interviewed without one or paragraphs 11.1, 11.18 to 11.20 apply.

13.6   An interpreter should also be called if a juvenile is interviewed and the parent or guardian present as the appropriate adult appears to be deaf or there is doubt about their hearing or speaking ability, unless they agree in writing to the interview proceeding without one or paragraphs 11.1, 11.18 to 11.20 apply.

13.7   The interviewer shall make sure the interpreter is allowed to read the interview record and certify its accuracy in the event of the interpreter being called to give evidence. If the interview is tape-recorded or visually recorded, the arrangements in Code E or F apply.

(d)   Additional rules for detained persons

13.8   All reasonable attempts should be made to make the detainee understand that interpreters will be provided at public expense.

13.9　If paragraph 6.1 applies and the detainee cannot communicate with the solicitor because of language, hearing or speech difficulties, an interpreter must be called. The interpreter may not be a police officer or civilian support staff when interpretation is needed for the purposes of obtaining legal advice. In all other cases a police officer or civilian support staff may only interpret if the detainee and the appropriate adult, if applicable, give their agreement in writing or if the interview is tape-recorded or visually recorded as in Code E or F.

13.10　When the custody officer cannot establish effective communication with a person charged with an offence who appears deaf or there is doubt about their ability to hear, speak or to understand English, arrangements must be made as soon as practicable for an interpreter to explain the offence and any other information given by the custody officer.

(e)　Documentation

13.11　Action taken to call an interpreter under this section and any agreement to be interviewed in the absence of an interpreter must be recorded.

14　Questioning—special restrictions

14.1　If a person is arrested by one police force on behalf of another and the lawful period of detention in respect of that offence has not yet commenced in accordance with PACE, section 41 no questions may be put to them about the offence while they are in transit between the forces except to clarify any voluntary statement they make.

14.2　If a person is in police detention at a hospital they may not be questioned without the agreement of a responsible doctor. See Note 14A

Note for guidance

14A　If questioning takes place at a hospital under paragraph 14.2, or on the way to or from a hospital, the period of questioning concerned counts towards the total period of detention permitted.

15　Reviews and extensions of detention

(a)　Persons detained under PACE

15.1　The review officer is responsible under PACE, section 40 for periodically determining if a person's detention, before or after charge, continues to be necessary. This requirement continues throughout the detention period and except as in paragraph 15.10, the review officer must be present at the police station holding the detainee. See Notes 15A and 15B

15.2　Under PACE, section 42, an officer of superintendent rank or above who is responsible for the station holding the detainee may give authority any time after the second review to extend the maximum period the person may be detained without charge by up to 12 hours. Further detention without charge may be authorised only by a magistrates' court in accordance with PACE, sections 43 and 44. See Notes 15C, 15D and 15E

15.2A　Section 42(1) of PACE as amended extends the maximum period of detention for arrestable offences from 24 hours to 36 hours. Detaining a juvenile or mentally vulnerable person for longer than 24 hours will de dependent on the circumstances of the case and with regard to the person's:

(a) special vulnerability;

(b) the legal obligation to provide an opportunity for representations to be made prior to a decision about extending detention;

(c) the need to consult and consider the views of any appropriate adult; and

(d) any alternatives to police custody.

15.3[72] Before deciding whether to authorise continued detention the officer responsible under paragraphs 15.1 or 15.2 shall give an opportunity to make representations about the detention to:

(a) the detainee, unless in the case of a review as in paragraph 15.1, the detainee is asleep;

(b) the detainee's solicitor if available at the time; and

(c) the appropriate adult if available at the time.

15.3A[73] Other people having an interest in the detainee's welfare may also make representations at the authorising officer's discretion.

15.3B Subject to paragraph 15.10, the representations may be made orally in person or by telephone or in writing. The authorising officer may, however, refuse to hear oral representations from the detainee if the officer considers them unfit to make representations because of their condition or behaviour. See Note 15C

15.3C The decision on whether the review takes place in person or by telephone or by video conferencing (see Note 15G) is a matter for the review officer. In determining the form the review may take, the review officer must always take full account of the needs of the person in custody. The benefits of carrying out a review in person should always be considered, based on the individual circumstances of each case with specific additional consideration if the person is:

(a) a juvenile (and the age of the juvenile); or

(b) mentally vulnerable; or

(c) has been subject to medical attention for other than routine minor ailments; or

there are presentational or community issues around the person's detention.

15.4[74] Before conducting a review or determining whether to extend the maximum period of detention without charge, the officer responsible must make sure the detainee is reminded of their entitlement to free legal advice, see paragraph 6.5, unless in the case of a review the person is asleep.

15.5[75] If, after considering any representations, the officer decides to keep the detainee in detention or extend the maximum period they may be detained without charge, any comment made by the detainee shall be recorded. If applicable, the officer responsible under paragraph 15.1 or 15.2 shall be informed of the comment as soon as practicable. See also paragraphs 11.4 and 11.13

15.6[76] No officer shall put specific questions to the detainee:

● regarding their involvement in any offence; or

● in respect of any comments they may make;

~ when given the opportunity to make representations; or

~ in response to a decision to keep them in detention or extend the maximum period of detention.

[72] From pre-2003 para.15.1.

[73] From pre-2003 para.15.1.

[74] Pre-2003 para.15.3.

[75] Based on para.15.2A.

[76] Based on para.15.2A.

Such an exchange could constitute an interview as in paragraph 11.1A and would be subject to the associated safeguards in section 11 and, in respect of a person who has been charged, paragraph 16.5. See also paragraph 11.13

15.7   A detainee who is asleep at a review, see paragraph 15.1, and whose continued detention is authorised must be informed about the decision and reason as soon as practicable after waking.

(b)   Persons detained under the Terrorism Act 2000

15.8   In terrorism cases:
    (a)   the powers and duties of the review officer are in the Terrorism Act 2000, Schedule 8, Part II;
    (b)   a police officer of at least superintendent rank may apply to a judicial authority for a warrant of further detention under the Terrorism Act 2000, Schedule 8, Part III.

(c)   Telephone review of detention

15.9   PACE, section 40A provides that the officer responsible under section 40 for reviewing the detention of a person who has not been charged, need not attend the police station holding the detainee and may carry out the review by telephone.

15.9A   PACE, section 45A(2) provides that the officer responsible under section 40 for reviewing the detention of a person who has not been charged, need not attend the police station holding the detainee and may carry out the review by video conferencing facilities (See Note 15G).

15.9B   A telephone review is not permitted where facilities for review by video conferencing exist and it is practicable to use them.

15.9C   The review officer can decide at any stage that a telephone review or review by video conferencing should be terminated and that the review will be conducted in person. The reasons for doing so should be noted in the custody record.
See Note 15F

15.10   When a telephone review is carried out, an officer at the station holding the detainee shall be required by the review officer to fulfil that officer's obligations under PACE section 40 or this Code by:
    (a)   making any record connected with the review in the detainee's custody record;
    (b)   if applicable, making a record in (a) in the presence of the detainee; and
    (c)   giving the detainee information about the review.

15.11   When a telephone review is carried out, the requirement in paragraph 15.3 will be satisfied:
    (a)   if facilities exist for the immediate transmission of written representations to the review officer, e.g. fax or email message, by giving the detainee an opportunity to make representations:
        (i)   orally by telephone; or
        (ii)   in writing using those facilities; and
    (b)   in all other cases, by giving the detainee an opportunity to make their representations orally by telephone.

(d)   Documentation

15.12[77]   It is the officer's responsibility to make sure all reminders given under paragraph 15.4 are noted in the custody record.

15.13[78]   The grounds for, and extent of, any delay in conducting a review shall be recorded.

15.14   When a telephone review is carried out, a record shall be made of:

(a)   the reason the review officer did not attend the station holding the detainee;

(b)   the place the review officer was;

(c)   the method representations, oral or written, were made to the review officer, see paragraph 15.11.

15.15[79]   Any written representations shall be retained.

15.16[80]   A record shall be made as soon as practicable about the outcome of each review or determination whether to extend the maximum detention period without charge or an application for a warrant of further detention or its extension. If paragraph 15.7 applies, a record shall also be made of when the person was informed and by whom. If an authorisation is given under PACE, section 42, the record shall state the number of hours and minutes by which the detention period is extended or further extended. If a warrant for further detention, or exten sion, is granted under section 43 or 44, the record shall state the detention period authorised by the warrant and the date and time it was granted.

Notes for guidance

15A   *Review officer for the purposes of:*

- *PACE, sections 40 and 40A means, in the case of a person arrested but not charged, an officer of at least inspector rank not directly involved in the investigation and, if a person has been arrested and charged, the custody officer;*

- *the Terrorism Act 2000, means an officer not directly involved in the investigation connected with the detention and of at least inspector rank, for reviews within 24 hours of the detainee's arrest or superintendent for all other reviews.*

15B   *The detention of persons in police custody not subject to the statutory review requirement in paragraph 15.1 should still be reviewed periodically as a matter of good practice. Such reviews can be carried out by an officer of the rank of sergeant or above.The purpose of such reviews is to check the particular power under which a detainee is held continues to apply, any associated conditions are complied with and to make sure appropriate action is taken to deal with any changes. This includes the detainee's prompt release when the power no longer applies, or their transfer if the power requires the detainee be taken elsewhere as soon as the necessary arrangements are made. Examples include persons:*

(a)   *arrested on warrant because they failed to answer bail to appear at court or failed to answer street bail;*

---

[77] From para.15.3.
[78] Pre-2003 para.15.4.
[79] Pre-2003 para.15.5.
[80] First sentence from para.15.6.

    (b) *arrested under the Bail Act 1976, section 7(3) for breaching a con-dition of bail granted after charge;*

    (c) *in police custody for specific purposes and periods under the Crime (Sentences) Act 1997, Schedule 1;*

    (d) *convicted, or remand prisoners, held in police stations on behalf of the Prison Service under the Imprisonment (Temporary Provisions) Act 1980, section 6;*

    (e) *being detained to prevent them causing a breach of the peace;*

    (f) *detained at police stations on behalf of the Immigration Service.*

    The detention of persons remanded into police detention by order of a court under the Magistrates' Courts Act 1980, section 128 is subject to a statutory requirement to review that detention. This is to make sure the detainee is taken back to court no later than the end of the period autho-rised by the court or when the need for their detention by police ceases, whichever is the sooner.

15C *In the case of a review of detention, but not an extension, the detainee need not be woken for the review. However, if the detainee is likely to be asleep, e.g. during a period of rest allowed as in paragraph 12.2, at the latest time a review or authorisation to extend detention may take place, the officer should, if the legal obligations and time constraints permit, bring forward the procedure to allow the detainee to make representa-tions. A detainee not asleep during the review must be present when the grounds for their continued detention are recorded and must at the same time be informed of those grounds unless the review officer considers the person is incapable of understanding what is said, violent or likely to become violent or in urgent need of medical attention.*

15D[81] *An application to a Magistrates' Court under PACE, sections 43 or 44 for a warrant of further detention or its extension should be made between 10am and 9pm, and if possible during normal court hours. It will not usually be practicable to arrange for a court to sit specially out-side the hours of 10am to 9pm. If it appears a special sitting may be needed outside normal court hours but between 10am and 9pm, the clerk to the justices should be given notice and informed of this possibility, while the court is sitting if possible.*

15E *In paragraph 15.2, the officer responsible for the station holding the detainee includes a superintendent or above who, in accordance with their force operational policy or police regulations, is given that respon-sibility on a temporary basis whilst the appointed long-term holder is off duty or otherwise unavailable.*

15F *The provisions of PACE, section 40A allowing telephone reviews do not apply to reviews of detention after charge by the custody officer or to reviews under the Terrorism Act 2000, Schedule 8, Part II in terror-ism cases. When video conferencing is not required, they allow the use of a telephone to carry out a review of detention before charge. The procedure under PACE, section 42 must be done in person.*

15G *The use of video conferencing facilities for decisions about detention under section 45A of PACE is subject to the introduction of regulations by the Secretary of State*

---

[81] Pre-2003 Note 15B.

16   Charging detained persons

(a)   Action

16.1   When the officer in charge of the investigation reasonably believes there is sufficient evidence to provide a realistic prospect of conviction, see paragraph 11.6, they shall without delay, and subject to the following qualification, inform the custody officer who will be responsible for considering whether the detainee should be charged. See Notes 11B and 16A. When a person is detained in respect of more than one offence it is permissible to delay informing the custody officer until the above conditions are satisfied in respect of all the offences, but see paragraph 11.6. If the detainee is a juvenile, mentally disordered or otherwise mentally vulnerable, any resulting action shall be taken in the presence of the appropriate adult if they are present at the time. See Note 16B and 16C

16.1A   'Where guidance issued by the Director of Public Prosecutions under section 37A is in force the custody officer must comply with that Guidance in deciding how to act in dealing with the detainee. See Note 16AB.'

16.1B   Where in compliance with the DPP's Guidance the custody officer decides that the case should be immediately referred to the CPS to make the charging decision, consultation should take place with a Crown Prosecutor as soon as is reasonably practicable. Where the Crown Prosecutor is unable to make the charging decision on the information available at that time, the detainee may be released without charge and on bail (with conditions if necessary) under section 37(7)(a). In such circumstances, the detainee should be informed that they are being released to enable the Director of Public Prosecutions to make a decision under section 37B.

16.2   When a detainee is charged with or informed they may be prosecuted for an offence, see Note 16B, they shall, unless the restriction on drawing adverse inferences from silence applies, see Annex C, be cautioned as follows:

'You do not have to say anything. But it may harm your defence if you do not mention now something which you later rely on in court. Anything you do say may be given in evidence.'

Annex C, paragraph 2 sets out the alternative terms of the caution to be used when the restriction on drawing adverse inferences from silence applies.

16.3   When a detainee is charged they shall be given a written notice showing particulars of the offence and, subject to paragraph 2.6A, the officer's name and the case reference number. As far as possible the particulars of the charge shall be stated in simple terms, but they shall also show the precise offence in law with which the detainee is charged. The notice shall begin:

'You are charged with the offence(s) shown below.' Followed by the caution.

If the detainee is a juvenile, mentally disordered or otherwise mentally vulnerable, the notice should be given to the appropriate adult.

16.4   If, after a detainee has been charged with or informed they may be prosecuted for an offence, an officer wants to tell them about any written statement or interview with another person relating to such an offence, the detainee shall either be handed a true copy of the written statement or the content of the interview record brought to their attention. Nothing shall be done to invite any reply or comment except to:

(a)   caution the detainee, 'You do not have to say anything, but anything you do say may be given in evidence.'; and

(b)   remind the detainee about their right to legal advice.

16.4A[82]   If the detainee:
- cannot read, the document may be read to them
- is a juvenile, mentally disordered or otherwise mentally vulnerable, the appropriate adult shall also be given a copy, or the interview record shall be brought to their attention

16.5   A detainee may not be interviewed about an offence after they have been charged with, or informed they may be prosecuted for it, unless the interview is necessary:
- to prevent or minimise harm or loss to some other person, or the public
- to clear up an ambiguity in a previous answer or statement
- in the interests of justice for the detainee to have put to them, and have an opportunity to comment on, information concerning the offence which has come to light since they were charged or informed they might be prosecuted

Before any such interview, the interviewer shall:
- (a)   caution the detainee, 'You do not have to say anything, but anything you do say may be given in evidence.';
- (b)   remind the detainee about their right to legal advice.

See Note 16B

16.6   The provisions of paragraphs 16.2 to 16.5 must be complied with in the appropriate adult's presence if they are already at the police station. If they are not at the police station then these provisions must be complied with again in their presence when they arrive unless the detainee has been released.

See Note 16C

16.7[83]   When a juvenile is charged with an offence and the custody officer authorises their continued detention after charge, the custody officer must try to make arrangements for the juvenile to be taken into the care of a local authority to be detained pending appearance in court unless the custody officer certifies it is impracticable to do so or, in the case of a juvenile of at least 12 years old, no secure accommodation is available and there is a risk to the public of serious harm from that juvenile, in accordance with PACE, section 38(6). See Note 16D

(b)   Documentation

16.8[84]   A record shall be made of anything a detainee says when charged.

16.9[85]   Any questions put in an interview after charge and answers given relating to the offence shall be recorded in full during the interview on forms for that purpose and the record signed by the detainee or, if they refuse, by the interviewer and any third parties present. If the questions are tape recorded or visually recorded the arrangements in Code E or F apply.

16.10[86]   If it is not practicable to make arrangements for a juvenile's transfer into local authority care as in paragraph 16.7, the custody officer must record the reasons and complete a certificate to be produced before the court with the juvenile. See Note 16D

---

[82] From pre-2003 para.16.4.
[83] Pre-2003 para.16.7.
[84] Pre-2003 para.16.7.
[85] Pre-2003 para.16.8.
[86] Pre-2003 para.16.9.

Notes for guidance

16AB Where Guidance issued by the Director of Public Prosecutions under section 37B is in force, custody officers are entitled (notwithstanding section 37(1)) to take reasonable time to apply that guidance in deciding how a detained person is to be dealt with in accordance with section 37(7), as amended by Schedule 2 of the Criminal Justice Act 2003, including where appropriate consultation with a Duty Prosecutor. Where in accordance with the Guidance the case is referred to the CPS for decision, the custody officer should ensure that an officer involved in the investigation sends to the CPS such information as is specified in the Guidance.

16A The custody officer must take into account alternatives to prosecution under the Crime and Disorder Act 1998, reprimands and warning applicable to persons under 18, and in national guidance on the cautioning of offenders, for persons aged 18 and over.

16B The giving of a warning or the service of the Notice of Intended Prosecution required by the Road Traffic Offenders Act 1988, section 1 does not amount to informing a detainee they may be prosecuted for an offence and so does not preclude further questioning in relation to that offence.

16C There is no power under PACE to detain a person and delay action under paragraphs 16.2 to 16.5 solely to await the arrival of the appropriate adult. After charge, bail cannot be refused, or release on bail delayed, simply because an appropriate adult is not available, unless the absence of that adult provides the custody officer with the necessary grounds to authorise detention after charge under PACE, section 38.

16D[87] Except as in paragraph 16.7, neither a juvenile's behaviour nor the nature of the offence provides grounds for the custody officer to decide it is impracticable to arrange the juvenile's transfer to local authority care. Similarly, the lack of secure local authority accommodation does not make it impracticable to transfer the juvenile. The availability of secure accommodation is only a factor in relation to a juvenile aged 12 or over when the local authority accommodation would not be adequate to protect the public from serious harm from them. The obligation to transfer a juvenile to local authority accommodation applies as much to a juvenile charged during the daytime as to a juvenile to be held overnight, subject to a requirement to bring the juvenile before a court under PACE, section 46.

17[88] Testing persons for the presence of specified Class A drugs

(a) Action

17.1   A sample of urine or a non-intimate sample may be taken from a person in police detention for the purpose of ascertaining whether he has any specified Class A drugs in his body if:

(a)   he has been charged with a trigger offence; or

(b)   he has been charged with any offence and a police officer of inspector rank or above, who has reasonable grounds for suspecting that the

---

[87] Pre-2003 Note 16B.

[88] s.17 was only in force in certain areas—see para.5–12 and Annexes I and J.

misuse by that person of any specified Class A drug caused or contributed to the offence, has authorised the sample to be taken.

17.2 The person from whom the sample is taken must have attained the minimum age for drug testing under the provisions in force in the police area or police station concerned (14 or 18 years of age). See Note 17F..

17.3 A police officer must have requested the person concerned to give the sample.

17.4 Before requesting a sample from the person concerned, an officer must:

    (a) inform him that the purpose of taking the sample is for drug testing under PACE. This is to ascertain whether he has a specified Class A drug present in his body;

    (b) warn him that if, when so requested, he fails without good cause to provide a sample he may be liable to prosecution;

    (c) where the taking of the sample has been authorised by an inspector or above under paragraph 17.1(b) of this Code, inform him that the authorisation has been given and the grounds for giving it;

    (d) remind him of the following rights, which may be exercised at any stage during the period in custody:

      (i) the right to have someone informed of his arrest; [See section 5]

      (ii) the right to consult privately with a solicitor and the fact that free independent legal advice is available ; [See section 6] and

      (iii) the right to consult these Codes of Practice. [See section 3]

17.5 In the case of a person who has not attained the age of 17 —

    (a) the making of the request for a sample under paragraph 17.3 above;

    (b) the giving of the warning and the information under paragraph 17.4 above; and

    (c) the taking of the sample,

may not take place except in the presence of an appropriate adult. (see Note 17G)

17.6 Authorisation by an officer of the rank of inspector or above within paragraph 17.1(b) may be given orally or in writing, but if it is given orally it must be confirmed in writing as soon as practicable.

17.7 Custody officers may authorise continued detention for up to six hours from the time of charge to enable a sample to be taken.

(b) Documentation

17.8 If a sample is taken following authorisation by an officer of the rank of inspector or above, the authorisation and the grounds for suspicion must be recorded in the custody record.

17.9 The giving of a warning on the consequences of failure to provide a specimen must be recorded in the custody record.

17.10 The time of charge and the time at which the sample was given must be recorded in the custody record.

(c) General

17.11 A sample may only be taken by a prescribed person.

17.12 Force may not be used to take any sample for the purpose of drug testing.

17.13 The terms 'Class A drug' and 'misuse' have the same meaning as in the Misuse of Drugs Act 1971. 'Specified' (in relation to a Class A drug) and 'trigger offence' have the same meanings as in Part III of the Criminal Justice and Court Services Act 2000.

17.14   Any sample taken:

(a)   may not be used for any purpose other than to ascertain whether the person concerned has a specified Class A drug present in his body; and

(b)   must be retained until court proceedings have been concluded.

Notes for guidance

17A   When warning a person who is asked to provide a urine or non-intimate sample in accordance with paragraph 17.1, the following form of words may be used:

'You do not have to provide a sample, but I must warn you that if you fail or refuse without good cause to do so, you will commit an offence for which you may be imprisoned, or fined, or both.'

17B   A sample has to be sufficient and suitable. A sufficient sample is sufficient in quantity and quality to enable drug testing analysis to take place. A suitable sample is one which, by its nature, is suitable for a particular form of drug analysis.

17C   A prescribed person in paragraph 17.11 is one who is prescribed in regulations made by the Secretary of State under section 63B(6) of the Police and Criminal Evidence Act 1984. [The regulations are currently contained in regulation SI 2001 No. 2645, the Police and Criminal Evidence Act 1984 (Drug Testing Persons in Police Detention) (Prescribed Persons) Regulations 2001.]

17D   The retention of the sample in paragraph 17.14(b) allows for the sample to be sent for confirmatory testing and analysis if the detainee disputes the test. But such samples, and the information derived from them, may not be subsequently used in the investigation of any offence or in evidence against the persons from whom they were taken.

17E   The trigger offences include: from the Theft Act 1968—theft, robbery, burglary, aggravated burglary, taking a motor vehicle (or other conveyance) without authority, aggravated vehicle-taking, obtaining property by deception, going equipped for stealing etc.; and from the Misuse of Drugs Act 1971 (but only if committed in respect of a specified Class A drug)—producing and supplying a controlled drug, possessing a controlled drug, possessing a controlled drug with intent to supply.]

17F   Section 17 is applicable only within certain police areas, where the relevant provisions for drug testing under section 63B of PACE have been brought into force. The areas where testing for persons aged 18 or over has been introduced are listed at Annex I. The minimum age of 14 will apply only in those police areas where:

● new provisions introduced by section 5 of the Criminal Justice Act 2003 to test persons aged 14 or over have been brought into force

AND

● the relevant chief officer of police has been notified by the Secretary of State that arrangements for the taking of samples from persons under the age of 18 have been made for the police area as a whole, or for a particular police station within that area and the notice has not been withdrawn.

The police areas where section 5 of the Criminal Justice Act 2003 is in force and where drug testing of persons aged 14–17 applies, if such notification is in force, are set out in Annex J.

17G *Appropriate adult in paragraph 17.5 means the person's—*

(a) *parent or guardian or, if he is in the care of a local authority or voluntary organisation, a person representing that authority or organisation; or*

(b) *a social worker of a local authority social services department; or*

(c) *if no person falling within (a) or (b) above is available, any responsible person aged 18 or over who is not a police officer or a person employed by the police.*

ANNEX A

INTIMATE AND STRIP SEARCHES

A Intimate search

1.   An intimate search consists of the physical examination of a person's body orifices other than the mouth. The intrusive nature of such searches means the actual and potential risks associated with intimate searches must never be underestimated.

(a) Action

2.   Body orifices other than the mouth may be searched only if authorised by an officer of inspector rank or above who has reasonable grounds for believing that:

(a) the person may have concealed on themselves

  (i) anything which they could and might use to cause physical injury to themself or others at the station; or

  (ii) a Class A drug which they intended to supply to another or to export; and

(b) an intimate search is the only means of removing those items.

2A.   The reasons an intimate search is considered necessary shall be explained to the person before the search begins.

3.   An intimate search may only be carried out by a registered medical practitioner or registered nurse, unless an officer of at least inspector rank considers this is not practicable and the search is to take place under paragraph 2(a)(i), in which case a police officer may carry out the search. See Notes A1 to A5

3A.   Any proposal for a search under paragraph 2(a)(i) to be carried out by someone other than a registered medical practitioner or registered nurse must only be considered as a last resort and when the authorising officer is satisfied the risks associated with allowing the item to remain with the detainee outweigh the risks associated with removing it. See Notes A1 to A5

4.   An intimate search under:

  • paragraph 2(a)(i) may take place only at a hospital, surgery, other medical premises or police station

  • paragraph 2(a)(ii) may take place only at a hospital, surgery or other medical premises and must be carried out by a registered medical practitioner or a registered nurse

5.   An intimate search at a police station of a juvenile or mentally disordered or otherwise mentally vulnerable person may take place only in the presence of an appropriate adult of the same sex, unless the detainee specifically requests a particular adult of the opposite sex who is readily available. In the case of a juvenile the search may take place in the absence of the appropriate adult only if the juvenile signifies in the presence of the appropriate adult they do not want the adult present during the search and the adult agrees. A record shall be made of the juvenile's decision and signed by the appropriate adult.

6.   When an intimate search under paragraph 2(a)(i) is carried out by a police officer, the officer must be of the same sex as the detainee. A minimum of two people, other than the detainee, must be present during the search. Subject to paragraph 5, no person of the opposite sex who is not a medical practitioner or nurse shall be present, nor shall anyone whose presence is unnecessary. The search shall be conducted with proper regard to the sensitivity and vulnerability of the detainee.

(b)   Documentation

7.   In the case of an intimate search the custody officer shall as soon as practicable, record:
- which parts of the detainee's body were searched
- who carried out the search
- who was present
- the reasons for the search including the reasons to believe the article could not otherwise be removed
- the result.

8.   If an intimate search is carried out by a police officer, the reason why it was impracticable for a registered medical practitioner or registered nurse to conduct it must be recorded.

B   Strip search

9.   A strip search is a search involving the removal of more than outer clothing. In this Code, outer clothing includes shoes and socks.

(a)   Action

10.   A strip search may take place only if it is considered necessary to remove an article which a detainee would not be allowed to keep, and the officer reasonably considers the detainee might have concealed such an article. Strip searches shall not be routinely carried out if there is no reason to consider that articles are concealed.

The conduct of strip searches

11.   When strip searches are conducted:
- (a)   a police officer carrying out a strip search must be the same sex as the detainee;
- (b)   the search shall take place in an area where the detainee cannot be seen by anyone who does not need to be present, nor by a member of the

opposite sex except an appropriate adult who has been specifically requested by the detainee;

(c) except in cases of urgency, where there is risk of serious harm to the detainee or to others, whenever a strip search involves exposure of intimate body parts, there must be at least two people present other than the detainee, and if the search is of a juvenile or mentally disordered or otherwise mentally vulnerable person, one of the people must be the appropriate adult. Except in urgent cases as above, a search of a juvenile may take place in the absence of the appropriate adult only if the juvenile signifies in the presence of the appropriate adult that they do not want the adult to be present during the search and the adult agrees. A record shall be made of the juvenile's decision and signed by the appropriate adult. The presence of more than two people, other than an appropriate adult, shall be permitted only in the most exceptional circumstances;

(d) the search shall be conducted with proper regard to the sensitivity and vulnerability of the detainee in these circumstances and every reasonable effort shall be made to secure the detainee's co-operation and minimise embarrassment. Detainees who are searched shall not normally be required to remove all their clothes at the same time, e.g. a person should be allowed to remove clothing above the waist and redress before removing further clothing;

(e) if necessary to assist the search, the detainee may be required to hold their arms in the air or to stand with their legs apart and bend forward so a visual examination may be made of the genital and anal areas provided no physical contact is made with any body orifice;

(f) if articles are found, the detainee shall be asked to hand them over. If articles are found within any body orifice other than the mouth, and the detainee refuses to hand them over, their removal would constitute an intimate search, which must be carried out as in Part A;

(g) a strip search shall be conducted as quickly as possible, and the detainee allowed to dress as soon as the procedure is complete.

(b) Documentation

12. A record shall be made on the custody record of a strip search including the reason it was considered necessary, those present and any result.

Notes for guidance

A1 *Before authorising any intimate search, the authorising officer must make every reasonable effort to persuade the detainee to hand the article over without a search. If the detainee agrees, a registered medical practitioner or registered nurse should whenever possible be asked to assess the risks involved and, if necessary, attend to assist the detainee.*

A2 *If the detainee does not agree to hand the article over without a search, the authorising officer must carefully review all the relevant factors before authorising an intimate search. In particular, the officer must consider whether the grounds for believing an article may be concealed are reasonable.*

A3   *If authority is given for a search under paragraph 2(a)(i), a registered medical practitioner or registered nurse shall be consulted whenever possible. The presumption should be that the search will be conducted by the registered medical practitioner or registered nurse and the authorising officer must make every reasonable effort to persuade the detainee to allow the medical practitioner or nurse to conduct the search.*

A4   *A constable should only be authorised to carry out a search as a last resort and when all other approaches have failed. In these circumstances, the authorising officer must be satisfied the detainee might use the article for one or more of the purposes in paragraph 2(a)(i) and the physical injury likely to be caused is sufficiently severe to justify authorising a constable to carry out the search.*

A5   *If an officer has any doubts whether to authorise an intimate search by a constable, the officer should seek advice from an officer of superintendent rank or above.*

ANNEX B

DELAY IN NOTIFYING ARREST OR ALLOWING ACCESS TO LEGAL ADVICE

A   Persons detained under PACE

1.   The exercise of the rights in Section 5 or Section 6, or both, may be delayed if the person is in police detention, as in PACE, section 118(2), in connection with a serious arrestable offence, has not yet been charged with an offence and an officer of superintendent rank or above, or inspector rank or above only for the rights in Section 5, has reasonable grounds for believing their exercise will:

   (i) lead to:
   - interference with, or harm to, evidence connected with a serious arrestable offence; or
   - interference with, or physical harm to, other people; or
   (ii) lead to alerting other people suspected of having committed a serious arrestable offence but not yet arrested for it; or
   (iii) hinder the recovery of property obtained in consequence of the commission of such an offence.

2.   These rights may also be delayed if the serious arrestable offence is:

   (i) a drug trafficking offence and the officer has reasonable grounds for believing the detainee has benefited from drug trafficking, and the recovery of the value of the detainee's proceeds from drug trafficking will be hindered by the exercise of either right;
   (ii) an offence to which the Criminal Justice Act 1988, Part VI (confiscation orders) applies and the officer has reasonable grounds for believing the detainee has benefited from the offence, and the exercise of either right will hinder the recovery of the value of the:
   - property obtained by the detainee from or in connection with the offence
   - pecuniary advantage derived by the detainee from or in connection with it.

3.   Authority to delay a detainee's right to consult privately with a solicitor may be given only if the authorising officer has reasonable grounds to believe the solicitor the detainee wants to consult will, inadvertently or otherwise, pass on a message from the detainee or act in some other way which will have any of the consequences specified under paragraphs 1 or 2. In these circumstances the detainee must be allowed to choose another solicitor. See Note B3

4.[89]   If the detainee wishes to see a solicitor, access to that solicitor may not be delayed on the grounds they might advise the detainee not to answer questions or the solicitor was initially asked to attend the police station by someone else. In the latter case the detainee must be told the solicitor has come to the police station at another person's request, and must be asked to sign the custody record to signify whether they want to see the solicitor.

5.[90]   The fact the grounds for delaying notification of arrest may be satisfied does not automatically mean the grounds for delaying access to legal advice will also be satisfied.

6.[91]   These rights may be delayed only for as long as grounds exist and in no case beyond 36 hours after the relevant time as in PACE, section 41. If the grounds cease to apply within this time, the detainee must, as soon as practicable, be asked if they want to exercise either right, the custody record must be noted accordingly, and action taken in accordance with the relevant section of the Code.

7.[92]   A detained person must be permitted to consult a solicitor for a reasonable time before any court hearing.

B   Persons detained under the Terrorism Act 2000

8.   The rights as in sections 5 or 6, may be delayed if the person is detained under the Terrorism Act 2000, section 41 or Schedule 7, has not yet been charged with an offence and an officer of superintendent rank or above has reasonable grounds for believing the exercise of either right will:

   (i) lead to:
   - interference with, or harm to, evidence connected with a serious arrestable offence;
   - interference with, or physical harm to, other people; or

   (ii) lead to the alerting of other people suspected of having committed a serious arrestable offence but not yet arrested for it; or

   (iii) hinder the recovery of property:
   - obtained in consequence of the commission of such an offence; or
   - in respect of which a forfeiture order could be made under that Act, section 23;

   (iv) lead to interference with the gathering of information about the commission, preparation or instigation of acts of terrorism; or

   (v) by alerting any person, make it more difficult to prevent an act of terrorism or secure the apprehension, prosecution or conviction of any person in connection with the commission, preparation or instigation of an act of terrorism.

---

[89] Pre-2003 Annex B, para. 3.
[90] Pre-2003 Annex B, Note B5.
[91] Pre-2003 Annex B, para.4.
[92] Pre-2003 Annex B, para.5.

9.   These rights may also be delayed if the officer has reasonable grounds for believing:

   (a) the detainee:

      (i) has committed an offence to which the Criminal Justice Act 1988, Part VI (confiscation orders) applies;

      (ii) has benefited from the offence; and

   (b) the exercise of either right will hinder the recovery of the value of that benefit.

10.   In these cases paragraphs 3 (with regards to the consequences specified at paragraphs 8 and 9), 4 and 5 apply.

11.[93]   These rights may be delayed only for as long as is necessary but not beyond 48 hours from the time of arrest if arrested under section 41, or if detained under the Terrorism Act 2000, Schedule 7 when arrested under section 41, from the beginning of their examination. If the above grounds cease to apply within this time the detainee must as soon as practicable be asked if they wish to exercise either right, the custody record noted accordingly, and action taken in accordance with the relevant section of this Code.

12.   In this case paragraph 7 applies.

C   Documentation

13.[94]   The grounds for action under this Annex shall be recorded and the detainee informed of them as soon as practicable.

14.[95]   Any reply given by a detainee under paragraphs 6 or 11 must be recorded and the detainee asked to endorse the record in relation to whether they want to receive legal advice at this point.

D   Cautions and special warnings

15.   When a suspect detained at a police station is interviewed during any period for which access to legal advice has been delayed under this Annex, the court or jury may not draw adverse inferences from their silence.

Notes for guidance

B1   Even if Annex B applies in the case of a juvenile, or a person who is mentally disordered or otherwise mentally vulnerable, action to inform the appropriate adult and the person responsible for a juvenile's welfare if that is a different person, must nevertheless be taken as in paragraph 3.13 and 3.15.

B2   In the case of Commonwealth citizens and foreign nationals, see Note 7A.

B3[96] A decision to delay access to a specific solicitor is likely to be a rare occurrence and only when it can be shown the suspect is capable of misleading that particular solicitor and there is more than a substantial risk that the suspect will succeed in causing information to be conveyed which will lead to one or more of the specified consequences.

---

[93] Based on pre-2003 Annex B, para.9.

[94] Pre-2003 Annex B, para.6.

[95] Pre-2003 Annex B, para.7.

[96] Based on pre-2003 Annex B, Note B4.

ANNEX C

RESTRICTION ON DRAWING ADVERSE INFERENCES FROM SILENCE AND TERMS OF THE
CAUTION WHEN THE RESTRICTION APPLIES

(a) The restriction on drawing adverse inferences from silence

1.   The Criminal Justice and Public Order Act 1994, sections 34, 36 and 37 as amended by the Youth Justice and Criminal Evidence Act 1999, section 58 describe the conditions under which adverse inferences may be drawn from a person's failure or refusal to say anything about their involvement in the offence when interviewed, after being charged or informed they may be prosecuted. These provisions are subject to an overriding restriction on the ability of a court or jury to draw adverse inferences from a person's silence. This restriction applies:

   (a)   to any detainee at a police station, see Note 10C who, before being interviewed, see section 11 or being charged or informed they may be prosecuted, see section 16, has:

   (i)   asked for legal advice, see section 6, paragraph 6.1;

   (ii)   not been allowed an opportunity to consult a solicitor, including the duty solicitor, as in this Code: and

   (iii)   not changed their mind about wanting legal advice, see section 6, paragraph 6.6(d)

   Note the condition in (ii) will

   ~ apply when a detainee who has asked for legal advice is interviewed before speaking to a solicitor as in section 6, paragraph 6.6(a) or (b);

   ~ not apply if the detained person declines to ask for the duty solicitor, see section 6, paragraphs 6.6(c) and (d);

   (b)   to any person charged with, or informed they may be prosecuted for, an offence who:

   (i)   has had brought to their notice a written statement made by another person or the content of an interview with another person which relates to that offence, see section 16, paragraph 16.4;

   (ii)   is interviewed about that offence, see section 16, paragraph 16.5; or

   (iii)   makes a written statement about that offence, see Annex D paragraphs 4 and 9.

(b) Terms of the caution when the restriction applies

2.   When a requirement to caution arises at a time when the restriction on drawing adverse inferences from silence applies, the caution shall be:

'You do not have to say anything, but anything you do say may be given in evidence.'

3.   Whenever the restriction either begins to apply or ceases to apply after a caution has already been given, the person shall be re-cautioned in the appropriate terms. The changed position on drawing inferences and that the previous caution no longer applies shall also be explained to the detainee in ordinary language. See Note C2

748

Notes for guidance

C1   The restriction on drawing inferences from silence does not apply to a
person who has not been detained and who therefore cannot be prevented
from seeking legal advice if they want to, see paragraphs 10.2 and 3.15.

C2   The following is suggested as a framework to help explain changes in
the position on drawing adverse inferences if the restriction on drawing
adverse inferences from silence:

(a)   begins to apply:

'The caution you were previously given no longer applies. This is
because after that caution:

(i)   you asked to speak to a solicitor but have not yet been allowed
an opportunity to speak to a solicitor. See paragraph 1(a); or

(ii)   you have been charged with/informed you may be prosecuted.'
See paragraph 1(b).

'This means that from now on, adverse inferences cannot be
drawn at court and your defence will not be harmed just
because you choose to say nothing. Please listen carefully to the
caution I am about to give you because it will apply from now
on. You will see that it does not say anything about your defence
being harmed.'

(b)   ceases to apply before or at the time the person is charged or
informed they may be prosecuted, see paragraph 1(a);

'The caution you were previously given no longer applies. This is
because after that caution you have been allowed an opportunity to
speak to a solicitor. Please listen carefully to the caution I am about
to give you because it will apply from now on. It explains how your
defence at court may be affected if you choose to say nothing.'

ANNEX D

WRITTEN STATEMENTS UNDER CAUTION

(a)   Written by a person under caution

1.   A person shall always be invited to write down what they want to say.

2.   A person who has not been charged with, or informed they may be prosecuted
for, any offence to which the statement they want to write relates, shall:

(a)   unless the statement is made at a time when the restriction on drawing
adverse inferences from silence applies, see Annex C, be asked to write
out and sign the following before writing what they want to say:

'I make this statement of my own free will. I understand that I do not
have to say anything but that it may harm my defence if I do not mention when questioned something which I later rely on in court. This
statement may be given in evidence.';

(b)   if the statement is made at a time when the restriction on drawing
adverse inferences from silence applies, be asked to write out and sign
the following before writing what they want to say;

'I make this statement of my own free will. I understand that I do not
have to say anything. This statement may be given in evidence.'

3.   When a person, on the occasion of being charged with or informed they may be prosecuted for any offence, asks to make a statement which relates to any such offence and wants to write it they shall:

(a)   unless the restriction on drawing adverse inferences from silence, see Annex C, applied when they were so charged or informed they may be prosecuted, be asked to write out and sign the following before writing what they want to say:

'I make this statement of my own free will. I understand that I do not have to say anything but that it may harm my defence if I do not mention when questioned something which I later rely on in court. This statement may be given in evidence.';

(b)   if the restriction on drawing adverse inferences from silence applied when they were so charged or informed they may be prosecuted, be asked to write out and sign the following before writing what they want to say:

'I make this statement of my own free will. I understand that I do not have to say anything. This statement may be given in evidence.'

4.   When a person, who has already been charged with or informed they may be prosecuted for any offence, asks to make a statement which relates to any such offence and wants to write it they shall be asked to write out and sign the following before writing what they want to say:

'I make this statement of my own free will. I understand that I do not have to say anything. This statement may be given in evidence.';

5.[97]   Any person writing their own statement shall be allowed to do so without any prompting except a police officer or other police staff may indicate to them which matters are material or question any ambiguity in the statement.

(b)   Written by a police officer or other police staff

6.[98]   If a person says they would like someone to write the statement for them, a police officer, or other police staff shall write the statement.

7.   If the person has not been charged with, or informed they may be prosecuted for, any offence to which the statement they want to make relates they shall, before starting, be asked to sign, or make their mark, to the following:

(a)   unless the statement is made at a time when the restriction on drawing adverse inferences from silence applies, see Annex C:

'I, ... , wish to make a statement. I want someone to write down what I say. I understand that I do not have to say anything but that it may harm my defence if I do not mention when questioned something which I later rely on in court. This statement may be given in evidence.';

(b)   if the statement is made at a time when the restriction on drawing adverse inferences from silence applies:

'I, ... , wish to make a statement. I want someone to write down what I say. I understand that I do not have to say anything This statement may be given in evidence.'

8.   If, on the occasion of being charged with or informed they may be prosecuted for any offence, the person asks to make a statement which relates to any

---

[97] Pre-2003 Annex D, para.3.
[98] Pre-2003 Annex D, para.4.

such offence they shall before starting be asked to sign, or make their mark to, the following:

(a)   unless the restriction on drawing adverse inferences from silence applied, see Annex C, when they were so charged or informed they may be prosecuted:

'I, ... , wish to make a statement. I want someone to write down what I say. I understand that I do not have to say anything but that it may harm my defence if I do not mention when questioned something which I later rely on in court. This statement may be given in evidence.';

(b)   if the restriction on drawing adverse inferences from silence applied when they were so charged or informed they may be prosecuted:

'I, ... , wish to make a statement. I want someone to write down what I say. I understand that I do not have to say anything This statement may be given in evidence.'

9.   If, having already been charged with or informed they may be prosecuted for any offence, a person asks to make a statement which relates to any such offence they shall before starting, be asked to sign, or make their mark to:

'I, ... , wish to make a statement. I want someone to write down what I say. I understand that I do not have to say anything This statement may be given in evidence.'

10.[99]   The person writing the statement must take down the exact words spoken by the person making it and must not edit or paraphrase it. Any questions that are necessary, e.g. to make it more intelligible, and the answers given must be recorded at the same time on the statement form.

11.[1]   When the writing of a statement is finished the person making it shall be asked to read it and to make any corrections, alterations or additions they want. When they have finished reading they shall be asked to write and sign or make their mark on the following certificate at the end of the statement:

'I have read the above statement, and I have been able to correct, alter or add anything I wish. This statement is true. I have made it of my own free will.'

12.[2]   If the person making the statement cannot read, or refuses to read it, or to write the above mentioned certificate at the end of it or to sign it, the person taking the statement shall read it to them and ask them if they would like to correct, alter or add anything and to put their signature or make their mark at the end. The person taking the statement shall certify on the statement itself what has occurred.

ANNEX E

SUMMARY OF PROVISIONS RELATING TO MENTALLY DISORDERED AND OTHERWISE MENTALLY VULNERABLE PEOPLE

1.   If an officer has any suspicion, or is told in good faith, that a person of any age may be mentally disordered or otherwise mentally vulnerable, or mentally incapable of understanding the significance of questions or their replies that

---

[99] Pre-2003 Annex D, para.5.

[1] Pre-2003 Annex D, para.6.

[2] Pre-2003 Annex D, para.7.

person shall be treated as mentally disordered or otherwise mentally vulnerable for the purposes of this Code. See paragraph 1.4

2.   In the case of a person who is mentally disordered or otherwise mentally vulnerable, 'the appropriate adult' means:

(a)   a relative, guardian or other person responsible for their care or custody;

(b)   someone experienced in dealing with mentally disordered or mentally vulnerable people but who is not a police officer or employed by the police;

(c)   failing these, some other responsible adult aged 18 or over who is not a police officer or employed by the police.

See paragraph 1.7(b) and Note 1D

3.   If the custody officer authorises the detention of a person who is mentally vulnerable or appears to be suffering from a mental disorder, the custody officer must as soon as practicable inform the appropriate adult of the grounds for detention and the person's whereabouts, and ask the adult to come to the police station to see them. If the appropriate adult:

- is already at the station when information is given as in paragraphs 3.1 to 3.5 the information must be given in their presence

- is not at the station when the provisions of paragraph 3.1 to 3.5 are complied with these provisions must be complied with again in their presence once they arrive.

See paragraphs 3.15 to 3.17

4.   If the appropriate adult, having been informed of the right to legal advice, considers legal advice should be taken, the provisions of section 6 apply as if the mentally disordered or otherwise mentally vulnerable person had requested access to legal advice. See paragraph 3.19 and Note E1

5.   The custody officer must make sure a person receives appropriate clinical attention as soon as reasonably practicable if the person appears to be suffering from a mental disorder or in urgent cases immediately call the nearest health care professional or an ambulance. It is not intended these provisions delay the transfer of a detainee to a place of safety under the Mental Health Act 1983, section 136 if that is applicable. If an assessment under that Act is to take place at a police station, the custody officer must consider whether an appropriate health care professional should be called to conduct an initial clinical check on the detainee. See paragraph 9.5 and 9.6

6.   It is imperative a mentally disordered or otherwise mentally vulnerable person detained under the Mental Health Act 1983, section 136 be assessed as soon as possible. If that assessment is to take place at the police station, an approved social worker and registered medical practitioner shall be called to the station as soon as possible in order to interview and examine the detainee. Once the detainee has been interviewed, examined and suitable arrangements been made for their treatment or care, they can no longer be detained under section 136. A detainee should be immediately discharged from detention if a registered medical practitioner having examined them, concludes they are not mentally disordered within the meaning of the Act. See paragraph 3.16

7.   If a mentally disordered or otherwise mentally vulnerable person is cautioned in the absence of the appropriate adult, the caution must be repeated in the appropriate adult's presence. See paragraph 10.12

8.   A mentally disordered or otherwise mentally vulnerable person must not be interviewed or asked to provide or sign a written statement in the absence of the

appropriate adult unless the provisions of paragraphs 11.1 or 11.18 to 11.20 apply. Questioning in these circumstances may not continue in the absence of the appropriate adult once sufficient information to avert the risk has been obtained. A record shall be made of the grounds for any decision to begin an interview in these circumstances. See paragraphs 11.1, 11.15 and 11.18 to 11.20

9.   If the appropriate adult is present at an interview, they shall be informed they are not expected to act simply as an observer and the purposes of their presence are to:

- advise the interviewee
- observe whether or not the interview is being conducted properly and fairly
- facilitate communication with the interviewee

See paragraph 11.17

10.   If the detention of a mentally disordered or otherwise mentally vulnerable person is reviewed by a review officer or a superintendent, the appropriate adult must, if available at the time, be given an opportunity to make representations to the officer about the need for continuing detention. See paragraph 15.3

11.   If the custody officer charges a mentally disordered or otherwise mentally vulnerable person with an offence or takes such other action as is appropriate when there is sufficient evidence for a prosecution this must be done in the presence of the appropriate adult. The written notice embodying any charge must be given to the appropriate adult. See paragraphs 16.1 to 16.4A

12.   An intimate or strip search of a mentally disordered or otherwise mentally vulnerable person may take place only in the presence of the appropriate adult of the same sex, unless the detainee specifically requests the presence of a particular adult of the opposite sex. A strip search may take place in the absence of an appropriate adult only in cases of urgency when there is a risk of serious harm to the detainee or others. See Annex A, paragraphs 5 and 11(c)

13.   Particular care must be taken when deciding whether to use any form of approved restraints on a mentally disordered or otherwise mentally vulnerable person in a locked cell. See paragraph 8.2

Notes for guidance

E1[3]   *The purpose of the provision at paragraph 3.19 is to protect the rights of a mentally disordered or otherwise mentally vulnerable detained person who does not understand the significance of what is said to them. If the detained person wants to exercise the right to legal advice, the appropriate action should be taken and not delayed until the appropriate adult arrives. A mentally disordered or otherwise mentally vulnerable detained person should always be given an opportunity, when an appropriate adult is called to the police station, to consult privately with a solicitor in the absence of the appropriate adult if they want.*

E2[4]   *Although people who are mentally disordered or otherwise mentally vulnerable are often capable of providing reliable evidence, they may, without knowing or wanting to do so, be particularly prone in certain circumstances to provide information that may be unreliable, misleading or self-incriminating. Special care should always be taken when*

---

[3] Pre-2003 Annex E, Note E2.
[4] Pre-2003 Annex E, Note E3.

questioning such a person, and the appropriate adult should be involved if there is any doubt about a person's mental state or capacity. Because of the risk of unreliable evidence, it is important to obtain corroboration of any facts admitted whenever possible.

E3[5]   *Because of the risks referred to in Note E2, which the presence of the appropriate adult is intended to minimise, officers of superintendent rank or above should exercise their discretion to authorise the commencement of an interview in the appropriate adult's absence only in exceptional cases, if it is necessary to avert an immediate risk of serious harm. See paragraphs 11.1, 11.18 to 11.20*

ANNEX F

COUNTRIES WITH WHICH BILATERAL CONSULAR CONVENTIONS OR AGREEMENTS REQUIRING NOTIFICATION OF THE ARREST AND DETENTION OF THEIR NATIONALS ARE IN FORCE AS AT 1 APRIL 2003

Armenia	France	Poland
Austria	Georgia	Romania
Azerbaijan	German Federal Republic	Russia
Belarus	Greece	Slovak Republic
Belgium	Hungary	Slovenia
Bosnia-Herzegovina	Italy	Spain
Bulgaria	Japan	Sweden
China*	Kazakhstan	Tajikistan
Croatia	Macedonia	Turkmenistan
Cuba	Mexico	Ukraine
Czech Republic	Moldova	USA
Denmark	Mongolia	Uzbekistan
Egypt	Norway	Yugoslavia

* Police are required to inform Chinese officials of arrest/detention in the Manchester consular district only. This comprises Derbyshire, Durham, Greater Manchester, Lancashire, Merseyside, North South and West Yorkshire, and Tyne and Wear

ANNEX G

FITNESS TO BE INTERVIEWED

1.   This Annex contains general guidance to help police officers and health care professionals assess whether a detainee might be at risk in an interview.

2.   A detainee may be at risk in a interview if it is considered that:

    (a)   conducting the interview could significantly harm the detainee's physical or mental state;

    (b)   anything the detainee says in the interview about their involvement or suspected involvement in the offence about which they are being interviewed might be considered unreliable in subsequent court proceedings because of their physical or mental state.

---

[5] Pre-2003 Annex E, Note E4.

3. In assessing whether the detainee should be interviewed, the following must be considered:

    (a) how the detainee's physical or mental state might affect their ability to understand the nature and purpose of the interview, to comprehend what is being asked and to appreciate the significance of any answers given and make rational decisions about whether they want to say anything;

    (b) the extent to which the detainee's replies may be affected by their physical or mental condition rather than representing a rational and accurate explanation of their involvement in the offence;

    (c) how the nature of the interview, which could include particularly probing questions, might affect the detainee.

4. It is essential health care professionals who are consulted consider the functional ability of the detainee rather than simply relying on a medical diagnosis, e.g. it is possible for a person with severe mental illness to be fit for interview.

5. Health care professionals should advise on the need for an appropriate adult to be present, whether reassessment of the person's fitness for interview may be necessary if the interview lasts beyond a specified time, and whether a further specialist opinion may be required.

6. When health care professionals identify risks they should be asked to quantify the risks. They should inform the custody officer:

    ● whether the person's condition:

      ~ is likely to improve

      ~ will require or be amenable to treatment; and

    ● indicate how long it may take for such improvement to take effect

7. The role of the health care professional is to consider the risks and advise the custody officer of the outcome of that consideration. The health care professional's determination and any advice or recommendations should be made in writing and form part of the custody record.

8. Once the health care professional has provided that information, it is a matter for the custody officer to decide whether or not to allow the interview to go ahead and if the interview is to proceed, to determine what safeguards are needed. Nothing prevents safeguards being provided in addition to those required under the Code. An example might be to have an appropriate health care professional present during the interview, in addition to an appropriate adult, in order constantly to monitor the person's condition and how it is being affected by the interview.

ANNEX H

DETAINED PERSON: OBSERVATION LIST

1. If any detainee fails to meet any of the following criteria, an appropriate health care professional or an ambulance must be called.

2. When assessing the level of rousability, consider:

    Rousability—can they be woken?

    ● go into the cell

    ● call their name

    ● shake gently

Response to questions—can they give appropriate answers to questions such as:

- What's your name?
- Where do you live?
- Where do you think you are?

Response to commands—can they respond appropriately to commands such as:

- Open your eyes!
- Lift one arm, now the other arm!

3.   Remember to take into account the possibility or presence of other illnesses, injury, or mental condition, a person who is drowsy and smells of alcohol may also have the following:

- Diabetes
- Epilepsy
- Head injury
- Drug intoxication or overdose
- Stroke

ANNEX I

POLICE AREAS WHERE THE POWER TO TEST PERSONS AGED 18 AND OVER FOR SPECIFIED CLASS A DRUGS UNDER SECTION 63B OF PACE HAS BEEN BROUGHT INTO FORCE*

Avon and Somerset	Metropolitan Police district
Bedfordshire	North Wales
Cambridgeshire	Northumbria
Cleveland	Nottinghamshire
Devon and Cornwall	South Yorkshire
Greater Manchester	Staffordshire
Humber	Thames Valley
Lancashire	West Midlands
Leicestershire	West Yorkshire
Merseyside	

* The provisions are being implemented in selected police stations within these police areas.

ANNEX J

POLICE AREAS WHERE THE POWER TO TEST PERSONS AGED 14 AND OVER FOR
SPECIFIED CLASS A DRUGS UNDER SECTION 63B OF PACE (AS AMENDED BY
SECTION 5 OF THE CRIMINAL JUSTICE ACT 2003) HAS BEEN BROUGHT INTO FORCE*

Cleveland
Humber
Greater Manchester
Metropolitan Police District

Nottinghamshire
Merseyside
West Yorkshire

This power is subject to notification by the Secretary of State that arrangements for the taking of samples from persons who have not attained the age of 18 (i.e. persons aged 14–17) are available in the police area as a whole or in the particular police station concerned. The minimum age of 14 will apply only following that notification and if the notice has not been withdrawn.

Testing in the case of those aged 14–17 cannot be carried out unless such notification is in force.

* The provisions are being implemented in selected police stations within these police areas.

CODE D

CODE OF PRACTICE FOR THE IDENTIFICATION OF PERSONS BY POLICE OFFICERS

Commencement—Transitional Arrangements

This code has effect in relation to any identification procedure carried out after midnight on 31 July 2003.

1 Introduction

1.1 This Code of Practice concerns the principal methods used by police to identify people in connection with the investigation of offences and the keeping of accurate and reliable criminal records.

1.2 Identification by witnesses arises, e.g., if the offender is seen committing the crime and a witness is given an opportunity to identify the suspect in a video identification, identification parade or similar procedure. The procedures are designed to:

- test the witness' ability to identify the person they saw on a previous occasion
- provide safeguards against mistaken identification.

While this Code concentrates on visual identification procedures, it does not preclude the police making use of aural identification procedures such as a "voice identification parade", where they judge that appropriate.

1.3 Identification by fingerprints applies when a person's fingerprints are taken to:

- compare with fingerprints found at the scene of a crime
- check and prove convictions
- help to ascertain a person's identity.

1.4 Identification by body samples and impressions includes taking samples such as blood or hair to generate a DNA profile for comparison with material obtained from the scene of a crime, or a victim.

1.5 Taking photographs of arrested people applies to recording and checking identity and locating and tracing persons who:

- are wanted for offences
- fail to answer their bail.

1.6 Another method of identification involves searching and examining detained suspects to find, e.g., marks such as tattoos or scars which may help establish their identity or whether they have been involved in committing an offence.

1.7 The provisions of the Police and Criminal Evidence Act 1984 (PACE) and this Code are designed to make sure fingerprints, samples, impressions and photographs are taken, used and retained, and identification procedures carried out, only when justified and necessary for preventing, detecting or investigating crime. If these provisions are not observed, the application of the relevant procedures in particular cases may be open to question.

2 General[1]

2.1 This Code must be readily available at all police stations for consultation by:
- police officers
- police staff
- detained persons
- members of the public .

2.2 The provisions of this Code:
- include the Annexes
- do not include the Notes for guidance.

2.3 Code C, paragraph 1.4, regarding a person who may be mentally disordered or otherwise mentally vulnerable and the Notes for guidance applicable to those provisions apply to this Code.

2.4 Code C, paragraph 1.5, regarding a person who appears to be under the age of 17 applies to this Code.

2.5 Code C, paragraph 1.6, regarding a person who appears blind, seriously visually impaired, deaf, unable to read or speak or has difficulty orally because of a speech impediment applies to this Code.

2.6 In this Code:
- 'appropriate adult' means the same as in Code C, paragraph 1.7,
- 'solicitor' means the same as in Code C, paragraph 6.12

and the Notes for guidance applicable to those provisions apply to this Code.

2.7 References to custody officers include those performing the functions of custody officer.

2.8 When a record of any action requiring the authority of an officer of a specified rank is made under this Code, subject to paragraph 2.18, the officer's name and rank must be recorded,

2.9 When this Code requires the prior authority or agreement of an officer of at least inspector or superintendent rank, that authority may be given by a sergeant or chief inspector who has been authorised to perform the functions of the higher rank under PACE, section 107.

2.10 Subject to paragraph 2.18, all records must be timed and signed by the maker.

2.11 Records must be made in the custody record, unless otherwise specified. References to 'pocket book' include any official report book issued to police officers or police staff.

2.12 If any procedure in this Code requires a person's consent, the consent of a:
- mentally disordered or otherwise mentally vulnerable person is only valid if given in the presence of the appropriate adult
- juvenile, is only valid if their parent's or guardian's consent is also obtained unless the juvenile is under 14, when their parent's or guardian's consent is sufficient in its own right. If the only obstacle to an identification procedure in section 3 is that a juvenile's parent or guardian refuses consent or reasonable efforts to obtain it have failed, the identification officer may apply the provisions of paragraph 3.21. See Note 2A

2.13 If a person is blind, seriously visually impaired or unable to read, the custody officer or identification officer shall make sure their solicitor, relative, appropriate adult or some other person likely to take an interest in them and not

---

[1] Pre-2003, as there was no Introduction, this was s.1.

involved in the investigation is available to help check any documentation. When this Code requires written consent or signing, the person assisting may be asked to sign instead, if the detainee prefers. This paragraph does not require an appropriate adult to be called solely to assist in checking and signing documentation for a person who is not a juvenile, or mentally disordered or otherwise mentally vulnerable (see Note 2B and Code C paragraph 3.15).

2.14　If any procedure in this Code requires information to be given to or sought from a suspect, it must be given or sought in the appropriate adult's presence if the suspect is mentally disordered, otherwise mentally vulnerable or a juvenile. If the appropriate adult is not present when the information is first given or sought, the procedure must be repeated in the presence of the appropriate adult when they arrive. If the suspect appears deaf or there is doubt about their hearing or speaking ability or ability to understand English, and effective communication cannot be established, the information must be given or sought through an interpreter.

2.15　Any procedure in this Code involving the participation of a person (whether as a suspect or a witness) who is mentally disordered, otherwise mentally vulnerable or a juvenile, must take place in the presence of the appropriate adult. However, the adult must not be allowed to prompt any identification of a suspect by a witness.

2.16　References to:

- 'taking a photograph', include the use of any process to produce a single, still, visual image
- 'photographing a person', should be construed accordingly
- 'photographs', 'films', 'negatives' and 'copies' include relevant visual images recorded, stored, or reproduced through any medium
- 'destruction' includes the deletion of computer data relating to such images or making access to that data impossible

2.17　Except as described, nothing in this Code affects the powers and procedures:

(i) for requiring and taking samples of breath, blood and urine in relation to driving offences, etc, when under the influence of drink, drugs or excess alcohol under the:
- Road Traffic Act 1988, sections 4 to 11
- Road Traffic Offenders Act 1988, sections 15 and 16
- Transport and Works Act 1992, sections 26 to 38;

(ii) under the Immigration Act 1971, Schedule 2, paragraph 18, for taking photographs and fingerprints from persons detained under that Act, Schedule 2, paragraph 16 (Administrative Controls as to Control on Entry etc.); for taking fingerprints in accordance with the Immigration and Asylum Act 1999; sections 141 and 142(3), or other methods for collecting information about a person's external physical characteristics provided for by regulations made under that Act, section 144;

(iii) under the Terrorism Act 2000, Schedule 8, for taking photographs, fingerprints, skin impressions, body samples or impressions from people:
- arrested under that Act, section 41,
- detained for the purposes of examination under that Act, Schedule 7, and to whom the Code of Practice issued under that Act, Schedule 14, paragraph 6, applies ('the terrorism provisions'); See Note 2C

(iv) for taking photographs, fingerprints, skin impressions, body samples or impressions from people who have been:
- arrested on warrants issued in Scotland, by officers exercising

powers under the Criminal Justice and Public Order Act 1994, section 136(2)

- arrested or detained without warrant by officers from a police force in Scotland exercising their powers of arrest or detention under the Criminal Justice and Public Order Act 1994, section 137(2), (Cross Border powers of arrest etc.).

Note: In these cases, police powers and duties and the person's rights and entitlements whilst at a police station in England and Wales are the same as if the person had been arrested in Scotland by a Scottish police officer.

2.18   Nothing in this Code requires the identity of officers or police staff to be recorded or disclosed:

    (a)   in the case of enquiries linked to the investigation of terrorism;

    (b)   if the officers or police staff reasonably believe recording or disclosing their names might put them in danger.

In these cases, they shall use warrant or other identification numbers and the name of their police station. See Note 2D

2.19   In this Code:

    (a)   'designated person' means a person other than a police officer, designated under the Police Reform Act 2002, Part 4, who has specified powers and duties of police officers conferred or imposed on them;

    (b)   any reference to a police officer includes a designated person acting in the exercise or performance of the powers and duties conferred or imposed on them by their designation.

2.20   If a power conferred on a designated person:

    (a)   allows reasonable force to be used when exercised by a police officer, a designated person exercising that power has the same entitlement to use force;

    (b)   includes power to use force to enter any premises, that power is not exercisable by that designated person except:

        (i)   in the company, and under the supervision, of a police officer; or

        (ii)   for the purpose of:

- saving life or limb; or
- preventing serious damage to property.

2.21   Nothing in this Code prevents the custody officer, or other officer given custody of the detainee, from allowing police staff who are not designated persons to carry out individual procedures or tasks at the police station if the law allows. However, the officer remains responsible for making sure the procedures and tasks are carried out correctly in accordance with the Codes of Practice. Any such civilian must be:

    (a)   a person employed by a police authority maintaining a police force and under the control and direction of the Chief Officer of that force;

    (b)   employed by a person with whom a police authority has a contract for the provision of services relating to persons arrested or otherwise in custody.

2.22   Designated persons and other police staff must have regard to any relevant provisions of the Codes of Practice.

Notes for guidance

  2A   *For the purposes of paragraph 2.12, the consent required from a parent or guardian may, for a juvenile in the care of a local authority or voluntary organisation, be given by that authority or organisation. In the case of a juvenile, nothing in paragraph 2.12 requires the parent, guardian or representative of a local authority or voluntary organisation to be present to give their consent, unless they are acting as the appropriate adult under paragraphs 2.14 or 2.15. However, it is important that a parent or guardian not present is fully informed before being asked to consent. They must be given the same information about the procedure and the juvenile's suspected involvement in the offence as the juvenile and appropriate adult. The parent or guardian must also be allowed to speak to the juvenile and the appropriate adult if they wish. Provided the consent is fully informed and is not withdrawn, it may be obtained at any time before the procedure takes place.*

2B *People who are seriously visually impaired or unable to read may be unwilling to sign police documents. The alternative, i.e. their representative signing on their behalf, seeks to protect the interests of both police and suspects.*

2C *Photographs, fingerprints, samples and impressions may be taken from a person detained under the terrorism provisions to help determine whether they are, or have been, involved in terrorism, as well as when there are reasonable grounds for suspecting their involvement in a particular offence.*

2D *The purpose of paragraph 2.18(b) is to protect those involved in serious organised crime investigations or arrests of particularly violent suspects when there is reliable information that those arrested or their associates may threaten or cause harm to the officers. In cases of doubt, an officer of inspector rank or above should be consulted.*

3   Identification by witnesses[2]

3.1[3]   A record shall be made of the suspect's description as first given by a potential witness. This record must:
  (a)   be made and kept in a form which enables details of that description to be accurately produced from it, in a visible and legible form, which can be given to the suspect or the suspect's solicitor in accordance with this Code; and
  (b)   unless otherwise specified, be made before the witness takes part in any identification procedures under paragraphs 3.5 to 3.10, 3.21 or 3.23.
A copy of the record shall where practicable, be given to the suspect or their solicitor before any procedures under paragraphs 3.5 to 3.10, 3.21 or 3.23 are carried out. See Note 3E

(a)   Cases when the suspect's identity is not known

3.2   In cases when the suspect's identity is not known, a witness may be taken to a particular neighbourhood or place to see whether they can identify the person they saw. Although the number, age, sex, race, general description and style of clothing of other people present at the location and the way in which any iden-

---

[2] Pre-2003 this was s.2. The section was drastically amended in March 2002. "Pre-2002" in this section refers to the pre-March 2002 text.
[3] Pre-2003 para.2.0.

tification is made cannot be controlled, the principles applicable to the formal procedures under paragraphs 3.5 to 3.10 shall be followed as far as practicable. For example:

(a) where it is practicable to do so, a record should be made of the witness' description of the suspect, as in paragraph 3.1 (a), before asking the witness to make an identification;

(b) care must be taken not to direct the witness' attention to any individual unless, taking into account all the circumstances, this cannot be avoided. However, this does not prevent a witness being asked to look carefully at the people around at the time or to look towards a group or in a particular direction, if this appears necessary to make sure that the witness does not overlook a possible suspect simply because the witness is looking in the opposite direction and also to enable the witness to make comparisons between any suspect and others who are in the area; See Note 3F

(c) where there is more than one witness, every effort should be made to keep them separate and witnesses should be taken to see whether they can identify a person independently;

(d) once there is sufficient information to justify the arrest of a particular individual for suspected involvement in the offence, e.g., after a witness makes a positive identification, the provisions set out from paragraph 3.4 onwards shall apply for any other witnesses in relation to that individual. Subject to paragraphs 3.12 and 3.13, it is not necessary for the witness who makes such a positive identification to take part in a further procedure;

(c) the officer or police staff accompanying the witness must record, in their pocket book, the action taken as soon as, and in as much detail, as possible. The record should include: the date, time and place of the relevant occasion the witness claims to have previously seen the suspect; where any identification was made; how it was made and the conditions at the time (e.g., the distance the witness was from the suspect, the weather and light); if the witness's attention was drawn to the suspect; the reason for this; and anything said by the witness or the suspect about the identification or the conduct of the procedure.

3.3[4] A witness must not be shown photographs, computerised or artist's composite likenesses or similar likenesses or pictures (including 'E-fit' images) if the identity of the suspect is known to the police and the suspect is available to take part in a video identification, an identification parade or a group identification. If the suspect's identity is not known, the showing of such images to a witness to obtain identification evidence must be done in accordance with Annex E.

(b) Cases when the suspect is known and available

3.4[5] If the suspect's identity is known to the police and they are available, the identification procedures set out in paragraphs 3.5 to 3.10 may be used. References in this section to a suspect being 'known' mean there is sufficient information known to the police to justify the arrest of a particular person for suspected

---

[4] Based on pre-2002 para.2.18.
[5] Pre-2002 para.2.1.

involvement in the offence. A suspect being 'available' means they are immediately available or will be within a reasonably short time and willing to take an effective part in at least one of the following which it is practicable to arrange:

- video identification;
- identification parade; or
- group identification.

Video identification

3.5   A 'video identification' is when the witness is shown moving images of a known suspect, together with similar images of others who resemble the suspect. See paragraph 3.21 for circumstances in which still images may be used.

3.6   Video identifications must be carried out in accordance with Annex A.

Identification parade

3.7   An 'identification parade' is when the witness sees the suspect in a line of others who resemble the suspect.

3.8   Identification parades must be carried out in accordance with Annex B.

Group identification

3.9   A 'group identification' is when the witness sees the suspect in an informal group of people.

3.10   Group identifications must be carried out in accordance with Annex C.

Arranging identification procedures

3.11   Except for the provisions in paragraph 3.19, the arrangements for, and conduct of, the identification procedures in paragraphs 3.5 to 3.10 and circumstances in which an identification procedure must be held shall be the responsibility of an officer not below inspector rank who is not involved with the investigation, 'the identification officer'. Unless otherwise specified, the identification officer may allow another officer or police staff, see paragraph 2.21, to make arrangements for, and conduct, any of these identification procedures. In delegating these procedures, the identification officer must be able to supervise effectively and either intervene or be contacted for advice. No officer or any other person involved with the investigation of the case against the suspect, beyond the extent required by these procedures, may take any part in these procedures or act as the identification officer. This does not prevent the identification officer from consulting the officer in charge of the investigation to determine which procedure to use. When an identification procedure is required, in the interest of fairness to suspects and witnesses, it must be held as soon as practicable.

Circumstances in which an identification procedure must be held

3.12   Whenever:
    (i)   a witness has identified a suspect or purported to have identified them prior to any identification procedure set out in paragraphs 3.5 to 3.10 having been held; or

    (ii)   there is a witness available, who expresses an ability to identify the suspect, or where there is a reasonable chance of the witness being able to do so, and they have not been given an opportunity to identify the suspect in any of the procedures set out in paragraphs 3.5 to 3.10,

and the suspect disputes being the person the witness claims to have seen, an identification procedure shall be held unless it is not practicable or it would serve no useful purpose in proving or disproving whether the suspect was involved in committing the offence. For example, when it is not disputed that the suspect is already well known to the witness who claims to have seen them commit the crime.

3.13[6] Such a procedure may also be held if the officer in charge of the investigation considers it would be useful.

Selecting an identification procedure

3.14   If, because of paragraph 3.12, an identification procedure is to be held, the suspect shall initially be offered a video identification unless:

    (a)   a video identification is not practicable; or

    (b)   an identification parade is both practicable and more suitable than a video identification;

        or

    (c)   paragraphs 3.16 applies.

The identification officer and the officer in charge of the investigation shall consult each other to determine which option is to be offered. An identification parade may not be practicable because of factors relating to the witnesses, such as their number, state of health, availability and travelling requirements. A video identification would normally be more suitable if it could be arranged and completed sooner than an identification parade.

3.15   A suspect who refuses the identification procedure first offered shall be asked to state their reason for refusing and may get advice from their solicitor and/or if present, their appropriate adult . The suspect, solicitor and/or appropriate adult shall be allowed to make representations about why another procedure should be used. A record should be made of the reasons for refusal and any representations made. After considering any reasons given, and representations made, the identification officer shall, if appropriate, arrange for the suspect to be offered an alternative which the officer considers suitable and practicable. If the officer decides it is not suitable and practicable to offer an alternative identification procedure, the reasons for that decision shall be recorded.

3.16   A group identification may initially be offered if the officer in charge of the investigation considers it is more suitable than a video identification or an identification parade and the identification officer considers it practicable to arrange.

Notice to suspect

3.17[7] Unless paragraph 3.20 applies, before a video identification, an identification parade or group identification is arranged, the following shall be explained to the suspect:

    (i)   the purposes of the video identification, identification parade or group identification;

    (ii)   their entitlement to free legal advice; see Code C, paragraph 6.5;

---

[6] Pre-2002 from para.2.3.

[7] Pre-2002 para.2.15.

(iii) the procedures for holding it, including their right to have a solicitor or friend present;

(iv) that they do not have to consent to or co-operate in a video identification, identification parade or group identification;

(v) that if they do not consent to, and co-operate in, a video identification, identification parade or group identification, their refusal may be given in evidence in any subsequent trial and police may proceed covertly without their consent or make other arrangements to test whether a witness can identify them, see paragraph 3.21;

(vi) whether, for the purposes of the video identification procedure, images of them have previously been obtained, see paragraph 3.20, and if so, that they may co-operate in providing further, suitable images to be used instead;

(vii) if appropriate, the special arrangements for juveniles;

(viii) if appropriate, the special arrangements for mentally disordered or otherwise mentally vulnerable people;

(ix) that if they significantly alter their appearance between being offered an identification procedure and any attempt to hold an identification procedure, this may be given in evidence if the case comes to trial, and the identification officer may then consider other forms of identification, see paragraph 3.21 and Note 3C;

(x) that a moving image or photograph may be taken of them when they attend for any identification procedure;

(xi) whether, before their identity became known, the witness was shown photographs, a computerised or artist's composite likeness or similar likeness or image by the police, see Note 3B

(xii) that if they change their appearance before an identification parade, it may not be practicable to arrange one on the day or subsequently and, because of the appearance change, the identification officer may consider alternative methods of identification, see Note 3C;

(xiii) that they or their solicitor will be provided with details of the description of the suspect as first given by any witnesses who are to attend the video identification, identification parade, group identification or confrontation, see paragraph 3.1.

3.18[8] This information must also be recorded in a written notice handed to the suspect. The suspect must be given a reasonable opportunity to read the notice, after which, they should be asked to sign a second copy to indicate if they are willing to co-operate with the making of a video or take part in the identification parade or group identification. The signed copy shall be retained by the identification officer.

3.19 The duties of the identification officer under paragraphs 3.17 and 3.18 may be performed by the custody officer or other officer not involved in the investigation if:

(a) it is proposed to hold an identification procedure at a later date, e.g., if the suspect is to be bailed to attend an identification parade; and

(b) an inspector is not available to act as the identification officer, see paragraph 3.11, before the suspect leaves the station.

---

[8] Pre-2002 para.2.16.

The officer concerned shall inform the identification officer of the action taken and give them the signed copy of the notice. See Note 3C

3.20 If the identification officer and officer in charge of the investigation suspect, on reasonable grounds that if the suspect was given the information and notice as in paragraphs 3.17 and 3.18, they would then take steps to avoid being seen by a witness in any identification procedure, the identification officer may arrange for images of the suspect suitable for use in a video identification procedure to be obtained before giving the information and notice. If suspect's images are obtained in these circumstances, the suspect may, for the purposes of a video identification procedure, co-operate in providing suitable new images to be used instead, see paragraph 3.17(vi).

(c) Cases when the suspect is known but not available

3.21 When a known suspect is not available or has ceased to be available, see paragraph 3.4, the identification officer may make arrangements for a video identification (see Annex A). If necessary, the identification officer may follow the video identification procedures but using still images. Any suitable moving or still images may be used and these may be obtained covertly if necessary. Alternatively, the identification officer may make arrangements for a group identification. See Note 3D These provisions may also be applied to juveniles where the consent of their parent or guardian is either refused or reasonable efforts to obtain that consent have failed. (see paragraph 2.12)

3.22 Any covert activity should be strictly limited to that necessary to test the ability of the witness to identify the suspect.

3.23 The identification officer may arrange for the suspect to be confronted by the witness if none of the options referred to in paragraphs 3.5 to 3.10 or 3.21 are practicable. A 'confrontation' is when the suspect is directly confronted by the witness. A confrontation does not require the suspect's consent. Confrontations must be carried out in accordance with Annex D.

3.24 Requirements for information to be given to, or sought from, a suspect or for the suspect to be given an opportunity to view images before they are shown to a witness, do not apply if the suspect's lack of co-operation prevents the necessary action.

(d) Documentation[9]

3.25 A record shall be made of the video identification, identification parade, group identification or confrontation on forms provided for the purpose.

3.26 If the identification officer considers it is not practicable to hold a video identification or identification parade requested by the suspect, the reasons shall be recorded and explained to the suspect.

3.27 A record shall be made of a person's failure or refusal to co-operate in a video identification, identification parade or group identification and, if applicable, of the grounds for obtaining images in accordance with paragraph 3.20.

---

[9] This section restates pre-2002 paras 2.19 to 2.21.

(e) Showing films and photographs of incidents and information released to the media

3.28[10] Nothing in this Code inhibits showing films or photographs to the public through the national or local media, or to police officers for the purposes of recognition and tracing suspects. However, when such material is shown to potential witnesses, including police officers, see Note 3A, to obtain identification evidence, it shall be shown on an individual basis to avoid any possibility of collusion, and, as far as possible, the showing shall follow the principles for video identification if the suspect is known, see Annex A, or identification by photographs if the suspect is not known, see Annex E.

3.29[11] When a broadcast or publication is made, see paragraph 3.28, a copy of the relevant material released to the media for the purposes of recognising or tracing the suspect, shall be kept. The suspect or their solicitor shall be allowed to view such material before any procedures under paragraphs 3.5 to 3.10, 3.21 or 3.23 are carried out, provided it is practicable and would not unreasonably delay the investigation. Each witness involved in the procedure shall be asked, after they have taken part, whether they have seen any broadcast or published films or photographs relating to the offence or any description of the suspect and their replies shall be recorded. This paragraph does not affect any separate requirement under the Criminal Procedure and Investigations Act 1996 to retain material in connection with criminal investigations.

(f) Destruction and retention of photographs and images taken or used in identification procedures

3.30 PACE, section 64A, provides powers to take photographs of suspects detained at police stations and allows these photographs to be used or disclosed only for purposes related to the prevention or detection of crime, the investigation of offences or the conduct of prosecutions by, or on behalf of, police or other law enforcement and prosecuting authorities inside and outside the United Kingdom. After being so used or disclosed, they may be retained but can only be used or disclosed for the same purposes.

3.31 Subject to paragraph 3.33, the photographs (and all negatives and copies), of suspects not detained and any moving images, (and copies), of suspects whether or not they have been detained which are taken for the purposes of, or in connection with, the identification procedures in paragraphs 3.5 to 3.10, 3.21 or 3.23 must be destroyed unless the suspect:

    (a) is charged with, or informed they may be prosecuted for, a recordable offence;

    (b) is prosecuted for a recordable offence;

    (c) is cautioned for a recordable offence or given a warning or reprimand in accordance with the Crime and Disorder Act 1998 for a recordable offence; or

    (d) gives informed consent, in writing, for the photograph or images to be retained for purposes described in paragraph 3.30.

---

[10] Pre-2002 para.2.21A.
[11] Pre-2002 para.2.21B.

3.32 When paragraph 3.31 requires the destruction of any photograph or images, the person must be given an opportunity to witness the destruction or to have a certificate confirming the destruction if they request one within five days of being informed that the destruction is required.

3.33 Nothing in paragraph 3.31 affects any separate requirement under the Criminal Procedure and Investigations Act 1996 to retain material in connection with criminal investigations.

Notes for guidance

3A[12] *Except for the provisions of Annex E, paragraph 1, a police officer who is a witness for the purposes of this part of the Code is subject to the same principles and procedures as a civilian witness.*

3B[13] *When a witness attending an identification procedure has previously been shown photographs, or been shown or provided with computerised or artist's composite likenesses, or similar likenesses or pictures, it is the officer in charge of the investigation's responsibility to make the identification officer aware of this.*

3C *The purpose of paragraph 3.19 is to avoid or reduce delay in arranging identification procedures by enabling the required information and warnings, see sub-paragraphs 3.17(ix) and 3.17(xii), to be given at the earliest opportunity.*

3D *Paragraph 3.21 would apply when a known suspect deliberately makes themself 'unavailable' in order to delay or frustrate arrangements for obtaining identification evidence. It also applies when a suspect refuses or fails to take part in a video identification, an identification parade or a group identification, or refuses or fails to take part in the only practicable options from that list. It enables any suitable images of the suspect, moving or still, which are available or can be obtained, to be used in an identification procedure.*

3E[14] *When it is proposed to show photographs to a witness in accordance with Annex E, it is the responsibility of the officer in charge of the investigation to confirm to the officer responsible for supervising and directing the showing, that the first description of the suspect given by that witness has been recorded. If this description has not been recorded, the procedure under Annex E must be postponed. See Annex E paragraph 2*

3F *The admissibility and value of identification evidence obtained when carrying out the procedure under paragraph 3.2 may be compromised if:*

    (a) before a person is identified, the witness' attention is specifically drawn to that person; or

    (b) the suspect's identity becomes known before the procedure.

[12] Pre-2002 Note 2A.
[13] Pre-2002 Note 2B.
[14] Pre-2002 Note 2D.

4   Identification by fingerprints[15]

(A)   Taking fingerprints in connection with a criminal investigation

(a)   General

4.1   References to 'fingerprints' means any record, produced by any method, of the skin pattern and other physical characteristics or features of a person's:
- (i)   fingers; or
- (ii)   palms.

(b)   Action

4.2[16]   A person's fingerprints may be taken in connection with the investigation of an offence only with their consent or if paragraph 4.3 applies. If the person is at a police station consent must be in writing.

4.3[17]   PACE, section 61, provides powers to take fingerprints without consent from any person over the age of ten years:

- (a)   under section 61(3), from a person detained at a police station in consequence of being arrested for a recordable offence, see Note 4A, if they have not had their fingerprints taken in the course of the investigation of the offence unless those previously taken fingerprints are not a complete set or some or all of those fingerprints are not of sufficient quality to allow satisfactory analysis, comparison or matching.
- (b)   under section 61(4), from a person detained at a police station who has been charged with a recordable offence, see Note 4A, or informed they will be reported for such an offence if they have not had their fingerprints taken in the course of the investigation of the offence unless those previously taken fingerprints are not a complete set or some or all of those fingerprints are not of sufficient quality to allow satisfactory analysis, comparison or matching.
- (c)   under section 61(4A), from a person who has been bailed to appear at a court or police station if the person:
  - (i)   has answered to bail for a person whose fingerprints were taken previously and there are reasonable grounds for believing they are not the same person; or
  - (ii)   who has answered to bail claims to be a different person from a person whose fingerprints were previously taken;

  and in either case, the court or an officer of inspector rank or above, authorises the fingerprints to be taken at the court or police station;
- (d)   under section 61(6), from a person who has been:
  - (i)   convicted of a recordable offence;
  - (ii)   given a caution in respect of a recordable offence which, at the time of the caution, the person admitted; or
  - (iii)   warned or reprimanded under the Crime and Disorder Act 1998, section 65, for a recordable offence.

---

[15] Pre-2003 para.5.3.
[16] Pre-2003 para.3.1.
[17] Pre-2003 para.3.2.

4.4 PACE, section 27, provides power to:

    (a) require the person as in paragraph 4.3(d) to attend a police station to have their fingerprints taken if the:

        (i) person has not been in police detention for the offence and has not had their fingerprints taken in the course of the investigation of that offence; or

        (ii) fingerprints that were taken from the person in the course of the investigation of that offence, do not constitute a complete set or some, or all, of the fingerprints are not of sufficient quality to allow satisfactory analysis, comparison or matching; and

    (b) arrest, without warrant, a person who fails to comply with the requirement.

Note: The requirement must be made within one month of the date the person is convicted, cautioned, warned or reprimanded and the person must be given a period of at least 7 days within which to attend. This 7 day period need not fall during the month allowed for making the requirement

4.5 A person's fingerprints may be taken, as above, electronically.

4.6[18] Reasonable force may be used, if necessary, to take a person's fingerprints without their consent under the powers as in paragraphs 4.3 and 4.4.

4.7[19] Before any fingerprints are taken with, or without, consent as above, the person must be informed:

    (a) of the reason their fingerprints are to be taken;

    (b) of the grounds on which the relevant authority has been given if the powers mentioned in paragraph 4.3 (c) applies;

    (c) that their fingerprints may be retained and may be subject of a speculative search against other fingerprints, see Note 4B, unless destruction of the fingerprints is required in accordance with Annex F, Part (a); and

    (d) that if their fingerprints are required to be destroyed, they may witness their destruction as provided for in Annex F, Part (a).

(c) Documentation

4.8[20] A record must be made as soon as possible, of the reason for taking a person's fingerprints without consent. If force is used, a record shall be made of the circumstances and those present.

4.9[21] A record shall be made when a person has been informed under the terms of paragraph 4.7(c), of the possibility that their fingerprints may be subject of a speculative search.

(B) Taking fingerprints in connection with immigration enquiries

Action

4.10 A person's fingerprints may be taken for the purposes of Immigration Service enquiries in accordance with powers and procedures other than under PACE

---

[18] Pre-2003 from para.3.2.
[19] Based on pre-2003 Note 2A.
[20] Pre-2003 para.3.7.
[21] Pre-2003 para.3.8.

and for which the Immigration Service (not the police) are responsible, only with the person's consent in writing or if paragraph 4.11 applies.

4.11   Powers to take fingerprints for these purposes without consent are given to police and immigration officers under the:

    (a)   Immigration Act 1971, Schedule 2, paragraph 18(2), when it is reasonably necessary for the purposes of identifying a person detained under the Immigration Act 1971, Schedule 2, paragraph 16 (Detention of person liable to examination or removal);

    (b)   Immigration and Asylum Act 1999, section 141(7)(a), from a person who fails to produce, on arrival, a valid passport with a photograph or some other document satisfactorily establishing their identity and nationality if an immigration officer does not consider the person has a reasonable excuse for the failure;

    (c)   Immigration and Asylum Act 1999, section 141(7)(b), from a person who has been refused entry to the UK but has been temporarily admitted if an immigration officer reasonably suspects the person might break a condition imposed on them relating to residence or reporting to a police or immigration officer, and their decision is confirmed by a chief immigration officer;

    (d)   Immigration and Asylum Act 1999, section 141(7)(c), when directions are given to remove a person:

-    as an illegal entrant,
-    liable to removal under the Immigration and Asylum Act 1999, section 10,
-    who is the subject of a deportation order from the UK;

    (e)   Immigration and Asylum Act 1999, section 141(7)(d), from a person arrested under UK immigration laws under the Immigration Act 1971, Schedule 2, paragraph 17;

    (f)   Immigration and Asylum Act 1999, section 141(7)(e), from a person who has made a claim:

-    for asylum
-    under Article 3 of the European Convention on Human Rights; or

    (g)   Immigration and Asylum Act 1999, section 141(7)(f), from a person who is a dependant of someone who falls into (b) to (f) above.

4.12   The Immigration and Asylum Act 1999, section 142(3), gives a police and immigration officer power to arrest, without warrant, a person who fails to comply with a requirement imposed by the Secretary of State to attend a specified place for fingerprinting.

4.13   Before any fingerprints are taken, with or without consent, the person must be informed:

    (a)   of the reason their fingerprints are to be taken;

    (b)   the fingerprints, and all copies of them, will be destroyed in accordance with Annex F, Part B.

4.14 Reasonable force may be used, if necessary, to take a person's fingerprints without their consent under powers as in paragraph 4.11.

4.15 Paragraphs 4.1 and 4.8 apply.

Notes for guidance

4A[22] *References to 'recordable offences' in this Code relate to those offences for which convictions, cautions, reprimands and warnings may be recorded in national police records. See PACE, section 27(4). The recordable offences current at the time when this Code was prepared, are any offences which carry a sentence of imprisonment on conviction (irrespective of the period, or the age of the offender or actual sentence passed) as well as the non-imprisonable offences under the Street Offences Act 1959, section 1 (loitering or soliciting for purposes of prostitution), the Telecommunications Act 1984, section 43 (improper use of public telecommunications systems), the Road Traffic Act 1988, section 25 (tampering with motor vehicles), the Malicious Communications Act 1988, section 1 (sending letters, etc. with intent to cause distress or anxiety) and others listed in the National Police Records (Recordable Offences) Regulations 2000.*

4B *Fingerprints or a DNA sample (and the information derived from it) taken from a person arrested on suspicion of being involved in a recordable offence, or charged with such an offence, or informed they will be reported for such an offence, may be subject of a speculative search. This means the fingerprints or DNA sample may be checked against other fingerprints and DNA records held by, or on behalf of, the police and other law enforcement authorities in, or outside, the UK, or held in connection with, or as a result of, an investigation of an offence inside or outside the UK. Fingerprints and samples taken from a person suspected of committing a recordable offence but not arrested, charged or informed they will be reported for it, may be subject to a speculative search only if the person consents in writing. The following is an example of a basic form of words:*

'I consent to my fingerprints and DNA sample and information derived from it being retained and used only for purposes related to the prevention and detection of a crime, the investigation of an offence or the conduct of a prosecution either nationally or internationally.

I understand that my fingerprints or this sample may be checked against other fingerprint and DNA records held by or on behalf of relevant law enforcement authorities, either nationally or internationally.

I understand that once I have given my consent for the sample to be retained and used I cannot withdraw this consent.'

See Annex F regarding the retention and use of fingerprints taken with consent for elimination purposes.

5   Examinations to establish identity and the taking of photographs

(A)   Detainees at police stations

(a)   Searching or examination of detainees at police stations

5.1   PACE, section 54A (1), allows a detainee at a police station to be searched or examined or both, to establish:

---

[22] Based on pre-2003 Note 3A.

(a) whether they have any marks, features or injuries that would tend to identify them as a person involved in the commission of an offence and to photograph any identifying marks, see paragraph 5.5; or

(b) their identity, see Note 5A.

A person detained at a police station to be searched under a stop and search power, see Code A, is not a detainee for the purposes of these powers.

5.2   A search and/or examination to find marks under section 54A (1) (a) may be carried out without the detainee's consent, see paragraph 2.12, only if authorised by an officer of at least inspector rank when consent has been withheld or it is not practicable to obtain consent, see Note 5D.

5.3   A search or examination to establish a suspect's identity under section 54A (1) (b) may be carried out without the detainee's consent, see paragraph 2.12, only if authorised by an officer of at least inspector rank when the detainee has refused to identify themselves or the authorising officer has reasonable grounds for suspecting the person is not who they claim to be.

5.4   Any marks that assist in establishing the detainee's identity, or their identification as a person involved in the commission of an offence, are identifying marks. Such marks may be photographed with the detainee's consent, see paragraph 2.12; or without their consent if it is withheld or it is not practicable to obtain it, see Note 5D.

5.5   A detainee may only be searched, examined and photographed under section 54A, by a police officer of the same sex.

5.6   Any photographs of identifying marks, taken under section 54A, may be used or disclosed only for purposes related to the prevention or detection of crime, the investigation of offences or the conduct of prosecutions by, or on behalf of, police or other law enforcement and prosecuting authorities inside, and outside, the UK. After being so used or disclosed, the photograph may be retained but must not be used or disclosed except for these purposes, see Note 5B.

5.7   The powers, as in paragraph 5.1, do not affect any separate requirement under the Criminal Procedure and Investigations Act 1996 to retain material in connection with criminal investigations.

5.8   Authority for the search and/or examination for the purposes of paragraphs 5.2 and 5.3 may be given orally or in writing. If given orally, the authorising officer must confirm it in writing as soon as practicable. A separate authority is required for each purpose which applies.

5.9   If it is established a person is unwilling to co-operate sufficiently to enable a search and/or examination to take place or a suitable photograph to be taken, an officer may use reasonable force to:

(a) search and/or examine a detainee without their consent; and

(b) photograph any identifying marks without their consent.

5.10   The thoroughness and extent of any search or examination carried out in accordance with the powers in section 54A must be no more than the officer considers necessary to achieve the required purpose. Any search or examination which involves the removal of more than the person's outer clothing shall be conducted in accordance with Code C, Annex A, paragraph 11.

5.11   An intimate search may not be carried out under the powers in section 54A.

(b)   Photographing detainees at police stations

5.12   Under PACE, section 64A, an officer may photograph a detainee at a police station:

(a)   with their consent; or

(b)   without their consent if it is:

   (i)   withheld; or

   (ii)   not practicable to obtain their consent.

   See Note 5E

and paragraph 5.6 applies to the retention and use of photographs taken under this section as it applies to the retention and use of photographs taken under section 54A, see Note 5B.

5.13   The officer proposing to take a detainee's photograph may, for this purpose, require the person to remove any item or substance worn on, or over, all, or any part of, their head or face. If they do not comply with such a requirement, the officer may remove the item or substance.

5.14   If it is established the detainee is unwilling to co-operate sufficiently to enable a suitable photograph to be taken and it is not reasonably practicable to take the photograph covertly, an officer may use reasonable force:

(a)   to take their photograph without their consent; and

(b)   for the purpose of taking the photograph, remove any item or substance worn on, or over, all, or any part of, the person's head or face which they have failed to remove when asked.

5.15   For the purposes of this Code, a photograph may be obtained without the person's consent by making a copy of an image of them taken at any time on a camera system installed anywhere in the police station.

(c)   Information to be given

5.16   When a person is searched, examined or photographed under the provisions as in paragraph 5.1 and 5.12, or their photograph obtained as in paragraph 5.15, they must be informed of the:

(a)   purpose of the search, examination or photograph;

(b)   grounds on which the relevant authority, if applicable, has been given; and

(c)   purposes for which the photograph may be used, disclosed or retained.

This information must be given before the search or examination commences or the photograph is taken, except if the photograph is:

   (i)   to be taken covertly;

   (ii)   obtained as in paragraph 5.15, in which case the person must be informed as soon as practicable after the photograph is taken or obtained.

(d)   Documentation

5.17   A record must be made when a detainee is searched, examined, or a photograph of the person, or any identifying marks found on them, are taken. The record must include the:

(a)   identity, subject to paragraph 2.18, of the officer carrying out the search, examination or taking the photograph;

(b)   purpose of the search, examination or photograph and the outcome;

(c)   detainee's consent to the search, examination or photograph, or the reason the person was searched, examined or photographed without consent;

(d)   giving of any authority as in paragraphs 5.2 and 5.3, the grounds for giving it and the authorising officer.

5.18   If force is used when searching, examining or taking a photograph in accordance with this section, a record shall be made of the circumstances and those present.

(B)   Persons at police stations not detained

5.19   When there are reasonable grounds for suspecting the involvement of a person in a criminal offence, but that person is at a police station voluntarily and not detained, the provisions of paragraphs 5.1 to 5.18 should apply, subject to the modifications in the following paragraphs.

5.20   References to the 'person being detained' and to the powers mentioned in paragraph 5.1 which apply only to detainees at police stations shall be omitted.

5.21   Force may not be used to:
   (a)   search and/or examine the person to:
      (i)   discover whether they have any marks that would tend to identify them as a person involved in the commission of an offence; or
      (ii)   establish their identity, see Note 5A;
   (b)   take photographs of any identifying marks, see paragraph 5.4; or
   (c)   take a photograph of the person.

5.22   Subject to paragraph 5.24, the photographs or images, of persons not detained, or of their identifying marks, must be destroyed (together with any negatives and copies) unless the person:
   (a)   is charged with, or informed they may be prosecuted for, a recordable offence;
   (b)   is prosecuted for a recordable offence;
   (c)   is cautioned for a recordable offence or given a warning or reprimand in accordance with the Crime and Disorder Act 1998 for a recordable offence; or
   (d)   gives informed consent, in writing, for the photograph or image to be retained as in paragraph 5.6.

5.23   When paragraph 5.22 requires the destruction of any photograph or image, the person must be given an opportunity to witness the destruction or to have a certificate confirming the destruction provided they so request the certificate within five days of being informed the destruction is required.

5.24   Nothing in paragraph 5.22 affects any separate requirement under the Criminal Procedure and Investigations Act 1996 to retain material in connection with criminal investigations.

Notes for guidance

5A   *The conditions under which fingerprints may be taken to assist in establishing a person's identity, are described in Section 4.*

5B   *Examples of purposes related to the prevention or detection of crime, the investigation of offences or the conduct of prosecutions include:*
   (a)   checking the photograph against other photographs held in records or in connection with, or as a result of, an investigation of an offence to establish whether the person is liable to arrest for other offences;
   (b)   when the person is arrested at the same time as other people, or at a time when it is likely that other people will be arrested, using the photograph to help establish who was arrested, at what time and where;

(c)   when the real identity of the person is not known and cannot be readily ascertained or there are reasonable grounds for doubting a name and other personal details given by the person, are their real name and personal details. In these circumstances, using or disclosing the photograph to help to establish or verify their real identity or determine whether they are liable to arrest for some other offence, e.g. by checking it against other photographs held in records or in connection with, or as a result of, an investigation of an offence;

(d)   when it appears any identification procedure in section 3 may need to be arranged for which the person's photograph would assist;

(e)   when the person's release without charge may be required, and if the release is:

(i)   on bail to appear at a police station, using the photograph to help verify the person's identity when they answer their bail and if the person does not answer their bail, to assist in arresting them; or

(ii)   without bail, using the photograph to help verify their identity or assist in locating them for the purposes of serving them with a summons to appear at court in criminal proceedings;

(f)   when the person has answered to bail at a police station and there are reasonable grounds for doubting they are the person who was previously granted bail, using the photograph to help establish or verify their identity;

(g)   when the person arrested on a warrant claims to be a different person from the person named on the warrant and a photograph would help to confirm or disprove their claim;

(h)   when the person has been charged with, reported for, or convicted of, a recordable offence and their photograph is not already on record as a result of (a) to (f) or their photograph is on record but their appearance has changed since it was taken and the person has not yet been released or brought before a court.

5C   There is no power to arrest a person convicted of a recordable offence solely to take their photograph. The power to take photographs in this section applies only where the person is in custody as a result of the exercise of another power, e.g. arrest for fingerprinting under PACE, section 27.

5D   Examples of when it would not be practicable to obtain a detainee's consent, see paragraph 2.12, to a search, examination or the taking of a photograph of an identifying mark include:

(a)   when the person is drunk or otherwise unfit to give consent;

(b)   when there are reasonable grounds to suspect that if the person became aware a search or examination was to take place or an identifying mark was to be photographed, they would take steps to prevent this happening, e.g. by violently resisting, covering or concealing the mark etc and it would not otherwise be possible to carry out the search or examination or to photograph any identifying mark;

(c)   in the case of a juvenile, if the parent or guardian cannot be contacted in sufficient time to allow the search or examination to be carried out or the photograph to be taken.

5E Examples of when it would not be practicable to obtain the person's consent, see paragraph 2.12, to a photograph being taken include:

(a) when the person is drunk or otherwise unfit to give consent;

(b) when there are reasonable grounds to suspect that if the person became aware a photograph, suitable to be used or disclosed for the use and disclosure described in paragraph 5.6, was to be taken, they would take steps to prevent it being taken, e.g. by violently resisting, covering or distorting their face etc, and it would not otherwise be possible to take a suitable photograph;

(c) when, in order to obtain a suitable photograph, it is necessary to take it covertly; and

(d) in the case of a juvenile, if the parent or guardian cannot be contacted in sufficient time to allow the photograph to be taken.

6 Identification by body samples and impressions[23]

(A) General

6.1 References to:

(a) an 'intimate sample' mean a dental impression or sample of blood, semen or any other tissue fluid, urine, or pubic hair, or a swab taken from a person's body orifice other than the mouth;

(b) a 'non-intimate sample' means:

(i) a sample of hair, other than pubic hair, which includes hair plucked with the root, see Note 6A;

(ii) a sample taken from a nail or from under a nail;

(iii) a swab taken from any part of a person's body including the mouth but not any other body orifice;

(iv) saliva;

(v) a skin impression which means any record, other than a finger-print, which is a record, in any form and produced by any method, of the skin pattern and other physical characteristics or features of the whole, or any part of, a person's foot or of any other part of their body.

(B) Action

(a) Intimate samples

6.2[24] PACE, section 62, provides that intimate samples may be taken under:

(a) section 62(1), from a person in police detention only:

(i) if a police officer of inspector rank or above has reasonable grounds to believe such an impression or sample will tend to confirm or disprove the suspect's involvement in a recordable offence, see Note 4A, and gives authorisation for a sample to be taken; and

(ii) with the suspect's written consent;

[23] Pre-2003 para.5.5.

[24] Based on pre-2003 paras 5.1 and 5.1A.

(b) section 62(1A), from a person not in police detention but from whom two or more non-intimate samples have been taken in the course of an investigation of an offence and the samples, though suitable, have proved insufficient if:

(i) a police officer of inspector rank or above authorises it to be taken; and

(ii) the person concerned gives their written consent. See Notes 6B and 6C

6.3[25] Before a suspect is asked to provide an intimate sample, they must be warned that if they refuse without good cause their refusal may harm their case if it comes to trial, see Note 6D. If the suspect is in police detention and not legally represented, they must also be reminded of their entitlement to have free legal advice, see Code C, paragraph 6.5, and the reminder noted in the custody record. If paragraph 6.2(b) applies and the person is attending a station voluntarily, their entitlement to free legal advice as in Code C, paragraph 3.21 shall be explained to them.

6.4[26] Dental impressions may only be taken by a registered dentist. Other intimate samples, except for samples of urine, may only be taken by a registered medical practitioner or registered nurse or paramedic.

(b)   Non-intimate samples

6.5[27] A non-intimate sample may be taken from a detainee only with their written consent or if paragraph 6.6 applies.

6.6[28] (a) Under section 63 a non-intimate sample may **not** be taken from a person without consent and the consent must be in writing

(aa) a non-intimate sample may be taken from a person without the appropriate consent in the following circumstances:

(i) under section 63(2A) where the person is in police detention as a consequence of his arrest for a recordable offence and he has not had a non-intimate sample of the same type and from the same part of the body taken in the course of the investigation of the offence by the police or he has had such a sample taken but it proved insufficient.

(ii) Under section 63(3)(a) where he is being held in custody by the police on the authority of a court and an officer of at least the rank of inspector authorises it to be taken.

(b) under section 63(3A), from a person charged with a recordable offence or informed they will be reported for such an offence: and

(i) that person has not had a non-intimate sample taken from them in the course of the investigation; or

(ii) if they have had a sample taken, it proved unsuitable or insufficient for the same form of analysis, see Note 6B; or

(c) under section 63(3B), from a person convicted of a recordable offence after the date on which that provision came into effect. PACE, section 63A, describes the circumstances in which a police officer may require

---

[25] Pre-2003 para.5.2.
[26] Based on pre-2003 para.5.3.
[27] Pre-2003 para.5.4.
[28] Based on pre-2003 para.5.5.

a person convicted of a recordable offence to attend a police station for a non-intimate sample to be taken.

6.7[29]   Reasonable force may be used, if necessary, to take a non-intimate sample from a person without their consent under the powers mentioned in paragraph 6.6.

6.8[30]   Before any intimate sample is taken with consent or non-intimate sample is taken with, or without, consent, the person must be informed:

(a)   of the reason for taking the sample;

(b)   of the grounds on which the relevant authority has been given;

(c)   that the sample or information derived from the sample may be retained and subject of a speculative search, see Note 6E, unless their destruction is required as in Annex F, Part A.

6.9[31]   When clothing needs to be removed in circumstances likely to cause embarrassment to the person, no person of the opposite sex who is not a registered medical practitioner or registered health care professional shall be present, (unless in the case of a juvenile, mentally disordered or mentally vulnerable person, that person specifically requests the presence of an appropriate adult of the opposite sex who is readily available) nor shall anyone whose presence is unnecessary. However, in the case of a juvenile, this is subject to the overriding proviso that such a removal of clothing may take place in the absence of the appropriate adult only if the juvenile signifies, in their presence, that they prefer the adult's absence and they agree.

(c)   Documentation[32]

6.10   A record of the reasons for taking a sample or impression and, if applicable, of its destruction must be made as soon as practicable. If force is used, a record shall be made of the circumstances and those present. If written consent is given to the taking of a sample or impression, the fact must be recorded in writing.

6.11   A record must be made of a warning given as required by paragraph 6.3.

6.12   A record shall be made of the fact that a person has been informed as in paragraph 6.8(c) that samples may be subject of a speculative search.

Notes for guidance

6A[33]   *When hair samples are taken for the purpose of DNA analysis (rather than for other purposes such as making a visual match), the suspect should be permitted a reasonable choice as to what part of the body the hairs are taken from. When hairs are plucked, they should be plucked individually, unless the suspect prefers otherwise and no more should be plucked than the person taking them reasonably considers necessary for a sufficient sample.*

6B[34] *(a) An insufficient sample is one which is not sufficient either in quantity or quality to provide information for a particular form of analy-*

---

[29]   Pre-2003 para.5.6.

[30]   Based on pre-2003 paras 5.11A and 5.11B.

[31]   Pre-2003 para.5.12.

[32]   This section restates pre-2003 paras 5.9, 5.10.

[33]   Pre-2003 Note 5C.

[34]   Based on pre-2003 Note 5B.

sis, such as DNA analysis. A sample may also be insufficient if enough information cannot be obtained from it by analysis because of loss, destruction, damage or contamination of the sample or as a result of an earlier, unsuccessful attempt at analysis.

(b) *An unsuitable sample is one which, by its nature, is not suitable for a particular form of analysis.*

6C[35] *Nothing in paragraph 6.2 prevents intimate samples being taken for elimination purposes with the consent of the person concerned but the provisions of paragraph 2.12 relating to the role of the appropriate adult, should be applied. Paragraph 6.2(b) does not, however, apply where the non-intimate samples were previously taken under the Terrorism Act 2000, Schedule 8, paragraph 10.*

6D[36] *In warning a person who is asked to provide an intimate sample as in paragraph 6.3, the following form of words may be used:*

'You do not have to provide this sample/allow this swab or impression to be taken, but I must warn you that if you refuse without good cause, your refusal may harm your case if it comes to trial.'

6E *Fingerprints or a DNA sample and the information derived from it taken from a person arrested on suspicion of being involved in a recordable offence, or charged with such an offence, or informed they will be reported for such an offence, may be subject of a speculative search. This means they may be checked against other fingerprints and DNA records held by, or on behalf of, the police and other law enforcement authorities in or outside the UK or held in connection with, or as a result of, an investigation of an offence inside or outside the UK. Fingerprints and samples taken from any other person, e.g. a person suspected of committing a recordable offence but who has not been arrested, charged or informed they will be reported for it, may be subject to a speculative search only if the person consents in writing to their fingerprints being subject of such a search. The following is an example of a basic form of words:*

'I consent to my fingerprints/DNA sample and information derived from it being retained and used only for purposes related to the prevention and detection of a crime, the investigation of an offence or the conduct of a prosecution either nationally or internationally.

I understand that this sample may be checked against other fingerprint/DNA records held by or on behalf of relevant law enforcement authorities, either nationally or internationally.

I understand that once I have given my consent for the sample to be retained and used I cannot withdraw this consent.'

See Annex F regarding the retention and use of fingerprints and samples taken with consent for elimination purposes.

6F *Samples of urine and non-intimate samples taken in accordance with sections 63B and 63C of PACE may not be used for identification purposes in accordance with this Code. See Code C note for guidance 17D.*

---

[35] Based on pre-2003 Note 5E.
[36] Pre-2003 Note 5A.

ANNEX A

VIDEO IDENTIFICATION[37]

(a) General

1.[38] The arrangements for obtaining and ensuring the availability of a suitable set of images to be used in a video identification must be the responsibility of an identification officer, who has no direct involvement with the case.

2.[39] The set of images must include the suspect and at least eight other people who, so far as possible, resemble the suspect in age, height, general appearance and position in life. Only one suspect shall appear in any set unless there are two suspects of roughly similar appearance, in which case they may be shown together with at least twelve other people.

3.[40] The images used to conduct a video identification shall, as far as possible, show the suspect and other people in the same positions or carrying out the same sequence of movements. They shall also show the suspect and other people under identical conditions unless the identification officer reasonably believes:

    (a) because of the suspect's failure or refusal to co-operate or other reasons, it is not practicable for the conditions to be identical; and

    (b) any difference in the conditions would not direct a witness' attention to any individual image.

4. The reasons identical conditions are not practicable shall be recorded on forms provided for the purpose.

5. Provision must be made for each person shown to be identified by number.

6. If police officers are shown, any numerals or other identifying badges must be concealed. If a prison inmate is shown, either as a suspect or not, then either all, or none of, the people shown should be in prison clothing.

7. The suspect or their solicitor, friend, or appropriate adult must be given a reasonable opportunity to see the complete set of images before it is shown to any witness. If the suspect has a reasonable objection to the set of images or any of the participants, the suspect shall be asked to state the reasons for the objection. Steps shall, if practicable, be taken to remove the grounds for objection. If this is not practicable, the suspect and/or their representative shall be told why their objections cannot be met and the objection, the reason given for it and why it cannot be met shall be recorded on forms provided for the purpose.

8.[41] Before the images are shown in accordance with paragraph 7, the suspect or their solicitor shall be provided with details of the first description of the suspect by any witnesses who are to attend the video identification. When a broadcast or publication is made, as in paragraph 3.28, the suspect or their solicitor must also be allowed to view any material released to the media by the police for the purpose of recognising or tracing the suspect, provided it is practicable and would not unreasonably delay the investigation.

---

[37] Pre-2002 this was Annex B.
[38] Pre-2002 para.2.
[39] Pre-2002 para.3.
[40] Based on pre-2002 para.4.
[41] Pre-2002 Note 8A.

9.[42]   The suspect's solicitor, if practicable, shall be given reasonable notification of the time and place the video identification is to be conducted so a representative may attend on behalf of the suspect. If a solicitor has not been instructed, this information shall be given to the suspect. The suspect may not be present when the images are shown to the witness(es). In the absence of the suspect's representative, the viewing itself shall be recorded on video. No unauthorised people may be present.

(b)   Conducting the video identification[43]

10.   The identification officer is responsible for making the appropriate arrangements to make sure, before they see the set of images, witnesses are not able to communicate with each other about the case or overhear a witness who has already seen the material. There must be no discussion with the witness about the composition of the set of images and they must not be told whether a previous witness has made any identification.

11.   Only one witness may see the set of images at a time. Immediately before the images are shown, the witness shall be told that the person they saw on a specified earlier occasion may, or may not, appear in the images they are shown and that if they cannot make a positive identification, they should say so. The witness shall be advised that at any point, they may ask to see a particular part of the set of images or to have a particular image frozen for them to study. Furthermore, it should be pointed out to the witness that there is no limit on how many times they can view the whole set of images or any part of them. However, they should be asked not to make any decision as to whether the person they saw is on the set of images until they have seen the whole set at least twice.

12.   Once the witness has seen the whole set of images at least twice and has indicated that they do not want to view the images, or any part of them, again, the witness shall be asked to say whether the individual they saw in person on a specified earlier occasion has been shown and, if so, to identify them by number of the image. The witness will then be shown that image to confirm the identification, see paragraph 17.

13.   Care must be taken not to direct the witness' attention to any one individual image or give any indication of the suspect's identity. Where a witness has previously made an identification by photographs, or a computerised or artist's composite or similar likeness, the witness must not be reminded of such a photograph or composite likeness once a suspect is available for identification by other means in accordance with this Code. Nor must the witness be reminded of any description of the suspect.

14.   After the procedure, each witness shall be asked whether they have seen any broadcast or published films or photographs, or any descriptions of suspects relating to the offence and their reply shall be recorded.

(c)   Image security and destruction

15.   Arrangements shall be made for all relevant material containing sets of images used for specific identification procedures to be kept securely and their

---

[42] Pre-2002 para.8.
[43] Pre-2002, the paragraphs in this section were numbered 9–16.

movements accounted for. In particular, no-one involved in the investigation shall be permitted to view the material prior to it being shown to any witness.
16.   As appropriate, paragraph 3.30 or 3.31 applies to the destruction or retention of relevant sets of images.

(d) Documentation

17.   A record must be made of all those participating in, or seeing, the set of images whose names are known to the police.
18.   A record of the conduct of the video identification must be made on forms provided for the purpose. This shall include anything said by the witness about any identifications or the conduct of the procedure and any reasons it was not practicable to comply with any of the provisions of this Code governing the conduct of video identifications.

ANNEX B

IDENTIFICATION PARADES[44]

(a) General

1.   A suspect must be given a reasonable opportunity to have a solicitor or friend present, and the suspect shall be asked to indicate on a second copy of the notice whether or not they wish to do so.
2.   An identification parade may take place either in a normal room or one equipped with a screen permitting witnesses to see members of the identification parade without being seen. The procedures for the composition and conduct of the identification parade are the same in both cases, subject to paragraph 8 (except that an identification parade involving a screen may take place only when the suspect's solicitor, friend or appropriate adult is present or the identification parade is recorded on video).
3.   Before the identification parade takes place, the suspect or their solicitor shall be provided with details of the first description of the suspect by any witnesses who are attending the identification parade. When a broadcast or publication is made as in paragraph 3.28, the suspect or their solicitor should also be allowed to view any material released to the media by the police for the purpose of recognising or tracing the suspect, provided it is practicable to do so and would not unreasonably delay the investigation.

(b) Identification parades involving prison inmates

4.   If a prison inmate is required for identification, and there are no security problems about the person leaving the establishment, they may be asked to participate in an identification parade or video identification.
5.   An identification parade may be held in a Prison Department establishment but shall be conducted, as far as practicable under normal identification parade rules. Members of the public shall make up the identification parade

---

[44] Pre-2002 this was Annex A.

unless there are serious security, or control, objections to their admission to the establishment. In such cases, or if a group or video identification is arranged within the establishment, other inmates may participate. If an inmate is the suspect, they are not required to wear prison clothing for the identification parade unless the other people taking part are other inmates in similar clothing, or are members of the public who are prepared to wear prison clothing for the occasion.

(c)   Conduct of the identification parade

6.   Immediately before the identification parade, the suspect must be reminded of the procedures governing its conduct and cautioned in the terms of Code C, paragraphs 10.5 or 10.6, as appropriate.

7.   All unauthorised people must be excluded from the place where the identification parade is held.

8.   Once the identification parade has been formed, everything afterwards, in respect of it, shall take place in the presence and hearing of the suspect and any interpreter, solicitor, friend or appropriate adult who is present (unless the identification parade involves a screen, in which case everything said to, or by, any witness at the place where the identification parade is held, must be said in the hearing and presence of the suspect's solicitor, friend or appropriate adult or be recorded on video).

9.   The identification parade shall consist of at least eight people (in addition to the suspect) who, so far as possible, resemble the suspect in age, height, general appearance and position in life. Only one suspect shall be included in an identification parade unless there are two suspects of roughly similar appearance, in which case they may be paraded together with at least twelve other people. In no circumstances shall more than two suspects be included in one identification parade and where there are separate identification parades, they shall be made up of different people.

10.   If the suspect has an unusual physical feature, e.g., a facial scar, tattoo or distinctive hairstyle or hair colour which cannot be replicated on other members of the identification parade, steps may be taken to conceal the location of that feature on the suspect and the other members of the identification parade if the suspect and their solicitor, or appropriate adult, agree. For example, by use of a plaster or a hat, so that all members of the identification parade resemble each other in general appearance.

11.   When all members of a similar group are possible suspects, separate identification parades shall be held for each unless there are two suspects of similar appearance when they may appear on the same identification parade with at least twelve other members of the group who are not suspects. When police officers in uniform form an identification parade any numerals or other identifying badges shall be concealed.

12.   When the suspect is brought to the place where the identification parade is to be held, they shall be asked if they have any objection to the arrangements for the identification parade or to any of the other participants in it and to state the reasons for the objection. The suspect may obtain advice from their solicitor or friend, if present, before the identification parade proceeds. If the suspect has a reasonable objection to the arrangements or any of the participants, steps shall, if practicable, be taken to remove the grounds for objection. When it is not practicable to do so, the suspect shall be told why their objections cannot be met and

the objection, the reason given for it and why it cannot be met, shall be recorded on forms provided for the purpose.

13.　The suspect may select their own position in the line, but may not otherwise interfere with the order of the people forming the line. When there is more than one witness, the suspect must be told, after each witness has left the room, that they can, if they wish, change position in the line. Each position in the line must be clearly numbered, whether by means of a number laid on the floor in front of each identification parade member or by other means.

14.　Appropriate arrangements must be made to make sure, before witnesses attend the identification parade, they are not able to:

    (i)　communicate with each other about the case or overhear a witness who has already seen the identification parade;

   (ii)　see any member of the identification parade;

  (iii)　see, or be reminded of, any photograph or description of the suspect or be given any other indication as to the suspect's identity; or

  (iv)　see the suspect before or after the identification parade.

15.　The person conducting a witness to an identification parade must not discuss with them the composition of the identification parade and, in particular, must not disclose whether a previous witness has made any identification.

16.　Witnesses shall be brought in one at a time. Immediately before the witness inspects the identification parade, they shall be told the person they saw on a specified earlier occasion may, or may not, be present and if they cannot make a positive identification, they should say so. The witness must also be told they should not make any decision about whether the person they saw is on the identification parade until they have looked at each member at least twice.

17.　When the officer or civilian support staff (see paragraph 3.11) conducting the identification procedure is satisfied the witness has properly looked at each member of the identification parade, they shall ask the witness whether the person they saw on a specified earlier occasion is on the identification parade and, if so, to indicate the number of the person concerned, see paragraph 28.

18.　If the witness wishes to hear any identification parade member speak, adopt any specified posture or move, they shall first be asked whether they can identify any person(s) on the identification parade on the basis of appearance only. When the request is to hear members of the identification parade speak, the witness shall be reminded that the participants in the identification parade have been chosen on the basis of physical appearance only. Members of the identification parade may then be asked to comply with the witness' request to hear them speak, see them move or adopt any specified posture.

19.　If the witness requests that the person they have indicated remove anything used for the purposes of paragraph 10 to conceal the location of an unusual physical feature, that person may be asked to remove it.

20.　If the witness makes an identification after the identification parade has ended, the suspect and, if present, their solicitor, interpreter or friend shall be informed. When this occurs, consideration should be given to allowing the witness a second opportunity to identify the suspect.

21.　After the procedure, each witness shall be asked whether they have seen any broadcast or published films or photographs or any descriptions of suspects relating to the offence and their reply shall be recorded.

22.　When the last witness has left, the suspect shall be asked whether they wish to make any comments on the conduct of the identification parade.

(d)   Documentation

23.   A video recording must normally be taken of the identification parade. If that is impracticable, a colour photograph must be taken. A copy of the video recording or photograph shall be supplied, on request, to the suspect or their solicitor within a reasonable time.

24.   As appropriate, paragraph 3.30 or 3.31, should apply to any photograph or video taken as in paragraph 23.

25.   If any person is asked to leave an identification parade because they are interfering with its conduct, the circumstances shall be recorded.

26.   A record must be made of all those present at an identification parade whose names are known to the police.

27.   If prison inmates make up an identification parade, the circumstances must be recorded.

28.   A record of the conduct of any identification parade must be made on forms provided for the purpose. This shall include anything said by the witness or the suspect about any identifications or the conduct of the procedure, and any reasons it was not practicable to comply with any of this Code's provisions.

ANNEX C

GROUP IDENTIFICATION[45]

(a)   General

1.   The purpose of this Annex is to make sure, as far as possible, group identifications follow the principles and procedures for identification parades so the conditions are fair to the suspect in the way they test the witness' ability to make an identification.

2.   Group identifications may take place either with the suspect's consent and co-operation or covertly without their consent.

3.   The location of the group identification is a matter for the identification officer, although the officer may take into account any representations made by the suspect, appropriate adult, their solicitor or friend.

4.   The place where the group identification is held should be one where other people are either passing by or waiting around informally, in groups such that the suspect is able to join them and be capable of being seen by the witness at the same time as others in the group. For example people leaving an escalator, pedestrians walking through a shopping centre, passengers on railway and bus stations, waiting in queues or groups or where people are standing or sitting in groups in other public places.

5.   If the group identification is to be held covertly, the choice of locations will be limited by the places where the suspect can be found and the number of other people present at that time. In these cases, suitable locations might be along regular routes travelled by the suspect, including buses or trains or public places frequented by the suspect.

---

[45] Pre-2002 this Annex was Annex E. Former para.3 has been divided into two paras. The only addition is para.10. There is consequential renumbering.

6.   Although the number, age, sex, race and general description and style of clothing of other people present at the location cannot be controlled by the identification officer, in selecting the location the officer must consider the general appearance and numbers of people likely to be present. In particular, the officer must reasonably expect that over the period the witness observes the group, they will be able to see, from time to time, a number of others whose appearance is broadly similar to that of the suspect.

7.   A group identification need not be held if the identification officer believes, because of the unusual appearance of the suspect, none of the locations it would be practicable to use, satisfy the requirements of paragraph 6 necessary to make the identification fair.

8.   Immediately after a group identification procedure has taken place (with or without the suspect's consent), a colour photograph or video should be taken of the general scene, if practicable, to give a general impression of the scene and the number of people present. Alternatively, if it is practicable, the group identification may be video recorded.

9.   If it is not practicable to take the photograph or video in accordance with paragraph 8, a photograph or film of the scene should be taken later at a time determined by the identification officer if the officer considers it practicable to do so.

10.   An identification carried out in accordance with this Code remains a group identification even though, at the time of being seen by the witness, the suspect was on their own rather than in a group.

11.   Before the group identification takes place, the suspect or their solicitor shall be provided with details of the first description of the suspect by any witnesses who are to attend the identification. When a broadcast or publication is made, as in paragraph 3.28, the suspect or their solicitor should also be allowed to view any material released by the police to the media for the purposes of recognising or tracing the suspect, provided that it is practicable and would not unreasonably delay the investigation.

12.   After the procedure, each witness shall be asked whether they have seen any broadcast or published films or photographs or any descriptions of suspects relating to the offence and their reply recorded.

(b)   Identification with the consent of the suspect

13.   A suspect must be given a reasonable opportunity to have a solicitor or friend present. They shall be asked to indicate on a second copy of the notice whether or not they wish to do so.

14.   The witness, the person carrying out the procedure and the suspect's solicitor, appropriate adult, friend or any interpreter for the witness, may be concealed from the sight of the individuals in the group they are observing, if the person carrying out the procedure considers this assists the conduct of the identification.

15.   The person conducting a witness to a group identification must not discuss with them the forthcoming group identification and, in particular, must not disclose whether a previous witness has made any identification.

16.   Anything said to, or by, the witness during the procedure about the identification should be said in the presence and hearing of those present at the procedure.

17.   Appropriate arrangements must be made to make sure, before witnesses attend the group identification, they are not able to:

(i) communicate with each other about the case or overhear a witness who has already been given an opportunity to see the suspect in the group;

(ii) see the suspect; or

(iii) see, or be reminded of, any photographs or description of the suspect or be given any other indication of the suspect's identity.

18. Witnesses shall be brought one at a time to the place where they are to observe the group. Immediately before the witness is asked to look at the group, the person conducting the procedure shall tell them that the person they saw may, or may not, be in the group and that if they cannot make a positive identification, they should say so. The witness shall be asked to observe the group in which the suspect is to appear. The way in which the witness should do this will depend on whether the group is moving or stationary.

Moving group

19. When the group in which the suspect is to appear is moving, e.g. leaving an escalator, the provisions of paragraphs 20 to 24 should be followed.

20. If two or more suspects consent to a group identification, each should be the subject of separate identification procedures. These may be conducted consecutively on the same occasion.

21. The person conducting the procedure shall tell the witness to observe the group and ask them to point out any person they think they saw on the specified earlier occasion.

22. Once the witness has been informed as in paragraph 21 the suspect should be allowed to take whatever position in the group they wish.

23. When the witness points out a person as in paragraph 21 they shall, if practicable, be asked to take a closer look at the person to confirm the identification. If this is not practicable, or they cannot confirm the identification, they shall be asked how sure they are that the person they have indicated is the relevant person.

24. The witness should continue to observe the group for the period which the person conducting the procedure reasonably believes is necessary in the circumstances for them to be able to make comparisons between the suspect and other individuals of broadly similar appearance to the suspect as in paragraph 6.

Stationary groups

25. When the group in which the suspect is to appear is stationary, e.g. people waiting in a queue, the provisions of paragraphs 26 to 29 should be followed.

26. If two or more suspects consent to a group identification, each should be subject to separate identification procedures unless they are of broadly similar appearance when they may appear in the same group. When separate group identifications are held, the groups must be made up of different people.

27. The suspect may take whatever position in the group they wish. If there is more than one witness, the suspect must be told, out of the sight and hearing of any witness, that they can, if they wish, change their position in the group.

28. The witness shall be asked to pass along, or amongst, the group and to look at each person in the group at least twice, taking as much care and time as possible according to the circumstances, before making an identification. Once the witness has done this, they shall be asked whether the person they saw on the specified earlier occasion is in the group and to indicate any such person by whatever means the person conducting the procedure considers appropriate in

the circumstances. If this is not practicable, the witness shall be asked to point out any person they think they saw on the earlier occasion.

29. When the witness makes an indication as in paragraph 28, arrangements shall be made, if practicable, for the witness to take a closer look at the person to confirm the identification. If this is not practicable, or the witness is unable to confirm the identification, they shall be asked how sure they are that the person they have indicated is the relevant person.

All cases

30. If the suspect unreasonably delays joining the group, or having joined the group, deliberately conceals themselves from the sight of the witness, this may be treated as a refusal to co-operate in a group identification.

31. If the witness identifies a person other than the suspect, that person should be informed what has happened and asked if they are prepared to give their name and address. There is no obligation upon any member of the public to give these details. There shall be no duty to record any details of any other member of the public present in the group or at the place where the procedure is conducted.

32. When the group identification has been completed, the suspect shall be asked whether they wish to make any comments on the conduct of the procedure.

33. If the suspect has not been previously informed, they shall be told of any identifications made by the witnesses.

(c) Identification without the suspect's consent

34. Group identifications held covertly without the suspect's consent should, as far as practicable, follow the rules for conduct of group identification by consent.

35. A suspect has no right to have a solicitor, appropriate adult or friend present as the identification will take place without the knowledge of the suspect.

36. Any number of suspects may be identified at the same time.

(d) Identifications in police stations

37. Group identifications should only take place in police stations for reasons of safety, security or because it is not practicable to hold them elsewhere.

38. The group identification may take place either in a room equipped with a screen permitting witnesses to see members of the group without being seen, or anywhere else in the police station that the identification officer considers appropriate.

39. Any of the additional safeguards applicable to identification parades should be followed if the identification officer considers it is practicable to do so in the circumstances.

(e) Identifications involving prison inmates

40. A group identification involving a prison inmate may only be arranged in the prison or at a police station.

41. When a group identification takes place involving a prison inmate, whether in a prison or in a police station, the arrangements should follow those in paragraphs 37 to 39. If a group identification takes place within a prison, other inmates may participate. If an inmate is the suspect, they do not have to

wear prison clothing for the group identification unless the other participants are wearing the same clothing.

(f) Documentation

42.   When a photograph or video is taken as in paragraph 8 or 9, a copy of the photograph or video shall be supplied on request to the suspect or their solicitor within a reasonable time.

43.   Paragraph 3.30 or 3.31, as appropriate, shall apply when the photograph or film taken in accordance with paragraph 8 or 9 includes the suspect.

44.   A record of the conduct of any group identification must be made on forms provided for the purpose. This shall include anything said by the witness or suspect about any identifications or the conduct of the procedure and any reasons why it was not practicable to comply with any of the provisions of this Code governing the conduct of group identifications.

ANNEX D

CONFRONTATION BY A WITNESS[46]

1,   Before the confrontation takes place, the witness must be told that the person they saw may, or may not, be the person they are to confront and that if they are not that person, then the witness should say so.

2.   Before the confrontation takes place the suspect or their solicitor shall be provided with details of the first description of the suspect given by any witness who is to attend. When a broadcast or publication is made, as in paragraph 3.28, the suspect or their solicitor should also be allowed to view any material released to the media for the purposes of recognising or tracing the suspect, provided it is practicable to do so and would not unreasonably delay the investigation.

3.   Force may not be used to make the suspect's face visible to the witness.

4.   Confrontation must take place in the presence of the suspect's solicitor, interpreter or friend unless this would cause unreasonable delay.

5.   The suspect shall be confronted independently by each witness, who shall be asked 'Is this the person?'. If the witness identifies the person but is unable to confirm the identification, they shall be asked how sure they are that the person is the one they saw on the earlier occasion.

6.   The confrontation should normally take place in the police station, either in a normal room or one equipped with a screen permitting a witness to see the suspect without being seen. In both cases, the procedures are the same except that a room equipped with a screen may be used only when the suspect's solicitor, friend or appropriate adult is present or the confrontation is recorded on video.

7.   After the procedure, each witness shall be asked whether they have seen any broadcast or published films or photographs or any descriptions of suspects relating to the offence and their reply shall be recorded.

---

[46] Pre-2002 this was Annex C.

ANNEX E

SHOWING PHOTOGRAPHS[47]

(a)   Action

1.   An officer of sergeant rank or above shall be responsible for supervising and directing the showing of photographs. The actual showing may be done by another officer or civilian support staff, see paragraph 3.11.

2.   The supervising officer must confirm the first description of the suspect given by the witness has been recorded before they are shown the photographs. If the supervising officer is unable to confirm the description has been recorded they shall postpone showing the photographs.

3.   Only one witness shall be shown photographs at any one time. Each witness shall be given as much privacy as practicable and shall not be allowed to communicate with any other witness in the case.

4.   The witness shall be shown not less than twelve photographs at a time, which shall, as far as possible, all be of a similar type.

5.   When the witness is shown the photographs, they shall be told the photograph of the person they saw may, or may not, be amongst them and if they cannot make a positive identification, they should say so. The witness shall also be told they should not make a decision until they have viewed at least twelve photographs. The witness shall not be prompted or guided in any way but shall be left to make any selection without help.

6.   If a witness makes a positive identification from photographs, unless the person identified is otherwise eliminated from enquiries or is not available, other witnesses shall not be shown photographs. But both they, and the witness who has made the identification, shall be asked to attend a video identification, an identification parade or group identification unless there is no dispute about the suspect's identification.

7.   If the witness makes a selection but is unable to confirm the identification, the person showing the photographs shall ask them how sure they are that the photograph they have indicated is the person they saw on the specified earlier occasion.

8.   When the use of a computerised or artist's composite or similar likeness has led to there being a known suspect who can be asked to participate in a video identification, appear on an identification parade or participate in a group identification, that likeness shall not be shown to other potential witnesses.

9.   When a witness attending a video identification, an identification parade or group identification has previously been shown photographs or computerised or artist's composite or similar likeness (and it is the responsibility of the officer in charge of the investigation to make the identification officer aware that this is the case), the suspect and their solicitor must be informed of this fact before the identification procedure takes place.

10.   None of the photographs shown shall be destroyed, whether or not an identification is made, since they may be required for production in court. The photographs shall be numbered and a separate photograph taken of the frame or

---

[47] Pre-2002 this was Annex D.

part of the album from which the witness made an identification as an aid to reconstituting it.

(b)   Documentation

11.   Whether or not an identification is made, a record shall be kept of the showing of photographs on forms provided for the purpose. This shall include anything said by the witness about any identification or the conduct of the procedure, any reasons it was not practicable to comply with any of the provisions of this Code governing the showing of photographs and the name and rank of the supervising officer.

12.   The supervising officer shall inspect and sign the record as soon as practicable.

ANNEX F

FINGERPRINTS AND SAMPLES—DESTRUCTION AND SPECULATIVE SEARCHES

(a)   Fingerprints and samples taken in connection with a criminal investigation

1.   When fingerprints or DNA samples are taken from a person in connection with an investigation and the person is not suspected of having committed the offence, see Note F1, they must be destroyed as soon as they have fulfilled the purpose for which they were taken unless:

   (a)   they were taken for the purposes of an investigation of an offence for which a person has been convicted; and

   (b)   fingerprints or samples were also taken from the convicted person for the purposes of that investigation.

However, subject to paragraph 2, the fingerprints and samples, and the information derived from samples, may not be used in the investigation of any offence or in evidence against the person who is, or would be, entitled to the destruction of the fingerprints and samples, see Note F2.

2.   The requirement to destroy fingerprints and DNA samples, and information derived from samples, and restrictions on their retention and use in paragraph 1 do not apply if the person gives their written consent for their fingerprints or sample to be retained and used after they have fulfilled the purpose for which they were taken, see Note F1.

3.   When a person's fingerprints or sample are to be destroyed:

   (a)   any copies of the fingerprints must also be destroyed;

   (b)   the person may witness the destruction of their fingerprints or copies if they ask to do so within five days of being informed destruction is required;

   (c)   access to relevant computer fingerprint data shall be made impossible as soon as it is practicable to do so and the person shall be given a certificate to this effect within three months of asking; and

   (d)   neither the fingerprints, the sample, or any information derived from the sample, may be used in the investigation of any offence or in evidence against the person who is, or would be, entitled to its destruction.

4. Fingerprints or samples, and the information derived from samples, taken in connection with the investigation of an offence which are not required to be destroyed, may be retained after they have fulfilled the purposes for which they were taken but may be used only for purposes related to the prevention or detection of crime, the investigation of an offence or the conduct of a prosecution in, as well as outside, the UK and may also be subject to a speculative search. This includes checking them against other fingerprints and DNA records held by, or on behalf of, the police and other law enforcement authorities in, as well as outside, the UK.

(b)   Fingerprints taken in connection with Immigration Service enquiries

5.   Fingerprints taken for Immigration Service enquiries in accordance with powers and procedures other than under PACE and for which the Immigration Service, not the police, are responsible, must be destroyed as follows:

(a)   fingerprints and all copies must be destroyed as soon as practicable if the person from whom they were taken proves they are a British or Commonwealth citizen who has the right of abode in the UK under the Immigration Act 1971, section 2(1)(b);

(b)   fingerprints taken under the power as in paragraph 4.11(g) from a dependant of a person in 4.11 (b) to (f) must be destroyed when that person's fingerprints are to be destroyed;

(c)   fingerprints taken from a person under any power as in paragraph 4.11 or with the person's consent which have not already been destroyed as above, must be destroyed within ten years of being taken or within such period specified by the Secretary of State under the Immigration and Asylum Act 1999, section 143(5).

Notes for guidance

F1   Fingerprints and samples given voluntarily for the purposes of elimination play an important part in many police investigations. It is, therefore, important to make sure innocent volunteers are not deterred from participating and their consent to their fingerprints and DNA being used for the purposes of a specific investigation is fully informed and voluntary. If the police or volunteer seek to have the sample or fingerprints retained for use after the specific investigation ends, it is important the volunteer's consent to this is also fully informed and voluntary. Examples of consent for:

- *DNA/fingerprints—to be used only for the purposes of a specific investigation;*
- *DNA/fingerprints—to be used in the specific investigation and retained by the police for future use.*

To minimise the risk of confusion, each consent should be physically separate and the volunteer should be asked to sign one or the other, not both.

(a)   DNA:

(i)   DNA sample taken for the purposes of elimination or as part of an intelligence-led screen and to be used only for the purposes of that investigation and destroyed afterwards:
'I consent to my DNA/mouth swab being taken for forensic

analysis. I understand that the sample will be destroyed at the end of the case and that my profile will only be compared to the crime stain profile from this enquiry. I have been advised that the person taking the sample may be required to give evidence and/or provide a written statement to the police in relation to the taking of it'.

(ii) *DNA sample to be retained on the National DNA database and used in the future:*

'I consent to my DNA sample and information derived from it being retained and used only for purposes related to the prevention and detection of a crime, the investigation of an offence or the conduct of a prosecution either nationally or internationally.'

'I understand that this sample may be checked against other DNA records held by, or on behalf of, relevant law enforcement authorities, either nationally or internationally'.

'I understand that once I have given my consent for the sample to be retained and used I cannot withdraw this consent.'

(b) *Fingerprints:*

(i) *Fingerprints taken for the purposes of elimination or as part of an intelligence led screen and to be used only for the purposes of that investigation and destroyed afterwards:*

'I consent to my fingerprints being taken for elimination purposes. I understand that the fingerprints will be destroyed at the end of the case and that my fingerprints will only be compared to the fingerprints from this enquiry. I have been advised that the person taking the fingerprints may be required to give evidence and/or provide a written statement to the police in relation to the taking of it.'

(ii) *Fingerprints to be retained for future use:*

'I consent to my fingerprints being retained and used only for purposes related to the prevention and detection of a crime, the investigation of an offence or the conduct of a prosecution either nationally or internationally'.

'I understand that my fingerprints may be checked against other records held by, or on behalf of, relevant law enforcement authorities, either nationally or internationally.'

'I understand that once I have given my consent for my fingerprints to be retained and used I cannot withdraw this consent.'

F2   The provisions for the retention of fingerprints and samples in paragraph 1 allow for all fingerprints and samples in a case to be available for any subsequent miscarriage of justice investigation.

CODE E

CODE OF PRACTICE ON TAPE RECORDING INTERVIEWS WITH SUSPECTS

Commencement—Transitional Arrangements

This code applies to interviews carried out after midnight on 31 July 2004, notwithstanding that the interview may have commenced before that time.

1 General

1.1   This Code of Practice must be readily available for consultation by:
- police officers
- police staff
- detained persons
- members of the public.

1.2   The Notes for Guidance included are not provisions of this Code.

1.3   Nothing in this Code shall detract from the requirements of Code C, the Code of Practice for the detention, treatment and questioning of persons by police officers.

1.4   This Code does not apply to those people listed in Code C, paragraph 1.12.

1.5   The term:
- 'appropriate adult' has the same meaning as in Code C, paragraph 1.7
- 'solicitor' has the same meaning as in Code C, paragraph 6.12.

1.6   In this Code:
  (a)   'designated person' means a person other than a police officer, designated under the Police Reform Act 2002, Part 4 who has specified powers and duties of police officers conferred or imposed on them;
  (b)   any reference to a police officer includes a designated person acting in the exercise or performance of the powers and duties conferred or imposed on them by their designation.

1.7   If a power conferred on a designated person:
  (a)   allows reasonable force to be used when exercised by a police officer, a designated person exercising that power has the same entitlement to use force;
  (b)   includes power to use force to enter any premises, that power is not exercisable by that designated person except:
    (i)   in the company, and under the supervision, of a police officer; or
    (ii)   for the purpose of:
      saving life or limb; or
      preventing serious damage to property.

1.8   Nothing in this Code prevents the custody officer, or other officer given custody of the detainee, from allowing police staff who are not designated persons to carry out individual procedures or tasks at the police station if the law allows. However, the officer remains responsible for making sure the procedures and tasks are carried out correctly in accordance with these Codes. Any such civilian must be:
  (a)   a person employed by a police authority maintaining a police force and under the control and direction of the Chief Officer of that force; or

    (b) employed by a person with whom a police authority has a contract for the provision of services relating to persons arrested or otherwise in custody.

1.9 Designated persons and other police staff must have regard to any relevant provisions of the Codes of Practice.

1.10 References to pocket book include any official report book issued to police officers or police staff.

1.11 References to a custody officer include those performing the functions of a custody officer.

2 Recording and sealing master tapes

2.1 Tape recording of interviews shall be carried out openly to instil confidence in its reliability as an impartial and accurate record of the interview.

2.2 One tape, the master tape, will be sealed in the suspect's presence. A second tape will be used as a working copy. The master tape is either of the two tapes used in a twin deck machine or the only tape in a single deck machine. The working copy is either the second/third tape used in a twin/triple deck machine or a copy of the master tape made by a single deck machine. See Notes 2A and 2B

2.3 Nothing in this Code requires the identity of officers or police staff conducting interviews to be recorded or disclosed:

    (a) in the case of enquiries linked to the investigation of terrorism; or

    (b) if the interviewer reasonably believes recording or disclosing their name might put them in danger.

In these cases interviewers should use warrant or other identification numbers and the name of their police station.
See Note 2C

Notes for guidance

2A   *The purpose of sealing the master tape in the suspect's presence is to show the tape's integrity is preserved. If a single deck machine is used the working copy of the master tape must be made in the suspect's presence and without the master tape leaving their sight. The working copy shall be used for making further copies if needed.*

2B   *Reference to 'tapes' includes 'tape', if a single deck machine is used.*

2C   *The purpose of paragraph 2.3(b) is to protect those involved in serious organised crime investigations or arrests of particularly violent suspects when there is reliable information that those arrested or their associates may threaten or cause harm to those involved. In cases of doubt, an officer of inspector rank or above should be consulted.*

3 Interviews to be tape recorded

3.1 Subject to paragraphs 3.3 and 3.4, tape recording shall be used at police stations for any interview:

    (a) with a person cautioned under Code C, section 10 in respect of any indictable offence, including an offence triable either way, see Note 3A

   (b)   which takes place as a result of an interviewer exceptionally putting further questions to a suspect about an offence described in paragraph 3.1(a) after they have been charged with, or told they may be prosecuted for, that offence, see Code C, paragraph 16.5

   (c)   when an interviewer wants to tell a person, after they have been charged with, or informed they may be prosecuted for, an offence described in paragraph 3.1(a), about any written statement or interview with another person, see Code C, paragraph 16.4.

3.2   The Terrorism Act 2000 makes separate provision for a Code of Practice for the tape recording of interviews of those arrested under Section 41 or detained under Schedule 7 of the Act. The provisions of this Code do not apply to such interviews.

3.3   The custody officer may authorise the interviewer not to tape record the interview when it is:

   (a)   not reasonably practicable because of equipment failure or the unavailability of a suitable interview room or recorder and the authorising officer considers, on reasonable grounds, that the interview should not be delayed; or

   (b)   clear from the outset there will not be a prosecution.

Note: In these cases the interview should be recorded in writing in accordance with Code C, section 11. In all cases the custody officer shall record the specific reasons for not tape recording. See Note 3B

3.4   If a person refuses to go into or remain in a suitable interview room, see Code C paragraph 12.5, and the custody officer considers, on reasonable grounds, that the interview should not be delayed the interview may, at the custody officer's discretion, be conducted in a cell using portable recording equipment or, if none is available, recorded in writing as in Code C, section 11. The reasons for this shall be recorded.

3.5   The whole of each interview shall be tape recorded, including the taking and reading back of any statement.

Notes for guidance

   3A   *Nothing in this Code is intended to preclude tape recording at police discretion of interviews at police stations with people cautioned in respect of offences not covered by paragraph 3.1, or responses made by persons after. they have been charged with, or told they may be prosecuted for, an offence, provided this Code is complied with.*

   3B   *A decision not to tape record an interview for any reason may be the subject of comment in court. The authorising officer should be prepared to justify that decision.*

4   The interview

(a)   General

4.1   The provisions of Code C:

- sections 10 and 11, and the applicable Notes for Guidance apply to the conduct of interviews to which this Code applies
- paragraphs 11.7 to 11.14 apply only when a written record is needed.

4.2   Code C, paragraphs 10.10, 10.11 and Annex C describe the restriction on drawing adverse inferences from a suspect's failure or refusal to say anything about their involvement in the offence when interviewed or after being charged or informed they may be prosecuted, and how it affects the terms of the caution and determines if and by whom a special warning under sections 36 and 37 can be given.

(b)   Commencement of interviews

4.3   When the suspect is brought into the interview room the interviewer shall, without delay but in the suspect's sight, load the recorder with clean tapes and set it to record. The tapes must be unwrapped or opened in the suspect's presence.

4.4   The interviewer should tell the suspect about the tape recording. The interviewer shall:

(a)   say the interview is being tape recorded

(b)   subject to paragraph 2.3, give their name and rank and that of any other interviewer present

(c)   ask the suspect and any other party present, e.g. a solicitor, to identify themselves

(d)   state the date, time of commencement and place of the interview

(e)   state the suspect will be given a notice about what will happen to the tapes.

See Note 4A

4.5   The interviewer shall:

● caution the suspect, see Code C, section 10

● remind the suspect of their entitlement to free legal advice, see Code C, paragraph 11.2.

4.6   The interviewer shall put to the suspect any significant statement or silence, see Code C, paragraph 11.4.

(c)   Interviews with deaf persons

4.7   If the suspect is deaf or is suspected of having impaired hearing, the interviewer shall make a written note of the interview in accordance with Code C, at the same time as tape recording it in accordance with this Code. See Notes 4B and 4C

(d)   Objections and complaints by the suspect

4.8   If the suspect objects to the interview being tape recorded at the outset, during the interview or during a break, the interviewer shall explain that the interview is being tape recorded and that this Code requires the suspect's objections be recorded on tape. When any objections have been tape recorded or the suspect has refused to have their objections recorded, the interviewer shall say they are turning off the recorder, give their reasons and turn it off. The interviewer shall then make a written record of the interview as in Code C, section 11. If, however, the interviewer reasonably considers they may proceed to question the suspect with the tape still on, the interviewer may do so. See Note 4D

4.9   If in the course of an interview a complaint is made by or on behalf of the person being questioned concerning the provisions of this Code or Code C, the interviewer shall act as in Code C, paragraph 12.9. See Notes 4E and 4F

4.10   If the suspect indicates they want to tell the interviewer about matters not directly connected with the offence and they are unwilling for these matters to be tape recorded, the suspect should be given the opportunity to tell the interviewer at the end of the formal interview.

(e)   Changing tapes

4.11   When the recorder shows the tapes have only a short time left, the interviewer shall tell the suspect the tapes are coming to an end and round off that part of the interview. If the interviewer leaves the room for a second set of tapes, the suspect shall not be left unattended. The interviewer will remove the tapes from the tape recorder and insert the new tapes which shall be unwrapped or opened in the suspect's presence. The tape recorder should be set to record on the new tapes. To avoid confusion between the tapes, the interviewer shall mark the tapes with an identification number immediately they are removed from the tape recorder.

(f)   Taking a break during interview

4.12   When a break is taken, the fact that a break is to be taken, the reason for it and the time shall be recorded on tape.

4.12A   When the break is taken and the interview room vacated by the suspect, the tapes shall be removed from the tape recorder and the procedures for the conclusion of an interview followed, see paragraph 4.18.

4.13   When a break is a short one and both the suspect and an interviewer remain in the interview room, the tape recorder may be turned off. There is no need to remove the tapes and when the interview recommences the tape recording should continue on the same tapes. The time the interview recommences shall be recorded on tape.

4.14   After any break in the interview the interviewer must, before resuming the interview, remind the person being questioned that they remain under caution or, if there is any doubt, give the caution in full again. See Note 4G

(g)   Failure of recording equipment

4.15   If there is an equipment failure which can be rectified quickly, e.g. by inserting new tapes, the interviewer shall follow the appropriate procedures as in paragraph 4.11. When the recording is resumed the interviewer shall explain what happened and record the time the interview recommences. If, however, it will not be possible to continue recording on that tape recorder and no replacement recorder is readily available, the interview may continue without being tape recorded. If this happens, the interviewer shall seek the custody officer's authority as in paragraph 3.3. See Note 4H

(h)   Removing tapes from the recorder

4.16   When tapes are removed from the recorder during the interview, they shall be retained and the procedures in paragraph 4.18 followed.

(i)   Conclusion of interview

4.17   At the conclusion of the interview, the suspect shall be offered the opportunity to clarify anything he or she has said and asked if there is anything they want to add.

4.18   At the conclusion of the interview, including the taking and reading back of any written statement, the time shall be recorded and the tape recorder switched off. The interviewer shall seal the master tape with a master tape label and treat it as an exhibit in accordance with force standing orders. The interviewer shall sign the label and ask the suspect and any third party present during the interview to sign it. If the suspect or third party refuse to sign the label an officer of at least inspector rank, or if not available the custody officer, shall be called into the interview room and asked, subject to paragraph 2.3, to sign it.

4.19   The suspect shall be handed a notice which explains:

- how the tape recording will be used
- the arrangements for access to it
- that if the person is charged or informed they will be prosecuted, a copy of the tape will be supplied as soon as practicable or as otherwise agreed between the suspect and the police.

Notes for guidance

4A   *For the purpose of voice identification the interviewer should ask the suspect and any other people present to identify themselves.*

4B   *This provision is to give a person who is deaf or has impaired hearing equivalent rights of access to the full interview record as far as this is possible using audio recording.*

4C   *The provisions of Code C, section 13 on interpreters for deaf persons or for interviews with suspects who have difficulty understanding English continue to apply. However, in a tape recorded interview the requirement on the interviewer to make sure the interpreter makes a separate note of the interview applies only to paragraph 4.7 (interviews with deaf persons).*

4D   *The interviewer should remember that a decision to continue recording against the wishes of the suspect may be the subject of comment in court.*

4E   *If the custody officer is called to deal with the complaint, the tape recorder should, if possible, be left on until the custody officer has entered the room and spoken to the person being interviewed. Continuation or termination of the interview should be at the interviewer's discretion pending action by an inspector under Code C, paragraph 9.2.*

4F   *If the complaint is about a matter not connected with this Code or Code C, the decision to continue is at the interviewer's discretion. When the interviewer decides to continue the interview, they shall tell the suspect the complaint will be brought to the custody officer's attention at the conclusion of the interview. When the interview is concluded the interviewer must, as soon as practicable, inform the custody officer about the existence and nature of the complaint made.*

4G   *The interviewer should remember that it may be necessary to show to the court that nothing occurred during a break or between interviews which influenced the suspect's recorded evidence. After a break or at the beginning of a subsequent interview, the interviewer should consider summarising on tape the reason for the break and confirming this with the suspect.*

4H   *If one of the tapes snaps during the interview it should be sealed as a master tape in the suspect's presence and the interview resumed where it left off. The unbroken tape should be copied and the original sealed as a master tape in the suspect's presence, if necessary after the interview. If equipment for copying the unbroken tape is not readily available, both tapes should be sealed in the suspect's presence and the interview begun again. If the tape breaks when a single deck machine is being used and the machine is one where a broken tape cannot be copied on available equipment, the tape should·be sealed as a master tape in the suspect's presence and the interview begun again.*

5   After the interview

5.1   The interviewer shall make a note in their pocket book that the interview has taken place, was tape recorded, its time, duration and date and the master tape's identification number.

5.2   If no proceedings follow in respect of the person whose interview was recorded, the tapes must be kept securely as in paragraph 6.1 and Note 6A.

Note for guidance

5A   *Any written record of a tape ˙recorded interview should be made in accordance with national guidelines approved by the Secretary of State.*

6   Tape security

6.1   The officer in charge of each police station at which interviews with suspects are recorded shall make arrangements for master tapes to be kept securely and their movements accounted for on the same basis as material which may be used for evidential purposes, in accordance with force standing orders. See Note 6A

6.2   A police officer has no authority to break the seal on a master tape required for criminal trial or appeal proceedings. If it is necessary to gain access to the master tape, the police officer shall arrange for its seal to be broken in the presence of a representative of the Crown Prosecution Service. The defendant or their legal adviser should be informed and given a reasonable opportunity to be present. If the defendant or their legal representative is present they shall be invited to reseal and sign the master tape. If either refuses or neither is present this should be done by the representative of the Crown Prosecution Service. See Notes 6B and 6C

6.3   If no criminal proceedings result or the criminal trial and, if applicable, appeal proceedings to which the interview relates have been concluded, the chief officer of police is responsible for establishing arrangements for breaking the seal on the master tape, if necessary.

6.4   When the master tape seal is broken, a record must be made of the procedure followed, including the date, time, place and persons present.

Notes for guidance

6A　*This section is concerned with the security of the master tape sealed at the conclusion of the interview. Care must be taken of working copies of tapes because their loss or destruction may lead to the need to access master tapes.*

6B　*If the tape has been delivered to the crown court for their keeping after committal for trial the crown prosecutor will apply to the chief clerk of the crown court centre for the release of the tape for unsealing by the crown prosecutor.*

6C　*Reference to the Crown Prosecution Service or to the crown prosecutor in this part of the Code should be taken to include any other body or person with a statutory responsibility for prosecution for whom the police conduct any tape recorded interviews.*

CODE F

CODE OF PRACTICE ON VISUAL RECORDING WITH SOUND OF INTERVIEWS WITH SUSPECTS[1]

Commencement

The contents of this code should be considered if an interviewing officer decides to make a visual recording with sound of an interview with a suspect. There is no statutory requirement to visually record interviews

1 August 2004

1 General

1.1   This code of practice must be readily available for consultation by police officers and other police staff, detained persons and members of the public.
1.2   The notes for guidance included are not provisions of this code. They form guidance to police officers and others about its application and interpretation.
1.3   Nothing in this Code shall be taken as detracting in any way from the requirements of the Code of Practice for the Detention, Treatment and Questioning of Persons by Police Officers (Code C). [See Note 1A].
1.4   The interviews to which this Code applies are set out in paragraphs 3.1 to 3.3.
1.5   In this Code, the terms "appropriate adult", "solicitor" and "interview" have the same meaning as those set out in Code C. The corresponding provisions and notes for guidance in Code C applicable to those terms shall also apply where appropriate.
1.6   Any reference in this Code to visual recording shall be taken to mean visual recording with sound.
1.7   References to "pocket book" in this Code include any official report book issued to police officers.

Note for guidance

1A   As in Code C, references to custody officers include those carrying out the functions of a custody officer.

2 Recording and sealing of master tapes

2.1   The visual recording of interviews shall be carried out openly to instil confidence in its reliability as an impartial and accurate record of the interview. [See Note 2A]
2.2   The camera(s) shall be placed in the interview room so as to ensure coverage of as much of the room as is practicably possible whilst the interviews are taking place.

---

[1] Code F was introduced on a pilot basis in April 2002. It was made part of the national system as from August 1, 2004.

2.3   The certified recording medium will be of a high quality, new and previously unused. When the certified recording medium is placed in the recorder and switched on to record, the correct date and time, in hours, minutes and seconds, will be superimposed automatically, second by second, during the whole recording. [See Note 2B]

2.4   One copy of the certified recording medium, referred to in this Code as the master copy, will be sealed before it leaves the presence of the suspect. A second copy will be used as a working copy. [See Notes 2C and 2D]

2.5   Nothing in this code requires the identity of an officer to be recorded or disclosed if:

   (a)   the interview or record relates to a person detained under the Terrorism Act 2000; or

   (b)   otherwise where the officer reasonably believes that recording or disclosing their name might put them in danger.

In these cases, the officer will have their back to the camera and shall use their warrant or other identification number and the name of the police station to which they are attached. Such instances and the reasons for them shall be recorded in the custody record. [See Note 2E]

Notes for guidance

2A   *Interviewing officers will wish to arrange that, as far as possible, visual recording arrangements are unobtrusive. It must be clear to the suspect, however, that there is no opportunity to interfere with the recording equipment or the recording media.*

2B   *In this context, the certified recording media will be of either a VHS or digital CD format and should be capable of having an image of the date and time superimposed upon them as they record the interview.*

2C   *The purpose of sealing the master copy before it leaves the presence of the suspect is to establish their confidence that the integrity of the copy is preserved.*

2D   *The recording of the interview is not to be used for any identification purpose.*

2E   *The purpose of the paragraph 2.5 is to protect police officers and others involved in the investigation of serious organised crime or the arrest of particularly violent suspects when there is reliable information that those arrested or their associates may threaten or cause harm to the officers, their families or their personal property.*

3   Interviews to be visually recorded

3.1   Subject to paragraph 3.2 below, if an interviewing officer decides to make a visual recording these are the areas where it might be appropriate::

   (a)   with a suspect in respect of an indictable offence (including an offence triable either way) [see Notes 3A and 3B];

   (b)   which takes place as a result of an interviewer exceptionally putting further questions to a suspect about an offence described in sub-paragraph (a) above after they have been charged with, or informed they may be prosecuted for, that offence [see Note 3C];

   (c)   in which an interviewer wishes to bring to the notice of a person, after that person has been charged with, or informed they may be prosecuted

for an offence described in sub-paragraph (a) above, any written statement made by another person, or the content of an interview with
another person [see Note 3D];

(d) with, or in the presence of, a deaf or deaf/blind or speech impaired
person who uses sign language to communicate;

(e) with, or in the presence of anyone who requires an "appropriate adult";
or

(f) in any case where the suspect or their representative requests that the
interview be recorded visually.

3.2   The Terrorism Act 2000 makes separate provision for a Code of Practice for
the video recording of interviews in a police station of those detained under
Schedule 7 or section 41 of the Act. The provisions of this Code do not therefore
apply to such interviews. [See Note 3E]

3.3   The custody officer may authorise the interviewing officer not to record the
interview visually:

(a) where it is not reasonably practicable to do so because of failure of
the equipment, or the non-availability of a suitable interview room or
recorder, and the authorising officer considers on reasonable grounds
that the interview should not be delayed until the failure has been
rectified or a suitable room or recorder becomes available. In such
cases the custody officer may authorise the interviewing officer to
audio record the interview in accordance with the guidance set out
in Code E;

(b) where it is clear from the outset that no prosecution will ensue; or

(c) where it is not practicable to do so because at the time the person resists
being taken to a suitable interview room or other location which would
enable the interview to be recorded, or otherwise fails or refuses to go
into such a room or location, and the authorising officer considers on
reasonable grounds that the interview should not be delayed until these
conditions cease to apply.

In all cases the custody officer shall make a Note in the custody records of the
reasons for not taking a visual record. [See Note 3F]

3.4   When a person who is voluntarily attending the police station is required to
be cautioned in accordance with Code C prior to being interviewed, the subsequent interview shall be recorded, unless the custody officer gives authority in
accordance with the provisions of paragraph 3.3 above for the interview not to be
so recorded.

3.5   The whole of each interview shall be recorded visually, including the taking
and reading back of any statement.

3.6   A visible illuminated sign or indicator will light and remain on at all times
when the recording equipment is activated or capable of recording or transmitting
any signal or information.

Notes for guidance

3A   *Nothing in the Code is intended to preclude visual recording at police
discretion of interviews at police stations with people cautioned in
respect of offences not covered by paragraph 3.1, or responses made
by interviewees after they have been charged with, or informed they
may be prosecuted for, an offence, provided that this code is complied
with.*

3B   Attention is drawn to the provisions set out in Code C about the matters to be considered when deciding whether a detained person is fit to be interviewed.

3C   Code C sets out the circumstances in which a suspect may be questioned about an offence after being charged with it.

3D   Code C sets out the procedures to be followed when a person's attention is drawn after charge, to a statement made by another person. One method of bringing the content of an interview with another person to the notice of a suspect may be to play him a recording of that interview.

3E   When it only becomes clear during the course of an interview which is being visually recorded that the interviewee may have committed an offence to which paragraph 3.2 applies, the interviewing officer should turn off the recording equipment and the interview should continue in accordance with the provisions of the Terrorism Act 2000.

3F   A decision not to record an interview visually for any reason may be the subject of comment in court. The authorising officer should therefore be prepared to justify their decision in each case.

4   The Interview

(a)   General

4.1   The provisions of Code C in relation to cautions and interviews and the notes for guidance applicable to those provisions shall apply to the conduct of interviews to which this Code applies.

4.2   Particular attention is drawn to those parts of Code C that describe the restrictions on drawing adverse inferences from a suspect's failure or refusal to say anything about their involvement in the offence when interviewed, or after being charged or informed they may be prosecuted and how those restrictions affect the terms of the caution and determines whether a special warning under sections 36 and 37 of the Criminal Justice and Public Order Act 1994 can be given.

(b)   Commencement of interviews

4.3   When the suspect is brought into the interview room the interviewer shall without delay, but in sight of the suspect, load the recording equipment and set it to record. The recording media must be unwrapped or otherwise opened in the presence of the suspect. [See Note 4A]

4.4   The interviewer shall then tell the suspect formally about the visual recording. The interviewer shall:

(a)   explain the interview is being visually recorded;

(b)   subject to paragraph 2.5, give his or her name and rank, and that of any other interviewer present;

(c)   ask the suspect and any other party present (e.g. his solicitor) to identify themselves;

(d)   state the date, time of commencement and place of the interview; and

(e)   state that the suspect will be given a notice about what will happen to the recording.

4.5   The interviewer shall then caution the suspect, which should follow that set out in Code C, and remind the suspect of their entitlement to free and independent legal advice and that they can speak to a solicitor on the telephone.

4.6   The interviewer shall then put to the suspect any significant statement or silence (i.e. failure or refusal to answer a question or to answer it satisfactorily) which occurred before the start of the interview, and shall ask the suspect whether they wish to confirm or deny that earlier statement or silence or whether they wish to add anything. The definition of a "significant" statement or silence is the same as that set out in Code C.

(c)   Interviews with the deaf

4.7   If the suspect is deaf or there is doubt about their hearing ability, the provisions of Code C on interpreters for the deaf or for interviews with suspects who have difficulty in understanding English continue to apply.

(d)   Objections and complaints by the suspect

4.8   If the suspect raises objections to the interview being visually recorded either at the outset or during the interview or during a break in the interview, the interviewer shall explain the fact that the interview is being visually recorded and that the provisions of this Code require that the suspect's objections shall be recorded. The suspect's objections shall be noted.
4.9   If in the course of an interview a complaint is made by the person being questioned, or on their behalf, concerning the provisions of this Code or of Code C, then the interviewer shall act in accordance with Code C, record it in the interview record and inform the custody officer. [See Notes 4B and 4C]
4.10   If the suspect indicates that they wish to tell the interviewer about matters not directly connected with the offence of which they are suspected and that they are unwilling for these matters to be recorded, the suspect shall be given the opportunity to tell the interviewer about these matters after the conclusion of the formal interview.

(e)   Changing the recording media

4.11   In instances where the recording medium is not of sufficient length to record all of the interview with the suspect, further certified recording media will be used. When the recording equipment indicates that the recording medium has only a short time left to run, the interviewer shall advise the suspect and round off that part of the interview. If the interviewer wishes to continue the interview but does not already have further certified recording media with him, they shall obtain a set. The suspect should not be left unattended in the interview room. The interviewer will remove the recording media from the recording equipment and insert the new ones which have been unwrapped or otherwise opened in the suspect's presence. The recording equipment shall then be set to record. Care must be taken, particularly when a number of sets of recording media have been used, to ensure that there is no confusion between them. This could be achieved by marking the sets of recording media with consecutive identification numbers.

(f)   Taking a break during the interview

4.12   When a break is to be taken during the course of an interview and the interview room is to be vacated by the suspect, the fact that a break is to be taken, the reason for it and the time shall be recorded. The recording equipment must be turned off and the recording media removed. The procedures for the conclusion of an interview set out in paragraph 4.19, below, should be followed.

4.13 When a break is to be a short one, and both the suspect and a police officer are to remain in the interview room, the fact that a break is to be taken, the reasons for it and the time shall be recorded on the recording media. The recording equipment may be turned off, but there is no need to remove the recording media. When the interview is recommenced the recording shall continue on the same recording media and the time at which the interview recommences shall be recorded.

4.14 When there is a break in questioning under caution, the interviewing officer must ensure that the person being questioned is aware that they remain under caution. If there is any doubt, the caution must be given again in full when the interview resumes. [See Notes 4 D and 4E].

(g) Failure of recording equipment

4.15 If there is a failure of equipment which can be rectified quickly, the appropriate procedures set out in paragraph 4.12 shall be followed. When the recording is resumed the interviewer shall explain what has happened and record the time the interview recommences. If, however, it is not possible to continue recording on that particular recorder and no alternative equipment is readily available, the interview may continue without being recorded visually. In such circumstances, the procedures set out in paragraph 3.3 of this Code for seeking the authority of the custody officer will be followed. [See Note 4F]

(h) Removing used recording media from recording equipment

4.16 Where used recording media are removed from the recording equipment during the course of an interview, they shall be retained and the procedures set out in paragraph 4.18 below followed.

(i) Conclusion of interview

4.17 Before the conclusion of the interview, the suspect shall be offered the opportunity to clarify anything he or she has said and asked if there is anything that they wish to add.

4.18 At the conclusion of the interview, including the taking and reading back of any written statement, the time shall be recorded and the recording equipment switched off. The master tape or CD shall be removed from the recording equipment, sealed with a master copy label and treated as an exhibit in accordance with the force standing orders. The interviewer shall sign the label and also ask the suspect and any appropriate adults or other third party present during the interview to sign it. If the suspect or third party refuses to sign the label, an officer of at least the rank of inspector, or if one is not available, the custody officer, shall be called into the interview room and asked to sign it.

4.19 The suspect shall be handed a notice which explains the use which will be made of the recording and the arrangements for access to it. The notice will also advise the suspect that a copy of the tape or CD shall be supplied as soon as practicable if the person is charged or informed that he will be prosecuted.

Notes for guidance

4A   *The interviewer should attempt to estimate the likely length of the interview and ensure that an appropriate quantity of certified recording media and labels with which to seal the master copies are available in the interview room.*

4B   *Where the custody officer is called immediately to deal with the complaint, wherever possible the recording equipment should be left to run until the custody officer has entered the interview room and spoken to the person being interviewed. Continuation or termination of the interview should be at the discretion of the interviewing officer pending action by an inspector as set out in Code C.*

4C   *Where the complaint is about a matter not connected with this Code of Practice or Code C, the decision to continue with the interview is at the discretion of the interviewing officer. Where the interviewing officer decides to continue with the interview, the person being interviewed shall be told that the complaint will be brought to the attention of the custody officer at the conclusion of the interview. When the interview is concluded, the interviewing officer must, as soon as practicable, inform the custody officer of the existence and nature of the complaint made.*

4D   *In considering whether to caution again after a break, the officer should bear in mind that he may have to satisfy a court that the person understood that he was still under caution when the interview resumed.*

4E   *The officer should bear in mind that it may be necessary to satisfy the court that nothing occurred during a break in an interview or between interviews which influenced the suspect's recorded evidence. On the recommencement of an interview, the officer should consider summarising on the tape or CD the reason for the break and confirming this with the suspect.*

4F   *If any part of the recording media breaks or is otherwise damaged during the interview, it should be sealed as a master copy in the presence of the suspect and the interview resumed where it left off. The undamaged part should be copied and the original sealed as a master copy in the suspect's presence, if necessary after the interview. If equipment for copying is not readily available, both parts should be sealed in the suspect's presence and the interview begun again.*

5   After the Interview

5.1   The interviewer shall make a note in his or her pocket book of the fact that the interview has taken place and has been recorded, its time, duration and date and the identification number of the master copy of the recording media.

5.2   Where no proceedings follow in respect of the person whose interview was recorded, the recording media must nevertheless be kept securely in accordance with paragraph 6.1 and Note 6A.

Note for guidance

5A   *Any written record of a recorded interview shall be made in accordance with national guidelines approved by the Secretary of State, and with regard to the advice contained in the Manual of Guidance for the preparation, processing and submission of files.*

6   Tape Security

(a)   General

6.1   The officer in charge of the police station at which interviews with suspects are recorded shall make arrangements for the master copies to be kept securely and their movements accounted for on the same basis as other material which may be used for evidential purposes, in accordance with force standing orders [See Note 6A]

(b)   Breaking master copy seal for criminal proceedings

6.2   A police officer has no authority to break the seal on a master copy which is required for criminal trial or appeal proceedings. If it is necessary to gain access to the master copy, the police officer shall arrange for its seal to be broken in the presence of a representative of the Crown Prosecution Service. The defendant or their legal adviser shall be informed and given a reasonable opportunity to be present. If the defendant or their legal representative is present they shall be invited to reseal and sign the master copy. If either refuses or neither is present, this shall be done by the representative of the Crown Prosecution Service. [See Notes 6B and 6C]

(c)   Breaking master copy seal: other cases

6.3   The chief officer of police is responsible for establishing arrangements for breaking the seal of the master copy where no criminal proceedings result, or the criminal proceedings, to which the interview relates, have been concluded and it becomes necessary to break the seal. These arrangements should be those which the chief officer considers are reasonably necessary to demonstrate to the person interviewed and any other party who may wish to use or refer to the interview record that the master copy has not been tampered with and that the interview record remains accurate. [See Note 6D]

6.4   Subject to paragraph 6.6, a representative of each party must be given a reasonable opportunity to be present when the seal is broken, the master copy copied and re-sealed.

6.5   If one or more of the parties is not present when the master copy seal is broken because they cannot be contacted or refuse to attend or paragraph 6.6 applies, arrangements should be made for an independent person such as a custody visitor to be present. Alternatively, or as an additional safeguard, arrangement should be made for a film or photographs to be taken of the procedure.

6.6   Paragraph 6.5 does not require a person to be given an opportunity to be present when:

(a)   it is necessary to break the master copy seal for the proper and effective further investigation of the original offence or the investigation of some other offence; and

(b) the officer in charge of the investigation has reasonable grounds to suspect that allowing an opportunity might prejudice any such an investigation or criminal proceedings which may be brought as a result or endanger any person. [See Note 6E]

(e) Documentation

6.7   When the master copy seal is broken, copied and re-sealed, a record must be made of the procedure followed, including the date, time and place and persons present.

Notes for guidance

6A   *This section is concerned with the security of the master copy which will have been sealed at the conclusion of the interview. Care should, however, be taken of working copies since their loss or destruction may lead unnecessarily to the need to have access to master copies.*

6B   *If the master copy has been delivered to the crown court for their keeping after committal for trial the crown prosecutor will apply to the chief clerk of the crown court centre for its release for unsealing by the crown prosecutor.*

6C   *Reference to the Crown Prosecution Service or to the crown prosecutor in this part of the Code shall be taken to include any other body or person with a statutory responsibility for prosecution for whom the police conduct any recorded interviews.*

6D   *The most common reasons for needing access to master copies that are not required for criminal proceedings arise from civil actions and complaints against police and civil actions between individuals arising out of allegations of crime investigated by police.*

6E   *Paragraph 6.6 could apply, for example, when one or more of the outcomes or likely outcomes of the investigation might be: (i) the prosecution of one or more of the original suspects; (ii) the prosecution of someone previously not suspected, including someone who was originally a witness; and (iii) any original suspect being treated as a prosecution witness and when premature disclosure of any police action, particularly through contact with any parties involved, could lead to a real risk of compromising the investigation and endangering witnesses.*

APPENDIX 1

THE DIRECTOR'S GUIDANCE ON CHARGING

Guidance to Police Officers and Crown Prosecutors Issued by the Director of Public Prosecutions under Section 37A of the Police and Criminal Evidence Act 1984

What this Guidance is for, where it applies and when it comes into effect.

1.1 This Guidance[1] is to enable Custody Officers to decide how a person should be dealt with when:
- The Custody Officer determines there is sufficient evidence (in accordance with the Threshold Test) to charge a person with an offence,[2] or
- A person has been arrested for breach of bail who had previously been released on bail for a charging decision.[3]

1.2 This Guidance also specifies what information must be sent to a Crown Prosecutor to enable a charging or other decision to be made.[4]

1.3 This Guidance applies to those cases the Director of Public Prosecutions is required to take over in accordance with Section 3 of the Prosecution of Offences Act 1985.

1.4 This Guidance will come into effect in those Local Criminal Justice Board Areas and on the dates specified in the schedule hereto [not included here. (ed.)].

2. Key Provisions and Principles of this Guidance

Statutory provisions and key principles that under-pin this Guidance.

- Crown Prosecutors will determine whether a person is to be charged in all indictable only, either way or summary offences subject to those cases specified in this Guidance which the police may continue to charge.
- Charging decisions by Crown Prosecutors will be made following a review of evidence in cases and will be in accordance with this Guidance.

[1] Issued by the Director of Public Prosecutions under Section 37(A)(1)(a) of the Police and Criminal Evidence Act 1984, as inserted by the Criminal Justice Act 2003.
[2] PACE, Section 37(7) as amended.
[3] PACE, Section 37C.
[4] PACE, Section 37A(1)(b).

- Custody Officers must comply with this Guidance in deciding how a person is to be dealt with in accordance with Section 37(7) PACE, as amended by Schedule 2 to the Criminal Justice Act 2003.
- Crown Prosecutors will seek to identify and resolve cases that are clearly not appropriate for prosecution at the earliest opportunity on consideration of whatever material is available.
- Crown Prosecutors will provide guidance and advice to investigators throughout the investigative and prosecuting process. This may include lines of enquiry, evidential requirements and assistance in any pre-charge procedures. Crown Prosecutors will be pro-active in identifying, and where possible, rectifying evidential deficiencies and in bringing to an early conclusion those cases that cannot be strengthened by further investigation.
- Crown Prosecutors will only require "evidential reports" (see Paragraph 7.2 (i) below) where it is clear that the case will proceed to the Crown Court or is likely to be a contested summary trial or where it appears to the Crown Prosecutor that the case is so complex or sensitive that a decision to charge cannot be made without an evidential report.
- Where it is necessary, pre-charge bail arrangements will be utilised to facilitate the gathering of evidence, including, in appropriate cases, all the key evidence on which the prosecution will rely, prior to the charging decision being taken (Section 37(7)(a) and Section 47(1A) PACE).
- Crown Prosecutors will notify the officer involved in the investigation of any advice and charging or other decision in writing using the form MG3 (Section 37B(4) PACE).
- Persons may be charged whilst in police detention, or in accordance with Section 29 of the Criminal Justice Act 2003 (charging by post) when it is brought into force. [The summons procedure may be used until that change in the process arrangements.]
- Where a Crown Prosecutor notifies a Custody Officers that there is insufficient evidence to charge, or that though there is sufficient evidence to charge, a person should not be charged or given a caution, the Custody Officer shall give notice in writing to that person that he is not to be prosecuted (Section 37B(5) PACE).

- Where Crown Prosecutors decide that a person should be charged with an offence or given a caution, conditional caution, a reprimand or final warning in respect of an offence, the person shall be charged or cautioned, or conditionally cautioned, or given a reprimand or final warning accordingly (Section 37B(6) PACE).
- Where Crown Prosecutors decide that a person should be cautioned but it proves not to be possible to give the person such a caution, the person shall instead be charged with the offence (Section 37B(7) PACE.)
- In order to facilitate efficient and effective early consultations and make charging decisions, Crown Prosecutors will be deployed, as Duty Prosecutors for such hours as shall be agreed locally to provide guidance and make charging decisions. This service will be complemented by a centrally managed out of hours duty prosecutor arrangement to ensure a continuous 24 hour service.

3. Responsibility for determining charges

Duty of Crown Prosecutors to determine charge cases.

3.1 Charging by Crown Prosecutors—the principle

(i) Crown Prosecutors will be responsible for the decision to charge and the specifying or drafting of the charges in all indictable only, either way or summary offences where a Custody Officer determines that the Threshold Test is met in any case, except for those offences specified in this Guidance which may be charged or cautioned by the police without reference to a Crown Prosecutor.

Transitional arrangements for charging some likely guilty plea cases

3.2 Charging by Crown Prosecutors—transitional arrangements

(ii) Establishment of the principle set out in Paragraph 3.1 above will be achieved incrementally and will be notified by further editions of this Guidance.

(iii) Until such notification, the police may determine the charge in any either way or summary offences where it appears to the Custody Officer that a guilty plea is likely and that the case is suitable for sentencing in the magistrates' court, but excluding those specified in Annex A to this Guidance.

(iv) Where the Custody Officer is uncertain whether a case falls under 3.2(iii) above, early consultation with a Duty Prosecutor should be undertaken to clarify whether the charging decision is one that should be made by a Crown Prosecutor.

Details, with exceptions, of cases the police may charge	3.3	**Charging by the Police**

The Police may determine the charge in the following cases:

(i) Any offence under the Road Traffic Acts or any other offence arising from the presence of a motor vehicle, trailer, or pedal cycle on a road or other public place, except where (and the charge must therefore be determined by a Crown Prosecutor):

- The circumstances have resulted in the death of any person; or
- There is an allegation of dangerous driving; or
- The allegation is one of driving whilst disqualified and there has been no admission in a PACE interview to both the driving and the disqualification; or
- The statutory defence to being in charge of a motor vehicle (unfit through drink or drugs or excess alcohol) may be raised under Section 4(3) or 5(2) of the Road Traffic Act 1988; or
- There is an allegation of the unlawful taking of a motor vehicle or the aggravated unlawful taking of a motor vehicle (unless the case is suitable for disposal as an early guilty plea in the magistrates' court).

(ii) Any offence of absconding under the Bail Act 1976 and any offence contrary to Section 5 of the Public Order Act 1986 and any offence under the Town Police Clauses Act 1847, the Metropolitan Police Act 1839, the Vagrancy Act 1824, the Street Offences Act 1959, under Section 91 of the Criminal Justice Act 1967, Section 12 of the Licensing Act 1872, any offence under any bylaw and any summary offence punishable on conviction with a term of imprisonment of 3 months or less except where (and the charge must therefore be determined by a Crown Prosecutor):

- The Director of Public Prosecutions publishes other arrangements for the charging and prosecution of these offences.

Cases charged by the police to be reviewed by a Crown Prosecutor.	3.4	**Review by Crown Prosecutors under Section 10 of the Prosecution of Offences Act 1985**

Where by virtue of this Guidance the police determine the charge, that determination and the charge will be subject to a review by a Crown Prosecutor acting under Section 10 of the Prosecution of Offences Act 1985 and under Section 37B of the Police and Criminal Evidence Act 1984 (as amended).

CPS to charge cases delegated to police in certain circumstances.	3.5	<u>Combinations of persons and offences</u> Where the charges or joint charges to be preferred against one or more persons include a combination of offences, some of which may be determined by the police, and others that must be determined by a Crown Prosecutor, the Custody Officer shall refer all charges to a Crown Prosecutor for determination.
Application of Code for Crown Prosecutors to Custody Officers.	3.6	<u>The application of the Code for Crown Prosecutors</u> When determining charges, Crown Prosecutors and Custody Officers will apply the principles contained in the latest edition of the Code for Crown Prosecutors.
Charge selection, range and number of charges.	3.7	<u>Number and seriousness of charge(s)</u> In determining the totality of charges to proceed, the selection of charges should seek to reflect the seriousness and the extent of the offending. It should also provide the court with adequate sentencing powers, and enable the case to be presented in a clear and simple way. Where appropriate, a schedule of other admitted offences may be listed on an MG18 for the charged person to ask the Court to take into consideration.
General application of full Code Test.	3.8	<u>Application of the Full Code Test</u> In any case where the charging decision is to be made, and the information required to be considered under Paragraph 7.2 (below) of this Guidance is available for review, the standard to be applied in reaching the charging decision will be the Full Test under the Code for Crown Prosecutors: namely (following a review of the evidential material provided) that there is enough evidence to provide a realistic prospect of conviction and that it is in the public interest to proceed.
	3.9	<u>Application of the Threshold Test to Charging decisions</u> In cases where it is determined that it would not be appropriate for the person to be released on bail after charge and where the information referred to in Paragraph 7.2 (below) of this Guidance is not available at the time the charging decision has to be taken, a staged approach will then apply:
The Threshold Test for charging in custody cases where an evidential file is unavailable.		(i) Where the evidential material required under Paragraph 7.2 (below) is not available, the Crown Prosecutor (or Custody Officer) will assess the case against the Threshold Test set out in Paragraph 3.10. This should be noted on the MG3 and a review date for a Full Code Test agreed as part of the action plan.

When to apply a Full Code Test for Crown Prosecutors in custody cases.

(ii) Subsequently, upon receipt of further evidence or a Report to Crown Prosecutor for a Charging Decision (MG3) accompanied by the information required in accordance with Paragraph 7.2 of this Guidance, the Crown Prosecutor will review the case in accordance with the Full Code Test before deciding whether it is appropriate to continue with the offence(s) charged or prefer additional or alternative charges.

A decision to charge and withhold bail must be kept under review. The evidence gathered must be regularly assessed to ensure the charge is still appropriate and that continued objection to bail is justified. Crown Prosecutors will only apply the Threshold Test for a limited period. The Full Code Test must be applied as soon as reasonably practicable, taking into account the progress of the investigation.

Where however the information specified in Paragraph 7.2 is available at the time that the initial Report to Crown Prosecutor is made, the Full Code Test will be applied.

The Threshold Test

3.10 The Threshold Test

Application of the Threshold Test will require an overall assessment of whether in all the circumstances of the case there is at least a reasonable suspicion against the person of having committed an offence (in accordance with Article 5 of the European Convention on Human Rights) and that at that stage it is in the public interest to proceed.

The evidential decision in each case will require consideration of a number of factors including: the evidence available at the time and the likelihood and nature of further evidence being obtained; the reasonableness for believing that evidence will become available; the time that will take and the steps being taken to gather it; the impact of the expected evidence on the case, and the charges the totality of the evidence will support.

The public interest means the same as under the Full Code Test, but will be based on the information available at the time of charge, which will often be limited.

Application of the above Tests to police charged cases.

3.11 Where, in accordance with this Guidance, Custody Officers make the charging decision without referral to Crown Prosecutors, they will apply the Full Code Test. Where the case is one in which it is not proposed to release the person on bail after charge and the evidential material required to apply the Full Code Test is not available, the Custody

Officer will proceed to apply the Threshold Test in accordance with Paragraph 3.10 above.

Emergency charging by the police of CPS cases.

3.12 Emergency Cases—Expiry of PACE Time Limits
 In cases where the charging responsibility lies with a Crown Prosecutor in accordance with this Guidance and it is proposed to withhold bail for the purposes of making an application to a court for a remand in custody (or for bail conditions that may only be imposed by a court) but it proves not to be possible to consult with a Crown Prosecutor in person or by telephone before the expiry of any PACE custody time limit applicable before charge, a Custody Officer may proceed to charge, but only on the authority of a Duty Inspector. The Duty Inspector shall note the custody record and MG3 to confirm that it is appropriate to charge under this emergency provision. The case must be referred to a Crown Prosecutor as soon as is practicable for authority to proceed with the prosecution.

4. Decisions ancillary to the charging decision

Consultations prior to applications to with-hold bail at court and short remands to police custody

4.1 Consultations where it is proposed to withhold bail or impose conditions
 Whilst decisions to detain or bail persons are exclusively matters for a Custody Officer, where it appears that a person in police detention should not be released and should be detained for the purposes of an application being made to a court for a remand in custody, including short periods in police custody for the purpose of enquiries into other offences, the Custody Officer may wish to consult a Duty Prosecutor to confirm that any proposed application for a remand in custody or the imposition of bail conditions which can only be imposed by a court is justified in accordance with the Bail Act 1976, is proportionate, is likely to be ordered by the court and that sufficient detail to support any such application is recorded on the MG7.

Court selection

4.2 Determination of the court for first appearance
 When Crown Prosecutors make charging decisions concerning cases that are to be bailed directly to an initial hearing, the Crown Prosecutor will determine whether the case is appropriate for an Early First Hearing Court or an Early Administrative Hearing Court. This will be indicated on the form MG3 with the charge decision.

Special provisions for PYO cases

4.3 Special procedure for Persistent Young Offenders
 Crown Prosecutors will be responsible for the decision to charge in all cases involving Persistent

Young Offenders unless the charge is one specified in Paragraph 3.3 of this Guidance.

Whenever a person who is, or appears to be, under 18 years of age is taken into custody, the Custody Officer will undertake an immediate check to ascertain whether the person is a Persistent Young Offender.

Where it appears to an Investigating or Custody Officer that the person under investigation may be a Persistent Young Offender, early consultation will be undertaken with the Duty Prosecutor to confirm the likely charges and the evidential requirements in the case. Early consultation will be utilised to proactively manage all Persistent Young Offender cases to secure consistent performance in progressing these cases.

Where it appears that the case will be contested, the Duty Prosecutor and Investigating Officer will agree, as soon as practicable and in any case within 3 days of the arrest on the evidential requirements to progress the case and on a date for the completion of the agreed work, including any pre-charge bail period, taking into account the 71 day target from arrest to sentence for concluding such cases.

5. Deployment of and role of Duty Prosecutor

Deployment and duty of Crown Prosecutors

5.1 Deployment

Chief Crown Prosecutors will make arrangements for the deployment of Crown Prosecutors to act as Duty Prosecutor in locally agreed locations having regard to the area business and wherever possible on a face-to-face basis, or to be otherwise available for the purposes of fulfilling the CPS's statutory duty. Duty Prosecutors will be available for consultation and will render such early legal advice and guidance, including where appropriate the making of charging decisions as will facilitate the efficient and effective preparation and disposal of criminal prosecutions.

When early advice may be sought by the police

5.2 Early Consultations

Early consultation and advice may be sought and given in any case (including those in which the police may themselves determine the charge) and may include lines of enquiry, evidential requirements and any pre-charge procedures. In exercising this function, Crown Prosecutors will be pro-active in identifying and, where possible, rectifying evidential deficiencies and identify those cases that can proceed to court for an early guilty plea as an expedited report.

Stopping weak cases early	5.3	Early consultation should also seek to identify evidentially weak cases, which cannot be rectified by further investigation, either at that stage or at all, so that these investigations may, where appropriate, be brought to an early conclusion.
Duty Prosecutor's action on receipt of a case	5.4	Reviewing the Report to Crown Prosecutor for a Charging Decision (MG3) and evidence. Where Crown Prosecutors receive a 'Report to Crown Prosecutor for a Charging Decision' (MG3) accompanied by the information specified in Paragraph 7.2 below, it is the duty of the Crown Prosecutor to review the evidence as soon as is practicable, having regard to any bail return dates, and decide whether it is appropriate or not, at that stage, to charge the person with an offence or divert them from the criminal justice system.
Written notice of charging or other decision	5.5	Once a charging (or other) decision has been made, Crown Prosecutors will give written notice of the decision by completing the second part of the Report to Crown Prosecutor for a Charging Decision (MG3) which will be provided to an officer involved in the investigation of the offence. A copy will be retained by the Crown Prosecutor.
Agreeing an action plan to build a case file	5.6	Where during the course of a consultation or following receipt of the Report to Crown Prosecutor for a Charging Decision (MG3) it is clear that a charging decision in the case cannot be reached at that stage, the Crown Prosecutor consulted will advise on the further steps to be taken, including the evidence to be gathered or the statements to be obtained before the decision can be reached and will agree with the investigating officer the action to be taken and the time in which that is to be achieved. This agreement will be recorded on the MG3 and a copy will be provided to an officer involved in the investigation. A copy will be retained by the Crown Prosecutor. In providing such advice, Crown Prosecutors should avoid simply requiring full files to be produced but will specify the precise evidence required or to be sought in accordance with Paragraph 7.2 below. Persons will not be charged until all agreed actions have been completed.
Referrals of cases in special circumstances	5.7	Where it appears at an early consultation that the case is of such complexity or sensitivity that it is more appropriate for referral to a specialist unit or prosecutor, or for an individual prosecutor to be allocated to the case from the outset, the Duty Prosecutor, or any Crown Prosecutor consulted,

will contact the appropriate Area Unit Head forthwith to make the necessary arrangements.

Building evidential files: use of police pre-charge bail   5.8   In cases identified as likely to be contested or to be sent to the Crown Court, Crown Prosecutors will detail the requirements for preparation of an evidential report where that information is not immediately available before a full charging decision can be taken. Where the person is suitable for release on bail the Custody Officer will then bail the person for such a period as is sufficient to allow any agreed action to be completed and the case to be reported to a Crown Prosecutor for a charging decision.

6. Decisions not to prosecute

Written notice by Custody Officer of no prosecution   6.1   <u>Insufficient evidence or not in the public interest to charge</u>
Where the Crown Prosecutor notifies a Custody Officer that there is not sufficient evidence to charge the person with an offence or that there is sufficient evidence but the public interest does not require the person to be charged or given a caution in respect of an offence, the Custody Officer will notify the person in writing to that effect.

Written notice by Custody Officer of no prosecution, but possible further action   6.2   Where however it appears to the Crown Prosecutor that should further evidence or information come to light in the future the case may be re-considered under the Code for Crown Prosecutors, the Crown Prosecutor will notify the Custody Officer to that effect who will notify the person in writing accordingly.

7. Information to be sent to Crown Prosecutors for charging decisions

Evidence needed to make a charging decision   7.1   In making charging decisions, Crown Prosecutors will examine and assess the evidence available before reaching a decision. Wherever possible, Crown Prosecutors will seek to make the decision on the evidence presented to them by the investigator. Where however this is not possible, Custody Officers will arrange for persons to be released on bail, if it is necessary and appropriate to do so, to permit the required information to be provided as soon as is practicable.

Form of reports   7.2   The information to be provided by an officer involved in the investigation to a Crown Prosecutor to determine charges will be in the form of the 'Report to a Crown Prosecutor for a Charging Decision' (MG3) and must be accompanied by the following:

Crown Court and likely
not guilty cases

(i)   All cases proceeding to the Crown Court or
expected to be contested: Evidential Report.
Where it is clear that the case is likely to or will proceed to the Crown Court or is likely to be contested,
the Report to Crown Prosecutor for a Charging
Decision (MG3) must be accompanied by an
Evidential Report containing the key evidence upon
which the prosecution will rely together with
any unused material which may undermine the
prosecution case or assist the defence (including
crime reports, initial descriptions and any previous
convictions of key witnesses).

The Evidential Report must also be accompanied
by suggested charge(s), a record of convictions and
cautions of the person, and any observations of the
reporting or supervising officer.

All other cases

(ii)   Other cases referred to a Crown Prosecutor
for a charging decision
In any other case to be referred to a Crown Prosecutor
for a charging decision, the Report to Crown
Prosecutor must be accompanied by an Expedited
Report containing key witness statements, any other
compelling evidence[5] and a summary of an interview.
Where the offence has been witnessed by no more
than 4 police officers, a key witness statement and a
summary of the other evidence may suffice. Whether
the summary of the interview or of other police witnesses is to be oral or written will be at the discretion
of the Duty Prosecutor concerned.

The Expedited Report must be accompanied by
any other information that may have a bearing on
the evidential or public interest test, a record of
convictions and cautions and any observations of
the reporting or supervising officer.

File information in
custody cases

7.3   Custody cases—Threshold Test—expedited report
Where in accordance with this Guidance and in order
to facilitate the making of an application to a court
for a remand in custody, a charging decision is to be
taken in accordance with Paragraph 3.9 (i) above,
the Report to Crown Prosecutor (MG3) must be
accompanied by an Expedited Report containing sufficient material then available and brief details of any
previous convictions or cautions of the person to
allow the Threshold Test to be applied. The Manual
of Guidance remand file will be provided for the first
and subsequent interim hearings, until the completed

---

[5] For example, visually recorded evidence of the crime taking place from which it is possible to
clearly identify the offender.

Report to Crown Prosecutor, or further evidence referred to in Paragraph 3.9 (ii) above is submitted.

Early consultation in evidential report cases

7.4 Requirement for early consultation in Evidential Report Cases

Early consultation with a Duty Prosecutor should be undertaken to identify those cases in which an evidential file will be required and to agree the timescales for the completion and submission of the Report to Crown Prosecutor for a Charging Decision (MG3). An officer involved in the investigation must submit the completed Report to Crown Prosecutor for a Charging Decision (MG3) within the agreed timescale together with the evidential material referred to in Paragraphs 5.6 and 7.2(i) above.

Complex or sensitive cases

7.5 Complex or sensitive cases—evidential report

In any case where it appears to a Duty Prosecutor that the case is so complex or sensitive that a decision to charge, or not as the case may be, cannot be made without fuller information, the Report to Crown Prosecutor for a Charging Decision (MG3) must be accompanied by an evidential file and the material mentioned in Paragraphs 5.6 and 7.2(i) above.

When police uncertain about the information required

7.6 Case requirements unclear—consult with a Duty Prosecutor

Where an Investigating Officer considers that a defence may have been raised by a person in interview, or is uncertain whether a person has fully admitted an offence and requires clarification of the information required to accompany the report for a charging decision, early consultation with a Duty Prosecutor should occur to determine whether the case is likely to proceed and to establish the report requirements to facilitate the making of the charging decision.

8. Roles and Responsibilities of Custody Officers under Section 37(7) (a) to (d) PACE, as amended by Schedule 2 to the Criminal Justice Act 2003

Early consultation where offence to be charged by CPS

8.1 Requirement for early consultations

Where it appears likely that a charge will be determined by Crown Prosecutors, Custody Officers must direct investigating officers to consult a Duty Prosecutor as soon as is practicable after a person is taken into custody. This will enable early agreement to be reached as to the Report and evidential requirements and, where appropriate, for any period of bail to be determined to permit submission of the Report to the Crown Prosecutor for a Charging Decision (MG3).

Early decisions

8.2 Early consultation with a Duty Prosecutor will allow the early identification of weak cases and those where the charging decision may be made upon consideration of limited information.

Referrals where police do not wish to prosecute where sufficient to charge on Threshold Test

8.3 Referrals where the police do not wish to proceed
In any indictable only case in which the Threshold Test is met and in which an investigating or supervisory officer decides that he does not wish to proceed with a prosecution, the case must be referred to a Crown Prosecutor to confirm whether or not the case is to proceed. Early consultation in such a case may allow the investigation and preparation of case papers to be curtailed unless the complexity or sensitivity of the case determines otherwise.

Stage at which cases must be referred to a Crown Prosecutor

8.4 The standard to be applied in determining whether the case is to be referred to a Crown Prosecutor or the person released on bail.
In determining whether there is sufficient evidence to charge in accordance with Section 37(7) PACE, Custody Officers will apply the Threshold Test set out in Paragraph 3.10 above. Where, in any case, it appears that there is manifestly no evidence and the Threshold Test is not met in respect of a detained person, the Custody Officer need not refer the case to a Crown Prosecutor before releasing that person, whether on bail or otherwise. In any case where this Guidance requires charges to be determined by Crown Prosecutors and a Custody Officer concludes that the Threshold Test is met, the Custody Officer will ensure that the case is referred to a Crown Prosecutor as soon as is practicable, or, where the person is suitable for bail, release the person detained on pre-charge bail, with or without conditions, in accordance with Section 37(7)(a).

Application of police pre-charge bail

8.5 Delaying charging and releasing persons suitable on bail
In any case where this Guidance requires charging decisions to be made by Crown Prosecutors and the required information is not then available, Custody Officers will release those persons suitable for bail (with or without conditions as appropriate) to allow for consultation with a Crown Prosecutor and the submission of an evidential report for a Charging Decision (MG3) in accordance with this Guidance.

Early disclosure to defence

8.6 The period of bail should be such as to allow the completion of the investigation, submission of a Report to a Crown Prosecutor for a Charging Decision (MG3), for the person to be charged, and for early disclosure of the evidence and any unused material referred to in Paragraph 7.2 to be provided to the defence prior to the first appearance.

| Delayed charges—other reasons | 8.7 | Where a Custody Officer determines that there is sufficient evidence to charge a person but concludes that it is not appropriate at that stage to charge the person with an offence or to seek a charging decision from a Crown Prosecutor and proposes to release the person from police custody in accordance with Section 37 (7)(b) PACE, the person may only be released on unconditional bail. The Custody Officer should record the reasons for so acting. |

9. Cautions, reprimands and final warnings

Diversion from prosecution, police to caution, reprimand etc	9.1	Where the police consider that the Threshold Test is met in a case, other than an indictable only offence, and determine that it is in the public interest instead to administer a simple caution, or to administer a reprimand or final warning in the case of a youth, the police may issue that caution, reprimand or final warning as appropriate, without referring the case to a Crown Prosecutor.
Consultation on decision to caution	9.2	Notwithstanding the above, an investigating officer may wish to consult with a Crown Prosecutor in respect of any case in which it is proposed to deal with a person by way of a caution, reprimand or final warning.
Actions on conditional caution cases	9.3	Where a conditional cautioning scheme is in force locally and the police wish to conditionally caution any person for an offence, the Custody Officer must refer the case to a Crown Prosecutor for decision.
Review by Crown Prosecutors	9.4	Where in accordance with this Guidance, the police have determined to initiate proceedings against a person by way of a charge, and a Crown Prosecutor, acting under Section 10 of the Prosecution of Offences Act 1985 and Section 37B of the Police and Criminal Evidence Act 1984 (as amended) notifies a Custody Officer that it is more appropriate to proceed by way of a conditional caution (if a scheme is in force locally), simple caution, reprimand or final warning, the Custody Officer will ensure that the person is given a conditional caution, simple caution, reprimand or final warning as appropriate.
Decisions to charge or caution by Crown Prosecutors	9.5	Crown Prosecutors, when undertaking a charging review in accordance with this Guidance, may determine that a charge, conditional caution (if a scheme is in force locally), simple caution, reprimand or final warning is appropriate. Written notice of the decision will be given to the Custody Officer on an MG3. Where it subsequently proves not to be possible to give the person a conditional caution (if

this scheme is enforced locally), simple caution, reprimand, or final warning, the matter will be referred back to the Crown Prosecutor to determine whether the person is instead to be charged with the offence.

10. Breach of Pre-Charge Bail Conditions

Action on breach of bail conditions pending CPS charging decision

10.1 Where a person is released on bail pending a CPS decision on charge or re-released following arrest for breach of a condition of bail for that purpose [under Section 37(7)(a) or 37C(2)(b) PACE,] and that person is subsequently arrested under Section 46A (1A) PACE on reasonable grounds of having broken any of the conditions of bail, or for failing to surrender to bail at the police station, and a Custody Officer concludes that the person should be detained in custody for the purpose of an application to the court for a remand in custody, the Custody Officer will consult a Crown Prosecutor for a decision as to whether to charge with the offence for which the person had previously been released on bail or with any other offence or be released without charge either on bail or without bail.

Charging breach of bail—emergency situations

10.2 In any such case where it has proved not to be possible to consult with a Crown Prosecutor in person or by telephone before the expiry of any PACE custody time limit and it is proposed to withhold bail for the purposes of an application for a remand into custody (or for bail conditions that may only be imposed by the court) a Custody Officer may proceed to charge, but only on the authority of a Duty Inspector. The Duty Inspector shall note the custody record and MG3 to confirm that it is appropriate to charge under the emergency provisions. The case must be referred to a Crown Prosecutor as soon as is practicable for authority to proceed with the prosecution.

11. Police action post referral and escalation procedure.

Police action post referral

11.1 In any case where the Threshold is met and the case has been referred to a Crown Prosecutor for a charging decision, and the decision of the Crown Prosecutor is to charge, caution, obtain additional evidence, or take no action, the police will not proceed in any other way without first referring the matter back to a Crown Prosecutor.

Dispute resolution

11.2 Where in any case an Investigating or Custody Officer is not in agreement with the charging decision, the Report requirements or any diversion proposal of a Crown Prosecutor and wishes to have the case referred for further review, the case must be referred to the BCU Crime Manager (normally Detective Chief Inspector), or appointed Deputy, for consultation with a CPS Unit Head, or appointed Deputy for resolution. If further escalation is required, the involvement of the Divisional Commander and the Level E Unit Head or Chief Crown Prosecutor should be obtained. Procedures should be in place for this review to be conducted speedily.

12. Form of Report to Crown Prosecutor for a Charging Decision (MG3)

Form of MG3   12.1   The Report to Crown Prosecutor for a Charging Decision to be used will be the form MG3, a copy of which is attached at Annex B to this Guidance. The Manual of Guidance Editorial Board may vary this form from time to time.

13. Requirements to Comply with the Manual of Guidance Provisions

Form of MG3   13.1   All consultation arrangements and procedures for the preparation, processing and submission of prosecution files and the disclosure of unused material will be carried out in accordance with the provisions of the latest edition of the Manual of Guidance as agreed between the Home Office, Association of Chief Police Officers and the Crown Prosecution Service.

Ken Macdonald Q.C.
Director of Public Prosecutions

ANNEX A

Offences or circumstances, which must always be referred to a crown prosecutor for early consultation and charging decision—whether admitted or not

- Offences requiring the Attorney General's or Director of Public Prosecution's consent.
- Any indictable only offence.
- Any either way offence triable only on indictment due to the surrounding circumstances of the commission of the offence or the previous convictions of the person.

In so far as not covered by the above:

- Offences under the Terrorism Act 2000 or any other offence linked with terrorist activity.

- Offences under the Anti-Terrorism, Crime and Security Act 2001.
- Offences under the Explosive Substances Act 1883.
- Offences under any of the Official Secrets Acts.
- Offences involving any racial, religious or homophobic aggravation.
- Offences classified as Domestic Violence.
- Offences under the Sexual Offences Act 2003 committed by or upon persons under the age of 18 years.
- Offences involving Persistent Young Offenders, unless chargeable by the police under Paragraph 3.3.
- Offences arising directly or indirectly out of activities associated with hunting wild mammals with dogs under the Hunting Act 2004.
- The following specific offences[6]:
  - Wounding or inflicting grievous bodily harm, contrary to Section 20 of the Offences Against the Person Act 1861.
  - Assault occasioning actual bodily harm, contrary to Section 47 of the Offences Against the Person Act 1861.
  - Violent Disorder contrary to Section 2 of the Public Order Act 1986.
  - Affray, contrary to Section 3 of the Public Order Act 1986.
  - Offences involving deception, contrary to the Theft Acts 1968 & 1978.
  - Handling stolen goods, contrary to Section 22 of the Theft Act 1968.

---

[6] File requirements for these cases will be in accordance with the Manual of Guidance expedited file, to include key witness statements or other compelling evidence and a short descriptive note of any interview conducted.

PACE PROVISIONS NOT IN FORCE AS AT JANUARY 1, 2005

PACE PROVISION	THE AMENDING OR REPEALING OF STATUTORY PROVISION
s.9(2A)	Courts Act 2003, s.65, Sch.4, para.5
s.16(10)(i)	Courts Act 2003, s.109(1), Sch.8, para.281(1), (2)
s.16(11)(i)	Courts Act 2003, s.109(1), Sch.8, para.281(1), (4)
s.24(1)	Criminal Justice and Court Services Act 2000, s.74, Sch.7, Pt II, paras 76, 77
s.37B(8)	Criminal Justice Act 2003, s.28, Sch.2, para.(3)
s.38(6A)	Criminal Justice Act 2003, s.5(1), 2(b), Sch.32, Pt 1, para.44
s.46(2)	Courts Act 2003, s.109, Sch.8, para.282(1), (2)
s.46(3)	Courts Act 2003, s.109, Sch.8, para.282(1), (3)(a)
s.46(3)	Courts Act 2003, s.109, Sch.8, para.282(1), (3)(b)
s.46(4)	Courts Act 2003, s.109, Sch.8, para.282(1), (4)(a)
s.46(5)	Courts Act 2003, s.109, Sch.8, para.282(1), (5)(a), (b)
s.46(6)	Courts Act 2003, s.109, Sch.8, para.282(1), (6)(a), (b)
s.46(7)	Courts Act 2003, s.109, Sch.8, para.282(1), (7)(a), (b)
s.46(8)	Courts Act 2003, s.109, Sch.8, para.282(1), (8)
s.47(3A)	Courts Act 2003, s.109, Sch.8, para.283
s.47(7)	Courts Act 2003, s.109, Sch.8, para.284
s.61(8A)	Criminal Justice and Police Act, 2001, s.78(7)
s.61(9)(a)	Immigration and Asylum Act 1999, s.169(1), Sch.14, para.80(1), (4)
s.62(10)(a)(i)	Criminal Justice Act 2003, ss.41, 332, Sch.3, Pt 2, para.56(1), (2)(a), Sch.37, Pt 4

PACE PROVISION	THE AMENDING OR REPEALING OF STATUTORY PROVISION
s.62(10)(aa)(i),(ii)	Criminal Justice Act 2003, s.41, Sch.3, Pt 2, para.56(1), (2)(b)
s.63(9A)	Criminal Justice and Police Act 2001, s.80(4)
s.71	Criminal Justice Act 2003, ss.41, 332, Sch.3, Pt 2, para.56(1), (3), Sch.37, Pt 4
s.73(3)	Courts Act 2003, s.109(1), Sch.8, para.285
s.76(9)	Criminal Justice Act 2003, ss.41, 332, Sch.3, Pt 2, para.56(1), (4), Sch.37, Pt 4
s.76A	Criminal Justice Act 2003, s.128(1)
s.78(3)	Criminal Justice Act 2003, ss.41, 332, Sch.3, Pt 2, para.56(1), (5), Sch.37, Pt 4
s.82(1)	Youth Justice and Criminal Evidence Act 1999, s.67(3), Sch.6
Sch.1	(replacement of "circuit judge") Courts Act 2003, s.65, Sch.4, para.6
Sch.1A, para.27	Licensing Act 2003, s.198(1), Sch.6, para.93

PACE BIBLIOGRAPHY[1]

ALLEN, C.J.W. (1990) "Discretion and security: excluding evidence under s.78(1) of the Police and Criminal Evidence Act 1984", 49 *Cambridge Law Journal* 80.

BALDWIN, J. (1992a) *Preparing the record of taped interviews* (Royal Commission on Criminal Justice, Research Study No.2).

BALDWIN, J. (1992b) *The role of legal representatives at the police station* (Royal Commission on Criminal Justice, Research Study No.3).

BALDWIN, J. and BEDWARD, J. (1991) "Summarising tape recordings of police interviews", *Criminal Law Review* 671–679.

BALDWIN, J. and MOLONEY, T. (1992) *Supervision of criminal investigations* (Royal Commission on Criminal Justice, Research Study No.4).

BIRCH, D.J. (1989) "The PACE hots up: confessions and confusions under the 1984 Act", *Criminal Law Review* 95–116.

BLAND, N., MILLER, J. and QUINTON, P. (2000) *Managing the Use and Impact of Searches: A review of force interventions* (Home Office Policing and Reducing Crime Unit, Paper No.132).

BLAND, N., MILLER, J. and QUINTON, P. (2000) *Upping the PACE? An evaluation of the recommendations of the Stephen Lawrence Inquiry on stops and searches* (Home Office Policing and Reducing Crime Unit, Paper No.128).

BOTTOMLEY, A.K., COLEMAN, C.A., DIXON, D., GILL, M. and WALL, D. (1991a) *The Impact of PACE: Policing in a Northern Force* (Hull University, Centre for Criminological Research).

BOTTOMLEY, A.K., COLEMAN, C.A., DIXON, D., GILL, M. and WALL, D. (1991b) "The Detention of Suspects in Police Custody", 31 *British Journal of Criminology* 347–364.

BROWN, D. (1987) *The Police Complaints Procedure: A Survey of Complainants' Views* (Home Office Research Study No.93, HMSO).

BROWN, D. (1989) *Detention at the Police Station under the Police and Criminal Evidence Act 1984* (Home Office Research Study No.104, HMSO).

BROWN, D. (1991) *Investigating Burglary: the effects of PACE* (Home Office Research Study No.123, HMSO).

BROWN, D. (1993) *Detention under the Prevention of Terrorism Provisions Act 1989: Legal Advice and Outside Contact* (Home Office Research and Planning Unit, Paper No.75).

BROWN, D. (1997) *PACE ten years on: a review of the research* (Home Office Research Study No.155).

BROWN, D., ELLIS, T. and LARCOMBE, K. (1992) *Changing the Code: Police Detention under the Revised PACE Codes of Practice* (Home Office Research

---

[1] This bibliography drew heavily, with his permission, on one prepared by David Brown in *PACE ten years on: a review of the research*, 1997 (Home Office Research Study No.155).

Study No.129, HMSO). (For a summary, see *Research Findings No.5* (Home Office Research and Statistics Department, March 1993).)

BUCKE, T. and BROWN, D. (1997) *In police custody: police powers and suspects' rights under the revised PACE codes of practice* (Home Office Research Study No.174).

BUCKE, T., STREET, R. and BROWN, D. (2000) *The right of silence: the impact of the Criminal Justice and Public Order Act* (Home Office Research Study No.199).

CLARE, I. and GUDJONNSON, G. (1993) *Devising and piloting an experimental version of the 'notice to detained persons'* (Royal Commission on Criminal Justice, Research Study No.7).

COLEMAN, C.A., DIXON, D. and BOTTOMLEY, A.K. (1993) "Police Investigative Procedures: Researching the Impact of PACE", in C. Walker and K. Starmer (eds.) *Justice in Error* (Blackstone Press), pp.17–36.

CORBETT, C. (1991) "Complaints against the police: the new procedure of informal resolution", 2(1) *Policing and Society*.

CRAWFORD, A., JONES, T. and YOUNG, J. (1990) *The Second Islington Crime Survey* (London: Middlesex Polytechnic Centre for Criminology).

DIXON, D. (1990) "Juvenile suspects and the Police and Criminal Evidence Act", in D.A.C. Freestone (ed.) *Children and the Law* (Hull University Press), pp.107–29.

DIXON, D., COLEMAN, C.A. and BOTTOMLEY, A.K. (1990) "Consent and the legal regulation of policing", 17 *Journal of Law and Society* 345–362.

DIXON, D., BOTTOMLEY, A.K., COLEMAN, C.A., GILL, M. and WALL, D. (1989a) "Safeguarding the rights of suspects in police custody", 1 *Policing and Society* 115–140.

DIXON, D., BOTTOMLEY, A.K., COLEMAN, C.A., GILL, M. and WALL, D. (1989b) "Reality and rules in the construction and regulation of police suspicion", 17 *International Journal of the Sociology of Law* 185–206.

EVANS, R. (1993) *The conduct of police interviews with juveniles* (Royal Commission on Criminal Justice, Research Study No.8).

FITZGERALD, M. (1999) *Searches in London under s.1 of the Police and Criminal Evidence Act 1984* (Metropolitan Police).

GELOWITZ, M. (1990) "Section 78 of the Police and Criminal Evidence Act 1984", 106 *Law Quarterly Review* 327.

GEMMILL, R. and MORGAN-GILES, R.F. (1980) *Arrest, Charge and Summons: Current Practice and Resource Implications* (Royal Commission on Criminal Procedure, Research Study No.9).

GREER, S. (1990) "The right to silence: a review of the current debate", 53 *Modern Law Review* 709–721.

GUDJONSSON, G. (1992) *The Psychology of Interrogations, Confessions and Testimony* (John Wiley).

IRVING, B.L. (1980) *Police Interrogation* (Royal Commission on Criminal Procedure, Research Study No.1, HMSO).

IRVING, B.L. and McKENZIE, I. (1989) *Police Interrogation: the effects of the Police and Criminal Evidence Act 1984* (Police Foundation).

JORDAN, P. (2000) *Stop/Search: Impact on crime and impact on public opinion* (Police Foundation).

LENG, R. (1993) *The right to silence in police interrogation: a study of some of the issues underlying the debate* (Royal Commission on Criminal Justice, Research Study No.10).

LIDSTONE, K. (1989) "The Police and Criminal Evidence (Northern Ireland) Order 1989: Powers of Entry, Search and Seizure", *Northern Ireland Legal Quarterly* 333–362.

LITTLECHILD, B. (1996) *The Police and Criminal Evidence Act 1984: The Role of the Appropriate Adult* (British Association of Social Workers).

McCONVILLE, M. and HODGSON, J. (1993) *Custodial legal advice and the right to silence* (Royal Commission on Criminal Justice, Research Study No.16).

McCONVILLE, M., SANDERS, A. and LENG, R. (1991) *The Case for the Prosecution* (Routledge).

McCONVILLE, M., HODGSON, J., BRIDGES, L. and PAVLOVIC, A. (1994) *Standing Accused* (Clarendon, Oxford).

McKENZIE, I., MORGAN, R. and REINER, R. (1990) "Helping the police with their enquiries: the necessity principle and voluntary attendance at the police station", *Criminal Law Review* 22–33.

MACPHERSON, SIR WILLIAM OF CLUNY (1999) Report of the Inquiry into the Matters Arising from the Death of Stephen Lawrence (Cm.4262, Home Office).

MAGUIRE, M. (1998) "Effects of the PACE provisions on detention and questioning:some preliminary findings", 28(1) *British Journal of Criminology* 19–43

MAGUIRE, M. and CORBETT, C. (1989) "Patterns and profiles of complaints against the police", in R. Morgan and D.J. Smith (eds.) *Coming to Terms with Policing* (Routledge).

MAGUIRE, M. and CORBETT, C. (1991) *A Study of the Police Complaints System* (HMSO).

MAGUIRE, M. and NORRIS, C. (1993) *The conduct and supervision of criminal investigations* (Royal Commission on Criminal Justice, Research Study No.5).

MEAD, D. (2002) "Informed Consent to Police Searches in England and Wales—A Critical (Re-) Appraisal in the Light of the Human Rights Act" *Criminal Law Review* 791–804.

MILLER, J. and MVA (2000) *Profiling Populations Available for Stops and Searches* (Home Office Policing and Reducing Crime Unit, Paper No.131).

MILLER, J. BLAND, P. and QUINTON, P. (2000) *The Impact of Stops and Searches on Crime and Community* (Home Office Policing and Reducing Crime Unit, Paper No.127).

MORGAN, R. (1987) "The local determinants of policing policy", in P. Willmott (ed.) *Policing and the Community* (Policy Studies Institute Discussion Paper No.16).

MORGAN, R. (1989) "Policing by consent: legitimating the doctrine", in R. Morgan and D.J. Smith (eds.) *Coming to Terms with Policing* (Routledge), pp.217–234.

MORGAN, R. (1992) "Talking about Policing", in D. Downes (ed.) *Unravelling Criminal Justice* (Macmillan), pp.165–83.

MORGAN, R. and MAGGS, C. (1985) *Setting and PACE: Police Community Consultation Arrangements in England and Wales* (University of Bath, Bath Social Policy Paper No.4).

MORGAN, R., REINER, R. and McKENZIE, I.K. (1991) "Police Powers and Police: a study of the work of custody officers" (Final report to the ESRC, unpublished).

MOSTON, S. and STEPHENSON, G. (1993) *The questioning and interviewing of suspects outside the police station* (Royal Commission on Criminal Justice, Research Study No.22).

MOSTON, S., STEPHENSON, G. and WILLIAMSON, T. (1990) *Police Interrogation Styles and Suspect Behaviour* (Final Report to the Police Requirements Support Unit, University of Kent Institute of Social Applied Psychology, unpublished).

MOSTON, S., STEPHENSON, G. and WILLIAMSON, T. (1992) "The incidence, antecedents and consequences of suspects' use of the right of silence", 3 *Criminal Behaviour and Mental Health* 30–47.

PAINTER, K., LEA, J., WOODHOUSE, T. and YOUNG, J. (1989) *Hammersmith and Fulham crime and police survey* (Centre for Criminology, Middlesex Polytechnic).

PHILLIPS, C. and BROWN, D. (1998) *Entry into the Criminal Justice System: a survey of police arrests and their outcomes* (Home Office Research Study No.185).

QUINTON, P., BLAND, N. and MILLER, J. (2000) *Police Stops, Decision-making and Practice* (Home Office Policing and Reducing Crime Unit, Paper No.130).

ROYAL COMMISSION ON CRIMINAL PROCEDURE (1981) Report (Cmnd.8092, HMSO).

ROYAL COMMISSION ON CRIMINAL PROCEDURE (1981) *The Investigation and Prosecution of Criminal Offences in England and Wales: the Law and Procedure* (Cmnd.8092–1, HMSO).

ROYAL COMMISSION ON CRIMINAL JUSTICE (1993) Report (Cm.2263).

SANDERS, A., BRIDGES, L., MULVANEY, A. and CROZIER, G. (1989) *Advice and Assistance at Police Stations and the 24–hour Duty Solicitor Scheme* (Lord Chancellor's Department).

SCARMAN (1981) *The Brixton Disorders 10–12 April 1981, Report of an Inquiry by the Rt. Hon. Lord Scarman* (Cmnd.8427, HMSO).

SMITH, D. and GRAY, J. (1985) *Police and People in London: The PSI Report* (Gower, Aldershot).

SOFTLEY, P. with BROWN, D., FORDE, B., MAIR, G. and MOXON, D. (1980) *Police Interrogation:an observational study in four police stations* (Home Office Research Study No.61, HMSO).

STONE, V. and PETTIGREW, N. (2000) *The Views of the Public on Stops and Searches* (Home Office Policing and Reducing Crime Unit, Paper No.129).

TULLY, B. and CAHILL, D. (1984) *Police Interviewing of the Mentally Handicapped: an experimental study* (Police Foundation).

WILLIS, C.F. (1983) *The Use, Effectiveness and Impact of Police Stop and Search Powers* (Home Office Research and Planning Unit, Paper 15).

WILLIS, C.F., MACLEOD, J. and NAISH, P. (1988) *The Tape-recordings of Police Interviews with Suspects: a second interim report* (Home Office Research Study No.97, HMSO).

WOLCHOVER, D. (2001) *Silence and Guilt: An assessment of case law on the Criminal Justice and Public Order Act 1994* (Lion Court Lawyers).

YOUNG, J. (1994) *Policing the Streets: stops and search in North London* (Centre for Criminology, Middlesex University).

ZUCKERMAN, A.A.S. (1989) "Trial by unfair means—the Report of the Working Group on the Right of Silence", *Criminal Law Review* 855.

INDEX

Note—Roman type is used to indicate pages in the Commentary and Appendices, **bold** type to indicate sections of the Police and Criminal Evidence Act and *italic* type to indicate paragraphs in the Codes of Practice (A to F). The abbreviation *N.* stands for Notes for Guidance. The abbreviation A,B,C,D,E,F stands for Code A, Code B etc. (*B6.9* and *N.B6A* means therefore Code B, para. 6.9 and Note for Guidance 6A of Code B).